AA Lifestyle Guides

in association with **Hilton Hot**

are giving away

18 **Fam** **Wee**

in 6 free prize draws.

3 winners will be drawn every 2 months:-

- **December 1998**
- **February 1999**
- **April 1999**
- **June 1999**
- **August 1999**
- **October 1999**

Hilton have 11 Family Fun! hotels dedicated to families across the UK, all providing the perfect base for local attractions and family days out. Based on the Yogi Bear theme, these very special hotels are equipped with fun-filled activities, services and special accommodation to ensure the whole family enjoys their Hilton Weekend.

Features include the Yogi Bear Fun Park, Children's Welcome packs, Yogi Bear Menu, Thirst Buster Beaker offering unlimited soft drink refills, Sony Playstation hire and much more.

All Hilton hotels offer superb dining, and most have beautifully appointed Health clubs with heated indoor pools.

For more information on Hilton Weekends, and for your complimentary copy of their 'Time to Unwind' leisure brochure, FREEPHONE 0800 856 8000.

HOW TO ENTER

Just complete (in capitals, please) and send off this card or, alternatively, send your name and address on a **stamped** postcard to the address overleaf (no purchase required). Entries limited to one per household and to residents of the UK and Republic of Ireland. This card will require a stamp if posted in the Republic of Ireland.

MR/MRS/MISS/MS/OTHER, PLEASE STATE:

NAME:

ADDRESS:

POSTCODE:

TEL. NOS:

Are you an AA Member ?   Yes/No

Have you bought this or any other AA Lifestyle Guide before?   Yes/No

If yes, please indicate the year of the last edition you bought:

The AA Hotel Guide	19____	**AA Camping and Caravanning (Europe)**	19____
AA Best Restaurants	19____	**AA Hotels in France**	19____
AA Bed and Breakfast Guide	19____	**AA Bed & Breakfast in France**	19____
AA Camping & Caravanning (Britain & Ireland)	19____	**AA Best Pubs & Inns**	19____

If you do not wish to receive further information or special offers from

AA Publishing ☐   Hilton Hotels ☐   please tick the box

CCE99

Terms and Conditions

1. Three winners will be drawn for each of the six prize draws to take place on 31st December, 1998, 26 February, 30 April, 30 June, 27 August, 29 October, 1999.

2. Closing date for receipt of entries is midday on the relevant draw date. Final close date for receipt of entries is 31 October 1999

3. Entries received after any draw date except the final one will go forward into the next available draw. Entries will be placed in one draw only. Only one entry per household accepted.

4. Winners will be notified by post within 14 days of the relevant draw date. Prizes must be booked within 3 months from the relevant draw date. Prizes are not transferable and there will be no cash alternative.

5. This offer cannot be used in conjunction with any other discount, promotion or special offer.

6. Each prize consists of a 2 night "Family Fun!" weekend break at a Hilton National hotel in the UK. The prize includes 2 nights accommodation and full breakfast for two

adults and 2 children (aged 16 and under) sharing a twin or double room. Plus dinner on the first night. The prize does not include dinner on the second night, lunch or additional expenses such as drinks or travelling expenses. Any additional expenses will be charged as taken and payable on departure.

7. All hotel accommodation, services and facilities are provided by Hilton Hotels and AA Publishing is not party to your agreement with Hilton Hotels in this regard.

8. The prize draw is open to anyone resident in the UK or the Republic of Ireland over the age of 18 other than employees of the Automobile Association or Hilton Hotels, their subsidiary companies, their families or agents.

9. For a list of winners, please send a stamped, self-addressed envelope to AA Lifestyle Guides Winners, Publishing Admin, Fanum House, Basing View, Basingstoke, Hants, RG21 4EA.

10. If this card is posted in the Republic of Ireland it must have a stamp.

AA Lifestyle Guide Prize Draw

AA PUBLISHING

FANUM HOUSE

BASING VIEW

BASINGSTOKE

HANTS RG21 4EA

CARAVAN
AND
CAMPING
EUROPE
1999

This edition published March 1999
© The Automobile Association 1999
The Automobile Association retains the copyright in the current edition © 1999 and in all subsequent
editions, reprints and amendments to editions

Mapping is produced by the Cartographic Department of the Automobile Association from the
Automaps database using electronic and computer technology.
Maps © The Automobile Association 1999

The directory is compiled by the AA's Hotels and Touring Services Department
and generated from the AA's establishment database

Filmset by Avonset, Bath
Printed and bound in Great Britain by Bemrose Security Printing, Derby

Advertisement Sales
Advertisement Sales: telephone 01256 491544 or 491545

The cover photographs:
Berchtesgaden, Konigsee, Bavaria, Germany

Country introduction photographs: AA Picture Library (©AA Photo Library)
Luxembourg photograph, Spectrum Colour Library Andorra photograph, Pictures Colour Library

A CIP catalogue record for this book is available from the British Library
ISBN 0 7495 2020 5
Published by AA Publishing, a trading name of
Automobile Association Developments Limited, whose registered office is
Norfolk House, Priestley Road, Basingstoke, Hampshire RG24 9NY.
Registered number 1878835

CONTENTS

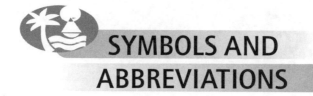

SYMBOLS AND ABBREVIATIONS

For a more detailed explanation refer to How to Use the Guide (see contents page).

● **ENGLISH** ●

🕺 adult
🚗 car
pp per person ⎫ charge
🚐 caravan or motor caravan ⎬ per night
🕺 tent ⎭
☎ telephone
HEC 1 hectare (equals approx 2 acres)
〰〰 grass
∷∷∷ sand
⬦ stone
🌿 little shade
🌤 partly shaded
🌳 mainly shaded
🚿 shower
🛒 shop
✕ cafe/restaurant
🍸 bar
🐕 no dogs
☺ electric points for razors
🔌 electric points for caravans
⌀ Camping Gaz International
🔥 gas other than Camping Gaz
🏠 bungalows for hire
🚐 caravans for hire
⛺ tents for hire
🏊 swimming:
   L lake
   P pool
   R river
   S sea
🚗 parking by tents permitted
🅿 compulsory separate car park
➡ facilities not on site, but within 2km
➕ first-aid facilities
🏰 site belongs to 'Castels & Camping Caravanning' chain (France only)
CM camping municipal, parque municipal de campismo, or parque de la camara municipal (local authority site)
KC Kommunens Campingplads (local authority site)
lau laundry
pitch pitch charge per night for car with tent or caravan (there is usually a charge per adult in addition to this)
☞ Entry continued overleaf

Entries in italics indicate that particulars have not been confirmed by management.

Pour plus amples informations veuillez vous referer a How to Use the Guide (voir la table de matieres).

● **FRANCAIS** ●

🕺 Adulte
🚗 Voiture
pp par personne ⎫ tarif pour
🚐 Caravane ou camping car ⎬ une nuit
🕺 Tente ⎭
☎ Telephone
HEC 1 hectare (correspond a environ 2 acres (mesures imperiales))
〰〰 Gazon
∷∷∷ Sable
⬦ Pierres
🌿 Peu ombrage
🌤 En partie ombrage
🌳 Surtout ombrage
🚿 Douches
🛒 Magasin
✕ Cafe/restaurant
🍸 Bar
🐕 Chiens non admis
☺ Prises de courant pour rasoirs electriques
🔌 Branchements electriques pour caravanes
⌀ Camping Gaz International
🔥 Gaz autre que Camping Gaz
🏠 Bungalows a louer
🚐 Caravanes a louer
⛺ Tentes a louer
🏊 Natation:
   L Lac
   P Piscine
   R Rivere
   S Mer
🚗 Stationnement voiture pres des tentes autorise
🅿 Utilisation des parkings voitures obligatoire
➡ Amenities pas sur le terrain, mais au plus, a 2km
➕ Poste de premiers-secours

🏰 Terrain fait partie de la chaine 'Castels & Camping Caravanning' (en France seulement)
CM Camping municipal
KC Kommunens Campingplads (camping municipal)
lau Blanchisserie
pitch Tarif d'un emplacement pour une nuit pour voiture avec tente ou caravane (en general s'ajoute un tarif par adulte)
☞ Suite au verso

Une insertion imprime en italiques indique que la direction de l'etablissement n'a pas confirme les precisions.

Fur weitere Angaben beziehen Sie sich auf How to Use the Guide (siehe Inhaltsverzeichnis).

● **DEUTSCH** ●

🕺 Erwachsene (r) ⎫
🚗 Auto ⎪
pp Pro person ⎬ Preis pro
🚐 Caravan bzw. Campingbus ⎪ nacht
🕺 Zelt ⎭
☎ Telefon
HEC 1 Hektar (ca 2 acres)
〰〰 Grasboden
∷∷∷ Sandgelande
⬦ Steiniges Gelande
🌿 Wenig Schatten
🌤 Teilschattig
🌳 Grosstenteilsschattig
🚿 Dusche
🛒 Laden
✕ Imbiss/Restaurant
🍸 Bar
🐕 Hundeverbot
☺ Stromanschlusse fur Rasierapparate
🔌 Stromanschlusse fur Caravans
⌀ Camping Gaz International
🔥 Gas ausser Camping Gaz International
🏠 Mietbungalows
🚐 Mietcaravans
⛺ Mietzelte
🏊 Schwimmen
   L See
   P Schwimmbad

4

R Fluss
S Meer
⌂ Abstellen des PKWs neben dem Zelt gestattet
▣ Separates Abstellen des PKWs obligatorisch
➡ Einrichtungen nicht an Ort und Stelle aber nicht weiter als 2 Kilometer entfernt
⊞ Unfallstation
☪ Platz gehort der 'Castels & Camping Caravanning' (nur Frankreich)
CM Stadischer Campingplatz
KC Kommunens Campingplads (stadis cher Campingplatz)
lau Wascherei
pitch Stellplatzpreis pro Nacht fur Auto mit Zelt bzw. Caravan (normaler weise eine zusatzliche Berechnung pro Erwachsener)
☞ siehe umseitig

Eine kursiv gedruckte Eintragung zeigt an, dass die entsprechenden Angaben nicht von der Direktion bestatigt worden sind.

Per una spiegazione piu dettagliata, consultare la sezione How to Use the Guide (vedi indice).

● ITALIANO ●

🜨 Adulto
🚗 Vettura
pp a persona ⎫ Prezzo per
🚐 Roulotte o ⎬ notte
   camper ⎭
▲ Tenda
☎ Telefono
HEC 1 ettaro (pari a 2 acri circa)
⼐ Erba
⠿ Sabbia
♦ Pietra
⚵ Poca ombra
♘ Ombreggiato in parte
♠ Ombreggiato in gran parte
♣ Doccia
⚑ Negozio
✕ Caffe ristorante
♟ Bar
⊗ Proibito ai cani
☉ Prese elettriche rasoi
⚏ Prese elettriche roulotte
⌀ Camping Gaz Internatioal
⚕ Altri tipi di gas che non siano il Camping Gaz
⚏ Alffittansi bungalows
🚐 Affitansi roulotte
⚠ Affitansi tende
⚓ Nuoto

L Lago
P Piscina
R Fiume
S Mare
⌂ E permesso parcheggiare vicino alle tende
▣ E obbligatorio parcheggiare nel posteggio apposito
➡ Le attrezzature non sono nel campeggio, bensi in un raggio di 2km
⊞ Proto soccorso
☪ If campeggio appartienne alla cate na 'Castels & Camping Caravanning' (per la Francia sola mente)
CM Camping municipal (campeggio municipale)
KC Kommunens Campingplads (Campeggio municipale)
lau Lavanderia
pitch Prezzo pe notte di un posto macchina e tenda o roulotte (di solito ciascun adulto paga un extra oltre al posto macchina)
☞ La lista delle voci continua a tergo

Le voci in corsivo stanno a indicare che i particolari non sono stati confermati dalla Direzione.

Para una explicacion mas detallada, consultese la section How to Use the Guide (vease el indice de materias).

● ESPANOL ●

🜨 Adulto
🚗 Automovil ⎫ Precio por
pp Por persona ⎬ noche
🚐 Rulota o ⎭
   coche-rulota
▲ Tienda
☎ Telefono
HEC 1 hectarea (igual a 2 acres aproxi madamente)
⼐ Hierba
⠿ Arena
♦ Piedra
⚵ Poca sombra
♘ Sombreado en parte
♠ Sombreado en su mayor parte
♣ Ducha
⚑ Almacen
✕ Cafe/restaurante
♟ Bar
⊗ Se prohiben los perros
☉ Tomas de corriente para maquinil las electricas
⚏ Tomas de corriente para rulotas
⌀ Camping Gaz International

⚕ Otros tipos de gas que no sean el Gaz International
⚏ Se alquilan bungalows
🚐 Se alquiln rulotas
⚠ Se alquin tiendas
⚓ Natacion:
   L Lago
   P Piscina
   R Rio
   S Mar
⌂ Se permite estacionar el coche junto a las tiendas
▣ Prohibido estacionarse fuera del aparacamiento
➡ Los servicios no estan en el camp ing, sino en un radio de 2km
⊞ Puesto de socorro
☪ Este camping pertenece al grupo 'Castle & Camping Caravanning' (para Francia solamente)
CM Camping municipal
KC Kommunens Campingplads (camping municipal)
lau Lavanderia
pitch Precio por noche de un puesto para coche y tienda o rulota (cada adulto paga un suplemento ade mas del precio susodicho)
☞ La lista de simbolos continua a la vuelta

Los articulos en bastardilla indican que los detalles no han sido confirmados por la Direccion.

HOW TO USE THIS GUIDE

Each country in this guide is divided into regions, so that you can easily find all the sites in your chosen holiday area. Within the regions, place names are listed in alphabetical order, and details of regional boundaries and site locations can be found on the country maps at the back of this book. If you need overnight stops on the way to your destination, the country maps should help you find something in the right place. Please remember that these maps are for site location purposes only and not for finding your way around. For route planning and use on the road, you should have a road atlas, such as the AA Road Atlas of Europe. Individual atlases of France, Germany and Italy are also available in the series.

ADVANCE BOOKING
Despite the carefree nature of a camping or caravanning holiday, it is best to book well in advance for peak holiday seasons, or for your first and last stop close to a ferry crossing point. However, we do find that some sites will not accept reservations. Although the AA cannot undertake to find sites or make reservations for you, we do include in this guide specimen booking letters in English, French, German, Italian and Spanish.

Please note that, although it is not common practice, some campsites may regard your deposit as a booking fee which is not deductible from the final account.

ON ARRIVAL
Look over the site if possible before you decide to stay. The information for any publication must be collected some time in advance, and ownership and standards may well have changed since our research was done. Even where standards are of the expected quality, the site may be very crowded and you may prefer to look elsewhere for more space and less noise.

When you look over a site, consider the following:

- Pleasant general situation, clean and tidy with plenty of refuse bins, site fenced and guarded.

- Sufficient and clean lavatories, washing facilities and showers with hot water. Well defined roads on site, preferably lit at night.

- Pitches should not be cramped.

- If you have a tent, make sure the surface is suitable for pegs; if you have a caravan, make sure the ground is firm enough.

- In hot weather there should be suitable shade, and if the weather is damp the ground should appear well drained.

- A good supply of safe drinking water.

- If you need the following facilities, confirm that they exist on the site: electric point for razors, Camping Gaz, a well stocked shop, laundry facilities, restaurant serving reasonably priced food, ice for sale.

Although most of the sites in this guide have been selected for the high standards they maintain, we have included, at the request of AA members, a number of sites along touring routes and others near the Channel ports which are suitable for overnight stops. These transit sites tend to become crowded at the height of the season, but provide the necessary amenities.

If you require information on additional sites, lists are free from most national tourist offices. In the introductions for each country we give details of local organisations which either publish a camping guide or provide more detailed information.

CAMPSITE ENTRIES
In order to update our information we send out questionnaires each year to every campsite. Inevitably a number of the questionnaires are not returned to us in time for publication, and where this is the case the campsite name is printed in italics. Most of the sites listed here take both tents and caravans unless otherwise stated.

PRICES

Prices are given in local currencies and are detailed per night, per adult, car, caravan and tent. We do not give charges relating to children, as these vary, but generally a 50 per cent reduction is made for children aged 3-14. To determine the cost of one night, simply add up the prices that apply to your party.

Some campsites do have different ways of structuring their prices. Whatever the variations may be, all will be reflected in the entry. Exceptions are:

pp Campsite charges per person. The charge for the vehicle and caravan/tent is included in the price for each person. For a party of four people, multiply the **pp** price by four for the total cost per night.

pitch This is the price per pitch, regardless of whether it is a caravan or a tent. Where the word pitch follows the 'A' for adult price, you should multiply the 'A' price by the number of adults in the party, then add the pitch price to that total obtain the cost per night for your party.

OPENING TIMES

Dates shown are inclusive of opening dates. If the site is open all year, then 'All year' is written in the entry. All information was correct at the time of going to press, but we recommend you to check with the site before arriving. Changes of date often occur because of demand and/or weather. Sometimes only restricted facilities are available between October and April.

COMPLAINTS

If you have any complaint about a site, do discuss the problem with the site proprietor immediately so that the matter can be dealt with promptly. If a personal approach fails, inform the AA when you return home.

We regret, however, that the AA cannot act as intermediary in any dispute, or attempt to gain refunds or compensation. Your comments, however, help us to prepare new editions.

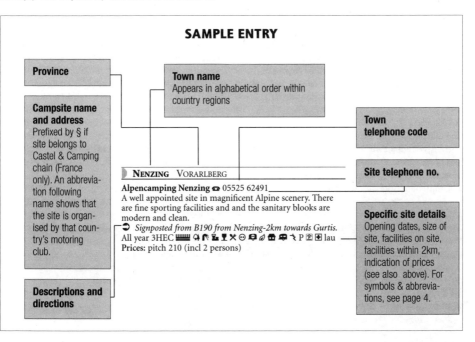

SAMPLE ENTRY

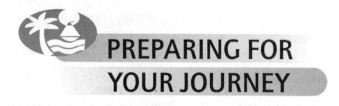

PREPARING FOR YOUR JOURNEY

PLEASE DO READ THIS SECTION BEFORE YOU SET OFF ON YOUR JOURNEY, EVEN IF YOU ARE AN EXPERIENCED TRAVELLER, AND DO ALSO READ THE FOLLOWING SECTION ON MOTORING INFORMATION, AND THE APPROPRIATE COUNTRY INTRODUCTIONS.

Before setting off on your Continental holiday, there are certain preparations you should make and some regulations you should know about. Experienced campers and caravanners will, of course, be familiar with most of this, but we hope it will be a useful chapter for newcomers.

PREPARING YOUR CARAVAN
Your caravan should of course be regularly serviced, but the following tips should be useful, specially for the first trip after winter storage.

Just before your trip give the caravan a good airing and, if you have a water pump fitted, check the flow and flush with clean water to get rid of any staleness. Make sure that there are no leaks and replace any doubtful washers. Examine all potential leak spots, especially around window rubbers, rear light clusters and roof lights, applying sealing compound as necessary. Test all window, cupboard and locker catches to make sure that they shut firmly. Outside, clean rain gutters and make sure down-spouts and window channel drainpipes are clear.

BRAKES
Check that the caravan braking mechanism is correctly adjusted. If it has a breakaway safety mechanism, the cable between car and caravan must be firmly anchored so that the trailer brakes act immediately if the two part company.

LIGHTS
Make sure that all the lights are working - rear lights, stop lights, number-plate lights, rear fog guard lamps and flashers (check that the flasher rate is correct: 60-120 times a minute).

TYRES
Both tyres on the caravan should be of the same size and type. Make sure that the tread depth is well above the legal minimum (see Continental ABC) and that there is no uneven wear. Look also for cuts and for cracks that might have developed during the winter. Replace any suspect tyres and any tyres over five years old, irrespective of the amount of tread remaining. Remember, caravan tyres rarely wear out but do deteriorate with age.

PREPARING YOUR TENT
Some weeks before your holiday, choose a fine day, spread the tent on the lawn or some other space so that you can make a close inspection of all potential stress points: where guylines attach, where the ground sheet meets tent walls, and where the frame poles come into contact with fabric. The fabric of the tent can be damaged by branches or sharp objects and by mildew if it has not been stored correctly. Additionally, it can lose its proofing through long exposure to the weather, as a result of being splashed by cooking fat or by washing-up water containing detergent. If your tent is damaged in this way, consult a specialist camping supplier. Patch kits of different colours and materials are available, as are proofing preparations and sprays.

PREPARING YOUR CAMPING EQUIPMENT
Use this camping equipment check list when you are planning what to take:
- Air mattress and pump, or camp beds
- All-purpose knife
- Bucket
- Camp stove and fuel
- Clothes-line and pegs
- Cutlery, including cooking utensils
- Dishcloths, scouring pad, and tea towels
- First-aid kit
- Folding chairs or stools
- Folding table

- Food containers
- Ground sheet
- Icebox (portable)
- Kettle
- Mallet
- Matches
- Plastic bags or bags for litter
- Plates, cups and saucers, or mugs
- Rope
- Saucepans, frying pan
- Sleeping bags
- Small brush (useful when camping on sand)
- Teapot
- Tent, poles, tent pegs (spares), sand pegs and discs
- Tent-tidy (for scissors, string, needles, thread, etc.)
- Tin-opener, bottle-opener, and corkscrew
- Torch and batteries
- Washing powder
- Washing-up bowl and washing-up liquid
- Water and milk containers
- Water-purifying tablets
- Windshield

HOW TO ENSURE GOOD ROAD HANDLING

Before you load all your luggage and equipment into the caravan, check on the weight restrictions that apply to it and to the towing vehicle. The laden weight of the caravan should always be less than, and ideally no more than 85 per cent of the kerbside weight of the towing vehicle.

The kerbside weight is defined as: the weight of the vehicle plus fuel and of other necessary liquids (e.g. water, oil, brake fluid, etc.) but with no passengers and no load other than normal tools and equipment.

The weight of the caravan is normally specified in the purchase literature, and usually refers to the weight 'ex works' or 'delivered'. This can be misleading because it is normally based on the standard model and may not take into account any fitted extras; one way to be certain is to take the unladen caravan to your local public weighbridge. Once you have the accurate unladen weight, subtract that from the manufacturer's recommended gross weight, and the figure you arrive at will be the amount of equipment you can safely load into the caravan.

Remember that, ideally, the gross weight of the caravan should not exceed 85 per cent of the kerbside weight of your car as given in the manufacturer's handbook.

Loading can greatly affect the stability of the car-caravan combination on the road. Keep as much weight as possible near the trailer axle, and store heavy equipment on the caravan floor. Never store heavy items at the rear of the caravan in an attempt to counterbalance an excessive nose weight - this causes instability and can be very dangerous. Keep the roof lockers free of luggage if possible and ensure lockers, drawers and cupboards are securely closed so there are no loose items that could roll about.

After loading, check that the caravan, when coupled to the car, is level with the ground, or slightly nose down. If the nose is up, this can be corrected by a hitch height adjuster, available from caravan manufacturers or dealers. An adapter plate can be used to lower the tow-ball mounting, but it does put extra pressure on the bracket.

Check that the nose weight of the trailer complies with the car manufacturer's recommendations. As a guide, the nose weight should be heavier than the rear by about 40-50kg (90-119lbs). Check the nose weight of the laden caravan with bathroom scales and blocks of wood or a spring balance. A twin-axle trailer must be weighed when the coupling is at the exact towing height. Obtaining the ideal weight and weight distribution of the car-trailer combination helps prevent pitching and snaking. Pitching can also be prevented by stiffening the towing car's rear suspension - either fit a supplementary rubber or air spring unit to the rear spring, or use heavier duty shock absorbers. (more expensive) but always ensure first that the car's front and rear shock absorbers are in good condition.

Excessive pitching and/or bad weight distribution can lead to snaking as the vertical movement sways the caravan sideways. This can be particularly dangerous, since the first instinct is to steer against the movement, which only makes matters worse. The best course is to steer straight and gently decelerate. Stabilisers are available, but it is far better to cure the cause. When choosing a car with which you intend to tow a caravan or trailer, remember that the amount of overhang - the distance between the car's rear axle and the towing ball - has an effect on the handling. The greater the overhang the more difficult handling will be.

A FEW FINAL CHECKS

- corner steadies are fully wound up and the brace is handy for when you arrive on site;
- windows, vents and doors are firmly shut;
- any fires or flames are extinguished and the tap on the gas cylinder is turned off;
- the coupling is firmly in position and the breakaway cable is attached;
- the over-run brake is working correctly;
- both car wing mirrors give good visibility ;
- all the car and caravan lights are working;
- the safety catch on the hitch is on;
- the jockey wheel is raised and secured, the handbrake is released, and the fire extinguishers are operational and close at hand.

Much of the art of towing comes with experience, but many of the problems can be eliminated by being aware:

- Know your car well before attempting to tow.
- Stop before you get tired.
- Plan to use roads suitable for towing.
- Have the appropriate mirrors and use them.
- If traffic builds up behind you, pull up safely and let it pass.
- Keep a safe stopping distance between you and the vehicle in front.
- Switch on your headlights whenever visibility becomes poor.
- Make good use of the gears on hills.
- Allow plenty of time when overtaking or pulling across a main road.
- Never stop on narrow roads, bends, crests of hills, or anywhere that could be dangerous
- In case of breakdown or accident, use hazard flashers and warning triangle(s).

OFF-ROAD HANDLING

On site you may encounter difficult ground. Try to avoid pitches liable to be waterlogged; sand that will not take the force of a driving wheel; and stone and shingle that provide no grip.

If you have to drive over difficult ground, keep moving slowly with a very light throttle. If you

stop, do not accelerate hard or the wheels will spin and dig in. Move gently backwards and forwards to get out of a dip. If the driving wheels do dig in, put brushwood or sacks in front of and behind the wheels. To move the trailer manually, pull sideways on the drawbar and then work the trailer forwards by chocking alternate wheels.

CAMPING FUELS

Gas in cylinders or bottles, as used in caravans, is mainly of two types, butane and propane. Both are kept as liquid under pressure and become a combustible gas once the pressure is released. They are available on the Continent, but propane is more widely distributed in countries with low winter temperatures. Propane has a higher pressure than butane. See also the paragraph on Branded Gases, below.

CARRIAGE OF GAS BY CAR FERRIES

Vehicles carrying unsealed cylinders of liquefied petroleum gas (LPG) must report at both United Kingdom and European ports for a leakage test at least 30 minutes before the published reporting time. A maximum of three Home Office approved cylinders, not exceeding 35lb net weight each, or up to 12 small expendable cartridges, sealed and packed in an outer container, are allowed for each caravan. Cylinders should be securely fixed in or on the caravan as intended by the caravan manufacturer.

New users of LPG particularly should follow safety instructions and experienced people sometimes need reminding of the safety rules:

- change cylinders with care
- provide fresh air for safe combustion
- don't improvise or tamper with equipment
- have regular maintenance carried out by qualified engineers

GAS SAFETY RULES

1 Always use the right type and length of hose for connections If in doubt, ask the dealer's advice.
2 Replace worn hose. Never try repairs.
3 When fitting the hose, where applicable use worm-drive clips and ensure they are tight.
4 Always use a spanner when fitting connections - finger tightness is not enough. Before fitting a regulator or other screwed

connection to a butane cylinder, always
ensure that the sealing washer is there and in
good condition. When fitting to switch-on or
clip-on valves, refer to the manufacturer's or
supplier's instructions.

5 Check for leaks by applying soapy water. Any
leaks will be shown by bubbles.

6 *Never* check for leaks with a naked flame.

7 Always keep containers away from excessive
heat or naked flames.

8 When starting, open container valve slowly.

9 If the container is not to be used for a while
close the valve, remove the pressure regulator
and replace the valve cover if fitted.

10 When changing a cartridge or container, keep
away from any naked light, flame or source of
ignition. Ensure good ventilation. With car
tridge appliances, check that the sealing
washer, usually housed in the appliance inlet
connection, is in position and in good condi
tion. Make sure that the valve on the con
tainer, where fitted, and the tap on the regula
tor are fully closed. Never try to change a
pierceable cartridge (such as the Camping
Gaz type) until you are sure all the gas has
been expended. You can usually hear any gas
remaining by gently shaking.

11 Once the pressure regulators are set they
should not be tampered with. Adjustments or
repairs should be left to a dealer.

12 Containers must always stand upright, valves
uppermost, whether in use or not. Carry them
upright, but not by the valve.

13 Whether full or empty, never store the
containers below ground or near drains, as all
these gases are heavier than air and will
collect at the lowest point in the event of a leak.

14 Good ventilation is essential where gas burn
ing appliances are used. Un-flued appliances
must not be installed in sleeping areas. Only
room-sealed appliances should be installed in
bath or shower rooms.

15 When moving, turn off all appliances and
cylinder valves.

16 Do not sleep in a room where gas cylinders
are in use.

17 Permanent storage must always be outdoors.

18 When fitting cylinders, always check that the
cylinder valve is fully closed in a clockwise
direction before removing the valve-sealing
cap or plug.

BRANDED GASES

Shell Gas BUTANE This product is marketed in
5.5kg, 7kg, 13kg and 15kg cylinders, with a
variety of connecting systems, by eight local
subsidiary companies operating in England and
Wales. Details of these companies, who will also
advise on the location of stockists, can be
obtained by ringing Freephone Shell Gas.
However, because of differing official standards
and regulations to which cylinders must conform,
butane cylinders cannot be exchanged for
Continental ones, nor can they be refilled abroad.
Foreign cylinders must not be brought back to
the United Kingdom, nor British cylinders left on
the Continent. For these reasons it is wise to take
enough gas to last throughout the holiday.

A list of main agents can be obtained from
Shell Gas, West Riverside, Immingham,
Humberside DN40 1AA telephone 01496
578076. Main agents will be able to give you
names and addresses of local sub-agents.

Butane is, however, marketed by Shell in France,
the Netherlands, Switzerland, Belgium, Portugal
and Luxembourg, usually in cylinders of 13kg
capacity (approximately 29lb). British butane
regulators will not connect directly with
cylinders obtained in these countries because of
differing connections. A regulator must be
obtained on loan. Deposits on cylinders are
payable on purchase; you must ensure that you
obtain a receipt in order to get your deposit
refunded. If your burner is specifically designed
for use with butane gas it is inadvisable to use it
with any other gas, such as propane or a
propane-butane mixture.

Shell Gas (PROPANE): Marketed by Shell Gas
in 3.9kg, 11kg, 18.5kg and 46kg cylinders in
Britain.
Calor Gas (BUTANE): Marketed by Calor Gas
Ltd, Appleton Park, Datchet, Slough, Berks SL3
9JG tel 0800 626626. Although Calor Gas refills
are not available abroad, You can take sufficient
with you to last for a short holiday, as follows:

Camping: Single-burner picnic set or double-
burner camp stove with 4.5kg butane cylinder.

Motor Caravan: Two-burner hotplate or two-burner hotplate grill with 4.5kg butane cylinder.

Caravan: Two-burner hotplate or small cooker, with 4.5kg butane cylinder with screw-on connections or 15kg butane cylinder or 7kg butane cylinder which will both accept the switch-on regulator. Take two 4.5kg or two 7kg.

If you follow the instructions a 4.5kg cylinder will last a month on either single or double-burner units.

If you cannot take enough Calor Gas cylinders in your outfit, you are advised to buy a Camping Gaz connecting tap before leaving this country. This enables a Calor Gas regulator or flow-control valve (or just the Calor Gas connecting nut in the case of appliances not using regulating equipment) to be connected to a Camping Gaz 904 or 907 cylinder (the exception to this is the quick-boiling ring or single burner, which fits directly to the 4.5kg cylinder shroud). The connecting tap is available from Calor Gas dealers.

Calor Gas (PROPANE): Marketed by Calor Gas Ltd, in 3.9kg, 6kg, 13kg and 19kg cylinders. This is suitable for those undertaking all-year-round camping and caravanning.

Primus (PROPANE): Primus cylinders are available in three sizes - 2000 (0.34kg), 2005 (0.8kg) and 2012 (1.98kg) - to complement the company's extensive range of leisure, DIY and industrial appliances. Cylinders are filled and distributed in this country by Calor Gas Ltd, and are available from most Calor Dealers.

Primus (BUTANE): Cartridges nos. 2201 (200g), 2202 (420g) and the new 2207 (220g) low profile, are widely available in Britain and on the Continent (except in Spain and Eastern Europe). French legislation makes it advisable to carry enough cartridges for passage through France.

Camping Gaz International (BUTANE): Marketed in the United Kingdom by Camping Gaz (GB) Ltd, 9 Albert Street, Slough, Berks SL1 2BH tel 0753 691707. This product is widely marketed throughout the Continent (see below) but prices can vary considerably in different countries. A list of their general agents is available from the company. Please contact them direct.

The cartridges are expendable, but cylinders are fully interchangeable for use with cooking, lighting and heater units. A special connecting tap unit is available to fit Shell Gas or Calor Gas regulators to Camping Gaz 904 or 907 cylinders. Gas is available in the following European countries: Andorra, Austria, Belgium, France, Germany, Italy, Luxembourg, Netherlands, Portugal, Spain including Majorca and Ibiza (cartridge 206 and 901 and 907 only), Switzerland and the United Kingdom.

PARAFFIN
Paraffin (pétrole or kerosene) is not easily obtainable in country districts in Europe and you are advised to get supplies on arrival in large towns. Methylated spirit (alcoöl à brûler) is easier to get.

SAFETY

•

Always make sure you have the right size and type of gas cartridge for the appliance.

•

Never put a cartridge in a cartridge holder unless the upper part of the appliance has been unscrewed and completely removed.

•

A cartridge with gas in it must never be removed from an appliance nor must the upper part of the appliance be unscrewed.

CONTINENTAL ABC MOTORING AND GENERAL INFORMATION

This ABC provides a general background of motoring regulations and general information, and is designed to be read in conjunction with the relevant country introductions.

Motoring laws on the Continent should cause little difficulty to British motorists, but drivers should take more care and extend greater courtesy then they would normally do at home, and bear in mind the essentials of good motoring - avoiding any action likely to obstruct traffic, endanger persons or cause damage to property.

Road signs are mainly the familiar international ones, but in every country there are a few exceptions; watch especially for signs showing crossings and speed limits. Probably the most unfamiliar aspect of motoring abroad to British motorists is the rule giving priority to traffic coming from the right, and unless this priority is varied by signs, it must be strictly observed.

A tourist driving abroad should always carry a current passport, a full valid national driving licence (even when an International Driving Permit is held), the vehicle registration document and certificate of motor insurance. The proper international distinguishing sign should be displayed on the rear of the vehicle and any caravan or trailer. The appropriate papers must be carried at all times. The practice of spot checks on foreign cars is widespread; to avoid inconvenience or a police fine, be sure that your papers are in order and that the international distinguishing sign is of the approved standard design.

Make sure that you have clear all-round vision. See that your seat belts are securely mounted and undamaged, and remember that in most Continental countries their use is compulsory. If you carry skis remember that their tips should point to the rear. You must be sure that your vehicle complies with the regulations concerning dimensions for all the countries you intend to pass through (see

below and relevant country introductions). This is particularly necessary if you are towing a trailer of any sort.

Mechanical repairs and replacement parts can be very expensive abroad and many breakdowns occur because the vehicle has not been properly prepared before the journey, which may involve many miles of hard driving over unfamiliar roads.

We recommend a major service by a franchised dealer before you go abroad. You should also carry out your own general check for any audible or visible defects. It is not practicable to provide a complete check list, but consult the ABC below under the following headings:

Automatic gearboxes
Automatic transmission fluid
Brakes
Cold-weather touring
Direction indicators
Electrical
Engine and mechanical
Lights
Spares
Tyres
Warm-climate touring

Also consult your manufacturer's handbook. AA members can arrange a thorough check of their car by one of the AA's experienced engineers who will submit a written report, complete with a list of repairs required. There is a fee for this service. For more information or, if you wish to book an inspection, please telephone 0345 500610.

A

ACCIDENTS

The country introductions give telephone numbers for the fire, police and ambulance services. International regulations are similar to those in the UK; the following action is usually required or advisable:

If you are involved in an accident you must stop. A warning triangle should be placed on the road at a suitable distance to warn following traffic of the obstruction. The use of hazard warning lights in no way affects the regulations governing the use of warning triangles. Get medical assistance for anyone injured in the accident. If the accident necessitates calling the police, leave the vehicle in the position in which it came to rest. If it seriously obstructs other traffic, mark the position of the vehicle on the road and get the details confirmed by independent witnesses before moving it.

The accident must be reported to the police in the following circumstances: if it is required by law, if the accident has caused death or bodily injury, or if an unoccupied vehicle or property has been damaged and there is no one present to represent the interests of the party suffering damage.

Be sure to notify your insurance company (by letter if possible), within 24 hours of the accident (see the conditions of your policy). If a third party is injured, contact your insurers for advice or, if you have a Green Card, notify the company or bureau, given on the back of your Green Card; this company or bureau will deal with any compensation claim from the injured party. AA policy holders should refer to 'AA Policy Holders Driving Abroad' statement for advice.

Make sure that all essential particulars are noted, especially details concerning third parties, and co-operate with police or other officials taking on-the-spot notes by supplying your name, address or other personal details as required. It is also a good idea to take photographs of the scene. Try to get good shots of other vehicles involved, their registration plates and any background which

might help later enquiries. This record may be useful when completing the insurance company's accident form.

AUTOMATIC GEARBOXES

The fluid in an automatic gearbox does more work when it has to cope with the extra weight of a caravan. It becomes hotter and thinner, so there is more slip and more heat generated in the gearbox. Many manufacturers recommend the fitting of a gearbox oil cooler. Check with the manufacturer as to what is suitable for your car.

Automatic transmission fluid

Automatic transmission fluid is not always readily available, especially in some of the more remote areas of Western Europe, and tourists are advised to carry an emergency supply.

B

BBC WORLD SERVICE

The international radio arm of the BBC. It broadcasts in 44 languages, including a 24-hour-a-day English Service. World news is on the hour every hour and there are regular bulletins of British news.

If you want to listen to World Service when you are abroad, write for information and a free programme guide to: BBC World Service, Audience Relations, Bush House, London WC2B 4PH. Remember to state the country or countries you are visiting.

A monthly magazine, BBC On Air, provides details of all World Service programmes and frequencies, with background information about features and personalities. It costs £18.00 for an annual subscription. If you would like to receive a sample copy, please write to the above address, quoting 'Free Issue, BBC On Air Magazine', or for more information, call 0171 557 2211.

If you are buying a new radio to listen to the BBC abroad, the World Service recommends that you choose a digitally tuned radio because it makes finding frequencies easier. Make sure your short-wave set can receive some of the key European frequencies such as 9410 and 12095 kHz.

BOATS

The completion of the Single Market on 1 January 1993 abolished temporary importation, permitting free movement of privately owned boats between member states provided VAT has been paid. Boat owners are now able to use their boats throughout the year in all EU countries, instead of being limited to a specified period of, for example, only six months of the year.

However all boats taken abroad by road should be registered in the UK, except for very small craft to be used close inshore in France. In France such craft are exempt from registration and the dividing line falls approximately between a Laser dinghy (which should be registered) and a Topper (which need not be); however, to avoid any confusion, registration is recommended. See also Identification Plate. Registration is carried out by the Small Ships Register at the RSS. Currently the fee is £10 and provides registration for five years. The original Certificate of Registry is required, not a photocopy. Application forms for Small Ships Registration, accompanied by notes on the purpose of the Register and eligibility for registration, are available from the Small Ships Register, PO Box 508, Cardiff CF4 5FH telephone 01222 761911. Application forms are also available from some yacht/boat clubs, marinas and shipyards.

Of the countries in this guide, an International Certificate of Competence (ICC) is required for Germany, Portugal and some parts of Italy; it is also required on French inland waters for vessels with an engine of more than 5HP. On Belgian and Dutch inland waters the certificate is required for vessels over 15 metres in length or capable of more than 20km per hour. The ICC is only acceptable for vessels on lakes, rivers and canals. For vessels over 15 metres in length or capable of more than 20 km per hour using the Schelde estuary, Ijsselmeer or Waddensee, an RYA (shore-based) day skipper course is required as well as the ICC. For further information, contact the

Royal Yachting Association, RYA House, Romsey Road, Eastleigh, Hampshire SO50 9YA telephone 01703 627400.

On 16 June 1998 the Recreational Craft Directirve came fully into force. This requires the CE mark on new boats, but has no retrospective effect. Proof of use in EU waters before this date may become a useful document when visiting other EU countries.

Third party insurance is compulsory for boats in Italy and Switzerland (see country introductions) and advisable elsewhere on the Continent.

BRAKES

Car brakes must always be in peak condition. Check both the level in the brake fluid reservoir and the thickness of the brake lining/pad material. The brake fluid should be completely changed according to the manufacturer's instructions or at intervals of not more than 18 months or 18,000 miles. However, it is always advisable to change the brake fluid before starting a Continental holiday, particularly if the journey includes travelling through a hilly or mountainous area.

BREAKDOWN

If your car breaks down, try to move it to the side of the road, or to a position where it will obstruct the traffic flow as little as possible. Place a warning triangle at the appropriate distance on the road behind the obstruction. Bear in mind road conditions and, if near or on a bend, the triangle should be placed where it is clearly visible to following traffic. If the car is fitted with hazard warning lights these may only be effective on straight roads, and will have no effect at bends or rises in the road. If the fault is electrical, the lights may not operate, which is why they cannot take the place of a triangle.

Motorists are advised to take out AA Five Star Europe, the overseas motoring emergency service. You can purchase breakdown and accident benefits, and personal travel insurance. It is available to all motorists travelling in Europe, although non-AA members pay a small additional premium. The AA and/or the insurer may also ask for an indemnity or guarantee if the proposer is under 18 or not permanently resident within the British Isles/Republic of Ireland. For further information and/or brochures call 0800 444500 (Republic of Ireland 1850 456789).

NOTE: AA Members with UK relay entitlement have the free benefit of 72-hour European Breakdown cover in specified European countries.
Of the countries dealt with in this guide, cover is available in: Belgium, France, Germany, Luxembourg and the Netherlands for any number of trips of up to 72 hours. You must, however, register before each trip by phoning the AA on 0800 731 70 72.

BRITISH EMBASSIES/CONSULATES (SEE ALSO COUNTRY INTRODUCTIONS)

In most Continental countries there is usually more than one British Consulate. The functions and office hours of Vice-Consulates and Honorary Consuls can be more restricted than those of full Consulates.

Consulates (and consular sections of the embassy) are ready to help British travellers overseas, but there are limits to what they can do. A consulate cannot pay your hotel, medical or any other bills, nor will they do the work of travel agents, information bureaux or police. Any loss or theft should first be reported to the local police, not the consulate, and a statement obtained confirming the loss or theft. If you still need help, such as the issue of an emergency passport or guidance on how to transfer funds, contact the consulate. See respective country introductions for addresses and locations of British Embassies and British Consulates.

C

CAMPING CARD INTERNATIONAL

A Camping Card International is valid for 12 months from the date of issue. It may be purchased from the AA by anyone over 18 who is a member of the AA; AA five Star Europe policies provide temporary membership for the period of cover. Recognised at most campsites

in Europe, the camping card is essential in some cases and you will not be allowed to camp without it. At certain campsites a reduction to the advertised charge may be allowed on presentation of the camping card. An application form may be obtained from the AA.

The camping card provides third-party insurance cover for up to 11 people camping away from home or staying in rented accommodation or at a hotel. Although the card is valid for 12 months, expiry of your AA membership invalidates the insurance coverage. Each card purchased is accompanied by a summary of the third-party insurance cover, conditions of use and details of the campers' code. A CCI Information and Discount booklet will also be provided.

On arrival at the campsite, report to the campsite manager who will tell you where you may pitch your tent or caravan. You may be asked to pay in advance, or alternatively, to give into charge the camping card for the length of your stay. Some campsite managers may also insist upon the retention of all passports.

CARAVAN AND LUGGAGE TRAILERS

Take a list of contents, especially if any valuable or unusual equipment is being carried, as this may be required at a frontier. A towed vehicle should be readily identifiable by a plate in an accessible position showing the name of the maker of the vehicle and the production or serial number. See Identification plate and also Principal mountain passes.

CHANNEL TUNNEL (SEE EUROTUNNEL)

CLAIMS AGAINST THIRD PARTIES

The law and levels of damages in foreign countries are different to our own. Some types of claim present difficulties, the most common relating to recovery of car hire charges. Rarely are they fully recoverable, and in some countries they may be drastically reduced or not recoverable at all. General damages for pain and suffering may not be recoverable in certain countries but even in countries where they are, the level of damages will often be considerably less than awards made in the UK.

The negotiation of claims against foreign insurers is extremely protracted and translation of documents slows the process. A delay of three months between sending a letter and getting a reply is not uncommon.

Legal costs and expenses are not recoverable in many Continental countries. The AA's overseas motoring emergency packages, such as Five Star Europe, include a discretionary service in certain matters arising abroad requiring legal assistance. This includes the pursuit of uninsured loss claims against third parties arising from an accident involving the insured vehicle. Policy holders should seek assistance from the AA.

COLD-WEATHER TOURING

If you are planning a winter tour, make sure that the strength of your antifreeze mixture is correct for low temperatures.

If travelling through snow-bound regions, it is important to remember that for many resorts and passes the authorities insist on wheel chains and/or winter tyres. However, chains should only be used when compulsory or necessary, prolonged use on hard surfaces may damage both the vehicle and the chains.

In fair weather, wheel chains are only necessary on the higher passes, but (as a rough guide) in severe weather you will probably need them at altitudes exceeding 610 metres (2000ft). Signposts usually indicate if wheelchains are compulsory.

Wheel chains fit over the driving wheels to enable them to grip on snow or icy surfaces. Full-length chains which fit tightly round a tyre are the most satisfactory, but they must be fitted correctly. Check that they do not foul your vehicle bodywork; if your vehicle has front-wheel drive put the steering on full lock while checking. It is essential that you also check the vehicle's handbook for the manufacturer's recommendations. On some vehicles there is insufficient clearance between the tyre and bodywork and wheel chains cannot be used. Winter or snow tyres are tyres with rugged treads which provide extra grip on

snow and ice. Some are designed to take spikes or studs which require specialist fitting and removal limiting their use. In practice, although regulations exist, spikes or studs are seldom used in countries such as Austria and Switzerland. A vehicle equipped with winter tyres without spikes or studs may be used all conditions. However, the use of winter tyres does not remove the need to carry chains; such tyres are generally more effective, reducing the need to fit chains. If you travel regularly to Alpine regions it may be worth considering a set of winter tyres. Contact your local tyre dealer for more information.

NOTE: The above guidelines do not apply where extreme winter conditions prevail. For extreme conditions it is doubtful whether the cost of preparing a car normally used in the UK would be justified for a short period. However, the AA's Technical Advice Department can advise on specific enquiries.

COMPULSORY EQUIPMENT

All countries have differing regulations as to how vehicles circulating on their roads should be equipped, but generally domestic laws are not enforced on visiting foreigners. However, where a country considers aspects of safety or other factors are involved, they will impose some regulations on visitors and these will be mentioned in the country introductions.

CRASH (SAFETY) HELMETS

All countries in this guide require visiting motorcyclists and their passengers to wear crash or safety helmets.

CREDIT AND CHARGE CARDS

See under Payment Cards.

CURRENCY NOTES
(SEE ALSO COUNTRY INTRODUCTIONS)

There is no limit to the amount of sterling notes you may take abroad. It is better, however, to take enough currency notes of the country you are visiting for immediate expenses. Some countries have regulations controlling the import and export of their currency. You are advised to consult your bank for information before making final arrangements.

CUSTOMS REGULATIONS FOR CONTINENTAL COUNTRIES

The completion of the European single market on 1 January 1993 abolished temporary importation, permitting free movement between member states. Consequently, persons travelling from one member state to another will be free to take not only their personal belongings, but a motor vehicle, boat (see also Boats), caravan or trailer across the internal frontiers without being subject to any Customs control or formality. Bona fide visitors to non-EU countries may generally assume that they may temporarily import personal articles duty free, providing the following conditions are met:

- that the articles are for personal use, and are not to be sold or otherwise disposed of;

- that they may be considered as being in use, and in keeping with the personal status of the importer;

- that they are taken out when the importer leaves the country;

- that the goods stay for no more than 6 months in any 12 month period, whichever is the earlier.

All dutiable articles must be declared when you enter a country, or you will be liable to penalties. If you will be taking a large number of personal effects with you, it would be wise to prepare an inventory to present to the Customs authorities on entry. Customs officers may withhold concessions at any time and ask travellers to deposit enough money to cover possible duty, especially on portable items of apparent high value such as television sets, radios, cassette recorders, portable computers, musical instruments, etc., all of which must be declared. Any deposit paid (for which a receipt must be obtained) is likely to be high: it is recoverable on leaving the country and

exporting the item but only at the entry point at which it was paid. Alternatively the Customs may enter the item in the traveller's passport; if this happens it is important to get the entry cancelled when the item is exported. Duty and tax-free allowances may not apply if travellers enter the country more than once a month, or are under 17 years of age (other ages may apply in some countries). Residents of the Channel Islands and the Isle of Man do not benefit from EU allowances because of their fiscal policies.

A temporarily imported motor vehicle, boat, caravan, or any other type of trailer is subject to strict control on entering a country, attracting Customs duty and a variety of taxes: much depends upon the circumstances and the period of the import, and also upon the status of the importer. Non-residents entering a country with a private vehicle for holiday or recreational purposes who intend to export the vehicle within a short period enjoy special privileges, and minimal formalities in the interests of tourism.

A temporarily imported vehicle, etc., should not:

- be left in the country after the importer has left;

- be put at the disposal of a resident of the country;

- be retained in the country longer than the permitted period; or

- be lent, sold, hired, given away, exchanged or otherwise disposed of.

Generally, people entering a country with a motor vehicle to stay for a period of more than six months (see also Visa), or who intend to take up residence, employment, any commercial activity or who intend to dispose of the vehicle should seek advice concerning their position well in advance of their departure. The AA Information Centre can give advice to members; for assistance, telephone 0990 500600.

CUSTOMS REGULATIONS FOR THE UNITED KINGDOM

If, when leaving Britain, you take any items bought in the UK which look very new, for example, watches, jewellery, cameras etc., particularly of foreign manufacture, it is a good idea to carry the retailer's receipts with you. In the absence of such receipts, you may be asked for a written declaration of where the goods were obtained. And remember, there are prohibitions and restrictions on taking certain goods out of the UK.

When you enter the UK from **another EC country without having travelled to or through a non-EC country** you do not need to go through the red or green channels. Look for the **blue channel** or **blue exit** reserved for EC travellers. But please remember that, although the limits on duty and tax paid goods bought within the EC ended on 30 December 1992, EC law sets out limits on purchases from duty-free and tax-free shops. It also establishes guidance levels for tobacco goods and wines and spirits bought elsewhere within the EC. Additionally the importation of certain goods into the UK is prohibited or restricted.

The quantities shown below may be bought from duty-free and tax-free shops for personal use. This is your entitlement each time you travel to and from another EC country until at least the end of June 1999, the deadline for the abolition of duty-free sales within the EU.

TOBACCO GOODS: 200 cigarettes; or 100 cigarillos; or 50 cigars; or 250gms of tobacco

---

WINES & SPIRITS: 2 litres of still table wine and 1 litre of spirits or strong liqueurs over 22% volume; or 2 litres of fortified spirits, sparkling wine or other liqueurs

---

PERFUME: 60cc/ml of perfume and 250cc/ml of toilet water

OTHER GOODS: £75 worth of all other goods including gifts and souvenirs

---

NOTE: under 17's cannot have tobacco or alcohol allowance

The guidance levels, which include any duty-free purchases, are the amounts you may bring in for your personal use. If you bring in more and cannot prove that the goods are for your personal use, they may be seized. The levels for tobacco goods are 800 cigarettes, 400 cigarillos, 200 cigars and 1kg of smoking tobacco; for wines and spirits 10 litres of spirits, 20 litres of fortified wine (such as port and sherry), 90 litres of wine (of which not more than 60 litres are sparkling) and 110 litres of beer. Prohibited or restricted goods include drugs, firearms, ammunition, offensive weapons (such as flick knives), explosives, obscene material, indecent and obscene material featuring children, unlicensed animals that could be carrying rabies (such as cats, dogs and mice) and endangered species or products made from them.

When you enter the UK from **a non-EC country or and EC country having travelled to or through a non-EC country,** you must go to Customs. If you have more than the customs allowances or any prohibited, restricted or commercial goods, go through the **red channel.** Only go through the **green channel** if you are sure that you have "nothing to declare".

Don't be tempted to hide anything or to mislead the Customs. Penalties are severe and articles not properly declared may be forfeit. If articles are hidden in a vehicle, that too becomes liable to forfeiture. Customs officers are legally entitled to examine your luggage. You are responsible for opening, unpacking and repackaging it. If you require more information obtain copy of Customs Notice 1, available at UK points of entry and exit, or telephone an Excise and Inland Customs Advice Centre (see Customs & Excise in the telephone directory.

CYCLE CARRIERS

If you intend taking your bicycles on a rear-mounted cycle rack, make sure that they do not obstruct rear lights and/or number plate, or you risk an on-the-spot fine. The AA recommends roof-mounted racks.

D

DIMENSIONS AND WEIGHT RESTRICTIONS

For an ordinary private car, a height limit of 4 metres and a width limit of 2.50 metres are generally imposed. However, see country introductions for full details. Apart from a laden-weight limit imposed on commercial vehicles, every vehicle has an individual weight limit. See Overloading and also Major road and rail tunnels as some dimensions are restricted by the shape of the tunnels.

DIRECTION INDICATORS

All direction indicators should be working at between 60 and 120 flashes per minute. Most standard car-flasher units will be overloaded by the extra lamps of a caravan or trailer, and a special heavy duty unit or relay device should be fitted.

DRINKING AND DRIVING

There is only one safe rule - if you drink, don't drive. The laws are strict and the penalties severe.

DRIVING LICENCE AND INTERNATIONAL DRIVING PERMIT

You should always carry your national driving licence with you even when you hold an International Driving Permit. A driving licence issued in the UK or Republic of Ireland is generally acceptable, subject to the minimum age requirements of the country concerned, but see also individual country introductions. If you wish to drive a hired or borrowed car in the country you are visiting, make local enquiries. If your licence is due to expire before your return, renew it in good time prior to your departure. The Driver and Vehicle Licensing Agency (in Northern Ireland, Driver and Vehicle Licensing Northern Ireland, DVLNI) will accept an application two months before the expiry of your old licence; in the Republic of Ireland, one month before expiry.

An International Driving Permit (IDP) is an internationally recognised document which enables the holder to drive for a limited period in countries where their national licences are not recognised (see Italy and Spain country introductions under Driving licence). The permit, for which a statutory charge is made, is issued by the AA to an applicant who holds a valid full British driving licence and who is over 18. For advice on the procedure to follow for personal or postal applications, or to obtain an application form, call the AA Information Centre on 0990 500 600. The permit cannot be issued to holders of foreign licences.

E

ELECTRICAL

General: The public electricity supply in Europe is predominantly 220 volts (50 cycles) AC (alternating current), but can be as low as 110 volts. In some isolated areas, low voltage DC (direct current) is provided. Continental circular two-pin plugs and screw-type bulbs are usually the rule.

Electrical adapters (not voltage transformers) which can be used in Continental power sockets, shaver points and light bulb sockets are available in the United Kingdom from electrical retailers.

Vehicle: Check that all connections are sound, and wiring is in good condition. If problems arise with the charging system, you must obtain the services of a qualified auto-electrician.

EMERGENCY MESSAGES TO TOURISTS

In emergencies, the AA will assist in the passing on of messages to tourists whenever possible. Members wishing to use this service should telephone the AA Information Centre on 0990 500600.

The AA can arrange for messages to be published in overseas editions of the Daily Mail, and in an extreme emergency (death or serious illness of next-of-kin) undertake to pass on messages to the appropriate authorities so that they can be broadcast on overseas radio networks. Obviously the AA cannot guarantee that messages will be broadcast, nor can the AA or the Daily Mail accept any responsibility for the authenticity of messages.

If you have any reason to expect a message from home, it is best to contact the tourist office or the motoring club of the country in which you are staying. They will be able to advise you on appropriate radio frequencies, and at what time messages are normally broadcast. Before you leave home, make sure your relatives understand what to do if an emergency occurs.

Emergency 'SOS' messages about dangerous illness of a close relative may be broadcast on BBC Radio 4's long wave transmitters on 1515m/198Hz at 06.59 and 17.59hrs BST. These should be arranged through the local police or hospital authorities.

ENGINE AND MECHANICAL

Consult your vehicle handbook for servicing intervals. Unless the engine oil has been changed recently, drain and refill it with fresh oil and fit a new filter. Deal with any significant leaks.

Brands and grades of engine oil familiar to the British motorist are usually available in Western Europe, but may be difficult to find in remote country areas. When available, they will be much more expensive than in the UK and are generally packed in 2-litre cans (3.5 pints). Motorists are strongly advised to carry a sufficient supply of oil.

If you suspect that there is anything wrong with the engine - even if it seems insignificant - it should be dealt with immediately. And do not neglect such common-sense precautions as checking valve clearances, sparking plugs, and contact breaker points where fitted, and make sure that the distributor cap is sound, and all drive belts in good condition.

Any obvious mechanical defects should be attended to at once. Look particularly for play in steering connections and wheel bearings and, where applicable, ensure that they are adequately greased. A car that has covered many miles will have absorbed a certain amount of dirt into the fuel system, and as breakdowns are often caused by dirt, it is essential that all filters (fuel and air) should be cleaned or renewed.

The cooling system should be checked for leaks and the correct proportion of anti-freeze, and any perished hoses or suspect parts replaced.

Owners should seriously reconsider towing a caravan with a car that has already given appreciable service. Hard driving on motorways and in mountainous country puts an extra strain on ageing parts, and items such as a burnt-out clutch can be very expensive.

EUROCHEQUES

The Eurocheque scheme is a flexible money-transfer system operated by a network of European banks. All the major UK banks are part of the Eurocheque scheme and they can provide a chequebook enabling you to write cheques in the local currency. Most European banks will cash Eurocheques * and retailer acceptance is widespread. Some UK banks issue cards which allow access to over 150,000 automatic cash dispensers in 40 countries. A Personal Identification Number (PIN) is required. This can be obtained from the account-holding branch of your bank.
* **Note:** Most French banks are no longer encashing Eurocheques. However, retail acceptance is unaffected and cash can be withdrawn from a network of about 20,000 automatic cash dispensers.

EUROTUNNEL

Eurotunnel provides fast, frequent, reliable travel between Folkestone and Coquelles/Calais for cars, coaches, motorcycles, campervans and cars with caravans or trailers. Eurotunnel operates 24 hours a day, 365 days a year, with up to four departures per hour at peak times. The journey takes 35 minutes platform to platform (approximately 45 minutes at night), and just over one hour from the M20 motorway in Kent to the A16 autoroute in France.

Motorists leave the M20 at Exit 11a (clearly signposted to the Channel Tunnel) and arive directly at the Eurotunnel check-in. Tickets can be purchased in advance by calling the "Eurotunnel Call Centre on 0990 353535; those booking less than 7 days in advance pick up their tickets at check-in. Eurotunnel also offers the facility for travellers to buy a ticket on arrival at the tollbooths by cash, cheque or credit card. Prices are charged per vehicle, and not by the number of passengers.

Once checked in, passengers can either follow the signs to take the next available departure, or visit the Passenger Terminal which has shops and cafés, as well as toilets, telephones, and bureau de change. Duty-free and tax-free shopping will also be available until at least the end of June 1999. Passengers pass through both UK and French frontier controls before boarding Eurotunnel shuttles, so there are no delays on arrival and motorists drive straight onto the French Autoroute network.

The shuttles are spacious, air-conditioned and well lit. Passengers stay with their vehicles for the short journey, although they can get out and walk around, and use the toilet facilities. The on-board radio station and visual display panels keep passengers informed during the journey.

Driving off takes a matter of minutes and - since the A16 autoroute was completed in the spring of 1998, the west of France is much more accessible to Eurotunnel passengers. For example, it is now only two hours to Rouen.

For further information and details of the latest special offers, telephone the Eurotunnel Call Centre on 0990 353535, or see your Travel Agent.

F

FERRY CROSSINGS
Before making ferry bookings, remember that the shortest sea crossing from a southern port to the Continent is not always the best choice; consider the roads and ease of travel from your home to a British port (an eastern British port might be easier if you are starting from the north of the country). Similarly consider the roads and travel from the Continental port to your final destination. Motorail services may be worth considering to save time and possibly an overnight stop.

FIRE EXTINGUISHER
It is a wise precaution to take a fire extinguisher when motoring abroad.

FIRST-AID KIT
It is a wise precaution (compulsory in Austria) to carry a first-aid kit when motoring abroad.

FOODS (SEE ALSO COUNTRY INTRODUCTIONS)
Countries do have regulations governing the types and quantities of foodstuffs which may be imported. Although they are usually not strictly applied, visitors should know that they exist and only take reasonable quantities of food with them. Where specific regulations exist they are listed under the country introductions.

Tinned, frozen and dehydrated foods offer great variety and are useful for camping. It is best to take only as much as you need until you can shop locally. Good value for money will be found in supermarkets or in the open markets in towns.

H

HORN
In built-up areas, the general rule is that you should not use it unless safety demands it: in many large towns and resorts, and in areas indicated by the international sign (a horn inside a red circle, crossed through) use of the horn is totally banned.

I

IDENTIFICATION PLATE
If a boat, caravan or trailer is taken abroad, it must have a unique chassis number for identification purposes. If yours does not have a number, you can buy an identification plate from the AA. Boats registered on the Small Ships Register (see Boats) have a unique number which must be permanently displayed.

INSURANCE, INCLUDING CARAVAN INSURANCE
See under Motor Insurance.

INTERNATIONAL DISTINGUISHING SIGN

An international distinguishing sign of the approved pattern, and size (oval with black letters on a white background; GB at least 6.9in by 4.5in), must be displayed on a vertical surface at the rear of your vehicle (and caravan or trailer if you are towing one). These signs indicate the country of registration of the vehicle. On the Continent, fines are imposed for failing to display a nationality plate, or for not displaying the correct nationality plate. See also Police fines.

L

LEVEL CROSSINGS

Practically all level crossings are indicated by international signs. Most guarded ones are the lifting barrier type, sometimes with bells or flashing lights to warn of an approaching train.

LIGHTS (SEE ALSO COUNTRY INTRODUCTIONS)

For driving abroad headlights should be altered so that the dipped beam does not dazzle oncoming drivers. This can easily be done by using headlamp or beam converter kits. However, don't forget to remove them as soon as you return to the UK. Remember to have the lamps set to compensate for the load being carried.

Dipped headlights should also be used in fog, snowfall, heavy rain and in a tunnel, irrespective of its length and lighting. Police may wait at the end of a tunnel to check vehicles.

Headlight flashing is used only to signal approach or as an overtaking signal at night. In other circumstances, it is taken as a sign of irritation, and could lead to misunderstandings. It is a wise precaution (compulsory in Spain and recommended in France, Germany and Italy) to carry a set of replacement bulbs.

LUGGAGE OR ROOF RACKS

Only use equipment suitable for your vehicle, i.e., approved by the vehicle manufacturer. Distribute the load evenly, taking care not to exceed the vehicle manufacturer's roof rack load limit. A roof rack laden with luggage increases fuel consumption, so remember this when calculating mileage per gallon, and it also reduces stability, especially when cornering.

M

MEDICAL TREATMENT

Travellers who normally take certain medicines should ensure they have a sufficient supply since they may be very difficult to get abroad.

Those with certain medical conditions (diabetes or coronary artery diseases, for example) should get a letter from their doctor giving treatment details. Some Continental doctors will understand a letter written in English, but it is better to have it translated into the language of the country you intend to visit. The AA cannot make translations.

Travellers who, for legitimate health reasons, carry drugs (see also Customs regulations for the United Kingdom) or appliances (e.g., a hypodermic syringe), may have difficulty with Customs or other authorities. They should carry translations which describe their special condition and appropriate treatment in the language of the country they intend to visit to present to Customs. Similarly, people with special dietary requirements may find translations helpful in hotels and restaurants.

The National Health Service is available in the UK only, and medical expenses incurred overseas cannot be reimbursed by the UK Government. There are reciprocal health agreements with most of the countries in this guide, but you should not rely exclusively on these arrangements, as the cover provided under the respective national schemes is not always comprehensive. (For instance, the cost of bringing a person back to the UK in the event of illness or death is never covered). The full costs of medical care must be paid in Andorra and Switzerland. Therefore, you are strongly advised to take out adequate insurance cover before leaving the UK, such as the AA's Personal Travel Insurance.

Urgent medical treatment in the event of an accident or unforeseen illness is available for most visitors at reduced costs, from the health care schemes of those countries with whom the UK has health-care arrangements. Details are in the Department of Health booklet T6 which also gives advice about health precautions and vaccinations. Free copies are available from main post offices or by ringing the Health Literature Line on 0800 555 777 any time, free of charge. In some of these countries, visitors can obtain urgently needed treatment by showing their UK passport, but in some an NHS medical card must be produced, and in most European Economic Area countries a certificate of entitlement (E111) is necessary. The E111 can be obtained over the counter of the post office on completion of the forms incorporated in booklet T6. However, the E111 must be stamped and signed by the post office clerk to be valid. Residents of the Republic of Ireland must apply to their Regional Health Board for an E111.

MINIBUS

A minibus constructed and equipped to carry 10 or more persons (including the driver) and used outside the UK is subject to the regulations governing international bus and coach journeys, including controls on drivers' hours. Such vehicles must weigh no more than 3.5 tonnes (gross vehicle weight) or 4.25 tonnes including any specialist equipment for the carriage of disabled passengers. The vehicle must be fitted with a tachograph (except for journeys between UK and Republic of Ireland) and carry documentation to show the type of journey being made. The documentation requirements are determined by whether the vehicle is owned or hired and countries to be visited, as follows:

a Outside EU (except Norway and Switzerland)- ASOR waybills for closed door tours (round trips carrying same group of passengers) and model control document. For other kinds of tours or journeys to countries outside the EU, contact:

The Department of the Environment, Transport and the Regions, Road Haulage Division, Great Minster House, 76 Marsham

Street, London SW1P 4DR, phone 0171 676 2766 for advice.

b Inside EU - own account certificate (owned vehicle); EU passenger waybills (hired vehicle).

For vehicles registered and driven by holders of licences issued in UK (England, Scotland, Wales and Northern Ireland), contact:

a Confederation of Passenger Transport UK, Imperial House, 15-19 Kingsway, London WC2B 6UN, (tel 0171-240 3131) for model control document and waybills.

b Department of the Environment, Transport and the Regions, International Road Freight Office, Westgate House, Westgate Road, Newcastle-upon-Tyne NE1 1TW(0191 201 4090) for own account certificate.

A person of 21 years or over and holding a car driving licence with D1 restricted entitlement (i.e. not for hire or reward) may drive a minibus with up to 16 passenger seats abroad, provided it is not a hire or reward operation. See Section 1 (5) of the Public Passenger Vehicles Act 1981 for a definition of 'hire or reward'. As a result of subsequent court rulings, that definition has been further refined to encompass situations in which there is payment:
of cash or kind - whether paid directly or indirectly
- whether paid by the passenger or someone else on their behalf
- even when paid in the course of an arrangement which is a business activity or an activity which has a 'business-like' nature (i.e. rather more than a social arrangement).
The effect of this is that most trips abroad by school or scout troops or similar organisations, running a minibus, could very likely be classed by the courts as 'hire or reward' operations for which full D1 entitlement is needed. Drivers involved in such operations are, therefore, advised to obtain a D1 licence; to do this they will need to pass a separate driving test for mimibus. Drivers or organisers are also advised

in any event to check the position with their insurance company.

For vehicles registered in the Republic of Ireland, contact the Department of Transport, Road Haulage Section, Setanta Centre, South Frederick Street, Dublin 2 for details about tachographs, and the Government Publications Sales Office, Molesworth Street, Dublin 2 for information about documentation.

MIRRORS

When driving or towing on the Continent on the right, it is essential to have clear all-round vision. Ideally, external rear-view mirrors should be fitted to both sides of your vehicle, but certainly on the left, to allow for driving on the right.

When towing a caravan it is essential to fit mirror accessories for better rear vision. The accessories available include clip-on extensions, arms to extend wing mirrors; long-arm wing or door mirror, and periscopes fitted on the car roof to reflect the rear view through the caravan window. A periscope and wing mirrors used together are best. The longer the mirror arm is, the more rigid its mounting has to be. Some mirrors have supporting legs or extra brackets to minimise vibration. A mirror mounted on the door pillar gives a wide field of vision because it is close to the driver, but it is at a greater angle to the forward line of sight. Convex mirrors give an even wider field of vision, but practice is needed in judging distance due to the diminished image.

MOTOR INSURANCE

When driving abroad you must carry your certificate of motor insurance with you at all times. Third-party is the minimum legal requirement in most countries. Therefore, before taking a motor vehicle, caravan or trailer abroad, contact your motor insurer or broker to notify them of your intentions and ask their advice. Some insurers will extend your UK or Republic of Ireland motor policy to apply in the countries you plan to visit free of charge, others may charge an additional premium. It is most important to know the level of cover you will actually have and what documents you will

need to prove it. If visiting Spain, see also the country introduction under 'Bail Bond'.

Of the countries covered by this guide, a Green Card is compulsory in Andorra. This document is issued by your motor insurer and provides internationally recognised proof of insurance. The Green Card must be signed on receipt as it will not be accepted without the signature of the insured.

Motorists can obtain expert advice through AA Insurance Services for all types of insurance. Several special schemes have been arranged with leading insurers at economic premiums. More information is available from AA Insurance Services Ltd, PO Box 2AA, Newcastle upon Tyne NE99 2AA.

Finally, do check to make sure that you are covered against damage in transit (e.g. on the ferry) when the vehicle is not being driven.

MOTORING CLUBS ON THE CONTINENT

The Alliance Internationale de Tourisme (AIT) is the largest federation of touring and motoring associations in the world, and it is through this network that the AA is able to offer its members the widest possible information service. Tourists visiting a country where there is an AIT club may use its advisory services on proof of membership of their home AIT club. AA members should seek the advice of the AA before setting out overseas and should approach the overseas AIT club for information on arrival.

OFF-SITE CAMPING

Off-site camping may contravene local regulations. You are strongly advised never to camp by the roadside and in isolated areas.

ORANGE BADGE SCHEME FOR DRIVERS WITH DISABILITIES AND PASSENGERS

Some European countries which operate national schemes of parking concessions for the disabled have reciprocal arrangements whereby visitors with disabilities get the same concessions by displaying their national badge. In some countries responsibility for the concessions rests with individual local authorities and in some cases they may not be generally available. You will have to enquire locally to find out about specific requirements.

As in the UK, these arrangements apply only to badge-holders themselves, and the concessions are not for the benefit of able-bodied companions. Wrongful display of the orange badge may incur whatever local penalties are imposed.

OVERLOADING

This can create risks, and in most countries the offence can involve on-the-spot fines (see Police fines). You would also be made to reduce the load to an acceptable level before being allowed to continue your journey.

The maximum loaded weight, and its distribution between front and rear axles, is decided by the vehicle manufacturer, and if your owner's handbook does not give these facts, contact the manufacturer direct. There is a public weighbridge in all districts, and when the car is fully loaded (including driver and passengers) use this to check that the vehicle is within the limits.

Load your vehicle carefully so that no lights, reflectors, or number plates are masked, and the driver's view is not impaired. All luggage loaded on a roof-rack must be tightly secured, and should not exceed the vehicle manufacturer's recommended maximum limit. Any projections beyond the front, rear, or sides of a vehicle, that may not be noticed by other drivers, must be clearly marked. Specific limits apply to projections and may vary from country to country.

OVERTAKING

When overtaking on roads with two lanes or more in each direction, signal in good time, and also signal your return to the inside lane. Do not remain in any other lane. Failure to comply with this regulation, particularly in France, will incur an on-the-spot fine (immediate deposit in France) - see Police fines.

Always overtake on the left and use your horn to warn the driver (except where the use of a horn is banned). Do check the vehicles behind before overtaking. Do not overtake at level crossings, intersections, the crest of a hill or pedestrian crossings. When being overtaken, keep to the right and reduce speed if necessary.

PARKING

Parking is a problem everywhere in Europe, and the police are extremely strict with offenders. Heavy fines are imposed and unaccompanied offending cars can be towed away. Besides being inconvenient, heavy charges are imposed for the recovery of impounded vehicles. Find out about local parking regulations and make sure you understand all relative signs. As a rule, always park on the right-hand side of the road or at an authorised place. As far as possible, park off the main carriageway, but not in cycle or bus lanes.

PASSENGERS

In many countries outside the UK, it is an offence to carry more passengers in a car than the vehicle is constructed to seat, and some have regulations as to how the passengers should be seated. For information about regulations applied to visiting foreigners, see country introductions.

Special regulations (see Minibus) apply to passenger-carrying vehicles constructed and equipped to carry more than 10 passengers, including the driver.

PASSPORTS

Each person must hold, or be named on, a valid passport. Carry your passport at all times and, as an extra precaution, a separate note of the number, date and place of issue. There is now only one type of passport, the standard 10-year passport.

Standard UK passports are issued to British Nationals, i.e. British Citizens, British Dependent Territories Citizens, British Overseas Citizens, British Nationals (Overseas), British Subjects, and British Protected Persons. A standard UK passport is valid for travel to all countries in the world - but you must check whether a visa is also required. From 5 October 1998 it has been necessary for all children to have their own passports; children entered on the existing passport of a parent before 5 October 1998 may of course remain until the passport expires. All passports issued to children under the age of 16 years are issued for 5 years only. After 5 years a new application must be made and the full fee paid.

Full information and application forms are available, on the UK mainland, from main Post Offices, branches of Lloyds Bank, World Choice Travel Agents, or from one of the Passport Offices in Belfast, Douglas (Isle of Man), Glasgow, Liverpool, London, Newport (Gwent), Peterborough, St Helier (Jersey) and St Peter Port (Guernsey). Application for a standard passport should be made to the appropriate area Passport Office. Allow 15 working days Apr-Aug, when demand is at its highest, and 10 working days for the rest of the year.

Irish citizens who require an Irish Passport, and who are resident either in the Dublin metropolitan area or in Northern Ireland should apply to the Passport Office, Dublin; if, however, they are resident elsewhere in the Irish Republic, they should apply through the nearest Garda station. Irish citizens resident in Britain should apply to the Irish Embassy in London.

PAYMENT CARDS

Credit, debit and charge cards are as convenient to use abroad as they are at home. Their use is subject to the conditions set out by the issuing company which, on request, will provide full information. Establishments display the symbols of cards which they accept.

PETROL/DIESEL

You will find familiar brands and comparable grades of petrol along the main routes in most countries. However, some countries no longer sell leaded petrol (see Germany and Netherlands country introductions under Petrol). You will normally have to buy a minimum of 5 litres (just over a gallon) but it is wise to keep the tank topped up, particularly in more remote areas. Remember when

calculating mileage per gallon that the extra weight of a caravan or roof rack increases petrol consumption. It is best to use a locking filler cap. Some garages may close between 12.00hrs and 15.00hrs, but petrol is generally available, with 24-hour service on motorways. Prices for petrol on motorways will normally be higher than elsewhere; self-service pumps will be slightly cheaper. The current position on petrol prices can be checked with the AA. Make sure you know the fuel requirement of the vehicle before you go (leaded petrol, unleaded premium, unleaded super or diesel) and whether or not the car has an exhaust catalyst. Catalyst-equipped petrol cars will usually have a small fuel filler neck, to prevent the use of the larger sized nozzle dispensing leaded petrol. If in doubt, check with a franchised dealer, or with the AA.

Some countries are supplying 98 octane unleaded petrol either in addition to, or instead of, 95 octane. The name may be 'super plus' or 'premium' but look for the octane rating 98. You should be careful to use the recommended type of fuel, particularly if your car has a catalytic converter, and the octane grade should be the same or higher. If you accidentally fill the tank of a catalyst-equipped car with leaded fuel, the best course, to avoid any possible reduction in the effectiveness of the catalyst, will be to have the tank drained and refilled with unleaded. However, if your car doesn't have a catalyst but is designed or converted for unleaded petrol, an accidental filling with leaded fuel will do no harm; simply go back to unleaded at the next fill. If your car requires leaded fuel and you fill with unleaded, avoid hard use of the engine until about half the tank is used, then fill with leaded or an additised lead-substitute petrol.

Diesel fuel is generally known as 'diesel' or 'gas-oil'. Although readily available it is probably more inconvenient to run out of diesel, and it is wise to keep the tank topped up. If more than about a gallon of petrol is put into the tank of a diesel car (or vice versa) you must drain the tank and refill with the correct fuel before the engine is started.

NOTE: **Importing fuel.** While you may wish to carry a reserve supply of fuel in a can, remember that all operators (ferry, motorail etc.) will either forbid the carriage of fuel in spare cans or insist that spare cans must be empty. In Italy and Luxembourg motorists are forbidden to carry petrol in cans in the vehicle. If your vehicle has LPG or a dual fuel system, check also with rail, ferry and tunnel operators.

POLICE FINES

Some countries impose on-the-spot fines for minor traffic offences, which vary in amount according to the offence and the country concerned. Others (e.g. France) impose an immediate deposit, and subsequently levy a fine which may be the same as, or greater or lesser than, this sum. Fines are normally paid in cash in the local currency, either to the police or at a local post office against a ticket issued by the police. The amount can exceed the equivalent of £1000 for the most serious offences. The reason for the fines is to penalise, and to keep minor motoring offences out of the law courts.

Disputing the fine usually leads to a court appearance, delays and extra expense. If the fine is not paid, legal proceedings will usually follow. Some countries immobilise vehicles until a fine is paid, and may sell it to pay the penalty imposed.

Once paid, a fine cannot be recovered, but a receipt should always be obtained as proof of payment. AA members who need assistance in any motoring matter involving local police should apply to the legal department of the relevant national motoring organisation.

POLLUTION

Pollution of seawater at certain Continental coastal resorts, including the Mediterranean, may still represent a health hazard, although the general situation is improving. Countries of the European Union publish detailed information on the quality of their bathing beaches, including maps, which are available from national authorities and the European Union. In many (though not all) popular resorts where the water quality may present risk, signs (generally small) are erected which forbid bathing:

FRENCH

| No bathing | Défense de se baigner |
| Bathing prohibited | Il est défendu de se baigner |

ITALIAN

| No bathing | Vietato bagnarsi |
| Bathing prohibited | Evietato bagnarsi |

SPANISH

| No bathing | Prohibido bañarse |
| Bathing prohibited | Se prohibe bañarse |

POSTE RESTANTE

If you are uncertain of having a precise address, you can be contacted through the local poste restante. Before leaving the UK notify your approximate whereabouts abroad at given times. If you expect mail, call with your passport at the main post office of the town where you are staying. To ensure that the arrival of correspondence will coincide with your stay, your correspondent should check with the post office before posting, as delivery times differ throughout Europe, and appropriate allowances must be made. It is important that the recipient's name be written in full: Mr John Smith, Poste Restante, Sintra, Portugal. Do not use 'Esq'.

The Italian equivalent of 'Poste Restante' is 'Fermo in Posta' plus the name of the town or village and the province or region, if necessary. The Spanish equivalent is 'Lista de Correos'. Correspondence will be lodged at the main post office, and you will need proof of identity (e.g. a passport) to collect it.

For all other countries, correspondence should be addressed as in the 'Mr John Smith' example.

PRIORITY INCLUDING ROUNDABOUTS

(See also country introductions)
The general rule is to give way to traffic entering a junction from the right, but this is sometimes varied at roundabouts (see below). This is one aspect of Continental driving which may cause British drivers the most confusion. Road signs indicate priority or loss of priority, and tourists must be sure that they understand such signs.

Great care should be taken at intersections, and tourists should never rely on being ceded the right of way, particularly in small towns and villages where local, often slow moving, traffic - farm tractors etc., will assume right of way regardless of oncoming traffic. Always give way to public services and military vehicles, blind and disabled people, funerals and marching columns. Vehicles such as buses and coaches will expect, and should be allowed, priority.

Generally, priority at roundabouts is given to vehicles entering the roundabout unless signposted to the contrary (see France). This is a reversal of the UK and Republic of Ireland rule, and particular care should be exercised when circulating in an anti-clockwise direction on a roundabout. It is advisable to keep to the outside lane if possible, to make your exit easier.

R

RADIO TELEPHONE/CITIZENS' BAND RADIOS, TRANSMITTERS AND DETECTION DEVICES

Many countries control the temporary importation and use of radio telephones and radio transmitters. If your vehicle contains such equipment, whether fitted or portable, approach the AA for guidance before departure.

The use or even possession of devices, whether inside or outside vehicles, to detect police radar speed traps is illegal in most countries. Penalties are severe, including confiscation of the equipment, payment of an immediate deposit to serve as collateral against any fine subsequently levied, and/or a driving ban. Finally, if the case is viewed sufficiently seriously, confiscation of vehicle and even imprisonment may result.

REGISTRATION DOCUMENT

You must take the registration document with you. The document should be in your name

and kept with you. If you do not have a registration document, apply to a Vehicle Registration Office (in Northern Ireland, a Local Vehicle Licensing Office) for a temporary certificate of registration (V379) to cover the period away. The address of your nearest Vehicle Registration Office is in the local telephone directory or in leaflet V100, available from post offices. You should apply well in advance of your journey, as it may take up to two weeks to issue the document if you are not already recorded as the vehicle keeper. Proof of identity (e.g. driving licence) and proof of ownership (e.g. bill of sale), should be produced for the Vehicle Registration Office.

If you plan to use a borrowed vehicle, the V5 must be accompanied by a letter of authority to use the vehicle from the registered keeper. If you plan to use a hired/leased or company vehicle, the V5 will not normally be available and you will need a Vehicle on Hire Certificate (VE103A). Generally the hiring/leasing operator or company transport will provide the certificate, but individual users may apply direct if necessary. For advice on the procedure to follow for personal or postal applications or to obtain an application form, call the AA Information Centre on 0990 500 600.

ROAD SIGNS

Most road signs throughout Europe conform to international standards and most will be familiar. Watch for road markings - do not cross a solid white or yellow line marked on the road centre. In Belgium there are three official languages, and signs will be in Dutch, French or German, see Belgian country information under Roads for further information. In the Basque and Catalonian areas of Spain local and national place names appear on signposts, see the country introduction for Spain for further information.

RULE OF THE ROAD

In all countries in this guide, drive on the right and overtake on the left.

S

SEAT BELTS
All countries in this guide require wearing of seat belts.

SPARES
The spares you should carry depend on the vehicle and how long you are likely to be away. Useful items include a pair of windscreen wiper blades, a length of electrical cable and a torch.

Remember that when ordering spare parts for dispatch abroad, you must be able to identify them clearly - by the manufacturer's part numbers if known. Always quote your engine and vehicle identification (VIN). See also Lights.

SPEED LIMITS
It is important to observe speed limits at all times. Remember that it can be an offence to travel so slowly as to obstruct traffic flow without good reason. Offenders may be fined, and driving licences confiscated on the spot, causing great inconvenience and possible expense.

The standard legal limits are given in the appropriate country introductions for private cars and for car-caravan-trailer combinations, but these may be varied by road signs, and where such signs are displayed the lower limit applies. At certain times, limits may also be temporarily varied, so watch out for the appropriate signs.

T

TOLLS
Tolls are payable on most motorways in France, Italy, Portugal, Spain and on sections in Austria. Over long distances, the toll charges can be quite considerable. Compare the cost against time and convenience (e.g., overnight stops), particularly as some of the all-purpose roads are often fast.

Always have some local currency ready to pay the tolls, as travellers cheques etc. are not acceptable at toll booths. Credit cards are accepted at toll booths in France and Spain. In Austria and Switzerland authorities levy a tax for use of motorway networks. See under Motorway tax in the respective country introduction for further information.

TOURIST INFORMATION
National tourist offices are well equipped to deal with enquiries relating to their countries. They are particularly useful for information on current events, tourist attractions, car hire, equipment hire and specific activities such as skin-diving, gliding, horse-riding, etc. The offices in London (see country introductions for addresses) are helpful, but the local offices overseas merit a visit when you arrive at your destination for information not available elsewhere.

TRAFFIC LIGHTS
In principal cities and towns, traffic lights operate in a way similar to those in the United Kingdom, although they are sometimes suspended over the roadway. The density of the light may be so poor that lights could be missed - especially those overhead. There is usually only one set on the right-hand side of the road some distance before the road junction, and if you stop too close to the corner the lights will not be visible. Look out for 'filter' lights enabling you to turn right at a junction against the main lights. If you wish to go straight ahead, do not enter a lane leading to 'filter' lights or you may obstruct traffic trying to turn right.

TRAMS
Trams take priority over other vehicles. Always give way to passengers boarding and alighting. Never position a vehicle so that it impedes the free passage of a tram. Trams must be overtaken on the right, except in one-way streets.

TRAVELLERS CHEQUES
We recommend that you take travellers cheques. Local currency cheques can often be

used like cash. Sterling cheques may be changed for local currency notes at banks. Your bank will be able to recommend currency travellers cheques for the countries your are visiting.

TYRES

Inspect your tyres carefully: if you think they are likely to be worn down to below 2mm before you get back, replace them before you leave. If you notice uneven wear, scuffed treads, or damaged walls, get expert advice on whether the tyres are suitable for further use.

The regulations in the UK governing tyres requires a minimum tread depth of 1.6mm over the central three-quarters of the tyre around the whole circumference. As many countries have similar requirements, the AA recommends at least 2mm of tread.

Check the car handbook for recommended tyre pressures. Different tyre pressures will be recommended for a fully loaded car travelling at motorway speeds. Remember pressures can only be checked accurately when the tyres are cold, and don't forget the spare wheel.

If towing a caravan find out the recommended tyre pressures from the caravan manufacturer. These will vary with the type and size of tyre. For winter or snow tyres see cold-weather touring.

V

VEHICLE EXCISE LICENCE

When taking a vehicle out of the UK for a temporary visit remember that the vehicle excise licence (tax disc) needs to be valid on your return*. Therefore, if it will expire while you are abroad, you can apply by post to a Head Post Office for a tax disc up to 42 days in advance of the expiry date of your present disc. You should explain why you want it in advance, and ask for it to be posted to you before you leave, or to your address abroad. However, your application form must always be completed with your UK address.

To find out which post office in your area offers this service, you should contact Post Office Customer Services Unit listed in your local telephone directory. Residents of the Republic of Ireland should contact their Local Vehicle Registration Office.

Residents of Northern Ireland must apply to Driver and Vehicle Licensing Northern Ireland, Vehicle Licensing Division, County Hall, Coleraine BT51 3HS.

*Agreement within the EU provides for the temporary use of foreign-registered vehicles within the member states. A vehicle which is properly registered and taxed in its home country should not be subject to the domestic taxation and registration laws of the host country during a temporary stay.

VISA

EU citizens travelling within the EU do not require visas. A visa is not normally required by United Kingdom and Republic of Ireland passport holders when visiting non-EU countries within Western Europe for periods of three months or less. However, if you hold a passport of any other nationality, a UK passport not issued in this country, or if you are in any doubt at all, check with the embassies or consulates of the countries you intend to visit.

VISITORS' REGISTRATION

In most countries registration formalities are to be undertaken by visitors spending up to three months. However, this formality is usually satisfied by completing a card or certificate when booking into a hotel, campsite or other accommodation. If you are staying with friends or relatives it is usually the responsibility of the host to seek advice from the police within 24 hours of the arrival of guests.

If you intend visiting a country for longer than three months and/or the circumstances are not as described above, then you should make the appropriate enquiries before your departure from the UK.

W

WARM-CLIMATE TOURING

In hot weather, and at high altitudes excessive heat in the engine compartment can cause fuel problems. If you are towing a caravan consult the manufacturers of your towing vehicle about the limitations of the cooling system, and the operating temperature of the gearbox fluid if automatic transmission is fitted (see Automatic gearboxes).

WARNING TRIANGLES/
HAZARD WARNING LIGHTS

The use of a warning triangle is compulsory in most Continental countries. It should be placed on the road behind a stopped vehicle to warn traffic approaching from the rear of an obstruction ahead. The triangle should be used when a vehicle has stopped for any reason - not just breakdowns. It should be placed in such a position as to be clearly visible up to 100m (109yds) by day and night, about 60cm (2ft) from the edge of the road, but not in such a position as to present a danger to oncoming traffic. It should be set up about 30m (33yds) behind the obstruction, but this distance should be increased to 100m (109yds) on motorways. A warning triangle is not required for two-wheeled vehicles.

Although four flashing indicators are allowed in the countries covered by this guide, they in no way affect the regulations governing the use of warning triangles. Generally, hazard warning lights should not be used in place of a triangle, although they may complement it. See the country introductions for France, Netherlands and Switzerland. See also Breakdown.

WEATHER INFORMATION

UK regional weather reports are provided direct from the Met. Office by the AA Weatherwatch recorded information service. By calling the following premium rate numbers you will hear the weather report for your chosen area followed by a report for the next four days:

National Forecast	* 0336 401 130
London & SE England	0336 401 131
West Country	0336 401 132
Wales	0336 401 133
Midlands	0336 401 134
East Anglia	0336 401 135
NW England	0336 401 136
NE England	0336 401 137
Scotland	0336 401 138
Northern Ireland	0336 401 139

For weather reports for crossing the Channel and northern France, call 0336 401 361, whilst Continental Roadwatch on 0336 401 904 provides information on traffic conditions to and from ferry ports, ferry news and details of major European events. A world-wide, city-by-city six-day weather forecast is also available on 0336 411 212.

For other weather information for the UK and the Continent (but not road conditions) please contact:

> The Met Office
> Enquiries Officer
> London Road
> Bracknell
> Berkshire RG12 2SZ

or telephone 01344 854455 during normal office hours.

* Calls are charged at 50p per minute at all times.

WHEEL OR SNOW CHAINS

See under Cold-weather touring.

Taking your own tent, caravan or motorhome abroad?

Eurocamp Independent
FREEPOST ALM 1584
Hartford Manor
NORTHWICH
Cheshire
CW8 1BF

Eurocamp
Independent

The easy way to take your own tent, trailer tent, caravan or motorhome to Europe.

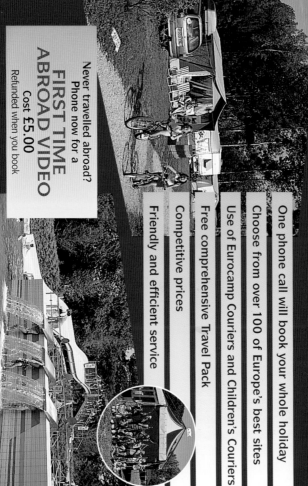

- One phone call will book your whole holiday
- Choose from over 100 of Europe's best sites
- Use of Eurocamp Couriers and Children's Couriers
- Free comprehensive Travel Pack
- Competitive prices
- Friendly and efficient service

Mr/Mrs/Miss _____ Initials _____

Surname _____

Address _____

_____ Postcode _____

How many adults are in your party? _____

If applicable what are the ages of your children? _____

Do you have a:

tent ☐ trailer tent ☐ caravan ☐ motorhome ☐

How many times have you taken your own equipment abroad? _____

Tick if you do not wish to receive direct mail from other carefully screened companies whose products or services we feel may be of interest ☐

Eurocamp
Independent

AA

YOUR Holiday Park

PARC DE VACANCES
Sanguli Salou
CAMPING & BUNGALOW PARK

IPING & BUNGALOW PARK SANGULÍ, situated in Salou in the heart of the
ta Daurada and only 50 m from the beach, offers all amenities only a
-class camping site can offer.

animation programme for young and old; daily entertainment in an
eptional amphitheatre with a capacity of 2000 seats.

swimming pools, 2 supermarkets, 4 bars, 2 children's playgrounds,
shop, restaurant, take-away-meals, launderette, etc.

orts facilities, such as tennis, mini-golf, squash, indoor football, basketball,
nque, volleyball, etc.

modern ablution blocks, offering the highest level of hygiene and comfort (facilities for the disabled
babies etc.).

his, surrounded by a unique nature and precious gardens, makes CAMPING & BUNGALOW
K SANGULÍ your ideal holiday destination.

ial prices in low season

ded "Camp Site of the Year 1988" by the Catalan Government, "Camp Site of the
1992" by the Royal Dutch Touring Club ANWB, "Camp Site of the Year 1994"
e French magazine "Caravanier" .

Prolongació carrer E, s/n. - Apartado de Correos 123.
43840 SALOU (Tarragona) España
: 977 38 16 41 - 977 38 16 98 - Fax: 977 38 46 16
/www.sanguli.es   e-mail: mail@sanguli.es

"This one I can recommend"

Please send further information

Name ....
Street ....
Town ....
Country ....

AA CAMPING
& CARAVANING

5 ha. meadow with shade. The site has good access for caravans and has convenient pitches, free hot water in showers and washing basins, electric connections 220V, washing machines, air conditioned bar and restaurant meals to take away, grocer's, leisure room, sports and games grounds. Tennis and swimming pools.
Mobile homes for hire.
Reduction: 20% June & September, 30% off-season.
Open: 28.3 – 20.9. We speak English.
07150 VALLON PONT D'ARC Tel: 04.75.88.06.63. Fax: 04.75.37.14.97
Internet: http://www.ardechois-camping.com

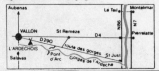

Only 40 km from Santander (ferry) and 70 km from Bilbao (ferry), easily and quickly reached along the magnificent, new, toll-free autovia and the coast roads.

A 25 ha. holiday site with a large (4 ha) recreation and sports area and a precious, 8 ha natural park with animals in semiliberty.

Modern, first category installations. Beautifull surroundings with direct access to wide, clean beaches. Surrounded by meadows and woods.

Service and comfort for the most exacting guests.Properly marked pitches.

English spoken. Open from Easter to 30th September.

Your beautiful holiday destination in SPAIN

CAMPING
PLAYA JOYEL

E-39180 NOJA
(SANTANDER, CANTABRIA)
SPAIN
Tel. (34) 942 63 00 81
Fax (34) 942 63 12 94

CAMPING + BUNGALOWS
"PARK PLAYA BARÁ"

Subtropical exotica on Spain's golden coast - Costa Daurada.

A botanical garden • A campers paradise. Spanish order for Touristic Merits and Catalan Government Tourism Diploma. Officially recommended by the leading European Automobile and Camping Clubs. ANWB Camp Site of the Year 1991. Garden like, terraced site with excellent installations.
Sand and rock beach with camp owned bar, near elegant holiday village - no high buildings, ideal for walks, not far from typical fishing village and holiday resort with many shopping possibilities. Dry, sunny climate throughout. Large, garden like pitches with conn. f. electr., water and waste water disposal, many w. own marble washing basins. The most modern sanatary install. w. free hot water, individual wash cabins, compl. children's baths, install. f. disabled, chem. toilets. Car wash. Heated swimming pool (23°), solarium. Large, compl. sports area (tennis, squash, volley, basket, large football ground, roller skating, minigolf, bicycle track, table tennis). Children's playground, medical service, safe deposit, money exchange. Bar, grill, restaurant, superm., souvenirs. Animation for all ages - Roman amphitheatre (dance, folklore, cultural progr. and many surprises). A 100% family camp with nice atmosphere for nature loving guests. Radio and tv forbidden on part of camp. Bungalows for hire. Open: 10.3 - 30.9. Special fees in off-season. 10% P/N reduction in main season if you stay at least 10 days. English spoken. Ask for our brochure and more inf. and/or reservation. Acces: A-7 (Barcelona-Tarragona), exit (sortida) nr. 31 (Vendrell-Coma-ruga), on the N-340 direct. Tarragona till Roman Arch, turn around arch and entrance on your right.

From 10.3-20.6 &1.9.-30.9.
50% reduction P/N
90% on tennis, minigolf, surf P/N penioners.
NEW, heated (26°) swimming pools with free jacuzzi.
At only 15 min. from the attraction park "PORT AVENTURA"

E-43883 RODA DE BERÀ (TARRAGONA) • Tel. (34) 977 802 701 • Fax (34) 977 800 456 • www.barapark.es • E-mail: barapark@lix.intercom.es

Lauterbrunnen "Jungfrau"

The ideal family campsite for both summer and winter, at the foot of those mountain giants the Eiger, Mönch and Jungfrau. Set in the heart of the "Jungfrau" region, famous throughout the world for its walking and skiing. Open throughout the year. Ticket sales for all cable cars. We shall be pleased to provide information on reduced-rate excursions (eg. Jungfraujoch, Schilthorn). Modern facilities with separate facilities for the disabled. Restaurant, large grocery shop/kiosk and children's playground. Mountain bikes for hire. Ideal for touring caravans (disposal facilities). Bungalows, caravans and inexpensive rooms for rent. During the winter free practice ski lift and cross-country loipe on the site plus free ski bus to cable car valley stations. Winter season sites. Ask for our brochure.

Important!!! Turn right 100m before the church
Families von Allmen, Nolan and Fuchs
Tel: 0041 33 856 20 10, Fax 33 856 20 20

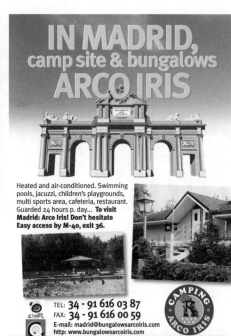

COSTA DAURADA –SPAIN–

An ideal camp site to enjoy nature, the sun, a shallow beach and aquatic sports. The mild climate permits you to swim in the sea from April to October. Good location for visits to the numerous important Roman ruins in and around Tarragona - Tarraco was the provincial capital of the ancient empire. Also nearby are the old monasteries of Poblet, Santes Creus, Montserrat and other places of cultural interest.

THEME PARK "PORT AVENTURA" AT 14 KM.

CAMPING BUNGALOWS
TAMARIT Park
TARRAGONA

Unusually beautiful, quiet and isolated location (1km distance from the N-340 road and the railway line). Over 350-metre-long front to the beach. Restaurant-bar directly on the beach. Original CHILDREN' S programmes. 2 play grounds, ping-pong, we organize games constantly. Sports area with floodlit tennis courts, sports fields, etc. Now also swimming-pool of 500 m2.

OPEN THROUGHOUT THE YEAR. Off-season special prices and discounts of 35% for pensioners and students with students card. We speak English.

Access: A-7, exit (salida) no. 32, then take the N-340 towards Tarragona, at km. 1172 towards to the beach and turn left at the end of the road.

NATURE • SUN BEACH • AQUATIC SPORTS

CAMPING BUNGALOWS
TAMARIT Park
TARRAGONA

Tel. (34) 977 650 128
Fax (34) 977 650 451
E-43893 **TARRAGONA**
TAMARIT- **COSTA DAURADA**
Internet: http://www.tamarit.com
E-Mail: tamaritpark@tamarit.com

erkende camping
ANWB

BUNGALOWS

No other city has its lungs as close to its heart as Lisbon

900 hectares of green just a stone's throw away from the city centre.

800 camping accommodation units

170 equipped lots

A forest site - totally refurbished and open all the year round.

Swimming pool, restaurant, outdoor cafés, 2 multi-purpose sport centres, mini golf, shopping area, and games rooms.

70 bungalows

Swimming pool

For further information please contact us at:
Estrada da Circunvalação
1500 - 171 - LISBOA
Tel: 351-1-7609620
Fax: 351-1-7609633

Turismo de Lisboa

Portugal

LISBOA CAMPING

A camping or caravanning holiday in Europe can bring a closer insight into another country through the simple necessity of having to shop for food, whether it be in a supermarket, local shop or traditional market.

Every country has its own preferences and specialities, and there is an enormous range of regional cooking methods. Germany, Austria and Switzerland, for instance, have a taste for soured cabbage and vinegar pickles. In many parts of Austria, dumplings are a top favourite, while Vienna is noted for rich pastries. Then there is cheese; every country, and often every region, specially France, prides itself on the glory of its many types of cheeses, some made from goats' or sheeps' milk, or in Italy from buffalo milk as well as cows' milk. Dishes may be based on every imaginable portion of the inside of an edible animal and perhaps sometimes it's best not to ask! You will come across locally-made wines rarely seen elsewhere, and often delicious sweets, pastries and cakes.

Discovering these different foods is as much part of a holiday as visiting historic sites or soaking up the sun on beaches.

From Kaiserschmarrn
Discovering European

AUSTRIA:
Austria is bordered by Germany, Italy and Hungary, and its cuisine tends to reflect these many culinary influences. Charcuterie, ragoûts, and fresh water fish classics such as stuffed pike, fried carp and trout *au bleu*, as well as dishes based on poultry, cabbage, cream cheeses, onion and paprika are to be found throughout the country. The Tirol, in particular, is renowned for charcuterie and sauerkraut, Styria for spiced ragoûts (served with potatoes and mushrooms with bread or liver *knödel),* and roast meats with dumplings, whilst from Carinthia come *nudln,* a form of ravioli. *Tafelspitz* (boiled best beef) is the pride of Austrian cooks, but undoubtedly the most famous Austrian meat dish is *Wiener schnitzel* (escalope of veal, thinly beaten then rolled in egg and breadcrumbs before being pan fried and served with lemon). Austria is also famous for its pâtisserie: Linz offers *linzertorte,* a very rich, short pastry with ground nuts, flavoured with lemon and cinnamon, and topped with raspberry jam, *Nockerln* is a sweet soufflé from Salzburg, whence come also *Mozartkugeln,* delicious little chocolate balls. Famous Viennese pâtisserie includes *Sachertorte,* a rich chocolate cake, and *strudel,* wafer-thin pastry encasing a sweet filling. *Kaiserschmarrn,* 'Emperor's rubbish', was created when the Kaiser's chef was unable to serve a single whole pancake out of the frying pan and in despair created a new dish with chopped pancakes, currants and lemon juice.

BELGIUM:
Although famous for giving the world exquisite chocolates, and *moules et frites* (mussels and chips), Belgian cuisine does have other great classics and Belgians are great connoisseurs of shellfish of all sorts. *Hotchpotch* is a Flemish stew, made nowadays with oxtail cooked with cabbage, carrots, onions, leeks and potatoes. *Waterzooï,* another Flemish speciality, consists of fresh water fish and eel cooked in stock with herbs and vegetables, and finished with butter and cream; in Ghent the same dish is made with chicken. *Carbonnade,* slices of beef cooked in

o clafouti:

pecialities...

beer and onions, incorporates the Belgian national drink; *Chimay, Krieck, Orval, Trappistes, Gueuze,* are just a few of the many beers to be explored - try them with Belgian cheeses *Herve* or *boulettes de Charleroi.* The Belgians are also great pastry lovers, look out for Ghent *moques,* almond bread and gingerbread, Verviers brioches with sugar candy, Namur and Brussels waffles, and the wonderful *flamiche,* a cheese tart from Dimant.

FRANCE:
Alps/East - A cheese producing region with *Reblochon* the best known cheese and cheese fondue the best known traditional dish (made with *Gruyère,* dry white wine and Kirsch).

Alsace/Lorraine - An area of gastronomic importance taking in *tarte à l'oignon,* onion tart, or sauerkraut cooked with Riesling and Kirsch, and wonderful terrines, pâtés de foie gras with truffles, turkey cooked with chestnuts, or fricassée of chicken with cream. Famous *eaux de vies* of Kirsch, Mirabelle and Framboise are well worth sampling, and Alsace white wines include Riesling, Pinot Blanc, spicy Gewürztraminer, and Muscat.
Burgundy/Champagne - The gastronomy of Champagne, in contrast to its celebrated wine, is largely rustic - meat loaves, pâtés, and terrines of chicken, hare, goose or pigeon, blood sausages, and cheese fritters. However, wine-rich Burgundy considers itself to be the

very centre of French cuisine. Dijon mustard, Dijon blackcurrant liqueur (cassis), Dijon gingerbread, are famous, as are such classics as ham with parsley, coq au vin, boeuf à la Bourguignonne, chicken from Bresse, sausages, pâtés, and cheeses that include *Epoisses,* its orange crust washed in white wine. And delicious savoury cheese pastries, *gougères,* are found in many pastry and cake shops.
South West/Pyrénées - *Cassoulet,* the region's most famous dish, offers ingredients that vary from fresh pork to smoked pork sausages, garlic sausages, bacon, smoked ham, preserved goose or pork, duck, calves' feet, the rind of pork and pig's cheek, all cooked with white haricot beans.
Loire/Central - Throughout the region, charcuterie of rillettes, terrines and pâtés of game and foie gras with truffles, are well known. Cognac and candied fruits come from the Charente, whilst Limousin provides hare *en cabessal* and *clafouti* (a dessert of cherries in batter).

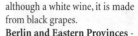

Brittany/Normandy - Breton crêpes, spread with butter and jam, or with chocolate, lemon or liqueur are justly famous. But look out for leg of lamb *à la Bretonne, boudin blanc* from Rennes, potted pork from Vallet, and fish cooked in the excellent Breton cider. Normandy, famous for dairy products, brings

studded with cloves of garlic and braised slowly in white wine with potatoes.
South Coast/Riviera - A vibrant cuisine best summed up by *pistou*, a thick vegetable soup with a spoonful of crushed basil and garlic mixed with oil, *bouillabaisse*, a fish stew served with *rouille* (red pepper,

although a white wine, it is made from black grapes.
Berlin and Eastern Provinces - Popular dishes in Berlin include boiled pork knuckle cooked with sour cream, and a Huguenot dish, chicken cooked in a fricassee with asparagus and mushrooms. At Christmas look out for *Baumkuchen* (huge Christmas cakes in the shape of trees), and that great classic cake, *Stollen* which originated in Dresden.
Central - Beer, ham, and rye bread flavoured with linseed, sesame or cumin, are justly famous in the Rhinelands. Dishes to look out for include Rhine salmon, game such as venison cutlets with mushrooms, and stuffed pheasant.
North - Dutch, Scandinavian and Polish influences dominate the cuisine here, with thick soups very popular - in Hamburg try the sweet and savoury cherry soup, or eel soup made with carrots, peas, asparagus, prunes and dried apricots. Chicken ragoût cooked with white wine, mushrooms and oysters or mussels is another speciality. Seafood is popular, especially herring, served smoked, marinated, fried, with horseradish, with mustard, with beer, or as rollmops, as well as turbot, oysters and eels.

chicken with cream and Calvados, and *tripe à la mode de Caen*. *Camembert* and *Pont l'Evêque* head a list of cheeses, Calvados, Benedictine and cider are the famous drinks.
Paris/North - Pork specialities from the Isle de France include *andouillettes, friandes Parisiens, fromage de tête de porc,* and *rillettes*; sweet or savoury vol-au-vents, and tarts have long been regarded as specialities of Paris. From Picardy comes *flamique à porions* , a leek tart, and from Amiens, macaroons.
Auvergne - The pork of the Auvergne is renowned - providing outstanding charcuterie of dried and smoked hams, sausages and black puddings. *Coq au vin* cooked with Chanturgues, a local red wine, is worth seeking out, as is *gigot Brayaude,* in which a leg of lamb is

garlic, olive oil), *tapenade*, a rich mixture based on olives, anchovy, capers and olive oil, and *pissaladière*, an onion tart from Nice.

GERMANY:
South East - Bavaria is noted for its charcuterie, especially hams, and for an astonishing array of sausages - for grilling, for sandwich spreads, for poaching - plus saveloys, black puddings and brawns. *Knödeln* are dumplings usually served with cream or melted butter. In Munich, during the Beer Festival, chickens are spit-roasted by the thousand.
South West - Black Forest saddle of venison served with apples stuffed with whortleberries is worth looking out for, as is Black Forest trout served *en papillotes*. In Baden, seek out a local wine, Weissherbst;

ITALY:
North West/Alps & Lakes - An important rice growing region, so expect a variety of risottos, some flavoured with white Piedmontese truffles, and drunk with the red wine, Barolo. Local pasta dishes are scarce, but *ravioli di zucca* (pumpkin ravioli) comes from Lombardy, as does minestrone soup. *Ossobucco*, shin of veal cooked with tomato, wine and vegetables, and *vitello tonnato,* veal with tuna, are typical Milanese dishes.

Venice/North - Polenta dressed with butter and cheese, and risottos are popular- look out for *risi e bisi* (rice with peas). Few native pasta dishes but try *pasta e fasoi* (pasta and beans) and *bigoli* - thick spaghetti, the only pasta made traditionally with whole-wheat flour. The ubiquitous tiramisu was created at Treviso.

North West/Med Coast - Roast meats are important here- look out for *bistecca alla Fiorentina*. Olive oil appears in everything including sweet fritters and in *castagnaccio*, a chestnut cake. *Panforte* is a speciality of Sienna, and *marzolino del chianti* is the best pecorino cheese of the area.

North East/Adriatic - Pasta, pasta, pasta - maccheroni, cavatieddi, laganelle, tiny gnocchi and recchietelle reign supreme. The olive oil of Bitonto in Puglia is of great repute, *pecorino* cheese is a speciality, and from Bari comes a pasta and fish dish called *ciambotto*. *Brodetto*, made all along the Adriatic coast, is the best fish soup in Italy,

Rome - Pasta features prominently in Roman cooking, and includes some of the most famous dishes, especially *carbonara*, and *amatriciana*. A classic is *saltimbocca alla Romana*, veal escallops with *prosciutto* ham and sage.

South - Pizza is part of the street life of Naples (never eaten at home), and the regions classic pasta sauces are based on the sweet, intensely flavoured plum tomato called San Marzano. *Fritto misto Napoletano* and *fritto misto di pesce* are other great Neapolitan delights. *Mustica* is a Calabrian speciality of salted, dried baby anchovies, stored in oil with lots of chilli . Here pasta is often dressed with a rich pork and chilli sauce.

The Islands - Sardinia is famous for *bottarga*, dried roe of tuna or grey mullet, served thinly sliced with olive oil and lemon juice; and *cassoeula*, fish cooked in tomatoes, wine and chilli. In Sicily, pasta is the mainstay of the local cuisine, the best known is *pasta con le sarde*, and cooling, delicious ice creams, *gellati*, and sorbets, *sorbetti*, are both made to perfection here.

colonies, is a frequent ingredient, and *rijsttafel* (rice table) - different dishes of spicy meat, fish, dipping sauces, and vegetables directly influenced by Indonesian cookery - is worth trying and offers a real banquet. Genever (Dutch gin, drunk neat and available as Young, Old, and in various fruit flavoured versions), Curaçao and Advocaat are well-known liqueurs.

NETHERLANDS:

The consumption of herring is treated seriously by the Dutch. Herring is often the centrepiece of meals - *haringsla*, a herring salad, and *Harlinger haringschotel*, Harlingen baked herring, are typical examples. However, the cuisine as a whole is based on a wide variety of salted and smoked meats and fish. Together with different breads, these make up the famous *koffietafel*, a cold lunchtime buffet - the main meal is served in the evening. One popular fish dish is *gebakken paling* fried fillets of eel, and split pea soup, *hazepepper*, jugged hare, and knuckle of veal with *sauerkraut*, are also worth seeking out. Rice, imported from former Dutch

SPAIN:

An old Spanish saying neatly sums up the climate and cuisine of Spain: *In the north they stew, in the middle they roast, in the south they fry*.

North East Coast - Fish dominates the cuisine here, with dishes such as the Catalan *zarzuela*, a fish and shellfish ragoût, and *arroz negro* (black rice), a Catalan version of paella, the rice blackened by cuttlefish ink. Interesting sauces compliment both meat and fish - especially the pungent garlic sauce *all-i-oli*, and the fiery red sauce, *romesco*. Charcuterie, especially air-dried hams, and delicious, slightly spicy black puddings, *butifarrones*, are also popular. *Crema catalana* is not dissimilar to crème brûlée.

Central - The central plains of Spain are famous for their roast meats - especially lambs and suckling pigs. But *pisto la Mancha*, a traditional form of ratatouille, but with the addition of chicken, ham or bacon. *Olla podrida,* a Madrid speciality, is a soup that combines meat and vegetables and where the different constituents are served separately, rather like the French *pot-au-feu.*

South East Coast - Valencia is the birthplace of the *paella,* Spain's national dish, and the only place, some say, to sample it. An Aragon speciality, also worth trying, is *carbonade de carne*, a pot-roasted beef whose sauce is enriched with the addition of dark chocolate.

North Coast - Asturias produces a special black smoked sausage, *morcilla,* used in the famous stew *fabada Asturiana,* whilst wild boar appears in dishes such as *jabali estofado.*

North East - This is the richest area from a culinary point of view with unusual dishes such as *marmitako* (fresh tuna fish), *bacaloa al pil-pil* (a salt cod dish), *piparrada,* an egg dish, *chocha a la Vizcaina,* woodcock, Basque style, and *lechona asada vasca* (roast suckling pig cooked in the Basque style), reflecting a varied cuisine.

North West - Galicia is home to Spain's greatest fishing ports, and is the place to eat seafood, whether as *tapas* (appetizers) especially of shell fish, considered to be the best in Spain, or in dishes such as *caldereta,* a northern Spanish fish stew, or *lubina al Santanderina,* Santander-style sea bass. Small red crabs, *necoras,* are a speciality of La Coruña, while scallops are a speciality of Santiago de Compostela.

Empanadas are little pies made with chicken, onions and peppers, sometimes seafood, and always eaten cold. The best known meat dish of the region is *lacon con grelos*, hand of pork boiled with green turnip tops served with potatoes and corn bread.

South - The best known Andalucian dish is *gazpacho,* a chilled soup based on oil, garlic, onion, bread and tomatoes, but look out for *ajo blanco* - the famous white *gazpacho* of Malaga. Because of the extreme heat in the south, the frying pan dominates the cuisine, and fried fish and meats appear ubiquitous, but dishes such as *carne machada a la Andaluza* (beef with almonds and olives), and *pollo al Jerez* (chicken with sherry), are worth seeking out.

PORTUGAL:

Salt cod (*bacalhão*) is the national fish of Portugal, there are said to be 1,000 recipes, but the best known are fried cod croquettes, salt cod and mussels cooked in wine with and tomatoes, and salt cod cooked in the oven on a bed of potatoes and onions and garnished with black olives and hard boiled eggs. In Lisbon and the south seafood predominates, especially lobster, but look out for *caldeirada,* a kind of bouillabaisse, and shellfish escabèche. On the sweet side, *Lampreia de ovos* is a cake made with egg yolks and decorated with crystallized fruit, and *lardo celeste* is made with almonds, lemon and cinnamon. Not often seen on wine lists outside Portugal is *Colares,* full bodied, agreeable red and white wine from the Lisbon area, and the rarer *Bucelas,* a white wine from the same area. In the north, Minho is famous for lively young *vinhos verdes* - green wines.

SWITZERLAND:

There is no typical Swiss cuisine, but Swiss chocolate requires no introduction, especially the quality of its milk chocolate bars. The country produces some 150 cheeses, the best known being *Gruyère, Emmental*, and *Vacherin.* Cheese fondue is a Swiss speciality, consisting of one or more cheeses melted in a special fondue dish. *Raclette*, from the canton of Valais in the south west, is a more rustic version of fondue made with *Bagnes, Conches* or *Orsières* cheese, and traditionally served with boiled potatoes and pickles and the local white wine, *Fendant. Swiss potée* shows off good regional charcuterie, especially smoked sausages, cooked here with cabbage and potatoes. *Rösti,* from Berne, is a large cake of grated potato, fried until golden and flavoured with bacon or sliced onion, in the Valais look out for *sil,* a dessert formerly served at weddings, and Thurgau produces an outstanding, unusual apple tart.

AA Hotel Booking Service

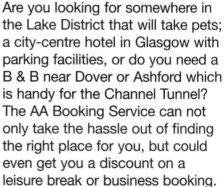

The AA Hotel Booking Service - Now AA Members have a free, simple way to find a place in the UK to stay for a week, weekend, or a one-night stopover.

Are you looking for somewhere in the Lake District that will take pets; a city-centre hotel in Glasgow with parking facilities, or do you need a B & B near Dover or Ashford which is handy for the Channel Tunnel? The AA Booking Service can not only take the hassle out of finding the right place for you, but could even get you a discount on a leisure break or business booking.

And if you are touring round the UK or Ireland, simply give the AA Hotel Booking Service your list of overnight stops, and from one phone call all your accommodation can be booked for you.

Telephone 0990 050505
to make a booking.
Office hours 8.30am - 7.30pm
Monday - Saturday.

Full listings of the 8,140 hotels and B & Bs available through the Hotel Booking Service can be found and booked at the AA's Internet Site:

http://www.theaa.co.uk/hotels

PRINCIPAL MOUNTAIN PASSES

It is best not to attempt to cross mountain passes at night, and daily schedules should make allowances for the comparatively slow speeds inevitable in mountainous areas.

Gravel surfaces (such as dirt and stone chips) vary considerably; they are dusty when dry, slippery when wet. Where known to exist, this type of surface has been noted. Road repairs can be carried out only during the summer, and may interrupt traffic. Precipitous road sides are rarely, if ever, totally unguarded; on the older roads, stone pillars are placed at close intervals. Gradient figures take the mean figure on hairpin bends, and may be steeper on the inside of the curves, particularly on the older roads.

CONVERSION TABLE GRADIENTS

All steep hill signs show the grade in percentage terms. The following conversion table may be used as a guide:

30%=1 in 3	14%=1 in 7
25%=1 in 4	12%=1 in 8
20%=1 in 5	11%=1 in 9
16%=1 in 6	10%=1 in 10

Before attempting late evening or early morning journeys across frontier passes, check the times of opening of the frontier controls. A number close at night; for example the Timmelsjoch border is closed between 20.00 and 07.00hrs and throughout the winter.

Always engage a low gear before either ascending or descending steep gradients, and keep well to the right-hand side of the road and avoid cutting corners. Avoid excessive use of brakes. If the engine overheats, pull off the road, making sure that you do not cause an obstruction, leave the engine idling, and put the heater controls (including the fan) into the maximum heat position. Under no circumstances should you remove the radiator cap until the engine has cooled down. Do not fill the coolant system of a hot engine with cold water.

Always engage a lower gear before taking a hairpin bend, give priority to vehicles ascending and remember that as your altitude increases, so your engine power decreases. Always give priority to postal coaches travelling in either direction. Their route is usually signposted.

CARAVANS

Passes suitable for caravans are indicated in the table on the following pages. Those shown to be negotiable by caravans are best used only by experienced drivers in cars with ample power; the rest are probably best avoided. A correct power-to-load ratio is always essential.

CONDITIONS IN WINTER

Winter conditions are given in italics in the last column. *UO* means usually open, although a severe fall of snow may temporarily obstruct the road for 24 to 48 hours, and wheel chains are often necessary; *OC* means occasionally closed, *UC*, usually closed, between the dates stated. Dates for opening and closing the passes are approximate only. Warning notices are usually posted at the foot of a pass if it is closed, or if chains or snow tyres should or must be used.

Wheel chains may be needed early and late in the season, and between short spells (a few hours) of obstruction. At these times, conditions are usually more difficult for caravans.

In fair weather, wheel chains or snow tyres are only necessary on the higher passes, but in severe weather you will probably need to use them (as a rough guide) at altitudes exceeding 610 metres (2000ft).

Pass and height	From To	Distances from summit and max gradient	Min width of road	Conditions (see previous page for key to abbreviations)
*Albula 2312 metres (7585ft) Switzerland	Tiefencastel 851 metres (2792ft) La Punt 1687 metres (5535ft)	30km 1 in 10 18.6 miles 9km 1 in 10 5.6 miles	3.5 metres 11ft 6in	UC Nov - early Jun. An inferior alternative to the Julier; tar and gravel, fine scenery. Alternative rail tunnel.
Allos 2250 metres (7382ft) France	Barcelonnette 1132 metres (3714ft) Colmars 1235 metres (4052ft)	20km 1 in 10 12.4 miles 24km 1 in 12 14.9 miles	4.0 metres 13ft 1n	UC Early Nov - early Jun. Very winding, narrow mostly unguarded but not difficult otherwise; passing bays on southern slope, poor surface (maximum width vehicles 1.8 metres, 5ft 11in).
Aprica 1176 metres (3858ft) Italy	Tresenda 375 metres(1230ft) Edolo 699 metres (2293ft)	14km 1 in 11 8.7 miles 15km 1 in 16 9.3 miles	4.0 metres 13ft 1in	UO Fine scenery, good surface, well graded; suitable for caravans.
Aravis 1498 metres (4915ft) France	La Clusaz 1040 metres (3412ft) Flumet 917 metres (3009ft)	8km 1 in 11 5.0 miles 12km 1 in 11 7.4 miles	4.0 metres 13ft 1in	OC Dec - Mar. Outstanding scenery, and a fairly easy road.
Arlberg 1802 metres (5912ft) Austria	Bludenz 581 metres (1905ft) Landeck 816 metres (2677ft)	35km 1 in 8 21.7 miles 32km 1 in 7.5 20 miles	6 metres 19ft 8in	OC Dec - Apr. Modern road; short, steep stretch from west easing towards the summit; heavy traffic; parallel toll road tunnel. Suitable for caravans; using tunnel (see chapter on Major Road and Rail Tunnels). Pass road closed to vehicles towing trailers.
Aubisque 1710 metres (5610ft) France	Eaux Bonnes 750 metres (2461ft) Argelés-Gazost 463 metres (1519ft)	12km 1 in 10 7 miles 30km 1 in 10 19 miles	3.5 metres 11ft 6in	UC Mid Oct - Jun. A very winding road; continuous but easy ascent; the descent incorporates the Col de Soulor (1450 metres, 4757ft); 8km (5 miles) of very narrow, rough unguarded road, with a steep drop.
Ballon d'Alsace 1178 metres (3865ft) France	Giromagny 476metres (1562ft) St-Maurice-sur-Moselle 549 metres (1801ft)	17km 1 in 9 10.6 miles 9km 1 in 9 5.6 miles	4.0 metres 13ft 1in	OC Dec - Mar. A fairly straightforward ascent and descent, but numerous bends; negotiable by caravans.
Bayard 1248 metres (4094ft) France	Chauffayer 911 metres (2989ft) Gap 733 metres (2405ft)	18km 1 in 12 11.2 miles 8km 1 in 7 5.0 miles	6 metres 19ft 8in	UO Part of the Route Napoléon. Fairly easy, steepest on the southern side with several hairpin bends; negotiable by caravans from north to south.
*Bernina 2330 metres (7644ft) Switzerland	Pontresina 1805 metres (5922ft) Poschiavo 1019 metres (3343ft)	15.5km 1 in 10 10.5 miles 18.5km 1 in 8 11.5 miles	5 metres 16ft 5in	OC Dec - Mar. A good road on both sides; negotiable by caravans.
Bonaigua 2072 metres (6797ft) Spain	Viella 974 metres (3195ft) Esterri d'Aneu 957 metres (3140ft)	23km 1 in 12 14 miles 23km 1 in 12 14 miles	4.3 metres 14ft 1in	UC Nov - Apr. A sinuous and narrow road with many hairpin bends and some precipitous drops; the alternative route to Lleida (Lérida) through the Viella tunnel is open in winter.
Bracco 613 metres (2011ft) Italy	Riva Trigoso 43 metres (141ft) Borghetto di Vara 104metres (341ft)	15km 1 in 7 9.3 miles 18km 1 in 7 11.2 miles	5 metres 16ft 5in	UO A two-lane road with continuous bends; passing usually difficult; negotiable by caravans; alternative toll motorway available.
Brenner 1374 metres (4508ft) Austria - Italy	Innsbruck 574 metres (1883ft) Vipiteno 948 metres (3110ft)	36km 1 in 12 22miles 15km 1 in 7 9.3 miles	6 metres 19ft 8in	UO Parallel toll motorway open; heavy traffic; suitable for caravans using toll motorway. Pass road closed to vehicles towing trailers.
+Brünig 1007 metres (3304ft) Switzerland	Brienzwiler Station 575 metres (1886ft) Giswil 485 metres (1591ft)	6km 1 in 12 3.7 miles 13km 1 in 12 8.1 miles	6 metres 19ft 8in	UO An easy but winding road, heavy traffic at weekends; suitable for caravans.

* Permitted maximum width of vehicles 7ft 6in   + Permitted maximum width of vehicles 8ft 2.5in   ++ Maximum length of vehicle 30ft

Pass and height	From To	Distances from summit and max gradient	Min width of road	Conditions (see page 51 for key to abbreviations)
Bussang 721 metres (2365ft) France	Thann 340 metres (1115ft) St Maurice-sur-Moselle 549 metres (1801ft)	24km 1 in 14 15 miles 8km 1 in 14 5.0 miles	4 metres 13ft 1in	UO A very easy road over the Vosges; beautiful scenery; suitable for caravans.
Cabre 1180 metres (3871ft) France	Luc-en-Diois 580 metres (1903ft) Aspres sur Buëch 764 metres (2507ft)	24km 1 in 11 15 miles 17km 1 in 14 10.6 miles	5.5 metres 18ft	UO An easy pleasant road; suitable for caravans.
Campolongo 1875 metres (6152ft) Italy	Corvara in Badia 1568 metres (5144ft) Arabba 1602 metres (5256ft)	6km 1 in 8 3.7 miles 4km 1 in 8 2.5 miles	5 metres 16ft 5in	OC Dec - Mar. A winding but easy ascent; long level stretch on summit followed by easy descent; good surface; suitable for caravans.
Cayolle 2326 metres (7631ft) France	Barcelonnette 1132 metres (3714ft) Guillaumes 819 metres (2687ft)	30km 1 in 10 19 miles 33km 1 in 10 20.5 miles	4 metres 13ft 1in	UC early Nov - early Jun. Narrow and winding road with hairpin bends; poor surface and broken edges; steep drops. Long stretches of single-track road with passing places.
Costalunga (Karer) 1753 metres (5751ft) Italy	Cardano 282 metres (925ft) Pozza 1290 metres (4232ft)	24km 1 in 6 14.9 miles 11km 1 in 8 7 miles	5 metres 16ft 5in	OC Dec - Apr. A good well-engineered road but mostly winding; caravans prohibited.
Croix 1778 metres (5833ft) Switzerland	Villars-sur-Ollon 1253 metres (4111ft) Les Diablerets 1155 metres (3789ft)	8km 1 in 7.5 5.0 miles 9km 1 in 11 5.6 miles	3.5 metres 11ft 6in	UC Nov - May. A narrow and winding route but extremely picturesque.
Croix-Haute 1179 metres (3868ft) France	Monestier-de-Clermont 832 metres (2730ft) Aspres-sur-Buëch 764 metres (2507ft)	34km 1 in 14 21 miles 29km 1 in 14 18 miles	5.5 metres 18ft	UO Well engineered; several hairpin bends on the north side; suitable for caravans.
Envalira 2407 metres (7897ft) Andorra	Pas de la Casa 2091 metres (6860ft) Andorra 1029 metres (3376ft)	5km 1 in 10 3.1 miles 25km 1 in 8 16 miles	6 metres 19ft 8in	OC Nov - Apr. A good road with wide bends on ascent and descent; fine views; negotiable by caravans (maximum height vehicles 3.5 metres, 11ft 6in on northern approach near L'Hospitalet).
Falzárego 2117 metres (6945ft) Italy	Cortina d'Ampezzo 1224 metres (4016ft) Andraz 1428 metres (4685ft)	17km 1 in 12 10.6 miles 9km 1 in 12 5.6 miles	5 metres 16ft 5in	OC Dec - Apr. Well engineered bitumen surface; many hairpin bends on both sides; negotiable by caravans.
Faucille 1323 metres (4341ft) France	Gex 628 metres (2060ft) Morez 702 metres (2303ft)	11km 1 in 10 6.8 miles 27km 1 in 12 17miles	5 metres 16ft 5in	UO Fairly wide, winding road across the Jura mountains; negotiable by caravans, but it is probably better to follow La Cure-St-Cergue-Nyon.
Fern 1209 metres (3967ft) Austria	Nassereith 843 metres (2766ft) Lermoos 995 metres (3264ft)	10km 1 in 10 6 miles 10km 1 in 10 6 miles	6 metres 19ft 8in	UO An easy pass, but slippery when wet; heavy traffic at summer weekends; suitable for caravans.
Flexen 1784 metres (5853ft) Austria	Lech 1447 metres (4747ft) Rauzalpe (near Arlberg Pass) 1628 metres (5341ft)	6.5km 1 in 10 4 miles 3.5km 1 in 10 2.2 miles	5.5 metres 18ft	UO The magnificent 'Flexenstrasse', a well engineered mountain road with tunnels and galleries. The road from Lech to Warth, north of the pass, is usually closed between November and April due to danger of avalanches.

* **Permitted maximum width of vehicles 7ft 6in**   + **Permitted maximum width of vehicles 8ft 2.5in**   ++ **Maximum length of vehicle 30ft**

PRINCIPAL MOUNTAIN PASSES

Pass and height	From To	Distances from summit and max gradient	Min width of road	Conditions (see page 51 for key to abbreviations)
*Flüela 2383 metres (7818ft) Switzerland	Davos-Dorf 1563 metres (5128ft) Susch 1438 metres (4718ft)	14km 1 in 10 9 miles 14km 1 in 8 9 miles	5metres 16ft 5in	OC Nov - May. Easy ascent from Davos; some acute hairpin bends on the eastern side; bitumen surface; negotiable by caravans.
+Forclaz 1527 metres (5010ft) Switzerland France	Martigny 476 metres (1562ft) Argentière 1253 metres (4111ft)	13km 1 in 12 8.1 miles 19km 1 in 12 11.8 miles	5 metres 16ft 5in	UO Forclaz; OC Montets Dec - early Apr. A good road over the pass and to the frontier; in France, narrow and rough over Col des Montets (1461 metres, 4793ft); negotiable by caravans.
Foscagno 2291 metres (7516ft) Italy	Bormio 1225 metres (4019ft) Livigno 1816 metres (5958ft)	24km 1 in 8 14.9 miles 14km 1 in 8 8.7 miles	3.3 metres 10ft 10in	OC Nov - May. Narrow and winding through lonely mountains, generally poor surface. Long winding ascent with many blind bends; not always well guarded. The descent includes winding rise and fall over the Passo d'Eira (2200 metres, 7218ft).
Fugazze 1159 metres (3802ft) Italy	Rovereto 201 metres (660ft) Valli del Pasubio 350 metres (1148ft)	27km 1 in 7 16.4 miles 12km 1 in 7 7.4 miles	3.5 metres 11ft 6in	UO Very winding with some narrow sections, particularly on northern side. The many blind bends and several hairpin bends call for extra care.
*Furka 2431 metres (7976ft) Switzerland	Gletsch 1757 metres (5764ft) Realp 1538 metres (5046ft)	10km 1 in 9 6.2 miles 13km 1 in 10 8.1 miles	4 metres 13ft 1in	UC Oct - Jun. A well graded road, with narrow sections and several sharp hairpin bends on both ascent and descent. Fine views of the Rhône glacier. Alternative rail route available.
Galibier 2645 metres (8678ft) France	Lautaret Pass 2058 metres (6752ft) St-Michel-de-Maurienne 712 metres (2336ft)	7km 1 in 9 4.4 miles 34km 1 in 8 21.1 miles	3 metres 9ft 10in	UC Oct - Jun. Mainly wide, well surfaced but unguarded. Ten hairpin bends on descent then 5km (3.1 miles) narrow and rough. Rise over the Col du Télégraphe (1600 metres, 5249ft), then 11 more hairpin bends. (The tunnel under the Galibier summit is closed.)
Gardena (Grödner-Joch) 2121 metres (6959ft) Italy	Val Gardena 1862 metres (6109ft) Corvara in Badia 1568 metres (5144ft)	6km 1 in 8 3.7 miles 10km 1 in 8 6.2 miles	5 metres 16ft 5in	OC Dec - Jun. A well engineered road, very winding on descent.
Gavia 2621 metres (8599ft) Italy	Bormio 1225 metres (4019ft) Ponte di Legno 1258 metres (4127ft)	25km 1 in 5.5 15.5 miles 18km 1 in 5.5 11 miles	3 metres 9ft 10in	UC Oct - Jul. Steep and narrow, but with frequent passing bays; many hairpin bends and a gravel surface; not for the faint-hearted; extra care necessary. (Maximum width for vehicles 1.8 metres, 5ft 11in.)
Gerlos 1628 metres (5341ft) Austria	Zell am Ziller 575 metres (1886ft) Wald 885 metres (2904ft)	29km 1 in 12 18 miles 15km 1 in 11 9.3 miles	4 metres 13ft 1in	UO Hairpin ascent out of Zell to modern toll road; the old, steep, narrow, and winding route with passing bays and 1-in-7 gradient is not recommended, but is negotiable with care; caravans prohibited.
+Grand St Bernard 2473 metres (8114ft) Switzerland - Italy	Martigny 476 metres (1562ft) Aosta 583 metres (1913ft)	46km 1 in 9 29 miles 34km 1 in 9 21 miles	4 metres 13ft 1in	UC Oct - Jun. Modern road to entrance of road tunnel (usually open; see chapter on Major Road and Rail Tunnels) then narrow over summit to frontier; also goodsurface in Italy; suitable for caravans using tunnel. Pass road closed to vehicles towing trailers.
*Grimsel 2164 metres (7100ft) Switzerland	Innerkirchen 630 metres (2067ft) Gletsch 1757 metres (5764ft)	26km 1 in 10 16.1 miles 6km 1 in 10 3.7 miles	5 metres 16ft 5in	UC mid Oct - late Jun. A fairly easy road, but heavy traffic weekends. A long winding ascent, finally hairpin bends; then a terraced descent (six hairpins) into the Rhône valley. Negotiable by caravans.
Grossglockner 2503 metres (8212ft) Austria	Bruck an der Glocknerstrasse 755 metres (2477ft) Heiligenblut 1301 metres (4268ft)	34km 1 in 8 21 miles 15m 1 in 8 9.3 miles	5.5 metres 18ft	UC late Oct - early May. Numerous well engineered hairpin bends; moderate but very long ascent, toll road; very fine scenery; heavy tourist traffic; negotiable preferably from south to north, by caravans. Road closed at night, 22.00 to 05.00 hrs.

* Permitted maximum width of vehicles 7ft 6in   + Permitted maximum width of vehicles 8ft 2.5in   ++ Maximum length of vehicle 30ft

Pass and height	From To	Distances from summit and max gradient	Min width of road	Conditions (see page 51 for key to abbreviations)
Hochtannberg 1679 metres (5509ft) Austria	Schröcken 1269 metres(4163ft) Warth (near Lech) 1500 metres (4921ft)	5.5km 1 in 7 3.4 miles 4.5km 1 in 11 2.8 miles	4 metres 13ft 1in	OC Jan - Mar. A reconstructed modern road.
Ibañeta (Roncesvalles) 1057 metres (3468ft) France - Spain	St-Jean-Pied-de-Port 163 metres (535ft) Pamplona 415 metres (1362ft)	27km 1 in 10 17 miles 49km 1 in 10 30 miles	4 metres 13ft 1in	UO A slow and winding, scenic route; negotiable by caravans.
Iseran 2770 metres (9088ft) France	Bourg-St-Maurice 840 metres (2756ft) Lanslebourg 1399 metres (4590ft)	47km 1 in 12 29 miles 33km 1 in 9 20.5 miles	4 metres 13ft 1in	UC Mid Oct - late Jun. The second highest pass in the Alps. Well graded with reasonable bends, average surface; several unlit tunnels on northern approach.
Izoard 2360 metres (7743ft) France	Guillestre 1000 metres (3281ft) Briançon 1321 metres (4334ft)	32km 1 in 8 20 miles 22km 1 in 8 14 miles	5 metres 16ft 5in	UC Late Oct - mid Jun. A winding and sometimes narrow road with many hairpin bends. Care is required at several unlit tunnels near Guillestre.
*Jaun 1509 metres (4951ft) Switzerland	Broc 718 metres (2356ft) Reidenbach 845 metres (2772ft)	25km 1 in 10 15.5 miles 8km 1 in 10 5 miles	4 metres 13ft 1in	UO A modernised but generally narrow road; some poor sections on ascent, and several hairpin bends on descent; negotiable by caravans.
+Julier 2284 metres (7493ft) Switzerland	Tiefencastel 851 metres (2792ft) Silvaplana 1815 metres (5955ft)	35km 1 in 10 22miles 7km 1 in 7.5 4.4 miles	4 metres 13ft 1in	UO Well engineered road, approached from Chur by Lenzerheide Pass (1549 metres, 5082ft); negotiable by caravans, preferably from north to south.
Katschberg 1641 metres (5384ft) Austria	Spittal 554 metres (1818ft) St Michael 1068 metres (3504ft)	37km 1 in 5 23 miles 6km 1 in 6 3.7 miles	6 metres 19ft 8in	UO Steep though not particularly difficult, parallel toll motorway, including tunnel available; negotiable by light caravans, using tunnel (see chapter on Major Road and Rail Tunnels, Tauern Autobahn).
*Klausen 1948 metres (6391ft) Switzerland	Altdorf 458 metres (1503ft) Linthal 662 metres (2172ft)	25km 1 in 10 15.5 miles 23km 1 in 11 14.3 miles	5 metres 16ft 5in	UC Late Oct - early Jun. Narrow and winding in places, but generally easy, in spite of a number of sharp bends; no through route for caravans as they are prohibited from using the road between Unterschächen and Linthal.
Larche (della Maddalena) 1994 metres (6542ft) France - Italy	La Condamine-Châtelard 1308 metres (4291ft) Vinadio 910 metres (2986ft)	19km 1 in 12 11.8 miles 32km 1 in 12 19.8 miles	3.5 metres 11ft 6in	OC Dec - Mar. An easy, well graded road; narrow ascent, wider on descent; suitable for caravans.
Lautaret 2058 metres (6752ft) France	Le Bourg-d'Oisans 719 metres (2359ft) Briançon 1321 metres (4334ft)	38km 1 in 8 23.6 miles 28km 1 in 10 17.4 miles	4 metres 13ft 1in	OC Dec - Mar. Modern, evenly graded, but winding, and unguarded in places; very fine scenery; suitable for caravans.
Loibl (Ljubelj) 1067 metres (3500ft) Austria - Slovenia	Unterloibl 518 metres (1699ft) Kranj 385 metres (1263ft)	10km 1 in 5.5 6.2 miles 26km 1 in 8 16miles	6 metres 19ft 8in	UO Steep rise and fall over Little Loibl pass to tunnel (1.6km, 1 mile long) under summit. The old road over the summit is closed to through traffic.
*Lukmanier (Lucomagno) 1916 metres (6286ft) Switzerland	Olivone 893 metres (2930ft) Disentis 1133 metres (3717ft)	20km 1 in 11 12 miles 20km 1 in 11 12 miles	5 metres 16ft 5in	UC early Nov - late May. Rebuilt, modern road; suitable for caravans.

* Permitted maximum width of vehicles 7ft 6in   + Permitted maximum width of vehicles 8ft 2.5in   ++ Maximum length of vehicle 30ft

Pass and height	From To	Distances from summit and max gradient	Min width of road	Conditions (see page 51 for key to abbreviations)
+Maloja 1815 metres (5955ft) Switzerland	Silvaplana 1815 metres (5955ft) Chiavenna 333 metres (1093ft)	11km level 6.8 miles 32km 1 in 11 19.8 miles	4 metres 13ft 1in	UO Escarpment facing south; fairly easy, but many hairpin bends on descent; negotiable by caravans, possibly difficult on ascent.
Mauria 1298 metres (4258ft) Italy	Lozzo Cadore 753 metres (2470ft) Ampezzo 560 metres (1837ft)	13km 1 in 14 8 miles 31km 1 in 14 19.2 miles	5 metres 16ft 5in	UO A well designed road with easy, winding ascent and descent; suitable for caravans.
Mendola 1363 metres (4472ft) Italy	Appiano (Eppan) 411 metres (1348ft) Sarnonico 978 metres (3208ft)	15km 1 in 8 9.3 miles 9km 1 in 10 6 miles	5 metres 16ft 5in	UO A fairly straightforward but winding road, well guarded; suitable for caravans.
Mont Cenis 2083 metres (6834ft) France - Italy	Lanslebourg 1399 metres (4590ft) Susa 503 metres (1650ft)	11km 1 in 10 6.8 miles 28km 1 in 8 17.4 miles	5 metres 16ft 5in	UC Nov - May. Approach by industrial valley. An easy highway, but with poor surface in places; suitable for caravans. Alternative Fréjus road tunnel (see chapter on Major Road and Rail Tunnels).
Monte Croce di Comélico (Kreuzberg) 1636 metres (5368ft) Italy	San Candido 1174metres (3852ft) Santo Stefano di Cadore 908 metres (2979ft)	15km 1 in 12 9.3 miles 21km 1 in 12 13miles	5 metres 16ft 5in	UO A winding road with moderate gradients, beautiful scenery; suitable for caravans.
Montgenèvre 1850m (6070ft) France - Italy	Briançon 1321 metres (4334ft) Cesana Torinese 1344 metres (4409ft)	12km 1 in 14 7.4 miles 8km 1 in 11 5miles	5 metres 16ft 5in	UO An easy, modern road; suitable for caravans.
Monte Giovo (Jaufen) 2094 metres (6870ft) Italy	Merano 324 metres (1063ft) Vipiteno 948 metres (3110ft)	40km 1 in 8 24.8 miles 19km 1 in 11 11.8 miles	4 metres 13ft 1in	UC Nov - May. Many well engineered hairpin bends; caravans prohibited.
Montets (see Forclaz)				
Morgins 1369 metres (4491ft) France - Switzerland	Abondance 930 metres (3051ft) Monthey 424 metres (1391ft)	14km 1 in 11 8.7 miles 15km 1 in 7 9.3 miles	4 metres 13ft 1in	UO A lesser used route through pleasant, forested countryside crossing the French-Swiss border.
*Mosses 1445m (4740ft) Switzerland	Aigle 417 metres (1368ft) Château d'Oex 958 metres (3143ft)	16km 1 in 12 10 miles 15km 1 in 12 9.3 miles	4 metres 13ft 1in	UO A modern road; suitable for caravans.
Nassfeld (Pramollo) 1530m (5020ft) Austria - Italy	Tröpolach 601 metres (1972ft) Pontebba 568 metres (1864ft)	10km 1 in 5 6.2 miles 10km 1 in 10 6.2 miles	4 metres 13ft 1in	OC Late Nov - Mar. The winding descent in Italy has been improved.
*Nufenen (Novena) 2478 metres (8130ft) Switzerland	Ulrichen 1346 metres (4416ft) Airolo 1142 metres (3747ft)	13km 1 in 10 8.1 miles 24km 1 in 10 14.9 miles	4.0 metres 13ft 1in	UC Mid Oct - mid Jun. The approach roads are narrow, with tight bends, but the road over the pass is good; negotiable by caravans.
*Oberalp 2044 metres (6706ft) Switzerland	Andermatt 1447 metres (4747ft) Disentis 1133 metres (3717ft)	10km 1 in 10 6.2 miles 21km 1 in 10 13miles	5 metres 16ft 5in	UC Nov - late May. A widened road with a modern surface; many hairpin bends, but long level stretch on summit; negotiable by caravans. Alternative rail tunnel for winter (see chapter on Major Roadand Rail Tunnels).

* Permitted maximum width of vehicles 7ft 6in   + Permitted maximum width of vehicles 8ft 2.5in   ++ Maximum length of vehicle 30ft

Pass and height	From To	Distances from summit and max gradient	Min width of road	Conditions (see page 51 for key to abbreviations)
*Ofen (Fuorn) 2149 metres (7051ft) Switzerland	Zernez 1474 metres (4836ft) Santa Maria im Münstertal 1375 metres (4511ft)	22km 1 in 10 13.6 miles 14km 1 in 8 8.7 miles	4 metres 13ft 1in	UO Good, fairly easy road through the Swiss National Park; negotiable by caravans.
Petit St Bernard 2188 metres (7178ft) France - Italy	Bourg-St-Maurice 840 metres (2756ft) Pré St-Didier 1000 metres (3281ft)	30km 1 in 16 19 miles 23km 1 in 12 14.3 miles	5 metres 16ft 5in	UC Mid Oct - Jun. Outstanding scenery; a fairly easy approach, but poor surface and unguarded broken edges near the summit; good on the descent in Italy; negotiable by light caravans.
Peyresourde 1563 metres (5128ft) France	Arreau 704 metres (2310ft) Luchon 630 metres (2067ft)	18km 1 in 10 11.2 miles 14km 1 in 10 8.7 miles	4 metres 13ft 1in	UO Somewhat narrow with several hairpin bends, though not difficult.
*Pillon 1546 metres (5072ft) Switzerland	Le Sépey 974 metres (3196ft) Gsteig 1184 metres (3885ft)	15km 1 in 11 9 miles 7km 1 in 11 4.4 miles	4 metres 13ft 1in	OC Jan - Feb. A comparatively easy modern road; suitable for caravans.
Plöcken (Monte Croce-Carnico) 1362 metres (4468ft) Austria - Italy	Kötschach 706 metres (2316ft) Paluzza 600 metres (1968ft)	16km 1 in 7 10 miles 16km 1 in 14 10 miles	5 metres 16ft 5in	OC Dec - Apr. A modern road with long, reconstructed sections; heavy traffic at summer weekends; delay likely at the frontier; negotiable by caravans, best used only by experienced drivers in cars with ample power.
Pordoi 2239 metres (7346ft) Italy	Arabba 1602 metres (5256ft) Canazei 1465 metres (4806ft)	9km 1 in 10 5.6 miles 12km 1 in 10 7.4 miles	5 metres 16ft 5in	OC Dec - Apr. An excellent modern road with numerous hairpin bends; negotiable by caravans.
Port 1249 metres (4098ft) France	Tarascon 474 metres (1555ft) Massat 650 metres (2133ft)	18km 1 in 10 11.2 miles 12km 1 in 10 7.4 miles	4 metres 13ft 1in	OC Nov - Mar. A fairly easy road, but narrow on some bends; negotiable by caravans.
Portet-d'Aspet 1069 metres (3507ft) France	Audressein 508 metres (1667ft) Fronsac 472 metres (1548ft)	18km 1 in 7 11.2 miles 29km 1 in 7 18miles	3.5 metres 11ft 6in	UO Approached from the west by the easy Col des Ares (797 metres, 2615ft) and Col de Buret (599 metres, 1965ft); well engineered road, but calls for particular care on hairpin bends; rather narrow.
Pötschen 982 metres (3222ft) Austria	Bad Ischl 469 metres (1539ft) Bad Aussee 659 metres (2162ft)	19km 1 in 11 11.8 miles 9 km 1 in 11 5.6 miles	7 metres 23ft	UO A modern road; suitable for caravans.
Pourtalet 1792 metres (5879ft) France - Spain	Eaux-Chaudes 656 metres (2152ft) Biescas 860 metres (2822ft)	23km 1 in 10 14.3 miles 32km 1 in 10 20 miles	3.5 metres 11ft 6in	UC late Oct - early Jun. A fairly easy, unguarded road, but narrow in places.
Puymorens 1915 metres (6283ft) France	Ax-les-Thermes 720 metres (2362ft) Bourg-Madame 1130 metres (3707ft)	28km 1 in 10 17.4 miles 27km 1 in 10 16.8 miles	5.5 metres 18ft	OC Nov - Apr. A generally easy, modern tarmac road, but narrow, winding and with a poor surface in places; not suitable for night driving; suitable for caravans (max height vehicles 3.5 metres, 11ft 6in). Parallel toll road tunnel available.
Quillane 1714 metres (5623ft) France	Quillan 291 metres (955ft) Mont-Louis 1600 metres (5249ft)	63km 1 in 12 39.1 miles 6 km 1 in 12 3.5 miles	5 metres 16ft 5in	OC Nov - Mar. An easy, straightforward ascent and descent; suitable for caravans.

* Permitted maximum width of vehicles 7ft 6in   **+ Permitted maximum width of vehicles** 8ft 2.5in   **++ Maximum length of vehicle** 30ft

Pass and height	From To	Distances from summit and max gradient	Min width of road	Conditions (see page 51 for key to abbreviations)
Radstädter-Tauern 1738 metres (5702ft) Austria	Radstadt 862 metres (2828ft) Mauterndorf 1122 metres (3681ft)	21km 1 in 6 13.0 miles 17km 1 in 7 10.6 miles	5 metres 16ft 5in	OC Jan - Mar. Northern ascent steep, but not difficult otherwise; parallel toll motorway including tunnel; negotiable by light caravans, using tunnel (see chapter on Major Road and Rail Tunnels).
Résia (Reschen) 1504 metres (4934ft) Italy - Austria	Spondigna 885 metres (2903ft) Pfunds 970 metres (3182ft)	29km 1 in 10 18 miles 21km 1 in 10 13miles	6 metres 19ft 8in	UO A good, straightforward alternative to the Brenner Pass; suitable for caravans.
Restefond (La Bonette) 2802 metres (9193ft) France	Jausiers (near Barcelonnette) 1220 metres (4003ft) St-Etienne-de-Tinée 1144 metres (3753ft)	23km 1 in 8 14.3 miles 27km 1 in 6 16.8 miles	3 metres 9ft 10in	UC Oct - Jun. The highest pass in the Alps, completed in 1962. Narrow, rough, unguarded ascent with many blind bends, and nine hairpins. Descent easier, winding with 12 hairpin bends. Not for the faint-hearted; extra care required.
Rolle 1970 metres (6463ft) Italy	Predazzo 1018 metres (3340ft) Mezzano 637 metres (2090ft)	21km 1 in 11 13.0 miles 27km 1 in 14 17 miles	5 metres 16ft 5in	OC Dec - Mar. A well engineered road with many hairpin bends on both sides; very beautiful scenery; good surface; negotiable by caravans.
Rombo (see Timmelsjoch)				
Routes des Crêtes 1283 metres (4210ft) France	St-Dié 343 metres (1125ft) Cernay 296 metres (971ft)	- 1 in 8 - 1 in 8	4 metres 13ft 1in	UC Nov - Apr. A renowned scenic route crossing seven ridges, with the highest point at 'Hôtel du Grand Ballon'.
+St Gotthard (San Gottardo) 2108 metres (6916ft) Switzerland	Göschenen 1106 metres (3629ft) Airolo 1142 metres (3747ft)	18km 1 in 10 11miles 15km 1 in 10 9.3 miles	6 metres 19ft 8in	UC Mid Oct - early Jun. Modern, fairly easy two to three-lane road. Heavy traffic; negotiable by caravans. Alternative road tunnel (see chapter on Major Road and Rail Tunnels).
*San Bernardino 2066 metres (6778ft) Switzerland	Mesocco 790 metres (2592ft) Hinterrhein 1620 metres (5315ft)	21km 1 in 10 13miles 9.5km 1 in 10 5.9 miles	4 metres 13ft 1in	UC Oct - late Jun. Easy, modern roads on northern and southern approaches to tunnel(see chapter on Major Road and Rail Tunnels). Narrow and winding over summit, via tunnel suitable for caravans.
Schlucht 1139 metres (3737ft) France	Gérardmer 665 metres (2182ft) Munster 381 metres (1250ft)	15km 1 in 14 9.3 miles 18km 1 in 14 11miles	5 metres 16ft 5in	UO An extremely picturesque route crossing the Vosges mountains, with easy, wide bends on the descent; suitable for caravans.
Seeberg (Jezersko) 1218 metres (3996ft) Austria - Slovenia	Eisenkappel 555 metres (1821ft) Kranj 385 metres (1263ft)	14km 1 in 8 8.7 miles 33km 1 in 10 20.5 miles	5 metres 16ft 5in	UO An alternative to the steeper Loibl and Wurzen passes; moderate climb with winding, hairpin ascent and descent.
Sella 2240 metres (7349ft) Italy	Plan 1606 metres (5269ft) Canazei 1465 metres (4806ft)	9km 1 in 9 5.6 miles 12km 1 in 9 7 miles	5 metres 16ft 5in	OC Dec - Jun. A finely engineered, winding road; exceptional views of the Dolomites.
Semmering 985 metres (3232ft) Austria	Mürzzuschlag im Mürztal 672 metres (2205ft) Gloggnitz 457 metres (1499ft)	14km 1 in 16 8.7 miles 17km 1 in 10 10.6 miles	6 metres 19ft 8in	UO A fine, well engineered highway; suitable for caravans.
Sestriere 2033 metres (6670ft) Italy	Cesana Torinese 1344 metres (4409ft) Pinerolo 376 metres (1234ft)	12km 1 in 10 7.4 miles 55km 1 in 10 34.2 miles	6 metres 19ft 8in	UO Mostly bitumen surface; negotiable by caravans.

* Permitted maximum width of vehicles 7ft 6in + Permitted maximum width of vehicles 8ft 2.5in ++ Maximum length of vehicle 30ft

PRINCIPAL MOUNTAIN PASSES

Pass and height	From To	Distances from summit and max gradient	Min width of road	Conditions (see page 51 for key to abbreviations)
Silvretta (Bielerhöhe) 2032 metres (6666ft) Austria	Partenen 1051 metres (3448ft) Galtür 1584 metres (5197ft)	16km 1 in 9 9.9 miles 10km 1 in 9 6.2 miles	5 metres 16ft 5in	UC Late Oct - early Jun. For the most part reconstructed; 32 easy hairpin bends on western ascent; eastern side more straightforward. Toll road; caravans prohibited.
+Simplon 2005 metres (6578ft) Switzerland - Italy	Brig 681 metres (2234ft) Domodóssola 280 metres (919ft)	22km 1 in 9 13.6 miles 41km 1 in 11 25.5 miles	7 metres 23ft	OC Nov - Apr. An easy, reconstructed modern road, but 13 miles long, continuous ascent to summit; suitable for caravans.
Somport 1632 metres (5354ft) France - Spain	Bedous 416 metres (1365ft) Jaca 820 metres (2690ft)	31km 1 in 10 19.2 miles 32km 1 in 10 20miles	3.5 metres 11ft 6in	UO A favoured, old-established route; generally easy, but in parts narrow and unguarded; fairly well surfaced road; suitable for caravans.
*Splügen 2113 metres (6932ft) Switzerland - Italy	Splügen 1457 metres (4780ft) Chiavenna 330 metres (1083ft)	9km 1 in 9 5.6 miles 30km 1 in 7.5 18.6 miles	3.5 metres 11ft 6in	UC Nov - Jun. Mostly narrow and winding, with many hairpin bends, and not well guarded; care is also required at many tunnels and galleries (max height vehicles 9ft 2in).
++Stelvio 2757 metres (9045ft) Italy	Bormio 1225 metres (4019ft) Spondigna 885 metres (2903ft)	22km 1 in 8 13.6 miles 28km 1 in 8 12.9 miles	4 metres 13ft 1in	UC Oct - late Jun. the third highest pass in the Alps; the number of acute hairpin bends, all well engineered, is exceptional - from 40 to 50 on either side; the surface is good, the traffic heavy. Hairpin bends are too acute for long vehicles.
+Susten 2224 metres (7297ft) Switzerland	Innertkirchen 630 metres (2067ft) Wassen 916 metres (3005ft)	28km 1 in 11 12.9 miles 19km 1 in 11 11.8 miles	6 metres 19ft 8in	UC Nov - Jun. A very scenic and well guarded mountain road; easy gradients and turns; heavy traffic at weekends; caravans prohibited.
Tenda (Tende) 1321 metres (4334ft) Italy - France	Borgo S Dalmazzo 641 metres (2103ft) La Giandola 308 metres (1010ft)	24km 1 in 11 14.9 miles 29km 1 in 11 18miles	6 metres 19ft 8in	UO Well guarded, modern road with several hairpin bends; road tunnel at summit; suitable for caravans; but prohibited during the winter.
+Thurn 1274 metres (4180ft) Austria	Kitzbühel 762 metres (2500ft) Mittersill 789 metres (2588ft)	19km 1 in 12 11.8 miles 10km 1 in 16 6.2 miles	5 metres 16ft 5in	UO A good road with narrow stretches; northern approach rebuilt; suitable for caravans.
Timmelsjoch (Rombo) 2509 metres (8232ft) Austria - Italy	Obergurgl 1910 metres (6266ft) Moso 1007 metres (3304ft)	14km 1 in 7 8.7 miles 23km 1 in 8 14miles	3.5 metres 11ft 6in	UC mid Oct - late Jun. Pass open to private cars (without trailers) only as some tunnels on the Italian side are too narrow for larger vehicles; toll road. Border closed at night 20.00 -07.00 hrs.
Tonale 1883 metres (6178ft) Italy	Edolo 699 metres (2293ft) Dimaro 766 metres (2513ft)	30km 1 in 12 18.6 miles 27km 1 in 10 16.7 miles	5 metres 16ft 5in	UO A relatively easy road; suitable for caravans.
Toses (Tosas) 1800 metres (5906ft) Spain	Puigcerdá 1152 metres (3780ft) Ribes de Freser 920 metres (3018ft)	26km 1 in 10 16miles 25km 1 in 10 15.5 miles	5 metres 16ft 5in	UO Now a fairly straightforward, but continuously winding, two-lane road with many sharp bends; negotiable by caravans.
Tourmalet 2114 metres (6936ft) France	Luz 711 metres (2333ft) Ste-Marie-de-Campan 857 metres (2812ft)	18km 1 in 8 11miles 17km 1 in 8 10.6 miles	4 metres 13ft 1in	UC Oct - mid Jun. The highest of the French Pyrenean routes; the approaches are good, though winding and exacting over summit; sufficiently guarded.
Tre Croci 1809 metres (5935ft) Italy	Cortina d'Ampezzo 1224 metres (4016ft) Auronzo di Cadore 864 metres (2835ft).	7km 1 in 9 4.4 miles 26 km 1 in 9 16 miles	6 metres 19ft 8in	OC Dec - Mar. An easy pass; very fine scenery; suitable for caravans.

* Permitted maximum width of vehicles 7ft 6in   + Permitted maximum width of vehicles 8ft 2.5in   ++ Maximum length of vehicle 30ft

Pass and height	From To	Distances from summit and max gradient	Min width of road	Conditions (see page 51 for key to abbreviations)
Turracher Höhe 1763 metres (5784ft) Austria	Predlitz 922 metres (3024ft) Ebene-Reichenau 1062 metres (3484ft)	20km 1 in 5.5 12.4 miles 8km 1 in 4.5 5miles	4 metres 13ft 1in	UO Formerly one of the steepest mountain roads in Austria; now much improved. A steep, fairly straightforward ascent is followed by a very steep descent; good surface and mainly two-lane width; fine scenery.
***Umbrail** 2501 metres (8205ft) Switzerland - Italy	Santa Maria im Münstertal 1375 metres (4511ft) Bormio 1225 metres (4019ft)	14km 1 in 11 9 miles 19km 1 in 11 11.8 miles	4.3 metres 14ft 1in	UC Early Nov - early Jun. Highest of the Swiss passes; narrow; mostly gravel surfaced with 34 hairpin bends, but not too difficult.
Vars 2109 metres (6919ft) France	St-Paul-sur-Ubaye 1470 metres (4823ft) Guillestre 1000 metres (3281ft)	8km 1 in 10 5miles 20km 1 in 10 12.4 miles	5 metres 16ft 5in	OC Dec - Mar. Easy winding ascent with seven hairpin bends; gradual winding descent with another seven hairpin bends; good surface; negotiable by caravans.
Wurzen (Koren) 1073 metres (3520ft) Austria - Slovenia	Riegersdorf 541 metres (1775ft) Kranjska Gora 810 metres (2657ft)	7km 1 in 5.5 4.5miles 6km 1 in 5.5 3.5 miles	4 metres 13ft 1in	UO A steep two-lane road, which otherwise is not particularly difficult; heavy traffic at summer weekends; delay likely at the frontier; caravans prohibited.
Zirler Berg 1009 metres (3310ft) Austria	Seefeld 1180 metres (3871ft) Zirl 622 metres (2041ft)	6km 1 in 7 3.5 miles 5km 1 in 6 3.1 miles	7 metres 23ft	UO An escarpment facing south, part of the route from Garmisch to Innsbruck; a good, modern road, but heavy tourist traffic and a long steep descent, with one hairpin bend, into the Inn Valley. Steepest section from the hairpin bend down to Zirl; caravans prohibited northbound.

* **Permitted maximum width of vehicles** 7ft 6in   + **Permitted maximum width of vehicles** 8ft 2.5in   ++ **Maximum length of vehicle** 30ft

KEY TO REGIONS

The country directories, with the exception of Andorra and Luxembourg, are divided into regions, each introduced by a brief description, to help people to plan their touring holidays. Below is a list of the regional headings used in each country directory, followed by a list of the departments, districts or administrative areas that may be included within each region. See also the country maps at the end of the book.

AUSTRIA

TIROL
CARINTHIA = Kärnten
STYRIA = Steiermark
LOWER AUSTRIA - Niederösterreich, Burgenland
UPPER AUSTRIA - Oberösterreich, Salzburg
VORARLBERG
VIENNA = Wien

BELGIUM

SOUTH WEST/COAST - Hainaut, West-Vlaanderen
NORTH/CENTRAL - Brabant, Oost-Vlaanderen
NORTH EAST - Antwerpen, Limburg
SOUTH EAST - Liège, Luxembourg, Namur

FRANCE

ALPS/EAST - Ain, Doubs, Hautes-Alpes, Haute Saône, Haute Savoie, Jura, Isère, Savoie, Territoire-de-Belfort
ALSACE/LORRAINE - Bas-Rhin, Haut-Rhin, Meurthe-et-Moselle, Meuse, Moselle, Vosges
BURGUNDY/CHAMPAGNE - Aube, Ardennes, Côte-d'Or, Haute-Marne, Marne, Nièvre, Saône-et-Loire, Yonne
SOUTH WEST/ PYRENEES - Ariège, Dordogne, Gers, Gironde, Haute-Garonne, Hautes-Pyrénées, Landes, Lot, Lot-et-Garonne, Pyrénées-Atlantiques, Tarn, Tarn-et-Garonne
LOIRE/CENTRAL - Charente, Charente-Maritime, Cher, Corrèze, Creuse, Deux-Sèvres, Eure-et-Loir, Haute-Vienne, Indre, Indre-et-Loire, Loire-Atlantique, Loiret, Loir-et-Cher, Maine-et-Loire, Mayenne, Sarthe, Vendée, Vienne
BRITTANY/NORMANDY - Calvados, Côtes-d'Armor, Eure, Finistère, Ille-et-Vilaine, Manche, Morbihan, Orne, Seine-Maritime
PARIS/NORTH - Aisne, Essonne, Hauts-de-Seine, Nord, Oise, Paris, Pas-de-Calais, Seine-et-Marne, Seine-St-Denis, Somme, Val-de-Marne, Val d'Oise, Yvelines
AUVERGNE - Allier, Aveyron, Cantal, Haute-Loire, Loire, Lozère, Puy-de-Dôme, Rhône
SOUTH COAST/RIVIERA - Alpes-Maritimes, Alpes-de-Haute-Provence, Ardèche, Aude, Bouches-du-Rhône, Drôme, Gard, Hérault, Monaco, Pyrénées-Orientales, Var, Vaucluse
CORSICA - Corse-du-Sud, Haute-Corse

GERMANY

SOUTH EAST - Bayern
SOUTH WEST - Baden-Württemberg
BERLIN AND EASTERN PROVINCES - Brandenburg, Sachsen, Thüringen
CENTRAL - Hessen, Nordrhein-Westfalen, Rheinland-Pfalz, Saarland
NORTH - Bremen, Hamburg, Niedersachsen, Schleswig-Holstein

ITALY

NORTH WEST/ALPS/LAKES - Aosta, Alessandria, Asti, Beramo, Bolzano, Brescia, Como, Cremona, Cuneo, Mantova, Milano, Novara, Pavia, Sondrio, Trento, Torino, Varese, Vercelli
VENICE/NORTH - Belluno, Gorizia, Padova, Pordenone, Rovigo, Treviso, Trieste, Udine, Venezia, Verona, Vicenza,
NORTH WEST/MED COAST - Arezzo, Firenze, Genova, Grosseto, Imperia, Livorno, Lucca, Massa Carrara, Pisa, Pistoia, Savona, Siena, La Spezia
NORTH EAST/ADRIATIC - Ancona, L'Aquila, Ascoli Piceno, Bologna, Campobasso, Chieti, Ferrara, Forli, Iserina, Macerata, Modena, Parma, Perugia, Pescara, Pesaro & Urbino, Piacenza, Ravenna, Reggio nell'Emilia, Teramo, Terni
ROME - Frosinone, Latina, Roma, Rieti, Viterbo
SOUTH - Avellino, Bari, Benevento, Brindisi,

Caserta, Catanzaro, Cosenza, Foggia, Lecce, Matera, Napoli, Potenza, Reggio di Calabria, Salerno, Taranto
SARDINIA - Cagliari, Nuoro, Oristano, Sassari
SICILY - Agrigento, Caltanissetta, Catania, Enna, Messina, Palermo, Ragusa, Siracusa, Trapani

NETHERLANDS

NORTH - Ameland, Drenthe, Friesland, Groningen
CENTRAL - Flevoland, Gelderland, Noord-Holland, Overijssel, Utrecht
SOUTH - Limburg, Noord-Brabant, Zeeland, Zuid-Holland

PORTUGAL

SOUTH - Algarve, Baixo-Alentejo
NORTH - Costa Verde, Douro Litoral, Minho, Tras os Montes, Alto Douro
CENTRAL - Alto Alentejo, Beira Alta, Beira Baixo, Beira Litoral, Costa de Prata, Estremadura, Ribatejo

SPAIN

NORTH EAST COAST - Barcelona, Girona
CENTRAL - Albacete, Avila, Badajoz, Cáceres, Ciudad Real, Cuenca, Guadalajara, Madrid, Salamanca, Segovia, Soria, Teruel, Toledo
SOUTH EAST COAST - Alicante, Castellón, Tarragona, Valencia
NORTH COAST - Asturias, Cantabria, Guipúzcoa, La Coruña, Lugo, Vizcaya
NORTH EAST - Alava, Burgos, Huesca, Lleida, La Rioja, Navarra, Zaragoza
NORTH WEST - Léon, Logrono Orense, Palencia, Pontevedra, Valladolid, Zamora
SOUTH - Almeria, Cádiz, Cordoba, Granada, Huelva, Jaén, Málaga, Murcia, Sevilla
ISLANDS - Ibiza, Mallorca Menorca

SWITZERLAND

NORTH - Aargau, Basel, Solothurn
NORTH EAST - Appenzell, Liechtenstein, St Gallen, Schaffhausen, Thurgau, Zürich
NORTH WEST/CENTRAL - Bern, Jura, Luzern, Neuchâtel, Nidwalden, Obwalden, Schwyz, Uri, Zug
EAST - Glarus, Graubünden
SOUTH - Ticino
SOUTH WEST - Fribourg, Genève, Valais, Vaud

AUSTRIA

Austria is a land of chalet villages and beautiful cities
bordered by eight countries: the Czech Republic,
Germany, Hungary, Italy, Liechtenstein, Switzerland,
Slovakia and Slovenia.

FACTS AND FIGURES

Capital: Wien (Vienna)
Language: German
IDD Code: 43.
To dial the UK, dial 00 44
Currency: Schilling (Schilling
(ATS)=100 Groschen) At the
time of going to press
£1=ATS 19.01

Local time: GMT + 1
(Summer GMT + 2)
Emergency services:
Police 133; Fire 122;
Ambulance 144
Business hours -
Banks: 08.00-12.30,
13.30-15.00 (extended to
17.30 Thu)
Shops: Mon-Fri 08.00-

18.00; Sat 08.00-12.30
**Average daily
temperatures:**
Jan -1°C   Mar 3°C
May 15°C   Jul 20°C
Sep 16°C   Nov 5°C
Tourist information:
Austrian National Tourist
Office
UK 14 Cork Street

London W1X 1PF
Tel 0171 629 0461
USA 500 Fifth Avenue
Suite 800, New York
NY 10110
Tel (212) 944 6880
Camping card:
recommended; some
reductions on site fees

The scenery is predominantly Alpine, an
inspiring mix of mountains, lakes and pine
forests. The splendour of the mountains is seen in
the imposing Dachstein region of upper Austria
and the massive Tyrolean peaks. The lakes of
Burgenland and Salzkammergut, the river
Danube, the forests and woods of Styria and the
world-famous city of Wien (Vienna) are
outstanding features of the landscape.

Most of the country enjoys a moderate
climate during the summer, although eastern areas
are sometimes very hot. The heaviest rainfall
occurs in midsummer. The language of Austria is
German, and English is not widely spoken.

Austria offers a variety of outdoor activities to
suit everyone and there are numerous campsites
throughout the country. Most are open from May
to September, although a number remain open all
year.

Off-site camping or caravanning is generally
prohibited. In areas with no campsites contact
local police to find out whether an overnight stay
is possible. If permission is granted, no camping
activity must be seen from outside, eg chairs,
awnings etc. Open fires are generally prohibited
in woodland areas. Campers not on an official
site, eg private property, staying in Austria for
more than three days should report to the police
as soon as possible, and also inform them of

subsequent changes of location. Within Wien
(Vienna) and Tirol (Tyrol) any form of off-site
camping or caravanning is prohibited.

HOW TO GET THERE
Apart from the crossing via the Channel Tunnel,
the usual Continental Channel ports for this
journey are Calais or Oostende (Ostend). From
Calais drive through eastern France to Strasbourg,
then via Karlsruhe and Stuttgart, crossing into
Austria at Füssen for **Innsbruck and the Tirol**, and
beyond München (Munich) for **Salzburg and
central Austria.**

From Ostend, drive through Belgium to
Aachen, then via Köln (Cologne), Frankfurt,
Nürnberg and München (Munich).

As an alternative, you could cross to Dieppe,
Le Havre, Caen or Cherbourg and drive through
northern France via **Strasbourg** and **Stuttgart**, or
via **Basel** and northern Switzerland. But see
'Motorway tax' in this and the Swiss section. For
details of the AA European Routes Service please
consult the Contents Page.

Distance
From the Continental Channel ports, Salzburg
is about 1140km (708 miles) and Vienna is
about 1320km (820 miles), and you would
normally need one overnight stop on the way.

Car sleeper trains
Services are available in summer from **Denderleeuw** in Belgium to Innsbruck and 's-Hertogenbosch in the Netherlands to Innsbruck and Villach.

MOTORING AND GENERAL INFORMATION
The information given here is specific to Austria. It **must** be read in conjunction with the European ABC at the front of the book, which covers those regulations which are common to many countries.

Air pollution alarm
Restrictions on the circulation of tourist vehicles may apply at certain times in those areas where the level of air pollution exceeds certain limits. However, these restrictions do not apply to tourists using non-polluting vehicles, i.e. those fitted with a catalytic converter system or low-pollution vehicles, i.e. all diesel-engines vehicles put on the road after 1 January 1990. Drivers of exempt vehicles must purchase a permit from the ÖAMTC and display a white test plaque on the windscreen in the event of a pollution alarm.

Boats*
Motorboats are not allowed on most of Austria's lakes. It is advisable to check with the Tourist Office before taking a boat in Austria (see *Tourist information* above for address).

British Embassy/Consulates*
The British Embassy is located at 1030 Wien, Jaurèsgasse 12 ☎ (01) 716130; consular section, Jaurèsgasse 10 ☎(01) 71613 5151. There are British Consulates in Bregenz, Graz, Innsbruck and Salzburg.

Children in cars
Children under 12 and 1.5 metres in height are not permitted to travel as front or rear seat passengers unless using a suitable restraint system.

Currency
There are no restrictions on the amount of foreign or Austrian currency that a *bona fide* tourist can take into or out of the country. during office hours. Exchange offices at some main railway stations are open Saturdays, Sundays and public holidays.

Dimension and weight restrictions
Private **cars** and towed **trailers** or **caravans** are restricted to the following dimensions - height, 4 metres; width 2.50 metres; length, 12 metres. The maximum permitted overall length of vehicle/trailer or caravan combination is 18.75 metres.

Trailers without brakes may weigh up to 750kg and may have a total weight of up to 50% of the towing vehicles.

Driving licence
A valid UK or Republic of Ireland licence is acceptable in Austria. However, those licences which do not incorporate a photograph will not be recognised unless accompanied by photographic proof of identity, eg. a passport. The minimum age at which a visitor may use a temporarily imported motorcycle (exceeding 50cc) or car is 18 years.

First-aid kit*
In Austria all vehicles (including motorcycles) must be equipped with a first-aid kit by law and visitors are expected to comply. This item will not be checked at the frontier, but motorists can be stopped at the scene of an accident and their first-aid kit demanded; if this is not forthcoming the police may take action.

Foodstuffs*
Visitors may import tea, coffee and foodstuffs for their own personal use but raw meat (fresh or frozen) from hoofed animals (*eg.* beef, pork) and shellfish (*eg.* mussels, crab) cannot be imported.

Motoring club*
The **Österreichischer Automobil-, Motorrad- und Touring Club** (ÖAMTC) which has its headquarters at 1010 Wien, Schubertring 1-3 ☎ (01)71199-0 has offices at the major frontier crossings, and is represented in most towns

either direct or through provincial motoring clubs. The offices are usually open between 09.00 to 18.00hrs weekdays, 09.00 to 12.00hrs on Saturdays and are closed on Sundays and public holidays.

Motorway tax

All vehicles using Austrian motorways must display a motorway tax sticker (vignette). Stickers may be purchased at the frontier and from ÖAMTC offices, post offices and petrol stations for periods of 10 days, 2 months or 1 year. The cost of a 10-day sticker (i.e. Friday to Sunday) for vehicles up to 3.5 tonnes in weight, with or without a trailer is ATS70.

Petrol*

Only unleaded petrol is sold in Austria. However, the 98 octane 'Super Plus' petrol contains an anti-wear additive making it suitable for vehicles designed to run on leaded petrol.

Roads

The motorist crossing into Austria from any frontier enters a network of well-engineered roads.

The main traffic artery runs from Bregenz in the west to Wien (Vienna) in the east, via the Arlberg Tunnel (Toll: see *Major Road and Rail Tunnels*), Innsbruck, Salzburg, and Linz. Most of the major alpine roads are excellent, and a comprehensive tour can be made through the Tirol, Salzkammergut and Carinthia without difficulty. Service stations are fairly frequent, even on mountain roads.

In July and August, several roads across the frontier become congested. The main points are on the Lindau-Bregenz road; at the Brenner Pass (possible alternative - the Résia (Reschen) Pass); at Kufstein; on the München (Munich)-Salzburg *Autobahn* and on the Villach-Tarvisio road. Additionally, because of increasing traffic from Germany, Klingenbach and Nickelsdorf on the Austro/Hungarian border are very busy. For details of mountain passes consult the Contents page.

Austria has some 1000 miles of motorway (*autobahn*) with additional tolls payable on the

Brenner, Karawanken Tunnel, Tauern, Pyhrn (Gleinalm and Bosruck Tunnels). Triangles marked on motorway posts indicate the nearest emergency telephone (every 2km). A flashing orange/yellow light at the top of telephone posts indicated danger ahead.

Speed limits*

Car

Built-up areas 50kph (31mph)
Other roads 100kph (62mph)
Motorways 130kph (80mph)
Car towing caravan not exceeding 750kg (1,650lb)†
Built-up areas 50kph (31mph)
Other roads 100kph (62mph)
Motorways 100kph (62mph)
Car towing caravan exceeding 750kg (1,650lb)†
Built-up areas 50kph (31mph)
Other roads 80kph (49mph)
Motorways 100kph (62mph)
† If the total weight of the two vehicles exceeds 3,500kg the following speed limits apply:
Built-up areas 50kph (31mph)
Other roads 70kph (43mph)
Motorways 100kph (62mph)

Notes

i. *To tow a caravan/trailer, the maximum weight of any caravan/trailer equipped with over-run brakes must not exceed the weight of towing vehicle.*
ii. *Driving licence must show entitlement to drive this kind of combination.*

Warning triangle*

The use of a warning triangle is compulsory outside built-up areas in the event of an accident or breakdown. The triangle must be placed 50 metres (55yds) behind the vehicle on ordinary roads and 100 metres (109yds) on motorways to warn following traffic of any obstruction; it must visible at a distance of 50 metres (55yds).

* Additional information will be found in the Continental ABC at the front of the book.

Prices are in Austrian Schillings. Abbreviation: str strasse. Each placename preceded by 'Bad' is listed under the name that follows it.

  TIROL

Magnificent lofty peaks, crystal-clear mountain lakes, peaceful forests and tranquil valleys characterise this internationally-famous corner of Austria. The high mountain regions, reaching altitudes of over 10,000ft (4,000 metres), are accessible by mountain road passes and dozens of cable-cars and chair lifts, and for the climbing and walking enthusiast this is a wonderland of opportunity. The Tirol has a long architectural heritage; even the trim little provincial towns and villages have dignified burgher houses with impressive façades; there are mosaics on public buildings and private houses, and medieval castles and castle ruins command some of the finest settings in the Tirol. The cheerful hospitality of the region is renowned, and folk festivals, dancing and yodelling are colourful local traditions. Innsbruck, the capital of the region, still boasts its medieval old town, with handsome houses facing narrow, irregular streets. Highlights here include the Golden Roof (Goldenes Dachl), with its gilded copper tiles; the Cathedral (Dom), with its imposing west front and rich interior; and the fascinating and extensive displays in the Museum of Folk Art (Tiroler Volkskunstmuseum).

ASCHAU TIROL

Aufenfeld Distelberg 1 ☎ 05282 2916
Level meadowland on forest slope.
➲ *Signposted.*
Closed 2 Nov-7 Dec 4HEC ⬛⬛⬛ ♨ ⚓ 🏪 ⚑ ⚌ ✕ ⊙ ⚑ ∅ ☴ ⚑ ⚡
LPR 🅿 lau ➡ ⊞
Prices: ⚡55-69 pitch 80-110

EHRWALD TIROL

International Dr-Ing E Lauth Zugspitzstr 34
☎ 05673 2666
On undulating grassland, surrounded by high conifers, below the Wetterstein mountain range. Cars may park by tents in winter.
➲ *To the right of the access road to the Zugspitz funicular.*
All year 1HEC ⬛⬛⬛ ♨ ⚓ 🏪 ⚑ ⚌ ✕ ⊙ ⚑ ∅ ☴ ⊞ lau ➡ ⚌
Prices: ⚡70-80 pitch 70-80

Tiroler Zugspitzcamp ☎ 05673 2309
Several grassy terraces. Modern sanitary installations with bathrooms.
➲ *Near the Zugspitz funicular station.*
All year 4HEC ⬛⬛⬛ ∴∴ ♨ ⚓ 🏪 ⚑ ⚌ ✕ ⊙ ⚑ ⚡ P 🅿 ⊞
Prices: ⚡137 pitch 75

FERNSTEINSEE TIROL

Schloss Fernsteinsee ☎ 05265 5210-157
A shady wooded meadowland site.
➲ *Approx. 3km from Nasserieth towards the Fernpass. Signposted.*
Mar-Oct 8HEC ⬛⬛⬛ ♦ ⚓ 🏪 ⚑ ✕ ⊙ ⚑ ∅ ⚡ LR 🅿 ⊞ lau ➡ ⚑ ✕
☴ ⚡P

FIEBERBRUNN TIROL

Tirol-Camp ☎ 05354 56666
A summer and winter site in pleasant Alpine surroundings.
All year 4.7HEC ⬛⬛⬛ ♨ ⚓ 🏪 ⚑ ⚑ ✕ ⊙ ⚑ ∅ ⚡ P 🅿 ⊞ ➡ ⚡L
Prices: ⚡50-100 pitch 55-142

FÜGEN TIROL

Hell ☎ 05288 62203
In a meadow surrounding a farm.
➲ *1km N of Fügen on the B169.*
All year 2.2HEC ⬛⬛⬛ ♨ ⚓ 🏪 ⚑ ⚑ ✕ ⊙ ⚑ ∅ ☴ ⚑ ⚡ P 🅿 ⊞ ⊗
lau ➡ ✕
Prices: ⚡65-70 pitch 65-80

GRÄN TIROL

Tannheimer Tal ☎ 05675 6570
Dogs allowed summer only.
➲ *1km N of the village centre on the Pfronten-Tannheimer Tal road.*
Closed 3 Nov-15 Dec 3HEC ⬛⬛⬛ ∴∴ ☀ ♨ ⚓ 🏪 ⚑ ⚑ ✕ ⊙ ⚑ ∅
☴ ⚑ ⚑ 🅿 ⊞ lau ➡ ⚡LPR

HAIMING TIROL

Center Oberland Bundestr 9 ☎ 05266 88294
On a sloping meadow behind the BP garage.
➲ *Off B171 at Km485.*
All year 1HEC ⬛⬛⬛ ♨ ⚓ 🏪 ⚑ ⚑ ✕ ⊙ ⚑ ∅ ⚡ P 🅿 ⊞ ➡ ⚡R
Prices: ⚡55 ⚑40 ⚑40 ⚓40

HÄSELGEHR TIROL

Rudi Luxnach 122 ☎ 05634 6425
Camping Card Compulsory.
➲ *By the church. Approach from B198.*
All year 1HEC ⬛⬛⬛ ♨ ⚓ ⚑ ⊙ ⚑ ∅ ⚑ ⚡ R 🅿 ⊞ lau
➡ ⚑ ✕ ⚡PR

HEITERWANG TIROL

Heiterwangersee ☎ 05674 5116
In a quiet situation in a meadow beside lake.
➲ *By Hotel Fischer am See.*
All year 1HEC ♨ ♦ ⚓ 🏪 ✕ ⊙ ⚑ ∅ ☴ ⚡ L 🅿 ⊞ lau ➡ ⚑
Prices: ⚡95 pitch 65

HOPFGARTEN TIROL

Reiterhof Penningberg 90 ☎ 05335 3512
➲ *Take B170 towards Kitzbühel and branch off in Kelschauer Tal.*
All year 2HEC ⬛⬛⬛ ♨ ⚓ ✕ ⊙ ⚑ ∅ ☴ ⚡ R ⊞ lau ➡ ⚑ ⚑ ✕

Schlossberg-Itter Itter 140 ☎ 05335 2181
In terraced meadowland below Schloss Itter on the Brixental Ache.
➲ *2km W on B170.*
All year 4HEC ⬛⬛⬛ ∴∴ ♨ ⚓ 🏪 ⚑ ⚑ ✕ ⊙ ⚑ ∅ ☴ ⚡ PR 🅿 lau
➡ ⊞
Prices: ⚡68 ⚑22-45 ⚑22-45 ⚓22-45

HUBEN TIROL

Ötztaler Naturcamping ☎ 05253 5855
A well kept site in a beautiful wooded location beside a mountain stream.
➲ *S of the town. Signposted from Km27 on B186.*
All year 1HEC ♨ ♦ ⚓ 🏪 ⚑ ✕ ⊙ ⚑ ∅ ☴ 🅿 ⊞ lau ➡ ⚑ ✕
Prices: ⚡47-49 ⚑27 ⚑51 ⚓35-51

IMST TIROL

Imst-West Langgasse 62 ☎ 05412 66293
On open meadowland in the Langgasse area.
➲ *Off the bypass near the turn for the Pitztal.*
All year 1HEC ⬛⬛⬛ ♨ ⚓ 🏪 ⚑ ⚑ ⊙ ⚑ ∅ ☴ ⊞ lau ➡ ✕ ⚡PR ⊞
Prices: ⚡55 pitch 70

INNSBRUCK TIROL

Innsbruck-Kranebitten Kranebitter Allee 214
☎ 0512 284180

In a pleasant location close to the city. An 'Innsbruck Card' giving reductions to many places of interest and some forms of public transport is available at the site.
➲ *Signposted from A12/E60 (Innsbruck-Arlberg).*
All year 3HEC ⚏ ⌕ ⋔ ⚞ ⚟ ✗ ⊙ ⬛ ⬤ ≞ ⚐ ↘ R 🕾 ⊞ lau
Prices: ⋔75 ⇔40 ⊕45 ⚑40

▶ KITZBÜHEL TIROL

Schwarzsee Reitherstr 24 ☎ 05356 62806
In meadowland on the edge of a wood behind a large restaurant.
➲ *2km from town on B170 towards Wörgl turn right, 400m after Schwarzsee railway station.*
All year 5HEC ⚏ ↘ ⌕ ⋔ ⚞ ⚟ ✗ ⊙ ⬛ ⬤ ⚐ ↘ L 🕾 ⊞ lau
Prices: ⋔88-99 pitch 95-107

▶ KÖSSEN TIROL

Wilder Kaiser Kranebittau 18 ☎ 05375 6444
Situated in a lovely position below Unterberg, this level site is adjoined on three sides by woodland.
➲ *For access follow road to Unterberg Lift, then turn right and continue for 200m.*
All year 5HEC ⚏ ⌕ ⌂ ⚞ ⚟ ✗ ⊙ ⬛ ⬤ ↘ P 🕾 ⊞ lau

▶ KRAMSACH TIROL

Ferien Comfort Seeblick Toni Brantlhof ☎ 05337 63544
Rural site near the Brantlhof above Lake Reintaler.
Camping Card Compulsory.
➲ *From Inntal Motorway (Rattenberg/Kramsach exit) follow signs 'Zu den Seen' for about 3km, then drive through Seehof site.*
All year 3HEC ⚏ ⌕ ⌂ ⚞ ✗ ⊙ ⬛ ⬤ ↘ L 🕾 ⊞ lau

Stadlerhof ☎ 05337 63371
A pleasant, year-round site on the Reintaler See.
➲ *Access via A12.*
All year 3HEC ⚏ ⌕ ⌂ ⚞ ⚟ ✗ ⊙ ⬛ ⬤ ≞ ⬤ ⚐ ↘ LP 🕾 ⊞ lau
Prices: ⋔56-71 pitch 79-89

▶ KUFSTEIN TIROL

Hager Langkampfen 326 ☎ 05372 64170
Site situated on level meadowland.
All year 0.8HEC ⚏ ⌕ ⌂ ⚞ ✗ ⊙ ⬛ ⬤ 🕾 ⊞ lau ↘ ↘LPR

Kufstein Salurner Str 36 ☎ 05372 62229
In a pleasant location with a good variety of sporting facilities.
➲ *1km W of Kufstein between River Inn and B171.*
May-Oct 1HEC ⚏ ⌕ ⌂ ⚞ ⚟ ✗ ⊙ ⬛ ⬤ ≞ 🕾 ⊞ lau ↘ ↘LPR
Prices: ⋔48-49 ⇔40-41 ⊕40-41 ⚑35-36

▶ LANDECK TIROL

See also Zams

Riffler ☎ 05442 624774
Site on meadowland between residential housing and banks of Sanna.
Closed May 0.3HEC ⚏ ⌕ ⌂ ⊙ ⬛ ↘ R 🕾 ⊞ lau ↘ ⚟ ✗ ⬤ ↘P
Prices: ⋔55 ⇔30 ⊕90-105 ⚑55-90

Sport Camp Tirol Mühlkanal 1 ☎ 05442 64636
Meadowland site with many fruit trees.
➲ *On B316.*
All year 1.3HEC ⚏ ⌕ ⌂ ⚞ ⚟ ✗ ⊙ ⬛ ⬤ ≞ ⬤ ↘ R 🕾 ⊞ lau ↘ ↘P

▶ LÄNGENFELD TIROL

Ötztal ☎ 05253 5348
In meadowland with some tall trees on the edge of woodland.

➲ *Turn right off E186 at fire station.*
All year 2.8HEC ⚏ ⌕ ⌂ ⚞ ⚟ ✗ ⊙ ⬛ ⬤ ≞ ⚐ 🕾 ⊞ lau ↘ ↘PR

▶ LERMOOS TIROL

Happy Camp Hofherr Garmischer Str 21
☎ 05673 2980
Well equipped site in a wooded location.
➲ *500mtrs from the town, off B187 towards Ehrwald.*
Closed 1-31 May & 1 Nov-14 Dec 0.8HEC ⚏ ⌕ ⌂ ⚟ ✗ ⊙ ⬛ ≞ 🕾 lau ↘ ⌂ ↘ ↘P ⊞
Prices: ⋔69.50-81.50 pitch 85-105

▶ LEUTASCH TIROL

Holiday ☎ 05214 65700
A modern site on level grassland screened by trees on the Leutascher Ache.
➲ *Turn off B313 (Mittenwald-Scharnitz) towards Leutasch.*
Closed Nov 2.6HEC ⚏ ⌕ ⌂ ⚞ ⚟ ✗ ⊙ ⬛ ⬤ ≞ ⬤ ↘ PR 🕾 ⊞ lau
Prices: ⋔85 pitch 70-150

▶ LIENZ TIROL

Falken Eichholz 7 ☎ 04852 64022
➲ *S of Lienz. Signposted from B100.*
Closed 21 Nov-15 Dec 2HEC ⚏ ↘ ⌕ ⌂ ⚞ ⚟ ✗ ⊙ ⬛ ⬤ ≞ 🕾 lau ↘ ↘PR ⊞

▶ MAURACH TIROL

Karwendel ☎ 05243 6116
➲ *In town turn off the B181 and follow the Pertisau road.*
All year 2HEC ⚏ ⌕ ⌂ ⚞ ⚟ ✗ ⊙ ⬛ ⬤ ≞ ⬤ ⚐ lau ↘ ⌂ ↘LP ⊞
Prices: ⋔50-60 ⇔30 ⊕60 ⚑40-50

▶ MAYRHOFEN TIROL

Laubichl ☎ 05285 2580
On a gently sloping meadow near a farm at N entrance to village.
All year 2HEC ⚏ ↘ ⌕ ⌂ ✗ ⊙ ⬛ ⬤ ≞ 🕾 ⊞ lau ↘ ↘P

▶ NASSEREITH TIROL

Rossbach ☎ 05265 5154
All year 1HEC ⚏ ↘ ⌕ ⌂ ⚞ ✗ ⊙ ⬛ ⬤ ≞ ↘ P 🕾 ⊞

▶ NATTERS TIROL

Natterer See Natterer See 1 ☎ 0512 546732
A terraced site beautifully situated amidst woodland and mountains on the shore of Natterersee.
➲ *Approach via Brenner Motorway, exit 'Innsbruck Süd', via Natters, onto B182 and follow signs.*
Closed Oct-15 Dec 7HEC ⚏ ⌕ ⌂ ⚞ ⚟ ✗ ⊙ ⬛ ⬤ ≞ ⬤ ⚐ ⚑ ↘ L 🕾 ⊞ lau
Prices: ⋔72-93 pitch 98-125

▶ NAUDERS TIROL

Alpencamping Nauders ☎ 05473 268
A year-round family site in a delightful Alpine location with good recreational facilities.
➲ *Access via B315.*
Closed 3 Nov-18 Dec 0.3HEC ⚏ ↘ ⌕ ⌂ ✗ ⊙ ⬛ ⬤ 🕾 lau

▶ NEUSTIFT TIROL

Hochstubai ☎ 05226 3484
On slightly sloping meadowland.
➲ *Near the Geier Alm approximately 5km S of town on the road towards the Gletscher bahn.*
All year 2.7HEC ⚏ ⌕ ⌂ ⚟ ✗ ⊙ ⬛ ⬤ ≞ ↘ R 🕾 ⊞ lau ↘ ↘LP

❯ Pfunds Tirol

Sonnen ☎ 05474 5232
Site in meadowland with some fruit trees.
➲ *On road B315 between SHELL Garage and Gasthof Sonne.*
All year 1HEC ⟂ 🚽🏠🛁🍴✕⊙🖪🚿🏢⊞➤ ⚡LP

❯ Pill Tirol

Plankenhof ☎ 05242 641950
Site in meadow.
➲ *On B171 near Gasthof Plankenhof.*
May-Oct 0.6HEC ⟂ 🚽🏠🍴⊙🖪⚡ P 🏢⊞ lau ➤ 🛁✕
Prices: 🏕46 🚐40 🚙40 🛖40

❯ Prutz Tirol

Prutz ☎ 05472 2648
A pleasant site in a beautiful mountain setting with good, modern facilities.
All year 2.5HEC ⟂ ➤🏠🛁🍴✕⊙🖪🚿⚡ R 🏢⊞ lau ➤ ⚡LP
Prices: pitch 125-140

❯ Reutte Tirol

Reutte Ehrenbergstr 53 ☎ 05672 62809
Well kept site on a meadow on the edge of a forest near the sports centre. Modern swimming pool in town.
➲ *Turn right towards Waldrast.*
Closed May 2.2HEC ⟂ 🏊🏠🛁⊙🖪🚿🏢⊞ lau ➤🛁✕ ⚡P
Prices: 🏕71-81 pitch 73-109

Seespitze ☎ 05672 78121
May-15 Oct 2HEC ⟂ 🚽🏠🛁✕⊙🖪🚿⚡ L 🏢⊞ lau ➤✕

Sennalpe ☎ 05672 78115
In a quiet situation next to the lake.
➲ *On Reutte-Oberammergau road 200m from the Hotel Forelle.*
Closed 16 Oct-14 Dec 3HEC ⟂ 🚽🏠🛁⊙🖪🚿🚿⚡ L 🏢⊞ lau ➤🛁✕

❯ Ried bei Landeck Tirol

Dreiländereck ☎ 05472 6025
Level site in centre of village beside a lake with spectacular views.
All year 1HEC ⟂ 🚽🏠🛁🍴✕⊙🖪🚿🏢🚐🏢⊞ lau ➤✕ ⚡LPR

❯ Rinn Tirol

Judenstein Judenstein 40 ☎ 05223 78620
In a wooded location with fine views.
➲ *Access via motorway exit Hall.*
Apr-15 Oct 0.6HEC ⟂ 🚽🏠⊙🖪🚿🏢⊞ lau ➤🛁🍴✕
Prices: 🏕40 🚐25 🚙40 🛖30

❯ St Johann Tirol

Michelnhof Weiberndorf 6 ☎ 05352 62584
➲ *1.5km S via B161 (St-Johann-Kitzbühel).*
All year 2HEC ⟂ 🚽🏠🛁✕⊙🖪🚿⚡🏢⊞ lau ➤🍴⚡R

❯ Scharnitz Tirol

Alm
On level, open grassland. Near B177.
➲ *Access from S outskirts.*
1 Nov-15 Dec & 15-30 Apr 0.8HEC ⟂ 🚽🏠✕⊙🖪🚿🚿 🚐🏢⊞ lau ➤🛁✕ ⚡R
Prices: 🏕45-50 pitch 40-50

❯ Schwaz Tirol
❯ At Weer (6km W)

Alpencamping Mark Maholmhof ☎ 05224 68146
Situated on meadowland by a farm on the edge of a forest.
➲ *Off B171.*
Apr-30 Oct 2HEC ⟂ ➤🏠🛁🍴✕⊙🖪🚿🏢🏢🛖 ⚡ P 🏢⊞ lau

❯ Sölden Tirol

Sölden ☎ 05254 2672
Situated on meadowland on left bank of Ötztaler tributary. Beautiful views of the surrounding mountains.
➲ *By Grauer Bär Inn at Km36 on the B186.*
Closed May-15 Jun 1.2HEC ⟂ 🏊🏠⊙🖪🚿🚿🏢⊞ lau ➤ 🛁✕⚡P

❯ Stams Tirol

Eichenwald Schiessstand weg 10 ☎ 05263 6159
Well managed terraced site in oak wood.
➲ *Turn off B171 at ESSO filling station in direction of abbey, onto a steep, narrow access road.*
May-Sep 2HEC ⟂ 🚽🏠🛁🍴✕⊙🖪🚿🏢🏢🚐🛖 ⚡ P 🏢⊞ lau ➤ ⚡R

❯ Thiersee Tirol

Rueppenhof Seebauern 8 ☎ 05376 5694
Site made up of several meadows surrounding a farm that lies on the banks of a lake.
Apr-Oct 1.5HEC ⟂ 🚽🏠⊙🖪⚡ L 🏢⊞➤🛁🍴✕🚿🚿

❯ Umhausen Tirol

Ötztal Arena Camp Krismer ☎ 05255 5390
➲ *Signposted from B186.*
All year 1HEC ⟂ 🚽🏠⊙🖪🚿🚿🚐🏢⊞ lau ➤🛁🍴✕

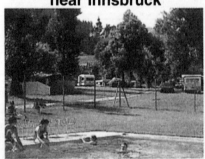

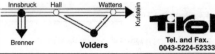

UNTERPERFUSS TIROL

Farm ☎ 05232 2209
Modern site on gently sloping meadow in a beautiful
mountain setting.
➔ *W end of village near Amberg railway and main road.*
All year 2HEC ⸗ ▢◖◗♨✕☉▢◒⸚▥⊞➔▨✕
Prices: ♦60 pitch 78

VOLDERS TIROL

Schloss ☎ 05224 52333
A pleasant site in the grounds of a castle surrounded by thick
woods.
Camping Card Compulsory.
➔ *Access from the B171 by ARAL filling station or from
motorway exit Schwaz or Wattens.*
15 May-15 Oct 2.5HEC ◖◗♨✕☉▢◒♨▲ ⸗ P⊞ lau
Prices: ♦65 ♠40 ♣40 ▲40

VÖLS TIROL

Völs Bahnhofstr 10 ☎ 0512 303533
➔ *Access via motorway exit Innsbruck-Kranebitten.*
May-Sep 0.4HEC ⸗ ▢◖◗♨✕☉▢⊞ lau➔▨◒ ⸗PR

WAIDRING TIROL

Steinplatte Unterwasser 43 ☎ 05353 5345
All year 4HEC ⸗ ▢◖▨♨✕☉▢◒⸚◍ ⸗L⊞➔ ⸗P

WALCHSEE TIROL

Seespitz Wassersportzentrum ☎ 05374 5359
Site made up of several plots of land.
➔ *Between B172 and bank of lake.*
All year 3HEC ⸗ ▢◖▨♨✕☉▢◒ ⸗L⊞ lau
Prices: ♦65-70 pitch 65-100

Terrassencamping Süd-See Seestr 76 ☎ 05374 5339
Extensively terraced site, the lowest are reserved for tourers.
➔ *500m W on B172 turn into 'no through road' and continue
for 1500m.*
All year 10HEC ⸗ ◍▢◖▨♨✕☉▢◒⸚ ⸗L⊞ lau

WESTENDORF TIROL

Panorama Mühltal 26 ☎ 05334 6166
In a beautiful Alpine setting with good modern facilities,
including well furnished studio appartments.
➔ *W towards Wörgl via B170.*
All year 2.2HEC ⸗ ▢◖▨♨✕☉▢◒⸚▥ ▣⊞ lau➔ ⸗P
Prices: ♦65-95 ♠42-66 ♣42-66 ▲42

ZAMS TIROL

See also Landeck

Zams Magdalenaweg 1 ☎ 05442 63289
A comfortable family site in a central location.
➔ *2km NE of Landeck. Access via A12 and B171.*
Jun-20 Sep 0.3HEC ⸗ ▢◖☉▢▢⊞➔▨♨✕☉⸚ ⸗R
Prices: ♦46 ♠19 ♣49 ▲49

ZELL AM ZILLER TIROL

Hofer Gerlossasstr 33 ☎ 05282 2248
On meadowland with some fruit trees.
➔ *Site lies to the end of Zillertal off the road leading to the
Gerlos Pass.*
All year 1.5HEC ⸗ ▢◖♨✕☉▢◒ ⸗P⊞ lau
Prices: ♦50-60 pitch 65

ZIRL TIROL

Alpenfrieden Eigenhofen 11 ☎ 05238 53520
➔ *Near the B171.*
May-Sep 1HEC ⸗ ◍◖♨✕☉▢◒ ⸗P⊞➔⸚ ⸗R
Prices: ♦45 pitch 80

● ● ● ● ● **CARINTHIA** ● ● ● ●

High mountains on all sides tumble down to this sunny,
southern, gentle land of soft light and over a thousand
warm, clear lakes. The climate is kind to holiday-makers -
most of the weather troughs are broken up by the
surrounding mountains, so this province gets many more
sunny days than the rest of the country. The lakes provide a
wealth of water sports in the summer, frequently reaching
temperatures of over 75 degrees F (24 degrees C) - ideal
for swimmers, wind-surfers and sailors. Anglers can fish for
pike, whitefish and carp, and hot springs in the region have
been channelled into waterpark complexes with chutes and
whirling currents, or health spas offering the 'gift of youth'.
But the mild summers are complemented by sharp winters,
making Nassfeld and the Nock district popular areas for
winter sports.
There is a relaxed Mediterranean atmosphere in this region,
and a substantial Slovene minority, dating back to the 6th
century, adds its own distinct character and language to
southern parts.
The capital of Carinthia is Klagenfurt which, according to
legend, was built on a swamp once dominated by a dragon.
The centre of the town now is the Dragon Fountain
(Lindwurmbrunnen), with its huge grim 16th-century
sculpture of the town's heraldic emblem. Now an important
junction and commercial centre, Klagenfurt's old quarter
has many handsome baroque buildings set in attractive
lanes and passageways.
....

ANNENHEIM KÄRNTEN

Bad Ossiacher See ☎ 04248 2757
An extensive level site with adjoining meadow.
➔ *Situated on B94 Villach-Wien road.*
15 May-15 Sep 5.4HEC ⸗ ▢◖▨♨✕☉▢◒ ⸗L⊞➔⸚
lau

DELLACH KÄRNTEN

Neubauer ☎ 04766 2530
A terraced site with direct access to the Millstättersee.
➔ *Access from B100, Leinz-Spittal road. The turn-off is well
signposted in the village.*
14 Apr-15 Oct 1.5HEC ⸗ ▢◖♨✕☉▢◒ ⸗L⊞ lau
➔▨✕⸚
Prices: ♦68.50-83.50 pitch 60-70

DELLACH IM DRAUTAL KÄRNTEN

Waldbad ☎ 04714 288 & 234
A small site in a delightful wooded setting with two large
swimming pools.
➔ *Leave A10 at Spittal & turn onto B100.*
May-Sep 2HEC ⸗ ▢◖▨✕☉▢◒ ⸗P⊞ lau
➔♨ ⸗R
Prices: pitch 150-230 (incl 2 persons)

DÖBRIACH KÄRNTEN

Brunner am See Glanzerstr 108 ☎ 04246 7189
Tidily arranged with poplar trees. Private bathing area.
➔ *The access road is at the E end of Lake Millstatt.*
All year 2.5HEC ⸗ ⸚⸚ ▢◖▨♨✕☉▢◒⸚◍ ⸗L⊞
lau
Prices: ♦65-95 pitch 85-140 (incl 2 persons)

Burgstaller Seefeldstr 16 ☎ 04246 7774
A quiet site situated 100m from the lake, with good modern
facilities.
➔ *At SE end of lake. From B98 continue towards Lake
Millstatt for 1km.*   *Contd.*

All year 7.5HEC ⬛ 🔌🚿🛒🍴✕⊙🚮🅿🚻 LP
📷➕ lau
Prices: ⚑65-98 pitch 65-120

Ebner's Seefeldstr 1 ☎ 04246 7735
➲ *On either side of the Seefeldstr, beyond Camping Burgstaller, at E end of Lake Millstatt.*
1HEC ⬛ 🔌🚿🛒🍴✕⊙🚮🅿🚻 P📷➕ lau ➤ L

Winkler Strandweg 26 ☎ 04246 7187
Family site on level ground, divided into sections and surrounded by woodland close to the Millstättersee.
➲ *Approx. 200m E of the lake.*
15 Apr-15 Oct 2HEC ⬛ 🔌🚿🛒🍴✕⊙🚮🅿🚻
LPR
Prices: ⚑45-90 pitch 100-110

▶ **DÖLLACH** KÄRNTEN

Zirknitzer ☎ 04825 451
Beside the River Möu.
➲ *Between Km8 and Km9 on the Glocknerstr (B107).*
All year 0.6HEC ⬛ 🔌🚿🛒🍴✕⊙🚮🅿🚻 R📷➕ lau
➤ P
Prices: ⚑38.50-49.50 🚗20-27.50 🚐24-27.50 ⚑13-17

▶ **DROBOLLACH** KÄRNTEN

Mittewald Fuchsbichlweg 9 ☎ 04242 27392
In a hollow on slightly rising ground surrounded by trees and divided into pitches. Large children's playground.
➲ *Off Villach-Faaker See road. Signposted 'Serai'.*
All year 2.5HEC ⬛ 🔌🚿🍴✕⊙🚮🚻 P📷 lau ➤

▶ **EBERNDORF** KÄRNTEN

Rutar Lido ☎ 04236 2262-0
On an open meadow at the edge of a forest. A popular family site with good facilities.
All year 15HEC ⬛ 🔌🚿🛒✕⊙🚮🚻 LP📷➕ lau
➤ 🍴

▶ **FELDKIRCHEN** KÄRNTEN

Maltschach Briefelsdorf 7 ☎ 04277 2644
Near the lake, next to Sotour Holiday Village.
➲ *On B95 take exit 'Radweg', then follow signposts.*
May-Sep 7HEC ⬛ 🔌🚿⊙🚮🚻📷➕ lau ➤🛒🍴✕ LP

▶ **GNESAU** KÄRNTEN

Hobitsch Sonnleiten 24 ☎ 04278 368
➲ *From B95, drive N towards Gnesau.*
31 May-Sep 0.6HEC ⬛ 🔌🚿⊙🚮 P📷➕ lau ➤🛒✕

▶ **HEILIGENBLUT** KÄRNTEN

Grossglockner Hadergasse 11 ☎ 04824 2048
In a location on a meadow surrounded by woodland within the National Park.
➲ *Signposted.*
May-Oct & Dec-Etr 2.5HEC ⬛ ☼🚿🛒🍴✕⊙🚮
R📷 lau ➤ P➕
Prices: ⚑60-70 🚗30 🚐30

▶ **HERMAGOR** KÄRNTEN

Flaschberger ☎ 04282 2020
Camping Card Compulsory
➲ *2km E via B111.*
All year 2HEC ⬛ 🔌⊙🚮🚻 LP📷➕ lau ➤🛒🍴
✕

Schluga Seecamping ☎ 04282 2051
Approx. 800m N of lake in meadowland with some terraces and fine views.
➲ *6km E of Hermagor.*

20 May-20 Sep 8.8HEC ⬛ ➤🚿🛒🍴✕⊙🚮🚻⚓ L
📷➕
Prices: ⚑41.50-83 pitch 47.50-95

▶ **KEUTSCHACH** KÄRNTEN

Strandcamping Süd ☎ 04273 2773
On south side of the Keutschachersee.
➲ *Access via motorway exit Valden towards Kreutschacher-Seental.*
May-Sep 2HEC ⬛ 🔌🚿✕⊙🚮🚻 L📷➕ lau
Prices: ⚑60-70 pitch 80-90

▶ **KLAGENFURT** KÄRNTEN

Strandbad ☎ 0463 21169
Large site divided into sections by trees and bushes.
➲ *From town centre take B83 towards Velden. Turn left just outside town in direction of bathing area.*
May-Sep 4HEC ⬛ ➤🚿🛒🍴✕⊙🚮🚻📷➕ lau ➤ L
Prices: ⚑50-80 pitch 100

▶ **KÖTSCHACH-MAUTHEN** KÄRNTEN

Alpen ☎ 04715 429
On level meadowland beside River Gail with good facilities for water sports.
➲ *Turn off B110 in the S part of the village on the road to the Plöcken Pass and drive 800m towards Lesachtal.*
Closed Nov-14 Dec 1.4HEC ⬛ ➤🚿🛒🍴✕⊙🚮🚻
➕ lau ➤ ✕ PR
Prices: ⚑41-65 pitch 47-75

▶ **MALTA** KÄRNTEN

Maltatal ☎ 0043 4733 234
On a gently rising alpine meadow with breathtaking views of the surrounding mountains.
➲ *In Gmünd turn off B99 and drive 5.5km through Malta valley.*
27 Mar-31 Oct 3.5HEC ⬛ ➤🚿🛒🍴✕⊙🚮🚻 PR📷
➕ lau
Prices: ⚑69-89 pitch 68-138

▶ **MÖLLBRÜCKE** KÄRNTEN

Rheingold Mölltalstr 65 ☎ 04769 2338
➲ *Site on main road from Spittal to Mallnitz, next to swimming pool.*
All year 2HEC ⬛ 🔌🚿🍴✕⊙🚮 P📷➤🛒

▶ **OBERVELLACH** KÄRNTEN

Sport Erlebnis ☎ 04782 2727
May-Sep 10HEC ⬛ 🔌🚿🍴✕⊙🚮⚓ R📷➕ lau ➤🛒

▶ **OSSIACH** KÄRNTEN

Ossiach ☎ 04243 436
Divided into pitches with generally well-situated terraces.
➲ *Off B94 on E bank of Kale Ossiacher.*
May-30 Sep 10HEC ⬛ 🔌🚿🛒🍴✕⊙🚮🚻⚓ L📷
➕🏊 lau
Prices: ⚑59-89 pitch 80-130

Parth ☎ 04243 2744
On hilly ground on S shore of the lake. Steep, but there are some terraces.
➲ *Off B94 on S bank of Lake Ossiach.*
Apr-Oct 2HEC ⬛ ➤🚿🛒✕⊙🚮🚻⚓ L📷➕🏊
lau
Prices: ⚑55-84 pitch 42-108

▶ At **HEILIGEN GESTADE** (5km SW)

Seecamping Berghof Ossiachersee-Süduferstr 241
☎ 04242 41133

Terraced meadowland in attractive setting. 800m long promenade with bathing areas. Dogs not allowed Jul-Aug
➲ *E shore of Lake Ossiacher.*
24 Apr-15 Oct 10HEC ⚏ ⋮⋮⋮ ⚶ ♠ ⚑ ♈ ✕ ⊙ ⚑ ∅ ⚒ ⚑ ⚑ ⚘ L ⚐
Prices: ♦64-92 pitch 99-160

SCHIEFLING KÄRNTEN

Weisses Rössl ☎ 04274 2898
In a wooded setting with fine views of the surrounding mountains on the shore of the Wôrther See.
May-Sep 2.5HEC ⚏ ♦ ♠ ⚑ ♈ ✕ ⊙ ⚑ ∅ ⚒ ⚑ ⚐ ⚘ lau ♦ ⚘L
Prices: ♦76-90 ♠20 ⚑35-42 ♠35-42

SEEBODEN KÄRNTEN

Ferienpark Lieseregg Lieseregg ☎ 04762 2723
On large level meadows; some terraces and asphalt drives.
➲ *B99 from Spittal north to B98, then left for 1.5km.*
May-15 Oct 4HEC ⚏ ⚶ ♠ ⚑ ♈ ✕ ⊙ ⚑ ∅ ⚒ ⚑ ⚘ ⚘ P ⚐ ⊞ lau
Prices: ♦75-90 pitch 90

Seecamping Penker ☎ 04762 81267
Site situated on meadowland and divided into fields on both sides of the lakeside promenade. There are some rows of poplars and the lower part of the site is terraced.
➲ *For access turn off opposite ADEG store and continue for 300m.*
May-Oct 1.2HEC ⚏ ⚶ ♠ ⚑ ♈ ✕ ⊙ ⚑ ∅ ⚘ LP ⚐ ⊞

SPITTAL AN DER DRAU KÄRNTEN

Draufluss ☎ 04762 2466
A long, narrow riverside site, partly surrounded by a hedge.
➲ *From town centre follow road to river towards Goldeckbahn.*
Apr-Oct 0.7HEC ⚏ ⚶ ♠ ♈ ✕ ⊙ ⚑ ⚘ P ⚐ ⊞ lau ♦ ⚘ ∅
Prices: ♦50-60 ♠30-40 ⚑30-40 ♠30-40

STOCKENBOI KÄRNTEN

Ronacher ☎ 04761 256
Situated on meadow between forest slopes, gently sloping to the shore of Lake Weissensee.
Camping Card compulsory.
➲ *Approach for caravans via Weissensee.*
May-Sep 1.7HEC ⚏ ♦ ♠ ⚑ ♈ ✕ ⊙ ⚑ ∅ ⚘ L ⚐ ⊞ lau

TECHENDORF KÄRNTEN

Strandcamping Knaller ☎ 04713 2234
➲ *From B87, drive towards Weissensee.*
May-Oct 1.5HEC ⚏ ♠ ⚑ ♈ ✕ ⊙ ⚑ ∅ ⚘ L ⚐ ⊞ ♦ ♈ ✕

UNTERNARRACH KÄRNTEN

Strandcamping Turner See St Primus ☎ 04239 2350
A quiet site in a picturesque mountain setting with a good variety of recreational facilities.
24 Apr-3 Oct 6.8HEC ⚏ ♦ ♠ ⚑ ♈ ✕ ⊙ ⚑ ∅ ⚒ ⚑ ⚑ ⚘ L ⚐ ♦ ⊞
Prices: ♦50-87 pitch 74-110

At VELLACH(2km W)

Schluga ☎ 04282 2051
Well equipped family site in a rural setting 4km from Presseger See.
All year 5.8HEC ⚏ ⚶ ♠ ⚑ ♈ ✕ ⊙ ⚑ ∅ ⚒ ⚑ ⚘ LP ⚐ ⊞
Prices: ♦41.50-83 pitch 47.50-95

VILLACH KÄRNTEN

Gerli St Georgenerstr 140 ☎ 04242 57402
Level, quiet, isolated site, with heated swimming pool annexed to it which is open to the public.

➲ *From Spittal/Drau turn off B100, turn right just before Villach and continue for 2km.*
All year 2.3HEC ⚏ ⚶ ♠ ⚑ ♈ ✕ ⊙ ⚑ ∅ ⚒ ⚑ ⚑ ⚘ P ⚐ ⊞ lau ♦ ♈
Prices: ♦45-54 pitch 45-54

At FAAK AM SEE(10km SE)

Komfortcamping Poglitsch ☎ 04254 2718
Mar-Oct 7HEC ⚏ ⚶ ♠ ⚑ ♈ ✕ ⊙ ⚑ ∅ ⚒ ⚘ L ⚐ ⊞ lau

Strandcamping Arneitz ☎ 04254 2137
On a wooded peninsula jutting into the Faakersee with good sporting facilities.
28 Apr-1 Oct 6HEC ⚏ ⋮⋮⋮ ⚶ ♠ ⚑ ♈ ✕ ⊙ ⚑ ∅ ⚒ ⚑ ⚘ L ⚐ ⊞ ⚑ lau
Prices: ♦88-96 pitch 120-150

Strandcamping Florian Badeweg 3 ☎ 04254 2261
A partially shaded site between the lakeside and the road.
➲ *Access from road by Hotel Fürst.*
May-25 Sep 3.5HEC ⚏ ⚶ ♠ ⚑ ♈ ✕ ⊙ ⚑ ∅ ⚒ ⚑ ⚘ L ⚐ ⊞ lau ♦ ⚘
Prices: ♦65-80 ♠30-30 ⚑50-70 ♠50-70 pitch 80-100

Strandcamping Gruber ☎ 04254 2298
On level ground beside the lake with fine views of the surrounding mountains.
May-Sep 2.5HEC ⚏ ⋮⋮⋮ ⚶ ♠ ⚑ ♈ ✕ ⊙ ⚑ ⚘ L ⚐ ⊞ lau ♦ ∅
Prices: pitch 250-400 (incl 4 persons)

WERTSCHACH KÄRNTEN

Alpenfreude ☎ 04256 2708
May-Sep 5HEC ⚏ ⚶ ♠ ⚑ ♈ ✕ ⊙ ⚑ ∅ ⚒ ⚑ ⚑ ⚘ P ⚐ ⊞ lau

● ● ● ● ● **STYRIA** ● ● ● ● ●

Styria is a mosaic; soft hills in the southern wine-growing area, wide forest areas which have given the province the name of the 'green march', and the grand rocky massifs of the upper Styria. Between the high Alps, crossed by dramatic mountain passes, and the lowland regions, is a spectrum of beautiful scenery, with pleasant summer resorts as well as winter sports areas. The region is rich in beautiful gorges and waterfalls, the largest and the best known of which is the Gesause, where the River Enns has carved its way through the mountains. Caves are a feature of Styria - the large Lurgrotten at Peggau is well equipped for visitors - and some caves have revealed evidence of prehistoric occupation. Austria's second largest city and Styria's capital, the lively city of Graz is in the south-east corner of the province. A major industrial and university town, Graz boasts many interesting historic buildings, and above the attractive old town, a funicular leads to the 1,552ft (473 metres) Schlossberg which is dominated by the town's distinctive landmark, the 92ft (28 metre) clock tower (Uhrturm).

AUSSEE, BAD STEIERMARK

Traun Grundlseer Str 21 ☎ 03622 54565
In pleasant wooded surroundings.
➲ *2.5km from Bad Aussee towards Grundlsee.*
All year 0.4HEC ⚏ ⚶ ♠ ♈ ✕ ⊙ ⚑ ∅ ⚒ ⚑ ⚘ R ⚐ lau ♦ ⚘⚘
Prices: ♦55 pitch 40

▶ **GRAZ** STEIERMARK

S C Central Martinhofstr 3 ☎ 0316 281831
A site with many lawns separated by asphalt paths and partly
divided into pitches.
⊃ *Turn off the B70 in Strassgang S of Graz and continue for
300m.*
Mar-Oct 4HEC ⏚ ♣ ⋔ ⛟ ⵉ ✕ ⊙ ⚑ ⛴ 🏕 ⚑ ⵋ P 🅿 ⊞ lau
Prices: pitch 180-220

▶ At **MANTSCHA**

Tenniscamping Reiderhof ☎ 0316 284380
A peaceful, terraced site surrounded by woodlands.
⊃ *From Graz take Reininghausstr and Steinbergstr towards
Mantscha signposted from railway station.*
All year 5HEC ⏚ ⊲ ⋔ ⛟ ⵉ ✕ ⊙ ⚑ 🅿 lau ♦ ⵋPR

▶ **HIRSCHEGG** STEIERMARK

Hirschegg ☎ 03141 2201
In a delightful Alpine setting.
⊃ *Access via A2 towards Klagenfurt, exit Modriach.*
All year 2HEC ⏚ ⋔ ⊙ ⚑ ⚑ 🏕 lau ♦ ⛟ ⵉ ✕ ⵋLR ⊞
Prices: ♦38 ⇔25 ⚑25 ▲25

▶ **LANGENWANG-MÜRTZAL** STEIERMARK

Europa Siglstr 5 ☎ 03854 2950
On level meadow with some trees, surrounded by hedges.
⊃ *The B306 (E7) by-passes the town, so be careful not to miss
the exit 6km S of Mürzzuschlag.*
All year 0.6HEC ⏚ ⊲ ⋔ ⊙ ⚑ ⵣ ⵉ lau ♦ ⛟ ⵉ ✕ ⵋR ⊞
Prices: ♦47 ⇔37 ⚑37 ▲37

▶ **LEIBNITZ** STEIERMARK

Leibnitz R-H-Bartsch-Gasse 33 ☎ 03452 82463
⊃ *W of town. Signposted.*
May-Sep 0.7HEC ⏚ ♣ ⋔ ✕ ⊙ ⚑ ⵋ PR 🅿 ⊞ ♦ ⛟ ⵉ ⵣ ⵣ

▶ **LIEBOCH** STEIERMARK

Graz-Lieboch ☎ 03136 61797
In a picturesque wooded location with good modern
facilities.
⊃ *Access via A2, exit Lieboch.*
May-Oct 0.3HEC ⏚ ♣ ⋔ ⊙ ⚑ ⵣ 🏕 ⵋ P 🅿 ⊞ lau ♦ ⛟ ⵣ
Prices: ♦50 ⇔50 ⚑50 ▲40-50

▶ **MÜHLEN** STEIERMARK

Badsee Hitzmannsdorf 2 ☎ 03586 2418
⊃ *N via B92.*
May-Sep 1.5HEC ⏚ ⊲ ⋔ ⛟ ⵉ ✕ ⊙ ⚑ ⚑ ⵋ LP 🅿 lau ♦ ✕
Prices: ♦45 ⇔30 ⚑70 ▲40

▶ **OBERWÖLZ** STEIERMARK

Schloss Rothenfels ☎ 03581 8208
In picturesque Alpine surroundings with good recreational
facilities.
Apr-Oct 8HEC ⏚ ⊲ ⋔ ⊙ ⚑ 🏕 ⵋ LR 🅿 lau ♦ ⛟ ⵉ ✕ ⵣ ⵋP
⊞
Prices: ♦50 ⇔45 ⚑45 ▲35

▶ **ST GEORGEN** STEIERMARK

Olachgut ☎ 03532 2162
Camping Card Compulsory.
⊃ *Signposted.*
All year 10HEC ⏚ ⊲ ⋔ ⛟ ✕ ⊙ ⚑ ⵣ ⵣ 🏕 ⚑ ⵋ L 🅿 lau ♦
ⵋR
Prices: ♦50-55 pitch 180-190

▶ **ST SEBASTIAN** STEIERMARK

Erlaufsee Erlaufseestr 3 ☎ 03882 4937
In a picturesque Alpine setting in woodland, 100mtrs from
the lake.
⊃ *Signposted.*
May-15 Sep 0.5HEC ⏚ ♣ ⋔ ⊙ ⚑ 🅿 ♦ ✕ ⵋL
Prices: ♦45 ⇔30 ⚑40 ▲40

▶ **SCHLADMING** STEIERMARK

Zirngast Linke Ennsau 633 ☎ 03687 23195
Site in meadow on left bank of River Enns next to railway.
⊃ *Turn off B308 towards town as far as the MOBIL filling
station.*
All year 1.5HEC ⏚ ⊲ ⋔ ⛟ ⵉ ✕ ⊙ ⚑ ⵣ ⵣ 🏕 ⵋ R 🅿 lau
♦ ⵋP ⊞
Prices: ♦70-90 pitch 75-85

▶ **STUBENBERG** STEIERMARK

Steinmann ☎ 03176 8390
⊃ *5km towards Hirnsdorf towards the lake.*
All year 4HEC ⏚ ♣ ⋔ ⛟ ⵉ ✕ ⊙ ⚑ ⵣ ⵋ L 🅿 ⊞

▶ **UNGERSDORF BEI FROHNLEITEN** STEIERMARK

Lanzmaierhof Ungersdorf 16 ☎ 03126 2360
⊃ *Signposted 2km S of Frohnleiten on the Graz road.*
Apr-15 Oct 0.5HEC ⏚ ⊲ ⋔ ⛟ ✕ ⊙ ⚑ ⵣ ⵣ 🅿 ⊞
Prices: ♦45 ⇔25 ⚑25 ▲14-28

▶ **WEISSKIRCHEN** STEIERMARK

Fisching Fisching 9 ☎ 03577 82284
A modern site with fine sanitary and sporting facilities, 6km
from the Formula 1 circuit (A1-Ring) in Zeltweg.
⊃ *Leave S36 at Zeltweg-Ost exit, head towards Obdach and
follow signs for B78. Site well signposted in centre of Fisching.*
Apr-15 Oct 1.5HEC ⏚ ⊲ ⋔ ⵉ ✕ ⊙ ⚑ ⵣ 🏕 ⚑ 🅿 ⊞ lau ♦ ⵣ
ⵋP
Prices: ♦60 ⇔40 ⚑80 ▲20

▶ **WILDALPEN** STEIERMARK

Wildalpen ☎ 03636 342 & 341
Located in a nature reserve beside the River Salza with good
canoeing facilities.
Apr-Oct 0.8HEC ⏚ ⵈ ⊲ ⋔ ⊙ ⚑ ⵣ ⵋ R 🅿 lau ♦ ⛟ ⵉ ✕
ⵋP ⊞

● ● ●　**LOWER AUSTRIA**　● ● ● ●

Lower Austria, by far the largest of the nine provinces,
wraps itself around the federal capital of Vienna, itself a
separate province. The Danube divides Lower Austria
roughly in half, and has been central to the development of
the area for centuries: prehistoric and Roman remains have
been found, castles and fortified churches testify to the
Romanesque and Gothic periods and great monasteries and
pilgrimage churches celebrate the Baroque. North of the
river the countryside, flat in the west, becomes hilly towards
the Czechoslovak border; south of the river the land rises
into wooded hills (including the well-known Vienna Woods
- Wienerwald), and climbs to over 6,560ft (2,000 metres) in
the Schneeberg and Rax regions - popular holiday areas for
the Viennese.
Good communications have promoted industrial
development in the Vienna basin and it is now the largest
industrial area in the country. But agriculture is also
important in the province, and vineyards around Krems and
Weinviertel produce excellent wines.
The south of the province, Burgenland the 'land of castles',
has many monuments to a valiant past in what was for

centuries a frontier area, occupied by the Romans and later vulnerable to attack from the Huns and the Turks. It is now a peaceful landscape of wooded hills, pastures, fruit orchards and vineyards.

In dramatic contrast is the impressive expanse of the 'paszta' plain in the north east, and the vast Neusiedler See - the only steppe lake in central Europe, and well known for unique flora and fauna - providing good opportunities for bathing and yachting.

Eisenstadt, the provincial capital is dominated by the Schloss Esterhazy, where this aristocratic family had its seat in the 17th and 18th centuries. There is an attractive old town, a cathedral, and the Haydnhaus (now a museum) where Haydn lived during the 30 years he was Kapellmeister here.

....

ANDAU BURGENLAND

Pusstasse ☎ 02176 3512 & 2301
A family site with good modern sanitary installations.
➲ *Access via A4, exit Mönchhof/Halbturn/Andau towards Tadten.*
15 Apr-15 Oct 1HEC ▦ ⊞ 𝕣 ✕ ⊙ ☒ ⹁ L 🏠 lau ➧ 🅿 ⚑ ✕ 𝘢

BREITENBRUNN BURGENLAND

Seebad ☎ 02683 5252
May-Sep 1HEC ▦ ⊞ 𝕣 ⊙ ☒ ⹁ L 🏠 ⊞ ⊘ lau ➧ 🅿 ✕
Prices: ⛺48 ⛟18 ⛺40 ▲25-40

GMÜND NIEDERÖSTERREICH

Assangteich Albrechtser Str 10 ☎ 02852 52506
In a pleasant location with a good variety of recreational facilities.
➲ *Signposted from B41.*
23 Apr-3 Oct 0.5HEC ▦ ⊞ 𝕣 🅿 ⚑ ✕ ⊙ ☒ 🏠 lau ➧ 𝘢 ⛱ ⹁LP ⊞
Prices: ⛺55.50 pitch 85

HIRTENBERG NIEDERÖSTERREICH

Hirtenberg Leobersdorfefstr ☎ 02256 81111
➲ *Take exit Leobersdorf on A2/E59 and continue W on B18 for approx. 0.8km.*
15 May-15 Sep 1.5HEC ▦ ➧ 𝕣 ⊙ ☒ 🏠 ⊘ lau ➧ 🅿 ✕ ⊞
Prices: ⛺50 pitch 70

INPRUGG NIEDERÖSTERREICH

Finsterhof ☎ 02772 52130
➲ *N towards Tulln.*
All year 2HEC ▦ ⊞ 𝕣 🅿 ⚑ ⊙ ☒ 𝘢 ⛱ ☒ 🏠 ⊞ lau ➧ ✕

JENNERSDORF BURGENLAND

Jennersdorf Freizeitzentrum 3 ☎ 03329 46133
A pleasant site in wooded surroundings.
➲ *Access via A2 exit Fürstenfeld.*
16 Mar-Oct 1HEC ▦ ⊞ 𝕣 ⊙ ☒ ⹁ P ⊞ ⊘ lau ➧ 🅿 ⚑ ✕ 𝘢
Prices: ⛺55 pitch 60

KREMS NIEDERÖSTERREICH

Donau (ÖAMTC) Wiedengasse 7 ☎ 02732 84455
➲ *By river opposite SHELL filling station.*
May-Sep 1HEC ▦ ⊁ 𝕣 ✕ ⊙ ☒ ⛱ ⹁ R 🏠 ⊘

LAXENBURG NIEDERÖSTERREICH

Schlosspark Laxenburg Münchendorfer Str ☎ 02236 71333
On level meadowland with surfaced roads. The site lies in a recreation centre within the grounds of the historic Laxenburg Castle.

➲ *Access 600m S on the road leading to the B16.*
Apr-Oct 2.4HEC ▦ ⊞ 𝕣 ⚑ 🅿 ✕ ⊙ ☒ 𝘢 🏠 ⊞ lau ➧ ✕ ⹁P
Prices: ⛺74-80 ⛺62-69 ▲37-42

MARBACH NIEDERÖSTERREICH

Marbach ☎ 07413 466
➲ *Access via A1 exit Ybbs.*
Apr-Oct 0.3HEC ▦ ⊞ 𝕣 ⚑ ✕ ⊙ ☒ ⹁ R 🏠 ⊞ lau ➧ 🅿 ✕ 𝘢
Prices: ⛺55 ⛟38 ⛺55 ▲55

MARKT ST MARTIN BURGENLAND

Markt St Martin Mühlweg 2 ☎ 02618 2239
May-Sep 0.5HEC ▦ ➧ 𝕣 🅿 ✕ ⊙ ☒ ⹁ PR 🏠 ⊞ ⊘ ➧ 🅿 ✕

OBERRETZBACH NIEDERÖSTERREICH

Hubertus ☎ 02942 3238
Camping Card Compulsory.
➲ *Signposted.*
All year 1HEC ▦ ⊞ 𝕣 ✕ ⊙ ☒ 🏠 ⊞ lau ➧ 🅿 ▼

PODERSDORF BURGENLAND

Strandcamping Podersdorf am See Strandpl ☎ 02177 2279
Directly on the Neusiedler See next to the sportsground.
Apr-Oct 7HEC ▦ ⠿ 𝕣 🅿 ⊙ ☒ 🅿 ⹁ L 🏠 lau ➧ 🅿 ✕ 𝘢 ⊞
Prices: ⛺80 ⛟62 ⛺70 ▲52

PURGSTALL NIEDERÖSTERREICH

Erlauftal-Camp Purgstall Augasse 8-12 ☎ 07489 2015
All year 1.5HEC ▦ ⊞ 𝕣 🅿 ✕ ⊙ ☒ 🅿 ▲ ⹁ L 🏠 ⊞ lau ➧ 𝘢 ⛱ ⹁P

RAPPOLTENKIRCHEN NIEDERÖSTERREICH

Rappoltenkirchen ☎ 02274 8425
➲ *Turn off B1 at Sieghartskirchen and continue S for 3km.*
Closed Jan 2.2HEC ▦ ➧ 𝕣 ⊙ ☒ 𝘢 ⛱ ☒ 🏠 ⊞ lau ➧ ✕
Prices: ⛺44 ⛟20 ⛺60 ▲30

RECHNITZ BURGENLAND

GC Hauptpl 10 ☎ 03363 79202
On an artificial lake in the heart of the beautiful Faludi Valley.
Jun-Aug 1HEC ▦ ⊁ 𝕣 ✕ ⊙ ☒ ⹁ L 🏠 ⊞ ➧ 🅿 ✕ 𝘢 ⛱
Prices: ⛺35 ⛺70 ▲40

RUST BURGENLAND

Rust ☎ 02685 4595
Situated on level meadowland with young trees.
➲ *From Rust follow the lake road.*
Etr-26 Oct 56HEC ▦ ⊞ 𝕣 🅿 ✕ ⊙ ☒ 🅿 🅿 ⹁ L 🏠 ⊞ lau ➧ ⹁P
Prices: ⛺44-55 ⛟38-44 ⛺44-55 ▲33-44

SCHÖNBÜHEL NIEDERÖSTERREICH

Stumpfer Schönbühel 7 ☎ 02752 8510
A small site in a wooded location attached to a guesthouse close to the River Donau.
➲ *SW of town.*
Apr-Oct 1HEC ▦ ➧ 𝕣 🅿 ✕ ⊙ ☒ 𝘢 ⹁ R 🏠 ⊞ lau
Prices: ⛺44.50 ▲30-50 pitch 50-70

TRAISEN NIEDERÖSTERREICH

Kulmhof Kulmhof 1 ☎ 02762 62900
Set out in a circular formation around the main buildings with plenty of trees around the pitches.
➲ *0.6km W via B20.*
All year 1.7HEC ▦ ⊞ 𝕣 ⊙ ☒ 𝘢 ⛱ 🅿 ⹁ P 🏠 ⊞ lau ➧ ▼ ✕
Prices: ⛺60 pitch 60

COME AND SEE
COME AND ENJOY
The best campsites nearby
VIENNA (Motorway A1/Exit 41)
Information/prospects/reservation:
Donaupark Camps:
Klosterneuburg Tel: +43-1-2272-65200
Fax: +43-1-2272-65201
Tulln Tel: +43-1-2243-25877
Fax: +43-1-2243-25878

TULLN NIEDERÖSTERREICH

Donaupark-Camping Tulln Hafenstr ☎ 02272 65200
A modern site in a peaceful location with good facilities close
to the River Danube with a high season bus service to
Vienna.
May-Sep 10HEC ⚏ 🏠 👫 🏊 🍴 ✗ ⊙ 🚻 🖋 ⚒ 🏕 🅿 Å ⤵ L 🏪 ⊞
lau ⤵ ⟿PR
Prices: ⚑60 pitch 110-130

TÜRNITZ NIEDERÖSTERREICH

Gravogl Pichlrotte 16 ☎ 02769 201
All year 0.9HEC ⚏ 🏠 🏠 👫 🏊 🍴 ✗ ⊙ 🚻 🖋 🏪 ⊞ lau ⤵ ⟿P

● ● ● UPPER AUSTRIA/SALZBURG ● ● ●

The province of Salzburg is wonderfully diverse: in the
north mighty massifs fall away to rolling uplands and plains,
and to the east the hills of the Salzkammergut merge into
the Alpine landscape of Upper Austria. Visitors are drawn
to the province by the natural landscape; dozens of
attractive summer resorts, from smart cosmopolitan spas to
picturesque mountain hamlets; and facilities for winter
sports in almost every part of the province.
A magnificent setting and a wealth of beautiful buildings
and attractive streets have given Salzburg an international
reputation as one of the most beautiful cities in the world. It
contains a rich heritage of architecture and the arts, and
Mozart was born here in 1756. The city is still a major
musical centre, and hosts an annual music festival every
summer, with performances of the highest quality.
The scenic facets of Upper Austria (Oberösterreich) stretch
from the wooded Mühlviertel area north of the Danube to
the lake-studded Salzkammergut and the glacier region of
the Dachstein - all dotted with lively holiday centres,
peaceful villages and idyllic spas and health resorts.
The provincial capital Linz, Austria's third-largest city, spans
both banks of the Danube in the Linz basin. The old town's
original market square is flanked by impressive buildings,
and the city has many attractive streets and arcaded
courtyards.
....

ABERSEE SALZBURG

Wolfgangblick Seestr 24 ☎ 06227 3475
In a pleasant position directly on the Wolfgangsee.
Camping Card Compulsory.
⮕ *Access via B1598 6km from St Gilgen. Signposted from
village.*
May-Sep 2HEC ⚏ 🏠 🏠 👫 🏊 🍴 ✗ ⊙ 🚻 🖋 ⟿ LR 🏪 ⊞ lau
⤵ ⚒ ⊞
Prices: ⚑48-52 ⚑30-40 ⚑30-44 Å30-40

ABTENAU SALZBURG

Oberwötzhof Erlfeld 37 ☎ 06243 2698
All year 2HEC ⚏ 🏠 🏠 👫 🏊 🍴 ✗ ⊙ 🚻 🖋 ⚒ 🏕 ⟿ P 🏪 ⊞ ⤵ ⟿R
Prices: ⚑60 ⚑35 ⚑60 Å40-60

ALTENMARKT SALZBURG

Götschl-Au Palfen 386 ☎ 06452 7821
⮕ *S towards the Zauchensee*
All year 10HEC ⚏ ⤵ 🏠 👫 🏊 🍴 ✗ ⊙ 🚻 🖋 ⚒ 🏪 lau ⤵ ⟿P

ALTMÜNSTER OBERÖSTERREICH

Schweizerhof Hauptstr 17 ☎ 07612 89313
A modern site on the shore of Lake Traunsee with plenty of
sporting facilities.
⮕ *Signposted from the motorway.*
May-Sep 0.6HEC ⚏ ⸬⸬ 🏠 🏠 👫 🏊 🍴 ✗ ⊙ 🚻 ⟿ L 🏪 ⊞ lau ⤵ 🚢
🖋 ⟿P
Prices: ⚑62 ⚑30 ⚑80-125 Å48-75

BADGASTEIN SALZBURG

Kurcamping 'Erlengrund' Miesbichlstr 20 ☎ 06434 2790
On meadowland below the road leading to the Tauern
railway tunnel.
⮕ *From Hofgastein turn left off B167 and descend for 100m.*
All year 4.5HEC ⚏ 🏠 🏠 👫 ⊙ 🚻 🖋 ⚒ ⟿ P 🏪 ⊞ lau ⤵ ⚒ ✗
⟿LR
Prices: ⚑61-68 pitch 68-88

BRUCK AN DER GROSSGLOCKNERSTRASSE SALZBURG

Woferlgut Kroessenbach 40 ☎ 06545 7303-0
In a beautiful valley beside a lake with good recreational
facilities.
⮕ *Access via Bruck-Süd or Grossglockner on B311.*
All year 16HEC ⚏ 🏠 🏠 👫 🏊 🍴 ✗ ⊙ 🚻 🖋 ⚒ 🏕 🏠 Å ⟿ LP 🏪
⊞ lau ⤵ ⟿R ⊞
Prices: ⚑48-70 ⚑43-64 ⚑53-74 Å53-74

BURGAU SALZBURG

Burgau ☎ 07663 266
Mainly level site surrounded by trees between the road and
the Attersee at Weissenbach.
⮕ *On B152 at Km 27.6 opposite Hotel Burgau.*
May-Oct 100HEC ⚏ 🏠 🏠 👫 🏊 🍴 ✗ ⊙ 🚻 🖋 ⚒ ⟿ LR 🏪 ⊞

Eitzinger Burgau 4 ☎ 07663 769
In a fine situation directly on the Attersee with good
recreational facilities.
⮕ *Access from 'Mondsee' exit on Autobahn.*
Apr-Sep ⚏ 🏠 🏠 👫 ✗ ⊙ 🚻 🖋 ⟿ L 🏪 ⊞

ESTERNBERG OBERÖSTERREICH

Pyrawang ☎ 07714 6504
⮕ *At Km45.5 on B130 (Passau-Linz).*
Apr-Oct 3HEC ⚏ 🏠 🏠 👫 🏊 ✗ ⊙ 🚻 🖋 ⊞ ⤵ ⟿R

GLEINKERAU OBERÖSTERREICH

Air Pyhrn Priel ☎ 07562 7066
A year-round site with a wide variety of facilities.
⮕ *Signposted from Windischgarsten towards Gleinkersee.
2.5km from town.*
All year 1HEC ⚏ ⤵ 🏠 👫 ✗ ⊙ 🚻 🖋 🏪 lau

GOLLING SALZBURG

Torrener Hof Torren 24 ☎ 06244 5522
⮕ *On the outskirts of the village on the B159.*
All year 2HEC ⚏ ⸬⸬ 🏠 🏠 👫 ✗ ⊙ 🚻 🖋 🏪 ⊞ lau
Prices: ⚑50 ⚑30 ⚑50 Å50

HAIBACH OBERÖSTERREICH

Schlögen ☎ 0043 72788241
In wooded surroundings on the shore of the marina.
Camping Card Compulsory.
➾ *Access via B139.*
All year 2.2HEC ⟱ 🛒 🏕 🏪 ✕ ⊙ ♨ 🔧 L 🏚 ⊞ lau ✦ 🍴

KAPRUN SALZBURG

Mühle ☎ 06547 8254
On long stretch of meadow by the Kapruner Ache. S end of
village towards cable lift.
All year 1.5HEC ⟱ 🛒 🏕 🏪 🍴 ✕ ⊙ ♨ 🔧 🔧 PR 🏚 ⊞ lau ✦ 🛖
Prices: ♦65-70 pitch 90-100

MAISHOFEN SALZBURG

Kammerlander Oberreit 18 ☎ 06542 68755
➾ *On B168.*
15 Apr-1 Oct ⟱ 🛒 🏕 🍴 ✕ ⊙ ♨ 🏚 ✦ 🛒 🔧L
Prices: ♦30 ✦20 ♨20 ▲20

MITTERSILL SALZBURG

Mittersill Klausgasse 49 ☎ 06562 4811
A modern, well-equipped site suitable for both summer and
winter holidays.
➾ *0.5km from the centre of the town on the shores of the lake.*
All year 1.7HEC ⟱ 🛒 🏕 🏪 🍴 ✕ ⊙ ♨ 🔧 🛖 🏚 ⊞ lau
Prices: ♦70-90 pitch 70-100

NEUSTIFT OBERÖSTERREICH

Gasthof Weiss Puhret 5 ☎ 07284 8104
➾ *Leave the motorway at Passau-Nord and take B388.*
Apr-Nov 1HEC ⟱ 🛒 🏕 🍴 ✕ ⊙ ♨ 🛖 🔧 LPR 🏚 lau
✦ 🛒 🔧 ⊞

FREEDOM, FITNESS & HOLIDAYS

We offer more concerning comfort: the most modern
sanitary facilities, heated swimming pool (25°C),
fitness studio, sauna and a huge animation
programme – everything you need
for a successful holiday!

Seecamping Gruber
A-4865 Nussdorf / Attersee
Telephone 07666-80450
Telefax 07666-80456

NUSSDORF OBERÖSTERREICH

See Camping Gruber Dortstr 63 ☎ 07666 80450
On fairly long meadow parallel to the promenade.
➾ *S of village, access is at Km19.7. Turn off B151 towards the
lake (Attersee).*
15 Apr-15 Oct 2.6HEC ⟱ 🛒 🏕 🏪 🍴 ✕ ⊙ ♨ 🔧 LP 🏚 ⊞ lau
✦ ⊘

Strandcamping Graus Dorfstr 55 ☎ 07666 8008
Site on long meadow with fruit trees, sloping towards lake
and bathing area. Access is within the village.
➾ *Turn off main road B151 at Km19.5 towards the lake
(Attersee).*
May-Sep 2.7HEC ⟱ ✦ 🏕 🍴 ✕ ⊙ ♨ ⊘ 🛖 ♨ 🔧 L 🏚 ⊞ 🏊
lau ✦ 🛒

PERWANG AM GRABENSEE OBERÖSTERREICH

Perwang ☎ 06217 8288
Site beside lake.
May-Oct 1.5HEC ⟱ 🛒 🏕 🍴 ✕ ⊙ ♨ 🏚 ⊞ 🏊 lau ✦ 🛒 🔧L

PETTENBACH OBERÖSTERREICH

Almtal ☎ 07586 8627
On a level meadow in the grounds of a former castle,with
good, modern facilities.
➾ *Leave A1/E55/E60 at Sattledt exit and continue towards Graz.*
All year 12HEC ⟱ 🛒 🏕 🏪 🍴 ✕ ⊙ ♨ ⊘ 🛖 ♨ 🔧 P 🏚 ⊞ lau
Prices: ♦45 pitch 70

RADSTADT SALZBURG

Forellencamp Gaismairallee 51 ☎ 06452 7861
Flat meadowland near town
➾ *SW via B99.*
All year 1HEC ⟱ ⋮⋮⋮ 🛒 🏕 🏪 🍴 ✕ ⊙ ♨ 🛖 🏚 ⊞ lau
Prices: ♦50 ✦30 ♨50 ▲25

ST JOHANN IM PONGAU SALZBURG

Hirschenwirt Bundesstr 1 ☎ 06412 6012
A small, pleasant site with good, modern facilities.
➾ *Access via Bischofshofen and B311.*
All year 0.8HEC ⟱ 🛒 🏕 🍴 ✕ ⊙ ♨ 🛖 🔧 P lau
Prices: ♦50-70 pitch 80-100

Wieshof Wieshofgasse 8 ☎ 06412 8292
On gently sloping meadow behind pension and farmhouse.
Modern facilities. Big spa house with sauna, massage facilities
and health bars, adjacent to site.
➾ *Off B311 towards Zell am Zee.*
All year 1.2HEC ⟱ 🌿 🏕 ⊙ ♨ ⊘ 🏚 lau ✦ 🛒 ✕ 🔧P ⊞
Prices: ♦60 pitch 60

ST LORENZ OBERÖSTERREICH

Alten Ischler Bahn St Lorenz 88 ☎ 06232 2902
Clean orderly site, easily accessible in the beautiful Mondsee
Valley.
All year 1HEC ⟱ 🌿 🏕 ⊙ ♨ ♨ 🔧 P 🏚 ⊞ lau ✦ 🔧L

Austria-Camp St Lorenz 229 ☎ 06232 2927
Level site on grassland bordered by trees and hedges and
divided into fields by internal roads. Separate field for young
people.
➾ *4km from Mondsee, beside the lake.*
May-Sep 3.7HEC ⟱ ✦ 🏕 🏪 🍴 ✕ ⊙ ♨ ▲ 🔧 L 🏚 lau

ST MARTIN BEI LOFER SALZBURG

Park Grubhof ☎ 06588 8237
Situated in meadowland on the banks of the River Saalach.
Separate sections for dog owners, families, teenagers and
groups.

Contd.

1.5km S of Lofer turn left off B311.
May-Sep 10HEC ⸺ ♦ ⋔ ⛺ ☕ ♉ ✕ ⊙ ⊟ ⊘ ⊞ ⊡ Å ⸮ R ⊞ ⊞
♦ ⸮P
Prices: ⵠ60 ⛶30 ⛺44-55 Å30-44

ST WOLFGANG OBERÖSTERREICH

Appesbach Au 99 ☎ 06138 2206
On sloping meadow facing lake with no shade at upper end.
0.8km E of St Wolfgang between lake and Strobl road.
Apr-Oct 2HEC ⸺ ⚶ ⋔ ⛺ ♉ ✕ ⊙ ⊟ ⊘ ⊞ ⊞ ⸮ L ⊞ lau
♦ ⊞

Berau Schwarzenbach 16 ☎ 06138 2543
A family-run site in a picturesque setting on the edge of the
Wolfgangsee. Spacious, level pitches and good, modern
facilities.
*From A1 exit 'Talgau' folloe signs for Hof and Bad Ischl on
N158 through Strobl village towards St Wolfgang and follow signs.*
All year 1.5HEC ⸺ ⚶ ⚶ ⋔ ⛺ ♉ ✕ ⊙ ⊟ ⊘ ⊞ ⊞ ⸮ L ⊞ ⊞
lau
Prices: ⵠ54-65 pitch 97-128

SALZBURG SALZBURG

Kasern C-Zuckmayerstr 26 ☎ 0662 450576
Access via exit 'Salzburg-Nord' on the A1.
Apr-Oct 1.1HEC ⸺ ⚶ ⋔ ⛺ ✕ ⊙ ⊟ ⊞ ⊞ lau ♦ ♉ ✕ ⊘
Prices: ⵠ60 ⛶35 ⛺35 Å35

Nord Sam Samstr 22A ☎ 0662 660611
Site divided into pitches.
400m from Salzburg Nord Autobahn Exit.
May-Sep 2HEC ⸺ ⸬ ⚶ ⋔ ⛺ ✕ ⊙ ⊟ ⊘ ⸮ P ⊞ ⊞ lau ♦ ⊞
Prices: ⵠ50-60 pitch 79-99

Schloss Aigen ☎ 0662 622079
Site divided into pitches in partial clearing on mountain
slope.
*From Salzburg-Süd motorway exit through Anif and
Glasenbach.*
May-Sep 25HEC ⸺ ⚶ ⋔ ⛺ ♉ ✕ ⊙ ⊟ ⊘ ⊞ ⊞ ⊞ lau
Prices: ⵠ54 pitch 60-72

Stadtblick Rauchenbichlerstr 21 ☎ 0662 450652
Leave motorway at exit Salzburg-Nord and follow signs.
20 Mar-15 Nov 0.8HEC ⸺ ⸬ ♦ ⋔ ⛺ ♉ ✕ ⊙ ⊟ ⊘ ⊞ ⊞ Å
⊞ ⊞ lau

SCHLÖGEN OBERÖSTERREICH

Terrassencamping Pension Schlögen ☎ 07279 8241
On level ground beside the River Donau, backed by woods
and mountains.
20 Mar-28 Oct 2.8HEC ⸺ ♦ ⋔ ⛺ ♉ ✕ ⊙ ⊟ ⸮ PR ⊞ lau

SEEKIRCHEN SALZBURG

Strand Seestr 2 ☎ 06212 4088
Beside the Wallersee in beautiful meadow.
Apr-Oct 2HEC ⸺ ⚶ ⋔ ⛺ ♉ ✕ ⊙ ⊟ ⊘ ⸮ LP ⊞ ⊞ lau ♦ ⛺

Zell am Wallersee ☎ 06212 4080
Level meadowland separated from the lake by the Lido.
Access from A1 exit Wallersee then via Seekirchen to Zell.
May-Oct 3HEC ⸺ ⚶ ⋔ ⛺ ✕ ⊙ ⊟ ⸮ L ⊞ ⊞ lau
Prices: ⵠ60 pitch 120

STEINBACH OBERÖSTERREICH

Seefeld ☎ 07663 342
On meadowland sloping gently towards lake, behind Gasthof
Föttinger.
Near MOBIL garage on B152 at Km13.6.
May-Oct 1.2HEC ⸺ ⚶ ⋔ ⛺ ✕ ⊙ ⊟ ⸮ LP ⊞ lau ♦ ⊘

TIEFGRABEN OBERÖSTERREICH

Fohlenhof Hof 17 ☎ 06232 2600
In a picturesque, peaceful location between Lake Mondsee
and Lake Irrsee with good facilities.
*From Mondsee exit on A1/E55/E60 take B154 towards
Strasswalden for 1.5km, then take Haider-Mühle road for 2km.*
Apr-10 Oct 2.5HEC ⸺ ⚶ ⋔ ⛺ ♉ ✕ ⊙ ⊟ ⊘ ⊞ ⊞ ⸮ P ⊞ ⊞
lau
Prices: ⵠ50 ⛶30 ⛺36 Å36

UNTERACH OBERÖSTERREICH

Insel ☎ 07665 8311
Quiet site on shore of Lake Attersee; divided into two
sections by River Seeache. Family site.
*Entrance below B152 towards Steinbach at Km24.5; about
300m from fork with B151.*
15 May-15 Sep 1.8HEC ⸺ ⚶ ⋔ ⛺ ⊙ ⊟ ⸮ LR ⊞ lau ♦ ♉ ✕ ⊞
Prices: ⵠ58 ⛶25 ⛺43 Å30

WALD SALZBURG

S.N.P Lahn 65 ☎ 06565 8446
A small family site in a beautiful Alpine setting.
W of town.
All year 6HEC ⸺ ⚶ ⋔ ⛺ ⊙ ⊟ ⊘ ⊞ ⊞ lau ♦ ⸮P

WESENUFER OBERÖSTERREICH

Nibelungen ☎ 07718 7589
Beside the River Donau, 500m from B130.
Apr-Sep 1.2HEC ⸺ ⚶ ⋔ ✕ ⊙ ⊟ ⸮ R ⊞ ⊞ lau ♦ ♉ ✕ ⸮P
Prices: ⵠ35 pitch 50

ZELL AM SEE SALZBURG

Seecamp Zell am See Thumersbacherstr 34 ☎ 06542 72115
In a pleasant wooded location beside the lake with excellent
site and recreational facilities.
Access via B311, N of lake towards Thumersbach. Signposted.
All year 2.8HEC ⸺ ⚶ ⚶ ⋔ ⛺ ♉ ✕ ⊙ ⊟ ⊘ ⊞ ⊞ ⊞ ⸮ L ⊞
⊞ lau ♦ ⸮P

Südufer Thumersbach, Seeuferstr 196 ☎ 06542 56228
A family site on level ground in a picturesque spot on the
southern bank of the Zeller See.
S via B311 towards Thumersbach.
All year 0.6HEC ⸺ ♦ ⋔ ⛺ ✕ ⊙ ⊟ ⊘ ⊞ ⊞ lau ♦ ✕ ⸮LR
Prices: ⵠ55-60 ⛶25 ⛺75 Å45-75

● ● ● ● VORARLBERG ● ● ●

Austria's most western province, Vorarlberg is small but
very beautiful. The gardens and orchards in the Rhine
valley and on the shores of Lake Constance give way to a
forested upland region, and finally to the peaks and glaciers
of the Silvretta, rising to over 9,800ft (3,000 metres). With
its lovely old towns and villages, clear mountain lakes and
rivers, quiet bays on Lake Constance, pastures and
meadowlands, steep-sided valleys and peaks, Vorarlberg is
a province of special charm. Watersports are popular on
Lake Constance, but there is good access to the
mountainous regions, making them popular in the summer
with walkers and climbers, as well as in winter for skiers.
The onion-domed St Martin's tower (Martinstrum), dating
back from 1602, distinguishes the skyline of Bregenz, the
provincial capital. The newer districts of the town, on the
shores of Lake Constance, have modern well-equipped
tourist facilities - an open air-pool, lakeside gardens, a
floating stage and a Festspielhaus for festivals and
conferences.

Au VORARLBERG

Au ☎ 05515 2331
➲ *On B200 (Dornbirn-Wath)*
Closed 7 Apr-8 May & 22 Sep-Oct 0.3HEC ▦ ⚡ ♠ ✕ ☉ ⬛◔⊞⊞⌁ lau ➧ ⚡ ♉ ✕ ⅃PR

Bezau VORARLBERG

Bezau Ach 206 ☎ 05514 2964
Small family-owned site with modern sanitary facilities.
➲ *S via B200 (Dornbirn-Warth).*
All year 0.5HEC ▦ ⚡ ♠ ☉ ⬛▣⊞ ➧ ♉ ✕ ⅃PR
Prices: ♠58 pitch 70-90

Bludenz VORARLBERG

At **Braz**(7km SE)

Traube ☎ 05552 8103
On sloping grassland in the picturesque Klostertal valley with good, modern facilities.
➲ *7km SE of Bludenz via E17, S16 (Bludenz-Arlberg-Innsbruck). Signposted. Near railway.*
All year 2HEC ▦ ➧ ♠ ♉ ✕ ☉ ⬛◔◚ ⅃ P ▣⊞⌁ ➧ ⅃R

Bregenz VORARLBERG

See Bodangasse 7 ☎ 05574 71895
Quiet site on level meadow beside lake.
➲ *From town centre (Bahnhofplatz) follow signs towards 'Seecamping'.*
15 May-15 Sep 8HEC ▦ ◑ ♠ ♉ ✕ ☉ ⬛◔ ⅃ L ▣⊞ lau ➧ ◔ ⅃P

Dalaas VORARLBERG

Erne ☎ 05585 7223
In the town, attached to a guesthouse and next to the swimming pool.
➲ *Access via S16, exit 'Dalaas'.*
All year 0.6HEC ▦ ◑ ♠ ☉ ⬛◔◚ ⅃ R▣ ➧ ♉ ✕ ⅃P ⊞
Prices: pitch 240 (incl 2 persons)

Dornbirn VORARLBERG

In der Enz ☎ 05572 29119
A municipal site beside a public park, in a wooded area some 100m beyond the Karren cable lift.
➲ *Access via autobahn exit Dornbirn-Süd.*
May-Sep 10HEC ▦ ◑ ♠ ♉ ✕ ☉ ⬛◔ ▣⊞ lau ➧ ✕ ⅃PR ⊞
Prices: ♠54-60 ⬤22 ⬛60 ▲60

Langen VORARLBERG

At **Klösterle**(2km W)

Alpencamping ☎ 05582 269
➲ *Well signposted.*
All year 1.5HEC ▦ ◑ ♠ ♉ ✕ ☉ ⬛◔ ⅃ R ⊞ lau ➧ ⅃P

Lingenau VORARLBERG

Feurstein Haidach 185 ☎ 05513 6114
A small site located in a meadow adjacent to some farm buildings with sufficient facilities for a pleasant stay.
All year 1HEC ▦ ◑ ♠ ☉ ⬛◔◚ ⬛▣⊞ lau ➧ ✕
Prices: ♠60 ⬤15 ⬛35 ▲35

Nenzing VORARLBERG

Alpencamping Nenzing ☎ 05525 62491
A well appointed site in magnificent Alpine scenery. There are fine sporting facilities and and the sanitary blooks are modern and clean.
➲ *Signposted from B190 from Nenzing-2km towards Gurtis.*
All year 3HEC ▦ ◑ ♠ ♉ ✕ ☉ ⬛◔ ⬛⬛ ⅃ P ▣⊞ lau
Prices: pitch 210 (incl 2 persons)

At **Nüziders**(2.5km NW)

Sonnenberg Hintenofeust 12 ☎ 05552 64035
Clean site with modern facilities in gently sloping meadowland and splendid mountain scenery.
➲ *Access from Bludenz-Nüziders road, at first fork follow up hill.*
17 May-5 Oct 1.9HEC ▦ ⚡ ♠ ♉ ☉ ⬛◔ ⬛ ▣⊞⌁ lau ➧ ♉ ✕ ◚ ⅃R
Prices: ♠50 pitch 90-130

Raggal-Plazera VORARLBERG

Grosswalsertal ☎ 05553 209
Situated in a quiet location on gently sloping terrain, with pleasant views.
15 May-Sep 0.8HEC ▦ ⚡ ♠ ☉ ⬛◔ ⬛ ⅃ P ▣ lau ➧ ♉ ♉ ✕ ⊞

Tschagguns VORARLBERG

Zelfen ☎ 05556 7103-0
Partly uneven, grassy site beside River Ill.
All year 2HEC ▦ ◑ ♠ ♉ ✕ ☉ ⬛◔◚ ⅃ R ▣⊞ lau ➧ ⅃P
Prices: ♠65-75 pitch 85-95

VIENNA (WIEN)

For hundreds of years Vienna was the heart of a vast empire and cultural focus of central Europe. Today Vienna is very much one of the world's great modern tourist cities with a confident and cosmopolitan atmosphere, but it still keeps a distinctive charm and native flair. The mighty façades of the buildings and palaces of the city bear witness to the tall, grand Baroque buildings that earn it the name 'Vienna gloriosa'. And it retains and builds on its traditions of the finest music; many of the world's great composers lived and worked here, and the Opera House (Staatsoper) plays a prominent part in the social, cultural and political life of the city.

Vienna's cultural district is encircled by the wide boulevard, the Ringstrasse, on which many of the city's main buildings stand: the Opera House, the Burg Theatre, the Hofburg, the Parliament, and the neo-Gothic City Hall (Rathaus), as well as churches, museums and lovely parks, gardens and squares.

There is a full programme of events in the city - everything from operas and concerts to sporting events. For more casual entertainment, though, the Viennese cafés are a famous and historic institution - popular meeting places for the Viennese and a delight for the tourists - with tables outside in the summer, newspapers and magazines always available, and of course, the traditional strong, aromatic Viennese coffee.

....

Wien (vienna) WIEN

Donaupark Klosterneuburg In der Au ☎ 02243 85877
A modern site in delightful wooded surroundings with fine recreational facilities and within easy reach of the city centre.
➲ *Signposted from A1.*
All year 2HEC ▦ ⚡ ♠ ♉ ✕ ☉ ⬛◔◚ ⬛⬛ ▲ ▣ lau ➧ ⅃PR ⊞

Neue Donau Am Kaisermuehlendamm 119 ☎ 0043 12024010
Situated in a meadow surrounded by trees on the banks of the Danube within a leisure park.
May-Sep ▦ ◑ ♠ ♉ ✕ ☉ ⬛◔ ▣ lau ➧ ⅃LPR ⊞

Contd.

Wien-West 2 Hüttelbergstr 80 ☎ 1 9142314
On slightly rising meadow with asphalt paths.
⊃ *From end of A1/E5 (Linz-Wien) to Bräuhausbrücke, then*
turn left and across road to Linz, continue for approx. 1.8km.
Closed Feb 2HEC ▦ ♣ ↿ ⅃ ⌶ ✕ ☺ ⊞ ⌀ ⊕ ▣ lau
Prices: ♣67-73 pitch 62-69

❱ At **RODAUN**(4km SW)

Schwimmbad Camping Rodaun An der Au 2 ☎ 0222 884154
⊃ *Between An der Austr and Leising River dam. Access from*
Breitenfürter Str N492.
25 Mar-10 Nov 0.6HEC ▦ ♦ ♣ ↿ ☺ ⊞ ⌀ ⅂ P ☒ ⊞ lau ♦ ⅃
⅃ ✕

BELGIUM

❖

Belgium is a small, densely populated country
bordered by France, Germany, Luxembourg and
The Netherlands.

❖

FACTS AND FIGURES
Capital: Bruxelles (Brussel, Brussels)
Language: French, Dutch, German
IDD code: 32. To call the UK dial 00 44
Currency: Franc (*BEF*) = 100 centimes). £1 = *BEF* 55.93
Local time: GMT + 1

(summer GMT + 2)
Emergency Services: Police 101; Fire 100; Ambulance 100. From a mobile phone dial 112 and ask for the service required.
Business hours:
Banks: Mon-Fri 09.00-12.00, 14.00-16.00
Shops: Mon-Sat 09.00-18.00. (Supermarkets

20.00)
Average daily temperatures:
Bruxelles (Brussel, Brussels)
Jan 3°C   Jul 17°C
Mar 5°C   Sep 14°C
May 13°C   Nov 5°C
Tourist Information:
Belgian National Tourist Office
UK 31 Pepper St
London E14 9RW

Tel 0891 887799 (premium rate information line)
USA Suite 1501,
780 Third Ave,
New York,
NY10017
Tel (212) 758 8130
Camping Card
recommended; some reductions on site fees.

Despite the fact that it is heavily industrialised, it possesses some beautiful scenery, notably the great forest of the Ardennes. The resorts in the Oostende (Ostend) area offer a selection of wide, safe, sandy beaches and cover about forty miles of coastline.

The climate is temperate and similar to that of Britain: the variation between summer and winter lessened by the effects of the Gulf Stream. Three languages are spoken: French, Dutch and German. See *language* below.

Belgium is a varied, charming country in which to spend a camping holiday - the rivers and gorges of the Ardennes contrasting sharply with the rolling plains which make up the rest of the countryside. There are now over 800 campsites officially authorised by local authorities. They are normally open from April to October, but many are open throughout the year. Coastal sites tend to be very crowded at the height of the season.

Off-site camping (including sleeping) is prohibited beside public roads for more than 24 consecutive hours; on seashores; within a 100-metre radius of a main water point; or on a site classified for the conservation of monuments. Elsewhere, camping is permitted free of charge, as long as the stay does not exceed 24 hours and the

camper has obtained authorisation from the landowner.

HOW TO GET THERE
There are direct ferry services to Belgium:
To **Oostende** (Ostend) from **Dover** takes 2 hours by catamaran; from **Ramsgate** 4 hours by ferry; to **Zeebrugge** from **Hull** takes 13 hrs 15 mins.

Alternatively, you could use Eurotunnel, or take a shorter crossing by ferry or Hoverspeed to Calais, France, and drive along the coast road to Belgium.

For details of the *AA European Routes Service* please consult the Contents Page.

MOTORING & GENERAL INFORMATION
The information given here is specific to Belgium. It **must** be read in conjunction with the Continental ABC at the front of the book, which covers those regulations which are common to many countries.

Accidents
The police must also be called if an unoccupied, stationary vehicle is damaged, or if injuries are caused to persons; in the latter case, the car must

not be moved; see recommendations under
Accidents (also *Warning triangle*) in the European
ABC.

British Embassy/Consulates*
The British Embassy is located at 1040 Bruxelles,
rue d'Arlon 85 ☎ (02) 2876211. There are
British Consulates with Honorary Consuls in
Antwerpen (Antwerp) and Liège.

Children in cars
Child under 3 must be in suitable restraint when
travelling in the front and, if such a system is
fitted, when travelling in the rear. Children over 3
and under 12 seated in front or rear must use seat-
belt or child restraint appropriate to their size and
weight.

Currency
There are no restrictions on the amount of
Belgian or foreign currency which may be taken
into or out of Belgium.

Dimensions and weight restrictions
Private **cars** and towed **trailers** or **caravans** are
restricted to the following dimensions: height,
4 metres; width, 2.5 metres; length, 8 metres. The
maximum permitted overall length of vehicle/
trailer or caravan combination is 18 metres.

Trailers without brakes may have a total
maximum weight of 750kg.

Driving Licence*
A valid UK or Republic of Ireland licence is
acceptable in Belgium. The minimum age at
which visitors from UK or Republic of Ireland
may use a temporarily imported car or
motorcycle is 18 years.

Foodstuffs*
There are no limits on the importation of
foodstuffs obtained duty and tax paid within the
EC. Up to 500g of coffee (200g of coffee extract)
and 100g of tea (40g of tea extract) purchased
duty free or outside the EC may be imported free

The Grand Place, Brussels

of duty and tax. However, coffee bought duty free or outside the EC cannot be imported by visitors under 15 years of age.

Language
There are *three* official languages in Belgium - Dutch, French and German. Dutch is spoken in the north, French in the south and, in the eastern provinces, German. Both Dutch and French are spoken in Brussels. These divisions are administrative but act as a rough guide to the areas in which the various languages are spoken.

Some of the town names in the directory are shown in both Dutch and French, and that shown first is the one used locally. However, Brussels (Bruxelles-Brussel) is officially bi-lingual.

Motoring club*
The **Touring Club Royal de Belgique** (TCB) has its head office at 1040 Bruxelles, 44 rue de la Loi ☎(02) 2332211 and branch offices in most towns. The Bruxelles (Brussels) head office is open weekly 08.30-17.30hrs; Saturday 09.00-12.00hrs. Regional offices are open weekdays 09.00-12.30hrs (Monday from 09.30hrs) and 14.00-18.00hrs; Saturday 09.00-12.00hrs. All offices are closed on Saturday afternoons and Sundays.

Petrol
At the time of going to press both leaded and unleaded petrol are available in Belgium. However, only one grade of leaded petrol is sold, 98 octane 'Super'.

Roads
A good road system is available. However, one international route that has given more cause for complaints than any other is, without doubt, that from Calais (France) through Belgium to Köln/Cologne (Germany). The problem is aggravated by the fact that there are three official languages in Belgium (see *language* above). In the Flemish part of Belgium the destination place names are in Dutch, in Wallonia, in French and in the German part of Belgium they are in German and Fench or just in German. Brussels (Bruxelles-

Brussel) seems to be the only neutral ground where the signs show the two alternative spellings of placenames (Antwerpen-Anvers; Gent-Gand; Liège-Luik; Mons-Bergen; Namur-Namen; Oostend-Ostende; Tournai-Doornik.) From the Flemish part of the country, Dunkirk (Dunkerque) in France is signposted *Duinkerke* and Lille is referred to as *Rijsel*, and even Paris is shown as *Parijs*.

Belgium has a comprehensive system of toll-free motorways linking major towns and adjoining countries. Generally, signposts leading to and on motorways show foreign destination place-names in the language of the country concerned. The exceptions to this are on the E40 and E314 where cities such as Aachen and Köln may be given as Aken (Dutch) and Cologne (French).

Speed limits*
Car/caravan/trailer
Built-up areas 50kph (31mph)
Other roads 90kph (56pmh)
Motorways and 4-lane roads separated by central reservation 120kph (74mph)†. Minimum speed on motorways on straight level stretches is 70kph (43mph).
Vehicles being towed due to accident or breakdown are limited to 25kph (15mph) on all roads and, if on a motorway, must leave at the first exit.
†On dual carriageways separated only by road markings the limit is 90kph (55mph).

Warning triangle*
The use of a warning triangle is compulsory in the event of accident or breakdown. The triangle must be placed 30 metres (33yds) behind the vehicle on ordinary roads and 100 metres (109yds) on motorways to warn following traffic of any obstruction; it must be visible at a distance of 50 metres (55yds). In built-up areas the triangle may be placed close to or even on the vehicle if the 30 metre rule cannot be obeyed.
*Additional information on these topics will be found in the Continental ABC at the front of the book.

● ● ● SOUTH WEST/COAST ● ● ●

The coastline of Belgium is one of fine sandy beaches
backed by dunes, with few openings to the sea. The coast is
lined with resorts: De Panne; Nieuwpoort; Ostende, with its
port, is also a fashionable resort; Blankenberge; Zeebrugge;
and popular Knokke-Heist. Bruges, once connected to
the sea by an inlet, was a great medieval port. When the
inlet silted up, the city declined, preserving a city whose
architecture and unique atmosphere has survived until
today, to the delight of the increasing number of
visitors.

Ypres is historically an important textile centre. Reduced to
rubble in World War I, the town has been almost
completely restored, and now has its lovely Cloth Hall and
cathedral. There are hundreds of war cemeteries and
memorials near by, recalling the massive war casualties
suffered in the area. Tournai is one of the oldest cities in
Belgium and an important ecclesiastical centre, evidenced
by the remarkable Cathedral of Notre Dame, with its rich
interior and wealth of treasures.

....

▶ BELOEIL HAINAUT

Orangerie r du Major 3 ☎ 069 689190
Behind the Château de Beloeil.
Apr-Oct 3HEC ▦ ⚥ ⋔ ☎ ✗ ⊙ ⬚ ⚐ ⊞ lau ✦ ✗

▶ BLANKENBERGE WEST-VLAANDEREN

Bonanza I & III Zeebruggelaan 137 ☎ 050 416658
A family site in wooded surroundings 1km from both the
village and the sea.
15 Mar-Sep 4.5HEC ▦ ⚥ ⋔ ☎ ✗ ⊙ ⬚ ⚐ ⋔ P ⊞
lau ✦ ⋏S
Prices: ♦130-130 ⬛550-550 ▲350-600

Dallas Ruzettelaan 191 ☎ 050 418157
Well equipped family site near a large department store
50mtrs from the beach.
Apr-15 Sep 3HEC ▦ ⋔ ☎ ⬚ ⚐ ⊞ lau ✦ ☎ ✗ ⋏PS
Prices: ♦150 ⬛50 ⬛150 ▲100-150

▶ BRUGELETTE HAINAUT

Parc et Loisirs r de Bolignies 20 ☎ 068 455422
A quiet site in wooded surroundings with well defined
pitches and good facilities.
All year 6HEC ▦ ⚥ ⋔ ⊙ ⬚ ⋏ LPR ⊞ lau ✦ ☎ ✗

▶ HAAN, DE WEST-VLAANDEREN

Tropical Bredeweg 76A ☎ 050 236341
A quiet, well kept site in wooded surroundings close to the
beach.
⭢ *Signposted from A10/E40.*
Apr-Sep 2.6HEC ▦ ⚥ ⋔ ⊙ ⬚ ⚐ ⊞ ✦ ☎ ✗ ⋏S
Prices: pitch 600-660 (incl 2 persons)

▶ KNOKKE-HEIST WEST-VLAANDEREN

Vuurtoren Heistlaan 168 ☎ 050 511782
On level meadow with tarred roads.
⭢ *Turn S off Knokke-Oostende road 4km from Knokke and
follow signposts.*
15 Mar-15 Oct 6.6HEC ▦ ⋔ ☎ ✗ ⊙ ⬚ ⊞ lau ✦ ⚐
⋏PS
Prices: ♦115 pitch 270-580

Zilvermeeuw Heistlaan 166 ☎ 050 512726
Level site in wooded surroundings.
⭢ *SW via N300.*

Mar-10 Nov 7HEC ▦ ⋔ ☎ ✗ ⊙ ⬚ ⚐ ⋏ ⬛ ⊞ lau ✦
✗ ⋏LPS
Prices: pitch 375-575 (incl 2 persons)

▶ At WESTKAPELLE(3km S)

Holiday Natienlaan 70-72 ☎ 050 601203
A quiet family site with good modern facilities within easy
reach of the sea.
⭢ *On S outskirts near the railway station.*
Apr-Sep 1.5HEC ▦ ⋔ ⊙ ⬚ ⚐ ⊞ ⊞ ⊘ lau ✦ ☎ ✗ ⋏PS
Prices: ♦150 pitch 250

▶ KOKSIJDE WEST-VLAANDEREN

Blekker & Blekkerdal Jachtwakerstr 12 ☎ 058 511633
In a peaceful location, surrounded by trees, with good
modern facilities.
⭢ *Situated between Dunkerque and Oostende, 5km from the
Belgian frontier. Leave motorway and head towards Veurne.*
All year 2.3HEC ▦ ⋔ ☎ ✗ ⊙ ⬚ ⊞ ⊞ lau ✦ ☎ ⚐ ⋏PS
Prices: pitch 650-875

▶ LOMBARDSIJDE WEST-VLAANDEREN

Lombarde Elisabethlaan 4 ☎ 058 236839
A well equipped family site 400mtrs from the sea and close to
the centre of the village.
All year 8.5HEC ▦ ⋔ ☎ ✗ ✗ ⊙ ⬚ ⚐ ⬛ ⋏ L ⬛ ⊞ lau ✦ ⋏S
Prices: pitch 380-835 (incl 6 persons)

Zomerzon Elisabethlaan 1 ☎ 058 237396
All year 10HEC ▦ ⚥ ⋔ ☎ ⊙ ⬚ ⋏ ⬛ ⊞ ⊞ ⊘ lau ✦ ☎ ✗
⚐ ⋏PS

▶ LOPPEM WEST-VLAANDEREN

Lac Loppem ☎ 050 824262
Surrounded by fir trees on the edge of a lake.
⭢ *Leave A10/E40 at Torhout exit and turn right by the ESSO
service station.*
All year 14HEC ▦ ⋔ ☎ ✗ ⊙ ⬚ ⚐ ⋏ L ⬛ ⬛ ⊞
Prices: ♦90 ⬛90 ⬛90 ▲90

▶ MIDDELKERKE WEST-VLAANDEREN

Myn Plezier Duinenweg 489 ☎ 059 300279
In wooded surroundings close to the castle. The camp shop
only operates during high season.
Apr-10 Sep 3HEC ▦ ⚥ ⋔ ☎ ✗ ⊙ ⬚ ⚐ ⊞ lau ✦ ⋏S

▶ MONS HAINAUT

Waux-Hall av St-Pierre 17 ☎ 065 337923
In a secluded position with direct access to the Parc du
Waux-Hall.
All year 1.4HEC ▦ ⋔ ☎ ⊙ ⬚ ⬛ ⊞ lau ✦ ☎ ✗ ⚐ ⋏ ⋏LP
Prices: ♦135 ⬛35 ⬛35 ▲35

▶ NIEUWPOORT WEST-VLAANDEREN

Info Bruggesteenweg 49 ☎ 058 236037
A family site. Facilities for watersports.
⭢ *On N67 between St Joris and Nieuwpoort.*
26 Mar-14 Nov 24HEC ▦ ⋔ ☎ ✗ ⊙ ⬚ ⚐ ⋏ P ⬛ ⊞
lau ✦ ⋏LRS
Prices: pitch 695-975 (incl 4 persons)

▶ OOSTENDE (OSTENDE) WEST-VLAANDEREN

▶ At BREDENE(5km NE)

Asterix Duinenstr 200 ☎ 059 331000
A family site in wooded surroundings, 500m from the sea.
Camping Card Compulsory.
All year 3HEC ⠿ ⋔ ☎ ✗ ⊙ ⬚ ⚐ ⋏ ⬛ ⚐ ⋏ LPS ⬛ ⬛
⊞ lau
Prices: ♦110 ⬛50 ⬛330 ▲330

ST SAUVEUR HAINAUT

Hauts r des Vertes Feuilles 13 ☎ 3269 768672
In a secluded, wooded situation within the Flemish Ardennes
with fine facilities.
➡ *Signposted from Renaix.*
All year 1HEC 💦 ♦ 🏠 ☉ 🕑 🦢 ᖯ 🏕 🚐 🖱 🎫 lau ➡ 🍴 🏆 ✗
Prices: 🏝60 🚙60 ▲250 pitch 250-300

TOURNAI HAINAUT

Orient Vieux Chemin de Mons 8 ☎ 069 222635
A pleasant site with good recreational facilities.
➡ *From motorway exit 'Tournai Est' head towards the town
centre. Turn left at first crossroads and follow signs.*
All year 20HEC 💦 🕑 🏠 ☉ 🕑 🏆 ᖯ P 🖱 🎫 lau ➡ 🦢 ᖰ

WAREGEM WEST-VLAANDEREN

Gemeentelijk Sportstadion Zuiderlaan 13 ☎ 056 609532
In a sports and leisure centre SE of the town centre.
➡ *Access via E17 (Kortrijk-Gent).*
Apr-Sep 1HEC 💦 🕑 🏠 ☉ 🕑 🖱 🎫 ➡ 🍴 🏆 ✗ 🦢 ᖰ ↝PR

WAUDREZ HAINAUT

Gloriettes r de la Résistance 92 ☎ 064 332611
Apr-Oct 3HEC 💦 🕑 🏠 🏆 ✗ ☉ 🕑 🖱 🎫 lau
Prices: 🏝90 🚙90 🚐90 ▲90 pitch 90

WESTENDE WEST-VLAANDEREN

KACB Bassevillestr 81 ☎ 058 237343
A well appointed site close to the beach.
Camping Card Compulsory.
➡ *Situated between Westende and Lombardsijde towards the
sea.*
All year 6.5HEC 💦 🕑 🏠 🦢 🏆 ✗ ☉ 🕑 🦢 ᖯ 🚐 🖱 🎫 lau ➡ ᖰ
↝LPS

WIERS HAINAUT

Château du Biez r du Prince d'Espinoy 11 ☎ 069 772126
A quiet site in a forested area with good recreational
facilities.
➡ *Access via E42 exit 30.*
All year 5HEC 💦 🕑 🏠 ✗ ☉ 🕑 🦢 ᖰ ↝ R 🖱 🎫 ➡ ᖯ
Prices: pitch 200

NORTH/CENTRAL

Most of this central region of Belgium is intensely
agricultural, vast open plains are covered in crops, with
large, compact villages in the valleys. Gent is the capital of
the province of East Flanders - one of the most beautiful of
Belgian cities with a wonderful medieval heart. Rivers and
canals dissect the city, and it buzzes with commerce and
industry, lively shopping streets and markets. Imposing
buildings are reminders of a colourful past: the view from
St Michael's Bridge takes in the towers of St Nicholas'
Church (13th to 15th century), the Belfry (13th to 14th
century) and the Cathedral of St Bavo (dating from the 10th
century). Also in East Flanders, Oodenaarde is historically a
textile centre; its tapestries are still renowned, and the town
has many beautiful buildings dating from the late Middle
Ages.
The centre of the south of this region, and capital of
Belgium, is Brussels. Although some parts of the old
Brussels remain intact, today it is essentially a modern
cosmopolitan centre, the cultural and educational capital of
Belgium, headquarters of the EC and NATO and many
other international organisations. The city exudes vitality
and prosperity, in keeping with its position as an
international centre.

BACHTE-MARIA-LEERNE OOST-VLAANDEREN

Groeneveld Groenevelddreef ☎ 09 3801014
Well equipped site beside a lake.
➡ *Approach via E17 or E40.*
Apr-13 Nov 1.7HEC 💦 🕑 🏠 ᖯ 🏆 ✗ ☉ 🕑 🦢 ᖯ ᖱ 🖱 🎫 ➡ ✗ ᖰ
Prices: pitch 515-655

BEAUVECHAIN BRABANT

Arpents Verts r Longue 115 ☎ 010 866993
➡ *Access via E411 exit 8 towards Louvain or E40 exit 23
towards Bevekom.*
May-Aug 1HEC 💦 🕑 🏠 ᖯ 🏆 ✗ ☉ 🕑 🦢 ᖰ 🖱 🎫 ⌀ lau
Prices: pitch 450-900 (incl 2 persons)

BEGYNENDYK BRABANT

Roygaerden Betekomsesteenweg 75 ☎ 016 531087
Pitches are in wooded surroundings beside a lake.
All year 5HEC 💦 🕑 🏠 🏆 ✗ ☉ 🕑 🦢 🚐 🖱 🎫 🖱 lau ➡ ᖯ ↝LP
Prices: 🏝150 🚐350 ▲100

BEVERE OOST-VLAANDEREN

Vlaamse Ardennen Kortrijkstr 342 ☎ 055 315473
A family site with good recreational facilities.
6 Jan-12 Dec 23HEC 💦 🕑 🏠 ᖯ 🏆 ✗ ☉ 🕑 🦢 ᖯ ᖱ ↝ LP 🖱 🎫
lau

GENT (GAND) OOST-VLAANDEREN

Blaarmeersen Zuiderlaan 12 ☎ 09 2215399
In pleasant wooded surroundings SW of Gent towards the
railway station.
Mar-15 Oct 5HEC 💦 🕑 🏠 ᖯ 🏆 ✗ ☉ 🕑 🦢 ᖯ ᖰ 🖱 L 🖱 🎫 lau
➡ ᖰP
Prices: 🏝110-120 🚙60-65 🚐120-130 ▲120-130

GRIMBERGEN BRABANT

Grimbergen Veldkanstr 64 ☎ 02 2709597
➡ *Access via exit 7 on Bruxelles ringroad.*
Apr-Oct 1.5HEC 💦 ♦ 🕑 🏠 ☉ 🕑 🖱 🎫 lau ➡ ᖯ 🏆 ✗ ᖰP
Prices: 🏝100 🚙50 🚐100 ▲100

HEVERLEE BRABANT

Ter Munck Kampingweg ☎ 016 238668
12 Jun-11 Sep 1.5HEC 💦 🕑 🏠 🏆 ✗ ☉ 🕑 🖱 🎫 lau ➡ ᖯ ✗ 🦢
ᖰ ᖰP
Prices: pitch 360 (incl 2 persons)

LOONBEEK BRABANT

Bergendal Biezen Str 81 ☎ 016 403904 & 470169
Camping Card Compulsory.
➡ *Access via E411 and RN253.*
15 Mar-15 Nov 9HEC 💦 🕑 🏠 ☉ 🕑 🖱 🎫 lau ➡ 🦢

ONKERZELE OOST-VLAANDEREN

Gavers Onkerzelestr 280 ☎ 054 416324
A quiet, well equipped site beside a lake between the Dendre
Valley and the foothills of the Ardennes. There are good
sporting and sanitary facilities.
All year 10HEC 💦 🕑 🏠 ᖯ 🏆 ✗ ☉ 🕑 🦢 🖱 🎫 lau
Prices: pitch 490

STEKENE OOST-VLAANDEREN

Eurocamping Baudeloo Heirweg 159 ☎ 03 7890663
All year 4.5HEC 💦 ♦ 🕑 🏠 🏆 ✗ ☉ 🕑 🏆 ᖰ P 🖱 🎫 lau ➡ ᖯ ✗ 🦢
Prices: 🏝70 🚙70 🚐70 ▲70 pitch 100

Reinaert Lunterbergstr 4 ☎ 03 7798525
Apr-Oct 5HEC 💦 🕑 🏠 ᖯ 🏆 ✗ ☉ 🕑 🖱 🎫 lau ➡ ᖯ
Prices: 🏝70 🚙60 🚐60 ▲60

▶ **WACHTEBEKE** OOST-VLAANDEREN

Puyenbroeck Puyenbrug 1A ☎ 09 3557607
Apr-Sep 8HEC ⚏ 🔆 ♠ ⊙ 🖾 🖻 ⊞ 🛇 lau ➡ 🖫 ✗ ⚲LPR

● ● ● ● **NORTH EAST** ● ● ●

The natural entrance to this region is Antwerp. One of the
great ports of Europe and a fascinating city to visit, it is
dominated by the elegant tower of its cathedral. The
cathedral's graceful exterior is complemented by a spacious
and rich interior, with some fine Rubens masterpieces. Near
the cathedral is the Grote Markt, with an impressive town
hall, and several guildhalls with wonderful façades. The
extensive old city contains many fine old buildings and
some fascinating museums, including the Plantin Moretus
Museum, and Rubens' House.
Other interesting towns in this region include Turnhout, a
commercial centre with a modern town hall and lovely
church in the market place; Mechelen - an ecclesiastical
centre with a particularly well preserved old town;
Tongeren, known as the oldest town in Belgium and
containing many interesting reminders of the past; The
quiet picturesque town of Zoutleeuw, with its lovely 13th-
century church; Lier, with its attractive market place; and
the old abbey town of Averbode.
....

▶ **ANTWERPEN (ANVERS)** ANTWERPEN

De Molen Thonetlaan ☎ 03 2196090
Apr-Sep 1.3HEC ⚏ ⚶ ♠ ⊙ 🖾 🖻 ⊞ lau ➡ 🖫 🍸 ✗ ⚲PR

▶ **BRECHT** ANTWERPEN

Floreal Het Veen Eekhoornlaan 1, St-Job In't Goor
☎ 03 6361327
A comfortable site in a pleasant wooded setting with
residential and touring pitches.
➲ *Leave Autoroute E19 at exit St Job In't Goor.*
Apr-Sep 7.5HEC ⚏ ⚶ ♠ ✗ ⊙ 🖾 🖻 ⚲ R 🖻 ⊞ lau ➡ 🍸 ⚱
🖾
Prices: ♦105 ☞270 ▲265

▶ **EKSEL** LIMBURG

Lage Kempen Kiefhoeki str 19 ☎ 011 402243
Situated in the middle of a forest with a variety of
recreational facilities.
➲ *From route 67 from Hasselt follow signs 'Lage Kampen' to
the left.*
Etr-2 Nov 3.5HEC ⚏ 🔆 ♠ 🖫 🍸 ✗ ⊙ 🖾 ⚱ 🖾 ⚲ P lau
Prices: ♦120 ☞70 ☞110 ▲110

▶ **GIERLE** ANTWERPEN

Lilse Bergen Strandweg 6 ☎ 014 557901
A very well equipped family site surrounding a private lake.
➲ *E39 exit 22.*
All year 60HEC ⚬⚬⚬ ➡ ♠ 🖫 🍸 ✗ ⊙ 🖾 ⚱ 🖾 ⚲ L 🖻 ⊞ lau
Prices: pitch 400-550

▶ **HOUTHALEN** LIMBURG

Hengelhoef ☎ 089 382500
A family site in pleasant wooded surroundings with good,
modern facilities.
Apr-Nov 15HEC ⚏ ➡ ♠ 🖫 🍸 ✗ ⊙ 🖾 ⚱ 🖾 ⚲ LP 🖻 ⊞ ⚘
lau ➡ ⚲LP

▶ **KASTERLEE** ANTWERPEN

Houtum Houtum 51 ☎ 014 852365
An extensive site with well defined pitches shaded by trees
and bushes.

➲ *On S outskirts of Kasterlee.*
All year 9HEC ⚏ 🔆 ♠ 🍸 ✗ ⊙ 🖾 🖾 ⚲ R 🖻 ⊞ ⚘ ➡ ⚱

▶ **MOL** ANTWERPEN

Zilvermeer Zilvermeerlaan 2 ☎ 014 829500
A pleasant lakeside site with good recreational facilities.
Closed 16 Nov-15 Dec 45HEC ⚏ ⋮⋮⋮ ♠ ♠ 🖫 🍸 ✗ ⊙ 🖾 ⚱
🖾 🖾 ⚲ L 🖻 🖻 ⊞ lau
Prices: pitch 300-440 (incl 4 persons)

▶ **OPGLABBEEK** LIMBURG

Jeugdparadijs Speeltuinstr 8 ☎ 089 854347
Apr-Sep 8HEC ⚏ ♠ ♠ 🖫 🍸 ✗ ⊙ 🖾 ⚲ P 🖻 ➡ ⚱

▶ **REKEM** LIMBURG

Sonnevijer Heidestr 103 ☎ 089 713048
➲ *4km S of Autoroute E39, exit 'Lanaken'.*
All year 30HEC ⚏ ➡ ♠ 🖫 🍸 ✗ ⊙ 🖾 ⚱ 🖾 ⚲ LP 🖻 ⊞ lau

▶ **RETIE** ANTWERPEN

Berkenstrand Brand 78 ☎ 014 377590
In wooded surroundings beside a lake.
➲ *3km NE on road to Postel.*
All year 10HEC ⚏ ♠ ♠ 🖫 🍸 ✗ ⊙ 🖾 ⚱ 🖾 🖾 🖾 ⚲ L 🖻 ⊞
lau
Prices: ♦100 ☞75 ☞75 ▲75

▶ **VORST-LAAKDAL** ANTWERPEN

Kasteel Meerlaer Verboekt 105 ☎ 013 661420
➲ *E313 exit 24 towards Hosselt or exit 24 towards Antwerp.*
All year 6HEC ⚏ ➡ ♠ 🍸 ✗ ⊙ 🖾 ⚱ 🖾 🖾 🖾 🖾 ⊞ lau ➡ 🖫 ✗

▶ **ZONHOVEN** LIMBURG

Berkenhof Teutseweg 33 ☎ 011 814439
Apr-Oct 3.5HEC ⚏ ➡ ♠ 🍸 ✗ ⊙ 🖾 ⚱ 🖾 🖾 🖻 ⊞ ➡ 🖫

Holsteenbron Hengelhoelseweg 9 ☎ 04 81 71 40
Apr-15 Nov 6HEC ⚏ ♠ ♠ 🍸 ✗ ⊙ 🖾 ⚱ 🖾 🖻 ⊞ lau ➡ 🖫

● ● ● ● **SOUTH EAST** ● ● ● ●

This region is known as the great garden of the Ardennes -
dense forests, hills rising to over 2,000ft, imposing chalk
cliffs, deep, wide valleys and serene reservoirs. Small
villages, ancient monasteries, high fortress citadels and
picturesque towns - with imposing civic buildings and half-
timbered dwellings, dot the countryside. The graceful
Meuse flows through the north of this area; historically an
important north-south artery. Today barges frequent its
waters, and the 'castles of Namur' adorn its banks. There
are a number of impressive caves in the region - the caves
at Han-sur-Lesse are remarkable, stretching some miles
underground, with fantastic formations.
Towns set on the River Meuse include Dinant, overlooked
by the mass of its castle; picturesque Namur, between the
banks of the Meuse and the Sambre, also dominated by its
castle; and cosmopolitan Liège, a bustling mix of culture
and industry. La Roche-en-Ardenne is beautifully set in its
deep valley on a loop of the Ourthe, and Spa is a traditional
resort with thermal springs.
....

▶ **AISCHE-EN-REFAIL** NAMUR

Manoir de lá Bas rte de Gembloux 180 ☎ 081 655353
In a beautiful situation within the wooded grounds of a
former manor house.
➲ *5km W of Eghezée.*
Apr-Oct 22HEC ⚏ 🔆 ♠ 🍸 ✗ ⊙ 🖾 ⚱ 🖾 ⚲ P 🖻 lau ➡ 🖫 ⊞
Prices: ♦80 pitch 130

▷ **AMBERLOUP** LUXEMBOURG

Tonny r Tonny 35-36 ☎ 061 688285
In a pleasant valley beside the River Ourthe with fine
sporting facilities.
All year 3HEC ⚏ ⬗ ⋔ ⚌ ⚑ ✕ ⊙ ⊖ ⊘ 📷 ♨ ⊞ ⚐ ⟨ R ⊡ ⊞ lau

▷ **AMONINES** LUXEMBOURG

Val de l'Aisne Blier ☎ 086 477053
All year 15HEC ⚏ ⚡ ⬗ ⋔ ⚑ ✕ ⊙ ⊖ ⚑ ⟨ R ⊡ ⊞ lau

▷ **AVE-ET-AUFFE** NAMUR

Roptai r Roptai 34 ☎ 084 388319
The site is located in a hilly situation in pretty clearings
amidst a large forest about 1km from the village.
All year 10HEC ⚏ ⬗ ⋔ ⚌ ⚑ ✕ ⊙ ⊖ ⚑ ⊘ ♨ ⊞ ⚑ ⟨ P ⊡ ⊞
lau ⟶ ✕

▷ **BARVAUX-SUR-OURTHE** LUXEMBOURG

Hazalles Chainrue 77a ☎ 086 211642
Situated in an orchard, 600mtrs from the village beside a
stream with well maintained facilities.
Apr-Oct 0.3HEC ⚏ ⬗ ⋔ ⊙ ⚑ ⚑ ⊡ ⊞ lau ⟶ ⚌ ⚑ ✕ ⊘ ♨
⟨PR
Prices: ⚲65 🚐40 ⚑100 ⚑100

Rives de l'Ourthe r Inzespres 70 ☎ 086 211730
A large site with plenty of touring pitches beside the River
Ourthe.
➲ *200mtrs from the village towards the river.*
Apr-Sep 2HEC ⚏ ⬗ ⚌ ⚑ ✕ ⊙ ⊖ ⚑ ⟨ R ⊡ ⊞ ⟶ ⚌ ✕ ⊘ ♨ ⟨LP
Prices: ⚲70 ⚑140 ⚑140

▷ **BERTRIX** LUXEMBOURG

Info rte de Mortehan ☎ 061 412281
Well equipped family site in a pleasant wooded setting.
➲ *S of town beyond the church. Signposted from N884.*
12 Feb-21 Feb/2 Apr-14 Nov 14HEC ⚏ ⬗ ⋔ ⚌ ⚑ ✕ ⊙ ⊖ ⊘
♨ ⚑ ⟨ P ⊡ ⊞ lau
Prices: ⚑200 pitch 900 (incl 6 persons)

▷ **BONNERT** LUXEMBOURG

Officiel rte de Bastogne 373 ☎ 063 226582
➲ *E of E9-N4.*
All year 1.4HEC ⚏ ⬗ ⋔ ✕ ⊙ ⊖ ⚑ ⊘ ♨ ⚑ ⟨ P ⊡ ⊞ ⊞ lau
⟶ ⟨LP

▷ **BÜLLINGEN (BULLANGE)** LIÈGE

Hêtraie Rotheck 264 ☎ 080 642413
This site is situated on a sloping meadow near a fish pond
and is surrounded by groups of beautiful beech trees and
conifers.
➲ *Leave village in direction of Amel then left and continue for
2km. Signposted.*
Apr-15 Nov 3HEC ⚏ ⬗ ⋔ ⊙ ⊖ ⚑ ⚑ ⚑ ⟨ P ⊡ ⊞ lau

▷ **BURE** LUXEMBOURG

Parc la Clusure 30 chemin de la Clusure ☎ 084 366080
Pleasant site with good facilities in the centre of the
Ardennes.
➲ *Access from E411 and N846 via Tellin.*
All year 13HEC ⚏ ⬗ ⋔ ⚌ ⚑ ✕ ⊙ ⊖ ♨ ⚑ ⚑ ⚑ ⟨ PR ⊡ ⊞
lau

▷ **BÜTGENBACH** LIÈGE

Worriken Worriken Center 1 ☎ 080 446358
Situated on the shores of a lake.
14 Dec-13 Nov 8HEC ⚏ ⬗ ⋔ ⚌ ⚑ ✕ ⊙ ⊖ ⚑ ⟨ L ⊡ ⊞ lau ⟶ ⚌
⊘ ♨ ⟨PR
Prices: ⚑340 pitch 580 (incl 4 persons)

▷ **CHEVETOGNE** NAMUR

Domaine Provincial ☎ 083 688821
All year 0.5HEC ⚏ ⬗ ⋔ ⚌ ⚑ ✕ ⊙ ⊖ ⚑ ⚑ ⟨ P ⊡ ⊞ ⊞ ⟶ ⊘ ♨

▷ **COO-STAVELOT** LIÈGE

Cascade Chemin des Faravennes 5 ☎ 080 684312
A small family and holiday site beside the River Amblève.
➲ *3km from Trois-Ponts via motorway exit 10 or 11.*
Mar-Oct 0.8HEC ⚏ ⚡ ⬗ ⋔ ⊙ ⊖ ⟨ R ⊡ ⊞ lau ⟶ ✕ ⟨L

▷ **EUPEN** LIÈGE

'An der Hill' Hutte 46 ☎ 087 744617
➲ *SW of town via N67 towards Monschau.*
All year 0.6HEC ⚏ ⬗ ⋔ ⚌ ⚑ ✕ ⊙ ⊖ ⚑ ⊘ ⊡ ⊞ ⊞ lau ⟶ ⚌ ⟨P

▷ **FLORENVILLE** LUXEMBOURG

Rosière Rive Gauche de la Semois ☎ 061 311937
In wooded surroundings close to the town centre.
Apr-Oct 10HEC ⚏ ⬗ ⋔ ⚌ ⚑ ✕ ⊙ ⊖ ⚑ ⊘ ⟨ PR ⊡ ⊞ lau
Prices: ⚲75-85 🚐40-50 ⚑260-310 ⚑210-230

▷ **FORRIÈRES** LUXEMBOURG

Pré du Blason r de la Ramée 30 ☎ 084 212867
This well-kept site lies on a meadow surrounded by wooded
hills and is completely divided into pitches and crossed by
rough gravel drives.
➲ *Off N49 Masbourg road.*
Apr-Oct 3HEC ⚏ ⬗ ⋔ ⚌ ⚑ ✕ ⊙ ⊖ ⊘ ♨ ⚑ ⟨ R ⊡ ⊞ lau
Prices: ⚲80 ⚑270

▷ **GEDINNE** NAMUR

Mélèzes Hameau Station, 2 rte Dinant-Bouillon ☎ 061
588560
In pleasant wooded surroundings. Area for tents and
caravans, also modern timber chalets for hire.
➲ *Access via E411 Brussels-Namur.*
All year 2HEC ⚏ ⬗ ⋔ ⚌ ⚑ ✕ ⊙ ⊖ ⚑ ⊘ ⚑ ⚑ ⊞ ⊞ lau

▷ **GEMMENICH** LIÈGE

Kon Tiki Terstraeten 141 ☎ 087 785973
All year 12HEC ⚏ ⬗ ⋔ ⚌ ⚑ ✕ ⊙ ⊖ ⚑ ⊘ ♨ ⟨ PR ⊡ ⊞ lau

▷ **GOUVY** LUXEMBOURG

Lac de Cherapont Cherapont 2 ☎ 080 517082
On an extensive lakeside tourist complex with a wide variety
of recreational facilities.
➲ *Access via E25 exit 51 or E42 exit 15.*
Mar-Dec 10HEC ⚏ ⟶ ⋔ ⚌ ⚑ ✕ ⊙ ⊖ ⚑ ♨ ⚑ ⚑ ⟨ L ⊡ ⊞ lau

▷ **GRAND-HALLEUX** LUXEMBOURG

Neuf Prés av de la Résistance ☎ 080 216882
Apr-Sep 4HEC ⚏ ⬗ ⋔ ⚌ ✕ ⊙ ⊖ ⟨ PR ⊡ lau ⟶ ⚌ ✕ ⊘ ♨
Prices: ⚲82 🚐45 ⚑120 ⚑90

▷ **HABAY-LA-NEUVE** LUXEMBOURG

Portail de la Forêt r du Bon-Bois 3 ☎ 063 422312
Parkline, terraced site on a hill surrounded by woodland.
➲ *Turn off N48 and follow signs.*
Closed 15 Dec-Jan 5HEC ⚏ ⬗ ⋔ ⚌ ⚑ ✕ ⊙ ⊖ ⊘ ♨ ⟨ P ⊡
lau ⟶ ⊞
Prices: pitch 600

▷ **HAMOIR-SUR-OURTHE** LIÈGE

CM Dessous Hamoir r du Moulin ☎ 086 388925
A municipal site with well equipped pitches and good
facilities for children beside the River Ourthe.
➲ *From the Liège-Luxembourg motorway take exit
Werbomont and continue for 15km.*

Contd.

15 Mar-15 Nov 3.5HEC ⬛ ⌁ ⌂ ☉ ⌁ ⟡ R 🔳 ⊞ lau ➡ ⚓ ▼ ✗ ⌀
Prices: ♠80 ♣50 ⬛100 ▲90

HOGNE NAMUR

Relais 16 r de Serinchamps ☎ 084 311580
A pleasant site in a wooded park beside a lake.
➲ *Take N4 from Courrière to Hogne via Marche.*
Closed Jan-15 Feb 10HEC ⬛ ⌁ ⌂ ▼ ✗ ☉ ⌁ ⌀ ♨ 🏠 ⌁ ⟡
L 🔳 ⊞ lau
Prices: pitch 275-500 (incl 4 persons)

HOUFFALIZE LUXEMBOURG

Chasse et Pêche r de la Roche 63 ☎ 061 288314
A pleasant site attached to a café-restaurant with good
recreational facilities.
➲ *3km NW off E25.*
All year 2HEC ➡ ⌂ ⚓ ▼ ✗ ☉ ⌀ ⌁ ⟡ R 🔳 🅿 ⊞ lau
Prices: ♠120 ♣90 ⬛100 ▲100

Moulin de Rensiwez Moulin de Rensiwez 1 ☎ 061 289027
Isolated terraced site by the River Ourthe around an old
water-mill. Shop open July and August only.
All year 8HEC ⬛ ⌁ ⌂ ⚓ ☉ ⌁ ⌀ 🏠 ⟡ R 🔳 🅿 ⊞ ✗ lau
Prices: pitch 450 (incl 4 persons)

JAMOIGNE LUXEMBOURG

Faing ☎ 061 330272
A municipal camp on a meadow situated behind a sports
ground which separates the site from the road.
➲ *400m W on N44.*
Jan 3.5HEC ⬛ ⌁ ⌂ ⚓ ▼ ✗ ☉ ⌁ ⟡ R 🔳 lau ➡ ⚓ ⌀ ♨ ⟡P ⊞

LOUVEIGNÉ LIÈGE

Moulin du Rouge-Thier Rouge-Thier 8 ☎ 04 3608341
A well equipped site in a pleasant wooded location.
➲ *S of town towards Deigné.*
Apr-Oct 7HEC ⬛ ✂ ⌂ ⚓ ▼ ✗ ☉ ⌁ ⌀ ♨ ⟡ P 🔳 ⊞ lau
Prices: pitch 410 (incl 4 persons)

MALONNE NAMUR

Trieux r des Três 99 ☎ 081 445583
Apr-Oct 2HEC ⬛ ⌁ ⌂ ⚓ ☉ ⌁ ⌀ ⌁ ⊞ lau ➡ ▼ ✗
Prices: ♠80 ♣100 ⬛100 ▲100

MARCHE-EN-FAMENNE LUXEMBOURG

Euro Camping Paola r du Panorama 10 ☎ 084 311704
A long site on a hill with a beautiful view. The only noise
comes from a railway line, which passes right by the site.
➲ *Take road towards Hotton, turn right after cemetery and
continue 1km.*
All year 13HEC ⬛ ⌀ ⌁ ⌂ ▼ ✗ ☉ ⌁ ⌀ ♨ 🔳 ⊞
Prices: pitch 420

NEUFCHÂTEAU LUXEMBOURG

International Spineuse rte de Florenville ☎ 061 277320
Camp shop operates July-Aug only.
➲ *Situated 2km from Florenville in the direction of
Neufchâteau.*
All year 2.5HEC ⬛ ⌁ ⌂ ⚓ ▼ ✗ ☉ ⌁ ⌀ ♨ ⟡ LR 🔳 ⊞
lau
Prices: ♠85 pitch 250-300

OLLOY-SUR-VIROIN NAMUR

Try des Baudets r de la Champagne ☎ 060 390108
In a peaceful situation on the edge of a forest.
All year 12HEC ⬛ ⌀ ⌁ ⌂ ⚓ ▼ ✗ ☉ ⌁ ♨ 🔳 ⊞ lau ➡ ⚓ ✗
⟡R
Prices: ♠20 ⬛430 ▲220

OTEPPE LIÈGE

Hirondelle r du Château 1 ☎ 085 711131
Ideal family site with modern facilities.
➲ *N of town between E40 and E42. Signposted.*
Apr-Oct 65HEC ⬛ ⌁ ⌂ ⚓ ▼ ✗ ☉ ⌀ 🏠 ⟡ P 🔳 ⊞ lau
Prices: ♠90-110 ♣40 ⬛180-260 ▲180-260

POLLEUR LIÈGE

Polleur r de Congrès 90 ☎ 087 541033
A family site in a pleasant wooded location.
➲ *Signposted from A27/E42.*
Apr-1 Nov 4HEC ⬛ ✂ ⌂ ⚓ ▼ ✗ ☉ ⌁ ⌀ ♨ ⟡ PR 🔳 ⊞ lau
Prices: ♠110-135 ♣110-135 ⬛110-135 ▲110-135

PURNODE NAMUR

Bocq av de la Vallée ☎ 082 612269
In a beautiful wooded location beside the river.
Apr-Sep 2HEC ⬛ ⌁ ⌂ ▼ ✗ ☉ ⌁ ⟡ PR 🔳 ➡ ⊞
Prices: ♠100 ♣100 ⬛100 ▲100

REMOUCHAMPS LIÈGE

Eden r de Trois Ponts 92 ☎ 041 3844165
Apr-Oct 3.2HEC ⬛ ⌁ ➡ ⌂ ⚓ ☉ ⌁ ⌀ ⌁ ⟡ R 🔳 ⊞ ➡ ▼
✗
Prices: ♠70 pitch 300

RENDEUX LUXEMBOURG

Festival rte de la Roche 89 ☎ 084 477371
In unspoiled surroundings beside the River Ourthe.
15 Mar-Sep 12HEC ⬛ ⌁ ⌂ ⚓ ▼ ✗ ☉ ⌁ ⌀ ♨ ⟡ R 🔳 🅿 ⊞
lau
Prices: pitch 400-770 (incl 4 persons)

ROBERTVILLE LIÈGE

Plage 33 rte des Bains ☎ 080 446658
All year 1.8HEC ▦ ⌖ ⋒ ⧉ ✕ ⊙ ⬤ ⌀ ⛺ ⬢ ⤳ LPR ⊡ ⊞

ROCHE-EN-ARDENNE, LA LUXEMBOURG

Grillon r des Echarées ☎ 084 412062
Well equipped family site in a pleasant wooded setting.
Etr-Oct 3.5HEC ▦ ⌖ ⋒ ⧉ ⍩ ⊙ ⬤ ⌀ ⛺ ⤳ R ⊡ ⊞ lau ➧ ✕ ⤳P
Prices: ♠80 pitch 240

Lohan 20a rte de Houffalize ☎ 084 411545
In a park, on N bank of the River Ourthe.
Apr-Oct 4HEC ▦ ⌖ ⋒ ⧉ ✕ ⊙ ⬤ ⌀ ⤳ LR ⊡ ⊞ ⌀ lau
Prices: ♠75 pitch 220-250

Ourthe ☎ 084 411459
Well kept site, beside the River Ourthe.
➲ *On SW bank of the Ourthe below the N34.*
15 Mar-15 Oct 2HEC ▦ ➧ ⋒ ⧉ ⊙ ⬤ ⌀ ⛺ ⬢ ⤳ R ⊡ ⊞
lau ➧ ⊞
Prices: ♠70 pitch 210

ROCHEHAUT LUXEMBOURG

Laviot r Laviot 6 ☎ 061 466314
Apr-15 Oct 6HEC ▦ ⍟ ⋒ ⧉ ⍩ ✕ ⊙ ⬤ ⌀ ⬢ ⤳ R ⊡ lau ➧
✕ ⛺

SART-LEZ-SPA LIÈGE

Touring Club Stockay 17 ☎ 087 474400
➲ *Signposted. The site lies to the E of Spa.*
All year 6HEC ▦ ⌖ ⋒ ⧉ ⍩ ✕ ⊙ ⬤ ⌀ ⛺ ⬢ ⤳ R ⊡ ⊞ lau ➧
⤳L
Prices: pitch 383 (incl 2 persons)

SIPPENAEKEN LIÈGE

Vieux Moulin 114 Tebruggen ☎ 087 784255
A family site in a pleasant wooded location close to a nature
reserve with good recreational facilities.
Apr-Sep 6HEC ▦ ⌖ ⋒ ⧉ ✕ ⊙ ⬤ ⌀ ⛺ ⬢ ⤳ PR ⊡ ⊞ lau
Prices: ♠100 pitch 140

SPA LIÈGE

Parc des Sources r de la Sauvenière 141 ☎ 087 772311
➲ *S of town centre on N32.*
Apr-Oct 2.5HEC ▦ ⌖ ⋒ ⧉ ✕ ⊙ ⬤ ⌀ ⊡ lau ➧ ⧉ ⍩ ✕ ⛺
⤳P ⊞
Prices: ♠105 ➧75 ⬤145 ⛺145

SPRIMONT LIÈGE

Tultay r de Tultay 22 ☎ 04 3821162
All year 1.5HEC ▦ ⌖ ⋒ ⍩ ✕ ⊙ ⬤ ⊡ ⊞ lau ➧ ⧉ ✕ ⌀ ⛺
Prices: ♠100 pitch 150

STAVELOT LIÈGE

Domaine de l'Eau Rouge Cheneux 25 ☎ 0032-80 863075
A pleasant riverside site with good sporting facilities.
➲ *Access via E42 to Francorchamps or Malmedy.*
All year 4HEC ▦ ⌖ ⋒ ⧉ ⍩ ✕ ⊙ ⬤ ⌀ ⛺ ⬢ ⤳ PR ⊡ ⊟ ⊞
lau
Prices: ♠50 pitch 320-500

TENNEVILLE LUXEMBOURG

Pont de Berguème r Berguème 9 ☎ 084 455443
In a peaceful, wooded setting in the beautiful Ardennes area
with good, modern facilities.
➲ *Turn off E40/N4 towards Berguème then turn right.*
All year 3HEC ▦ ⌖ ⋒ ⧉ ⍩ ✕ ⊙ ⬤ ⌀ ⛺ ⬢ ⤳ PR ⊟ ⊞
lau
Prices: ♠85 pitch 150

THOMMEN-REULAND LIÈGE

Hohenbusch Grüfflingen 44 ☎ 080 227523
A well appointed family site on a wooded meadow with
plenty of recreational facilities.
➲ *Off N26 SW of St-Vith.*
All year 5HEC ▦ ⌖ ⋒ ⧉ ⍩ ✕ ⊙ ⬤ ⌀ ⬢ ⤳ P ⊡ lau

VIELSALM LUXEMBOURG

Salm chemin de la Vallée ☎ 080 216241
All year 2.5HEC ▦ ➧ ⧉ ⍩ ✕ ⊙ ⬤ ⛺ ⬢ ⤳ R ⊡ ⊞ lau ➧ ⧉
✕ ⌀ ⤳LP
Prices: ♠45 ➧45 ⬤280

VIRTON LUXEMBOURG

Vallée de Rabais r du Bonlieu ☎ 063 570144
A secluded family site in the heart of the Gaume region close
to a lake with good recreational facilities.
All year 8HEC ▦ ⌖ ⋒ ⍩ ✕ ⊙ ⬤ ⌀ ⬢ ⊡ ⊞ lau ➧ ⧉ ✕ ⤳L

WAIMES LIÈGE

Anderegg Bruyerès 4 ☎ 080 679393
In a peaceful situation beside the Lac de Robertville.
All year 1HEC ▦ ⌖ ⋒ ⧉ ⍩ ✕ ⊙ ⬤ ⌀ ⛺ ⤳ R ⊡ ⊞
Prices: ♠70 pitch 140

FRANCE

France, rich in history and natural beauty, is bordered by six countries: Belgium, Germany, Italy, Luxembourg, Spain and Switzerland.

FACTS AND FIGURES

Capital: Paris
Language: French
IDD code: 33.
To call the UK dial 00 44
Currency: Franc *(FRF)* =
100 centimes). At the time
of going to press
£1 = *FRF 9.05*.
Local time: GMT + 1
(summer GMT + 2)
Emergency Services:
Police 17; Fire 18;

Ambulance 15. Alternatively,
dial the European
emergency call number
112, and request the
service you require.
Business hours-
Banks: Mon-Fri 09.00-
12.00 & 14.00-16.00
Shops: Mon-Sat 09.00-
18.00 (times may vary for
food shops)
Average daily
temperature: Paris
Jan 3°C   Jul 18°C

Mar 6°C   Sep 15°C
May 13°C   Nov 6°C
Tourist Information:
UK French Government
Tourist Office
178 Piccadilly
London W1V 0AL
Tel 0891 244123 (08.30 -
20.00 weekdays, 09.00 -
17.00 Saturdays. calls are
charged at 50p per minute
at all times)
Monaco Government Tourist
and Convention Office

The Chambers,
Chelsea Harbour
London SW10 0XF
Tel 0171-352 9962
USA French Government
Tourist Office
444 Madison Ave
New York, NY 10020
Tel (212) 838 7800
Camping Card: not
compulsory, but advisable
when using *Castels et
Camping* sites and also the
forts domaniales.

The country offers a great variety of scenery from the mountain ranges of the Alps and the Pyrénées to the attractive river valleys of the Loire, Rhône and Dordogne. And with some 1,800 miles of coastline, which includes the golden sands of the Côte-d'Azur, there is a landscape appealing to everyone's taste.

The climate of France is temperate but varies considerably. The Mediterranean coast enjoys a sub-tropical climate with hot summers, whilst along the coast of Brittany the climate is very similar to that of Devon and Cornwall. The language is, of course, French and this is spoken throughout the country, although there are many local dialects and variations.

France has an enormous number of campsites, over 10,000 of them, under the auspices of the *French Federation of Camping and Caravanning*. During July and August, however, they are heavily booked, specially on the Mediterranean coast and other popular holiday destinations.

There are *castels et camping* caravanning sites in the grounds of châteaux (castles) and many are included in this guide. On sites in state forests, *forêts domaniales*, it is necessary to apply to the *garde forestier* for permission to camp and evidence of insurance must be produced (such as the *camping card*). Opening periods vary widely and some sites are open all year. Local information offices (see *Tourist information* above) can supply detailed information about sites in their locality.

All graded sites must display their official classification, site regulations, capacity and current charges at the site entrance. Some sites have inclusive charges per pitch, others show basic prices per person, vehicle and space, with extra facilities like showers, swimming pools and ironing incurring additional charges. In practice, most campsites charge from midday to midday, with each part day being counted as a full day. Reductions for children are usually allowed up to 7 years of age; there is generally no charge for children under 3.

Off-site camping in the South of France is restricted because of the danger of fire; in other parts, camping is possible, provided that permission has been obtained, although camping is seldom allowed near the water's edge, or at a large seaside resort. Casual camping is prohibited in state forests, national parks in the Landes and Gironde *départements* and in the Camargue. Camping in an unauthorised place renders offenders liable to prosecution or confiscation of equipment, or both, especially in the South.

However, an overnight stop on parking areas of some motorways is tolerated, but make sure you do not contravene local regulations; overnight stops in a lay-by are not permitted. Camping is not permitted in *Monaco*. Caravans in transit are allowed but it is forbidden to park them.

HOW TO GET THERE

For details of the *AA European Routes Service* please consult the Contents page.

Apart from the direct crossing by Eurotunnel (Folkestone-Calais, 35 mins by day or 45 mins by night), the following ferry services are available:

Short ferry crossings
From **Dover** to **Calais** takes 75-90min.
Longer ferry crossings
From **Newhaven** to **Dieppe** takes 4hrs or 2hrs 15 by catamaran.
From **Portsmouth** to **Le Havre** takes 5hrs 30mins (day) - 7hrs 30mins (night): to **Caen** takes 6hrs; to **Cherbourg** takes 5hrs (day) – 7 hrs (night): to **St Malo** takes 8hrs 45mins (day) – 10hrs 30 mins (night). From **Poole** to **Cherbourg** takes 4hrs 15mins (day) – 5hrs 45mins (night). From **Plymouth** to **Roscoff** takes 6 hrs; to **St Malo** (winter only) takes 8hrs.

Fast Hoverspeed services

Hoverspeed/Hovercraft from Dover to Calais takes 35 mins. Hoverspeed/Seacat catamaran from Folkestone to Boulogne takes 55 mins.

Car sleeper trains

A daily service operates from **Calais** to the south of the country.

MOTORING & GENERAL INFORMATION

The information given here is specific to France. It **must** be read in conjunction with the European ABC at the front of the book, which covers those regulations which are common to many countries.

British Embassy/Consulates*

The British Embassy is located at 75383 Paris Cedex 08, 35 rue du Faubourg St-Honoré ☎0144513100; consular section 18 bis, rue d'Anjou as for Embassy.
There are British Consulates in Bordeaux, Lille,

Lyon and Marseille.
There are British Consulates with Honorary Consuls in Amiens, Biarritz, Boulogne-sur-Mer, Calais, Cherbourg, Dunkerque (Dunkirk), Le Havre, Montpellier, Nantes, Nice, Perpignan, St Malo-Dinard and Toulouse.

Childen in cars

Child under 10 not permitted to travel as front seat passenger, with the exception of baby - up to 9 months and less than 9kg weight - in rear-facing seat. Children under 10 in rear must use restraint system appropriate to age and weight. **Note**: Under no circumstances should a rear facing restraint be used in a front seat with an airbag.

Currency

There are no restrictions on the amount of French or foreign currency that can be taken in or out of France. However, amounts over *FRF*50,000 should be declared if re-exportation likely.

Banks close at midday on the day prior to a national holiday, and all day on Monday if the holiday falls on a Tuesday.

Dimensions and weight restrictions

Private **cars** and towed **trailers** or **caravans** are restricted to the following dimensions - height, no restrictions, but 4 metres is a recommended maximum; width, 2.5 metres; length, 12 metres (excluding tow-bar). The maximum permitted overall length of vehicle/trailer or caravan combination is 18.35 metres.
Traliers without brakes have a maximum authorised weight of 750kg or 50% of unladen weight of the towing vehicle, whichever is lower. If the weight of the trailer exceeds that of the towing.vehicle, see also *Speed limits* below.

Driving licence*

(see also *Speed limits* below)
A valid UK or Republic of Ireland licence is acceptable in France. The minimum age at which visitors from UK or Republic of Ireland may use a temporarily imported motorcycle (over 80cc) or car is 18. Visitors may use temporarily imported motorcycles of up to 80cc at 16.

Foodstuffs*
There are no limits on the importation of foodstuffs obtained duty and tax paid within the EC. Up to 500g of coffee (200g of coffee extract) and 100g of tea (40g of tea extract) purchased duty free or outside the EC may be imported free of duty and tax. However, coffee bought duty-free outside the EC cannot be imported by visitors under 15 years of age. Visitors may also import up to 10kg of fully cooked meat and meat products including poultry (if from EC) for personal consumption and not for resale. Meat and meat products from Africa are prohibited

Lights*
It is obligatory to use headlights, as driving on sidelights only is not permitted. In fog, mist or poor visibility during the day, either two fog lamps or two dipped headlights must be switched on in addition to two sidelights. It is also compulsory for motorcyclists riding machines exceeding 125cc to use dipped headlights during the day. Failure to comply with these regulations will lead to an on-the-spot deposit(see *Police fines* in the Continental ABC).

It is recommended that visiting motorists equip their vehicles with a set of replacement bulbs. Drivers able to replace a faulty bulb when requested to do so by the police will not avoid a fine, but may avoid the cost and inconvenience of a garage call out. Yellow tinted headlights are no longer necessary in France.

Motoring club*
The AA is affiliated to the **Fédération Française des Automobile-Clubs et des Usagers de la Route (FFAC)** whose office is at 8 place de la Concorde, 75008 Paris.
☎0153308930

Parking*
Parking restrictions are indicated by signs or yellow lines on the kerb. Stopping and parking is prohibited if the yellow line is continuous; parking if it is broken. In Paris parking is forbidden in many city centre streets, and wheelclamps are in use. It is absolutely forbidden to stop or park on a *red route*. The east-west route includes the left bank of the Seine and the Quai

de la Megisserie; the north-south route includes the Avenue du Général Leclerc, part of the Boulevard St Michel, the Rue de Rivoli, the Boulevards Sébastopol, Strasbourg, Barbès and Ornano, Rue Lafayette and Avenue Jean Jaurès.

Priority including Roundabouts*
In built-up areas, you must give way to traffic coming from the right - *priorit droite*. However, at roundabouts with signs bearing the words *"Vous n'avez pas la priorité"* or *"Cédez le passage"* traffic on the roundabout has priority. Where no such sign exists, traffic **entering** the roundabout has priority. Outside built-up areas, all main roads of any importance have right of way. This is indicated by a red-bordered triangle showing a black cross on a white background with the words *"Passage Protégé"* underneath; or a red-bordered triangle showing a pointed black upright with horizontal bar on a white background; or a
yellow square within a white square with points vertical.

Petrol
At the time of going to press, leaded and unleaded petrol are both available in France, but only one grade of leaded petrol is sold, 98 octane 'Super'.

Roads
France has a very comprehensive network of roads, and surfaces are generally good; exceptions are usually signposted *Chauseé deformeé*. The camber is often severe and the edges rough.

During July and August, and especially at weekends, traffic on main roads is likely to be very heavy. Special signs are erected to indicate alternative routes with the least traffic congestion. Wherever they appear, it is usually advantageous to follow them, although you cannot be absolutely sure of gaining time. The alternative routes are quiet, but they are not as wide as the main roads. They are **not** suitable for caravans.

A free road map showing the marked alternative routes, plus information centres and petrol stations open 24 hours, is available from service stations displaying the *Bison Futé* poster (a Red Indian chief in full war bonnet). These maps are also available from *Syndicats d'Initiative* and information offices.

Speed limits*

Built-up areas 50kph (31mph)
Outside built-up areas on normal roads 90kph (55mph); on dual-carriageways separated by a central reservation 110kph (69mph).
On Motorways 130kph (80mph). **Note** The minimum speed in the fast lane on a level stretch of motorway during good daytime visibility is 80kph (49mph), and drivers travelling below this speed are liable to be fined. The maximum speed on the Paris ring road is 80kph (49mph) and, on other urban stretches of motorway, 110kph (69mph).

In **fog**, when visibility is reduced to 50 metres (55yds), the speed limit on all roads is 50kph (31mph). In **wet weather** speed limits outside built-up areas are reduced to 80kph (49mph), 100kph (62mph) and 110kph (69mph) on motorways.

These limits also apply to private cars towing a trailer or caravan, if the latter's weight does not exceed that of the car and the total weight is less than 3.5 tonnes. However, if the weight of the trailer exceeds that of the car by less than 30%, the speed limit is 65kph (40mph), if more than 30% the speed limit is 45kph (28mph).

Additionally these combinations must:

i Display a disc at the rear of the caravan/trailer showing the maximum speed.

ii Not be driven in the fast lane of a 3-lane motorway.

Both French residents and visitors to France who have held a full driving licence for less than two years, must not exceed 80kph (49mph) outside built-up areas, 100kph (62mph) on dual carriageways separated by a central reservation and 110kph (69mph) on motorways.

Warning triangle/Hazard-warning lights*

The use of a warning triangle or hazard-warning lights† is compulsory in the event of accident or breakdown. As hazard-warning lights may be damaged or inoperative, it is recommended that a warning triangle be carried. The triangle must be placed on the road 30 metres (33yds) behind the vehicle and clearly visible from 100 metres (109yds).

†If your vehicle is equipped with hazard warning lights, it is also complusory to use them if you are forced to drive temporarily at a greatly reduced speed. However, when slow moving traffic is established in an uninterrupted lane or lanes, this only applies to the last vehicle in the lane(s).

*Additional information will be found in the Continental ABC at the front of the book.

Beynac-et-Cezenac

● ● ● ● **ALPS/EAST** ● ● ● ●

Within the French Alps is the old Duchy of Savoie, which only became part of France in the middle of the last century, and which still retains a distinctive character. The Alps is a region of clear air, majestic mountain peaks, peaceful valleys and meadows. Good roads link the valleys; steep winding mountain roads lead to delightful villages and spectacular viewpoints, but cable cars offer a unique alternative. A cable car goes up to the 12,000ft Aiguille du Midi, and a funicular railway leads to the spectacular 'Mer de Glace'. Annecy has a delightful, bustling medieval centre, and Lake Annecy, with its backdrop of mountains, provides opportunities for watersports and cruising. There are a number of attractive Alpine resorts - La Clusaz, Morzine, and the sophisticated Chamonix, and Savoy's ancient capital, Chambéry, has a fascinating old town and castle.

A well-kept secret is the Jura - a land of thickly wooded hills and plateaux and lush meadows grazed by sheep, goats and cattle. The rivers Rhône, Doubs and Ain flow through the region, and the many smaller rivers and lakes make this a fisherman's paradise.

....

▶ **ABRETS, LES** ISÈRE

Coin Tranquille ☎ 476321348
Completely divided into pitches with attractive flower beds in rural surroundings.
➲ *2 km E of village, 500m off N6.*
Apr-Oct 6HEC ⬛ ♠ ⛺ 🛁 ⚡ ☉ 🚿 ⌀ 🏪 🍴 ⚡ P ⊞ lau
Prices: pitch 85-129 (incl 2 persons)

▶ **AILLON-LE-JEUNE** SAVOIE

Jeanne et Georges Cher ☎ 479546032
On a level meadow with heated sanitary installations. Situated close to the local ski station.
All year 2HEC ⬛ ⛷ ⛺ ☉ 🚿 lau ♦ 🛒 ✕
Prices: ♠8.40-13.50 pitch 8.40-13.50

▶ **ALBENS** SAVOIE

Beauséjour rte de la Rippe ☎ 479541520
In a delightfully peaceful, wooded setting between Aix-les-Bains and Annecy.
➲ *SW via rte de la Chambotte. Signposted*
Jun-20 Sep 2HEC ⬛ ♠ ⛺ ☉ 🚿 ⌀ ⊞ lau ♦ 🛒 🍴 ✕ ⛏ ⁌R ⊞
Prices: ♠9 ♠10 ♠10 ♠10

▶ **ALLEVARD** ISÈRE

Clair Matin rte de Pommiers ☎ 476975519
Gently sloping terraced area divided into pitches.
➲ *S of village, 300m off D525.*
May-10 Oct 3.5HEC ⬛ 🔌 ⛺ ☉ 🚿 🅿 ⛏ 🏪 🍴 ⁌ P ⊞ lau
♦ 🛒 🍴 ✕
Prices: pitch 71-94.95

▶ **ANNECY** HAUTE-SAVOIE

Belvédère 8 rte du Semnoz ☎ 450454830
➲ *On S outskirts, on the Semnoz road.*
Closed 16 Oct-19 Dec 2.7HEC ⬛ 🔌 ⛺ 🛒 ✕ ☉ 🚿 ⌀ ⊞
lau ♦ 🍴 ✕ ⁌LP

▶ **ANTHY-SUR-LÉMAN** HAUTE-SAVOIE

Pays Léman r des Pêcheurs ☎ 450760195
In a quiet situation 200m from the beach on Lake Geneva.
Apr-20 Oct 1.5HEC ⬛ ♠ ⛺ 🛒 ☉ 🚿 🅿 🏪 🍴 ⊞ lau ♦ 🍴
✕ ⛏ ⁌LP

▶ **ARBOIS** JURA

CM Vignes av Gl-Leclerc ☎ 384661412
Terraced site. Shop open Jul-Aug only.
➲ *E on D107 Mesnay road at stadium.*
Apr-Sep 5HEC ⬛ ♠ ⛺ 🛒 🍴 ☉ 🚿 ⌀ ⌀ ⊞ ⊞ lau ♦ ✕ ⛏ ⁌P
Prices: pitch 60-67.50

▶ **ARGENTIÈRE** HAUTE-SAVOIE

Glacier d'Argentière 161 chemin des Chosalets ☎ 450541736
Clean site on sloping meadowland in beautiful quiet situation at the foot of the Mont Blanc Massif.
➲ *Access is 1km S of Argentière, turn off N506 towards Cableway Lognan et de Grandes Montets, then a further 200m to site.*
15 May-Sep 1.5HEC ⬛ 🔌 ⛺ ☉ 🚿 ⌀ ⌀ ⊞ ⊞ lau ♦ 🛒 🍴 ✕ ⛏
Prices: ♠24 ♠8 ♠18 ♠12

▶ **ARS-SUR-FORMANS** AIN

Bois de la Dame Chemin du Bois de la Dame ☎ 474007723
Compulsory separate car park for arrivals after 22.00hrs.
➲ *From A6, exit Villefranche and continue towards Jassans-Riottier.*
May-Sep 1.5HEC ⬛ ♠ ☉ 🚿 🅿 ⊞ ⊞ lau ♦ 🛒 🍴 ✕ ⛏
Prices: pitch 42 (incl 2 persons)

▶ **AUTRANS** ISÈRE

Caravaneige du Vercors Les Gaillards ☎ 476953188
Ideal for summer or winter holidays, situated in the heart of the Vercors with easy access to ski lifts and skiing tracks.
➲ *0.6km S via D106 towards Méaudre.*
Closed last 2 wks May & last 2 wks Sep 1HEC ⬛ ⛷ ⛺ ☉
🅿 ⌀ ⁌ P ⊞ ⊞ lau ♦ 🛒 🍴 ✕ ⛏
Prices: pitch 63 (incl 2 persons)

Joyeux Réveil ☎ 476953344
In a beautiful location surrounded by woodland, with fine mountain views.
➲ *NE of town via rte de Montaud.*
All year 1.5HEC ⬛ ⛷ ⛺ ☉ 🚿 ⛏ 🏪 🍴 ⁌ P ⊞ ⊞ lau ♦ 🛒
🍴 ✕ ⌀

▶ **BARATIER** HAUTES-ALPES

Verger ☎ 492431587
Terraced site in plantation of fruit trees with fine views of Alps. Divided into pitches. Rest room.
➲ *From N94 drive 2.5km S of Embrun, 1.5km E on D40.*
All year 2.5HEC ⬛ 🔌 ⛺ ☉ 🚿 ⌀ ⛏ 🏪 🍴 ⁌ P ⊞ ⊞ lau ♦ 🍴
✕ ⁌LR

▶ **BELLEGARDE-SUR-VALSERINE** AIN

Crêt d'Eau 2 av de Lattre-de-Tassigny ☎ 450566081
In a pleasant mountain setting with good facilities.
➲ *3km N of town, 200m from N84.*
15 May-15 Sep 5HEC ⬛ ♠ ⛺ 🍴 ✕ ☉ 🚿 ⌀ ⌀ 🍴 ⁌ PR ⊞ ⊞
lau ♦ 🛒
Prices: ♠21 pitch 17-28

▶ **BOURG-D'OISANS, LE** ISÈRE

Caravaneige le Vernis ☎ 476800268
Well-kept site with modern sanitary facilities. At foot of mountain in summer ski-ing area.
➲ *2.5km of N91, rte de Briançon.*
Closed 15 Sep-1 Dec 1.2HEC ⬛ ♠ ⛺ ☉ 🚿 🍴 ⁌ P ⊞ ⊞ ⌀ lau
♦ 🛒 🍴 ✕ ⌀ ⛏
Prices: pitch 85 (incl 2 persons)

Cascade rte de l'Alpe-d'Huez ☎ 476800242
Completely divided into pitches at the foot of a mountain with a waterfall and modern, very well-kept sanitary

arrangements. Television lounge with library, open fireplace. Booking essential.
➲ *From Grenoble follow signs 'Stations de l'Oisans' then from Bourg-d'Oisans continue towards Alpe-d'Huez.*
Feb-Sep 2.5HEC ⨆⨆⨆ ♣ ⋔ ⍶ ⊙ ⋦ ⌀ ⌂ ⋆ PR 🖾 lau ➨ ⤶ ✕⊞
Prices: pitch 125 (incl 2 persons) pp30

Rencontre du Soleil rte de l'Alpe-d'Huez ☎ 476800033
Charming site in a lovely setting in the Dauphiny Alps at the foot of a mountain. Fine rustic common room with open fireplace. TV, playroom for children.
➲ *At the foot of the hairpin road to L'Alp-d'Huez, leave N91 (Grenoble-Briançon road) in Le Bourg d'Osians.*
25 May-14 Sep 1.6HEC ⨆⨆⨆ ⍶ ⋔ ⍶ ✕ ⊙ ⋦ ⋆ P 🖾 lau ➨ ⤶ ✕ ⌀ ⍰ ⋆R
Prices: pitch 90-130 (incl 2 persons)

At VENOSC(10km SE on N91 and D530)

Champ de Moulin ☎ 476800738
In a picturesque location with fine views of the surrounding mountains and a direct cablecar connection to local ski slopes. Separate car park for late arrivals.
All year 1HEC ⨆⨆⨆ ⍶ ⍶ ⋔ ⊙ ⋦ ⌀ ⌂ ⋆ R 🖾 ⊞ lau ➨ ⍰ ⋆P
Prices: pitch 102 (incl 2 persons)

BOURG-EN-BRESSE AIN

CM de Challes 5 allée du Centre Nautique ☎ 474453721
In football ground near swimming pool.
➲ *Well signposted from outskirts of town.*
Apr-15 Oct 23HEC ⨆⨆⨆ ⠿⠿ ⍶ ⋔ ⤶ ✕ ⊙ ⋦ ⋆ P 🖾 🖾 ⊞ lau ➨ ⌀ ⍰
Prices: ♠17 ⊞37 ▲31

BOURGET-DU-LAC, LE SAVOIE

CM Ile aux Cygnes ☎ 479250176
A family site on the shore of the Lac Bourdeau with plenty of recreational facilities.
➲ *Access via N514.*
May-24 Sep 4.3HEC ⨆⨆⨆ ♣ ⋔ ⊙ ⋦ ⌀ ⋆ LR 🖾 ⊞ lau ➨ ⍶ ✕ ⍰
Prices: ♠15.50-23 pitch 27-32

BOURG-ST-MAURICE SAVOIE

Versoyen rte des Arcs ☎ 479070345
Two communal sanitary blocks - one heated. Ski-ing facilities. Many secluded pitches in a wood.
➲ *On S outskirts of town. Access via N90.*
Closed 3 Nov-15 Dec & 3-5 May 4HEC ⨆⨆⨆ ⍶ ⋔ ⊙ ⋦ ⌀ ⍰
⌂ ⋦ 🖾 ⊞ lau ➨ ⤶ ⍶ ✕ ⌀ ⍰ ⋆PR
Prices: ♠22-25 pitch 23.50

BOUT-DU-LAC HAUTE-SAVOIE

International du Lac Bleu rte d'Albertville ☎ 450443018
Modern, well-kept site. Overflow area with own sanitary blocks.
➲ *On the southern shores of Lake Annecy via the N508, opposite ANTAR Garage.*
Apr-10 Oct 3.3HEC ⨆⨆⨆ ♣ ⋔ ⍶ ✕ ⊙ ⋦ ⌂ ⋆ L 🖾 ⊞ lau ➨ ⤶ ⌀ ⍰

Nublière ☎ 450443344
Extensive site divided into pitches in attractive surroundings.
➲ *150m off N508 at S end of Lac d'Annecy.*
Jun-Sep 9HEC ⨆⨆⨆ ♣ ⋔ ⊙ ⋦ ⌀ ⌂ ▲ ⍰ ⊞ lau ➨ ⍶ ✕ ⍰ ⋆LR

CHAMONIX-MONT-BLANC HAUTE-SAVOIE

Mer de Glace 200 Chemin de la Bagna ☎ 450530863
In a forested setting with pitches divided by hedges and fine mountain views.
➲ *2km NE to Les Praz. On approach to village (from Chamonix) turn right under railway bridge.*
25 Apr-Sep 2.2HEC ⨆⨆⨆ ⠿⠿ ⍶ ⋔ ⍶ ⍶ ✕ ⊙ ⋦ 🖾 ⊞ lau ➨ ⤶ ✕ ⌀ ⍰ ⋆P
Prices: ♠28-33 pitch 27-38

Rosières 121 Clos des Rosières ☎ 450531042
Picturesque site at the foot of the Mont Blanc range.
➲ *1.2km NE via N506.*
15 Oct-16 Dec 1.6HEC ⨆⨆⨆ ♣ ⋔ ⍶ ⋔ ✕ ⊙ ⋦ ⌀ ⌂ 🖾 lau ➨ ⤶ ⋆P
Prices: ♠26-30 pitch 24-31

At BOSSONS, LES(3km W)

Cimes 28 rte des Tissieres ☎ 450535893
In a wooded meadow at the foot of Mont Blanc Massif. Ideal for hiking and mountain tours.
Jun-Sep 1HEC ⨆⨆⨆ ⍶ ⋔ ⊙ ⋦ ⌀ ⋔ ⋆ R 🖾 lau ➨ ⤶ ⍶ ✕ ⍰ ⋆LP ⊞

Deux Glaciers 80 rte des Tissières ☎ 450531584
A glacial stream runs through the site. Pitches shaded by trees, very modern, well-kept sanitary installations. Rustic common room with open fires.
➲ *Leave N506 towards road underpass. 250m to site.*
All year 16HEC ⨆⨆⨆ ⍶ ⋔ ⍶ ✕ ⊙ ⋦ ⌀ ⍰ 🖾 ⊞ lau ➨ ⤶ ⍶

CHAMPAGNOLE JURA

CM Boyse r G-Vallery ☎ 384520032
Clean and tidy site with asphalt drives and completely divided into pitches. In grounds of municipal swimming pool.
➲ *Turn onto D5 just before town and continue 1.3km to site.*
15 Jun-15 Sep 7HEC ⨆⨆⨆ ♣ ⋔ ⍶ ✕ ⊙ ⋦ ⌀ ⋆ PR 🖾 ⊞ lau

CHÂTEAUROUX-LES-ALPES HAUTES-ALPES

Cariamas Font-Molines ☎ 492432263
On a meadow in an attractive mountain setting beside the River Durance.
➲ *1.5km SE.*
Jul-Aug 10HEC ⨆⨆⨆ ♣ ⋔ ⤶ ⊙ ⋦ ⌂ ⋔ ⋆ P 🖾 lau ➨ ⍶ ✕ ⌀ ⋆R
Prices: ♠24 pitch 32

CHOISY HAUTE-SAVOIE

Chez Langin ☎ 450774165
In pleasant wooded surroundings.
➲ *1.3km NE via D3.*
15 Apr-15 Oct 3HEC ⨆⨆⨆ ⍶ ⋔ ⤶ ⍶ ✕ ⊙ ⋦ ⌀ ⍰ ⌂ ⋆ P 🖾 lau
Prices: pitch 80 (incl 2 persons)

CLAIRVAUX-LES-LACS JURA

Fayolan ☎ 384252619
In a wooded location beside the lake.
➲ *1.2km SE via D118.*
May-19 Sep 17HEC ⨆⨆⨆ ⍶ ⋔ ⤶ ⍶ ✕ ⊙ ⋦ ⌀ ⌂ ▲ ⋆ LP 🖾 lau ➨ ⍰ ⋆R ⊞
Prices: pitch 65-135 (incl 2 persons)

Grisière et Europe Vacances ☎ 384258048
Fenced in meadowland with some trees, sloping down to the Grand Lac. The site is guarded during July and August.
➲ *From village centre turn off N78, follow D118 towards*

Contd.

Châtel-de-Joux for 800m to the site.
May-Sep 11HEC ⟋⟍ ⌂ ♠ ⚭ ♨ ♀ ✕ ⊙ ⊟ ⌀ ♥ ⚡ L ☎ ⊞ lau
Prices: ♦16.50 pitch 29

CLUSAZ, LA HAUTE-SAVOIE

Plan du Fernuy route des Confins ☎ 450024475
Airing rooms. 30 ski-lifts nearby. Several cable cars. Well-situated for skiing or walking.
➦ *At the road fork E of La Clusaz leave N50 the Col des Aravis road, and drive towards Les Confins from road fork 2km to site.*
Jun-15 Sep 1.3HEC ⟋⟍ ⚴ ⌂ ♠ ⚭ ♨ ♀ ✕ ⊙ ⊟ ⊞ ♥ ⚡ P ☎ lau
♦ ✕ ⌀ ⊞
Prices: pitch 74-99 (incl 2 persons)

DIVONNE-LES-BAINS AIN

Fleutron Quartier Villard ☎ 450200195
In wooded surroundings with large individual pitches.
➦ *3 km N.*
3 Apr-1 Nov 8HEC ⟋⟍ ⌂ ♠ ⚭ ♨ ♀ ✕ ⊙ ⊟ ⊞ ♀ ⚡ Å ⚡ P ☎ lau
♦ ⌀ ⚭
Prices: ♦23-29 pitch 25-39

DOLE JURA

Pasquier 18 Chemin Theremot ☎ 384720261
Clean meadow site near River Doubs.
➦ *900m SE of town centre.*
15 Mar-15 Oct 1.8HEC ⟋⟍ ⚴ ♠ ⚭ ♨ ♀ ✕ ⊙ ⊟ ⌀ ⊟ ☎ ⊞
lau ♦ ✕ ⚭ ⚡R
Prices: pitch 63-68 (incl 2 persons)

DOUCIER JURA

Domaine de Chalain ☎ 384242900
A large site beside Lake Chalain with a wide variety of recreational facilities.
➦ *3km NE.*
May-22 Sep 20HEC ⟋⟍ ⌂ ♠ ⚭ ♨ ♀ ✕ ⊙ ⊟ ⚭ ⊟ ⚡ L ☎ ⊞ lau
Prices: pitch 70-135 (incl 3 persons)

DOUSSARD HAUTE-SAVOIE

Serraz r de la Poste ☎ 450443068
Modern site divided into pitches. Cosy bar in rustic style.
➦ *At E end of village 500m from N508 on D181.*
15 May-30 Sep 4HEC ⟋⟍ ⌂ ♠ ⚭ ✕ ⊙ ⊟ ⌀ ⊟ ⚡ P ☎ ⊞ lau
♦ ⚭ ⚭ ⚡L
Prices: pitch 89-112 (incl 2 persons)

EGATS, LES ISÈRE

Belvédère de l'Obiou ☎ 476304080
Situated in beautiful scenery; modern sanitary installations and good recreational facilities.
➦ *Access via N85 S of Grenoble.*
May-Sep 1HEC ⟋⟍ ⌂ ♠ ⚭ ♀ ✕ ⊙ ⊟ ⌀ ⚭ ⊟ ⚡ P ☎ ⊞ lau
♦ ⚭

EMBRUN HAUTES-ALPES

CM Clapière av du Lac ☎ 492430183
Well-managed site with shaded pitches on stony ground, on N shore of lake. Site shop open during summer only.
➦ *2.5km SW on N94.*
10 Apr-Sep 6HEC ⟋⟍ ⌂ ♠ ⊙ ⊟ ⊟ ☎ ⊞ lau ♦ ⚭ ♀ ✕ ⌀ ⚭
⚡LP

ENTRE-DEUX-GUIERS ISÈRE

Arc en Ciel Le Bourg ☎ 476660697
In a wooded location on the river bank with well shaded pitches.
➦ *On D520 300m from N6.*

Mar-Oct 1.2HEC ⟋⟍ ♠ ⚭ ⊙ ⊟ ⌀ ⚭ ⊟ ⚭ ⚡ R ☎ ⊞ lau ♦
⚭ ♀ ✕ ⚡P
Prices: ♦16 pitch 13.50

ÉVIAN-LES-BAINS HAUTE-SAVOIE

At AMPHION-LES-BAINS(3.5km W on N5)

Plage Amphion les Bains ☎ 450700046
A pleasant site with direct access to the lake. There are good recreational facilities and modern, well equipped bungalows and chalets are available for hire.
➦ *NW of town on N5, 150m from lake.*
Apr-Nov 1.5HEC ⟍⟍ ⌂ ♠ ⚭ ♀ ✕ ⊙ ⊟ ⊟ ⚡ LP ☎ ⊞ lau ♦ ⚭
✕ ⌀ ⊞
Prices: pitch 80-110 (incl 2 persons)

At MAXILLY(2.5km E on N5)

Clos Savoyard Maxilly sur Ciman ☎ 450752584
Very clean and tidy site with fine views of the lake and the mountains.
➦ *Turn onto D21 in town 1200m after Hôtel le Maximillien and continue uphill.*
Apr-Sep 2HEC ⟋⟍ ⌂ ♠ ⚭ ⊙ ⊟ ⊟ ⚭ ⊞ lau ♦ ♀ ✕ ⌀ ⚡L
Prices: ♦20 pitch 55

GRESSE-EN-VERCORS ISÈRE

4 Saisons ☎ 476343027
In a picturesque mountain setting with good facilities.
➦ *1.3km SW*
21 May-5 Sep 2.2HEC ⟋⟍ ⚴ ⚒ ♠ ⊙ ⊟ ⌀ ⚭ ⚡ PR ☎ lau
♦ ⚭ ♀ ✕ ⊞
Prices: pitch 71 (incl 2 persons)

GUILLESTRE HAUTES-ALPES

Villard Le Villard ☎ 492450654
In a magnificent location between the Ecrins national park and Queyras regional park. Good facilities, but bar and café operate July-Aug only.
➦ *2km W via D902A and N4, rte de Gap.*
All year 3HEC ⟋⟍ ⌂ ♠ ⚭ ♀ ✕ ⊙ ⊟ ⌀ ⚭ ⚭ ⚡ PR ☎ lau ♦
⌀ ⊞
Prices: pitch 60-105 (incl 2 persons)

HUANNE-MONTMARTIN DOUBS

Étangs du Bois de Reveuge ☎ 381843860
A terraced site in a 20 hectare park surrounded by the Vosges and Jura mountains with good recreational facilities.
➦ *Access via A36 exit 'Baumes-les-Dames'.*
May-Sep 20HEC ⟋⟍ ⟍⟍ ⚴ ⌂ ♠ ⚭ ♀ ✕ ⊙ ⊟ ⌀ ⚭ ⚭ ⚡ LP
☎ ⊞ lau

ISLE-SUR-LE-DOUBS, L' DOUBS

CM Lumes 10 r des Lumes ☎ 381927305
The site lies close to the town. Common room with TV.
➦ *Off N83. Entrance near bridge over the Doubs.*
15 May-15 Sep 1.5HEC ⟋⟍ ⌂ ♠ ⊙ ⊟ ⚭ ⚡ R ☎ lau ♦ ⚭ ♀
✕ ⌀ ⚭
Prices: ♦17 ♦10 pitch 24

LANDRY SAVOIE

Eden ☎ 479076181
A modern site with excellent sports and sanitary facilities, situated in the heart of the Savoie Olympic area.
18 Dec-26 Apr & 21 May-15 Sep 2.7HEC ⟋⟍ ⌂ ♠ ⚭ ♀ ✕ ⊙
⊟ ⚭ ⚡ PR ☎ ⊞ lau ♦ ✕ ⌀ ⚭
Prices: ♦28 ♦10 ♦30 Å30

LONS-LE-SAUNIER JURA

Majorie 640 bd de l'Europe ☎ 384242694
Clean, tidy site with tent and caravan sections separated by a
stream. Caravan pitches (80 sq m) are gravelled and
surrounded by hedges. Heated common room with TV,
reading area, kitchen. Swimming pool free to campers.
➲ *Near swimming stadium on outskirts of town.*
Apr-15 Oct 7.5HEC ⬛⬛⬛⬛ ♦ ⚬ ⋔ ⅏ ⚑ ❢ ✕ ⊙ ⬛ ⌀ ⬛ ⬛ ⊞ lau ➡
⅏ ❢ ✕ ⌀ 👖 ⅃P
Prices: pitch 69-84 (incl 2 persons)

LUGRIN HAUTE-SAVOIE

Myosotis 28 chemin du Grand Tronc ☎ 450760759
A terraced site with fine views over the lake and of the
surrounding mountains.
➲ *W of town. Signposted. 1km from Lac Leman*
20 Apr-Sep 8.8HEC ⬛⬛⬛⬛ ⚬ ⋔ ⊙ ⬛ ⌀ ⬛ ⊞ lau ➡ ⅏ ❢ ✕ 👖
⅃L
Prices: ⭓14-17 pitch 21-23

Rys Route le Rys ☎ 450760575
Calm shady site with panoramic views of the lake and
mountains. 10min walk from the beach
➲ *W of town. Signposted.*
Apr-Oct 1.5HEC ⬛⬛⬛⬛ ♦ ⋔ ⊙ ⬛ ⌀ ⬛ ⊞ lau ➡ ⅏ ❢ ✕ 👖
⅃L

Vieille Église ☎ 450760195
On rising meadow between lake and mountains with good
views. Close to lake Léman and its beaches.
➲ *D24 to Neuvecelle, then take D21, 1km after Maxilly on
right.*
01/04-15/10 1.6HEC ⬛⬛⬛⬛ ♦ ⋔ ⚬ ⊙ ⬛ ⌀ ⬛ ⬛ ⅃ LP ⬛ ⊞ lau
➡ ⅏ ❢ ✕ 👖 ⅃L
Prices: ⭓23 ⛟10 ⛺22 ⛁22

MALBUISSON DOUBS

Fuvettes ☎ 381693150
Mainly level site with some terraces, gently sloping towards
lake. At an altitude of 900mtrs in the Jura mountains.
➲ *500m S on D437.*
Apr-Oct 6HEC ⬛⬛⬛⬛ ⚬ ⋔ ⅏ ❢ ✕ ⊙ ⬛ ⌀ 👖 ⬛ ⅃ L ⬛ ⬛ ⊞ lau
➡ ⅃PR
Prices: pitch 60-82 (incl 2 persons)

MARIGNY JURA

Pergola ☎ 384257003
A well equipped, terraced site with direct access to the lake.
➲ *S of Marigny off D27.*
May-Sep 12HEC ⬛⬛⬛⬛ ⠴⠴⠴ ⚬ ⋔ ⅏ ❢ ✕ ⊙ ⬛ ⌀ ⬛ ⛁ ⅃ LP ⬛
⊞ lau
Prices: pitch 90-228.50 (incl 2 persons)

MÉAUDRE ISÈRE

Buissonnets ☎ 476952104
A quiet, friendly site in the heart of the Vercors Regional Parc
with modern sanitary blocks and a wide range of summer
and winter recreational facilities.
➲ *200m from village centre.*
All year 2HEC ⬛⬛⬛⬛ ⚬ ⋔ ⅏ ⚑ ⊙ ⬛ ⌀ 👖 ⬛ ⅃ P ⬛ ⬛ lau ➡ ❢ ✕
⅃R
Prices: pitch 59 (incl 2 persons)

MEGÈVE HAUTE-SAVOIE

Ripaille 395 rte de Vauray ☎ 450214724
Facing Mont-Blanc.
➲ *On N212, 800m from Pont d'Arbon.*
All year 0.9HEC ⬛⬛⬛⬛ ⚬ ⋔ ⅏ ✕ ⊙ ⬛ ⌀ 👖 ⬛ ⬛ ⅃ P ⬛ ⊞ lau

MESSERY HAUTE-SAVOIE

Relais du Léman ☎ 450947111
Well equipped site in a wooded location on the shore of Lac
Léman.
➲ *1.5km SW via D25.*
May-Aug 3.5HEC ⬛⬛⬛⬛ ♦ ⋔ ❢ ✕ ⊙ ⬛ ⌀ ⬛ ⬛ ⅃ P ⬛ lau ➡
⅏ ⅃L ⊞
Prices: ⭓30 ⛺35 ▲35

MEYRIEU-LES-ÉTANGS ISÈRE

Moulin ☎ 474593034
In a quiet, rural setting with good recreational facilities.
➲ *On D552 between Vienne and Bourgoin-Jallieu.*
Apr-Oct 1.5HEC ⬛⬛⬛⬛ ⚬ ⋔ ⅏ ❢ ✕ ⊙ ⬛ ⬛ ⅃ L ⬛ ⊞ lau
Prices: ⭓19-22 pitch 28-32

MIRIBEL-LES-ÉCHELLES ISÈRE

Bourdons ☎ 476552853
A peaceful site in the heart of the Parc Régional de Chartreuse, with fine views of the surrounding mountains.
➲ *400m from village centre.*
Feb-Oct 2HEC ⚏ ♠ ↿ ⅃ ⅄ × ⊙ ⬤ ⦿ ⚄ ⬛ ⬤ ⇃ P ☎ ⊞
lau

MONTMAUR HAUTES-ALPES

Mon Repos ☎ 592580314
Generally well-kept site on wooded terrain with shaded pitches.
➲ *1km E on D937 and D994.*
May-Oct 7HEC ⚏ ♠ ↿ ⊙ ⬤ ⦿ ⬛ ⬤ ⇃ L ☎ ⊞ lau
Prices: pitch 62 (incl 2 persons)

MONTMÉLIAN SAVOIE

Manoir av du Prés E-Herriot ☎ 0479652238
Situated close to the historical area of the town with 90 pitches divided by hedges.
Closed 25 Oct-Nov 2.8HEC ⚏ ♠ ↿ ⊙ ⬤ ☎ ⊞ ⇃ ↿ ⅄ × ⦿ ⚏

MONTREVEL-EN-BRESSE AIN

Plaine Tonique Base de Plein Air ☎ 474308052
A well equipped site divided into a series of self contained sections beside the lake. Entrance closed between 22.00 & 07.00 hrs. Booking advisable in July and August.
➲ *0.5km E on D28.*
10 May- 25 Sep 17HEC ⚏ ♠ ↿ ⅃ ⅄ × ⊙ ⬤ ⦿ ⚄ ⬛ ⇃ LPR
☎ ⊞ lau
Prices: ↿18-22 pitch 40-55

MOUCHARD JURA

Halte Jurassienne Bel Air ☎ 384378392
Camping Card Compulsory.
➲ *NE, near the service station.*
15 Apr-15 Oct 0.5HEC ⚏ ↿ ↿ ⊙ ⬤ ⦿ ⬛ ☎ ⊞ lau ⇃ ↿ ⅄ ×

NEYDENS HAUTE-SAVOIE

Colombière ☎ 450351314
A pleasant, friendly site with good recreational facilities.
➲ *Access via A40.*
Apr-1 Nov 2.2HEC ⚏ ↿ ♠ ↿ ↿ ⅄ × ⊙ ⬤ ⦿ ⬛ ⬤ ⇃ P
☎ ⊞ lau
Prices: pitch 81-90 (incl 2 persons)

NOVALAISE SAVOIE

Charmilles Lac d'Aiguebelette ☎ 479360467
A terraced site in a beautiful mountain setting, 150m from the lake.
➲ *On W shore of the lake on D941 towards St-Alban-de-Montbel.*
Jul-Aug 2.3HEC ⚏ ⸪ ↿ ↿ ↿ ⊙ ⬤ ⦿ ☎ ⊞ lau ⇃ ↿ × ⇃L
Prices: pitch 60-74 (incl 2 persons)

ORNANS DOUBS

Chanet rte de Chassagne ☎ 381622344
Comfortable site with good facilities in the peaceful Loue Valley.
➲ *1.5km SW on D241. Follow green signs.*
Mar-15 Nov 1.5HEC ⚏ ♠ ↿ ⊙ ⬤ ⦿ ⬛ ☎ ⊞ lau ⇃ ⅄ ×
⚏ ⇃PR
Prices: ↿20 pitch 21

ORPIERRE HAUTES-ALPES

Princes d'Orange ☎ 492662253
The site lies on a meadow with terraces.

➲ *Exit N75 at Eyguians and take D30.*
Apr-Oct 2.5HEC ⚏ ◊ ↿ ↿ ⅄ ⊙ ⬤ ⦿ ⚏ ⬤ ⬛ Å ⇃ PR ☎ ⊞
lau ⇃ ↿

OUNANS JURA

Plage Blanche 3 r de la Plage ☎ 384376963
In a pleasant location beside the River Loue with good recreational facilities.
➲ *1.5km S via D71 (rte de Montbarcy).*
15 Mar-Oct 5HEC ⚏ ↿ ↿ ⅄ × ⊙ ⬤ ⬤ ⦿ ⇃ R ☎ lau ⇃ ↿
⇃P ⊞
Prices: ↿25 pitch 31

PARCEY JURA

Bords de Loue Chemin du Val d'Amour ☎ 384710382
A quiet site on the River Loue.
➲ *1.5km from the centre of the village via N5. Signposted.*
15 Apr-15 Sep 18HEC ⚏ ↿ ↿ ↿ ⅄ × ⊙ ⬤ ⦿ ⬤ ⦿ Å ⇃ PR
☎ ⊞ lau ⇃ ↿ Å ⇃
Prices: ↿22 pitch 26

PATORNAY JURA

Moulin ☎ 384483121
A modern site on a level meadow in a peaceful, wooded location on the banks of the River Ain.
➲ *Access is NE via N78, rte de Clairvaux-les-Lacs.*
May-15 Sep 5HEC ⚏ ♠ ↿ ↿ ⅄ × ⊙ ⬤ ⦿ ⇃ PR ☎ ⊞ lau ⇃
⇃L

PLAGNE-MONTCHAVIN SAVOIE

Montchavin les Coches ☎ 479078323
A summer and winter site overlooking the Tarentaise Valley with good, modern facilities.
Nov-Sep 1.3HEC ⚏ ♠ ↿ ⊙ ⬤ ☎ ⊞ lau ⇃ ↿ ⅄ × ⦿ ⚏ ⇃P
Prices: ↿20 pitch 17

PONTARLIER DOUBS

Larmont r du Toulombief ☎ 381462333
A mountain site with good facilities in an area associated with winter sports.
All year ⚏ ◊ ⅄ ↿ ↿ ⅄ × ⊙ ⬤ ⦿ ⚏ ⬤ ☎ ⊞ lau ⇃ × ⇃R

PORT-SUR-SAÔNE HAUTE-SAÔNE

CM Maladière ☎ 384915132
A quiet, comfortable site with modern facilities, close to the River Saône.
➲ *S on the D6, between the River Saône and the Canal*
15 May-15 Sep 2HEC ⚏ ↿ ↿ ⊙ ⬤ ☎ ⊞ lau ⇃ ↿ × ⦿ ⚏
⇃PR
Prices: ↿10 ⬤6 ⬤10 Å10

PRESLE SAVOIE

Combe Léat ☎ 479255402
A quiet mountain site.
➲ *Access via A43 and D207.*
15 Jun-Aug 3.5HEC ⚏ ♠ ↿ ⅄ × ⊙ ⬤ ⬤ ⬤ ☎ ⊞ lau
Prices: ↿15 pitch 15

RENAGE ISÈRE

Verdon 185 av de la Piscine ☎ 476914802
➲ *5km N of Tullins on D45.*
1 Apr-15 Oct 1.5HEC ⚏ ♠ ↿ ⊙ ⬤ ⦿ ☎ ⊞ lau ⇃ ↿ ⅄ × ⚏
⇃P
Prices: ↿17 pitch 16

ROCHETTE, LA SAVOIE

Lac St-Clair ☎ 479257355
At the foot of the Belledonne mountains, 1km from a lake with good fishing.

⮑ *Access via D925B Grenoble-Albertville.*
Jun-15 Sep 2.2HEC ᴟ ⚙ ⋔ ⊙ ⬛ ⊞ lau ➜ ⤋ ⤋ ✗ ⊘ ⛺
↝P

▶ **ROSIÈRE-DE-MONTVALEZAN, LA** SAVOIE

Forêt ☎ 479068621
A peaceful site in pleasant wooded surroundings, with good,
modern facilities.
⮑ *2km S via N90 towards Bourg-St-Maurice.*
15 Jun-15 Sep & 15 Dec-1 May 2.7HEC ᴟ ➜ ⋔ ✗ ⊙ ⬛
⛺ ⬛ ⊞ lau ➜ ⤋ ⊘

▶ **ROUGEMONT** DOUBS
At **BONNAL**(3.5km N on D18)
◀Val de Bonnal ☎ 381869087
Quiet woodland site beside the River Ognon. Supervised
swimming in lake with beach.
8 May-15 Sep 15HEC ᴟ ⚙ ⋔ ⤋ ✗ ⊙ ⬛ ⊘ ↝ LPR ⊞ ⊞
lau
Prices: ♠37 pitch 70

▶ **ST-AVRE** SAVOIE

Bois Joli St Martin-sur-la-Chambre ☎ 479562128
Well kept site with pitches and individual washing cabins.
⮑ *1km N of St-Avre, off N6-E70 via La Chambre.*
Apr-15 Sep 4HEC ᴟ ➜ ⋔ ⤋ ✗ ⊙ ⬛ ⛺ ⬛ ↝ P ⊞ ⊞ lau ➜
↝R
Prices: pitch 60-75 (incl 2 persons)

▶ **ST-CLAIR-DU-RHÔNE** ISÈRE

Daxia rte du Péage ☎ 474563920
A riverside site with good sanitary and recreational facilities.
⮑ *Access via N7/A7.*
Apr-Sep 7.5HEC ᴟ ⚙ ⋔ ✗ ⊙ ⬛ ⛺ ⬛ ↝ PR ⊞ lau

▶ **ST-CLAUDE** JURA

Martinet ☎ 384450040
⮑ *2km SE, beside the river*
May-Sep 3HEC ᴟ ⚙ ⋔ ⤋ ✗ ⊙ ⬛ ⊘ ↝ PR ⊞ lau

▶ **ST-DISDILLE** HAUTE-SAVOIE

St-Disdille av de St-Disdille ☎ 450711411
In a peaceful, wooded location in the heart of the Chablais
region.
⮑ *N of N5. Signposted.*
Apr-Sep 12HEC ᴟ ➜ ⋔ ⤋ ✗ ⊙ ⬛ ⊘ ⛺ ⊞ lau ➜
↝LPR
Prices: pitch 84 (incl 3 persons)

▶ **ST-GERVAIS-LES-BAINS** HAUTE-SAVOIE

Dômes de Miage 197 rte des Contamines ☎ 450934596
On a beautiful wooded plateau with fine views of the
surrounding mountains.
⮑ *2km S on D902.*
20 May-30 Sep 2.5HEC ᴟ ⚙ ⋔ ⤋ ✗ ⊙ ⬛ ⊘ ⊞ ⊞ lau
➜ ⛺ ↝P
Prices: pitch 79-84 (incl 2 persons)

▶ **ST-INNOCENT-BRISON** SAVOIE

Rolande 24 chemin des Berthets ☎ 479543685
Situated on gently sloping terrain.
⮑ *Signposted from village centre.*
May-Sep 1.5HEC ᴟ ⚙ ⋔ ⤋ ✗ ⊙ ⬛ ⊘ ⊞ ⊞ lau ➜ ↝L
Prices: pitch 48.60-63 (incl 2 persons)

▶ **ST-JEAN-DE-COUZ** SAVOIE

International la Bruyère ☎ 479657427
In wooded surroundings close to the Grande Chartreuse
range with a variety of sporting facilities.

⮑ *2km S via N6, towards Côte-Barrier*
Apr-Oct 1HEC ᴟ ⚙ ⋔ ⤋ ✗ ⊙ ⬛ ⊘ ⛺ ⬛ ⬛ ⊞ ⊞ lau ➜
⊘ ↝R
Prices: ♠16 pitch 15

▶ **ST-JEAN-ST-NICOLAS** HAUTES-ALPES

CM le Châtelard Pont-du-Fossé ☎ 492559431
15 Jun-15 Sep 4HEC ᴟ ➜ ⋔ ⊙ ⬛ ↝ R ⊞ ⊞ lau ➜ ⤋ ✗ ⊘
⛺

▶ **ST-JORIOZ** HAUTE-SAVOIE

Europa 1444 rte d'Albertville ☎ 450685101
Well equipped site in picturesque surroundings close to Lake
Annecy.
⮑ *1.4km SE*
15 May-15 Sep 3.5HEC ᴟ ☼ ⋔ ⤋ ⤋ ✗ ⊙ ⬛ ⛺ ⬛ ↝ P ⬛
⊞ lau ➜ ⊘ ↝L
Prices: pitch 86-108 (incl 2 persons)

International du Lac d'Annecy ☎ 450686793
⮑ *N508 towards Albertville.*
Jun-15 Sep 2.5HEC ᴟ ➜ ⋔ ⤋ ✗ ⊙ ⬛ ⊘ ⛺ ↝ LP ⊞ ⊞
lau

▶ **ST-PIERRE-DE-CHARTREUSE** ISÈRE

Martinière rte du Col de Porte ☎ 476886036
In pleasant position surrounded by the Chartreuse
mountains and close to the famous monastry.
⮑ *2km SW off D512.*
Closed 20 Sep-1 Nov & 30 Apr-16 May 2HEC ᴟ ⚙ ⋔ ⤋
✗ ⊙ ⬛ ⊘ ⛺ ⬛ ↝ P ⊞ ⊞ lau
Prices: ♠69-78 ⬤10.50-12 ⬛10.50-12 ▲10.50-12

▶ **SALLE-EN-BEAUMONT, LA** ISÈRE

Champ-Long ☎ 476304181
In a beautiful Alpine setting at the entrance to the Ecrins
Park at an altitude of 700mtrs.
⮑ *1.5km NW off N85.*
May-30 Oct 3.5HEC ᴟ ◊ ⚙ ⋔ ⤋ ✗ ⊙ ⬛ ⛺ ⬛ ↝ P ⬛
⊞ lau ➜ ↝R

▶ **SÉEZ** SAVOIE

Reclus rte de Tignes ☎ 479410105
In a pleasant wooded location within easy reach of the ski
slopes.
⮑ *NW on N90.*
¨ All year 1.8HEC ᴟ ➜ ⋔ ⊙ ⬛ ⬛ ↝ R ⊞ ⊞ lau ➜ ⤋ ✗ ⊘
⛺
Prices: ♠21-22 pitch 19-20

▶ **SERRES** HAUTES-ALPES

Barillons ☎ 492670116
Well-laid out with terraces.
⮑ *1km SE on N75.*
May-Sep 3HEC ᴟ ➜ ⋔ ⤋ ✗ ⊙ ⬛ ⊘ ⬛ ↝ L ⊞ ⊞ lau ➜ ⤋ ✗
↝R
Prices: pitch 75.50 (incl 2 persons)

Domaine des 2 Soleils ☎ 492670133
Well-kept terraced site in Buéch Valley.
⮑ *S of town off N75. Signposted.*
May-Sep 12HEC ᴟ ⚙ ⋔ ⤋ ✗ ⊙ ⬛ ⊘ ⛺ ⬛ ↝ P ⊞ ⊞ lau
➜ ↝LR
Prices: pitch 109-123 (incl 2 persons) pp22.95

▶ **SEYSSEL** AIN

International de Seyssel chemin de la Barotte ☎ 450592847
A quiet site on steep, terraced meadowland, with individual
washbasins and clean sanitary installations.
⮑ *1km SW off Culoz road.* *Contd.*

Jun-15 Sep 1.5HEC ⚏ ♦ ♠ ♥ ✕ ☉ ▣ ⊘ ♨ ♨ ♨ ⚲ P ☎ ⊞
lau ♦ ⚱ ♥ ✕ ⚲LR
Prices: pitch 62-78 (incl 2 persons)

▶ TALLOIRES HAUTE-SAVOIE

Lanfonnet Angon ☎ 450607212
A well equipped site 100mtrs from the lake.
➲ 1.5km SE.
May-25 Sep 2.4HEC ⚏ ♦ ♠ ⚱ ♥ ✕ ☉ ▣ ⊘ ♨ ⚲ L ☎ ⊞ lau
♦ ⚲L
Prices: pitch 123 (incl 2 persons)

▶ THOISSEY AIN

CM ☎ 474040425
Situated between two rivers, the Saône and the Chalaronne.
➲ 1km SW on D7.
Apr-Sep 15HEC ⚏ ⠿ ◗ ♠ ♥ ✕ ☉ ▣ ⚲ PR ☎ lau ♦ ⚱ ⊘
♨ ⊞

▶ THONON-LES-BAINS HAUTE-SAVOIE

Morcy ☎ 450704487
In a quiet location close to Lac Léman and the thermal spa.
➲ 2.5km W of town.
Etr-15 Sep 1HEC ⚏ ♦ ♠ ♥ ☉ ▣ ⊘ ♨ ⚲ L ☎ ⊞ lau ♦ ⚱ ✕
⚲L
Prices: ⚑22 pitch 22

▶ TIGNES-LES-BRÉVIÈRES SAVOIE

Escapade rte des Boisses ☎ 479064127
A well equipped site 1km from the centre of the village.
➲ Signposted from D902.
15 Jun-Sep 4.5HEC ⚏ ♨ ◗ ♠ ⚱ ♥ ✕ ☉ ▣ ⊘ ⚲ P ☎ ⊞ lau

▶ TREPT ISÈRE

3 Lac La Plaine ☎ 474929206
Situated at the gateway to the Alps, an undulating woody
area with small lakes.
➲ On D517, 2.5km W.
15 Apr-15 Sep 4HEC ⚏ ◗ ♠ ⚱ ♥ ✕ ☉ ▣ ♨ ♨ ⚲ LP ☎ ⊞
lau
Prices: ⚑30 pitch 40

▶ VERNIOZ ISÈRE

Bontemps ☎ 474578352
A pleasantly landscaped site beside the River Varèze.
➲ Access via N7 and D131.
Apr-Sep 7HEC ⚏ ♦ ♠ ⚱ ♥ ✕ ☉ ▣ ⊘ ♨ ♨ ⚲ PR ☎ ⊞ lau
Prices: ⚑25 ♠10 ♨35 ▲35

▶ VILLARS-LES-DOMBES AIN

CM Autières 164 av des Nations ☎ 474980021
Clean and tidy park-like site divided into plots and pitches.
Part reserved for overnight campers. Clean, modern sanitary
installations.
➲ SW off N83.
4 Apr-27 Sep 4.5HEC ⚏ ◗ ♠ ⚱ ♥ ✕ ☉ ▣ ♨ ⚲ PR ☎ ⊞ lau
♦ ⚱ ⊘ ♨

▶ VOIRON ISÈRE

Porte de la Chartreuse 33 av du 8 Mai 45 ☎ 476051420
On level terrain with some trees, divided into pitches. Much
traffic noise from nearby N75. Clean and modern sanitary
installations.
➲ Access is NW of town next to the ESSO garage.
All year 1.5HEC ⚏ ♨ ♦ ♠ ☉ ▣ ♨ ☎ ⊞ ♦ ⚱ ♥ ✕ ⊘ ♨ ⚲P
Prices: ⚑20 ♠12 ♨20 ▲12-16

In its natural border position next to Germany, Alsace
enjoys a special identity, neither German nor completely
French. And, with Lorraine, it shares some of the most
turbulent chapters in French history. They also share the
impressive Vosges mountains, with great wooded slopes,
gentle pastures, fertile plains, enchanting lakes and famous
thermal spas. In the summer this region is ablaze with
colour - there are brilliant displays of wild flowers in the
Vosges, and in the towns and cities, flowers cascade from
every available ledge. Gerardmer is at the heart of the
Vosges, and La Bresse is also popular with visitors.
Nancy, the capital of Lorraine, and Metz, with its lovely old
town and fine Gothic cathedral, are great centres for the
area, but Strasbourg is a delight to discover. The waterways
of the 'Petit France' district are charming, and the splendid
soaring spine of the cathedral of Notre Dame is
unforgettable.
In the countryside, vineyards surround pretty villages with
half-timbered houses and cobbled streets, and produce the
fine wines of the area, but hops are also grown in the
region, and famous beers are brewed in Strasbourg.
....

▶ ANOULD VOSGES

Acacias ☎ 329571106
In pleasant surroundings with well defined pitches in the
heart of the Hautes-Vosges region.
➲ NE of town centre towards the ski slopes.
10 Oct-1 Dec 2.5HEC ⚏ ♦ ♠ ⚱ ♥ ✕ ☉ ▣ ⊘ ♨ ♨ ♨ ⚲ P
☎ ⊞ lau ♦ ⚲R
Prices: ⚑18 pitch 20

▶ AUBURE HAUT-RHIN

CM La Ménère ☎ 389739299
A peaceful site at an altitude of 800mtrs.
➲ Access via N415 or D416, then D11.
15 May-20 Sep 1.5HEC ⚏ ⠿ ◗ ♠ ♥ ☉ ▣ ⊘ ☎ ⊞ lau ♦ ⚱ ♥
✕

▶ BAERENTHAL MOSELLE

Ramstein Plage Base De Baerenthal, Ramstein Plage
☎ 387065073
The River Zinsel runs through this rural wooded site close to
the border with Germany.
➲ W via r du Ramstein.
Apr-Sep 13HEC ⚏ ◗ ♠ ♥ ✕ ☉ ▣ ⊘ ♨ ♨ ♨ ⚲ L ☎ ⊞ lau
♦ ⚱
Prices: ⚑18 pitch 20

▶ BIESHEIM HAUT-RHIN

Ile du Rhin Zone Turistique ☎ 389725795
On the Ile du Rhin, between the Canal d'Alsace and the River
Rhine in pleasant wooded surroundings.
➲ From Colmar take N415 towards Germany as far as the
Rhine bridge.
All year 4.3HEC ⚏ ◗ ♠ ⚱ ☉ ▣ ⊘ ☎ ⊞ lau ♦ ♥ ✕ ♨ ⚲PR

▶ BRESSE, LA VOSGES

Belle Hutte Belle Hutte ☎ 329254975
Terraced site beside the River Moselotte.
➲ Access via D34 towards Col de la Schlucht.
All year 3HEC ⚏ ◗ ♠ ⚱ ☉ ▣ ⊘ ♨ ♨ ⚲ PR ☎ lau ♦ ♥ ✕
⚲L ⊞
Prices: ⚑13.50-23 ♠8-9.50 ♨9-12

▶ **BRUYÈRES** Vosges

▶ At **CHAPELLE-DEVANT-BRUYÈRES, LA**
(5km SE via N423)
Pinasses 215 rte de Bruyères ☎ 329585110
➲ *1.2km NW on D60 towards Bruyères*
Apr-10 Sep 3HEC ⛺ ♦ ♠ ☎ ♀ ✗ ☉ ♀ ⌀ ♣ ♬ ⇃ P ☎ ⊞ lau

▶ **BUSSANG** Vosges

Domaine de Champé 14 Les Champs Navés ☎ 329858645
In pleasant surroundings beside the River Moselle.
➲ *On N57.*
Apr-Oct 1.5HEC ⛺ ⚶ ♠ ☉ ♀ ☎ ⊞ lau ♦ ♠ ♀ ✗ ⌀ ♨ ⇃L

▶ **CELLES-SUR-PLAINE** Vosges

Lac Base de Loisirs, Les Lacs de Pierre-Percée ☎ 329411925
Set among wooded hills in an extensive natural leisure area around the Lakes of Pierre-Percée.
➲ *Access via D392A.*
Apr-Sep 3HEC ⛺ ⚶ ♠ ☎ ♀ ✗ ☉ ♀ ⌀ ♣ ⇃ PR ☎ ⊞ lau ♦ ✗ ♨ ⇃L

▶ **CERNAY** Haut-Rhin

CM *Acacias* 16 rue Ré-Guilbert ☎ 389755697
Clean, quiet site on right bank of the River Thur.
➲ *Off N83 between Colmar and Belfort.*
Apr-Sep 4HEC ⛺ ♀ ♠ ☎ ♀ ✗ ☉ ♀ ⌀ ♀ lau ♦ ✗ ⇃P ⊞
Prices: pitch 19-22

▶ **COLMAR** Haut-Rhin

Intercommunal de l'Ill ☎ 389411594
On a meadow beside the river with good, modern facilities.
Separate sections for campers in transit.
➲ *2km E on N415.*
Feb-Nov 2.2HEC ⛺ ♀ ♠ ☎ ♀ ✗ ☉ ♀ ⌀ ⇃ R ☎ ⊞ lau
Prices: ♠17 pitch 19

▶ **CORCIEUX** Vosges

▦ *Domaine des Bains* r J-Wiese ☎ 329516467
On meadowland divided into pitches with a variety of recreational facilities.
➲ *E of village off D8.*
May-Sep 15HEC ⛺ ⚶ ♦ ♀ ♠ ☎ ♀ ✗ ☉ ♀ ⌀ ♨ ♣ ♬ ⇃ LP ☎ ⊞ lau ♦ ✗
Prices: ♠26-32 pitch 63-78

▶ **CORNY-SUR-MOSELLE** Moselle

Paquis ☎ 387520359
➲ *0.7km via N57.*
Mar-Sep 1.2HEC ⛺ ♀ ♠ ☎ ✗ ☉ ♀ ⌀ ⇃ R ☎ ⊞ ♦ ☎ ♀ ✗ ♨

▶ **DABO** Moselle

Rocher 10 pl de l'Église ☎ 387074452
In a beautiful position close to the historic town of Dabo in the Voges mountains.
➲ *1.5km SW via D45.*
Etr-1 Nov 0.5HEC ⛺ ♀ ♠ ☉ ♀ ☎ lau ♦ ♀ ✗ ⊞
Prices: ♠11 ♠6 ♀14 ♠6

▶ **DAMBACH-LA-VILLE** Bas-Rhin

CM rte d'Ebersheim ☎ 388924860
In a wooded location close to the town centre. Advance booking recommended during July and August.
➲ *1km E via D120.*
15 May-15 Sep 1.8HEC ⛺ ♀ ♠ ☉ ♀ ☎ lau ♦ ☎ ♀ ✗ ⌀ ♨ ⊞
Prices: ♠14 ♠7 ♀12 ♠10

▶ **EGUISHEIM** Haut-Rhin

CM *Aux Trois Châteaux* 10 r du Bassin ☎ 389231939
In a peaceful location at an altitude of 210mtrs and surrounded by vineyards.
➲ *6km S of Colmar on N83.*
Etr-15 Oct 1.8HEC ⛺ ♀ ♠ ☉ ♀ ⌀ ☎ ♀ ⊞ lau ♦ ☎ ♀ ✗ ♨
Prices: ♠18 pitch 17

▶ **FERDRUPT** Vosges

Pommiers ☎ 329259835
A peaceful site at the foot of the mountains, beside the river.
May-Aug 1.2HEC ⛺ ♀ ♠ ☉ ♀ ♣ ☎ lau ♦ ☎ ♀ ✗ ♨ ⇃R ⊞

▶ **FONTENOY-LE-CHÂTEAU** Vosges

Fontenoy rte de la Vierge ☎ 329363474
Set on a hill in peaceful, wooded surroundings.
➲ *2.2km via D40.*
15 Apr-15 Sep 1.2HEC ⛺ ♦ ♠ ☎ ♀ ✗ ☉ ♀ ⌀ ♀ ⇃ P ☎ ⊞ lau ♦ ♨ ⇃R
Prices: ♠14 ♠11 ♀13 ♠12 pitch 13

▶ **GEMAINGOUTTE** Vosges

CM *'Le Violu'* ☎ 329577202
➲ *W, beside the river, via N59.*
May-Oct 0.9HEC ⛺ ♀ ♠ ☉ ♀ ♣ ⇃ R ☎ ⊞ lau ♦ ☎ ♀ ✗
Prices: ♠12 ♠10 ♀10 ♠10

▶ **GÉRARDMER** Vosges

Ramberchamp 21 chemin du Tour du Lac ☎ 329630382
On a level meadow on S side of Lac de Gérardmer.
➲ *2km from the village centre via N417 or 486.*
Etr-15 Sept 3.5HEC ⛺ ♦ ♠ ☎ ♀ ✗ ☉ ♀ ⌀ ♣ ⇃ L ☎ lau

▶ **GERSTHEIM** Bas-Rhin

Clair Ruisseau r du Ried ☎ 388983004
➲ *NE on the shore of a lake, near the river.*
Apr-Sep 3HEC ⛺ ♀ ♠ ☉ ♀ ♣ ⇃ L ☎ ⊞ lau ♦ ♨

▶ **GRANGES-SUR-VOLOGNE** Vosges

Château 2 Les Chappes ☎ 329575083
A terraced site with good sports facilities 1km from the village,
16 Jun-14 Sep 2HEC ⛺ ♀ ♠ ☎ ♀ ♣ ♬ ⇃ P ☎ lau ♦ ♀ ✗ ⌀ ♨ ⇃R ⊞
Prices: ♠17.50 pitch 20

Gina-Park ☎ 329514195
In a pleasant park at the foot of a wooded mountain. Streams cross the site and there is a lake and facilities for a variety of sports.
➲ *1km SE of town centre.*
All year 4.5HEC ⛺ ♦ ♠ ☎ ♀ ✗ ☉ ♀ ⌀ ♨ ♣ ♬ ⇃ LP ☎ lau ♦ ⇃R

▶ **GUEWENHEIM** Haut-Rhin

Doller ☎ 389825690
Camping Card Compulsory
➲ *1km N via D34.*
Apr-Oct 0.8HEC ⛺ ♦ ♠ ♀ ✗ ☉ ♀ ⇃ PR ☎ ⊞ lau ♦ ☎

▶ **HARSKIRCHEN** Bas-Rhin

Étang Zone de Loisirs, r du Canal ☎ 388009365
➲ *0.8km NW via D23 beside the lake.*
All year 12HEC ⛺ ⚶ ♠ ♀ ✗ ☉ ♀ ☎ ⊞ lau ♦ ☎ ✗ ⌀ ♨

▶ **HEIMSBRUNN** Haut-Rhin

Chaumière 62 r de la Galfingue ☎ 389819343
In a pleasant wooded location with good, modern facilities.
➲ *Signposted from village centre.*
All year 1.1HEC ⛺ ⚶ ♦ ♠ ☉ ♀ ⌀ ♀ ☎ ⊞ ♦ ✗ ⇃L

Contd.

HOHWALD, LE BAS-RHIN

CM ☎ 388083090
A well equipped terraced site in beautiful wooded surroundings.
➲ *W via D425*
All year 3HEC ⸺ ♀ ♠ ⊙ ♥ 🏠 lau ➧ ☒ ♘ ✗ ∅ 🏔 ⊞

KAYSERSBERG HAUT-RHIN

CM r des Acacias ☎ 389471447
Between a sports ground and the River Weiss. Subdivided by low hedges.
Camping Card Recommended.
➲ *200m from N415. Signposted.*
Apr-Sep 1.5HEC ⸺ ➧ ♠ ⊙ ♥ ⱳ R ⓐ ⊞ lau ➧ ☒ ♘ ✗ ∅ 🏔 ⱳP
Prices: ♦22 pitch 14

KRUTH HAUT-RHIN

Schlossberg r du Bourbach ☎ 389822676
In a quiet location in the heart of the Parc des Ballons with good, modern facilities.
➲ *2.3km NW via D13b.*
Etr-Sep 5.2HEC ⸺ ➧ ♠ ♘ ♘ ✗ ⊙ ∅ ♥ ⱳ R ⓐ ⊞ lau ➧ ✗ 🏔 ⱳL
Prices: ♦20 pitch 17

LAUTERBOURG BAS-RHIN

CM des Mouettes chemin des Mouettes ☎ 388546860
A level site on the shores of a lake.
➲ *Access via D63 from Haguenau.*
3 Mar-10 Dec 2.7HEC ⸺ ⅏ ♠ ✗ ⊙ ♥ ∅ 🏔 ⱳ L ⓐ ⊞ ⅏ lau ➧ ☒ ✗ ⱳR

LUTTENBACH HAUT-RHIN

Amis de la Nature r du Château ☎ 389773860
Situated on a long strip of land, in the heart of Luttenbach countryside. Site is divided into pitches.
➲ *From Munster follow D10 for 1km.*
10 Feb-20 Nov 7HEC ⸺ ♀ ♠ ☒ ✗ ⊙ ♥ ∅ ⱳ R ⓐ ⊞ lau ➧ 🏔

MASEVAUX HAUT-RHIN

CM 3 r du Stade ☎ 389824229
In wooded surroundings beside the River Doller.
➲ *Off the main road to Ballon-d'Alsace.*
Etr-Sep 3.5HEC ⸺ ♀ ♠ ⊙ ♥ ⓐ ⊞ lau ➧ ☒ ♘ ✗ ∅ 🏔 ⱳPR
Prices: ♦15.30 pitch 15.30

METZERAL HAUT-RHIN
At MITTLACH(3km SW)

CM ☎ 389776377
Situated in forested area in small village, very quiet.
➲ *From Munster follow signs for Metzeral then Mittlach D10.*
May-Oct ♠ ⊙ ♥ ∅ ⱳ R ⓐ lau

MOOSCH HAUT-RHIN

Mine d'Argent r de la Mine d'Argent ☎ 389823066
A well established site in a peaceful wooded setting.
➲ *1.5km SW off N66.*
May-Sep 2HEC ⸺ ♀ ♠ ⊙ ♥ ∅ ⱳ R ⓐ ⊞ lau ➧ ☒ ♘ ✗
Prices: ♦14 pitch 14

MUNSTER HAUT-RHIN

CM Parc de la Fecht rte de Gunsbach ☎ 389773108
Well maintained site close to the town centre within a park-like area surrounded by high walls and trees.
➲ *Access on D417, 200m after entering Munster town centre, near the swimming pool.*

Apr-Sep 4HEC ⸺ ♀ ♠ ♘ ♘ ⊙ ♥ ∅ ⱳ R ⓐ ⊞ lau ➧ ✗ 🏔 ⱳP
Prices: ♦14.20 pitch 20.60

OBERBRONN BAS-RHIN

CM Eichelgarten r de Zinswiller ☎ 388097196
➲ *Follow signposts W from D28 (Oberbronn-Zinswiller).*
16 Mar-14 Nov 4HEC ⸺ ♀ ♠ ♘ ⊙ ♥ ∅ 🏠 ♥ ⱳ P ⓐ lau ➧ ♘ ✗ 🏔 ⱳR ⊞
Prices: ♦17.40 ♠8.20 ♥11.20 ♠11.20

OBERNAI BAS-RHIN

CM 204 rte d'Ottrott ☎ 388953848
Partly terraced site, situated in park.
➲ *W on D426 towards Ottrott.*
Apr-Oct 2.5HEC ⸺ ⅏ ➧ ♠ ⊙ ♥ ⓐ ⊞ ⅏ lau ➧ ♘ ♘ ✗ ∅ 🏔 ⱳP

PHALSBOURG MOSELLE

CM Vieux Château r de la Manutention ☎ 387241372
Site within walls of ancient castle close to the town centre.
➲ *E on rte de Saverne.*
All year 4HEC ⸺ ♀ ♠ ⊙ ♥ ⓐ ⊞ ➧ ♘ ♘ ✗ ∅ 🏔

RHINAU BAS-RHIN

Ferme des Tuileries ☎ 388746045
➲ *Approach from Germany via ferry across River Rhine.*
Apr-Sep 1HEC ⸺ ♀ ♠ ♘ ♘ ✗ ⊙ ♥ ∅ ⓐ ⊞ ⅏ lau ➧ ⱳP

RIBEAUVILLE HAUT-RHIN

Pierre de Coubertin 23 r de Landau ☎ 389736671
In a peaceful location. Shop open in summer only.
➲ *Access via D106.*
Mar-1 Nov 3.4HEC ⸺ ➧ ♠ ♘ ⊙ ♥ ∅ ⓐ ⊞ lau ➧ ♘ ✗ ⱳP

RIQUEWIHR HAUT-RHIN

Inter Communal rte des Vins ☎ 389479008
Extensive site overlooking vineyards.
➲ *2km E on D16. Turn W off N83 (Colmar-Strasbourg) at Ostheim.*
Etr-Oct 4HEC ⸺ ♀ ♠ ⊙ ♥ ⓐ ⊞ lau ➧ ♘ ♘ ✗ ∅ 🏔 ⊞
Prices: ♦21 pitch 26

ROMBACH-LE-FRANC HAUT-RHIN

Bouleaux ☎ 389589399
➲ *1.5km NW beside the river.*
May-Sep 1HEC ⸺ ♀ ♠ ⊙ ♥ ⱳ R ⓐ lau ➧ ♘ 🏔 ⊞

ST-MAURICE-SUR-MOSELLE VOSGES

Deux Ballons 17 r du Stade ☎ 329251714
Well maintained site beside a stream and surrounded by woodland and mountains.
➲ *1km W on N66.*
15 Feb-Sep 4HEC ⸺ ♀ ♠ ⊙ ♥ 🏔 🏠 ⱳ P ⓐ ⊞ lau ➧ ∅
Prices: ♦22-23 pitch 25-26

ST-PIERRE BAS-RHIN

Beau Séjour ☎ 388085224
Situated midway between Strasbourg and Colmar with good modern facilities.
15 May-3 Oct 0.6HEC ⸺ ♀ ♠ ⊙ ♥ ⓐ ⊞ lau ➧ ♘ ♘ ✗ 🏔
Prices: ♦12 ♠8 ♥12 ♠12

SAVERNE BAS-RHIN

CM ☎ 388913565
➲ *1.3km SW via D171.*
Apr-Sep 1.6HEC ⸺ ⅏ ♠ ⊙ ♥ ∅ ⓐ ⊞ lau ➧ ✗ ⱳP

◗ **SCHIRMECK** BAS-RHIN

Schirmeck 26 rte de Strasbourg ☎ 388970161
➥ *5km NE. Beside Strasbourg road and railway, on level ground.*
Mar-Oct 2.5HEC ⏛ ⌇ ♠ 🏕 ⊙ 🚐 ⌀ 🔾 ↴ R 🏧 ⊞ lau ➧ 🦺 🍽 ✗ 🚿

◗ **SÉLESTAT** BAS-RHIN

CM Cigognes r de la 1-er DFL ☎ 388920398
In a rural setting at an altitude of 175mtrs.
➥ *900mtrs from the town centre.*
May-15 Oct 0.7HEC ⏛ ⌇ ♠ 🏕 ⊙ 🚐 🏧 ⊞ lau ➧ 🦺 🍽 ✗ 🚿 ↴LPR
Prices: pitch 70-80 (incl 3 persons)

◗ **SEPPOIS-LE-BAS** HAUT-RHIN

CM les Lupins r de l'Ancienne Gare ☎ 389256537
Picturesque site close to the German and Swiss borders.
➥ *Access via A36, exit 'Burnhaupt' and continue towards Dannemarie.*
Apr-Oct 4HEC ⏛ ⌇ ♠ 🏕 ⊙ 🚐 ⌀ ↴ P 🏧 ⊞ lau ➧ 🦺 🍽 ✗ 🚿 ↴R
Prices: ♦21 pitch 21

◗ **SIVRY-SUR-MEUSE** MEUSE

Brouzel 26 r du Moulin ☎ 329858645
May-Sep 1.5HEC ⏛ 🌿 🏕 ⊙ 🚐 ↴ R 🏧 ⊞ lau ➧ 🦺 🍽 ✗ ⌀ 🚿
Prices: ♦12 ♠8 🚐12 ▲12

◗ **THILLOT, LE** VOSGES

Étang de Chaume 36 r de la Chaume ☎ 329251030
➥ *1.3km NW via N66.*
All year ⏛ ⌇ ♠ 🏕 ⊙ 🚐 🏧 lau ➧ 🦺 🍽 ✗ ⌀ 🚿 ↴PR

◗ **THIONVILLE** MOSELLE

CM 6 r du Parc ☎ 382538375
On the edge of River Moselle, adjacent to the Napoléon Park.
Apr-Sep 2HEC ⏛ ⌇ ♠ 🏕 ⊙ 🚐 🏧 ⊞ lau ➧ 🦺 🍽 ✗ ↴R

◗ **THOLY, LE** VOSGES

Noir Rupt chemin de l'Étang de Noirrupt ☎ 229618127
A peaceful site in a beautiful wooded location. Plenty of facilities.
➥ *2km SE on D417.*
15 Apr-15 Oct 3HEC ⏛ ⌇ ♠ 🦺 🍽 ✗ ⊙ 🚐 🏡 ↴ P 🏧 🄿 lau ➧ ✗ ⊞
Prices: ♦18.90-27 pitch 31.50-45

◗ **TONNOY** MEURTHE-ET-MOSELLE

Grande Vanné ☎ 383266236
➥ *W via D74, beside the River Moselle*
29 May-4 Sep 7HEC ⏛ ⌇ ♠ 🍽 ✗ ⊙ 🚐 ⌀ 🚿 ↴ R 🏧 ⊞ lau ➧ 🦺

◗ **TURCKHEIM** HAUT-RHIN

Cigognes 7 quai de la Gare ☎ 389270200
Camping Card Compulsory.
➥ *From Colmar follow N417 to Wintzenheim, then to Turckheim. Before bridge turn left, continue past railway station and stadium.*
15 May-Oct 2.5HEC ⏛ ♠ 🏕 🦺 🍽 ✗ ⊙ 🚐 ⌀ ↴ R 🏧 🄿 ⊞ lau ➧ ✗
Prices: ♦18 pitch 21

◗ **URBÈS** HAUT-RHIN

CM Benelux Bâle ☎ 389827876
A well maintained site with good facilities.
➥ *W of rte de Bussang.*
Apr-Oct 2.4HEC ⏛ ⌇ ♠ ⊙ 🚐 🏧 ⊞ lau ➧ 🦺 ⌀ 🚿 ↴R
Prices: ♦15-22 ♠8 🚐8

◗ **VAGNEY** VOSGES

CM du Mettey ☎ 329248135
➥ *1.3km E on Gérardmer road.*
15 Jun-15 Sep 2HEC ⏛ ♦ 🏕 ⊙ 🚐 🏧 ⊞ lau ➧ 🦺 🍽 ✗ ⌀ 🚿 ↴PR

◗ **VERDUN** MEUSE

Breuils allée des Breuils ☎ 329861531
A family site in peaceful surroundings. Pitches are divided by trees and bushes and the sanitary facilities are well maintained.
➥ *SW via D34. Signposted.*
Apr-15 Oct 5HEC ⏛ ♦ 🏕 🦺 🍽 ✗ ⊙ 🚐 ⌀ 🚿 🏡 🚐 ↴ P 🏧 lau ➧ ↴L
Prices: ♦21 🚐18 ▲15

◗ **VILLERS-LÈS-NANCY** MEURTHE-ET-MOSELLE

Touristique International de Nancy-Brabois av P-Muller ☎ 383271828
In beautiful wooded surroundings with well defined pitches and good recreational facilities.
➥ *SW in Brabois park.*
Apr-15 Oct 6HEC ⏛ ⌇ ♠ 🏕 🦺 🍽 ✗ ⊙ 🚐 ⌀ 🏧 lau ➧ ⌀
Prices: pitch 55 (incl 2 persons)

◗ **VITTEL** VOSGES

CM r C-Bassot ☎ 329080271
➥ *NE via D68 rte de Domjulien.*
Etr-Oct ⏛ ⌇ ♦ ♠ 🏕 ⊙ 🚐 🏧 lau ➧ 🦺 🍽 ✗ ⌀ 🚿 ↴P ⊞

◗ **WASSELONNE** BAS-RHIN

CM rte de Romanswiller ☎ 388870008
On a level meadow adjoining the local sports complex.
➥ *1km W on D224.*
Apr-15 Oct 2.5HEC ⏛ ⌇ ♠ 🦺 🍽 ✗ ⊙ 🚐 ⌀ ↴ P 🏧 🄿 ⊞ lau ➧ ✗ 🚿
Prices: ♦15.65 pitch 11.55

◗ **WATTWILLER** HAUT-RHIN

Sources rte des Crêtes ☎ 389754494
A family site on the edge of the Vosges forest close to the Route du Vin.
➥ *Approach via N83 exit Cernay Nord.*
1 Apr-15 Oct 14HEC ⏛ ⌇ ⁝⁝⁝ ♠ 🏕 🦺 🍽 ✗ ⊙ 🚐 ⌀ 🚿 🏡 🚐 ↴ P 🏧 🄿 ⊞ lau
Prices: ♦30 pitch 45

◗ **WIHR-AU-VAL** HAUT-RHIN

Route Verte 13 r de la Gare ☎ 389711010
Near the centre of the village at an altitude of 320mtrs.
➥ *Approach via D10.* *Contd.*

Jul-Aug 1HEC ⚏ ⚥ ⚦ ⊙ ⚘ ∅ 🅿 lau ➧ ⚌ ⚍ ✕ ↺R ⊞
Prices: ♠14.50 pitch 11

▶ XONRUPT/LONGEMER VOSGES

L'Eau-Vive rte de Colmar ☎ 329630737
On a meadow surrounded by trees, close to the ski slopes.
⤷ *2km SE on D67A next to Lac de Longemer.*
All year 1HEC ⚏ ⚥ ⚦ ✕ ⊙ ⚘ ∅ ⚏ ⚌ 🅿 ↺ R 🅿 ⊞ lau ➧
⚌ ↺L

Jonquilles rte du Lac ☎ 329633401
In a delightful wooded lakeside setting. Advance booking
necessary in July and August.
⤷ *2km SE on D67A beside Lac de Longemer.*
Apr-15 Oct 4HEC ⚏ ⚥ ⚌ ⚍ ✕ ⊙ ⚘ ∅ ↺ L 🅿 ⊞ lau
Prices: pitch 38.20-56.20 (incl 2 persons)

● ● BURGUNDY/CHAMPAGNE ● ●

The Champagne region is one of the rich greens and huge
landscapes of the Ardennes and the wide meadows of the
River Marne. Its former capital, Laon, has a rich medieval
heritage and a lovely 12th-century cathedral, while, to the
south , Troyes boasts wonderful Renaissance treasures. But
the jewel of the area is Reims, with its magnificent Gothic
cathedral - an important centre for the region and the
whole of France for centuries.
The local wine of Champagne needs no introduction, and
pre-arranged visits and regular tours are available from the
famous names - Mercier, Moët, Veuve Cliquot - and there
is a Champagne Museum (Musée du Champagne) in
Épernay.
The representatives of Burgundy also travel the world -
names such as Chablis, Mâcon and Nuits St Georges. A
wonderful surprise of the area, though, is the network of
hundreds of miles of navigable waterways, accessing a
wealth of Romanesque churches, abbeys, castles, and
medieval fortress towns, exquisite small villages and quiet
rolling expanses of rich pastures and vineyards - the
quintessential provincial France. Visitors should include a
visit to Beaune, famous for its 14th-century hospice.

▶ ACCOLAY YONNE

Moulin Jacquot r du Moulin Jacquot ☎ 386815648
A well equipped site in a pleasant rural setting, close to the
village.
⤷ *W, beside the Canal du Nivernais.*
Apr-15 Oct 1HEC ⚏ ➧⚦ ⊙ ⚘ 🅿 lau ➧ ⚌ ⚍ ✕ ⚌ ↺R ⊞
Prices: ♠9 ⇆7 ⚏12 ▲7

▶ ANCY-LE-FRANC YONNE

CM rte de Cusy ☎ 386751321
In a sheltered position just beyond the village.
⤷ *Access via Montbard road.*
Jun-15 Sep 0.8HEC ⚏ ➧⚦ ⊙ ⚘ 🅿 lau ➧ ⚌ ⚍ ✕ ∅ ⚍ ↺R
⊞
Prices: ♠12 ⇆6 ⚏12 ▲6

▶ ANDRYES YONNE

Bois Joli ☎ 386817048
A small site in pleasant Burgundian countryside.
⤷ *0.6km SW via N151.*
Apr-Oct 5HEC ⚏ ➧⚦ ⚍ ✕ ⊙ ⚘ ⚏ ⚏ ↺ P ⊞ lau ➧ ⚌ ∅
⚍ ↺R
Prices: pitch 56.50-85.50 (incl 2 persons)

▶ ARNAY-LE-DUC CÔTE-D'OR

CM de Fouché ☎ 380900223
In a quiet location beside a lake with good recreational
facilities close to the medieval town of Arnay-le-Duc.
⤷ *0.7km E on CD17.*
All year 5HEC ⚏ ⚥ ⚦ ⚌ ⚍ ⊙ ⚘ ∅ ↺ L 🅿 ⊞ lau ➧ ✕ ⚍

▶ AUXERRE YONNE

CM 8 rte de Vaux ☎ 386521115
⤷ *SE towards Vaux*
Apr-Sep 5HEC ⚏ ➧⚦ ⚍ ✕ ⊙ ⚘ ∅ ⚍ 🅿 ⊞ lau ➧ ⚌ ✕ ↺PR

▶ AUXONNE CÔTE-D'OR

Arquebuse rte d'Athée ☎ 380373436
Clean, well-equipped site on right bank of River Saône near
bathing area.
⤷ *From Auxonne travel W on N5 for 3km. Then turn
northwards on D24 towards Athée and Pontailler-sur-Saône.*
15 Jun-15 Sep 3HEC ⚏ ⚥ ⚦ ⚍ ✕ ⊙ ⚘ ⚏ 🅿 lau ➧ ⚌ ✕ ∅
⚍ ↺PR
Prices: ♠20 pitch 24

▶ AVALLON YONNE

CM Sous Roche 1 r Sous-Roche ☎ 386341039
⤷ *2km SE by D944 and D427.*
15 Mar-15 Oct 2HEC ⚏ ⚥ ⚦ ⚌ ✕ ⊙ ⚘ ↺ R 🅿 ⊞ lau ➧ ↺P
Prices: ♠18 pitch 13

▶ BAR-SUR-AUBE AUBE

Gravière av du Parc ☎ 325271294
⤷ *0.5km E of D13.*
Apr-15 Oct 2.8HEC ⚏ ➧⚦ ⊙ ⚘ ⚏ ↺ PR 🅿 lau ➧ ⚌ ⚍ ✕ ∅
⚍ ↺P
Prices: ♠5.60 ⇆3.30 ⚏3.40 ▲3.20

▶ BAZOLLES NIÈVRE

Baye ☎ 386389033
Apr-Oct 1.5HEC ⚏ ⚥ ⚦ ⊙ ⚘ ⚏ ↺ L 🅿 ⊞ lau ➧ ⚌ ⚍ ✕
∅ ⚍

▶ BEAUNE CÔTE-D'OR

CM Cent Vignes 10 rue August Dubois ☎ 380220391
On outskirts of town. Site divided into pitches, clean, well-
looked after sanitary installations. From 20 Jun-31 Aug it is
advisable to arrive before 1600 hrs.
⤷ *On N74 on Savigny-les-Beaune road.*
15 Mar-30 Oct 2HEC ⚏ ♠ ⚥ ⚦ ⚌ ✕ ⊙ ⚘ ∅ 🅿 ⊞ lau ➧
⚍ ↺P
Prices: ♠16 pitch 23

▶ BOURBON-LANCY SAÔNE-ET-LOIRE

St-Prix r du St-Prix ☎ 385891485
A well equipped family site close to an extensive water sports
centre.
⤷ *By the swimming pool off the D979a.*
15 Apr-15 Oct 2.5HEC ⚏ ⚥ ⚦ ⚌ ⚍ ⊙ ⚘ ⚏ lau ➧ ⚌ ✕ ∅ ⚍
↺LP ⊞
Prices: ♠14.50 ⇆12 ⚏13-21 ▲12

▶ BOURBONNE-LES-BAINS HAUTE-MARNE

Montmorency r du Stade ☎ 325900864
A well equipped site in a pleasant natural setting.
Apr-Oct 2HEC ⚏ ⚥ ⚦ ⚍ ⚍ ⊙ ⚘ ∅ ⚏ ↺ P 🅿 ⊞ lau
Prices: ♠14 pitch 13

BOURG HAUTE-MARNE

Croix d'Arles ☎ 325882402
A peaceful site in wooded surroundings close to Langres.
➲ *Access via N74 or A31.*
13 Mar-Oct 7HEC ⟱ ⌘ ⋔ ⋤ ⟐ ✕ ⊙ ⬛ 🏠 ⬚ ⁊ P 🏛 ⊞ lau
Prices: ♠16 pitch 32

BOURG-FIDÈLE ARDENNES

Murée rte de Rocroi ☎ 324542445
A lakeside site in wooded surroundings.
➲ *1km N via D22.*
All year 1.3HEC ⟱ ⌘ ⋔ ⋤ ✕ ⊙ ⬛ ⬚ 🏛 lau ➤ ⋤ ∅ ⚲ ⊞

CHAGNY SAÔNE-ET-LOIRE

CM Pâquier Fané ☎ 385872142
A clean site 600m W of the church.
➲ *Follow the D974 from town centre.*
13 May-4 Sep 1.5HEC ⟱ ⌘ ⋔ ⋤ ✕ ⊙ ⬛ ∅ ⁊ R 🏛 ⊞ lau ➤
⁊P

CHÂLONS-SUR-MARNE (CHÂLONS-EN-CHAMPAGNE)
MARNE

CM r de Plaisance ☎ 326683800
In a pleasant wooded location with good recreational
facilities.
Mar-Oct 7HEC ⟱ ⌘ ⋔ ✕ ⊙ ⬛ ∅ 🏛 ⊞ lau ➤ ⋤
Prices: ♠25 pitch 21

CHARLEVILLE-MÉZIÈRES ARDENNES

CM Mont Olympe r des Paquis ☎ 324332360
Level meadowland near the town centre and 100m from
municipal indoor swimming pool.
➲ *Well signed from town centre.*
Etr-15 Oct 2HEC ⟱ ⌘ ⋔ ⋤ ⟐ ✕ ⊙ ⬛ ∅ ⚲ ⁊ PR 🏛 ⊞ lau
➤ ✕

CHAROLLES SAÔNE-ET-LOIRE

CM rte de Viny ☎ 385240490
In pleasant wooded surroundings with good, modern
sanitary facilities.
➲ *NE of town via D33 towards Viry. Follow signs.*
1 Apr-15 Oct 0.6HEC ⟱ ⌘ ⋔ ⟐ ⊙ ⬛ ⁊ PR 🏛 ⊞ lau ➤ ⋤ ✕
∅ ⚲
Prices: ♠12 ⬛7.50 ⬛11

CHÂTILLON-SUR-SEINE CÔTE-D'OR

CM espl St-Vorles ☎ 380910305
Hilly shaded site near the historic Renaissance church of St
Vorles.
➲ *SE of town off rte de Langres (D928).*
May-Sep 0.8HEC ⟱ ⬥ ⋔ ⋤ ⟐ ⊙ ⬛ ∅ 🏛 ⊞ lau ➤ ⋤ ✕ ⚲ ⁊P
Prices: ♠15 pitch 12

CHATONRUPT HAUTE-MARNE

CM ☎ 25948182
15 Apr-Sep 1.1HEC ⟱ ⋇ ⋔ ⊙ ⬛ ⁊ R 🏛 ⊞ lau ➤ ⋤ ⟐ ✕ ⚲

CHEVIGNY NIÈVRE

Hermitage de Chevigny ☎ 386845097
A pleasant site with good facilities in wooded surroundings
within the Morvan Nature Reserve. There is direct access to
the lake and most watersports are available.
Apr-Sep 2.2HEC ⟱ ⬥ ⋔ ⋤ ⟐ ✕ ⊙ ⬛ ∅ 🏠 ⁊ L 🏛 ⊞ lau
Prices: ♠24 ⬛15 ⬛15

CLAMECY NIÈVRE

Pont Picot rte de Chenoches ☎ 386270597
In a pleasant situation between the River Yonne and the
Canal du Nivernais.
May-Sep 1.2HEC ⟱ ⋇ ⋔ ⊙ ⬛ ⁊ R 🏛 lau ➤ ⋤ ⟐ ✕ ⚲ ⚲
⁊P ⊞

CONFLANS-SUR-SEINE MARNE

Vieille Seine rue du Port ☎ 326426159
On the outskirts of the village, beside the River Seine.
➲ *3km from Romilly.*
Apr-Sep 6HEC ⟱ ⬥ ⋔ ⟐ ✕ ⊙ ⬛ 🏠 ⬚ ⚲ ▲ ⁊ R 🏛 ⊞ lau ➤
⋤ ⟐ ✕ ⚲ ⚲ ⁊R

COSNE-SUR-LOIRE NIÈVRE

Loire & Nohain Ile de Cosne ☎ 386282792
Site borders River Loire.
➲ *Follow D955 W towards Sancerre.*
15 Sep-15 Oct 4HEC ⟱ ⋮⋮ ⬥ ⌘ ⋔ ⋤ ⟐ ✕ ⊙ ⬛ ∅ ⬚ 🏛 ⊞
lau ➤ ⚲ ⁊P
Prices: ♠15 ⬛22 ▲17

CRÊCHES-SUR-SAÔNE SAÔNE-ET-LOIRE

CM Le Port d'Arciat ☎ 385371183
In a wooded location beside the River Saône.
➲ *1.5km E via D31.*
May-Sep 6HEC ⟱ ⬥ ⋔ ⋤ ⟐ ✕ ⊙ ⬛ ∅ ⁊ LR 🏛 ⊞ lau ➤ ⚲
Prices: ♠16 pitch 34

DIGOIN SAÔNE-ET-LOIRE

CM Chevrette r de la Chevrette ☎ 385531149
➲ *W of village on N79.*
Apr-Oct 1.6HEC ⟱ ⬥ ⌘ ⋔ ⋤ ⟐ ✕ ⊙ ⬛ 🏠 ⬚ ⁊ P 🏛 lau
➤ ∅
Prices: ♠16 pitch 32

DIJON CÔTE-D'OR

Lac 3 bd Chanoine Kir ☎ 380435472
A well maintained site in natural surroundings, an ideal base
for exploring the historic town of Dijon.
➲ *1.5km W on N5.*
Apr-15 Oct 3HEC ⟱ ⋮⋮ ⬥ ⌘ ⋔ ⋤ ⟐ ✕ ⊙ ⬛ 🏛 ⊞ lau ➤ ∅
⚲ ⁊LPR

ÉCLARON-BRAUCOURT HAUTE-MARNE

Presqu'île de Champaubert ☎ 325041320
Situated on lake peninsula.
Apr-15 Oct 3.5HEC ⟱ ⌘ ⋔ ⋤ ⟐ ✕ ⊙ ⬛ ∅ 🏛 ⊞ lau ➤ ⁊L
Prices: ♠26 ⬛20 ⬛26 ▲26

EPINAC SAÔNE-ET-LOIRE

Pont Vert ☎ 385820026
➲ *S via D43 beside the River Drée.*
Apr-Sep 3HEC ⟱ ⬥ ⋔ ⋤ ⟐ ✕ ⊙ ⬛ 🏠 ⁊ R 🏛 lau ➤ ∅ ⚲

FRONCLES HAUTE-MARNE

Deux Ponts r des Ponts ☎ 325023121
In a peaceful location beside the River Marne.
15 Mar-15 Oct 3HEC ⌘ ⋔ ⟐ ⊙ ⁊ R 🏛 ⊞ ➤ ⋤ ⟐ ✕ ⊞
Prices: ♠7 pitch 10.60

GIBLES SAÔNE-ET-LOIRE

Château de Montrouant Montrouant ☎ 385845113
A small site situated in the Charollais hill region with access
to extensive parkland.
➲ *1.6km NE beside the lake.*
20 Jun-Aug 1HEC ⟱ ⋮⋮ ⌘ ⋔ ⋤ ⟐ ✕ ⊙ ⬛ 🏠 ▲ ⁊ LPR 🏛
⊞ lau ➤ ∅ ⚲

▶ **GIFFAUMONT** MARNE

Plage Chemin de la Cachotte, Station Nautique
☎ 326726184
A well maintained site situated at the Station Nautique.
➲ *2km from the village.*
May-10 Sep 1.5HEC ⊞ ♠ 🏠 ♀ ⊙ ▣ ∅ 🏢 ⊞ lau ➧ 🖳 ✕ 🏛
🔫L

▶ **GIGNY-SUR-SAÔNE** SAÔNE-ET-LOIRE

🏚 Château de l'Epervière ☎ 385448323
Quiet site in park surrounding 16th-century château. Close
to the River Saône for fishing and sailing.
➲ *N6 to Sennecey-le-Grand, then follow signs.*
12 Apr-Sep 10HEC ⊞ ♠ 🏠 🖳 ♀ ⊙ ▣ ∅ 🔫 P ▣ ⊞ lau
Prices: ⚲26-32 ➕10-10 ➘37-48 ⚑37-48

▶ **GRANDPRÉ** ARDENNES

CM ☎ 324305071
A peaceful riverside site.
➲ *150m from village centre on D6.*
Apr-Sep 1HEC ⊞ ♠ 🏠 ⊙ ▣ 🔫 R ▣ ⊞ lau ➧ 🖳 ✕ ∅ 🏛

▶ **GUEUGNON** SAÔNE-ET-LOIRE

CM rte de Digoin, Chazey ☎ 385855050
A quiet site in wooded surroundings near a lake.
Jun-Sep 3HEC ⊞ 🍴 🏠 🖳 ⊙ ▣ ∅ 🏛 🏢 🔫 L ▣ ⊞ lau ➧ ♀ ✕

▶ **ISSY-L'ÉVÊQUE** SAÔNE-ET-LOIRE

CM de l'Étang Neuf ☎ 385249605
In a fine position beside the lake, overlooking the château.
May-15 Sep 4HEC ⊞ 🍴 🏠 🖳 ✕ ⊙ ▣ ∅ 🔫 P ▣ ▣ ⊞ lau ➧
🖳 🏛 🔫L
Prices: ⚲16 pitch 16

▶ **LAIVES** SAÔNE-ET-LOIRE

Lacs 'La Heronnière' Les Bois de Laives ☎ 385448967
Compulsory separate car park for arrivals after 2200hrs.
➲ *Access via 'Châlon Sud' autoroute exit towards Mâcon.*
15 May-15 Sep 1.5HEC ⊞ 🍴 🏠 🖳 ♀ ✕ ⊙ ▣ ∅ ▣ ⊞ lau
➧ 🔫LR
Prices: ⚲18 pitch 20

▶ **MÂCON** SAÔNE-ET-LOIRE

CM ☎ 385381622
Divided into pitches. Water sports centre and pool nearby.
➲ *2km N on N6.*
15 Mar-Oct 5HEC ⊞ 🍴 🏠 🖳 ♀ ✕ ⊙ ▣ ∅ 🔫 P ▣ lau ➧ 🏛
🔫R
Prices: pitch 58-82 (incl 2 persons)

▶ **MARCENAY** CÔTE-D'OR

Grebes Laignes ☎ 380816172
A peaceful site in unspoiled contryside with separate hedged
pitches. Direct access to lake.
All year 2.4HEC ⊞ 🍴 🏠 🖳 ⊙ ▣ ∅ ▣ 🔫 L ▣ ⊞ lau ➧ ♀ ✕

▶ **MAS-CABARDÈS** AUDE

Eaux Vives ∅ 468263105
➲ *1km E via D101, beside the river.*
Apr-Sep 1HEC ⊞ ♠ 🏠 ⊙ ▣ ∅ ▣ ▣ ⊞ lau ➧ 🖳 ✕

▶ **MATOUR** SAÔNE-ET-LOIRE

CM Le Paluet Le Paluet ☎ 385597058
In pleasant countryside beside the river.
May-Sep 0.2HEC ⊞ ⁙⁙ ♠ 🏠 ♀ ✕ ⊙ ▣ 🔫 PR ▣ ⊞ lau ➧ 🖳
∅ 🏛
Prices: ⚲14 pitch 20

▶ **MESNIL-ST PÈRE** AUBE

Voie Colette ☎ 325412715
Grassland, with trees, ornamental shrubs and flower beds.
Slightly sloping, with a man-made lake nearby.
➲ *About 2km from Mesnil-St-Père; signposted from centre.*
Apr-15 Oct 4HEC ⊞ 🍴 🏠 🖳 ✕ ⊙ ▣ ∅ 🏢 ⊞ lau ➧ 🖳 ✕ 🔫L
Prices: pitch 60 (incl 2 persons)

▶ **MEURSAULT** CÔTE-D'OR

Grappe d'Or 2 rte de Volnay ☎ 380212248
Clean terraced site on an open meadow. Mountain bikes are
available for hire.
➲ *700m NE on D11b.*
23 Mar-1 Nov 4.5HEC ⊞ ♠ ♠ 🏠 🖳 ♀ ⊙ ▣ ∅ 🏢 🔫 P ▣
lau ➧ ⊞
Prices: pitch 21.50-26.50 (incl 2 persons)

▶ **MONTAPAS** NIÈVRE

CM La Chênaie La Chênaie ☎ 386583432
In a wooded location beside a lake with plenty of recreational
facilities.
➲ *500m from town centre, beside the lake, via D259.*
Apr-Oct 1HEC ⊞ 🍴 🏠 🖳 ✕ ⊙ ▣ 🔫 L ▣ ➧ 🖳
Prices: ⚲8 ➕8 ⚑8 ⚲8

▶ **MONTBARD** CÔTE-D'OR

CM r M-Servet ☎ 380922160
➲ *NW via rte de Laignes.*
Feb-Oct 2.5HEC ⊞ ♠ 🏠 ♀ ⊙ ▣ 🏢 ▣ lau ➧ 🖳 ✕ ∅ 🏛 🔫PR
⊞

▶ **MONTHERMÉ** ARDENNES

Base de Loisirs Départementale ☎ 324328161
In a pleasant wooded situation.
➲ *0.8km NE beside the River Semoy.*
All year 16HEC ⊞ 🍴 🏠 ⊙ ▣ 🏢 🔫 R ▣ lau

▶ **MONTSAUCHE** NIÈVRE

Mesanges Lac des Settons, Rive Gauche ☎ 386845577
On the left bank of Lac des Settons.
May-15 Sep 5HEC ⊞ 🍴 🏠 ⊙ ▣ 🏢 ▣ ⊞ lau ➧ ♀ ✕ ∅ 🏛
🔫LPR
Prices: ⚲22 pitch 15

Plage du Midi ☎ 386845197
In a wooded setting directly on the Lac des Settons with good
facilities.
➲ *From Salieu (on N6) follow D977. From town centre follow
D193 to Les Sultons, then to site.*
Etr-Sep 4HEC ⊞ 🍴 🏠 🖳 ♀ ✕ ⊙ ▣ ∅ 🔫 L ▣ ⊞ lau ➧ ✕
Prices: ⚲23 pitch 15

▶ **PARAY-LE-MONIAL** SAÔNE-ET-LOIRE

Mambré rte du Gué-Léger ☎ 385888920
On a level meadow with good, modern facilities.
➲ *Well signposted from outskirts of town.*
Apr-Oct 4HEC ⊞ 🍴 🏠 🖳 ♀ ✕ ⊙ ▣ 🏛 🏢 🏢 🔫 PR ▣ lau ➧
🖳 ✕ ∅ 🏛
Prices: ⚲14-19 pitch 34-38

▶ **POUGUES-LES-EAUX** NIÈVRE

CM Chanternes ☎ 386688618
➲ *On N7 approx. 7km N of Nevers.*
Etr-Oct 1.4HEC ⊞ 🍴 🏠 ⊙ ▣ ⊞ lau ➧ 🖳 ♀ ✕ 🔫P

▶ **PREMEAUX** CÔTE-D'OR

Saule Guillaume ☎ 380612799
Pleasant site beside a lake.
➲ *1.5km E via D109G.*

15 Jun-Sep 2.1HEC ⬛⬛⬛ ♦ ⋔ ▦ ⊙ ⊡ ⛺ ♨ ⚓ ⟲ L ⊞ ⊞ lau ➧ ▼ ✕ ⊘ ⟲P
Prices: ⭓12.50 pitch 10.50-25

▶ Radonvilliers Aube

Garillon ☎ 325922146
Beside the river,250m from the lake.
Jun-15 Sep 1HEC ⬛⬛⬛ ⊕ ⋔ ⊙ ⊡ ⊞ lau ➧ ✕

▶ Riel-les-eaux Côte-d'or

Riel-les-Eaux ☎ 380937276
A lakeside site with fishing and boating facilities.
➩ *2.2km W via D13.*
Apr-Oct 0.2HEC ⬛⬛⬛ ⊕ ⋔ ▦ ▼ ✕ ⊙ ⊡ ⊘ ⟲ L ⊞ lau ➧ ▦
Prices: ⭓9 pitch 12

▶ Romilly-sur-seine Aube

Cerisiers Voie Herbesace ☎ 325249398
A comfortable family site with plenty of recreational facilities.
➩ *E of town, 250m from N19 Troyes road.*
15 Jun-5 Sep 1.7HEC ⬛⬛⬛ ♦ ⋔ ⊙ ⊡ ⊘ ♨ ⚓ ⟲ P ⊞ ⊞ lau ➧
▦ ▼ ✕ ⟲R
Prices: pitch 45-60 (incl 2 persons)

▶ St-hilaire-sous-romilly Aube

Airotel La Noue des Rois chemin des Brayes ☎ 325244160
A quiet site in a pine forrest on the Basin d'Arcachon.
Booking recommended in July and August.
➩ *2km NE.*
All year 30HEC ⬛⬛⬛ ⊕ ⋔ ▼ ✕ ⊙ ⊡ ♨ ⚓ ⚓ ⟲ LR ⊞ ⊞ ⊞ ⊞ ⚡
lau ➧ ▦

▶ St-honoré Nièvre

Bains 15 av J-Mermoz ☎ 386307344
A family site with good facilities close to the Morvan National Park.
➩ *Access via A6 and D985.*
May-Sep 4.5HEC ⬛⬛⬛ ⊕ ⋔ ▦ ▼ ✕ ⊙ ⊡ ⊘ ⚓ ⟲ P ⊞ ⊞ lau ➧ ▦
Prices: pitch 64-92 (incl 2 persons)

▶ St-marcel Saône-et-loire

Butte r J-Lenevev ☎ 385482686
All year 5HEC ⬛⬛⬛ ⊕ ⋔ ▦ ▼ ✕ ⊙ ⊡ ⊘ ⟲ R ⊞ ⊞ lau ➧ ▦
⟲P

▶ St-péreuse Nièvre

🏔 **Manoir de Bezolle** ☎ 386844255
Situated in grounds of a manor house, at the edge of a National Park. Well-kept site divided by hedges.
➩ *At 'X' roads of D11 and D978.*
15 Mar-15 Oct 8HEC ⬛⬛⬛ ♦ ⋔ ▦ ▼ ✕ ⊙ ⊡ ⊘ ♨ ⚓ ⟲ P ⊞
⊞ lau
Prices: pitch 80-115 (incl 2 persons)

▶ Ste-menehould Marne

CM de la Grelette ☎ 326608021
A well equipped municipal site.
➩ *E of town towards Metz, beside the River Aisne*
May-Sep 0.5HEC ⬛⬛⬛ ⊕ ⋔ ⊙ ⊡ ⟲ P ⊞ lau ➧ ▦ ▼ ✕ ⊘ ⊞
Prices: pitch 27.50 (incl 2 persons)

▶ Saulieu Côte-d'or

CM Perron ☎ 380641619
On level, open ground with good recreational facilities.
➩ *1 km NW on N6.*
Apr-20 Oct 8HEC ⬛⬛⬛ ⊕ ⋔ ▦ ▼ ⊙ ⊡ ⊘ ⚓ ⟲ P ⊞ ⊞ lau ➧ ✕
Prices: ⭓13 pitch 20-25

▶ Sedan Ardennes

CM de la Prairie bd Fabert ☎ 324271305
A well equipped municipal site on the banks of the River Meuse, close to the centre of the village.
Etr-15 Oct 1.5HEC ⬛⬛⬛ ⊕ ⋔ ⊙ ⊡ ⊞ lau ➧ ▦ ▼ ✕ ⊘ ▦ ⟲LP
Prices: ⭓15 pitch 15

▶ Selongy Côte-d'or

CM Les Courvelles r H-Jevain ☎ 380757074
In a rural location close to the river.
➩ *Access via A31 and N74.*
May-Sep 0.4HEC ⬛⬛⬛ ⊕ ⋔ ⊙ ⊡ ⊞ lau ➧ ▦ ▼ ✕ ⟲P ⊞

▶ Seurre Côte-d'or

Piscine ☎ 380204922
A well equipped municipal site with direct access to the river.
➩ *From town centre follow N73 W for 600m in the direction of Beaune.*
Jun-Sep ⬛⬛⬛ ⊕ ⋔ ▼ ✕ ⊙ ⊡ ⊘ ⊞ ⊞ lau ➧ ▦ ✕ ⟲PR

▶ Sézanne Marne

CM rte de Launat ☎ 326805700
➩ *1.5km W on D239, rte de Launat.*
Etr-11 Oct 1HEC ⬛⬛⬛ ⊕ ⋔ ⊙ ⊡ ⟲ P ⊞ lau ➧ ▦ ▼ ✕ ⊘ ▦

▶ Signy-le-petit Ardennes

Pré Hugon Base de Loisirs ☎ 0324535101
A pleasant site in wooded surroundings.
➩ *Access via N43.*
May-15 Oct 0.8HEC ⬛⬛⬛ ♦ ⋔ ⊙ ⊡ ⊞ lau ➧ ▦ ▼ ✕ ⊘ ▦ ⟲LR ⊞

▶ Soulaines-dhuys Aube

CM La Croix Badeau ☎ 325927744
May-Sep 0.5HEC ♦ ⊕ ⋔ ⊙ ⊡ ⊞ lau ➧ ▦ ▼ ✕ ▦ ⊞
Prices: ⭓8 ⬤8 ⊡20 ▲20

▶ Tazilly Nièvre

Château de Chigy ☎ 386301080
In a beautiful location within the extensive grounds of a magnificent chateau. Good sporting facilities and entertainment programme.
➩ *4km from Luzy on D973 Luzy-Moulins.*
Apr-Sep 7HEC ⬛⬛⬛ ⊕ ⋔ ▦ ▼ ✕ ⊙ ⊡ ⊘ ⚓ ⟲ LP ⊞ ⊞ lau
Prices: ⭓21-30 pitch 25-37

▶ Thonnance-les-moulins Haute-marne

🏔 **Forge de Ste-Marie** ☎ 325944200
Partially terraced, on the site of an 18th century forge containing a lake.
➩ *Access via N67 and D427.*
May-Sep 11HEC ⬛⬛⬛ ⊕ ⋔ ⊙ ⊡ ✕ ⊙ ⊡ ⊘ ♨ ⚓ ⟲ P ⊞ lau
Prices: ⭓32-32 ⊡78 pitch 63

▶ Toulon-sur-arroux Saône-et-loire

CM du Val d'Arroux rte d'Uxeau ☎ 385795122
On W outskirts beside the River Arroux.
➩ *Access via D985 then take Uxeau road.*
Etr-1 Nov 1.3HEC ⬛⬛⬛ ♦ ⋔ ⊙ ⊡ ⟲ R ⊞ ⊞ lau ➧ ▦ ▼ ✕ ⊘ ▦
Prices: ⭓8.50 pitch 7.50

▶ Uchizy Saône-et-loire

National 6 ☎ 385405390
Site surrounded by poplar trees on banks of river.
➩ *Turn off N6 towards Saône 6km S of Tournus and continue 0.8km.*
Apr-1 Oct 6HEC ⬛⬛⬛ ♦ ⋔ ▦ ▼ ✕ ⊙ ⊡ ♨ ⚓ ⚓ ⟲ PR ⊞
⊞ lau
Prices: ⭓24 pitch 30

> **VAL-DES-PRÉS** MARNE

Gentianes La Vachette ☎ 492212141
In a delightful wooded location backed by imposing
mountains and bordered by a river.
⊃ *On the edge of the village, 3km SE of Briançon.*
All year 2HEC ⛺ ⬛⬛⬛⬛⬛⬛⬛⬛⬛⬛ PR ⬛⬛
lau ➧ ⬛
Prices: ⭡25 pitch 26

> **VANDENESSE-EN-AUXOIS** CÔTE-D'OR

Lac de Panthier ☎ 380492194
In a wooded location beside Lake Panthier with a wide
variety of sporting facilities.
⊃ *5km SE from Pouilly-en-Auxois on A6.*
15 May-Sep 5HEC ⛺ ⬛⬛⬛⬛⬛⬛⬛⬛⬛ LP ⬛⬛ lau
Prices: ⭡26 pitch 30

Voiliers ☎ 380492194
In a pleasant situation beside a lake with plenty of facilities
for families.
⊃ *2.5km NE via D977.*
15 Apr-Sep 7HEC ⛺ ⬛⬛⬛⬛⬛⬛⬛⬛⬛⬛⬛ LP ⬛
lau
Prices: ⭡30 pitch 38-40

> **VENAREY-LES-LAUMES** CÔTE-D'OR

Alésia r Dr-Roux ☎ 380960776
A peaceful site close to the lake and river.
All year 2HEC ⛺ ⬛⬛⬛⬛⬛⬛➧⬛⬛⬛⬛⬛LR

> **VERMENTON** YONNE

Coulemières ☎ 386815302
A peaceful site with good facilities set amongst the meadows
of Burgundy.

⊃ *On the N6 S of Auxerre.*
10 Apr-10 Oct 1.5HEC ⛺ ⬛⬛⬛⬛⬛⬛⬛⬛⬛⬛⬛ R ⬛ lau ➧ ⬛

> **VILLENEUVE-LES-GENÊTS** YONNE

Bois Guillaume ☎ 386454541
In wooded surroundings with good, modern facilities.
⊃ *2.7km NE.*
All year 8HEC ⛺ ⬛⬛⬛⬛⬛⬛⬛⬛⬛⬛⬛⬛ P ⬛⬛ lau
➧ ⬛R
Prices: ⭡19 pitch 12

● ● ● ● **SOUTH WEST/PYRÉNÉES** ● ● ●

One of the largest regions of France, Aquitaine stretches
from the lower plateaus of the Massif Central, west to the
Atlantic and south to the foothills of the Pyrénées.
This is a land of sunshine, and the three main rivers - the
Lot, the Garonne and the Dordogne - wind through valleys
and meander through orchards and vineyards, occasionally
flowing between high cliffs with castles perched on rocky
ledges. Along the Vézère valley in the Dordogne are the
impressive caves and grottos with prehistoric remains - the
remarkable Lascaux paintings can be admired in Lascaux II
- a full-scale replica of the original. On the coast in the
south of the region, holidaymakers are attracted by the
sophisticated chic of Biarritz, colourful resorts like St-Jean-
de-Luz, and Atlantic rollers offering some of the best
surfing in Europe. At the foothills of the Pyrénées is Basque
country, with charming white houses and timbered
cottages, colourful cascading flowers, and rich heritage of
festivals and folklore.
Inland, popular centres include Lourdes, which has attracted
pilgrims for centuries, and the fascinating Pyrénées National
Park with its wild flora and fauna. The Renaissance city of

Toulouse has a wonderful heritage, with some of the finest examples of Romanesque architecture in Europe. The region is internationally famous for wonderful cuisine. Here you can find duck liver paté, "fois gras", Armagnac, and the succulent Toulouse sausage.
....

ABZAC GIRONDE

Paradis rte de Périgueux ☎ 557490510
In a centre of gastronomic importance, this site stands on meadowland near an artificial lake. Pedal boats and fishing nearby.
➲ *Drive W on N89 from the direction of Périgueux. After St-Médard-de-Guizières turn onto D17E and follow signposts.*
15-31 Dec 5HEC ⬜ 🔱 🏕 🛒 🍽 ✕ ⊙ 🚻 🖉 🚿 🏠 🚽 ⁀ LR 🏷 ⊞ lau
Prices: ♙16-18 pitch 25-30

AIGUES-VIVES ARIÈGE

Serre ☎ 561030616
All year 5HEC ⬜ 🔱 🏕 ✕ ⊙ 🚿 🚽 🏠 🔱 Å ⁀ P 🏷 lau ➟ 🛒 ✕ 🖉 🚻

AIRE-SUR-L'ADOUR LANDES

Ombrages de l'Adour ☎ 558717510
A clean, tidy site next to a sports stadium beside the river. Clean sanitary installations.
May-Oct 2HEC ⬜ 🔱 🏕 ⊙ 🚿 🏠 Å ⁀ R 🏷 ⊞ lau ➟ 🛒 🍽 ✕ ⁀P

ALBI TARN

Languedoc allée du Camping Caussels ☎ 563603706
The site is owned by the local automobile club. It lies on terraced land in a forest next to municipal swimming pools.
Camping Card Compulsory.
➲ *From village take N99 towards Millau, then turn left onto D100 and left again into site.*
Apr-Oct 1HEC ⬜ 🔱 ⊙ 🚿 🖉 ⊞ lau ➟ 🛒 🍽 ✕ ⁀P

ANDERNOS-LES-BAINS GIRONDE

Fontaine-Vieille 4 bd du Colonel Wurtz ☎ 556820167
On level ground in sparse forest.
➲ *S of village centre.*
Apr-Sep 12.6HEC ⬜ ∷ 🔱 🏕 🛒 ✕ ⊙ 🚿 🖉 🚻 🏠 🚽 PS 🏷 ⊞ lau
Prices: pitch 60-85 (incl 2 persons)

Pleine Forêt ☎ 556821718
Situated in a quiet location among pines.
➲ *Off D106E or D106 Andernos-les-Bains-Bordeaux road.*
All year 6HEC ⬜ ∷ 🔱 🏕 ✕ ⊙ 🚿 🏠 🚻 🚽 ⁀ P 🏷 ⊞ lau ➟ ✕ 🖉 ⁀S

ANGLARS-JUILLAC LOT

Floiras ☎ 565362739
A quiet, level site beside the River Lot surrounded by vineyards in a hilly landscape dotted with villages, castles and caves. Good facilities for boating etc.
➲ *SW via D8.*
Apr-15 Oct 1HEC ⬜ 🔱 🏕 🍽 ✕ ⊙ 🚿 🖉 Å ⁀ R 🏷 ⊞ lau ➟ ✕
Prices: ♙17-19 pitch 25-30

ANGLES TARN

▮Manoir de Boutaric rte de Lacabarede ☎ 563709606
Site lies in the grounds of an old Manor House in the heart of the Haute Languedoc region.
➲ *S of village, on D52 towards Lacabarède.*
Etr-mid Oct 3HEC ⬜ 🔱 🏕 🍽 ✕ ⊙ 🚿 🏠 🚽 ⁀ P 🏷 ⊞ lau ➟ 🛒 🖉 🚻 ⁀LR
Prices: pitch 130 (incl 2 persons)

ANGLET PYRÉNÉES-ATLANTIQUES

Parme Quartier Brindos ☎ 559230300
In a wooded area with good facilities on the outskirts of Biarritz.
➲ *3km SW off N10*
All year 4HEC ⬜ 🔱 🏕 🛒 🍽 ✕ ⊙ 🚿 🖉 🚻 🏠 🚽 ⁀ P 🏷 ⊞ lau ➟ ⁀L

ANGOISSE DORGOGNE

Rouffiac en Périgord ☎ 553526879
May-Sep 6HEC ⬜ 🔱 🏕 🛒 🍽 ✕ ⊙ 🚿 🖉 🚻 ⁀ L 🏷 lau

ARCACHON GIRONDE

Camping Club d'Arcachon av de la Galaxie, Les Abatilles ☎ 556832415
In a delightful wooded position 800mtrs from the town and 1km from the beaches.
➲ *1.5 km S.*
All year 6HEC ∷ 🔱 🏕 🛒 🍽 ✕ ⊙ 🚿 🖉 🚻 🏠 🚽 ⁀ P 🏷 ⊞ lau ➟ ⁀S

ARCIZANS-AVANT HAUTES-PYRÉNÉES

Lac ☎ 562970188
Set in delightful Pyrenean surroundings on outskirts of village. Lakeside site close to a château.
➲ *S on N21 take D13 through St-Savin.*
Jun-Sep 2.7HEC ⬜ 🔱 🏕 ⊙ 🚿 🚽 ⁀ P 🏷 ⊞ lau ➟ 🍽 ✕ 🚻
Prices: ♙25 pitch 26

ARÈS GIRONDE

Abberts ☎ 556602680
Camping Card Compulsory.
➲ *Follow signs from D106.*
10 May-Sep 2HEC ⬜ ∷ 🔱 🏕 🛒 🍽 ✕ ⊙ 🚿 🖉 🚽 ⊞ lau ➟ 🖉 🚻 ⁀LPS

Canadienne rte de Lège, 82 r du Gl-de-Gaulle ☎ 556602491
A family site surrounded by pine and oak trees with good
facilities.
➲ *1 km N off D106.*
Apr-20 Oct 2HEC ⊷ ♦♠⚓♥✗⊙🅿🅿∅⚏🏠🏪⚡ P 🎫⊞
lau ♦🔥⚓S
Prices: pitch 72-120 (incl 2 persons)

Cigale rte de Lège ☎ 556602259
Clean tidy site with good recreational facilities amongst pine
trees. Grassy pitches.
➲ *0.5 km N on D106 between the sea and the Arcachon Basin.*
Apr-10 Oct 2.5HEC ⊷ ⚓♠⚓♥✗⊙🅿🅿⚡ P 🎫⊞ lau ♦
∅⚏⚓L
Prices: ♠50-60

CM Goëlands av de la Libération ☎ 556825564
Situated among oak trees 200mtrs from the beach with good
facilities.
➲ *1.7km SE*
Apr-Sep 10HEC ⊷ ⋮⋮⋮ ♦♠⚓♥✗⊙🅿🅿∅⚏🅰🎫⊞ lau ♦
⚓LP
Prices: pitch 30.50-56.50 (incl 2 persons)
See advertisement on page 107

Pasteur 1 r du Pilote ☎ 556603333
➲ *S of D3, 300m from the sea.*
Apr-Sep 1HEC ⊷ ⚓♠⚓✗⊙🅿⚏🏠🏪⚡ P 🎫⊞ lau ♦⚓S
Prices: pitch 69-88 (incl 2 persons)

▶ ARGELÈS-GAZOST HAUTES-PYRÉNÉES
At AGOS-VIDALOS(5km NE)

Soleil du Pibeste ☎ 562975323
In a beautiful wooded setting in the heart of the Pyrenees.
➲ *S on N21.*
All year 1.5HEC ⊷ ♦♠⚓♥✗⊙🅿🅿⚏🏠⚡ P 🎫⊞ lau
♦✗⚓R
Prices: pitch 80-86

▶ ARREAU HAUTES-PYRÉNÉES

Refuge International rte Internationale ☎ 562986334
Enclosed terrace site.
➲ *2km N on D929.*
All year 15HEC ⊷ ♦♠✗⊙🅿🏠🏪⚡ PR 🎫⊞ lau ♦🔥
✗∅⚏⚓L

▶ ASCAIN PYRÉNÉES-ATLANTIQUES

Nivelle ☎ 559540194
➲ *2km N of town on D918 to St-Jean-de-Luz.*
15 Jun-15 Sep 3HEC ⊷ ♦♠⚓♥✗⊙🅿🅿∅🏠⚡ R 🎫⊞
lau ♦ ⚓LPS
Prices: ♠18.50 pitch 30

▶ ASCARAT PYRÉNÉES-ATLANTIQUES

Europ' Camping ☎ 559371278
In rustic surroundings of mountains and vineyards, 300m
from the River Nive.
➲ *1km W of St-Jean-Pied-de-Port on D918.*
10 Apr-15 Oct 1.7HEC ⊷ ⚓♠⚓♥✗⊙🅿∅⚓ P 🎫⊞ lau
♦⚓RS
Prices: ♠32 pitch 46

▶ AUREILHAN LANDES

CM 1001 promenade de l'Étang ☎ 558091088
Quiet site separated by a small road on the banks of Lake
Aureilhan.
➲ *D626, 2km before Mimizan, on the right.*
17 May-21 Sep 7HEC ⊷ ⚓♠⚓♥⊙🅿🅿⚓ L 🎫⊞ lau ♦
✗

Parc Saint James Eurolac Promenade de l'Étang
☎ 558090287
Well tended site under deciduous trees providing shade,
partially on open meadow.
➲ *Turn right at Labouheyre off N10 on D626 to Aureilhan.
Follow signs.*
Apr-29 Sep 13HEC ⊷ ♦🔥⚓♥✗⊙🅿🅿∅🏠🏪🅰⚓ LP 🎫
⊞ lau
Prices: pitch 65-120 (incl 2 persons)
See advertisement under Colour Section

▶ AZUR LANDES

CM d'Azur Au bord du lac ☎ 558483072
A family site in wooded surroundings close to the Lac de
Soustons and 8km form the coast.
➲ *2 km S of Azur.*
Jun-15 Sep 7HEC ⊷ ⋮⋮⋮ ⚓♠⚓♥✗⊙🅿🅿∅⚏🏠🏪⚓
LR 🎫⊞ lau
Prices: ♠15.50 pitch 27

▶ BAGNÈRES-DE-BIGORRE HAUTES-PYRÉNÉES

Bigourdan rte de Tarbes ☎ 562951357
A level site recommended for caravans in a beautiful
Pyrenean setting.
➲ *2.5km NW at Pouzac.*
All year 1HEC ⊷ ♦♠⊙🅿🏠🏪⚓ P 🎫⊞ lau ♦🔥✗∅⚏
⚓R⊞
Prices: ♠20.50 pitch 21

Tilleuls rte de Sabassère ☎ 562952604
May-Sep 2.6HEC ⊷ ♦♠⊙🅿∅⚏🏠 lau ♦⚓P⊞
Prices: pitch 83.20 (incl 2 persons)

▶ At TRÉBONS(4km N on D935)

Parc des Oiseaux ☎ 562953026
Clean, well-kept site with large pitches.
All year 2.8HEC ⊷ ♦♠⚓♥✗⊙🅿🅿∅⚏🏠🏪🎫⊞ lau ♦🔥✗⚓P
Prices: ♠18-20 🚗9-10 🚐9-10 ▲9-10

▶ BASTIDE-DE-SEROU, LA ARIÈGE

Arize rte de Nescus ☎ 561658151
A well run site with a wide range of facilities in a peaceful,
wooded location at the foot of the Pyrénées.
Mar-Oct 1.4HEC ⊷ ⚓♠⊙🅿🏠🏪⚓ PR 🎫⊞ lau ♦🔥♥
✗∅⚏
Prices: pitch 67-95 (incl 2 persons)

▶ BAYONNE PYRÉNÉES-ATLANTIQUES

Airotel la Chêneraie chemin de Cazenare ☎ 559550131
On gently sloping field divided by hedges.
➲ *4km NE off N117 (Pau) road.*
Etr-1 Oct 10HEC ⊷ ♦♠♥✗⊙🅿🅿∅🏠🅰⚓ LP 🎫 lau
Prices: ♠18-26 pitch 43-80

▶ BEAUCENS-LES-BAINS HAUTES-PYRÉNÉES

Viscos ☎ 562970545
In a secluded location at the foot of the Pyrénées.
➲ *1km N on D13, rte de Lourdes.*
15 May-Sep 2HEC ⊷ ♦♠⚓⊙🅿∅🎫⊞ lau ♦♥✗
Prices: ♠17 pitch 16

▶ BELVÈS DORDOGNE

🏠 Hauts de Ratebout ☎ 553290210
A well equipped site on an old Périgord farm, set in extensive
grounds on top of a hill.
➲ *D710 to Fumel. After Vaurez-de-Belvès, take D54 to Casals.*
May-11 Sep 12HEC ⊷ ⚓♠⚓♥✗⊙🅿🅿∅⚏🏠🏪⚓ P 🎫⊞
🍴 lau
Prices: pitch 81-135 (incl 2 persons)

Moulin de la Pique ☎ 553290115
A quiet well equipped site set out around an imposing villa and a small lake. There are fine entertainment facilities and modern sanitary installations.
➲ *500m S on D710.*
24 Apr-31-Oct 12HEC ⊞ ♣ ↑ 🐟 ♥ ✕ ⊙ 🖵 🖉 ⛺ 🛒 ▲ ↘ P ☎ ⊞ lau
Prices: ↑26.40-33 pitch 43.60-54.50

Nauves Bos Rouge ☎ 553291264
Located on a site of 40 hectares surrounded by forest
➲ *4.5km SW via D53.*
May-15 Sep 40HEC ⊞ ♀ ↑ ♥ ✕ ⊙ 🖵 🛒 ↘ P ☎ ⊞ lau
Prices: ↑20-23 pitch 30-35

▶ **BEYNAC-ET-CAZENAC** DORDOGNE

Capeyrou ☎ 553295495
Situated beside the River Dordogne close to the gates of the picturesque medieval town of Beynac.
➲ *Access via D703.*
15 May-15 Sep 5HEC ⊞ ♣ ↑ ♥ ✕ ⊙ 🖵 ↘ P ☎ ⊞ lau ♣ 🐟 🖉 ⛱ ↘R
Prices: ↑22 pitch 30

▶ **BEZ, LE** TARN

Plô ☎ 563740082
A pleasant site in wooded surroundings.
➲ *0.9km W via D30.*
2 Jul-Sep 2HEC ⊞ ♀ ↑ ⊙ 🖵 🖲 ☎ ⊞ lau ♣ 🐟 ♥ ✕ ⛱
Prices: ↑11 ♣5 🚐15 ▲10

▶ **BIARRITZ** PYRÉNÉES-ATLANTIQUES

Biarritz 28 r d'Harcet ☎ 559230012
A pleasant site with spacious pitches 200m from beach.
➲ *2km from town centre on N10, follow signs 'Espagne'.*
May-28 Sep 3HEC ⊞ ♣ ↑ 🐟 ♥ ✕ ⊙ 🖵 🖉 ↘ P ☎ ⊞ ⊗ lau ♣ ⛱ ↘S

▶ At **ARCANGUES**(4km S on D254)

Aldabénia ☎ 559430730
➲ *4km from beaches.*
Jun-Sep 1HEC ⊞ ♣ ↑ ⊙ 🖵 🖉 🛒 ▲ ☎ ⊞ lau ♣ ♥ ✕ ⛱ ↘R

▶ At **BIDART**(4km SW)

Berrua rte d'Arbonne ☎ 59549666
A well equipped family site 1km from the beach and 500mtrs from the village.
Apr-Sep 5HEC ⊞ ♣ ↑ 🐟 ♥ ✕ ⊙ 🖵 🖉 ⛺ 🛒 ↘ P ☎ ⊞ lau ♣ ↘LS
Prices: pitch 70-112 (incl 2 persons)

Jean Paris Quartier M-Pierre ☎ 559265558
600m from beaches.
➲ *S of town, cross railway line, site on S side of N10.*
Jun-Sep 1HEC ⊞ ♣ ↑ 🐟 ♥ ✕ ⊙ 🖵 🛒 ☎ ⊞ lau ♣ ✕ ⛱ ↘S

Oyam Ferme Oyamburua ☎ 359549161
Level meadow site near farm. Views of the Pyrénées. Simple but pleasant site.
➲ *Turn off beyond the church in the direction of Arbonne, via N10, for a pprox 1km.*
Jun-Sep 5HEC ⊞ ♣ ↑ ♥ ✕ ⊙ 🖵 ⛺ 🛒 ↘ P ☎ ⊞ lau ♣ 🐟 🖉 ↘S
Prices: pitch 60-106 (incl 2 persons)

Pavillon Royal av Prince de Galles ☎ 559230054
Beautiful, well-kept site, divided into pitches, most of which have open view of sea. Beside rocky beach.

➲ *2 km N.*
15 May-25 Sep 5HEC ░░░ ♀ ↑ 🐟 ♥ ✕ ⊙ 🖵 🖉 ↘ PS ☎ ⊞ ⊗ lau

Résidence des Pins rte de Biarritz ☎ 559230029
Terraced site with numbered pitches, 800m from sea.
➲ *2km N on N106 Biarritz road.*
25 May-Sep 6HEC ⊞ ♣ ↑ 🐟 ♥ ✕ ⊙ 🖵 🛒 ↘ P ☎ ⊞ lau ♣ ↘LS
Prices: pitch 80-128 (incl 2 persons)

▶ **Ruisseau** rte d'Arbonne ☎ 559419450
A well equipped site in wooded surroundings set out around two lakes.
➲ *2km E on D255.*
8 May-9 Sep 15HEC ⊞ ♀ ↑ 🐟 ♥ ✕ ⊙ 🖵 🖉 ⛺ 🛒 ↘ LP ☎ ⊞ lau
Prices: pitch 115 (incl 2 persons)

Ur-Onéa r de la Chapelle ☎ 559265361
A well equipped site lying at the foot of the Pyrénées with good recreational facilities.
➲ *0.6km E.*
4 Apr-27 Sep 5HEC ⊞ ♣ ↑ 🐟 ♥ ✕ ⊙ 🖵 🖉 ⛺ 🛒 ↘ P ☎ ☎ ⊞ lau ♣ ✕ ⛱ ↘RS
Prices: pitch 59-125 (incl 2 persons)

▶ **BIAS** LANDES

CM Le Tatiou ☎ 558090476
➲ *2km W towards Lespecier*
Etr-Oct 10HEC ⊞ ♣ ↑ 🐟 ♥ ✕ ⊙ 🖵 ⛺ 🛒 ↘ P ☎ ⊞ lau
Prices: pitch 67 (incl 2 persons)

▶ **BIRON** DORDOGNE

Moulinal ☎ 553408460
In a pleasant situation beside a lake close to the former mill of Biron Castle. This is a modern holiday village with a wide variety of recreational facilities.
➲ *2km S on the Lacapelle-Biron road.*
11 May-12 Sep 10HEC ⊞ ♀ ↑ 🐟 ♥ ✕ ⊙ 🖵 ⛱ 🛒 ▲ ↘ LP ☎ ⊞ lau

▶ **BISCARROSSE** LANDES

Bimbo 176 chemin de Bimbo ☎ 558098233
In delightful wooded surroundings 500mtrs from the lake and 10 minutes from the sea. Reservations recommended.
➲ *3.5km N towards Sanguinet.*
All year 6HEC ⊞ ♣ ↑ 🐟 ♥ ✕ ⊙ 🖵 🖉 ⛺ 🛒 ↘ P ☎ ⊞ lau ♣ ↘L
Prices: ↑30 pitch 40

Rive rte de Bordeaux ☎ 558781233
Level site in tall pine forest on E side of lake. Private port and beach.
➲ *N of town off D652 Sanguinet road.*
Apr-Oct 15HEC ⊞ ░░░ ♣ ↑ 🐟 ♥ ✕ ⊙ 🖵 ⛱ ⛺ 🛒 ↘ LP ⊞ lau
Prices: pitch 135-145 (incl 2 persons)

▶ **BLAYE** GIRONDE

▶ At **MAZION**(5.5km NE on N937)

Tilleuls ☎ 557421813
Camping Card Compulsory.
➲ *5.5km NE on N937.*
May-Oct 0.5HEC ⊞ ♣ ↑ ⊙ 🖵 ☎ ⊞ lau
Prices: ↑20-22 ♣15-16 🚐15-16 ▲12

▶ **BOURNEL** LOT-ET-GARONNE

Ferme de Bourgade ☎ 553366715
A small, tranquil site with good, clean facilities. *Contd.*

➡ *Signposted from N21 between Castillonnès and Villeréal.*
15 Apr-15 Oct 1HEC ⛭ ♦ ⋒ 🚻 ⚑ ☷ ⊞ lau ➡ ♀ ✗
Prices: ♠10 ⇢10 ⊡10 ▲10

❱ BRETENOUX LOT

Bourgnatelle ☎ 565384407
In a pleasant location beside the River Cére. Separate car
park for arrivals after 22.30hrs.
➡ *Access via D940 towards Rocamadour.*
May-15 Sep 2HEC ⛭ ♦ ⋒ ⊙ ⚑ ∅ ⚑ ⅞ R ☷ ⊞ lau ➡ ⅞ ♀
✗ ⅜ ⅞P

❱ BUGUE, LE DORDOGNE

St-Avit Loisirs St-Avit-de-Vialard ☎ 553026400
A pleasant site in natural wooded surroundings.
➡ *W of town via C201.*
11 Apr-Sep 42HEC ⛭ ⅌ ⋒ 🚻 ♀ ✗ ⊙ ⚑ ∅ ⅜ ⚑ ⅞ P ☷ ⊞
lau ➡ ⅞R
Prices: ♠22-37 pitch 34.60-95

❱ At LIMEUIL(5.5km SW by D703 and D31)

Port de Limeuil allés sur Dordogne ☎ 553632976
In a wooded area adjacent to the confluence of the Rivers
Dordogne and Vezère and facing Limeuil.
May-15 Oct 7HEC ∷∵ ♦ ⋒ 🚻 ♀ ✗ ⊙ ⚑ ∅ ⚑ ⅞ R ☷ ⊞ lau
➡ ✗ ⅜
Prices: pitch 99 (incl 2 persons)

❱ CAHORS LOT

Rivière de Cabessut r de la Rivière ☎ 565300630
➡ *N of town via the Cabessut Bridge over the River Lot.*
Apr-Oct 3HEC ⛭ ♦ ⋒ 🚻 ♀ ✗ ⊙ ⚑ ∅ ⚑ ⅞ PR ☷ ⊞ lau ➡
✗ ⅜
Prices: ♠12 pitch 50

❱ At ESCLAUZELS(18km SE)

Pompit ☎ 565315340
Situated in the heart of a large forest close to the magnificent
Lot Valley.
➡ *5km NW of Esclauzels village.*
Apr-15 Sep 4HEC ⛭ ⚴ ♦ ⋒ 🚻 ♀ ✗ ⊙ ⚑ ∅ ⚑ ⚑ ⅞ P ☷ ⊞
lau
Prices: ♠22 pitch 22

❱ CALVIAC LOT

Chênes Verts rte de Sarlat, Souillac ☎ 553592107
May-Sep 6HEC ⛭ ♦ ⋒ 🚻 ♀ ✗ ⊙ ⚑ ∅ ⚑ ⅞ P ☷ ⊞ lau ➡
⅞LR
Prices: ♠20-25 pitch 33.60-42

Trois Sources Le Peyratel ☎ 565330301
Wooded location, family site with plenty of leisure facilities.
➡ *Access via D653, then D25 to Calviac.*
May-Sep 6.4HEC ⛭ ∷∵ ♦ ⋒ 🚻 ♀ ✗ ⊙ ⚑ ∅ ⚑ ⅞ LPR ☷
⊞ lau
Prices: ♠32 pitch 37

❱ CAMBO-LES-BAINS PYRÉNÉES-ATLANTIQUES

Brixta Eder rte de St-Jean-de-Luz ☎ 559299423
Modern site with good sports facilities.
➡ *Near the junction of D932 and D10.*
15 Apr-15 Oct 1HEC ⛭ ⚴ ♦ ⋒ ⊙ ⚑ ☷ lau ➡ ⅞ ♀ ✗ ∅
⅞LP ⊞

❱ CAPBRETON LANDES

Pointe av J-Castigan ☎ 558721498
Family site in a wooded location on the banks of a river,
800mtrs from the sea. Good recreational facilities.
➡ *2km S towards Labenne on N652.*

Jun-Sep 4.5HEC ∷∵ ♦ ⋒ 🚻 ♀ ✗ ⊙ ⚑ ∅ ⅞ R ☷ ⚑ ⊞ lau ➡
⅞S

❱ CAP FERRET GIRONDE

Truc Vert rte Forestière ☎ 556608955
In a very pleasant location on a slope in a pine wood.
➡ *On D106 in the direction of Cap Ferret to Petit Piquey.*
Turn right and follow signs.
May-Sep 11HEC ∷∵ ⅌ ⋒ 🚻 ♀ ✗ ⊙ ⚑ ∅ ⅜ ⊞ lau ➡ ⅞S
Prices: ♠25 ⊡58 ▲58

❱ CARLUCET LOT

Château de Lacomté ☎ 565387546
In wooded surroundings with good sized pitches and a
variety of recreational facilities.
➡ *Follow signposts from D677/D32.*
Feb 11HEC ⛭ ⚴ ⅌ ⋒ 🚻 ♀ ✗ ⊙ ⚑ ⚑ ▲ ⅞ P ☷ ⊞ lau

❱ CASTELJALOUX LOT-ET-GARONNE

Club de Clarens rte de Mont-de-Marsan ☎ 553930745
A large site with direct access to a 17 hectare Lac de Clarens
and good recreational facilities.
Apr-Sep 2HEC ∷∵ ⅌ ⋒ ♀ ✗ ⊙ ⚑ ⚑ ⚑ ⅞ LR ☷ ⊞ lau
➡ ⅞ ✗

Prices: pitch 26

CM de la Piscine rte de Marmande ☎ 553935468
➡ *NW on D933 Marmande road.*
Mar-Oct 1HEC ⛭ ♦ ⋒ ⊙ ⚑ ⅞ P ☷ lau ➡ ⅞ ♀ ✗ ∅ ⅜
⅞LR ⊞
Prices: ♠11 pitch 21

❱ CASTELNAUD-LA-CHAPELLE DORDOGNE

Maisonneuve ☎ 553295129
In picturesque surroundings, 800mtrs from the village, close
to the River Céou in the heart of the Périgord Noir region.
➡ *10kms S of Sarlat on D57.*
Apr-Oct 6HEC ⛭ ♦ ⋒ 🚻 ♀ ✗ ⊙ ⚑ ∅ ⚑ ⅞ PR ☷ ⊞ lau
Prices: pitch 26.60-38

❱ CAUNEILLE LANDES

Sources ☎ 558730440
➡ *N of town, 200m from N117.*
May-Sep 1.5HEC ⛭ ⚴ ⋒ 🚻 ♀ ✗ ⊙ ⚑ ⅜ ⚑ ⚑ ⅞ P ☷ ⊞
lau ➡ ✗ ⅞LR

❱ CAUTERETS HAUTES-PYRÉNÉES

Mamelon-Vert 32 av du Mamelon-Vert ☎ 562925156
In a beautiful wooded mountain setting close to the local
winter sports facilities.
Closed Oct-10 Nov 2HEC ⛭ ⅌ ⊙ ⚑ ☷ ⊞ lau ➡ ⅞ ♀ ✗
∅ ⅜ ⅞PR
Prices: pitch 53-67 (incl 2 persons)

❱ CLAOUEY GIRONDE

Airotel les Viviers rte du Cap Ferret ☎ 56607004
Beautiful, widespread site in a forest divided by seawater
channels.
➡ *On the D106, 1km S of the town.*
May-Sep 33HEC ∷∵ ♦ ⋒ 🚻 ♀ ✗ ⊙ ⚑ ⚑ ⚑ ⅞ L ☷ ⊞ lau
➡ 🚻 ♀ ✗ ∅
Prices: pitch 85-166 (incl 3 persons)

See advertisement under Colour Section

❱ CONTIS-PLAGE LANDES

Lous Seurrots ☎ 558428582
Well equipped site in a pine forest on outskirts of village
between road and stream.
➡ *Access via D41.*

Apr-Sep 15HEC ∷ ♦ ↿ ⚍ ⚑ ✗ ☉ ⛊ ⌀ ⛺ ⛫ ⚓ PRS ⊡ ⊞ lau
Prices: pitch 78-128 (incl 2 persons)

▶ CORDES TARN

Moulin de Julien ☎ 563561110
In a beautiful valley with good pitches for caravans and tents and plenty of modern facilities.
➔ *900m E on D600 and D922.*
Apr-Sep 7HEC ⚏ ♦ ↿ ⚑ ☉ ⛊ ⌀ ⛺ ⛫ ⚓ P ⊡ ⊞ lau

▶ COUX-ET-BIGAROUQE DORDOGNE

Valades Les Valades ☎ 553291427
In wooded surroundings within a pleasant valley. Well equipped pitches available.
➔ *5km N of town off N703.*
Mar-Nov 11HEC ⚏ ♦ ↿ ⚍ ⚑ ✗ ☉ ⛊ ⛺ ⛫ ⚓ L ⊡ ⊞ lau
Prices: ♦20 pitch 28

▶ DAGLAN DORDOGNE

Moulin de Paulhiac ☎ 553282088
In picturesque wooded surroundings with wide, well marked pitches and good, modern facilities.
➔ *4km N via D57 beside the Céou*
20 May-15 Sep 5HEC ⚏ ♦ ↿ ⚍ ⚑ ✗ ☉ ⛊ ⌀ ⛺ ⛫ ⚓ PR ⊡ ⊞ lau
Prices: ♦21-30 pitch 30.10-43

▶ DAX LANDES

Chênes Au Bois-de-Boulogne ☎ 558900553
In a wooded park on the edge of the Bois de Boulogne with good facilities.
➔ *1.5km W of town beside River Adour.*
End Mar-early Nov 5HEC ⚏ ♦ ↿ ⚍ ☉ ⛊ ⌀ ⛺ ⚓ P ⊡ ⊞ lau ♦ ⚍ ✗
Prices: ♦18 pitch 41-69

▶ DURAS LOT-ET-GARONNE

Moulin de Borie Neuve Moulin de Borie Neuve ☎ 553947657
A pleasant site in the Dourdèze valley close to an old mill.
➔ *Access via D244 towards St-Astier-de-Duras.*
15 Apr-15 Oct 1HEC ⚏ ⚎ ↿ ☉ ⛊ ⛫ ⚓ R ⊡ ⊞ lau ♦ ⚍ ✗ ⌀ ⚓LP
Prices: ♦14 pitch 16

▶ DURAVEL LOT

Club de Vacances Port de Vire ☎ 565246506
A pleasant site with good facilities beside the River Lot.
Camping Card Compulsory
➔ *2.3km S via D58.*
26 Apr-Sep 7HEC ⚏ ⚎ ↿ ⚍ ✗ ☉ ⛊ ⌀ ⚍ ⛺ ⛫ ⚓ PR ⊡ ⊞ lau

▶ DURFORT ARIÈGE

Bourdieu ☎ 561673017
Well equipped site in a picturesque setting with fine views over the Pyrénées.
➔ *Off D14 Le Fossat-Saverdun.*
All year 20HEC ⚏ ♦ ↿ ⚍ ✗ ☉ ⛊ ⛺ ⛫ ⚓ P ⊡ ⊞ lau

▶ ÉYZIES-DE-TAYAC, LES DORDOGNE

▶ At SIREUIL(7km E off D47)

Mas ☎ 553296806
Forested site on a farm with a direct sales shop selling farm and local produce.
➔ *N of D47 (Sarlat-Les Éyzies).*
15 May-Sep 5HEC ⚏ ⚎ ↿ ⚍ ✗ ☉ ⛊ ⌀ ⛺ ⚓ P ⊡ ⊞ lau

▶ FOIX ARIÈGE

Lac RN 20 ☎ 561651158
On well-kept meadow beside the Lac de Labarre.
➔ *3km N on N20.*
Apr-Oct 5HEC ⚏ ♦ ↿ ☉ ⛊ ⌀ ⚓ LPR ⊡ lau ♦ ⚍
Prices: pitch 45-65 (incl 2 persons)

▶ GAUGEAC DORDOGNE

Moulin de David ☎ 553226525
Situated in a wooded valley alongside a small stream with well defined pitches and good recreational facilities.
➔ *3km from town towards Villeréal.*
16 May-12 Sep 14HEC ⚏ ♦ ↿ ⚍ ✗ ☉ ⛊ ⌀ ⛺ ⛫ ⚓ LPR ⊡ ⊞ lau
Prices: ♦20-33.50 pitch 24.50-45

▶ GOURDON LOT

Paradis La Peyrugue ☎ 565416501
On a pleasant wooded meadow surrounded by hills.
➔ *1.6km SW off N673.*
Jun-15 Sep 2HEC ⚏ ⚎ ↿ ☉ ⛊ ⛺ ⛫ ⚓ LP ⊡ ⊞ lau ♦ ⚍ ⚍ ✗ ⌀ ⚎ ⚓L
Prices: ♦27 pitch 17

▶ At GROLÉJAC(15km N on D704)

Granges ☎ 553281115
Beautifully situated terraces on a hill with big pitches. The site has been constructed around a disused railway station, incorporating the old ticket office and the bridge into its modern design. Facilities for sports and entertainment.
➔ *Turn off D704 in village towards Domme.*
2 May-20 Sep 6.5HEC ⚏ ⚎ ↿ ✗ ☉ ⛊ ⛺ ⚓ PR ⊡ ⊞ lau ♦ ⚍ ⚓L
Prices: pitch 149-189 (incl 2 persons)

▶ At ST-MARTIAL-DE-NABIRAT(6km W)

Carbonnier ☎ 553284253
Family site in a small, wooded valley with a variety of recreational facilities.
➔ *Off the D46.*
Etr-15 Sep 8HEC ⚏ ♦ ↿ ⚍ ✗ ☉ ⛊ ⌀ ⛺ ⛫ ⚓ LP ⊡ ⊞ lau
Prices: ♦21-33 pitch 30-42

▶ GOURETTE PYRÉNÉES-ATLANTIQUES

Ley ☎ 559051147
Terraced site with gravel and asphalt caravan pitches. TV, common room.
➔ *From Laruns drive E to Eaux-Bonnes and drive uphill to Gourette.*

Contd.

15 Dec-30 Apr & Jun-15 Sep 2HEC ▥ ☀ ⋔ ⚤ ✕ ⊙ ⌺ ♨
♠ ⌺ ⁎ R ▣ ⊞ lau ➡ ⅃ ∅
Prices: pitch 50 (incl 2 persons) pp20

▶ **GRAULGES, LES** DORDOGNE

Graulges ☎ 553607473
In a picturesque setting in woodland beside a lake.
➲ *Off D939 between Angoulême and Périgueux.*
Mar-Oct 8HEC ▥ ♠ ⋔ ⚤ ⚥ ✕ ⊙ ⌺ ♨ ⁎ P ▣ ⊞
Prices: ♠16 pitch 27

▶ **GRISOLLES** TARN-ET-GARONNE

Aquitaine rte Nationale 20 ☎ 563673322
➲ *1.5km N off 'X' roads N20/N113.*
15 May-15 Oct 3HEC ▥ ♠ ⋔ ⊙ ⌺ ♨ ⌺ ⁎ P ▣ ⊞ lau ➡ ⅃
⚥ ✕ ∅ ⋒ ⁎LR

▶ **GUJAN-MESTRAS** GIRONDE

Plage La Hume ☎ 556661215
May-Sep 3.5HEC ▥ ⍾ ⋔ ⚥ ✕ ⊙ ⌺ ♨ ▣ ⊞ lau ➡ ⅃ ✕ ∅
⁎S

▶ **HASPARREN** PYRÉNÉES-ATLANTIQUES

Chapital rte de Cambo ☎ 559296294
➲ *0.5km W via D22.*
Etr-Oct 2.6HEC ▥ ⍾ ⋔ ⊙ ⌺ ∅ ♨ ▣ ⊞ lau ➡ ⅃ ⌬ ⁎P

▶ **HAUTEFORT** DORDOGNE

Moulin des Loisirs Le Coucou ☎ 553504655
➲ *2km SW via D72 & D71, 100m from Coucou lake.*
Etr-Sep 4HEC ▥ ♠ ⋔ ⚤ ⚥ ✕ ⊙ ⌺ ♨ ⁎ P ▣ ⊞ lau ➡ ∅

▶ **HENDAYE** PYRÉNÉES-ATLANTIQUES

Acacias ☎ 559207876
A pleasant family site in parkland, 5 minutes from the beach.
➲ *1.8km E (rte de la Glacière).*
Apr-Sep 5HEC ▥ ♠ ⋔ ⚥ ✕ ⊙ ⌺ ♨ ⌬ ⌺ ⁎ LP ▣ ⊞ lau ➡ ⅃
✕ ⁎S
Prices: pitch 79-92 (incl 2 persons)

Airotel Eskualduna rte de la Corniche (D-912) ☎ 559200464
On gently sloping meadow.
➲ *2km from village on N10c.*
15 Jun-Sep 8HEC ▥ ♠ ⋔ ⚤ ⚥ ✕ ⊙ ⌺ ∅ ⌺ ⁎ R ▣ lau ➡ ✕
⌬ ⁎PS ⊞

▶ **HOURTIN** GIRONDE

Acacia Ste-Hélène ☎ 556738080
Pleasant, quiet site on the edge of a forest with good sanitary
facilities. Compulsory car park for arrivals after 2330hrs.
➲ *Off D3 towards the lake.*
15 Jun-15 Sep 5HEC ▥ ⍾ ⋔ ⊙ ⌺ ♨ ▣ ⊞ 🄿 lau ➡ ⁎L
Prices: ♠17 pitch 15

Mariflaude ☎ 556091197
Level meadowland, shaded by pines, in rural setting 2km
from one of the biggest lakes in the country.
➲ *Turn onto D4 at the chemist and continue E towards
Pauillac.*
15 May-15 Sep 6.5HEC ▥ ⍾ ⋔ ⚤ ⚥ ✕ ⊙ ⌺ ∅ ⌬ ⁎ P
⊞ lau ➡ ⁎L
Prices: ♠16-20 pitch 48-60

Orée du Bois rte d'Aquitaine ☎ 556091588
In a quiet, wooded location with good facilities.
➲ *1500m from town centre beside the lake.*
Jun-15 Sep 2HEC ⫶⫶⫶ ⍾ ⋔ ⚤ ⚥ ✕ ⊙ ⌺ ∅ ⌬ ⁎ P ▣ ⊞ lau
➡ ⁎LR

Ourmes av du Lac ☎ 556091276
In wooded surroundings close to the beach and 500mtrs
from the largest freshwater lake in France.
➲ *Follow D4 towards lake.*
Apr-Sep 7HEC ▥ ⍾ ⋔ ⚤ ⚥ ✕ ⊙ ⌺ ∅ ⌬ ⌺ ⁎ P ▣ lau ➡ ⌬
⁎L ⊞
Prices: pitch 110 (incl 2 persons)

▶ **HOURTIN-PLAGE** GIRONDE

Côte d'Argent ☎ 556091025
In a pine and oak forest 500m from beach with good
facilities.
➲ *Access via D101 from Hourtin.*
15 May-15 Sep 20HEC ⫶⫶⫶ ♠ ⋔ ⚤ ⚥ ✕ ⊙ ⌺ ∅ ⌬ ⌺ ⁎ S ▣
⊞ lau

▶ **HUME, LA** GIRONDE
▶ At **TESTE, LA** (3km SW)

Village de Loisirs Domaine de la Forge rte Sanguinet
☎ 556660772
Secluded site in very quiet woodland.
➲ *3km S on D652.*
All year 8.5HEC ▥ ⫶⫶⫶ ♠ ⋔ ⚤ ⚥ ✕ ⊙ ⌺ ⌬ ⌺ ⁎ P ▣ 🄿 ⊞ lau
➡ ⁎R

▶ **LABENNE** LANDES

Savane av de l'Océan ☎ 559454113
➲ *On RN10.*
All year 7HEC ▥ ♠ ⋔ ⚥ ✕ ⊙ ⌺ ⌬ Å ▣ lau ➡ ⅃ ∅ ⌬
⁎LRS ⊞

▶ **LABENNE-OCÉAN** LANDES

Boudigau ☎ 559454207
Situated in pine forest.
➲ *Turn right into site after bridge.*
15 May-15 Sep 6HEC ▥ ⍾ ⋔ ⚤ ⚥ ✕ ⊙ ⌺ ∅ ⌬ ⌺ ⁎ P
⊞ lau ➡ ⁎S
Prices: pitch 80-145

Côte d'Argent av de l'Océan ☎ 559454202
Very well-managed modern site attached to holiday village.
➲ *3km W on D126.*
Apr-Oct 4HEC ▥ ⫶⫶⫶ ♠ ⋔ ⚤ ⚥ ✕ ⊙ ⌺ ⌬ ⌬ ⌺ ⁎ P ▣ 🄿 ⊞
lau ➡ ⅃ ∅ ⁎RS
Prices: pitch 50-101 (incl 2 persons)

Mer rte de la Plage ☎ 559454209
In a pine forest 700mtrs from the beach.
➲ *On D126 (rte de la Plage).*
May-Sep 5.5HEC ▥ ⫶⫶⫶ ♠ ⋔ ⚥ ✕ ⊙ ⌺ ∅ ⌬ ⁎ PR ▣ ⊞
lau ➡ ⁎S
Prices: pitch 45-92 (incl 2 persons)

Sylvamar av de l'Océan ☎ 559457516
➲ *Access via D126.*
20 May-20 Sep 14.5HEC ▥ ⫶⫶⫶ ♠ ⋔ ⚥ ✕ ⊙ ⌺ ⌬ ⌺ ⁎ P
▣ lau ➡ ⅃ ∅ ⁎S

▶ **LACANAU-OCÉAN** GIRONDE

Airotel de l'Océan 24 r du Répos ☎ 556032445
On rising ground in pine forest. 800m from beach.
May-Sep 9.5HEC ⫶⫶⫶ ♠ ⋔ ⚤ ⚥ ✕ ⊙ ⌺ ∅ ⌬ ⌬ ⌺ Å ⁎ P
🄿 🄿 lau ➡ ⁎S
Prices: pitch 130-155 (incl 2 persons)

Grands Pins Plages Nord ☎ 556032077
On very hilly terrain in woodland. 350m from the beach,
access to which is through dunes.
➲ *Approach via exit 7 on A10, then D6 to Lacanau.*

CAMPING LE TEDEY
★★★

Route de Longarisse - 33680 Lacanau
Tel: 05.56.03.00.15 Fax: 05.56.03.01.90

Situated in 34 acres of pine forest, peace and quiet on the edge of the Lake of Lacanau. Sandy beaches, exceptional situation for children, sailing paradise, cycling paths and fishing.

Post • change • information • shop • newspapers • swimming • windsurfing • volley-ball • ping-pong • entertainment for children • bar • cinema • music garden • supermarket • take away meals • butcher's • fishmonger's • sanitary installations for disabled • mobile homes to let.

Open: 30.04 – 19.09

May-15 Sep 11HEC ⠇∴ ♣ ♠ ⛱ ♨ ✕ ☉ ♨ ∅ ⚓ ⛫ ₹ P ▣ ⊞ lau ♦ ₹S
Prices: pitch 125-166 (incl 2 persons)

▶ At **MEDOC**(8km E)

Talaris Route de l'Océan ☎ 556030415
A family site in delightful wooded surroundings 1.2km from the lake. Separate car park for arrivals after 22.30hrs.
➲ *2km E on rte de Lacanau.*
1 Jun-15 Sep 6.3HEC ⠇ ♣ ♠ ⛱ ♨ ✕ ☉ ♨ ∅ ⚓ ⛫ Å ₹ P ▣ lau ♦ ₹L ⊞
Prices: pitch 98-140 (incl 2 persons)

▶ At **MOUTCHIC**(5km E)

Lac ☎ 556030026
➲ *On D6 rte de Lacanau, 60m from lake.*
Apr-15 Oct 0.7HEC ⠇ ♣ ♠ ⛱ ♨ ✕ ☉ ♨ ∅ ⛫ ▣ ⊞ lau ♦ ✕ ₹L

Tedey rte de Longarisse ☎ 55603015
Quiet site in pine forest, on edge of Lake Lacanau. Private bathing area.
➲ *Turn off D6 and continue along narrow track through forest for 0.5km.*
30 Apr-19 Sep 14HEC ⠇∴ ♣ ♠ ⛱ ♨ ✕ ☉ ♨ ∅ ⛫ ₹L ▣ ⊞ lau
Prices: pitch 86-101 (incl 2 persons)

▶ **LACAPELLE-MARIVAL** LOT

CM Bois de Sophie Route d'Aymac ☎ 565408259
In a pleasant wooded location with a variety of sporting facilities.
➲ *1km NW via D940*

---

15 May-Sep 1HEC ⠇ ♣ ♠ ☉ ♨ ⛫ ₹ P ▣ lau ♦ ⛱ ♨ ✕ ∅ ⚓ ₹LR ⊞
Prices: ♠11-14 pitch 16-22

▶ **LANTON** GIRONDE

Roumingue ☎ 556829748
Level terrain under a few deciduous trees partially in open meadow on the Bassin d'Arcachon.
➲ *1km NW of village towards sea.*
All year 33HEC ⠇∴ ♨ ♠ ⛱ ♨ ✕ ☉ ♨ ∅ ⚓ ⛫ ₹ PS ▣ ⊞ lau ♦ ⛱ ♨
Prices: pitch 54-105 (incl 2 persons)

▶ **LARNAGOL** LOT

Ruisseau de Treil Le Ruisseau ☎ 565312339
➲ *0.6km E via D662*
Etr-Nov 4.3HEC ⠇ ♣ ♠ ⛱ ♨ ✕ ☉ ♨ ⚓ ₹ P ▣ lau ♦ ₹R
Prices: ♠29 pitch 44

▶ **LARUNS** PYRÉNÉES-ATLANTIQUES

Gaves ☎ 559053237
On the bank of the Gave d'Ossan amid beautiful Pyrenean scenery. Some pitches reserved for caravans.
➲ *1km S.*
All year 2HEC ⠇ ♨ ♠ ♨ ✕ ☉ ♨ ∅ ⚓ ⛫ ▣ ⊞ lau ♦ ⛱ ✕ ₹PR
Prices: ♠21 pitch 56

▶ **LARUSCADE** GIRONDE

Relais du Chavan ☎ 557686305
On well-kept meadow edged by a strip of forest. Some traffic noise.
➲ *6.5km NW on N10 near Km20.3.*
15 May-15 Sep 3.6HEC ⠇∴ ♨ ♠ ⛱ ♨ ✕ ☉ ♨ ∅ ⚓ ⛫ ₹ P ▣ ⊞ lau
Prices: ♠18 pitch 20

▶ **LECTOURE** GERS

Lac des Trois Vallées ☎ 562688233
This rural site is part of a large park and lies next to a lake. It has spacious marked pitches.
➲ *3km SE on N21.*
Apr-15 Sep 8HEC ⠇ ♣ ♠ ⛱ ♨ ✕ ☉ ♨ ∅ ⛫ ⚓ Å ₹ LP ▣ ⊞ lau
Prices: pitch 40-56

▶ **LÉON** LANDES

Lou Puntaou ☎ 558487430
In oak wood with separate sections for caravans.
➲ *Turn off N652 in village and continue towards lake for 1.5km on D142.*

Contd.

15 Apr-Sep 14HEC ⚏ ∷ ♠♪⚓♀♈✕⊙☺⌀⚑ ₹ P ☎⊞
lau ➤ 🛏 ₹LR

St-Antoine St-Michel-Escalus ☎ 500890033
A pleasant, well equipped site beside a river in peaceful
wooded surroundings.
Mar-Sep 6HEC ⚏ ♠♪⚓♀♈✕⊙☺⌀🏕⚑₹ R☎⊞ lau
Prices: ↟15 ♨11 ⚑17 ▲16

LESCAR PYRÉNÉES-ATLANTIQUES

Terrier av du Vert Galant ☎ 559810182
On meadowland split in two with pitches surrounded by
hedges in foreground.
➲ *From Pau take N117 towards Bayonne for approx. 6.5km,
then turn left onto D501 towards Monein to site towards
bridge.*
All year 5.2HEC ⚏ ⚴♠♪♈✕⊙☺⌀🏕⚑₹ PR ☎
lau ➤ ⚓ ₹L ⊞
Prices: ↟22 pitch 31

LINXE LANDES

CM Le Grandjean rte de Mixe ☎ 558429000
A modern site situated on the edge of a forest. Ideal for
family holidays.
➲ *From the Castets road, take the D42 towards Linxe.*
28 Jun-6 Sep 2.7HEC ⚏ ∷ ♠♪⊙☺🏕☎ lau ➤⚓✕
Prices: ↟16 ⚑32 ▲19

LIT-ET-MIXE LANDES

Vignes rte du Cap de l'Homy ☎ 558428560
In a pine forest with good sanitary and sports facilities.
➲ *3km S via D652 and D89.*
Apr-Oct 15HEC ⚏ ∷ ⚴♪⚓♀♈✕⊙☺⌀🏕⚑▲₹ P
☎⊞ lau ➤⌀
Prices: pitch 69-125 (incl 2 persons)

LIVERS-CAZELLES TARN

Rédon ☎ 563561464
A quiet site with fine views over the surrounding area and
good modern facilities.
➲ *4km SE of Cordes on D600.*
Apr-27 Oct 1.5HEC ⚏ ♠♪⚓⊙☺⌀⚑₹ P ☎⊞ lau ➤♈
✕
Prices: pitch 60 (incl 2 persons)

LOUPIAC LOT

Hirondelles ☎ 55376625
➲ *3km N via N20.*
Apr-Oct 2.5HEC ⚏ ♠♪⚓♀♈✕⊙☺⌀🏕⚑▲₹ P☎
⊞ lau

LOURDES HAUTES-PYRÉNÉES

Arrouach 9 r des Trois Archanges, Quartier Biscaye
☎ 62421143
In pleasant wooded surroundings on N outskirts.
➲ *Situated on D947 Soumoulou road.*
All year 13HEC ⚏ ♠♪♈⊙☺⌀☎⊞ lau ➤⚓🛏 ₹LR
Prices: ↟19 pitch 22

Domec rte de Julos ☎ 562940879
➲ *Off N21 Tarbes road N of town centre.*
Etr-Oct 2HEC ⚏ ♠♪⚓♀⊙☺⌀⚑☎⊞ lau ➤♈✕ ₹PR
Prices: ↟13 pitch 14

LUCHON HAUTE-GARONNE

Frênes Garin ☎ 561798844
All year 1HEC ⚏ ⚴♪⚓♀✕⊙☺⌀🏕⚑☎ lau ➤✕

LUZ-ST-SAUVEUR HAUTES-PYRÉNÉES

Bergons rte de Barèges ☎ 562929077
In a beautiful setting on a level meadow surrounded by
woodland close to the main Pyrenean ski resorts.
➲ *600m E on D618 Barèges road.*
15 Dec-20 Oct 1HEC ⚏ ♠♪⊙☺⌀⚑ lau ➤⚓♈✕ ⚏
₹PR ⊞
Prices: ↟16.50 pitch 16

Pyrénées International rte de Lourdes ☎ 562928202
In a wooded valley at an altitude of 700mtrs with panoramic
views of the surrounding mountains.
➲ *1.3km NW on N21.*
15/12-20/04 and 01/06-30/09 4HEC ⚏ ⚴♪⚓♀✕⊙☺⌀
🛏🏕⚑₹ P ☎⊞ lau

Pyrénévasion rte de Luz-Ardiden, Sazos ☎ 562929154
A quiet site in an idyllic mountain setting close to the ski-
runs. The pitches are well defined and all facilities are clean
and modern.
➲ *2km from town on Luz-Ardiden road.*
All year 3HEC ⚏ ⚴♪⚓♀✕⊙☺⌀🛏🏕☎⊞ lau ➤✕ ₹R
⊞
Prices: ↟20 pitch 60

MARCILLAC-ST-QUENTIN DORDOGNE

Tailladis ☎ 553591095
Well maintained family site with good recreational facilities.
➲ *2km N near D48.*
15 Mar-25 Oct 23HEC ⚏ ♠♪⚓♀♈✕⊙☺⌀🏕⚑▲₹
LP ☎⊞ lau
Prices: ↟26.50-28 pitch 36-39

MAREUIL DORDOGNE

Étang Bleu Vieux Mareuil ☎ 553609270
Very large shaded site on level ground.
➲ *Half way between Angoulême and Périgueux on D939.*
Apr-Oct 9.8HEC ⚏ ♠♪⚓♀♈✕⊙☺⌀🛏🏕⚑₹ LP ☎
⊞ lau

MARTRES-TOLOSANE HAUTE-GARONNE

Moulin ☎ 561988640
In a beautiful wooded location beside the River Garonne at
the foot of the Pyrénées. Well maintained, with a wide variety
of recreational facilities.
➲ *1.5km SE off N117.*
15 Mar-15 Oct 0.6HEC ⚏ ♠♪⚓♀♈⊙☺⌀⚑₹ PR ☎
lau ➤✕🛏⊞

MAULÉON-LICHARRE PYRÉNÉES-ATLANTIQUES

Saison rte de Libarrenx ☎ 559281879
A peaceful site beside the river, near the town centre.
➲ *1.5km S on D918.*
Apr-Sep 1.1HEC ⚏ ♠♪⚓♀♈✕⊙☺⌀⚑₹ R☎⊞ lau ➤
✕🛏₹P
Prices: ↟18.50 pitch 21

MESSANGES LANDES

Côte rte de Vieux Boucau ☎ 558489494
In a picturesque wooded area 1km from the beach.
➲ *2.3km S via D652.*
Apr-Sep 3HEC ⚏ ⚴♪⚓♀⊙☺🛏🏕⚑☎⊞ lau ➤♈✕⌀
₹LPS
Prices: pitch 52-60 (incl 2 persons)

Moïsan rte de la Plage ☎ 558489206
In a pine forest, 800mtrs from the sea with good modern
facilities.

15 May-Sep 7HEC ▦ ⁘ ♦ ⋔ 🏊 ✗ ⊙ 🛒 🅿 🚻 🚐 🚱 ⁒ S 🔒 ⊞
lau ♦ 🍴 ⛐ ⁒PS
Prices: pitch 50-72 (incl 2 persons)

Vieux Port Plage Sud ☎ 558482200
A family site in the heart of the Landes forest with direct
access to the beach. Good recreational facilities.
⟳ *2.5 km SW via D652.*
Apr-Sep 40HEC ⁘ ♦ ⋔ 🏊 🍴 ✗ ⊙ 🛒 🅿 ⛐ 🚐 🚱 ⁒ PS 🔒 🅿
⊞ lau ♦ ⛐ ⁒L
Prices: pitch 150-195 (incl 3 persons)

❱ **MÉZOS** LANDES

Sen Yan ☎ 558426005
A pleasant site in exotic tropical gardens, surrounded by a
pine wood.
⟳ *1km E*
15 Jun-15 Sep 7.7HEC ▦ ⁘ 🍴 ⋔ 🏊 🍴 ✗ ⊙ 🛒 🚐 🚱 ⁒
PRS 🔒 🅿 ⊞ lau ♦ � ⛐ ⁒R
Prices: pitch 135 (incl 2 persons)

❱ **MIERS** LOT

Pigeonnier ☎ 565337195
Peaceful, shady site close to the River Dordogne amid some
of France's most spectacular scenery.
⟳ *400m E via D91.*
Etr-Sep 1HEC ▦ 🍴 ⋔ 🍴 ✗ ⊙ 🛒 🚐 🚱 ⁒ P 🔒 ⊞ lau ♦ 🏊 ✗
⁒L
Prices: ♦16-18 pitch 18-19

❱ **MILLAC** LOT

Millac Lieu dit Combe de Lafon ☎ 553297793
Terraced site.
Apr-Sep 2HEC ▦ 🌊 🌿 ⋔ 🏊 🍴 ✗ ⊙ 🛒 🝙 ⛐ 🚱 ⁒ P 🔒 ⊞
lau

❱ **MIMIZAN** LANDES

❱ At **MIMIZAN-PLAGE**(6km E by D626)

Marina ☎ 558091266
In a pinewood. 500m from beach.
15 May-15 Sep 9HEC ▦ 🍴 ⋔ 🏊 ✗ ⊙ 🛒 🚐 🚱 Å ⁒ P
🔒 ⊞ lau ♦ ⁒RS
Prices: pitch 76-190 (incl 3 persons)

See advertisement under Colour Section

❱ **MIRANDOL** TARN

Clots Les Clots ☎ 563769278
In a wooded area within the Viaur Valley with good facilities.
⟳ *5.5km N via D905, rte de Rieupeyroux.*
Etr-Oct 3.5HEC ▦ ♦ ⋔ 🏊 🍴 ⊙ 🛒 🚐 🚱 Å ⁒ PR 🔒 lau ♦ ⊞
Prices: ♦18-24 pitch 16-18

❱ **MIREPOIX** GERS

Mousquetaires ☎ 562643264
Situated on a hill in the heart of Gascony.
⟳ *2km SE.*
Jun-Sep 1HEC ▦ 🍴 ⋔ 🍴 ✗ ⊙ 🛒 🚐 🚱 Å ⁒ P 🔒 ⊞ lau ♦
⁒L
Prices: pitch 75 (incl 2 persons)

❱ **MOLIÈRES** DORDOGNE

Grande Veyière ☎ 553632584
Wooded site with good sporting facilities in the heart of
Périgord's Bastides country.
⟳ *2.4km SE.*
1 Apr-5 Nov 4HEC ▦ 🍴 ⋔ 🏊 🍴 ✗ ⊙ 🛒 🚐 🚱 ⁒ P 🔒 lau
Prices: ♦18.50-22 pitch 25-32

❱ **MOLIÈRES** TARN-ET-GARONNE

Les Amis du Lac du Malivert Centre de Loisirs du Malivert
☎ 563677637
In a pleasant lakeside setting.
⟳ *Approaching Molières from the south, head towards Centre
de Loisirs and Lac Malivert.*
Jul-Aug 0.7HEC ▦ 🍴 ⋔ ⊙ 🛒 🚱 ⁒ L 🔒 lau ♦ 🏊 🍴 ✗ ⊞
Prices: ♦12 pitch 14

❱ **MOLIETS-PLAGE** LANDES

Airotel St-Martin av de l'Océan ☎ 558485230
Large site on the Atlantic coast with direct access to the
largest sandy beach in the region.
⟳ *Between the village and the beach.*
Etr-mid Oct 18.5HEC ▦ ⁘ 🍴 ⋔ 🏊 🍴 ✗ ⊙ 🛒 🚐 ⁒ PS
🔒 lau ♦ 🏊 🍴 ✗ ⊞
Prices: pitch 132-180 (incl 3 persons)

Cigales av de l'Océan ☎ 558485118
On undulating ground in pine trees.
⟳ *300m from beach.*
15 Apr-Sep 23HEC ▦ ⁘ ♦ ⋔ 🏊 🍴 ✗ ⊙ 🛒 🚐 🚱 ⁒ 🔒 ⊞ lau
♦ � ⛐ ⁒RS

❱ **MONCRABEAU** LOT-ET-GARONNE

CM Mouliat ☎ 553654279
A small site in a wooded location on the banks of the River
La Baïse.
⟳ *On D219, 200m from D930.*
15 Jun-15 Sep 1.3HEC ▦ ♦ ⊙ 🛒 🚱 ⊞ lau ♦ 🏊 🍴 ✗
⛐ ⁒PR
Prices: ♦12.50 pitch 10.50

❱ **MONTAUBAN-DE-LUCHON** HAUTE-GARONNE

Lanette ☎ 561790038
On gently sloping ground surrounded by pastures.
⟳ *1.5km E of Luchon. Off D27.*
All year 4.3HEC ▦ 🍴 ⋔ 🏊 🍴 ✗ ⊙ 🛒 🚐 🚱 🔒 ⊞ lau ♦
⁒PR
Prices: pitch 82-99 (incl 3 persons)

❱ **MONTESQUIOU** GERS

Château le Haget ☎ 562709580
In grounds of Château.
May-Oct 11HEC ▦ ♦ ⋔ 🏊 🍴 ✗ ⊙ 🛒 🝙 ⛐ 🚐 🚱 ⁒ P 🔒
lau ♦ ⁒R
Prices: ♦25 pitch 27-35

❱ **MUSSIDAN** DORDOGNE

CM Le Port ☎ 553812009
15 Jun-15 Sep 0.5HEC ▦ ♦ ⋔ ⊙ 🛒 🚱 ⊞ lau ♦ 🏊 🍴 ✗ 🝙 ⛐
⁒PR

❱ **NAGES** TARN

Rieu Montagné Lac du Laouzas ☎ 563374052
In a wooded location beside the Laouzas lake with good
recreational facilities.
⟳ *4.5km S via D62*
15 Mar-15 Nov 4HEC ▦ ♦ ⋔ 🏊 🍴 ✗ ⊙ 🛒 🚐 ⛐ ⁒ P 🔒
⊞ lau ♦ ⁒L

❱ **NONTRON** DORDOGNE

❱ At **ABJAT**(15km NE)

Moulin de Masfrolet ☎ 553568270
⟳ *2.4km N.*
Jun-15 Sep 12HEC ▦ ♦ ⋔ 🏊 🍴 ✗ ⊙ 🛒 🚱 ⁒ LPR 🔒 ⊞
lau

OLORON-STE-MARIE PYRÉNÉES-ATLANTIQUES

Val du Gave-d'Aspe rte du Somport, Guermençon
☎ 559360507
A pleasant site situated in the Aspe Valley amid picturesque
Pyrenean scenery.
All year 0.5HEC ⸋⸋⸋⸋ ♦ ⋔ ⍾ ⍾ ⊙ ◘ ◙ ♨ ⍾ P ₽ 田 lau ➡ ✕ ♨ ⍾R

ONDRES LANDES

Lou Pignada av de la Plage ☎ 559453045
In a forest 3 minutes walk from the sea.
➲ *Turn off the N10 in the village onto rte de la Plage.*
Apr-20 Sep 2HEC ⸋⸋⸋⸋ ⠿ ♦ ⋔ ⍾ ⍾ ✕ ⊙ ◘ ⍾ ♨ ◙ ⍾ P 田
田 lau ➡ ◿ ⍾LRS

ONESSE-ET-LAHARIE LANDES

CM *Bienvenu* ☎ 558073049
A family site situated within a forest.
➲ *500m from village centre on D38.*
15 Jun-15 Sep 1.5HEC ⍾ ⋔ ⊙ ◘ ◙ 田 lau ➡ ♨ ⍾ ✕
Prices: ⋔14.50 ♨8 ◙13 ▲13

OUSSE PYRÉNÉES-ATLANTIQUES

Sapins ☎ 559817421
➲ *Access via N117, exit 'Pau' or A64, exit Soumoulou.*
All year 0.8HEC ⸋⸋⸋⸋ ⍾ ⋔ ⍾ ⍾ ✕ ⊙ ◘ ◙ ♨ 田 lau ➡ ♨ ✕
Prices: ⋔18 pitch 22

PADIRAC LOT

Chênes rte du Gouffre ☎ 565336554
➲ *1.5km NE via D90 towards Gouffre.*
May-Sep 5HEC ⸋⸋⸋⸋ ♦ ⋔ ⍾ ⍾ ✕ ⊙ ◘ ◿ ♨ ♨ ◙ ▲ ⍾ P 田 田
lau

PAMIERS ARIÈGE

Ombrages Route d'Escosse ☎ 561671224
A pleasant site in wooded surroundings beside the River
Ariège, 1.5km from the town centre.
➲ *NW on D119 beside river.*
All year 2.5HEC ⸋⸋⸋⸋ ♦ ⋔ ⍾ ⍾ ✕ ⊙ ◘ ◿ ♨ ◙ 田 lau ➡
⍾PR
Prices: ⋔10 ♨6 ◙10 ▲10

PARENTIS-EN-BORN LANDES

Arbre d'Or 75 rte du Lac ☎ 558784156
A level site in pine wood on S shore of the Étang de
Biscarosse.
➲ *Turn off D652 2km S of Gastes.*
All year 4.5HEC ⠿ ♦ ⋔ ⍾ ⍾ ✕ ⊙ ◘ ◿ ♨ ♨ ◙ ♨ ⍾ P 田 田
lau ➡ ⍾LP

At GASTES(7.5km SW)

Réserve ☎ 558097596
A large, popular site situated in one of the largest forests in
Europe. Plenty of sporting and entertainment facilities.
➲ *3km SW via D652*
15 May-19 Sep 32HEC ⸋⸋⸋⸋ ⠿ ♦ ⋔ ⍾ ⍾ ✕ ⊙ ◘ ◿ ♨ ♨ ▲
⍾ LP 田 田 lau
Prices: pitch 71.50-143 (incl 2 persons)

PAUILLAC GIRONDE

CM *Les Gabarreys* rte de la Rivière ☎ 556591003
A municipal site with good sports facilities.
➲ *S of town. Follow signposts.*
2 Apr-10 Oct 2HEC ⸋⸋⸋⸋ ♨ ⍾ ⋔ ⊙ ◘ ⍾ R lau ➡ ♨ ⍾ ✕ ◿ ♨
⍾P
Prices: pitch 58.50-65 (incl 2 persons)

PAYRAC LOT

Panoramic rte de Loupiac ☎ 565379845
A peaceful family site 5km from the River Dordogne with
good recreational facilities.
➲ *Off N20 N of Payrac.*
All year 1.5HEC ⸋⸋⸋⸋ ♦ ⋔ ⍾ ✕ ⊙ ◘ ◿ ♨ ♨ ▲ 田 田 lau ➡ ♨
◿ ⍾P
Prices: ⋔13 ◙18 ▲18

Pins rte de Cahors ☎ 565379632
A well-managed site, partly in forest, partly on meadowland.
Sheltered from traffic noise.
➲ *S of village off N20.*
Apr-15 Sep 4HEC ⸋⸋⸋⸋ ⍾ ⋔ ⍾ ⍾ ✕ ⊙ ◘ ◿ ♨ ♨ ⍾ P 田 lau
Prices: ⋔16-32 pitch 24-48

PÉRIGUEUX DORDOGNE

Barnabé-Plage 80 r des Bains, Boulazac ☎ 553534145
A well appointed site in a wooded park-like location beside
the river.
➲ *Signposted from N89, 2km E of town centre.*
All year 1.5HEC ⸋⸋⸋⸋ ⍾ ⋔ ⍾ ✕ ⊙ ◘ 田 田 lau ➡ ♨
Prices: ⋔16.50 ♨10 ◙16 ▲16

At BOULAZAC(4km SE)

Isle rte de Brive ☎ 553535775
A family site in wooded surroundings.
➲ *3km from Périgueux in the direction of Brive on D5.*
15 May-15 Sep 3HEC ⸋⸋⸋⸋ ⍾ ⋔ ⍾ ⍾ ✕ ⊙ ◘ ◿ ♨ ⍾ PR 田 田 ➡
♨ ✕ ♨

PETIT-PALAIS GIRONDE

Pressoir Queyrai Petit-Palais ☎ 557697325
An old farm in the rolling countryside around St-Emilion.
➲ *On N89 Bordeaux-Périgueux road, exit at St-Médard de
Guizières & follow signs.*
May-Sep 2.5HEC ⸋⸋⸋⸋ ♦ ⋔ ⍾ ✕ ⊙ ◘ ▲ ⍾ P 田 田 ⍒ lau
Prices: ⋔31 pitch 41

PEZULS DORDOGNE

Forêt ☎ 553227169
In extensive grounds on the edge of the forest with modern
facilities.
➲ *600m off D703. 3km from the village centre.*
Apr-Oct 8HEC ⸋⸋⸋⸋ ♨ ♦ ⋔ ⍾ ⍾ ✕ ⊙ ◘ ◿ ♨ ♨ ◙ ♨ ⍾ P 田 田
lau
Prices: ⋔21-27.80 pitch 19-26.40

PONT-ST-MAMET DORDOGNE

Lestaubière Pont-St-Mamet ☎ 553829815
Peaceful and secluded site in attractive part of the Dordogne,
occupying the former outbuildings and wooded grounds of
the adjacent château. Site commands fine views of the
surrounding countryside.
➲ *Off N21.*
Jun-Aug 5HEC ⸋⸋⸋⸋ ⍾ ⋔ ⍾ ⍾ ✕ ⊙ ◘ ◿ ⍾ LP 田 田 ⍒ lau ➡
✕
Prices: ⋔26 pitch 28.50

PUYBRUN LOT

Sole ☎ 565385237
A well run site in pleasant wooded surroundings with good
facilities.
➲ *On D703 leave village in the direction of Bretenoux and
take the first turning after the garage.*
Apr-Sep 3HEC ⸋⸋⸋⸋ ♦ ⋔ ⍾ ✕ ⊙ ◘ ◿ ♨ ♨ ◙ ♨ ▲ ⍾ PR 田 田
lau ➡ ♨
Prices: ⋔20.90-25 pitch 26

PUY-L'ÉVÊQUE LOT

At MONTCABRIER(7 km NW)

Moulin de Laborde ☎ 565246206
Well equipped site surrounded by woods and hills, in a picturesque valley on the River Thèze.
➲ *NW off D673.*
1 May-14 Sep 9HEC ⚊ 🔥 🏕 🛒 🍴 ✕ ⊙ 🚿 ∅ ⟟ LPR ⌂ ⊞ ⌖
lau ➡ 🏔
Prices: ⚑30 pitch 35

PYLA-SUR-MER GIRONDE

Dune rte de Biscarrosse ☎ 556227217
A beautifully situated and quiet site partly on terraced sandy fields. Opposite a dune of over 100m in height, which separates the site from the sea.
➲ *Follow the road between Pilat-Plage.*
May-Sep 6HEC ⚌ 🔥 🔥 🏕 🛒 🍴 ✕ ⊙ 🚿 ∅ 🚲 ⟟ P ⌂ ⊞ lau ➡
⟟S
Prices: pitch 75-115 (incl 2 persons)

Forêt rte de Biscarrosse ☎ 556227328
A well equipped site surrounded by pine trees and with direct access to the fine sandy beaches at the mouth of the Arcachon Basin. There are good sporting facilities and evening entertainment is provided on a regular basis.
➲ *Access via N250 then D218.*
Etr-Oct 12HEC ⚊ 🔥 🔥 🏕 🛒 🍴 ✕ ⊙ 🚿 ∅ 🏔 🚲 🛖 🏕 ⟟ PS ⌂ ⊞
lau
Prices: pitch 75-150 (incl 2 persons)

Panorama rte de Biscarrosse ☎ 556221044
Partially terraced site amongst dunes, on the edge of the 100m high 'Dune de Pyla'. Views of the sea from some pitches.
➲ *On the D218. Signposted.*
May-Sep 15HEC ⚌ 🔥 🔥 🏕 🛒 🍴 ✕ ⊙ 🚿 ∅ 🏔 🛖 🏕 🞀 ⟟ PS ⌂
⊞ lau
Prices: ⚑19-28 pitch 55-93

Petit Nice rte de Biscarrosse ☎ 556227403
Sandy terraced site, mainly suitable for tents; in parts sloping steeply in pine woodland. Paths and standings are strengthened with timber. 220 steps down to the beach.
➲ *6 km S on D218.*
Apr-10 Oct 5.5HEC ⚊ 🔥 🔥 🏕 🛒 🍴 ✕ ⊙ 🚿 ∅ 🏔 🛖 🏕 ⟟ PS
⌂ ⊞ lau
Prices: pitch 32-75 (incl 4 persons)

Pyla rte de Biscarrosse ☎ 556227456
A well equipped family site with good recreational facilities and direct access to the sea.
May-Sep 8HEC ⚊ ⚌ 🔥 🔥 🏕 🛒 🍴 ✕ ⊙ 🚿 ∅ 🏔 🛖 ⟟ PS ⌂ ⊞
lau
Prices: pitch 76-130 (incl 2 persons)

RAUZAN GIRONDE

Vieux Château ☎ 557841538
A family site sitauted in a peaceful valley surrounded by vineyards and overlooked by the ruined 12th century Rauzan castle.
➲ *200mtrs N, 1500mtrs from N670.*
All year 2HEC ⚊ 🔥 🔥 🛒 🍴 ⊙ 🚿 🏔 ⟟ P ⌂ lau
Prices: ⚑20 pitch 30

REYREVIGNES LOT

Papillon ☎ 565401240
In a wooded park in the heart of the Haut-Quercy region with good, modern facilities.
➲ *Access via N653.*

1 Apr-1 Nov 3HEC ⚊ 🔥 🔥 🏕 🛒 🍴 ✕ ⊙ 🚿 ∅ 🏔 🛖 🏕 🞀 ⟟ P ⌂
⊞ lau ➡ 🛒 ⟟LR
Prices: ⚑20 pitch 30

ROCAMADOUR LOT

Cigales ☎ 565336444
A peaceful, well equipped site with shaded pitches and good, modern facilities. Fine views of Rocamadour.
27 Jun-4 Sep 3HEC ⚊ 🔥 🔥 🏕 🛒 🍴 ✕ ⊙ 🚿 ∅ 🚲 ⌂ 🖩 ⊞ lau
Prices: pitch 85 (incl 2 persons)

Relais du Campeur l'Hospitalet ☎ 565336328
Shady, level site with well marked pitches and good facilities. Fine views of Rocamadour.
➲ *On D36.*
Etr-Sep 1.7HEC ⚊ 🔥 🔥 🏕 🛒 🍴 ✕ ⊙ 🚿 ∅ ⟟ P ⌂ ⊞ lau ➡ 🏔
Prices: pitch 60 (incl 2 persons)

ROCHE-CHALAIS, LA DORDOGNE

Gerbes r de la Dronne ☎ 553914065
Well appointed family site on banks of River Dronne.
➲ *Off D674 in village centre. Signposted.*
Apr-Oct 3HEC ⚊ 🔥 🔥 ⊙ 🚿 ⟟ R ⌂ ⊞ lau ➡ 🏕 🛒 🍴 ✕ ∅ ⟟P
Prices: ⚑12 pitch 16

ROMIEU, LA GERS

Camp de Florence ☎ 562281558
Well equipped site in rural surroundings.
➲ *Take D931 in direction Agen-Condom. 3km before Condom turn left to La Romieu.*
Apr-Oct 10HEC ⚊ 🔥 🔥 🏕 ✕ ⊙ 🚿 🛖 🏕 🞀 🛡 ⟟ P ⌂ ⊞ lau ➡
🏕
Prices: pitch 85-112 (incl 2 persons)

ROQUEFORT LANDES

CM de Nauton Cité Nauton ☎ 558455046
A small municipal site with good facilities.
➲ *1.6km N via D932 towards Bordeaux.*
Apr-Oct 1.4HEC ⚊ ⚌ 🔥 🔥 ⊙ 🚿 ➡ 🏕 🛒 🍴 ✕ ⟟R
Prices: ⚑12.50

ROQUELAURE GERS

Talouch ☎ 562655243
A family site in picturesque wooded surroundings, situated in the heart of Gascony. There are fine sports and entertainment facilities.
➲ *Access via N21 and D148.*
Apr-Sep 8HEC ⚊ 🔥 🔥 🏕 🛒 🍴 ✕ ⊙ 🚿 ∅ 🏔 🛖 🏕 🛡 ⟟ P ⌂ ⊞ lau
Prices: pitch 84 (incl 2 persons)

ROUFFIGNAC DORDOGNE

Cantegrel ☎ 553054830
In a peaceful location in the heart of the Périgord Noir, with good recreational facilities.
➲ *1.5km N via D31, rte de Thenon.*
Apr-15 Oct 45HEC ⚊ 🔥 🔥 🏕 🛒 🍴 ✕ ⊙ 🚿 ∅ 🏔 🛖 🏕 🞀 ⟟ P ⌂
⊞ lau
Prices: ⚑12-17 pitch 40-65

SADIRAC GIRONDE

Bel Air ☎ 556230190
A well equipped, roomy site on a level meadow shaded by tall trees.
➲ *1 mile W of Créon on D671.*
All year 2HEC ⚊ 🔥 🔥 🏕 🛒 🍴 ✕ ⊙ 🚿 ∅ 🏔 🞀 ⟟ P ⌂ ⊞ ➡ ✕
Prices: ⚑15 pitch 27-35

ST-ANTOINE-DE-BREUILH DORDOGNE

CM St-Aulaye ☎ 553248280
⮕ *Access via D936. Take a right turn before the village and travel 3kms in the direction of the Dordogne.*
Apr-Sep 2.5HEC ⏛ ♦ ⋔ ⅏ ♀ ✕ ⊙ ◉ ⬛ ⬛ ⤚ P ▣ ⊞ ➡ ⤚R
Prices: ♦15 pitch 20

ST-ANTONIN-NOBLE-VAL TARN-ET-GARONNE

Trois Cantons ☎ 563319857
Divided into pitches, partly on sloping ground within an oak forest. Separate section for teenagers.
⮕ *8.5km NW near D926. Signposted.*
5 Apr-Sep 5HEC ⏛ ▲ ⅏ ⋔ ⅏ ♀ ✕ ⊙ ◉ ⬛ ⬛ ⤚ P ▣ ⊞ lau
Prices: ♦30 pitch 39

ST-BERTRAND-DE-COMMINGES HAUTE-GARONNE

Es Pibous chemin de St-Just ☎ 561989420
A quiet, shaded site in an elevated position with good facilities.
May-Sep 2HEC ⏛ ♦ ⋔ ⅏ ⊙ ◉ ⬛ ⬛ ⬛ ▣ lau ➡ ♀ ✕ ≞
Prices: ♦15 pitch 15

ST-CÉRÉ LOT

CM de Soulhol quai A-Salesse ☎ 565381237
A family site bordered by two rivers with good recreational facilities.
⮕ *200m SE on D940.*
Apr-Sep 3.5HEC ⏛ ♦ ⋔ ⊙ ◉ ⬛ ⬛ ⬛ ⤚ R ▣ ⊞ lau ➡ ⅏ ✕ ⅆ ≞ ⤚P

ST-CIRQ DORDOGNE

Brin d'Amour Saint Cirq ☎ 553072373
In a fine location overlooking the Vézère Valley with good facilities.
Mar-Nov 3.8HEC ⏛ ♦ ⋔ ⅏ ♀ ✕ ⊙ ◉ ⅆ ≞ ⬛ ⬛ ⤚ LP ▣ ▣ ⊞ lau
Prices: ♦25 pitch 30-35

ST-CRICQ GERS

Lac de Thoux ☎ 562657129
A family site with good facilities situated on the edge of the lake, 50mtrs from the beach.
⮕ *On D654 between Cologne and L'Isle Jourdain.*
15 Apr-15 Oct 3HEC ⏛ ⅏ ⋔ ⅏ ♀ ✕ ⊙ ◉ ⬛ ⅆ ≞ ⬛ ⤚ L ▣ ⊞ lau

ST-CYBRANET DORDOGNE

Bel Ombrage ☎ 553283414
Quiet holiday site in wooded valley.
Jun-5 Sep 6HEC ⏛ ♦ ⋔ ⊙ ◉ ⤚ PR ▣ ⊞ lau ➡ ⅏ ✕ ⅆ ≞
Prices: ♦26 pitch 38

ST-CYPRIEN DORDOGNE

Ferme de Campagnac Castels ☎ 553292603
A quiet site situated 200mtrs from the farm in a sheltered position.
⮕ *Access from town on D25. Signposted*
Apr-Oct 0.8HEC ⏛ ♦ ⋔ ⊙ ◉ ⬛ ⬛ lau ➡ ⅏ ✕ ⅆ ≞ ⤚R ⊞
Prices: ♦8 ▲25 pitch 25

CM Garrit ☎ 553292056
In a peaceful location beside the River Dordogne with safe bathing.
⮕ *1.5km S on D48.*
Apr-Oct ⏛ ⅏ ⋔ ⅏ ✕ ⊙ ◉ ⬛ ▣ ⊞ lau ➡ ⅆ ≞ ⤚R
Prices: pitch 61 (incl 2 persons)

Plage Vezac ☎ 553295083
Modest but attractive site in a pleasant riverside setting.
⮕ *Access via D703 beyond La Roque Gageac.*
Apr-Sep 2.5HEC ⏛ ♦ ⋔ ⅏ ⊙ ◉ ⅆ ⤚ R ▣ ⊞ lau ➡ ⅏ ✕
Prices: ♦19-20 ⬤9.50-10 ⬛9.50-10 ▲9.50-10

ST-ÉMILION GIRONDE

Barbanne ☎ 557247580
⮕ *A peaceful country setting among vineyards, close to a 12 acre lake.*
3km N via D122
01-APR/17-OCT 10HEC ⏛ ⅏ ⋔ ⅏ ✕ ⊙ ◉ ⅆ ⬛ ⤚ P ▣ ⊞ lau
Prices: ♦22-25 pitch 36-40

ST-GENIES DORDOGNE

Bouquerie ☎ 553289822
A family site in wooded surroundings with a good variety of facilities.
⮕ *N of village on D704.*
15 May-15 Sep 8HEC ⏛ ♦ ⋔ ⅏ ✕ ⊙ ◉ ⅆ ≞ ⬛ ⤚ LP ▣ ⊞ lau
Prices: ♦36.60 pitch 51.50

ST-GIRONS ARIÈGE

Pont du Nert rte de Lacourt (D33) ☎ 561665848
Grassy site between road and woodland.
⮕ *Approx 3km SE at the junction of the D33 and the D3.*
1 Jun-15 Sep 1.5HEC ⏛ ♦ ⋔ ⊙ ◉ ⬛ ▣ ➡ ⤚R
Prices: ♦15 ⬛10 ▲10-13

ST-JEAN-DE-LUZ PYRÉNÉES-ATLANTIQUES

International d'Erromardie ☎ 559263426
Site is situated by the sea and consists of several sections divided by roads and low hedges. Take away food.
⮕ *If approached from N to N10, cross railway bridge and turn immediately right and follow signs.*
15 Mar-15 Oct 2HEC ⏛ ⅏ ⋔ ⅏ ♀ ✕ ⊙ ◉ ≞ ⬛ ⬛ ⤚ RS ▣ ⊞ lau
Prices: pitch 66-105 (incl 2 persons)

Iratzia ☎ 559261489
⮕ *1km NE off N10. Leave autoroute, signed St-Jean-de-Luz Nord and follow directions for Plage d'Erromardie.*
15 Mar-Sep 4HEC ⏛ ♦ ⋔ ⅏ ♀ ✕ ⊙ ◉ ⅆ ⬛ ▣ ⊞ lau ➡ ⤚S

Tamaris Plage Quartier d'Acotz ☎ 559265590
Level family site with good facilities divided into sections by drives and hedges.
⮕ *Signposted from N10 towards the sea.*
Apr-Sep 1.2HEC ⏛ ⅏ ⋔ ⊙ ◉ ⬛ ⬛ ⬛ ▣ lau ➡ ⅏ ✕ ⅆ ⤚S ⊞

At SOCOA(3km SW)

Juantcho rte de la Corniche ☎ 559471197
⮕ *2km W on D912.*
14 May-Sep 6HEC ⏛ ⅏ ⋔ ⊙ ◉ ⬛ ⬛ ▣ ▣ lau ➡ ⅏ ♀ ✕ ⅆ ⤚RS ⊞
Prices: ♦19 pitch 28

ST-JEAN-PIED-DE-PORT PYRÉNÉES-ATLANTIQUES

Narbaïtz rte de Bayonne, Ascarat ☎ 559371013
A quiet, comfortable site beside the River Berroua.
⮕ *2km NW towards Bayonne.*
15 Mar-30 Sept 2.5HEC ⏛ ♦ ⋔ ⅏ ✕ ⊙ ◉ ⅆ ⬛ ⤚ PR ▣ lau ➡ ⅏ ✕ ≞ ⊞
Prices: pitch 72 (incl 2 persons)

ST-JULIEN-EN-BORN LANDES

Lette Fleurie ☎ 558427409
On undulating ground in a pine wood with good facilities, 5 minutes from the beach.
Apr-Sep 15.5HEC ⟡ ♦♠☎♈✕☉♨⌂☄⊟⌷ P ☎⊞ lau
Prices: ↑13.60-17 ♣5.20-6.50 ⊞16-20 ▲16-20

ST-JUSTIN LANDES

Pin rte de Roquefort ☎ 358448891
A quiet family site beside the lake. Bar and café open May to 15 September only.
➱ 2.3km N on D626.
Mar-Nov 3HEC ⟡ ⟡ ♦♠✕☉♨⌂☄⌷ P ☎⊞ lau
Prices: ↑15-25 ♣5-10 ⊞10 ▲5-10

ST-LÉON-SUR-VÉZÈRE DORDOGNE

Paradis ☎ 553507264
Situated on the river bank in the picturesque Vézère valley.
➱ S of village off D706 Les Éyzies road.
Apr-25 Oct 6HEC ⟡ ⌘♠☎☀✕☉♨⌂☄⌷ PR ☎⊞ lau
Prices: ↑25-35.50 pitch 39.50-56

At TURSAC(7km SW)

Pigeonnier ☎ 553069690
A small, peaceful site in the heart of the Dordogne countryside.
➱ Acces via D706 between Le Moustier and Les Éyzies.
Jun-Sep 1.1HEC ⟡ ♦♠☎☀✕☉♨⌂☄⌷ P ☎⊞ lau ♦ ✕ ⌷R
Prices: ↑20 pitch 20

Vézère Périgord ☎ 553069631
A well equipped site in wooded surroundings close to the river.
➱ 0.8km NE on D706.
May-Sep 5HEC ⟡ ⌘♠☎☀✕☉♨⌂☄⌷ P ☎⊞ lau ♦⌷R

ST-MARTIN-DE-SEIGNANX LANDES

Lou P'tit Poun ☎ 559565579
A quiet site with well defined pitches on terraces.
➱ Access via A63 exit Bayonne Nord towards Pau.
Jun-Sep 7HEC ⟡ ⌘♠☎☀✕☉♨⌂☄⊞☄▲⌷ P ☎⊞ lau
Prices: ↑26-29 pitch 53-59

ST-MARTORY HAUTE-GARONNE

CM rte de St-Girons ☎ 561902224
All year ⟡ ⌘♠☎☉♨⊞⌷ lau ♦☎✕☄⌷ ⌷R

ST-NICOLAS-DE-LA-GRAVE TARN-ET-GARONNE

Plan d'Eau Base de Plein Air, et de Loisirs ☎ 563955002
➱ 2.5km N via D15.
15 Jun-15 Sep 1.5HEC ⟡ ⌘♠☉♨⌂⊟⊞ lau ♦☀✕⌷P
Prices: ↑56

ST-PARDOUX-LA-RIVIÈRE DORDOGNE

🏰 **Château le Verdoyer** ☎ 553569464
A small, well equipped site in the grounds of a restored castle.
➱ 3km N via D96.
May-Sep 17HEC ⟡ ⌘♠☎☀✕☉♨⌂☄⌷▲⌷ LP ☎⊞ lau
Prices: ↑25-35 pitch 32-46

ST-PAUL-LES-DAX LANDES

Pins du Soleil ☎ 558913791
On a hotel complex with good modern facilities.
➱ SW via D954.
3 Apr-Oct 6HEC ⟡ ♦♠☎☀✕☉♨⌂☄⊟⌷ P ☎⊞ lau ♦☎✕☄⌷ ⌷R
Prices: pitch 60-115 (incl 2 persons)

ST-PÉE-SUR-NIVELLE PYRÉNÉES-ATLANTIQUES

Goyetchea ☎ 559541959
Quiet, peaceful site in a wooded location at the foot of the Pyrénées.
➱ 0.8km N on rte d'Ahetze.
Jun-27 Sep 3HEC ⟡ ⌘♠☎☀✕☉♨⌂☄⌷ P ☎⊞ lau ♦☀✕☄ ⌷R
Prices: ↑73-91

At IBARRON(2km W)

Ibarron ☎ 559541043
In a pleasant wooded location with level pitches and good, modern facilities.
➱ 2km W on D918.
15 May-20 Sep 2.8HEC ⟡ ♦♠☉♨⌂☄⊞⊞ lau ♦☎ ☀✕☄⌷ ⌷LPR
Prices: pitch 63 (incl 2 persons)

ST-PIERRE-LAFEUILLE LOT

Quercy-Vacances Le Mas de Lacombe ☎ 565368715
A well equipped site in pleasant wooded surroundings.
➱ On N20. 12km N of Cahors.
May-Sep 3HEC ⟡ ⌘♠☎☀✕☉♨⌂☄⌷ P ☎⊞ lau

ST-RÉMY-SUR-LIDOIRE DORDOGNE

Tuilière ☎ 553824729
In pleasant wooded surroundings beside a lake. Separate car park for arrivals after 22.00hrs.
➱ 6km from Montpon on D708 towards Ste-Foy-la-Grande.
15 Apr-15 Sep 8HEC ⟡ ♦♠☎☀✕☉♨⌂☄⌷ LP ☎⊞ lau
Prices: ↑16-20 pitch 20.80-26

ST-SEURIN-DE-PRATS DORDOGNE

Plage ☎ 553586107
In a peaceful, wooded setting beside the Dordogne with a variety of recreational facilities.
➱ 0.7kms on D11.
May-27 Sep 3.9HEC ⟡ ♦♠☎☀✕☉♨⌂☄⌷ PR ☎ lau ♦☄☄⊞

STE-EULALIE-EN-BORN LANDES

Bruyères chemin Laffont ☎ 558097336
In the middle of the Landes forest close to the lakes and the sea.
➱ 2.5km N via D652.
Etr-Sep 3HEC ⟡ ♦♠☎☀✕☉♨⌂☄⊞⌷ P ☎⊞ lau ♦⌷LR
Prices: pitch 98 (incl 2 persons)

SALIGNAC DORDOGNE

'Les Peneyrals' Le Poujol, Sy-Crépin Carlucet ☎ 553288571
Quiet site among trees between the Vézère and Dordogne rivers.
➱ 10 km N of Sarlat on D60.
15 May-15 Sep 12HEC ⟡ ⌘♠☎☀✕☉♨⌂☄⊞⌷ P ☎P⊞ lau
Prices: ↑27-36 pitch 37.50-50

SALLES (GIRONDE) GIRONDE

Val de l'Eyre 8 rte de Minoy ☎ 556884703
A well equipped family site in a pleasant wooded location between the Landes forests and the Bordeaux vineyards.
➪ *SW on D108, rte de Lugos.*
Apr-Oct 13HEC ⋯ ⌖ ⋔ ⋚ ⟟ ✕ ☉ ◨ ⊘ ≞ ⌂ ⋒ 🅰 ⚲ LR ⌹ ⊞
lau ➧ ⋚ ⚲P
Prices: pitch 59-86

SALLES (LOT-ET-GARONNE) LOT-ET-GARONNE

Bastides ☎ 553408309
In peaceful wooded surroundings overlooking the Lède Valley with good sporting and entertainment facilities.
➪ *1km N via D150.*
May-Sep 6.1HEC ⟱ ⋔ ⋚ ⟟ ✕ ☉ ◨ ⌂ ⋒ ⚲ P ⌹ ⊞ lau

SARE PYRÉNÉES-ATLANTIQUES

Goyenetche rte des Grottes ☎ 559542171
In a peaceful location in a wooded valley close to the Caves of Sarre.
➪ *3.5km S via D306.*
15 Jun-15 Sep 1HEC ⟱ ⌖ ⋔ ☉ ◨ ⚲ ⚲ R ⌹ ⊞ lau ➧ ⋚ ⟟ ✕

SARLAT-LA-CANÉDA DORDOGNE

Maillac Ste-Nathalène ☎ 553592212
In wooded surroundings in the heart of the Périgord Noir region with good facilities for a family holiday. Separate car park for arrivals after 23.00hrs.
➪ *7km NE on D47.*
15 May-Sep 6HEC ⟱ ⌖ ⋔ ⋚ ⟟ ✕ ☉ ◨ ⊘ ≞ ⌂ ⋒ ⚲ P ⌹
⊞ lau ➧ ⚲L

▥ Moulin du Roch rtes des Eyzies ☎ 553592027
In a picturesque location between the Dordogne and Vézère valleys.
➪ *10km NW via D704-D6-D47.*
May-19 Sep 8HEC ⟱ ⌖ ⋔ ⋚ ⟟ ✕ ☉ ◨ ⊘ ⚲ P ⌹ ⊞ ⌸ lau
Prices: pitch 70-124 (incl 2 persons)

Périères ☎ 553590584
Very well kept terraced site situated in 12 acres of parkland and woods in the heart of the Périgord Noir with fine views over the Sarlat valley. There are good recreational facilities and modern, well equipped bungalows are available for hire.
➪ *1km N of town on D47.*
Etr-Sep 11HEC ⟱ ⌖ ⋔ ⋚ ⟟ ✕ ☉ ◨ ⊘ ⋒ ⚲ P ⌹ ⊞ lau
Prices: pitch 111-167 (incl 2 persons)

At CARSAC-AILLAC(7km SE via D704A)

Aqua Viva ☎ 553314600
Site with numerous terraces in beautiful wooded surroundings in the heart of the Dordogne.
➪ *Along the main road Sarlat/Souillac D704A*
Etr-Sep 11HEC ⟱ ⋯ ⌖ ⋔ ⋔ ⋚ ⟟ ✕ ☉ ◨ ⊘ ⌂ ⚲ L ⌹ ⊞
lau
Prices: ⚑18-33 pitch 22-47

Rocher de la Cave ☎ 553281426
Pleasant family site on a level meadow beside the river.
➪ *Access via D703 & D704.*
May-15 Sep 4HEC ⟱ ⋯ ⌖ ⋔ ⋚ ⟟ ✕ ☉ ◨ ⊘ ⌂ ⋒ 🅰 ⚲ R
⌹ ⊞ lau
Prices: ⚑21 pitch 29

At PROISSANS(6km NE)

Val d'Ussel La Fond d'Ussel ☎ 553592873
A well equipped site in woodland in the heart of the Périgord Noir region. Separate car park for late arrivals.
➪ *Off D704 or D56.*
May-25 Sep 6.5HEC ⟱ ⌖ ⋔ ⋚ ⟟ ✕ ☉ ◨ ⊘ ⌂ ⋒ 🅰 ⚲ P ⌹
lau
Prices: ⚑20-30 pitch 22-40

SAUVETERRE-DE-BÉARN PYRÉNÉES-ATLANTIQUES

CM Gave av de la Gare ☎ 559385330
➪ *Turn left before bridge on St-Palais road.*
Jun-Sep 1.5HEC ⟱ ⌖ ⋔ ☉ ◨ ⚲ R ⌹ ⊞ lau ➧ ⋚ ⟟ ✕ ⊘ ≞
Prices: ⚑10 ⚙14.10 ⋒10.60 🅰7

SAUVETERRE-LA-LÉMANCE LOT-ET-GARONNE

Moulin du Périé rte de Loubejac ☎ 553406726
In a wooded valley close to an 18th century watermill with good, modern facilities.
➪ *3km E of town off D710. Follow signposts from the entrance to the village and keep to the valley road.*
Apr-Sept 5HEC ⟱ ⌖ ⋔ ⋚ ⟟ ✕ ☉ ◨ ⊘ ≞ ⌂ ⋒ 🅰 ⚲ PR ⌹
⊞ lau ➧ ⚲L
Prices: ⚑22-35 pitch 24-47.50

SEIGNOSSE LANDES

Chevreuils rte de Hossegor ☎ 558433280
In a pine forest close to the sea with good recreational facilities.
➪ *On CD79 rte de Hossegor.*
Jun-15 Sep 8HEC ⟱ ⋯ ⌖ ⋔ ⋚ ⟟ ✕ ☉ ◨ ⊘ ≞ ⌂ ⋒ ⚲ P
⊞ lau ➧ ⚲S
Prices: ⚑21.60-28 ⚙9.20-11.50 ⋒42.80-53.50

CM Hourn Naou av des Tucs ☎ 558433030
Very clean and tidy site situated in a pine forest 600mtrs from the sea.
➪ *200mtrs from Seignosse town centre.*
6 Apr-Sep 16HEC ⋯ ⌖ ⋔ ⋚ ⟟ ✕ ☉ ◨ ⊘ ⌂ ⋒ ⌹ ⊞ lau ➧ ≞
⚲LPS
Prices: ⚑18-25 ⚙9.50-9.50 ⋒48-48

At SEIGNOSSE-LE-PENON(5km W)

Forêt ☎ 558433020
A pleasant, quiet site 300m from the sea.
13 Jun-13 Sep 11HEC ⋯ ⌖ ⋔ ⋚ ✕ ☉ ◨ ⚲ P ⌹ ⊞ ⌸ lau
➧ ⋚ ≞ ⚲S

SEIX ARIÈGE

Haut Salat ☎ 561668178
Very clean, well kept site beside stream. Big gravel pitches for caravans. Common room with TV.
➪ *0.8km NE on D3.*
All year 2.5HEC ⟱ ⌖ ⋔ ⋚ ⟟ ✕ ☉ ◨ ⊘ ≞ ⋒ ⚲ R ⊞ lau ➧
✕
Prices: ⚑22 pitch 22

SIORAC-EN-PÉRIGORD DORDOGNE

At COUX-ET-BIGAROQUE(2.5 km NW by D710/D703)

Clou Meynard Haut ☎ 553316332
Separate section for dog owners.
➪ *Access via D703 (Le Bugue-Delve road).*
Apr-1 Oct 3HEC ⟱ ⌖ ⋔ ⋚ ⟟ ✕ ☉ ◨ ⊘ ≞ ⌂ ⚲ P ⌹ ⊞ lau
Prices: ⚑26 pitch 32

Faval ☎ 553316044
In a wooded location 200m from River Dordogne. A family site with good recreational facilities.
➪ *1km E of village on D703, near junction with D710.*
Apr-Sep 3HEC ⟱ ⌖ ⋔ ⋚ ⟟ ✕ ☉ ◨ ⊘ ⌂ ⋒ ⚲ P ⌹ ⊞ lau ➧
✕ ≞ ⚲R

SORE LANDES

CM Zone de Loisirs 'La Piscine' ☎ 558076006
➲ *1.2km S via D651.*
15 Jun-15 Sep 1HEC ⸺ ⚐ ⋔ ⊙ ⊟ ⋨ PR ⊡ lau ➡ ⚑ ⚏ ✕ ∅ ㎡ ⊞

SOUILLAC LOT

CM les Ondines r des Ondines ☎ 565378644
Camping Card Compulsory.
May-Sep ⋔ ⊙ ⊟ ⋨ R ⊡ ⊞ lau ➡ ⚑ ⚏ ✕

⚐ Domaine de la Paille Basse ☎ 565378548
A family site in a picturesque wooded location in the grounds of a former château.
➲ *6.5km NW off D15 Salignac-Eyvignes road.*
15 May-15 Sep 10HEC ⸺ ⚐ ➡ ⋔ ⚑ ⚏ ✕ ⊙ ⊟ ∅ ⊟ ⋨ P ⊡ ⊞ lau
Prices: ⚑33 pitch 53-65

SOULAC-SUR-MER GIRONDE

Océan L'Amélie ☎ 556097610
A level site in a pine forest, 300mtrs from the beach.
➲ *3.5km S.*
Jun-15 Sep 6HEC ⸺ ⋯ ⚐ ⋔ ⚑ ⚏ ✕ ⊙ ∅ ⊟ ⊡ ⊞ lau ➡ ⚑ ⚏ ✕ ⋨S
Prices: pitch 72 pp19

Sables d'Argent r de l'Amélie ☎ 556098287
In a pine forest, bordered by sand dunes with direct access to the beach.
➲ *1.5km SW of village.*
Etr-Sep 2.6HEC ⸺ ⋯ ⚐ ⋔ ⚑ ⚏ ✕ ⊙ ⊟ ∅ ㎡ ⊟ ⋨S ⊡ ⊞ lau ➡ ⋨P

At AMÉLIE-SUR-MER, L'(4.5km S)

Amélie-Plage ☎ 556098727
In hilly wooded terrain. Lovely sandy beach.
➲ *3km S on the Soulac road.*
Apr-30 Oct 8.5HEC ⸺ ⋯ ➡ ⋔ ⚑ ⚏ ✕ ⊙ ⊟ ∅ ㎡ ⊟ ⊟ ⋨ S ⊡ ⊞ lau
Prices: pitch 90 (incl 2 persons)

At LILIAN(4.5km S)

Pins ☎ 556098252
Situated in beautiful pine forest close to the beach with plenty of sporting facilities.
➲ *S on D101.*
Jun-Sep 3.2HEC ⋯ ➡ ⋔ ⊙ ⊟ ∅ ㎡ ⊟ ⊡ ⊞ lau ➡ ⋨S
Prices: pitch 58-68 (incl 2 persons)

SOUSTONS LANDES

CM **Airial** ☎ 558411248
➲ *2km W on D652.*
Etr-15 Oct 12HEC ⸺ ➡ ⋔ ⚑ ⚏ ✕ ⊙ ⊟ ∅ ⋨ P ⊡ ⊞ lau

TARASCON-SUR-ARIÈGE ARIÈGE

Pré Lombard rte d'Ussat ☎ 561056194
In beautiful wooded surroundings beside the River Ariège with good, modern facilities.
➲ *1.5km SE on D23.*
Feb-Dec 3.5HEC ⸺ ➡ ⋔ ⚏ ✕ ⊙ ⊟ ∅ ㎡ ⊟ ⊟ ⋨ PR ⊡ ⊞ lau ➡ ⚑ ⋨L
Prices: pitch 60-90 (incl 2 persons)

TEILLET TARN

Relais de l'Entre Deux Lacs ☎ 563557445
Shady terraced site. Various activities arranged. Beautiful views.

➲ *Off D81 towards Lacaune.*
All year 4HEC ⸺ ➡ ⋔ ⚏ ✕ ⊙ ⊟ ⊟ ⊟ ⋨ P ⊡ ⊞ lau ➡ ⚑ ∅ ㎡

TERRASSON-LA-VILLEDIEU DORDOGNE

Ile de France pl de la Vergne ☎ 553500882
➲ *500m E.*
15 Mar-Oct 0.7HEC ⸺ ➡ ⋔ ⊙ ⊟ ⊟ ⊡ ⊞ lau ➡ ⚑ ⚏ ✕ ⋨P

THIVIERS DORDOGNE

CM **Le Repaire** ☎ 553526975
In a wooded valley, this well appointed family site lies in the 'Périgord Vert' region of the Dordogne some ten minutes walk from the ancient village of Thiviers.
➲ *1500mtrs along D707 towards Lanouaille.*
May-Sep 11HEC ⸺ ⚐ ⋔ ⚑ ⚏ ⚏ ⊙ ⊟ ⊟ ⋨ P ⊡ lau ➡ ∅ ㎡ ⋨L ⊞
Prices: ⚑20-25 pitch 25-35

TONNEINS LOT-ET-GARONNE

CM **Robinson** ☎ 553790228
➲ *500m from town centre on N113 Agen road.*
Jun-Sep 0.7HEC ⸺ ➡ ⋔ ⊙ ⊟ ⊟ ⋨ R ⊡ lau ➡ ⚑ ⚏ ✕ ∅ ㎡ ⋨P ⊞

TOUZAC LOT

Ch'Timi ☎ 565365236
A well equipped site overlooking the River Lot. Entertainment available in high season.
➲ *800m from Touzac on D8.*
Apr-Sep 3.5HEC ⸺ ➡ ⋔ ⚑ ⚏ ✕ ⊙ ⊟ ∅ ⊟ ⋨ PR ⊡ ⊞ lau
Prices: ⚑18.75-25 pitch 22.75-35

Clos Bouyssac ☎ 565365221
On the fringe of a wooded hillside by the sandy shore of the River Lot. Good for walking.
➲ *S of Touzac on D65.*
May-20 Sep 5HEC ⸺ ➡ ⋔ ⚑ ⚏ ✕ ⊙ ⊟ ∅ ㎡ ⊟ ▲ ⋨ PR ⊡ ⊞ lau

URRUGNE PYRÉNÉES-ATLANTIQUES

Larrouleta ☎ 559473784
Hilly meadow with young trees.
➲ *1.5 km N of Urrugne on N1 to Spain.*
All year 5HEC ⸺ ➡ ⋔ ⚑ ⚏ ✕ ⊙ ⊟ ⋨ LR ⊡ ⊞ lau ➡ ∅ ㎡ ⋨
Prices: ⚑24 ⛺10 ⛟17 ▲17

VALEUIL DORDOGNE

Bas Meygnaud D393 Brantôme ☎ 553055844
A quiet, shady site in the Dronne Valley.
➲ *Access via D939, turning off at Lasserre.*
Apr-Sep 1.7HEC ⸺ ⋔ ⚑ ⚏ ⚏ ⊙ ⊟ ⊟ ⋨ P ⊡ ⊞ lau ➡ ⋨R
Prices: ⚑15 ⛺9 ⛟24 ▲23

VARILHES ARIÈGE

CM **Parc du Château** av du 8 Mai 45 ☎ 561674284
On the banks of the river and close to the town.
➲ *N on N20.*
All year 1HEC ⸺ ➡ ⋔ ⊙ ⊟ ⊡ ⊞ lau ➡ ⚑ ⚏ ✕ ∅ ㎡ ⋨P

VAYRAC LOT

Domaine de Bourzolles Condat ☎ 565321632
➲ *Off D20 between Condat and Vayrac.*
Jun-15 Sep 4HEC ⸺ ➡ ⋔ ⊙ ⊟ ⋨ P ⊡ ⊞ lau ➡ ⚏ ✕ ∅ ㎡

VENDAYS-MONTALIVET GIRONDE

Mayan ☎ 556417651
A small site situated in a pine wood.
➲ *Access from Bordeaux direction via N215 and D102.*
Contd.

Jul-Aug 1HEC ⬛ 🏠 🅿 ⊙ 🏪 🏢 lau
Prices: ⛺8.90 pitch 8.90

VERDON-SUR-MER, LE GIRONDE

Cordouan 📞 556097142
Clean, pleasant meadowland with some pines and deciduous trees. 1km to sea.
➲ *N of Soulac-sur-Mer via D1.*
All year 4.5HEC ⬛ ♣ 🏠 🅿 ⍢ ✕ ⊙ 🏪 🏢 🏢 ⊞ lau ➡ ✕ ⤳S

Royannais 88 rte de Soulac 📞 556096112
Level, sandy terrain under high pine and deciduous trees.
➲ *S of Le Verdon-sur-Mer in Le Royannais district on D1.*
15 Jun-15 Sep 2HEC ⬛ ⌁⌁ ♣ 🏠 🅿 ⍢ ✕ ⊙ 🏪 🏢 ⍩ 🏢 🏢 ⊞ lau ➡ ⤳S
Prices: pitch 58 (incl 2 persons) pp18

VERGT-DE-BIRON DORDOGNE

Patrasses 📞 553630587
Situated in the heart of the Périgord Noir region with good facilities.
➲ *3.6km S via D2E.*
Jun-15 Sep 3HEC ⬛ 🏠 🅿 ⍢ ✕ ⊙ 🏪 🏢 🏢 ⤳ P 🏢 ⊞ lau
Prices: ⛺20 🚐45 ⛺30

VEYRINES-DE-DOMME DORDOGNE

Pastourels Le Brouillet 📞 553295249
A quiet site in a pleasant rural setting near the Château des Milandes.
➲ *3.6km N off D53 towards Belvès.*
Apr-Sep 2.5HEC ⬛ ⌁⌁ ♣ 🏠 🅿 ⊙ 🏪 ⍢ 🏢 ⛺ ⤳ R 🏢 ⊞ lau

VÉZAC DORDOGNE

Deux Vallées 📞 553295355
A level site in a picturesque location in the Dordogne Valley. Good facilities for families.
➲ *Access via D57 from Sarlat or D703 from Bergerac.*
All year 3.6HEC ⬛ ♣ 🏠 🅿 ⍢ ✕ ⊙ 🏪 ⍢ 🏢 ⛺ ⤳ P lau ➡ ⤳R
Prices: ⛺16-26 pitch 23-36

VIELLE-ST-GIRONS LANDES

Col Vert Lac de Léon 📞 558429406
Quiet site on lakeside in sparse pine woodland. Small natural harbour in the mouth of a stream.
➲ *Turn off D652 on N side of village and continue towards lake.*
Apr-Sep 30HEC ⬛ 🏠 🏠 🅿 ⍢ ✕ ⊙ 🏪 ⍢ 🏢 🏢 ⛺ ⤳ LPS 🏢 ⊞ lau
Prices: ⛺12-25 pitch 24.50-96

Eurosol rte de la Plage 📞 558479014
Well maintained family site in a pine forest, 700mtrs from one of the finest beaches in the country.
➲ *Access via A63 exit Castets.*
Jun-15 Sep 18HEC ⬛ ⌁⌁ ♣ 🏠 🅿 ⍢ ✕ ⊙ 🏪 ⍢ ⛺ ⤳ P 🏢 ⊞ lau ➡ ⤳S
Prices: ⛺25-25 pitch 50-82

VIEUX-BOUCAU-LES-BAINS LANDES

CM des Sablères bd du Marensin 📞 558481229
A family site with modern facilities and direct access to the beach.
➲ *Access via N10 and D652.*
Apr-15 Oct 11HEC ⬛ 🏠 🏠 ⊙ 🏪 🏢 🏢 ⊞ lau ➡ ⍢ ✕ ⍢ ⍢ ⤳LS

VIGAN, LE LOT

Rêve Revers 📞 565412520
A modern family site in wooded surroundings.
➲ *From Payrac take D673 towards Le Vigan and follow signs.*
24 Apr-23 Sep 8HEC ⬛ ⌁⌁ 🏠 🏠 ⍢ 🅿 ✕ ⊙ 🏪 ⍢ 🏢 ⤳ P 🏢 ⊞ lau
Prices: ⛺16.10-23 pitch 19.60-28

VILLEFRANCHE-DU-QUEYRAN LOT-ET-GARONNE

Moulin de Campech 📞 553887243
A beautiful site in a peaceful location beside a small lake stocked with trout.
➲ *Access via D11 towards Casteljaloux.*
Apr-Sep 4HEC ⬛ ♣ 🏠 🅿 ⍢ ✕ ⊙ 🏪 ⍢ ⛺ ⤳ LPR 🏢 lau
Prices: ⛺20-28 pitch 37-47

VILLENAVE-D'ORNON GIRONDE

Gravières chemin de Macau 📞 556870036
➲ *2km NE*
All year 3.5HEC ⬛ ♠ ♣ 🏠 🅿 ⍢ ✕ ⊙ 🏪 ⍢ 🏢 🏢 ⛺ ⤳ L 🏢 ⊞ lau ➡ ⍢
Prices: ⛺19 🚐8 🚐30-38 ⛺22-30

VILLERÉAL LOT-ET-GARONNE

🏠 Château de Fonrives Rives 📞 553366338
In a beautiful natural park in the grounds of a château with good facilities for all ages.
➲ *2.2km NW via D207*
9 May-19 Sep 20HEC ⬛ ⌁⌁ ♠ ♣ 🏠 🅿 ⍢ ✕ ⊙ 🏪 ⍢ 🏢 ⛺ 🏢 ⤳ P 🏢 ⊞ lau
Prices: pitch 81-120

VITRAC DORDOGNE

Bouysse Caudon 📞 553283305
Well appointed site in a wooded valley beside the Dordogne.
➲ *2km E, near the River Dordogne.*
Etr-Sep 3HEC ⬛ ♣ 🏠 🅿 ✕ ⊙ 🏪 ⍢ ⛺ ⤳ PR 🏢 lau ➡ ⊞
Prices: ⛺27 pitch 32

Soleil Plage 📞 553283333
Set out around an old farmhouse bordering the Dordogne with excellent facilities.
➲ *4km E on D703, turn by 'Camping Clos Bernard'.*
Apr-Sep 9HEC ⬛ 🏠 🏠 🅿 ⍢ ✕ ⊙ 🏪 ⍢ ⛺ ⤳ PR 🏢 ⊞ lau
Prices: ⛺22-33 pitch 36-53

● ● ● ● LOIRE/CENTRAL ● ● ● ●

The undoubted highlight of this area is the Loire, France's longest river, which winds its unhurried way through green valleys, vine-covered hills, meadows, and, of course, past the remarkable châteaux and medieval citadels which are masterpieces spanning the changing architectural style of seven centuries. The western Loire region unites a countryside of soft hills little farms and vineyards, and historic châteaux and abbeys with the sea. North of the river the coastline meets the Atlantic at rocky cliffs; south of the river great sandy beaches are backed by great pine woods. Still farther south, the province of Charente-Maritime boasts sunshine totals to rival the Mediterranean, and 150 miles of coastline with busy ports, family resorts - both on the mainland and off-lying islands, and harbours bustling with colourful life. La Rochelle, with its ancient harbour and fine old houses, is a popular resort. Inland, there are literally hundreds of interesting churches and abbeys, and vineyards whose grapes mature into Cognac. Inland still further, the region of Limousin is a charming backwater of rolling hills, with Limoges a fascinating porcelain centre.

AIGUILLON-SUR-MER, L' VENDÉE

Bel Air ☎ 251564405
A long, level stretch of meadowland in rural surroundings.
⊃ *1.5 km NW on D44 then turn left.*
Etr-9 Sep 7HEC ⬛ ⌂ ⋔ ⅃ ♥ ⊙ ⌷ ⌀ ▬ ⌸ ⛺ ⅄ P ☎
⊞ lau ➧ ⅄LR
Prices: pitch 77-110 (incl 2 persons)

AIRVAULT DEUX-SÈVRES

Courte Vallée Courte Vallée ☎ 549647065
A modern site, situated in a river valley, with large pitches and good facilities.
⊃ *On the outskirts of the town, 0.5km NW towards Availles.*
May-Sep 3.5HEC ⬛ ⌂ ⋔ ⊙ ⌷ ⌀ ⛺ ⅄ P ☎ ⊞ lau ➧ ⅃ ⅄ ✕ ⌀ ⅄P
Prices: ⅄20 pitch 40

ALLONNES MAINE-ET-LOIRE

Pô Doré Le Pô Doré ☎ 241387880
A family site in a pleasant rural setting in the heart of the Anjou region with good recreational facilities. Separate car park for arrivals 22.00hrs.
⊃ *Access via D35 from Tours or N147 from Angers.*
3 Apr-Oct 2HEC ⬛ ⌂ ⋔ ⅃ ✕ ⊙ ⌷ ⛺ ⅄ P ☎ lau
Prices: ⅄13-18 pitch 60-80

ANDONVILLE LOIRET

Domaine de la Joullière rte de Richerelles ☎ 238395846
Spread over a series of small, wooded valleys with good sports and leisure facilities.
⊃ *1km E on road to Richerelles.*
Jan 10HEC ⬛ ⌂ ⋔ ⅃ ✕ ⊙ ⌷ ⌀ ⅄ P ☎ ⊞ lau
Prices: ⅄32 ⌷32 ⅄20

ANGERS MAINE-ET-LOIRE

Lac de Maine av du Lac de Maine ☎ 241730503
In pleasant rural surroundings on the shore of the 100 hectares Lac de Maine. There are fine sporting and entertainment facilities and the historic town of Angers is within easy reach.
⊃ *Access via A11 (Angers/Nantes) at Lac de Maine exit.*
25 Mar-10 Oct 4HEC ⬛ ⋮⋮⋮ ⌂ ⋔ ✕ ⊙ ⌷ ⌀ ⌸ ⅄ P ☎ lau ➧ ⅃ ⅄LR ⊞
Prices: pitch 58.50-73 (incl 2 persons)

ANGLES VENDÉE

Moncalm-Atlantique ☎ 251975550
Two distinct sites, but sharing the same recreational facilities in a wooded setting close to the beach.
Apr-Sep 10HEC ⬛ ♣ ⌂ ⅃ ✕ ⊙ ⌷ ⌀ ⌸ ⛺ ⌸ ⅄ P ☎ ⊞ lau ➧ ⅄R
Prices: pitch 105-130

ANGOULINS-SUR-MER CHARENTE-MARITIME

Chirats rte de la Platère ☎ 546569416
Modern site with good facilities 100m from a small sandy beach and providing panoramic views over the Bay of Fouras. The more popular, larger beaches of the area are some 3km away. Reservations are strongly recommended.
⊃ *7km S of La Rochelle.*
Etr-Sep 4.5HEC ⬛ ♣ ⌂ ⋔ ⅃ ✕ ⊙ ⌷ ⌀ ⌸ ⛺ ⅄ P ☎ ⊞ lau ➧ ⅄S
Prices: ⅄24-25 pitch 15-30

ARDILLIÈRES CHARENTE-MARITIME

Ferme Toucherit ☎ 546277306
Camping Card Compulsory.
Jun-Sep 0.8HEC ⬛ ♣ ⌂ ⊙ ⌷ ⛺ ☎ ⊞ lau ➧ ⅃ ⅄ ✕ ⌀ ⅄R

ARGENTAT CORRÈZE

Gibanel Le Gibanel ☎ 555281011
Pleasant site situated in grounds of a château next to a lake. Some facilities are only available in high season.
⊃ *S from Tulle on N120.*
Jun-14 Sep 60HEC ⬛ ⌂ ⋔ ⅃ ✕ ⊙ ⌷ ⌀ ⅄ LP ☎ ⊞ lau ➧ ⛺
Prices: ⅄21.60-27 pitch 23.20-29

Saulou Vergnolles ☎ 555281233
A peaceful site in a wooded location beside the River Dordogne. Ideal for families.
⊃ *6km S on D116.*
10 Apr-05 Sep 7HEC ⬛ ♣ ⌂ ⅃ ✕ ⊙ ⌷ ⌀ ⛺ ⅄ PR ☎ ⊞ lau
Prices: pitch 59-105 (incl 2 persons)

At MONCEAUX-SUR-DORDOGNE(3km SW)

Vaurette ☎ 555280967
On the banks of the River Dordogne with a beach, swimming pool & tennis court.
⊃ *On D12 between Argentat and Beaulieu.*
May-21 Sep 4HEC ⬛ ⌂ ⋔ ⅃ ✕ ⊙ ⌷ ⌀ ⛺ ⅄ PR ☎ ⊞ lau
Prices: ⅄21.60-27 pitch 26.40-33

ARGENTON-CHÂTEAU DEUX-SÈVRES

CM du Lac d'Hautibus ☎ 549657022
⊃ *0.4km S on D748.*
15 Jun-15 Sep 1HEC ⬛ ⌂ ⋔ ⊙ ⌷ ⛺ ☎ ⊞ lau ➧ ⅃ ✕ ⅄P

ASSERAC LOIRE-ATLANTIQUE

Traverno ☎ 240017335
⊃ *500m from the village, towards Pont-Mahé on D82.*
Jul-Sep 2HEC ⬛ ⌂ ⋔ ⊙ ⌷ ⌸ ☎ ⊞ lau ➧ ⅃ ✕ ⌀ ⛺

AVRILLÉ VENDÉE

Forges Domaine Les Forges ☎ 251223885
In a pleasant position beside a lake, 300m from the town centre. Close to beach, the site has a variety of leisure facilities.
Etr-Sep 15HEC ⬛ ⌂ ⋔ ⅃ ✕ ⊙ ⌷ ⛺ ⌸ ⅄ LP ☎ lau ➧ ⌀ ⊞
Prices: pitch 78 (incl 2 persons)

Mancelières rte de Longeville-sur-Mer ☎ 251903597
A pleasant site in a wooded park approx. 5km from the fine beaches of South Vendée. Separate car park for arrivals after 23.00hrs.
⊃ *1.7km S via D105 towards Longeville*
May-Sep 2.6HEC ⬛ ♣ ⌂ ⅃ ✕ ⊙ ⌷ ⌀ ⛺ ⌸ ⅄ P ☎ ⊞ lau ➧ ⅃ ✕
Prices: pitch 89 (incl 2 persons)

AZAY-LE-RIDEAU INDRE-ET-LOIRE

Parc du Sabot r du Stade ☎ 247454272
Site lies in large meadow on bank of River Indre.
⊃ *Near château in town centre.*
Etr-Oct 9HEC ⬛ ♣ ⌂ ⊙ ⌷ ⅄ R ☎ ⊞ lau ➧ ⅄P

BARDÉCILLE CHARENTE-MARITIME

Ferme de Chez Filleux Arces-sur-Gironde ☎ 546908433
On a level meadow partly shaded by trees and bushes with good, modern facilities. 10 minutes from the local beaches.
May-15 Sep 3HEC ⬛ ⌂ ⋔ ⅃ ✕ ⊙ ⌷ ⌀ ⌸ ⅄ P ☎ ⊞ lau ➧ ✕

BATZ-SUR-MER LOIRE-ATLANTIQUE

Govelle rte de la Côte Sauvage ☎ 240239163
Direct access to the sea. Supervised beach and sea-fishing nearby.
➲ *On D45 between Le Pouliguen and Batz.*
Apr-Sep 0.7HEC ⊞ ∷ ⚤ ⋔ ♀ ✕ ⊙ ♥ ♠ ♠ ⋞ S 🏧 🅿 ⊞ lau ➡ 🛒 ⌀ ⋞

BAULE, LA LOIRE-ATLANTIQUE

Ajoncs d'Or chemin du Rocher ☎ 240603329
In a large wooded park, close to the beach with well defined pitches.
➲ *Signposted from the entrance to the town.*
Apr-Sep 6HEC ⊞ ➡ ⋔ 🛒 ♀ ✕ ⊙ ♥ ⌀ 📛 ♠ ♠ ⋞ P 🏧 ⊞ lau ➡ ⋞S
Prices: pitch 73.50-98 (incl 2 persons)

CM av de Diane ☎ 240601740
Site consists of two sections, one for caravans, one for tents, each with separate entrance.
➲ *On NE outskirts near the railway.*
Mar-Oct 5HEC ⊞ ∷ ⚐ ⋔ 🛒 ♀ ✕ ⊙ ♥ ⌀ 📛 ♠ 🏧 ⊞ ⌀ lau ➡ ⋞PS
Prices: pitch 56-78 (incl 2 persons)

Eden St-Servais D.99 ☎ 240600323
In pleasant rural surroundings with good sports and sanitary facilities.
➲ *1km NW via N171 exit 'La Baule-Escoublac'.*
Etr-Sep 4.7HEC ⊞ ⚐ ⋔ 🛒 ♀ ✕ ⊙ ♥ ♠ ⋞ LP 🏧 ⊞ lau ➡ ✕ ⌀

Roseraie 20 av J-Sohier ☎ 240604666
A well planned site in wooded surroundings with good recreational facilities.
➲ *E of N171 towards the bay.*
Apr-Sep 5HEC ⋔ 🛒 ♀ ✕ ⊙ ♥ ⌀ 📛 ♠ ♠ ⋞ P 🏧 ⊞ lau ➡ ⋞S

BAZOUGES-SUR-LE-LOIR SARTHE

CM rte de Cré-sur-Loir ☎ 243459580
On the bank of the River Loir with well defined pitches.
➲ *Approach off A11 towards La Flèche.*
15 May-15 Oct 0.8HEC ⊞ ⚐ ⋔ ⊙ ♥ ⋞ R 🏧 lau ➡ 🛒 ♀ ✕ ⌀ 📛
Prices: ⋔7.50 pitch 15.50

BEAULIEU-SUR-DORDOGNE CORRÈZE

Îles ☎ 555910265
On an island in the River Dordogne, within easy reach of all facilities.
May-Sep 4HEC ⊞ ∷ ➡ ⋔ ♀ ♥ ⋞ R 🏧 ⊞ lau ➡ ⌀

BESSINES-SUR-GARTEMPE HAUTE-VIENNE

At MORTEROLLES-SUR-SEMME(4.5km N on N20)

CM ☎ 555766018
➲ *100m from N20; in town centre.*
All year 8HEC ⊞ ⚐ ⋔ ⊙ ♥ 🏧 ⊞ lau ➡ 🛒 ♀ ✕ ⌀ ⋞R

BEYNAT CORRÈZE

Étang de Miel ☎ 555855066
A family site in a picturesque wooded setting close to the lake within the 'Green Valley'.
➲ *4km E on N121 Argentat road.*
Jul-Aug 9HEC ⊞ ⚐ ⋔ 🛒 ♀ ✕ ⊙ ♥ ⌀ 📛 ♠ ⋞ L 🏧 ⊞ lau
Prices: ⋔24 pitch 26

BIGNAC CHARENTE

Marco de Bignac Lieudit "Les Sablons" ☎ 545217841
In a beautiful wooded location set out around the shore of a 5 acre lake with fine entertainment and sporting facilities.
➲ *N of Angoulême off N10. Take D11 W at La Touche through Vars to Basse then right onto D117 to Bignac. Site well signposted close to the River Charente.*
Apr-Sep 8.5HEC ⊞ ➡ ⋔ 🛒 ♀ ✕ ⊙ ♥ ♠ ⋞ LP 🏧 ⊞ lau ➡ ⋞R
Prices: pitch 65-80 (incl 2 persons)

BLÉRÉ INDRE-ET-LOIRE

CM r de la Gatine ☎ 247579260
Well-kept site beside River Cher. Two entrances.
Apr-15 Oct 4HEC ⊞ ⚐ ⋔ ⊙ ♥ 🏧 🅿 lau ➡ 🛒 ♀ ✕ ⋞P ⊞

BLOIS LOIR-ET-CHER

CM Boire bd A-Carrel ☎ 254742278
➲ *1.5km E on D751.*
Mar-Nov 10HEC ⊞ ⚐ ⋔ ⊙ ♥ 🏧 ⊞ lau ➡ 🛒 ♀ ✕ ⋞LP

BONNAC-LA-CÔTE HAUTE-VIENNE

🏰 *Château de Leychoisier* ☎ 555399343
Well-managed site on ground sloping gently towards the woods. Divided into roomy pitches.
➲ *1km S off N20.*
15 Apr-20 Sep 2HEC ⊞ ⚐ ⋔ 🛒 ♀ ✕ ⊙ ♥ ⌀ ⋞ LP 🏧 ⊞ lau

BONNES VIENNE

CM r de la Varenne ☎ 549564434
A quiet site with plenty of recreational facilities.
➲ *S beside the River Vienne.*
May-Sep 1HEC ⊞ ⚐ ⋔ ⊙ ♥ ♠ ⋞ R 🏧 lau ➡ 🛒 ♀ ✕ 📛 ⋞L ⊞
Prices: ⋔17 ➡6 ♠11 ▲8

BONNY-SUR-LOIRE LOIRET

Val ☎ 238315771
Woodland site situated by the side of the Loire, near the town centre
➲ *At the junction of N7 and D965.*
5 Apr-1 Nov 0.8HEC ⊞ ⚐ ⋔ ⊙ ♥ ⋞ R 🏧 lau ➡ 🛒 ♀ ✕ 📛
Prices: ⋔7 pitch 7

BOURGES CHER

CM de Bourges 26 bd de l'Industrie ☎ 248201685
In the town near Lake Auron.
➲ *Access via A71, N144 or N76.*
15 Mar-15 Nov 2.2HEC ⊞ ∷ ⚐ ⋔ ⊙ ♥ 🏧 ⊞ lau ➡ 🛒 ♀ ✕ ⌀ 📛 ⋞LPR
Prices: ⋔18 ♠26 ▲18

BOUSSAC-BOURG CREUSE

🏰 *Château de Poinsouze* rte de La Châtre ☎ 5555650121
In a picturesque location in the grounds of a château with good, modern facilities.
➲ *2km N via D917.*
May-19 Sep 22HEC ⊞ ⚐ ⋔ 🛒 ♀ ✕ ⊙ ♥ ⌀ 📛 ♠ ⋞ LP 🏧 ⊞ lau ➡ ⋞R
Prices: pitch 80-145 (incl 2 persons)

BOUZONVILLE-AUX-BOIS LOIRET

Clos des Tourterelles 29 r des Rendillons ☎ 238330100
➲ *8km S of Pithiviers on D921.*
All year 0.5HEC ⊞ ➡ ⋔ 🛒 ♀ ⊙ ♥ ⌀ 📛 ♠ 🏧 lau ➡ ♀ ✕

BRACIEUX LOIR-ET-CHER

CM des Châteaux rte de Blois ☎ 254464184
In a pleasant, shady park close to the town centre and conveniently situated for visiting the castles of Chambord, Cheverny and Villesavin.
Apr-15 Oct 14HEC ▦ ♣ ♠ ⌂ ⊙ ▯ ⌀ ▯ ▦ ⚑ ⇃ PR ☎ ⊞ lau ➡ ⛴ ♟ ✕
Prices: pitch 43-53

BRAIN-SUR-L'AUTHION MAINE-ET-LOIRE

CM Caroline ☎ 241804218
A modern site in a pleasant wooded setting close to the river.
15 Mar-Oct 3.5HEC ▦ ♣ ♠ ⊙ ▯ ☎ ⊞ lau ➡ ⛴ ♟ ✕ ⌀ ⚏ ⇃R
Prices: ♟12 ⚐9 ⚑10 ⛺10

BRETIGNOLLES-SUR-MER VENDÉE

Dunes Plage des Dunes ☎ 251905532
Direct access to the beach. All plots surrounded by hedges.
⮡ *2km S turn right off D38 and proceed for 1km across the dunes. 150m from beach.*
Apr-Oct 12HEC ⋇ 🏊 ♠ ⛴ ♟ ✕ ⊙ ▯ ⌀ ⚏ ⚑ ⇃ P ☎ ⊞ lau ➡ ⇃S
Prices: ♟15-27 pitch 80-130

Motine 4 r des Morinières ☎ 251900442
Pleasant site situated 350m from the town centre and 400m from the beach with good facilities.
Apr-Sep 1.8HEC ▦ ♠ ♟ ✕ ✕ ⊙ ▯ ⌀ ⚏ ⚑ ☎ ⊞ lau ➡ ⛴ ⇃LS

Vagues 20 bd du Centre ☎ 251901948
A family site situated on the Côte de Lumière in a delightful rural setting.
⮡ *N on D38 towards St-Gilles-Croix-de-Vie.*
Apr-Sep 4.3HEC ▦ ♣ ♠ ♟ ⊙ ▯ ⚏ ⚑ ⇃ P ☎ ⊞ lau ➡ ⛴ ✕ ⌀ ⇃RS
Prices: pitch 112-128 (incl 3 persons)

BRISSAC-QUINCÉ MAINE-ET-LOIRE

Domaine de l'Étang ☎ 241917061
A lakeside site in the heart of the Anjou countryside with good recreational facilities.
⮡ *Access via D748 towards Poitiers.*
15 May-15 Sep 3.5HEC ▦ ♠ ♠ ⛴ ♟ ✕ ⊙ ▯ ⌀ ⚏ ⚑ ⇃ P ☎ ⊞ lau ➡ ✕
Prices: ♟21.20-26.50 pitch 50.40-63

BRÛLON SARTHE

Brûlon-le-Lac ☎ 243956896
May-Sep 3HEC ▦ ♣ ♠ ⛴ ♟ ✕ ⊙ ▯ ⌀ ⛺ ⇃ LP ☎ ⊞ lau ➡ ⚏ ⇃R
Prices: pitch 65 (incl 2 persons)

CANDÉ-SUR-BEUVRON LOIR-ET-CHER

Grande Tortue 3 rte de Pontlevoy ☎ 254441520
A family site in a peaceful wooded setting.
⮡ *D751, between Blois and Amboise, on the left bank of the river.*
Etr-Sep 5.8HEC ▦ ♣ ♠ ⛴ ♟ ✕ ⊙ ▯ ⌀ ⚏ ⚑ ⇃ P ☎ ⊞ lau
Prices: pitch 56-97 (incl 2 persons)

CHALARD, LE HAUTE-VIENNE

Vigères Les Vigères ☎ 555093722
Generally level site in peaceful surroundings in an elevated position with fine views. English management.
⮡ *Between Châlus and Le Chalard on D901.*
All year 20HEC ▦ ♠ ♠ ⊙ ▯ ▯ ⚑ ⛺ ⇃ L ☎ ⊞ lau ➡ ♟ ✕
Prices: ♟13-15 pitch 12-16

CHALONNES-SUR-LOIRE MAINE-ET-LOIRE

CM Candais rte de Rochefort ☎ 241780227
On the banks of the River Loire at its confluence with the River Louet.
⮡ *NE off D751 towards Rochefort.*
15 May-Sep 3HEC ▦ ♣ ♠ ⊙ ▯ ☎ ⊞ lau ➡ ⛴ ♟ ✕ ⌀ ⇃P
Prices: pitch 47 (incl 2 persons)

CHARTRES EURE-ET-LOIR

CM des Bords de l'Eure 9 r de Launay ☎ 237287943
In wooded surroundings beside the river.
⮡ *Signposted towards Orléans.*
21 Apr-3 Sep 3.9HEC ▦ ♠ ♠ ⛴ ⊙ ▯ ▯ ☎ ⊞ lau ➡ ♟ ✕ ⇃PR
Prices: pitch 49-71 (incl 3 persons)

CHARTRE-SUR-LE-LOIR, LA SARTHE

Vieux Moulin av des Déportés ☎ 243444118
15 Apr-Sep 2.4HEC ▦ ♠ ♠ ⊙ ▯ ⚑ ⇃ PR ☎ ⊞ lau ➡ ⛴ ♟ ✕ ⌀ ⚏ ⇃LP

CHASSENEUIL-SUR-BONNIEURE CHARENTE

CM r des Ecoles ☎ 45395536
⮡ *W of town via D27, beside the River Bonnieure.*
15 Jun-15 Sep 2HEC ▦ ♠ ♠ ⊙ ▯ ⚑ lau ➡ ⛴ ♟ ✕ ⌀ ⇃P ⊞
Prices: ♟7.50 pitch 5.20

CHÂTEAU-DU-LOIR SARTHE

CM de Coemont ☎ 243794463
Shady site on the bank of the Loir.
15 May-15 Sep 0.6HEC ▦ ♠ ♠ ⊙ ▯ ⇃ R ☎ lau ➡ ⛴ ♟ ✕ ⌀ ⇃P ⊞

CHÂTEAULONG VENDÉE

Pin Parasol Lac du Jaunay ☎ 251346472
In the heart of the Vendée countryside on the shore of Lac du Jaunay with good, modern facilities.
⮡ *Between D6 and D12.*
May-15 Sep 5HEC ▦ ♠ ♠ ⛴ ♟ ✕ ⊙ ▯ ⌀ ⚏ ⛺ ⚑ ⇃ P ☎ ⊞ lau ➡ ⇃L

CHÂTELAILLON-PLAGE CHARENTE-MARITIME

Clos des Rivages av des Boucholeurs ☎ 546562609
Level, well-kept site with pitches divided by trees and bushes, 500mtrs from the sea.
⮡ *500mtrs from the village. Signposted.*
15 Jun-10 Sep 2.5HEC ▦ ♠ ♠ ⊙ ▯ ⌀ ⊞ lau ➡ ⛴ ♟ ✕ ⚏ ⇃S

Deux Plages ☎ 546562753
In pleasant wooded surroundings 200mtrs from the beach.
May-15 Sep 4.5HEC ▦ ⋇ ♣ ♠ ⛴ ♟ ✕ ⊙ ▯ ⛺ ⚏ ☎ ⊞ lau ➡ ⛴ ⌀ ⚏ ⇃S
Prices: pitch 80 (incl 3 persons)

CHÂTELLERAULT VIENNE

Relais du Miel rte d'Antran ☎ 549020627
In the grounds of the Château de Valette, beside the River Vienne.
⮡ *Access via A10 exit 26 (Châtellerault Nord).*
May-Sep 7HEC ▦ ⋇ ♠ ♠ ⛴ ♟ ✕ ⊙ ▯ ⚑ ⇃ PR ☎ ⊞ lau ➡ ⌀ ⚏
Prices: pitch 130 (incl 2 persons)

CHÂTRES-SUR-CHER LOIR-ET-CHER

CM des Saules ☎ 254980455
⮡ *On N76 near bridge.*
May-Sep 1.8HEC ▦ ♠ ♠ ⊙ ▯ ⇃ R ☎ lau ➡ ⛴ ♟ ✕ ⌀ ⚏ ⇃P ⊞

CHAUFFOUR-SUR-VELL CORRÈZE

Feneyrolles ☎ 555253143
In a quiet, wooded location with good facilities. Ideal for exploring the Dordogne Valley and surrounding area.
➲ *2.2km E.*
15 Apr-15 Sep 4HEC ⏚⏚⏚ ♣ ⋔ ⍾ ⍨ ❤ ✕ ☉ ⊟ ⏠ ⊞ ⋌ P ⌧ ⊞
lau
Prices: ⋔20 pitch 20

CHEF-BOUTONNE DEUX-SÈVRES

Moulin Treneuillet, rte de Brioux ☎ 549297346
Small, secluded family site in a rural setting.
➲ *1km NE via D740.*
All year 2HEC ⏚⏚⏚ ⊶ ⋔ ⍾ ⍨ ✕ ☉ ⊟ ⏠ ⏠ ⛺ ⋌ P ⌧ ⊞ lau
Prices: ⋔12-14 pitch 30-45

CHÉNIERS CREUSE

Moulin de Piot ☎ 555621320
In beautiful natural surroundings in the heart of the Creuse region.
➲ *Access via D6. In Chéniers turn left by the bakers in the village square.*
Mar-Oct 1HEC ⏚⏚⏚ ♣ ⋔ ☉ ⊟ ⏠ ⛺ ⋌ R ⌧ ⊞ lau ♦ ⍾ ⍨ ✕ ⌀ ⍙

CHENONCEAUX INDRE-ET-LOIRE

Moulin Fort ☎ 247238622
➲ *2km SE*
May-15 Sep 3HEC ⏚⏚⏚ ⊶ ⋔ ⍾ ⍨ ✕ ☉ ⊟ ⌀ ⋌ PR ⌧ ⊞ lau

CHÉVERNY LOIR-ET-CHER

Les Saules rte de Contres ☎ 254799001
In the heart of the Châteaux-du-Val-de-Loire, bordered by a golf course and the Cheverny forest.
➲ *1.5km from town towards Contres on D102.*
Etr-22 Sep 10HEC ⏚⏚⏚ ♣ ⋔ ⍾ ⍨ ✕ ☉ ⊟ ⏠ ⏠ ⛺ ⋌ P ⌧ ⊞ lau
Prices: ⋔29-30 ⛺43-44 ⋔37-38

CHINON INDRE-ET-LOIRE

CM ☎ 247930835
On the banks of the river opposite the Château.
➲ *Off D951.*
Apr-Oct 6HEC ⏚⏚⏚ ⠿⠿ ⊶ ⋔ ☉ ⊟ ⛺ ⋌ PR ⌧ ⊞ lau ♦ ⍾ ⍨ ✕ ⋌S

CHOLET MAINE-ET-LOIRE

Lac de Ribou av L-Mandin ☎ 241587474
Well set-out site bordering a lake, with fishing, boating, tennis and volleyball.
➲ *3km from town centre.*
Apr-Oct 5HEC ⏚⏚⏚ ♣ ⋔ ⍾ ⍨ ✕ ☉ ⊟ ⏠ ⛺ ⋌ P lau ♦ ⋌L

CLOYES-SUR-LE-LOIR EURE-ET-LOIR

Parc des Loisirs rte du Montigny ☎ 237985053
On the bank of the River Loir. Extensive leisure facilities. Separate section for teenagers. Shop only available in July and August, bar and restaurant only May-September.
➲ *Access from Châteaudun S on N10 towards Cloyes, then right onto Montigny-le-Gamelon road.*
15 Mar-14 Nov 5HEC ⏚⏚⏚ ⊶ ⋔ ⍾ ⍨ ✕ ☉ ⊟ ⌀ ⏠ ⋌ P ⌧ ⊞ lau
Prices: ⋔25 ⛺40 ⛺40 ⋔40

COGNAC CHARENTE

Cognac rte de Ste-Sévère, bd de Chatenay ☎ 545321332
In wooded surroundings beside the River Charente with good, modern facilities.

➲ *2km N on D24.*
May-15 Oct 1.6HEC ⏚⏚⏚ ⊶ ⋔ ⍾ ⍨ ✕ ☉ ⊟ ⋌ PR ⌧ lau ♦ ⍨ ✕ ⋌P ⊞
Prices: ⋔33-39 pitch 44-50

CONTRES LOIR-ET-CHER

Charmoise Sassay ☎ 154795515
On a level meadow with good facilities.
➲ *N956.*
Apr-Oct 1HEC ⏚⏚⏚ ⊶ ⋔ ☉ ⊟ ⌧ lau ♦ ⍾ ⍨ ✕ ⌀ ⍙

Prices: pp15

COUHÉ-VERAC VIENNE

Peupliers ☎ 549592116
A family site in a forest beside the river.
➲ *N of village on N10 Poitiers road.*
2 May-Sep 8HEC ⏚⏚⏚ ⊶ ⋔ ⍾ ⍨ ✕ ☉ ⊟ ⏠ ⏠ ⛺ ⋌ PR ⌧ ⊞ lau ♦ ⍙
Prices: ⋔23.20-29 pitch 31.20-39

COURÇON-D'AUNIS CHARENTE-MARITIME

Garenne 21 r du Stade ☎ 546016050
15 Mar-Oct ⏚⏚⏚ ♣ ⋔ ☉ ⊟ ⌧ lau ♦ ⍾ ⍨ ✕ ⌀ ⍙ ⋌P ⊞

COUTURES MAINE-ET-LOIRE

Européen Montsabert ☎ 241579163
In a picturesque wooded park with mature trees.
➲ *Access via left bank of the River Loire (D751) between Angers and Saumur.*
May-Sep 10HEC ⏚⏚⏚ ⊶ ⋔ ✕ ☉ ⊟ ⏠ ⛺ ⋌ P ⌧ ⊞ lau ♦ ⍾ ✕ ⌀ ⍙

CROISIC, LE LOIRE-ATLANTIQUE

Océan ☎ 240230769
A quiet, well appointed site situated 150m from the sea.
➲ *1.5km NW via D45*
Apr-Sep 7.5HEC ⏚⏚⏚ ⊶ ⋔ ⍾ ⍨ ✕ ☉ ⊟ ⌀ ⍙ ⏠ ⛺ ⋌ P ⌧ ⊞ lau ♦ ⋌S

DISSAY VIENNE

Bois de Chaume Chemin des Meuniers ☎ 549623630
Situated on N10 within easy reach of the Futuroscope.
Mar-Oct 1.7HEC ⏚⏚⏚ ⊶ ⋔ ☉ ⊟ ⏠ ⛺ ⌧ lau ♦ ✕ ⋌R
Prices: pitch 32-50 (incl 2 persons)

DURTAL MAINE-ET-LOIRE

CM 9 r du Camping ☎ 241763180
A pleasant site beside the River Loire.
➲ *Near the centre of the town. Access via N23 or A11.*
Etr-Sep 3HEC ⏚⏚⏚ ⊶ ⋔ ☉ ⊟ ⌀ ⛺ ⌧ ⊞ lau ♦ ⍾ ⍨ ✕ ⍙ ⋌P
Prices: pitch 50 (incl 2 persons)

EGLETONS CORRÈZE

Egletons-Lac ☎ 555931475
A lakeside site in wooded surroundings with a fine range of recreational facilities.
➲ *2km from Egletons towards Ussel.*
All year 9HEC ⏚⏚⏚ ♣ ⋔ ⍨ ✕ ☉ ⊟ ⌀ ⍙ ⏠ ⊞ lau ♦ ⋌LP
Prices: ⋔20 ⛺8 ⛺10 ⋔10

EYMOUTHIERS CHARENTE

⛺Gorges du Chambon ☎ 545707170
In a beautiful location on a wooded hilltop.
➲ *3km N via D163.*
15 May-15 Sep 7HEC ⏚⏚⏚ ♣ ⋔ ⍾ ⍨ ✕ ☉ ⊟ ⌀ ⏠ ⋌ PR ⌧ ⊞ lau
Prices: ⋔24-28 pitch 34-38

❯ FAUTE-SUR-MER, LA VENDÉE

Fautais 18 rte de la Tranche ☎ 251564196
Situated in centre of village. Numbered pitches.
➲ *On D46.*
Jul-Aug 1HEC ⊞ ♦ ↾ ☉ ◨ ☎ ⊞ lau ➡ ﹗ ✗ ∅ ⚡LRS
Prices: pitch 80 (incl 3 persons)

Flots Bleus av des Chardons ☎ 251271111
Family site only 100m from the sea.
➲ *In La Faute, cross Pont de l'Aiguillons-sur-Mer and follow Route de la Pointe d'Arçay to site.*
Apr-8 Sep 1.5HEC ⊞ ♦ ↾ ﹗ ✗ ☉ ◨ ∅ ☶ ☎ ◨ ⚑ ⊞ lau ➡ ﹗ ✗ ⚡RS
Prices: pitch 70-106 (incl 3 persons)

❯ FENOUILLER, LE VENDÉE

Domaine le Pas Opton rte de Nantes ☎ 251551198
Well equipped family site a few minutes from the beach and close to the "Des Vallées" sailing centre.
➲ *2km N beside the River Vie on D754.*
20 May-10 Sep 6.5HEC ⊞ ♦ ↾ ﹗ ✗ ☉ ◨ ∅ ☎ ⚡ PR ◨ ⊞ ⚑ lau

❯ FLÈCHE, LA SARTHE

Route d'Or allée de la Providence ☎ 243945590
➲ *Beside the River Loir*
Closed 15 Nov-15 Feb 4.5HEC ⊞ ♦ ↾ ☉ ◨ ∅ ◨ ⚡ R ◨ lau ➡ ﹗ ✗ ⚡LP ⊞

❯ FRESNAY-SUR-SARTHE SARTHE

CM Sans Souci r de Haut Ary ☎ 243973287
Pool open weekends June and all July-Aug
➲ *1km SE on D310.*
Apr-Sep 2HEC ⊞ ↾ ☉ ◨ ∅ ⚡ PR ◨ lau ➡ ﹗ ✗ ☶
Prices: ♠12 pitch 42

❯ FRIDAUDOUR HAUTE-VIENNE

Freaudour ☎ 555765722
A well equipped site beside Lac de St-Pardoux.
➲ *Access via A20 exit 25.*
5 Jun-13 Sep 4.5HEC ⊞ ↾ ﹗ ✗ ☉ ◨ ∅ ☎ ⚡ LP ◨ ⊞ lau
Prices: pitch 70-102 (incl 2 persons)

❯ GENNES MAINE-ET-LOIRE

Européen Montsabert ☎ 241579163
In wooded surroundings close to the River Loire with good facilities.
➲ *Access via D751.*
May-Sep 10HEC ⊞ ♦ ↾ ﹗ ✗ ☉ ◨ ☎ ⚡ P ◨ ⊞ lau ➡ ﹗ ∅ ☶
Prices: pitch 95 (incl 3 persons)

Your holiday in the Loire Valley

LES BOIS DU BARDELET

Lake, water slide, 3 swimming pools

All activities with club-card. Tennis, canoe, archery,
Mini golf, fishing, recreation programme.
Open Easter – 30.9.
NEW: indoor swimming pool, body-building, jacuzzi.

Route de Bourges D940 • POILLY • F-45500 GIEN
Tel: 0033 238 67 47 39 • Fax 0033 238 38 27 16

Chalets and mobile homes for hire
per week or weekend

Bord de l'Eau r des Cadets de Saumur ☎ 241380467
In a peaceful location on the river bank.
➲ *N beside the River Loire*
May-Oct 2.5HEC ⊞ ↾ ↾ ☉ ◨ ⚡ R ◨ lau ➡ ﹗ ✗ ∅ ⚡P ⊞
Prices: ♠14 pitch 11

❯ GIEN LOIRET

Bois du Bardelet rte de Bourges, Poilly ☎ 238674739
A family site with a good variety of sporting facilities.
➲ *Access via D940 SW of Gien.*
Apr-Sep 12HEC ⊞ ↾ ↾ ﹗ ✗ ☉ ◨ ∅ ☎ ⚡ LP ◨ ⊞ lau
Prices: pitch 72-120 (incl 2 persons)

❯ GIVRAND VENDÉE

Europa Le Petit Bois ☎ 251553268
A pleasant family site with a wide variety of recreational facilities and modern sanitary blocks.
➲ *W from St-Gilles-Croix-de-Vie via D6 for 2.5km, then S for 0.2km.*
Apr-Sep 4HEC ⊞ ↾ ↾ ﹗ ✗ ☉ ◨ ∅ ☶ ☎ ⚡ P ◨ ⊞ lau ➡ ⚡LRS
Prices: ♠19-27 pitch 44-79

❯ GRIÈRE VENDÉE

Préveils av Ste-Anne-la-Grière ☎ 3251304052
A pleasant site in wooded surroundings 200m from the beach.
15 May-15 Sep 4HEC ⁂ ↾ ↾ ﹗ ✗ ☉ ◨ ∅ ☶ ☎ ⚡ P ◨ ⊞ lau ➡ ⚡S

❯ GUÉMENÉ-PENFAO LOIRE-ATLANTIQUE

Hermitage 36 av du Paradis ☎ 240792348
➲ *1.5km N on rte de Châteaubriant.*
Apr-Oct 2.5HEC ⊞ ↾ ↾ ☉ ◨ ☎ ▲ ⚡ P ◨ lau ➡ ﹗ ✗ ∅ ☶ ⚡R ⊞
Prices: pitch 45-52 (incl 2 persons)

❯ GUÉRANDE LOIRE-ATLANTIQUE

Bréhadour ☎ 240249312
➲ *2km NE on D51, rte de St-Lyphard.*
3 Apr-26 Sep 7HEC ⊞ ↾ ↾ ﹗ ✗ ☉ ◨ ☎ ▲ ⚡ P ◨ lau ➡ ∅ ☶ ⊞
Prices: ♠23-29 pitch 25-39

Parc de Lévéno rte de l'Étang de Sandun ☎ 240247930
In a pleasant location with good facilities.
➲ *3km E via rte de Sandun.*
May-25 Sep 12HEC ⊞ ↾ ↾ ﹗ ✗ ☉ ◨ ∅ ☶ ☎ ☎ ⚡ P ◨ ⊞ lau
Prices: ♠17.50-25 pitch 44.80-81

Pré du Château de Careil Careil ☎ 240602299
Divided into pitches. Caravans only. Booking recommended for Jul & Aug.
➲ *2km N of La Baule on D92.*
May-27 Sep 2HEC ⊞ ↾ ↾ ☉ ◨ ⚡ P ◨ ⊞ lau ➡ ﹗ ✗ ∅ ☶
Prices: pitch 110-125 (incl 2 persons)

❯ HÉRIC LOIRE-ATLANTIQUE

Pindière ☎ 240576541
A family site on a level meadow with good facilities.
➲ *1km from town on D16.*
All year 3HEC ⊞ ↾ ↾ ﹗ ✗ ☉ ◨ ☶ ☎ ☎ ⚡ P ◨ ⊞ lau ➡ ﹗
Prices: ♠16 pitch 25

⟩ **HOUMEAU, L'** CHARENTE-MARITIME

Trépied au Plomb ☎ 546509082
⤷ *NE via D106*
20 May-25 Sep 2HEC ⱲⱲ 🖴 🏕 ⊙ 🍴 🖈 ⊞ lau ➡ 🛒 🍴 ✕ ⊘ 🚿
ᚬS

⟩ **INGRANDES** VIENNE

⟩ At **ST-USTRE**(2km NE)

🏠 **Petit Trianon de St-Ustre** ☎ 549026147
In a beautiful park surrounding a small 18th-century castle,
the site has good entertainment and recreational facilities.
⤷ *Turn off N10 at signpost N of Ingrandes and continue for
1km.*
15 May-20 Sep 7HEC ⱲⱲ 🖴 🏕 🛒 ⊙ 🍴 ⊘ 🏕 🚐 ᚬ P 🏧 ⊞ lau
➡ 🍴 ✕
Prices: 🏠36 pitch 22

⟩ **JARD-SUR-MER** VENDÉE

Curtys r de la Perpoise ☎ 251336342
May-Sep 4.4HEC ⱲⱲ 🌿 🏕 🛒 ✕ ⊙ 🍴 ⊘ 🏕 🚐 ᚬ P 🏧 lau
➡ 🛒 ᚬS

Écureuils rte des Goffineaux ☎ 251334274
Quiet woodland terrain 500yds from the sea. Large pitches
surrounded by hedges.
⤷ *Signposted.*
21 May-12 Sep 4.3HEC ⱲⱲ ⫶⫶⫶ 🖴 🏕 🛒 🍴 ✕ ⊙ 🍴 ⊘ 🏕 🚐 ᚬ
P 🏧 ⊞ ⌇ lau ➡ ✕ ᚬS
Prices: 🏠30 pitch 66

Océano d'Or r G-Clemenceau ☎ 251334385
A well maintained site 1km from the beach and 500mtrs
from the town centre.
⤷ *Access via D19.*
Apr-25 Sep 8HEC ⱲⱲ 🌿 🏕 🛒 🍴 ✕ ⊙ 🍴 ⊘ 🏕 🚐 🛆 ᚬ P
⊞ lau ➡ ᚬS
Prices: pitch 70-123 (incl 2 persons)

⟩ **JARGEAU** LOIRET

Isle aux Moulins r du 44ème RI ☎ 238597004
In a wooded location on the bank of the Loire.
Mar-Nov 7.2HEC ⱲⱲ 🖴 🏕 🛒 ⊙ 🍴 ⊘ 🏕 🚐 ᚬ R 🏧 ⊞ lau
➡ 🍴 ✕ ᚬP
Prices: 🏠14 pitch 18-20

⟩ **JAUNAY CLAN** VIENNE

Croix du Sud rte de Neuville ☎ 549625814
Within easy reach of 'Futuroscope', the European Park of the
Moving Image.
⤷ *Access via A10 and D62.*
Feb-10 Nov 4HEC ⱲⱲ 🌿 🛒 🍴 ✕ ⊙ 🍴 🏕 🚐 ᚬ P 🏧 lau ➡
⊞
Prices: 🏠22 pitch 40

⟩ **JAVRON** MAYENNE

CM rte de Bagnoles-de-l'Orne ☎ 243034067
⤷ *200m SW of town off N12. On the road to Mayenne after
the little lake take road for Bagnoles-de-l'Orne, then take first
on left. Signposted.*
Jul-Aug 1.5HEC ⱲⱲ 🖴 🏕 ⊙ 🍴 ᚬ R 🏧 ⊞ lau ➡ 🛒 🍴 ✕ ⊘ 🏕

⟩ **LAGORD** CHARENTE-MARITIME

CM Parc r du Parc ☎ 546676154
Pleasant municipal site within easy reach of the coast.
⤷ *Access via N137/D735.*
15 May-Sep ⱲⱲ 🖴 🏕 ⊙ 🍴 🏧 ⊞ lau ➡ 🛒 🍴 ✕ ⊘ 🏕
Prices: pitch 44 (incl 2 persons)

⟩ **LANDEVIEILLE** VENDÉE

Pong r du Stade ☎ 251229263
A family site with spacious pitches surrounded by trees and
bushes. Good recreational facilities.
Etr-Sep 3HEC ⱲⱲ ➡ 🏕 🛒 🍴 ✕ ⊙ 🍴 ⊘ 🏕 🏕 🚐 ᚬ P 🏧 ⊞ lau
➡ ⊞
Prices: pitch 75-90 (incl 3 persons)

⟩ **LINDOIS, LE** CHARENTE

Étang ☎ 545650267
Well shaded site with a natural lake, ideal for swimming and
fishing with a small beach.
⤷ *From Rochefoucauld take D13 towards Montemboeuf.*
All year 9.7HEC ⱲⱲ 🖴 🏕 🛒 ✕ ⊙ 🍴 ᚬ L 🏧 ⊞ lau ➡ 🛒 ⊘ 🏕
Prices: 🏠22 pitch 40

⟩ **LION D'ANGERS, LE** MAINE-ET-LOIRE

CM Frénes ☎ 241953156
A municipal site on the banks of the River Oudon, 300mtrs
from the town centre.
⤷ *NE on N162.*
15 May-Aug 2HEC ⱲⱲ 🖴 🏕 ⊙ 🍴 🏧 lau ➡ 🛒 🍴 ✕ ᚬP ⊞

⟩ **LISSAC-SUR-COUZE** CORRÈZE

Prairie ☎ 555853797
Jun-13 Sep 3HEC ⱲⱲ ⫶⫶⫶ 🖴 🏕 🛒 ⊙ 🍴 🏕 🏧 ⊞ lau ➡ 🍴 ✕

⟩ **LONGEVILLE** VENDÉE

Brunelles Le Bouil ☎ 251335075
A well appointed site in a wooded location 700mtrs from the
beach.
⤷ *On the coast between Longeville and Jard-sur-Mer.*
Etr-Sep 4.8HEC ⱲⱲ 🖴 🏕 ⊙ 🍴 ⊘ 🏕 🏕 🚐 ᚬ P 🏧 ⊞ lau ➡ 🛒
🍴 ✕ ᚬS
Prices: pitch 67-120 (incl 2 persons)

Jarny Océan Le Bouil ☎ 251335819
Subdivided well tended meadow, with a holiday complex of
the same name where shopping facilities are provided. 800m
to sea via forest path.
⤷ *Turn off D105 about 3km S of Longeville.*
May-15 Sep 7.6HEC ⱲⱲ 🖴 🏕 🛒 🍴 ✕ ⊙ 🍴 ⊘ ᚬ P 🏧 lau ➡ ✕
🏕 ᚬS
Prices: pitch 58-144 (incl 2 persons)

⟩ At **CONCHES, LES**(4km S)

Dunes av de la Plage ☎ 251333293
Well-kept site amongst sand dunes in pine forest.
⤷ *6km S of Longeville on D105.*
May-Sep 5HEC ⫶⫶⫶ ➡ 🏕 🛒 🍴 ✕ ⊙ 🍴 ⊘ 🚐 ᚬ P 🏧 ⊞ lau
ᚬPRS

⟩ **LUCHÉ-PRINGÉ** SARTHE

CM de la Chabotière Place des Tilleuls ☎ 243451000
Site by a river just 100 metres from the village and a short
drive from several Loire chateaux. Large marked sites are set
on terraces above the river and most cars are kept in a private
car park to ensure play areas are safe for children.
Apr-15 Oct 1.7HEC ⱲⱲ 🖴 🏕 ⊙ 🍴 🏕 ᚬ P 🏧 🏧 ⊞ lau ➡ 🛒 🍴
✕ ⊘ 🏕
Prices: 🏠8.50-16 pitch 10

⟩ **LUDE, LE** SARTHE

CM rte du Mans ☎ 243946770
Shady site in a rural location with direct access to the River
Loir.
⤷ *400m from town centre, direct from N307.*
Apr-Sep 4.5HEC ⱲⱲ ➡ 🏕 ⊙ 🍴 🏕 ᚬ PR 🏧 ⊞ lau ➡ 🛒 🍴 ✕

▶ **LUSIGNAN** VIENNE

CM Vauchiron Vauchiron ☎ 549433008
➲ *500m NE on N11.*
15 Apr-15 Oct 4HEC ⬛ 🔾🏠💧✕⊙🔌⌇R 🏧⊞ lau ➡ 🏧
✕🔌🛏
Prices: 🛝8 ➡5 🚐5 🛆5

▶ **LUYNES** INDRE-ET-LOIRE

CM Granges Les Granges ☎ 247556085
Quiet site close to the village. Ideal for visiting historical sites,
fishing, and wine tasting
➲ *S via D49.*
8 May-15 Sep 0.8HEC ⬛ 🔾🏠⊙🔌🔌⌇🏧⊞ lau ➡ 🏧💧✕
⌇P
Prices: 🛝11 pitch 11-12

▶ **MAGNAC-BOURG** HAUTE-VIENNE

Écureuils rte de Limoges ☎ 555008028
A grassy site close to the historic village
➲ *25 kms S on N20.*
Apr-Sep 1.3HEC ⬛ 🔾🏠⊙🔌🏧 lau ➡ 🏧💧✕🔌🛏⊞
Prices: 🛝12 pitch 12

▶ **MANSIGNÉ** SARTHE

CM de la Plage rte du Plessis ☎ 243461417
A holiday complex set in extensive parkland around a 60 acre
lake with good recreational facilities.
➲ *On D13, 4km from D307 (Le Mans-Le Lude).*
Etr-Oct 3.4HEC ⬛ 🔾🏠💧✕⊙🔌🔌🔌⌇LP🏧⊞ lau ➡
🏧🔌🛏

▶ **MARANS** CHARENTE-MARITIME

CM Le Bois Dinot rte de Nantes ☎ 546011051
Separate car park for arrivals after 22.00hrs.
➲ *Access via N137 (Nantes-Bordeaux).*
Apr-15 Nov 6HEC ⬛ 🔾🏠⊙🔌🔌⌇P🏧⊞ lau ➡ 🏧💧✕
🔌🛏⌇R
Prices: 🛝16 pitch 10

▶ **MARÇON** SARTHE

Lac des Varennes ☎ 243441372
15 Mar-15 Nov 5HEC ⬛ 🔾🏠🏧💧⊙🔌🔌🔌⌇LR🏧⊞
lau ➡🔌

▶ **MATHES, LES** CHARENTE-MARITIME

Charmettes av de la Palmyre ☎ 546225096
Large site with plenty of organised activities. 5km from the beach.
➲ *1km SW via D141.*
4 Apr-Sep 34HEC ⬛ ⠏ ⌇🏠💧✕⊙🔌🛏🔌🛆⌇PS
🏧🅿🔌⌇ lau
Prices: pitch 134-232 (incl 6 persons)

Orée du Bois 225 rte de la Bouverie, La Fouasse
☎ 546224243
A family site situated in a pine and oak forest, 5 minutes
from the beach.
➲ *3.5km NW.*
12 May-14 Sep 6HEC ⬛ ⠏ ⠿🏠💧✕⊙🔌🔌🛏🔌🔌
⌇P🏧🅿⊞ lau
Prices: pitch 90-160 (incl 2 persons)

Pinède rte de la Fouasse ☎ 546224513
A modern family site in a wooded area around the large
Aquatic Park. Excellent sporting facilities. Entertainment
available in July and August.
➲ *3km NW.*
Apr-Sep 7HEC ⬛ ⠏ ⠿🏠💧✕⊙🔌🔌🛏🔌⌇P🏧⊞
lau
Prices: pitch 100-200 (incl 3 persons)

▶ **MAYENNE** MAYENNE

CM Raymond Fauque r St-Léonard ☎ 243045714
In a wooded location on the banks of the River Mayenne.
➲ *800m from town centre near N12.*
15 Mar-Sep 1.8HEC ⬛ ⠏🏠🔌⊙🔌🔌⌇P🏧⊞ lau ➡🏧💧✕
🔌🛏⊞
Prices: pitch 53 (incl 3 persons)

▶ **MEMBROLLE-SUR-CHOISILLE, LA** INDRE-ET-LOIRE

CM rte de Foudettes ☎ 247412040
On level meadow in sports ground beside River Choisille.
➲ *N on N138 Le Mans road.*
May-Sep 1.3HEC ⬛ 🔾🏠⊙🔌🔌⌇R🏧⊞ lau ➡🏧💧✕

▶ **MESLAND** LOIR-ET-CHER

Parc du Val de Loire rte de Fleuray ☎ 254702718
In a sheltered position in the heart of the Touraine vineyards
with good recreational facilities.
Camping Card Compulsory.
➲ *1.5km W between the A10 and the N152.*
May-15 Sep 15HEC ⬛ 🔾🏠🏧💧✕⊙🔌🔌🛏🔌⌇P🏧🅿
⊞ lau
Prices: pp27-35

▶ **MESQUER** LOIRE-ATLANTIQUE

Beaupré rte de Kervarin, Kercabellec ☎ 240426748
Well equipped site 500mtrs from the beach.
➲ *On road between Mesquer and Quimiac. Entrance
signposted.*
Jun-Aug 0.6HEC ⬛ 🔾🏠⊙🔌🔌🛏🔌🔌⊞◇ lau ➡🏧💧✕
🔌🛏⌇S
Prices: pitch 64 (incl 2 persons)

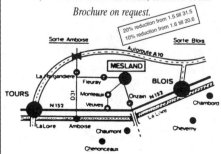

Le PARC du VAL de LOIRE
★ ★ ★ ★ NN
41150 MESLAND
A PARADISE FOR CHILDREN

An ideal starting point from where to visit the famous
castles of the Loire.

Mobile homes and chalets for hire.

3 swimming pools and tennis.

Tel: 02.54.70.27.18   Fax: 02.54.70.21.71

Open 1st May to 15th September. Highway A10, exit
'Blois', from there follow the N152, direction Tours.

Brochure on request.

20% reduction from 1.5 till 31.5
10% reduction from 1.6 till 20.6

Château de Petit Bois ☎ 240426877
In the extensive grounds of an 18th century castle with shaded, well defined pitches.
Apr-Oct 10HEC ⭢ ♦ ⋒ ⅃ ⍟ ⊙ ▣ ⩲ ⊞ ⤢ ⤳ P ▦ lau ➤ ⌀ ⤳S ⊞

Praderoi alleé des Barges, Quimiac ☎ 240426672
On level ground 70mtrs from Lanseria Beach.
➩ *300mtrs from Quimiac.*
15 Jun-15 Sep 0.5HEC ⭢ ♦ ⋒ ⊙ ▣ ⤢ ▦ ⊞ ⤳ ⚡ lau ➤ ⌁ ⅃ ✕ ⌀ ⤳S
Prices: pitch 66-85 (incl 2 persons)

Welcome r de Bel-Air ☎ 240425085
Separate car park for arrivals after 22.30 hrs.
➩ *1.8km NW via D352*
Apr-Sep 2HEC ⭢ ♦ ⋒ ⌁ ⊙ ▣ ⌀ ⩲ ⊞ ⤢ ▦ lau ➤ ⅃ ✕ ⤳S ⊞

MISSILLAC LOIRE-ATLANTIQUE

CM des Platanes 10 r du Château ☎ 240883888
➩ *1km W via D2, 50m from the lake.*
Jul-Aug 2HEC ⭢ ⌀ ⋒ ⊙ ▣ ⊞ lau ➤ ⌁ ⅃ ✕ ⊞
Prices: pitch 37 (incl 2 persons)

MONTARGIS LOIRET

CM de la Forêt rte de Paucourt ☎ 238980020
In the Forest of Montargis.
➩ *1.5km NE near the station and the stadium.*
Closed 20 Dec-10 Jan 5.5HEC ⭢ ⡂⡂⡂ ⌀ ⋒ ⊙ ▣ ▦ ⊞ lau ➤ ⌁ ⅃ ✕ ⌀ ⤢ ⤳LPR

MONTGIVRAY INDRE

CM Solange Sand r du Pont ☎ 254483783
A pleasant, riverside site in the grounds of a château.
15 Mar-15 Oct 1HEC ⭢ ⌀ ⋒ ⊙ ▣ ⌀ ⤳ R ⊞ lau ➤ ⅃ ✕ ⌀ ⤢ ⤳P
Prices: ⋔11.60 pitch 10.50

MONTLOUIS-SUR-LOIRE INDRE-ET-LOIRE

CM Peupliers ☎ 247458585
On level meadow.
➩ *1.5km W on N751, next to swimming pool near railway bridge.*
15 Mar-15 Oct 6HEC ⭢ ♦ ⋒ ⌁ ✕ ⊙ ▣ ⌀ ⤳ P ▦ ⊞ lau ➤ ⤳R
Prices: pitch 43.25 (incl 2 persons)

MONTMORILLON VIENNE

CM Allochon av F-Tribot ☎ 549910233
A well equipped municipal site close to the river and 1.5km from the town centre.
➩ *SE via D54*
All year 2HEC ⭢ ♦ ⋒ ⊙ ▣ ▦ lau ➤ ⌁ ⅃ ✕ ⤳PR ⊞

MONTSOREAU MAINE-ET-LOIRE

Isle Verte av de la Loire ☎ 241517660
➩ *On D947 between road and river.*
May-Sep 3HEC ⭢ ♦ ⌁ ⋒ ⅃ ✕ ⊙ ▣ ⩲ ⊞ ⤢ ⤳ P ▦ ⊞ lau ➤ ⌀
Prices: pitch 63-75 (incl 2 persons)

NANTES LOIRE-ATLANTIQUE

Petit Port bd du Petit Port 21 ☎ 240744794
On modern well kept park by a river.
➩ *In N part of town near Parc du Petit Port. From town centre follow Rennes road (N137) then signs to camp site.*
All year 6.5HEC ⭢ ⋒ ⌁ ⊙ ▣ ▦ ⊞ lau ➤ ⅃ ✕ ⤢ ⤳PR

NEUVILLE-SUR-SARTHE SARTHE

Vieux Moulin ☎ 243253182
A pleasant site with good recreational facilities, close to the village.
➩ *Access via N138 and D197.*
May-Oct 4.8HEC ⭢ ♦ ⋒ ⌁ ⊙ ▣ ⌀ ⤢ ⊞ ⤳ PR ⊞ ⊞ lau ➤ ⅃ ✕
Prices: pitch 65 (incl 2 persons)

NIBELLE LOIRET

Nibelle rte de Boiscommun ☎ 238322355
Level site in the clearing of an oak woodland.
➩ *Access via D921 turning off to Nibelle in an easterly direction. Signposted.*
Mar-Nov 6HEC ⭢ ⌀ ⋒ ⅃ ✕ ⊙ ▣ ⤢ ⊞ ⩲ ⤳ P ▦ ⊞ lau
Prices: ⋔50 ➤10 ⚑20 ⚐10

NIORT DEUX-SÈVRES

Niort-Noron 21 bd Salvador-Allendé ☎ 549790506
Shady site by a river.
Apr-Sep 3HEC ⭢ ♦ ⋒ ⅃ ✕ ⊙ ▣ ⤳ R ⊞ ⊞ lau ➤ ⌁ ✕ ⌀ ⤢
Prices: ⋔17 ➤7 ⚑9 ⚐7

NOIRMOUTIER, ILE DE VENDÉE
BARBÂTRE

Onchères ☎ 251398131
In quiet setting on sand dunes. S of village on D95.
Apr-Sep Oct-Mar 10HEC ⋰⋰ ⌀ ⋒ ⌁ ⅃ ✕ ⊙ ▣ ⌀ ⤳ S ⊞ ⊞ lau
Prices: ⋔16-24.50 pitch 16-24.50

NOIRMOUTIER-EN-L'ILE

Vendette rte des Sableaux ☎ 251390624
A well equipped site in a pine wood close to the beach.
➩ *From town centre continue towards Plage des Sableaux.*
27 Mar-Sep 12HEC ⭢ ⋰⋰ ♦ ⋒ ⅃ ✕ ⊙ ▣ ⤳ S ⊞ ⊞ lau ➤ ⌁ ⌀ ⤢ ⤳P
Prices: ⋔15-17 pitch 15-17

NOTRE-DAME-DE-MONTS VENDÉE

Beauséjour ☎ 251588388
➩ *2km NW on D38.*
Etr-Sep 1.3HEC ⭢ ⌀ ⋒ ⊙ ▣ ⌀ ⤢ ⊞ ⊞ lau ➤ ⌁ ⤳S

Grand Jardin Le Grand Jardin, 50 r de la Barre ☎ 228112175
A family site in a picturesque location facing the Ile d'Yeu. Modern sanitary installations and plenty of sporting facilities. 1km from the beach.
➩ *0.6km N*
All year 2HEC ⭢ ♦ ⋒ ⅃ ✕ ⊙ ▣ ⤢ ⤳ S ⊞ ▣ lau ➤ ⌁ ⌀
Prices: pitch 95 (incl 3 persons)

OLÉRON, ILE D' CHARENTE-MARITIME
BOYARDVILLE

Signol ☎ 546470122
In attractive surroundings within a pine forest, close to the village centre and 800mtrs from the beach.
➩ *W of town, leave D126 by the AVIA service station and follow signs for 0.6km.*
May-Sep 7HEC ⋰⋰ ⌀ ⋒ ⅃ ⊙ ▣ ⤢ ⊞ ⩲ ⤳ P ▦ ⊞ ⚡ lau ➤ ⌁ ⅃ ⤳S

CHÂTEAU-D'OLÉRON, LE

Airotel d'Oléron Domaine de Montreavail ☎ 546176182
In a peaceful, parklike setting 1km from the beach and the town centre.
➩ *Signposted from town centre.*
Etr-10 Oct 4HEC ⭢ ♦ ⋒ ⌁ ⅃ ✕ ⊙ ▣ ⌀ ⤢ ⊞ ⤳ LPS ⊞ ⊞ lau

Brande rte des Huîtres ☎ 546476237
A family site with good facilities in beautiful surroundings.
➲ *2.5km NW, 250m from the sea.*
15 Mar-15 Nov 4HEC ⬛ ∷∵ 🚰 🏪 🛒 ⚑ ✕ ⊙ 🍴 🅐 ⛺ 🏕 ⌇ P
🏧 ⊞ lau ➡ ⌇S
Prices: pitch 70-119 (incl 2 persons)

COTINIÈRE, LA

Tamaris 72 av des Pins ☎ 546471051
About 150m from sea. Level site in pleasant olive grove.
➲ *W side of island. N of town.*
15 Mar-15 Oct 5HEC ⬛ ⚑ 🏪 🛒 ⚑ ✕ ⊙ 🍴 ⌇ P 🏧 ⊞ lau ➡ 🛒
🅐 ⌇S
Prices: pitch 139 (incl 3 persons)

DOLUS-D'OLÉRON

Ostréa rte des Huîtres ☎ 546476236
A well equipped site in wooded surroundings close to the beach.
➲ *3.5km NE*
Apr-Sep 2HEC ⬛ ∷∵ ⚑ 🏪 🛒 ⚑ ✕ ⊙ 🍴 🅐 🅐 ⛺ 🏕 ⌇ S 🏧
⊞ lau
Prices: pitch 85-90 (incl 2 persons)

DOMINO

International Rex Domino ☎ 546765597
Pleasant seaside site with good recreational facilities and access to the beach.
May-14 Sep 0.8HEC ∷∵ ⚑ 🚰 🏪 🛒 ⚑ ✕ ⊙ 🍴 🅐 ⌇ PS 🏧 ⊞
lau ➡ ✕

ST-DENIS-D'OLÉRON

Phare Ouest 7 Impasse des Beaupins ☎ 546479000
➲ *1km NW*
Etr-Sep 3.5HEC ⬛ 🚰 🏪 🛒 🛒 ⚑ ⊙ 🍴 ⛺ 🏕 ⌇ S 🏧 lau ➡ ✕ 🅐
🅐 ⊞
Prices: pitch 65 (incl 3 persons)

Soleil Levant ☎ 546478303
Quiet site beside sea.
➲ *1km from village adjacent to D734.*
All year 7HEC ⬛ 🌿 🏪 🛒 ⚑ ✕ ⊙ 🍴 🅐 🅐 ⛺ 🏕 ⌇ S 🏧 ⊞
lau

ST-GEORGES-D'OLÉRON

Gautrelle Plage des Saumonards ☎ 546472157
In a pine wood close to the beach.
27 Mar-Sep 6HEC ∷∵ 🚰 🏪 ⊙ 🍴 ⌇ S 🏧 ⊞ lau
Prices: ⚑14.30-16.30 pitch 14.30-16.30

Quatre Vents Le Jousselinière ☎ 546756547
A peaceful site with good facilities.
➲ *3km E via N739.*
15 Apr-15 Sep 1.2HEC ⬛ 🚰 🏪 🛒 ⊙ 🍴 🅐 🅐 ⛺ 🏕 🅐 🏧 ⊞
lau ➡ 🛒 ✕

Suroît rte Touristique Côte Ouest, l'Ileau ☎ 546470725
On level ground, sheltered by sand dunes with fine, modern facilities.
➲ *5km SW of town.*
Apr-Sep 5HEC ⬛ ∷∵ ⚑ 🏪 🛒 ⚑ ✕ ⊙ 🍴 🅐 ⌇ S 🏧 ⊞ lau ➡
🅐
Prices: pitch 77-96 (incl 2 persons)

Verébleu La Jousselinière ☎ 546765770
➲ *1.7km SE via D273*
3 Apr-20 Sep 7.5HEC ⬛ 🚰 🏪 🛒 🛒 ⚑ ✕ ⊙ 🍴 🅐 ⛺ ⌇ P 🏧 🔲
⊞ lau ➡ ✕ 🅐
Prices: pitch 110 (incl 2 persons)

Gros Joncs ☎ 546765229
Quiet location on undulating land in the midst of lovely pine woodland.
➲ *On tourist route from La Cotinière about 5km NW in the direction of Domino, 1km SW of St-Georges-d'Oléron.*
All year 5.2HEC ⬛ ∷∵ 🚰 🏪 🛒 ⚑ ✕ ⊙ 🍴 🅐 🅐 ⛺ ⌇ PS 🏧
⊞ lau
Prices: pitch 72-185 (incl 2 persons)

ST-PIERRE-D'OLÉRON

Pierrière 18 rte de St-Georges ☎ 546470829
A pleasant site in wooded surroundings with well defined pitches.
➲ *NW towards St-Georges-d'Oléron*
7 May-26 Sep 4HEC ⬛ 🚰 🏪 🛒 ⚑ ✕ ⊙ 🍴 ⌇ P 🏧 lau ➡ 🛒 🅐 🅐
⊞
Prices: pitch 88-115 (incl 2 persons)

Trois Masses Le Marais Doux ☎ 546472396
A well equipped site in a picturesque location 2.5 km from the beach.
Etr-Sep 3HEC ⬛ 🚰 🏪 🛒 ⚑ ✕ ⊙ 🍴 🅐 ⛺ 🏕 🅐 ⌇ P 🏧 ⊞ lau
➡ 🛒 ⌇S
Prices: pitch 69-87 (incl 2 persons)

OLIVET LOIRET

CM Olivet r du Pont Bouchet ☎ 238635394
Site lies partly on shaded peninsula, partly on open lawns beside river.
➲ *2km E. Signposted from village.*
Apr-15 Oct 1HEC ⬛ ⚑ 🏪 ⊙ 🍴 🅐 ⊞ lau ➡ 🅐 🅐
Prices: ⚑15.50 ⚑10 🏕11 🅐11

OLONNE-SUR-MER VENDÉE

Loubine 1 rte de la Mer ☎ 0251331292
Situated on the edge of a forest bordering the beach.
➲ N via D87/D80.
Apr-Sep 7.5HEC ▦ ♣ ⋔ ⌷ ⚍ ♀ ✕ ⊙ ◲ ⌀ ☎ ⟨ P ⓐ ⊞ ✍
lau ➡ ⟨S

Moulin de la Salle r des Rabaudières ☎ 251959910
In pleasant surroundings close to the beach with good facilities.
➲ 2.7km W.
Apr-Oct 3.1HEC ▦ ♣ ⋔ ⌷ ⚍ ♀ ✕ ⊙ ◲ ⌀ ☎ ⟨ P ⓐ lau ➡ ⟨RS
Prices: pitch 65-110 (incl 2 persons)

Oreé rte des Amis de la Nature ☎ 251331059
➲ 3km N
Apr-Sep 5.5HEC ▦ ♣ ⋔ ⌷ ⚍ ♀ ✕ ⊙ ◲ ⌀ ☎ ⟨ P ⓐ ⊞ lau ➡ ⟨R

ONZAIN LOIR-ET-CHER

Dugny rte de Chambon-sur-Cisse ☎ 254207066
On a small lake, surrounded by farmland with well marked pitches shaded by poplars.
➲ From Onzain follow direction Chambon-sur-Cisse (CD45).
All year 8HEC ▦ ⋔ ⌷ ♀ ⊙ ◲ ⌀ ⚍ ☎ ⟨ P ⓐ ⊞ lau
Prices: ⋔29-52
See advertisement on page 131

PALMYRE, LA CHARENTE-MARITIME

Bonne Anse Plage ☎ 546224090
An extensive, gently undulating site in a pine wood, 400m from the beach.
➲ 1km from La Palmyre roundabout. Follow signs for Ronce-les-Bains.
22 May-5 Sep 17HEC ▦ ⋮⋮ ♣ ⋔ ⌷ ⚍ ♀ ✕ ⊙ ◲ ⌀ ☎ ⟨ P ⓐ ⊞ ✍ lau ➡ ⌀ ⚍ ⟨S
Prices: pitch 163 (incl 3 persons)

Palmyre Loisirs 28 des Mathes ☎ 546236766
Well equipped family site with plenty of recreational facilities and well supervised activities for children.
➲ From Les Mathes take the La Palmyre road.
16 May-12 Sep 20HEC ▦ ⋮⋮ ♣ ⋔ ⌷ ⚍ ♀ ✕ ⊙ ◲ ⌀ ⚍ ☎ ☎ ⟨ P ⓐ ⊞ lau

Palmyr Océana 26 av des Mathes ☎ 546224035
A well equipped family site in a delightful wooded setting close to the beach. A wide variety of recreational facilities are available.
Apr-Sep 17HEC ♣ ⋔ ⌷ ⚍ ♀ ✕ ⊙ ◲ ⌀ ⚍ ☎ ☎ ⟨ P ⓐ ⊞ lau ➡ ⟨RS
Prices: pitch 67-101 (incl 2 persons)

PERRIER, LE VENDÉE

CM de la Maison Blanche ☎ 151493923
Jul-15 Sep 3.2HEC ▦ ♣ ⋔ ⊙ ◲ ☎ ☎ ⟨ R ⓐ lau ➡ ⌷ ♀ ✕ ⌀ ⚍ ⊞
Prices: pitch 42-47 (incl 2 persons)

PEZOU LOIR-ET-CHER

CM "Les Ilots" rte de Renay ☎ 254234069
A well equipped site 400mtrs from the town centre.
➲ SE via D12, 50m from the River Loir
7 May-13 Sep 1HEC ▦ ⋔ ⋔ ⊙ ◲ ☎ lau ➡ ⌷ ♀ ✕ ⌀ ⚍ ⊞
Prices: ⋔12 pitch 12-24

PIERREFITTE-SUR-SAULDRE LOIR-ET-CHER

Sologne Parc des Alicourts Domaine des Alicourts
☎ 254886334

In wooded surroundings at the heart of an extensive park, this family site is exceptionally well equipped and provides a wide variety of recreational facilities.
➲ 6km NE via D126 beside the lake.
May-15 Sep 25HEC ▦ ⋮⋮ ⋇ ⋔ ⌷ ♀ ✕ ⊙ ◲ ⌀ ☎ ⟨ LP ⓐ lau ➡ ⟨R

PIRIAC-SUR-MER LOIRE-ATLANTIQUE

Parc du Guibel ☎ 240235267
On level ground in a delightful wooded setting with good recreational facilities.
➲ 3.5km E via D52
Etr-Sep 10HEC ▦ ♣ ⋔ ⌷ ⚍ ♀ ✕ ⊙ ◲ ⌀ ⚍ ☎ ☎ ⟨ P ⓐ ⊞ lau ➡ ⟨PS
Prices: ⋔19-24 pitch 18-23

Pouldroit 247 rte de Mesquer ☎ 240235091
A pleasant site in wooded surroundings 300m from the sea and 600m from the village.
➲ 500m E on D52.
Apr-15 Sep 12HEC ▦ ♣ ⋔ ⌷ ⚍ ♀ ✕ ⊙ ◲ ⌀ ⚍ ☎ ⟨ P ⓐ ⊞ lau ➡ ⟨S

PLAINE-SUR-MER, LA LOIRE-ATLANTIQUE

Tabardière ☎ 603003417
A wooded, terraced site 3km from the sea.
➲ Situated between Pornic and La Plaine-sur-Mer off D13.
Apr-Sep 4HEC ▦ ⋔ ⌷ ⚍ ♀ ✕ ⊙ ◲ ⌀ ⚍ ☎ ⟨ P ⓐ ⊞ lau ➡ ✕

POIRÉ-SUR-VELLUIRE, LE VENDÉE

Petits Prés ☎ 251523777
➲ On S outskirts beside the River Vendée. Well signposted.
All year 2.6HEC ▦ ⋔ ⋔ ⊙ ◲ ☎ ☎ ⟨ R ⓐ ⊞ lau ➡ ⌷ ♀ ✕ ⌀ ⚍

PONS CHARENTE-MARITIME

Chardon Chardon ☎ 546940486
Quietly situated on the edge of a small village next to a farm.
➲ From Pons take D732 westwards towards Royan. The site is 2.5km on the left. Alternatively from exit 36 of the Autoroute A10 and turn towards Pons. Site is 800m on right.
Apr-Oct 1.6HEC ▦ ⋔ ⋔ ⊙ ◲ ☎ lau ➡ ⟨R ⊞

PONTS-DE-CÉ, LES MAINE-ET-LOIRE

Ile du Château r de la Boire Salée ☎ 241446205
Situated on a small island in the River Loire close to the Château des Ponts-de-Cé. Separate car park for arrivals after 9pm.
➲ SW of Angers towards Cholet.
Etr-Sep 2.3HEC ▦ ♣ ⋔ ⊙ ◲ ⚍ ☎ ⟨ PR ⓐ ⊞ lau ➡ ⌷ ♀ ✕ ⌀ ⚍
Prices: pitch 60-72 (incl 2 persons)

PORNIC LOIRE-ATLANTIQUE

Patisseau Le Patisseau ☎ 240821039
In wooded surroundings close to the beach with fine recreational facilities.
➲ 3km E via D751.
May-11 Sep 4HEC ▦ ⋔ ⌷ ⚍ ♀ ✕ ⊙ ◲ ⌀ ⚍ ☎ ☎ ⟨ P ⓐ ⊞ lau
Prices: pitch 81-145 (incl 2 persons)

PORNICHET LOIRE-ATLANTIQUE

Bel Air 150 av de Bonne Source ☎ 240611078
In a pleasant, wooded location 50m from the beach.
Apr-Oct 6HEC ⋮⋮ ⋔ ⌷ ⚍ ♀ ✕ ⊙ ◲ ⌀ ⚍ ☎ ☎ ⓐ lau ➡ ⚍ ⟨S ⊞
Prices: pitch 43-85 (incl 2 persons)

Forges 98 rte de Villes Blais ☎ 240611884
In wooded surroundings with well defined pitches and good recreational facilities.
➲ *Access via N171.*
Jun-Sep 2HEC ⊞ ♣ ♠ ☎ ⊙ 🏳 ∅ ⚏ ⚑ ⇥ P ☎ ⊞ lau ♦ ⇤LS
Prices: ♠20-25 pitch 35-42

▶ PORT-DE-PILES VIENNE

Bec des Deux Eaux rte de Marigny ☎ 247650271
Wooded family site located close to the confluence of the Vienne and Creuse rivers with quite easy access to the Futuroscope.
➲ *E off N10.*
Apr-Sep 3.5HEC ⊞ ♣ ♠ ☎ ✕ ⊙ 🏳 ⚑ ⇥ PR ☎ lau
Prices: ♠22 pitch 28

▶ POUANCÉ MAINE-ET-LOIRE

CM Roche Martin 23 r des Étangs ☎ 241924397
On the edge of a lake.
➲ *On D72, in the direction of La Guerche. Site is on left, bordering Étang de St Aubin and is well signposted.*
15 Apr-Sep ⊞ ♣ ♠ ⊙ 🏳 ⚑ ▲ ☎ ⊞ lau ♦ ✕ ∅ ⇤L

▶ PRÉFAILLES LOIRE-ATLANTIQUE

Lambertianas Vallée Mouraud, r St Dominique
☎ 240216105
➲ *E of town, 450m from the sea*
15 Apr-15 Sep 1.7HEC ⊞ ♣ ♠ ⊙ 🏳 ☎ lau ♦ ☎ ✕ ∅ ⇤S ⊞

▶ RÉ, ILE DE CHARENTE-MARITIME
▶ ARS-EN-RÉ

Soleil 57 r de la Plage ☎ 546294062
On level, shaded meadow 150mtrs from the beach and 500mtrs from the village.
➲ *Signposted from the N735 shortly before reaching Ars.*
Mar-16 Nov 2HEC ⊞ ♣ ♠ ☎ ✕ ⊙ 🏳 ∅ ☎ ⊞ lau ♦ ⇤S
Prices: pitch 120 (incl 3 persons)

▶ BOIS-PLAGE-EN-RÉ, LE

Antioche ☎ 546092386
In quiet, wooded area among dunes with direct access to the beach.
➲ *3.5km SE of village towards the beach.*
27 Mar-Sep 2.7HEC ∴∷ ♠ ☎ ✕ ⊙ 🏳 ∅ ⚑ ⇥S ☎ ⊞ lau

Camping Interlude-Gros-Jonc rte de Gros Jonc
☎ 546091822
In a pleasant, wooded location 50m from the beach, this site has a fitness centre and can arrange guided tours of the area.
28 Mar-21 Sep 6.5HEC ∴∷ ♠ ☎ ✕ ⊙ 🏳 ∅ ⚏ ⚑ ▲ ⇥ P ☎ lau ♦ ⇤S ⊞
Prices: ♠28-50 pitch 36-64

▶ COUARDE-SUR-MER, LA

Océan La Passe ☎ 546298770
In a fine position facing the sea with good modern facilities.
➲ *3km NW on N735.*
Apr-Sep 7HEC ⊞ ∴∷ ♣ ♠ ☎ ✕ ⊙ 🏳 ⚏ ☎ ⇥ P ☎ ⊞ lau ♦ ⇤S
Prices: pitch 82-175 (incl 3 persons)

▶ FLOTTE, LA

Blanche Deviation de la Flotte ☎ 546095243
A popular family site in a wooded location.
➲ *N on D735 towards St-Martin.*
Apr-11 Nov 4HEC ∴∷ ♣ ♠ ☎ ✕ ⊙ 🏳 ∅ ⚏ ⚑ ⇥ P ☎ ⊞ lau ♦ ⇤S
Prices: ♠27-39 pitch 40-73

Peupliers ☎ 546096235
Siutated in a large, wooded park 800m from the sea with good sporting facilities.
➲ *1.3km SE*
Apr-18 Sep 4.4HEC ∴∷ ♠ ☎ ☎ ✕ ⊙ 🏳 ∅ ⚏ ⚑ ⇥ P ☎ ⊞ lau ♦ ⇤S

▶ LOIX

Ilattes Le Petit Boucheau, rte du Grouin ☎ 546290543
➲ *Access E towards Pointe du Grouin, 500m from the sea.*
All year 4.5HEC ⊞ 🌿 ♠ ☎ ✕ ⊙ 🏳 ⚑ ⇥ P ☎ ⊞ lau ♦ ☎ ∅ ⚏

▶ ST-CLÉMENT-DES-BALEINES '

Plage ☎ 546294262
Meadow subdivided by hedges, close by lighthouse. Access to sea via sand dunes. Mobile shop during peak season.
➲ *NW on D735.*
Etr-Sep 2.4HEC ⊞ 🌿 ♠ ⊙ 🏳 lau ♦ ⇤S

▶ ST-MARTIN-DE-RÉ

CM r du Rempart ☎ 546092196
In pleasant wooded surroundings at the foot of the 17th century ramparts.
➲ *N, beyond La Flotte.*
Mar-15 Oct 3HEC ⊞ ♣ ♠ ⊙ 🏳 ⚑ ☎ lau ♦ ☎ ⇤S ⊞
Prices: pitch 67 (incl 3 persons)

▶ RONCE-LES-BAINS CHARENTE-MARITIME

Pignade av des Monards ☎ 546362525
A family site with good recreational facilities.
➲ *1.5km S*
15 May-18 Sep 16HEC ⊞ ∴∷ ♣ ♠ ☎ ✕ ⊙ 🏳 ∅ ⚏ ⚑ ⇥ P ☎ ⊞ lau
Prices: ♠15.50-31 pitch 61.50-123

▶ ROSIERS, LES MAINE-ET-LOIRE

Val de Loire 6 r Ste-Baudruche ☎ 241519433
A comfortable site partly on the banks of the River Loire with good recreational facilities.
➲ *N via D59*
Etr-Sep 4HEC ⊞ ♠ ☎ ✕ ⊙ 🏳 ⚑ ⇥ P ☎ 🏳 ⊞ lau ♦ ☎ ✕ ∅ ⚏ ⇤R
Prices: pitch 60-75 (incl 2 persons)

▶ ROYAN CHARENTE-MARITIME
▶ At MÉDIS(4km NE)

Chênes La Verdonneric ☎ 546067138
In a wooded location with good facilities. Separate late arrivals car park after 22.00hrs.
➲ *2km from Royan on the Saintes-Royan road.*
15 Mar-Oct 6.5HEC ⊞ ♠ ☎ ✕ ⊙ 🏳 ∅ ⚏ ☎ 🏳 ⇥ P ☎ ⊞ lau

▶ At PONTAILLAC(2km NE on D25)

Clairfontaine allée des Peupliers ☎ 546390811
A well equipped site in wooded surroundings 300m from the beach with a variety of recreational facilities.
13 May-13 Sep 5HEC ⊞ ♠ ☎ ✕ ⊙ 🏳 ∅ ⚏ ⇥ PS ☎ 🏳 ⊞ lau
Prices: pitch 162 (incl 3 persons)

▶ SABLES-D'OLONNE, LES VENDÉE

Roses 1 r des Roses ☎ 251951042
A level site, shaded by trees and bushes, 500mtrs from the Remblai beach.
Contd.

⊃ *Close to the town centre off D949.*
Apr-Oct 3.3HEC ⊞ ♣ ♠ ⛺ 🏊 ⛾ ✕ ⊙ 🖵 ⊘ 🛒 🏠 🛏 ⊀ P ⓐ ⊞
lau ➧ ⊀S
Prices: pitch 75-145 (incl 2 persons)

Trianon ☎ 251953050
A spacious site in a pleasant situation with good sporting
facilities.
⊃ *Access via N160 and CD80.*
Etr-Sep 12HEC ⊞ 🏕 ♠ ⛺ ⛾ ✕ ⊙ 🖵 ⊘ 🛒 ⊀ P ⓐ ⊞ lau

◗ SABLÉ-SUR-SARTHE SARTHE

Hippodrome allée du Quebec ☎ 243954261
In a peaceful wooded setting with a great variety of
recreational facilities.
⊃ *Situated 450 yards from the town.*
Apr-Sep 3HEC ⊞ 🏕 ♠ ⛺ ⊙ 🖵 ⊘ 🛒 ⊀ PR ⓐ ⊞ lau ➧ ⛺ ✕
⊀P
Prices: ♠12.90 pitch 24.80

◗ ST-AIGNAN-SUR-CHER LOIR-ET-CHER

CM Cochards ☎ 254751559
On beautiful meadowland, completely surrounded by
hedges.
⊃ *1km from bridge on D17 towards Selles.*
Apr-Sep 4HEC ⊞ ♣ ♠ ⛺ ⊙ 🖵 ⊘ 🏠 ⓐ ⊞ lau ➧ ⛺ ✕ ⛾
⊀R
Prices: ♠14.50 pitch 14.50

◗ ST-AMAND-MONTROND CHER

CM Roche chemin de la Roche ☎ 248960936
In a lovely wooded location between the River Cher and the
Berry Canal with good modern facilities.
⊃ *1.5km SW near river and canal.*
Apr-Sep 4HEC ⊞ ♣ ♠ ⛺ ⊙ 🖵 ⊘ ⓐ ⊞ lau ➧ ⛺ ✕ ⛾ ⊀PR
Prices: ♠14 pitch 20.30

◗ ST-ANDRÉ-DES-EAUX LOIRE-ATLANTIQUE

CM Les Chalands Fleuris r du Stade ☎ 240012040
A peaceful site with good facilities in the middle of a natural
park.
⊃ *1km NE.*
Apr-15 Oct 3HEC ⊞ 🌾 ♠ ⛺ 🏊 ✕ ⊙ 🖵 🏠 🛒 🛏 ⊀ P ⓐ
⊞ lau ➧ ⊘
Prices: ♠22 ⊕12 🚐35 🛆29

◗ ST-AVERTIN INDRE-ET-LOIRE

CM Rives du Cher 61 r de Rochepinard ☎ 247272760
Municipal site on the banks of the River Cher. Only caravans
weighing less than 1000kg accepted.
⊃ *400mtrs N of the town centre and 4km from Tours.*
Apr-15 Oct 3HEC ⊞ 🏕 ♠ ⊙ 🖵 ⓐ ⊞ lau ➧ ⛺ ✕ ⊘ ⛾ PR
Prices: ♠14 pitch 14

◗ ST-BRÉVIN-LES-PINS LOIRE-ATLANTIQUE

CM Courance 100/110 av Ml-Foch ☎ 240272291
In a pine forest with direct access to the beach.
⊃ *S off D305.*
All year 4HEC ⁑ ♣ ♠ ⛺ 🏊 ✕ ⊙ 🖵 🛒 ⊀ S ⓐ ⊞ lau
➧ ✕ ⊘ ⛾ ⊀P

Fief 57 chemin du Fief ☎ 240272386
A family site adjacent to a long sandy beach. The pitches are
surrounded by trees and bushes and there are good modern
facilities.
⊃ *In town follow 'Route Bleue' to Centre Leclerc then take 2nd
on right to site.*
1 Apr-15 Oct 7HEC ⊞ 🏕 ♠ ⛺ 🏊 ✕ ⊙ 🖵 ⊘ ⛾ 🏠 🛆 ⊀ P ⓐ
⊞ lau ➧ ⊀S
Prices: pitch 65-120 (incl 2 persons)

◗ ST-BRÉVIN-L'OCÉAN LOIRE-ATLANTIQUE

Village Club des Pierres Couchées L'Ermitage ☎ 240278564
Extensive, well screened terrain made up of 3 sites, 2 of
which are open all year.
⊃ *300m from the sea, 2km on D213 toward Pornic.*
All year 14HEC ⊞ ⁑ ♣ ♠ ⛺ 🏊 ✕ ⊙ 🖵 🏠 🛒 ⊀ P ⊞
lau ➧ ⊀S

◗ ST-CYR VIENNE

Parc de Loisirs ☎ 549625722
In a delightful setting in a spacious park beside a lake. The
Futuroscope is within easy reach via the A10.
⊃ *1.5km NE via D4/D82.*
Apr-Sep 5HEC ⊞ 🏕 ♠ ⛺ 🏊 ✕ ⊙ 🖵 🛒 ⊀ L ⓐ ⊞ lau
Prices: ♠15-25 pitch 30-60

◗ SAINTES CHARENTE-MARITIME

Au Fill de l'Eau 6 r de Courbiac ☎ 546930800
On the banks of the River Charente, 900mtrs from the town
centre.
⊃ *1km on D128.*
7 May-15 Sep 7HEC ⊞ ♣ ♠ ⛺ 🏊 ✕ ⊙ 🖵 ⊘ 🛒 ⊀ PR ⓐ ⊞
lau ➧ ⛾
Prices: ♠22 pitch 23

◗ ST-FLORENT-LE-VIEIL MAINE-ET-LOIRE

Ile Batailleuse ☎ 240834501
⊃ *6km SE. N of Lac du Boudon.*
May-25 Sep 2.5HEC ⊞ 🏕 ♠ ⊙ 🖵 ⊀ R ⓐ lau ➧ ⛺ ✕ ⊀P ⊞

◗ ST-GAULTIER INDRE

Village Vacances 'La Matronnerie' r de la Pierre Plate
☎ 254471704
Feb-Nov 2.5HEC ⊞ 🏕 ♠ ⛺ ✕ ⊙ 🖵 🏠 🛒 ⊀ P ⓐ ⊞ lau ➧ ⛺
⊘ ⊀R
Prices: 🛆68 pitch 80-96 (incl 2 persons)

◗ ST-GEORGES-DE-BAILLARGEAUX VIENNE

Futuriste ☎ 549524752
In an elevated position offering fine views over the Parc du
Furturoscope and the Clain valley. Advance booking is
advisable from June to August.
All year 32HEC ⊞ ♣ ♠ ⛺ ⊙ 🖵 🛒 ⊀ P ⓐ lau ➧ ⛺ ✕ ⊘
⊞
Prices: pitch 73-99 (incl 3 persons)

◗ ST-GEORGES-DE-DIDONNE CHARENTE-MARITIME

Bois Soleil 2 av de Suzac ☎ 546050594
Pitches lie on different levels. Direct access to the beach.
⊃ *2.5km S of town on Meschers road (D25).*
Apr-Sep 8.5HEC ⊞ ⁑ 🏕 ♠ ⛺ ✕ ⊙ 🖵 ⊘ ⛾ 🏠 🛒 ⊀ S
ⓐ ℗ ⓐ ⊘ lau
Prices: pitch 110-143 (incl 3 persons)

Ideal Camping No 1 Suzac ☎ 546052904
A well equipped, peaceful site in a pine forest 200mtrs from
Suzac beach.
⊃ *W of St-Georges-de-Didonne via D25.*
May-15 Sep 8HEC ⁑ ♣ ♠ ⛺ 🏊 ✕ ⊙ 🖵 ⊘ 🛒 ⓐ ⊞ ⊘ lau ➧
⊀S
Prices: pitch 76.60-99.50 (incl 3 persons)

◗ ST-GILLES-CROIX-DE-VIE VENDÉE

Pas Opton rte de Nantes, Le Fenouiller ☎ 251551198
Well tended garden-like site in rural surroundings.
⊃ *On D754 Nantes Road.*
20 May-10 Sep 6.5HEC ⊞ 🏕 ♠ ⛺ 🏊 ✕ ⊙ 🖵 ⊘ 🛒 ⊀ PR ⓐ
⊞ ⊘ lau
Prices: pitch 94 (incl 2 persons)

❯ St-Hilaire-de-Riez Vendée

Biches rte de Notre-Dame-de-Riez ☎ 251543882
A well equipped site in a pine forest and close to the sea.
⤷ *2km N*
15 May-15 Sep 11HEC ▦ ∴ ♠ ⋒ ⚼ ♨ 🍴 ✕ ☺ 🅿 🖉 ⛺ ⋟ P
🏤 ⊞ lau ➧ ⋟R
Prices: pitch 173-200 (incl 3 persons)

Bois Tordu 84 av de la Pège ☎ 251543378
In a wooded location with good facilities.
⤷ *5.3km NW.*
15 May-15 Sep 1.7HEC ▦ ♠ ⋒ ⚼ ♨ 🍴 ✕ ☺ 🅿 🖉 ⛺ ⋟ P 🏤
⊞ lau ➧ ✕ ⋟S
Prices: pitch 134.40-168 (incl 3 persons)

Chouans 108 av de la Faye ☎ 251543490
In a wooded location on the edge of the National Forest.
⤷ *2.5 km NW.*
Etr-15 Oct 5HEC ▦ 🔌 ⋒ ⚼ ♨ 🍴 ✕ ☺ 🅿 🖉 ⚌ ⛺ ⋟ P 🏤 lau ➧
⋟S
Prices: pitch 108 (incl 3 persons)

Ecureuils 100 av de la Pège ☎ 251543371
In pleasant surroundings, 250m from a fine sandy beach,
with good recreational facilities.
⤷ *From A11 to Nantes, then via D178 and D753 to St-Hilaire-de-Riez.*
15 May-15 Sep 4HEC ▦ 🔌 ⋒ ⚼ ♨ 🍴 ✕ ☺ 🅿 ⋟ P 🏤 ⊞
lau ➧ 🖉 ⋟S
Prices: pitch 139 (incl 2 persons)

Padrelle 1 r Prévot, La Corniche de Sion/l'Océan
☎ 251553203
In a rural setting 50mtrs from the beach and within 5
minutes of the town.
May-Sep 1.5HEC ▦ ⚡ ⋒ ☺ 🅿 🅿 🏤 lau ➧ ⚼ 🍴 ✕ 🖉 ⚌
⋟S
Prices: pitch 58-70 (incl 2 persons)

Plage 106 av de la Pège ☎ 251543393
On a meadow with trees. Access to beach via dunes.
⤷ *5.7km NW.*
15 May-15 Sep 5.5HEC ▦ ∴ 🔌 ⋒ ⚼ 🍴 ✕ ☺ 🅿 ⚌ ⛺ 🅿 ⚓
⋟ PS 🏤 ⊞ lau ➧ ⚼
Prices: pitch (incl persons)

Prairie chemin des Roselières ☎ 251540856
⤷ *5.5km NW, 500m from the beach*
15 May-15 Sep 4HEC ▦ ♠ ⋒ ⚼ 🍴 ✕ ☺ 🅿 🖉 ⚌ ⛺ 🅿 PS
🏤 ⊞ lau

Puerta del Sol Les Borderies - D59 ☎ 251491010
A peaceful site with well defined pitches in a wooded
location. Good facilities for family recreation.
⤷ *4.5km N.*
Apr-Sep 5HEC ▦ ♠ ⋒ ⚼ 🍴 ✕ ☺ 🅿 ⛺ 🅿 ⋟ P 🏤 ⊞ lau ➧
⊞
Prices: pitch 65-180 (incl 3 persons)

Riez à la Vie 9 av Parée Preneau ☎ 251543049
Flat site, divided into pitches. Popular with families.
⤷ *3km NW.*
Etr-15 Sep 3HEC ▦ ∴ ♠ ⋒ ⚼ 🍴 ✕ ☺ 🅿 🖉 ⛺ 🅿 ⋟ P 🏤
lau ➧ ✕ ⚌ ⋟S ⊞

Sapinière chemin de Bellevue ☎ 251544574
A family site in natural, wooded surroundings 5 minutes
from the beach.
⤷ *2km NE*
15 May-15 Sep 3.6HEC ▦ ∴ ♠ ⋒ ⚼ 🍴 ✕ ☺ 🅿 🖉 ⛺ ⋟ P
🏤 ⊞ lau

Sol-à-Gogo 61 Av de la Pège ☎ 251542900
A family site with good recreational facilities, including an
aquaslide, with direct access to the beach.
⤷ *4.8km NW of St-Hilaire, 6km S of St-Jean-de-Monts.*
15 May-15 Sep 4HEC ▦ ∴ 🔌 ⋒ ⚼ 🍴 ✕ ☺ 🅿 ⛺ ⋟ PS 🏤
⊞ lau ➧ 🖉 ⚌
Prices: pitch 134-168 (incl 3 persons)

❯ St-Jean-de-Monts Vendée

Abri des Pins rte de Notre-Dame-de-Monts ☎ 251588386
A family site on level grassland with pitches subdivided by
hedges, bushes and trees. 10 minutes walk from the beach.
⤷ *4km N on D38 Notre-Dame-de-Monts road.*
Jun-15 Sep 3HEC ▦ 🔌 ⋒ ⚼ 🍴 ✕ ☺ 🅿 🆎 ⛺ ⚓ ⋟ P 🏤 ⊞ lau
➧ ⋟S
Prices: pitch 116-159 (incl 3 persons)

Amiaux 223 rte de Notre-Dame de Monts ☎ 251582222
A well equipped site on the edge of a forest, 700mtrs from
the beach.
⤷ *3.5km NW of D38.*
Etr-15 Sep 15HEC ▦ ∴ ⚡ ⋒ ⚼ 🍴 ✕ ☺ 🅿 🖉 ⋟ P 🏤 ⊞
lau ➧ ⋟S

Avenhiriers de la Calypso rte de Notre-Dame-de-Monts, Les
Tonnelles ☎ 251560878
A holiday village with good, modern facilities, 700mtrs from
Tonnelles beach.
Apr-Sep 5HEC ▦ ⋒ ⚼ 🍴 ✕ ☺ 🅿 🖉 ⚌ ⛺ 🆎 🅿 ⚓ ⊞ lau ➧
⋟S
Prices: pitch 91.50-150 (incl 2 persons)

Bois Joly 46 r de Notre-Dame-de-Monts ☎ 251591163
A pleasantly landscaped, terraced site set among pine trees.
Good facilities. Close to the beach and the town centre.
4 Apr-27 Sep 5.5HEC ▦ 🔌 ⋒ ⚼ 🍴 ✕ ☺ 🅿 🖉 ⛺ 🅿 ⋟ PR 🏤
⊞ lau ➧ ⋟S

Clarys Plage av des Epines ☎ 251581024
A family site with good facilities including an indoor
swimming pool and an outdoor pool with a water slide.
⤷ *S of town 300mtrs from the beach.*
15 May-15 Sep 7HEC ▦ ∴ 🔌 ⋒ ⚼ 🍴 ✕ ☺ 🅿 🖉 ⛺ ⋟ P 🏤
⊞ lau ➧ ⚌ ⋟S
Prices: pitch 116-145 (incl 2 persons)

Sirenes av des Demoiselles ☎ 251580131
In a forested location 500m from the beach with good
facilities.
⤷ *SE off D38.*
27 Mar-Oct 15HEC ▦ ∴ ♠ ⋒ ☺ 🅿 🏤 🅿 ⊞ lau ➧ ⚼ 🍴 ✕
🖉 ⚌ ⋟PS
Prices: pitch 15.50-17 (incl 2 persons)

Forêt 190 chemin de la Rive ☎ 251588463
A well equipped family site in a pleasant rural setting.
⤷ *5.5km NW.*
15 May-15 Sep 1HEC ▦ ∴ 🔌 ⋒ ☺ 🅿 🖉 ⛺ ⋟ P 🏤 lau ➧
⚼ 🍴 ✕ ⚌ ⋟S ⊞

❯ At Orouet(6km SE)

Yole chemin des Bosses ☎ 251586717
In rural surroundings 1km from a fine sandy beach.
⤷ *Signposted from D38 in Orouet.*
May-15 Sep 6HEC ▦ ∴ 🔌 ⋒ ⚼ 🍴 ✕ ☺ 🅿 🖉 🅿 ⋟ P 🏤 ⊞
⊗ lau ➧ ⋟S
Prices: pitch 98-146 (incl 2 persons)

ST-JULIEN-DES-LANDES VENDÉE

Fôret ☎ 251466211
In a picturesque setting in the grounds of a château with well defined pitches and modern facilities.
➲ *NE on D55, rte de Martinet.*
15 May-15 Sep 50HEC ⚏ ♣ ⋔ ⛟ ⵌ ✕ ☉ 🛒 ⊘ 🚐 ⵢ P 🏕 ⊞ lau
♣ ⵤ
Prices: pitch 104-139 (incl 3 persons)

▥ Garangeoire ☎ 251466539
Family site set in 200 hectare estate. Pitches separated by hedges. A good variety of recreational facilities.
➲ *2km N of the village.*
15 May-15 Sep 15HEC ⚏ ⵄ ⋔ ⛟ ⵌ ✕ ☉ 🛒 ⊘ 🚐 ⵢ LP 🏕 ⊞ lau
Prices: pitch 87-165 (incl 2 persons)

Guyonnière La Guyonnière ☎ 251466259
A pleasant site with pitches divided by hedges with good sanitary and recreational facilities.
➲ *2km from the town centre towards St-Gilles-Croix-de-Vie.*
May-1 Oct 30HEC ⚏ ⵄ ⋔ ⛟ ⵌ ✕ ☉ 🛒 ⊘ ⵗ 🚐 ⵙ ⵢ LP 🏕 ⊞ lau ♣ ⵤL
Prices: ⟑20 pitch 35

ST-JUST-LUZAC CHARENTE-MARITIME

▥ Séquoia Parc ☎ 546855555
Situated in a spacious park on the 'La Josephtrie' estate containing an attractive château some 5km from the coast.
➲ *Access via A10 exit 'Saintes' then D728 towards Ile d'Oléron and follow signs from St-Just.*
May-15 Sep 45HEC ⚏ ♣ ⋔ ⛟ ⵌ ✕ ☉ 🛒 ⊘ 🚐 ⵢ P 🏕 lau

ST-LÉONARD-DE-NOBLAT HAUTE-VIENNE

CM Beaufort ☎ 555560279
In pleasant wooded surroundings with good facilities.
➲ *Access from the D39.*
15 Jun-15 Sep 2HEC ⚏ ⵄ ⋔ ⛟ ☉ 🛒 ⊘ 🚐 ⵢ R 🏕 ⊞ lau
Prices: pitch 41-48 (incl 2 persons)

ST-MALÔ-DU-BOIS VENDÉE

Plein Air de Poupet ☎ 251923145
In a picturesque location beside the River Sèvre Nantaise, surrounded by woodland.
➲ *From village take D72 for 1km, then take left fork and follow signs.*
May-Sep 3HEC ⚏ ⵄ ⋔ ☉ 🛒 🚐 ⵢ R 🏕 ⊞ lau ♣ ⛟ ✕
Prices: pitch 49.50 (incl 2 persons)

ST-PALAIS-SUR-MER CHARENTE-MARITIME

Ormeaux 44 av de Bernezac ☎ 546390207
Well equipped site in wooded surroundings, 500m from the beach.
➲ *1km N.*
15 May-15 Sep 3.5HEC ⚏ ⵄ ⋔ ⛟ ⵌ ✕ ☉ 🛒 ⊘ ⵗ 🚐 ⵢ P 🏕 ⊞ lau ♣ ⵤLS

Puits de l'Auture La Grande Côte ☎ 546232031
A family site in a picturesque location at the edge of a forest facing the sea.
➲ *2km NW on D25 La Palmyre road.*
May-Sep 5HEC ⚏ ♣ ⋔ ⛟ ⵌ ✕ ☉ 🛒 ⊘ 🚐 ⵢ P 🏕 ⊞ ✍ lau ♣ ⵤS
Prices: pitch 105-160 (incl 3 persons)

ST-PRIEST-DE-GIMEL CORRÈZE

Étang-de-Ruffaud ☎ 555212665
On hilly wooded ground beside lake. Common room with TV.

➲ *2.5km N on D53.*
15 Jun-15 Sep 5HEC ⚏ ♣ ⋔ ⛟ ⵌ ✕ ☉ 🛒 🚐 ⵢ LR 🏕 ⊞ lau

ST-VINCENT-SUR-JARD VENDÉE

'Bolée d'Air' rte du Bouil ☎ 251903605
A family site on level ground with pitches divided by hedges. Good recreational facilities, including a water slide, and 900mtrs from Bouil beach.
➲ *2km E via D21.*
Apr-25 Sep 5.7HEC ⚏ ⵄ ⋔ ⛟ ⵌ ✕ ☉ 🛒 ⊘ ⵗ 🚐 🚐 ⵙ ⵢ P 🏕 ⊞ lau ♣ ⵤS
Prices: pitch 70-123 (incl 2 persons)

STE-CATHERINE-DE-FIERBOIS INDRE-ET-LOIRE

▥ Parc de Fierbois ☎ 247654335
Beside artificial lake; good bathing area.
➲ *Follow D101 off N10, 1.5km SE.*
15 May-14 Sep 20HEC ⚏ ♣ ⋔ ⛟ ⵌ ✕ ☉ 🛒 ⊘ ⵗ 🚐 ⵢ LP 🏕 ⊞ lau
Prices: pitch 95-144 (incl 2 persons)

STE-GEMME CHARENTE-MARITIME

Jamica la Sablière Ferme de Magne ☎ 546229099
In a pleasant situation beside a lake within a country park.
➲ *Access via A10 exit 25 (Saintes) and D728 towards Ile d'Oléron.*
May-15 Oct ⚏ ♣ ⋔ ⛟ ⵌ ✕ ☉ 🛒 ⊘ ⵗ 🚐 🚐 ⵢ L 🏕 🏕 ⊞ lau

STE-REINE-DE-BRETAGNE LOIRE-ATLANTIQUE

▥ Château du Deffay BP 18 ☎ 240880057
Situated in the beautiful Parc de Brière providing fishing, walking and horse riding. Games and TV rooms.
➲ *4.5km W on D33 rte de Pontchâteau.*
May-25 Sep 12HEC ⚏ ⵄ ⋔ ⛟ ⵌ ✕ ☉ 🛒 🚐 ⵢ P 🏕 ⊞ lau
Prices: ⟑16-23 pitch 39-95

SANTROP HAUTE-VIENNE

Santrop ☎ 555710808
A well equipped family site on the shore of Lac de St-Pardoux with good facilities for water sports.
➲ *Access via A20 exit 25.*
19 May-20 Sep 5.5HEC ⚏ ⚭ ♣ ⋔ ⛟ ⵌ ✕ ☉ 🛒 🚐 ⵢ L 🏕 ⊞ lau
Prices: pitch 61-89 (incl 2 persons)

SAUMUR MAINE-ET-LOIRE

Chantepie ☎ 241679534
A pleasant site with a fine view over the River Loire.
➲ *Access via D751 towards Gennes.*
May-15 Sep 10HEC ⚏ ⵄ ⋔ ⛟ ⵌ ✕ ☉ 🛒 ⊘ ⵙ ⵢ P 🏕 ⊞ lau
Prices: ⟑20.80-26 pitch 50.50-63

Ile d'Offard r de Verden ☎ 241403000
On island in the middle of the Loire near municipal stadium.
Some facilities are only available during the high season.
15 Jan-15 Dec 4.5HEC ⬛ 🅶 ☏ ⌷ ♥ ✗ ⊙ 🔲 🅾 ↳ PR 🔳 ⊞
lau

SELLE CRAONNAISE, LA MAYENNE

Rincerie Base de Loisirs la Rincerie ☎ 243061752
A modern site offering a good selection of sporting facilities.
Separate carpark for arrivals after 22.00hrs.
⮕ *N of La Selle-Craonnaise towards Ballots.*
All year 5HEC ⬛ ⋇ ☏ ✗ ⊙ 🔲 🔳 ⊞ lau
Prices: pitch 30-50 (incl 2 persons)

SILLÉ-LE-GUILLAUME SARTHE

Privé du Landereau ☎ 243201269
⮕ *1.5km NW via D304*
Etr-15 Oct 2.5HEC ⬛ 🅶 ☏ ✗ ⊙ 🔲 🅾 🎪 🔳 ⊞ lau ➤ ✗
♨ ↳L

SILLÉ-LE-PHILIPPE SARTHE

🏚Château de Chanteloup ☎ 243275107
Set partly in wooded clearings and open ground within the
park surrounding an old mansion. Good sanitary
installations.
⮕ *17km NE of Le Mans on D301.*
Jun-4 Sep 22HEC ⬛ 🅶 ☏ ♥ ✗ ⊙ 🔲 🎪 Å ↳ P 🔳 ⊞ lau
Prices: ⋔32 pitch 55

SOUTERRAINE, LA CREUSE

Suisse Océan Le Cheix ☎ 555633332
⮕ *1.8km E via D912 near the lake.*
All year 2HEC ⬛ 🅶 ☏ ♥ ✗ ⊙ 🔲 🎪 🔳 ⊞ lau ➤ ♥ ↳L

SUÈVRES LOIR-ET-CHER

🏚Château de la Grenouillère ☎ 254878037
Completely divided into pitches. Castle now hotel with
common room for campers. Each pitch 150sq m. Separate
area for overnight campers.
⮕ *3km from village towards Orléans.*
15 May-15 Sep 11HEC ⬛ 🅶 ☏ ♥ ✗ ⊙ 🔲 🅾 🎪 ↳ P 🔳 ⊞
lau

SULLY-SUR-LOIRE LOIRET

CM chemin de la Salle Verte ☎ 238362393
Near Château, adjacent to River Loire.
⮕ *100m from town.*
27 Mar-Oct 3.4HEC ⬛ ⋰⋰ 🅶 ☏ ⊙ 🔲 🔳 ⊞ lau ➤ ♥ ✗
↳P
Prices: ⋔11.70 pitch 7.30

At ST-PÈRE-SUR-LOIRE

St-Père rte d'Orléans ☎ 238363594
On a level meadow on the right bank of the River Loire.
⮕ *W on D60 towards St-Benoît-sur-Loire.*
Apr-Oct 2.7HEC ⬛ 🅶 ☏ ⊙ 🔲 🎪 🔳 ⊞ lau ➤ ♥ ✗ 🅾 ♨
↳P

TALMONT-ST-HILAIRE VENDÉE

Littoral Le Porteau ☎ 251220464
Situated near Port Bourgenay, 80m from the sea. Good
facilities and entertainment available during the season.
Apr-Sep 8.5HEC ⬛ 🅶 ☏ ♥ ✗ ⊙ 🔲 🅾 ♨ ↳ P 🔳 ⊞ lau
➤ ↳S
Prices: pitch 105-165 (incl 2 persons)

At ST-HILAIRE-LA-FORÊT(7km SE)

Batardières ☎ 251333385
⮕ *W on D70*
Jul-8 Sep 1.6HEC ⬛ 🅶 ☏ ⊙ 🔲 🎪 🔳 lau ➤ ♥ ☏ ✗

TOURS INDRE-ET-LOIRE

At BALLAN-MIRÉ(8.5km W D751)

Mignardière 22 av des Aubepines ☎ 247733100
A well maintained site with a variety of sporting facilities.
⮕ *2.5km NE.*
10 Apr-Sep 3.5HEC ⬛ 🅶 ☏ ♥ ⊙ 🔲 🅾 🎪 🎪 Å ↳ P 🔳 ⊞
lau ➤ ♥ ☏ ✗
Prices: pitch 86-106 (incl 2 persons)

TRANCHE-SUR-MER, LA VENDÉE

Bale d'Aunis 10 r du Pertuis ☎ 251274736
On level land on sea-shore, 50mtrs from the beach and
400mtrs from the town centre with a variety of leisure
activities.
⮕ *300m E on D46.*
Apr-Sep 24.5HEC ⋰⋰ ♥ 🅶 ☏ ♥ ✗ ⊙ 🔲 🅾 🎪 🎪 ↳ PS 🔳
lau ➤ ♨ ↳S
Prices: pitch 38-120 (incl 2 persons)

Bel r du Bottereau ☎ 251304739
A quiet, family-run site 500yds from a magnificent beach and
a marine lake. Plenty of sports and entertainment facilities.
⮕ *400m from town centre.*
25 May-12 Sep 3.5HEC ⬛ ⋰⋰ ♥ 🅶 ☏ ♥ ✗ ⊙ 🔲 ↳ PS 🔳 ⊞
♨ lau ➤ ✗ 🅾 ♨ ↳S ⊞
Prices: pitch 110 (incl 2 persons)

Cottage Fleuri La Grière-Plage ☎ 251303457
A level site with modern facilities.
⮕ *2.5km E, 500m from the beach*
Apr-Sep 7.5HEC ⬛ 🅶 ☏ ♥ ✗ ⊙ 🔲 🅾 ♨ 🎪 ↳ PR 🔳 ⊞ lau
➤ ♥ ↳S
Prices: pitch 70-130 (incl 2 persons)

Jard 123 bd de Lattre-de-Tassigny ☎ 251274379
25 May-15 Sep 6HEC ⬛ ⋇ 🅶 ☏ ♥ ✗ ⊙ 🔲 🅾 ♨ 🎪 ↳ P 🔳 ⊞
♨ lau ➤ 🅾
Prices: pitch 60-80 (incl 2 persons)

Repos du Pêcheur rte de la Roche-sur-Yon ☎ 251303694
Situated on the banks of a canal approx 3km from the sea.
May-Sep 6HEC ⬛ 🅶 ☏ ✗ ⊙ 🔲 🅾 🎪 🎪 ↳ PR 🔳 ⊞ lau
Prices: pitch 60-80 (incl 2 persons)

Savinière ☎ 251274270
Set in a beautiful natural park with good, modern facilities.
⮕ *1.5km NW via D105.*
Apr-Sep 2.5HEC ⬛ ⋰⋰ ♥ 🅶 ☏ ♥ ⊙ 🔲 🎪 ↳ PS 🔳 ⊞ lau ➤

TURBALLE, LA LOIRE-ATLANTIQUE

🏚Parc Ste-Brigitte Domaine de Bréhet ☎ 240248891
Site in grounds of old Château. Parkland divided into pitches
and surrounded by hedges.
⮕ *E of village on D99 Guérande road.*
Apr-1 Oct 10HEC ⬛ 🅶 ♥ 🅶 ☏ ♥ ✗ ⊙ 🔲 🅾 ↳ LP 🔳 ⊞ lau
➤ ↳S
Prices: ⋔26.50 ♥15 🚐57 Å28.50

VALENÇAY INDRE

CM Chênes rte de Loches ☎ 254000392
A quiet site on level ground with well defined pitches.
⮕ *1km W on D960*
Apr-Sep 5HEC ⬛ 🅶 ☏ ⊙ 🔲 🔳 ⊞ lau ➤ ☏ ✗ 🅾 ♨ ↳P

▶ **VARENNES-SUR-LOIRE** MAINE-ET-LOIRE

Étang de la Brèche 5 Impasse de la Brèche ☎ 241512292
Relaxing site in the heart of the Loire Valley, ideal base for
visiting sites of historical interest.
➲ *4.5km NW via N152.*
15 May-17 Sep 12HEC ⊞ ∷∴ ♠ ⋔ ⅗ ⓧ ⓧ ⊙ ♥ ∅ ≷ P ⊠
⊞ lau
Prices: pitch 105-150 (incl 3 persons)

▶ **VEILLON, LE** VENDÉE

St-Hubert av de la Plage, Bourgenay Le Veillon ☎ 251222230
In a wooded location with well defined pitches, 300mtrs
from the sea.
➲ *From Talmont-St-Hilaire head towards Bourgenay and
Veillon.*
Apr-Sep 1HEC ⊞ ♠ ⋔ ⅗ ⊙ ♥ ∅ ☷ ⊞ ⊠ ⊞ lau ♦ ⅗ ✗
≷LPS

▶ **VELLES** INDRE

Grands Pins Les Maisons Neuves ☎ 254366193
The site has individual pitches and has easy access to the
countryside. Swimming pool available July-August only.
➲ *7km S of Châteauroux on N20.*
5HEC ⊞ ∷∴ ♠ ⋔ ⅗ ✗ ⊙ ♥ ⊞ ≷ P ⊠ lau
Prices: ♠18 pitch 20

▶ **VENDÔME** LOIR-ET-CHER

Grand Prés r G-Martel ☎ 254770027
Site lies on a meadow, next to a sports ground.
➲ *E of town on right bank of Loire.*
Etr-Sep ⊞ ⅗ ⋔ ⅗ ⊙ ♥ ≷ P ⊠ lau
Prices: pitch 43 (incl 2 persons)

▶ **VINEUIL** LOIR-ET-CHER

Châteaux ☎ 254788205
Level site on left bank of River Loire with modern buildings.
Boating. Bathing not recommended.
➲ *From Blois drive towards St-Dye. After modern bridge
continue towards 'Lac de Loire' for 1.5km.*
Apr-15 Oct 30HEC ⊞ ⅗ ⋔ ⅗ ✗ ⊙ ♥ ∅ ☷ ♥ ≷ P ⊠ ⊞ lau
Prices: pitch 38-45

● ● ● BRITTANY/NORMANDY ● ● ●

France's most westerly province, Brittany's 750 miles of
splendid coastline juts proudly out into the Atlantic. This is
a wild and rugged coastline, with great rollers crashing into
magnificent cliffs and headlands, the unique wooded
estuaries, "abers", and sheltered harbour coves and
picturesque fine-sand beaches in the south to rival the best
in Europe. The sea dominates the province, and the popular
and chic coastal resorts, as well as the charming fishing
ports, abound in friendly family-run restaurants serving a
wonderful variety of fresh seafood. Away from the sea, this
is a land of gentle hills, narrow, wooded valleys, wild moors
of gorse and heather, and sunken lanes linking sleepy
villages and quaint farmhouses.
Behind the Normandy coastline of splendid sandy beaches
and sheer chalk cliffs is a lush agricultural countryside
which makes a rich contribution to the region's distinctive
cuisine. Apple orchards - a splendid sight in spring - result
in the ciders and strong Calvados, and from the dairy farms
come the famous fine dairy produce and excellent cheeses.
But the region is also rich in history - the beaches recalling
the Allied landings, feudal castles, elegant châteaux; and
the great religious buildings - Mont St Michel, and the
cathedrals at Bayeux, Coutances, Evreux, Lisieux, and the
great Cathedral of Notre Dame at Rouen.

▶ **ALENÇON** ORNE

CM de Guéramé r de Guéramé ☎ 233263495
Situated in open country near a stream, 500m from town centre.
➲ *Access via the Boulevard Périphérique in the SW part of town.*
May-Sep 1.5HEC ⊞ ♠ ⋔ ⊙ ♥ ≷ R ⊞ ⊠ lau ♦ ⅗ ✗ ∅ ☷
≷P
Prices: ♠11.50 ♠♦12.50 ♥12.50 ▲12.50

Jacques Fould av H-Chanteloup ☎ 233292329
➲ *On N12.*
All year 1HEC ⊞ ♠ ⋔ ⊙ ♥ ⊞ ⊠ lau ♦ ⅗ ✗ ∅ ≷PR
Prices: ♠9 ♠♦7 ♥7 ▲7

▶ **ARRADON** MORBIHAN

Penboch 9 chemin de Penboch ☎ 297447129
An exceptionally well appointed site in a pleasant wooded
location 200mtrs from the beaches of the Gulf of Morbihan.
➲ *Signposted from N165.*
30 Apr-20 Sep 4HEC ⊞ ⅗ ⋔ ⅗ ⅗ ⊙ ♥ ∅ ☷ ⊞ ♥ ≷ PS ⊠
⊞ lau ♦ ≷S
Prices: ♠24-24 pitch 30-82

▶ **ARZANO** FINISTÈRE

Ty Nadan rte d'Arzano ☎ 298717547
A quiet riverside site in attractive parkland in the Ellé valley.
➲ *3km W. Leave N165 at Quimperlé exit and drive towards
Arzano.*
8 May-5 Sep 12HEC ⊞ ♠ ⅗ ⅗ ✗ ⊙ ♥ ∅ ☷ ♥ ≷ PR
⊠ ⊞ lau
Prices: ♠24-30 pitch 48-60

▶ **AUMALE** SEINE-MARITIME

CM Grand Mail 2 le Grand Mail ☎ 562050022
➲ *In the town centre*
May-Sep 0.5HEC ⊞ ⅗ ⋔ ⊙ ♥ ⊞ ⊠ lau ♦ ⅗ ✗ ∅ ☷ ≷PR

▶ **AVRANCHES** MANCHE

At GENÊTS (10km W on D911)

Coques d'Or 14 rte du Bec d'Andaine ☎ 233708257
A well equipped site 1km from the sea.
Apr-Sep 4.6HEC ⊞ ♠ ⋔ ⅗ ✗ ⊙ ♥ ♥ ≷ P ⊠ ⊞ lau ♦ ⅗ ✗
∅ ☷

▶ **BADEN** MORBIHAN

Mané Guernehué ☎ 297570206
In a pleasant situation at the head of the Gulf of Morbihan
with good recreational facilities.
➲ *1km SW via Mériadec road.*
Apr-Sep 5.3HEC ⊞ ⅗ ⋔ ⅗ ✗ ⊙ ♥ ∅ ☷ ♥ ≷ P ⊠ ⊞ lau ♦
∅ ☷ ≷RS
Prices: ♠15-27 pitch 47-75

BARNEVILLE-CARTERET MANCHE

Bosquets La Plage ☎ 233047362
A quiet site in wooded surroundings, 400mtrs from the beach with views of the Channel Islands.
Apr-Sep 11HEC ⸎⸎⸎ ⸎ ⸎ P ⸎ ⸎
lau ✦ ⸎ ⸎RS
Prices: ⸎23 pitch 23

At BARNEVILLE-PLAGE

Pré Normand St Jean de la Rivière ☎ 233538564
On slightly hilly meadow away from traffic noise but exposed to sea winds. Vehicles allowed on beach but beware of tide. Separate carpark for arrivals after 22.30hrs.
⮕ Off D166.
Etr-15 Sep 2HEC ⸎⸎⸎ ⸎ ⸎ P ⸎ ⸎
lau ✦ ⸎ ⸎S
Prices: ⸎22 pitch 141

BAYEUX CALVADOS

CM Calvados bd d'Eindhoven ☎ 231920843
Very clean and tidy site with tarmac drive and hardstanding for caravans. Adjoins football field.
⮕ N side of town on Boulevard Circulaire.
15 Mar-Oct 2.9HEC ⸎⸎⸎ ⸎ lau ✦ ⸎ ⸎
⸎P
Prices: ⸎17.10 pitch 21

BEG-MEIL FINISTÈRE

Roche Percée ☎ 298949415
Wooded family site 400mtrs from the Roche Percée beach.
⮕ 1km from Beg Meil towards Fouesnant.
2 Apr-6 Sep 2HEC ⸎⸎⸎ ✦ ⸎ P ⸎ lau
✦ ⸎ ⸎S
Prices: ⸎16-23 pitch 49-69

BÉNODET FINISTÈRE

Letty ☎ 298570469
Site bordering beach, divided into sectors. Good sanitary installations, ironing rooms and games room. Good beach for children. Use of car park compulsory after 11pm.
⮕ By the sea 1km SE.
15 Jun-6 Sep 10HEC ⸎⸎⸎ ⸎ lau
Prices: ⸎25 ⸎11 ⸎38 ⸎37

Plage Kéranbechenner ☎ 298570055
400m from the town centre and close to the beaches, with good, modern facilities.
⮕ Follow signs from town centre.
15 May-Sep 5HEC ⸎⸎⸎ ⸎ PR ⸎ ⸎
lau ✦ ⸎S

Pointe St-Gilles r du Poulmic ☎ 298570537
Holiday site south of village, on fields by beach. Divided into several sectors; individual pitches. Well-equipped sanitary blocks.
May-Sep 7HEC ⸎⸎⸎ ⸎ PS ⸎ ⸎ ⸎ lau
✦ ⸎
Prices: ⸎29 ⸎15 ⸎52 ⸎52

Port de Plaisance 7 rte de Quimper, Prad Puollou
☎ 298570238
A well equipped family site on the outskirts of the town, 500mtrs from the harbour.
⮕ NE off D34 at the entrance to the town.
Apr-Sep 5HEC ⸎⸎⸎ ✦ ⸎ P ⸎ ⸎ lau
✦ ⸎RS

BÉNOUVILLE CALVADOS

Hautes Coutures rte de Ouistréham ☎ 231447308
Pleasant site with good facilities near the Canal Maritime and within easy reach of the Caen-Portsmouth ferry.
Apr-Sep 9HEC ⸎⸎⸎ ⸎ P ⸎ lau ✦ ⸎ ⸎
Prices: ⸎32 pitch 34

BERNIÈRES-SUR-SEINE EURE

Château-Gaillard ☎ 232541820
⮕ 0.8km SW
Jan 24HEC ⸎⸎⸎ ⸎ P ⸎ lau

BINIC CÔTES-D'ARMOR

Palmiers Kerviarc'h ☎ 296737259
A well equipped site within the Parc Tropical de Bretagne, just over one kilometre from the town centre.
⮕ Access via N12/D786.
Jun-Sep 2HEC ⸎⸎⸎ ⸎ PRS ⸎ lau
Prices: ⸎22 ⸎11 ⸎20 ⸎14

Panoramic r Gasselin ☎ 296736043
On a meadow divided into pitches, on a hill above the town.
⮕ On S outskirts of village.
All year 5HEC ⸎⸎⸎ ⸎ P ⸎ lau
✦ ⸎ ⸎S

BLAINVILLE-SUR-MER MANCHE

Mélette ☎ 233471484
⮕ 1km W on D651.
15 Jun-15 Sep 6HEC ⸎⸎⸎ ⸎ lau ✦ ⸎ ⸎
⸎PS

Senéquet ☎ 233472311
⮕ 2km NW on D651.
Mar-early Dec 13HEC ⸎⸎⸎ ⸎ PS ⸎
⸎ lau ✦ ⸎
Prices: ⸎19 pitch 55

BLANGY-LE-CHÂTEAU CALVADOS

Brévedent ☎ 32647288
Situated in the grounds of an 18th century manor house with good facilities.
⮕ 3km SE on D51 beside lake.
15 May-21 Sep 5.5HEC ⸎⸎⸎ ⸎ P ⸎ ⸎ ⸎
lau ✦ ⸎
Prices: ⸎30 pitch 45

Domaine du Lac ☎ 231646200
Apr-Oct 4HEC ⸎⸎⸎ ⸎ lau
Prices: ⸎25 pitch 25-25

BLANGY-SUR-BRESLE SEINE-MARITIME

CM r des Étangs ☎ 235945565
⮕ 300m on N28.
15 Mar-15 Oct 7HEC ⸎⸎⸎ ⸎ lau ✦ ⸎ ⸎
⸎ ⸎R
Prices: ⸎11.75 pitch 9.10

BLONVILLE-SUR-MER CALVADOS

Village Club le Lieu Bill rte de Beaumont-en-Auge, Le Lieu Bill ☎ 231879727
Apr-Sep 7HEC ⸎⸎⸎ ⸎ P ⸎ ⸎ lau
✦ ⸎S

BOURG-ACHARD EURE

Clos Normand 235 rte de Pont-Audemer ☎ 232563484
⮕ Access via N175 (Rouen-Caen).
Apr-Sep 1.5HEC ⸎⸎⸎ ⸎ P ⸎ lau ✦ ⸎ ⸎ ⸎
Prices: ⸎20-23 ⸎8 ⸎19 ⸎19

▶ **CABOURG** CALVADOS

Vert Pré rte de Caen ☎ 231242119
➲ *2km SW on D513.*
Apr-Sep 5HEC ⁙ ⚪ ⋔ ⚑ ♥ × ⊙ ⚐ ⌀ ⬛ ⬛ ⬛ ⅋ P ⊡ ⊞
lau ➧ ⬛ × ⅋S

▶ **CALLAC** CÔTES-D'ARMOR

CM Verte Vallée ☎ 296455850
➲ *W via D28 towards Morlaix*
15 Jun-15 Sep 1HEC ⁙ ⚪ ⋔ ⊙ ⚐ ⊡ lau ➧ ⬛ ♥ × ⌀ ⅋L

▶ **CAMARET-SUR-MER** FINISTÈRE

Lambézen ☎ 298279141
Situated beside the sea on the edge of the Armorican Natural Park with a wide variety of recreational facilities.
➲ *3km NE on rte de Roscanvel (D355).*
Apr-Sep 2.8HEC ⁙ ⚪ ⋔ ⚑ ♥ × ⊙ ⚐ ⌀ ⬛ ⬛ ⬛ ⅋ P ⊡ ⊞
lau ➧ ⅋S
Prices: ♦20-28.50 pitch 40-60

Plage de Trez Rouz ☎ 298279396
On level ground 50mtrs from the beach.
➲ *3km from Camaret-sur-Mer via D355 towards Pointe-des-Espagnols.*
Etr-Sep 1.1HEC ⁙ ⚪ ⋔ ♥ ⊙ ⚐ ⌀ ⬛ ⊡ ⊞ lau ➧ ⅋S
Prices: ♦24-25 pitch 18-20

▶ **CAMPNEUSEVILLE** SEINE-MARITIME

Monchy-le-Preux ☎ 235937703
➲ *2km N on D260.*
Jun-Sep 2HEC ⁙ ⚪ ⋔ ⚑ ⊙ ⚐ ⌀ ⊡ ⊞ lau ➧ ⅋LPRS

▶ **CANCALE** ILLE-ET-VILAINE

Notre Dame du Verger ☎ 299897284
Terraced site overlooking the sea with direct access to the beach.
➲ *2km from Pointe-du-Grouin on D201.*
Apr-Sep 2.2HEC ⁙ ⚪ ⋔ ⚑ ⊙ ⚐ ⌀ ⊡ ⊞ lau ➧ ⅋S

▶ **CARANTEC** FINISTÈRE

Mouettes Grande Grève ☎ 298670246
Level site divided by low shrubs and trees.
➲ *1.5km SW on rte de St-Pol-de-Léon, towards the sea.*
Etr-20 Sep 7HEC ⁙ ⚪ ⋔ ⚑ ♥ ⊙ ⚐ ⌀ ⬛ Å ⅋ LP ⊡ ⊞ lau
➧ ⅋S
Prices: ♦21.75-32 pitch 61.50-87

▶ **CARENTAN** MANCHE

CM le Haut Dyck chemin du Grand-Bas Pays ☎ 233421689
A level site in wooded surroundings with well defined pitches.
➲ *Take village road off N13 towards Le Port.*
All year 2.5HEC ⁙ ⚪ ⋔ ⊙ ⚐ ⌀ ⊡ ⊞ lau ➧ ⬛ ♥ × ⌀ ⬛ ⅋PR
Prices: ♦13-14 ⬛24-25 ▲16-17

▶ **CARNAC** MORBIHAN

Bruyères Kerogile ☎ 297523057
Partly wooded site with modern facilities.
➲ *N of Carnac on C4, 2km from Plouharnel.*
3 Apr-15 Oct 1.8HEC ⁙ ⚪ ⋔ ⚑ ⊙ ⚐ ⌀ ⬛ ⬛ ⬛ ⊡ ⊞ lau ➧ ♥
×
Prices: ♦14-17.50 pitch 28.50-35

Étang 67 rte de Kerlann ☎ 297521406
In a rural setting with pitches divided by hedges, 2.5km from the coast.
➲ *2km N at Kerlann on D119.*
Apr-Oct 2.8HEC ⁙ ⚪ ⋔ ⚑ ♥ × ⊙ ⚐ ⌀ ⬛ ⬛ ⬛ ⅋ P ⊡ ⊞
lau ➧ × ⅋S
Prices: ♦18-23 pitch 28-39

Grande Métairie rte des Alignements, de Kermario
☎ 297522401
Holiday site with modern amenities, completely divided into pitches. Country-style bar, terraced restaurant, TV. Swimming pools.
➲ *2.5km NE on D196.*
27 Mar-18 Sep 15HEC ⁙ ⚪ ⋔ ⚑ ♥ × ⊙ ⚐ ⌀ ⬛ ⬛ ⬛ ⅋ PS
⊡ ⊞ lau
Prices: ♦18-30 pitch 76.80-128

Moulin de Kermaux ☎ 297521590
In a quiet location, surrounded by trees and bushes, with good facilities. Within easy reach of the coast and the local megaliths.
➲ *2.5km NE.*
Etr-15 Sep 3HEC ⁙ ⚪ ⋔ ⚑ ♥ ⊙ ⚐ ⌀ ⬛ ⅋ P ⊡ lau ➧ × ⌀
⅋L
Prices: ♦12-23 pitch 42-70

Moustoir rte du Moustoir ☎ 297521618
Well equipped site in a rural setting close to the sea.
➲ *3 km NE of Carnac.*
Apr-Sep 5HEC ⁙ ⚪ ⋔ ⚑ ♥ × ⊙ ⚐ ⌀ ⬛ ⅋ P ⊡ ⊞ lau ➧ ×
⬛ ⅋RS
Prices: ♦15.50-24 pitch 39-60

Ombrages ☎ 297521652
In a wooded location with shaded pitches divided by hedges.
➲ *Take rte Carnac to Auray and turn left at SHELL filling station.*
15 Jun-15 Sep 1HEC ⁙ ⚪ ⋔ ⚑ ⊙ ⚐ ⌀ ⊡ ⊞ lau ➧ ♥ × ⅋L
Prices: ♦18 pitch 28

Rosnual rte d'Auray ☎ 297521457
A pleasant site in a wooded rural setting with good recreational facilities.
➲ *1.5km from village, 2.5km from the sea.*
Apr-Sep 4HEC ⁙ ⚪ ⋔ ⚑ ♥ × ⊙ ⚐ ⌀ ⬛ ⬛ ⬛ ⅋ P ⊡ ⊞ ⌀
lau ➧ ⌀
Prices: ♦26 pitch 92

Saules rte de Rosnual ☎ 297521498
Grassland site between road and deciduous woodland, subdivided by hedges and shrubs.
➲ *2.5km N on D119.*
Apr-Sep 2.5HEC ⁙ ⚪ ⋔ ⚑ ⊙ ⚐ ⌀ ⬛ ⬛ Å ⅋ P ⊡ ⊞ lau ➧
♥ × ⬛
Prices: ♦16-22 pitch 22-30

▶ At **CARNAC-PLAGE**(1km S)

Druides 55 chemin de Beaumer ☎ 297520818
Family site with well defined pitches, 400m from a fine sandy beach.
➲ *SE of town centre. Approach via D781 or D119.*
20 May-10 Sep 2.5HEC ⁙ ⚪ ⋔ ♥ ⊙ ⚐ ⊡ ⊞ lau ➧ ⬛ × ⌀ ⬛ ⅋S
Prices: pitch 129 (incl 3 persons)

Men Dû r de Beaumer ☎ 297520423
Peaceful site in a wooded setting close to the beach.
➲ *1km from Carnac Plage via D781 and D186.*
Etr-Sep 1.5HEC ⁙ ⚪ ⋔ × ⊙ ⚐ ⬛ ⬛ ⬛ ⊡ ⊞ lau ➧ ⬛ ♥ ×
⌀ ⅋PS
Prices: pitch 75-100 (incl 2 persons)

Menhirs allée St-Michel ☎ 297529467
A family site near the beach and shops with good recreational facilities and modern sanitary blocks, including toilets suitable for the disabled.
May-Sep 6HEC ⁙ ⚪ ⋔ ♥ ⬛ × ⊙ ⚐ ⬛ ⅋ P ⊡ ⊞ lau ➧ ⌀
⬛ ⅋S
Prices: ♦21.50-43 pitch 82-164

CAUREL CÔTES-D'ARMOR

Nautic International rte de Beau Rivage ☎ 296285794
A terraced site in woodland on the edge of Lake Guerlédan
with a variety of recreational facilities.
➲ *N164 in the direction of Beau Rivage.*
Apr-25 Sep 3.6HEC ⸬ 🏕 🚻 ⊙ 🚿 🏪 🍴 LP 🏧 ⊞ lau ➡
🍴 ✕
Prices: ⋔21-26 pitch 35-45

CHAPELLE-AUX-FILZMÉENS, LA ILLE-ET-VILAINE

Camping du Logis ☎ 299452155
A quiet, pleasant site in the wooded grounds of an 18th
century château.
➲ *NE of town towards Combourg.*
All year 20HEC ⸬ 🏕 🚻 🍴 ✕ ⊙ 🚿 🌂 🏖 🏪 Å P 🏧 ⊞
lau ➡ ⇌R
Prices: ⋔29 pitch 45-60

CLÉDER FINISTÈRE

CV Roguennic Roguennic ☎ 298696388
➲ *5km N on coast.*
Apr-Sep 8HEC ⸬ 🌾 🚻 🍴 ✕ ⊙ 🚿 🌂 🏪 ⇌ PS
🏧 ⊞ lau

CLOÎTRE-ST-THEGONNEC, LE FINISTÈRE

Bruyères ☎ 298797176
A small, secluded site in a picturesque setting within the
Amorique Nature Park.
➲ *12km S of Morlaix via D769.*
Jun-Sep 2.5HEC ⸬ 🏕 🌂 🏖 🏧 lau ➡ 🚻 🍴 ✕ 🛁
Prices: ⋔15 ⇌7 pitch 18

COMBOURG ILLE-ET-VILAINE

Bois Coudrais Cuguen ☎ 299732745
A small, level site with fine views.
➲ *Access via D83 (Combourg-Mont-St-Michel).*
Etr-mid Oct 1HEC ⸬ 🌾 🚻 ✕ ⊙ 🚿 🏪 🏧 ⊞ lau ➡ 🚻

CONCARNEAU FINISTÈRE

Prés Verts Kernous Plage ☎ 298970974
A landscaped site with good facilities overlooking
Concarneau Bay.
➲ *1.2km NW.*
May-11 Sep 3HEC ⸬ 🏕 🚻 ⊙ 🚿 🏪 ⇌ PS 🏧 🅿 lau
➡ 🚻
Prices: pitch 33.60-42 (incl 2 persons)

COUTERNE ORNE

Clos Normand rte de Bagnoles ☎ 233379243
A pleasant site in rural surroundings in a sheltered position
close to the thermal spa of Bagnoles-de-l'Orne.
➲ *Approach D916.*
May-Sep 1.3HEC ⸬ 🏕 🌾 ⊙ 🚿 🏪 🏧 lau ➡ 🚻 🍴 🌂 🛁
⇌PR
Prices: pitch 39 (incl 2 persons)

CRACH MORBIHAN

Fort Espagnol rte de Fort Espagnol ☎ 297551488
In a secluded, wooded location, this is a family site with a
wide variety of recreational facilities.
➲ *Due E of Crac'h towards the coast.*
Apr-15 Sep 4.5HEC ⸬ 🏕 🚻 🍴 ✕ ⊙ 🚿 🌂 🏪 🍴 Å ⇌ P 🏧
lau

CRIEL-SUR-MER SEINE-MARITIME

Mouettes r de la Plage ☎ 235867073
Small grassy site overlooking the sea.
Etr-Oct 2HEC ⸬ 🌾 🚻 🍴 ⊙ 🚿 🌂 🏪 🏧 lau ➡ ✕ ⇌RS ⊞

CROZON FINISTÈRE

Pen ar Menez bd de Pralognan ☎ 298271236
On fringe of a pinewood. Water sport facilities 5km away.
Cycles for hire.
Apr-Sep 2.6HEC ⸬ 🏕 🍴 ✕ ⊙ 🚿 🏪 🏧 lau ➡ 🚻 ✕ 🌂 🛁
⇌S ⊞

Plage de Goulien Kernaveèno ☎ 298271710
Grassy site in wooded surroundings 150m from the sea.
➲ *5km W on D308.*
10 Jun-20 Sep 2.5HEC ⸬ 🏕 🍴 ⊙ 🚿 🏪 🏧 ⊞ lau ➡ ⇌S

At ST-FIACRE(5km NW)

Pieds dans l'Eau ☎ 298276243
Site on several meadows divided by trees. In quiet secluded
situation reaching as far as a pebbly beach. Bathing is
dependent on tides.
15 Jun-15 Sep 3HEC ⸬ 🏕 🍴 ⊙ 🚿 🏪 ⇌ S 🏧 lau ➡ 🚻 🍴 ✕ 🌂

DEAUVILLE CALVADOS

At ST-ARNOULT(3km S)

Vallée route de Beaumont ☎ 231885817
In a pleasant wooded setting with plenty of recreational
facilities.
➲ *1km S via D27 and D275.*
Etr-Oct 19HEC ⸬ 🌾 🚻 🍴 🍴 ✕ ⊙ 🚿 🌂 🛁 🏪 🍴 ⇌ P 🏧 🅿
lau
Prices: ⋔32.50 pitch 36.50

At TOUQUES(3km SE)

Haras chemin du Calvaire ☎ 231884484
A partially residential site in pleasant surroundings. Ideal for
overnight stops, but reservations recommended in July and
August.
➲ *N on D62, to Honfleur.*
All year 4HEC ⸬ 🏕 🚻 🍴 🍴 ⊙ 🚿 🌂 🏧 🏧 lau ➡ ⇌PRS

DÉVILLE-LÈS-ROUEN SEINE-MARITIME

CM r Jules-Ferry ☎ 235740759
All year 1HEC ⸬ 🌾 🔆 🍴 ⊙ 🚿 🏧 ⊞ lau ➡ 🚻 🍴 ✕ ⇌PR
Prices: ⋔24.50 ⇌8.50 🏕16 Å8.50

DIEPPE SEINE-MARITIME

At HAUTOT-SUR-MER(6km SW)

Source Petit Appeville ☎ 235842704
15 Mar-15 Oct 2.5HEC ⸬ 🏕 🍴 ✕ ⊙ 🚿 🌂 ⇌ R 🏧 ⊞ lau
➡ 🚻
Prices: ⋔20 pitch 34

DINAN CÔTES-D'ARMOR

At TADEN(3.5km NE)

CM Hallerais ☎ 296391593
Beautiful clean site with level pitches on gentle slope near a
country estate. Asphalt drives. Good sanitary installations.
Shop, bar and restaurant are only open in July and August.
➲ *SW of Taden off D12.*
15 Mar-Oct 8HEC ⸬ 🏕 🚻 🍴 ✕ ⊙ 🚿 🌂 🛁 🏪 🍴 ⇌ P 🅿
⊞ lau

DINARD ILLE-ET-VILAINE

See also St-Lunaire

Mauny ☎ 299469473
A pleasant site in pleasant wooded surroundings with a variety
of recreational facilities.
➲ *Off St-Briac road (CD603).*
3 Mar-25 Sep 5HEC ⸬ 🏕 🍴 🚻 🍴 ✕ ⊙ 🚿 🌂 🏪 ⇌ P 🏧 🏧
lau ➡ ⇌S
Prices: ⋔25 pitch 60

Prieuré 20 av Vicomte ☎ 299462004
➲ *SE via D114*
Etr-Oct 1.4HEC ⬛ 🏕 ♿ ♃ ☎ ♨ ✕ ⊙ ⊟ ∅ ⚊ ▦ ⬛ ↖ S ⬜ ⊞
lau ➡ ↖P

▶ DOL-DE-BRETAGNE ILLE-ET-VILAINE

🏯 **Château des Ormes** ☎ 299734959
Site in grounds of château, within a large leisure complex
with excellent facilities.
➲ *7km S on N795 Rennes road.*
20 May-10 Sep 160HEC ⬛ ➡ ♃ ☎ ♨ ✕ ⊙ ⊟ ∅ ⬛ ↖ LP ⬜
lau

CM r de Dinan ☎ 299481468
On level meadow.
➲ *SW on rte de Dinan 400m from town centre.*
15 May-15 Sep 1.7HEC ⬛ ♿ 🏕 ⊙ ⊟ ⬜ lau ➡ ♨ ♃ ✕
Prices: ♦11.90 ➡5.35 ⬛5.35 ▲5.35

▷ At BAGUER-PICAN(4km E on N176)

Camping du Vieux Chêne ☎ 299480955
Spacious site in pleasant lakeside situation. Farm produce
available.
➲ *5km E of Dol-de-Bretagne on D576.*
3 Apr-18 Sep 8HEC ⬛ ♿ 🏕 ♃ ☎ ✕ ⊙ ⊟ ∅ ⬛ ▲ ↖ LP ⬜ ⊞
lau
Prices: ♦28 pitch 40-75

▶ DOUARNENEZ FINISTÈRE

Kerleyou Tréboul ☎ 298741303
Family site in wooded surroundings near the beach. Separate
car park for arrivals after 23.00hrs.
➲ *1km W on r de Préfet-Collignon towards the sea.*
Apr-Sep 3HEC ⬛ ♿ 🏕 ♃ ☎ ♨ ♃ ⊙ ⊟ ∅ ⬛ ▦ ⬛ ⬜ ⊞ lau ➡ ⚊
↖LPS

▷ At POULLAN-SUR-MER(5km W on D765)

Pil Koad ☎ 298742639
In a natural wooded setting with a variety of recreational
facilities.
➲ *E via D7 towards Douarnenez.*
Apr-Sep 5.5HEC ⬛ ♿ 🏕 ☎ ♃ ✕ ⊙ ⊟ ∅ ⚊ ▦ ⬛ ⬛ ↖ P ⬜ ⊞
lau ➡ ✕
Prices: ♦20-29 pitch 37-79

▶ ERDEVEN MORBIHAN

Sept Saints ☎ 297555265
In wooded surroundings with good recreational facilities.
➲ *2km NW via D781 rte de Plouhinec.*
15 May-15 Sep 5HEC ⬛ ➡ 🏕 ☎ ♃ ♨ ⊙ ⊟ ∅ ⬛ ↖ P ⬜ ⊞
lau ➡ ✕ ↖LRS
Prices: ♦18-28 pitch 50-79

▶ ERQUY CÔTES-D'ARMOR

Hautes Greés 123 r St-Michel ☎ 296723478
Good family site, 2km from the town centre and 400mtrs
from the beach.
➲ *500m from the sea.*
15 Apr-15 Sep 2.5HEC ⬛ ♿ 🏕 ☎ ⊙ ⊟ ⬛ ⬛ ⬜ ⊞ lau ➡ ♃
✕ ∅ ⚊ ↖S
Prices: ♦19 pitch 34

Roches Caroual Village ☎ 296723290
In a rural setting with well marked pitches, 800mtrs from the
beach.
➲ *3km SW.*
Apr-Sep 3.1HEC ⬛ ♿ 🏕 ⊙ ⊟ ∅ ⚊ ▦ ⬛ ⬛ ⬜ ⊞ lau ➡ ♃ ✕
↖S
Prices: ♦15-16 pitch 14-15

St-Pabu ☎ 296722465
On big open meadow with several terraces in beautiful,
isolated situation by sea. Divided into pitches.
➲ *W on D786 then follow signposts from La Coutre.*
Apr-10 Oct 5.5HEC ⬛ ⟡ 🏕 ♃ ☎ ♃ ✕ ⊙ ⊟ ∅ ⬛ ⬛ ↖ R ⬜
⊞ lau
Prices: ♦20 pitch 40

Vieux Moulin r des Moulins ☎ 296723423
Clean tidy site divided into pitches and surrounded by a pine
forest. Suitable for children.
➲ *On D783.*
May-20 Sep 4.5HEC ⬛ ➡ 🏕 ☎ ♃ ✕ ⊙ ⊟ ∅ ⬛ ↖ P ⬜ ⊞ lau
➡ ⚊ ↖S
Prices: ♦29 ➡22 ⬛55 ▲55

▶ ÉTABLES-SUR-MER CÔTES-D'ARMOR

Abri Côtier ☎ 296706157
➲ *1km N of town centre on D786.*
6 May-20 Sep 2HEC ⬛ ♿ 🏕 ☎ ♃ ✕ ⊙ ⊟ ∅ ⚊ ⬛ ↖ P ⬜
lau ➡ ✕
Prices: ♦28-31 pitch 42-46

▶ ETRÉHAM CALVADOS

Reine Mathilde ☎ 231217655
In a quiet rural setting 4km from the sea.
➲ *1km W via D123*
Apr-Sep 6HEC ⬛ ♿ 🏕 ✕ ⊙ ⊟ ∅ ⚊ ▦ ⬛ ⬛ ↖ P ⬜ ⊞ lau
Prices: ♦23 pitch 24

▶ EU SEINE-MARITIME

CM r Mozart ☎ 235503017
➲ *About 7km SE of town at Incheville, on the road to
Beauchamps.*
Apr-Sep 2HEC ⬛ ♿ 🏕 ☎ ⊙ ⊟ ∅ ⬜ ⊞ lau ➡ ♃ ✕ ↖LPR

▶ FAOUËT, LE MORBIHAN

Beg Er Roch rte de Lorient ☎ 297231511
In pleasant surroundings on the banks of a river. A popular
site with modern sanitary facilities and a wealth of
opportunities for all kinds of sport.
7 Mar-15 Sep 3.5HEC ⬛ ♿ ⊙ ⊟ ⬛ ⬛ ↖ R ⬜ lau ➡ ♃ ♃
✕ ∅ ⚊ ↖LP ⊞
Prices: ♦14-20 pitch 10-18

▶ FORÊT-FOUESNANT, LA FINISTÈRE

Kérantérec ☎ 298569811
Well-kept terraced site, divided into sections by hedges and
extending to the sea.
➲ *3km SE.*
3 Apr-26 Sep 6.5HEC ⬛ ♿ 🏕 ✕ ⊙ ⊟ ∅ ⚊ ⬛ ⬛ ↖ PS ⬜
⬜ ⊞ lau ➡ ♃ ✕
Prices: ♦30 pitch 35

Manoir de Pen Ar Steir ☎ 298569775
Well-tended site close to Port La Forêt, a major yachting arena.
➲ *NE off D44.*
All year 3HEC ⬛ ♿ 🏕 ⊙ ⊟ ⚊ ⬛ ⬛ ⬛ ⬜ ⊞ lau ➡ ♃ ✕ ∅
↖S

Plage Plage de Kerleven, rte de Port la Forêt ☎ 298569625
➲ *2.5km SE on D783.*
Mar-Dec 1HEC ⬛ ⟡ ⟡ ♃ ♃ ⊙ ⊟ ⬜ lau ➡ ♃ ✕ ∅ ⚊ ↖S ⊞

Pontérec Pontérec ☎ 298569833
A modern site with well defined pitches separated by hedges,
2.5km from the beach.
➲ *0.5km on D44 towards Bénodet.*
Apr-Sep 3HEC ⬛ ♿ 🏕 ⊙ ⊟ ⬛ ⬛ ⬜ ⊞ lau ➡ ♃ ♃ ✕ ∅
Prices: ♦17-18 pitch 18-19

St-Laurent Kerleven ☎ 298569765
On rocky coast. Divided into pitches.
➲ *3.5km SE of village.*
Apr-Sep 5.3HEC ⌂ ⌂ ⌂ ⌂ ⌂ ⌂ ⊙ ⌂ ⌂ ⌂ PS ⌂ lau ♦ ⌂ ⌂
⌂

FOUESNANT FINISTÈRE

Atlantique rte de Mousterlin ☎ 298561444
Modern site with plenty of amenities 400mtrs from the beach.
➲ *4.5km S on the road to Mousterlin.*
May-15 Sep 9HEC ⌂ ⌂ ⌂ ⌂ ⌂ ⌂ ⊙ ⌂ ⌂ ⌂ ⌂ ⌂ ⌂ P ⌂
⌂⌂ lau ♦ ✗ ⌂S

Piscine Kerleya ☎ 298565606
In a beautiful location 1.5km from the baech.
➲ *4km NW towards Kerleya.*
15 May-15 Sep 3.8HEC ⌂ ⌂ ⌂ ⌂ ⊙ ⌂ ⌂ ⌂ ⌂ P ⌂ lau ♦ ⌂S
Prices: ⌂17.50-25 pitch 34.50-49.50

FOUGÈRES ILLE-ET-VILAINE

CM Paron rte de la Chapelle Janson ☎ 299994081
A well managed site suitable for overnight stays.
➲ *1.5km E via D17*
Mar-Nov 2.5HEC ⌂ ♦ ⌂ ⊙ ⌂ ⌂ lau ♦ ⌂ ⌂ ✗ ⌂ ⌂

GLACERIE, LA MANCHE

Clos à Froment r P & M Curie ☎ 233542599
A modern site near the Cherbourg ferry terminal and the Auchan hypermarket.
All year 1.7HEC ⌂ ⌂ ⌂ ✗ ⊙ ⌂ ⌂ ⌂ ⌂ ⌂ lau ♦ ⌂ ✗ ⌂
⌂

GOUVILLE-SUR-MER MANCHE

Belle Étoile ☎ 233478687
Terraced site among sand dunes.
➲ *20m from the beach.*
May-Aug 2.8HEC ⌂ ⌂ ⌂ ⌂ ⌂ ✗ ⊙ ⌂ ⌂ ⌂ ⌂ ⌂ ⌂ ⌂
lau ♦ ⌂S

GUIDEL-PLAGES MORBIHAN

Kergal ☎ 297059818
➲ *3km SW*
Apr-Sep 5HEC ⌂ ⌂ ⌂ ⌂ ⊙ ⌂ ⌂ ⌂ ⌂ ⌂ ⌂ ⌂ lau ♦ ⌂ ✗
⌂RS

GUILLIGOMARC'H FINISTÈRE

Bois des Ecureuils ☎ 298717098
Tranquil four acre wooded site set among oak, chestnut and beech trees. An ideal base for walking, cycling, horse-riding and fishing.

➲ *2km W from D769 (Roscoff to Lorient).*
15 May-15 Sep 1.5HEC ⌂ ♦ ⌂ ⌂ ⊙ ⌂ ⌂ ⌂ ⌂ ⌂ ⌂ lau
Prices: ⌂14 ♦8 ⌂14 ⌂14

GUILVINEC FINISTÈRE

Plage rte de Penmarc'h ☎ 298586190
On level meadow. Divided into pitches. Flat beach suitable for children.
➲ *2km W of village on the Corniche towards Penmarc'h.*
11 Apr-15 Sep 14HEC ⌂ ⌂ ⌂ ⌂ ⌂ ✗ ⊙ ⌂ ⌂ ⌂ ⌂ ⌂
⌂ PS ⌂ ⌂ lau

HAYE-DU-PUITS, LA MANCHE

Étang des Haizes ☎ 233460116
A well equipped family site bordering a lake, shaded by apple trees.
➲ *Access via D903 from Carentan.*
15 Apr-15 Oct 5HEC ⌂ ⌂ ⌂ ⌂ ✗ ⊙ ⌂ ⌂ ⌂ ⌂ LP ⌂ ⌂
lau
Prices: ⌂30 pitch 45

HOULGATE CALVADOS

Vallée 88 r de la Vallée ☎ 231244069
Site with good recreational facilities, 900m from the beach.
➲ *1km S.*
Apr-Sep 11HEC ⌂ ⌂ ⌂ ⌂ ⌂ ⊙ ⌂ ⌂ ⌂ ⌂ ⌂ ⌂ P ⌂ ⌂ ⌂ lau
♦ ⌂S
Prices: ⌂30 pitch 45

IFFENDIC ILLE-ET-VILAINE

Domaine de Trémelin ☎ 299097379
A lakeside site in beautiful wooded surroundings with good sports and entertainment facilities.
➲ *S of town towards Plélan-le-Grand.* Contd.

BAIE DU MONT-SAINT-MICHEL • 80 metres from the beach

LA CHAUSSEE ★★★
50610-JULLOUVILLE
Tel: 00 33/2 33 61 80 18 Fax: 00 33/2 33 61 45 26
Perfect for family holidays in peaceful, flowery surroundings. Children's playground, leisure programme, archery, satellite-television. Grocery, bar, take away meals, multilingual library. MOBILE HOMES FOR HIRE. Motor caravans are also welcome. Permanently guarded campsite. Animals are allowed. The reception closes at 20.00 h

Apr-Sep 2HEC ⬛ ⚐ ♠ ⚏ ✕ ⊙ ⚑ ⚅ ⌕ L ⚐ ⊞
Prices: ♦9-13 ♣5-6 ⚑7-9 ▲7-9

JULLOUVILLE MANCHE

Chaussée 1 av de la Libération ☎ 233618018
On large meadow, completely divided into pitches. Separated from beach and coast road by row of houses.
3 Apr-19 Sep 6HEC ⬛ ⚐ ♠ ⚏ ✕ ⊙ ⚑ ⚅ ⚏ ⚑ ⚐ ⊞ lau ➡ ✕ ⅞S
Prices: pitch 95 (incl 2 persons)

At ST-MICHEL-DES-LOUPS(4km SE)

Chaumière ☎ 233488293
⮕ *4km SE on D21 via Bouillon.*
Jul-Aug 2HEC ⬛ ⚐ ♠ ⚏ ✕ ⊙ ⚑ ⚅ ⌕ ⚐ ⚑ ▲ ⅞ L ⚐ ⊞ lau ➡ ⅞
Prices: ♦18 pitch 18

KERLIN FINISTÈRE

Étangs de Trévignon Pointe de Trévignon ☎ 298500041
A family site with good, modern facilities 800mtrs from the beach, reached by a short pathway.
Jun-15 Sep 3.5HEC ⬛ ⚐ ♠ ⚏ ✕ ⊙ ⚑ ⚅ ⚏ ⊞ lau ➡ ⅞S
Prices: ♦28 pitch 31

LANDAUL MORBIHAN

Pied-à-Terre Branzého ☎ 297246715
In a pleasant, quiet location, 15 minutes from the sea.
1km from N165. Signposted from Landaul.
Jun-Aug 5HEC ⬛ ⚐ ♠ ⊙ ⚑ ▲ ⚐ ⊞ lau ➡ ⅞ ⚏ ✕ ⚑ ⌕
Prices: ♦15-20 ♣10 ⚑10 ▲8

LANDÉDA FINISTÈRE

Abers Dunes de Ste-Marguerite ☎ 298049335
Very quiet beautiful site among dunes. Ideal for children.
⮕ *2.5km NW on a peninsula between bays of Aber-Wrac'h and Aber Bernoît.*
Apr-Sep 4.5HEC ⬛ ⚐ ♠ ⊙ ⚑ ⚅ ⚏ ⚑ ⅞ S ⚐ ⊞ lau ➡ ⚏
Prices: ♦12.80-16 pitch 20-25

LARMOR-PLAGE MORBIHAN

Fontaine Kerderff ☎ 297337128
800m from the beach, near the leisure centre.
⮕ *300m from D152.*
2 May-15 Sep 4HEC ⬛ ⚐ ♠ ⚏ ⊙ ⚑ ⚐ ⊞ lau ➡ ⚏ ✕ ⅞S

LESCONIL FINISTÈRE

Dunes 7 r P-Langevin ☎ 298878178
A family site on slightly sloping landscaped ground, 800mtrs from the town centre and the harbour.

Direct access to the beach

GRAND CAMPING DE LA PLAGE
★ ★ ★
F-29730 Le Guilvinec

Tel: (00-33)-2.98.58.61.90
Fax: (00-33)-2.98.58.89.06

ACTIVE HOLIDAYS
FOR THE WHOLE FAMILY
Tentbungalows, mobile homes and chalets for hire • swimming pool • sauna • tennis • organised activities • grocery • take away meals • open air game of chess • bikes to let • miniclub.
NEW: Waterslide
(Grand Camping La Plage)
RESERVATION RECOMMENDED
SOUTH BRITTANY

2 km from the beaches

CAMPING MANOIR DE KERLUT
★ ★ ★ ★
F-29740 Plobannalec le Lesconil

Tel: (00-33)-2.98.82.23.89
Fax: (00-33)-2.98.82.26.49

⮕ *Access via D53, turning S in Plobannalac. Signposted.*
25 May-15 Sep 2.8HEC ⬛ ⚐ ♠ ⊙ ⚑ ⚐ ⊞ lau ➡ ⚏ ⚏ ✕ ⅞S
Prices: ♦25.40 pitch 38.50

Grande Plage 71 r P-Langevin ☎ 298878827
Well equipped site on level ground, surrounded by woodland, 300mtrs from the sea.
May-10 Sep 2.5HEC ⬛ ⚐ ♠ ⊙ ⚑ ⚅ ⚑ ⚐ ⊞ lau ➡ ⚏ ✕ ⅞S
Prices: ♦22.50 pitch 32.80

LION-SUR-MER CALVADOS

Roches av de Blagny ☎ 231972115
⮕ *NW on D514.*
Apr-Sep 1.3HEC ⬛ ⚶ ♠ ⚏ ✕ ⊙ ⚑ ⚅ ⚑ ⅞ S ⚐ ⊞ lau

LOUARGAT CÔTES-D'ARMOR

At ST-ELOI(5km N)

Cleuziou ☎ 296431490
In the grounds of a château with pitches marked out by hedges.
⮕ *Between Guingamp and Morlaix, the site is signposted from the church in Louargat.*
17 Mar-12 Nov 7HEC ⬛ ⚐ ♠ ⚏ ✕ ⊙ ⚑ ⚅ ⌕ ⚑ ⅞ P ⚐ ⊞ lau

LOUVIERS EURE

Bel Air Hameau de St-Lubin, rte de la Haye Malherbe ☎ 232401077
Small site on the edge of a forest with landscaped pitches and good facilities.
⮕ *3km from the town centre via D81.*
Mar-Nov 2.5HEC ⬛ ⚐ ♠ ⚏ ⊙ ⚑ ⌕ ⚏ ⚑ ⅞ P ⚐ ⊞
Prices: ♦21.50 pitch 26.50

LUC-SUR-MER CALVADOS

Capricieuse 2 r Brummel ☎ 231973443
A large family site 100mtrs from the beach.
➲ *On W outskirts, access via A13 exit Douvres.*
Apr-Sep 4.5HEC 〰 ⚡🏠⊙🍴🏕🚐🖂⊞ lau ➧ 🛒🍷✕∅⛱
🏊PS
Prices: ⚑22 pitch 20-28.50

See advertisement under Colour Section

MARTIGNY SEINE-MARITIME

CM ☎ 235856082
On the shore of a lake in pleasant surroundings 8km from
Dieppe.
➲ *Access via D154.*
27 Mar-10 Oct 6.8HEC 〰 ⚡🏠🛒⊙🍴🏕 🏊 R 🖂⊞ lau ➧ 🏊P
Prices: pitch 67-81

MARTRAGNY CALVADOS

🏰**Château de Martragny** ☎ 231802140
Family site in grounds of a château which also offers
accommodation.
➲ *From N13 take exit for Martragny. Drive through St-Léger
and campsite is on the right as you leave the village.*
1 May-15 Sep 15HEC 〰 ⚡🏠🛒🍷✕⊙🍴∅ 🏊 P 🖂⊞ lau
➧ 🏊RS
Prices: ⚑28 pitch 57

MAUPERTUS-SUR-MER MANCHE

Anse du Brick ☎ 233543357
Terraced site in a landscaped park between the sea and the
forest.
➲ *200m from beach.*
1 Apr-15 Sep 17HEC 〰 ⚡🏠🛒🍷✕⊙🍴∅⛱🏕🚐🏊 P
🖂⊞ lau ➧ 🏊S
Prices: ⚑23-26 pitch 35-47

MONT-ST-MICHEL, LE MANCHE

Gué de Beauvoir 5 rte du Mont-St-Michel, Beauvoir
☎ 233600923
A level site in an orchard close to the River Couesnon.
➲ *4km S of Abbey on D776 Pontorson road.*
Etr-Sep 0.6HEC 〰 ⚡🏠🛒🍷✕⊙🍴🖂⊞ lau ➧ 🛒✕
Prices: ⚑15 🚐8-8 🚐15 🛖10

MORGAT FINISTÈRE

Bouis ☎ 298261253
On a meadow surrounded by woodland with pitches divided
by hedges on the extremity of the Parc Naturel Régional
d'Armorique.
➲ *From Morgat follow D255 towards Cap de la Chèvre for
1.5km then right towards Bouis.*
Etr-Sep 3HEC 〰 ⚡🏠🛒⊙🍴∅🚐🖂⊞ lau ➧🍷✕⛱ 🏊S

MOYAUX CALVADOS

🏰**Colombier** ☎ 231636308
Well-kept site in grounds of manor house.
Camping Card Compulsory.
➲ *3km NE on D143.*
May-15 Sep 10HEC 〰 ⚡🏠🛒🍷✕⊙🍴∅🏊 P 🖂⊞ lau

NÉVEZ FINISTÈRE

Deux Fontaine Raguènes ☎ 298068191
Mainly level site, subdivided into several fields surrounded by
woodland with good recreational facilities including an
aquaslide.
➲ *700m from Ragunès Beach.*
15 May-15 Sep 7HEC 〰 ⚡🏠🛒🍷✕⊙🍴∅🏕🏊 P 🖂⊞
lau ➧ 🏊S

NOYAL-MUZILLAC MORBIHAN

Moulin de Cadillac Moulin de Cadillac ☎ 297670347
A well equipped family site in a pleasant wooded location
with good facilities.
➲ *Access via N165, N through Muzillac.*
May-Sep 3HEC 〰 ⚡🏠🛒⊙🍴⛱🏕🚐🛖🏊 P 🖂 lau
Prices: ⚑18 pitch 26

OUISTREHAM CALVADOS

Prairies de la Mer rte de Lion, Riva-Bella ☎ 231976161
A camping area attached to a larger static caravan site with
good recreational facilities, 400mtrs from the sea.
➲ *Access via D514.*
13 Mar-17 Oct 80HEC 〰 ⚡🏠🛒🍷✕⊙🍴∅🏕🚐🏊 P 🖂
⊞ lau ➧ 🛒✕🏊S
Prices: ⚑20-22 pitch 35

PÉNESTIN-SUR-MER MORBIHAN

Airotel-Inly ☎ 299903509
Situated in the centre of a nature reserve and close to the
coast, with good recreational facilities.
➲ *2km SE via D201.*
Apr-Sep 20HEC 〰 ⚡🏠🛒🍷✕⊙🍴🏊 LP 🖂 lau ➧ ∅⛱
🏊S ⊞
Prices: ⚑26 pitch 50

Cénic ☎ 299904565
In a forested area 2km from the sea. Spacious grassy pitches
ideal for families.
➲ *Access via D34 from La Roche-Bernard.*
Apr-Sep 7HEC 〰 ⚡🏠🛒🍷✕⊙🍴∅⛱🏕🚐🛖🏊 P 🖂⊞
lau ➧✕🏊S
Prices: ⚑18-22 pitch 27-35

Iles La Pointe du Bile ☎ 299903024
A family site with direct access to the beach and a separate
residential section.
➲ *3km S on D201.*
1 Apr-Sep 4HEC 〰 ⚡🏠🛒🍷✕⊙🍴∅🏕🏊 S 🖂⊞ lau
Prices: pitch 78-150 (incl 2 persons)

PENTREZ-PLAGE FINISTÈRE

Tamaris ☎ 298265395
Level site divided into pitches 20m from the beach.
➲ *Access via D887.*
May-11 Sep 3HEC 〰 ⚡🏠🛒⊙🍴∅⛱🏕🚐🖂🅿⊞ lau ➧
🍷✕🏊PS
Prices: ⚑19 pitch 20

PERROS-GUIREC CÔTES-D'ARMOR

Claire Fontaine Toul ar Lann ☎ 296230355
Spacious, level site in a rural setting.
➲ *1.2km SW of town centre, 800m from Trestraou beach.*
May-Sep 3HEC 〰 ⚡🏠🍷⊙🍴∅🏕🚐🖂⊞ lau ➧ 🛒✕🏊S
Prices: ⚑32 pitch 20-34

At **LOUANNEC**(3km SE)

CM Ernest Renan rte de Perros-Guirec ☎ 296231178
Well situated site next to the sea. Take away food, games
room.
➲ *1km W.*
1 Jun-30 Sep 4.5HEC 〰 ⚡🏠🛒🍷✕⊙🍴∅🚐🏊 LS 🖂
lau ➧⛱
Prices: ⚑13-14.30 pitch 25.30-29

At **PLOUMANACH**(2km NW)

🏰**Ranolien** ☎ 296914358
The site is divided into pitches by hedges; separate sections
for caravans. *Contd.*

145

➲ *500m from the village.*
2 Mar-14 Nov 16HEC ⚏ 🔧 🏠 🛒 🍽 ✕ ☉ 🚿 ⊘ ⛺ 🚐 ⚓ P 🔲 ⊞ lau ➡ ⚓S
Prices: pitch 75-130 (incl 2 persons)

▶ PIEUX, LES MANCHE

Grand Large ☎ 233524075
In an unspoilt location with direct access to the beach.
➲ *3km from the town centre on D117.*
3 Apr-19 Sep 4HEC ⚏ ⠿ 🔧 🏠 🛒 🍽 ✕ ☉ 🚿 ⊘ ⛺ 🚐 ⚓ PS 🔲 ⊞ lau
Prices: pitch 84-105 (incl 2 persons)

▶ PLÉRIN CÔTES-D'ARMOR

Mouettes Les Rosaires les Mouettes ☎ 296745148
Jul-Sep 1HEC ⚏ 🔧 🏠 ☉ 🚿 🚐 🔲 ⊞ lau ➡ ⊘ ⚓PS
Prices: ⫪16 pitch 10

▶ PLEUBIAN CÔTES-D'ARMOR

Port la Chaîne ☎ 296229238
A peaceful, terraced site on the 'Wild Peninsula', with direct access to the sea, with good facilities.
➲ *2km N via D20.*
Apr-Sep 5HEC ⚏ 🏠 🏠 🛒 🍽 ✕ ☉ 🚿 ⊘ ⛺ 🚐 ⚓ S 🔲 ⊞ lau
Prices: ⫪22 pitch 38

▶ PLEUMEUR-BODOU CÔTES-D'ARMOR

Port Landrellec ☎ 296238779
Beautiful site by the sea with numbered pitches surrounded by hedges.
➲ *3km from Trégastel turn towards Tréburden.*
Apr-Sep 2HEC ⚏ 🏊 🏠 🍽 ☉ 🚿 ⊘ 🚐 ⚓ S 🔲 ⊞ lau ➡ 🏠 🛒 ✕

▶ PLOBANNALEC FINISTÈRE

Manoir de Kerlut ☎ 298822389
A peaceful site located in the grounds of a manor house some 2km from the beach.
➲ *1.6km S via D102.*
May-15 Sep 14HEC ⚏ 🔧 🏠 🛒 🍽 ✕ ☉ 🚿 ⊘ ⛺ 🚐 ⚓ PS 🔲 ⊞ lau ➡ ✕
Prices: ⫪20-29 pitch 50-96

▶ PLOËMEL MORBIHAN

Kergo ☎ 297568066
In pleasant wooded surroundings, close to the neighbouring beaches.
➲ *2km SE via D186.*
15 May-15 Sep 2.5HEC ⚏ 🔧 🏠 🛒 ✕ ☉ 🚿 🚐 🔲 ⊞ lau
Prices: ⫪20 🛏11 🚐20 ▲20

▶ PLOEMEUR MORBIHAN

Ajoncs Beg Minio ☎ 297863011
A rural site situated in an orchard.
➲ *From town centre continue towards Fort-Bloqué.*
27 Mar-Sep 2HEC ⚏ 🔧 🏠 ☉ 🚐 🔲 ⊞ lau ➡ ⚓P
Prices: ⫪11.25 🛏11.25 🚐11.25 ▲11.25

▶ PLOËRMEL MORBIHAN

Lac Les Belles Rives, Taupont ☎ 297740122
A lakeside family site with plenty of facilities for water sports.
➲ *2km from village centre, beside the lake.*
Apr-Oct 3.5HEC ⚏ 🔧 🏠 🛒 🍽 ☉ 🚿 ⊘ ⛺ 🚐 ⚓ L 🔲 ⊞ lau ➡ ✕ ⛺
Prices: ⫪16.50 pitch 20

Vallée du Ninian Le Rocher ☎ 297935301
Peaceful family site at the heart of Brittany which specialises in homemade cider beside the River Ninian.

➲ *W of Taupont towards the river.*
May-Sep 2.7HEC ⚏ 🔧 🏠 🛒 🍽 ☉ 🚿 ⊘ ⛺ 🚐 ⚓ PR 🔲 ⊞ lau ➡ ✕
Prices: ⫪12.60-15 pitch 28.80-35

▶ PLOMEUR FINISTÈRE

Torche Pointe de la Torche ☎ 298586282
A family site with pitches surrounded by trees and bushes, 1.5km from the beach.
➲ *3.5km W*
Apr-Sep 4HEC ⚏ 🏊 🏠 🛒 🍽 ✕ ☉ 🚿 ⊘ ⛺ 🚐 ⚓ P 🔲 ⊞ lau ➡ ✕ ⚓S
Prices: pitch 65-94 (incl 2 persons)

▶ PLOMODIERN FINISTÈRE

Iroise Plage de Pors-ar-Vag ☎ 298815272
A family site with fine recreational facilities, providing magnificent views over the Bay of Douarnenez.
➲ *5km SW, 150m from the beach.*
Apr-Sep 2.5HEC ⚏ 🔧 🏠 🛒 🍽 ✕ ☉ 🚿 ⊘ ⛺ 🚐 ⚓ P 🔲 ⊞ lau ➡ ✕ ⚓S
Prices: ⫪21.60-27 pitch 41.60-52

▶ PLONÉVEZ-PORZAY FINISTÈRE

International de Kervel ☎ 298925154
One of the best sites in the region. Ideal for families. 800m from the sea.
➲ *SW of the village on the D107 Douarnenez road for 3km, then towards coast at 'X' roads.*
1 May-12 Sep 7HEC ⚏ 🔧 🏠 🛒 🍽 ✕ ☉ 🚿 ⊘ ⛺ 🚐 ▲ ⚓ P 🔲 ⊞ lau ➡ ⚓S
Prices: ⫪26 pitch 76

Tréguer-Plage Ste-Anne-la-Palud ☎ 298925352
A level site with direct access to the beach.
➲ *1.3km N*
Apr-Sep 6HEC ⚏ ⠿ 🏊 🏠 🛒 🍽 ✕ ☉ 🚿 ⊘ ⛺ 🚐 ⚓ S 🔲 lau ➡ ⊞
Prices: ⫪17 pitch 16

▶ PLOUÉZEC CÔTES-D'ARMOR

Cap Horn Port Lazo ☎ 296206428
In an elevated position overlooking the Ile de Bréhat with direct access to the beach.
➲ *2.3km NE via D77 at Port-Lazo.*
Apr-Sep 5HEC ⚏ 🏊 🏠 🛒 🍽 ✕ ☉ 🚿 ⊘ ⛺ ⚓ P 🔲 lau ➡ ✕ ⛺ ⚓S
Prices: ⫪26 pitch 41

PLOUEZOCH FINISTÈRE

Baie de Térénez ☎ 298672680
A well equipped site in a pleasant rural setting.
➲ *3.5km NW via D76.*
2 Apr-Sep 3HEC ⌂⌂⌂⌂ ⚐🏕🏪🍴✕☉🟥🅿⛺🚿🔌🚻 ⚡ P 🏛⊞ lau
➡ ⚡S
Prices: ⚑17-25 pitch 23-35

PLOUGASNOU FINISTÈRE

CM Mélin-ar-Mésqueau ☎ 298673745
Large municipal site with good recreational facilities.
➲ *3.5km S via D46*
May-15 Sep 15HEC ⌂⌂⌂⌂ ⚐🏕🏪🍴✕☉🟥🚿 ⚡ LR 🏛🅿⊞ lau
Prices: ⚑9 🚗4 🚌4 ⛺4

Trégor Kerjean ☎ 298673764
A sheltered site with numbered, grassy pitches. Surrounded by hedges.
➲ *Off D46 towards Morlaix.*
Jul-Sep 1HEC ⌂⌂⌂⌂ ⚐🏕☉🟥🏕🚻🚌🏛 lau ➡ 🏪🍴✕⊞

PLOUHA CÔTES-D'ARMOR

At TRINITÉ, LA(2km NE)

Domaine de Keravel rte de Port Moguer ☎ 296224913
Forested site built around an elegant country mansion, 1km from the sea.
15 May-Sep 5HEC ⌂⌂⌂⌂ ⚐🏕🏪✕☉🟥🚌🚻 ⚡ P 🏛⊞ lau ➡ ⚡S
Prices: ⚑22.40-28 pitch 38.40-48

PLOUHARNEL MORBIHAN

Étang de Loperhet ☎ 297523468
➲ *1km NW via D781*
Apr-Oct 6HEC ⌂⌂⌂⌂ ⚐⚐⚐ ⚐🏕🏪🍴✕☉🟥🚌🚻 ⚡ P 🏛 lau ➡✕🚻 ⚡S⊞

Kersily Ste-Barbe ☎ 297523965
Etr-Oct 3HEC ⌂⌂⌂⌂ ⚐🏕🏪🍴✕☉🟥🚌🚻 ⚡ P 🏛⊞ lau
Prices: ⚑16-23 pitch 22-32

Lande Kerzivienne ☎ 297523148
On partially shaded terrain, 600mtrs from the beach.
Jun-Sep 1.2HEC ⌂⌂⌂⌂ ⚐🏕☉🟥🚌🚻🏛⊞ lau ➡🏪🍴✕🟥

PLOUHINEC MORBIHAN

Moténo rte du Magouer ☎ 297367663
On slightly sloping ground, subdivided into several fields in a wooded area 600mtrs from the beach.
➲ *S beside the Mer d'Etel.*
Apr-Sep 4HEC ⌂⌂⌂⌂ ⚐🏕🏪🍴✕☉🟥🚌🚻 ⚡ P 🏛⊞ lau ➡ ⚡RS

PLOZÉVET FINISTÈRE

Corniche rte de la Corniche ☎ 298913394
Peaceful rural site 1.5km from the sea.
15 May-15 Sep 2HEC ⌂⌂⌂⌂ ⚐🏕🏪🍴✕☉🟥🚌 ⚡ P 🏛⊞ lau ➡✕🚻 ⚡S
Prices: ⚑25 pitch 34

PONTAUBAULT MANCHE

Vallée de la Sélune 7 r du Ml-Leclerc ☎ 233603900
This site is in a quiet village near the River Sélune. Ideal base for exploring the Normandy/Brittany area.
➲ *Access via N175 Portorson-Caen.*
Etr-20 Oct 1.6HEC ⌂⌂⌂⌂ ⚐🏕🏪✕☉🟥🚌🚻 ⚡ R 🏛➡🍴 ✕🚻 ⚡S
Prices: ⚑15 🚗10 🚌15 ⛺15

PONT-AVEN FINISTÈRE

Domaine de Ker Lann Land Rosted ☎ 298060273
The site covers a large area, well wooded. Good leisure facilities.
➲ *Signposted from main road.*
27 Apr-28 Sep 17HEC ⌂⌂⌂⌂ ➡🏪🏕🍴✕☉🟥🚌🚻🚻 ⚡ P 🏛⊞ lau

PONT-L'ABBÉ FINISTÈRE

Écureuil ☎ 298870339
Shady site set in a wooded park with good recreational facilities.
➲ *3.5km NE onD44.*
15 Jun-15 Sep 3HEC ⌂⌂⌂⌂ ⚐🏕🏪🍴✕☉🟥🚌🚻🚻 🏛⊞ lau
Prices: ⚑20 pitch 26

PORDIC CÔTES-D'ARMOR

Madières rte de Vau Madec ☎ 296790248
A quiet coastal site in a well shaded position.
➲ *1500m from village on St-Brieuc road (D786).*
May-Sep 2HEC ⌂⌂⌂⌂ ⚐🏕🏪🍴✕☉🟥🚌🚻🚻 ⚡ S 🏛 lau

PORT-MANECH FINISTÈRE

St-Nicolas ☎ 298068975
Divided into hedge-lined pitches in beautiful surroundings close to the beach.
May-Sep 3.5HEC ⌂⌂⌂⌂ ⚐🏕☉🟥🚌🚻 ⚡ RS 🏛⊞ lau ➡🏪🍴 ✕🟥
Prices: ⚑22.50 pitch 25

POULDU, LE FINISTÈRE

Embruns r du Philosophe Alain ☎ 298399107
A pleasant site with good facilities and easy access to the beach. Separate car park for arrivals after 22.00hrs.
Apr-20 Sep 4HEC ⌂⌂⌂⌂ ⚐🏕🏪🍴✕☉🟥🚌🚻🚻 ⚡ P 🅿⊞ lau ➡✕ ⚡RS

POURVILLE-SUR-MER SEINE-MARITIME

Marqueval rte de la Mer ☎ 235826646
15 Mar-Sep 8HEC ⌂⌂⌂⌂ ⚐🏕☉🟥🚌🚻 ⚡ PRS 🏛⊞ lau

QUETTEHOU MANCHE

Rivage rte de Morsalines ☎ 233541376
Quiet, sheltered site, 400m from the sea.
➲ *Access via D14.*
Apr-Oct 1.8HEC ⌂⌂⌂⌂ ⚡🏕☉🟥🚻🚌🚻🏛 lau ➡🏪🍴✕ ⚡S⊞
Prices: ⚑13 pitch 20

QUIBERON MORBIHAN

Bois d'Amour rte St-Clement ☎ 297501352
➲ *1.5 km SE at La Pointe de la Presqu'ile, 100m from beach.*
03 Apr-26 Sept 4.5HEC ⌂⌂⌂⌂ ⚐⚐⚐ ⚡🏕🏪☉🟥🚌 ⚡ P 🏛 lau ➡🏪🍴✕🟥🚻 ⚡S
Prices: ⚑23-37 pitch 37-69

Conguel bd Teignouse ☎ 297501911
Directly on the beach, with fine recreational facilities.
➲ *Near the aerodrome towards Pointe de Conguel.*
Apr-Oct 5HEC ⌂⌂⌂⌂ ⚐🏕🏪🍴✕☉🟥🚌 ⚡ P 🏛⊞ lau ➡ ⚡S

QUIMPER FINISTÈRE

⛺Orangerie de Lanniron Château de Lanniron ☎ 298906202
In the grounds of the former residence of the Bishops of Quimper, beside the River Odet and surrounded by tropical vegetation.
➲ *2.5km from town centre via D34.*
15 May-15 Sep 17HEC ⌂⌂⌂⌂ ⚐🏕🏪🍴✕☉🟥🚌🚻🚌 ⚡ PR 🏛⊞ lau
Prices: ⚑26.10-29 pitch 44.10-49

147

RAGUENÈS-PLAGE FINISTÈRE

Airotel International Raguenès-Plage 19 r des Iles, Ragunes
☎ 298068069
Asphalt drives; 400m from beaches.
➲ *Leave Pont-Aven and take the road to Nevez. At Nevez follow directions to Raguenès.*
Apr-Sep 6HEC ▦ ♣ ⋔ ﹗ ⊙ ⬛ ⌀ 🚿 🏠 🚐 ⌇ P 🏧 P 🎫
lau ➧ ⌇S
Prices: pitch 42-60 (incl 2 persons)

RENNES ILLE-ET-VILAINE

CM Gayeulles r du Prof-M-Audin ☎ 299369122
➲ *NE via N12*
Apr-Sep 2HEC ▦ ⋇ ⋔ ⊙ ⬛ 🏧 🎫 lau ➧ ﹗ ✕ ⌇P

RIEC-SUR-BÉLON FINISTÈRE

Château de Bélon Port de Bélon ☎ 298064143
Situated in wooded parkland by the sea with facilities for sailing and fishing.
➲ *3.5km S*
Apr-15 Nov 8HEC ▦ ♣ ⋔ ﹗ ⊙ ⬛ ⌀ 🚿 ⌇ S 🏧 🎫 lau ➧ ﹗
✕
Prices: pitch 20

ROCHE-BERNARD, LA MORBIHAN

CM Patïs 3 chemin du Patis ☎ 299906013
On banks of River Vilaine.
➲ *100m from village centre.*
Etr-Sep 1HEC ▦ 🔌 ⋔ ⊙ ⬛ 🚐 🏧 🎫 lau ➧ ﹗ ✕ ⌀ ⌇P
Prices: ♦16 pitch 20

ROCHEFORT-EN-TERRE MORBIHAN

Moulin Neuf ☎ 297433752
A well equipped site in wooded surroundings. The shop contains only basic items but there is a supermarket nearby.
Camping Card compulsory.
➲ *Signposted from D744 in village.*
Apr-Sep 2.5HEC ▦ 🔌 ⋔ ﹗ ✕ ⊙ ⬛ ⌇ P 🏧 🎫 lau ➧ ⌀
⌇LR 🎫
Prices: ♦18-21 pitch 42-49

ROSTRENEN CÔTES-D'ARMOR

Fleur de Bretagne Kerandouaron ☎ 296291645
A spacious site in a picturesque, sheltered valley with good, modern facilities.
➲ *1.5km from Rostrenen on D764 towards Pontivy.*
1 Apr-16 Oct 6HEC ▦ ⋔ ﹗ ✕ ⊙ ⬛ ⌇ P 🏧 lau ➧ ﹗ 🚿 🎫
Prices: ♦14 ⬥6 ⬛25

ST-ALBAN CÔTES-D'ARMOR

St-Vrêguet St-Vréguet ☎ 296329021
A peaceful site in a pleasant park with good sanitary and recreational facilities.
Jun-Sep 1HEC ▦ 🔌 ⋔ ﹗ ⊙ ⬛ ⌀ 🚐 ▲ 🏧 🎫 lau ➧ ⌇R
Prices: ♦17 pitch 10

ST-AUBIN-SUR-MER CALVADOS

Côte de Nacre 17 r du Major Moulton ☎ 231971445
A pleasant site with good recreational facilities. Reservations recommended in high season. Separate car park for arrivals after 22.00hrs.
Apr-Oct 6HEC ▦ ⋇ ⋔ ﹗ ✕ ⊙ ⬛ ⌀ 🚿 ⌇ P 🏧 🎫 lau ➧
⌇S

CM Mesnil ☎ 235830283
A family site attached to a typical Norman farm.
➲ *2 km W on D68.*
Apr-Oct 2.3HEC ▦ 🔌 ⋔ ✕ ⊙ ⬛ 🎫 lau ➧ ﹗ ✕ ⌀ 🚿 ⌇S
Prices: ♦22.70 pitch 15.80

ST-BRIEUC CÔTES-D'ARMOR

Vallées Parc de Brézillet ☎ 296940505
Situated on the edge of the town in a plateau criss-crossed by wooded valleys. Restaurant open July and August only.
All year 4.8HEC ▦ ♣ ⋔ ﹗ ✕ ⊙ ⬛ 🚐 🚐 ⌇ PR 🏧 🎫 lau
➧ ⌀ 🚿
Prices: ♦15-19 pitch 39-49

ST-CAST-LE-GUILDO CÔTES-D'ARMOR

Château de Galinée ☎ 296411056
A family site in a 5 acre wood incorporating the buildings of an old farm, 3km from the local beaches.
➲ *1km from CD786. Well signposted.*
Etr-12 Sep 14HEC ▦ 🔌 ⋔ ﹗ ✕ ⊙ ⬛ ⌀ 🚐 ⌇ P 🏧 lau
Prices: ♦22-28 pitch 45-60

Châtelet r des Nouettes ☎ 296419633
In superb landscaped surroundings overlooking the sea with good sporting facilities.
➲ *1km W, 250m from the beach*
May-12 Sep 8HEC ▦ 🔌 ⋔ ﹗ ✕ ⊙ ⬛ 🚿 ⌇ LPS 🏧 🎫 lau
➧ ⌀
Prices: ♦23-29 pitch 70-90

ST-COULOMB ILLE-ET-VILAINE

Chevrets La Guimorais ☎ 299890190
On Lupin Bay near Chevrets beach.
➲ *3km NW.*
Apr-Sep 10HEC ▦ ⋰⋰ ⋇ ⋔ ﹗ ✕ ⊙ ⬛ ⌀ 🚐 🚐 ⌇ S 🏧
🎫 lau

ST-EFFLAM CÔTES-D'ARMOR

CM r de Ian-Carré ☎ 296356215
On a level meadow with well defined pitches 100mtrs from a magnificent beach.
Apr-Sep 4HEC ▦ 🔌 ⋔ ﹗ ✕ ⊙ ⬛ 🏠 🏧 lau ➧ ﹗ ✕ ⌀ ⌇S
Prices: ♦16 ⬥9 ⬛21 ▲20

ST-ÉVARZEC FINISTÈRE

Keromen ☎ 298562063
Children's playground and fishing facilities on site.
Jul-Aug 2HEC ▦ 🔌 ⋔ ⊙ ⬛ 🏧 🎫 lau ➧ ﹗ ﹗ ✕ ⌀ 🚿

ST-GERMAIN-SUR-AY MANCHE

Aux Grands Espaces ☎ 233071014
On slightly sloping ground among dunes. Children's play area. Lunchtime siesta 12.30-14.30 hrs. 500m from sea.
➲ *Leave D650 W of town and follow signs 'Plage' on D306.*
May-15 Sep 15HEC ▦ 🔌 ⋔ ﹗ ✕ ⊙ ⬛ ⌀ ▲ ⌇ P 🏧 🎫
lau ➧ ⌇S
Prices: ♦24 🚐29 ▲29

ST-GILDAS-DE-RHUYS MORBIHAN

Menhir rte de Port Crouesty ☎ 297452288
A family site with good facilities situated 1km from the beach.
➲ *3.5km N.*
15/05-12/09 3HEC ▦ ♣ ⋔ ﹗ ✕ ⊙ ⬛ ⌀ 🚐 ⌇ PS 🏧 🎫 lau
➧ ⌇S
Prices: ♦28 pitch 80

ST-JOUAN-DES-GUÉRÊTS ILLE-ET-VILAINE

P'tit Bois ☎ 299211430
A pleasant family site in quiet wooded surroundings.
➲ *Access via N137.*
May-12 Sep 6HEC ▦ 🔌 ⋔ ﹗ ✕ ⊙ ⬛ ⌀ 🚐 🚐 ▲ ⌇ P 🏧
🎫 lau ➧ 🚿 ⌇RS

ST-LÉGER-DU-BOURG-DENIS SEINE-MARITIME

Aubette 23 r Vert Buisson ☎ 235084769
In a wooded valley, 3km E of Rouen.
All year 0.8HEC 〰 ⌁ ⌂ ⌿ ⌘ ⊙ ⌶ ⌸ ⌹ ⌺ P ⊞ lau ✦ ⌀
⌇R
Prices: ♦15 pitch 16

ST-LUNAIRE ILLE-ET-VILAINE

Longchamp bd de St-Cast ☎ 299463398
In a beautiful wooded setting in the heart of the Emerald
coast with a good range of facilities.
➲ Turn off D786 towards St-Briac at end of village, site is on
left. 100m from the sea.
15 May-10 Sep 5HEC 〰 ⌁ ⌂ ⌿ ⌘ ⌶ ✕ ⊙ ⌶ ⌸ ⌺ ⊞ lau
✦ ⌇S
Prices: ♦27 ⇐15 ⇔25 ▲25

Touesse ☎ 299466113
A well equipped family site, 300mtrs from the beach.
➲ 2km E via D786.
Apr-Sep 2.5HEC 〰 ⌁ ⌂ ⌿ ⌘ ⌶ ✕ ⊙ ⌶ ⌀ ⌸ ⌺ ⌹ ⊞ lau
✦ ⌇S
Prices: ♦20-26 ⇐15-19 ⇔27-34 ▲27-34

ST-MALO ILLE-ET-VILAINE

CM le Nicet av de la Varde ☎ 299402632
100m from the beach; direct access via staircase. Water sports
and other activities available.
7 Jun-7 Sep 2.9HEC 〰 ⌁ ⌂ ⌿ ⊙ ⌶ ⌇ S ⌺ ⊞ lau ✦ ⌘ ⌿ ✕ ⌀
⌶ ⌇S

Ville Huchet rte de la Passagère ☎ 299811183
➲ 5km S via N137.
Etr-Sep 6HEC 〰 ⌁ ⌂ ⌿ ⌘ ⌿ ✕ ⊙ ⌶ ⌀ ▲ ⌺ ⊞ lau ✦ ⌀ ⌇R
Prices: ♦18.50 ⇐11 ⇔30 ▲19

ST-MARCAN ILLE-ET-VILAINE

Balcon de la Baie ☎ 299802295
In a beautiful location overlooking the bay of Mont-St-Michel.
➲ 10km NW of Pontorson on D797.
May-Oct 2.7HEC 〰 ⌁ ⌂ ⌘ ⌿ ✕ ⊙ ⌶ ⌀ ⌸ ⌺ lau ✦ ✕
Prices: pitch 65 (incl 2 persons)

ST-MARTIN-EN-CAMPAGNE SEINE-MARITIME

Goelands r des Grèbes ☎ 235838290
Site with good recreational facilities in an area of woodland,
100mtrs from a small lake. Shop and bar open in high season
only.
➲ NE of Dieppe, 2km from D925.
15 Mar-Oct 4HEC 〰 ⌇ ⌂ ⌿ ⊙ ⌶ ⌀ ⌸ ⌺ ⊞ lau ✦ ✕ ⌇PS
Prices: pitch 102-108

ST-MICHEL-EN-GRÈVE CÔTES-D'ARMOR

Capucines Kervourdon ☎ 296357228
In a peaceful setting near the beach with a large variety of
facilities.
➲ On D786 Lannion-Morlaix road.
8 May-10 Sep 4HEC 〰 ⌁ ⌂ ⌿ ⌘ ⌿ ✕ ⊙ ⌶ ⌀ ⌸ ⌺ ⌇ P ⌺ ⊞
⌇⌀ lau ✦ ⌿ ✕ ⌇S
Prices: ♦23.40-26 pitch 49.50-55

ST-PAIR-SUR-MER MANCHE

Château de Lez-Eaux St-Aubin-des-Preaux ☎ 233516609
Situated in grounds of an old Château. Bank, TV and reading
room. Fishing available.
➲ 7km SE via D973 rte d'Avranches.
May-15 Sep 13HEC 〰 ⌁ ⌂ ⌘ ⌿ ✕ ⊙ ⌶ ⌀ ⌸ ⌺ ⌇ P ⌺ ⊞
lau
Prices: pitch 105-125 (incl 2 persons)

Ecutot ☎ 233502629
Situated in an orchard 1km from the sea.
➲ On the main road between Granville and Avranches.
Apr-Sep 4HEC 〰 ✦ ⌿ ⌘ ⌿ ✕ ⊙ ⌶ ⌀ ⌸ ⌇ P ⌺ ⊞ lau ✦ ⌀ ⌶
⌇S

Mariénée ☎ 233500571
2km from sea; situated in grounds of old farm.
➲ 2km S of town on D21.
Etr-Sep 1.2HEC 〰 ⌁ ⌂ ⌿ ⊙ ⌶ ⌺ ⊞ lau ✦ ⌘ ⌿ ✕ ⌀ ⌶ ⌇PS

ST-PHILIBERT-SUR-MER MORBIHAN

Vieux Logis ☎ 297550117
Beautiful, well-kept site divided by hedges.
➲ 2km W via D781.
4 Apr-29 Sep 2.1HEC 〰 ⌁ ⌂ ⌿ ✕ ⊙ ⌶ ⌀ ⌸ ⌺ ⊞ lau ✦ ⌿ ✕
Prices: pitch 86 (incl 2 persons)

ST-PIERRE-DU-VAUVRAY EURE

St-Pierre 1 r du Château ☎ 232610155
In wooded surroundings with pitches divided by hedges,
50mtrs from the River Seine.
➲ Access via A13/N15.
All year 3HEC 〰 ⌁ ⌂ ⊙ ⌶ ⌺ lau ✦ ⌘ ⌿ ✕ ⌀ ⌶ ⌇R

ST-PIERRE-QUIBERON MORBIHAN

Park-er-Lann ☎ 297502493
➲ 1.5km S on D768.
Etr-Sep 1.6HEC 〰 ✦ ⌿ ⌘ ⌿ ✕ ⊙ ⌶ ⌀ ⌸ ⌺ ⌹ ⊞ lau ✦ ⌘ ⌀
⌶ ⌇S
Prices: ♦25 pitch 35

ST-QUAY-PORTRIEUX CÔTES-D'ARMOR

Bellevue 68 bd du Littoral ☎ 296704184
A terraced site adjacent to the sea with numbered pitches.
➲ 800m from town centre off D786.
May-20 Sep 5HEC 〰 ⌁ ⌂ ⌿ ⊙ ⌶ ⌀ ⌇ PS ⌺ ⊞ lau ✦ ⌘ ⌿
✕ ⌀ ⌶
Prices: ♦21-23 pitch 30-35

ST-VAAST-LA-HOUGUE MANCHE

Gallouette r de la Gallouette ☎ 233542057
A well equipped site, 300mtrs from the town centre and with
direct access to the beach.
Apr-15 Oct 2.3HEC 〰 ⌁ ⌂ ⌿ ✕ ⊙ ⌶ ⌀ ⌸ ⌇ S ⌺ lau

STE-MARIE-DU-MONT MANCHE

Utah Beach La Madeleine ☎ 233715369
On a level meadow 100mtrs from the beach.
➲ 6km NE via D913 and D421. *Contd.*

Apr-Sep 3HEC ⊞ ∷ ⛺ ⋔ ℝ ⅏ ⅋ ✕ ⊙ � ⌀ ⌂ ⊞ ⊰ S ☒ lau
Prices: ⋔22 pitch 27

STE-MARINE FINISTÈRE

Hellès ☎ 298563146
⊃ *400m from the beach*
15 Jun-15 Sep 3HEC ⊞ ⊕ ℝ ⊙ George ⌀ ⌒ ☒ ⊞ lau ✦ ⊰S

STE-MÈRE-ÉGLISE MANCHE

Cormoran Ravenoville-Plage ☎ 233413394
A quiet site with well defined pitches, 20m from the sea.
⊃ *Drive towards Ravenoville Plage, then take Utah Beach road for 500m.*
Apr-Sep 6.5HEC ⊞ ⊕ ℝ ⅏ ⅋ ✕ ⊙ George ⌀ ⌂ George ⊰ P ☒ ⊞ lau ✦ ⊰S
Prices: ⋔20.80-26 pitch 27.20-34

SARZEAU MORBIHAN

Treste rte de la Plage du Roaliguen ☎ 297417960
A family site with good facilities 800mtrs from the Roaliguen beach.
⊃ *2.5km S*
end Apr-mid Sep 2.5HEC ⊞ ⛺ ℝ ⅏ ⊙ George ⌀ George ⛺ ☒ lau ✦ ✕ ⊰S
Prices: ⋔26 pitch 50

At PENVINS(7km SE D198)

Madone ☎ 297673330
Situated 400m from the sea. Extensive sites on edge of village near old country estate. Divided into several sections.
Jun-Sep 6HEC ⊞ ⊕ ℝ ⅏ ⅋ ✕ ⊙ George George ☒ ⊞ lau ✦ ✕ ⌀ ⌂ ⊰S

At POINTE-ST-JACQUES(5.5km S)

CM St-Jacques ☎ 297417929
On beach protected by dunes. Well kept site with asphalt drives in a pleasant wooded location.
Apr-Sep 7.6HEC ⊞ ⊕ ℝ ⅋ ✕ ⊙ George George ⛺ ⊰ S ☒ ⊞ lau ✦ ⅏ ✕ ⌀
Prices: ⋔14.40-18 pitch 24-30

SASSETOT-LE-MAUCONDUIT SEINE-MARITIME

Trois Plages ☎ 235274011
Well equipped site 3km from the coast.
⊃ *1.3km S near D925.*
25 Apr-15 Sep 4HEC ⊞ ⊕ ℝ ⅏ ⊙ ⌀ ⌂ ☒ ⊞ lau ✦ ✕
Prices: ⋔20 pitch 25

TELGRUC-SUR-MER FINISTÈRE

Panoramic rte de la Plage ☎ 298277841
Quiet terraced site with views across a wide sandy beach. Secluded pitches.
⊃ *W on D887 and then S on D208.*
15 May-15 Sep 4HEC ⊞ ⊕ ℝ ⅏ ⅋ ✕ ⊙ George ⌀ ⌂ ⊰ P ☒ ⊞ lau ✦ ⊰S
Prices: ⋔25 pitch 50

THEIX MORBIHAN

Rhuys Le Poteau Rouge, Atlantheix ☎ 297541477
Directly on the sea, with good modern facilities.
⊃ *3.5km NW via N165*
15 Apr-15 Oct 4HEC ⊞ ∷ ⊕ ℝ ⊙ George ⛺ George ⊰ P ☒ P ⊞ lau ✦ ⅏ ✕ ⌂ ⊰R
Prices: ⋔18-22 pitch 25-42

THURY-HARCOURT CALVADOS

Vallée du Traspy ☎ 231796180
Level meadow site near a small reservoir, 250mtrs from Centre Aquatique de la Suisse Normande.
15 Apr-15 Sep 1.5HEC ⊞ ⊕ ℝ ⊙ George ⊰ LPR ☒ ⊞ lau ✦ ⅏ ⅋ ✕ ⌀ ⌂

TINTÉNIAC ILLE-ET-VILAINE

Peupliers La Besnelais ☎ 299454975
A peaceful site in a wooded location with good facilities.
⊃ *2km SE via N137.*
Mar-Oct 4.3HEC ⊞ ✦ ℝ ⅏ ⅋ ✕ ⊙ George ⌀ ⌂ ⊰ P ☒ ⊞ lau ✦ ✕

TOLLEVAST MANCHE

Pins ☎ 233430078
A peaceful site situated in a pine grove within an extensive park.
⊃ *From Cherbourg car ferry terminal follow N13 to the Auchout Hypermarket and then continue for 200m for site on left-hand side of the road.*
All year 6HEC ⊞ ⊕ ℝ ⅏ ⊙ George George ☒ ⊞ ⊘ lau ✦ ⅏ ✕ ⌀ ⌂ ⊰R
Prices: ⋔16 pitch 18

TOURLAVILLE MANCHE

Espace Loisirs de Collignon ☎ 233201688
A pleasant site with good facilities, 1km from town centre.
May-Sep 2HEC ⊞ ✦ ℝ ⅏ ⊙ George ⌀ ⌂ George ☒ lau ✦ ⅏ ✕ ⌂ ⊰PS ⊞

TOURNIÈRES CALVADOS

Picard Holidays ☎ 231228244
A quiet site with pleasant, sheltered pitches conveniently situated between Cherbourg and Caen.
⊃ *Access via N13 and D15/D5.*
All year 1.9HEC ⊞ ⛺ ℝ ⊙ George George ⊰ LPR ☒ P ⊞ ⊘ lau ✦ ⅏
Prices: ⋔25 pitch 25

TRÉBEURDEN CÔTES-D'ARMOR

Armor-Loisirs rte de Pors Mabo ☎ 296235231
Modern site with individual pitches surrounded by hedges. Hardstandings for caravans.
⊃ *500m S of the Kernévez road.*
25 May-Sep 2.2HEC ⊞ ⊕ ℝ ⅏ ⅋ ✕ ⊙ George ⌀ ⌂ George ⊞ ⊞ ⊘ lau ✦ ⅏ ⊰S

TREGUNC FINISTÈRE

Pendruc ☎ 298976628
On level grassland subdivided by hedging. Separate section for young campers.
⊃ *From N165 Concarneau exit follow signs for Tregunc. Site is signposted from the village on Le Pendruc/Lambell road on right hand side.*
May-Sep 3.6HEC ⊞ ⊕ ℝ ⅏ ⊙ George ⌀ George ⊰ P ☒ ⊞ lau ✦ ⅏ ✕ ⊰S

Pommeraie St-Philibert ☎ 298500273
A well equipped site with good facilities for children, 1.2km from the beach.
⊃ *S via D1.*
3 Apr-11 Sep 6HEC ⊞ ⊕ ℝ ⅏ ⅋ ✕ ⊙ George ⌂ ☒ ⊞ ⊞ lau ✦ ⌀ ⊰S
Prices: ⋔19.50-28 pitch 28.50-40

TRÉLÉVERN CÔTES-D'ARMOR

Port l'Epine Pors-Garo ☎ 296237194
Well shaded site directly on the sea.
Apr-15 Oct 4HEC ⸺ 🟡🏕🛁🍽✕⊙🚮🅰🏠 🎿 PS 🏧⊞ lau
➡️⛺

TRÉPORT, LE SEINE-MARITIME

CM les Boucaniers r Mendes-France ☎ 235863547
Well-kept site on flat meadow on E edge of village. Sports and games nearby.
Apr-Sep 5.5HEC ⸺ ⚓🏕⊙🚮🏠🏧⊞ lau ➡️🛁🍽✕🅰⛺
🎿PRS

Parc International du Golf rte de Dieppe ☎ 235863380
In a park on the coast.
➲ *1km W on D940.*
Apr-20 Sep 5HEC ⸺ 🟡🏕🛁🍽✕⊙🚮🅰🏧⊞ lau ➡️✕ 🎿PS
Prices: pitch 64-85 (incl 2 persons)

At **MESNIL-VAL**

Parc Val d'Albion 1 r de la Mer ☎ 235862142
Terraced site in wooded parkland next to the sea.
➲ *3km S from Le Tréport on D126.*
1 Jun-15 Sep 3HEC ⸺ 🟡🏕⊙🚮🅰🏧⊞ lau ➡️🛁🍽✕🅰 🎿S
Prices: pitch 64-85 (incl 2 persons)

TRÉVOU-TRÉGUIGNEC CÔTES-D'ARMOR

Mât 38 r de Trestel ☎ 296237152
A family site on level ground, 50m from beach.
➲ *Access via D38.*
15 Jun-15 Sep 1.6HEC ⸺ 🟡🏕⊙🚮🅰🏧⊞ lau ➡️🛁🍽✕⛺
🎿S
Prices: ⚓26 pitch 35

TRINITÉ-SUR-MER, LA MORBIHAN

Baie Plage de Kervilan ☎ 297557342
Several strips of land divided by tall trees on the edge of a fine sandy beach.
➲ *Signposted in the direction of Kerbihan.*
15 May-15 Sep 2.3HEC ⸺ 🟡🏕🛁🍽✕⊙🚮🅰🚰🎿 P 🏧⊞
lau ➡️⛺ 🎿S
Prices: ⚓16-27 pitch 62-115

Kervilor ☎ 297557675
In a pleasant wooded location 1.5km from the port. Plenty of recreational facilities.
➲ *1.6km N*
15 May-15 Sep 4.5HEC ⸺ 🟡🏕🛁🍽✕⊙🚮🅰🎿 P 🏧⊞
lau ➡️✕⛺ 🎿S
Prices: ⚓18-24 pitch 42-56

Plage Plage de Kervilen ☎ 297557328
A family site divided into pitches and lying behind sand dunes which give direct access to the beach.
➲ *1km S towards Carnac-Plage.*
8 May-15 Sep 3HEC ⸺ 🟡🏕⊙🚮🚰 🎿 PS 🏧⊞ lau ➡️🛁🍽
✕🅰 🎿S
Prices: ⚓24-24.50 pitch 51-113

VEULES-LES-ROSES SEINE-MARITIME

Mouettes av J-Moulin ☎ 235976198
15 Feb-Nov 3.6HEC ⸺ 🟡🏕🛁⊙🚮🅰🏧⊞ lau ➡️🛁🍽✕🅰
🎿S
Prices: pitch 50-60 (incl 2 persons) pp16-18

Paradis chemin de Manneville ☎ 235976142
A municipal site on the southern outskirts of the town.
mid May-mid Sep 0.9HEC ⸺ 🟡🏕⊙🚮🏧⊞ lau ➡️🛁🍽✕
🅰 🎿RS
Prices: ⚓12-13 pitch 7-8

VILLERS-SUR-MER CALVADOS

Ammonites rte de la Corniche ☎ 231870606
➲ *4km SW on rte de Cabourg and D163 towards Auberville.*
Apr-15 Oct 2.6HEC ⸺ ⋯⋯ ⚓🏕🛁🍽✕⊙🚮🅰⛺🏠🚰
🎿 PS 🏧⊞ lau

⚫ ⚫ ⚫ ⚫ **PARIS/NORTH** ⚫ ⚫ ⚫ ⚫

The chalk cliffs and sands of the northern coast give way to the two beautiful regions of Picardy and Nord-Pas-de-Calais. Here quiet country roads meander through green wooded valleys and rolling farmland. The area has a wealth of neolithic sites, cathedrals, castles, abbeys, mansions and museums. Lille is an important centre for northern France, with its commercial and industrial interests, and has a bustling cosmopolitan centre. Amiens is the ancient capital of Picardy, and its remarkable 12th-century Cathedral of Notre Dame is one of the finest in France.
The Île de France, known as the garden of Paris, is a delightful region of famous palaces, parklands, forests and attractive little towns. Visit Fontainbleau, the town of kings and emperors, with its famous palace, and the dazzling palace and grounds at Versailles.
Paris has a wealth of things to do and see - rivalling any other city in the world. Visitors can choose from the traditional rich treasures of the Louvre or the ultra modern exhibits and setting of the Pompidou Centre, immerse themselves in Parisian life along the banks of the Seine or view it from the giddy heights of Monsieur Eiffel's famous tower, the Champ de Mars and the Champs Élysées or the buzzing streets of the city's famous districts - Montmartre and Marais. And night life , too, is for all tastes, with everything from the sophisticated entertainment of the Lido, to a small quiet restaurant on the Left Bank.
....

ABBEVILLE SOMME

At **PORT-LE-GRAND**(5km NW)

Airotels Château des Tilleuls
On gently sloping meadow surrounding a farm.
➲ *1 km SE on D940A.*
Mar-Oct 4.3HEC ⸺ 🟡🏕🛁🍽✕⊙🚮🅰⛺🏠🚰🅰 🎿 P 🏧
⊞ lau
Prices: ⚓22 🚗10 🚐30 ⛺30

ACY-EN-MULTIEN OISE

Ancien Moulin ☎ 344872128
Situated beside a river and a small lake with good sporting facilities.
All year 5HEC ⸺ ⚓🏕⊙🚮🏧⊞ lau ➡️🛁🍽✕🅰⛺⊞
Prices: ⚓18.60 🚗18.60 🚐18.60 ⛺18.60

AMBLETEUSE PAS-DE-CALAIS

Beaucamp 10 r de Ferquent ☎ 321326210
A useful overnight stop between Boulogne and Calais.
All year ⸺ 🟡🏕🛁🍽✕⊙🚮🅰⛺🏠🚰🏧 lau

AMPLIER PAS-DE-CALAIS

Val d'Authie 93 r du Marais ☎ 321485707
In wooded surroundings beside a small lake.
➲ *Access via D24 and D938.*
20 Dec-25 Jan 2HEC ⸺ ⚓🏕🛁🍽✕⊙🚮🅰 🎿 R 🏧 lau
Prices: ⚓17 pitch 20

ARDRES PAS-DE-CALAIS

At **AUTINGUES**(2km S)

St-Louis 223 r Leulène ☎ 321354683
A well equipped site in pleasant wooded surroundings.
⮑ *Turn off N43 approx 1km SE of Ardres onto D224 and follow signs.*
Mar-Oct 1.7HEC ⸫⸫⸫ ⚫ ⌂ ⛟ ⊙ ⬛ ⬛ ⬛ ☎ ⊞ lau ➧ ⌀ ⛱ ⛱LP

ATTICHY OISE

CM ☎ 344421597
⮑ *On SE outskirts near the swimming pool and the river.*
All year 1.5HEC ⸫⸫⸫ ⚫ ⌂ ⊙ ⬛ ⛱ L ⬜ lau ➧ ⛴ ⛌ ✕ ⛱P

AUDRUICQ PAS-DE-CALAIS

CM Les Pyramides ☎ 321355917
A site with good sanitary and sports facilities beside the canal.
Apr-Sep ⸫⸫⸫ ⚫ ⌂ ⊙ ⬛ ⬜ ⬜ ⊞ lau ➧ ⛴ ⛌ ✕ ⌀

BEAURAINVILLE PAS-DE-CALAIS

CM de la Source ☎ 321814071
Camping Card Compulsory.
⮑ *1.5km SE via D130*
All year 2.5HEC ⸫⸫⸫ ⚫ ⌂ ⊙ ⬛ ⬛ ⬛ ⛱ R ⬜ lau ➧ ⛴ ⛌ ✕

BEAUVAIS OISE

Clos Normand 1 r de l'Abbaye, St-Paul ☎ 344822730
A small site on a lake with facilities for fishing.
⮑ *6km W via N31 towards Rouen.*
All year 2HEC ⸫⸫⸫ ⚫ ⌂ ⊙ ⬛ ⬛ ⬜ ⬜ lau ➧ ⛌ ✕
Prices: ⚑11 pitch 30-36

BERCK-SUR-MER PAS-DE-CALAIS

Orée du Bois chemin Blanc 251, Rang-du-Fliers
☎ 321842851
A modern site in wooded surroundings with good sports facilities.
⮑ *2km NE.*
Apr-Oct 18HEC ⸫⸫⸫ ⚫ ⌂ ⛌ ✕ ⊙ ⬛ ⛱ ⬜ A ⬜ lau ➧ ⛴ ⌀
Prices: ⚑20-25 pitch 90-115

BERNY-RIVIÈRE AISNE

Croix du Vieux Pont ☎ 323555002
In wooded surroundings beside the River Aisne with ample facilities.
⮑ *N of N31; cross River Aisne, site is 500m E of Vic-sur-Aisne on D91.*
All year 19HEC ⸫⸫⸫ ⚫ ⌂ ⛴ ⛌ ✕ ⊙ ⬛ ⌀ ⛱ ⛱ P ⬜ lau
Prices: pitch 110 (incl 2 persons)

BERTANGLES SOMME

Château r du Château ☎ 322933773
Site in old orchard of Château.
⮑ *Signed off Amiens-Doullens road.*
23 Apr-6 Sep 0.8HEC ⸫⸫⸫ ⚫ ⌂ ⊙ ⬛ ⬜ ⬜ lau ➧ ✕ ⛱
Prices: ⚑17 ⬤10 ⬛16 A16

BEUVRY PAS-DE-CALAIS

CM r Victor-Dutériez ☎ 321650800
11 Apr-Oct 1HEC ⸫⸫⸫ ⚫ ⌂ ⊙ ⬛ ⬜ lau ➧ ⛴ ⛌ ✕ ⌀ ⛱ ⛱P
Prices: ⚑12 pitch 16-35

BOIRY-NOTRE-DAME PAS-DE-CALAIS

Flandres Artois 1 r Verte ☎ 321481540
On a level meadow with a good variety of recreational facilities.
⮑ *On D34. Access via A1 exit 15 towards Cambrai or A26 exit 8 towards Arras.*
21 Mar-Oct 3.2HEC ⸫⸫⸫ ⚫ ⌂ ⛌ ✕ ⊙ ⬛ ⬛ lau ➧ ⛴
Prices: pitch 80 (incl 2 persons)

BOISSY-LE-CUTTE ESSONNE

Boulinière La Boulinière ☎ 164576523
Situated in a wood 800mtrs from the village.
⮑ *Access via N20 and D148.*
All year 4HEC ⸫⸫⸫ ⚫ ⌂ ⊙ ⬛ ⬜ lau ➧ ⛴ ⛌ ✕ ⌀ ⛱ ⊞
Prices: ⚑10.50 ⬤10.50 ⬛10.50 A10.50

BOUBERS-SUR-CANCHE PAS-DE-CALAIS

Flore 7 rte de Frévent ☎ 321036576
⮑ *E via D340 towards Frévent.*
Apr-Oct 1HEC ⸫⸫⸫ ⚫ ⌂ ⊙ ⬛ ⬜ ⊞ ➧ ⛴ ✕ ⌀ ⛱ ⛱R

BOULANCOURT SEINE-ET-MARNE

Ile de Boulancourt 6 allée des Marronniers ☎ 164241338
A peaceful site shaded by mature trees in a convenient situation in the Essonne valley.
⮑ *Access via D410.*
All year 5HEC ⸫⸫⸫ ⚫ ⌂ ⊙ ⬛ ⛱ ⛱ R ⬜ lau ➧ ⛴ ⛌ ✕ ⌀ ⛱L
Prices: ⚑15 pitch 20

BRAY-DUNES NORD

Perroquet-Plage ☎ 328583737
An above average site situated among sand dunes with direct access to the beach.
⮑ *3km NE towards La Panne*
Apr-2 Oct 28HEC ⸫⸫⸫ ⦂⦂⦂ ⚫ ⌂ ⛴ ⛌ ✕ ⊙ ⬛ ⌀ ⛱ ⬛ ⬛ ⛱ S ⬜ ⊞ lau ➧ ⛱P
Prices: ⚑30 ⬤10 ⬛15 A12

CALAIS PAS-DE-CALAIS

Peupliers 394 r du Beau Marais ☎ 321340356
All year 1HEC ⸫⸫⸫ ⚫ ⌂ ⛴ ⛌ ✕ ⊙ ⬛ ⬜ ⊞ lau ➧ ⛴ ✕ ⌀ ⛱PRS

CAMIERS PAS-DE-CALAIS

Sables d'Or ☎ 321849515
In a wooded location with good recreational facilities.
All year 10HEC ⸫⸫⸫ ⦂⦂⦂ ⚫ ⌂ ⛌ ⊙ ⬛ ⛱ P ⬜ ⊞ lau ➧ ⛱S
Prices: ⚑15 ⬤15 ⬛15 A15

CAYEUX-SUR-MER SOMME

Voyeul rte des Canadiens ☎ 322266084
In pleasant surroundings, 400mtrs from the sea, with pitches enclosed by hedges and flowerbeds.
⮑ *1.5km S on D140.*
Apr-15 Oct 1.7HEC ⸫⸫⸫ ⚫ ⌂ ⛴ ⛌ ✕ ⊙ ⬛ ⌀ ⛱ ⬜ ⊞ lau ➧ ✕ ⛱S
Prices: ⚑13 pitch 13

CHAMOUILLE AISNE

Parc de l'Ailette Parc Nautique de l'Ailette
☎ 323246686
On the shore of a lake within an extensive leisure park and nature reserve.
⮑ *2km SW via D19.*
Apr-Sep 6.5HEC ⸫⸫⸫ ⚫ ⌂ ⛴ ⛌ ✕ ⊙ ⬛ ⌀ ⬛ ⛱ L ⬜ ⊞ lau ➧ ✕
Prices: pitch 58-98 (incl 2 persons)

CONDETTE PAS-DE-CALAIS

Château 21 r Nouvelle ☎ 321875959
On pleasant parkland, bordered by a forest, 500mtrs from the town centre. Separate car park for arrivals after 23.00hrs.
⮑ *Access via D940 towards Hardelot.*
Apr-Oct 1.2HEC ⸫⸫⸫ ⚫ ⌂ ⊙ ⬛ ⬛ ⬜ ⊞ lau ➧ ⛴ ⛌ ✕ ⌀ ⛱
Prices: pitch 68-88 (incl 2 persons)

COUDEKERQUE NORD

Bois des Forts ☎ 328610441
➲ *0.7km NW on D72.*
All year 3HEC ⢁⢁⢁ ⚙⚙⚙ lau ➧ ⚙⚙⚙ ⚙P

DUNKERQUE (DUNKIRK) NORD

CM bd de l'Europe ☎ 328692668
Apr-Nov 10HEC ⢁⢁⢁ ⚙⚙⚙ P ⚙⚙⚙ lau ➧
⚙⚙⚙ ⚙PS ⚙
Prices: ⚙26-27 ⚙12-13 ⚙25-26 ▲13-14

ÉPERLECQUES PAS-DE-CALAIS

Château de Gandspette ☎ 321934393
A peaceful site, surrounded by woodland.
➲ *11.5km NW on N43 and D207.*
Apr-Sep 8HEC ⢁⢁⢁ ⚙⚙⚙ P ⚙⚙⚙ lau ➧ ⚙
Prices: ⚙27 ⚙10 ⚙50 ▲50

EPISY SEINE-ET-MARNE

Peupliers rte de Sorques ☎ 64458000
A pleasant riverside site with facilities for fishing and
canoeing.
➲ *0.9km NW via D148 beside the Loing.*
All year 4HEC ⢁⢁⢁ ⚙⚙⚙ R ⚙⚙⚙ lau ➧ ⚙⚙⚙

EQUIHEN-PLAGE PAS-DE-CALAIS

CM la Falaise r C-Cazin ☎ 321312261
150mtrs between Boulogne and Le Touquet.
Apr-Oct 8HEC ⢁⢁⢁ ⚙⚙⚙ S ⚙⚙⚙ lau ➧ ⚙⚙⚙⚙

ESCALLES PAS-DE-CALAIS

Cap Blanc Nez r de la Mer ☎ 321852738
500m from the beach.
Apr-10 Nov 1.5HEC ⢁⢁⢁ ⚙⚙⚙ lau ➧
⚙S

ÉTAMPES ESSONNE

Vauvert Ormoy La Rivière ☎ 164942139
In a pleasant woodland situation beside the river.
➲ *2km S via D49.*
15 Dec-15 Jan 11HEC ⢁⢁⢁ ⚙⚙⚙ R ⚙⚙⚙ ➧
⚙LP
Prices: ⚙21 ⚙26 ▲26

ÉTAPLES PAS-DE-CALAIS

Pinède ☎ 321943451
A well equipped site situated amongst sand dunes and
surrounded by pine trees close to the yacht basin and local
shopping facilities.
All year ⢁⢁⢁ ⚙⚙⚙ lau ➧ ⚙⚙ ⚙PR ⚙

FELLERIES NORD

CM La Boissellerie r de la Place ☎ 327590650
15 Apr-Sep 1HEC ⢁⢁⢁ ⚙⚙⚙ ➧⚙⚙⚙⚙
Prices: ⚙11 ⚙4.50 ⚙4.50 ▲4.50

FERTÉ-GAUCHER, LA SEINE-ET-MARNE

Joël Teinturier rte de St-Martin-des-Camps ☎ 164202040
➲ *E via D14*
All year 4HEC ⢁⢁⢁ ⚙⚙⚙ R ⚙⚙⚙ lau ➧ ⚙⚙⚙⚙
⚙P

FERTÉ-SOUS-JOUARRE, LA SEINE-ET-MARNE

Bondons 47/49 r des Bondons ☎ 160220098
Set in a beautiful wooded park. Reserved for caravans.
➲ *2km NE via D402 & D70.*
All year 28HEC ⢁⢁⢁ ⚙⚙⚙ lau ➧ ⚙⚙⚙ ⚙PR
Prices: ⚙40 pitch 60

FILLIÈVRES PAS-DE-CALAIS

Trois Tilleuls ☎ 321479415
Apr-1 Oct 2.5HEC ⢁⢁⢁ ⚙⚙⚙ lau ➧ ⚙⚙⚙⚙ ⚙R

FORT-MAHON-PLAGE SOMME

Royon rte de Quend ☎ 322234030
A family site with good facilities and well marked pitches,
2.5km from the beach.
Mar-Oct 4HEC ⢁⢁⢁ ⚙⚙⚙ P ⚙⚙ lau
➧ ⚙RS
Prices: pitch 110-120 (incl 3 persons)

FRIAUCOURT SOMME

CM Au Chant des Oiseaux Ruelle du Grand Patis
☎ 322264954
In pleasant surroundings with good sanitary and sporting
facilities 2km from the sea. Separate carpark for arrivals after
22.00hrs.
➲ *NE via D63.*
Apr-15 Oct 1.4HEC ⢁⢁⢁ ⚙⚙⚙ lau ➧ ⚙⚙
Prices: ⚙10.20 ⚙7.30 ⚙8.60 ▲7.80

GOUVIEUX OISE

César rte de Toutevoie 10 ☎ 344571273
On a hill overlooking the River Oise.
➲ *Access via A1 to Gouvieux town centre, then towatds Creil.*
All year 6HEC ⢁⢁⢁ ⚙⚙⚙ ⚙⚙⚙ ⚙P
Prices: ⚙10.50 ⚙10.50 ⚙10.50 ▲10.50

GRAND-FORT-PHILIPPE NORD

CM de la Plage r Ml-Foch ☎ 328653195
Apr-Oct 1.5HEC ⢁⢁⢁ ⚙⚙⚙ lau ➧ ⚙⚙⚙⚙⚙

GREZ-SUR-LOING SEINE-ET-MARNE

CM Près chemin des Près ☎ 64457275
➲ *NE towards Loing*
20 Mar-11 Nov 6HEC ⢁⢁⢁ ⚙⚙⚙ lau ➧ ⚙⚙⚙⚙ ⚙R ⚙

GUINES PAS-DE-CALAIS

Bien Assise D231 ☎ 321352077
A nice site in the country near to a large forest and a
charming little town.
➲ *Access via D231 towards Marquise.*
25 Apr-25 Sep 12HEC ⢁⢁⢁ ⚙⚙⚙ ⚙⚙⚙ P ⚙
⚙ lau
Prices: ⚙25 pitch 59

GUISE AISNE

Vallée de l'Oise r du Camping ☎ 323611486
In a pleasant location with plenty of recreational facilities.
➲ *1km SE on D960.*
Apr-20 Oct 3.5HEC ⢁⢁⢁ ⚙⚙⚙ ⚙⚙⚙➧⚙⚙⚙⚙
⚙R

HIRSON AISNE

Cascade ☎ 323580391
In a picturesque woodland setting with good, modern
facilities.
➲ *1.8km N via N43 towards La Capelle.*
20 Apr-20 Sep 1.6HEC ⢁⢁⢁ ⚙⚙⚙ P ⚙⚙ lau ➧ ⚙
Prices: ⚙9 pitch 6-7

HOUDAIN PAS-DE-CALAIS

Parc d'Olhain Parc d'Olhain ☎ 321279179
Situated in an extensive leisure park on the edge of a forest.
➲ *1.5 km S.*
Apr-Sep 1HEC ⢁⢁⢁ ⚙⚙⚙ ⚙⚙⚙⚙ ➧ ⚙P
Prices: ⚙16 pitch 67

BASE DE PLEIN AIR ET DE LOISIRS ★★★

F-77450 JABLINES

Tel. 33 1.60.26.09.37 - Fax 33.1.60.26.52.43

9 km from **DISNEYLAND PARIS**, far away from the noise, in peaceful green surroundings and with the longest beach of the **ILE DE FRANCE**. Restaurant, tennis, mini golf, children's playground, fishing, sailing, mountain bikes to let, horse riding and all the comfort of a camp site, opened in July 1997.

Open all year • Reservation recommended • 150 pitches.

> **ISQUES** PAS-DE-CALAIS

Cytises r de l'Église ☎ 321311110
In a pleasant rural setting beside the River Liane.
⊃ *4km S of Boulogne-sur-Mer towards Abbeville, 100m from N1.*
Apr-15 Oct 2.5HEC ⊞ Ꭿ ᑭ ✗ ⊙ 🔲 🕼 ╲ R 🆎 ⊞ lau ➡ 🔝 🕼 ᐟ
Prices: ⋔16.50-18 pitch 16.50-18

> **JABLINES** SEINE-ET-MARNE

Base de Loisirs ☎ 160260937
Only 9km from Disneyland Paris.
⊃ *Access via A1 or A3 towards Marne-la-Vallée, then N3.*
Closed 10 Jan-Feb 3.5HEC ⊞ ⇶ ᑭ 🔝 ✗ ⊙ 🔲 🕼 ╲ LP 🆎
Prices: ⋔30 pitch 60-65

> **LAON** AISNE

CM La Chênaie allée de la Chênaie ☎ 323202556
A peaceful family site with good facilities close to the city centre.
⊃ *S of the city centre towards N44.*
Apr-Oct 3.3HEC ⊞ Ꭿ ᑭ ⊙ 🔲 🆎 lau ➡ 🔝 🕼 ✗ 🕼 ╲ L

> **LICQUES** PAS-DE-CALAIS

Canchy r de Canchy ☎ 321826341
A quiet site on an open, level meadow well situated for access to the ferries and the Channel Tunnel.
15 Mar-Oct 1HEC ⊞ Ꭿ ᑭ 🔝 ✗ ⊙ 🔲 🕼 ╲ R 🆎 ⊞ lau ➡ ✗ ᐟ
Prices: ⋔17 pitch 17

> **LYNDE** NORD

Becquerelle 1396 r du Becquerelle ☎ 328432037
In a rural setting surrounded by woodland and hedges.

Mar-Nov 1.5HEC ⊞ Ꭿ ᑭ 🔝 ✗ ⊙ 🔲 🆎
Prices: ⋔10 ⬛5 ⬛10 ▲10-15

> **MAISONS-LAFFITTE** YVELINES

International 1 r Johnson ☎ 139122191
A well-kept site in a residential area on the banks of the Seine. Modern installations, heated in cold weather.
⊃ *For access, 8 km N of St-Germain-en-Laye; alternatively follow N308 from Porte Champerret or from Colombos-Ouest exit of Autoroute A86.*
All year 7HEC ⊞ Ꭿ ᑭ 🔝 ✗ ⊙ 🔲 🕼 🕼 ╲ R 🆎 lau ➡ ᐟP ⊞
Prices: pitch 100-130 (incl 2 persons)

> **MAMETZ** PAS-DE-CALAIS

Château de Mametz 32 r du Moulin ☎ 32190525
All year 11HEC ⊞ Ꭿ ᑭ 🔝 ✗ ⊙ 🔲 🕼 ᖑ ╲ R 🆎 lau ➡ 🔝 ᐟLPS

> **MARNE-LA-VALLÉE** SEINE-ET-MARNE

🐾 **Davy Crockett Ranch Disneyland Paris** ☎ 160456900
A modern site in wooded surroundings on the Disneyland Paris complex.
⊃ *Access via A4 Serris exit (no 13).*
Mar-Oct 57HEC ⊞ Ꭿ ᑭ 🔝 🔝 ✗ ⊙ 🔲 🕼 ╲ P 🆎 ⊞ 🕼 lau
Prices: pitch 300-400

> **MAUBEUGE** NORD

CM rte de Mons ☎ 327622548
⊃ *1.5km N via N2 (Bruxelles road).*
All year 2.1HEC ⊞ Ꭿ ᑭ ⊙ 🔲 🆎 ⊞ lau ➡ 🔝 🔝 ✗ 🕼 ᖑ

> **MELUN** SEINE-ET-MARNE

Belle Étoile Quai Joffre ☎ 164394812
Pleasant grassy site with two central blocks.
⊃ *At La Rochette, on left bank of River Seine 1km from the town.*
Apr-Oct 3.5HEC ⊞ Ꭿ ᑭ 🔝 ✗ ⊙ 🔲 🕼 🕼 ╲ P 🆎 🔲 ⊞ lau ➡ ✗ 🕼 ᐟP
Prices: ⋔24 ⬛8 ⬛17-24 ▲17

> **MERLIMONT** PAS-DE-CALAIS

Parc Résidentiel du Château St-Hubert Bagatelle ☎ 321891010
In pleasant wooded surroundings with good recreational facilities.
⊃ *3km S via D940, near Parc de Bagatelle.*
Apr-Oct 16HEC ⊞ Ꭿ ᑭ 🔝 🔝 ✗ ⊙ 🔲 🕼 ╲ P 🆎 ⊞ lau

> **MILLY-LA-FORÊT** ESSONNE

Musardière rte des Grandes Vallées ☎ 164989191
In pleasant wooded surroundings.
⊃ *4km SE via D948.*
Closed 16 Dec-14 Feb 12HEC ⊞ ⠉⠉ Ꭿ ᑭ ⊙ 🔲 ╲ P 🆎 ⊞

> **MONNERVILLE** ESSONNE

Bois de la Justice ☎ 164950534
Pitches separated by trees and hedges in beautiful natural woodland with good facilities.
⊃ *N20 Orléans to Étampes.*
Mar-Nov 5.5HEC ⊞ ➡ ᑭ 🔝 ✗ ⊙ 🔲 🕼 🕼 ╲ P 🆎 ⊞ lau
Prices: ⋔30 ⬛15 ⬛30 ▲15-30

> **MONTIGNY-LE-BRETONNEUX** YVELINES

Parc Étang Base de Loisirs-de-St Quentin ☎ 130585620
In beautiful rural surroundings within a leisure centre with easy access to Paris and Versailles.
⊃ *SE of town centre towards the Centre de Volle.*
All year 12HEC ⊞ Ꭿ ᑭ 🔝 🔝 ✗ ⊙ 🔲 🕼 ᖑ 🔝 ▲ 🆎 ⊞ lau ➡ ✗ ᐟL

MONTREUIL-SUR-MER PAS-DE-CALAIS

CM ☎ 321060728
➲ N of town on N1.
All year 2HEC ⚏ ♠ ⋔ ☉ ♨ ⋌ R ☎ ⊞ lau ➧ ⊾ ⍟ ✕ ⌀ ⚏ ⋌P
Prices: pitch 44-45 (incl 2 persons)

MOYENNEVILLE SOMME

Val de Trie Bouillancourt-sous-Miannay ☎ 322314888
A small site in a picturesque wooded location with good
facilities including a lake for fishing.
➲ 1km from the D925 (Abbeville-Le Tréport).
Apr-Oct 2.6HEC ⚏ ⌂ ⋔ ⊾ ⍟ ☉ ♨ ⌀ ⋌ LPR ☎ ⊞ lau ➧ ✕
⚏
Prices: ♦18-19 pitch 15-17

NEMOURS SEINE-ET-MARNE

ACCCF ☎ 64281062
On well-kept meadow. Clean sanitary installations.
➲ 200m from N7.
15 Mar-11 Nov 4.8HEC ⚏ ⌂ ⋔ ☉ ♨ ⋌ R ☎ lau ➧ ⊾ ⍟ ✕
⌀ ⚏ ⊞
Prices: ♦23 ♨23

NESLES-LA-VALLÉE VAL-D'OISE

Parc de Séjour de l'Étang 10 Chemin des Belles Vues
☎ 134706289
Level site near a small lake.
➲ A15 exit 10, then D927 and D79. From N1 take exit for
L'Isle Adam.
Mar-15 Nov 6HEC ⚏ ⌂ ⋔ ☉ ♨ ♨ ☎ ⊞ lau ➧ ⊾ ⍟ ✕ ⌀ ⚏
Prices: ♦17.50-25 pitch 17.50-25

NEUVILLE, LA NORD

Leu Pindu 2 r du Gl-de-Gaulle ☎ 320865087
➲ N on D8.

All year 1.2HEC ⚏ ♠ ⋔ ☉ ♨ ☎ ⊞ lau ➧ ⊾ ⍟ ✕ ⌀ ⚏ ⋌L
Prices: pitch 55 (incl 2 persons)

. ORVILLERS-SOREL OISE

Sorel ☎ 344850274
Divided into pitches. Local tradesmen supply provisions.
➲ Leave A1 at N17, turn right and continue 400mtrs.
Feb-15 Dec 3HEC ⚏ ⌂ ⋔ ✕ ☉ ♨ ⌀ ⚏ ♨ Å ☎ lau ➧ ⍟
✕

OYE-PLAGE PAS-DE-CALAIS

Oyats 272 Digue Vert ☎ 321851540
4.5km NW directly on the beach.
May-1 Oct 4HEC ⚏ ⌂ ⋔ ✕ ☉ ♨ ☎ ⊞ lau

PARIS

Bois de Boulogne 2 allée du Bord de l'Eau ☎ 145243000
Much of this site's popularity stems from its location close to
the city centre and it can become crowded during high
season as it is the only site actually in Paris.
All year 7HEC ⚏ ⌀ ♠ ⋔ ⊾ ⍟ ✕ ☉ ♨ ⌀ ♨ ☎ ⊞ lau
Prices: pitch 60-138 (incl 2 persons)

At CHAMPIGNY-SUR-MARNE(12km SE)

Tremblay bd des Alliés ☎ 143974397
Site tends to become full during peak season. Good
transportation into city and well placed for visiting
Disneyland Paris.
Reserved mainly for International Camping Card holders.
➲ Take N4 and turn left 350m after Joinville bridge.
All year 8HEC ⚏ ⌂ ⋔ ⊾ ⍟ ✕ ☉ ♨ ⌀ ♨ ☎ ⊞ lau ➧ ⚏ ⋌P

At CHOISY-LE-ROI(14km SE)

Paris Sud 125 av de V-St-Georges ☎ 148909230
Located in an attractive sports and leisure park with plenty of
facilities. Popular with student groups on visits to the Paris area.
Contd.

⮑ *Signposted from A86 SE of Paris.*
All year 9HEC ⏚⏚⏚ ♀ ╠ ⚚ ⛢ ✕ ⊙ ⚒ ⊘ 🚿 🏠 🔁 ⊞ lau ➡
⮑LPR

PLESSIS-FEU-AUSSOUX SEINE-ET-MARNE

Château-de-Chambonnières ☎ 164041585
⮑ *On D231 towards Provins, some 23km from Diseyland Paris.*
All year 5HEC ⏚⏚⏚ ♀ ╠ ⚚ ⊙ ⚒ ⊘ 🔁 ⊞ lau

POIX-DE-PICARDIE SOMME

Bois des Pêcheurs rte de Forges-les-Eaux ☎ 322901171
In a quiet riverside location with a high standard of sanitary facilities.
⮑ *W via D919 towards Forges-les-Eaux.*
Apr-Sep 2.4HEC ⏚⏚⏚ ⚞ ╠ ⊙ ⚒ ⊘ 🚿 🔁 ⊞ lau ➡ ⚚ ⛢ ✕
⮑PR
Prices: pitch 65 (incl 4 persons)

POTELLE NORD

Pré Vert Chemin du Moulin ☎ 327491987
Apr-20 Sep 2HEC ⏚⏚⏚ ♀ ╠ ⚚ ⊙ ⚒ 🏠 🔁 ⊞ lau ➡ ⚚ ✕ ⊘
⮑LR

PRESLES-VAILLY-SUR-AISNE AISNE

Domaine de la Nature chemin de Boufaud ☎ 323547455
⮑ *4km W via D144 near the canal and lake.*
All year 3HEC ⏚⏚⏚ ♀ ╠ ⚚ ✕ ⊙ ⚒ ⚒ ⛰ ⚛ ꜀ R 🔁 ⊞ lau ➡ ⚚ ⚚
✕ ⊘ ⮑L
Prices: pitch 72-88 (incl 2 persons)

PROYART SOMME

Loisir la Violette rte de Mericourt ☎ 322858136
Mar-30 Oct 1.8HEC ⏚⏚⏚ ♀ ╠ ⊙ ⚒ 🏠 🔁 lau ➡ ⚚ ⚚ ✕ 🚿 ⊞
Prices: ↟10 🚘5 🚐11-20 ▲6

QUEND-PLAGE-LES-PINS SOMME

At **MONCHAUX-LES-QUEND**(3.5km E via D102E)

Roses ☎ 322277617
Well-kept site with trees and hedges surrounding individual pitches. Only recommended site in area.
⮑ *Turn off D940 at Quend, site 500m on left of D102.*
15 Mar-Oct 9HEC ⏚⏚⏚ ♀ ╠ ⚚ ✕ ⊙ ⚒ ⚒ 🔁 ⊞ lau ➡ ⚚ ⊘

RAMBOUILLET YVELINES

CM de l'Étang d'Or r du Château d'Eau ☎ 130410734
In a pleasant situation. Shop, bar etc only open Jun-Aug.
⮑ *From railway station follow road SE for 1.3km passing Camping Pont Hardy.*
All year 5HEC ⏚⏚⏚ ➡ ╠ ⚚ ✕ ⊙ ⚒ 🔁 ⊞ lau ➡ ⮑P
Prices: ↟20 pitch 23

RUE SOMME

Garenne de Moncourt ☎ 322250693
⮑ *On D85 towards Montreuil-sur-Mer.*
Apr-Oct 8HEC ⏚⏚⏚ ♀ ╠ ⊙ ⚒ ⊘ ꜀ PR 🔁 lau ➡ 🚿

ST-AMAND-LES-EAUX NORD

Mont des Bruyères 806 r Basly ☎ 327485687
⮑ *3.5km SE in the forest of St-Amand*
Mar-Nov 3.5HEC ⏚⏚⏚ ➡ ╠ ⚚ ⛢ ✕ ⊙ ⚒ 🚿 🏠 🔁 ⊞ lau ➡ ✕
⊘ ꜀P
Prices: pitch 51 (incl 2 persons)

ST-CHÉRON ESSONNE

Parc des Roches La Petite Beauce ☎ 164566550
In a wooded park.
Apr-Oct 23HEC ⏚⏚⏚ ♀ ╠ ⛢ ✕ ⊙ ⚒ ꜀ P 🔁 ⊞ lau ➡ ⊘

ST-CYR-SUR-MORIN SEINE-ET-MARNE

Choisel rte de Rebais ☎ 160238493
In a pleasant situation. Separate carpark for arrivals after 22.00hrs.
⮑ *2km W via D31.*
Mar-Nov 3.5HEC ⏚⏚⏚ ♀ ╠ ⛢ ✕ ⊙ ⚒ ⊘ 🚿 🔁 ⊞ lau

ST-JANS-CAPPEL NORD

Domaine de la Sablière Le Mont Noir ☎ 328494634
A pleasant family site in a wooded location with large, well defined pitches.
⮑ *3.5km NE via D10 and D318.*
Apr-Oct 3.6HEC ⏚⏚⏚ ➡ ╠ ⚚ ✕ ⊙ ⚒ 🚿 🔁 ⊞ lau ➡ ⚚ ✕ ꜀P

ST-LEU-D'ESSERENT OISE

Campix ☎ 44560848
In wooded surroundings, within easy reach of Chantilly.
⮑ *3.5km NE via D12.*
7 Mar-1 Dec 6HEC ⏚⏚⏚ ꞉꞉꞉ ➡ ╠ ⊙ ⚒ ⊘ 🔁 ⊞ lau ➡ ⚚ ⚚ ✕
⮑L

ST-QUENTIN AISNE

CM bd J-Bouin ☎ 323626866
A good site in pleasant wooded surroundings near the canal.
Mar-Nov 1HEC ⏚⏚⏚ ꞉꞉꞉ ♀ ╠ ⚒ ⚒ ➡ ⚚ ⚚ ✕ ⊘ 🚿 ⮑LPR ⊞

ST-VALÉRY-SUR-SOMME SOMME

🏨 **Domaine du Château de Drancourt** ☎ 322269345
In open countryside, surrounded by woods, fields and lakes, within the grounds of a former hunting lodge.
⮑ *3.5km S via D48.*
Apr-Sep 15HEC ⏚⏚⏚ ♀ ╠ ⚚ ⛢ ✕ ⊙ ⚒ ⊘ 🚿 🏠 ꜀ P 🔁 ⊞ lau
➡ ✕ ⮑L
Prices: ↟30 pitch 48-48

SALENCY OISE

Étang du Moulin 54 r du Moulin ☎ 344099981
A small site opposite a trout fishing lake and recreational area under the ownership of the site proprietors.
➲ *3km from Noyon on the N32 towards Chauny.*
All year 0.4HEC ⬛ 🔧 🌳 ⊙ 🚿 ⛺ 🏪
Prices: ⛺10 🚗15 🚐20 🏕20

SERAUCOURT-LE-GRAND AISNE

Pêche du Vivier aux Carpes 10 r Ch-Voyeux ☎ 323605102
A peaceful site bordered by lakes. Separate car park for arrivals after 22.00hrs.
➲ *A26 exit 11-left on D1 exit Essigny-D72.*
23 Dec-4 Jan 3HEC ⬛ 🔧 🌳 🏪 ⊙ 🚿 ⌀ 🏪 🏢 lau ➤ 🍽 ✕ ⛱
Prices: pitch 90 (incl 2 persons)

SERQUES PAS-DE-CALAIS

Frémont rte Nationale 9 ☎ 321930115
A pleasant site near the Éperlecques Forest.
➲ *1.5km SW on N43*
Apr-15 Oct 2HEC ⬛ 🔧 🌳 🏪 ⊙ 🚿 🏪 🏢 lau ➤ ✕

SOISSONS AISNE

CM av du Mail ☎ 323745269
In pleasant surroundings with good, modern facilities.
All year 1.8HEC ⬛ 🔧 🌳 ⊙ 🚿 🏪 🏢 lau ➤ 🏪 🍽 ✕ ⌀ ⛱ ₹P 🏢
Prices: ⛺14 🚗10 🚐10 🏕10

STEENBECQUE NORD

Paradiso r du Bois
➲ *1.2km SE, 400m from the canal.*
Apr-15 Oct 1.6HEC ⬛ 🔧 🌳 🍽 ✕ ⊙ 🚿 ⛱ 🏪 🏢 lau ➤ ₹R

THIEMBRONNE PAS-DE-CALAIS

Pommiers rte de Desvres ☎ 321395019
A family site in pleasant wooded surroundings
➲ *NW on D132.*
15 Mar-15 Oct 1.8HEC ⬛ 🔧 🌳 ⊙ 🚿 ⌀ 🏪 ₹ P 🏢 lau ➤ 🏪 🍽 ✕ ₹R

TOLLENT PAS-DE-CALAIS

Val d'Authie ☎ 321471427
In a pleasant wooded location with wide, well marked pitches.
➲ *SE via D119*
Apr-Sep 3HEC ⬛ 🔧 🌳 🏪 🍽 ✕ ⊙ 🚿 ₹ LP 🏢 lau ➤ ⛱ ₹R
Prices: pitch 25-50 (incl 2 persons)

TORCY SEINE-ET-MARNE

Parc de la Colline rte de Lagny ☎ 160054232
An ideal base for visiting Paris (30 minutes from the centre by Metro). Separate car park for arrivals after 22.00 hrs.
➲ *Access via exit 10 on the A104 and D10E.*
All year 10HEC ⬛ ➤ 🔧 🌳 🏪 🍽 ✕ ⊙ 🚿 ⌀ 🏪 🏕 A 🏢 lau ➤ ₹LP

TOUQUIN SEINE-ET-MARNE

Étangs Fleuris rte de la Couture ☎ 164041636
In wooded surroundings with well defined pitches and modern facilities.
➲ *E of town towards Provins.*
Mar-Oct 5.5HEC ⬛ ➤ 🔧 🌳 🏪 🍽 ✕ ⊙ 🚿 ₹ P 🏢 lau
Prices: pitch 34-39

TOURNEHEM PAS-DE-CALAIS

Bal Parc 500 r du Vieux Château ☎ 321356590
A peaceful site in rural surroundings with good, modern facilities.

By the A104 towards Roissy – Charles de Gaulle, then A1 towards St Denis – Paris

CAMPING LE PARC
Montjay la Tour – 77410 VILLEVAUDE
Tel: 01 60 26 20 79 Fax: 01 60 27 02 75

Marylise welcomes you in her park full of flowers and trees. Ideal for visits to Paris and region. You will find rest and comfort to spend your weekends or holidays. Marked pitches, with sun or shadow. Comfortable sanitary installations. Free brochure. Open all year. Ping-pong – French boules – volleyball – handball – fishing – playground – tennis 200m.

20 min. from EuroDisney (shuttle-service possible with reservation)
30 min. from Paris. 40 min. from Parc Asterix.

➲ *Access via D218 from village centre.*
All year 1.6HEC ⬛ 🔧 🌳 🏪 🍽 ✕ ⊙ 🚿 ⌀ ⛱ 🏕 🏪 ₹R 🏢 🏢 lau
Prices: ⛺18 pitch 32

VILLENNES-SUR-SEINE YVELINES

Club des Renardières rte de Vernouillet ☎ 139758897
Site for caravans only, in beautiful hilly park laid out with hedges, lawns and flower beds. Fully divided into completely separated pitches.
➲ *Follow D113 to Maison Blanche turn right and continue 3km.*
All year 6.5HEC ⬛ ➤ 🌳 ⊙ 🚿 ₹ L lau ➤ 🏪 🍽 ✕

VILLERS-HÉLON AISNE

Castel des Biches 4 r Duchateau ☎ 323960499
Attractive site in grounds of an old castle.
➲ *Turn off N2 onto D2 between Soissons and Villers-Cotterêts and continue for 7km via Longport.*
All year 7HEC ⬛ 🔧 🌳 🍽 ⊙ 🚿 🏕 A ₹ P 🏢 lau ➤ ⌀ ⛱ ₹S

VILLERS-SUR-AUTHIE SOMME

Val d'Authie 20 rte de Vercourt ☎ 322299247
A well designed site situated between the Forest of Crécy and the sea. Bar and café open in high season only.
➲ *Access via N1.*
Apr-Oct 7HEC ⬛ 🔧 🌳 🏪 🍽 ✕ ⊙ 🚿 ⛱ ₹ P 🏢 lau
Prices: ⛺24 🚗10 🚐15 🏕15

VILLEVAUDE SEINE-ET-MARNE

Parc Montjay-la-Tour ☎ 160262079
Bar and restaurant facilities open summer only.
➲ *Access via A104 exit 6B, Marne-la-Vallée.*
All year 10HEC ⬛ ➤ 🌳 🍽 ✕ ⊙ 🚿 🏪 🏢 lau

VIRONCHAUX SOMME

Peupliers 221 r du Cornet ☎ 322235427
A peaceful site 3km form the Forest of Crécy.
➲ *Approach via N1 and D938.*
Apr-Sep 1.2HEC ⬛ 🔧 🌳 🏪 ⊙ 🚿 ⌀ ⛱ 🏪 🏢 lau ➤ 🍽 ✕
Prices: ⛺12 pitch 12

WACQUINGHEM PAS-DE-CALAIS

Éscale ☎ 321320069
In a pleasantly landscaped park with modern facilities 5 minutes from the coastal resorts.
➲ *Access via A16 and D231.*
15 Mar-Oct 11HEC ⬛ 🔧 🌳 🏪 🍽 ✕ ⊙ 🚿 🏕 🏢 lau ➤ ⌀
Prices: ⛺19 🚗10 🚐17 🏕13

● ● ● ● AUVERGNE ● ● ● ●

The mountainous Massif Central characterises the Auvergne, giving an atmosphere of grandeur and tranquility to this ancient land. The rivers Dordogne and Allier begin in the region; on the banks of the Allier is the bustling town of Langeac - especially lively on market days. The rivers offer good fishing and recreational opportunities, many of these have been dammed, creating great placid lakes providing wonderful centres for watersports. A unique highlight of the area is the remarkable Parc de Volcans, where 80 extinct volcanos form a majestic line stretching some 20 miles.
South west of the Auvergne, the département of Aveyron is a little-known district with a turbulent past, and ancient abbeys, medieval citadels and fortified towns. Cordes and Villefranche-de-Rourgue are perfect 15th-century garrison towns, and Najac stands in a superb position on its 1,200ft rock. East from Aveyron is Lozère, an arid, rugged landscape. The highlight here is the well-known Gorges du Tarn, where the Tarn slices its way through the land for more than 50 miles, and twisting, narrow roads offer an unforgettable succession of spectacular views.

▶ **ALLANCHE** CANTAL

CM Pont Valat ☎ 471204587
➲ *1km S on D679 towards St-Flour.*
15 Jun-15 Sep 3HEC ⬛ ⚅ 🏕 ⊙ 🔌 🏕 lau ➡ 🛒 🍽 ✕ ⌀ 🍴 ⊞
Prices: 🏕7 pitch 4.50

▶ **ALLEYRAS** HAUTE-LOIRE

CM ☎ 471575686
➲ *2.5km NW.*
May-Sep 1HEC ⬛ 🏊 🏕 ⊙ 🔌 ⌀ 🏕 🏕 ⊞ lau ➡ 🛒 🍽 ✕ 🍴 ⚡R
Prices: pitch 49 (incl 2 persons)

▶ **ANSE** RHÔNE

Porte du Beaujolais chemin des Grandes Levées
☎ 474671287
A pleasant, modern site in the heart of the Beaujolais country beside the River Saône.
➲ *Access via A6 or N6 then D39.*
Dec-Feb 7HEC ⚅ 🏕 🛒 🍽 ⊙ 🔌 🏕 ⚡ PR 🏕 ⊞ lau ➡ ✕ ⌀ 🍴 ⚡L

▶ **ARNAC** CANTAL

Gineste ☎ 471629190
Situated on a peninsula in Lake Enchanet with good, modern facilities and access to local ski slopes.
All year 3HEC ⬛ ⚅ 🏕 🛒 🍽 ✕ ⊙ 🔌 🏕 🏕 ⚡ LP 🏕 lau
Prices: 🏕36-40

▶ **ARPAJON-SUR-CÈRE** CANTAL

Cère r F-Ramond ☎ 471645507
➲ *S towards Rodez via D920, beside the river.*
Jun-Sep 2HEC ⬛ ⚅ 🏕 ⊙ 🔌 ⚡ R 🏕 lau ➡ 🛒 🍽 ✕ ⌀ ⊞

▶ **AUBIN** AVEYRON

CM ☎ 565630386
➲ *100m from the lake.*
Apr-15 Sep 4HEC ⚙ ⚅ 🏕 ⊙ 🔌 🏕 lau ➡ 🛒 🍽 ✕ 🍴 ⚡P

▶ **BELMONT-SUR-RANCE** AVEYRON

Val Fleuri ☎ 565999513
A peaceful site beside the River Rance with good, modern facilities.

➲ *Access via N9 and D999.*
Jun Aug 1HEC ⬛ ⚅ 🏕 🛒 🍽 ✕ ⊙ 🔌 ⌀ 🍴 🏕 ⚡ R 🏕 ⊞ lau ➡ 🛒 ⚡P
Prices: pitch 68 (incl 2 persons)

▶ **BOURBON-L'ARCHAMBAULT** ALLIER

CM Parc Bignon Parc Jean Bignon ☎ 470670883
➲ *1km SW on N153, rte de Montluçon, turn right.*
Mar-Oct 3HEC ⬛ ⚅ 🏕 ⊙ 🔌 🏕 lau ➡ 🛒 🍽 ✕ ⚡P
Prices: 🏕13 ➡5 �'7.50 🛖6.5-7

▶ **BOURG-ARGENTAL** LOIRE

Astrée 'L'Allier' ☎ 477397297
In pleasant surroundings with good recreational facilities.
➲ *Access via N82.*
All year 2HEC ⬛ ⚅ 🏕 🛒 🍽 ✕ ⊙ 🔌 🏕 🏕 ⚡ R 🏕 lau ➡ 🛒 ✕ ⌀ 🍴 ⚡P ⊞

▶ **BRAIZE** ALLIER

Champ de la Chapelle ☎ 470061545
A family site in the centre of the Tronçais Forest with good recreational facilities.
➲ *7km SE via D28 and D978.*
May-15 Sep 5.6HEC ⬛ ⚅ 🏕 ✕ ⊙ 🔌 🏕 🏕 lau ➡ 🛒 🍽 ✕
Prices: pitch 46

▶ **BRUSQUE** AVEYRON

VAL Camping Les Pibouls Domaine de Céras ☎ 565495066
Jul-Aug 1HEC ⬛ ⚅ 🏕 🛒 🍽 ✕ ⊙ 🔌 ⚡ L 🏕 lau ➡ 🛒 ⊞
Prices: pitch 133 (incl 4 persons)

▶ **CANET-DE-SALARS** AVEYRON

Caussanel Lac de Pareloup ☎ 565468519
Well equipped site on the shore of Lake Pareloup.
➲ *Access via D911.*
All year 10HEC ⬛ ⚅ 🏕 🛒 🍽 ✕ ⊙ 🔌 ⌀ 🏕 🏕 ⚡ LP 🏕 ⊞ lau
Prices: pitch 60-95 (incl 2 persons)

▶ **CAPDENAC-GARE** AVEYRON

Diège Vallée de la Diège, Sonnac ☎ 565646125
Level, sub-divided terrain located in a narrow valley of La Diège river.
➲ *From Figeac on N140 travel 7km, in the direction of Capdenac-Gare. Turn sharp right after the bridge and continue on D558 for about 7km in the direction of Naussac.*
May-1 Nov 7HEC ⬛ ⚅ 🏕 🛒 🍽 ✕ ⊙ 🔌 ⌀ 🍴 🏕 🛖 ⚡ R 🏕 ⊞ lau
Prices: 🏕18 pitch 29

CM Rives d'Olt bd Paul-Ramadier ☎ 565808887
A quiet site on level ground with pitches divided by hedges.
➲ *7km from Figeac via N140 towards Rodez.*
Etr-Sep 1.3HEC ⬛ ⚅ 🏕 ⊙ 🔌 🏕 ⚡ R 🏕 ⊞ lau ➡ 🛒 🍽 ✕ ⌀ ⚡P
Prices: 🏕14 ➡9 �'14 🛖9

▶ **CEYRAT** PUY-DE-DÔME

CM av J-B-Marrou ☎ 473613073
On undulating meadow on partly terraced hill. Large common room with games. Supplies only available peak season.
All year 6HEC ⬛ ⚅ 🏕 🛒 🍽 ✕ ⊙ 🔌 🏕 🏕 🏕 ⊞ lau ➡ ⌀

▶ **CHAMPAGNAC-LE-VIEUX** HAUTE-LOIRE

Chanterelle Le Plan d'Eau ☎ 471763400
Situated in the heart of the Auvergne beside a wooded lake.
➲ *1km N via D5.*
15 Jun-15 Sep 4HEC ⬛ ⚅ 🏕 ⊙ 🔌 🏕 🛖 🛒 ⚡ L 🏕 lau ➡ 🛒 🍽 ✕ ⌀ 🍴 ⚡R ⊞

CHAMPS-SUR-TARENTAINE CANTAL

Tarentaine ☎ 471787275
➲ *1km SW via D679 and D22 beside the River Tarentaine.*
15 Jun-15 Sep 3HEC ⭤ 🏕 ⊙ 🖳 🖵 ⚲ R 🏚 lau ➧ 🏖 💺 ✕ 📷
⚲P

CHÂTEL-DE-NEUVRE ALLIER

Deneuvre Les Graves ☎ 470420451
In pleasant surroundings within a nature reserve beside the River Allier.
➲ *0.5km N via D9.*
1 Apr-1 Oct 1HEC ⭤ 🕏 🏕 🏖 💺 ✕ ⊙ 🖳 🖵 🐪 🅰 ⚲ R 🏚 🎛
lau
Prices: 🏕18-22 pitch 18-22

CHÂTEL GUYON PUY-DE-DÔME

Clos de Balanède r de la Piscine ☎ 473860247
A pleasant site, situated in an orchard.
➲ *Access via A71 and D685.*
10 Apr-5 Oct 4HEC ⭤ ➧ 🏕 🏖 💺 ✕ ⊙ 🖳 🐿 📷 🐪 ⚲ P 🏚
lau ➧ 🎛
Prices: 🏕14-20 pitch 10.50-15

CHÂTEL-MONTAGNE ALLIER

Croix Cognat ☎ 470593138
Well equipped site at an altitude of 540mtrs.
➲ *0.5km NW via D25 towards Vichy.*
May-Oct 1HEC ⭤ ➧ 🏕 🏖 💺 ✕ ⊙ 🖳 🐿 📷 🐪 ⚲ P 🏚 🎛
lau ➧ ⚲R

CHAUDES-AIGUES CANTAL

CM du Couffour ☎ 471235708
Tastefully sited around the town football pitch in the local leisure area.
➲ *2km S via D921.*
May-20 Oct 2.5HEC ⭤ 🕏 🏕 ⊙ 🖳 🖵 🏚 🎛 lau ➧ 🏖 💺 ✕ 🐿
📷 ⚲PR
Prices: 🏕11 ➡5 🖵5 🅰5

CHOUVIGNY ALLIER

Bel Le Soult ☎ 470904117
➲ *3km SE via D915 beside the River Sioule.*
Etr-Sep 1.5HEC ⭤ 🕏 🏕 ⊙ 🖵 ⚲ P 🏚 lau

CONDRIEU RHÔNE

Belle Rive La Plaine ☎ 474595108
In wooded surroundings bordering the Rhône.
➲ *11km S of Vienne on N86.*
Apr-Sep 5HEC ⭤ 🕏 🏕 🏖 💺 ✕ ⊙ 🖳 🐿 ⚲ PR 🏚 lau ➧ ⚲L
Prices: 🏕17 ➡10 🖵23 🅰23

CONQUES AVEYRON

Beau Rivage ☎ 565698223
Peaceful site beside the river with spacious, well marked pitches.
➲ *On D901.*
Apr-Sep 1HEC ⭤ ➧ 🕏 🏖 💺 ✕ ⊙ 🖳 🐿 📷 🐪 ⚲ PR 🏚 lau ➧
📷 🎛
Prices: 🏕20 pitch 16

COURNON-D'AUVERGNE PUY-DE-DÔME

CM Plage r de Laveuses ☎ 473848130
In a rural setting on the shore of a 7 hectare lake, close to the River Allier.
➲ *1.5km E towards Billom.*
All year 4.8HEC ⭤ 🐿 🕏 🏕 🏖 💺 ✕ ⊙ 🖳 🐪 ⚲ LR 🏚 lau ➧
🐿 📷
Prices: 🏕18-19 pitch 24.50-26.50

DALLET PUY-DE-DÔME

Ombrages rte de Pont-du-Château ☎ 473831097
In a wooded location beside the River Allier.
Jun-15 Sep 3.5HEC ⭤ 🕏 🏕 🏖 💺 ✕ ⊙ 🖳 🖵 ⚲ PR 🏚 🎛 lau
➧ 🏖 ✕
Prices: 🏕25 pitch 32

DARDILLY RHÔNE

Ville de Lyon ☎ 478356455
Generously arranged and equipped site divided into pitches. Ideal for overnight stays near motorway. Concrete platforms for caravans.
➲ *9km N of Lyon La Garde exit off A6.*
All year 6HEC ⭤ 🕏 🏕 🏖 💺 ✕ ⊙ 🖳 ⚲ P 🏚 🎛 lau ➧ 🏖 🐿 📷

EBREUIL ALLIER

Filature de la Sioule Ile de Nieres ☎ 470907201
A peaceful, well equipped site in an orchard beside the River Sioule.
➲ *Access signposted from exit 12 on A71.*
31 Mar-1 Oct 3.6HEC ⭤ ➧ 🕏 🏖 💺 ✕ ⊙ 🖳 🐿 📷 ⚲ R 🏚 🎛
lau ➧ ✕ 📷
Prices: pitch 80 (incl 2 persons)

FERRIÈRES-ST-MARY CANTAL

Vigeaires ☎ 471206147
A level site surrounded by woodland close to the River Allagnon with good, modern facilities.
➲ *Access via A75 exit Massiac towards Aurillac.*
15 Jun-Aug 1.5HEC ⭤ ➧ 🕏 ⊙ 🖳 ⚲ R 🏚 🎛 lau ➧ 🏖 💺 ✕ 🐿
📷

FIRMI AVEYRON

Étang r du Camping ☎ 565634302
In a pleasant situation close to the lake.
➲ *Off the main N140.*
Jul-Aug 1.4HEC ⭤ 🕏 🏕 ⊙ 🖳 🏚 🎛 lau ➧ 🏖 💺 ✕ 📷
⚲L 🎛

FLEURIE RHÔNE

CM la Grappe Fleurie ☎ 474698007
A good quality municipal site in a picturesque setting in the heart of the Beaujolais region.
➲ *0.6km SE on D119 E.*
14 Mar-24 Oct 2.5HEC ⭤ 🕏 🏕 ⊙ 🖳 🐿 🏚 lau ➧ 🏖 💺 ✕ 📷
⚲LPR 🎛

GOUDET HAUTE-LOIRE

Bord de l'Eau Plaine du Chambon ☎ 471571682
Well equipped site in wooded surroundings below the ruins of the castle.
➲ *W via D49, beside the River Loire.*
15 Jun-5 Oct 5HEC ⭤ 🕏 🏕 🏖 💺 ✕ ⊙ 🖳 🐿 🖵 ⚲ PR 🏚 🎛
lau
Prices: 🏕23 ➡23

ISLE-ET-BARDAIS ALLIER

Écossais ☎ 470666257
In a peaceful location in the heart of the Forest of Tronçais, beside the Pirot Lake.
➲ *Access via A71-E11.*
Apr-Sep 25HEC ⭤ 🕏 🏕 🏖 💺 ✕ ⊙ 🖳 🐿 📷 ⚲ L 🏚 🎛 lau
Prices: 🏕12.20-14.30 pitch 6.10-7.10

JABRUN CANTAL

Tillet ☎ 471738080
➲ *4km SW via D921.*
15 Jun-15 Sep 1.5HEC ➧ 🕏 ⊙ 🖵 🏚 lau ➧ 💺 ✕ 📷 ⚲PR

Contd.

JENZAT ALLIER

Champ de Sioule rte de Chantelle ☎ 470568635
29 May-26 Sep 1HEC ⸜⸝⸍ ⚬ ⚭ ⊙ ▣ 🅿 ⊞ lau ➧ ⚎ ⚍ ✕ ⌀ ⚏
⚑PR
Prices: ⚲10.50 ⚬4.50 ⚐4.50 ▲4.50

LACAPELLE-VIESCAMP CANTAL

Puech des Ouilhes ☎ 471464238
On a wooded peninsula on Lake St-Étienne-Cantalès.
10 Jun-10 Sep 2HEC ⸜⸝⸍ ➧ ⚭ ⚎ ⊙ ▣ ⌀ ⚏ ⚑ P ⚐ ⊞ ⚸ lau
➧ ⚍
Prices: ⚲20 ⚬9 ⚐10 ▲10

LANGEAC HAUTE-LOIRE

Gorges d'Allier 'Le Pradeau' Domaine du Prad'Eau
☎ 471770501
In wooded surroundings within a natural park, 800mtrs
from the river. Good recreational facilities.
➲ Access via N102.
Apr-Oct 12HEC ⸜⸝⸍ ⚬ ⚭ ⚎ ⊙ ▣ ⌀ ⚏ ⚓ ⚐ ▲ ⚑ PR ⚐ lau
➧ ⚍ ✕ ⊞
Prices: pitch 59

LAPEYROUSE PUY-DE-DÔME

CM Les Marins La Loge ☎ 473520273
A modern, lakeside site with good facilities set among the
rolling hills of the Combtaille.
➲ 2km E via D998.
15 Jun-1 Sep 2.5HEC ⸜⸝⸍ ⚬ ⚭ ⚎ ⚍ ⊙ ▣ ⚏ ⚑ L ⚐ lau ➧ ⚍
Prices: pitch 60 (incl 3 persons)

LOUBEYRAT PUY-DE-DÔME

Colombier ☎ 473866694
➲ 1.5km S via D16.
15 Apr-15 Oct 0.9HEC ⸜⸝⸍ ⚬ ⚭ ⊙ ▣ ⚏ ⚐ ⚑ P ⚐ ⊞ lau ➧
⚎ ⚍ ✕ ⌀ ⚏

MARTRES-DE-VEYRE, LES PUY-DE-DÔME

CM la Font de Bleix r des Roches ☎ 473392649
A pleasant site beside the River Allier. A good centre for
touring the surrounding area.
➲ SE via D225 beside the River Allier.
Jul-Aug 1.3HEC ⸜⸝⸍ ⚸ ⚭ ⊙ ▣ ⚏ ⚑ R ⚐ lau ➧ ⚎ ⚍ ✕ ⌀ ⚏
Prices: ⚲12 ⚬10 ⚐8-10

MASSIAC CANTAL

CM Allagnon av de Courcelles ☎ 471230393
A riverside site with plenty of facilities.
➲ 0.8km W on N122.
May-Sep 2.5HEC ⸜⸝⸍ ➧ ⚭ ⊙ ▣ ⌀ ⚑ R ⚐ ⊞ lau ➧ ⚎ ⚍ ✕ ⚏
⚑P

MAURS CANTAL

At **ST-CONSTANT**(4.5km SE via N663)

Moulin de Chaules rte de Calvinet ☎ 471491102
Terraced site in a valley by the stream of a former watermill
with good, modern facilities.
➲ 3km E via D28.
20 Apr-Oct 3HEC ⸜⸝⸍ ⚬ ⚭ ⚎ ⚍ ✕ ⊙ ▣ ⚏ ⚑ PR ⚐ ⊞ lau

MENDE LOZÈRE

Tivoli av des Gorges-du-Tarn ☎ 466650038
A level site in wooded surroundings beside the river.
➲ 2km from the town via A75 or N88.
All year 2HEC ⸜⸝⸍ ➧ ⚭ ⚎ ⊙ ▣ ⌀ ⚓ ⚏ ⚐ ⚑ PR ⚐ ⊞ ➧ ✕
Prices: ⚲23 ⚬12 ⚐14 ▲14

MEYRUEIS LOZÈRE

Ayres rte de la Brêze ☎ 466456051
On a wooded meadow with well defined pitches and modern
sanitary installations within easy reach of the picturesque
Gorges de la Jonte. Plenty of recreational facilities.
➲ 0.5km E via D57
1 Apr-20 Sep 1.5HEC ⸜⸝⸍ ⚬ ⚭ ⚍ ✕ ⊙ ▣ ⌀ ⚏ ⚑ P ⚐ ⊞ lau
➧ ⚎ ⚍ ⚑R
Prices: ⚲14-20 pitch 38

Capelan ☎ 466456050
In picturesque surroundings alongside the Gorges de la Jonte
with good sporting facilities.
➲ Access via D986 from Ste-Enimie.
May-19 Sep 4HEC ⸜⸝⸍ ➧ ⚭ ⚎ ⚍ ✕ ⊙ ▣ ⌀ ⚏ ⚑ PR ⚐ ⊞ lau
➧ ✕
Prices: pitch 58-79 (incl 2 persons)

MILLAU AVEYRON

Deux Rivières 61 av de l'Migoual ☎ 565600027
➲ 1.5km NE via D991, beside the River Tarn.
Apr-15 Oct 1.1HEC ⸜⸝⸍ ⸛⸛ ➧ ⚭ ⊙ ▣ ⌀ ⚏ ⚑ R ⚐ ⊞ lau
➧ ⚍

CM Millau Plage rte de Millau Plage ☎ 565601097
Beside the River Tarn, flat shady parkland.
➲ Access via D187.
Apr-Sep 5HEC ⸜⸝⸍ ➧ ⚭ ⚎ ⚍ ✕ ⊙ ▣ ⌀ ⚏ ⚑ PR ⚐ ⊞ lau

Rivages av de l'Aigoual ☎ 565610107
A family site with good facilities beside the River Dourbie.
➲ 1.7km E via D991.
May-Sep 7HEC ⸜⸝⸍ ⚬ ⚭ ⚎ ⚍ ✕ ⊙ ▣ ⌀ ⚏ ▲ ⚑ PR ⚐ ⊞ lau
➧ ⚍
Prices: pitch 85-125 (incl 2 persons)

MIREMONT PUY-DE-DÔME

Confolant ☎ 473799276
➲ 7km NE via D19 and D19E.
Jun-10 Sep 2.5HEC ⸜⸝⸍ ➧ ⚭ ⚎ ⚍ ✕ ⊙ ▣ ⌀ ⚏ ⚏ ⚑ L ⚐ ⊞
lau
Prices: ⚲18 pitch 23

MOLOMPIZE CANTAL

CM ☎ 471736006
In a wooded valley beside the River Alagnan.
➲ 0.5km NE via N122.
15 Jun-15 Sep 2HEC ⸜⸝⸍ ⸛⸛ ⚬ ⚭ ⊙ ▣ ⚑ R ⚐ lau ➧ ⚎ ⚍ ✕
⌀ ⚏

MONISTROL-SUR-LOIRE HAUTE-LOIRE

CM Beau Séjour chemin de Chaponas ☎ 471665390
➲ Adjacent to N88 near the municipal swimming pool.
Signposted from town centre.
Apr-Oct 1.5HEC ⸜⸝⸍ ➧ ⚭ ⊙ ▣ ⚑ P ⚐ ⊞ lau ➧ ⚎ ⚍ ✕ ⌀ ⚏
⚑S

MONTAIGUT-LE-BLANC PUY-DE-DÔME

CM Le Bourg ☎ 473967507
A quiet, level municipal site with good recreational facilities.
Jun-15 Sep 1.5HEC ⸜⸝⸍ ➧ ⚭ ⊙ ▣ ⚑ R ⚐ ⊞ lau ➧ ⚎ ⚍ ✕
Prices: ⚲14 pitch 18

MONT-DORE, LE PUY-DE-DÔME

CM du L'Esquiladou rte des Cascades ☎ 473652374
Mountainous situation in the heart of a national park region
10 May-15 Oct 2HEC ⸛⸛ ⚸ ⚭ ⊙ ▣ ⊞ lau ➧ ⚎ ⚍ ✕ ⌀ ⚏
⚑R
Prices: ⚲16 pitch 15

MORNANT RHÔNE

CM de la Trillonière bd du Général-de-Gaulle ☎ 478441647
In a rural setting on the southern outskirts of the town at an altitude of 333mtrs.
➲ *Off D30 towards La Condamine.*
May-Sep 1.6HEC ⬛ ⌕ ⌂ ⊙ ⬚ ☎ ⊞ ⌗ ✦ ⬛ ⍲ ✕ ⌀ ⛱ ⌇P
Prices: ⚑16-21 pitch 17

MOSTUÉJOUS AVEYRON

Aubigue ☎ 565626367
➲ *1.3km SE beside the River Tarn.*
Apr-Sep 1.5HEC ⬛ ✦ ⌂ ⬛ ⍲ ✕ ⊙ ⬚ ⌀ ⛱ ⬚ ⍭ ⚑ ⌇ R ⊞ ⊞
lau ✦ ✕

MUROL PUY-DE-DÔME

Europe ☎ 473886046
A family site in rural surroundings on the slopes of a forested valley close to the banks of Lake Chambon.
➲ *Access via A71/75 and D996.*
25 May-9 Sep 5.5HEC ⬛ ✦ ⌂ ⬛ ⍲ ✕ ⊙ ⬚ ⌀ ⛱ ⬚ ⌇P ⊞
lau ✦ ⌇LR ⊞

Plage Plage du Lac Chambon ☎ 473886027
Busy site beside lake. Caravan section divided into pitches, terraced area for tents. Asphalt drive.
➲ *1.2km from centre of village. Turn off into allée de Plage before entering village and follow signposts.*
May-Sep 7HEC ⬛ ⋯ ✦ ⌂ ⬛ ⍲ ✕ ⊙ ⬚ ⌀ ⛱ ⌇ L ⊞ ⊞ lau
✦ ⛱
Prices: ⚑20 ⇔10 ⬚10 ⚑10

Pré-Bas Lac Chambon ☎ 473886304
On the side of Lake Chambon with direct access to the beach and windsurf beach.
➲ *SW off D996.*
May-30 Sep 3.5HEC ⬛ ✦ ⌂ ⬛ ⍲ ✕ ⊙ ⬚ ⛱ ⌇ P ⊞ lau ✦ ⬛
✕ ⌀ ⌇LR
Prices: ⚑22 pitch 34

Ribeyre Jassat ☎ 473886429
A modern site in a beautiful mountain location 1km from Lac Chambon.
➲ *1.2km S on rte de Jassat.*
1 May-15 Sep 10HEC ⬛ ✦ ⌂ ⬛ ⍲ ✕ ⊙ ⬚ ⌀ ⛱ ⬚ ⌇ LPR
⊞ lau ✦ ⬛ ⊞
Prices: ⚑18-24 pitch 28-36

NANT AVEYRON

Val de Cantobre ☎ 565584300
Beside the river in the picturesque Gorges de la Dourbie with fine views from the terraced pitches.
➲ *4km N of Nant, towards Millau off D591.*
15 May-15 Sep 6.5HEC ⬛ ⌕ ⌂ ⬛ ⍲ ✕ ⊙ ⬚ ⌀ ⛱ ⌇ PR
⊞ ⊞ lau

NAUCELLE AVEYRON

Lac de Bonnefon ☎ 565470067
A peaceful site in a wooded location beside a lake with good modern facilities and well marked pitches.
➲ *NW of N88. Signposted.*
Jun-Sep 2.5HEC ⬛ ⌕ ⌂ ⍲ ✕ ⊙ ⬚ ⛱ ⌇ P ⊞ ⊞ lau ✦ ⬛ ⌀ ⛱
Prices: pitch 60 (incl 2 persons)

NAYRAC, LE AVEYRON

CM La Planque ☎ 565444450
In an ideal situation on the Viadène plateau between the Lot valley and the Aubrac mountains.
➲ *1.4km S via D97 beside the lake.*
Jul-Aug 4.6HEC ⬛ ✦ ⌂ ⊙ ⬚ ⌇ LR ⊞ lau ✦ ⬛ ✕ ⌇P

NÉBOUZAT PUY-DE-DÔME

Domes Les Quatre routes de Neébouzat ☎ 473871406
A comfortable site with hard-standing for caravans. Advance reservations recommended.
➲ *On D216 towards Orcival.*
15 May-15 Sep 1HEC ⬛ ⌕ ⌂ ⬛ ✕ ⊙ ⬚ ⌀ ⛱ ⬚ ⌇ P ⊞ ⊞
lau ✦ ✕ ⌇R
Prices: pitch 76.50 (incl 2 persons)

NEUVÉGLISE CANTAL

Belvédère du Pont de Lanau ☎ 471235050
➲ *5km S on D921.*
15 Jun-3 Sep 5HEC ⬛ ✦ ⌂ ⬛ ⍲ ✕ ⊙ ⬚ ⌀ ⛱ ⬚ ⌇ P ⊞ ⊞
lau ✦ ⌇LR

OLLIERGUES PUY-DE-DÔME

Chelles ☎ 473955434
➲ *5km from town centre.*
May-Oct 3.5HEC ⬛ ✦ ⌂ ⬛ ⍲ ✕ ⊙ ⬚ ⛱ ⬚ ⌇ P ⊞ ⊞ lau
Prices: pitch 54 (incl 2 persons)

ORCET PUY-DE-DÔME

Clos Auroy r de la Narse ☎ 473842697
Terraced site in a green valley next to a small river.
➲ *From Clermont-Ferrand take A75 towards Montpellier, then exit 5 to Orcet (signposted).*
All year 2.5HEC ⬛ ⌕ ⌂ ⬛ ⍲ ✕ ⊙ ⬚ ⌀ ⛱ ⌇ P ⊞ lau ✦ ✕
⛱ ⌇R
Prices: ⚑10.80-18 pitch 21-35

ORCIVAL PUY-DE-DÔME

Étang de Fléchat ☎ 473658296
A well equipped site in a pleasant location in a volcanic park beside a lake.
➲ *1.5km S via D27, then 2.5km via D74 towards Rochefort-Montagne.*
Jun-19 Sep 3HEC ⬛ ✦ ⌂ ✕ ⊙ ⬚ ⌀ ⛱ ⬚ ⌇ L ⊞ ⊞ ⊞
lau ✦ ⛱

PARAY-SOUS-BRIAILLES ALLIER

CM Le Moulin du Pré ☎ 470450514
A small municipal site beside the river.
➲ *N via D142.*
Etr-Sep 1.5HEC ⬛ ⌕ ⌂ ⊙ ⬚ ⌇ R ⊞ lau ✦ ⬛ ✕ ⌀ ⛱ ⊞
Prices: ⚑6.70 pitch 5.35

POLLIONNAY RHÔNE

Col de la Luère Col de la Luère ☎ 478458111
Situated in the Monts du Lyonnais, 20 minutes from Lyon.
All year 5HEC ⬛ ✦ ⌂ ⬛ ⍲ ✕ ⊙ ⬚ ⌀ ⛱ ⬚ ⌇ P ⊞ ⊞ ⌗
lau

PONT-DE-SALARS AVEYRON

Lac ☎ 565468486
A terraced site on the shore of a 200hect lake with good water sports facilities.
➲ *1.5km N via D523.*
15 Jun-15 Sep 5HEC ⬛ ✦ ⌂ ⬛ ⍲ ✕ ⊙ ⬚ ⌀ ⛱ ⬚ ⌇ LP ⊞
⊞ ⌗ lau
Prices: pitch 78-96 (incl 2 persons)

Terrasses du Lac rte du Vibal ☎ 565468818
Pleasant lake-side site with terraced pitches overlooking the Pont-de-Salars lake.
➲ *4km N via D523.*
15 Jun-15 Sep 6HEC ⬛ ✦ ⌂ ⬛ ⍲ ✕ ⊙ ⬚ ⌀ ⛱ ⬚ ⍭ ⌇
LP ⊞ lau
Prices: pitch 65-95 (incl 2 persons)

PONTGIBAUD PUY-DE-DÔME

CM rte de la Miouze ☎ 473889699
In a wooded area beside the River Sioule.
➲ 0.5km SW via D986 towards Rochefort-Montagne.
15 Apr-15 Oct 3.5HEC ⊞ ⚘ ⌂ ⊙ 🚿 🍴 🛒 ⤚ R 🅿 ⊞ lau ➧ 🛒 🍴 ✕ ⊘ ⚓
Prices: ⚑12 pitch 16

PRADEAUX, LES PUY-DE-DÔME

Châteaux la Grange Fort ☎ 473710593
Parklike area surrounding an old château on the bank of the River Allier.
➲ From A75 take exit 13 for Parentignat, then take D999. Signposted.
Mar-Oct 25HEC ⊞ ⋮⋮ ⚘ ⌂ ✕ ⊙ 🚿 ⊘ 🛒 ▲ ⤚ PR 🅿 ⊞ lau ➧ 🛒

PUY, LE HAUTE-LOIRE

CM Bouthezard ☎ 471095509
On a wooded meadow with a section reserved for motor caravans.
➲ From the town centre follow sign for Clermont-Ferrand; at traffic lights by church of St-Laurent, turn right following 'camping' signpost, site is 500m on left of road.
Apr-15 Oct 1HEC ⊞ ⚘ ⌂ ⊙ 🚿 ⊞ lau ➧ 🛒 ✕ ⊘ ⚓ ⤚P ⊞

At BLAVOZY(9km E)

Moulin de Barette ☎ 471030088
A pleasant site situated in woodland beside a picturesque stream.
➲ Access via D156 off N88.
Etr-Nov 1HEC ⊞ ⚘ ⌂ 🛒 ✕ ⊙ 🚿 ⊘ 🛒 ⤚ PR 🅿 lau
Prices: ⚑20 pitch 25

At BRIVES-CHARENSAC(4.5km E)

Audinet ☎ 471091018
➲ E on N88.
May-Oct 3HEC ⊞ ⚘ ⌂ 🛒 ⊙ 🚿 ⊘ ⚓ 🛒 ⤚ R 🅿 ⊞ lau ➧ 🍴 ✕ ⤚LPR

RIOM-ÈS-MONTAGNES CANTAL

Sédour rte de Condat ☎ 471780571
In a pleasant situation beside the River Véronne.
➲ Access via D678.
May-Sep ⊞ ⚘ ⌂ ⊙ 🚿 ⤚ R 🅿 lau ➧ 🛒 🍴 ✕ ⊘ ⚓ ⤚LP ⊞

RIVIÈRE-SUR-TARN AVEYRON

Peyrelade rte des Gorges-du-Tarn ☎ 565626254
In wooded surroundings close to the Gorges du Tarn.
➲ 2km E via D907, beside the River Tarn.
Etr-15 Sep 4HEC ⊞ ♦ ⌂ 🛒 🍴 ✕ ⊙ 🚿 ⊘ ⚓ 🛒 ⤚ PR 🅿 ⊞ lau

RODEZ AVEYRON

CM Layoule ☎ 565670952
Clean, tidy site in valley below town, completely divided into pitches.
➲ NE of town centre. Well signposted.
Jun-Sep 3HEC ⊞ ⋮⋮ ⚘ ⌂ ⊙ 🚿 🛒 🅿 ⊞ lau ➧ 🛒 🍴 ✕ ⊘ ⚓

ROYAT PUY-DE-DÔME

CM de l'Oclède rte de Gravenoire ☎ 473359705
Apr-Oct 7HEC ⊞ ⋮⋮ ♦ ⌂ 🛒 🍴 ✕ ⊙ 🚿 ⊘ ⚓ 🛒 🅿 lau ➧ ✕

RUYNES-EN-MARGERIDE CANTAL

CM Petit Bois ☎ 471234226
A pleasant, well equipped, parklike site on the bank of the River Charente.

➲ 0.5km SW on D13, rte de Garabit. Signposted.
May-Oct 7HEC ⊞ ♦ ⌂ ⊙ 🚿 🛒 ⤚ ⊞ lau ➧ 🛒 🍴 ✕ ⊘ ⚓ ⤚P
Prices: ⚑10·♦10 🚐10 ▲10

SAIGNES CANTAL

Bellevue ☎ 471406840
A pleasant rural site in the Sumène Valley.
Jul-Aug 0.9HEC ⊞ ⚘ ⌂ ⊙ 🚿 🛒 lau ➧ 🛒 🍴 ✕ ⊘ ⚓ ⤚P ⊞
Prices: ⚑10.50 pitch 6.40

ST-ALBAN-SUR-LIMAGNOLE LOZÈRE

Galier ☎ 466315880
Well equipped site beside the river.
➲ Access via A75 exit 34.
Mar-Nov 4HEC ⊞ ⚘ ⌂ 🛒 ✕ ⊙ 🚿 ⊘ ⚓ 🛒 ⤚ PR 🅿 ⊞ lau ➧ 🛒 ✕
Prices: pitch 51-63 (incl 2 persons)

ST-AMANT-ROCHE-SAVINE PUY-DE-DÔME

CM Saviloisirs ☎ 73957360
Run by the local tourist authoriry with plenty of sporting facilities within easy reach.
May-Sep 1.5HEC ⊞ ⚘ ⌂ ⊙ 🚿 ⚓ 🛒 🅿 ⊞ lau ➧ 🛒 🍴 ✕ ⤚R
Prices: ⚑15 ♦8 🚐10-15 ▲6

ST-BONNET-TRONÇAIS ALLIER

Champ-Fossé ☎ 470061130
In the Forest of Tronçais beside a lake with plenty of recreational facilities.
➲ Access via A71-E11.
Apr-Sep 35HEC ⊞ ⚘ 🛒 🍴 ⊙ 🚿 ⊘ 🛒 ⤚ L ⊞ lau
Prices: ⚑12.20-14.30 pitch 6.10-7.10

ST-CLÉMENT-DE-VALORGUE PUY-DE-DÔME

Narcisses ☎ 473954576
In a beautiful natural setting within the Livradois Forez national park area.
Jun-15 Sep 1.3HEC ⊞ ⚘ ⌂ 🛒 🍴 ⊙ 🚿 🛒 ⤚ R 🅿 ⊞ lau ➧ 🍴
Prices: ⚑13 pitch 17

ST-GAL-SUR-SIOULE PUY-DE-DÔME

Pont de St-Gal ☎ 473974471
➲ E via D16 towards Ebreuil, beside the River Sioule.
May-15 Sep 1HEC ⊞ ♦ ⌂ 🛒 🍴 ✕ ⊙ 🚿 ⊘ ⚓ 🛒 ⤚ R 🅿 ⊞ lau

ST-GENIEZ-D'OLT AVEYRON

Marmotel ☎ 565704651
Grassy family site on River Lot with a wide variety of recreational facilities.
➲ On D19 about 1km NW of St Geniez-d'Olt.
10 Jun-10 Sep 4HEC ⊞ ♦ ⌂ 🍴 ✕ ⊙ 🚿 ⊘ ⤚ PR 🅿 ⊞ lau ➧ 🛒 ⤚L
Prices: pitch 115 (incl 2 persons)

ST-GERMAIN-DE-CALBERTE LOZÈRE

Garde ☎ 466459482
In a pleasant situation on the edge of the Cevennes National Park.
➲ Access via A7 or A75.
15 Apr-Sep 1HEC ⊞ ⚘ ⌂ 🛒 ⤚ P ⊞ lau ➧ 🛒 🍴 ✕ ⊘ ⚓ ⤚R
Prices: pitch 65-90 (incl 2 persons)

ST-GÉRONS CANTAL

Presqu'île d'Espinet ☎ 471622890
On a wooded peninsula jutting into the lake with fine views of the Cantal mountains.

⊃ *8.5km SE, 300m from Lake St-Étienne-Cantalès.*
15 May-15 Sep 3HEC ⱶⱶ 🜨 🏕 🜨 🏕 ✕ ⊙ 🍴 🛒 🚐 🜨 LP 🏕
🏕 lau ➡ 🜨L
Prices: 🏕15 pitch 46

ST-GERVAIS-D'AUVERGNE PUY-DE-DÔME

CM de l'Étang Philippe rte de St-Eloy-les-Mines
🛒 473857484
A small municipal site beside a small lake.
⊃ *Access via N987.*
Etr-30 Sep 5HEC ⱶⱶ 🏕 🏕 ⊙ 🍴 🚐 🜨 L 🏕 lau ➡ 🜨 🍴 ✕
Prices: 🏕8 pitch 53

ST-HIPPOLYTE AVEYRON

CM La Rivière 🛒 565661450
A small site in wooded surroundings with good sporting facilities.
⊃ *Access via D904.*
15 Jun-15 Sep 0.9HEC ⱶⱶ 🏕 🏕 ⊙ 🍴 🚐 🜨 PR 🏕 lau ➡
🍴 ✕ 🛒

ST-JACQUES-DES-BLATS CANTAL

CM rte de la Gare 🛒 471470590
A small site on the banks of the River Cère. A good centre for exploring the surrounding Volcanic Park area.
Jun-Sep 1HEC ⱶⱶ 🜨 🏕 ⊙ 🍴 🜨 R 🏕 lau ➡ 🜨 🍴 ✕

ST-JODARD LOIRE

CM 🛒 477634242
May-Sep 0.3HEC ⱶⱶ 🏕 🏕 ⊙ 🍴 🜨 P 🏕 lau ➡ 🜨 🍴 ✕ 🛒
Prices: 🏕9.60 pitch 4.80

ST-JUST CANTAL

CM 🛒 471737257
In the centre of the village beside the river.
Apr-30Sep 2HEC ⱶⱶ 🜨 🏕 ⊙ 🍴 🛒 🚐 🜨 P 🏕 lau ➡ 🜨 🍴
✕ 🛒 🛒 🜨R
Prices: 🏕11 🛒7 🚐10 🏕10

ST-MARTIN-VALMEROUX CANTAL

Moulin du Teinturier rte de Loupiac 🛒 471694312
Wooded valley site close to medieval market town.
⊃ *Off D922 Aurillac-Mauriac.*
May-Oct 5HEC ⱶⱶ 🜨 🏕 ⊙ 🍴 🚐 🜨 R 🏕 lau ➡ 🜨 🍴 ✕ 🛒
🜨R 🏕

ST-NECTAIRE PUY-DE-DÔME

Oasis rte des Granges 🛒 473885268
In wooded surroundings by a river within the Auvergne Natural Volcanic Park.
⊃ *On R146, 400 mtrs from R996.*
15 Apr-30 Sept 2HEC ⱶⱶ 🏕 🏕 ⊙ 🍴 🜨 🛒 🚐 🜨 R 🏕 lau ➡
🜨 🍴 ✕
Prices: 🏕15-17 pitch 12.50-15

ST-OURS PUY-DE-DÔME

Bel-Air 🛒 473887214
⊃ *1km SW on D941.*
Jun-Aug 2HEC ⱶⱶ 🏕 🏕 🍴 ⊙ 🍴 🛒 🏕 🏕 lau ➡ ✕ 🜨
Prices: 🏕11 🛒6 🚐7 🏕7

ST-PAL-EN-CHALENÇON HAUTE-LOIRE

CM Ste-Reine chemin des Sources 🛒 471613387
Apr-Oct 0.8HEC ⱶⱶ 🜨 🏕 ⊙ 🍴 🜨 P 🏕 lau ➡ 🜨 🍴 ✕ 🛒 🛒 🏕

ST-PIERRE-COLAMINE PUY-DE-DÔME

Ombrage 🛒 473967787
A pleasant site in peaceful wooded surroundings at an altitude of 800 metres on the edge of the Auvergne Volcano

Park. All the usual services are provided and there are good recreational facilities.
⊃ *300m from D978.*
All year 2HEC ⱶⱶ 🏕 🏕 🜨 ⊙ 🍴 🜨 🛒 🚐 🜨 P 🏕 🏕 lau
➡ 🍴 ✕ 🜨R
Prices: 🏕19 pitch 15

ST-RÉMY-SUR-DUROLLE PUY-DE-DÔME

CM Chanterelles 🛒 473943171
In pleasant wooded surroundings close to the lake.
⊃ *3km via D201*
May-Sep 6HEC ⱶⱶ 🏕 🏕 ⊙ 🍴 🜨 🏕 🏕 lau ➡ 🜨 🍴 ✕ 🛒 🜨LP
Prices: 🏕15 🛒7.50 🚐9.50 🏕7.50

ST-ROME-DE-TARN AVEYRON

Cascade 🛒 565625659
Terraced site beside the River Tarn.
⊃ *0.3km N via D993.*
Apr-Sep 4HEC ⱶⱶ 🜨 🏕 🜨 🍴 ⊙ 🍴 🜨 🛒 🚐 🜨 LP 🏕 lau
➡ 🏕

ST-SALVADOU AVEYRON

Muret 🛒 565818069
A modern site in peaceful, rural surroundings beside the lake.
⊃ *3km SE.*
27 Jun-Aug 3HEC ⱶⱶ 🏕 🏕 🜨 🍴 ✕ ⊙ 🍴 🜨 🜨 L 🏕 🏕 lau
➡ 🜨
Prices: 🏕13 pitch 45

STE-CATHERINE RHÔNE

CM du Châtelard 🛒 478818060
A quiet, well equipped site providing magnificent views over the surrounding countryside.
⊃ *2km S.*
Mar-Nov 4HEC ⱶⱶ 🜨 🏕 ⊙ 🍴 🏕 🏕 lau ➡ 🜨 🍴 ✕ 🜨 🜨R
Prices: 🏕11 pitch 13

STE-SIGOLÈNE HAUTE-LOIRE

Vaubarlet Vaubarlet 🛒 471666495
In a beautiful wooded valley beside the River Dunières with a variety of supervised family activities.
⊃ *Exit for Ste-Sigolène on D44, then towards Grazac on D43.*
May-Sep 3.5HEC ⱶⱶ 🜨 🏕 🜨 🍴 ✕ ⊙ 🍴 🛒 🏕 🜨 PR 🏕 lau
Prices: pitch 72-80 (incl 2 persons)

SALLES-CURAN AVEYRON

Beau Rivage Lac de Pareloup 🛒 565463332
A terraced site located on the shore of Lac de Pareloup. There are facilities for all kinds of water sports and the site's popularity makes advance booking advisable.
⊃ *3.5km N via D993n and D243.*
Jun-Sep 2HEC ⱶⱶ 🜨 🏕 🜨 🍴 ✕ ⊙ 🍴 🜨 🛒 🚐 🜨 LP 🏕 🏕
lau ➡ 🜨R
Prices: pp30-40

Genêts 🛒 565463534
On the edge of the Papeloup lake.
⊃ *7 km W via D577.*
May-15 Sep 3HEC ⱶⱶ 🜨 🏕 🜨 🍴 ⊙ 🍴 🜨 🛒 🏕 🜨 LP 🏕 🏕 lau
➡ ✕

SEMBADEL-GARE HAUTE-LOIRE

Casses 🛒 471009062
A family site in a rural setting at an altitude of 1000mtrs, 2km from a lake.
⊃ *1km W via D22.*
15 Jun-Sep 2HEC ⱶⱶ 🜨 🏕 ⊙ 🍴 🏕 lau ➡ 🜨 🍴 ✕ 🛒 🜨L

> **Sénergues** Aveyron

Étang du Camp ☎ 565796225
Well equipped site in a wooded setting beside the lake.
➲ *6km SW via D242.*
Jun-15 Oct 3HEC ⊞ 🖙 📞 ⊙ 🖵 ⌀ 🛒 🖵 🖹 🔲 lau
Prices: pitch 70 (incl 2 persons)

> **Serverette** Lozère

CM ☎ 466483036
➲ *0.4km S beside the River Truyère.*
15 Jun-15 Sep 1HEC ⊞ 🖙 📞 ⊙ 🖵 ⁀ R 🖹 lau ➡ 🔜 💪 ✗ 🔲

> **Sévérac-le-château** Aveyron

CM av J-Moulin ☎ 565476482
A quiet, well equipped municipal site close to the town
centre. In a good location for visiting the Gorges du Tarn.
➲ *1.2km S via N9 towards Millau.*
Jun-Sep 1.3HEC ⊞ 🖙 📞 ⊙ 🖵 🖵 lau ➡ 🔜 💪 ✗ ⌀ 🛏 ⁀PR 🔲

> **Sévérac-l'église** Aveyron

Grange de Monteillac Monteillac ☎ 565702100
A family site in a quiet wooded location with good
recreational facilities.
➲ *Access via A75 and N88.*
May-15 Sep 4.5HEC ⊞ 🖙 📞 🖙 💪 💪 ✗ ⊙ 🖵 🛒 🖵 🛏 🅰 ⁀ P 🖹
lau
Prices: pitch 112 (incl 2 persons)

> **Singles** Puy-de-dôme

Moulin de Serre ☎ 473211606
A well equipped site beside the River Burande.
➲ *1.7km S of La Guinguette via D73.*
Apr-Oct 3HEC ⊞ 🖙 📞 💪 💪 ✗ ⊙ 🖵 ⌀ 🛒 🖵 🅰 ⁀ PR 🖹 🔲
lau

> **Thérondels** Aveyron

Source ☎ 565660562
In a beautiful situation beside Lake Sarrans.
mid Jun-mid Sep 4.5HEC ⊞ 🖙 📞 💪 💪 ✗ ⊙ 🖵 ⌀ 🛒 ⁀ LP
🖹 lau
Prices: pitch 65-121 (incl 2 persons)

> **Thizy** Rhône

CM ☎ 474640529
➲ *2km S on D504, rte de Tarare. Access difficult for caravans
(gradient of 18%).*
Jun-1 Sep ⊞ 🖙 📞 ⊙ 🖵 ⌀ 🖵 lau ➡ ✗ ⁀LP

> **Trizac** Cantal

Pioulat ☎ 471786420
15 Jun-15 Sep 4.7HEC ⊞ 🖑 📞 ⊙ 🖵 🛒 ⁀ LR 🖹 lau ➡ 🔜
💪 ✗ ⌀ 🛏 🔲
Prices: 🏕10 🚗7 🚐8 🅰8

> **Truel, le** Aveyron

Prade ☎ 565464146
In rural surroundings beside the River Tarn.
15 Jun-15 Sep 4HEC ⊞ 🖙 📞 ⊙ 🖵 ⌀ 🖵 lau ➡ 🔜 💪 ✗ 🛏
⁀PR

CM r de la Gare ☎ 470069402
Etr-Sep 0.7HEC ⊞ ⁙ 🖙 📞 ⊙ 🖵 ⁀ R 🖹 lau ➡ 🔜 💪 ✗ ⌀ 🛏
🔲

> **Urçay** Allier

> **Varennes-sur-allier** Allier

🏔 **Château de Chazeuil** ☎ 470450010
On well-kept meadow within the château park.
➲ *3km NW on N7.*

15 Apr-14 Oct 1.5HEC ⊞ 🖙 📞 ⊙ 🖵 ⁀ P 🖹 🔲 lau ➡ 🔜 💪 ✗
⌀ ⁀R
Prices: 🏕25-28 pitch 22.50-25

> **Verrières-en-forez** Loire

Ferme Le Soleillant Le Soleillant ☎ 477762273
A small terraced site within the grounds of a farm.
➲ *Access via A47.*
All year 4HEC ⊞ 🖙 📞 💪 ✗ ⊙ 🖵 🛒 🖹 🔲 lau ➡ 💪 ✗ 🛏 ⁀R

> **Vichy** Allier

> At **Bellerive**(3km W)

Acacias r Claude-Decloître ☎ 470323632
Well-managed site, sub-divided into numbered pitches by
hedges. Clean sanitary installations. Library, billiard room.
Water sports are available nearby on lake.
➲ *From Vichy turn left after bridge beside ESSO garage and
follow river for 500m.*
Apr-10 Oct 3HEC ⊞ 🖙 📞 💪 ✗ ⊙ 🖵 ⌀ 🛒 ⁀ LPR 🖹 🔲 lau
➡ 💪 ✗ 🛏

Prices: 🏕14-28 pitch 18-30

Beau Rivage r C-Decloître ☎ 470322685
Neat meadowland with marked out pitches. Well kept
sanitary installations. TV.
➲ *Watch for turning over bridge onto left bank of River Allier.*
May-Sep 1.5HEC ⊞ 🖙 📞 💪 ✗ ⊙ 🖵 ⌀ 🛒 🖵 ⁀ PR 🖹 🔲
lau
Prices: 🏕15-26 pitch 15-26

> **Vic-sur-cère** Cantal

Pommeraie ☎ 471475418
A well equipped family site in a peaceful situation with good
recreational facilities.
➲ *2km SE.*
Apr-Sep 4HEC ⊞ 🖙 📞 💪 ✗ ⊙ 🖵 ⌀ 🛏 🛒 🖵 🅰 ⁀ PR 🖹
🔲 lau
Prices: pitch 75-120 (incl 2 persons)

> **Vielle-brioude** Haute-Loire

Dintillat ☎ 471509336
A terraced site with good modern facilities at an altitude of
500mtrs.
➲ *Access via N102 and D16.*
Apr-Oct 1HEC ⊞ 🖙 📞 💪 ✗ ⊙ 🖵 🖵 🅰 🖹 lau ➡ ⁀RS
Prices: 🏕18 pitch 12

> **Villefort** Lozère

Palhère rte du Mas de la Banque ☎ 466468063
A well equipped, peaceful site on the edge of the Parc
National des Cévennes.
➲ *4km SW via D66 beside the river.*
May-Sep 2HEC ⊞ 🖙 📞 💪 ✗ ⊙ 🖵 ⁀ PR 🖵 🔲 lau
Prices: pitch 52-72 (incl 2 persons)

> **Villefranche-de-panat** Aveyron

Cantarelles Alrance ☎ 565464035
On level grassland by Lac de Villefranche-de-Panat.
➲ *On the D25 about 3km N.*
May-Sep 3.5HEC ⊞ 🖙 📞 💪 ✗ ⊙ 🖵 ⌀ 🛏 🛒 ⁀ L 🖹 🔲 lau
Prices: pitch 80 (incl 2 persons)

> **Villefranche-de-rouergue** Aveyron

Rouergue ☎ 565451624
A comfortable site in a pleasant, shady situation beside the
River Aveyron.
➲ *1.5km SW via D47 rte de Monteils.*
Etr-Sep 2HEC ⊞ 🖙 📞 ⊙ 🖵 🖵 lau ➡ 💪 ✗ ⌀ 🛏 ⁀PR 🔲
Prices: pitch 60-70 (incl 2 persons)

YSSINGEAUX HAUTE-LOIRE

CM Choumouroux ☎ 471655344
➲ *800m S of town off the rte de Puy.*
May-Sep 0.8HEC ⊞⊞⊞ ⚐ ⋒ ⊙ ⊟ ⊡ ⊞ lau ➨ ⚒ ⚏ ✕ ⌀ ⚟ ⚑P

 SOUTH COAST/RIVIERA

Stretching along the Golfe du Lion between the Pyrénées and Provence for 150 miles, the Languedoc-Rousillon region's vast stretches of beautiful sands are backed by a gentle countryside covered in vineyards and dotted with quiet villages. Inland are attractive Roman and medieval towns - Montpellier, Bézier and the splendid Carcassonne. High on the crags of the Corbières are the remarkable medieval castles of the Cathares.
Although away from the sea, the Rhône Valley region is undoubtedly a Mediterranean land - unparalleled sunshine warms this unspoilt countryside of vineyards, pastel villages and cypressus in the valleys, against dramatic backdrops of the Provençal Alps and Cévennés, with tumbling rivers running through spectacular gorges.
South again towards the coast is Provence - a land of blue clear skies, wonderful wines and superb food. The area's many rivers begin in the Alpine foothills, and these flow south and irrigate the rich plains below, filled with wonderful fruit and herbs.
Popular with visitors since the 18th century, the chic coastal resorts of Nice, Cannes and St Tropez are ablaze with palatial hotels and celebrated restaurants, and, in the summer, swarming with holidaymakers - an acknowledgement of the spectacular coastline where the Alps meet the sea. But there is still a quieter hinterland, with ancient villages perched on high peaks, spectacular deep valleys and canyons, fine lakes, and breathtaking views from high corniche roads.
The principality of Monaco, which is 350 acres in extent, is an independent enclave inside France. It consists of three adjacent towns - Monaco, the capital, la Condamine, along the harbour and Monte-Carlo, along the coast immediately to the north. It is a narrow ribbon of coastline backed by the foothills of the Alps Maritime - a wonderful natural ampitheatre overlooking the sea.

⋯⋯⋯⋯⋯⋯⋯⋯⋯

▶ **AGAY** VAR

Agay Soleil rte de Cannes RN 98 ☎ 494820079
A small site in a shady position directly on a sandy beach. The facilities are good and all kinds of watersports are available nearby.
➲ *Between N98 and the sea.*

15 Mar-15 Nov 0.7HEC ⊞⊞⊞ ⠿ ➨ ⋒ ⚏ ✕ ⊙ ⚑ ⌀ ⚟ ⚟ ⚑ S ⚐ ⊞ lau ➨ ⚒
Prices: pitch 168 (incl 3 persons)

🗹 **Estérel** rte de Valescure ☎ 494820328
A pleasant family-site of provincial architecture. There is plenty to entertain all age groups day and evening. Riding and cycling can be enjoyed in the nearby in the surrounding hills and woods.
➲ *3km from Agay-Plage towards Valescure. Nof Agay near the golf course.*
28 Mar-4 Oct 12.5HEC ⊞⊞⊞ ⌀ ⚐ ⋒ ⚒ ⚏ ✕ ⊙ ⚑ ⌀ ⚟ ⚟ ⚑ P ⚐ ⊞ lau
Prices: pitch 135-150 (incl 2 persons)

Rives de l'Agay av du Gratadis ☎ 494820274
A level site below a country road.
➲ *Turn off N98 at Agay beach and continue for 0.5km towards Valescure.*
15 Feb-4 Nov 3HEC ⊞⊞⊞ ⠿ ➨ ⋒ ⚒ ⚏ ✕ ⊙ ⚑ ⌀ ⚟ ⚟ ⚑ PR ⚐ ⊞ lau ➨ ⚑ S

Vallée du Paradis rte du Gratadis ☎ 494821600
On a large meadow and a narrow strip of land between the road and the river.
➲ *500m inland from N98.*
15 Mar-15 Oct 3HEC ⊞⊞⊞ ➨ ⋒ ⚒ ⚏ ✕ ⊙ ⚑ ⌀ ⚟ ⚟ ⚑ R ⚐ ⊞ lau ➨ ⚑ S

▶ **AGDE** HÉRAULT

Escale Rte de la Tamarissière ☎ 467212109
A riverside site, 900m from the sea, with good recreational facilities.
1 Apr-30 Sep 3HEC ⊞⊞⊞ ➨ ⋒ ⚒ ⚏ ✕ ⊙ ⚑ ⚟ ⚑ PRS ⚐ ⊞ lau ➨ ⌀ ⚑ S
Prices: pitch 130-130 (incl 2 persons)

International de l'Hérault rte de la Tamarissière ☎ 467941283
A grassy site on W bank of the River Hérault. There are fine sporting and recreational facilities and free transport is provided to the beach 3km away.
➲ *Take the exit for 'Agde' off autoroute A9, then continue via D13 and D32E.*
Etr-Sep 11HEC ⊞⊞⊞ ➨ ⋒ ⚒ ⚏ ✕ ⊙ ⚑ ⚟ ⚑ Å lau ➨ ⚑RS
Prices: pitch 85-128 (incl 2 persons)

Mer et Soliel rte de Rochelongue ☎ 467942114
A modern, well equipped family site within easy reach of the beach.
15 Mar-6 Nov 6.9HEC ⊞⊞⊞ ⠿ ➨ ⋒ ⚒ ⚏ ✕ ⊙ ⚑ ⌀ ⚟ ⚟ ⚑
Å ⚑ P ⚐ ⊞ lau ➨ ⚑RS
Prices: pitch 55-95 (incl 2 persons)

At ROCHELONGUE-PLAGE(4km S)

Champs Blancs rte de Rochelongue ☎ 467942342
Quiet shady site with hedged pitches and surrounded by
exotic vegetation. Good sporting and entertainment facilities.
➲ *Situated between Agde and Cap d'Agde on route de
Rochelongue.*
Apr-Sep 4HEC ⚏ ♣ ⋔ ⚓ ⚑ ⊙ ☺ ⚏ ⚏ ⋗ P ⚐ ⊞ lau

AIGUES MORTES GARD

Petite Camargue ☎ 466538477
A grassy site lying amongst vineyards on the D62. 3.5 km
from the sea.
➲ *Access via autoroute exit Gallargues in direction of La
Grande Motte.*
24 Apr-19 Sep 13HEC ⚏ ⋮⋮ ⚓ ⋔ ⚓ ⚑ ⚑ ⊙ ☺ ⚏ ⚏ ⋗
P ⚐ ⊞ lau
Prices: pitch 73-176 (incl 2 persons)

AIX-EN-PROVENCE BOUCHES-DU-RHÔNE

Arc en Ciel Pont de Trois Sautets, rte de Nice ☎ 442261428
A pleasant terraced site on both sides of a stream.
➲ *Near motorway exit 3 Sautets on N7 towards Toulon. 3km
SE near Pont des Trois Sautets.*
Apr-Oct 3HEC ♣ ⋔ ⊙ ☺ ⚏ ⚑ ⋗ P ⚐ ⊞ ≋ lau ♣ ⚓ ⚑ ✕ ⚑
Prices: ♣32 pitch 29

Chantecler Val St-André ☎ 442261298
A well equipped family site set out around an old Provençal
country house a short distance from the centre of Aix-en-
Provence.
➲ *Access via A8 exit Val-St-André.*
All year 8HEC ⚏ ♣ ⋔ ⚓ ⚑ ✕ ⊙ ☺ ⚑ ⚏ ⚑ ⚑ ⋗ P ⚐ ⊞ lau

ALET-LES-BAINS AUDE

Val d'Aleth chemin de la Paoulette ☎ 468699040
In picturesque surroundings beneath the ancient ramparts,
on the banks of the River Aude. English owners.
➲ *From Carcassonne take D118 towards Quillan. Site 8km
beyond Limoux.*
All year 0.5HEC ⚏ ♣ ⋔ ⚓ ⊙ ☺ ⚑ ⚑ ⚑ ⚑ ⚐ ⋗ R ⚐ ⊞ lau
♣ ⚑ ✕ ⋗P
Prices: pitch 54 (incl 2 persons)

ALLÈGRE GARD

Domaine des Fumades ☎ 466248078
On sloping meadow near the river. Extensive leisure facilities.
Liable to flooding at certain times.
➲ *Turn off D7 (Bourgot-les-Allrègre) at TOTAL filling station
and follow signs.*
15 May-15 Sep 15HEC ⚓ ⚓ ⋔ ⚓ ⚑ ✕ ⊙ ☺ ⚑ ⚑ ⚑ ⋗ PR ⚐
⊞ lau

ANDUZE GARD

Arche ☎ 466617408
In a beautiful situation on the River Gard with fine views of
the surrounding Cevennes scenery.
➲ *Access via A7 exit Bollène and D907.*
29 Mar-Sep 10HEC ⚏ ⋮⋮ ⚓ ⋔ ⚓ ⚑ ✕ ⊙ ☺ ⚑ ⚑ ⚑ ⋗ R
⚐ ⊞ lau
Prices: pitch 55-89 (incl 2 persons)

Castel Rose 610 chemin de Recoulin ☎ 466619005
A well equipped site on the banks of the River Gardon.
➲ *1 km NW on D907.*
15 Mar-Oct 6.5HEC ⚏ ⋮⋮ ♣ ⋔ ⚓ ⚑ ✕ ⊙ ☺ ⚑ ⚑ ⋗ R lau ♣ ⚓
⚑ ⚑

At ATTUECH(5km SE on D907)

Fief ☎ 466618171
On level meadow, divided by flowerbeds and shrubs.
➲ *Turn off D982 E of Attuech and continue for 400m on
partially rough track.*
Etr & Jun-Sep 4.5HEC ⚏ ⚓ ⋔ ⚓ ⚑ ✕ ⊙ ☺ ⚑ ⚑ ⚑ ⚑ ⋗ P ⚐
⊞ lau ♣ ⋗R

At CORBÈS(5km NW on D907)

Cévennes Provence ☎ 466617310
Situated in a valley bordered by two rivers and offering a
choice of pitches in varying levels of shade and terrain.
➲ *Near railway station.*
20 Mar-Oct 30HEC ⚏ ♣ ⋔ ⚓ ⚑ ✕ ⊙ ☺ ⚑ ⚑ ⚑ ⚑ ⚑ ⋗ R ⚐
⊞ lau
Prices: pitch 59.50-85 (incl 2 persons)

ANTHÉOR-PLAGE VAR

Azur Rivage RN 98 ☎ 494448312
Well-equipped site only a few metres from the sea and a
sandy beach.
Etr-Sep 1HEC ⚏ ♣ ⋔ ⚓ ⚑ ✕ ⊙ ☺ ⚑ ⚑ ⚑ ⋗ PS ⚐ ⚑ ⊞
lau
Prices: pitch 900-1400 (incl 3 persons)

Viaduc bd des Lucioles ☎ 494448231
A quiet site 150m from a sandy beach, with good facilities.
➲ *Access via N98.*
Etr-Sep 1.1HEC ⚏ ♣ ⋔ ⊙ ☺ ⚑ ⚐ ⊞ lau ♣ ⚓ ⚑ ✕ ⚑ ⋗S
Prices: pitch 145 (incl 3 persons)

ANTIBES ALPES-MARITIMES

Logis de la Brague 1221 rte de Nice ☎ 493335472
On a level meadow beside a small river.
➲ *On N7.*
2 May-Sep 1.7HEC ⚏ ⚓ ⋔ ⚓ ⚑ ✕ ⊙ ☺ ⚑ ⚑ ⋗ R ⚐ ⊞ lau ♣
⚑ ⋗S
Prices: pitch 65-110 (incl 2 persons)

At BIOT(7km N on N7 and A8)

Airotel Parc l'Eden chemin du Val-de-Pome ☎ 493656370
Site on level meadowland, no tents allowed.
➲ *On D4.*
Apr-Oct 2.5HEC ⚏ ♣ ⋔ ⚓ ⚑ ✕ ⊙ ☺ ⚑ ⚑ ⚑ ⋗ P ⚐ ⊞ lau ♣
⚑ ⋗S

Prés Quartier la Romaine ☎ 493656106
➲ *2km SE via D4*
15 May-25 Sep 11.8HEC ⚏ ♣ ⋔ ⊙ ☺ ⚑ ⚐ ⊞ lau ♣ ⚓ ⚑ ✕ ⚑
⋗S

At Brague, la(4km N on N7)

Frênes ☎ 493333652
➲ *Opposite Biot railway station.*
15 Jun-15 Sep 2.5HEC ⸾⸾⸾⸾ ♦ ⋔ ⛟ 🛒 🍴 ✕ ⊙ 🚻 ⌀ 🚐 🚫 ⚡ S 🏪
⊞ lau

Pylône av du Pylone ☎ 493335286
In an ideal location between Cannes and Nice, the Pylône is a family site with good facilities.
➲ *From N7 take D4 for Biot. First turning on left.*
All year 16HEC ⸾⸾⸾⸾ ♦ ⋔ ⛟ 🛒 🍴 ✕ ⊙ 🚻 ⌀ 🚐 🚫 ⚡ P 🏪 ⊞
♒ lau ♦ ⚡S
Prices: ⋏25-35 pitch 20-25

Arcs, les Var

Eau Vive Quartier du Pont d'Argens ☎ 494474066
Camping Card Compulsory.
➲ *2km S on N7.*
Mar-Nov 2.5HEC ⸾⸾⸾⸾ ♦ ⋔ 🛒 🍴 ✕ ⊙ 🚻 ⌀ 🚐 🚫 ⚡ PR 🏪 ⊞ lau ♦
🛒 ⌀ ♒

Argelès-sur-mer Pyrénées-orientales

Criques de Porteils rte de Collioure ☎ 468811273
Terraced site with beautiful view of sea.
➲ *4km S on N114 turn left through railway underpass and continue for 0.3km.*
Apr-Sep 5HEC ⸾⸾⸾⸾ 🄰 ⋔ 🛒 🍴 ✕ ⊙ 🚻 ⌀ ⚡ S 🏪 ⊞ lau

Dauphin rte de Taxo d'Avall ☎ 468811754
On a long stretch of grassland shaded by poplars, 1500m from sea.
➲ *3km N of town; at Taxo d'Avall turn right onto unclass road.*
25 May-Sep 5.5HEC ⸾⸾⸾⸾ ♦ ⋔ 🛒 🍴 ✕ ⊙ 🚻 ⌀ 🚐 ⚡ P 🏪 🄿 ⊞
lau ♦ ⚡RS
Prices: pitch 112-140 (incl 2 persons)

Galets rte de Taxo d'Avall ☎ 468810812
A well equipped family site with trees, bushes and exotic plants.
➲ *4km N*
21 Mar-8 Nov 5HEC ⸾⸾⸾⸾ 🄰 ⋔ 🛒 🍴 ✕ ⊙ 🚻 ⌀ 🚐 ⚡ P 🏪 ⊞
lau ♦ ⌀ ⚡S

Marsouins chemin du Tamariguer ☎ 468811481
A large family site with good facilities.
➲ *2km NE towards Plage Nord.*
5 Apr-Sep 10HEC ⸾⸾⸾⸾ ♦ ⋔ 🛒 🍴 ✕ ⊙ 🚻 ⌀ 🚐 🚫 ⚡ P 🏪 ⊞
lau ♦ ⚡S
Prices: pitch 75-138 (incl 2 persons)

Massane ☎ 468810685
Well laid-out site in shady garden 1km from sea.
➲ *Beside D618 near the municipal sports field.*
15 Mar-15 Oct 3.5HEC ⸾⸾⸾⸾ ⸾⸾⸾ 🄰 ♦ ⋔ 🛒 🍴 ⊙ 🚻 ⌀ 🚐 🚫
⚡ P 🏪 ⊞ lau ♦ 🛒 🍴 ✕ ⚡S
Prices: ⋏25 pitch 115

Neptune Plage Nord ☎ 468810298
Flat site with both sunny and shady pitches 350mtrs from the northern beach. Modern sanitary facilities. Water-slide. Separate car park for arrivals after 23.00 hrs.
May- 15 Sep 4HEC ⸾⸾⸾⸾ ♒ 🄰 ♦ ⋔ 🛒 🍴 ✕ ⊙ 🚻 ⌀ 🚐 ⚡ P
🏪 ⊞ lau ♦ ⌀ ⚡LS
Prices: pitch 145-169 (incl 2 persons)

Ombrages av du Général-de-Gaulle ☎ 468812983
In a picturesque wooded setting, 300mtrs from the beach. A well equipped site with good recreational facilities and clearly defined pitches.
Jun-Sep 4HEC ⸾⸾⸾⸾ ♦ ⋔ ⊙ 🚻 ⌀ 🚐 🚫 🏪 lau ♦ 🛒 🍴 ✕ ♒
⚡LPRS ⊞
Prices: pitch 75-100 (incl 2 persons)

Pujol rte du Tamariguer ☎ 468810025
Set amid rich vegetation with a wide variety of recreational facilities.
➲ *1km from the beach and 500m from the village.*
Jun-Sep 4.5HEC ⸾⸾⸾⸾ ♦ ⋔ 🛒 🍴 ✕ ⊙ 🚻 ⌀ 🚐 🚫 ⚡ P 🏪 ⊞ lau ♦
⚡S
Prices: pitch 110-130 (incl 2 persons)

CM Roussillonnais bd de la Mer ☎ 468811042
On a long stretch of sandy terrain adjoining a fine sandy beach.
➲ *In N part of town. Well signposted.*
mid Apr-mid Oct 10HEC ⸾⸾⸾⸾ ⸾⸾⸾ 🄰 ⋔ 🛒 🍴 ✕ ⊙ 🚻 ⌀ 🚐 🚫
⚡ S 🏪 ⊞ lau

Sirène rte de Taxo d'Avall ☎ 468810461
A well appointed family site with good facilities in a delightful wooded setting.
➲ *4km NE.*
Apr-26 Sep 17HEC ⸾⸾⸾⸾ ♦ ⋔ 🛒 🍴 ✕ ⊙ 🚻 ⌀ 🚐 🚫 ⚡ P 🏪
🄿 ⊞ lau ♦ ⚡S
Prices: pitch 120-205

At Argelès-plage(2.5km E via D618)

Pins Av du Tech, BP 46 ☎ 468811046
A peaceful family site situated on a narrow stretch of grassland with some poplar trees.
15 May-21 Sep 4HEC ⸾⸾⸾⸾ ♦ ⋔ ✕ ⊙ 🚻 ⌀ 🚐 🏪 lau ♦ 🛒 ⌀ 🍴
⚡PS
Prices: pitch 72-117 (incl 2 persons)

Soleil rte du Littoral, Plage Nord ☎ 468811448
Peaceful site in wide meadow surrounded by tall trees. Private beach, natural harbour. Best site in region, but pitches must be booked in advance.
➲ *Follow rte du Littoral N out of town then 1.5km towards beach.*
15 Sep-Sep 16HEC ⸾⸾⸾⸾ ♦ ⋔ 🛒 🍴 ✕ ⊙ 🚻 ⌀ 🚐 🚫 ⚡ PRS
🏪 ⊞ ♒
Prices: ⋏32-40 pitch 45-57

Arles Bouches-du-rhône

Rosiers Pont de Crau ☎ 490960212
On level ground, shaded by bushes.
➲ *Access via autoroute exit 'Arles Sud' or N443.*
15 Mar-30 Oct 3.8HEC ⸾⸾⸾⸾ 🄰 ⋔ 🛒 🍴 ✕ ⊙ 🚻 🚐 🚫 ⚡ P 🏪
⊞ lau ♦ 🍴
Prices: ⋏18 🚐5 🚫18 ⛺18

Arles-sur-tech Pyrénées-orientales

Riuferrer ☎ 468391106
Quiet holiday site on gently sloping ground in pleasant area. Clean sanitary installations. Separate area reserved for overnight stops. Bar, ice for iceboxes and nearby municipal swimming pool are available in summer only.
➲ *Signposted from N115.*
All year 4HEC ⸾⸾⸾ 🄰 ♦ ⋔ 🍴 ⊙ 🚻 ⌀ 🚐 🚫 ⚡ R 🏪 ⊞ lau
♦ 🛒 ✕
Prices: ⋏17-23 pitch 19-22

Arpaillargues Gard

Mas de Rey rte d'Anduze ☎ 466221827
In quiet wooded surroundings with pitches divided by trees and bushes. There are good facilities for sports and modern sanitary arrangements.
➲ *3km from Uzès towards Anduze.*
Apr-15 Oct 3HEC ⸾⸾⸾⸾ 🄰 ⋔ 🛒 🍴 ✕ ⊙ 🚻 ⌀ 🚐 🚫 ⚡ P 🏪 ⊞
lau
Prices: pitch 74-82 (incl 2 persons)

INTERNATIONAL CAMPING
83630 AUPS (Var)
Route de Fox-Amphoux
Tel: 04.94.70.06.80 & 04.94.70.06.47
Fax: 04.94.70.10.51
Open: 1/4 – 30/9

Family site, 40,000m², 5 min from the town centre and 15 min from the Lake Ste Croix and the Grand Canyon du Verdon. SWIMMING POOL – TENNIS – SHADED – NICE ATMOSPHERE – SOUNDPROOF DISCOTHEQUE – CARAVAN HIRE AND STORAGE. MOBILE HOMES TO LET. RESERVATIONS POSSIBLE

▶ **AUBIGNAN** VAUCLUSE

Intercommunal du Brégoux chemin du Vas ☎ 490626250
A level site with good views of Mt.Ventoux.
➲ *On southern outskirts of town turn off D7 onto D55 and continue towards Caromb for 0.5km.*
15 Mar-Oct 3.5HEC ⊞ ♦ ⋔ ⊙ ⊞ ⊞ ⊞ lau ♦ ⅃ ⊀ × ⊘ ≒
Prices: ♦14.50 pitch 14.50

▶ **AUPS** VAR

International rte de Fox-Amphoux ☎ 494700680
In wooded surroundings with well defined pitches and good recreational facilities. An ideal centre for exploring the magnificent Gorges du Verdon.
➲ *0.5km W via D60 towards Fox-Amphoux*
Apr-Sep 4HEC ⊕ ⋔ ⅃ × ⊙ ⊞ ⊞ ⊞ ⊀ P ⊞ lau ♦ ⅃ × ⊘ ≒ ⊞
Prices: ♦24 pitch 19

▶ **AURIBEAU** ALPES-MARITIMES

Parc des Monges 635 Chemin du Gabre ☎ 493609171
In a wooded setting on the banks of a 1st category fishing river, surrounded by mimosas fields.
➲ *Leave A8 at Mandelieu exit and head towards Grasse.*
20 May-1 Oct 1.4HEC ⊞ ⊕ ⋔ ⅃ × ⊙ ⊞ ⊞ ⊀ PR ⊞ lau ♦ ⅃ ⊘ ≒
Prices: pitch 75-92 (incl 2 persons)

▶ **AVIGNON** VAUCLUSE

Bagatelle Ile de la Barthelasse ☎ 490863039
Pleasant site with tall trees on the Isle of Barthelasse. All pitches are numbered; on hard standing and divided by hedges. Separate section for young people.
➲ *Travel alongside the old town wall and the Rhône onto the Rhône bridge (Nîmes road). About halfway along turn right and follow signs.*
All year 2.2HEC ⊞ ♦ ⋔ ⅃ × ⊙ ⊞ ⊘ ≒ ⊞ ⊞ lau ♦ ⊀P
Prices: ♦17.80-23.80 ⊕6.50-7 ⊞12.50-15 ▲8.50-11

CM Pont St-Bénézet Ile de la Barthelasse ☎ 490826350
On island opposite bridge with fine views of town. Several tiled sanitary blocks with individual wash cabins. Individual pitches. Common room with TV, souvenir shop, car wash. Several playing fields for volleyball and basketball. Definite divisions for tents and caravans.
➲ *NW of the town on the right bank of the Rhône, 370m upstream from bridge on right. (N100 leading to Nîmes).*
Mar-Oct 9HEC ⊞ ♦ ⋔ ⅃ ⅃ × ⊙ ⊞ ⊘ ⊞ ⊞ lau ♦ ⊀P

▶ **AXAT** AUDE

Crémade ☎ 468205064
A shady, peaceful site, ideal for water sports.
May-Sep 4HEC ⊞ ♦ ⋔ ⅃ × ⊙ ⊞ ⊘ ⊞ ⊞ ⊞ ⊞ lau ♦ ⊀R
Prices: pitch 52 (incl 2 persons)

Moulin du Pont d'Alies ☎ 468205327
In a picturesque location at the entrance to the Gorges de la Pierre.
➲ *Junction of D117 and D118, 800m from Axat.*
All year 2HEC ⊞ ♦ ⋔ ⅃ ⅃ × ⊙ ⊞ ⊘ ⊞ ⊀ PR ⊞ ⊞ lau
Prices: ♦18 ⊕10 ⊞49 ▲38

▶ **BANDOL** VAR

Vallongue ☎ 494294955
Terraced site, parts of which have lovely sea views.
Camping Card Compulsory.
Apr-Sep 1.5HEC ⊘ ⊕ ⋔ ⊙ ⊞ ⊞ ⊞ ⊞ lau ♦ ⅃ ⊘ ≒

▶ **BARCARÈS, LE** PYRÉNÉES-ORIENTALES

Bousigues av des Corbières ☎ 468861619
Well equipped family site approx. 1km from the sea. Bar and café etc open July and August only.
➲ *From D83 take exit 10.*
Apr-7 Nov 3HEC ⊞ ♦ ⋔ ⅃ ⅃ × ⊙ ⊞ ⊘ ⊞ ⊀ P ⊞ lau ♦ ⊀S
Prices: pitch 55-112 (incl 2 persons)

California rte de St-Laurent ☎ 468861608
A friendly family site with regular organised entertainment in a pleasant wooded location close to the beach.
➲ *1.5km SW via D90.*
25 Apr-25 Sep 5HEC ⊞ ⠸ ♦ ⋔ ⅃ ⅃ × ⊙ ⊞ ⊘ ≒ ⊞ ⊀ P ⊞ ⊞ lau ♦ ⊀RS
Prices: pitch 52.50-121 (incl 2 persons)

Europe rte de St-Laurent ☎ 468861536
A holiday village type of site with good recreational facilities, 500mtrs from the beach.
➲ *Via D90 2km SW, 200m from Agly.*
All year 6HEC ⊞ ♦ ⋔ ⅃ ⅃ × ⊙ ⊞ ⊘ ≒ ⊞ ⊞ ⊀ P ⊞ lau ♦ ⊀LRS

Presqu'île ☎ 468861280
A well equipped family site on the edge of the Leucate lake and close to the beach.
➲ *2km on rte de Leucate, turn right. Well-kept family site on strip of land between large inlet and the Mediterranean*
28 Mar-3 Nov 3HEC ⊞ ⠸ ♦ ⋔ ⅃ ⅃ × ⊙ ⊞ ⊘ ≒ ⊞ ⊞ LP ⊞ ⊞ lau ♦ × ⊀RS
Prices: pitch 67-110 (incl 2 persons)

Sable d'Or r des Palombes ☎ 468861841
A wooded site situated between the sea and the Lac Marin.
➲ *From Narbonne leave A9 at exit 40 and head towards Grand Plage.*
All year 4HEC ⊞ ♦ ⋔ ⅃ ⅃ × ⊙ ⊞ ⊞ ⊞ ⊀ PS ⊞ lau ♦ ⊘ ⊀L
Prices: pitch 95 (incl 2 persons)

▶ **BAR-SUR-LOUP, LE** ALPES-MARITIMES

Gorges du Loup 965 chemin des Vergers ☎ 493424506
Terraced site divided into pitches, in an olive grove. Very steep entrance.
➲ *Access from Grasse on D2085 towards Le Pré du Lac (NE), then turn left on D2210 in the direction of Vence.*
27 Mar-2 Oct 2HEC ⊞ ♦ ⋔ ⅃ ⅃ × ⊙ ⊞ ⊘ ⊞ ⊀ P ⊞ lau ♦ ⊀R
Prices: pitch 90-145 (incl 2 persons)

BEAUCHASTEL ARDÈCHE

CM Voiliers ☎ 475622404
In a wooded location beside the River Rhône with good recreational facilities.
➲ *1km E, 900m S of N86.*
Apr-Oct 1.5HEC ⸻ ♣ ♠ ⚶ ✕ ⊙ ▣ ↯ P ⊞ lau ♦ ⊘ ↯R
Prices: ↟18 pitch 14.50

BELGENTIER VAR

Tomasses Quartier les Tomasses ☎ 494489270
➲ *1.5km SE towards Toulon. Leave autoroute A6 at exit 'St-Maximin' and continue via D554.*
Apr-Sep 2.3HEC ⸻ ⚲ ♠ ▙ ⚶ ✕ ⊙ ▣ ⊘ ≕ ▣ ↯ PR ⊞ lau

BOISSERON HÉRAULT

Boisseron Domaine de Gajan ☎ 466809430
Mar-Oct 3HEC ♣ ♠ ▙ ⚶ ✕ ⊙ ▣ ⊘ ≕ ⊟ ▣ ↯ P ⊞ lau ♦ ↯R

BOISSON GARD

Château de Boisson ☎ 466248221
A peaceful, well equipped site in the beautiful Cevennes region. Painting, bridge and cookery courses are available.
Camping Card Compulsory.
➲ *D7 in direction Fumades. Boisson is 10km on the right and the campsite is signposted.*
May-Sep 7.5HEC ⸻ ⚲ ♠ ▙ ⚶ ✕ ⊙ ▣ ⊘ ⊟ ▣ ↯ P ⊞ ⊞ ⊘ lau
Prices: ↟26-35 pitch 45-55

BOLLÈNE VAUCLUSE

Barry Lieu Dit St-Pierre ☎ 490301320
Well-kept site near ruins of Barry troglodite village.
➲ *Signposted from Bollène via D26.*
All year 3HEC ⸻ ♣ ♠ ▙ ⚶ ✕ ⊙ ▣ ⊘ ≕ ▣ ↯ P ⊞ lau ♦ ↯LR
Prices: ↟20-27 pitch 26-33

Simioune Quartier Guffiage ☎ 490304462
In pleasant wooded surroundings close to the River Rhône
➲ *From A7 follow signs for Carpentras, at 3rd x-roads turn left towards Lambisque, then follow signposts to site.*
All year 1.5HEC ⠿ ♣ ♠ ⚶ ✕ ⊙ ▣ ⊘ ▣ ↯ P ⊞ lau
Prices: ↟20 pitch 20

BORMES-LES-MIMOSAS VAR

Clau Mar Jo 895 chemin de Benat ☎ 494715339
A well shaded site 1200mtrs from the sea with good facilities.
➲ *Access via N98, then D298.*
Apr-Sep 1HEC ⸻ ♣ ♠ ⊙ ▣ ▣ ⊞ lau ♦ ▙ ⚶ ✕ ⊘ ≕

Manjastre 150 Chemin des Girolles ☎ 494710328
A peaceful site 6km from the Mediterranean beaches.
➲ *5km NW via N98 on road to La Môle/Cogolin.*
All year 8HEC ⸻ ♣ ♠ ▙ ⚶ ⊙ ▣ ⊘ ↯ P ⊞ ⊞ ⊘ lau
Prices: pitch 123 (incl 3 persons)

At FAVIÈRE, LA(3km S)

Domaine ☎ 494710312
In a very attractive setting with a long sandy beach and numbered pitches. Fine views of sea. Sport facilities.
➲ *0.5km E of Bormes-Cap Bénat road.*
26 Mar-Oct 38HEC ⸻ ⠿ ♠ ♣ ♠ ▙ ⚶ ✕ ⊙ ▣ ⊘ ≕ ↯ S ⊞ ⊞ lau
Prices: ↟26-30 ▥80-93 ▲37-47

BOULOU, LE PYRÉNÉES-ORIENTALES

Mas Llinas ☎ 468832546
A family site in wooded surroundings with a good variety of leisure facilities.
➲ *3km N via N9.*
May-Dec 4HEC ⸻ ♣ ⚶ ♠ ▙ ⚶ ✕ ⊙ ▣ ⊟ ▣ ↯ P ⊞ lau ♦ ▙ ✕ ⊘ ↯LS ⊞
Prices: ↟25 pitch 30

BOULOURIS-SUR-MER VAR

Ile d'Or ☎ 494955213
In a quiet location, 50mtrs from a private beach with well equipped pitches.
➲ *E off N98.*
Mar-Oct 10HEC ⸻ ⚲ ♠ ▙ ⚶ ✕ ⊙ ▣ ⊘ ≕ ⊟ ▣ ↯ S ⊞ ⊞ lau
Prices: pitch 135 (incl 2 persons)

Val Fleury RN 98 ☎ 494952152
Terraced site with tarred drives set amongst pines and mimosas close to the beach.
➲ *Off N98 at Km 93.1.*
All year 1HEC ⸻ ♠ ⚶ ✕ ⊙ ▣ ▣ ↯ lau ♦ ▙ ⊘ ↯PS
Prices: pitch 120-220 (incl 4 persons)

BOURDEAUX DRÔME

At POËT-CÉLARD, LE(3km NW)

Couspeau Quartier Bellevue ☎ 475533014
In a beautiful natural setting with well maintained facilities.
➲ *1.3km SE via D328A.*
May-25 Sep 3HEC ⸻ ♣ ♠ ▙ ⚶ ✕ ⊙ ▣ ⊘ ⊟ ↯ P ⊞ lau
Prices: ↟72-110

BOURG-MADAME PYRÉNÉES-ORIENTALES

Ségre 8 av du Puymorens ☎ 468046587
➲ *100m N on N20.*
Closed Oct 1HEC ⸻ ♣ ♠ ⊙ ▣ ▣ ↯ R ⊞ lau ♦ ▙ ⚶ ⊘ ≕ ↯PR
BOURG-ST-ANDÉOL ARDÈCHE

Lion ☎ 475545320
Large well-shaped park in wooded terrain, beside River Rhône.
➲ *N86 in direction of Viviers, through the centre of town.*
Apr-15 Sep 8HEC ⸻ ♣ ♠ ▙ ⚶ ✕ ⊙ ▣ ⊘ ▣ ↯ PR ⊞ lau
Prices: pitch 57-82 (incl 2 persons)

BRISSAC HÉRAULT

Val d'Hérault St-Étienne d'Issensac ☎ 467737229
A terraced site in a quiet location. Bar and restaurant facilities available July and August only.
➲ *4km S via D4.*
15 Mar-30 Oct 3.4HEC ⠿ ♠ ♣ ♠ ▙ ⚶ ✕ ⊙ ▣ ⊘ ≕ ▣ ↯ R ⊞ lau ♦ ⊞

BROUSSES-ET-VILLARET AUDE

Martinet Rouge ☎ 468265198
A pleasant, well equipped site on gently sloping terrain. Terraced, with well marked pitches.
➲ *Access via D48.*
Apr-Oct 2.8HEC ⸻ ♣ ♠ ▙ ⚶ ✕ ⊙ ▣ ⊘ ⊟ ▣ ↯ P ⊞ lau ♦ ↯R
Prices: pitch 30 (incl 2 persons)

CADENET VAUCLUSE

Val de Durance Les Routes ☎ 490683775
A well equipped family site on the shore of a lake and close to the River Durance.
Contd.

LE TODOS ★★★

meeting point for the European youth. Vallon des Vaux
(Val Fleuri), 06800 Cagnes sur Mer
N8 exit Cagnes sur Mer. Follow N7 direction Nice. Follow arrows

- free swimming pool on site
- a very beautiful site with typical, shady vegetation of the Mediterranean Sea.
- Pitches 'great comfort' (water, waste, electr.)
- Caravans, mobile homes, bungalows and chalets with heating to let.
- Reservations recommended.
- **A large part of the site has been reserved for the young people with dance-evenings and meals with special prices for young people.**
- Restaurant, pizzeria.
- Volleyball, table tennis and French boules.
- Tennis 300m.
- Green Park planned for 1997.
- **Open: 1.2 - 31.10**
- **Tel: 04.93.31.20.05 Fax: 04.92.12.81.66**

CAMPING – CARAVANNING
"LA RIVIERE" ★★NN

06800 Cagnes sur Mer Chemin des Salles
(via Val de Cagnes, dir. Haut de Cagnes)
Tel/Fax: 04.93.20.62.27
A shady, flat, quiet site.
We offer, among other things grocery
shop, restaurant, bar, free swimming pool
and rent of caravans. Reservation of a
pitch is possible. Small sanitary block.
Cabin for disabled.

3 Apr-10 Oct 3.5HEC ⬛ ⚐ 🏕 🍴 ✕ ⊙ 🚫 🏪 🛈 Å ⤓ LP ⊞
lau
Prices: ↟23-29 pitch 25-39

CAGNES-SUR-MER ALPES-MARITIMES

Colombier 35 chemin de Ste-Colombe ☎ 493731277
Well equipped site in a wooded location 2km from the sea.
Apr-Sep 0.5HEC ⬛ ♣ 🏕 🍴 ✕ ⊙ 🚫 🏪 ⤓ P ⊞ lau ♣ 🛈 ✕ 🏕
Prices: ↟12-19 pitch 46-151

Green Park 159 Vallon-des-Vaux ☎ 493312005
A modern site with well defined pitches in pleasant wooded
surroundings with good recreational facilities.
➲ From A8 exit Cagnes-sur-Mer take N7 towards Nice.
May-Oct 3HEC ⬛ ⚐ 🏕 ⊙ 🚫 🏪 🛈 ⊞ lau ♣ 🛈 🍴 ✕ ⤓ P
Prices: ↟19 pitch 59-178

Rivière 168 chemin des Salles ☎ 493206227
In secluded wooded surroundings with good, modern
facilities.
➲ 4km N beside River Cagne.
All year 1.2HEC ⬛ ♣ 🏕 🍴 ✕ ⊙ 🚫 🏪 🏪 ⤓ PR ⊞
lau
Prices: pitch 71 (incl 2 persons)

Todos 159 Vallon des Vaux ☎ 493312005
In a beautiful Mediterranean setting. Exceptionally shady
with a mixture of flat and terraced sites. Evening
entertainment. Use of car park compulsory after 11pm.
➲ Access via N7 towards Nice.
Feb-Oct 6HEC ⬛ ♣ 🏕 🍴 ✕ ⊙ 🚫 🏪 🏪 ⤓ P ⊞ ⊞ ⊞
lau
Prices: ↟19 🏕75-178 Å59-156

At CROS-DE-CAGNES(2km S)

Panoramer 30 chemin des Gros Buaux ☎ 493311615
Pleasant terraced site with sea view. Separate sections for
tents and caravans.
➲ 2km N of town.
Mar-30 Oct 1.4HEC ⬛ ♣ 🏕 🍴 ✕ ⊙ 🚫 🏪 ⤓ P ⊞ lau
Prices: pitch 70-125

CAMURAC AUDE

Sapins ☎ 468203811
In a picturesque, wooded location on the edge of a forest
with excellent views of the surrounding mountains.
➲ 1.5km from village.
Apr-Oct 3HEC ⬛ ♣ 🏕 🍴 ✕ ⊙ 🚫 🏪 🛈 Å ⤓ P ⊞ lau ♣ 🛈
🏕 ⤓L
Prices: ↟19.50 🏕11 🏕11 Å11

CANET-PLAGE PYRÉNÉES-ORIENTALES

Domino r des Palmiers ☎ 468802725
In a wooded location 150mtrs from the sea.
Apr-Sep 6.8HEC ⬛ ♣ 🏕 🍴 ✕ ⊙ 🚫 🏪 🛈 ⊞ 🔀 lau ♣ 🛈
🏕 ⤓PRS
Prices: ↟20-26 🏕78 Å30-48

At CANET-VILLAGE(2km W)

Brasilia Voie de la Crouste, Zone Technique du Port
☎ 468802382
Near beach. Divided into pitches which are surrounded by
bushes and flowerbeds.
➲ Turn off main road in village and continue towards beach
for 2km.
Apr-Sep 15HEC ⬛ ♣ 🏕 🛈 🍴 ✕ ⊙ 🚫 🛈 🏪 🏪 ⤓ PRS ⊞
lau
Prices: pitch 80-150 (incl 2 persons)

Peupliers Voie de la Crouste ☎ 468803587
Quiet, level site divided into pitches by hedges with a variety
of leisure facilities. Reservations recommended for July and
August.
Jun-Sep 4HEC ⬛ ♣ 🏕 🛈 🍴 ✕ ⊙ 🚫 🏪 🏪 ⤓ P ⊞ 🏪 ⊞ lau ♣ 🛈
🏕 ⤓S
Prices: pitch 40-68 (incl 2 persons)

Ma Prairie rte de St-Nazaire ☎ 468732617
Grassland site in a hollow surrounded by vineyards.
➲ Access from D11 in the direction of Elne off N617
Perpignan-Canet-Plage road.
10 May-20 Sep 4.5HEC ⬛ ♣ 🏕 🛈 🍴 ✕ ⊙ 🚫 🏪 🏕 🏪 ⤓ P ⊞
⊞ lau
Prices: pitch 78-125 (incl 2 persons)

CANNES ALPES-MARITIMES

At CANNET, LE

Grand Saule 24 bd J-Moulin ☎ 493905510
Separate sections for families and groups of young people. 5
mins to beach in peaceful surroundings with fine views and a
variety of sports and leisure activities.
➲ Access via A8 towards Ranguin.
Apr-Sept 1HEC ⬛ ♣ 🏕 🍴 ✕ ⊙ 🚫 🏪 ⤓ P ⊞ lau ♣ 🛈
🏕 ⤓S
Prices: ↟89-127 🏕19

Ranch chemin St-Joseph, L'Aubarède ☎ 493460011
On a wooded hillside 2km from the local beaches with good
facilities.
➲ Access via A8 exit 41 & 42.
Apr-30 Oct 2HEC ⬚ ⚐ 🏕 🛈 ⊙ 🚫 🏪 🏪 ⤓ P ⊞ lau ♣
✕ ⤓S

CARCASSONNE AUDE

Breil d'Aude Le Breil D'Aude, rte de Limoux ☎ 468268818
In a wooded location beside a private lake where free fishing is allowed.
➲ *1.5km N via D118.*
Etr-Sep 10HEC ▥ ♦ ↑ ⚎ ♈ ✕ ☉ ◘ ∅ ⌂ ▲ ⁘ LPR 🕿 ⊞
lau
Prices: pitch 80-985 (incl 2 persons)

At PENNAUTIER(4km NW off N113)

Lavandières N113 ☎ 468254166
Apr-Oct 1HEC ▥ ♦ ↑ ⚎ ♈ ✕ ☉ ◘ 🕿 ⊞ lau ➜ ⚎ ∅ ≝ ⁘LPR

CARPENTRAS VAUCLUSE

Lou Comtadou 881 av P-de-Coubertin ☎ 490670316
Near the Carpentras swimming pool in pleasant surroundings with good, modern facilities.
28 Mar-2 Nov 2HEC ▥ ♦ ↑ ⚎ ♈ ✕ ☉ ◘ ∅ ⌂ ▲ ⁘ P 🕿 ⊞ lau ➜ ≝
Prices: ♠18-22 ⚎55-52 ▲27-29

CARQUEIRANNE VAR

⚑Beau-Vezé rte de la Moutonne ☎ 494576530
In a beautiful wooded park with good, modern facilities.
➲ *2.5km NW via N559 and then D76 between Hyères and Toulon.*
Jun-15 Sep 7HEC ▥ ♦ ↑ ⚎ ♈ ✕ ☉ ◘ ∅ ≝ ⌂ ⚐ ⁘ P 🕿 ⊞ lau

CASTELLANE ALPES-DE-HAUTE-PROVENCE

International rte Napoléon ☎ 492836667
Family site at the foot of the Col des Lèques and close to the Gorges du Verdon.
➲ *1km from the centre of the village. Signposted.*
15 Mar-15 Oct 6HEC ▥ ◈ ↑ ⚎ ♈ ✕ ☉ ◘ ∅ ≝ ⌂ ⚐ ⁘ P 🕿 lau ➜ ⁘R ⊞
Prices: ♠40-50

Nôtre Dame rte des Gorges du Verdon ☎ 492836302
In meadowland with deciduous and fruit trees.
➲ *200m W on D952.*
Apr-15 Oct 0.6HEC ▥ ♦ ↑ ⚎ ♈ ✕ ☉ ◘ ∅ ⌂ ⚐ 🕿 ⊞ lau ➜ ✕ ≝ ⁘PR
Prices: pitch 57 (incl 2 persons)

⚑Verdon Domain de la Salaou ☎ 492836129
Well-maintained site on meadowland on banks of River Verdon. Divided into pitches. Rooms in rustic style. Reservations recommended Jul-Aug.
➲ *Below the D952 towards the Gorges du Verdon.*
15 May-15 Sep 14HEC ▥ ♦ ↑ ⚎ ♈ ✕ ☉ ◘ ∅ ⌂ ⚐ ⁘ P 🕿 ⊞ lau
Prices: pitch 250-500 (incl 4 persons)

At CHASTEUIL(9km W on D952)

Gorges du Verdon Clos d'Arémus ☎ 492836364
Situated on bank of the Verdon, surrounded by mountains and at an altitude of 660 metres. Fully divided into pitches split into two by road. Bathing in river not advised due to strong current.
➲ *0.5km S of village.*
May-15 Sep 7HEC ▥ ∅ ♦ ↑ ⚎ ♈ ✕ ☉ ◘ ∅ ⌂ ⚐ ⁘ PR 🕿 ⊞ lau
Prices: pitch 60-110 (incl 3 persons)

At GARDE-CASTELLANE(7.5km SE)

Clavet rte de Grasse Napoleon ☎ 492836896
Terraced site on wooded grassland with mountain views.

➲ *On Grasse road beyond La Garde.*
15 May-15 Sep 7HEC ▥ ⊿ ↑ ⚎ ♈ ✕ ☉ ◘ ∅ ≝ ⌂ ⚐ ▲ ⁘ P 🕿 lau

CAVAILLON VAUCLUSE

Durance Digue des Grands Jardins ☎ 490711178
Situated in a shaded area with a wide variety of recreational facilities.
➲ *2km S.*
All year 4HEC ▥ ⊿ ♦ ↑ ☉ ◘ ⌂ ⚐ 🕿 ⊞ lau ➜ ⚎ ♈ ✕ ∅

CAVALAIRE-SUR-MER VAR

Cros de Mouton ☎ 494641087
Terraced site with individual pitches, separated for caravans and tents. Good view of sea, 1.5km distance.
➲ *Turn off N559 in town centre and continue inland for 1.5km.*
15 Mar-Oct 5HEC ⊿ ♦ ↑ ⚎ ♈ ✕ ☉ ◘ ∅ ⌂ ⚐ ⁘ P 🕿 lau ➜ ⁘S
Prices: ♠30-36 pitch 30-36

Pinède Chemin des Mannes ☎ 494641114
A family site with well defined pitches, 500mtrs from the sea.
➲ *300mtrs from the centre of the village.*
15 Mar-15 Oct 2HEC ▥ ♦ ↑ ⚎ ♈ ◘ ∅ ⌂ 🕿 ⊞ lau ➜ ⚎ ♈ ✕ ≝ ⁘S
Prices: pitch 105 (incl 2 persons)

Roux r Pardigon ☎ 494640547
A family site in a pine wood 800mtrs from the sea.
➲ *N of main coast road.*
23 Mar-30 Sep 5HEC ▥ ♦ ↑ ⚎ ♈ ✕ ☉ ◘ ∅ ⌂ 🕿 ⊞ lau ➜ ⁘S

CENDRAS GARD

Croix Clémentine ☎ 466865269
An extensive, partly terraced site, in wooded surroundings.
➲ *Signposted W of town towards La Baume via D160.*
Apr-20 Sep 12HEC ▥ ♦ ↑ ⚎ ♈ ✕ ☉ ◘ ∅ ≝ ⌂ ⚐ ⁘ P 🕿 ⊞ lau
Prices: ♠25-39 ⚎16-32 ▲32

CHABEUIL DRÔME

Grand Lierne ☎ 475598314
On the edge of the Vercors Regional Park.
➲ *Access via A7 exit 'Valence Sud' towards Chabeuil, then follow signs for site.*
Apr-Sep 4.8HEC ▥ ⊿ ↑ ⚎ ♈ ✕ ☉ ◘ ∅ ≝ ⌂ ⚐ ▲ ⁘ P 🕿 ⊞ ⌾ lau
Prices: ♠30 pitch 35-70

CHAPELLE-EN-VERCORS, LA DRÔME

Bruyères ☎ 475482146
A well appointed municipal site in the centre of the Parc Naturel Régional du Vercors.
All year 1HEC ▥ ⊿ ↑ ☉ ◘ ⚐ ▲ 🕿 ⊞ ➜ ⚎ ♈ ✕ ∅ ≝ ⁘P
Prices: ♠20 ⚎8 ⚎8 ▲8

CHARLEVAL BOUCHES-DU-RHÔNE

Orée des Bois av du Bois ☎ 442284175
Spacious, well shaded pitches. Approx. 500mtrs from the village.
➲ *Access via A7 exit Sénas. From Charleval follow road towards Cazan.*
All year 5HEC ▥ ⠿ ♦ ↑ ☉ ◘ ∅ ⌂ ⚐ 🕿 ⊞ lau ➜ ⚎ ♈ ✕ ≝ ⁘P 🕿
Prices: ♠16-22 pitch 22-30

CHÂTEAU-ARNOUX ALPES-DE-HAUTE-PROVENCE

Salettes ☎ 492640240
Some facilities (shop, café etc) available in summer only.
➲ *1km E beside the river.*
All year 4HEC ⸺ ♣ ⋔ ⅀ ⚍ ✕ ⊙ ◘ ◖ ⚡ P 🅿 ⊞ lau
Prices: ⚑22 pitch 22

CHÂTEAUNEUF-DU-RHÔNE DRÔME

CM ☎ 475908096
➲ *N end of village.*
Jun-Sep 0.6HEC ⸺ ⚐ ⋔ ⊙ ◘ ⚡ P 🅿 ⊞ lau ♦ ⅀ ⅄ ✕ ⚍ ⚌

CHAUZON ARDÈCHE

Digue ☎ 475396357
In a beautiful wooded location with good recreational facilities.
➲ *1km E, 100m from the River Ardèche*
20 Mar-Sep 2HEC ⸺ ♣ ⋔ ⅀ ⚍ ✕ ⊙ ◘ ⚡ ⚐ ⚡ PR 🅿 ⊞ lau
Prices: pitch 77-96 (incl 2 persons)

CIOTAT, LA BOUCHES-DU-RHÔNE

Oliviers rte du Bord de Mer ☎ 442831504
A terraced family site between the N559 and the railway line from Nice.
➲ *Turn inland off the N559 at Km34, some 5km E of the centre of the town and drive for 150m.*
Mar-Sep 10HEC ⸺ ⚐ ⋔ ⅀ ⚍ ✕ ⊙ ◘ ⚡ ⚌ ⚐ ⚡ P 🅿 ⊞ lau ♦ ⚡S
Prices: ⚑28 pitch 35

St Jean 30 av de St-Jean ☎ 442831301
Site on the right side of the coast road in an excellent position with direct access to the beach.
➲ *Between D559 and sea behind the motel in NE part of town.*
27 Mar-1 Oct 9.9HEC ⸺ ♣ ⋔ ⅀ ⅄ ✕ ⊙ ◘ ⚡ ◖ ⚡ 🅿 ⊞ lau ♦ ⚡S
Prices: pitch 85-155

Soleil rte de Cassis ☎ 442715532
A small site, divided into pitches, 1.5km from the beach.
➲ *Access via A50 exit 9 (La Ciotat).*
15 Mar-15 Oct 0.5HEC ⸺ ♣ ⋔ ✕ ⊙ ◘ ⚡ ⚌ 🅿 ⊞ lau ♦ ⅀ ⚡ ⚌ ⚡PS

COGOLIN VAR

Argentière chemin de l'Argentière ☎ 494546363
Landscaped, partly terraced site.
➲ *1500m NW along D48 rte de St-Maur.*
15 Apr-Sep 8HEC ⸺ ♣ ⋔ ⅀ ⅄ ✕ ⊙ ◘ ⚡ ⚌ ⚐ ⚡ P 🅿 ⊞ lau
Prices: ⚑20-22 pitch 88-98

COLLE-SUR-LOUP, LA ALPES-MARITIMES

Castellas rte de Roquefort ☎ 493329705
In a wooded location with direct access to the river.
All year 1.2HEC ⸺ ⚐ ♣ ⋔ ⅀ ✕ ⊙ ◘ ⚡ ⚌ ⚐ ⚡ R 🅿 ⊞ lau
Prices: ⚑17.50-25 pitch 24.50-50

Pinèdes rte du Pont de Pierre ☎ 493329894
Well-kept terraced site on steep slope with woodland providing shade, interesting walks and beautiful views.
➲ *By the motorway A8 exit 'Cagnes-sur-Mer' turn right off D6 towards La Colle-sur-Loup.*
Mar-15 Oct 3.8HEC ⸺ ♣ ⋔ ⅀ ⅄ ✕ ⊙ ◘ ⚡ ⚌ ⚐ ⚡ PR 🅿 ⊞ lau
Prices: ⚑20-25 ⚑⚑11.50-50 ⚑40-50 ▲26-41

Vallon Rouge rte Greolières ☎ 493328612
In a picturesque forested location, close to the river, with good facilities.
➲ *3km W of town, 100m to right of D6 towards Gréolières.*
Apr-Sep 3HEC ⸺ ♣ ⋔ ⅀ ⅄ ✕ ⊙ ◘ ⚡ ⚌ ⚐ ⚡ PR 🅿 ⊞ lau
Prices: pitch 50-95 (incl 2 persons)

COURONNE, LA BOUCHES-DU-RHÔNE

Mas Plage de Ste-Croix, La Couronne ☎ 442807034
A well equipped family site on a plateau with a fine view of the bay, and access to a sandy beach.
➲ *Access from A55, then D49.*
Apr-Sep 6HEC ⸺ ♣ ⋔ ⅀ ⅄ ✕ ⊙ ◘ ⚡ ⚌ ⚡ P 🅿 lau ♦ ⚡S
Prices: ⚑26.20-33 ⚑⚑17.70-22.10 ⚑26.20-33 ▲31.50

CRAU, LA VAR

Bois de Mont-Redon 480 chemin du Mont-Redon ☎ 494667334
Set among oak and pine trees with well defined pitches and plenty of recreational facilities.
➲ *3km NE via D29*
15 Jun-15 Sep 5HEC ⸺ ♣ ⋔ ⅀ ⅄ ✕ ⊙ ◘ ⚡ ⚐ ⚡ P 🅿 ⊞ lau
Prices: pitch 112 (incl 3 persons)

CRESPIAN GARD

🏕 **Mas de Reilhe** ☎ 466778212
In the grounds of a château, surrounded by pine trees with good recreational facilities.
➲ *On N110.*
Jun-Sep 3HEC ⸺ ♣ ⋔ ⅀ ⅄ ✕ ⊙ ◘ ⚡ ⚌ ▲ ⚡ P 🅿 ⊞ lau
Prices: ⚑25-31 pitch 40-50

DIE DRÔME

Pinède Quartier du Pont-Neuf ☎ 475221777
In a picturesque mountain setting beside the River Drôme.
➲ *W via D93 then cross railway line and the river to site.*
25 Apr-15 Sep 5HEC ⸺ ⁝⁝⁝ ♣ ⋔ ⅀ ⅄ ✕ ⊙ ◘ ⚡ ⚌ ⚡ PR 🅿 ⊞ lau ♦ ▲
Prices: ⚑32 pitch 70-117

DIEULEFIT DRÔME

Source du Jabron Jabron ☎ 475906130
A terraced site in a pleasant location beside the River Jabron.
➲ *N of town on D538.*
May-15 Sep 5HEC ⸺ ⚐ ⋔ ⅀ ⅄ ✕ ⊙ ◘ ⚌ ⚡ PR 🅿 lau
Prices: ⚑15-16 ⚑⚑9-10 ⚑17-22

ENTRECHAUX VAUCLUSE

Bon Crouzet rte de St-Marcelin ☎ 490460162
On level ground with modern facilities beside the river.

Camping AUX HAMACS
F-11560 Fleury d'Aude
Tel: 04.68.33.22.22 – Fax: 04.68.33.22.23
A spacious setting by the side of the Aude river. Far from the crowd yet only 1 km from unspoiled beaches (10km). Pizzeria, Latin Bar, night entertainment, Archaeologic excursions.
Open from 1.4 – 31.9.
Access: A9, exit Béziers Ouest.

➲ *From Vaison-la-Romaine exit follow road towards St-Marcelin-les-Vaison for 6km.*
Apr-Oct 1.3HEC ⸺ ⌾ ♠ ⟰ 🕏 ⟀ ✗ ⊙ ⬟ ⬤ ↘ R ▣ ⊞ lau ➡ ✗
Prices: ↟18 pitch 20

▶ **ESPARRON-DE-VERDON** ALPES-DE-HAUTE-PROVENCE

Soleil rte de la Teillière ☎ 492771378
In wooded surroundings beside Lake Esparron with well defined pitches.
Etr-Sep 1.5HEC ⸺ ⬧ ♠ ⟰ 🕏 ⟀ ✗ ⊙ ⬟ ⬤ ⬤ ↘ L ▣ ⊞ ⏿
lau
Prices: ↟25 ⬤34 ▲30

▶ **FLEURY** AUDE

Aux Hamacs Les Cabanes de Fleury ☎ 468332222
A large site beside the River Aude and 1km from the coast.
➲ *Access via A9 exit Béziers, then 15km W.*
Apr-Sep 10HEC ⸺ ⸬ ⸻ ⟰ 🕏 ⟀ ✗ ⊙ ⬟ ⬤ ⬤ ↘ L ▣
lau ➡ ↘S
Prices: pitch 52-135 (incl 3 persons)

▶ **FONTES** HÉRAULT

Clairettes ☎ 467250131
➲ *D9 10km N of Pézenas, access via Adissan D128.*
May-Oct 1.6HEC ⬧ ⌾ ⟰ 🕏 ⟀ ✗ ⊙ ⬟ ⬤ ⛢ ⬤ ⬤ ↘ P ▣ ⊞
lau

▶ **FONTVIEILLE** BOUCHES-DU-RHÔNE

CM Pins r Michelet ☎ 490547869
In a pine wood close to the Moulin d'Alphonse Daudet.
➲ *1km from village via D17.*
Apr-14 Oct 3.5HEC ⸺ ⬧ ♠ ⟰ ⊙ ⬟ ▣ ⊞ lau ➡ 🕏 ⟀ ✗ ⬤ ⛢
↘P
Prices: pitch 60 (incl 3 persons)

▶ **FOS-SUR-MER** BOUCHES-DU-RHÔNE

Estagnon Plage St-Gervais ☎ 442050119
Level, rather dusty site. Public beach on other side of road.
Camping Card Compulsory.
➲ *Situated S of an industrial zone-Quartier St-Gervais.*
May-Sep 2HEC ⸺ ⌾ ⟰ 🕏 ⟀ ✗ ⊙ ⬟ ⬤ ⬤ ⬤ ↘ S ▣ ⊞ lau

▶ **FRÉJUS** VAR

Dattier rte de Bagnols-en-Forêt ☎ 494408893
Laid out in terraces among typically Mediterranean vegetation this compact family site is well maintained and has good recreational facilities.
➲ *Access from A8 via RN7, then D4.*
Etr-Sep 4HEC ⸺ ♠ ⟰ 🕏 ⟀ ✗ ⊙ ⬟ ⬤ ⬤ ↘ P ▣ ⊞ lau

Domaine de Colombier rte de Bagnols ☎ 494515601
Widespread site on hill on some individual terraces under pine trees. Good recreational facilities.
➲ *Turn N off N7 onto D4 towards Bagnols and continue for 500m. Access also via A8 exit 38.*
30 Mar-Sep 10HEC ⸺ ♠ ⟰ 🕏 ⟀ ✗ ⊙ ⬟ ⬤ ⬤ ⬤ ↘ P ▣ ⊞
lau
Prices: pitch 120-197 (incl 2 persons)

See advertisement under Colour Section

Fréjus rte de Bagnols ☎ 494199460
Well equipped site in wooded surroundings.
➲ *Access via D4.*
15 Dec-15 Jan 4HEC ⸺ ⌾ ⟰ 🕏 ⟀ ✗ ⊙ ⬟ ⬤ ⬤ ⛢ ⬤ ⬤ ▲ ↘ P ▣
▣ ⊞ lau
Prices: ↟25-32 pitch 36-45

Holiday Green rte de Bagnols-en-Forêt ☎ 494408820
➲ *6km N via D4.*
3 Apr-23 Oct 15HEC ⸺ ♠ ⟰ 🕏 ⟀ ✗ ⊙ ⬟ ⬤ ⬤ ⬤ ↘ PS ▣
⊞ lau
Prices: ↟28-40 pitch 45.50-110

Montourey Quartier Montourey ☎ 494532641
Comfortable, well equipped site within 10 minutes of the beach.
➲ *2km N.*
Apr-Sep 5HEC ⸺ ⌾ ⟰ 🕏 ⟀ ✗ ⊙ ⬟ ⬤ ⬤ ⛢ ⬤ ↘ P ▣ ⊞ lau ➡
↘R
Prices: ↟26 pitch 98

Pierre Verte rte de Bagnols ☎ 494408830
A large family site in a pine forest 8km from the coast.
➲ *Access on A8 from Puget-sur-Argens.*
Apr-Oct 28HEC ⸺ ⬧ ♠ ⟰ 🕏 ⟀ ✗ ⊙ ⬟ ⬤ ⬤ ⛢ ⬤ ↘ P ▣ ⊞
lau
Prices: pitch 96 (incl 2 persons)

Pins Parasols rte de Bagnols-en-Forêt ☎ 494408843
A modern family site shaded by oaks and pines with spacious, well defined pitches and good recreational facilities.
➲ *4km N via D4.*
Etr-Sep 4.5HEC ⸺ ⌾ ⟰ 🕏 ⟀ ✗ ⊙ ⬟ ⬤ ⬤ ↘ P ▣ ⊞ lau ➡ ⛢
Prices: pitch 129 (incl 2 persons) pp34

▶ **FRONTIGNAN** HÉRAULT

Soleil ☎ 467430202
Family site bordering the beach.
➲ *NE via D60.*
May-Sep 1.5HEC ⸺ ⌾ ⟰ 🕏 ⟀ ✗ ⊙ ⬟ ⛢ ⬤ ⬤ ↘ PS ▣ ▣ ⊞
lau

Tamaris av d'Ingril ☎ 467434477
A family site on level ground with direct access to the beach. Good recreational facilities.
➲ *From N112 take D129 and D60/D50 for 6km.*
20 May-22 Sep 4.5HEC ⸬ ⌾ ⟰ 🕏 ⟀ ✗ ⊙ ⬟ ⬤ ⬤ ⬤ ↘ PS
▣ ⊞ lau
Prices: pitch 100-180 (incl 2 persons)

▶ **GALLARGUES-LE-MONTUEUX** GARD

Amandiers ☎ 466352802
A family site with good facilities in a beautiful wooded situation.
➲ *Along N113 heading away from Lunel towards Nîmes.*
May-12 Sep 3HEC ⸺ ⌾ ⟰ 🕏 ⟀ ✗ ⊙ ⬟ ⬤ ⛢ ⬤ ⬤ ▲ ↘ P ▣
lau ➡ ✗ ⛢ ↘R
Prices: pitch 75 (incl 2 persons)

‣ **GALLICIAN** GARD

Mourgues ☎ 466733088
Situated in an old vineyard with some vines retained to separate pitches. Views overlooking the Camargue.
➲ *On the N572 between St-Gilles and Vauvert at the junction with the road to Gallician.*
Apr-15 Sep 2HEC ⊷ ♨ 🏕 🏠 🖪 🍴 ⊙ 🚻 🛒 ♩ P 🅿 ⊞ lau ♦ 🛒 🍴 ✕
Prices: pitch 66 (incl 2 persons)

‣ **GASSIN** VAR

Moulin de Verdagne ☎ 494797821
Flat grassy site with a family atmosphere 4km from the beach.
➲ *SE of town towards the coast.*
Dec 5HEC ⊷ 🏠 🖪 🍴 ✕ ⊙ 🚻 🛒 🚿 ♩ P 🅿 ⊞ lau
Prices: pitch 89 (incl 2 persons)

Parc St-James Gassin rte du Bourrian ☎ 494552020
Park-like site on slopes of a hill.
➲ *2.5km E of N559. Access from main road at Km84.5 and 84.9 on D89.*
Closed 15 Nov-15 Dec 32HEC ⊷ ♦ 🏠 🖪 🍴 ✕ ⊙ 🚻 🚿 ♩ P 🅿 ⊞ lau

See advertisement under Colour Section

‣ **GAUJAC** GARD

Domaine de Gaujac Boisset ☎ 466605390
A family site in wooded surroundings on the banks of a river.
➲ *Access via D910.*
Apr-Sep 10HEC ⊷ ♦ 🏠 🖪 🍴 🍴 ✕ ⊙ 🚻 🚿 🛒 ♩ P 🅿 ⊞ lau ♦ ♩R
Prices: pitch 86 (incl 2 persons)

‣ **GIENS** VAR

Mediterranée-Les Cigales Quartier du Pousset, bd Alsace-Lorraine ☎ 494582106
A well-kept site with numbered pitches. Special places for caravans.
➲ *0.3km E of D97.*
Etr-Sep 1.5HEC ⊷ ♦ 🏠 🖪 🍴 ✕ ⊙ 🚻 🛒 🚿 ♩ A 🅿 lau ♦ 🚿 ♩S
Prices: pitch 68-133 (incl 2 persons)

‣ **GILETTE** ALPES-MARITIMES

Moulin Noù rte de Carros ☎ 493089240
In wooded surroundings between the sea and the mountains with good recreational facilities.
➲ *On the D2209, 1.8km SW of the Pont-Charles-Albert*
6 Apr-25 Sep 3HEC ⊷ 🏠 🖪 🍴 ✕ ⊙ 🚻 🚿 ♩ PR 🅿 lau

‣ **GRANDE-MOTTE, LA** HÉRAULT

Garden 44 pl des Tamaris ☎ 467565009
Completely divided into pitches separated by hedges and surrounded by a wall. 0.3km from beach.
➲ *Access from D62. Site by crossroads towards Palavas/Grand Travers.*
Mar-Oct 3HEC ⊷ ✂ ♦ 🏠 🖪 🍴 ✕ ⊙ 🚻 🚿 ♩ P 🅿 lau ♦ ♩S

Lou Gardian 603 allée de la Petite Motte ☎ 467561414
A well run site with well defined pitches, 0.5km from the beach. Advisable to book in advance in high season.
Etr-12 Oct 2.6HEC ⊷ ♦ 🏠 🖪 ✕ ⊙ 🚻 🅿 ⊞ lau ♦ 🚿 ♩LPS

Lous Pibols ☎ 467565008
Well-organised. Divided into level pitches.
➲ *W on D59, 0.4km from sea.*
Apr-Sep 3HEC ✂ ♦ 🏠 🖪 ⊙ 🚻 🚿 🚻 🛒 ♩ P 🅿 ⊞ lau ♦ ♩S

‣ **GRASSE** ALPES-MARITIMES

Paoute 160 rte de Cannes ☎ 493091142
A family site in a wooded location close to the town centre.
➲ *S of town centre, E of the Cannes road just beyond the Centre Commercial.*
Jun-Sep 3HEC ⊷ ♦ 🏠 🖪 🍴 ✕ ⊙ 🚻 🚿 🚻 🛒 ♩ P 🅿 🅿 ⊞ lau

‣ At **OPIO**(8km E via D2085 & D3)

Caravan Inn 18 rte de Cannes ☎ 493773200
A well equipped site in a wooded location between the sea and the mountains
➲ *1.5km S of Opio on D3.*
Jun-15 Sep 5HEC ⊷ ♦ 🏠 🖪 🍴 ✕ ⊙ 🚻 🚿 🚻 🛒 ♩ P 🅿 ⊞ lau ♦ 🛒
Prices: pitch 97-166 (incl 2 persons)

‣ **GRAU-DE-VENDRES** HÉRAULT

Foulègues ☎ 467373365
Camping Card Compulsory.
➲ *Signposted.*
Jun-Sep 4HEC ⊷ ✂ 🏠 🖪 🍴 ✕ ⊙ 🚻 🚿 🚻 🛒 ♩ PRS 🅿 ⊞ lau

‣ **GRAU-DU-ROI, LE** GARD

Abri de Camargue rte du Phare de l'Espiguette, Port Camargue ☎ 466515483
A pleasant site near the beach on the edge of the Camargue with well-marked pitches and modern installations.
➲ *2.5km S on L'Espiguette road.*
Apr-Oct 4HEC ⊷ ♦ 🏠 🖪 🍴 ✕ ⊙ 🚻 🚿 🚻 🛒 ♩ P 🅿 ⊞ lau ♦ ♩S
Prices: pitch 117-252

Bon Séjour ☎ 466514711
Clean, tidy, well-kept site.
➲ *3km E of village off road to lighthouse.*
Apr-Sep 5HEC ⊷ 🏠 🖪 🍴 ✕ ⊙ 🚻 🚿 🚻 🛒 ♩ L 🅿 ⊞ lau

Boucanet ☎ 466514148
Flat sandy site bordering beach.
➲ *3 km NW on D255.*
26 Apr-20 Sep 7.5HEC ✂ ♦ 🏠 🖪 🍴 ✕ ⊙ 🚻 🚿 🚻 A ♩ PS 🅿 ⊞ 🚿 lau

Eden Port-Camargue ☎ 466514981
Quiet site on both sides of access road. 300m from beach.
➲ *On D626 towards Espiguette.*
1 Apr-4 Oct 5.3HEC ⊷ ✂ ♦ 🏠 🖪 🍴 ✕ ⊙ 🚻 🚿 🚻 A ♩ P 🅿 ⊞ lau ♦ 🚿 ♩LS
Prices: pitch 90-199 (incl 2 persons)

Elysée Résidence 980 rte de l'Espiguette ☎ 466535400
Large family site on the edge of the Camargue with a good variety of sporting and entertainment facilities.
➲ *Access via A9.*
21 Mar-3 Oct 32HEC ✂ ♦ 🏠 🖪 🍴 ✕ ⊙ 🚻 🚿 🚻 🛒 ♩ LPS 🅿 ⊞ lau ♦ ♩S ⊞
Prices: pitch 50-150 (incl 2 persons)

Jardins de Tivoli rte de l'Éspiguette ☎ 466539700
A modern site with well marked pitches in a wooded setting 600mtrs from the baech. There are good recreational facilities including mountain bike hire.
➲ *Access via A9 continuing SE through Le Grau-du-Roi.*

Apr-Sep 7HEC [symbols] P [symbols] lau ♦
S
Prices: pitch 120-150 (incl 2 persons)

Mouettes av Jean-Jaurès ☎ 466514400
On level ground, shaded by olive and poplar trees, this site is well equipped and the beach is only 500mtrs away.
➲ 1.2km SE.
Apr-Sep 1HEC [symbols] lau ♦ [symbols]
S
Prices: pitch 60-80 (incl 2 persons)

Salonique rte du Phare de l'Espiguette ☎ 466531163
A comfortable family site in woodland with a wide range of recreational facilities. Close to the beach.
25 Apr-26 Sep 3.5HEC [symbols]
P [symbols] lau
Prices: pitch 78-137 (incl 2 persons)

GRIGNAN DRÔME

Truffières Lieu-dit Nachony ☎ 475469362
A family site opposite the Château Grignan with good facilities.
➲ Leave A7 at exit Montélimar Sud and follow N7 E.
Apr-Sep 2HEC [symbols] P [symbols] lau
♦ [symbols]
Prices: pitch 70-85 (incl 2 persons)

GRIMAUD VAR
At PORT-GRIMAUD(4km E)

Plage RN 98 ☎ 494563115
Wide area of land on both sides of road beside sea. Partly terraced and divided into pitches.
➲ N on N98.
15 Mar-Sep 18HEC [symbols] S [symbols]
lau
Prices: pitch 105 (incl 2 persons)

HYÈRES VAR
At AYGUADE-CEINTURON(4km SE)

Ceinturon II ☎ 494663966
A popular site on level meadowland divided into pitches. 300yds from the sea. Some individual washing cubicles.
➲ 4km SE of Hyères on D42.
Jun-Aug 4.8HEC [symbols] lau ♦ [symbols] PS
Prices: ♦24.20 pitch 25.70-34.70

Ceinturon III L'Ayguade ☎ 494663265
Well-kept site in wooded surroundings divided into numbered pitches. Individual washing cubicles.
➲ 4km SE of Hyères on D42.
Apr-Sep 2.8HEC [symbols] lau ♦ [symbols]
RS [symbols]
Prices: ♦27 pitch 34

At HYÈRES-PLAGE(4km SE)

Pins Maritimes 1633 bd de la Marine ☎ 494663357
Situated in a pine wood close to the beach.
➲ Turn off D42 between Hyères-Plage and L'Ayguade and continue inland for 200m.
Apr-Sep 37HEC [symbols] lau ♦ S

ISLE-SUR-LA-SORGUE, L' VAUCLUSE

CM Sorguette rte d'Apt ☎ 490380571
In tranquil wooded surroundings beside the River Sorguette with good sports and entertainment facilities.
➲ Access via N100 towards Apt.
15 Mar-24 Oct 2.5HEC [symbols]
R [symbols] lau
Prices: ♦27 pitch 24

ISTRES BOUCHES-DU-RHÔNE

Vitou 31 rte de St-Chamas ☎ 442565157
In a wooded location with a large area for tents.
➲ N of town on D16.
All year 6.5HEC [symbols] L [symbols] ♦ [symbols]
Prices: pitch 125 (incl 2 persons)

LAGORCE ARDÈCHE

Domaine de Chaussy ☎ 475939966
➲ On D559 near Ruoms.
4 Apr-4 Oct 18.5HEC [symbols] P
[symbols] lau

LAROQUE-DES-ALBÈRES PYRÉNÉES-ORIENTALES

Planes 117 Av du Vallespir, rte de Villelongue dels Monts ☎ 468892136
In a picturesque setting surrounded by trees, bushes and flowers.
➲ Approach via Laroque towards Villelongue-del-Monts.
15 Jun-Aug 2.5HEC [symbols] P [symbols] lau ♦ [symbols]
Prices: ♦18-20 pitch 38-40

LATTES HÉRAULT
See also Montpellier

Lac des Rêves rte de Pérols ☎ 467502600
Pleasant site with individual pitches, alongside a small lake.
➲ On the road between Pérols and Lattes.
15 Apr-15 Sep 33HEC [symbols] P [symbols]
lau ♦ [symbols]

LAURENS HÉRAULT

Oliveraie chemin de Bédarieux ☎ 467902436
Situated in the heart of the Faugères vineyards, this comfortable family site provides clearly marked pitches and a wide variety of sporting facilities.
➲ D909 from Bédarieux. 900m from village centre.
All year 7HEC [symbols] P [symbols]
Prices: pitch 36-120 (incl 2 persons)

LÉZIGNAN-CORBIÈRES AUDE

CM Pinède av Gaston-Bonheur ☎ 468270508
Well-kept terraced site with numbered pitches and tarred drives, decorated with bushes and flower beds. Shop available July and August only.
➲ Signposted from N113.
Mar-Oct 3.8HEC [symbols] P [symbols] lau ♦ [symbols]
Prices: ♦17-20 pitch 35-37

LONDE-LES-MAURES, LA VAR

Forge ☎ 494668265
Level meadow with good sanitary facilities.
Camping Card Compulsory.
➲ Turn off N98 into village, at traffic lights turn N for 1km to site on outskirts of village.
Jun-Sep 1.2HEC [symbols] lau ♦ [symbols]

Moulières ☎ 494015321
Well tended level meadowland in quiet location. 1km from the sea.
Camping Card Compulsory.
➲ On western outskirts towards the coast.
Jun-15 Sep 3HEC [symbols] lau ♦ S

Pansard ☎ 494668322
Beautiful, wide piece of land in a pine forest beside the beach.
➲ Turn off N98. *Contd.*

Facing the Golden Isles in a pine forest right on the seashore, the "CAMPING LE PANSARD" offers you an ideal setting for your Riviera holidays, from 1st April to 30th September and without booking, Its beach, protected environment, possibility for practicing many sports, shopping centre, its bar and its restaurant will make your stay an unforgettable one.

LE PANSARD
Camping-Caravanning ★★★
83250 LA LONDE DES MAURES
Tel: 00 33 494 66 83 22 Fax: 00 33 494 66 56 12

Apr-Sep 6HEC ⬛ ∴ ♠ ⋔ ⅀ ♥ ⅄ ✕ ⊙ ⊟ ⌀ ⌂ ⊞ ⌘ ⅀ S ☎ ✍ lau ♦ ⊞
Prices: pitch 115 (incl 3 persons)

Val Rose ☎ 494668136
In a rural setting at the foot of the Maures mountains, close to a golf course. Well defined pitches and good modern facilities.
➲ *4km NE on N98.*
Mar-Oct 2.4HEC ⬛ ♠ ⋔ ⅀ ♥ ⅄ ✕ ⊙ ⊟ ⌂ ⌘ ⅀ P ☎ ⊞ lau

▶ LUNEL HÉRAULT

Bon Port rte de la Petite Camargue ☎ 467711565
In a pleasant wooded location at the gateway to the Camargue.
➲ *Access via D24.*
Mar-Oct 5HEC ⬛ ♠ ⋔ ⅀ ♥ ⅄ ✕ ⊙ ⊟ ⌀ ⌂ ⌘ ⅀ P ☎ ⊞ lau
Prices: ⁂15-19 pitch 31-38

Mas de l'Isle 85 chemin du Clapas ☎ 467832652
A pleasant site between the Cévennes mountains and the Mediterranean.
➲ *1.5km SE via D34 near junction with the D61.*
1 Apr-30 Sep 3HEC ⬛ ♠ ⋔ ✕ ⊙ ⊟ ⌂ ⌘ ⅀ P ☎ ⊞ lau ♦ ⅂
Prices: ⁂19 ⬟15 ⌘15 ⛺15

▶ MALLEMORT BOUCHES-DU-RHÔNE

Durance et Luberon Domaine du Vergon ☎ 490591336
➲ *2.5 km on D23c, 200m from Canal.*
May-15 Sep 4HEC ⬛ ⅄ ⋔ ⊙ ⊟ ⅀ P ☎ lau ♦ ⌀ ⌂ ⅀R ⊞

▶ MANDELIEU-LA-NAPOULE ALPES-MARITIMES

Cigales 505 av de la Mer ☎ 493492353
A riverside site with well defined pitches, 800mtrs from the sea.
➲ *S on N7.*
All year 2HEC ⬛ ♠ ⋔ ⅄ ⊙ ⊟ ⌂ ⌘ ⅀ PR ☎ ⊞ lau ♦ ⅂ ⌀ ⅀S
Prices: ⁂22.50 ⬟25 ⌘45-120 ⛺30-120

Plateau des Chasses r J-Monnet ☎ 493492593
Terraced land, on hill in a park.
➲ *Turn off N7 at Km 4.2 and continue uphill for 1.2km.*
Apr-Sep 4HEC ⬛ ♠ ⋔ ⅄ ✕ ⊙ ⊟ ⌂ ⌘ ⅀ P ☎ ⊞ lau ♦ ⅂ ⌀ ⅀RS
Prices: pitch 132-165 (incl 4 persons)

▶ MARSEILLAN-PLAGE HÉRAULT

Charlemagne av du Camping ☎ 467219249
200m from the beach in quiet, wooded surroundings with good sanitary and sporting facilities.

➲ *Access via N112 at Marseillan Plage.*
26 Mar-3 Oct 6.6HEC ⬛ ∴ ♠ ⋔ ⅀ ♥ ⅄ ✕ ⊙ ⊟ ⌀ ⌂ ⌘ ⅀ PS ☎ ⊞ lau
Prices: pitch 90-195 (incl 3 persons)

Languedoc-Camping 117 chemin du Pairollet ☎ 467219255
A family site in wooded surroundings with direct access to the beach.
➲ *On the coast road between the Mediterranean and the Bassin de Thau.*
15 Mar-Oct 1.5HEC ⬛ ∴ ♠ ⋔ ⅀ ♥ ⅄ ✕ ⊙ ⊟ ⌂ ⌘ ⅀ S ⊞ lau ♦ ⌀
Prices: pitch 75-145 (incl 2 persons)

Plage 69 chemin du Pairollet ☎ 467219254
A family site with direct access to a sandy beach.
15 Mar-Oct 1.5HEC ∴ ♠ ⋔ ⅄ ✕ ⊙ ⊟ ⌀ ⅀ S ☎ lau ♦ ⅂
Prices: pitch 86-155 (incl 2 persons)

▶ MAUREILLAS PYRÉNÉES-ORIENTALES

Val Roma Park Les Thermas du Boulou ☎ 468831972
➲ *2.5km NE on N9.*
All year 3.5HEC ⬛ ♠ ⋔ ⅀ ♥ ⅄ ✕ ⊙ ⊟ ⌀ ⌂ ⌘ ⅀ PR ☎ ⊞ lau ♦ ⅀L
Prices: pitch 50-72 (incl 2 persons)

▶ MENTON ALPES-MARITIMES

Fleur de Mai 67 rte du Val de Gorbio ☎ 493572236
Terraced site in a peaceful situation by a stream in the heart of the Côte-d'Azur.
➲ *Exit from D23 at the Parc de la Madone.*
Apr-Sep 2HEC ⬛ ♠ ⋔ ⊙ ⊟ ☎ ⌂ ⊞ lau ♦ ⅂ ⅀ ⅄ ✕ ⌀ ⅀PS
Prices: ⁂20 pitch 60-70

▶ MÉOLANS-REVEL ALPES-DE-HAUTE-PROVENCE

Domaine de Loisirs de l'Ubaye ☎ 492810196
A large terraced site in a delightful wooded valley. There is a small lake and direct access to the river and good sporting and recreational facilities.*7km NW of Barcelonnette.*
All year 10HEC ⬛ ♠ ⋔ ⅀ ♥ ⅄ ✕ ⊙ ⊟ ⌂ ⌘ ⅀ LPR ☎ ⊞ lau
Prices: pitch 86 (incl 2 persons)

▶ MÉOUNES-LES-MONTRIEUX VAR

Aux Tonneaux ☎ 494339834
Site in wooded area, divided into pitches.
➲ *200m S of village off N554.*
All year 2.7HEC ⬛ ⅄ ⋔ ✕ ⊙ ⊟ ⌀ ⌂ ⌘ ⅀ PR ☎ ⊞ lau ♦ ⅂ ⅀

▶ MONDRAGON VAUCLUSE

CM La Pinède Quartier Les Massanes ☎ 490408298
➲ *1km SW via N7.*
All year 3HEC ⬛ ∴ ♠ ⋔ ⊙ ⊟ ☎ lau ♦ ⅂ ⅀ ⅄ ✕ ⌀ ⌂ ⊞

▶ MONTBLANC HÉRAULT

Rebau ☎ 467985078
Divided into pitches and surrounded by vineyards.
➲ *From Pézenas follow N113; in La Bégude de Jordy turn off main road and drive 2km on D18 towards Montblanc.*
01/04-30/10 3HEC ⬛ ♠ ⋔ ⅄ ♥ ⊙ ⊟ ⌀ ⌂ ⌘ ⅀ P ☎ ⊞ lau ⅂ ⅀

▶ MONTCLAR AUDE

Au Pin d'Arnauteille Domaine d'Arnauteille ☎ 468268453
In a natural wooded park with fine views of the surrounding mountains.
➲ *2.2km SE via D43*
Apr-Sep 7HEC ⬛ ♠ ⋔ ⅀ ♥ ⅄ ✕ ⊙ ⊟ ⌀ ⌂ ⌘ ⌂ ⅀ P ☎ ⊞ lau
Prices: ⁂18-25 ⬟11-15 ⌘30-32 ⛺30-32

▶ MONTÉLIMAR DRÔME

Deux Saisons Chemin des Alexis ☎ 475018899
A well equipped site on the bank of River Roubion.
⮕ *From town centre follow D540 across Pont de la Libération;
then first turning right into chemin des Alexis.*
Mar-Nov 1.5HEC ⬛ ⚏ ⊙ ⬛ ⬛ ⬛ ⬛ ⬛ ✕ ⊙ ⬛ ⬛ ⬛ ⬛ ⊞ lau ➡
⚏ ⭑P
Prices: ⭑20 ➡10 ⬛20 ⬛20

▶ MONTPELLIER HÉRAULT

See also Lattes

Floréal rte de Palavas ☎ 467929305
On level ground surrounded by vineyards.
⮕ *500m off Autoroute A9, exit Montpellier-Sud. From town
centre follow road for Palavas (D986).*
All year 1.5HEC ⬛ ⬛ ⚏ ⚏ ⊙ ⬛ ⬛ ⬛ ⊞ lau ➡ ✕ ⬛
⚏ ⭑PR
Prices: pitch 75 (incl 2 persons)

▶ MONTPEZAT ALPES-DE-HAUTE-PROVENCE

Coteau de la Marine ☎ 492775333
A pleasant wooded site, providing easy access to the Verdon
Gorges. There are good facilities, especially for boating.
⮕ *Access via D11 and D211.*
May-15 Sep 10HEC ⬛ ⬛ ⚏ ⚏ ✕ ⊙ ⬛ ⬛ ⚏ ⬛ ⬛ ⭑ LPR ⬛
⊞ lau
Prices: pitch 70-145 (incl 3 persons)

▶ MONTRÉAL ARDÈCHE

Moulinage rte des Défilés de Ruoms ☎ 475368620
Well-equipped family site with a variety of bungalows, caravans
and timber chalets. Close to the famous Gorges de l'Ardèche.
Apr-Sep 3.5HEC ⬛ ⚏ ⚏ ✕ ⊙ ⬛ ⬛ ⬛ ⬛ ⬛ ⭑ PR ⬛ ⊞ lau
Prices: ⭑18-22 ➡12

▶ MOURIÈS BOUCHES-DU-RHÔNE

Devenson ☎ 490475201
Terraced site amongst pine and olive trees in Provençal
countryside.
⮕ *Turn off N113 at La Samatane and continue N towards
Mouriès. Site is in N part of village.*
Etr-15 Sep 3.5HEC ⬛ ⬛ ➡ ⚏ ⚏ ⊙ ⬛ ⬛ ⬛ ⬛ ⭑ P ⬛ ⊞ lau ➡
⚏ ✕ ⚏
Prices: ⭑25 ⬛30

▶ MOUSTIERS-STE-MARIE ALPES-DE-HAUTE-PROVENCE

St-Jean rte de Riez ☎ 492746685
Quiet and relaxing site located at the gateway to the Gorges
du Verdon, 5 minutes from Ste-Croix Lake.
⮕ *Access D952.*
1 May-20 Sep 1.6HEC ⬛ ➡ ⚏ ⚏ ⊙ ⬛ ⬛ ⬛ ⭑ R ⬛ ⊞ lau ➡
⚏ ✕ ⚏
Prices: ⭑20 pitch 22

Vieux Colombier Quartier St-Michel ☎ 492746189
A family site near the entrance to the Gorges du Verdon at an
altitude of 630 metres.
⮕ *0.8km S via D952 towards Castellane.*
Apr-Sep 2.7HEC ⬛ ⚏ ⚏ ✕ ⊙ ⬛ ⬛ ⬛ ⬛ ⬛ ⊞ lau ➡ ⚏ ⚏
Prices: ⭑21 ⬛23 ⬛23

▶ MUY, LE VAR

Cigales ☎ 494451208
A family site set among Mediterranean vegetation with excellent
facilities and organised entertainment during the high season.
⮕ *Exit 'Draguignan' off A8 onto N7. 0.8km to site. Well
signposted.*

Apr-Oct 10HEC ⬛ ➡ ⚏ ⚏ ⚏ ✕ ⊙ ⬛ ⬛ ⬛ ⬛ ⭑ P ⬛ lau ➡ ⚏
Prices: ⭑18-30 pitch 18-42

Sellig 41 chemin des Valettes ☎ 494451171
A peaceful family site in a wooded location.
⮕ *1.5km W on N7.*
closed Nov-14 Feb 1.9HEC ⬛ ➡ ⚏ ⚏ ⚏ ✕ ⊙ ⬛ ⬛ ⬛ ⬛ ⭑
P ⬛ ⊞ lau

▶ NANS-LES-PINS VAR

Ste-Baume ☎ 494789268
A pleasant, landscaped site in the heart of the local lavender
region. There are modern sanitary installations and varied
recreational facilities.
⮕ *0.9km N via D80*
May-6 Sep 7HEC ⬛ ➡ ⚏ ⚏ ⚏ ✕ ⊙ ⬛ ⬛ ⬛ ⚏ ⬛ ⬛ ⬛ ⭑ P ⬛ ⊞ lau

▶ NAPOULE, LA ALPES-MARITIMES

Azur-Vacances bd du Bon Puits ☎ 493499112
Site with many long terraces, on edge of mountain slope in
mixed woodland.
⮕ *Turn inland 200m after fork at railway station and
continue 600m.*
Apr-Sep 10HEC ⬛ ➡ ⚏ ⚏ ⚏ ✕ ⊙ ⬛ ⬛ ⬛ ⊞ lau ➡ ⭑RS
Prices: pitch 88 (incl 2 persons)

▶ NARBONNE AUDE

Relais de Nautique La Nautique ☎ 468904819
Situated on the salt water lake 'Étang de Bages et de Sigean',
this site is particularly well appointed, each pitch having its
own washing and toilet facilities. There are good recreational
facilities and advance booking is recommended.
⮕ *Access via Narbonne Sud exit on A9.*
Mar-15 Nov 16HEC ⬛ ➡ ⚏ ⚏ ⚏ ✕ ⊙ ⬛ ⬛ ⬛ ⚏ ⬛ ⭑ P ⬛
⊞ lau
Prices: pitch 78-125 (incl 2 persons)

▶ At **NARBONNE-PLAGE**(15km E D168)

CM de la Côte des Roses ☎ 468498365
A modern site nestling at the foot of the Massif of the Calpe
close to the sea.
⮕ *3 km SW.*
Apr-Sep 8HEC ⬛ ➡ ⚏ ⚏ ⚏ ✕ ⊙ ⬛ ⬛ ⬛ ⬛ ⊞ lau ➡ ⭑S
Prices: pitch 51-71 (incl 2 persons)

CM Falaise av des Vacances ☎ 468498077
On level ground at the foot of the Massif of the Calpe with
good modern facilities.
⮕ *W of Narbonne Plage, 400m from beach.*
Apr-Sep 8HEC ⬛ ➡ ⚏ ⚏ ⚏ ✕ ⊙ ⬛ ⬛ ⬛ ⬛ ⊞ lau ➡ ⭑S
Prices: pitch 79-108 (incl 2 persons)

▶ NÉBIAS AUDE

Fontaulié-Sud ☎ 468201762
In a beautiful setting in the heart of the Cathare region.
⮕ *0.6km S via D117.*
Etr-Oct 3HEC ⬛ ⚏ ⚏ ⚏ ✕ ⊙ ⬛ ⬛ ⬛ ⚏ ⬛ ⬛ ⭑ P ⬛ ⊞ lau
Prices: pitch 19 (incl 2 persons)

▶ NÎMES GARD

Domaine de la Bastide Rte de Generac ☎ 466380921
In a rural setting with excellent facilities. Shop open summer
only.
⮕ *5km S of town centre on D13. Access via A9 exit 'Nîmes-
Ouest'.*
All year 5HEC ⬛ ➡ ⚏ ⚏ ⚏ ✕ ⊙ ⬛ ⬛ ⬛ ⚏ ⬛ ⬛ ⬛ ⊞ lau ➡
⭑LP
Prices: ⭑25 pitch 65-80

NIOZELLES Alpes-de-Haute-Provence

Moulin de Ventre ☎ 492786331
In a rural setting with good facilities.
⮩ *2.5km E via N100*
25 Mar-25 Oct 3HEC ⟨symbols⟩ LP
⟨symbols⟩ lau
Prices: pitch 79-138 (incl 2 persons)

NYONS Drôme

CM Promenade de la Digue ☎ 475262239
Situated on bank of river on level meadow with fruit trees.
Sports ground and golf course in town.
15 Mar-7 Nov 1.6HEC ⟨symbols⟩ lau ⟨symbols⟩
⟨symbols⟩PR
Prices: pitch 41 (incl 3 persons)

Sagittaire Vinsobres ☎ 475270000
Well-kept site divided by hedges in a beautiful Alpine setting.
⮩ *S of town on D538 road to Vaison-la-Romaine.*
All year 14HEC ⟨symbols⟩ LP ⟨symbols⟩ lau ⟨symbols⟩ ⟨symbols⟩R

OLLIÈRES-SUR-EYRIEUX, LES Ardèche

▨ Domaine des Plantas ☎ 475662153
Games room, discotheque and other leisure activities.
6 Apr-20 Sep 7HEC ⟨symbols⟩ R
⟨symbols⟩ lau

ORANGE Vaucluse

Jonquier 1321 r Alexis-Carrel ☎ 490341983
⮩ *On the NW outskirts*
1 Apr-15 Oct 5HEC ⟨symbols⟩ P ⟨symbols⟩
lau ⟨symbols⟩ ⟨symbols⟩R
Prices: ⟨symbol⟩30 pitch 30

ORGON Bouches-du-Rhône

Vallée Heureuse ☎ 490730278
A quiet transit site in a rocky valley.
⮩ *1.5km from the village on the N7. Access is past a non-working quarry.*
11 Jun-31 Aug 8HEC ⟨symbols⟩ P ⟨symbols⟩ lau ⟨symbols⟩
⟨symbols⟩L

PALAVAS-LES-FLOTS Hérault

Roquilles 267 bis av St-Maurice ☎ 467680347
An attractive site 50m from the sea.
15 Apr-25 Sep 15HEC ⟨symbols⟩
⟨symbols⟩ P ⟨symbols⟩ lau ⟨symbols⟩ ⟨symbols⟩S

PEYREMALE-SUR-CÈZE Gard

Drouilhédes ☎ 466250480
In a beautiful location beside the River Cèze surrounded by pine and chestnut trees.
⮩ *Access via A6 and D17.*
Mar-Sep 2HEC ⟨symbols⟩ R ⟨symbols⟩ lau ⟨symbols⟩

PONT-D'HÉRAULT Gard

Magnanarelles Le Rey ☎ 467824013
In a pleasant mountain setting with well defined pitches.
⮩ *0.3km W via D999, beside the river.*
All year 2HEC ⟨symbols⟩ PR ⟨symbols⟩ lau

PONT-DU-GARD Gard

International des Gorges du Gardon rte de Uzès
☎ 466228181
In a peaceful, wooded location beside the River Gardon.
⮩ *1km from aqueduct on D981 Uzès road.*
15 Mar-Sep 4.2HEC ⟨symbols⟩ PR
⟨symbols⟩ lau
Prices: pitch 66 (incl 2 persons)

PORTIRAGNES-PLAGE Hérault

Mimosas ☎ 467909292
A well equipped family site located in a leisure park on the banks of the Canal du Midi, 1.3km from the sea.
⮩ *Leave A9 at exit Béziers Est and continue towards coast via N112 and D37.*
May-15 Sep 7HEC ⟨symbols⟩ PR
⟨symbols⟩ lau ⟨symbols⟩ ⟨symbols⟩S
Prices: pitch 87-125 (incl 2 persons)

PRADET, LE Var

Mauvallon chemin de la Gavaresse ☎ 494213173
A well-kept site amidst young trees divided into pitches.
⮩ *Turn off the N559 in Le Pradet and take the D86 for 2.5km towards sea.*
Apr-Sep 0.9HEC ⟨symbols⟩ lau ⟨symbols⟩ ⟨symbols⟩S

Pin de Galle Quartier San Peyre ☎ 494212606
In a wooded location 200mtrs from the beach.
⮩ *On the Toulon road on the outskirts of Pradet.*
All year 1HEC ⟨symbols⟩ lau ⟨symbols⟩
⟨symbols⟩S

PRAMOUSQUIER Var

Pramousquier ☎ 494058395
A terraced site set in a wooded park 400mtrs from a fine sandy beach. Good recreational facilities.
⮩ *2km E via D559*
May-Sep 3HEC ⟨symbols⟩ lau ⟨symbols⟩ ⟨symbols⟩S
Prices: ⟨symbol⟩23-25 pitch 30.50-33.50

PRIVAS Ardèche

CM Espace Ouvèze rte de Montélimar ☎ 475640580
A comfortable municipal site with good facilities in the heart of the Ardèche region.
Etr-15 Oct Closed 2 wks in May & Sep 3.5HEC ⟨symbols⟩
⟨symbols⟩ lau ⟨symbols⟩ P ⟨symbols⟩

PUGET-SUR-ARGENS Var

Aubrèdes 408 chemin des Aubrèdes ☎ 494455146
Situated on undulating meadowland surrounded by pine trees with good, modern facilities.
⮩ *Leave autoroute A8 at exit Puget-sur-Argens, then site is 850m. If approaching from Fréjus on N7 turn left before Puget, cross motorway and follow road towards Lagourin.*
Etr-26 Sep 3.8HEC ⟨symbols⟩ P ⟨symbols⟩ lau

Bastiane chemin des Suvières ☎ 494455131
Hilly site divided into numbered pitches in pine and oak wood. Individual washing cubicles. Meals to take away. Separate car park for arrivals after 23.00hrs.
⮩ *Access from A8.*
15 Mar-15 Oct 3HEC ⟨symbols⟩ P
⟨symbols⟩ lau ⟨symbols⟩
Prices: pitch 67-149 (incl 3 persons)

Parc St-James Oasis rte de la Bouverie ☎ 494454464
27 Mar-25 Sep 42HEC ⟨symbols⟩ P

QUILLAN Aude

Sapinette 2 r René Delpech ☎ 468201352
⮩ *Access W via D79, rte de Ginoles.*
Mar-3 Nov 1.8HEC ⟨symbols⟩ lau ⟨symbols⟩
⟨symbols⟩PR

RAMATUELLE Var

Croix du Sud rte des Plages ☎ 494798084
Terraced site in beautiful pine forest divided into pitches with view of sea. Minimum stay 3 days.

➲ *3km NE of town, 80m N of D93.*
Apr-Oct 2.5HEC ⬛ ♦ 🛒 🛁 🍴 ✕ ⊙ 🚿 🅿 🚽 📷 🅿 ⊞ lau ♦
↖S

Tournels rte de Camarat ☎ 494559090
Lovely views to Pampelonne Bay from part of this site. 1km
to beach.
➲ *Access from D93 Croix-Valmer/St-Tropez road, follow the
signs to 'Cap Camarat'.*
Closed 10 Jan-10 Feb 20HEC ⬛ ♦ 🛒 🍴 ✕ ⊙ 🚿 🅿 🛒 ↖ P 📷
⊞ lau ♦ ↖S
Prices: ⚑28-38 pitch 44-77.50
See advertisement under Colour Section

▶ **REMOULINS** GARD

Soubeyranne rte de Beaucaire ☎ 466370321
In a picturesque location close to the river Gard with good,
modern facilities.
➲ *S on D986.*
2 Apr-13 Sep 6HEC ⬛ ∷ ♦ 🛒 🛁 🍴 ✕ ⊙ 🚿 🅿 🛒 ↖
P 📷 ⊞ lau ♦ ↖R
Prices: pitch 73-113 (incl 2 persons)

Sousta av du Pont-du-Gard ☎ 466371280
Picturesque forest site a short distance from the Pont du
Gard.
➲ *2km NW.*
Mar-Oct 12HEC ∷ ♦ 🛒 🛁 🍴 ✕ ⊙ 🚿 🅿 🛒 🏕 A ↖ PR 📷 ⊞
lau
Prices: pitch 64-83 (incl 2 persons)

▶ **REVENS** GARD

Lou Triadou Le Bourg ☎ 467827358
A well equipped site in the heart of the Causse Noir.
➲ *Access via D159/D151.*
mid Jun-mid Sep 0.7HEC ⬛ ⚒ 🛒 🛁 🍴 ✕ ⊙ 🚿 🅿 🛒 A
📷 ⊞ lau
Prices: ⚑15 pitch 25

▶ **RIA** PYRÉNÉES-ORIENTALES

Bellevue 8 r Bellevue ☎ 468964896
Beautifully situated terraced site. Very well kept. Beside
former vineyard.
➲ *2km S on N116, take road to Sirach, turn right and
continue 600m up drive which is difficult for caravans.*
Apr-Sep 2.2HEC ⬛ ♦ 🛒 🍴 ⊙ 🚿 🅿 🛒 📷 ⊞ lau ♦ 🛁 ✕ ↖R
Prices: ⚑16 pitch 16

▶ **ROQUEBRUNE-SUR-ARGENS** VAR

Domaine de la Bergerie Valleé du Fournel ☎ 494829011
A large, well run family site set in a beautiful Provençal
countryside with fine recreational facilities.
➲ *Access via A8 exit Le Muy N7 and D7.*
15 Feb-15 Nov 60HEC ⬛ ⚒ 🛒 🛁 🍴 ✕ ⊙ 🚿 🅿 🏕 🛒 🛒 ↖ P
📷 ⊞ lau ♦ ↖L

Domaine J J Bousquet rte de la Bouverie ☎ 494454251
In a quiet, wooded location with good, modern facilities.
➲ *Access via N7 towards Le Muy.*
All year 5HEC ⬛ ⚒ 🛒 🛁 🍴 ✕ ⊙ 🚿 🅿 🏕 🛒 ↖ P 📷 ⊞ lau
Prices: ⚑18.60 🚐18.60 🚗18.60 A18.60

Lei Suves Quartier du Blavet ☎ 494454395
In a picturesque forested area with good recreational
facilities.
➲ *4km N via N7.*
15 Mar-15 Oct 7HEC ⬛ ♦ 🛒 🛁 🍴 ✕ ⊙ 🚿 🅿 🛒 🛒 A ↖
P 📷 ⊞ lau
Prices: pitch 103-158 (incl 3 persons)

Moulin des Iscles Quartier La Valette ☎ 494457074
In a picturesque location beside the River Argens with good,
modern facilities.
➲ *Access via D7 towards St-Aygulf.*
Apr-Sep 1.2HEC ⬛ ♦ 🛒 🛁 🍴 ✕ ⊙ 🚿 🅿 🏕 🛒 🛒 ↖ R 📷 ⊞
lau ♦ ↖L
Prices: pitch 104 (incl 3 persons)

Pêcheurs ☎ 494457125
A pleasant site with direct access to the river in a wooded
location at the foot of the Roquebrune crag.
➲ *0.5km NW via D7, near the lake*
Etr-Sep 4HEC ⬛ ♦ 🛒 🛁 🍴 ✕ ⊙ 🚿 🅿 🛒 🛒 ↖ LPR 📷 ⊞ lau

▶ **ROQUE-D'ANTHÉRON, LA** BOUCHES-DU-RHÔNE

Domaine les Iscles ☎ 442504425
➲ *1.8km N via D67c.*
Mar-1 Oct 10HEC ⬛ ⚒ 🛒 🛁 🍴 ✕ ⊙ 🚿 🅿 🏕 🛒 🛒 ↖ LP 📷 ⊞ lau
Prices: ⚑17-27 pitch 22-62

Silvacane av de la Libération ☎ 442504054
Level gravelled ground with 100 sq m pitches. Heated
common room with TV. Water sports centre and stables
nearby. Site in wood on slopes of hill.
All year 6HEC ⬛ ⚒ ♦ 🛒 🛁 🍴 ✕ ⊙ 🚿 🅿 🛒 🛒 ↖ PR 📷 ⊞
lau ♦ 🛁 ✕ 🏕 🛒
Prices: ⚑17-27 pitch 22-62

▶ **ROQUETTE-SUR-SIAGNE, LA** ALPES-MARITIMES

Panoramic 1630 av de la République, Quartier St-Jean
☎ 492190777
A well equipped, modern site in a wooded location affording
magnificent views of the surrounding hills.
➲ *N of village off D9.*
All year 1HEC ⬛ ♦ 🛒 🍴 ✕ ⊙ 🚿 🅿 🏕 🛒 🛒 🛒 A ↖ P 📷 ⊞ lau
♦ 🛁 ↖R

St-Louis av de la République ☎ 493422667
Well equipped site in a pleasant rural setting, backed by hills.
➲ *On D9, 800m from Pégomas towards La Bocca.*
Apr-1 Oct 5HEC ⬛ ♦ 🛒 🛒 ⊙ 🚿 🅿 🛒 ↖ P 📷 🅿 ⊞ lau ♦ 🛁 🍴
🅿 🏕 ↖R ⊞
Prices: pitch 124-190 (incl 3 persons)

▶ **RUOMS** ARDÈCHE

🏠 **Bastide** ☎ 475396472
Well equipped family site in a pleasant wooded location.
➲ *4km SW on the banks of the Ardèche.*
20 Mar-14 Sep 7HEC ⬛ ♦ 🛒 🛁 🍴 ✕ ⊙ 🚿 🅿 🏕 🛒 🛒 A ↖
PR 📷 ⊞ lau
Prices: pitch 100-135 (incl 2 persons)

Ternis rte de Lagorce ☎ 475939315
A terraced site in a delightful setting in the southern Ardèche
region, with good recreational facilities. Separate car park for
arrivals between 22.00 and 08.00hrs.
➲ *Access via D559 towards Lagorce.*
Etr-20 Sep 6HEC ⬛ ♦ 🛒 🛁 🍴 ✕ ⊙ 🚿 🅿 🏕 🛒 🛒 ↖ P 📷 🅿
⊞ lau
Prices: pitch 70-98 (incl 2 persons) pp20-25

▶ At **SAMPZON**(6km S)

Aloha-Plage ☎ 475396762
In a fine situation beside the River Ardèche, midway between
Ruoms and Vallon-Pont-d'Arc. The site now has two private
swimming pools.
➲ *50m from the river.*
Apr-Sep 3HEC ⬛ ♦ 🛒 🍴 ✕ ⊙ 🚿 🅿 🏕 🛒 🛒 ↖ PR 📷 ⊞ lau
♦ 🛁
Prices: pitch 105 (incl 2 persons)

Soleil Vivarais ☎ 475396756
An exceptionally well appointed, terraced site surrounded by the imposing scenery of the Ardèche Gorge. An excellent canoeing centre with opportunities for all kinds of outdoor/water activities and regular organised entertainment.
⮕ *From Vallon drive towards Ruoms on D579 for 5km and cross bridge over River Ardèche.*
21 Mar-20 Sept 8HEC ⸺ ♣ ↑ ☟ ♀ ✕ ☉ 🕏 ⌀ ⊞ ♨ 🛦 ⁙
PR ☒ ⊞ lau
Prices: pitch 109-174 (incl 2 persons)

▶ **SAILLAGOUSE** PYRÉNÉES-ORIENTALES

Cerdan 11 r d'Estauar ☎ 468047046
Picturesque setting in meadow with some terraces. Hot meals served during peak season.
⮕ *Access via N116.*
Closed Oct 0.8HEC ⸺ ⌀ ↑ ♀ ☉ 🕏 ⌀ ♨ ☒ ☒ 🄿 lau ♦ ☟ ✕
⁙PR
Prices: pitch 64 (incl 2 persons)

▶ **ST-ALBAN-AURIOLLES** ARDÈCHE

Ranc Davaine ☎ 475396055
Well equipped, mainly level site with direct access to the River Chassezac and a variety of entertainment facilities.
⮕ *2.3km SW via D58.*
Apr-15 Sep 12HEC ⸺ ∷∷ ♣ ↑ ☟ ♀ ✕ ☉ 🕏 ⌀ ⊞ ⁙ R ☒ ⊞ lau
Prices: pitch 85-138 (incl 2 persons)

▶ **ST-AMBROIX** GARD

Beau-Rivage Le Moulinet ☎ 466241017
In a fine location between the sea and the Cevennes mountains beside the River Cèze.
⮕ *3.5km SE on D37.*
Apr-Sep 3.5HEC ⸺ ♣ ↑ ☉ 🕏 ⌀ ⁙ R ☒ ⊞ lau ♦ ☟ ♀ ✕
Prices: ⚑25.50 pitch 24

Clos ☎ 466241008
A quiet site in a pleasant setting beside the River Cèze with good, modern facilities.
⮕ *Access to the right of the church square.*
Apr-Oct 1.8HEC ⸺ ⌀ ↑ ♀ ☉ 🕏 ⌀ ♨ ⊞ ⊞ 🛦 ⁙ PR ☒
⊞ lau ♦ ☟
▶ **ST-ANDIOL** BOUCHES-DU-RHÔNE

St-Andiol ☎ 490950113
Well situated on the edge of the village. Divided into pitches.
⮕ *Access via A7.*
All year 1HEC ⸺ ⌀ ↑ ♀ ☉ 🕏 ⁙ P ☒ ⊞ lau ♦ ✕
Prices: ⚑20 pitch 25

▶ **ST-AYGULF** VAR

Étoile d'Argens chemin des Étangs ☎ 494810141
In pleasant wooded surroundings 2km from the beach which can be reached by a private boat service.
⮕ *5km NW, beside the River Argens.*
27 Mar-Sep 11HEC ⸺ ∷∷ ♣ ↑ ☟ ♀ ✕ ☉ 🕏 ⌀ ⊞ ⁙ PR
☒ ⊞ lau
Prices: pitch 185-212 (incl 3 persons)

Paradis des Campeurs La Gaillarde Plage ☎ 494969355
A quiet family site in a picturesque location with direct access to the beach.
⮕ *2.5km towards Gaillarde-Plage between St-Aygulf and Ste-Maxime.*
15 Mar-15 Oct 2.8HEC ⸺ ♣ ↑ ☟ ♀ ✕ ☉ 🕏 ⌀ ⊞ ⁙ S ☒
⊞ lau
Prices: pitch 78-146 (incl 3 persons)

Ideally located in the heart of the Côte d'Azur, exceptional site with friendly atmosphere on the banks of the Argens river with direct access to the fine sandy beaches (there is one for naturist). Bar, restaurant, take away food, swimming-pool which is heated in cool weather.
Entertainment: discotheque, giant barbecues, cabarets, concerts, excursions and a miniclub for children.
Mobile home and caravans available for hire.
Camping Caravanning Le Pont d'Argens
RN 98 Fréjus Saint Aygulf – FRANCE
Tél: 04 94 51 14 97 – Fax: 04 94 51 29 44

Pont d'Argens N98 ☎ 494511497
A pleasant site with good facilities beside the river.
Apr-15 Oct 7HEC ⸺ ♣ ↑ ☟ ♀ ✕ ☉ 🕏 ⌀ ⊞ ⁙ PR ☒ ⊞ lau
♦ ⁙S

St-Aygulf 270 av Salvarelli ☎ 494176249
A well equipped family site in wooded surroundings with direct access to the beach.
⮕ *Inland from N98 at Km881.3 N of town. Entrance on right of av Salvarelli.*
Apr-Oct 22HEC ⸺ ∷∷ ♣ ↑ ☟ ♀ ✕ ☉ 🕏 ⌀ ⊞ ⁙ LS
☒ ⊞ lau

▶ **ST-CHAMAS** BOUCHES-DU-RHÔNE

Canet Plage ☎ 490509689
A well equipped site beside the Étang de Berre with a wide range of recreational facilities.
⮕ *On D10, S of Salon-de-Provence towards La Fare les Oliviers.*
All year 3.9HEC ⸺ ⌀ ♣ ↑ ☟ ♀ ✕ ☉ 🕏 ⊞ ⁙ LP ☒ ⊞
lau ♦ ⌀
Prices: ⚑21 ♠15 ⊞20 🛦20

▶ **ST-JEAN-PLA-DE-CORTS** PYRÉNÉES-ORIENTALES

Deux Rivières rte de Maureillas ☎ 468832320
Situated on the banks of the River Tech with large roomy pitches.
⮕ *0.5km SE via D13, beside the River Tech*
May-Sep 4HEC ⸺ ⌀ ↑ ☟ ♀ ✕ ☉ 🕏 ⌀ ⊞ ⁙ PR ☒ ⊞
lau ♦ ⌀
Prices: ⚑20 pitch 37

▶ **ST-LAURENT-DU-VAR** ALPES-MARITIMES

Magali 1814 rte de la Baronne ☎ 493315700
A family site on level meadowland, surrounded by trees and bushes at the foot of the southern Alps.
⮕ *Leave A8 at 'St-Laurent-du-Var' exit, cross industrial zone turn left for 100m, then right and continue for 2km.*
Feb-Oct 1.2HEC ⸺ ⌀ ↑ ☟ ✕ ☉ 🕏 ⌀ ⊞ ⊞ ⁙ P ☒ ⊞ lau
♦ ♀ ✕
Prices: ⚑18-21 ♠13-15 ⊞89-129 🛦81-120

▶ **ST-LAURENT-DU-VERDON** ALPES-DE-HAUTE-PROVENCE

Farigoulette Lac de St Laurent ☎ 492744162
⮕ *1.5km NE near Verdon*
15 May-15 Sep 14HEC ⌀ ♣ ↑ ☟ ♀ ✕ ☉ 🕏 ⌀ ⊞ ⁙ LP ☒ ⊞
lau
Prices: 🛦10-10 pitch 80-80 (incl 2 persons)

▶ **ST-MARTIN-DE-LONDRES** HÉRAULT

Pic St-Loup rte du Pic St-Loup ☎ 467550053
⮕ *E via D122*
Apr-Sep 3HEC ⸺ ⌀ ⌀ ↑ ☟ ♀ ✕ ☉ 🕏 ⌀ ⊞ ⊞ ⁙ P ☒ lau ♦
⊞

ST-MAXIMIN-LA-STE-BAUME VAR

Provençal rte de Mazaugues ☎ 494781697
Bar, café and swimming pool are open Jul-Aug only.
➲ *2.5km S via D64.*
Apr-Sep 5HEC ⊞ ♦ ⋔ ⅃ ♥ ✗ ☉ ⬛ ⌀ ♨ ⬛ ⋞ P ☎ ⊞ lau ➡
⊞

ST-PAUL-EN-FORÊT VAR

Parc ☎ 494761535
Quiet, fairly isolated site surrounded by woodland.
➲ *3km N on D4.*
All year 5HEC ⊞ ♦ ⋔ ⅃ ♥ ✗ ☉ ⬛ ⌀ ⬛ ⬛ ⋞ P ☎ ⬛ ⊞ lau
➡ ⋞L

ST-PAUL-LES-ROMANS DRÔME

CM de Romans Les Chasses ☎ 475723527
Shady pitches separated by hedges.
May-Sep 1HEC ⊞ ♦ ⋔ ☉ ⬛ ⬛ ☎ ⊞ lau ➡ ⅃ ♥ ✗ ⌀ ♨

ST-RAPHAËL VAR

Douce Quiétude bd J-Baudino ☎ 494443000
Meadowland site in quiet location in attractively hilly
countryside with good facilities.
➲ *Approach from Agay Plage past Esterel Camping in
direction of Valescure.*
Apr-Sep 10HEC ⊞ ♦ ⋔ ⅃ ♥ ✗ ☉ ⬛ ⌀ ⬛ ⋞ P ☎ ⊞ lau
Prices: pitch 220 (incl 3 persons)

Royal Camp Long ☎ 494820020
Level site divided by walls and hedges. Ideal bathing for
children. Bar and hall next to site.
➲ *On N98 towards Cannes.*

15 Mar-24 Oct 0.6HEC ⊞ ⋮⋰⋱ ♦ ♦ ⋔ ⅃ ✗ ☉ ⬛ ⌀ ♨ ⬛
⋞ S ☎ ⊞ lau
Prices: pitch 140 (incl 3 persons)

ST-REMÈZE ARDÈCHE

Domaine de Briange rte de Gras ☎ 475041443
In a wooded location close to the Gorges de l'Ardèche.
➲ *1.5km NE.*
May-Sep 4HEC ⊞ ♦ ⋔ ⅃ ♥ ✗ ☉ ⬛ ⬛ ⋞ P ☎ ⊞ lau ➡ ⌀ ♨
Prices: pitch 63-75 (incl 2 persons)

ST-RÉMY-DE-PROVENCE BOUCHES-DU-RHÔNE

Pégomas ☎ 490920121
Well-tended grassland with trees and bushes. Divided into
several fields by high cedars providing shade.
➲ *500m E of village. Well signposted.*
Mar-Oct 2HEC ⊞ ♦ ⋔ ⅃ ♥ ✗ ☉ ⬛ ⌀ ⋞ P ☎ ⊞ lau ➡ ✗
Prices: pitch 75-89 (incl 2 persons)

ST-SAUVEUR-DE-MONTAGUT ARDÈCHE

Ardechois Le Chambon, Gluiras ☎ 475666187
In the grounds of a restored 18th-century farm set in rolling
countryside with fine views of the surrounding hills.
➲ *8.5km W on D102, beside the River Gluèyre.*
24 Apr-25 Sep 5HEC ⊞ ♦ ⋔ ⅃ ♥ ✗ ☉ ⬛ ⌀ ♨ ⬛ ⬛ ⋞ PR
☎ ⊞ lau
Prices: pitch 106-126 (incl 2 persons)

ST-SORLIN-EN-VALLOIRE DRÔME

Château de la Pérouze ☎ 475317021
A well appointed family site with a variety of recreational
facilities.
➲ *2.5km SE via D1.*
15 Jun-15 Sep 14HEC ⊞ ⋔ ⋔ ⅃ ✗ ☉ ⬛ ⌀ ♨ ⋞ LPR ⬛ ⊞
☼ lau ➡ ⌀
Prices: ⋞27 ⬛27 ⬛27

ST-THIBÉRY HÉRAULT

Tane Le Causse ☎ 467778429
In pleasant wooded surroundings, 1km from the River
Hérault.
➲ *Access via A9 exit Agde-Pézenas.*
Jun-Sep 2.4HEC ⊞ ⋔ ⋔ ⅃ ✗ ☉ ⬛ ⬛ ⬛ ⋞ P ☎ lau ➡ ⅃ ⌀
♨ ⋞R ⊞
Prices: pitch 70 (incl 2 persons)

ST-VALLIER-DE-THIEY ALPES-MARITIMES

Parc des Arboins RN85 ☎ 493426389
Pleasantly situated terraced site on hillside with some oak
trees.
➲ *Entrance at Km V36 on N85.*
All year 4HEC ⊞ ⋮⋰⋱ ♦ ⋔ ⅃ ♥ ✗ ☉ ⬛ ⬛ ⬛ ⋞ P ☎ ⊞ lau
➡ ⌀ ♨
Prices: pitch 88 (incl 2 persons)

STE-MARIE PYRÉNÉES-ORIENTALES

At TORREILLES(4km NW on D11)

Dunes de Torreilles ☎ 468283829
A well equipped site in wooded surroundings with direct
access to the beach.
➲ *E of the village off D81.*
15 Mar-15 Oct 16HEC ⋮⋰⋱ ♦ ⋔ ⋔ ⅃ ♥ ✗ ☉ ⬛ ♨ ⬛ ⋞ PS ☎
⊞ lau ➡ ⋞R

Mar-I-Sol Plage de Torreilles ☎ 468280407
A family site with a wide variety of sports and entertainment
facilities in a pleasant park-like setting 350 metres from the
beach.
➲ *Off D81 towards the sea.*
Contd.

All year 9HEC 🏕 ≈ 🚿 ⛽ 🛒 🍴 ⊙ 🛁 ⌷ 🏪 🚻 ⚓ ⚡ PS 🅿 ⊞ lau

Trivoly bd des Plages ☎ 468282028
A modern site with excellent facilities and well defined pitches, 800mtrs from the beach.
➲ *Access via autoroute exit 'Perpignan Nord' towards Le Barcarès.*
Apr-Sep 4.6HEC 🏕 ⚡ 🚿 🛒 🍴 ✕ ⊙ 🛁 ⌷ 🚻 ⚓ P 🅿 ⊞ lau ➤ ⚡S
Prices: pitch 70-123 (incl 2 persons)

STES-MARIES-DE-LA-MER BOUCHES-DU-RHÔNE

CM Brise ☎ 490978467
A well equipped family site with direct access to the beach, situated in the heart of the Canargue. The sanitary blocks are modern and there are facilities for a wide variety of sports.
➲ *NE via D85A, towards the beach*
All year 25HEC 🏕 ≈ ⚡ 🚿 🛒 🍴 ✕ ⊙ 🛁 ⌷ 🏪 ⚓ ⚡ PS 🅿 ⊞ lau ➤ 🍴
Prices: pitch 57-100 (incl 2 persons)

Clos-du-Rhône BP 74 ☎ 490978599
➲ *2km W via D38, near the beach*
Apr-Sep 7HEC 🏕 ≈ 🚿 🛒 🍴 ✕ ⊙ 🛁 ⌷ 🏪 🚻 ⚓ ⚡ PRS 🅿 ⊞ lau
Prices: pitch 85-105 (incl 2 persons)

SALAVAS ARDÈCHE

Chauvieux ☎ 475880537
A popular site in a wooded location close to the River Ardèche with plenty of recreational facilities. Advance booking recommended.
➲ *NE off D579.*
end Apr-mid Sep 1.8HEC 🏕 ≈ ⚡ 🚿 🛒 🍴 ✕ ⊙ 🛁 ⌷ 🏪 🚻 ⚓ R 🅿 ⊞ lau
Prices: pitch 90 (incl 2 persons)

Péquelet ☎ 475880449
➲ *Beside the River Ardèche*
Apr-Oct 2HEC 🏕 ⚡ 🚿 🛒 🍴 ✕ ⊙ 🛁 ⌷ 🚻 ⚓ R 🅿 lau ➤ ✕ 🍴
Prices: pitch 90 (incl 2 persons)

SALERNES VAR

Arnauds Quartier des Arnauds ☎ 494675195
Level site situated alongside a river and a lake.
➲ *Access via D560. Site entrance just beyond the village.*
May-Sep 3HEC 🏕 ⚡ 🚿 🍴 ✕ ⊙ 🛁 🏪 ⚓ R 🅿 ⊞ lau ➤ 🛒 ✕ ⌷ 🍴
Prices: ⚡22-27 pitch 38-48

SALINS-D'HYÈRES, LES VAR

Port Pothuau ☎ 494664117
A peaceful holiday village, completely divided into pitches with good leisure facilities.
➲ *6km E of Hyères on N98 and D12.*
03 Apr-15 Oct 6HEC 🏕 ⚡ 🚿 🛒 🍴 ✕ ⊙ 🛁 ⌷ 🏪 🚻 ⚓ P 🅿 ⊞ lau ➤ ⚡S
Prices: pitch 95-109 (incl 3 persons)

SALON-DE-PROVENCE BOUCHES-DU-RHÔNE

Nostradamus rte d'Eyguières ☎ 490560836
In pleasant, wooded surroundings with good sporting facilities.
➲ *5km W on D17 towards Eyguières and Arles.*
Mar-Oct 2.2HEC 🏕 ⚡ 🚿 🛒 🍴 ✕ ⊙ 🛁 🏪 ⚓ PR 🅿 ⊞ lau
Prices: pitch 78 (incl 2 persons)

SANARY-SUR-MER VAR

Girelles chemin de Beaucours ☎ 494741318
A modern family site with good facilities with direct access to the sea.

Camping Card Compulsory.
➲ *3km NW via D539, beside the sea.*
Etr-26 Sep 2HEC 🏕 ⚡ 🚿 🛒 🍴 ✕ ⊙ 🛁 ⌷ ⚓ S 🅿 ⊞ lau
Prices: ⚡31 pitch 116

Mogador ☎ 494745316
Situated 800m from the sea. The site, divided into pitches by hedges, is well managed and very well kept.
➲ *2km NW on N559 turn off at Km15 and take next left.*
Etr-5 Oct 2.7HEC 🏕 ⚡ 🚿 🛒 🍴 ✕ ⊙ 🛁 ⌷ 🏪 ⚓ P 🅿 ⊞ lau ➤ ⚡S

Pierredon r Raoul Coletta ☎ 494742502
A well equipped, wooded site providing a variety of family entertainment, 3km from the sea.
➲ *Access via A50 exit Bandol or Sanary.*
15 Mar-10 Oct 4HEC 🏕 ⚡ 🚿 🛒 🍴 ✕ ⊙ 🛁 ⌷ 🏪 🚻 ⚓ P 🅿 ⊞ lau ➤ 🛒 ⌷
Prices: ⚡23-31 pitch 31-55

SAUVE GARD

Domaine de Bagard rte de Nîmes ☎ 466775599
Shady site bordering the River Vidourle, surrounded by hedges.
➲ *1.2km SE via D999.*
Apr-Sep 16HEC 🏕 ⚡ 🚿 🛒 🍴 ✕ ⊙ 🛁 ⌷ 🏪 🚻 ⚓ P 🅿 lau ➤ 🚻
Prices: pitch 95-95 (incl 2 persons)

SAUVIAN HÉRAULT

Gabinelle ☎ 467395087
A modern site in pleasant wooded surroundings with good facilities.
➲ *Leave Sauvian in the direction of Valras Plage on D19.*
15 Jun-15 Sep 3HEC 🏕 🚿 🛒 🍴 ✕ ⊙ 🛁 🏪 ⚓ P 🅿 ⊞ lau ➤ 🛒 ✕ ⌷ 🍴

SÉRIGNAN-PLAGE HÉRAULT

Camargue ☎ 467321964
Situated in the edge of a wide sandy beach.
Arp-15 Oct 3.5HEC 🏕 🚿 🛒 🍴 ✕ ⊙ 🛁 ⌷ 🏪 🚻 ⚓ LPS 🅿 ⊞ lau

Clos Virgile ☎ 467322064
Situated 400m from the beach, the site is on level meadowland with large pitches and has two clean, well kept sanitary blocks.
15 Apr-15 Sep 5HEC 🏕 ⚡ 🚿 🛒 🍴 ✕ ⊙ 🛁 ⌷ 🏪 ⚓ PS 🅿 ⊞ lau ➤ ⚡S

Grand Large ☎ 467397130
Situated by the sea with private access to the beach. Good facilities. Entertainment during high season.
May-12 Sep 7HEC 🏕 ≈ 🚿 🛒 🍴 ✕ ⊙ 🛁 ⌷ 🏪 🚻 ⚓ PS 🅿 ⊞ lau
Prices: pitch 102-180 (incl 2 persons)

Sérignan-Plage ☎ 467323533
On a fine sandy beach, this is a family site with good recreational facilities.
➲ *Access via A9 exit Béziers Est.*
15 Apr-15 Sep 9HEC 🏕 ≈ 🚿 🛒 🍴 ✕ ⊙ 🛁 ⌷ 🏪 🚻 ⚓ PS 🅿 ⊞ lau
Prices: ⚡20-138 pitch 80-155

SEYNE-SUR-MER, LA VAR

Mimosas av M-Paul ☎ 494947315
Situated among pine trees facing the fortress of Six-Fours. Bar and café available during high season only.
➲ *Access via A50 exit 13 towards 'La Seyne Centre', then towards 'Sanary-Bandol'.*
All year 1HEC 🏕 🛁 🚿 🍴 ✕ ⊙ 🛁 🚻 🏪 🚻 🅿 lau ➤ 🛒 ⌷ ⊞
Prices: pitch 60-73 (incl 3 persons)

SILLANS-LA-CASCADE BOUCHES-DU-RHÔNE

Relais de la Bresque 15 chemin de la Piscine ☎ 494046489
In a beautiful setting among pine trees with good sanitary
and recreational facilities.
All year 1.3HEC ⸺ ♦♠↾↿×⊙ ♀⌂ ♥☎⊞ lau
Prices: ♠17-30 pitch 20

SIX-FOURS-LES-PLAGES VAR

Héliosports La Font de Fillol ☎ 494256276
Between the town centre and the beach.
➲ *1km W*
25 Mar-15 Oct 0.5HEC ⸺ ⇗♦↾⊙♀☎ lau ♦ 🛒♥×∅
⛺ ♜PS ⊞
Prices: pitch 74 (incl 3 persons)

International St-Jean av de la Collégiale ☎ 494875151
Site with pitches, separated by hedges and reeds. Well
managed, and lies just below the Fort Six-Fours.
➲ *Access from N559 and D63 via chemin de St-Jean.*
All year 3HEC ♦♠↾🛒♥×⊙ ♀⌂ ♥☎♜ P ☎⊞ lau ♦×

Playes 419 r Grand ☎ 494255757
Terraced site on north side of town. Trees abound in this
excellent location.
➲ *Access from N559 and D63 via chemin de St-Jean.*
Mar-Nov 1.5HEC ⸺ ♦↾🛒♥×⊙ ♀⌂∅⛺ ▲☎⊞ lau
Prices: pitch 79-91 (incl 3 persons)

SOSPEL ALPES-MARITIMES

Domaine St-Madeleine rte de Moulinet ☎ 493041048
A peaceful site in beautiful, unspoiled surroundings.
➲ *4.5km NW via D2566.*
Apr-Sept 3.5HEC ⸺ ⇗↾♥⊙♀∅⛺♜ PR ☎⊞ lau ♦
♜R
Prices: pitch 68-82 (incl 2 persons)

SOUBES HÉRAULT

Sources chemin d'Aubaygues ☎ 467443202
A small, friendly site in a quiet location beside a river.
➲ *5km NE. Signposted from N9.*
May-15 Sep 1HEC ⸺ ⇗↾♥×⊙♀♜ R ☎ lau ♦🛒×∅
⛺
Prices: pitch 80 (incl 2 persons)

TAIN-L'HERMITAGE DRÔME

CM Lucs 24 av Prés-Roosevelt ☎ 475083282
Good overnight stopping place but some traffic noise.
➲ *S of town near N7. Turn towards River Rhône at ESSO
garage.*
15 Mar-Oct 2HEC ⸺ ⇗↾⊙ ♀☎⊞ lau ♦🛒♥×∅♜P

TARASCON BOUCHES-DU-RHÔNE

Tartarin rte de Vallabrèques ☎ 490910146
Site lies on E bank of River Rhône.
➲ *Follow signs for 'Vallabrèques'.*
15 Mar-Sep 0.7HEC ⸺ ♦↾♥×⊙ ♀☎⊞ lau ♦🛒×∅
♜PR

THOR, LE VAUCLUSE

Jantou Quartier le Bourdis ☎ 490339007
In wooded surroundings beside a river. Separate car park for
arrivals after 22.00hrs.
➲ *Access via N100.*
Apr-Oct 6HEC ⸺ ♦↾🛒♥×⊙♀∅⛺♥☎♜ PR ☎⊞
lau ♦🛒♥×⊞
Prices: ♠20.75-25 pitch 25.30-30.50

TOURNON-SUR-RHÔNE ARDÈCHE

Manoir rte de Lamastre ☎ 475080250
In picturesque wooded surroundings with good, modern
facilities.
➲ *From N86 (Lyon-Valence) take Lamastre road for 3km.*
Etr-Sep 2HEC ⸺ ♦↾🛒♥×⊙ ♀∅⛺♜ LPR ☎ lau

Tournon 1 Promenade Roche de France ☎ 475080528
Well laid-out site in town centre beside River Rhône.
➲ *NW on N86.*
All year 1HEC ⸺ ♦↾⊙ ♀∅♜ R ☎⊞ lau
♦🛒×⛺♜P

TOURRETTES-SUR-LOUP ALPES-MARITIMES

Camassade 523 rte de Pie Lombard ☎ 493593154
Quiet site under oak trees and pines with several terraces.
➲ *From Vence turn left immediately beyond Tourette.*
All year 1.7HEC ⸺ ⁚⁚⁚♦♠↾♥⊙♀∅⛺♥☎♜ P ☎⊞
lau ♦♥
Prices: ♠22 ♠15 ♥68-72 ▲65-70

Rives du Loup rte de la Colle ☎ 493241565
In a wooded riverside setting with good, modern facilities
adjacent to a small hotel.
➲ *Between Vence and Grasse, 3km from Pont-du-Loup on the
road to La Colle-sur-Loup.*
Apr-15 Oct 2.2HEC ⸺ ⁚⁚⁚ ⇗↾🛒♥×⊙♀∅⛺♥☎♜
PR ☎⊞ lau
Prices: ♠25 ♠11 ♥29-44

UCEL ARDÈCHE

Domaine de Gil rte de Vals ☎ 0475946363
Pleasantly situated on the banks of the River Ardèche.
Surrounded by beautiful views of the countryside.
➲ *N of Aubenas off N104.*
1 May-15 Sep 4.8HEC ⸺ ⁚⁚⁚♦↾🛒♥×⊙ ♀∅♥☎♜ PR
☎⊞ lau
Prices: pitch 110 (incl 2 persons)

UR PYRÉNÉES-ORIENTALES

Gare d'Ur rte d'Espagne ☎ 468048095
In a pleasant mountainous setting with well defined pitches.
500mtrs from the village.
Oct 1HEC ⸺ ♦↾⊙ ♀∅ ♥☎⊞ lau ♦♥×⛺♜R ⊞
Prices: ♠17 pitch 16

UZÈS GARD

At ST-QUENTIN-LA-POTERIE(4km NE)

Moulin Neuf ☎ 466221721
Quiet site on extensive meadowland within an estate.
➲ *4 km NE on D982.*
Etr-Sep 5HEC ⸺ ⁚⁚⁚ ♦↾🛒♥×⊙♀∅⛺♜ P ☎⊞ lau
Prices: pitch 70-87 (incl 2 persons)

VAISON-LA-ROMAINE VAUCLUSE

International Carpe Diem rte de St-Narcellin ☎ 490360202
In wooded surroundings close to Mont Ventoux, with a wide
variety of leisure facilities.
➲ *S of town towards Malaucène.*
30 Mar-Oct 9HEC ⸺ ⁚⁚⁚ ⇗↾🛒♥×⊙♀⛺♥♥▲
♜ P ☎⊞ lau ♦∅♜R
Prices: ♠21-25 ♠18 ♥30-49 ▲30-42

Théâtre Romain Quartier des Arts, chemin du Brusquet
☎ 490287866
➲ *500mtrs from the town centre near the Roman Theatre.*
15 Mar-10 Oct 1.3HEC ⸺ ♦↾⊙♀♜ P ☎⊞ lau ♦🛒×
∅⛺♜R

VALENCE Drôme

CM chemin de l'Epervière ☎ 475423200
A well equipped site bordering the Rhône.
➲ *Access via exit Valence Sud off A7.*
All year 3.5HEC ▥ ♦ ⋔ ⴲ ♥ ✕ ☉ ◘ ⵣ P 🏕 lau ➧ ⵣ ⵁ ⴺ ⊞
Prices: pitch 60-78 (incl 2 persons)

VALLABRÈGUES Gard

Lou Vincen ☎ 466592129
In a pleasant shady location in the heart of a Provençal village.
15 Mar-15 Oct 1.4HEC ▥ ♦ ⋔ ☉ ◘ ⵣ ⵁ PR 🏕 ⊞ lau ➧ ⵣ
ⵀ ✕ ⴺ ⵁL ⊞
Prices: ⵀ20-22 pitch 24-26

VALLON-PONT-D'ARC Ardèche

Ardechois ☎ 475880663
In a pleasant situation in the Ardèche Gorge. Good access for caravans and plentiful sporting facilities.
➲ *From Vallon take D290 towards St-Martin. Signposted.*
27 Mar-20 Sep 6HEC ▥ ♦ ⋔ ⵣ ✕ ☉ ◘ ⵁ ⴲ ⵁ PR 🏕 ⊞
lau ➧ ⴺ
Prices: pitch 103-145 (incl 2 persons)

See advertisement under Colour Section

Mondial rte des Gorges de l'Ardèche ☎ 475880044
Modernised site on the bank of the Ardèche with good sanitary arrangements.
➲ *Access from Vallon-Pont-d'Arc D290. 800m towards Gorge d'Ardèche.*
15 Mar-10 Oct 4.2HEC ▥ ⵈⵈ ♦ ⋔ ⵣ ⴲ ✕ ☉ ◘ ⵁ ⴺ ⴲ ⵀ
ⵁ LPR 🏕 ⊞ lau
Prices: pitch 90-140 (incl 2 persons)

See advertisement under Colour Section

Plage Fleurie Les Mazes ☎ 475880115
Holiday site in unspoilt village beside river.
➲ *Take D579 towards Ruoms, turn left after 2.5km towards Les Mazes.*
Apr-Sep 12HEC ▥ ⵈⵈ ♦ ⋔ ⵣ ⴲ ✕ ☉ ◘ ⵁ ⵁ PR 🏕 P lau

VALRAS-PLAGE Hérault

Lou Village chemin des Montilles ☎ 467373379
Situated along a sandy beach, bordered by sand-dunes.
➲ *2km SW, 100m from the beach*
25 Apr-12 Sep 6HEC ▥ ♦ ⋔ ⵣ ⴲ ✕ ☉ ◘ ⵁ ⴺ ⴲ ⴱ ⵁ PS
🏕 ⊞ lau
Prices: pitch 80-130 (incl 2 persons)

Occitanie ☎ 467395906
Family site on rising ground to the north of town, 1km from the beach.
➲ *Access from A9 exit 'Béziers-Est' towards Valras.*
13 May-11 Sep 6HEC ▥ ♦ ⋔ ⵣ ⴲ ✕ ☉ ◘ ⵁ ⴱ Ⓐ ⵁ P 🏕
⊞ lau ➧ ⴺ ⵁRS
Prices: pitch 78-115 (incl 2 persons)

Vagues Vendres Plage ☎ 467373312
A well-organised family site 400m from the sea with a variety of sporting and entertainment facilities.
Etr-20 Sep 7HEC ⵈⵈ ⵉ ⋔ ⵣ ⴲ ✕ ☉ ◘ ⵁ ⴺ ⴲ ⴱ ⵁ P 🏕 ⊞
lau ➧ ⵁS

Yole ☎ 467373387
Very comfortable site divided into pitches. Good sanitary installations with individual washing cubicles. Hot water tap. Sailing boats for hire. Riding stables in village. Reservation recommended in July and August.
➲ *SW of D37E towards Vendres.*

May-25 Sep 20HEC ▥ ⵈⵈ ♦ ⋔ ⵣ ⴲ ✕ ☉ ◘ ⵁ ⴺ ⴲ ⴱ ⵁ
P 🏕 ⊞ lau ➧ ⵁS
Prices: pitch 102-167 (incl 2 persons)

VAUVERT Gard

Tourrades chemin des Canaux ☎ 466888020
A modern family site with a wide range of recreational facilities.
➲ *3km W via N572 and D135.*
All year 7.5HEC ▥ ♦ ⋔ ⵣ ⴲ ✕ ☉ ◘ ⵁ ⴺ ⴲ ⴱ ⵁ P 🏕 ⊞ lau
➧ ⵁ ⊞
Prices: pitch 59-85 (incl 2 persons)

VEDÈNE Vaucluse

Flory rte d'Entraigues ☎ 490310051
Well-kept site on a pine covered hill with good facilities.
➲ *From motorway, do not head for Vedène but follow D942 for 800m.*
15 Mar-15 Oct 6.5HEC ▥ ♦ ⋔ ⵣ ⴲ ✕ ☉ ◘ ⵁ ⴺ ⴲ ⵁ P 🏕
⊞ lau
Prices: ⵀ17.50-21.50 ⵆ17.50-21.50 ⵇ17.50-21.50 Ⓐ17.50-21.50

VENCE Alpes-maritimes

Domaine de la Bergerie rte de la Sine ☎ 493580936
Well-kept site on hilly land. Pitches near to a wood. Some facilities are only available in high season.
➲ *3km W on D2210.*
25 Mar-15 Oct 13HEC ▥ ♦ ⋔ ⵣ ⴲ ✕ ☉ ◘ ⵁ ⴺ ⴲ ⵁ P 🏕
⊞ lau
Prices: ⵆ18 pitch 70-141 (incl 2 persons) pp32

VERCHENY Drôme

Acacias ☎ 475217251
Pleasant site beside the River Drôme.
Camping Card Compulsory.
➲ *Access via D93.*
Apr-Sep 3HEC ▥ ♦ ⋔ ⵣ ✕ ☉ ◘ ⵁ ⴺ ⵁ R 🏕 P ⊞ lau ➧
ⵀ ✕

VÉREILLES Hérault

Sieste ☎ 467237296
In a rural setting on the River Orb.
➲ *NE of Bédarieux, 10km from Lodève.*
Jun-15 Sep 2HEC ▥ ⵇ ⋔ ⵣ ⴲ ✕ ☉ ◘ ⵁ ⴺ ⴲ ⴱ ⵁ PR 🏕
⊞ lau

VIAS Hérault

Air Marin ☎ 467216490
A well equipped family site in wooded surroundings 10 minutes walk from the beach.
➲ *E of Vias Plage.*
15 May-25 Sep 7HEC ▥ ♦ ⋔ ⵣ ⴲ ✕ ☉ ◘ ⵁ ⴺ ⴲ ⴱ ⵁ P 🏕
lau ➧ ⵣ ⵁ ⵁRS ⊞
Prices: pitch 135 (incl 2 persons)

Bourricot ☎ 467216427
In a delightful wooded setting beside a 7km stretch of beach. Plenty of recreational facilities.
➲ *3km S on D137; at Vias look for Farinette-Plage and in 100m before beach turn right.*
22 May-18 Sep 2HEC ▥ ♦ ⋔ ⵣ ⴲ ✕ ☉ ◘ ⵁ ⴺ ⵁ R 🏕 ⊞
lau ➧ ⵁS

Carabasse rte de la Mer ☎ 467216401
Clean modern well-kept site with a variety of recreational facilities.
➲ *2km S off D13.*
15 May-18 Sep 20HEC ▥ ♦ ⋔ ⵣ ⴲ ✕ ☉ ◘ ⵁ ⴲ ⴱ ⵁ Ⓐ ⵁ P
🏕 P ⊞ lau ➧ ⴺ ⵁRS

Farret ☎ 467216445
On level meadow beside flat sandy beach, ideal for children.
⤷ *Access via A9 exit Agde-Vias.*
25 Mar–Sep 6HEC ⊞ lau
Prices: pitch 110-185 (incl 2 persons)

Gai Soleil Côte Ouest ☎ 467216477
On level land near sea. Divided into pitches.
⤷ *Cross Canal du Midi, S of town, then turn W.*
All year 4HEC lau ⤷ ⚲S

Hélios Vias-Plage ☎ 467216366
On level ground divided into pitches.
⤷ *On D137 S of village signposted 'Farinette'.*
16 May–Sep 3HEC ⤷ ⚲S

Napoléon av de la Mediterranée ☎ 467010780
A well equipped family site surrounded by tropical vegetation with direct access to the beach.
⤷ *Access via A9 exit Agde-Vias.*
Apr–Sep 3HEC P ⊞ lau ⤷ ⚲RS
Prices: pitch 105-160 (incl 2 persons)

VIC-LA-GARDIOLE Hérault

Europe ☎ 467781150
A pleasant site in peaceful surroundings.
⤷ *1.5km W via D114.*
May–Sep 5HEC lau ⤷ ⚲L

VIGAN, LE Gard

Val de l'Arre rte de Ganges ☎ 467810277
In wooded surroundings beside the River Arre. Compulsory separate carpark for late arrivals.
⤷ *2.5km E on D999.*
Apr–Sep 4HEC lau ⤷

VILLARS-COLMARS Alpes-de-haute-provence

Haut-Verdon ☎ 492834009
A comfortable site in a picturesque wooded location beside the River Verdon.
⤷ *N on D908.*
26 Jun–29 Aug 3.5HEC ⊞ lau ⤷
Prices: ♠20-26 ♠40-56 ♠40-56 ▲40-56

VILLEMOUSTAUSSOU Aude

Pinhiers chemin du Pont Neuf ☎ 468478190
⤷ *A61 in the direction of Mazamet.*
Apr–Sep 2HEC P ⊞ lau ⤷

VILLENEUVE-DE-LA-RAHO Pyrénées-orientales

Rives-du-Lac chemin de la Serre ☎ 468558351
A quiet family site beside the lake.
⤷ *7km from Perpignan.*
Mar–Nov 2.5HEC lau ⤷
Prices: pitch 60-80 (incl 2 persons)

VILLENEUVE-LÈS-AVIGNON Gard

Île des Papes ☎ 490151590
A well equipped site situated on an island between the Rhône Canal and the River Rhône.
⤷ *Access via N7 and D228.*

Etr–2 Nov 20HEC
P ⊞ lau
Prices: pitch 95-140 (incl 2 persons)

VILLENEUVE-LOUBET-PLAGE Alpes-maritimes

Hippodrôme 5 av des Rives ☎ 493200200
In a spacious park with pitches divided by hedges with good facilities.
⤷ *Turn right off the N7 at ATLAS furniture store.*
All year 8HEC P ⊞ lau ⤷ ⚲S
Prices: pitch 69-120 (incl 2 persons)

Panorama ☎ 493209153
Small terraced site mainly for tents 0.8km from the sea.
⤷ *About 500m from the Nice-Cannes Autoroute.*
All year 1HEC ⊞ lau ⤷ ⚲RS
Prices: pitch 66-82 (incl 2 persons)

Parc des Maurettes 730 av du Dr-Lefebvre ☎ 493209191
Terraced site in a pine forest with good, modern facilities.
⤷ *Access via A8: From Cannes take exit 'Villeneuve-Loubet-Plage', then N7 towards Antibes for 1km. From Nice, take Villeneuve exit and A8 for 2km.*
10 Jan–15 Nov 2HEC ⊞ lau ⤷ ⚲S
Prices: pitch 75-117 (incl 2 persons)

Parc St-James Sourire La Tour de la Madone, La Vanade ☎ 493209611
Parkland dominated by an 11th-century monastery.
⤷ *2km W on D2085*
18 Mar–14 Oct 8HEC P ⊞ lau ⤷ ⚲R

See advertisement under Colour Section

Vieille Ferme 296 bd des Groules ☎ 493334144
In a wooded park close to the sea. Shop and café open in summer only.
⤷ *Access via A8/N7 from Antibes of Cagnes-sur-Mer.*
All year 2.9HEC P ⊞ lau ⤷ ⚲S
Prices: pitch 62-76 (incl 2 persons)

VILLEROUGE-LA-CRÉMADE Aude

Pinada ☎ 468436193
In pleasant rural surroundings on edge of forest.
⤷ *600m NW on D106.*
15 May–Sep 4.3HEC P ⊞ lau ⤷ ✕

▶ VILLES-SUR-AUZON VAUCLUSE

Verguettes rte de Carpentras ☎ 490618818
Lying at the foot of Mont Ventoux and Nesque Gorges in a
pine forest
➲ *W via D942.*
May-Sep 2HEC ⸺ ♠ ℝ ♀ ✕ ⊙ 🖳 🚐 ⚡ P 🏛 lau ➡ ⚓ ♀ ✕ ⊘
Prices: ♠26 ➡14 🚐23 ▲23

▶ VIOLS-LE-FORT HÉRAULT

Cantagrils ☎ 467550188
➲ *4.5km S on D127*
Apr-15 Oct 14HEC ◊ ♠ ℝ ⚓ ♀ ✕ ⊙ 🖳 🚐 ⊘ 🚐 🚐 ⚡ P 🏛 lau

▶ VITROLLES BOUCHES-DU-RHÔNE

Marina Plage ☎ 442893146
A family site in pleasant wooded surroundings with good
recreational facilities.
➲ *Access via N113 towards Rognac, then turn S at exit after
Marignane Airport.*
All year 6HEC ⸺ ◊ 🛇 ℝ ⚓ ♀ ✕ ⊙ 🖳 ♨ 🚐 ▲ ⚡ L 🏛 🔛 lau
Prices: pitch 61-92

▶ VIVIERS ARDÈCHE

Centre de Vacances d'Imbours ☎ 475543806
In wooded surroundings with a variety of recreational
facilities.
➲ *Access via N86 and D4.*
15 Jun-15 Sep 27HEC ⸺ ♠ ℝ ⚓ ♀ ✕ ⊙ 🖳 ⊘ ♨ 🚐 ⚡ P 🏛
🔛 lau
Prices: ♠15-30 pitch 16-32

Rochecondrie Loisirs ☎ 475527466
A level site with good facilities beside the River L'Escoutay.
➲ *N of town on N86.*
Apr-Oct 1.8HEC ⸺ ♠ ℝ ♀ ⊙ 🖳 🚐 ⚡ PR 🏛 🔛 lau ➡ ⚓ ✕
⊘
Prices: pitch 100 (incl 2 persons)

▶ VOGÜÉ ARDÈCHE

Domaine du Cros d'Auzon ☎ 475377586
In wooded surroundings close to the Gorges de l'Ardèche
with good recreational facilities.
➲ *2.5km via D579 bordering the river.*
Etr-15 Sep 20HEC ⸺ ⸛⸛ 🛇 ♠ ℝ ⚓ ♀ ✕ ⊙ 🖳 🚐 🚐 ▲ ⚡
PR 🏛 🔛 lau
Prices: pitch 110 (incl 2 persons)

▶ VOLONNE ALPES-DE-HAUTE-PROVENCE

Hippocampe rte Napoléon ☎ 492335000
Several strips of land, interspersed with trees, and running
down the edge of lake. Surrounded by fields and gardens.
➲ *On S edge of town. 2km E of N85.*
27 Mar-Sep 8HEC ⸺ ♠ ℝ ⚓ ♀ ✕ ⊙ 🖳 ⊘ 🚐 ▲ ⚡ P 🏛 🔛
lau
Prices: pitch 58-117 (incl 2 persons)

CORSICA

Corsica is a wonderful blend of green mountains, deep
valleys, and spectacular pink granite peaks where rain and
melting snow merge into torrents that rush down the
hillsides. In the spring the mountains are ablaze with wild
flowers and the maquis - the abundance of which gives the
island its name 'the scented isle'. This southernmost outpost
of France, is some 100 miles south of Toulon in the
Mediterranean. Beaches abound, and all kinds of
watersports are available in season, but in this relatively
undiscovered place it is still possible to find a quiet beach
on a summer day.

Corsica's capital is Ajaccio, birthplace of Napoleon, and
today a cosmopolitan centre with its busy harbour and
broad boulevards with smart shops. From Ajaccio there is a
railway to Bastia, in the north. This is a beautiful three-hour
trip, and ideal for drivers reluctant to venture onto more
tortuous minor roads.

▶ CORSE (CORSICA)

▶ ALÉRIA HAUTE-CORSE

Marina d'Aléria rte de la Mer ☎ 495570142
➲ *3km E of Cateraggio via RN200*
Apr-Oct 10HEC ⸛⸛⸛ ♠ ℝ ⚓ ♀ ✕ ⊙ 🖳 🚐 ⊘ 🚐 ⚡ S lau
Prices: ♠28-38 ➡10-12 🚐11-13 ▲8-10

▶ BONIFACIO CORSE-DU-SUD

Rondinara Suartone ☎ 495704315
In a beautiful situation 300mtrs from the beach with modern
facilities and fine opportunities for water sports.
➲ *Midway between Porto-Vecchio and Bonifacio on N198 in
the direction of Suartone-La Rondinara.*
15 May-Sept 6HEC ⸺ 🛇 ♠ ℝ ⚓ ♀ ✕ ⊙ 🖳 ⊘ ♨ 🚐 ⚡ PS 🏛 🔛
⊘ lau
Prices: ♠30-36 ➡15-17 🚐18-20 ▲15-17

▶ CALVI HAUTE-CORSE

Dolce Vita Ponte Bambino ☎ 495650599
In extensive woodland with well defined pitches and good,
modern facilities.
➲ *4km SW of Calvi between N197 to L'Ile Rousse and the sea.*
May-Sep 6HEC ⸺ ♠ ℝ ⚓ ♀ ✕ ⊙ 🖳 ⊘ 🚐 ⚡ RS 🏛 🔛 lau
Prices: ♠40 ➡16 🚐18 ▲16

▶ CARGESE CORSE-DU-SUD

Torraccia ☎ 495264239
➲ *4km N on N199.*
15 May-Sep 3.5HEC ◊ ♠ ℝ ⚓ ♀ ✕ ⊙ 🖳 ⊘ 🚐 🏛 🔛 lau
Prices: ♠30-34 pitch 12-14

▶ CENTURI HAUTE-CORSE

Isulottu ☎ 495356281
A peaceful, shady site, 200mtrs from the beach.
➲ *1km from Centuri-Port towards Morsiglia.*
20 Dec-22 Jan 3HEC ♠ ℝ ⚓ ♀ ✕ ⊙ 🖳 ⊘ 🏛 🔛 lau ➡ ⚡S
Prices: ♠28 ➡10 🚐20 ▲15

▶ CLOS-DU-MOUFLON HAUTE-CORSE

Mouflon ☎ 495650353
Terraced site, divided into pitches. Very steep access via partly
asphalted, winding road with gradient of 20%. **Tents and
motorised caravans only.**
➲ *15km from Calvi on D81 on the coastal road, in the
direction of Porto.*
6 Jun-25 Sep 2.5HEC ◊ 🛇 ♠ ℝ ⚓ ♀ ✕ ⊙ 🖳 ⊘ ⚡ S 🏛 🔛 lau ➡ ⚓

▶ FARINOLE, MARINE DE HAUTE-CORSE

A Stella ☎ 495371437
➲ *On D80 beside the sea*
Jun-15 Oct 5HEC ⸺ 🛇 ℝ ⚓ ♀ ✕ ⊙ 🖳 🚐 ⚡ S 🏛 🔛 lau

▶ GALÉRIA HAUTE-CORSE

Deux Torrents ☎ 495620067
A spacious, well equipped site nestling between two torrents
at the foot of the mountains.
➲ *5km E on D51 towards Calenzana.*
Jun-Sep 6.3HEC ⸺ ⸛⸛⸛ ♠ ℝ ⚓ ✕ ⊙ 🖳 ⊘ 🚐 🏛 🔛 lau
Prices: ♠27 ➡14 🚐16 ▲14

GHISONACCIA HAUTE-CORSE

Arinella-Bianca Arinella-Bianca ☎ 495560478
In wooded surroundings, directly on the beach with good recreational facilities.
Etr-Oct 12HEC ⚏ ♠ ⋔ ♨ ♀ ✕ ☉ ♥ ∅ ⌂ ♬ ↖ PS ☎ ⊞ lau
Prices: pitch 99-129 (incl 2 persons)

LOZARI HAUTE-CORSE

Clos des Chênes rte de Belgodère ☎ 495601513
In a delightful wooded setting, 1km from a fine sandy beach.
⤳ 1.5km S via N197 towards Belgodère
Etr-Sep 5.5HEC ⚏ ♠ ⋔ ♨ ♀ ✕ ☉ ♥ ∅ ⌂ ♬ ↖ P ☎ ⊞ lau
♦ ↖S
Prices: ⚑31.50-35 ♠12 ♬19 Å16

LUMIO HAUTE-CORSE

Panoramic rte de Lavataggio 1 ☎ 495607313
Very clean and tidy site divided into pitches.
⤳ From Calvi, 12km on N197, 200m from main road.
Jun-15 Sep 2.5HEC ⚏ ♠ ⋔ ♨ ♀ ✕ ☉ ♥ ∅ ♬ ↖ P ☎ ⊞

OLMETO-PLAGE CORSE-DU-SUD

Esplanade ☎ 495760503
In a pleasant natural park, 100mtrs from the sea.
All year 5HEC ⚏ ♠ ⋔ ♨ ♀ ✕ ☉ ♥ ⌂ ♬ ☎ ▣ ⊞ lau ♦ ∅ ⌕
↖S
Prices: ⚑28-34 ♠10-14 ♬15-19 Å14-18

PIANOTTOLI CORSE-DU-SUD

Kevano Plage Plage de Kevano ☎ 495718322
In a beautiful setting in the middle of woodland with modern facilities, 400mtrs from the beach.
15 Apr-15 Sep 6HEC ◈ ♠ ⋔ ♨ ♀ ✕ ☉ ♥ ⌂ ☎ ⊞ lau ♦ ∅ ↖S
Prices: ⚑28-39 ♠9-13 ♬17-20 Å9-13

PISCIATELLO CORSE-DU-SUD

Benista ☎ 495251930
In a beautiful wooded setting, 5 minutes from the local beaches. Pitches are divided by hedges and there are good sporting facilities.
Apr-Oct 5HEC ⚏ ⋔ ♨ ♀ ✕ ☉ ♥ ∅ ⌕ ⌂ ♬ ↖ PR ☎ ⊞ lau
♦ ↖S
Prices: pitch 105 (incl 2 persons)

PORTO-VECCHIO CORSE-DU-SUD

Pirellu rte de Palombaggia ☎ 495702344
A modern site situated in an oak grove 300mtrs from the beach.
⤳ S of Porto-Vecchio, take road for Bonifacio. After Pont du Stabiacco take first road on the left.
Apr-Oct 2.5HEC ⚏ ◈ ♠ ⋔ ♨ ♀ ✕ ☉ ♥ ∅ ⌕ ⌂ ↖ P ☎ lau
Prices: ⚑28-38 ♠12-15 ♬20-25 Å12-14

Vetta Trinité ☎ 495700986
In natural parkland with good, modern facilities 3km from the sea.
⤳ 5.5km N on N198.
1 Jun-20 Sep 8HEC ⚏ ♠ ⋔ ♨ ♀ ✕ ☉ ♥ ∅ ⌂ ♬ ↖ P ☎ ▣ lau
♦ ⌕
Prices: ⚑36 ♠12 ♬12 Å12

ST-FLORENT HAUTE-CORSE

U Pezzo chemin de la Plage ☎ 495370165
Pleasant site; partly level, partly terraced under eucalyptus trees. Private access to large beach.
⤳ S of town on road to beach.
15 Apr-15 Oct 2HEC ⚏ ♠ ⋔ ♨ ♀ ✕ ☉ ♥ ∅ ⌂ ↖ S ☎ ⊞ lau

SOTTA CORSE-DU-SUD

U Moru 20114 FIGARI ☎ 495712340
A quiet family site 5 minutes from the local beach.
⤳ 4km SW via D859.
Mar-Sep 6HEC ⚏ ♠ ⋔ ♨ ♀ ✕ ☉ ♥ ∅ ⌂ Å ☎ ⊞ lau

TIUCCIA CORSE-DU-SUD

Couchants rte de Casaglione ☎ 495522660
In a quiet location facing the vast Sagone Bay and close to the Liamone River.
⤳ 3km from the sea.
All year 5HEC ⚏ ♠ ⋔ ♀ ✕ ☉ ♥ ∅ ⌂ ⌂ ♬ Å ☎ ⊞ lau ♦
↖RS
Prices: ⚑23-25 ♠10-12 ♬15-20 Å10-12

U Sommalu rte de Casaglione ☎ 495522421
⤳ 2.5km N via D81 and D25.
15 Mar-Sep 6HEC ⚏ ♠ ⋔ ♨ ♀ ✕ ☉ ♥ ∅ ⌂ ♬ Å ☎ lau ♦
⌕ ↖RS ⊞

VICO CORSE-DU-SUD

Sposata Col Stantaine ☎ 495266155
On partly terraced, partly sloping ground.
⤳ 1km SW on N195.
Apr-Sept 2.5HEC ⚏ ♠ ⋔ ♀ ✕ ☉ ♥ ∅ ⌂ ☎ ⊞ lau ♦ ⌕
↖LRS

GERMANY

Germany, with its fairytale castles and ancient towns, is a country offering legend and tradition amongst its many attractions.

FACTS AND FIGURES
Capital: Berlin
Language: German
IDD code: 49. To call the UK dial 00 44.
Currency: Mark (*(DEM)* = 100 pfennigs). At the time of going to press £1 = DEM 2.71.
Local time: GMT + 1 (summer GMT + 2)
Emergency services:
Police and Ambulance 110; Fire 112.
Business hours-
Banks: 0830-1230 & 1330-1530 Mon-Wed and Fri, 0830-1230 & 1330-1730 Thur. These are approximate, there are no uniform banking hours.
Shops: 0900-2000 Mon-Fri and 0900-1600 Sat
These opening hours apply to city shops.
Average daily temperatures:Munich
Jan 2°C   Sep 15°C
Jul 18°C   May 13°C
Mar 4°C   Nov 3°C
Tourist Information:
German National Tourist Office
UK 65 Curzon Street
London W1Y 8NE
Tel 0171 493 0080 (0891 600100 premium rate information line)
USA 52nd Floor, 122 East 42nd Street, New York, NY10168-0072
Tel (212) 661-7200.
Camping card: generally recommended; some reductions on site fees.

Germany is bordered by nine countries: Austria, Belgium, Czech Republic, Denmark, France, Luxembourg, Netherlands, Poland and Switzerland. It is a country of forests, rivers and mountains. The Rhine Valley boasts magnificent cliffs and woods whilst the Black Forest has some fine valley scenery with countless waterfalls and gorges.

The climate is temperate and variable but Germany enjoys hotter summers than Britain.

Off-site camping Permission to camp off an official campsite must be obtained from the landowner or local police. Overnight parking at parking places is tolerated for one night, unless otherwise indicated, provided nearby campsites and hotels are fully booked. However, caravans must remain connected to the towing vehicle. Make sure you do not contravene local regulations.

HOW TO GET THERE

For western Germany use the Channel Tunnel, or one of the short Channel crossings and travel via Belgium. For northern Germany take a direct ferry from **Harwich** to **Hamburg** (20hrs approx) or **Newcastle** to **Hamburg** (23hrs approx) or one of the Channel crossings to the Netherlands. For southern Germany use Eurotunnel, or one of the short Channel crossings and drive through northern France entering Germany near

Strasbourg; this is also the route if using one of the longer Channel crossings to Caen, Cherbourg, Dieppe or Le Havre. For details of the *AA European Routes Service,* consult the Contents Page.

Distance

From the Continental Channel ports, Köln (Cologne) is about 414km (257 miles) and within a comfortable day's drive; routes to southern and eastern Germany usually require one or two overnight stops.

MOTORING & GENERAL INFORMATION

The information given here is specific to Germany. It **must** be read in conjunction with the European ABC at the front of the book, which covers those regulations which are common to many countries.

British Embassy/Consulates*

At the time of writing the British Embassy is located at 53113 Bonn, Friedrich-Ebert-Allee 77, ☎(0228) 9167-0; it has no Consular Section. The British Embassy Office is located at 0-10117 Berlin, Unter den Linden 32/34 ☎ (030) 201 840. There are British Consulates in Düsseldorf, Frankfurt/Main, Hamburg, München(Munich) and Stuttgart; there are British Consulates with

Honorary Consuls in Bremen, Hanover, Kiel and Nürnberg (Nurenberg).

Children in cars
Child under 12 and/or 1.5 metres in height are not permitted to travel as front or rear seat passengers unless using suitable restraint system, if fitted.

Currency
There are no restrictions on the amount of foreign or German currency that a *bona fide* tourist can import or export.

Banks and post offices provide exchange facilities for currency, Eurocheques and Travellers Cheques.

Dimensions and weight restrictions
Private **cars** and **trailers** or **caravans** are restricted to the following dimensions - height, 4 metres; width, 2.55 metres; length, 12 metres. The maximum permitted overall length of vehicle/trailer or caravan combinations is 18 metres. A fully-laden trailer without brakes may have a total maximum weight of 750kg.

Driving licence*
A valid UK or Republic of Ireland licence is acceptable in Germany. The minimum age at which visitors from UK or Republic of Ireland may use a temporarily imported car or motorcycle is 17 years.

First-aid kit*
The German authorities recommend that visiting motorists equip their vehicles with a first-aid kit.

Foodstuffs*
There are no limits on the importation of foodstuffs obtained duty and tax paid within the EC. Up to 500g of coffee (200g of coffee extract) and 100g of tea (40g of tea extract) purchased duty free or outside the EC may be imported free of duty and tax. However, coffee bought duty free or outside the EC cannot be imported by visitors under 15 years of age. Visitors may also import up to 1kg of fresh meat and meat products and up to 30kg of game and poultry. Sheep and goat's cheese and meat products from the CIS,

Turkey, and all African and Asian countries.

Lights*
The German authorities recommend that visiting motorists equip their vehicles with a spare set of vehicle bulbs.

Motoring clubs*
The principal German motoring club is the **Allgemeiner Deutscher Automobil Club e.V.** (ADAC) which has its headquarters at 81373 München, Am Westpark 8 ☎(089) 7676-0. ADAC has offices in the larger towns, and office hours are 09.00-18.00hrs Mon-Fri. ADAC also has offices at major frontier crossings.

Petrol*
Only unleaded petrol is sold in Germany. However, for vehicles deesigned to run on leaded petrol, a lead substitute additive may be purchased separately and added to the fuel tank each time the vehicle is filled with unleaded petrol. A precise quantity of additive is needed based upon the amount of unleaded petrol used. Petrol stations and accessory shops sell the additive.

Roads
The *Bundesstrassen*, or state roads, vary in quality. In the north and west, and in the touring areas of the Rhine Valley, Black Forest, and Bavaria, the roads are good and well-graded. Germany has a comprehensive motorway (*Autobahn*) network which dominates the road system and takes most of the long distance traffic. Emergency telephones are sited every 2km, the direction of the nearest telephone is indicated by the point of the black triangle on posts alongside the motorway. Traffic at weekends increases considerably during the school holidays, which are from July to mid September. In order to ease congestion, lorries of more than 7,500kg and lorries towing trailers are subject to restrictions. On all Saturdays from 1 July to 31 August such vehicles are not allowed on state roads or motorways betweeen 0700 and 1800 hours, and generally on all Sundays and public holidays between 0001 and 2200 hours.

The Eberhard Bridge, Tubingen

Speed limits*
Car
Built-up areas 50kph (31mph)
Other roads 100kph (62mph)
Motorways/dual carriageways †130kph (80mph)
Car/caravan/trailer
Built-up areas 50kph (31mph)
Other roads 80kph (49mph)
Motorways/dual-carriageways 80kph (49mph)
†unless a *different* maximum speed is signed.

Note:
Outside special built-up areas, motor vehicles to which a special speed limit applies, as well as vehicles with trailers with a combined length of more than 7 metres (23ft), must keep sufficient distance from the preceding vehicle so that an overtaking vehicle may pull in. Anyone driving so slowly that a line of vehicles has formed behind must permit the following vehicles to pass, by stopping at a suitable place if necessary.

Warning triangle
The use of a warning triangle is compulsory in the event of accident or breakdown. The triangle must be placed on the road behind the vehicle to warn following traffic of any obstruction: 100 metres (109yds) on ordinary roads and 150 metres (164yds) on motorways.

*Additional information will be found in the Continental ABC at the front of the book.

⦾ ⦾ ⦾ ⦿ **SOUTH EAST** ⦿ ⦾ ⦾ ⦾

The highest peak in Germany can be found in the Alps
along the southern border of Bavaria. Superb walks and
easy climbs bring rewarding views of lush meadows and
secluded lakes, and there are some rare and wonderful
species of Alpine fauna to be seen.
Bavaria is also a land of spruce, pine, and deciduous forests
impressively strewn with massive boulders and rock
labyrinths which are perfect for climbing, exploring and
caving. Many areas are also excellent for winter sports.
The Octoberfest and the Wagner festival are both held in
this region; other attractions include medieval tournaments,
Alpine horn-blowing, and Schuhplatter dancing.
To the south of the region, Munich is a most beautiful city
famed for art and learning, with an atmosphere and charm
of its own. Further north, be sure to visit Passau, which
possesses the largest church organ in the world, and the
former Imperial city of Regensburg.

....

⟩ **AACH BEI OBERSTAUFEN** BAYERN

Aach ☎ 08386 363
A terraced site with beautiful views of the mountains. Sauna,
solarium, games room.
⤴ *From Oberstaufen follow B308 for 7km towards the
Austrian border.*
All year 2HEC ⸺ ⇔♠☂⚑▯✕⊙⊟∅⛺🏕 ⟁ P ☎♦ ⟁R
Prices: ⇞7 ⊞10-14 ▲6-12

⟩ **AITRANG** BAYERN

Elbsee 3 Am Elbsee 3 ☎ 08343 248
On the E shore of the lake with good bathing facilities.
Section reserved for campers only.
⤴ *Take B12 from Marktoberdorf travel for 11km then turn N
to Aitrang.*
20 Dec-9 Nov 3.5HEC ⸺ ♠☂⊙⊟∅⛺🏕 ⟁ L ☎⊞ lau
♦✕
Prices: ⇞6 ⊖4 ⊞14 ▲14

⟩ **ARLACHING** BAYERN

Kupferschmiede Trostberger Str 4 ☎ 086671 446
On meadowland. Partially gravel.
⤴ *On Seebruck-Traunstein road.*
Apr-Oct 2HEC ⸺ ♦♠☂▯✕⊙⊟∅🏕 ⟁ L ☎⊞ lau ♦ ⟁PR
Prices: ⇞9.90-10.90 ⊖2.90 ⊞7 ▲7

⟩ **AUGSBURG** BAYERN

Augusta Mühlhauser Str 546 ☎ 0821 707575
Hard standings for caravans. Separate section for residential
caravans.
⤴ *Leave E11 by Augsburg-Ost exit. Continue N towards
Neuburg and turn right after 400m.*
All year 6.6HEC ⸺ ♠☂▯✕⊙⊟∅🏕⛺🚐▲⟁L☎♦▯

⟩ **BAMBERG** BAYERN

⟩ At **BUG**(5km S)

Insel ☎ 0951 56320
The site lies on the bank of the River Regnitz, S of Bamberg.
'Park & Ride' scheme into Bamberg.
⤴ *Leave A73 at Bamberg South exit and follow B505/B4
towards Bamberg until you see camping signs leading off left.*
All year 5HEC ⸺ ♠☂▯▯✕⊙⊟∅🏕 ⟁ R ☎⊞ lau
Prices: ⇞6.50 ⊖6-12 ⊞6-12 ▲6-12

⟩ **BERCHTESGADEN** BAYERN

Allwegiehen ☎ 08652 2396
A terraced site at the foot of the Untersalzberg Mountain

surrounded by bushy woods. There is also a steep and
narrow asphalt access road with passing places. A truck is
available for towing caravans. The camp is closed between
12.30 and 14.30 hrs and from 21.00 hrs.
⤴ *For access, take the B305, and drive approx. 3.5km towards
Schellenberg.*
All year 3HEC ⸺ ∷∷∴ ♦♠☂▯✕⊙⊟∅🏕 ⟁ P ☎⊞✖⤴
⟁LR
Prices: ⇞8 pitch 12

⟩ **BERGEN** BAYERN

Wagnerhof Campingstr 11 ☎ 08662 8557
Level site.
Camping Card Compulsory.
⤴ *Access from München-Salzburg motorway, Bergen exit.
Turn right at windmill just before entering town.*
All year 2.8HEC ♦♠☂▯⊙⊟∅🏕⛺♦▯✕ ⟁P ⊞

⟩ **BERNAU-AM-CHIEMSEE** BAYERN

⟩ At **FELDEN**(3km N)

Chiemsee-Süd ☎ 08051 7540 & 7175
Level meadowland shaded by trees, on lake shore.
⤴ *Leave the A8/E11 (München-Salzburg) at exit Felden,
continue W towards lake.*
01 Apr-15 Oct 2HEC ⸺ ∷∷∴ ♦♠☂▯✕⊙⊟∅🏕 ⟁ L
⊞

⟩ **BRUNNEN FORGGENSEE** BAYERN

Brunnen Seestr 81 ☎ 08362 8273
Situated on E shore of Lake Forggensee.
⤴ *From Füssen follow B17 to Schwangau, then continue N on
minor road.*
Closed 15 Nov-15 Dec 3.5HEC ⸺ ♦♠☂▯✕⊙⊟∅🏕 ⟁
L ☎⊞ lau ♦ ⟁P
Prices: ⇞10-12 pitch 8-10

⟩ **CHIEMING** BAYERN

Chieming Möwenplatz Haupstr 3 ☎ 08664 361 & 653
Small site on shore of lake, with gravelly terrain.
Camping Card Compulsory.
⤴ *5km S of Chieming.*
Apr-Sep 0.8HEC ⸺ ♠☂✕⊙⊟ ⟁ L ☎⊞ lau ♦☂▯✕∅
🏕 ⟁P
Prices: ⇞8-9 ⊖3-3 ⊞10 ▲8

⟩ **DIESSEN** BAYERN

St-Alban ☎ 08807 7305
Clean site next to St-Alban, lakeside with private bathing
beach and reserved section for residential campers. Good
sanitary installations when operated by the public.
⤴ *From München follow B12 towards Landsberg/Lech. Near
Greifenberg turn left, proceed via Utting to St-Alban.*
Apr-Oct 3.8HEC ⸺ ♠☂▯✕⊙⊟∅🏕 ⟁ L ☎⊞♦∅

⟩ **DINKELSBÜHL** BAYERN

Romantische Strasse ☎ 09851 7817
Terraced site with some hedges and trees. Separate field for
young people. Good sporting facilities.
⤴ *Signposted.*
All year 12HEC ⸺ ♠☂▯✕⊙⊟∅ ⟁ L ☎▯⊞ lau ♦▯

⟩ **ENDORF, BAD** BAYERN

Stein Hintersee 10 ☎ 08053 9349
A family site in wooded surroundings on the shore of the
Simsee.
15 May-15 Sep 2.5HEC ⸺ ∷∷∴ ✂♠☂⊙⊟ ⟁ L ☎ lau ♦
✕🏕
Prices: ⇞7.50 ⊖3.50 ⊞6 ▲6

ERLANGEN BAYERN

Rangau Campingstr 44 ☎ 091351 8866
Long stretch of land behind the sportsground and next to the Dechsendorfer Weiher Lake in nature reserve.
➲ *Leave motorway (A3/E5 Nürnberg-Würzburg) at exit Erlangen-West.*
Apr-Sep 1.8HEC ⟲ ⚌ ₲ ⟡ ✕ ⊙ ◘ ⊫ 🗐 ⊞ lau ➡ 🐃 ₹L
Prices: ♠7 ⊞8

ESCHERNDORF BAYERN

Escherndorf-Main Gaststatte ☎ 09381 2889
Site lies on meadowland by the River Main, next to the ferry station (River Ferry Northeim). Lunchtime siesta 13.00-15.00 hrs.
➲ *Site can be reached from motorway A7/E70 via exit Würzburg Estenfeld and follow road E towards 'Volkach'.*
Apr-30 Oct 1.5HEC ⟲ ➡ ₲ 🐃 ✕ ⊙ ◘ ⊫ ₹ R 🗐 ⊞
Prices: ♠9 ⊕9 ⊞9 ▲7-7

ESTENFELD BAYERN

Estenfeld Maidbronner Str 38 ☎ 09305 228
On meadowland next to sportsground.
➲ *From motorway A7/E70 leave at exit 'Würzburg/Estenfeld' and continue S on B19 for 1km.*
Mar-23 Dec 0.5HEC ⟲ ₲ ⟡ 🐃 ⟡ ✕ ⊙ ◘ ⊫ 🗐 ⊞ lau ➡ ✕ ∅ ₹LP
Prices: ♠7.50 pitch 6.50-13

FEILNBACH, BAD BAYERN

Tenda Reithof 2 ☎ 08066 533
Well organised site on level grassland with pitches laid out in circles and hardstandings for tourers near the entrance.
➲ *Leave München-Salzburg motorway (A8/E11) at 'Bad Aibling' exit and continue S for 4km on unclass road.*
All year 14HEC ⟲ ₲ 🐃 🐃 ✕ ⊙ ◘ ∅ ⊫ 🗐 ➡ P 🗐 ⊞ ➡ ⟡
₹L
Prices: ♠7.50-8 ▲6 pitch 5-12

FICHTELBERG BAYERN

Fichtelsee ☎ 09272 801
Gently sloping meadow amid pleasant woodland 100m from Lake Fichtelsee.
➲ *From A9/E6 Bad Berneck exit, take B303 to the Fichtelsee Leisure Centre turning.*
6 Nov-15 Dec 2.6HEC ⟲ ₲ ⟡ 🐃 ⊙ ◘ ∅ 🗐 ⊞ lau ➡ ⟡ ✕ ⊫
₹LP
Prices: ♠9 pitch 12

FINSTERAU BAYERN

Nationalpark-Ost ☎ 08557 768
Terraced site on edge of extensive woodland area at entrance to National Park.
➲ *N of Freyung towards the frontier.*
May-15 Sep 3HEC ⟲ ₲ ⟡ ✕ ⊙ ◘ ⊫ 🗐 ⊞ ➡ 🐃 ⟡ ₹LP
Prices: ♠6 pitch 7.50

FISCHBACH AM INN BAYERN

Inntal ☎ 08034 2869
On level grassland near a small forest lake.
➲ *Off B15 S of town.*
All year 6HEC ⟲ ₲ ⟡ ✕ ⊙ ◘ ∅ ₹ L 🗐 ⊞ lau
➡ 🐃 ⟡ ✕ ₹P
Prices: ♠7 ⊕6 ⊞8 ▲6

FRICKENHAUSEN BAYERN

KNAUS Frickenhausen ☎ 09331 3171
On level meadow in a small poplar wood beside River Main. Lunchtime siesta 13.00-15.00 hrs.

➲ *On N bank of Main 0.5km E of Oshsenfurt.*
Closed Nov 3.4HEC ⟲ ₲ ⟡ 🐃 ⟡ ✕ ⊙ ◘ ∅ ⊫ 🗐 ▲ ₹ PR
🗐 lau ➡ ⊞
Prices: ♠8.50 pitch 7.50-12

FÜRTH IM WALD BAYERN

SC Einberg Daberger Str ☎ 09973 1811
Municipal site in Dabergerstr, near swimming pool.
➲ *NE of Cham on B20.*
Mar-Oct 2HEC ⟲ ₲ ⟡ ⟡ ⊙ ◘ ⟡ ₹ R 🗐 ⊞ lau ➡ 🐃 ✕ ∅ ⊫
₹LP
Prices: ♠6 ⊕4.50 ⊞5 ▲3

GADEN BAYERN

Schwanenplatz Schwanenpl 1 ☎ 08681 281
Site lies on a meadow, divided into sections beside one of Bavaria's warmest lakes, Waginger See.
➲ *For access drive from Traunstein to Waging, then turn right in direction Freilassing 2km, then left to lake.*
May-20 Sep 3.8HEC ⟲ ₲ ⟡ ⟡ ✕ ⊙ ◘ ⊫ 🗐 ₹ L 🗐 ⊞ ⊗ ➡ 🐃
∅
Prices: ♠8-9.80 pitch 9.50

GARMISCH-PARTENKIRCHEN BAYERN

Zugspitze Griesener Str 4 ☎ 08821 3180
In beautiful setting at the foot of the Zugspitze between the road and the Loisach.
➲ *On the B24 towards the Austrian frontier.*
All year 2.9HEC ⟲ ₲ ⟡ ⟡ ✕ ⊙ ◘ ∅ ⊫ 🗐 ₹ R 🗐 ⊞ lau
➡ ⊞
Prices: ♠9.50 ⊕5 ⊞10 ▲7-10

GEMÜNDEN AM MAIN BAYERN

Saaleinsel Duivenallee 7 ☎ 09351 8574
This municipal site lies a short distance off the main road bordering the River Fränkische Saale. It is in the grounds of a sports field and has a swimming pool. Individual washing cubicles with curtains for the ladies.
➲ *Access signposted off main B26 road.*
Apr-15 Oct 5.1HEC ⟲ 💥 ⟡ ✕ ⊙ ◘ ⊫ 🗐 ₹ PR 🗐 ⊞ ➡ 🐃
∅

GEMÜNDEN-HOFSTETTEN BAYERN

Schönrain ☎ 09351 8645
Slightly sloping, partly terraced meadowland E of River Main. Lunchtime siesta 13.00-15.00 hrs.
➲ *From Gemünden/Main along the left bank of the River Main about 3km downstream. Turn left of B26 through Hofstetten to site.*
Apr-Sep 7HEC ⟲ ₲ ⟡ 🐃 ✕ ⊙ ◘ ∅ ⊫ 🗐 ₹ P 🗐 ⊞ lau
Prices: ♠8 pitch 10

GOTTSDORF BAYERN

AZUR-Ferienzentrum Bayerwald ☎ 08593 880
Extensive terrain in quiet location.
➲ *Access via A3 (Regensburg-Passau) and B388.*
15 Mar-15 Nov 12HEC ⟲ ₲ 🐃 ✕ ⊙ ◘ ∅ 🗐 🗐 ⊞ lau
➡ ₹LP
Prices: ♠6-9 pitch 8-12

GRIESBACH, BAD BAYERN

Kur-Und Feriencamping Dreiquellenbad ☎ 08532 96130
In pleasant wooded surroundings with good, modern facilities.
➲ *1km S of Griesbach Spa, on the Karpfham-Schwaim road.*
All year 2.5HEC ⟲ ⟡ ₲ ⟡ 🐃 ⟡ ✕ ⊙ ◘ ⊫
🗐 ₹ P 🗐 ⊞ lau
Prices: ♠8.50 ⊞10.50 ▲9.50

▶ HANAU BAYERN
At KAHL AM MAIN(9km SE)

Kahl am Main Königsberger Str ☎ 06188 94467
Extensive site on the lakeshore with public swimming
facilities.
➲ *Take B8 to Kahl, then turn off at ARAL petrol station.*
Apr-Sep 22HEC ⬛ ⫶⫶⫶ ⊕ ♠ ⟟ ⚐ ⚑ ✕ ⊙ ◨ ⬗ ♨ ⤳ L ⚏ ⊞ ⌀
➡ ⟍PR

▶ HASLACH BAYERN

Feriencenter Wertacher Hof ☎ 08361 770
Well-kept site on Lake Grüntensee.
➲ *Access road near the Wertach-Haslach railway station.*
All year 3.5HEC ⬛ ⬙ ⊕ ♠ ⟟ ✕ ⊙ ◨ ⬗ ♨ ⤳ L ⚏ lau

▶ HERSBRUCK BAYERN
At HOHENSTADT(6km E)

Pegnitz Eschenbacher Weg 4 ☎ 09154 1500
A quiet holiday site in set among wooded hills near the River
Pegnitz.
➲ *About 6km E of Hersbruck.*
Mar-Oct 1.1HEC ⬛ ➡ ⟟ ✕ ⊙ ◨ ⌀ ⤳ R ⚏ ⊞ lau ➡ ⟍ ⟟ ✕
♨ ⟍LP
Prices: ⟟5.20 pitch 11.60

▶ HOFHEIM BAYERN

Brugger am Riegsee ☎ 08847 728
A lakeside site in a rural setting with good, modern facilities.
20 Oct-14 Dec 6HEC ⬛ ⬙ ⊕ ♠ ⟟ ⚐ ⟟ ✕ ⊙ ◨ ⌀ ⤳ L ⚏ ⊞
lau

▶ HOHENWARTH BAYERN

Fritz-Berger-Comfort ☎ 09946 367
Meadowland in the valley of the Weissens Regens with views
of the mountain range and town above.
➲ *Access from Cham on the B85 S to Miltach and continue
via Kotzing to Hohenwarth.*
All year 12HEC ⬛ ⊕ ♠ ⟟ ✕ ⊙ ◨ ⌀ ♨ ◨ ⟍ LP ⚏

▶ HOPFEN AM SEE BAYERN

Hopfensee ☎ 08362 917710
In quiet situation beside lake. Private beach. Ski-ing lessons.
➲ *4km N of Füssen.*
12 Dec-7 Nov 8HEC ⬛ ⊕ ♠ ⟟ ⚐ ⟟ ✕ ⊙ ◨ ♨ ⤳ LP ⚏ ⊞ lau
Prices: ⟟13-14.80 pitch 19-21

▶ ILLERTISSEN BAYERN

Illertissen ☎ 07303 7888
Partially terraced site with plenty of trees.
➲ *Turn off towards Dietenheim at the ARAL filling station
and continue along road for 1.5km. Site on left hand side of
road.*
Apr-15 Oct 3HEC ⬛ ⊕ ♠ ⟟ ⚐ ⟟ ✕ ⊙ ◨ ⌀ ♨ ◨ ⤳ P ⚏ ⊞
lau

▶ INGOLSTADT BAYERN

AZUR Camping Auwaldsee ☎ 0841 9611616
Near to Auwaldsee, this site lies in a beautiful setting beside
the München-Ingolstadt motorway.
➲ *Access via the Ingolstadt-Süd exit off the A9/E6 (Müchen-
Nürnberg motorway).*
All year 10HEC ⬛ ⊕ ♠ ⟟ ⚐ ✕ ⊙ ◨ ♨ ⤳ L ⚏ ⊞ lau ➡ ⟍P
Prices: ⟟7-9 pitch 10-12

▶ ISSIGAU BAYERN

Schloss Issigau Altes Schloss 3 ☎ 09293 7173
➲ *About 5km W off A9/E6 (München-Berlin) road via the
Berg/Bad Steben exit.*

15 Mar-Oct 2HEC ⬛ ⊕ ♠ ⟟ ⟟ ✕ ⊙ ◨ ◨ ♨ ◨ ⚏ ⊞ lau ➡ ⟟ ⌀
⟍LP
Prices: ⟟7 ◨8-9 ⟟9

▶ JODITZ BAYERN

Auensee ☎ 09295 381
Municipal site on partly terraced meadowland above lake.
➲ *Leave München-Berlin motorway at Berg-Bad Steben exit
and drive E for 4km.*
All year 9HEC ⬛ ⊕ ♠ ⊙ ◨ ♨ ⤳ L ⚏ ⊞ lau ➡ ⟟ ✕ ⟍P
Prices: ⟟4 ◨2 ◨6 ⟟3-5

▶ KIPFENBERG BAYERN

AZUR-Camping Altmühltal Am Festpl 3 ☎ 08465 905167
Well equipped site in an unspoilt wooded location with good
canoeing facilities.
All year 5.5HEC ⬛ ➡ ⟟ ⊙ ◨ ◨ ⤳ R ⚏ ⊞ lau ➡ ⟟ ⟟ ✕ ♨
⟍P
Prices: ⟟8-10 ◨3-4 ◨11-13 ⟟3-4

▶ KIRCHAM BAYERN

Max ☎ 08537 356
On meadow divided into pitches and 1km from spa baths at
Bad Füssing.
➲ *Turn at Passau end of Tutling on B12 to Kircham then
follow signs to site on Egglfinger Strasse, 2km from Bad Füssing.*
All year 1.5HEC ⬛ ⊕ ♠ ⟟ ⟟ ✕ ⊙ ◨ ⌀ ⬚ ◨ ⚏ ⊞ lau ➡
⟍LPRS
Prices: ⟟8 pitch 9

▶ KIRCHZELL BAYERN

AZUR-Camping Odenwald ☎ 09373 566
In natural terraced meadowland in wooded hilly country. No
admission after 21.30 hrs. Lunchtime siesta 13.00-15.00 hrs.
➲ *From Amorbach follow the Eberbach road for 5km. Site
1km from town.*
All year 7HEC ⬛ ⊕ ♠ ⟟ ✕ ⊙ ◨ ♨ ◨ ⤳ P ⚏ ⊞ lau
Prices: ⟟8-10 pitch 11-13

▶ KISSINGEN, BAD BAYERN

Bad Kissingen Euerdorfer Str 1 ☎ 0971 5211
In park beside River Saale. Lunchtime siesta 13.00-15.00 hrs.
➲ *Access near the southern bridge over the Saale.*
Apr-15 Oct 1.8HEC ⬛ ⊕ ♠ ⟟ ⟟ ✕ ⊙ ◨ ⌀ ♨ ⚏ ⊞ lau ➡ ⟍P

▶ KITZINGEN BAYERN

Schiefer Turm Marktbreiter Str 20 ☎ 09321 33125
➲ *Access via A3 exit Biebelried/Kitzingen.*
Apr-15 Oct 2.5HEC ⬛ ⊕ ♠ ⟟ ⟟ ✕ ⊙ ◨ ♨ ◨ ⤳ R ⚏ lau ➡
⟍P

▶ KLINGENBRUNN BAYERN

NationalPark ☎ 08553 727
➲ *For access, leave the B85, which turns from Cham to
Passau, approx. 12km SE of Regen near Kirchdorf turn off E
and drive about 6km towards Klingenbrunn.*
All year 5HEC ⬛ ⊕ ♠ ⟟ ⟟ ✕ ⊙ ◨ ◨ ⬚ ◨ ⚏ ⊞ lau ➡ ⟟
⌀ ⟍LP
Prices: ⟟6.50 ◨1.50 ◨6 ⟟6

▶ KÖNIGSDORF BAYERN

Königsdorf Am Bibisee ☎ 08171 81580
Unspoilt site in natural setting in meadowland. A number of
individual pitches for tourers. Lunchtime siesta 12.30-14.30
hrs.
➲ *Off B11, 2km N of town just beyond the edge of the forest.*
All year 8.6HEC ⬛ ⊕ ♠ ⟟ ⟟ ✕ ⊙ ◨ ♨ ⤳ L ⚏ ⊞ lau ➡
⟍PRS
Prices: ⟟8-9 ◨3-4 ◨4-5 ⟟3-4

KÖNIGSSEE BAYERN

Mühlleiten ☎ 08652 4584
A pleasant site in wooded surroundings adjacent to a small guesthouse. Beautiful views of the Berchtesgaden mountains.
➲ *N of Königsee towards Berchtesgaden.*
All year 1.5HEC ⸽⸽⸽ ⚘ 🌳 ⚡ ✕ ⊙ 🚻 ∅ ⚓ R 🏪 lau ➡ 🍴 🎣LP

KRUN BAYERN

Tennsee ☎ 08825 170
A partially terraced site with fine views of the Karwendel and Zugspitz mountains.
➲ *From München-Garmisch-Partenkirchen motorway take B2 to Mittenwald and follow signs "Tennsee".*
Closed 16 Nov-13 Dec 5.2HEC ⸽⸽⸽ ⁖⁖⁖ ⚘ 🌳 ⚡ 🍴 ✕ ⊙ 🚻 ∅ ☲ 🏪 🏪 🖃 lau ➡ 🎣L

KÜHNHAUSEN BAYERN

Stadler Strandbadstr 10 ☎ 08686 8037
Level meadow on lake with private beach.
➲ *2m E shore of Lake Waginger.*
Apr-Sep 0.9HEC ⸽⸽⸽ ⚘ 🌳 ⊙ 🚻 ∅ ⚓ L 🖃 lau ➡ ⚡ 🍴 ✕ ∅ 🖃

LACKENHÄUSER BAYERN

KNAUS Lackenhäuser ☎ 08583 311
Extensive site with woodland parks, waterfalls. Siesta 13.00-15.00 hrs. Many health resort facilities. Garden chess. Curling.
Closed Nov 14.5HEC ⸽⸽⸽ ⚘ 🌳 ⚡ 🍴 ✕ ⊙ 🚻 ∅ ☲ 🏪 🏪 🔺 ⚓ P 🖃 🅿
Prices: ⚑8.50 pitch 7.50-12

LANDSBERG BAYERN

Romantik am Lech ☎ 08191 47505
Level site with some terraces on right bank of the Lech. Lunchtime siesta 13.00-15.00 hrs.
Camping Card Compulsory.
➲ *S towards Gut Pössing.*
All year 6.5HEC ⸽⸽⸽ ⁖⁖⁖ ⚘ ⚘ 🌳 ⚡ ⊙ 🚻 ∅ 🖃 🖃 lau ➡ 🍴 ✕ 🎣R

LANGLAU BAYERN

Langlau Seestr 30, Kleiner Brombachsee ☎ 09834 96969
On the shores of the Kleiner Brombachsee.
➲ *From Gunzevhausen 10km in the direction of Pleinfield.*
Mar-15 Nov 12.4HEC ⸽⸽⸽ ⚘ ⚡ 🌳 ⚡ 🍴 ✕ ⊙ 🚻 ∅ 🏪 🖃 lau ➡ ✕ 🎣L 🖃
Prices: ⚑10 pitch 11.50

LECHBRUCK BAYERN

DCC Stadt Essen Oberer Lechsee ☎ 08862 8426
Terraced site, very tidy and well maintained on Oberen Lech lake. Separate section for dog owners. Closed 13.00-15.00 hrs and 22.00-07.00 hrs.
➲ *Signposted from town centre.*
All year 16HEC ⸽⸽⸽ ⚘ 🌳 ⚡ ✕ ⊙ 🚻 ∅ 🎣 L 🖃 🖃 lau ➡ 🎣P

LINDAU IM BODENSEE BAYERN

At ZECH(4km SE)

Lindau-Zech Fraunhoferstr 20 ☎ 08382 72236
Site lies on meadowland with trees, reaching down to the lake. Very large sanitary blocks. Common room, reading room, field for ball games and a separate common room for young people.
➲ *From Lindau, take the B31 towards Bregenz and turn right (signposted) just before the level crossing. The site is 500m further down the road.*
Apr-15 Oct 5HEC ⸽⸽⸽ ⚘ ⚡ 🌳 ⚡ ✕ ⊙ 🚻 ∅ 🎣 L 🖃 🖃 ⚘ lau ➡ 🎣P
Prices: ⚑8.60-9.60 pitch 12-13

MEMMINGEN BAYERN

At BUXHEIM(5km NW)

See International Am Weiherhaus 7 ☎ 08331 71800
Terraced site beyond public bathing area.
➲ *Leave Um-Kempten motorway at Memminger Kreuz then right to Buxheim.*
May-Sep 42HEC ⸽⸽⸽ ➡ 🌳 ⚡ 🍴 ✕ ⊙ 🚻 ☲ 🏪 ⚓ L 🖃 lau ➡ ∅
Prices: ⚑7 ⚐13 🚗13 🔺4

MITTENWALD BAYERN

Isarhorn ☎ 08823 5216
In a loop of the River Isar with many pines. Lunchtime siesta 13.00-15.00 hrs.
➲ *3km N to the W of B2 (Garmisch-Partenkirchen-Mittenwald road).*
All year 7.5HEC ⸽⸽⸽ ⚘ ➡ 🌳 ⚡ ✕ ⊙ 🚻 ∅ ⚓ R 🖃 🖃 ➡ 🍴 ✕ 🎣LP
Prices: ⚑8-9 pitch 12-13

MÖRSLINGEN BAYERN

Mörslingen ☎ 09074 4024
Camping Card Compulsory.
➲ *6km N of Dillengen.*
All year 1HEC ⸽⸽⸽ ➡ 🌳 ⚡ ✕ ⊙ 🚻 ☲ 🏪 🏪 🎣 L 🖃 🖃 lau
Prices: ⚑8 pitch 15

MÜHLHAUSEN BEI AUGSBURG BAYERN

Lech Seeweg 6 ☎ 08207 2200
On level grassland with own swimming facilities on lakeside.
➲ *4km N in direction of Neuburg.*
All year 5HEC ⸽⸽⸽ ⚘ 🌳 ⚡ ✕ ⊙ 🚻 ∅ ☲ 🏪 🎣 L 🖃 🖃 lau ➡ 🍴 ✕ 🎣P
Prices: ⚑6.50 ⚐2 🚗12-14 🔺6-10

Waldcamping München-Obermenzing

To reach the site follow motorway signs for Stuttgart – coming from Salzburg direction follow Lindau signs and leave motorway at Pasing exit.
Set in a large park of 50,000 sq.m 900m from the end of the motorway Stuttgart-München.
350 spaces for caravans and tents, 130 with own electricity supply and separated by hedges. Individual washing cubicles, free hot water for washing, hot showers, washing machine, dryer. heated washrooms, self-service shop.
Opportunities for swimming 2.5km from site.
Locked from 22.00 hrs. Good connections to city centre by bus, tram or urban railway.
Open from 15.3-31.10.
Farmer: A. Blenck Telephone 089/8 11 22 35 Fax 089/8 14 48 07

Ludwigshof am See Augsburger Str 36 ☎ 08027 1077
Clean site with small lake away from motorway, near
restaurant of the same name. Separate section for residential
pitches.
➲ *1.5km from Augsburg Ost exit towards Neuberg.*
Apr-Oct 14HEC ⊔⊔⊔ ♠ ⋔ ⅊ ⅃ ✕ ⊙ ➋ ⌀ ≗ ⅃ ☒ ⊞ ⌘ lau
♦ ⅃P

MÜNCHEN (MUNICH) BAYERN
At OBERMENZING

München-Obermenzing Lochhausener Str 59 ☎ 089
8112235
Park-like site near motorway. Shop closed in winter and no
campers accepted after 31 Oct.
Camping Card or Identification papers Compulsory.
➲ *Approx 1km from the end of Stuttgart-München motorway.*
15 Mar-Oct 5.5HEC ⊔⊔⊔ ⠇⠇ ⋏ ♠ ⋔ ⅊ ✕ ⊙ ➋ ⌀ ☎ ⌘ Å ☒
⊞ lau ♦ ⅊ ⅃ ✕ ⅃LPR
Prices: ↟7.50 ♠5 ➋8 Å7.50

At THALKIRCHEN

SC München-Thalkirchen Zentrallandstr 49 ☎ 089 7231707
15 Mar-Oct 4.5HEC ⋏ ⋔ ⅊ ⅃ ✕ ⊙ ➋ ⌀ ➋ Å ☒ ⊞ lau
♦ ⅃P

NEBELBERG BAYERN

Waldhof ☎ 09922 1024
Partially terraced site on the Schwarzachback.
➲ *Turn off the B85 to Regen then N to Langdorf and continue
NE.*
All year 1HEC ⊔⊔⊔ ⋏ ⋔ ✕ ⊙ ➋ ≗ ☎ Å ⅃ L ☒ ⊞
♦ ⅃R

NEUBÄU BAYERN

Seecamping Seestr 4 ☎ 09469 331
Meadowland site along lakeshore.
➲ *Access from Schwandorf on the B85 in direction of Cham.*
Closed Nov 5HEC ⊔⊔⊔ ⋏ ⋔ ⅊ ⅃ ✕ ⊙ ➋ ⌀ ≗ ⅃ L ☒ ⊞ lau

NEUSTADT BAYERN

Main-Spessart-Camping-International ☎ 09393 639
Beautifully situated site along the River Main. Watersports,
including water skiing. Lunchtime siesta 12.00-14.00 hrs.
➲ *Access from Frankfurt-WÜrzburg motorway A3/E5, leave at
Marktheidenfeld exit, and follow local road towards Lohr.*
Apr-Sep 5.6HEC ⊔⊔⊔ ⋏ ⋔ ⅊ ✕ ⊙ ➋ ⌀ ≗ ⅃ PR ☒ lau
♦ ✕
Prices: ↟7.50 pitch 9.50

NÜRNBERG (NUREMBERG) BAYERN

SC Volkspark Dutzendteich Hans-Kalb-Str 56 ☎ 0911
811122
Well-kept municipal site in beautiful situation in a forest
between a stadium with a swimming pool and the Trade Fair
Centre.
➲ *Leave A9 München motorway at Nürnberg-Fischbach exit,
and continue towards the stadium.*
May-Sep 2.7HEC ⊔⊔⊔ ⋏ ⋔ ⅊ ✕ ⊙ ➋ ⌀ ⊞ lau ♦ ⅃LP
Prices: ↟9 ♠5 ➋10 Å5

OBERAMMERGAU BAYERN

Oberammergau Ettaler Str 56 ☎ 08822 94105
A year-round site with good, modern facilities providing fine
views of the Bavarian Alps.
➲ *Signposted from the town.*
All year 2.5HEC ⊔⊔⊔ ⋏ ☼ ⋔ ⅊ ⅃ ✕ ⊙ ➋ ⌀ ≗ ☎ ➋ ☒ ⊞
lau ♦ ⅃PR
Prices: ↟7-9 pitch 8-10

OBERNDORF BAYERN

Donau-Lech ☎ 09002 4044
A small site beside a lake on the SE outskirts of Donauwörth.
➲ *From Donauwörth follow B2 towards Augsburg for approx.
5km.*
All year 5HEC ⊔⊔⊔ ♠ ⋔ ⅊ ⅃ ✕ ⊙ ➋ ➋ ⅃ L ☒ lau ♦ ✕

OBERSTDORF BAYERN

Oberstdorf ☎ 08322 4022 & 6525
Level grassland site with fine mountain views.
➲ *800m N of town centre near railway line.*
All year 16HEC ⊔⊔⊔ ⋏ ⋔ ⋔ ⅊ ✕ ⊙ ➋ ⌀ ≗ ☒ ⊞ lau ♦ ⅊ ⅃P

OBERWÖSSEN BAYERN

Litzelau ☎ 08640 8704
Almost level meadowland surrounded by forested slopes.
➲ *Take B305 from Bernau exit on München-Salzburg
motorway and continue through Marquartstein and
Unterwössen.*
All year 4.5HEC ⊔⊔⊔ ⋏ ♠ ⋔ ⅊ ✕ ⊙ ➋ ⌀ ≗ ⅃ R ☒ ⊞ lau
Prices: ↟7 ➋12 Å6.50

OCHSENFURT BAYERN

Polisina Marktbreiter Str 265 ☎ 09331 8440
Terraced site at edge of wood.
➲ *From town centre follow road towards Markbreit and in
2km turn off under railway and continue uphill.*
All year 7.5HEC ⊔⊔⊔ ♠ ⋔ ⅊ ⅃ ✕ ➋ ⌀ ≗ ⅃ P ☒ ⊞ lau ♦ ⅊ ⅃L
Prices: ↟6 pitch 8

PASSAU BAYERN

Dreiflüsse ☎ 08546 633
A well equipped site in pleasant wooded surroundings.
➲ *From A3 'Passau-Nord' follow signposts.*
Apr-Oct 5HEC ⊔⊔⊔ ⠇⠇ ♠ ⋔ ⅊ ⅃ ✕ ⊙ ➋ ⌀ ≗ ☎ ➋ Å ⅃ P
☒ ⊞ lau
Prices: ↟7.50

PFAFFENHOFEN BAYERN

SC Warmbad Hauptpl 1 ☎ 08441 83543
The municipal site lies on the northern outskirts of the town
beside the River Lim.
➲ *Take the München-Nürnberg motorway, and leave at
Pfaffenhofen exit, or take the B13 which runs from München to
Ingolstadt.*
May-Sep 0.9HEC ⊔⊔⊔ ⋏ ⋔ ✕ ⊙ ➋ ⅃ P ☒ ⊞ lau ♦ ⅊ ⅃ ✕

PFRAUNDORF BAYERN

Kratzmühle ☎ 08461 64170
Terraced site, divided into pitches, on a wooded hillside
overlooking the River Altmühl.
➲ *In village turn off to Kratzmühle.*
All year 9.6HEC ⊔⊔⊔ ⋏ ⋔ ⅊ ✕ ⊙ ➋ ⌀ ☎ ⅃ LR ☒ ⊞ lau ♦
⅃LP
Prices: ↟9 ♠2 ➋8-10

PIDING BAYERN

Staufeneck ☎ 08651 2134
In beautiful and quiet situation beside River Saalach.
➲ *Leave motorway A8/E11 (München-Salzburg) via exit Bad
Reichenall road for 2.5km and then turn right.*
Apr-Oct 2.7HEC ⊔⊔⊔ ⋏ ⋔ ⅊ ⊙ ➋ ≗ ☒ ⊞ lau ♦ ⅊ ✕ ⌀ ⅃P
Prices: ↟8 pitch 9

PIELENHOFEN BAYERN

Naabtal ☎ 09409 373
The site is well-situated beside the River Nab, and has a
special section for overnight visitors.   *Contd.*

Camping Warsitzka GmbH, Rieden, Germany

Warsitzka Campsite
87669 Rieden-Roßhaupten/Forggensee
Telephone: 0049/8367/406 Fax 1256

Quiet site in wonderful location, right on Lake Forggen with a magnificent view of the Alps. Comfortable restaurant with kiosk, clean toilet facilities, children's play area, grassy area for sunbathing, water sports, fishing, walking, sites of interest, coach trips, cross-country skiing, ski paradise nearby, indoor swimming pools and much more. Price reductions in early and late season. Facilities for long-term camping from 1.10-30.4. Caravans bought and sold. Please ask for our brochure.

⊃ *Access from the Nittendorf turn off from A3/E5 Nürnberg-Regensburg N via Etterzhausen.*
All year 6HEC ⊞ 🔧 👤 🛒 👤 🍴 ✕ ⊙ 🚫 🌀 🚿 🏕 ⚡ ⅄ R 🏧 ⊞ lau
Prices: ⚡8.25 pitch 9.50

POTTENSTEIN BAYERN

Bärenschlucht ☎ 09243 206
The site lies on unspoilt meadowland in the narrow Püttlach valley and is surrounded by the rocky hills of the Fränkische Schweiz range.
⊃ *From the München-Berlin motorway leave at the Pegnitz exit and drive W for 10km on the B470 towards Forchheim.*
All year 5HEC ⊞ 🔧 🔦 🛒 ✕ ⊙ 🚫 🌀 🏕 ⚡ ⅄ R 🏧 ⊞ lau
Prices: ⚡8 🚗3 🛖8 ▲5-6

REGENSBURG BAYERN

AZUR-Regensburg Weinweg 40 ☎ 0941 270025
The municipal site lies on the western outskirts of the town, and the right bank of the Danube. Has a special section reserved for caravans.
⊃ *Access via the western by-pass, and over the Pfaffenstein Bridge.*
All year 2.6HEC ⊞ 🔧 🔦 🛒 ✕ ⊙ 🚫 🌀 🏧 lau ➡ ⅄LPR
Prices: ⚡8-10 🚗3-4 🛖11-13 ▲3-4

ROSSHAUPTEN BAYERN

Warsitzka ☎ 08367 406
A well-kept site with good installations.
⊃ *From Füssen follow road B16 for 10km towards Rosshaupten. About 2km before the village and before the bridge turn right.*
All year 4.5HEC ⊞ 🔧 🔦 🛒 ✕ ⊙ 🚫 🌀 ⅄ LR 🏧 ⊞ lau ➡ ⅄P
Prices: ⚡9-9.50 pitch 10-13.50

ROTHENBURG OB DER TAUBER BAYERN

Tauber-Idyll Detwang 28A ☎ 09861 3177
The well-kept site lies on a meadow scattered with trees and bushes, on the outskirts of the N suburb of Detwang and next to the River Tauber.
⊃ *Access from all main roads is well signposted. The best route is from Nordinger Str (B25) heading W along the River Tauber in the direction of Bad Mergentheim.*
28 Mar-Oct 0.5HEC ⊞ 🔧 🔦 🛒 ⊙ 🚫 🌀 🏧 ⊞ lau ➡ ✕ ⅄PR
Prices: ⚡7 🚗3 🛖6 ▲6

Tauber-Romantik Detwang 39 ☎ 09861 6191
Apr-Oct 1.2HEC ⊞ ➡ 🔦 🛒 👤 ✕ ⊙ 🚫 🌀 🏕 🏕 ⚡ lau ➡ ⅄R

ROTTENBUCH BAYERN

Terrassencamping am Richterbichl ☎ 08867 1500
Several pleasant terraces with good views.
⊃ *On S outskirts on B23.*
All year 1.2HEC ⊞ 🔧 🔦 👤 ⊙ 🚫 🌀 🍴 ⚡ ⅄ L 🏧 lau ➡ 👤 ✕ ⅄P ⊞
Prices: ⚡8.50 pitch 8

RUHPOLDING BAYERN

Ortnerhof Ort 5 ☎ 08663 1764
Well-kept site on a meadow at the foot of the Rauschberg Mountain, opposite the cable-car station.
⊃ *Off Deutsche Alpenstr.*
All year 2.4HEC ⊞ ❄ 🔧 🔦 ✕ ⊙ 🚫 🌀 🏧 ⊞ ➿ lau ➡ 👤
Prices: ⚡8-9 🚗2-2.50 🛖4-4.50 ▲4-4.50

SCHECHEN BAYERN

Erlensee Rosenheimer Str 63 ☎ 08039 1695
The site lies on the shores of an artificial lake.
⊃ *If approaching from Rosenheim, take the B15 approx 10km N of Rosenheim towards Wasserburg and turn right upon entering Schechen.*
All year 6HEC ⊞ 🔧 🔦 🛒 👤 ✕ ⊙ 🚫 🌀 ⚡ ⅄ L 🏧 ⊞ lau
Prices: ⚡7.50 🚗3.50 🛖9 ▲5-12

SCHWANGAU BAYERN

At BANNWALDSEE(4km N)

Bannwaldsee ☎ 08362 81001
Meadow gently sloping towards lake.
⊃ *Turn off the B17 about 4km NE of Schwangau, in westerly direction towards lake.*
All year 12HEC ⊞ ⛴ 🔧 ➡ 🔦 🛒 👤 ✕ ⊙ 🚫 🌀 🏕 ⅄ L 🏧 ⊞
SEEFELD BAYERN

Strandbad Pilsensee Graf Toerringstr 11 ☎ 08152 7232 or 7233
⊃ *S towards Pilsensee.*
All year 10HEC ⊞ 🔧 🔦 🛒 ✕ ⊙ 🚫 🌀 🏕 ⚡ ⅄ L 🏧 ⊞ lau
Prices: ⚡7-8 pitch 11-12

SOMMERACH AM MAIN BAYERN

Katzenkopf am See ☎ 09381 9215
On level ground beside the river Main. Pitches divided by bushes and good recreational facilities.
⊃ *Leave A3 (Würzburg-Nürbberg) at exit 'Kitzingen-Schwarzach-Volkach' and continue towards Volkach for 7km.*
7 Apr-25 Oct 4HEC ⊞ 🔧 🔦 🛒 ✕ ⊙ 🚫 🌀 🏕 ⅄ LR 🏧 ⊞ lau ➡ 👤 👤 ⅄P ⊞
Prices: ⚡8.50-9 pitch 9.50-11.50

SONTHOFEN BAYERN

Iller Sinwagstr 2 ☎ 08321 2350
Site lies on the shore of the River Iller (too dangerous for swimming) near a swimming pool.
⊃ *1km on the B19 towards Obersdorf, before the bridge over the River Iller.*
Closed Nov-20 Dec 2.1HEC ⊞ 🔧 🔦 🛒 ✕ ⊙ 🚫 🌀 ⅄ R 🏧 ⊞ lau ➡ ✕ ⅄P
Prices: pitch 30-35

STADTSTEINACH BAYERN

AZUR-Stadtsteinach Badstr 5 ☎ 09225 95401
Terraced site on SE facing slope with a view over the town and surrounding hills. Lunchtime siesta 13.00-15.00 hrs.
⊃ *Access via Badstr.*
All year 5HEC ⊞ 🔧 🔦 🛒 ✕ ⊙ 🚫 🌀 🏕 ⚡ ⅄ P 🏧 lau ➡ 👤 ⊞

▶ **TETTENHAUSEN** BAYERN

Gut Horn ☎ 08681 227
Quiet site, divided into pitches on lake shore, sheltered by forest. Lunchtime siesta 13.00-14.00 hrs.
⤳ *SE on Wagingersee.*
Mar-Nov 5HEC ⚏ ⌘ ↰ ⚑ ☉ ⚑ ⊟ ⚑ ↺ L ⚐ lau ➧ ⌀ ⊞
Prices: ⚑8.50 pitch 9

▶ **TITTMONING** BAYERN

Seebauer ☎ 08683 541
On meadow with a few terraces. Near a farm, beside a lake.
⤳ *3km NW towards Burghausen.*
All year 2.3HEC ⚏ ⌘ ↰ ⚑ ✕ ☉ ⚑ ⌀ ⊟ ↺ L ⚐ ⊞ lau ➧ ⚑
↺LP
Prices: ⚑7-9 pitch 8-10

▶ **TRAUSNITZ** BAYERN

Trausnitz ☎ 09655 1304
All year 3.5HEC ⚏ ⌘ ↰ ⚑ ✕ ☉ ⚑ ⌀ ↺ LR ⚐ ⊞ lau

▶ **TÜCHERSFELD** BAYERN

Fränkische Schweiz Tüchersfeld 57 ☎ 09242 1788
⤳ *Access from motorway A9/E6, leave at exit 'Pegnitz' then 12km W on B470 towards Forchheim.*
Apr-15 Oct 2HEC ⚏ ⌘ ↰ ⚑ ✕ ☉ ⚑ ⊟ ⚐ ⊞ lau ➧ ↺P
Prices: ⚑7.50-8.10 ⚐4.75-5.35 ⚐9.45-9.95 ▲8.05-8.65

▶ **VELBURG** BAYERN

Hauenstein ☎ 09182 454
A well-appointed site, lies on several terraces and is completely divided into individual pitches. All with electric points.
⤳ *From motorway A3 Nürnberg-Regensburg leave at exit Velberg, then continue through village towards the S following signs Naturbad.*
All year 5HEC ⚏ ⌘ ↰ ⚑ ☉ ⚑ ⚑ ⊟ ↺ lau ➧ ↺L
Prices: ⚑8.50 ⚐4 ⚐7 ▲6

▶ **VIECHTACH** BAYERN

KNAUS *Viechtach* ☎ 09942 1095
Site on slightly undulating meadow, divided by rows of trees. The site has modern installations.
⤳ *For access, take the B85 which runs from the junction with the road towards Freibad Viechtach, and follow the signposts.*
Closed Nov 5.7HEC ⚏ ⌘ ↰ ⚑ ✕ ☉ ⚑ ⌀ ⊟ ⚑ ▲ ↺ P ⚐
⊞ lau

▶ **WAGING** BAYERN

Strandcamping Am See 1 ☎ 08681 552
Extensive, level grassland site divided in two by access road to neighbouring sailing club. The site lies near the Strandbad and Kurhaus bathing area and spa, and the Casino. There is a Kneipp (hydrotherapeutic) pool in the camp.
⤳ *Follow the signposts leading to the Strandbad bathing area.*
Apr-Sep 15HEC ⚏ ➧ ↰ ⚑ ✕ ☉ ⚑ ⌀ ⊟ ↺ L ⚐ ✺ lau
Prices: ⚑6.90-10.90 pitch 10.10-19.80

▶ **WALTENHOFEN** BAYERN

Insel-Camping am See ☎ 08379 881
A well equipped site situated directly on the lake shore with access to neighbouring ski slopes.
⤳ *Off B19, S of Memhölz.*
All year 1.5HEC ⚏ ⌘ ↰ ⚑ ✕ ☉ ⚑ ⌀ ↺ L ⚐ ⊞ lau ➧ ⚑
Prices: ⚑7 ⚐1 ⚐8-10 ▲6-8

▶ **WEILER-SIMMERBERG** BAYERN

Alpenblick Schreckmanklitz 18 ☎ 08381 3447
Clean facilities on this site belonging to the Deutsche Alpenstrasse.

⤳ *Access from the B308 in Weiler. Signposted.*
Etr-4 Nov 2.5HEC ⚏ ⚒ ↰ ⚑ ✕ ☉ ⚑ ⌀ ⊟ ⚑ ↺ L ⚐ ⊞ ✺
lau ➧ ⚑ ✕

▶ **WEISSACH** BAYERN

Wallberg Rainerweg 10 ☎ 08022 5371
The well-kept site lies on a level meadow with a few trees beside a stream.
⤳ *For access take the B318 from Gmund to Tegernsee, drive through Bad Wiessee, and on to Wiessach, approx 9km further on.*
All year 3HEC ⚏ ⌘ ↰ ⚑ ✕ ☉ ⚑ ⌀ ⚑ ↺ R ⚐ ➧ ⚑ ↺LP
⊞
Prices: ⚑8-9 ⚐4 ⚐10-11.50 ▲8.50

▶ **WEISSENSTADT** BAYERN

Weissenstädter See Badstr 91 ☎ 09253 288
This municipal site is in close proximity to a swimming pool and a lake, so offering numerous sports facilities.
⤳ *1km NW of the town.*
All year 1.7HEC ⚏ ⌘ ↰ ✕ ☉ ⚑ ⌀ ↺ LP ⚐ lau ➧ ⚑
Prices: ⚑8 ⚐5.50 ⚐5.50 ▲5

▶ **WEMDING** BAYERN

AZUR Waldsee Wemding ☎ 09092 90101
In a wooded lakeside setting with excellent recreational facilities.
15 Mar-15 Nov 9HEC ⚏ ⌀ ⌘ ↰ ⚑ ✕ ☉ ⚑ ⌀ ⌀ ↺ L ⚑ ⊞
lau ➧ ⚑ ↺P
Prices: ⚑8-10 ⚐3-4 ⚐11-13 ▲3-4

▶ **WERTACH** BAYERN

Grüntensee Grüntenseestr 41 ☎ 08365 375
A modern site beside Lake Grünten.
⤳ *If approaching from Kempten, turn right entering Nesselwerg, and follow the signposts.*
All year 5HEC ⚏ ⌘ ↰ ⚑ ✕ ☉ ⚑ ⌀ ⌀ ↺ L ⚐ ⊞ lau ➧ ↺P
Prices: ⚑9.50-11 ⚐10-12 ▲6-7

▶ **WINKL BEI BISCHOFSWIESEN** BAYERN

Winkllandthal ☎ 08652 8164
In meadow between the B20 and edge of woodland.
⤳ *From Bad Reichenhall to Berchtesgaden about 8km.*
All year 2.5HEC ⚏ ⚒ ⌀ ⌘ ↰ ⚑ ✕ ☉ ⚑ ⌀ ⚑ ▲ ↺ R
⚐ ⊞ lau
Prices: ⚑9.50 ⚐3 ⚐7 ▲7

▶ **ZWIESEL** BAYERN

AZUR-Ferienzentrum Bayerischer Wald Waldesruhweg 34
☎ 09922 802595
A modern site. Clean sanitary installations.
All year 16HEC ⚏ ⌘ ↰ ⚑ ☉ ⚑ ⌀ ⊟ ⚑ ⊞ lau ➧ ↺P
Prices: ⚑7-10 ⚐3-4 ⚐9-13 ▲3-4

● ● ● ● **SOUTH WEST** ● ● ● ●

A rich variety of scenery both charming and grandiose, has led this magnificent area of Germany to become one of the most popular holiday regions.
In the far south, Lake Constance is a majestic expanse of water, ideal for watersports, fringed with historic towns and attractive villages.
The Black Forest is a perennial delight with its vast coniferous woodlands, rushing mountain streams, and glacier-cut valleys. Spectacular views are to be had from the popular Black Forest Ridgeway.
The Neckarland-Schwaben covers the rest of the region and is an exciting area to explore. There are castles and palaces, bustling towns and fascinating museums. At its
Contd.

core is Stuttgart, beautifully situated in a basin enclosed by forest-covered hills, orchards and vineyards that extend well into the city.
This undisputed cultural and commercial centre of the state, is a city of technical progress, while five castles remind us of its princely past.

··

▶ **ABTSGMÜND** BADEN-WÜRTTEMBERG
▶ At **POMMERTSWEILER**(6km N)

Hammerschmiede-See Hammerschmiede 6 ☎ 07963 1205 & 415
A terraced site in a wooded setting beside the lake. Partly divided into pitches with concrete paths.
⮕ *From Abtsgmünd travel for 3km then turn N to Pommertsweiler, site signposted.*
All year 4HEC ⸺ ⚐ ⌂ ✕ ⊙ ⬤ ∅ ⚒ ⅋ L ⊡ ⊞ lau

▶ **ACHERN** BADEN-WÜRTTEMBERG

SC am Achernsee ☎ 07841 25253
All year 6.5HEC ⸺ ⚐ ⌂ ⅊ ⊙ ⬤ ∅ ⚒ ⅋ L ⊡ ⊞ lau
Prices: ⚑9 pitch 12

▶ **ALPIRSBACH** BADEN-WÜRTTEMBERG

Wolpert ☎ 07444 6313
On level land beside the River Kinzig.
⮕ *1km N of town below B294.*
All year 1.2HEC ⸺ ⚐ ⌂ ⊙ ⬤ ∅ ⚒ ⅋ ⊡ ⊞ lau ▶ ⅊ ✕ ⅋R
Prices: ⚑6.50 ⬤4.50 ⬤5 ⚑3

▶ **ALTENSTEIG** BADEN-WÜRTTEMBERG

Schwarzwald ☎ 07453 8415
Parkland site of motor sport club Altensteig beside the River Nagold. Separate section for dog owners.
⮕ *On road to Garrweiler 1km from Altensteig.*
All year 3.3HEC ⸺ ⚐ ⌂ ✕ ⊙ ⬤ ∅ ⚒ ⬤ ⅋ R ⊡ ⊞ lau ▶ ⅋P
Prices: ⚑7.50 ⬤4 ⬤5 ⚑2.50

▶ **ALTNEUDORF** BADEN-WÜRTTEMBERG

Steinachperle ☎ 06228 467
The site lies in the narrow shady valley of the River Steinach. Lunchtime siesta 13.00-15.00 hrs.
⮕ *The entrance to the camp lies next to the Gasthaus zum Pflug, on the outskirts of Altneudorf.*
Apr-Sep 3.5HEC ⸺ ⚐ ⌂ ✕ ⊙ ⬤ ∅ ⚒ ⊡ ⊞ lau

▶ **BADENWEILER** BADEN-WÜRTTEMBERG

Badenweiler Weilertalstr 73 ☎ 07632 1550
On a level meadow surrounded by beautiful Black Forest scenery. Good facilities for local walking etc.
⮕ *Access via A5 exit Neuenburg.*
All year 1.6HEC ⸺ ⚐ ⥼ ⌂ ⅊ ⅊ ✕ ⊙ ⬤ ∅ ⚒ ⅋ P ⊡ ⊞ lau ▶ ✕ ⅋R
Prices: ⚑10.90 pitch 13.90

▶ **BUCHHORN BEI ÖHRINGEN** BADEN-WÜRTTEMBERG

Seewiese Seestr 11 ☎ 07941 61568
A well equipped site on a meadow beside a lake with fine views of the surrounding mountains. Good recreational facilities.
⮕ *7km S of Öhringen via Pfedelbach. Access via A6.*
All year 5.5HEC ⸺ ⚐ ⌂ ⅊ ⅊ ✕ ⊙ ⬤ ⚒ ⬤ ⅋ L ⊡ ⊞ lau ▶ ⅋PR
Prices: ⚑8 ⬤5 ⬤5-7 ⚑3-5

▶ **BÜHL** BADEN-WÜRTTEMBERG

Adam Campingstr 1 ☎ 07223 23194
On level grassland, by lake.
⮕ *1km from the Bühl exit of the A5/E4-E11 (Karlsruhe-Basel) in direction of Lichtenau.*
All year 16HEC ⸺ ⚐ ⌂ ⅊ ⅊ ✕ ⊙ ⬤ ∅ ⚒ ⅋ L ⊡ ⊞ lau ▶ ⅋P
Prices: ⚑8.50-11 ⬤9-11 ⚑7-9

▶ **CREGLINGEN** BADEN-WÜRTTEMBERG

AZUR Camping Romantische Strasse ☎ 07933 20289
A site completely divided into pitches, lying on the S outskirts of Münster. Children's playground. Individual washing cubicles.
⮕ *If approaching from Bad Mergentheim or from Rothenburg/Tauber, take the ' Romantic road' up to Creglingen. Then turn S and drive 3km up to Münster.*
15 Mar-15 Nov 6HEC ⸺ ⚐ ⌂ ⅊ ✕ ⊙ ⬤ ∅ ⅋ P ⊡ ⊞ lau ▶ ⅋L
Prices: ⚑6-9 ⬤3-4 ⬤8-12 ⚑3-4

▶ **DINGELSDORF** BADEN-WÜRTTEMBERG

Fliesshorn ☎ 07533 5262
At a farm, on meadowland with fine trees.
⮕ *In town turn off Stadd-Dettingen road and follow signs to NW for 1.3km.*
Apr-Sep 5HEC ⸺ ⚐ ⌂ ⅊ ✕ ⊙ ⬤ ∅ ⊞ lau ▶ ⅋LS

▶ **DONAUESCHINGEN** BADEN-WÜRTTEMBERG

Riedsee ☎ 07711 5511
Level meadow on lakeside.
⮕ *Turn off A81 exit 'Geisingen' and continue 13km on B31 towards Pfohren, then turn left and continue for 1km.*
All year 8HEC ⸺ ⚐ ⌂ ⅊ ⅊ ✕ ⊙ ⬤ ∅ ⚒ ⅋ L ⊡ ⊞ lau

▶ **DÜRRHEIM, BAD** BADEN-WÜRTTEMBERG

Sunthauersee ☎ 07706 712
Apr-Sep 10HEC ⸺ ⚐ ⌂ ⌂ ⊙ ⬤ ∅ ⬤ ⅋ LR ⊡ ⊞ lau ▶ ⅊ ✕ ⅋P
Prices: ⚑7 ⬤7.50 ⬤7.50 ⚑6

▶ **EBERBACH** BADEN-WÜRTTEMBERG

Eberbach ☎ 06271 1071
On slightly sloping meadow on left bank of the river. Separate field for young people. Some traffic noise and liable to flooding when river is high. Lunchtime siesta 13.00-15.00 hrs.
⮕ *For access head for the sportsground after crossing bridge from town centre.*
Apr-15 Oct ⸺ ⚐ ⌂ ⅊ ✕ ⊙ ⬤ ⊡ ⊞ lau ▶ ⅊ ∅ ⚒ ⅋P

▶ **ELLWANGEN-JAGST** BADEN-WÜRTTEMBERG

AZUR Ellwangen Rotenbacherstr 45 ☎ 07961 7921
A modern site with good facilities in a wooded loaction on the banks of the River Jagst.
All year ⸺ ⚐ ⌂ ⅊ ⅊ ✕ ⊙ ⬤ ∅ ⅋ R ⊡ ⊞ lau ▶ ⅋LPR

▶ **ERPFINGEN** BADEN-WÜRTTEMBERG

AZUR Schwäbische Alb (Rosencamping) ☎ 07128 466
Extensive site on a hill.
⮕ *Access from Reutlingen on B312 in south easterly direction to Grooengstingen, then S on Schwabische Albstr (B313) for 3.5km to Haid , then turn right to Erpfingen. Site on W outskirts.*
All year 9HEC ⸺ ⚐ ⥼ ⌂ ⅊ ⊙ ⬤ ∅ ⚒ ⬤ ⅋ P ⊡ ⊞ lau ▶ ✕ ⅋L
Prices: ⚑7-10 ⬤3-4 ⬤9-13 ⚑5-7

ETTENHEIM BADEN-WÜRTTEMBERG

Oase ☎ 07822 9881
In a wooded location with good, modern facilities.
➲ *Access via A5 exit Ettenheim.*
4 Apr-6 Oct 6HEC ▦ ♦ ⌕ ⌂ ⌂ ✕ ⊙ ⌀ ⌀ ≞ ☎ ⊞ lau ➡ ⇂P

FREIBURG IM BREISGAU BADEN-WÜRTTEMBERG

Breisgau Seestr 20 ☎ 07665 2346
Extensive level grassland site on outskirts of town. Section
reserved for campers with dogs.
➲ *500m E of autobahn exit 'Freiburg Nord'.*
All year 6.5HEC ▦ ♦ ⌕ ⌂ ✕ ⊙ ⌀ ⌀ ≞ ⇂ L ☎ lau

Ferien & Kurbad Mösle-Park Waldseestr 77 ☎ 0761 72938
On outskirts of town near 'Busse's Waldschänke' inn.
➲ *Turn right after town hall across railway and follow
Waldseestr towards Littenweiler.*
25 Mar-25 Oct 7HEC ▦ ♦ ⌕ ⌂ ✕ ⊙ ⌀ ⌀ ≞ ⌂ ☎ ⊞ lau
Prices: ⚑8 pitch 9

FREUDENSTADT BADEN-WÜRTTEMBERG

Langenwald Strassburgerstr 167 ☎ 07441 2862
The site consists of several sections and lies next to a former
mill beside the River Forbach.
➲ *4km W of Freudenstadt below the B28 (Freudenstadt-
Strasbourg).*
Apr-Nov 1.4HEC ▦ ⌕ ⌂ ⌂ ✕ ⊙ ⌀ ⌀ ≞ ⇂ PR ☎ ⊞
lau
Prices: ⚑9 ⇆5.50-6 ⌸6.50-6 ▲5-6

GAMMELSBACH BADEN-WÜRTTEMBERG

Freienstein Neckaltalstr 172 ☎ 06068 1306
The site lies just off the B45 in a landscaped preservation
area. It is terraced and divided into pitches. Lunchtime siesta
13.00-15.00 hrs.
Apr-Sep 5HEC ▦ ♦ ⌕ ⌂ ⌂ ✕ ⊙ ⌀ ⌀ ≞ ☎ lau ➡ ⌂⇂LPR
Prices: ⚑7.50 pitch 10

HALLWANGEN BADEN-WÜRTTEMBERG

Königskanzel ☎ 07443 6730
In an elvated position in the centre of the Black Forest.
➲ *Follow B28 from Freudenstadt towards Altensteig past the
Hallwangen junction to camping sign on left.*
All year 4HEC ▦ ⌕ ⌂ ⌂ ✕ ⊙ ⌀ ⌀ ≞ ⇂ P ☎ ⊞ lau ➡ ⇂L
Prices: ⚑8.50-9.50 pitch 12

HAUSEN BADEN-WÜRTTEMBERG

Wagenburg ☎ 07579 559
On meadowland between the railway bank and the Danube.
Site has spectacular view of surrounding landscape. Entrance
through subway.
15 Apr-15 Oct 1.2HEC ▦ ⌕ ⌂ ⌂ ✕ ⊙ ⌀ ⌀ ≞ ⇂ R ☎ ⊞
lau ➡ ✕
Prices: ⚑7 ⇆3 ⌸7.50 ▲5.50-7.50

HEIDELBERG BADEN-WÜRTTEMBERG

Heidelberg-Neckartal Schlierbacher Landstr 151 ☎ 06221
802506
Nov-14 Apr 3HEC ▦ ♦ ⌕ ⌂ ⌂ ✕ ⊙ ⌀ ≞ ⌂ ⌂ ▲ ⇂
R ☎ ⊞ lau

HERBOLZHEIM BADEN-WÜRTTEMBERG

Herbolzheim Im Laue 1 ☎ 07643 1460
Apr-15 Oct 2.5HEC ▦ ⌕ ⌂ ⊙ ⌀ ⌀ ☎ ⊞ ➡ ⌂ ⌂ ✕ ⇂P
Prices: ⚑9 pitch 10

HÖFEN AN DER ENZ BADEN-WÜRTTEMBERG

Quellgrund ☎ 07081 6984
Well maintained municipal site on grassland between the
B294 and the River Enz.
➲ *Access from Pforzheim on the B294 in SW direction to the
'Quelle' inn with entrance to ARAL petrol station at entrance to
Höfen, then turn right.*
All year 3.6HEC ▦ ⌕ ⌂ ⌂ ⊙ ⌀ ⌂ ☎ lau ➡ ✕ ⌂ ⇂P ⊞
Prices: ⚑7.50 pitch 9

HORB BADEN-WÜRTTEMBERG

Schüttehof ☎ 07451 3951
Situated on flat mountain top.
➲ *Access from Horb in direction of Freudenstadt. 1.5km
beyond the town boundary turn towards stables and site, and
onward for 1km.*
All year 6HEC ▦ ⌕ ⌂ ⌂ ✕ ⊙ ⌀ ⌀ ⇂ P ☎ ⊞ lau
Prices: ⚑9.50 pitch 11.50

HORN BODENSEE BADEN-WÜRTTEMBERG

Horn ☎ 07735 685
A large and well-managed municipal site with a pleasant
beach.
➲ *In Horn turn off the Radolfszell-Stein am Rhein road and
towards the lake.*
Apr-10 Oct 10HEC ▦ ⌕ ⌂ ⌂ ⌂ ✕ ⊙ ⌀ ⌀ ⌂ ▲ ⇂ LP ☎ ⊞
⌂ lau ➡ ⇂L

ISNY BADEN-WÜRTTEMBERG

Waldbad Isny ☎ 07562 2389
In wooded surroundings beside a lake.
➲ *S of town on B12. Signposted.*
All year 0.5HEC ▦ ⌕ ⌂ ⌂ ⊙ ⌀ ⌀ ⇂ LP ☎

KARLSRUHE BADEN-WÜRTTEMBERG

At DURLACH(8km SE)

AZUR Türmbergblick Tiegener Str 40 ☎ 0721 497206
On level ground amongst orchards. Lunchtime siesta 12.30-
15.00 hrs.
➲ *Access via Karlsruhe-Dürlach exit on A5/E4. Signposted.*
15 Mar-15 Nov 3.5HEC ▦ ⌕ ⌂ ⌂ ✕ ⊙ ⌀ ☎ ⊞ lau ➡ ⌂
✕ ≞ ⇂LP
Prices: ⚑7-10 ⇆3-4 ⌸9-13 ▲5.80-7

KEHL BADEN-WÜRTTEMBERG

Kehl-Strassburg ☎ 07851 2603
Park-like site divided into separate sections for young
campers, transit and holiday campers. Lunchtime siesta
13.00-15.00 hrs.
➲ *Turn left at the Rhine dam on the outskirts of the town.*
15 Mar-Oct 2.3HEC ▦ ⌕ ⌂ ⌂ ✕ ⊙ ⌀ ≞ ☎ ⊞ ➡ ⇂PR

ISNY CAMPING AM WALDBAD

Tel: 00 49 7562 2389 Fax: 00 49 7562 2004
Welcome to Isny-Siggi Ryssel, Manager awaits you. Situated
1.5km from Isny town centre and 1.2km to ALDI supermarket.
An attractive and peaceful campsite near a crystal clear,
spring lake. Experienced campers from all over the world are
enthusiastic about this beautiful site. Come and enjoy our
hospitality, even at breakfast a freshly baked roll, per person
is included in the overnight price. Separate tent area for
young people. Cosy atmosphere, shop, inn and modern toilet
facilities. The site has its own bathing lake with free
swimming, there is also an area for non swimmers. Children's
playground and many miles of footpaths. Separate grill house.
Ideal for touring or centre based campers. Excursions to
places of interest to suit all tastes. Only one hour to
Switzerland, Austria and Neuschwanstein near Füssen.

CAMP SITE

SOUTHERN BLACK FOREST

Comfortable holiday site in the southern Black Forest near Freiburg. New toilet facilities, 380 sites for visiting holiday-makers. Heated outdoor pool 23°C from 15.5-15.9 on the site itself. Wide range of facilities for sports and games. Walk in the magnificent countryside. Trips to the higher parts of the Black Forest, Switzerland and France.

**79199 Kirchzarten
Tel: 07661/39375
Fax 07661/61624**

KIRCHBERG BADEN-WÜRTTEMBERG

Christophorus ☎ 07354 663
Completely enclosed, clean site.
⮑ *Leave motorway A7 (Ulm-Memmingen) at exit Illereichen Allenstadt to town centre, then towards the railway station.*
All year 9.2HEC ⊞ ⊞ ⊞ ⊞ ⊞ ⊞ ⊞ ⊞ ⊞ ⊞ LP ⊞ ⊞

KIRCHZARTEN BADEN-WÜRTTEMBERG

Kirchzarten ☎ 07661 39375
Extensive site with trees providing shade.
⮑ *About 8km E of Freiburg im Breisgau off the B31.*
All year 5.6HEC ⊞ ⊞ ⊞ ⊞ ⊞ ⊞ ⊞ ⊞ ⊞ ⊞ ⊞ P ⊞ ⊞ ⊞ lau

KRESSBRONN BADEN-WÜRTTEMBERG

Gohren am See ☎ 07543 8656
A large site beside the lake. It has an older section divided by many hedges reserved for residential campers, and a newer section with fewer bushes.
⮑ *3km from Kressbronn. Well signposted from B31.*
26 Mar-15 Oct 40HEC ⊞ ⊞ ⊞ ⊞ ⊞ ⊞ ⊞ ⊞ ⊞ ⊞ ⊞ ⊞ L ⊞ ⊞ lau
Prices: ♦9 pitch 9

LAICHINGEN BADEN-WÜRTTEMBERG

Heidehof Blaubeurer str 50 ☎ 07333 6408
Well-cared for site on hillside with some high firs. Asphalt roads. Separate section outside enclosure for overnight campers.
⮑ *Leave Ulm-Stuttgart motorway at Merkingen exit, then continue S via Machtolsheim to camp 2km S.*
All year 25HEC ⊞ ⊞ ⊞ ⊞ ⊞ ⊞ ⊞ ⊞ ⊞ P ⊞ ⊞ lau
Prices: ♦8 pitch 10

LAUTERBURG BADEN-WÜRTTEMBERG

Hirtenteich ☎ 07365 296
This site lies on gently sloping terrain, near the Hirtenteich recreation area.
⮑ *Turn off the B29 (Aalen-Schwäbisch Gmünd) in Essingen and drive S for a pprox. 5km.*
All year 2HEC ⊞ ⊞ ⊞ ⊞ ⊞ ⊞ ⊞ ⊞ ⊞ ⊞ ⊞ ⊞ P ⊞ ⊞ lau
Prices: ♦6 ♦8 pitch 8-9

At **BARTHOLOMÄ**(3km S)

Feriendorf Amalienhof Haflinger Str 15 ☎ 07173 7542
Level site on high plateau of eastern Alps, partially surrounded by tall trees.
All year 4HEC ⊞ ⊞ ⊞ ⊞ ⊞ ⊞ ⊞ ⊞ ⊞ lau ➡ ⊞ ✕ ⊹P

LENGFURT BADEN-WÜRTTEMBERG

Main-Spessart-Park ☎ 09395 1079
Site lies partly on terraced meadowland and partly on the E slopes of the Main Valley. Lunchtime siesta 13.00-15.00 hrs, Possibilities for water sports, nearby private mooring on the River Main.
⮑ *From Frankfurt-Würzburg motorway A3/E5 leave at exit Markheidenfeld. N to Altfled then E for 6km to Lengfurt. Site lies at NW edge of village.*
All year 10HEC ⊞ ⊞ ⊞ ✕ ⊙ ⊞ ⊞ lau ➡ ⊞ ⊹PR ⊞
Prices: ♦9 ♦4 ♦6.50 ♦6

LENZKIRCH BADEN-WÜRTTEMBERG

Kreuzhof Bonndorfer Str 65 ☎ 07653 700
Grassland near former farm below the Rogg Brewery on the B315.
⮑ *Access from Freiburg on the B31 to Titisee, continue on the B317 towards Schaffhausen junction then take the B315 via Lenzkirch, site is some 2km from centre.*
All year 2HEC ⊞ ⊞ ⊞ ⊞ ⊞ ✕ ⊙ ⊞ ⊞ ⊹ P ⊞ ⊞ lau
Prices: ♦7.30-7.80 ♦5-5.50 ♦5-5.50 ♦5-5.50

LIEBELSBERG BADEN-WÜRTTEMBERG

Erbenwald Neubulach 3 ☎ 07053 7382
Pleasant site on edge of wood.
⮑ *Approach via Calw on the B463 for about 6km travelling S, then turn right and shortly before Neubulach continue N about 2km.*
All year 7.2HEC ⊞ ➡ ⊞ ⊞ ⊞ ✕ ⊙ ⊞ ⊞ ⊞ ⊞ ⊹ P ⊞ ⊞ lau ➡ ⊹S
Prices: ♦7 pitch 9

LIEBENZELL, BAD BADEN-WÜRTTEMBERG

Bad-Liebenzell Kurhausdamm 2 ☎ 07052 40460
Municipal site with trees near tennis courts. Divided by hedges and internal asphalt roads.
⮑ *Approach from Pforzheim on the B463 about 19km S. Turn left 500m before Bad Liebenzell to site on the banks of the Nagold.*
All year 3HEC ⊞ ⊞ ⊞ ⊞ ⊞ ✕ ⊙ ⊞ ⊞ ⊹ P ⊞ ⊞ ⊘ lau ➡ ✕

LÖRRACH BADEN-WÜRTTEMBERG

Grütt Grüttweg 8 ☎ 07621 82588
Level, grassy site near frontier.
⮑ *From motorway exit Lörrach on B316 then via Freiburger Str and bridge over the Wiesse and turn left after 100m.*
15 Mar-Oct 23.4HEC ⊞ ⊞ ✕ ⊙ ⊞ ⊞ lau ➡ ⊞ ✕ ⊹PR ⊞

LÖWENSTEIN BADEN-WÜRTTEMBERG

Heilbronn am Breitenauer See ☎ 07130 8558
⮑ *Exit at Weinsberg/Elhofen from A81/E41 (Stuttgart-Würzburg) and take B39 to Obersulm.*

All year 10HEC ⚏ ⌕ ⌂ ⌷ ✗ ⊙ ♨ ⌀ ⌇ L 🏤 lau
Prices: ⋔9 pitch 8-11

LUDWIGSHAFEN AM BODENSEE BADEN-WÜRTTEMBERG

See Ende ☎ 07773 5366
Meadowland with tall trees W of town, between railway and lake.
➯ *Access via Stuttgart-Singen-Lindau motorway. In Ludwigshafen turn off in direction of Radolfzell.*
May-Sep 2.6HEC ⚏ ⌕ ⌂ ⌷ ♀ ✗ ⊙ ♨ ⌀ ⌄ ⌇ L 🏤 ⊞ ⌿ lau

MANNHEIM BADEN-WÜRTTEMBERG
At NECKARAU(5.5km S)

Strandbad ☎ 0621 856240
A minicipal site in the grounds of a park beside the Rhine. At high water the site can get flooded.
➯ *From motorway exit 'Mannheim' to Neckarau, via the Freudenheim Bridge, then drive through Morchfeldstr, Friedrichstr, Rheingoldstr, Franzosenweg and Strandbadweg to the camp.*
Apr-15 Oct 0.9HEC ⚏ ⌕ ⌂ ⊙ ♨ ⌄ ♀ À ⌇ R 🏤 lau
⟿ ♀ ✗ ⌀ ⌇LP
Prices: ⋔9 ⛺2.50 ♨7.50 À6-8.50

MARKDORF BADEN-WÜRTTEMBERG

Wirthshof ☎ 07544 2325
15 Mar-30 Oct 8HEC ⚏ ⌕ ⌂ ⌷ ✗ ⊙ ♨ ⌀ ⌇ P 🏤 ⊞ lau ⟿
♀ ✗ ⌇L
Prices: ⋔9.50 pitch 15

MERGENTHEIM, BAD BADEN-WÜRTTEMBERG

Willingertal ☎ 07931 2177
Site lies on a meadow between high green bank and wooded hillside.
➯ *From Bad Mergentheim follow B19 S towards Stuttgart, then left towards Wachbach after 2km. then left to Gastätte.*
All year 15HEC ⚏ ⌽ ⌕ ⌂ ✗ ⊙ ♨ ⌀ ⌄ ♨ ⛺ À 🏤 ⊞
lau ⟿ ⌇P

MÖRTELSTEIN BADEN-WÜRTTEMBERG

Germania Mühlwiese 1 ☎ 06262 1795
Site is in Mörtelstein, 5km W of Obrigheim. Site lies between the left bank of the River Neckar and a wooded hillside.
➯ *Follow road B292 W towards 'Sinsheim' to just beyond Oberigheim, then N on a narrow, steep road into the Neckar Valley.*
Apr-Oct 0.8HEC ⚏ ⌕ ⌂ ✗ ⊙ ♨ ⌀ ⌄ ♨ ⌇ R 🏤 lau ⟿ ✗

MÜNSTERTAL BADEN-WÜRTTEMBERG

Münstertal ☎ 07636 353
Level, grassy site in pleasant situation with fine views. Lunchtime siesta 13.00-15.00 hrs.
➯ *Leave Karlsruhe-Basel motorway at Bad Kroningen exit and continue SE via Stauffen to W outskirts of Untermünstertal.*
All year 3.9HEC ⚏ ⌕ ⌂ ⌷ ✗ ⊙ ♨ ⌀ ⌄ ♨ ⌇ P 🏤 lau

MURRHARDT BADEN-WÜRTTEMBERG
At FORNSBACH(6km E)

Waldsee ☎ 07192 6436
The site lies near Lake Waldsee. Asphalt paths and pitches, with gravel surface.
➯ *Drive through Murrhardt towards Fornsbach and the camp, which is on the eastern shore of the lake.*
All year 2HEC ⚏ ⌕ ⌂ ⌷ ✗ ⊙ ♨ ⌀ ⌄ ⌇ L 🏤 ⊞ lau ⟿
⌇P
Prices: ⋔5-6 ⛺4-5.50 ♨5-5.50 À5-5.50

NECKARGEMÜND BADEN-WÜRTTEMBERG

Friedensbrücke ☎ 06223 2178
Campsite lies on the left bank of the River Neckar below the Frieden's bridge.
Mar-Sep 2.5HEC ⚏ ⌕ ⌂ ⌷ ✗ ⊙ ♨ ⌀ ⌄ ♨ ⌇ R 🏤 ⊟ ⊞ lau
⟿ ⌂ ✗ ⌇P ⊞
Prices: ⋔8 ⛺4 ♨6.50 À6

Haide ☎ 06223 2111
A well appointed site in the picturesque Neckar Valley, directly on the river on the outskirts of Heidelberg.
➯ *Follow the river towards the castle and Neckarsteinach.*
Apr-Oct 3.6HEC ⟿ ⌕ ⌂ ⌷ ✗ ⊙ ♨ ⌀ ⌄ ⛺ 🏤 ⊞ lau
Prices: ⋔8.50 ⛺2 ♨6-12 À6-12

NECKARZIMMERN BADEN-WÜRTTEMBERG

Cimbria ☎ 06261 2562
Site lies on level meadowland on the bank of the River Neckar.
➯ *Access to the site is signposted from road B27.*
Apr-Oct 3HEC ⚏ ⌕ ⌂ ✗ ⊙ ♨ ⌀ ⌄ ♨ ⌇ PR 🏤 lau ⟿ ⌂ ♀ ⊞
Prices: ⋔8 pitch 10

NEUENBURG BADEN-WÜRTTEMBERG

Dreiländer Camping und Freizeitpark Oberer Wald
☎ 07631 7719
An excellent site, very extensive, providing many entirely separate pitches.
➯ *Access via Karlsruhe-Basel motorway A5/E4, take the Müllheim/Neuenburg exit, then about 3km to site.*
All year 12.8HEC ⚏ ⌕ ⌂ ⌷ ✗ ⊙ ♨ ⌀ ⌄ ⌇ P 🏤 ⊞ lau ⟿
⌇L
Prices: ⋔8.90 ⛺7.60 ♨9.60 À6.60-9.60

NUSSDORF BADEN-WÜRTTEMBERG

Nell Uberlinger See ☎ 07551 4254
Site within orchard between farm of same name and the lakeside promenade. Small private beach.
➯ *Under railway bridge, then turn right.*
Apr-15 Oct 0.6HEC ⚏ ⌕ ⊙ ♨ ⌇ L 🏤 ⊞ ⌿ lau ⟿ ⌂ ♀ ✗
⌀ ♨ ⌇P
Prices: ⋔7 ⛺5 ♨10 À10

OSTRINGEN BADEN-WÜRTTEMBERG

Kraichgau Camping Wackerhof ☎ 07259 361
A modern terraced site. Lunchtime siesta 13.00-15.00 hrs (except Saturdays).
➯ *From motorway A5 exit 'Kronau/Bad Schönborn' follow road B292 to Östringen.*
15 Mar-15 Oct 3HEC ⚏ ⌕ ⌂ ⌷ ⊙ ♨ ⌀ ⌄ 🏤 lau
Prices: ⋔4.80 pitch 5.50

PFORZHEIM BADEN-WÜRTTEMBERG

International Schwarzwald Freibadweg 4 ☎ 07234 6517
Site on edge of wood with southerly aspect. Separate fields for residential, overnight and holiday campers.
➯ *S through Huchenfeld from Pforzheim to Schellbron (15km).*
All year 5HEC ⚏ ⌕ ⌂ ⌷ ✗ ⊙ ♨ ⌀ ⌄ ♨ ⌇ P 🏤 ⊞ ⌿ lau
⟿ ⌇R
Prices: ⋔7 ⛺9.50 ♨9.50 À4

RHEINMÜNSTER BADEN-WÜRTTEMBERG
At STOLLHOFEN

Freizeitcenter-Oberrhein ☎ 07227 2500
Modern leisure complex next to Rhine.
All year 36HEC ⚏ ⌕ ⌂ ⌷ ♀ ✗ ⊙ ♨ ⌀ ⌄ ♨ ⌇ L 🏤 ⊞ lau
Prices: ⋔8-13 pitch 8-12

ROSENBERG BADEN-WÜRTTEMBERG

Hüttenhof Hüttenhof 1 ☎ 07963 203
Flat meadow on incline in quiet woodland area, next to large farm.
➲ *From Ellwangen 3km N towards Crailsheim, turn W towards Adelmannsfelden and continue for 8km to turn off to N at Gaishardt.*
All year 4HEC ⊞ ♀ ♠ ⚍ ⊙ ◘ ⊘ ᗑ ⫯ LR ② ⊞ lau ➡ ⟐ ✗
Prices: ♦6 pitch 7

ST PETER BADEN-WÜRTTEMBERG

Steingrübenhof ☎ 07660 210
All year 2HEC ⊞ ♀ ♠ ⚍ ✗ ⊙ ◘ ⊘ ᗑ ② lau ➡ ⟐P
Prices: ♦7.50 pitch 8

SCHAPBACH BADEN-WÜRTTEMBERG

Alisehof ☎ 07839 203
The site lies on well-kept ground with several terraces and is separated from the road by the River Wolfach.
➲ *In Wolfach turn off the B924 at the Kinzighbrücke and drive N for about 8km to Schapbach. Site is 1km N of village.*
All year 3HEC ⊞ ➡ ♠ ⚍ ⟐ ⊙ ◘ ⊘ ᗑ ᗏ ⫯ R ② ⊞ lau ➡ ✗ ⟐P
Prices: ♦8.50-9.50 pitch 8-9

SCHILTACH BADEN-WÜRTTEMBERG

Schiltach ☎ 07836 7289
The site lies on meadowland on the banks of the River Kinzig and is well placed for excursions.
May-Oct 3.6HEC ⊞ ♀ ♠ ⚍ ✗ ⊙ ◘ ᗑ ᗏ ⫯ R ② ⊞ ⟨ lau ➡ ⊘
Prices: ♦6 ⟐4 ⟐5 ▲5

SCHÖMBERG BADEN-WÜRTTEMBERG

Höhen-Camping-Langenbrand ☎ 07084 6131
All year 1.6HEC ⊞ ♀ ♠ ⊙ ◘ ⊘ ② ⊞ lau ➡ ⚍ ⟐ ✗
Prices: ♦8-9 pitch 8-10

SCHWÄBISCH GMÜND BADEN-WÜRTTEMBERG
At RECHBERG(6km S)

Schurrenhof ☎ 07165 1625
The site lies in a beautiful setting on the edge of a forest, and has a lovely view of the surrounding countryside.
➲ *Drive S on the B29 from Schwäbisch Gmünd, through Strassdorf and Rechberg, and towards Reichenbach on the B10. Then turn towards Schurrenhof.*
All year 3HEC ⊞ ♀ ♠ ⚍ ✗ ⊙ ◘ ⊘ ᗑ ᗏ ⫯ P ② ⊞ ⟨ lau
Prices: ♦6-7.50 pitch 7.50-10

SCHWÄBISCH HALL BADEN-WÜRTTEMBERG

Steinbacher See Mühlsteige 26 ☎ 0791 2984
A modern site situated in the beautiful Kocher Valley. There are good sporting facilities and many places of interest nearby in the medieval town.
➲ *Access via B14/19 to Steinbach.*
Apr-15 Oct 1.4HEC ⊞ ♀ ♠ ⟐ ⊙ ◘ ᗑ ② lau ➡ ⚍ ✗ ⊘ ᗑ ⫯P ⊞

STAMMHEIM BADEN-WÜRTTEMBERG

Obere Mühle ☎ 07051 4844
The site is divided into two sections by the access road, and sub-divided into pitches.
➲ *Off B296 almost 3km S of Calw.*
All year 2.5HEC ⊞ ♀ ♠ ⚍ ⟐ ✗ ⊙ ◘ ⊘ ᗑ ᗏ ⫯ P ② ⊞ lau

STAUFEN BADEN-WÜRTTEMBERG

Belchenblick Münstertaler Str 43 ☎ 07633 7045
Well kept site on level ground.
➲ *Access from motorway exit Bad Krozingen/Staufen and continue 4km SE.*
All year 2.5HEC ⊞ ♀ ♠ ⚍ ⟐ ✗ ⊙ ◘ ⊘ ᗑ ⫯ PR ② ⊞ lau ➡ ✗

STEINACH BADEN-WÜRTTEMBERG

Kinzigtal ☎ 07832 8122
Site on level meadowland with tall trees, situated next to the municipal heated swimming pool.
➲ *Signposted from Steinach.*
All year 2.6HEC ⊞ ♀ ♠ ⚍ ⟐ ✗ ⊙ ◘ ⊘ ᗑ ② ⊞ lau ➡ ⟐P
Prices: ♦8 pitch 11

STUTTGART BADEN-WÜRTTEMBERG

Canstatter Wasen Mercedesstr 40 ☎ 0711 556696
Level site with tall poplar trees alongside the River Neckar. Lunchtime siesta 12.30-14.00 hrs.
➲ *Access from Bad Cannstatt near sports stadium.*
All year 1.7HEC ⊞ ⟐ ♀ ♠ ⚍ ✗ ⊙ ◘ ⊘ ᗑ ② ⊞ lau
Prices: ♦8 ⟐4 ⟐8.50 ▲8

SULZBURG BADEN-WÜRTTEMBERG

Alte Sägemuhle ☎ 07634 8550
Quiet holiday site in beautiful situation, surrounded by woodland. Partly terraced the site is divided into two sections by the approach road.
➲ *From autobahn exit 'Bad Krozingen' and B3 to Heitersheim. Here turn E for site in 6km.*
All year 2.5HEC ⊞ ♀ ♠ ⚍ ⊙ ◘ ⊘ ᗑ ⫯ P ② ⊞ ➡ ✗

TITISEE-NEUSTADT BADEN-WÜRTTEMBERG

Bankenhof Bruderhalde 31a ☎ 07652 1351
A family site in a wooded location close to the lake.
➲ *From Titisee village follow signs 'Camping platz'. Access road to site closed 22.00-06.00 hrs.*
All year 3.5HEC ⊞ ⁝⁝⁝ ♀ ♠ ⚍ ⟐ ✗ ⊙ ◘ ⊘ ᗑ ᗏ ▲ ⫯ R ② ⊞ lau ➡ ⟐LP
Prices: ♦6.50-8 pitch 11-13

Bühlhof Bühlhofweg 13 ☎ 07652 1606
In pleasant situation on hillside above lake. Lunchtime siesta 13.00-14.30 hrs.
➲ *Well signposted.*
Closed Nov-15 Dec 10HEC ⊞ ⁝⁝⁝ ♀ ♠ ⚍ ⟐ ✗ ⊙ ◘ ⊘ ᗑ ② lau ➡ ✗ ⟐LP ⊞
Prices: pitch 8.50-12

Sandbank ☎ 07651 8243 & 8166
On terrain rising from lakeside, upper part terraced, landscaped with trees.
➲ *Access from Titisee, N bank of lake, turn into old Feldbergstr. At SW end of lake turn left and continue along narrow private road through Camping 'Bankenhof' (closed 22.00-06.00 hrs) to the site about 700m on SE bank of lake.*
Apr-20 Oct 2HEC ⊞ ⟐ ♀ ♠ ⚍ ✗ ⊙ ◘ ⊘ ⫯ L ② ⊞ lau ➡ ⟐P
Prices: ♦6-8 pitch 9.60-12.10

Wellerhof ☎ 07652 1468
Mainly level site with trees, bordering on lake shore for about 400m.
➲ *Signposted from Titisee.*
15 May-Sep 2HEC ⊞ ⁝⁝⁝ ♀ ♠ ⚍ ✗ ⊙ ◘ ⊘ ⫯ L ② ⊞ lau

TODTNAU BADEN-WÜRTTEMBERG

Hochschwarzwald ☎ 07671 1288
Terraced site, partially grassland, by ski-lift.

6km NW of Todtnau.
All year 2.5HEC ⟁ ⋯ ♦ ⌺ ℾ ⊾ ✕ ⊙ ⬛ ∅ ⍓ R ⊞ lau ➡
⍓LP
Prices: ⋔6.50-7 ⬛8.50-9 ⒜6-9

TÜBINGEN BADEN-WÜRTTEMBERG

Tübingen ☎ 07071 43145
A quiet site, well situated on the left bank of the River
Neckar.
➲ *For access from the town centre, cross the Neckar bridge,
then turn right and drive S through Uhlandstr or Bahnhofstr to
next bridge. Cross bridge and drive upstream to the
Rappenberghalde hill.*
4 Mar-14 Oct 1HEC ⟁ ⚡ ℾ ⊾ ✕ ⊙ ⬛ ∅ ⍓ R ⊞ lau
➡ ⍓LP
Prices: ⋔9.50 ⬛4 ⬛7 ⒜5.50-7

ÜBERLINGEN BADEN-WÜRTTEMBERG

West Bahnhofstr 57 ☎ 07551 64583
The site lies on the western outskirts of the town, between
the railway line and the road on one side, and the concrete
shore wall on the other. It is divided into several sections by
low wooden barriers and has a very small beach. No
individual youths under 18.
➲ *Off B31 towards the lake.*
Apr-5 Oct 3HEC ⟁ ⌺ ℾ ⊾ ✕ ⊙ ⬛ ∅ ⍓ L ⊞ ⍓ lau ➡
⍓
Prices: ⋔10 pitch 17-19

UHLDINGEN BADEN-WÜRTTEMBERG
At SEEFELDEN(1km W)

Seeperle ☎ 07556 5454
This site has some large trees along the shore of the lake.
50m-long boat landing stage. It is one of the few camps that
does not reserve its best pitches for residential campers.
➲ *Turn off B31 at Oberuhldingen and head towards
Seefelden. Site 1km.*
Apr-3 Oct 0.7HEC ⟁ ⋯ ⌺ ℾ ⊾ ⊙ ⬛ ∅ ⍓ L ⊞ ➡ ⍓
✕ ⍓P
Prices: ⋔9.50 ⬛6.50 ⬛12.50-14 ⒜9-16

WALDBRONN BADEN-WÜRTTEMBERG

Albgau Herrenalbstr 2 ☎ 07243 61069
Extenisve meadowland adjacent to the little Alb river.
➲ *Near the Neurod Inn and the infrequent Ettingen-
Herrenalb railway.*
Closed 15 Oct-15 Nov 3.6HEC ⟁ ⌺ ℾ ⊾ ✕ ⊙ ⬛ ∅ ⬛ ⬛
⊞ lau ➡ ✕

WALDKIRCH BADEN-WÜRTTEMBERG

Elztalblick ☎ 07681 4212
A small site with terraced pitches in the heart of the Black
Forest.
➲ *Leave autobahn at 'Waldkirch/Ost' exit and follow signs for
3km.*
Mar-15 Nov 2HEC ⟁ ⌺ ℾ ⊾ ✕ ⊙ ⬛ ∅ ⍓ ⊞ lau
Prices: ⋔7.50 ⬛4.50 ⬛4.50 ⒜4.50

WALDSHUT BADEN-WÜRTTEMBERG

Rhein-Camping Jahnweg 22 ☎ 07751 3152
In wooded surroundings beside the River Rhein.
➲ *1km from Waldshut towards the Swiss border.*
All year 8HEC ⟁ ⌺ ℾ ⊾ ⍓ ✕ ⊙ ⬛ ∅ ⬛ ⍓ R ⊞ lau ➡
⍓P
Prices: ⋔7 ⬛15 ⒜8-15

WERTHEIM BADEN-WÜRTTEMBERG

AZUR Wertheim An den Christwiesen 35 ☎ 09342 83111
Site lies on a level, long stretch of meadowland on the banks

of the River Main next to a swimming pool. Lunchtime siesta
12.00-14.00 hrs.
➲ *Follow road towards 'Miltenberg', and in 1km turn right at
the ARAL petrol station and head towards the site.*
15 Mar-15 Nov 7HEC ⟁ ⌺ ℾ ⊾ ✕ ⊙ ⬛ ⬛ ⍓ R ⊞ lau
Prices: ⋔8-10 ⬛3-4 ⬛11-13 ⒜3-4

At BETTINGEN(5km E)

Wertheim-Bettingen Geiselbrunnweg 31 ☎ 09342 7077
In a peaceful wooded area on the bank of a river.
➲ *Motorway Frankfurt-Würzburg, exit Wertheim/Lengfurt,
1km.*
Apr-Oct 7HEC ⟁ ⌺ ℾ ⊾ ✕ ⊙ ⬛ ∅ ⍓ R ⊞ lau ➡ ⍓LP
Prices: ⋔7 ⬛2.50 ⬛4 ⒜4

WILDBAD IM SCHWARZWALD BADEN-WÜRTTEMBERG

AZUR-Camping Schwarzwald ☎ 07055 1320
Long narrow site with some terraces, set between the River Enz
and the wooded hillside. Separate section for young campers.
➲ *Access is from Pforzheim along B294 via Calmbach southwards.*
All year 3.5HEC ⟁ ⌺ ℾ ⊾ ✕ ⊙ ⬛ ∅ ⍓ R ⊞ lau ➡
⍓LP
Prices: ⋔6-7 pitch 8-9

Kleinenzhof ☎ 07081 3435
A family site with good, modern facilities.
➲ *Access via B294 3km S of Calmbach.*
All year 6HEC ⟁ ⌺ ℾ ⊾ ✕ ⊙ ⬛ ∅ ⬛ ⬛ ⍓ PR ⊞ lau
Prices: ⋔8.50 pitch 11.50

BERLIN AND EASTERN PROVINCES

This unique city has always been popular, but it surely must
now be the most exciting city to visit in the world.
The splendid palaces and monuments are the city's
architectural legacies of a rich and colourful history, of
many periods and many noble families, of events that have
rocked the world and made Berlin a focal point of political
and cultural life.
No longer divided, the city offers many contrasts; stroll
along the 'Unter den Linden' for an impression of "old"
Berlin; visit the 'Kurfstendamm' which packs no fewer than
1,000 shops, boutiques, restaurants and galleries, into an
elegant half-mile; relax in the delightful havens of parks,
forests and lakes, which make up one third of the city.
Berlin is alive, bursting with a vibrant energy that never
dies down; the nightlife offers everything from grand opera
to erotic nightclubs, and stays open longer than you can
stay up.

ALTENBERG SACHSEN

Kleiner Galgenteich ☎ 035056 31995
➲ *Leave E55 at exit Dresden-Nord and continue towards the
Czech border via B170/E55.*
All year 4HEC ⟁ ♦ ℾ ⊾ ✕ ⊙ ⬛ ∅ ⍓ P ⊞ lau ➡ ⍓

ALT SCHWERIN MEKLENBURG-VORPOMMERN

See Karower Chaussee ☎ 039932 42073
A pleasant lakeside site with good, modern facilities.
➲ *Access via B192.*
Apr-15 Oct 3.6HEC ⟁ ⚡ ℾ ⊾ ✕ ⊙ ⬛ ∅ ⬛ ⍓ L ⊞ lau

BERLIN
At KLADOW

DCC Else-Eckert-Platz Krampnitzer Weg 111-117
☎ 030 3652797
Large site in woodland close to the lake. Good, modern facilities.

⊃ *Access via B5 and B2 exit Berlin Spandau.*
All year 7HEC ⬛ ⫶⫶⫶ ♀ 🏕 🛁 ✕ ⊙ 🆒 🚻 🛒 🏪 lau ➜ ⇃L
Prices: ♠9.50 ⬛12.70 ♠7.20

At SCHMÖCKWITZ

Krosssinsee Wernsdorfer Str 45 ☎ 4930 6758687
In pleasant wooded surroundings on the shore of the
Krossinsee with plenty of recreational facilities.
⊃ *Access via A10 exit Berlin Köpenick.*
All year 7HEC ⬛ ➜ 🏕 🛁 ✕ ⊙ 🆒 🚻 ⇃ L 🏪 ⊞ lau

At WANNSEE

Kohlhasenbrück Neue Kreisstr 36 ☎ 4930 8051737
Very pleasantly situated site on shore of Lake Griebnitz,
owned by Deutscher Camping Club. Bathing area.
⊃ *From Wannsee railway station, drive through Königstr, past
Rathaus, through Chausseestr, Kohlhasenbrückerstr, and
Kreisstr.*
Mar-Oct 3HEC ⬛ ♀ 🏕 ✕ ⊙ 🆒 🏪 lau ➜ ⇃LP
Prices: ♠9.70 ⬛12.70 ♠7.20

BODSTEDT MECKLENBURG-VORPOMMERN

Bodstedt Damm 1 ☎ 038231 4226
A pleasant site on the shore of the Saaler Bodden with good
boating facilities.
⊃ *Access via B105 exit Zingst/Barth.*
Apr-Sep 3.5HEC ⬛ ➜ 🏕 ⊙ 🆒 🚻 🛒 ➜ ✕ ⇃LR

CAPUTH BRANDENBURG

Himmelreich Wentorfinsel, Geltow ☎ 033209 70475
All year 6HEC ⬛ ⫶⫶⫶ ♀ 🏕 🛁 ✕ ⊙ 🆒 🚻 ⇃ LR 🏪 ⊞ lau

CATTERFELD THÜRINGEN

Paulfeld ☎ 036253 5171
⊃ *Take E40 Frankfurt-Dresden and exit at Waltershausen.*
All year 7HEC ⬛ ⚡ 🏕 🛁 ✕ ⊙ 🆒 🚻 ⇃ L 🏪 ⊞ lau

COLDITZ SACHSEN

Waldbad ☎ 034381 43122
In wooded surroundings with some shaded pitches.
⊃ *Access via E176 exit Zschadras.*
28 May-7 Oct 2HEC ⬛ ♀ 🏕 ⊙ 🆒 🚻 🛒 ⇃ LPRS 🏪 lau
➜ 🛁 🍴 ✕ ⇃P
Prices: ♠5 ♠5 ⬛10-12 ♠8-13

DEUTSCHBASELITZ SACHSEN

AZUR Waldbad Deutschbaselitz Teichstr 30 ☎ 03578
301489
The site may close for a short time in the winter and the
shop and café are only open between May and September.
15 Mar-15 Nov 5HEC ⬛ ♀ 🏕 🛁 ✕ ⊙ 🆒 🚻 🛒 ⇃ L 🏪
Prices: ♠4.50-7 pitch 6.50-9

DRESDEN SACHSEN

Wostra Trieskestr 100 ☎ 0351 2013254
Café open May-Sep only.
⊃ *Access via B172 towards Heidenau. Signposted.*
Apr-Oct 1.8HEC ⬛ ♀ 🏕 ⊙ 🆒 🚻 🏪 ⊞ ➜ 🛁 ✕ ⇃P

FALKENBERG BRANDENBURG

Erholungsgebiet Kiebitz ☎ 035365 2135
⊃ *Access via E55 Duben exit, then B87/B101 towards
Herzberg.*
Apr-Oct 5.4HEC ⬛ ⫶⫶⫶ ♦ ♀ 🏕 ⊙ 🆒 🏪 ⇃ L 🖵 ⊞ lau ➜ 🛁
🍴 ✕ 🚻 ⇃PR
Prices: ♠3.60-6.10 ♠6.10 ⬛5.10-7.10 ♠2.60-10.10

FREEST MECKLENBURG-VORPOMMERN

Waldcamp ☎ 038370 20538
A modern site in wooded surroundings with good facilities.
⊃ *300mtrs from Freest centre.*
All year 1HEC ⬛ ⫶⫶⫶ ♀ 🏕 🍴 ✕ ⊙ 🆒 🚻 🛒 🏪 🖵 lau ➜ 🛁 ✕ ⊘
⇃S
Prices: ♠6.50 ♠3 ⬛9 ♠7-10

FÜRSTENBERG BRANDENBURG

Röblinsee Röblinsee Nord ☎ 033093 38278
All year 1.2HEC ⬛ ➜ 🏕 🛁 ✕ ⊙ 🆒 🚻 ⇃ P 🏪 ⊞ lau ➜ 🍴 ✕ ⊘

GEORGENTHAL THÜRINGEN

Georgenthal ☎ 036253 41314
Apr-Oct 1HEC ⬛ ♦ ⚡ 🏕 ✕ ⊙ 🆒 ⊘ 🚻 ⇃ P lau ➜ 🛁 🍴 🚻 ⊞

GROSS-LEUTHEN BRANDENBURG

Spreewaldtor ☎ 035471 303
On a level meadow beside the Gorss Leuthener See.
⊃ *N of town off B179.*
All year 9HEC ⬛ ♀ 🏕 🛁 ✕ ⊙ 🆒 🚻 🛒 🏪 ⇃ L 🏪 ⊞ lau ➜ 🍴
⊘ ⇃PR
Prices: ♠7-8 ♠3 ⬛7.50-11.50 ♠6-8.50

GROSS-QUASSOW MECKLENBURG-VORPOMMERN

Havelberge am Wobiltzsee ☎ 03981 24790
In a rural setting beside the lake. Restricted facilities during
March.
⊃ *1.5km S of town. Signposted.*
Mar-Oct 10HEC ⬛ ⫶⫶⫶ ♀ 🏕 ✕ ⊙ 🆒 ⇃ L lau

KELBRA THÜRINGEN

Stausee Kelbra Lange Str 150 ☎ 034651 6310
All year 6.5HEC ⬛ ⚡ 🏕 ✕ ⊙ 🆒 ⊘ 🚻 🛒 ⇃ LP 🏪 ⊞ ➜ 🍴
Prices: ♠6 ♠2 ⬛10 ♠8

KLEINMACHNOW BRANDENBURG

Yacht-Caravan-Club Bäkehang 9a ☎ 033203 79684
A riverside site with an hotel SW of town off A115.
All year 2.2HEC ⬛ ♀ 🏕 🍴 ✕ ⊙ 🆒 ⊘ ⇃ R 🏪 ⊞ lau ➜ 🛁 ✕
Prices: ♠8 ♠4 ⬛5 ♠4.50

KLEINRÖHRSDORF SACHSEN

Lux-Oase Arnsdorfer Str 1 ☎ 035952 56666
In beautiful, peaceful surroundings bordering a lake among
meadows and woods.
⊃ *Access via A4 (Dresden-Bautzen) exit Pulsnitz towards
Radeberg and continue for 4km through Leppersdorf then 1km
after the village turn right for site.*
All year 7.2HEC ⬛ ⚡ 🏕 🛁 🍴 ✕ ⊙ 🆒 ⊘ 🚻 ⇃ L 🏪 ⊞ lau
➜ 🛁 ⇃P
Prices: ♠6.50-7 ♠3 ⬛9.50-10 ♠8.50-10

KÖNIGSTEIN SACHSEN

Königstein Schandauer Str 23 ☎ 035021 68224
On level ground in a wooded location with fine views of the
surrounding mountains.
⊃ *Federal road B172 within Königstein near Dresden.*
Apr-Oct 2.5HEC ⬛ ♀ 🏕 🛁 🍴 ✕ ⊙ 🆒 🚻 🏪 🏪 lau ➜ ⇃P
Prices: ♠6.80 ♠6 ⬛4-6 ♠4-6

LASSAN MEKLENBURG-VORPOMMERN

Lassan Garthof 5-6 ☎ 038374 80373
A pleasant site on the Achterwasser.
⊃ *Access via B110.*
Etr-Sep 1.4HEC ⬛ ♀ 🏕 🛁 ✕ ⊙ 🆒 🚻 ⇃ LRS 🏪 lau ➜ 🛁 🍴 ✕
⇃P ⊞
Prices: ♠5-6 ♠3 ⬛7-9 ♠4-6

LEHNIN BRANDENBURG

Seeblick am Klostersee ☎ 03382 700274
➲ *50 miles from Berlin on E30.*
Apr-Sep 1 Oct - 31 Mar 1.5HEC ⬛ ⠿ ⌀♠♀⊙⬛⚡✦L⌖
⊞ lau ✦✗⌀
Prices: ⚹6 ⬌3 ⬛7 ▲4

MÜHLBERG THÜRINGEN

Drei Gleichen ☎ 0236256 22715
In pleasant wooded surroundings.
➲ *Access via A4 exit Wandersleben, then follow signs for Mühlberg.*
Apr-Oct 2.8HEC ⬛ ⛄♠♀✗⊙⬛⚡⌀⌖ lau ✦✗⊞
Prices: ⚹7 ⬌2 ⬛7 ▲5

NIESKY SACHSEN

Tonschächte ☎ 03588 205771
May-Sep 15HEC ⬛ ⠿ ♠♠♀⚹✗⊙⬛🚲⌖⌀✦L⌖lau✦
♀⌀⌖P⊞
Prices: ⚹5-6.50 ⬌3 ⬛5-7 ▲5-7

NIEWISCH BRANDENBURG

Schwielowsee-Camping Uferweg Nord 16 ☎ 033676 5186
A family site in pleasant wooded surroundings on the banks of the Schwielowsee.
All year 4.2HEC ⬛ ⠿ ⌀♠♀✗✗⊙⬛⬛⌖✦L⌖⊞lau
✦♀⌀
Prices: ⚹6.10-6.50 ⬌3.10 ⬛10.10-10.50 ▲4.90-8

PLÖTZKY SACHSEN

Waldsee ☎ 039200 50155
All year 8HEC ⬛ ⌀♠♀⚹✗⊙⬛⌀⌖✦L⌖⊞lau
Prices: ⚹4-5.50 ⬌3-4 ⬛8-9 ▲4-5

POTSDAM BRANDENBURG

Sanssouci-Gaisberg An der Pirscheide, Templiner See 41
☎ 03327 55680
In wooded surroundings close to the Templiner See.
➲ *Signposted from the B1.*
Apr-4 Nov 6HEC ⬛ ⠿ ⌀♠♀⚹✗⊙⬛⌀🚲⌖LR⌖
⊞
Prices: ⚹13.10 pitch 13.70

PRORA/RÜGEN MECKLENBURG-VORPOMMERN

Meier ☎ 038393 2085
Apr-Oct 2.5HEC ⬛ ⌀♠✗⊙⬛⚡⌖S⌖lau✦♀♀⌀⛄
⌖P⊞

REICHENBERG SACHSEN

Sonnenland Dresdner Str 115 ☎ 0351 4727788
Apr-30 Oct 18HEC ⬛ ⌀♠♀⚹✗⊙⬛⌀⌖✦L⌖⊞lau✦
♀⌖P
Prices: ⚹6.50-7 ⬌3-3 ⬛8.50-9 ▲4-5

SIETOW MECKLENBURG-VORPOMMERN

Sietower Bucht Dorfstr 21 ☎ 039931 52068
All year 0.9HEC ⬛ ⛄♠✗⊙⬛⌀⌖lau✦✗⌖L⊞

SUHRENDORF MECKLENBURG-VORPOMMERN

Suhrendorf ☎ 038305 82234
All year 90HEC ⬛ ⌀♠♀⚹✗⊙⬛⌀⛄⬛⌖S⌖lau

WAREN MECKLENBURG-VORPOMMERN

AZUR-Ferienpark Ecktannen Fontanestr ☎ 03991 668513
In an attractive situation on the shore of Lake Müritz.
➲ *Access via A19/E55 (Berlin-Rostock).*
15 Mar-15 Nov 17HEC ⬛ ⠿ ⌀♠✗⊙⬛⛄⬛⌖L⌖
lau ✦✗
Prices: ⚹6-9 ⬌8-12 ⬛8-12 ▲4.50-6

ZARRENTIN MECKLENBURG-VORPOMMERN

Schaalsee Wittenburger Chaussee ☎ 038851 3110
In a pleasant natural park 600mtrs from the lake.
Apr-Oct 8.5HEC ⬛ ⌀♠♀✗⊙⬛⌀⌖lau✦⌖L

ZINNOWITZ MECKLENBURG-VORPOMMERN

Pommerland ☎ 038377 40348 & 40177
In wooded surroundings on the north sea coast.
➲ *Access via B111.*
All year 7.7HEC ⬛ ⠿ ✦♠♀⚹✗⊙⬛⌀⛄⬛⌖S⌖⊞
lau ✦⌖P

◉ ◉ ◉ ◉ ◉ **CENTRAL** ◉ ◉ ◉ ◉ ◉

The centre of Germany incorporates an enormous range of different landscapes - from the heavily-wooded Saarland, to the gorge-like valleys of the Rhine, to the vine-covered slopes of the Moselle. There are castles perched above steeply scarped banks, and ancient but thriving towns nestling in open valleys, combining scenic beauty with architectural masterpieces and an historic past.
Contained within this region is Bonn, birthplace of Beethoven, now a busy commercial and political centre, and Cologne, a fine modern town centred around a majestic Gothic cathedral.
Trier is Germany's oldest city and one of the largest wine-producing communities in the region. Discover the vast network of cellars extending beneath the streets and passages - a city in itself!
One of the most important commercial and economic centres in Germany, by virtue of its central situation, is Frankfurt, birthplace of Goethe, and now home to over 5,000 animals in its famous zoo.

AACHEN NORDRHEIN-WESTFALEN

Passtrasse Pass Str.79 ☎ 0241 158502
Municipal site in town centre near the Kurplatz. Becomes very full during the peak season.
Apr-Oct 1.2HEC ⬛ ⌀♠♀⚹✗⊙⬛⌖⊞lau✦✗⌀⛄
⌖P

ASBACHERHÜTTE RHEINLAND-PFALZ

Harfenmühle ☎ 06786 7076
A quiet site, beautifully situated in Fischbach Valley. Level grassland, partly terraced.
➲ *3km NW of the B327 towards Kempfeld.*
All year 6.2HEC ⬛ ♠♠♀⚹✗⊙⬛⌀⛄⬛⌖L⌖⊞lau
Prices: ⚹6.50 ⬌3 pitch 10

ATTENDORN NORDRHEIN-WESTFALEN

Biggesee-Waldenburg ☎ 02722 95500
Generously sited recreational site on the northern shore of the Bigge Reservoir, with adjoining public bathing area. Private sunbathing area. Lunchtime siesta 13.00-15.00 hrs.
➲ *From Attendorn follow road towards Heldren. Shortly after the railway turn right and follow the signs to the site, about 1.5km on.*
All year 6.5HEC ⬛ ⌀♠♀⚹✗⊙⬛⌀⌖L⌖⊞lau✦♀
✗⌖P
Prices: ⚹5.50-7 ⬛18-24.50 ▲13-19

Hof Biggen Finnentroper Str 131 ☎ 02722 9553-0
Well-equipped terraced site, surrounded by woodlands. Lunchtime siesta 13.00-15.00 hrs.
➲ *Follow Atterdorn road to Ahauser Reservoir. Entrance near 'Haus am See' inn.*
All year 18HEC ⬛ ♠♠♀⚹✗⊙⬛⌀⌖lau✦⊞

BACHARACH RHEINLAND-PFALZ

Sonnenstrand Strandbadweg 9 ☎ 06743 1752
A beautifully situated site on grassland beside the Rhine with some high trees.
➲ *The turn off from B9 into the site can be difficult for caravans coming from the north, due to one way traffic.*
15 Mar-Oct 1.4HEC ⊞ ❄ ⌂ ♟ ❤ ✕ ⊙ ♥ ∅ ⌕ R ☎ ⊞ lau
Prices: ⍟8 ➡5 ⊟5 ▲5

BALHORN HESSEN

Erzeberg ☎ 05625 5274
Site lies on meadowland on slightly sloping ground above the village. Lunchtime siesta 13.00-15.00 hrs.
➲ *On B450 between Istha and Fritzlar.*
All year 5HEC ⊞ ♦ ⌂ ♟ ❤ ✕ ⊙ ♥ ∅ ♣ ⌕ P ☎ lau ➡ ⌕ ⊞

BARNTRUP NORDRHEIN-WESTFALEN

Schwimmbad Fischteiche 4 ☎ 05263 2221
This well-kept site lies next to an open-air swimming pool, which is covered over in autumn and winter.
➲ *Barntrup lies B66, near to junction with B1. Approach signposted from Barntrup.*
All year 2.4HEC ⊞ ⌂ ♟ ❤ ⊙ ♥ ∅ ♣ ▲ ⌕ P ☎ ⊞ lau ➡ ✕

BERNKASTEL-KUES RHEINLAND-PFALZ

Kueser Werth Am Hafen 2 ☎ 06531 8200
Grassy site near Mosel and boating marina, with view of Castle Landshut.
➲ *On S outskirts of town.*
Apr-Oct 2.2HEC ⊞ ⌂ ♟ ❤ ✕ ⊙ ♥ ∅ ⌕ R ☎ ⊞ lau
Prices: ⍟8 ➡3 ⊟8 ▲5-8

BIRKENFELD RHEINLAND-PFALZ

Waldwiesen ☎ 06782 5215
In a wooded location close to the lake.
➲ *Leave the B41 E of Birkenfeld. Signposted.*
15 Apr-15 Oct 4.5HEC ⊞ ⌂ ♟ ⊙ ♥ ∅ ⌕ ⊞ ♣ ⌕ L ☎ ⊞
lau ➡ ⌕ ♟ ✕
Prices: ⍟9.50 ➡12 ⊟12 ▲10

BÖMIGHAUSEN HESSEN

Barenberg ☎ 05632 1044
Beautifully terraced site at Neerdar reservoir.
➲ *Access from B251 between Korbach and Brilon.*
All year 1HEC ⊞ ❄ ⌂ ♟ ⊙ ♥ ∅ ⌕ LR ☎ lau

BORLEFZEN NORDRHEIN-WESTFALEN

Borlefzen ☎ 05733 80008
Apr-Oct 40HEC ⊞ ⌂ ♟ ❤ ✕ ⊙ ♥ ∅ ⊞ ♣ ⌕ LR ☎ ⊞
lau
Prices: ⍟8.50 pitch 11

BRAUNFELS HESSEN

Braunfels Am Weiherstieg 2 ☎ 06442 4366
A terraced site surrounded by a forest of pine and deciduous trees. Separate meadow for touring campers. Lunchtime siesta 12.30-14.30 hrs.
➲ *Access from Köln-Frankfurt motorway, exit 'Limburg', then B49 towards town.*
All year ⊞ ♦ ⌂ ♟ ✕ ⊙ ♥ ∅ ♣ ☎ lau ➡ ♟ ⌕ ⌕P

BREISIG, BAD RHEINLAND-PFALZ

Rheineck ☎ 02633 95645
A quiet, well-kept site on a level meadow in Vinxtbach Valley.
➲ *From Koblenz follow B9 NW to Bad Breisig, then turn left, cross railway and continue for 400m.*
All year 5HEC ⊞ ⌂ ♟ ♟ ❤ ⊙ ♥ ∅ ⌕ ☎ ⊞ lau ➡ ✕ ⌕R

BULLAY RHEINLAND-PFALZ

Bären-Camp Am Moselüfer 1/3 ☎ 06542 900097
On level meadow on right bank of the Mosel, next to the football ground. Fine view.
➲ *Access via B49 Cochem-Alf, then over the bridge and through the village. Signposted.*
15 Mar-5 Nov 1.8HEC ⊞ ⌂ ♟ ♟ ❤ ✕ ⊙ ♥ ∅ ⌕ R ☎ ⊞ lau ➡ ⌕P
Prices: ⍟7.20-8 ➡5 ⊟5 ▲5

BURGEN RHEINLAND-PFALZ

Burgen ☎ 02605 2396
A well maintained site with individual pitches set on level meadow with trees by the River Mosel. Site is broken up by shrubs and flower beds.
➲ *On the B49 (Kloblenz-Treis).*
7 Apr-22 Oct 4HEC ⊞ ⌂ ♟ ♟ ❤ ♟ ⊙ ♥ ∅ ⌕ PR ☎ ⊞ lau ➡ ✕

COBLENCE

See KOBLENZ

COCHEM RHEINLAND-PFALZ

Freizeitzentrum Stationstr ☎ 02671 4409
Site lies on level meadowland with trees. On right bank of the Mosel, downstream from the swimming pool and sports ground.
➲ *In town cross the Mosel bridge, turn sharp right, follow signs 'Wellenbad' along riverside road for 1km.*
end Mar-Oct 2.8HEC ⊞ ⌂ ♟ ♟ ✕ ⊙ ♥ ∅ ⌕ R ☎ ⊞ lau ➡ ✕ ⌕PS
Prices: ⍟6.50 ➡3.50 pitch 6.50-12

At LANDKERN(7km N)

Altes Forsthaus Haupstr 2 ☎ 02671 8701
The partly terraced site lies near woodland in the valley below Landkern.
➲ *From motorway A48 (Eifel motorway) leave at exit Kaisersesch, go S to Landkern, then follow signs to site.*
All year 10HEC ⊞ ⌂ ♟ ❤ ✕ ⊙ ♥ ∅ ⌕ P ☎ lau ➡ ♟ ✕ ⌕P
Prices: ⍟6 ➡3 ⊟8-11 ▲8-11

COLOGNE

See KÖLN

DAHN RHEINLAND-PFALZ

Büttelwoog ☎ 06391 5622
Site lies in a magnificent pine forest, partly surrounded by steep hills and rocks. Section reserved for young people with tents. Lunchtime siesta 12.00-14.00 hrs.
➲ *From Pirmasens follow B10 up to Hinterweidenthal then S on B427 to Dahn.*
All year 60HEC ⊞ ❄ ⌂ ♟ ♟ ❤ ✕ ⊙ ♥ ∅ ⌕ P ☎ ⊞ lau
Prices: ⍟9 pitch 11

DIEMELSEE-HERINGHAUSEN NORDRHEIN-WESTFALEN

AZUR-Camping Hohes Rad ☎ 05633 99099
A terraced site in the Sauerland hills overlooking Lake Diemel.
➲ *Access via B251 (Korbach-Beilon).*
All year 2.8HEC ⊞ ❄ ⌂ ♟ ✕ ⊙ ♥ ∅ ⌕ ☎ lau ➡ ✕ ⌕LP ⊞
Prices: ⍟7-10 pitch 9-13

CAMPING HOHENSYBURG

Weitkamp
D-44265 Dortmund-Hohensyburg
Tel: 0231/77 43 74 Fax: 0231/774 95 54

– Near the new casino   **Easy access**
– Easy access, road has been widened
Terraced design with all connection facilities – also available to touring vans. Modern washing facilities.
An attractive and quiet location on the Ruhr and Lake Hengstey.
Gateway to the Sauerland. Attractive bridleways and footpaths lead to places of historic interest and excellent day trip opportunities close by.
Access: Cologne-Bremen motorway (Hansa route) to the Hagen-Nord exit, A1 then to Hohensyburg.
A45 Dortmund-Frankfurt motorway (Sauerland route) to Dortmund-Süd and then the B54 to Hohensyburg.
B1 to Dortmund-Mitte exit and then the B54 to Hohensyburg.

Seeblick Arnold ☎ 05633 388
The fenced-in site lies next to the Diemel-Stausee (reservoir) at the Craststätte Seeblick.
↪ *From Brilon follow road B7 eastwards to Messinghausen, here turn off main road and follow road to Diemel-Stausee (8km).*
All year ⊞ 🛒 🏠 🍴 ✕ ⊙ 🅿 🧺 🚼 🔞 ⊞ lau ➡ 🍽 ⟲LP

DIEZ RHEINLAND-PFALZ

Ochsenwiese ☎ 06432 2122
On a meadow on the left bank of the River Lahn, below Schloss Oranienstein.
↪ *From N leave motorway A3 at Diez exit (from S at Limburg-Nord exit) then continue on B54 approx. 7km.*
Apr-Oct 7HEC ⊞ 🛒 🏠 🍴 ✕ ⊙ 🅿 🧺 🚼 🔞 🔞 ⟲ R ⊞ lau ➡ ⟲LP ⊞
Prices: ♦5 🚗4.80 🚐6 ▲3.50-6

DORSEL AN DER AHR RHEINLAND-PFALZ

Stahlhütte ☎ 02693 438
Site with individual pitches, on meadowland with trees near River Ahr.
↪ *Off B258 (Aachen-Koblenz) road.*
All year 5HEC 🛒 🏠 🍴 ✕ ⊙ 🅿 🧺 🔞 ⟲ R ⊞ ⊞ lau
Prices: ♦7.50 🚐15 ▲13-15

DORTMUND NORDRHEIN-WESTFALEN

Hohensyburg Syburger Dorfstr 69 ☎ 0231 774374
Terraced site on hilly grassland near Weitkamp inn.
↪ *Access via B54.*
All year 11.5HEC ⊞ 🐎 🛒 🏠 🍴 ✕ ⊙ 🅿 🧺 ⟲ LR ⊞ ⊞ lau
Prices: ♦8.50 🚗6 pitch 11

DREIEICH-OFFENTHAL HESSEN

Offenthal Bahnhofstr 77 ☎ 49 06074 5629
Camping Card Compulsory.
↪ *Exit B486 at Dreieich-Offenthal in direction of Dietzenbach.*
Apr-Oct 3HEC ⊞ 🛒 🏠 🍴 ⊙ 🅿 🚼 ⟲ P ⊞ ⊞ ⟲ ➡ 🍽 ✕ ⟲LR
Prices: ♦6 🚗1 🚐8 ▲8

DROLSHAGEN NORDRHEIN-WESTFALEN

Gut Kalberschnacke ☎ 00492763 7501
Terraced site above Bigge-Lister Reservoir in wooded area.
↪ *Turn off A45 (E41) autobahn at Wegringhausen exit and continue NE for approx. 4km.*
All year 13.5HEC ⊞ 🛒 🏠 🍴 ✕ ⊙ 🅿 🧺 🚼 ⟲ L ⊞ lau ➡ ⟲P
Prices: ♦9 🚗3.50 🚐13 ▲10

DÜLMEN NORDRHEIN-WESTFALEN

Tannenwiese Borkenbergestr 217 ☎ 02594 4795
The site lies on meadowland in a well wooded country area, near the gliderdrome. Lunchtime siesta 12.30-14.30 hrs.
↪ *Take the B51 from Recklinghausen towards Münster as far as Hausdülmen, then follow signpost 'Segelflügplatz Borkenberge'.*
Mar-Oct 3.7HEC ⊞ 🛒 🏠 🛒 ⊙ 🅿 🚼 🔞 ⊞ ➡ 🍽 ✕

DÜRKHEIM, BAD RHEINLAND-PFALZ

KNAUS Bad Dürkheim In den Almen 3 ☎ 06322 61356
Lakeside site on level meadow between vineyards, adjoining a sportsfield. Lunchtime siesta 12.00-15.00 hrs.
↪ *Access from E outskirts of town. Turn N at railway viaduct, near JET petrol station.*
Jan-30 Oct & Dec 16.3HEC ⊞ 🛒 🏠 🍴 ✕ ⊙ 🅿 🧺 ⟲ L
⊞ ⊞ ⟲ lau
Prices: ♦8.50 pitch 7.50-12

DÜSSELDORF NORDRHEIN-WESTFALEN

Unterbacher See Kleiner Torfbruch 31 ☎ 0211 89-92038
Site on sloping grassland.
↪ *From Düsseldorf B326 to 'Erkrath' exit. Turn left by Unterbacher lake.*
Mar-Sep 8HEC ⊞ 🛒 🏠 ✕ ⊙ 🅿 🧺 🚼 ⟲ L ⊞ ⊞ ⟲ ➡ 🍽 🍴 ✕
Prices: ♦7.50 🚐15 ▲10

EMS, BAD RHEINLAND-PFALZ

Bad Ems ☎ 02603 4679
Level grassy site with isolated trees by the River Lahn.
↪ *On E outskirts on B260.*
Apr-Oct 16HEC ⊞ 🛒 🏠 🍴 ✕ ⊙ 🅿 🧺 🚼 🔞 🔞 ⟲
PR ⊞ ⊞ lau
Prices: ♦7.50 🚗3-8 pitch 8

ESCHWEGE HESSEN

Fluss und Mineralbad Torwiese 4-5 ☎ 05651 3871
In grounds of mineral swimming pool at the foot of the Leuchberg with Bismarck Tower.
↪ *From B27 E take B452 or B249 to Eschwege then follow signs.*
Apr-Sep 1HEC ⊞ 🛒 🏠 ⊙ 🅿 🔞 ⟲ PR ⊞ ⊞ ⟲
➡ 🍽 ✕ 🚼

ESSEN NORDRHEIN-WESTFALEN

At WERDEN(10km S)

Essen-Werden Im Löwental 67 ☎ 0201 492978
Several fields divided by hedges, bank and surrounded by thick hedges. Lunchtime siesta 13.00-15.00 hrs.
↪ *From centre of Essen towards Werden, then turn towards railway station and follow signposts.*
All year 4HEC ⊞ 🛒 🏠 🍴 ✕ ⊙ 🅿 🧺 🚼 🔞 ⟲ R ⊞ ⟲ lau
➡ ⟲P
Prices: ♦7.50 pitch 15

FULDATAL-KNICKHAGEN HESSEN

Fulda-Freizeitzentrum ☎ 05607 340
On slightly sloping ground surrounded by woodland in a quiet, picturesque location. Lunchtime siesta 13.00-15.00 hrs.
↪ *From B3 Kassel-München turn towards Knickhagen and follow signs.*
All year 3.2HEC ⊞ 🛒 🏠 ✕ ⊙ 🅿 🚼 🔞 ⟲ P ⊞ ⊞ lau

FÜRTH IM ODENWALD HESSEN

Tiefertzwinkel Am Schwimmbad ☎ 06253 5804
Pleasantly landscaped site in beautiful setting next to the municipal open-air swimming pool. Lunchtime siesta 13.00-15.00 hrs.

Contd.

Mar-Nov 4.8HEC ⏛ ⛃ 🏪 🍴 ⊙ 🚑 🚿 🏛 🍴 ⊞ ⊘ lau
➡ 🛒 ✗ ⇃P
Prices: ⚑5.60 🚐10 ▲6-10

GEMÜNDEN RHEINLAND-PFALZ

Aumühle Auestr 26 ☎ 06453 7286
Well-kept meadowland site next to the municipal 'Freibad'
(swimming pool) in the valley of the River Wohra.
Lunchtime siesta 13.00-15.00 hrs.
➲ *From Road B3 (Marburg-Fritzlar) turn N in Halsdorf.*
All year 1HEC ⏛ ⛃ 🏪 🍴 ⊙ 🚑 ⇃ R 🏛
➡ 🛒 ✗ 🚿 🍴 ⇃P ⊞

GERBACH RHEINLAND-PFALZ

AZUR-Camping Pfalz ☎ 06361 8287
Lunchtime siesta 13.00-15.00 hrs.
➲ *Access from A8/E12 motorway at junction Enkenbach-
Hochspeyer. Then N on B48 via Rockenhausen and at
Dielkirchen continue E for 4.5km to Gerbach.*
All year 8.5HEC ⏛ ⛃ 🏪 🛒 ✗ ⊙ 🚑 🚿 🚐 🍴 ▲
⇃ P ⊞ 🍴 lau
Prices: ⚑7-9 pitch 10-12

GILLENFELD RHEINLAND-PFALZ

Feriedorf Pulvermaar ☎ 06573 996500
Partly terraced municipal site on a slightly sloping meadow
at Pulver Maar, surrounded by woods.
➲ *From motorway A48 (Eifel autobahn) leave at exit
Mehren/Daun, continue S o n B421 and take the first turning
into Gillenfeld. On near side of village turn off towards Pulver
Maar.*
All year 2HEC ⏛ ⛃ 🏪 🛒 🍴 ✗ ⊙ 🚑 🚿 🚐 🍴 🏛 lau ➡ ⇃LP ⊞
Prices: ⚑4.50-6 🚐14-16 ▲11-14

GRÜNBERG HESSEN

Spitzer Stein Alsfelderstr ☎ 06401 804
Beautifully situated site at a forest swimming pool.
➲ *From the Frankfurt-Kassel motorway (A5) leave at
Homberg junction. Campsite is 8km S.*
All year 4HEC ⏛ 🌿 🏪 🛒 🍴 ⊙ 🚑 🍴 ⊞ lau ➡ 🛒 🍴 ✗ 🚿
⇃P

GRUNDMÜHLE BEI QUENTEL HESSEN

Grundmühle Quentel ☎ 05602 3659
A forest camp site with a sunny location. Lunchtime siesta
13.00-15.00 hrs.
➲ *From Melsungen follow road B83 to Röhrenfurth. Here turn
right towards 'Furstenhagen' and follow road via Eiterhagen to
Quentel.*
All year 1.8HEC ⏛ 🌿 ⛃ 🏪 ⊙ 🚑 🚿 ⇃ P 🏛 lau ➡ 🛒 🍴 ✗
Prices: ⚑6.50 pitch 8.50

GULDENTAL RHEINLAND-PFALZ

Guldental ☎ 06707 633
Site lies in a valley of the Guldenbach Valley. Some terraces
are reserved for tourers and there is a lake suitable for
bathing.
Camping Card Compulsory.
➲ *From Bad Kreuznach N on road B48 to Langenlonsheim,
and on nearside turn left to Guldental.*
All year 8HEC ⏛ ⛃ 🏪 🍴 🛒 ✗ ⊙ 🚑 🚿 🏛 🏛 ⊞ ➡ 🛒 🚿 ⇃P
Prices: ⚑5 🚐11 ▲7.50

HALDERN NORDRHEIN-WESTFALEN

Strandhaus Sonsfeld ☎ 02857 2247
On meadowland at the 'Hagener-Meer' next to B8 and
railway line.
All year 15HEC ⏛ ⛃ 🏪 🍴 ✗ ⊙ 🚑 🚿 ⇃ L 🏛 ⊞ lau ➡ 🛒 🚿
Prices: ⚑4 🚐4 🚐4 ▲4

HAMMER NORDRHEIN-WESTFALEN

Hammer ☎ 02473 8115
In a quiet secluded valley.
Apr-Sep ⏛ 🌿 🏪 🛒 ✗ ⊙ 🚑 ⇃ R 🏛 ⊘ lau ➡ ✗

HAUSBAY RHEINLAND-PFALZ
At PFALZFELD-HAUSBAY

Schinderhannes ☎ 06746 1674
Terraced site on S facing slope, broken up by trees and shrubs
beside a small lake. Separate section for young people.
Lunchtime siesta 13.00-15.00 hrs.
➲ *E of B327. 29km S of Koblenz.*
All year 30HEC ⏛ 🌿 ⛃ 🏪 🛒 ✗ ⊙ 🚑 🚿 🍴 ⇃ L 🏛 lau ➡ 🍴 ✗
⇃P
Prices: ⚑7 pitch 14

HEIDENBURG RHEINLAND-PFALZ

Moselhöhe ☎ 06509 99016
A small, well appointed site on an open meadow.
➲ *Access via A1 exit Mehring towards Thalfang am Erbestopf.*
All year 3HEC ⏛ 🌿 🏪 🍴 ✗ ⊙ 🚑 🚿 🏛 lau ➡ 🛒 ✗ ⊞
Prices: ⚑6 🚐5 🚐6 ▲5

HEIMBACH NORDRHEIN-WESTFALEN

Rurthal-Burg Blens ☎ 02446 3377
Site with individual pitches on meadowland beside the River
Ruhr.
➲ *From Düren follow road S via Nideggen and Abenden to
Blens, then cross bridge and turn left.*
All year 7HEC ⏛ 🌿 🏪 🛒 ✗ ⊙ 🚑 🚿 🍴 🚐 ⇃ P 🏛 ⊘ lau ➡
✗ ⇃R

HEIMERTSHAUSEN HESSEN

Heimertshausen Ehringshauser Str ☎ 06635 206
Near swimming pool in extensive, grassy, wooded valley.
Lunchtime siesta 13.00-15.00 hrs.
⮩ *From Kassel-Frankfurt motorway take Alsfeld-West exit,*
then continue via Romrod and Zell.
Apr-Sep 3.6HEC ⊞ ⌖ ↾ ⅏ ♥ ✕ ⊙ ◘ ⌀ 丛 ⊠ ☎ ⊞ lau
➡ ₹P
Prices: ♠5 pitch 10-12

HELLENTHAL NORDRHEIN-WESTFALEN

Hellenthal ☎ 02482 1500
On extensive meadowland.
⮩ *0.5km S of town.*
All year 6HEC ⊞ ⌖ ↾ ⅏ ♥ ✕ ⊙ ◘ ⌀ 丛 ₹ P ☎ ⊞ lau
➡ ⅏
Prices: ♠6 pitch 15

HERINGEN HESSEN

Werra ☎ 06624 5127
Municipal site on slightly sloping ground at the swimming
pool. Lunchtime siesta 13.00-15.00 hrs.
All year 4HEC ⊞ ➡ ↾ ⅏ ✕ ⊙ ◘ ⌀ ☎ ⊞ lau ➡ ₹P
Prices: ♠5.50 ⊞4 ⊞4 ▲4

HIRSCHHORN AM NECKAR HESSEN

Odenwald Langenthalerstr 80 ☎ 06272 809
Extensive site in wooded valley. Divided by River Ülfenbach
and hedges.
⮩ *Turn off B37 towards Wald-Michelbach and continue for*
1.5km.
Apr-15 Nov 8HEC ⊞ ⌖ ↾ ⅏ ♥ ✕ ⊙ ◘ ⌀ 丛 ⊠ ₹ PR ☎ ⊞
lau

HOFGEISMAR HESSEN

Parkschwimmbad Schöneberger Str 16 ☎ 05671 1215
Municipal site, subdivided by trees. Next to a swimming
pool. Lunchtime siesta 13.00-15.00 hrs. Mobile shop.
All year 1.5HEC ⊞ ⌖ ↾ ✕ ⊙ ◘ 丛 ₹ P ☎ ⊞ lau ➡ ⅏ ⌀

At LIEBENAU-ZWERGEN(9km W)

Ponyhof Terrassen-Camping Wärmetal Warmetal
☎ 05676 1509
A terraced, south facing site, with magnificent scenery. 300m
from a swimming pool.
⮩ *Access from B83, at Hofgeismar turn W towards Liebenau,*
alternatively from B7 turn N at Obemeiser towards Liebenau.
15 Mar-1 Nov 7HEC ⊞ ⌖ ↾ ⅏ ♥ ✕ ⊙ ◘ ⌀ ₹ R ☎ ⊞
➡ ₹LP ⊞
Prices: ♠9 ⊞3 ⊞24 ▲24

HONNEF, BAD NORDRHEIN-WESTFALEN

At HONNEF-HIMBERG, BAD(7km E)

Jillieshof ☎ 02224 972066
All year 4HEC ⊞ ⌖ ↾ ⊙ ◘ ⌀ 丛 ☎ ⊞ ➡ ⅏ ✕ ₹P
Prices: ♠5 pitch 9

HORN-BAD MEINBERG NORDRHEIN-WESTFALEN

Eggewald Kempener Str 33 ☎ 05255 236
Site lies in well wooded countryside.
⮩ *Access via road B1. In Horn-Bad Meinberg turn off main*
road at the Waldschlosschen and follow the 'Altenbeken' road
for about 8km up to Kempen.
All year 2HEC ⊞ ⌖ ↾ ⅏ ✕ ⊙ ◘ ⌀ ₹ P ☎ ⊞ lau
Prices: ♠5 ⊞1 ⊞8-10 ▲7-10

IDSTEIN HESSEN

AZUR-Camping Idstein ☎ 06126 91299
In a peaceful rural setting close to the ancient town of
Idstein.
⮩ *Access via A3 (Frankfurt-Limburg).*
All year 2.6HEC ⊞ ⌖ ↾ ⅏ ✕ ⊙ ◘ ⌀ ₹ P ☎ ⊞ lau
➡ ✕
Prices: ♠8-10 ⊞3-4 ⊞11-13 ▲3-4

INGENHEIM RHEINLAND-PFALZ

SC Klingbachtal ☎ 06349 6278
Municipal site lies on level meadowland at the edge of the
village, next to the sports ground.
⮩ *8km S of Landau via B38. Final approach well signposted.*
Apr-Oct 1.5HEC ⊞ ⌖ ↾ ⊙ ◘ ⌀ ☎ ⊞ lau ➡ ⅏ ✕ ₹P
Prices: ♠6 ⊞4 ⊞8 ▲6-8

IRREL RHEINLAND-PFALZ

Nimseck ☎ 06525 314
Site on long grassy strip in wooded valley on the bank of
River Nims.
⮩ *Approach from Bitburg via B257/E42 in SW direction. At*
the turn-off from the bypass to Irrel, turn left.
Apr-Nov 7HEC ⊞ ⌖ ↾ ✕ ⊙ ◘ ⌀ 丛 ⊠ ₹ PR ☎ ⊞ lau ➡ ⅏
⅏

KALLETAL-VARENHOLZ NORDRHEIN-WESTFALEN

Ost/Weser/Freizeit-Zentrum ☎ 05755 444
Extensive site in Weser recreation area near River Weser N of
Schloss Varenholz. Separate field and common room for
young campers.
⮩ *Leave A2/E8 motorway at Exter exit then continue via*
Vlotho towards Rintein.
All year 12HEC ⊞ ⌖ ↾ ⅏ ♥ ✕ ⊙ ◘ ⌀ ⊠ ₹ L ☎ ⊞ ⅏ lau
Prices: ♠8-9 ▲10-13 pitch 10-13

KELL RHEINLAND-PFALZ

Freibad Hochwald ☎ 06589 1695
On meadow on slightly sloping wooded hillside, near a
public open-air swimming pool.**Advance booking necessary
in high season.**
⮩ *2km from B407 towards Trier.*
May-Sep 2.5HEC ⊞ ⌖ ↾ ⅏ ✕ ⊙ ◘ ₹ P ☎ ⊞ ➡ ⅏ ✕ ⌀ 丛

KIRCHHEIM HESSEN

Seepark Kirchheim ☎ 06628 1525
This terraced site, with individual pitches, is part of an
extensive and well equipped leisure and recreation centre.
All year 10HEC ⊞ ⌖ ↾ ⅏ ♥ ✕ ⊙ ◘ ⌀ ⊟ ⊠
₹ LP ☎ ⊞ lau

KIRN RHEINLAND-PFALZ

Papiermühle Krebsweilererstr 8 ☎ 06752 2267
⮩ *Access via B41 exit Meisenheim*
All year 6HEC ⊞ ⌖ ↾ ✕ ⊙ ◘ ⌀ 丛 ⊠ ₹ R ☎ ⊞
Prices: ♠5 pitch 10

KOBLENZ (COBLENCE) RHEINLAND-PFALZ

At WINNINGEN(9km SW)

Ziehfurt Fährstr 35 ☎ 02606 356
Site lies on level wooded meadowland.
⮩ *From Koblenz follow road B416 for 11km towards Trièr.*
Access to site at the Schwimmbad (swimming pool).
May-Sep 7HEC ⊞ ⌖ ↾ ⅏ ✕ ⊙ ◘ ⌀ ⌀ ₹ R ☎ ⊞ lau
➡ ₹P
Prices: ♠8 pitch 8

Contd.

KÖLN (COLOGNE) NORDRHEIN-WESTFALEN
At RODENKIRCHEN

Berger Ueferstr 71 ☎ 0221 9355240
Situated on a meadow beside the River Rhine, the campsite has fine views of the beautiful surrounding area and good, modern facilities. All year 6HEC ⟋⟋⟋ ⚘ ↿ ⋔ ⅀ ⅄ ⊙ ▣ ⌀ ⊡ ⟍ R ⊞ lau ➤ ⊞
Prices: ⚲8 ⇆4 ⊟4 ⅃4

KÖNEN RHEINLAND-PFALZ

Horsch Könenerstr 36 ☎ 06501 17571
Apr-Oct ⟋⟋⟋ ⚘ ↿ ⋔ ⅀ ⅄ ✕ ⊙ ▣ ⌀ ⨯ ⟍ P ⊡ ⊞
Prices: pitch 25 (incl 2 persons)

KÖNIGSTEIN IM TAUNUS HESSEN
At EPPSTEIN(8km SW)

Hubertushof Bezirksstr 2 ☎ 0177 456700
In the Taunus landscape preservation area.
⊃ *Follow B455 from Königstein.*
All year 3HEC ⟋⟋⟋ ⚘ ⬧ ↿ ⅀ ⊙ ▣ ⌀ ⨯ ⊡ ⊞ lau ➤ ⅀ ✕ ⟍P
Prices: ⚲9 pitch 10

KRÖV RHEINLAND-PFALZ

Kröver-Berg ☎ 06541 70040
All year 2HEC ⟋⟋⟋ ⚘ ↿ ⅀ ✕ ⊙ ▣ ⌀ ⊡ ⊞ lau

LADBERGEN NORDRHEIN-WESTFALEN

Waldsee Waldseestr 81 ☎ 05485 1816
Site lies at the inn, near the bathing area of the lake.
⊃ *2km N. From motorway leave at 'Ladbergen' exit following road towards Saerbeck/Emsdetten and after 100m turn right.*
All year 6HEC ⟋⟋⟋ ↿ ⅀ ⋔ ✕ ⊙ ▣ ⌀ ⨯ ⟍ L ⊡ ⊞ lau ➤ ⌀ ⟍LP
Prices: ⚲5 pitch 7

LAHNSTEIN RHEINLAND-PFALZ

Burg Lahneck ☎ 02621 2765
Level grassland site with sunny aspect and terraces which provide shade. Situated next to Lahneck Castle. Pleasant view of the Rhine Valley.
⊃ *From Koblenz (8km distance) follow road B42. In Lahnstein, leave main road and follow signs (Burg Lahneck), 1.5km to site.*
Apr-Oct 1.8HEC ⟋⟋⟋ ⚘ ↿ ⅀ ⊙ ▣ ⌀ ⊡ ⊞ lau ➤ ✕ ⟍P
Prices: ⚲9.50 ⇆6 ⊟9.50 ⅃7-9.50

LANGENSELBOLD HESSEN

GC Kinzigsee ☎ 06184 3589
Lakeside site on level meadowland. Lunchtime siesta 13.00-15.00 hrs.
⊃ *A66 between Hanau and Gelnhausen.*
Apr-Sep 6HEC ⟋⟋⟋ ⚶ ↿ ⅀ ✕ ⊙ ▣ ⌀ ⨯ ⟍ L ⊡ ⊞ lau

LEBACH SAARLAND

Lebach Dillingerstr 81 ☎ 06881 2764
Local authority site. Grassland, slightly sloping on edge of wood.
⊃ *Take B269, entrance 750m from sports field.*
All year 3.2HEC ⟋⟋⟋ ⚘ ↿ ⋔ ✕ ⊙ ▣ ⨯ ⟍ P ⊡ lau ➤ ⅀

LEIWEN RHEINLAND-PFALZ

AEGON-Ferienpark Sonnenberg ☎ 06507 93690
Extensive terraced site in one of the largest wine growing areas of this district. Lies above the River Mosel.
⊃ *Access from main B53 (Mosel Valley road) cross the River Mosel at Thornich then via Leiwen to site.*
20 Feb-1 Nov 25HEC ⟋⟋⟋ ⚘ ⚘ ↿ ⋔ ⅀ ⅄ ✕ ⊙ ▣ ⌀ ⨯ ⊟ ⟍ P ⊡ ⊞ lau
Prices: pitch 36-59 (incl 5 persons)

LEMGO NORDRHEIN-WESTFALEN

Alten Hansestadt Regenstorstr ☎ 05261 14858
The site lies by the swimming pool directly on the river.
All year 2HEC ⟋⟋⟋ ⚘ ↿ ⊙ ▣ ⌀ ⊟ ⟍ R ⊞ lau ➤ ⅀ ⅄ ✕ ⟍P
Prices: ⚲7 ⇆6 ⊟6 ⅃3-9

LIBLAR NORDRHEIN-WESTFALEN

Liblarer See ☎ 02235 3899
This site lies at Lake Liblar, with its own bathing area.
Camping Card Compulsory.
⊃ *Access SW from Cologne on the B265 (for approx 15km) 1km before Liblar turn left towards the lake.*
All year 10HEC ⟋⟋⟋ ∷ ⚘ ↿ ⋔ ⅀ ✕ ⊙ ▣ ⌀ ⟍ L ⊡ ⊞ lau ➤ ⅀

LICHTENBERG HESSEN

Odenwald Idyll Fischbachtal ☎ 06166 8577
In quiet and beautiful setting. Lunchtime siesta 13.00-15.00 hrs.
⊃ *Access from Darmstadt amd Gross-Bieberau.*
Apr-15 Oct 3.5HEC ⟋⟋⟋ ⚘ ↿ ⋔ ⅀ ✕ ⊙ ▣ ⨯ ⟍ P ⊡ ⊞

LINDENFELS HESSEN

Terrassencamping Schlierbach Am Zentbuckel 11 ☎ 06255 630
Site is fenced and lies on sloping terrain. Lunchtime siesta 13.00-15.00 hrs.
⊃ *From Bensheim-Michelstadt road B47, turn off in Lindenfels and go SW to Schlierbach.*
Apr-Oct 3.2HEC ⟋⟋⟋ ∷ ⚘ ↿ ⋔ ⅀ ⊙ ▣ ⌀ ⨯ ⊡ ⊞ ➤ ⅀ ✕ ⟍LP
Prices: ⚲5.20-7.40 pitch 6.80-8.50

LINGERHAHN RHEINLAND-PFALZ

Mühlenteich ☎ 067461 533
Site lies on slightly sloping meadowland, divided into sections by a group of trees. Isolated situation at the edge of woodland and adjoining the forest swimming pool (free entry for campers). Lunchtime siesta 13.00-15.00 hrs. Trout fishing.
⊃ *Access is from Koblenz-Bingen motorway A61 via exit 'Pfalzfeld' - or for caravans, an easier approach would be via exit 'Laudert'.*
All year 15HEC ⟋⟋⟋ ⚘ ↿ ⋔ ⅀ ⅄ ✕ ⊙ ▣ ⌀ ⨯ ⟍ P ⊡ ⊞ ➤ ⟍R
Prices: ⚲6 ⇆7 ⊟7 ⅃7

LORCH HESSEN

Suleika ☎ 06726 9464
Well laid out terraced site in an ideal location for exploring the historic Rhine Valley. Separate car park for users of the smaller pitches.
⊃ *From Assmannshausen take B42 for 3km towards Lorch then turn right into the Bodental - access to site through railway underpass. Approach for larger caravans - turn right 1km before Lorch.*
Apr-Oct 4HEC ⟋⟋⟋ ⚘ ↿ ⋔ ⅀ ⅄ ✕ ⊙ ▣ ⌀ ⨯ ⊞ ⊡ ⊞ lau ➤ ✕ ⟍LPR
Prices: ⚲7.50 ⇆2.50 ⊟8 ⅃5-8

LOSHEIM SAARLAND

AZUR-Camping Reiterhof Girtenmühle ☎ 06872 9024-0
⊃ *Access via B268 (Trier-Losheim).*
All year 5HEC ⟋⟋⟋ ↿ ✕ ⊙ ▣ ⌀ ⊡ ⊞ lau ➤ ⟍LP
Prices: ⚲7-9 pitch 10-12

MAINZ-KOSTHEIM HESSEN

Mainz-Wiesbaden Maarau ☎ 06134 4383
Shop closed in April.
15 Mar-Oct 2HEC ⬛ ♦ ⌂ ✗ ⊙ 🗐 🗑 lau ♦ ∅ ♨ ₹PR
Prices: ♠7.50 ⬅5 🚐7 ▲6-8

MARBURG AN DER LAHN HESSEN

GC Lahnaue Tro je damm 47 ☎ 06421 21331
Municipal site on level meadowland next to the 'Sommerbad'
(swimming pool) in the W part of this 'Town on the River
Lahn'.
Apr-Oct 1.2HEC ⬛ ⌂ ⌂ ▙ ✗ ⊙ 🗐 ∅ 🚐 ₹ R 🏧 lau ♦ ₹P
Prices: ♠7 ⬅3 🚐6 ▲5

MEERBUSCH NORDRHEIN-WESTFALEN

AZUR-Camping Meerbusch Zur Rheinfähre 21
☎ 02150 911817
In a peaceful location on the banks of the Rhine within easy
reach of Dusseldorf.
⤷ Access via A57 (Neuss-Krefeld).
Apr-Oct 6HEC ⬛ ⯆ ⌂ ▙ ▮ ✗ ⊙ ♨ ₹ R 🏧 lau
Prices: ♠7-9 ⬅3-4 🚐10-12 ▲3-4

MEHLEM NORDRHEIN-WESTFALEN

Genienau ☎ 0228 344949
The site lies opposite the Drachenfels.
All year 1.8HEC ⬛ ⌂ ⌂ ▮ ⊙ 🗐 ∅ ₹ R 🏧 lau ♦ ▙ ✗ ∅
♨ ₹P
Prices: ♠8 ⬅3 🚐5-8 ▲5-8

MEINHARD HESSEN

Werra-Meissner-Kreis ☎ 05651 6200
Apr-Oct 7HEC ⬛ ⌂ ⌂ ▮ ✗ ⊙ 🗐 ₹ L 🏧 ⊞ ⊘ lau ♦ ▙ ♨
₹P ⊞
Prices: ♠6 pitch 11

MESCHEDE NORDRHEIN-WESTFALEN

Sauerland-Camp Hennesee ☎ 0291 99950
In pleasant wooded surroundings beside the Hennesee. Shop
and café only open during high season.
⤷ S via B55.
All year 13HEC ⬛ ⌂ ⌂ ▙ ▮ ✗ ⊙ 🗐 ∅ ♨ ₹ LP 🏧 ⊞ lau
♦ ₹L

MICHELSTADT HESSEN

Odenwaldparadies ☎ 06061 74152
Site is partly fenced in and lies next to the station and
swimming pool in the NE part of town.
⤷ Site is well signposted from the by-pass road of Michelstadt.
May-Sep 1.2HEC ⬛ ⯆ ⌂ ✗ ⊙ 🗐 ∅ 🏧 ⊞ ⊘ ♦ ₹P

MITTELHOF RHEINLAND-PFALZ

Eichenwald ☎ 02742 931915
In oakwood, mainly divided into pitches.
Camping Card Compulsory.
⤷ From Siegen follow B62 towards Wissen. Turning to site
approximately 4km NE of Wissen.
All year 10HEC ⬛ ⌂ ⌂ ▙ ▮ ✗ ⊙ 🗐 ∅ 🏧 ⊞ lau

MONSCHAU NORDRHEIN-WESTFALEN

Perlenau ☎ 02472 4136
Apr-Oct 2.1HEC ⬛ ⌂ ⌂ ▙ ▮ ✗ ⊙ 🗐 ∅ ₹ R 🏧 ⊞ lau
Prices: ♠8 ⬅4 🚐8 ▲5.50-8

MONTABAUR RHEINLAND-PFALZ

At GIROD(4km E)

Eisenbachtal ☎ 06485 766
Situated in the 'Nassau Nature Park'.

⤷ From motorway exit 40 'Montabaur' turn right, before
Montabaur follow sign 5km towards Limburg. From motorway
exit 41 'Wallmerod/Diez' 5km towards Montabaur.
All year 3.5HEC ⬛ ⌂ ⌂ ▙ ▮ ✗ ⊙ 🗐 ∅ 🏧 ⊞ lau ♦ ₹P
Prices: ♠8 pitch 10

MÖRFELDEN-WALLDORF HESSEN

Arndt Mörfelden Am Zeltplatz 5 ☎ 06105 22289
Well laid out site in two sections near motorway. Lunchtime
siesta 13.00-15.00 hrs.
⤷ Well signposted 0.3km from Langen/Mörfelden exit on
A5/E4 Frankfurt-Darmstadt motorway.
All year 6HEC ⬛ ⌂ ⌂ ▙ ▮ ✗ ⊙ 🗐 ∅ 🏧 ⊞ lau
♦ ✗ ∅ ₹LP ⊞
Prices: ♠7 🚐10-15 ▲8

MÜLHEIM RHEINLAND-PFALZ

AZUR Camping Mülheim ☎ 06534 940157
Near Mülheim-Lieser bridge over the Mosel.
Camping Card Compulsory.
⤷ Access from Bernkastel, 5.5km along B53 towards Trier.
Mar-15 Nov 1.5HEC ⬛ ⌂ ⌂ ▮ ✗ ⊙ 🗐 ∅ ₹ R 🏧 ⊞ lau
♦ ▙ ₹P
Prices: ♠7-8.50 ⬅3 🚐10-12 ▲5-8.50

MÜLHEIM AN DER RUHR NORDRHEIN-WESTFALEN

Entenfangsee ☎ 0203 760111
Extensive site near lake. Touring pitches near railway line.
Adventure playground. Lunchtime siesta 13.00-15.00 hrs.
⤷ From motorway exit Duisburg-Wedau, continue towards
Bissingheim to lake.
All year 12.5HEC ⬛ ⌂ ⌂ ▙ ✗ ⊙ 🗐 ∅ ♨ ₹ L 🏧 ⊞ lau
♦ ₹P ⊞
Prices: ♠5 pitch 10

MÜLLENBACH RHEINLAND-PFALZ

Nürburgring ☎ 02692 224
A large, well equipped site in a wooded location with direct
access to the Nürburgring Grand-Prix circuit.
⤷ Access via A61/A48 and B412.
All year 30HEC ⬛ ⯌ ⌂ ⌂ ▙ ✗ ⊙ 🗐 ∅ ♨ 🚐 🏧 ⊞ lau
Prices: ♠18 pitch 14

NEHREN RHEINLAND-PFALZ

Nehren ☎ 02673 4612
On level terrain beside the River Moselle. Separate section for
teenagers. Lunchtime siesta 13.00-15.00 hrs. Liable to flood at
certain times of the year.
⤷ Turn off the B49 Cochem-Alf road in Nehren.
Apr-10 Oct 5HEC ⬛ ⌂ ⌂ ▙ ✗ ⊙ 🗐 ∅ ♨ ₹ R 🏧 ⊞ lau
♦ ₹LP
Prices: ♠6 🚐14 ▲8

NEUERBURG RHEINLAND-PFALZ

Neuerburg ☎ 06564 2660
Site divided by hedges, close to an open-air pool with a
smaller lake for inflatable boats.
⤷ Access via the B50 (Bitburg-Vianden). At Sinspett turn N
and continue to site on N outskirts (7km).
All year 1.5HEC ⬛ ⌂ ⌂ ▙ ▮ ✗ ⊙ 🗐 ∅ ♨ ₹ PRS 🏧 ⊘ lau ♦ ▙

NIEDERBERGHEIM NORDRHEIN-WESTFALEN

Niederbergheim Sauerlandstr 168 ☎ 02925 1842
Site lies on a meadow surrounded by woodland to the E of
the Möhne Dam.
⤷ From the Möhne Dam follow the B516 E to
Niederbergheim, here turn S towards Hirschberg. 2km to site.
All year 2.2HEC ⬛ ⌂ ⌂ ▙ ⊙ 🗐 ♨ 🏧 ⊞ lau ♦ ▮ ✗

NIEDEREISENHAUSEN HESSEN

Hinterland Ouotshauser Weg 32, Steffenberg ☎ 06464 7564
Lunchtime siesta 13.00-14.30 hrs.
➲ *Follow signs to 'Schwimmbad'.*
All year 2HEC ᛘᛘ ♠ ⋔ ✕ ☉ ⬛ ♨ ⬛ ⊞ lau ♦ ⬛ ⍦P

NIEDERKRÜCHTEN NORDRHEIN-WESTFALEN

Lelefeld Lelefeld 4 ☎ 02163 81203
In a quiet, wooded, location on the outskirts of the village.
➲ *Signposted from Elmpt.*
All year 1.5HEC ᛘᛘ ⍋ ⋔ ⬛ ⬤ ☉ ⬛ ⍺ ♨ ⬛ ⊞ lau
♦ ✕ ⍦LPR
Prices: ⋔6 ⬥3 ⬛6 ▲6

NIEDERWÖRRESBACH RHEINLAND-PFALZ

Fischbachtal ☎ 06785 7372
On level grassland in Fischbach valley. Lunchtime siesta 12.00-14.00 hrs.
➲ *6km N of Fischbach towards Herrsteij.*
All year 1.8HEC ᛘᛘ ⍋ ⋔ ⬛ ✕ ☉ ⬛ ⍺ ⬛ ⍦ R ⬛ ⊞ lau

OBERLAHR RHEINLAND-PFALZ

Lahrer Herrlichkeit In der Huth ☎ 02685 7326 & 8282
Holiday site with leisure park in wooded surroundings.
Lunchtime siesta 13.00-15.00 hrs.
➲ *From motorway A3 (Frankfurt-Köln) leave at exit 'Neuwied/Altenkirchen' then 5km on B256 towards Altenkirchen.*
All year 6.8HEC ᛘᛘ ⍋ ⋔ ✕ ☉ ⬛ ⍺ ♨ ⬛ ⬛ ⊞ lau ♦ ⬛ ✕ ⍦PR

OBERSGEGEN RHEINLAND-PFALZ

Reles-Mühle Kapellenstr 3 ☎ 06566 8741
In rural surroundings next to a farmhouse, set on a level meadow at a brook with trees and bushes.
➲ *From Bitburg on road B50 towards Vianden. Site lies near the Luxembourg frontier.*
All year 2HEC ᛘᛘ ⍋ ⋔ ☉ ⬛ ⬛ ⬛ ⊞ lau ♦ ⬛ ⬛ ✕ ⍺ ♨ ⍦LPRS
Prices: ⋔4 pitch 8

OBERWEIS RHEINLAND-PFALZ

Prümtal-Camping In der Klaus 5 ☎ 06527 92920
A family site in pleasant wooded surroundings with good sporting facilities.
➲ *Access from Bitburg on B50 towards Luxembourg border.*
All year 38HEC ᛘᛘ ⍋ ⋔ ⬛ ✕ ☉ ⬛ ⍺ ♨ ⬛ ⬛ ⍦ R ⬛ ⍦P ⊞
Prices: ⋔6.80-8.50 pitch 10.40-14.50

OLPE NORDRHEIN-WESTFALEN

At KESSENHAMMER

Biggesee-Kessenhammer ☎ 62761 24420
Long, narrow partly terraced site in quiet woodland setting on E shore of Bigge-Reservoir. Lunchtime siesta 13.00-15.00 hrs.
➲ *A45 exit Olpe continue B54 to Olpe eastwards on B55 and turn off at exit Rhode.*
All year 5.7HEC ᛘᛘ ⍋ ⋔ ⬛ ✕ ☉ ⬛ ⍺ ♨ ⍦ L ⬛ ⊞ lau ♦ ⬛ ✕ ⍦P
Prices: ⋔5.50-7 ⬛18-24 ▲11-17

At SONDERN

Biggesee-Sondern Sonderner Kopf 3 ☎ 02761 944111
A popular site in wooded surroundings on the shore of the Biggesee.
➲ *Exit Olpe A45 in direction Attendorn. In 6km turn off for Erholungsanlage Biggesee-Sondern.*

All year 6HEC ᛘᛘ ⍋ ♠ ⋔ ⬛ ✕ ☉ ⬛ ⍺ ♨ ⍦ L ⬛ ⊞ lau ♦ ⬛ ✕ ⍦P
Prices: ⋔5.50-7 pitch 19-25

OLSBERG NORDRHEIN-WESTFALEN

At BRUCHHAUSEN(7km SE)

Bruchhauser Steine Am Medebach 96 ☎ 02962 3000
The site lies on meadowland next to a brook. Lunchtime siesta 13.00-14.30 hrs.
➲ *From Meschede follow road B7 for 13 km eastwards, the turn off the 'Bigge' and continue via 'Olsberg' and 'Elleringhausen' to 'Bruchhausen' and finally follow signs to 'Skighebiet Sternrodt'.*
All year 2HEC ᛘᛘ ⍋ ⋔ ☉ ⬛ ⍺ ♨ ⬛ ⬛ ⊞ lau ♦ ⬛ ⬛ ✕

OSTRHAUDERFEHN NORDRHEIN-WESTFALEN

AZUR-Camping Idasee ☎ 04952 994297
Situated beside a lake between Oldenburg and the Dutch border with good water sports facilities.
➲ *Access via B27 (Cloppenburg-Aurich).*
15 Mar-15 Nov 5HEC ᛘᛘ ⍋ ⋔ ☉ ⬛ ⍺ ♨ ⍦ L ⬛ ⊞ lau

PORTA WESTFALICA NORDRHEIN-WESTFALEN

Grosser Weserbogen ☎ 05731 6188
➲ *From A2 (travelling towards Dortmund), take exit Porta Westfalica-Minden.*
All year 7HEC ᛘᛘ ⍒ ⋔ ✕ ☉ ⬛ ⍺ ⍦ L ⬛ ⊞ lau ♦ ⍦P
Prices: ⋔7.50-9.50 ⬛3-5 pitch 7-8

PRÜM RHEINLAND-PFALZ

Waldcampingplatz ☎ 06551 2481
Site lies on both side of the River Prüm and is surrounded by woods. Divided into three sections of level meadowland.
➲ *Situated at the NW of Prüm.*
All year 3HEC ᛘᛘ ⍋ ⋔ ✕ ☉ ⬛ ⍺ ♨ ⍦ R ⬛ ⊞ lau ♦ ⬛ ⬛ ✕ ⍦P
Prices: ⋔5 pitch 25

REINSFELD RHEINLAND-PFALZ

AZUR Camping Hunsrück ☎ 06503 95123
In a peaceful location close to Trier on the Luxembourg border, surrounded by hills.
➲ *Access via the B52 or B407.*
All year 20HEC ᛘᛘ ⍋ ⋔ ⬛ ⬤ ✕ ☉ ⬛ ⍺ ♨ ⍦ P ⬛ ⊞ lau
Prices: ⋔8-10 ⬛9-13

ROTENBURG-FULDA HESSEN

SC Campingweg ☎ 06623 5556
➲ *SE of town on River Fulda, follow 'DCC' signs.*
Apr-Oct 0.9HEC ᛘᛘ ⍋ ⋔ ⬛ ⬤ ✕ ☉ ⬛ ⬛ ⊞ lau ♦ ⬛ ✕ ⍺ ♨ ⍦P

ROTHEMANN HESSEN

Rothemann Maulkuppenstr 17 ☎ 06659 2285
A small, well-kept site surrounded by a hedge, lies next to the main Fulda road.
⮑ *From Fulda follow road B27 for 10km towards Bad Brükenau; can also be reached from the Kassel-Wüzburg motorway leaving exit Fulda Süd, then 3km along B27 towards Bad Brükenau.*
Apr-Oct 6.4HEC ⸬ ♠ ⋔ ⅀ ⊙ ▣ ∅ ⚊ 🅿 ⊞ ➹ ✕
Prices: ♠6.50 ➹4 ⛺4 ⛺4

RÜDESHEIM HESSEN

Landgut Ebental 'Ponyland' ☎ 06722 2518
On meadowland surrounded by woodlands. Ponies and carriages for hire. Private sports plane for pleasure flights.
⮑ *N towards Presberg. Steep approach road to Ebental. Signposted.*
15 May-15 Nov 2HEC ⸬ ⚘ ⋔ ✕ ⊙ ▣ ∅ ⚊ 🅿 ⊞ lau
➹ ⅀ ⅄

Rhein ☎ 06722 2528 & 2582
Near the open-air swimming pool and the River Rhine.
30 Apr-29 Oct 2.9HEC ⸬ ⚘ ⋔ ⅀ ⅄ ✕ ⊙ ▣ ∅ ⚊ 🅿 lau ➹ ✕
⤳P ⊞
Prices: ♠6.90 ➹5.60 ⛺7.30 ⛺6.30-8.30

RUNKEL AN DER LAHN HESSEN

Runkel Auf der Bleiche ☎ 06482 911022
⮑ *On road from Limburg.*
Apr-Sep 2HEC ⸬ ⚘ ⋔ ⅀ ✕ ⊙ ▣ ∅ ⚊ ▲ ⤳ R 🅿 ⊞
➹ ⅀ ✕

SAARBURG RHEINLAND-PFALZ

Landal Greenpark Warsberg ☎ 06581 91460
Open site in quiet situation on top of a hill. Chairlift (700m) leads down to the town.
⮑ *At N end of the town leave the B51 'Trier' road and follow signs ' Ferienpark Warsberg' 3km uphill on good road.*
3 Apr-6 Nov 11HEC ⸬ ⚘ ⋔ ⅀ ⅄ ✕ ⊙ ▣ ∅ ⚊ ⤳ P 🅿 ⊞
lau

Leukbachtal ☎ 06581 2228
Municipal site on level meadows on both sides of the Leuk-Bach (brook).
⮑ *Leave Saarburg on road B51 towards Trassen, then after crossroads, turn left off the B51.*
Etr-1 Nov 3HEC ⸬ ⚘ ⋔ ⅀ ✕ ⊙ ▣ ∅ ⚊ 🅿 ⊞ lau ➹ ⅀ ✕
⤳P
Prices: ♠6.50 pitch 16

Waldfrieden Im Fichtenhain 4 ☎ 06581 2255
Site lies next to the Café Waldfrieden on unspoilt, slightly rising meadowland in woods.
⮑ *S of town leave B51 or B407 and follow road towards Nennig (Luxembourg). 200m to site.*
Mar-Oct 2HEC ⸬ ⚘ ⚘ ⋔ ✕ ⊙ ▣ ∅ ⚊ 🅿 ⊞ lau ➹ ⅀ ✕
⤳PR ⊞
Prices: ♠5 ➹3 ⛺9-11 ▲6-9

SAARLOUIS SAARLAND

AZUR-Camping Saarlouis St-Nazairer Alle 23 ☎ 06831 3691
A municipal site, divided into pitches, and set on level meadowland with tall trees. Lunchtime siesta 13.00-14.30 hrs.
⮑ *Turn off road B51 in suburb of Roden, cross new bridge over the River Saar and continue to site, beyond sports hall.*
15 Mar-15 Nov 2HEC ⸬ ⚭ ⋔ ✕ ⊙ ▣ ∅ ⚊ 🅿 ⊞ lau
➹ ⤳P
Prices: ♠7-9 pitch 10-12

ST GOAR RHEINLAND-PFALZ

Friedenau Gruendelbach 103 ☎ 06741 368
On level, narrow stretch of meadowland at Gasthaus Friedenau.
⮑ *Leave B9 in St-Goar and continue through railway underpass towards Emmelshausen for approx 1km.*
Mar-Nov 1.2HEC ⸬ ♠ ⋔ ⅀ ⅄ ✕ ⊙ ▣ ∅ ⚊ ⤳ R ⊞ ⊞
lau ➹ ⅀ ⤳P
Prices: ♠6.50 ➹4.50 ⛺4.50 ▲3-4.50

ST GOARSHAUSEN RHEINLAND-PFALZ

Loreleystadt ☎ 06771 2592
Municipal site on level meadow beside the Rhine. Near a sportsfield and opposite Rheinfels Castle.
⮑ *Access via B42.*
15 Mar-Oct 1.5HEC ⸬ ⚘ ⋔ ⅀ ⅄ ⊙ ▣ ∅ ⤳ R 🅿 ⊞ lau
➹ ✕ ⊞
Prices: ♠6-7.50 ➹4 ⛺6 ▲5-8

SCHACHEN HESSEN

Hochrhön ☎ 06654 7836
Lies 1.5km from the Kneipp (hydrotherapeutic) Spa area of Gersfeld.
⮑ *2km N of Gersfeld.*
All year 3HEC ⸬ ⚘ ⋔ ⊙ ▣ ∅ ⚊ 🅿 lau ➹ ⅀ ⅄ ✕ ⤳LP ⊞
Prices: ♠6 pitch 8

SCHALKENMEHREN RHEINLAND-PFALZ

Camp am Maar Maarstr 22 ☎ 06592 551
Terraced lakeside site on meadowland at the Schalkenmehrener Maar (water-filled crater). Towing help for caravans.
⮑ *From A48 (Eifelautobahn) leave at 'Mehren/Daun' exit and follow B42 to Mehren. Turn off to the SW.*
All year 1HEC ⸬ ♠ ⋔ ⅀ ⅄ ✕ ⊙ ▣ ∅ ⚊ ⤳ LP 🅿 lau ➹ ⊞

SCHLEIDEN NORDRHEIN-WESTFALEN

Schleiden Im Wiesengrund 39 ☎ 02445 7030
Site lies on hilly, well-wooded country.
⮑ *On the B258 to Monschau, 1km to site.*
All year 5HEC ⸬ ⚘ ⋔ ✕ ⊙ ▣ ∅ ⚊ 🅿 ⊞ ⊘ lau ➹ ⅀ ⅄ ✕
⤳P
Prices: ♠7 ➹3 ⛺8 ▲9-12

SCHLÜCHTERN HESSEN

At **HUTTEN**(8km E)

Hutten Heiligenborn ☎ 06661 2424
Site lies at Heiligenborn and has a pleasant southerly aspect.
⮑ *Approach from Fulda on B40 towards Frankfurt to Flieden for 19km, then turn left via Rückers to Hutten (8km).*
All year 3.5HEC ⸬ ⚘ ⋔ ⅀ ⊙ ▣ ∅ ⚊ 🅿 ⊞ lau ➹ ⤳P
Prices: ♠7.20 pitch 8-10

SCHÖNENBERG SAARLAND

Ohmbachsee ☎ 06373 4001
Terraced site on sloping ground above E bank of the Ohmbachsee. Separate field for young people. Lunchtime siesta 13.00-15.00 hrs.
⮑ *Signposted.*
All year 7.8HEC ⸬ ⚘ ⋔ ⅀ ⅄ ✕ ⊙ ▣ ∅ ⚊ ⤳ P 🅿 ⊞ lau
➹ ⤳L

SCHOTTEN HESSEN

Nidda-Stausee Vogelsbergstr 184 ☎ 06044 1418
A pleasant family site on the shore of a lake.
⮑ *Access via B455.*
All year 3.8HEC ⸬ ⚘ ⋔ ⅀ ✕ ⊙ ▣ ∅ ⚊ ⤳ L 🅿 ⊞ lau

SCHWEICH RHEINLAND-PFALZ

Schweich ☎ 06502 91300
On level meadowland on the Mosel, next to a marina.
⮕ *Access via A48 (Eifelautobhan) exit 'Schweich' in direction of Trier. Continue through Schweich, turning left just before the Mosel bridge.*
15 Apr-15 Oct 3.5HEC ⛺ ⚐ ⛄ ✗ ⊙ ⬜ ∅ ☵ ⚲ R 🅿 lau ⮕ 🛒
⚲P ⊞

SECK RHEINLAND-PFALZ

Weiherhof ☎ 02664 8555
Site lies on level meadowland next to a small lake in a wooded nature reserve. Special section reserved for young people. Many bathers at weekends.
⮕ *Take the B255 from Rennerod and drive to Hellenbahn-Schellenberg. Then turn S and continue for approx 2km.*
All year 10HEC ⛺ ⚐ ⛄ 🛒 ⚲ ✗ ⊙ ⬜ ∅ ☵ ⚲ L 🅿 ⊞ lau

SENHEIM RHEINLAND-PFALZ

Internationaler Holländischer Hof ☎ 02673 4660
On level meadowland, divided into pitches beside the River Mosel which has boatmooring facilities.
⮕ *Access from Cochem via the B49 in direction of Zell as far as Senhals, then over the bridge and turn left.*
15 Apr-15 Oct 3HEC ⛺ ⚐ ⛄ 🛒 ✗ ⊙ ∅ ⚲ R
🅿 ⊞ 🛒 lau
Prices: ⚑6 pitch 12

SENSWEILER MÜHLE RHEINLAND-PFALZ

Bauernhof Bundestr 422 ☎ 06786 2395
On extenisve grassland beside the Idar, partially terraced, in rural area near a farm. Views of wooded range of hills. Next to Camping Oberes Idartal. Separate section for young groups.
⮕ *From Idar-Oberstein follow road B422 for about 10km to the NW. Site lies between Katzenloch and Allenbach.*
All year 2HEC ⛺ ⚐ ⚑ ⛄ 🛒 ⊙ ⬜ ∅ 🅿 ⊞ lau ⮕ 🛒

Oberes Idartal ☎ 06786 2114
Site lies on a farm by the Idar, set on several small meadows and partly on terraced terrain next to Camping Sensweiler Mühel. Blockhouse with facilities for spit-roasting.
⮕ *From Idar-Oberstein follow road B422 for about 10km to the NW. site lies between Katzenloch and Allenbach.*
All year 2.8HEC ⛺ ⚐ ⚑ ⛄ 🛒 ⊙ ∅ ☵ 🏠 ⚲ R 🅿 ⊞ lau
⮕ 🛒 ✗

SOLINGEN NORDRHEIN-WESTFALEN
At GLÜDER

Waldcamping Glüder ☎ 0212 242120
Site on level terrain surrounded by woodland on banks of the River Wupper.
⮕ *Access via Köln-Kamen Autobahn exit Burscheid, via Hilgen and Witzhelden to Glüder or from Solingen on B299/B224 in direction of Witzhelden via Burg Hohenscheid.*
All year 2HEC ⛺ ⚐ ⛄ 🛒 🛒 ✗ ⊙ ∅ ☵ 🅿 ⊞ lau
Prices: ⚑7 🚗12 ▲7-12

STADTKYLL RHEINLAND-PFALZ

AEGON Ferienpark Wirfttal ☎ 06597 92920
Extensive, level grassland beside the upper of two small reservoirs, approx 1km outside the town.
⮕ *Access S from Euskirchen on the A1, through Blankenheim and towards Stadtkyll.*
All year 2HEC ⛺ ⚑ ☀ ⚐ 🛒 🛒 ✗ ⊙ ∅ ☵ 🏠 ⚲ P ⊞
lau ⮕ ⚲L
Prices: pitch 29-52

STEINEN RHEINLAND-PFALZ

Hofgut Schönerlen ☎ 02666 207
Beautiful and quiet site at Lake Hausweiher, has a special section reserved for residential campers. Young campers under 18 years old not accepted unless with adults.
⮕ *Take the B8 Limburg-Altenkirchen road. In Steinen turn left to the site.*
All year 15HEC ⛺ ⮕ ⚐ ⊙ ⬜ ∅ ☵ ⚲ L 🅿 ⊞ ∅ lau ⮕ ✗
Prices: ⚑9 pitch 11

STUKENBROCK NORDRHEIN-WESTFALEN

Furlbach Am Furlbach 33 ☎ 05257 3373
Extensive site, partly on level, open meadow and partly in woodland. Separate section for dog owners. Old barn is used as a common room for young campers. Lunchtime siesta 12.30-14.30 hrs.
⮕ *From the Dortmund-Hannover motorway (A2/E73) leave at exit 'Bielefeld/Sennenstadt' then follow B68 for about 12km towards Paderborn. At Km44.2 turn off main road then 400m to site.*
Apr-Oct 9HEC ⛺ ⚐ ⛄ 🛒 ✗ ⊙ ☵ 🅿 ⊞ lau ⮕ ✗ ∅ ⚲P
Prices: ⚑7 🚗4.50 🚗6 ▲5-6

TANN HESSEN

Ulstertal Dippach 4 ☎ 06682 8292
Terraced site on slightly sloping meadowland.
⮕ *Leave the Bischofsheim-Tann road B278 in Wendershausen and go SE to Dippach.*
All year 2.4HEC ⛺ ⚐ ⛄ ✗ ⊙ ⬜ ∅ ☵ 🏠 🏠 🅿 ⊞ lau ⮕
⚲P
Prices: ⚑6.50-7.50 pitch 6-7

TECKLENBURG NORDRHEIN-WESTFALEN
At LEEDEN(12km E, also E of motorway)

Truma-Campingpark ☎ 05405 1007
Site lies on undulating meadowland, with asphalted roads. Four separate buildings. Separate section for dog owners. Lunchtime siesta 13.00-15.00 hrs.
⮕ *From A1-E3 Bremen-Münster motorway leave at Lengerich/Tecklenburg exit, then via Lengerich to Leeden (10km).*
All year 30HEC ⛺ ⚐ ⛄ ✗ ⊙ ∅ ☵ 🅿 ⊞ lau

TREIS-KARDEN RHEINLAND-PFALZ

Mosel-Islands ☎ 02672 2613
An extensive, level site on a grassy island in the Mosel next to a yacht marina.
⮕ *Turn off the B49 in Treis onto the southern coastal road.*
Apr-Oct 4.5HEC ⛺ ⚐ ⛄ ⊙ ☵ ⚲ R 🅿 lau ⮕ 🛒 🛒 ✗ ⚲P ⊞
Prices: ⚑7 🚗5 🚗10 ▲5

TRENDELBURG HESSEN

Trendelburg ☎ 05675 301
Site located at the foot of the castle, subdivided on the banks of the River Diemel. Covered tennis court.
⮕ *Access from Kessel N via Hofgeismar (B83) to Trendelburg cross the bridge and turn sharp left, down to site.*
All year 1.2HEC ⛺ ⚐ ⛄ 🛒 🛒 ✗ ⊙ ⬜ ∅ ☵ 🏠 ⚲ R 🅿 ⮕ ⚲P
Prices: ⚑5.20 pitch 7

TRIER RHEINLAND-PFALZ

Trier-City Luxemburger Str 81 ☎ 0651 86921
Level site owned by the Rowing Club Treviris, on left bank of the Mosel divided by an asphalt road.
⮕ *It lies between the Romer bridge and Adenauer bridge on road towards Luxembourg.*
Apr-Oct 1.5HEC ⛺ ⮕ ⚐ ⛄ ✗ ⊙ ⬜ 🚗 ⚲ R 🅿 ⮕ ∅ ☵
Prices: ⚑8 🚗4 🚗8 ▲4-8

TRIPPSTADT RHEINLAND-PFALZ

Sägmühle Sägmühle 1 ☎ 06306 1215
The site lies in a wooded valley beside the Sagmühle Lake
(Saw Mill Lake). It consists of several unconnected sections,
some of them terraced. Lunchtime siesta 12.30-14.00 hrs.
➲ *14km S of Kaiserslautern.*
All year 9HEC ▥ 🔌 🏕 ⛲ ✕ ⊙ 🅿 ⌀ ≞ 🔲 ⚡ L ⬚ ⊞ lau ➧ 🛒
⚡P

UTSCHEID RHEINLAND-PFALZ

Michelbach ☎ 06564 2097
A municipal site at the Michelbach, surrounded by meadows
and woods, 50% individual pitches.
➲ *From the B50 Bittburg-Vianden road turn N in Sinspelt.*
Then continue via Niederraden to Utscheid.
All year 1.5HEC 🏕 ✕ ⊙ 🅿 ⌀ lau ➧ 🛒 🛒 ⌀ ⚡LPR ⊞

VINKRATH BEI GREFRATH NORDRHEIN-WESTFALEN

SC Waldfrieden ☎ 02158 3855
Site within nature reserve.
➲ *From Grefrath N towards Wankum after 3km. Turn right.*
Apr-Oct 4.5HEC ▥ 🔌 🏕 ⊙ 🅿 ⌀ ≞ ⬚ ⊞ ⊘ lau ➧ 🛒 🛒 ✕
⚡LP
Prices: 🛏6.50 pitch 9.50-15

VORDERWEIDENTHAL RHEINLAND-PFALZ

Bethof Am Bethof 1 ☎ 06398 993011
Terraced site at the 'Naturefreudhaus' (hostel belonging to
Friends of Nature). Separate tent area for the young.
Camping Card Compulsory.
➲ *From Bad Bergzabern follow road B427 for 7km westwards,*
after Birkenhördt turn right, then 1.5km to site.
Apr-Oct 2HEC ▥ ⋮⋮ 🔌 🏕 ✕ ⊙ 🅿 ≞ ⬚ ⊞

WARBURG NORDRHEIN-WESTFALEN

Eversburg ☎ 05641 8668
Site lies next to restaurant of the same name on the SE
outskirts of the town.
All year 4.5HEC ▥ 🔌 🏕 ✕ ⊙ 🅿 ⚡ R ⬚ ⊞ lau ➧ 🛒 🛒 ⌀ ⚡P
Prices: 🛏8 🚐3 🚙12 🛆6

WASSERFALL NORDRHEIN-WESTFALEN

Wasserfall Aurorastr 9 ☎ 02905 332
Terraced site, surrounded by woodland, next to leisure centre
'Fort Fun'. Little room for touring campers during the winter.
➲ *About 10km E of Meschedes, between Bestwig and Nuttlar,*
turn S off the B7. Driver past Gevelinghausen and up to
Wasserfall.
All year 1HEC ▥ 🔌 🏕 ✕ ⊙ 🅿 ≞ 🏠 🅿 ⊞ ➧ 🛒

WAXWEILER RHEINLAND-PFALZ

AEGON-Ferienpark Im Prümtal ☎ 06554 427
Site lies on level terrain and is divided into pitches, with a
separate field on the opposite side of the River Prüm. Near
swimming pool. Lunchtime siesta between 13.00-15.00 hrs.
➲ *From N end of Waxweiler, turn off towards the River Prüm.*
31 Mar-5 Nov 3HEC ▥ 🔌 🏕 ⊙ 🅿 ⌀ ≞ 🏠 ⚡ P ⬚ ⊞ lau
➧ 🛒 ⚡P

WEHLEN RHEINLAND-PFALZ

Schenk Hauptstr 165 ☎ 06531 8176
A site in the Mosel valley, partly set on terraces. The site
approach can be difficult for caravans due to the steep
gradient.
➲ *From Bernkastel-Kues follow B53 for 4km NW towards*
'Koblenz' reaching Wehlen turn right.
Etr-Oct 1HEC ▥ 🔌 🏕 ⊙ 🅿 ≞ ⚡ PR ⬚ lau ➧ 🛒 ⌀ ⊞

WEILBURG HESSEN

At **ODERSBACH**

Odersbach Runkler Str 5A ☎ 06471 7620
In attractive setting beside the River Lahn, next to a public
swimming pool. Lunchtime siesta 12.00-14.00 hrs.
➲ *On S outskirts of town.*
Apr-Oct 5HEC ▥ 🔌 🏕 ✕ ⊙ 🅿 ⌀ ≞ ⚡ PR ⬚ ⊞ lau ➧ 🛒
🛒 ✕

WINTERBERG NORDRHEIN-WESTFALEN

At **NIEDERSFELD**(8.5km N)

Vossmecke ☎ 02985 8418
In a pleasant wooded location with facilities for winter
camping.
➲ *Off B480 towards Winterberg.*
All year 4HEC ▥ ♨ ❄ 🏕 🏕 ✕ ⊙ 🅿 ≞ 🅿 lau ➧ 🛒 ✕ ⊞
Prices: pitch 25.90-29.90 (incl 2 persons)

WISSEL NORDRHEIN-WESTFALEN

Wisseler See Am See 10 ☎ 02824 9631
Well-kept municipal site with modern equipment beside
Lake Wissel. There is a separate car park next to the open-air
swimming pool. The pool belongs to the camp. The
washrooms are closed during lunchtimes and at night.
➲ *From Kieve, take the B57 towards Xanten. After about 9km,*
turn left and drive a further 3km towards Wissel.
All year 40HEC ▥ 🔌 🛒 🛒 ✕ ⊙ 🅿 ⌀ ≞ 🏠 ⚡ L 🅿 ⊞ ⊘
lau ➧ ⚡P
Prices: 🛏8 🚐4 🚙10 🛆7

WITZENHAUSEN HESSEN

Werratal Am Sande 11 ☎ 05542 1465
The site lies on meadow between the outskirts of
Witzenhausen and the banks of the Werra.
➲ *For access, leave Hannover-Kassel motorway at Werratal.*
10km on B80 to Witzenhausen. From market place follow signs.
All year 30HEC ▥ ➧ 🛒 🛒 🛒 ⊙ 🅿 ⌀ 🏠 🏠 ⚡ R ⬚ ⊞ lau
➧ ✕ ⚡LP
Prices: 🛏6.30-7 pitch 6-8

WOLFSTEIN RHEINLAND-PFALZ

AZUR Camping Königsberg ☎ 06304 4143
Municipal site, beside small River Lauter next to open air
swimming pool.
➲ *Site lies at S end of Wolfstein to the right of B270 from*
Kaiserslautern.
All year 1.4HEC ▥ 🔌 🏕 🛒 ⊙ 🅿 ⚡ R ⬚ lau ➧ 🛒 ⌀ ⚡P ⊞
Prices: 🛏6-9 pitch 8-12

ZERF RHEINLAND-PFALZ

Rübezahl ☎ 06587 814
Meadowland site in natural grounds on wooded hillside.
➲ *Leave Zerf S on B268 towards Saarbrücken then turn*
towards Oberzerf 2.5km to site from turning. From Saarburg,
follow B407 beyond Vierherrenhorn, turn right and follow track
for 60m.
All year 3HEC ▥ 🔌 🏕 ⊙ 🅿 ⌀ ⚡ P ⬚ ⊞ ➧ 🛒 🛒 ✕
Prices: 🛏6 pitch 7

ZWESTEN HESSEN

Waldcamping Hinter dem Wasser ☎ 05626 379
Site in bend of River Schwalm. Lunchtime siesta 13.00-15.00
hrs. For touring campers there is also an overflow site outside
the actual campsite.
➲ *Access from Kassel in SW direction via Fritzlar to Zwesten.*
All year 3.2HEC ▥ 🔌 🏕 🛒 ✕ ⊙ 🅿 ≞ ⚡ PR ⬚ ⊞ lau
➧ 🛒 ✕

● ● ● ● **NORTH** ● ● ● ●

The northern finger of Germany has the bracing North Sea to the west, with a landscape of dykes, green beaches and pretty offshore islands. The gentle Baltic is to the east, and its coast is one continuous succession of delightful resorts. Excellent natural harbours have been formed by "forden" cut deep into the land between the ridges of wooded hills. Inland, there are tranquil lakes, stately homes and nature reserves.

The north of Germany is a land of mountains and plains, of estuaries and inlets, of forests and heaths. Delightful undulating landscape is scattered with fascinating towns and cities; Hamburg, whose beautiful skyline is characterised by the towers of its principal churches; Bremen, with its many parks and gardens, its fairytale streets and passages, and its cosy atmosphere; Hannover, whose flower-filled Royal Gardens at Herrenhausen have been a major attraction since 1666.

....

▶ **ALTENAU** NIEDERSACHSEN

Okertalsperre Kornhardtweg 1 ☎ 05328 702
On a long stretch of grassland at the S end of the Oker Reservoir. Lunchtime siesta 13.00-15.00 hrs.
➔ *Signposted from B498 (Oker-Altenau road).*
All year 4HEC ▦ ҈ ♠ ♠ ☕ ✕ ⊙ ❤ ∅ ≞ ☎ ♨ ⚡ L ☒ ⊞ ※ lau
Prices: ↟6 pitch 11

▶ **APEN-NORDLOH** NIEDERSACHSEN

Nordloh Schanzenweg 4 ☎ 04499 2625
All year 8HEC ▦ ☀ ♠ ✕ ⊙ ❤ ∅ ↟ L ☒ ⊞ lau ♦ ♨ ♥ ✕

▶ **BASSUM** NIEDERSACHSEN
▶ At **GROSS-RINGMAR**

Gross-Ringmar Dorfstr 15 ☎ 04241 5292
On level meadow with trees. Situated approx. 200m from the edge of the village.
➔ *Turn off B51 approx. 3km SW of Bassum.*
All year 10HEC ▦ ♠ ♠ ♨ ✕ ⊙ ❤ ♨ ↟ LP ☒ ⊞ lau

▶ **BLECKEDE** NIEDERSACHSEN

Alt-Garge (ADAC) Am Waldbad 23 ☎ 05854 311
A modern site surrounded by tall trees, lying at the SE end of Alt-Garge next to a heated swimming pool in the woods. The camp has its own gas-filling station. Archery butts. Lunchtime siesta 13.00-14.30 hrs.
➔ *5km SE of Bleckede.*
All year 6.6HEC ▦ ⁖⁖⁖ ♠ ♠ ⊙ ❤ ≞ ☒ ⊞ lau ♦ ✕ ∅ ↟PR
Prices: pitch 24-27 (incl 2 persons)

▶ **BODENWERDER** NIEDERSACHSEN

Himmelspforte Zigelerweg 1 ☎ 05533 4938
Site on grassland, with a fruit orchard, next to River Weser. Good possibilites for water sport. Separate section and common room for young campers.
➔ *Cross River Weser and turn right towards Rühle. Site is in about 2km.*
All year 8HEC ▦ ♦ ♠ ♨ ♥ ✕ ⊙ ❤ ≞ ↟ R ☒ ⊞ ♦ ↟P
Prices: ↟6 pitch 7

Rühler Schweiz ☎ 05533 2827
This site lies on well-kept meadowland by the River Weser.
➔ *From the Weser Bridge in Bodenwerder and follow road for 4km towards Rühle.*
Mar-Oct 5HEC ▦ ☀ ♠ ♥ ✕ ⊙ ❤ ≞ ↟ PR ☒ ⊞ lau
Prices: ↟6 ♠6 pitch 7

▶ **BOTHEL** NIEDERSACHSEN

Hanseat ☎ 04266 355
All year 20HEC ▦ ♠ ♠ ✕ ⊙ ❤ ∅ ☒ ⊞ lau ♦ ♨ ✕ ↟P
Prices: ↟6 ♠3 ♠9 ♠6

▶ **BRAUNLAGE** NIEDERSACHSEN

Ferien vom Ich ☎ 05520 413
Quiet site, partly on different levels, near woodland inn.
➔ *2km from town centre on B27 towards Lauterberg.*
All year 5.5HEC ▦ ♠ ♠ ♨ ✕ ⊙ ❤ ∅ ≞ ♨ ☒ ⊞ lau ♦ ↟P

▶ At **ZORGE**(14km S)

Waldwinkel ☎ 05586 1048
A site on different levels, surrounded by high trees, 200m from an open-air woodland pool in Kunzen Valley.
All year 1.5HEC ▦ ♦ ♠ ♠ ♨ ⊙ ❤ ∅ ≞ ☎ ♨ ☒ ⊞ lau ♦ ✕ ↟P
Prices: ↟9 ♠4 ♠5 ♠5

▶ **BREMEN** BREMEN

Freie Hansestadt Bremen Am Stadtwaldsee 1 ☎ 0421 212002
Situated in a Nature Reserve 700m from lake.
➔ *Access from autobahn A27 exit University Bremen.*
23 Mar-2 Nov 5.8HEC ▦ ♦ ♠ ♠ ♨ ♥ ✕ ⊙ ❤ ∅ ☒ lau ♦ ↟L

▶ **BRIETLINGEN-REIHERSEE** NIEDERSACHSEN

Reihersee 1 Alte Salzstr 8 ☎ 04133 3671 & 3577
Divided into pitches by hedges and pine trees. Private bathing area.
➔ *At car park, 2km beyond Brietlingen, turn E towards Reihersee and continue for 800m.*
All year 6.2HEC ▦ ♠ ♠ ✕ ⊙ ❤ ≞ ♨ ↟ LR ☒ ⊞ ♦ ♨

▶ **BÜCHEN** SCHLESWIG-HOLSTEIN

Waldschwimmbad ☎ 04155 5360
On gently sloping grassland. Lunchtime siesta 13.00-15.00 hrs.
➔ *From Lauenburg or Mölln follow road to Büchen then follow signposts to site.*
All year 1.6HEC ▦ ♠ ♠ ♨ ♥ ✕ ⊙ ❤ ∅ ≞ ☒ ⊞ lau ♦ ✕ ↟PR
Prices: ↟7.50 ♠10 ♠5

▶ **BURG (ISLAND OF FEHMARN)** SCHLESWIG-HOLSTEIN
▶ At **KLAUSDORF**(5km NW)

Klausdorf ☎ 04371 2549
A grassy site with sea views. Divided into pitches. Sandy beach. Lunchtime siesta 12.30-14.30 hrs.
➔ *From Burg turn off the main road 2.5km before Klausdorf onto a narrow asphalt road.*
15 Apr-15 Oct 12HEC ▦ ♦ ♠ ♠ ✕ ⊙ ❤ ∅ ≞ ♨ ↟ S ☒ ⊞ lau ♦ ↟L

▶ **BURGWEDEL** NIEDERSACHSEN

Erholungsgebiet Springhorstsee ☎ 05139 3232
All year 29HEC ▦ ☀ ♠ ♠ ♥ ✕ ⊙ ❤ ∅ ≞ ♨ ↟ LP ☒ ⊞ lau ♦ ♨ ∅
Prices: ↟7 ♠7-10 pitch 7

▶ **BÜSUM** SCHLESWIG-HOLSTEIN

Nordsee Nordseestr 90 ☎ 04834 2515
Situated immediately behind the high dyke. The site is divided into two and surrounded by tall bushes. Lunchtime siesta 12.30-14.00 hrs.
➔ *Leave A23 at Heide exit and follow signs.*
Mar-Oct 3.5HEC ▦ ♠ ♠ ♨ ♥ ✕ ⊙ ❤ ∅ ≞ ♨ ☒ ⊞ lau ♦ ↟S

CLAUSTHAL-ZELLERFELD NIEDERSACHSEN

Prahljust ☎ 05323 1300
The site lies on slightly sloping grassland in an area of woodland and lakes.
⤷ *Follow road B242 SE from outskirts 2km in direction of Braunlage, then turn right to site in 1.5km.*
All year 13HEC ⸺ ⌂ ♠ ⌱ ⚏ ⫶ ✕ ⊙ ⦿ ∅ ⫩ P 🕿 lau ➧ ≚ ⫩L
Prices: ⋔7.60-9.10 ▲4.10 pitch 7.70-9.30

Waldweben Spiegelthalerstr 31 ☎ 05323 81712
Holiday village with individual pitches in open meadow and coniferous woodland by three small lakes.
⤷ *Signposted from B241 in direction of Goslar.*
All year 4.5HEC ⸺ ⚸ ⌂ ♠ ⌱ ✕ ⊙ ⦿ ⫶ ⌸ 🕿 ⤇ ⫩LP ⊞

DAHRENHORST NIEDERSACHSEN

Irenensee ☎ 05173 98120
A lakeside site on meadowland, partly surrounded by woods, with separate section for tourers, statics and residentials. Lunchtime siesta 13.00-15.00 hrs.
⤷ *From Burgdorf follow road B188 for about 15km towards Uetze.*
All year 21HEC ⸺ ⌂ ♠ ✕ ⊙ ⦿ ∅ ⫶ ⦿ ⫩ L 🕿 ⊞ lau
Prices: ⋔9.10-11.90 ➬4-4.50 pitch 5.10-11.20

DETERN NIEDERSACHSEN

Jümmesee ☎ 04957 1808
⤷ *Access via B72 (Aurich-Cloppenburg).*
15 Mar-Oct 11.5HEC ⸺ ⌂ ♠ ✕ ⊙ ⦿ ⫩ LR 🕿 ⊞ ⟊ lau
➧ ⫩S
Prices: ⋔7.50 pitch 9

DORUM SCHLESWIG-HOLSTEIN

AZUR-Camping Dorumer Tief ☎ 04741 5020
Next to a small harbour. Separated from the beach by a dyke.
⤷ *Access via A27 (Bremerhaven-Cuxhaven).*
Apr-Sep 7HEC ⸺ ⌖ ♠ ⌱ ⚏ ✕ ⊙ ⦿ ⫶ ⫩ PS 🕿 ⊞ lau
Prices: ⋔4.50-7 ➬3-4 ▣8-9 ▲3-4

DRANSFELD NIEDERSACHSEN

Hohen Hagen ☎ 05502 2147
Well laid out municipal site. Lunchtime siesta 13.00-15.00 hrs.
⤷ *S of town off Hohen Hagen road.*
All year 10HEC ⸺ ⌖ ♠ ⌱ ⚏ ⫶ ✕ ⊙ ⦿ ∅ ⦿ 🕿 ⊞ lau ➧ ⫩P

EGESTORF NIEDERSACHSEN

AZUR-Camping Lüneburger Heide ☎ 04175 661
Modern site on wooded heathland on the edge of the Lüneburger Heath Nature Reserve 2km S of town on slightly sloping terrain with asphalt internal roads.
⤷ *Access via Hamburg-Hannover motorway A7/E4 Egestorf or Evendorf exits.*
All year 22HEC ⸺ ⋮⋮⋮ ⌂ ♠ ✕ ⊙ ⦿ ∅ ⦿ ⫩ P 🕿 ⊞ lau
➧ ⚏

EIMKE NIEDERSACHSEN

Eimke Im Extertal ☎ 05262 3307
Extensive, partly terraced site on slightly sloping meadowland with two ponds.
Camping Card Compulsory.
⤷ *From Dortmund-Hannover motorway (A2/E8) take 'Bad Eilsen' exit and follow B238 S. 1km beyond Rinteln, turn left and continue for 18km along External-Barntrup road.*
All year 20HEC ⸺ ⌂ ♠ ⌱ ⚏ ✕ ⊙ ⦿ ∅ ⫩ L 🕿 ⊞ lau
Prices: ⋔7 ⦿10 ▲8

ELISABETH SOPHIENKOOG (ISLAND OF NORDSTRAND)
SCHLESWIG-HOLSTEIN

Elisabeth-Sophienkoog ☎ 04842 8534
On meadowland behind the North Sea dyke. Lunchtime siesta 12.00-14.00 hrs.
⤷ *Access via Husum to Island of Nordstrand.*
Apr-Oct 1.7HEC ⸺ ⌖ ♠ ⌱ ⚏ ⫶ ✕ ⊙ ⦿ ∅ ⫩ S 🕿 ⊞ lau

ENGEHAUSEN NIEDERSACHSEN

AZUR-Camping Allertal Marschweg 1 ☎ 05071 912292
Useful as a first stop site, lying only 500m from Autobahn A7/E4. Situated on the Aller and surrounded by pine trees.
⤷ *For access, leave autobahn A7 at service area Allertal and follow road towards Celle.*
15 Mar-15 Nov 8HEC ⸺ ⌂ ♠ ⌱ ⚏ ✕ ⊙ ⦿ ⫶ ⫩ R 🕿 lau
Prices: ⋔7-9 ➬3-4 ▣8-12 ▲3-4

ESENS-BENSERSIEL NIEDERSACHSEN

Benersiel Kirchpl ☎ 04971 4906
Well-managed, extensive leisure centre with harbour, good fish restaurant and reading room. Swimming pools have sea water and artificial waves.
⤷ *Take B210 NE from Aurich to Ogenbargenn then via Esens.*
May-15 Sep 9HEC ⸺ ⋮⋮⋮ ⌖ ♠ ⌱ ⚏ ⫶ ✕ ⊙ ⦿ ⫶ ⦿ ⫩ S 🕿
⊞ ⟊ lau ➧ ∅ ⫶ ⫩P

EUTIN-FISSAU SCHLESWIG-HOLSTEIN

Prinzenholz Prinzenholzweg 20 ☎ 04521 5281
Terraced lakeside site divided by trees and bushes. Mobile shop.
⤷ *N of town take Malente road and turn right after 2km.*
Etr-Oct 2HEC ⸺ ⌂ ♠ ⌱ ⚏ ⊙ ⦿ ⫶ ⫩ L 🕿 lau ➧ ⚏ ✕ ⫩P
⊞

FALSHÖFT SCHLESWIG-HOLSTEIN

Seehof ☎ 04643 693
A partly sheltered site beside the Baltic Sea, near a lighthouse.
⤷ *Leave B199 at Gelting and travel N for 5km.*
Apr-Oct 2HEC ⸺ ⌖ ♠ ⌱ ⊙ ⦿ ⫶ 🕿 ⊞ lau ➧ ✕ ⫩S

FEHMARN (ISLAND OF)

See BURG, DÄNSCHENDORF, FEHMARNSUND,
MEESCHENDORF, WULFEN

FEHMARNSUND (ISLAND OF FEHMARN)
SCHLESWIG-HOLSTEIN

Miramar ☎ 04371 3220 & 2221
A family site on meadowland situated at the southern end of the island.
⤷ *Turn off the B207/E4 at the first turning after the Sundbrücke (bridge) and drive towards Svendorf.*
All year 12HEC ⸺ ⌂ ♠ ⌱ ⚏ ✕ ⊙ ⦿ ⫶ ⦿ ⫩ L 🕿 ⊞ lau ➧
∅ ⫩P
Prices: ⋔6-9.50 pitch 12-18

GANDERSHEIM, BAD NIEDERSACHSEN

DCC Kur-Campingpark Braunschweiger Str 12
☎ 05382 1595
On level meadow, divided in two by a brook beside a public park. Good sporting facilities. Separate section for young people.
⤷ *Access from Hannover-Kassel motorway via exit Soesen.*
All year 9HEC ⸺ ⌂ ♠ ⌱ ✕ ⊙ ⦿ ⫶ 🕿 ⊞ lau ➧ ∅ ⫩LPRS
Prices: ⋔7.50 pitch 16.50

GARTOW NIEDERSACHSEN

Gartow am See Springstr 14 ☎ 05846 2151
Situated in woodland with adjoining meadow.
Camping Card Compulsory

⮑ *NE on A493 from Lüchow.*
All year 14HEC ⚏ ⊞ ♠ ⟨ ✕ ☺ ⟩ ⟨ P ⛺ lau ⟩ ⟨ ⟨LR ⊞
Prices: ⚑7 ⟨5 ⟨9 ⚑6

GIFHORN NIEDERSACHSEN
At RÖTGESBÜTTEL(8km S)

Glockenheide ☎ 05304 1581
Tranquil site in heathland. Lunchtime siesta 13.00-15.00 hrs.
Camping Card Compulsory.
⮑ *In Rötgesbüttel turn left, then turn left again after level crossing.*
All year 5HEC ⚏ ⊞ ♠ ⟨ ✕ ☺ ⟩ ⟨ ⛺ ⊞ ⟩ ⟨
Prices: ⚑6 ⟨4 ⟨4 ⚑4

GLÜCKSBURG SCHLESWIG-HOLSTEIN

AZUR-Camping Glücksburg Am Kurstrand Holnis
☎ 04631 622071
Apr-Oct 6HEC ⚏ ⟨ ⟨ ⟨ ✕ ☺ ⟩ ⟨ ⛺ ⟩ lau ⟩ ⟨
Prices: ⚑7-9 ⟨3-4 ⟨10-12 ⚑3-4

Schwennau Stoebe ☎ 04631 2670
A watercourse divides the site into two sections which are linked by a bridge.
⮑ *In town centre make for Postplatz, then Hindenburgplatz, Collenburger Strasse. Schwennau-Strasse direct onto the site which lies adjacent to the Flensburger Förde.*
All year 1.5HEC ⚏ ⟨ ⟨ ✕ ☺ ⟩ ⟨ ⟨ RS ⛺ ⊞ lau ⟩ ⟨ ⟨
⟨PS

GOSLAR NIEDERSACHSEN

Sennhütte Clausthastr 28 ☎ 05321 22498
In woodland adjacent to the Hotel Sennhütte.
⮑ *3km S on B241 Clausthal-Zellerfeld road.*
All year 3HEC ⚏ ⟨ ♠ ⟨ ⟨ ✕ ☺ ⟩ ⟨ ⟨ ⛺ ⊞ lau ⟩ ⟨LP

At HAHNENKLEE(13km S on road B241 at turn-off to Hahnenklee)

Kreuzeck Goslar 2 ☎ 05325 2570
In the forest beside a lake. Terraces and a separate section for dog-owners.
⮑ *Beside Café am Kreuzeck at the junction of the B241 and the Hahnenklee road.*
All year 5HEC ⚏ ⚏ ⟨⟨ ⟨ ♠ ⟨ ⟨ ✕ ☺ ⟩ ⟨ ⟨ ⛺ ⟨ LP ⛺
⊞ lau

At WOLFSHAGEN(11km W on unclass road off B82)

SC Krähenberg Langelsheim ☎ 05326 4088
Situated in a quiet valley.
⮑ *S off the B82 between Langelsheim and Astfeld.*
All year 6.5HEC ⚏ ⟨ ♠ ⟨ ⟨ ☺ ⟩ ⟨ P ⛺ ⊞

GRUBE SCHLESWIG-HOLSTEIN

Rosenfelder Strand Textil Segeberger Str 17 ☎ 04365 412
Excellently managed family site beside the sea with a 1km long beach. Divided into separate fields by rows of bushes. Children's playground in woodland between site and sea. Strict observance of lunchtime siesta 13.00-15.00 hrs.
⮑ *Take the B207/E4 from Lübeck and drive N to Lensahn, then E to Grube.*
15 Apr-15 Oct 20HEC ⚏ ⟨ ♠ ⟨ ✕ ☺ ⟩ ⟨ ⛺ ⟨ S ⛺ ⊞ ⊞
Prices: ⚑6.50 pitch 16.50

HADDEBY SCHLESWIG-HOLSTEIN

Haithabu ☎ 04621 32450
Clean, tidy site beside River Schlei.
⮑ *From Schleswig follow B76 towards Eckernförde.*
Apr-Sep 5HEC ⚏ ⟨ ♠ ⟨ ✕ ☺ ⟩ ⟨ ⟨ R ⛺ ⊞
Prices: ⚑6 ⟨4 ⟨15 ⚑11

HADEMSTORF NIEDERSACHSEN

Waldhaus Allertal ☎ 05071 1872
Apr-Sep 2.5HEC ⚏ ⟨ ♠ ⟨ ⟨ ⟨ ✕ ☺ ⟩ ⟨ ⟨ ⟨ ⛺ lau ⟩ ⟨
⟨LPR ⊞
Prices: ⚑4 ⟨3.50 ⟨5.50 ⚑4.50

HAMBURG HAMBURG

Anders Kieler Str 650 ☎ 040 5704498
Useful transit site on a level meadow.
All year 2HEC ⚏ ⟨ ♠ ⟨ ⟨ ☺ ⟩ ⟨ ⟨ ⛺ ⛺ lau ⟩ ⟨ ✕ ⟨P

HAMELN NIEDERSACHSEN

Waldbad Pfedeweg 2 ☎ 05158 2774
A grassy terraced site on the edge of woodland beside a public swimming pool.
Camping Card Compulsory.
⮑ *Follow 'swimming pool' signs from Havelstorf.*
Apr-Oct 2.8HEC ⚏ ⟨ ♠ ⟨ ✕ ☺ ⟩ ⟨ ⟨ ⛺ ⛺ ⊞ lau ⟩ ⟨ ⟨P

HANNOVER NIEDERSACHSEN
At GARBSEN(10km W)

Blauer See ☎ 05137 8996-0
On a small lake beside the Garbsen service area on Hannover-Bielefeld motorway A2/E8.
All year 22HEC ⚏ ⟨ ♠ ⟨ ⟨ ☺ ⟩ ⟨ ⟨ ⟨ L ⛺ ⊞ lau ⟩ ⟨ ⟨
⟨P
Prices: ⚑9.50-9.90 ⟨3-3 ⟨5.90-9.90 ⚑3.90-6.90

At ISERNHAGEN(16km NE)

Parksee Lohne ☎ 05139 88260
Recreation area by a lake. On the flight approach path for Hannover Langenhagen airport. Separate section for tourers.
⮑ *From motorway exit 'Kirchorst' follow Altwarmbüchen road to Isernhagen.*
All year 16HEC ⚏ ⟨ ♠ ⟨ ⟨ ✕ ☺ ⟩ ⟨ ⟨ L ⛺ lau ⟩ ⟨ ⊞
Prices: ⚑7 pitch 13

HARDEGSEN NIEDERSACHSEN

Ferienpark Solling ☎ 05505 5585
Terraced site in forested area. Separate field for touring pitches. Lunchtime siesta 13.00-15.00 hrs.
⮑ *In town take 'Waldgebiet Gladeberg' road.*
All year 3HEC ⚏ ⟨ ♠ ⟨ ⟨ ☺ ⟩ ⟨ ⛺ ⊞ lau ⟩ ⟨ ✕ ⟨P
Prices: ⚑6 ⟨8 ⟨8 ⚑3-3

HARZBURG, BAD NIEDERSACHSEN

Wolfstein ☎ 05322 3585
Long, terraced site on edge of woodland.
⮑ *500m from town on B6 towards Eckertal.*
All year 20HEC ⟨ ⟨ ⟨ ✕ ☺ ⟩ ⟨ ⛺ ⊞ lau

At ORSTEIL GOTTINGERODE

Freizeit Oase Harz Camp Kreisstr 66 ☎ 05322 81215
On outskirts of village next to main road. Terraced site with separate touring field. Lunchtime siesta 13.00-15.00 hrs.
⮑ *On the B6 between Bad Harzburg and Goslar.*
All year 8HEC ⚏ ⟨ ♠ ⟨ ⟨ ✕ ☺ ⟩ ⟨ ⟨ ⛺ ⟨ P ⛺ ⊞ lau
Prices: ⚑7 pitch 9

HASELÜNNE NIEDERSACHSEN

Haseufer Andruper Str 1 ☎ 05961 1331
Beside the River Hase in an attractive area E of the town.
Camping Card Compulsory.
⮑ *Signposted from Andrup.*
Closed Nov-15 Dec 10HEC ⚏ ⟨ ♠ ⟨ ⟨ ✕ ☺ ⟩ ⟨ ⟨ ⛺ ⟨ L
⛺ ⊞ lau ⟩ ⟨PRS

HATTEN NIEDERSACHSEN

Freizeitzentrum Hatten Kreyenweg 8 ☎ 04482 677
All year 2HEC ▦ ⛟ ⛱ ⚓ ✕ ⊙ ◘ ⌀ ⌇ P ⌸ ⚑ lau

HATTORF NIEDERSACHSEN

Oderbrücke ☎ 05521 4359
In a pleasant wooded location with good recreational and
sanitary facilities.
➲ On the B27 towards Herzberg.
All year 2.5HEC ▦ ⚓ ⛱ ⚓ ⚐ ✕ ⊙ ◘ ⌀ ⌶ ⚑ ⌇ R ⌸ lau ✦
⌇LP ⊞
Prices: ⚑6 ⚗2 ⚘8 ⚠8

HEIKENDORF SCHLESWIG-HOLSTEIN

Möltenort ☎ 0431 241316
Terraced site by the Kieler Förde. 15km NE of Kiel to W of
road B502.
➲ Approach to site is via a narrow, winding road.
Apr-Oct 2HEC ▦ ⛟ ⛱ ⊙ ◘ ⌇ S ⌸ ⊞ lau ✦ ⚐ ✕ ⌀
Prices: ⚑7 ⚠10 pitch 10-13

HELMSTEDT NIEDERSACHSEN

Waldwinkel Maschweg 46 ☎ 05351 37161
In an orchard next to the Gasthaus Waldwinkel.
➲ Signposted from autobahn exit 'Helmstedt'.
All year 10HEC ▦ ⚓ ⛱ ⚓ ✕ ⊙ ◘ ⌀ ⌸ ⊞ lau ✦ ⛱ ⌇P
Prices: ⚑5.50 ⚗4.50 ⚘4.50 ⚠4.50

HEMELN NIEDERSACHSEN

Hemeln ☎ 05544 1414
Well-kept site on N outskirts of village, beside the River
Weser.
➲ From Autobahn A7 take the Gothenburg exit & follow B3 to
Dransfeld then follow signposts.
All year 20HEC ▦ ⚓ ⚐ ⛱ ⚓ ✕ ⊙ ◘ ⌀ ⌶ ⚏ ⚑ ⌇ R ⌸ ⊞
lau ✦ ⌇P
Prices: ⚑6 ⚗3.50 ⚘5.50 ⚠4

At REINHARDSHAGEN-VAAKE(2km W)

Ahletal ☎ 05544 408
Well kept municipal site about 500m from River Weser,
adjacent to a leisure centre with an indoor swimming pool.
Lunchtime siesta 13.00-15.00 hrs.
➲ From autobahn Kassel-Hannover leave at 'Hann-Münden'
exit. Then follow B80 N along W bank of Weser to
Reinhardshagen-Vaake then turn left.
All year 3.7HEC ▦ ⚓ ⛱ ⚓ ✕ ⊙ ◘ ⌀ ⌶ ⌇ P ⌸ ⊞ lau ✦ ✕

★ ★ ★ ★ ★
Ostseecampingplatz
Familie Heide
Strandweg 31, 24369 Kleinwaabs,
Tel. 04352/2530 und Fax 1398

Holiday in nature

Hollidys for the whold family

Located right at the coast - without health resort way ~
1,5 km coast with own bathing and nudist beach ~
heted indoor swimming pool (8x20 m), sauna und solarium ~
tennis, miniaturegolf, streethockey, beachvolleyball, basketball
and organized animation programm ~ BBQ with dance events,
and much more - ask for a brochure.

- 1992 - 1998 predicate of the ADAC:
One of the 12 best
campgrounds in Germany
- 1996 country winner of the competition:
" exenpary campgrounds in landscape "

See you soon
Familie Paul Heide

HERMANNSBURG NIEDERSACHSEN

Örtzetal ☎ 05052 3072 & 1555
Site lies on meadows on the E bank of the River Örtze, set in
unspoilt woodlands of the Lüneburg Heath. Boat landing
stage. Lunchtime siesta 13.00-15.00 hrs.
➲ From the B3 Celle-Soltau road turn off in Bergen and
follow road NE towards Hermannsburg, then continue towards
Eschwege.
15 Mar-Oct 4HEC ▦ ⫶⫶⫶ ⚓ ⛱ ⚐ ✕ ⊙ ◘ ⚏ ⚑ ⌇ R ⌸ ⊞
lau ✦ ⛱ ⚐ ⌇P

HOLLE NIEDERSACHSEN

At DERNEBURG(2km NW on unclass road)

Seecamp-Derneburg ☎ 05062 565
A terraced lakeside site on a hill slope with a southerly
aspect. Separate towing field. Useful transit site near
autobahn.
➲ From the motorway, leave at exit 'Derneburg' and continue
to road B6.
Apr-15 Sep 78HEC ▦ ⚓ ⛱ ⚓ ✕ ⊙ ◘ ⌀ ⚏ ⚑ ⌇ L ⌸ ⊞ lau
✦ ⌇R
Prices: ⚑7-6.50 ⚗3-3.50 ⚘7.50 ⚠6.50-7.50

KLEINWAABS SCHLESWIG-HOLSTEIN

Ostsee Heide ☎ 04352 2530
Divided into pitches and pleasantly landscaped. Large games
room for teenagers. Lunchtime siesta 13.00-14.30 hrs.
Mar-Oct 20HEC ▦ ⚓ ⛱ ⚓ ✕ ⊙ ◘ ⌀ ⌶ ⚏ ⚑ ⌇ PS ⌸ lau ✦ ⚠
Prices: ⚑4-7 pitch 16-28

KLINT-BEI-HECHTHAUSEN NIEDERSACHSEN

Geesthof Geesthofer Weg 37 ☎ 04774 512
On dry meadowland next to the River Oste, in quiet setting
with trees. Lunchtime siesta 13.00-15.00 hrs.
➲ In Hechthausen leave road B73 and drive W towards
'Lamstedt' for about 3 km.
All year 10HEC ▦ ⚐ ⛱ ⊙ ◘ ⌀ ⌶ ⚏ ⚑ ⌇ PR ⌸ ⊞ lau

LANGHOLZ ÜBER ECKERNFÖRDE
SCHLESWIG-HOLSTEIN

Langholz Fischerstr 9 ☎ 04352 2542
A holiday site surrounded by a belt of trees situated at a wide
natural beach, at the mouth of the Eckernförde Bay.
Camping Card Compulsory.
➲ From the Eckernförde take the B203 towards the NE to the
turn off for Langholz, then right and continue 3km to site.
Apr-Sep 20HEC ▦ ⚓ ⛱ ⚓ ✕ ⊙ ◘ ⚏ ⚑ ⌇ S ⌸ ⊞ lau ✦ ⌀
Prices: ⚑5 ⚘15 ⚠5

LAUTERBERG, BAD NIEDERSACHSEN

Wiesenbeker Teich ☎ 05524 2510
In wooded surroundings on the Wiesenbeker Teich.
➲ Approach via B243 SE of Bad Lauterberg.
All year 5.2HEC ▦ ⚒ ⛟ ⛱ ⚓ ✕ ⊙ ◘ ⌶ ⌇ LP ⌸ ⊞ ✦ ⛱ ⌀
Prices: ⚑7.50 ⚗2 ⚘8 ⚠8

LEER NIEDERSACHSEN

At BINGUM MARINA

Marina Bingum Marinastr ☎ 0491 64447
Camping Card Compulsory.
➲ On B75, over Ems bridge, 200m W of river.
All year ▦ ⚓ ⛱ ⚐ ✕ ⊙ ◘ ⌀ ⌸ ⌇ R ⌸ ⊞ lau

LOOSE SCHLESWIG-HOLSTEIN

Gut Ludwigsburg ☎ 04358 1068
This partly wooded holiday site lies between an inland lake
and the sea. 100m long private beach. It is divided into
pitches.

↪ *From Eckernförde, head towards Klein-Wabbs up to Gut Ludwigsburg, then follow a dirt track for 2km.*
Apr-Sep 10HEC ⚒ 🚶 🛁 ⚡ ✗ ⊙ 🚻 ⊘ ≛ 🏕 🚑 ⚡ L 🔲 ⊞ lau
◆ ⚡S

LÜBECK SCHLESWIG-HOLSTEIN
At RATEKAU(10km N)

Waldklause Badenstr ☎ 04504 3833
Divided by trees and shrubs. Noise from E4 (B207) partially absorbed by wood and motel.
↪ *Access from Lübeck-Puttgarden motorway exit Ratekau.*
Apr-Oct 10HEC ⸬ ⚒ 🚶 🛁 ⊙ 🚻 🔲 ⊞ lau ◆ ⚡ ✗

LÜNEBURG NIEDERSACHSEN

Rote Schleuse ☎ 04131 791500
In woodland clearing. Lunchtime siesta 13.00-15.00 hrs.
↪ *S of town off B4. Signposted.*
Mar-Oct 2HEC ⸬ ⚒ 🚶 🛁 ⚡ ✗ ⊙ 🚻 ≛ 🔲 ⊞ lau
◆ ✗ ⚡R

LÜRSCHAU BEI SCHLESWIG SCHLESWIG-HOLSTEIN

Lürschau am See ☎ 04621 41846
↪ *N of Schleswig off B76.*
All year 1.5HEC ⸬ ⚒ 🚶 🛁 ⚡ ✗ ⊙ 🚻 🚑 ⚡ LPS 🔲 ⊞ lau ◆ 🛁

MALENTE-GREMSMÜHLEN SCHLESWIG-HOLSTEIN

Schwentine Wiesenweg 14 ☎ 04523 4327
A park-like setting with trees and bushes, at a river within the village of Malente.
↪ *A17 18km NW of Eutin.*
Apr-18 Oct 2.5HEC ⸬ ⚒ 🚶 🛁 ✗ ⊙ 🚻 ≛ ⚡ R 🔲 ⊞ lau ◆ ⊘
⚡LP
Prices: ⚑7.50 ◆3 🚑10-12 ▲6-10

MELBECK NIEDERSACHSEN

Melbeck ☎ 04134 7311
Extensive site in woodland on the banks of the Ilmenau. Centre of site free of trees and reserved for tourers.
↪ *On B4, 9km Lüneburg.*
All year 20HEC ⸬ ⚒ 🚶 ✗ ⊙ 🚻 ⊘ 🏕 🚑 ⚡ R 🔲 lau
Prices: ⚑6 ◆6 🚑6 ▲6

MEPPEN NIEDERSACHSEN

Bleiche an der Bleiche ☎ 05931 16411
Level, grassy terrain between open air and indoor pool next to the River Ems. Lunchtime siesta 13.00-15.00 hrs.
↪ *From Lingen N on road B70, alongside the Dortmund-Ems canal.*
Apr-Sep 1.2HEC ⸬ ⚒ 🚶 ✗ ⊙ 🚻 ⚡ P 🔲 ⊞ lau ◆ 🛁 ✗

MÜNDEN NIEDERSACHSEN

Zella Im Werratal Zella im Werratal ☎ 05541 31310
Beautiful site on left bank of the River Werra near motel and restaurant of the same name.
↪ *7 km from town towards Laubach.*
Apr-10 Sep 2HEC ⸬ ⚒ ≉ 🚶 🛁 ✗ ⊙ 🚻 ≛ 🔲 ⊞

NEUSTADT SCHLESWIG-HOLSTEIN

Strande Pelzerhakenerstr ☎ 04561 4188
The site into small sections and slopes down to the sea. Narrow sandy beach.
↪ *Access from Neustadt towards Pelzerhaken, first site on the right after leaving Neustadt.*
Apr-Sep 4.5HEC ⸬ ⚒ 🚶 🛁 ⚡ ✗ ⊙ 🚻 ≛ ⚡ S 🔲 ⊞ lau ◆
✗ ⊘

NORDSTRAND (ISLAND OF)

See ELISABETH SOPHIENKOOG

NORTHEIM NIEDERSACHSEN

Sultmer Berg Sultmerberg 3 ☎ 05551 51559
Grassland site with views of surrounding hills. Lunchtime siesta 13.00-15.00 hrs.
↪ *Follow B3 from town centre.*
All year 5HEC ⸬ ⚒ 🚶 🛁 ⚡ ✗ ⊙ 🚻 ⊘ ≛ 🚑 ⚡ P 🔲 ⊞ lau ◆ ⚡
✗ ⚡LR
Prices: ⚑6.30-7 ◆5-8.50 🚑5.50-13.50 ▲4.50-7.50

OEHE-DRAECHT SCHLESWIG-HOLSTEIN

Oehe-Draecht ☎ 04642 6124 & 6029
Grassy site, divided into pitches, on sandy ground behind a sea dyke.
↪ *From Kappeln follow B199, turn towards Hasselberg and follow signs 'Strand'.*
Apr-Sep 6HEC ⸬ ⚒ ⸬⸬⸬ ≉ 🚶 🛁 ⚡ ✗ ⊙ 🚻 ⊘ ≛ 🏕 🚑 ⚡ LS
🔲 lau
Prices: ⚑6 pitch 13

OSNABRÜCK NIEDERSACHSEN

Niedersachsenhof Nordstr 109 ☎ 0541 77226
The site lies on a gently sloping meadow bordering a forest, near a converted farmhouse with an inn.
↪ *On outskirts of 5km from town centre NW on B51/65 towards Bremen, turn right and continue 300m.*
All year 3HEC ⸬ ⚒ 🚶 ✗ ⊙ 🚻 ≛ 🔲 ⊞ lau ◆ 🛁 ⚡ ✗ ⚡LPRS
⊞
Prices: ⚑6 pitch 11

OSTERODE NIEDERSACHSEN

Sösestausee ☎ 05522 3319
Terraced site on edge of woodland and by reservoir.
↪ *Follow road B498 from Osterode towards Altenau and after 3km turn right to the site.*
All year 4HEC ⸬ ⚒ 🚶 🛁 ⚡ ⊙ 🚻 ⊘ ≛ ⚡ LR 🔲 ⊞ lau ◆ ⚡ ✗
Prices: ⚑6 ◆2 🚑7 ▲7

OTTERNDORF NIEDERSACHSEN

See Achtern Diek Deichstr 14 ☎ 04751 2933
A family site with good facilities close to the North Sea coast.
↪ *Access via B73 Cuxhaven-Hamburg.*
Apr-Oct 1.4HEC ⸬ ⚒ 🚶 ✗ ⊙ 🚻 ⚡ L 🔲 lau ◆ 🛁 ⚡ ✗ ⊘ ≛
⚡LPRS ⊞
Prices: ⚑6 ◆3 🚑9 ▲4

PEINE NIEDERSACHSEN
At HÄMELERWALD(8km NW)

Waldsee ☎ 05175 05175
Near a woodland lake and a railway line. Lunchtime siesta 13.00-15.00 hrs.
↪ *From motorway A2/E8 (Hannover-Braunschweig) leave at exit 'Hämelerwald' and follow road S.*
All year 5HEC ⸬ ⚒ ≉ 🚶 🛁 ⚡ ✗ ⊙ 🚻 ⊘ 🚑 ⚡ L 🔲 🅿 ⊞ lau ◆ 🛁

PLÖN SCHLESWIG-HOLSTEIN

Spitzenort Ascheberger Str 76 ☎ 04522 2769
A pleasantly situated site with hedges on the shore of Lake Plön. Surrounded by the lake on three sides, it is ideal for water sports.
↪ *Access from Plön on B430 towards Neumünster.*
Apr-15 Oct 4.5HEC ⸬ ⚒ 🚶 🛁 ✗ ⊙ 🚻 ⊘ ≛ ⚡ L 🔲 ⊞ lau ◆ ✗
⚡P

PYRMONT, BAD NIEDERSACHSEN

Bad Pyrmont Im Schellental 1-3 ☎ 05281 8772
Site partially flat grassland, partially terraced with large building in the middle. Some tall trees, many bushes and flowers.

↪ *E from town centre to Dak-Kurcenter, then turn left towards Friedensthal.*
All year 5HEC ▦ ⚒ ⋔ ⛴ ⚡ ✕ ☉ ❊ ∅ ⛺ 🏪 🅿 🚻 lau ➡ ⤳P

▶ At LÜDGE-ELBRINXEN(3km S)

Eichwald Obere Dorfstr 80 ☎ 05283 335
Pleasantly situated grassy site near woodland and pool.
↪ *S of Lüdge in direction of Rischenau to Elbrinxen.*
All year 100HEC ▦ ⚒ ⋔ ⛴ ⚡ ✕ ☉ ❊ ∅ ⛺ ⤳ LRS 🏪 🅿 lau ➡ ⤳P

▶ RINTELN NIEDERSACHSEN

Doktor-See Hartler Str 6/7 ☎ 05751 2611
In a beautiful situation by a recreation area and beside the Doktor See bathing beach. Section for touring campers. Lunchtime siesta 13.00-15.00 hrs.
↪ *In town turn down stream at the River Weser bridge and continue along the left bank for 1.5km.*
All year 152HEC ▦ ⚒ ⋔ ⛴ ⚡ ✕ ☉ ❊ ∅ ⛺ 🏪 ⤳ L 🏪 🅿 lau

▶ ST ANDREASBERG NIEDERSACHSEN

Erikabrücke ☎ 05582 1431
↪ *Open site next to B27 NE of Oderstausee. Off B27 from Bad Lauterberg towards Braunlage.*
All year 5.5HEC ▦ ⚒ ⋔ ⛴ ⚡ ✕ ☉ ❊ ∅ ⛺ 🏪 ⤳ LR 🏪 🅿 lau
Prices: ♦5.80-8 ⛟2.10-3 ⛺5-7 ▲5-7

▶ SCHOBÜLL SCHLESWIG-HOLSTEIN

Seeblick ☎ 04841 3321
Beautifully situated beside the sea and divided into two sections.
↪ *Turn off the B5 on the northern outskirts of Husum, and drive towards Insel Nordstrand for 4km up to Schobüll.*
Apr-15 Oct 3.4HEC ▦ ⚒ ⋔ ✕ ☉ ❊ ∅ ⛺ 🏪 🅿 lau ➡ ⛴ ✕ ⤳P

▶ SCHÖNBERG SCHLESWIG-HOLSTEIN
▶ At KALIFORNIEN(5km N)

California Deichweg 46-47 ☎ 04344 9591
Family site behind the dyke, divided by numerous hedges.
↪ *Access through Schönberg, follow road to Kalifornien, then left at the dyke. Turn left and continue by rough track for 800m to site.*
Apr-Sep 8HEC ▦ ⚒ ⋔ ⛴ ⚡ ✕ ☉ ❊ ⛺ 🏪 ⤳ S 🏪 🅿 ⚙

▶ SOLTAU NIEDERSACHSEN

Scandinavia-Paradies ☎ 05191 2293
Heathland site in pine forest. Useful transit site 1km from motorway (from which there is some noise). Separate section for young campers. Lunchtime siesta 13.00-15.00 hrs.
↪ *Access from the Soltau Ost (East) motorway exit then 1km on the B209/71 towards Lüneberg.*
All year 25.5HEC ▦ ⋈ ⚒ ⋔ ⛴ ⚡ ✕ ☉ ❊ ∅ ⛺ ⤳ LP 🏪 🅿 lau

▶ STELLE NIEDERSACHSEN

Steller See Zum Steller See 15 ☎ 04206 6490
↪ *Delmenhorst-Ost eixt off motorway. Site 300m.*
Apr-Sep 16HEC ▦ ⚒ ⋔ ⛴ ⚡ ✕ ☉ ❊ ∅ ⛺ ⤳ L 🏪 🅿 lau
Prices: ♦7 ⛟2 ⛺7 ▲7

▶ SUDERBURG NIEDERSACHSEN
▶ At HÖSSERINGEN(5km SW)

Hardausee ☎ 05826 7676
Grassland site without firm internal roads. Statics have individual pitches and outbuildings. Separate fields for tourers.

↪ *Approach from Uelzen S on B4. In 9km turn right, continue via Suderburg to site on the right just before Hösseringen.*
All year 10HEC ▦ ⋈ ⋔ ⛴ ⚡ ✕ ☉ ❊ ∅ ⛺ 🏪 lau ➡ ⤳L

▶ SÜSSAU SCHLESWIG-HOLSTEIN

Minigolf ☎ 04365 284
The site lies on bushy meadowland behind a dyke next to the Süssauer beach.
↪ *Access from Neustadt N to Lensahn, then E to Goube, and then to Süssau. From there, follow the signposts to the site, 1km away.*
Apr-Sep 3HEC ▦ ⋈ ⋔ ☉ ❊ ⛺ 🏪 ⤳ S 🏪 🅿 lau ➡ ⛴ ✕ ∅

▶ TARMSTEDT NIEDERSACHSEN

Rethbergsee ☎ 04283 422
Level site on a grand scale. Lunchtime siesta 13.00-15.00 hrs.
↪ *About halfway between Bremen-Lilienthal and Zeven.*
All year 15HEC ▦ ⚒ ⋔ ⛴ ⚡ ✕ ☉ ❊ ∅ ⛺ 🏪 ⤳ L 🏪 🅿 lau
Prices: ♦8 ⛟8 ▲5

▶ TELLINGSTEDT SCHLESWIG-HOLSTEIN

Tellingstedt Teichstr ☎ 04838 657
Divided by a row of high shrubs.
↪ *Off B203 towards the swimming pool.*
May-15 Sep 3HEC ▦ ⚒ ⋔ ✕ ☉ ❊ ∅ ⛺ ⤳ P 🏪 🅿 lau ➡ ⛴ ✕

▶ TINNUM (ISLAND OF SYLT) SCHLESWIG-HOLSTEIN

Südhörn ☎ 04651 3607
Well-kept site divided into pitches.
↪ *Well signposted from railway unloading ramp. No road connections between the island and the mainland-rail from Niebüll to Westerland.*
All year 2HEC ▦ ⋈ ⋔ ⛴ ✕ ☉ ❊ ∅ ⛪ ⛺ 🏪 🅿 ➡ ⤳PS 🅿
Prices: ♦4-8 ⛟2.40-3 ⛺12-20 ▲8-20

▶ TÖNNING SCHLESWIG-HOLSTEIN

Lilienhof Katinger Landstr 5 ☎ 04861 439
Well-maintained site in the woodland grounds of an old manor house next to a quiet country road.
↪ *Leave B202 at far end of Tönning, then 2km W towards Welt.*
16 Mar-31 Dec 2HEC ▦ ⚒ ⋔ ☉ ❊ ⛪ ⛺ 🏪 🅿 lau

▶ USLAR NIEDERSACHSEN
▶ At DELLIEHAUSEN SOLLING(8km NE)

Bergsee Bergseestr 1 ☎ 05573 1217
Well-kept site on meadow beside lake, in Solling nature reserve. Separate section for young campers. Lunchtime siesta 13.00-15.00 hrs. Mobile shop.
↪ *Access from motorway exit Nörten-Hardenberg, take the B446 and then the B421 via Hardegsen to Volpriehausen, then right to Delliehausen (2.5km).*
All year 1HEC ▦ ⚒ ⋔ ☉ ❊ ⛺ ⛪ ⤳ L 🏪 lau ➡ ⛴ ✕ ∅ ⤳P
Prices: ♦7 ▲12 pitch 15

▶ WALKENREID NIEDERSACHSEN

KNAUS Walkenreid Ellricher Str 7 ☎ 05525 778
In an attractive location in the southern Harz area.
↪ *Access via A7 exit 'Seesen' and B243 via Herzberg and Bad Sachsa.*
Closed Nov 5.4HEC ▦ ⚡ ⋔ ✕ ☉ ❊ ∅ ⛺ ▲ ⤳ P 🏪 lau
Prices: ♦8.50 pitch 7.50-12

▶ WEENER NIEDERSACHSEN

Weener Am Erholungsgebiet 4 ☎ 04951 1740
A municpal site, pleasantly landscaped and set inside a leisure centre with swimming pool and harbour. Lunchtime siesta 13.00-15.00 hrs.

⮑ *From the main road B75 (E35) from Leer towards the Dutch frontier and turn off in the centre of Weener and follow signs to site.*
26 Mar-31 Oct 3.2HEC ⅏ ⊖ ⊙ ☺ ⚲ ⚡ ⚜ P ⊞ lau ⬥ ☺ ✕ ⊘
Prices: ⚐6-7 ☗6-8 ⚑4-6

WIETZENDORF NIEDERSACHSEN

Südsee Soltau-Süd ☎ 05196 98016
This site is beautifully situated in a forest beside lake.
⮑ *Leave the Hannover-Hamburg motorway at the Soltau-Süd exit, and take the B3 for 2km towards Bergen. At the underpass in Bokel, turn left and drive on for approx 4km towards Wietzendorf.*
All year 70HEC ⅏ ⊖ ⊙ ☺ ⚲ ☰ ✕ ⊙ ⊘ ⚡ ⚜ ⌂ ☗ ⚲ LP ⊞ lau ⬥ ⊞
Prices: pitch 35-54 (incl 2 persons)

WILSUM NIEDERSACHSEN

AZUR-Ferienpark Wilsumer Berge ☎ 05945 1029
Parts of the site adjoin a large lake. The separate section for touring campers has its own sanitary building.
⮑ *From Nordhorn follow road B403 via Uelsen to Wilsum. On nearside of Wilsum turn right.*
All year 88HEC ⅏ ⁝⁝⁝ ⊖ ⊖ ⊙ ☺ ⚲ ☰ ✕ ⊙ ⊘ ⚡ ⚜ ⚲ L ⊞ lau
Prices: ⚐6-9 ☗3-4 ☗8-12 ⚑3-4

WINGST NIEDERSACHSEN

KNAUS Wingst Schwimmbadallee 13 ☎ 04778 7044
This modern comfortable site extends over several terraces, above a small artificial lake on the northern edge of an extensive forested area. Lunchtime siesta 13.00-15.00 hrs. Municipal recreation centre across the road.
⮑ *Turn off the B73 between Stade and Cuxhaven, about 3km S of Cadenberge.*
Closed Nov 8.7HEC ⅏ ⊖ ⊖ ⊙ ✕ ⊙ ⊘ ⚡ ⚜ ⚲ L ⊞ ⊞ lau ⬥ ☺ ⚲P
Prices: ⚐8.50 pitch 7.50-12

WINSEN-ALLER NIEDERSACHSEN

AZUR Camping Winsen ☎ 05143 93199
Site lies on meadowland at the River Aller. Watersports available. Lunchtime siesta 13.00-15.00 hrs.
⮑ *From Celle go NW to Winsen.*
All year 12HEC ⅏ ⊖ ⊖ ⊖ ✕ ⊙ ⊙ ⊘ ⚲ R ⊞ ⊞ lau ⬥ ⚲P
Prices: ⚐6-9 pitch 8-12

WITTENBORN SCHLESWIG-HOLSTEIN

Weisser Brunnen ☎ 04554 1757 & 1413
A lakeside site consisting of several sections, hilly in parts, next to Lake Mözen. A public road, leading to the lake, passes through part of the site.
⮑ *Turn off B206 at Km23.6 towards lake.*
Apr-Oct 6.5HEC ⅏ ⊖ ⊖ ⚲ ☰ ✕ ⊙ ⊙ ⊘ ⚲ ⌂ ⚡ ⚜ L ⊞ ⊞ lau
Prices: ⚐7 ☗12 ☗12 ⚑6-10

WOLTERDINGEN NIEDERSACHSEN

Auf dem Simpel ☎ 05191 3651
The site lies in the Lüneberg Heath area in a very quiet setting of the main road. Densely wooded terrain. Separate section for touring campers. Lunchtime siesta 13.00-15.00 hrs.
⮑ *From Soltau head N on the B3 for about 4km towards 'Hamburg'. At the junction for Wolterdingen turn right and continue towards 'Harber'. Approach road is signposted.*
All year 4HEC ⁝⁝⁝ ⊖ ⚲ ☰ ✕ ⊙ ⊙ ⊘ ⚲ P ⊞ ⊞ lau ⬥ ✕

WULFEN (ISLAND OF FEHMARN)
SCHLESWIG-HOLSTEIN

Wulfener Hals ☎ 04371 8628-0
Meadowland site beside the Baltic Sea and an inland lake (Burger Binnensee). 1700m long private beach.
⮑ *Turn off B20/E4 (Vogelfluglinie) after the 'Sundbrücke' and follow roads towards 'Avendorf', then 'Wulfen' and 'Wulfener Hals'.*
All year 34HEC ⅏ ⊖ ⊖ ⚲ ☰ ✕ ⊙ ⊙ ⊘ ⚲ ⌂ ⚡ ⚜ PS ⊞ ⊞ lau

ZEVEN NIEDERSACHSEN

Sonnenkamp Zeven ☎ 04281 2876
The site lies mainly on open terrain, on the outskirts of town, opposite the swimming pool. For touring campers there is an open meadow near the entrance. Lunchtime siesta 13.00-15.00 hrs.
⮑ *From Zeven town centre follow road for 'Friebad' (swimming pool).*
May-Sep 8HEC ⅏ ⊖ ⚲ ☰ ✕ ⊙ ⊙ ⚲ ⊞ ⊞ lau ⬥ ⚲P

ITALY

Italy, with its many beautiful cities and rich architectural heritage, is bordered by four countries: from west to east, France, Switzerland, Austria and Slovenia.

FACTS AND FIGURES	Emergency Services:	Average daily	Tel 0171-408 1254
Capital: Roma (Rome)	Police 113, Ambulance 113	**temperatures:** Roma	**USA** 630 Fifth Avenue,
Language: Italian	or 118, Fire 115 (Carabinieri	Jan 8°C Jul 25°C	Suite 1565
IDD code: 39. To call the	112)	Mar 11°C Sep 21°C	New York, NY 10111
UK dial 00 44	**Business hours-**	May 18°C Nov 12°C	Tel(212) 245 4822
Currency: Lira (ITA). £1 =	**Banks:** Mon-Fri 08.30-	**Tourist Information:** Italian	**Camping card:** Not
ITL 2696 (at press date)	13.30 and 15.30-16.30	State Tourist Office (ENIT)	generally compulsory, but
Local time: GMT + 1	**Shops:** Mon-Sat 08.30-	**UK** 1 Princes Street	required on some sites.
(summer GMT + 2)	13.30 and 15.30-19.30	London W1R 8AY	Reductions available.

The approaches are all dominated by mountains. The lakes of the north present a striking contrast with the sun-parched lands of the south and there is some beautiful countryside in the central Appenines. There are fine, sandy beaches on both the Tyrrhenian and Adriatic coasts.

The north has a typically Continental climate whilst the south has a temperate Mediterranean climate with extremely hot summers. The language is Italian, a direct development of Latin. There are several dialect forms such as Sicilian and Sardinian, but the accepted standard derives from the vernacular spoken in Florence 700 years ago. German is spoken, to a small extent, near the Austrian frontier and French in Valle d'Aosta.

The International Reservation Centre in Calenzano (near Florence) *Federcampeggio* provides a campsite information and reservation service ☎ 055-882391.

The *Assessorati Regionali per il Turismo* (ART) and the *Azienda Promozione Turistica* (APT) have regional and local information offices and can provide details of campsites within their locality. In northern Italy, especially by the lakes and along the Adriatic coast, sites tend to become very crowded and it is advisable to book in advance during the season which extends from May to the end of August.

Off-site camping is permitted provided the landowner's permission has been obtained, but is strictly prohibited in State forests and national parks. In built-up areas, if parking is allowed, the towing vehicle must remain connected to the trailer or caravan and the corner steadies must not be used.

HOW TO GET THERE

Although there are several ways of getting to Italy, entry will most probably be by way of France and Switzerland. Some passes, which are closed in winter, are served by road or rail-tunnels. For details of these and the *AA European Routes Service* please consult the Contents Page.

Distance

From the Channel ports Milano (Milan) is about 1100km (684 miles) requiring one or two overnight stops. Roma (Rome) is about 580km (360 miles) further south.

Car-sleeper services operate during the summer from *Calais*, *'s-Hertogenbosch* and *Paris* to Bologna; from *Calais* and *Paris* to Milano(Milan) ; from *Calais* to Livorno and Roma; from *Paris* to Firenze (Florence) and Rimini.

MOTORING & GENERAL INFORMATION

The information given here is specific to Italy. It **must** be read in conjunction with the European ABC at the front of the book, which covers those regulations which are common to many countries.

Boats*
Third party insurance is compulsory in Italian waters for motorboats; an Italian translation of the insurance certificate must be carried.

British Embassy/Consulates*
The British Embassy together with its consular section is located at 00187 Roma, Via XX Settembre 80A ☎06-4825441 and 4825551. There are British Consulates in Firenze (Florence), Milano (Milan), and Napoli (Naples); there are British Consulates with honorary Consuls in Bari, Brindisi, Cagliari, Genova (Genoa), Messina, Palermo, Trieste, Torino (Turin) and Venezia (Venice).

Children in cars*
Child under 4 not permitted to travel as front or rear seat passenger unless using suitable restraint system. Child between 4 and 12 travelling in front seat must use suitable restraint system.

Currency
A visitor may *import* and *export* Italian and foreign currency up to ITL20,000,000 without formality. However, if you are entering or leaving Italy via a non-EU country and wish to export any amount in excess of this it must have been declared on arrival on Form V2 within the preceding 6 months. This form is then shown to the Customs when leaving Italy.

Dimensions and weight restrictions
Private cars and towed trailers or caravans are restricted to the following dimensions - car height, 4 metres: width, 2.5 metres: length (including tow-bar) 12 metres. Caravan/trailer height, must not exceed 1.8 times the distance between the wheels of the vehicle; width 2.3 metres; length (including tow-bar) with one axle 6.5 metres, with two axles 8 metres. The maximum permitted overall length of vehicle/ trailer or caravan combination is 18.75 metres. Trailers with an unladen weight of over 750kg or 50% of the weight of the towing vehicle must have service brakes on all wheels.

A load may only overhang at the rear and must be indicated by a special reflectorised square panel. The load must not exceed 30% of the length of the vehical nor should the combined length of vehicle and overhanging load exceed the length restrictions given above.

Driving Licence*
A valid UK or Republic of Ireland EC model licence is acceptable in Italy. The minimum age at which visitors from UK or Republic of Ireland may use a temporarily imported car is 18 years. The minimum age for using a temporarily imported motorcycle of up to 125cc, not transporting a passenger, is 16 years; to carry a passenger, or use a motorcycle over 125cc, the minimum age is 18 years.
Note The official Italian translation or 'Declaration', formerly issued to accompany older all-green UK licences (in Northern Ireland any licence issued before 1 April 1991) is no longer valid. If time allows, they should be changed for a new format licence. Alternatively if time is short,obtain an International Driving Permit to accompany the older licence.

Fiscal receipt
In Italy, the law provides for a special numbered fiscal receipt *(ricevuta fiscale)* to be issued after paying for a wide range of goods and services including meals and accommodation. This receipt indicates the cost of the various goods and services obtained, and the total charge after adding VAT. Tourists should ensure that this receipt is issued, as spot checks are made by the authorities, and both the proprietor and consumer are liable to an on-the-spot fine if the receipt cannot be produced.

Foodstuffs*
There are no limits on the importation of foodstuffs obtained duty and tax paid within the EC. Up to 500g of coffee (200g of coffee extract) and 100g of tea (40g of tea extract) purchased duty-free or outside the EC may be imported free of duty and tax. However, coffee bought duty-free or outside the EC cannot be imported by visitors under 15 years of age.

Lights*
Full-beam headlights can be used only outside cities and towns. Dipped headlights are compulsory when passing through tunnels, even if they are well-lit. The Italian authorities

recommend that visiting motorists equip their vehicles with a spare set of vehicle bulbs.

Motoring clubs*
There are two motoring organisations in Italy. The **Touring Club Italiano** (TCI) which has its head office at 20122 Milano, 10 Corso Italia ☎02-85261 and the **Automobile Club d'Italia** (ACI) whose head office is at 00185 Roma, 8 Via Marsala ☎06-4477. Both clubs have branch offices in most leading cities and towns.

Petrol*
At the time of going to press both leaded and unleaded petrol are available in Italy. However, only one grade pf leaded petrol is sold, 98-100 octane 'Super'.

Roads
Main and secondary roads are generally good, and there are an exceptional number of by-passes. Mountain roads are usually well engineered; for details of mountain passes, see the contents page.

Italy has some 4,000 miles of motorway (*autostrada*) with tolls payable on most sections. Emergency telephones are located every 2km on most motorways; there are two call buttons, one to call for technical assistance and one to alert the Red Cross services.

Speed limits*
The speed limit in *built-up areas* is 50kph (31mph); *outside built-up areas*, 90kph (55mph) on ordinary roads, 110kph (68mph) on main roads and 130kph (80mph) on motorways. Motorcycles under 150cc are not allowed on motorways.

For cars towing a caravan or trailer the speed limits are 70kph (43mph) outside built-up areas and 80kph (49mph) on motorways.

Warning triangle*
The use of a warning triangle is compulsory outside built-up areas in the event of accident or breakdown. The triangle must be placed 50 metres (55yds) behind the vehicle on ordinary roads and 100 metres (109yds) on motorways. Motorists who fail to do this are liable to an administrative fine of between ITA25,000 and 100,000.

*Additional information will be found in the Continental ABC at the front of the book.

Portofino

● ● NORTH WEST/ALPS & LAKES ● ●

The Gran Paradiso mountains on the French border, and the Matterhorn and Monte Rosa to the north on the Swiss border, give a dramatic glacier-topped backdrop to the steep-sided valleys and the distinctively Italian Lakes, below where decorated villas and medieval castles border the lakes, and palm trees and magnolias grow. The mountains provide winter skiing, and walking in the summer, and wood and stone chalets contribute to the Alpine landscape. On the lakes, boats take you from harbour to harbour, yet within an hour you can be in Lombardy's capital, Milan. Turin, to the west, is an elegant town with its Piazza San Carlo and many cafés. Nearby, in the Alba region, the vineyards produce the distinguished Barolo red wine and sparkling Asti Spumante.

To the north and eastwards in the Dolomites, roads are good in the summer and the scenery is dramatic with fortresses dominating high peaks. Through wooded countryside is the border town of Bolzano where you will hear German spoken (this was once the South Tyrol) and may be served sausage and sauerkraut and locally produced Reisling wine.

....

⟩ ANFO BRESCIA

Palafitte via Calcaterra ☎ 0365 809051
Pleasant site divided into plots, sloping towards the lake where there are some trees.
⟳ *Access as for Pilù, then turn right.*
22 Apr-18 Sep 20HEC ⸺ ♣ ♠ ㊙ ✗ ☉ ☻ ⌀ ♨ ⌇ LP ⌂
lau ➧ ✗

LAGO AZZURRO
CAMPING

Via E. Fermi 2
I-28040 Dormelletto-Arona (NO)
Tel: and Fax: 0039/0322497197
Tel: 0039/0322497877
Mobile 0039/347/9057827
http://www.xmedium./lagoazzurro/
E-mail:@clazzur intercom.it

Your ideal holiday location at any time of the year, lakeside location and own sandy beach with quiet and shady pitches set in open countryside and offering a range of leisure facilities: large swimming pool, tennis, beach volleyball, table tennis, children's play area, entertainment for children and adults, video games.

Ideal centre for excursions – including by boat – to places of interest on Lake Maggiore.

Also has a bar, restaurant, pizzeria, small shop, satellite TV, telephone boxes, Internet and Fax service. Modern toilet facilities with hot showers. Washing machines and ironing facilities are also available.

Pilù via Venturi 4 ☎ 0365 809037
Well-maintained, slightly sloping site subdivided by trees and rows of shrubs on pebble beach from which it is separated by narrow public footpath.
⟳ *On southern outskirts; well signed.*
Apr-5 Oct 2HEC ⸺ ♣ ♠ ㊙ ♈ ✗ ☉ ☻ ⌀ ♨ ⌂ ⌇ LPR ⌂ ⊞
lau ➧ ✗
Prices: ⋔6500-8100 pitch 10000-145000

⟩ ANGERA VARESE

Città di Angera via Bruschera 99 ☎ 0331 930736
Large family site with plenty of recreational facilities.
⟳ *Signposted.*
2 Feb-Dec 1HEC ⸺ ♀ ♠ ㊙ ♈ ✗ ☉ ☻ ⌀ ⌇ LP ⌂ ⊞ lau
Prices: ⋔8000-11000 pitch 14000-17000

⟩ ARONA NOVARA
⟩ At DORMELLETTO(5km S)

Lago Azzurro via E-Fermi 2 ☎ 0322 497197
A lakeside site in beautiful surroundings with fine sporting facilities.
⟳ *S of Arona off SS Sempione 33.*
All year 2.5HEC ⸺ ♣ ♠ ㊙ ♈ ✗ ☉ ☻ ⌀ ⌇ LP ⌂ ⊞ lau
Prices: ⋔8000 pitch 11500-14000

Lago Maggiore via L-da-Vinci 7 ☎ 0322 497193
Well-maintained site divided into plots, pleasantly landscaped by the lakeside.
⟳ *Access from SS33, well signposted.*
Apr-Sep 5HEC ⸺ ♣ ♠ ㊙ ♈ ✗ ☉ ☻ ⌀ ♨ ⌇ P ⌂ lau
Prices: ⋔7000-10000 pitch 10500-16000

Lido Holiday Inn via M-Polo 1 ☎ 0322 497047
Site on bank of the lake, with some trees.
⟳ *Turn off the SS33 at Km60/VII and the IP petrol station.*
Apr-Sep 3.5HEC ⸺ ♀ ♠ ㊙ ♈ ✗ ☉ ☻ ⌀ ♨ ⌇ LP lau ➧ ⌀
Prices: ⋔8000-9500 pitch 11000-14000

Smeraldo via Cavour 125 ☎ 0322 497031
Well-landscaped site, divided into plots and situated in woodland by lakeside.
⟳ *Access from SS33.*
Mar-Oct 24HEC ⸺ ♣ ♠ ㊙ ♈ ✗ ☉ ☻ ⌀ ♨ ⌂ ⌇ L ⌂ ⊞ lau
Prices: ⋔7900-9100 pitch 13300-15200

⟩ ARVIER AOSTA

Arvier via St Antoine 6 ☎ 0165 99088
Wooded quiet site close to mountains and a peaceful village
20 Jun-Aug 1HEC ⸺ ♣ ♠ ㊙ ☉ ☻ ⌇ P ⌂ ➧ ♈ ✗ ⌀ ♨ ⊞
Prices: ⋔8600 ♠4600 ☗7200 ▲7200

⟩ BASTIA MONDOVI CUNEO

Cascina via Pieve 27 ☎ 0174 60181
Closed Sep 4HEC ⸺ ♣ ♠ ㊙ ✗ ☉ ☻ ⌀ ⌇ PR ⌂ lau ➧ ✗
Prices: ⋔7500 pitch 6900

⟩ BAVENO NOVARA

Lido Bruno via Piase 66 ☎ 0323 924775
Etr-Oct 1.5HEC ⸺ ♀ ♠ ㊙ ✗ ☉ ☻ ⌀ ☻ ☗ ⌇ L ⌂ ⊞ lau
➧ ⌇P

Tranquilla via Cave 2 ☎ 0323 923452
In a peaceful location with fine panoramic views over the surrounding mountains and Lake Maggiore. Good, modern facilities.
⟳ *4 km from Stresa*
Mar-Oct 1.8HEC ⸺ ♣ ♠ ✗ ☉ ☻ ☗ ⌇ P ⌂ lau ➧ ㊙ ⌀ ♨
⊞
Prices: pitch 10500-13500

international camping

22100 Como (Italia)
tel. (031) 52.14.35 (summer)
tel. (02) 89513430 (winter)

Quiet position • Swimming pool • Pizzeria • Bar • Self
Service • Showers, warm and cold water • Bungalow •
5 minutes from the City • Nearest the Motor-Highway
Milan • Como • Chiasso

BELLAGIO COMO

Azienda Agricola Clarke via Valassina 170/c ☎ 031 951325
A small, secluded site situated on a horsebreeding farm on
the shores of Lake Bellagio.
Etr-Sep 0.5HEC 〰 ⚏ 🔆 ⛺ ❣ ⊙ 🔌 🛒 🔲 ✦ ❖ 🛒 ✕ ∅ ↘LP
Prices: ⚑7000 🚐16000 ▲16000

BOLZANO-BOZEN BOLZANO

Moosbauer Moritzingerweg 83 ☎ 0471 918492
Small site in attractive valley at the "Gateway to the
Dolomites."
All year 1HEC 〰 ❖ ❣ 🛒 🔅 ✕ ⊙ 🔌 ∅ ↘ P 🔲 lau ✦ 🔲
Prices: ⚑8000-9500 pitch 18000-23000

BRESCIA COMO

International via Cecilio ☎ 031 521435
On a level meadow near the motorway. Lunchtime siesta
13.00-15.30 hrs.
➲ *Off A9 Como-Milan motorway.*
28 Mar-15 Oct 1.8HEC 〰 ❖ ❣ 🛒 🔅 ✕ ⊙ 🔌 ∅ 🛒 🏕 🚐 ↘ P
🔲 🔲 lau
Prices: ⚑6500 🚗4500 🚐6500 ▲6000

BRESSANONE-BRIXEN BOLZANO

Löwenhof via Brennero 60 ☎ 0472 836216
Site offers rafting and canoeing school as well as sauna, pool
etc. which are avaliable in the Dolomiti resort 8km away.
➲ *Exit Bolzano/Brennero motorway at Varna. Site is just
before Brixen.*
All year 0.5HEC 〰 ⚏ ❣ 🛒 🔅 ✕ ⊙ 🔌 ∅ 🛒 ↘ PR 🔲 🔲 lau
Prices: ⚑10000-12000 🚗3000-6000 🚐10000-16000 ▲10000-
16000

BUISSON AOSTA

Cervino ☎ 0166 545111
All year 6HEC 〰 ⚏ ❣ 🛒 ✕ ⊙ 🔌 🛒 🏕 ↘ R lau ✦ 🔲

CALCERANICA TRENTO

Al Pescatore via dei Pescatori 1 ☎ 0461 723062
The site consists of several sections of meadowland, inland
from the lake shore road to Lago di Caldonazzo. Well
maintained with private beach.
30 May-15 Sep 3.8HEC 〰 ⚏ ❣ 🛒 🔅 ✕ ⊙ 🔌 ∅ ↘ L 🔲 lau

Fleiola via Trento 20 ☎ 0461 723153
Site is divided into sectors beside lake.
➲ *Exit the Verona/Brennero motorway at Trento, follow signs
for Pergine and Caldonazzo.*
Apr-5 Oct 1.2HEC 〰 ⚏ ❖ ❣ 🛒 🔅 ✕ ⊙ 🔌 ∅ 🛒 🏕 🚐 ↘ L 🔲
lau ✦ ✕ 🛒 🔲
Prices: ⚑5000-10000 pitch 7500-18000

Riviera viale Venezia 10 ☎ 0461 724464
All year 1.5HEC 〰 ❖ ❣ 🛒 🔅 ✕ ⊙ 🔌 ∅ ↘ L 🔲 lau ✦ 🛒 🔲
Prices: ⚑6800-10000 pitch 9400-13000

CAMPITELLO DI FASSA TRENTO

Miravalle via Camping 13 ☎ 0462 62002
In a wooded mountain setting beside the River Avisio and
close to the town centre.
➲ *Signposted.*
15 Dec-Apr & Jun-Sep 3HEC 〰 ⚏ ❣ 🔅 ✕ ⊙ 🔌 ∅ ↘ R 🔲 🔲
🔲 lau ✦ 🛒 ✕ 🛒 ↘P
Prices: ⚑12000-14000 ▲13500 pitch 13500-16000

CANAZEI TRENTO

Marmolada via Pareda ☎ 0462 61660
Grassland site extending to the river, part of it in spruce
woodland.
➲ *Located on S outskirts on the right of the road to Alba
Penia.*
All year 3HEC 〰 ⚏ ❣ 🛒 ✕ ⊙ 🔌 ∅ 🛒 🔲 lau ✦ 🛒 ✕ ↘P 🔲
Prices: ⚑13000 pitch 13000

CANNOBIO NOVARA

International Paradis via Casali Darbedo 12 ☎ 0323 71227
A level site on the bank of a lake.
➲ *Access from the SS34 at Km35/V.*
20 Mar-15 Oct 1.2HEC 〰 ❖ ❣ 🛒 🔅 ✕ ⊙ 🔌 ∅ 🛒 🔲 ↘ L 🔲
🔲 lau ✦ ✕ ↘R

Residence Campagna via Casali Darbedo 20/22 ☎ 0323
70100
A well equipped site in a pleasant lakeside location.
➲ *Turn off SS34 to Locarno at Km35/V on N outskirts of
village. W of lake on road 21.*
15 Mar-20 Oct 1.2HEC 〰 ❖ ❣ 🛒 🔅 ✕ ⊙ 🔌 ∅ 🛒 🏕 🚐 ↘ L
🔲 lau
Prices: ⚑10000-11000 pitch 16000-18000

Valle Romantica via Valle Cannobina ☎ 0323 71249
A pleasant site with trees, shrubs and flowers. Internal roads
are asphalted and a mountain stream provides bathing
facilities.
➲ *1.5km w off road to Malesco.*
28 Mar-Sep 25HEC 〰 ❖ ❣ 🛒 🔅 ✕ ⊙ 🔌 ∅ 🛒 🏕 🚐 ↘ PR 🔲 ✦
🛒 ↘L 🔲
Prices: ⚑10000-11000 pitch 16000-20000

CASTELLETTO TICINO NOVARA

Italia Lido via Cicognola 88 ☎ 0331 923032
A large family site with its own private beach on Lake
Maggiore. The site is popular with families and there are
good recreational facilities.
➲ *From A8 then join A26 is then signposted.*
Mar-Oct 22HEC 〰 ⋯ ❖ ❣ 🛒 🔅 ✕ ⊙ 🔌 ∅ 🛒 ↘ L 🔲 🔲
lau
Prices: ⚑7000-8000 🚐9000-11000 ▲7000-9000

CHIUSA-KLAUSEN BOLZANO

Gamp Griesbruck 10 ☎ 0472 847425
The site lies next to the Gasthof Gamp, between the Brenner
railway line and the motorway bridge, which passes high
above the camp.
➲ *Access from the motorway exit and the SS12 is well
signposted.*
All year 0.6HEC 〰 ❖ ❣ 🛒 🔅 ✕ ⊙ 🔌 ↘ P 🔲 lau
✦ ∅ ↘ 🛒
Prices: ⚑9000-9500 🚗14000-15000 🚐9500-10500
▲7000-9500

COLFOSCO BOLZANO

Colfosco via Sonegau ☎ 0471 836515
In a beautiful setting at the foot of the Sella mountains.
Jun-Oct & Dec-15 Apr 2.5HEC ⛺ ⋯ ☀ ♠ ⛱ ♨ ♀ ✕ ⊙ ⬛
∅ ⛌ ☎ ⌇ R ⛁ lau ♦ ⌇LP ⊞
Prices: ⋏8000-10000 ♠8000-10000 ⬛15000-25000 ⚑7000-25000

COLOMBARE BRESCIA

Sirmione via Sirmioncino 9 ☎ 030 919045
A well equipped site in a beautiful location on the Sirmione peninsula, with direct access to Lake Garda.
⟳ *From SS11 drive towards Sirmione and turn right after approx. 0.4km.*
15 Mar-15 Oct 3.5HEC ⛺ ∅ ♠ ⛱ ♨ ♀ ✕ ⊙ ⬛ ☎ ⌇ LP ⛁
⊞ lau ♦ ⛌ ∅ ⛌
Prices: ⋏8500-11000 pitch 9000-22000

CUNEO CUNEO

Turistico Comunale Bisalta San Rocco Castagnaretta ☎ 0171 491334
Large site with well defined pitches and a wide variety of sporting and recreational facilities.
⟳ *SW of town towards the French border.*
All year 4HEC ⛺ ♠ ⛱ ♨ ♀ ✕ ⊙ ⬛ ☎ ⌇ P ⛁ lau ♦ ⛌ ⊞

DESENZANO DEL GARDA BRESCIA

Vò via Vò 9 ☎ 030 9121325
Situated on Lake Garda, 1500m from Desenzano, surrounded by meadows and woods.
⟳ *On the banks of Lake Garda 2km from Desenzano, between Padenghe and Sirmione.*
Apr-Sep 5HEC ⛺ ♠ ⛱ ♨ ♀ ✕ ⊙ ⬛ ☎ ⌇ LP ⛁ lau ♦ ∅ ⊞
Prices: ⋏6000-8000 pitch 12000-18000

DIMARO TRENTO

Dolomiti di Brenta via Gole 105 ☎ 0463 974332
The campsite has large flat plots which are surrounded by tall pine trees. The facilities for sport are excellent with special a special lessons and tuition for canoeing and white water rafting.
⟳ *Turn off SS42, at Km173.5.*
Jun-10 Oct & 8 Dec-Apr 3HEC ⛺ ♠ ⛱ ♨ ♀ ✕ ⊙ ⬛ ∅ ⛌
☎ ⌇ P ⛁ ⊞ lau ♦ ⌇R
Prices: ⋏8000-12000 pitch 13000-19000

DOMASO COMO

Gardenia via Case Sparse 138 ☎ 0344 96262
⟳ *N at Case Sparse*
Apr-Sep 2HEC ⛺ ⋯ ♠ ⛱ ♨ ♀ ✕ ⊙ ⬛ ∅ ⛌ ☎ ⌇ L ⛁ ⊞ ✿
lau

EDOLO BRESCIA

Adamello via Campeggio 10 ☎ 0364 71694
A terraced site in wooded surroundings, 1km from the lake.
⟳ *1.5km W of SS39.*
All year 1.2HEC ⛺ ♠ ⛱ ♨ ♀ ✕ ⊙ ⬛ ∅ ⛌ ⬛ ☎ ⊞ lau ♦ ✕
⌇LPR
Prices: ⋏8500 ♠3500 ⬛12000 ⚑8000-12000

FERIOLO NOVARA

Orchidea via Repubblica dell' Ossola ☎ 0323 28257
A modern site on the extremity of Lake Maggiore with good sports and entertainment facilities.
⟳ *Access via SS33.*
Mar-Oct 4HEC ⛺ ♠ ⛱ ♨ ♀ ✕ ⊙ ⬛ ∅ ⬛ ⚑ ⌇ L ⛁ lau ♦
⊞

FONDOTOCE NOVARA

Continental Lido via 42 Martiri 156 ☎ 0323 496300
By Lake Mergozzo and 1km from Lake Maggiore.
⟳ *On right hand side of road from Verbania Fondotoce to Gravellona.*
30 Mar-22 Sep 8HEC ⛺ ⋯ ⊕ ♠ ⛱ ♨ ♀ ✕ ⊙ ⬛ ∅ ⬛ ⚑ ⚑
⌇ L ⛁ lau ♦ ⛌

Lido Toce via per Feriolo 41 ☎ 0323 496298
In a beautiful location on the eastern shore of the lake offering spectacular views. Good recreational facilities.
May-Sep 2HEC ⛺ ⋯ ⊕ ♠ ⛱ ♨ ♀ ✕ ⊙ ⬛ ☎ ⌇ LR ⛁ ⊞ lau
♦ ∅ ⬛
Prices: ⋏6500-8000 pitch 12000-15000

Village Isolino via Per Feriolo 25 ☎ 0323 496080
20 Mar-26 Sep 12HEC ⛺ ♠ ⛱ ♨ ♀ ✕ ⊙ ⬛ ∅ ⛌ ⬛ ⚑ ⚑ ⌇
LR ⛁ ⊞ lau ♦ ⌇R
Prices: ⋏7000-9000 pitch 15000-19000

FUCINE DI OSSANA TRENTO

Cevedale ☎ 0463 751630
A well equipped site in a peaceful location at an altitude of 900mtrs, close to the local ski resorts.
⟳ *4km W of Savona.*
All year 2.8HEC ⛺ ⊕ ♠ ⛱ ♨ ♀ ✕ ⊙ ⬛ ☎ ⛁ ⊞ ✿ lau
♦ ✕ ∅ ⛌
Prices: ⋏8000-12000 pitch 11000-16000

GERMIGNAGA VARESE

Il Boschetto via Mameli ☎ 0334 534740
In a pleasant location beside Lake Maggiore with a good variety of facilities and opportunities for water sports.
Apr-Sep 1HEC ⛺ ♠ ⛱ ♀ ✕ ⊙ ⬛ ∅ ⛌ ⬛ ⚑ ⚑ P ⛁ ♦ ⛱
Prices: ⋏7500-9000 ♠3500-4000 ⬛12000-16000
⚑7000-8000

IDRO BRESCIA

AZUR Idro Rio Vantone ☎ 0365 83125
The site lies at the mouth of the river of same name beside Lake Idro. Subdivided into pitches (separate pitches for youths) on grass and woodland at the foot of strange rock formations.
⟳ *Approach from Idro direction of Vantone, well signed from there.*
15 Mar-15 Nov 4.6HEC ⛺ ⊕ ♠ ⛱ ♨ ♀ ✕ ⊙ ⬛ ∅ ⛌ ⬛ ⌇ LP
⛁ ⊞ lau
Prices: ⋏5500-10000 pitch 6500-14000

Vantone Pineta Via Capovalle 11 ☎ 0365 823385
On eastern shore of lake. Grassland enclosed by rush and willow fencing. Part of site in a small wood on the bank of a stream.
⟳ *Approach from Idro and follow signs for Camping Idro Rio Vantone.*
31 Mar-Oct 2HEC ⛺ ♠ ⛱ ♨ ♀ ✕ ⊙ ⬛ ⌇ LP ⛁ lau ♦ ∅ ⊞

ISEO BRESCIA

Punta d'Oro via Antonioli 51/53 ☎ 030 980084
A well set out campsite with roads and paths reaching every pitch.
⟳ *From A4 exit at Rovato and follow signs Iseo.*
Apr-Oct 6.4HEC ⛺ ♠ ⛱ ♨ ♀ ✕ ⊙ ⬛ ⚑ ⌇ L ⛁ lau ♦ ✕ ∅
⛌ ⌇P ⊞
Prices: ⋏6500-9000 pitch 14000-19000

Quai via Antonioli 73 ☎ 030 981161
Shady site close to the edge of Lake D'Iseo.
⟳ *W of town. Signposted.*

Apr-26 Sept 1.3HEC ⚏ ♦ ⋔ 🏊 🍴 ✕ ⊙ 🚻 🛒 ⤳ L 🏠 🅿 ⊞
⚘ lau ♦ 🏊 ✕ ∅ ⤳P ⊞
Prices: ⋔6000-8000 pitch 12000-18000

Sassabanek via Colombera 2 ☎ 030 980300
Apr-Oct 3.5HEC ⚏ ♦ ⋔ 🏊 🍴 ✕ ⊙ 🚻 ∅ 🛒 ⤳ LP 🅿 ⊞ ⚘
lau ♦ ⛺

KALTERN BOLZANO

St Josef am Kalterer See Welnstr 75 ☎ 0471 960170
On level ground surrounded by trees close to the lake.
⮑ *Signposted from the Kalten-Tramin road.*
15 Mar-10 Nov 1.4HEC ⚏ ⋯ 🏊 ⋔ 🏊 🍴 ✕ ⊙ 🚻 ∅ ⤳ L 🏠
⊞ lau
Prices: ⋔7300-9000 ⮕5500-6000 ⛟6000-7000 ⛺5000-6500

LAIVES-LEIFERS BOLZANO

Steiner Kennedystr 34 ☎ 0471 950105
The site lies behind the Gasthof Steiner, the AGIP petrol station and a bungalow estate.
⮑ *Off the SS12 on the northern outskirts of the village.*
28 Mar-7 Nov 2.5HEC ⚏ ⋔ ♦ ⋔ 🏊 🍴 ✕ ⊙ 🚻 ∅ ⛺ 🛒 ⤳ P
🏠 ⊞ ⚘ lau ♦ 🏊

LATSCH BOLZANO

Latsch an der Etsch Reichstr 4 ☎ 0473 623217
A terraced site beside the river.
⮑ *Campsite is signposted on SS38.*
Jan-10 Nov & 20 Dec-Jan 1.6HEC ⚏ ♦ ⋔ 🏊 🍴 ✕ ⊙ 🚻 ∅
🛒 ⤳ R 🏠 ⊞ lau
Prices: ⋔7500-9000 ⮕7500-8000 ⛟8000-9000 ⛺7000-9000

LECCO COMO

Rivabella via Alla Spiaggia 35 ☎ 0341 421143
On a private, guarded beach on the shore of Lake Como.
⮑ *3km S towards Bergamo.*
25 Apr-Sep 2HEC ⚏ ♦ ⋔ 🏊 🍴 ✕ ⊙ 🚻 ∅ ⤳ L 🏠 lau ♦ ✕
⤳P ⊞
Prices: ⋔7500 pitch 13500

LEVICO TERME TRENTO

Due Laghi Loc Costa 3 ☎ 0461 512707
Aimed mainly at families this site offers 400 large flat grass pitches.
⮑ *From Trento follow signs for Pergine and Lake Caldonazza.*
25 May-Sep 11HEC ⚏ 🏊 ⋔ 🏊 🍴 ✕ ⊙ 🚻 ∅ ⛺ ⤳ LP 🏠 ⊞
lau
Prices: ⋔10000-12500 pitch 16000-17000

Jolly Loc Pleina ☎ 0461 706934 & 234351
The site is divided into plots and lies 200 metres from the lake with three inside swimming pools.
15 May-15 Sep 2HEC ⚏ 🏊 ⋔ 🏊 🍴 ✕ ⊙ 🚻 ∅ ⛟ ⤳ P 🏠
⊞ lau ♦ ✕ ⤳L

Levico ☎ 0461 706491
Site is by a lake with a private beach.
⮑ *Signposted on the Levico/Caldonazzo exit on SS47.*
Apr-Sep 4HEC ⚏ ♦ ⋔ 🏊 🍴 ⊙ ∅ 🚻 ∅ ⛺ ⤳ LR 🏠 ⊞ lau ♦ ✕
⤳P

LILLAZ AOSTA

Salasses ☎ 0165 74252
Pleasant site surrounded by mountains, grassland and conifers.
⮑ *Entrance to site before Camping al Sole.*
All year 1HEC ⚏ ⋯ 🏊 ⋔ 🏊 🍴 ✕ ⊙ 🚻 ⛟ ⤳ R 🏠 🅿 ♦ 🏊 ✕ ∅
⛺ ⊞
Prices: ⋔7500 ⮕5000 ⛟7500 ⛺5500-7500

LIMONE PIEMONTE CUNEO

Luis Matlas ☎ 0171 927565
This tidy site offers winter facilities and skiing lessons are provided by the owner. Fishing is also available.
⮑ *It lies to the north of the town, off the Limone-Nice road.*
Closed 1-15 Sep 1.5HEC ⚏ 🏊 ⚘ ⋔ 🏊 ✕ ⊙ 🚻 ∅ ⛺ 🏠 lau
♦ 🏊 ✕ ⤳R ⊞

LIMONE SUL GARDA BRESCIA

Nanzel via 4 Novembre 3 ☎ 0365 954155
Well managed site, with low terraces in olive grove.
⮑ *Access from Km101.2 (Hotel Giorgiol).*
Apr-Oct 0.7HEC ⚏ 🏊 ⋔ 🏊 🍴 ✕ ⊙ 🚻 ∅ ⤳ L lau ♦ ✕ ⛺ ⊞
Prices: ⋔8500 ⮕9500 ⛺9500

LINFANO D'ARCO TRENTO

Bellavista via Gardesana 31 ☎ 0464 505644
Apr-20 Oct 1HEC ⚏ ♦ ⋔ 🏊 🍴 ✕ ⊙ 🚻 ⤳ L 🏠 lau ♦ ✕

MACCAGNO VARESE

AZUR-Lago Maggiore ☎ 0332 560203
A popular site on the shore of the lake.
⮑ *In village turn off SS394 at Km43/III towards lake and after 500 m turn right.*
15 Mar-15 Nov 1.5HEC ⚏ 🏊 ⋔ 🏊 🍴 ✕ ⊙ 🚻 ∅ 🛒 ⤳ L 🏠 ⊞
lau ♦ ✕

Lido via 6 Pietraperzia 13 ☎ 0332 560250
Lakeside site with good facilities, 200mtrs from the river.
Apr-Sep 0.8HEC ⚏ ♦ ⋔ 🏊 🍴 ✕ ⊙ 🚻 ∅ ⤳ LR 🏠 ⚘ lau ♦ ✕
∅ ⤳R ⊞
Prices: ⋔8500-9500 ⮕3500-4000 ⛟11000-16000 ⛺11000-16000

MADERNO BRESCIA

Riviera SAS via Promontoorio 59 ☎ 0365 643039
Apr-Sep 3.8HEC ⚏ ♦ ⋔ 🏊 🍴 ✕ ⊙ 🚻 ∅ ⛺ ⤳ LR 🏠 ⊞ lau

MAGGIORE (LAGO)

See ARONA, BAVENO, CANNOBIO, FONDOTOCE, MACCAGNO

MANERBA DEL GARDA BRESCIA

Belvedere via Cavalle 5 ☎ 0365 551175
Terraced site by Lake Garda.
⮑ *Signposted from SS572.*
Etr-13 Oct 2.1HEC ⚏ ⋯ 🏊 ⋔ 🏊 ✕ ⊙ 🚻 🛒 ⤳ L 🏠
♦ 🍴 ✕ ⊞

Rio Ferienglück via del Rio 37 ☎ 0365 551450
⮑ *Follow SS572 Desenzano-Salo road, turn off between Km8 and 9, site 4km N.*
Apr-Sep 5HEC ⚏ ♦ ⋔ 🏊 🍴 ✕ ⊙ 🚻 ∅ ⛺ 🛒 ⤳ L 🏠 ⊞
lau

Rocca via Cavalle 22 ☎ 0365 551738
In a picturesque location with fine views over the Gulf of Manerba.
Apr-Sep 5HEC ⚏ ♦ ⋔ 🏊 🍴 ✕ ⊙ 🚻 ⛺ 🛒 ⤳ LP 🏠 ⊞ ♦ ✕

Zocco via del Zocco 43 ☎ 0365 551605
The site consists of several, terraced sections. The section below the maintenance/supply building lies on a sloping olive grove and is somewhat obstructed by bungalows.
⮑ *500m S of Gardonicino di Manerba.*
Apr-26 Sep 5HEC ⚏ ♦ ⋔ 🏊 🍴 ✕ ⊙ 🚻 ∅ ⛟ ⛺ ⛺ ⤳ L 🏠 ⊞
lau
Prices: ⋔7200-9500 pitch 15500-20000

MOLINA DI LEDRO TRENTO

International Camping Al Sole via Maffei ☎ 0464 508496
A family site with good, modern facilities situated on the
shore of Lake Ledro at an altitude of 655mtrs.
➲ *W of Molina beside the lake.*
May-Sep 3HEC ⏚⏚⏚⏚ ⌁ ♠ ♘ ⛱ ❡ ✗ ⊙ ⊟ ∅ ⟋ LP 🄿 ⊞ ♦ 🛆
Prices: ⚑8000-9000 pitch 9000-12000

MOLVENO TRENTO

Spiaggia-Lago di Molveno via Lungolago 27 ☎ 0461 586978
In a picturesque setting on the lake shore, at the foot of the
Brenta Dolomites.
➲ *Signposted from SS421.*
All year 4HEC ⏚⏚⏚⏚ ♦ ♠ ♘ ⛱ ❡ ✗ ⊙ ⊟ ∅ ⟋ LP 🄿 🄿 lau ♦ ⊞
Prices: ⚑6000-12000 ♠10000-20000 🚐10000-20000
🛆10000-20000

MONIGA DEL GARDA BRESCIA

Fontanelle via del Magone 13 ☎ 0365 502079
Peaceful site on the shores of Lake Garda shaded by olive
trees. All staff speak English.
May-19 Sep 4.5HEC ⏚⏚⏚⏚ ⌁ ♠ ♘ ⛱ ❡ ✗ ⊙ ⊟ ∅ ⟋ 🛆 ⟋ LP 🄿
⊞ lau
Prices: ⚑7500-10700 pitch 16000-21500

San Michele via San Michele 8 ☎ 0365 502026
A family site with good facilities and direct access to the lake
via a private beach.
➲ *Exit A4 at Desenzano. Site is 8km from Desenzano in
direction of Salo.*
Apr-Sep 3HEC ⏚⏚⏚⏚ ♦ ♠ ♘ ⛱ ❡ ✗ ⊙ ⊟ ∅ ⟋ LP 🄿 ⊞ lau ♦ ∅ 🛆
Prices: ⚑6500-9000 pitch 16500-21000

NATURNO-NATURNS BOLZANO

Wald Dornsbergweg 8 ☎ 0473 667298
The site lies on gently rising ground, in a forest of pine and
deciduous trees.
➲ *For access, turn off the SS38 near the Gasthof Alderwirt in
the village, and drive 0.8km S over the railway line.*
15 Mar-Oct 1.5HEC ⏚⏚⏚⏚ ⌁ ♠ ⊙ ⊟ ⟋ 🛆 ⟋ P ⊞ lau ♦ ❡ ✗
∅ ⟋R

NOVATE MEZZOLA SONDRIO

El Ranchero via Nazionale 3 ☎ 0343 44169
Located on the edge of the Mezzola lake in front of a
spectacular view of the mountains.
Apr-Sep 1HEC ⏚⏚⏚⏚ ⌁ ♠ ♘ ✗ ⊙ ⊟ ∅ 🐟 ⟋ LR 🄿 🄿 ✍ ♦ ♘ ✗
∅ 🛆 ⟋P ⊞

ORA-AUER BOLZANO

Wasserfall ☎ 0471 810519
Sloping site in front of the Gasthaus Wasserfall, between
wooded rocky hills and the River Schwarzbach.
➲ *For access turn off Fleimstralstrasse (SS48) E of the bridge
over the River Schwarzbach and drive N for 300m.*
Apr-5 Nov 1HEC ⏚⏚⏚⏚ ∴ ♦ ⌁ ♠ ⊙ ⊟ ∅ ⟋ P ⊞ ⊞ ✍ lau
♦ ♘ ❡ ✗

ORTA SAN GIULIO NOVARA

Cusio Lago d'Orta ☎ 0322 90290
Apr-Nov 2HEC ⏚⏚⏚⏚ ♦ ♠ ♘ ⛱ ⟋ P ⊟ lau ♦ ⟋L
Prices: ⚑6000-8000 ♠4000-5000 🚐7000-10000

PADENGHE BRESCIA

Cá via S.Cassiano 12 ☎ 030 9907006
The site lies in a park-like setting on terraced ground.
➲ *For access, turn off the road along Lake Garda, 1.5km N
turn for Padenghe, and drive down a very steep road towards
the lake.*

Mar-Oct 2HEC ⏚⏚⏚⏚ ♦ ♠ ♘ ⛱ ❡ ✗ ⊙ ⊟ ∅ ⊞ 🚐 ⟋ L 🄿 lau
Prices: ⚑6000-9900 pitch 11000-18700

Campagnola via Marconi 99 ☎ 030 9907523
In a beautiful position on the shores of Lake Garda with
good, modern facilities.
➲ *4km from Desenzano on the road to Salo.*
May-Sep 5HEC ⏚⏚⏚⏚ ♦ ♠ ♘ ⛱ ❡ ✗ ⊙ ⊟ ∅ ⟋ LP 🄿 ⊞ ✍ lau

PEIO TRENTO

Val di Sole Loc Dossi di Cavia ☎ 0463 753177
The site lies on terraced slopes at the foot of the Ortier
mountain range.
➲ *400m off SP87.*
Jun-Sep & Nov-Apr 2.3HEC ⏚⏚⏚⏚ ⌁ ♠ ♘ ⛱ ❡ ✗ ⊙ ⊟ ∅ 🛆 ⊞ 🄿
lau ♦ ✗ ⟋P ⊞
Prices: ⚑7000-9000 pitch 9000-12000

PERA DI FASSA TRENTO

Soal via Dolomiti 32 ☎ 0462 764519
Breath-taking location among the Dolomites, ideal for skiing
and walking.
All year 30HEC ⏚⏚⏚⏚ ◊ ⌁ ♠ ♘ ⛱ ❡ ✗ ⊙ ⊟ ∅ 🛆 ⟋ R ⊞ ⊞ lau
Prices: ⚑11000-14000 pitch 13000-16000

PERGINE TRENTO

Punta Indiani Lago di Caldonazzo ☎ 0461 548062
On level ground surrounded by trees with direct access to
400mtrs of private beach on the banks of the lake.
➲ *From the A22 exit at Trento follow signs for Pergine, S.
Cristoforo and Caldonazzo.*
May-Sep 1.5HEC ⏚⏚⏚⏚ ⌁ ♠ ⊙ ⊟ ⟋ L 🄿 ✍ lau
♦ ♘ ❡ ✗ ∅ 🛆 ⊞
Prices: ⚑10000-10000 pitch 12000-22000

San Cristoforo via dei Pescatori ☎ 0461 706290
A family-run site in a prime position on the sunniest side of
lake. Owned and run by family Oss with regular guests
helping as staff.
➲ *Follow road 47 from Trento towards Venice for 14km. Site is
in centre of S. Cristoforo village.*
25 May-15 Sept 2.5HEC ⏚⏚⏚⏚ ⌁ ♠ ♘ ⛱ ❡ ✗ ⊙ ⊟ ∅ 🛆 ⟋ LP 🄿
⊞ lau
Prices: ⚑10000-12000 pitch 16000-17000

PETTENASCO NOVARA

Punta di Crabbia via Crabbia 2/A ☎ 0323 89117
A well equipped site in a pleasant situation providing
panoramic views over the surrounding area.
Apr-Sep 2HEC ⏚⏚⏚⏚ ⌁ ♠ ♘ ⛱ ❡ ✗ ⊙ ⊟ ⟋ L 🄿 ⊞ lau ♦ ✗ ∅
⟋L
Prices: ⚑7500 ♠2000 🚐9000 🛆7000

PIEVE DI MANERBA BRESCIA

Faro via Repubblica 52 ☎ 0365 651704
Situated in a peaceful rural area close to the sea.
➲ *Leave A4 at Desenzano and take N572 to Manerba del
Garda.*
15 Apr-15 Sep 1HEC ⏚⏚⏚⏚ ♦ ⌁ ♠ ⊙ ⊟ 🚐 ⟋ P 🄿 ♦ ♘ ❡ ✗ ∅ 🛆
⟋L ⊞

PISOGNE BRESCIA

Eden via Piangrande 3 ☎ 0364 880500
The site lies on eastern lake shore with tall trees and a level
beach.
➲ *Turn off SS510 at Km37/VII, over railway line and towards
lake.*
2 Apr-28 Sep 2.5HEC ⏚⏚⏚⏚ ♦ ♠ ♘ ⛱ ❡ ⊙ ⊟ 🚐 ⟋ L 🄿 ⊞ lau
♦ ♘ ∅ 🛆 ⟋P ⊞
Prices: ⚑6500-7500 ♠4000 🚐16000-20000

▶ PONTE TRESA VARESE

Trelago via trelago 20 ☎ 0332 716583
Lakeside campsite with grassy pitches shaded by tall trees.
⤷ *Follow signs from Milan to Varese and Ghirla. Site is 15km from Varese.*
3 Apr-6 Sep 3HEC ▦ ⚓ ⚘ ⋔ ⌂ ♥ ⟳ ⊙ ♨ ⌀ ☵ ☎ ☭ ⟲ LP ⚐ ⊞ lau ➡ ✕
Prices: ⬆7000 pitch 11000

▶ PORLEZZA COMO

Paradiso Via Calbiga,30 ☎ 01243220132
The site lies in meadowland on the north eastern lake shore.
⤷ *S from SS340.*
15 Mar-15 Nov 5HEC ▦ ⚘ ⋔ ⌂ ♥ ✕ ⊙ ♨ ☎ ⟲ LP ⚐ ➡ ✕
Prices: ⬆7000-9000 pitch 12000-15000

▶ PORTESE BRESCIA

Eden via Preone 45 ☎ 0365 62093
Site with good facilities on the shore of Lake Garda.
Apr-Sep 4.4HEC ▦ ♥ ⋔ ⌂ ♥ ✕ ⊙ ♨ ⌀ ☵ ☎ ⟲ LP ⚐ lau ➡ ⊞

▶ POZZA DI FASSA TRENTO

Rosengarten via Avisio 15, Loc Puccia ☎ 0462 763305
In the heart of the Dolomites this well-tended site is an ideal base for a skiing or walking holiday.
⤷ *Signposted from SS48.*
Closed May & Oct 3.5HEC ▦ ⚘ ⋔ ⌂ ✕ ⊙ ♨ ⌀ ☵ ☎ ☭ ⟲ R ⚐ ⊞ lau ➡ ⚘ ✕

Vidor via Valle S Nicolo ☎ 0462 763247
This traditional family run site is set in a pine forest. Ideal for skiers, nature lovers and families all year round.
⤷ *Signposted from SS48.*
Jan-Apr, 15-Dec Closed May 1.5HEC ▦ ⚶ ⋔ ⚘ ⌂ ♥ ✕ ⊙ ♨ ⌀ ☵ ☭ ⚐ ⊞ lau ➡ ✕ ⟲R

▶ PRAD AM STILFSERJOCH BOLZANO

Kiefernhain ☎ 0473 616422
Apr-Oct 3HEC ▦ ⋮⋮ ♥ ⋔ ⌂ ✕ ⊙ ♨ ⟲ PR ⚐ ➡ ⚘ ⌀ ☵ ⟲L ⊞

▶ PRATO ALLO STELVIO BOLZANO

Sägomühle via delle Spine ☎ 0473 616078
Closed 10 Nov-10 Dec 1.2HEC ▦ ⚘ ⋔ ⌂ ♥ ⌂ ✕ ⊙ ♨ ☵ ☭ ♨ ⟲ P ⚐ ⊞ lau ➡ ⌀ ⟲LR

▶ RASUN BOLZANO

Corones ☎ 0474 496490
A modern site in an ideal mountain location with good sporting facilities.
⤷ *Exit Milan/Brenner motorway at Val Pusteria. Through Brunico and Valdaora to Rasun.*
All year 2.7HEC ▦ ⚓ ⚶ ⋔ ⌂ ♥ ⚘ ✕ ⊙ ♨ ⌀ ☵ ⟲ P ⊞ lau
Prices: pitch 30000-39500 (incl 2 persons)

▶ RHÊMES ST GEORGES AOSTA

Val di Rhêmes ☎ 0165 907648
Jun-10 Sep 18HEC ▦ ⚘ ⋔ ⌂ ♥ ✕ ⊙ ♨ ⌀ ☵ ☎ ☭ A ⟲ R ⚐ ⊞ lau

▶ RIVA DEL GARDA TRENTO

Bavaria viale Rovereto 100 ☎ 0464 552524
⤷ *On SS240 towards Rovereto.*
Apr-Oct 0.6HEC ▦ ⋮⋮ ⚘ ⋔ ⌂ ♥ ✕ ⊙ ♨ ⟲ L ⚐ ⊞ ➡ ⚘ ☵
Prices: ⬆10000 pitch 12000

Monte Brione via Brione 32 ☎ 0464 520885
This site is at the foot of a hill covered with olive trees with good sports facilities.

⤷ *250mtrs from San Nicolo' tourist centre.*
Etr-early Oct 3.3HEC ▦ ♥ ⋔ ⌂ ♥ ⌂ ✕ ⊙ ♨ ⟲ P ⚐ lau ➡ ✕ ⌀ ☵ ⟲L ⊞
Prices: ⬆12500 pitch 18500

▶ RIVOLTELLA BRESCIA

San Francesco strada Vicinale San Francesco ☎ 030 9110245
This well-kept site is divided into many sections by drives, vineyards and orchards and has a private gravel beach.
⤷ *At Km268 on SSN11.*
Apr-Sep 10.4HEC ▦ ♥ ⋔ ⌂ ♥ ⌂ ✕ ⊙ ♨ ⌀ ⟲ LP ⚐ lau ➡ ☵
Prices: ⬆8450-12300 pitch 18000-26200

▶ ST-ANSELME AOSTA

Village la Grolla Challand ☎ 0125 929587
⤷ *Access via SS506 Km116.*
All year 1.3HEC ▦ ⚘ ⋔ ⌂ ♥ ✕ ⊙ ♨ ☵ ☭ ⟲ R lau ➡ ⚘ ✕ ⌀ ⊞

▶ SALLE, LA AOSTA

Green Park via dei Romani 4 ☎ 0165 861300
Partly terraced site in a shaded location with good, modern facilities.
⤷ *Access via SS26.*
All year 7HEC ▦ ⚓ ♥ ⋔ ⌂ ♥ ⌂ ✕ ⊙ ♨ ☵ ⟲ P ⚐ lau ➡ ⚘ ⌀ ⟲R ⊞

▶ SAN ANTONIO DI MAVIGNOLA TRENTO

Faé ☎ 0465 507178
Situated in famous winter skiing region of Madonna di Campiglio. Good base for climbing in Brenta mountain range. On four gravel terraces, and alpine meadow in hollow next to SS239.
Camping Card Compulsory.
15 Jun-Sep & Dec-Apr 2.1HEC ▦ ⚘ ⋔ ⌂ ♥ ✕ ⊙ ♨ ⌀ ⚐ lau ➡ ⚘ ✕
Prices: ⬆13000 pitch 14000-15000

▶ SAN FELICE DEL BENACO BRESCIA

Europa-Silvella via Silvella ☎ 0365 651095
One site separated in two parts by the joint approach road. The beach is situated about 80m below.
⤷ *Signposted.*
19 Apr-30 Sep 7.4HEC ▦ ♥ ⋔ ⌂ ♥ ⌂ ✕ ⊙ ♨ ⌀ ☎ ☭ ⟲ LP ⚐ ⊞ lau

Fornella via Fornella 1 ☎ 0365 62294
A quiet site in an ideal location on the shore of Lake Garda.
⤷ *Signposted from SS572 (Salo-Desenzano).*
May-26 Sep 7HEC ▦ ⚘ ⋔ ⌂ ♥ ⌂ ✕ ⊙ ♨ ⌀ ☎ A ⟲ LP ⚐ ⊞ lau ➡ ⚘
Prices: ⬆7500-10700 pitch 16000-21500

Gardiola via Gardiola 36 ☎ 0365 559240
A terraced site with a wide variety of good facilities on the shore of Lake Garda.
⤷ *S of San Felice del Benaco off SS572.*
26 Mar-Sep 0.4HEC ▦ ⚘ ⋔ ⌂ ♥ ⌂ ⊙ ♨ ⌀ ☵ ☭ ⟲ L ⚐ lau ➡ ⚘ ✕ ⟲P
Prices: ⬆6000-10000 pitch 16000-27000

Ideal Molino ☎ 0365 62023
Situated right beside Lake Garda amid beautiful scenery. Charming and quiet site 1km from S. Felice. On the beach there is a pier and boat moorings. Pedal boats can be hired for lake trips.
15 Mar-28 Sept 1.7HEC ▦ ♥ ⋔ ⌂ ♥ ⌂ ✕ ⊙ ♨ ☎ ☭ ♨ ⟲ L ⚐ ⊞ ✍ lau ➡ ⌀ ☵
Prices: ⬆11300 pitch 22000

Weekend via Vallone della Selva 2 ☎ 0365 43712
A quiet family site with modern facilities, situated in a olive
grove overlooking Lake Garda.
↪ *Exit A4 at Desenzano following road to Cisano. Signposted
S.Felice D/B.*
25 Apr-25 Sept 9HEC ⬜ ⚒ ⟡ ▙ ⚻ ✗ ⊙ ☻ 🚿 ☕ ▲ ⟑ P ☎
⊞ lau ➡ ⊘ ♨ ⟑L

▶ **SAN LORENZEN** BOLZANO

Wildberg ☎ 0474 474080
All year 1.2HEC ⬜ 🌿 ⟡ ▙ ⟡ ⊙ 🚿 ⊘ ♨ ☕ ⟑ PR ☎ ⊞ lau
➡ ▙ ✗

▶ **SAN MARTINO DI CASTROZZA** TRENTO

Sass Maor via Laghetto 46 ☎ 0439 68347
A winter sports site in a beautiful mountain setting.
↪ *From Trento travel to Ora, Cavalese and S.Martino di
Castrozza.*
All year 0.2HEC ⟡ ▙ ⚻ ✗ ⊙ 🚿 ⊘ 🖳 lau ➡ ⟑LR ⊞
Prices: ♠10000-15000 🚐18000-25000 ▲10000-15000

▶ **SAN PIETRO DI CORTENO GOLGI** BRESCIA

Villaggio Aprica via Nazionale 507 ☎ 0342 710001
A small natural park ideal for winter skiing and summer
walking.
↪ *On SS39 (Aprica-Edolo).*
All year 2.1HEC ⬜ ⚒ ⟡ ▙ ⚻ ✗ ⊙ 🚿 ⊘ ☕ 🚐 ⟑ LPR ☎ lau
➡ ⊞
Prices: ♠8000-10000 pitch 9200-19000

▶ **SARRÈ** AOSTA

International Touring ☎ 0165 257061 & 35187
Flat, wooded site set among the highest mountains in
Europe.
↪ *4km W of Aosta on SS26.*
15 May-15 Sep 6HEC ⬜ ⚒ ⟡ ▙ ⚻ ✗ ⊙ 🚿 ⊘ ☕ 🚐 ⟑ PR ☎
⊞ lau
Prices: ♠7600-7900 🚐4600-4800 🚐6600-6800 ▲5500-6800

Monte Bianco Fraz St Maurice 3 ☎ 0165 257523
↪ *Access via SS26 towards Aosta and Courmayer.*
Apr-Sep 7.5HEC ⬜ ⚒ 🌿 ⊙ 🚿 ☎ 🖳 ⊞ ➡ ▙ ✗ ⊘ ♨
Prices: ♠6500-7000 🚐3500-3800 🚐5500-5900 ▲5500-5900

▶ **SORICO** COMO

Au Lac De Como via C-Battisti 18 ☎ 0344 84035
The well-kept site lies on the right of the River Mera as it
flows into Lake Como.
↪ *Turn off the SS340d at Km25 near TOTAL petrol station
and drive 200m towards the lake.*
All year 17HEC ⬜ ⚒ 🌿 ▙ ⚻ ✗ ⊙ 🚿 ⊘ ♨ 🚐 ⟑ LR ⊞ lau
Prices: ♠5000-10000 pitch 7500-15000

▶ **TORBOLE** TRENTO

Porto ☎ 0464 505891
A new site with modern facilities, situated in a quiet position
near the lake. Ideal for sports and families.
↪ *At Torbole join SS240 from there it is signposted.*
Apr-3 Nov 1HEC ⬜ ⚒ 🌿 ⚻ ✗ ⊙ 🚿 ⟑ R ☎ lau ➡ ▙ ✗ ⊘ ♨
⟑LPR ⊞
Prices: ♠9000-10000 pitch 13000-15000

▶ **TORRE DANIELE** TORINO

Mombarone via Nazionale 54 ☎ 0125 757907
↪ *13km N of Ivrea on SS26. Very close to River.*
All year 1.2HEC ⬜ ⚒ 🌿 ⊙ 🚿 ☕ 🚐 ⟑ PR ☎ lau ➡ ▙ ✗
⊘
Prices: ♠5000 🚐2000 🚐5000 ▲4000

▶ **TOSCOLANO MADERNO** BRESCIA

Chiaro di Luna via Statale 218 ☎ 0365 641179
Apr-Sep 9HEC ⬜ ⚒ ▙ ⚻ ✗ ⊙ 🚿 ♨ ⟑ L 🖳 lau ➡ ✗
Prices: ♠7000-8500 pitch 12000-16000

▶ **VALNONTEY** AOSTA

Lo Stambecco ☎ 0165 74152
25 May-20 Sep 1.6HEC ⬜ ⚒ 🌿 ⟡ ⊙ 🚿 ⊘ ♨ ☎ lau ➡ ▙ ✗
⊞
Prices: ♠8000 🚐4000 🚐7000

▶ **VIPITENO** BOLZANO

Sadobre Autoporto ☎ 0472 721793
In a wooded, mountain setting.
↪ *Access via A22.*
All year 1HEC ⊘ ⚒ 🌿 ▙ ⚻ ✗ ⊙ 🚿 ☎ ➡ ⟑R ⊞

▶ **VIVERONE** VERCELLI

Rocca via Lungo Lago 35 ☎ 0161 987479
Apr-Sep 1HEC ⬜ ⚒ 🌿 ▙ ⚻ ✗ ⊙ 🚿 ⟑ P ☎ lau ➡ ⊘ ♨
⟑L
Prices: ♠8000 pitch 11000

▶ **VOLS** BOLZANO

Seiseralm St Konstantin 16 ☎ 0471 706459
The site is avaliable all year round for skiers and climbers.
Horse riding/trekking is a major activity.
↪ *From Bolzano motorway site is signposted from Fie.*
All year 2.5HEC ⬜ ⚒ ⊘ ⟡ 🌿 ▙ ⚻ ✗ ⊙ 🚿 ⊘ ☕ 🚐 ☎ lau ➡ ⟑L
Prices: ♠9000-11500 pitch 11000-15000

• • • ● **VENICE/NORTH** ● • • •

Venice dominates this region. It is an ancient centre of arts and trade and is unique in having waterways as roads and many architectural splendours, as well as producing fine glass and lace and, due to the revival of the carnival, masks. Venetian influence is apparent in towns like Udine with its Piazza della Libertà surrounded by Renaissance buildings or at Treviso, with its own canal system, and where concerts and theatre performances are held in the main square. Echoes of Rome can be found in Palladio's architecture in Vicenza or in Verona where the amphitheatre is the setting for the July-September opera season.

Art lovers can enjoy Giotto's frescoes and Donatello's sculptures in the university town of Padua, and at Rovigo are paintings by Bellini and Tiepolo.

Trieste, on the Yugoslav border is the major port and contains handsome 19th-century architecture and there are attractive villages like Bellini on the southern edge of the Dolomites built overlooking two rivers. Vineyards and wineries (Soave and Valpolicella) welcome tourists.

....

▶ **ARSIE** BELLUNO
Gajole Loc Soravigo ☎ 0439 58505
➲ *Access from SS50 bis.*
Apr-Sep 15HEC ⊞ ♣ ℟ ⅃ ⅄ ⊙ ◻ ⌀ ♨ ⌂ ⅂ ⌂ lau
Prices: ⅄4200-4500 pitch 9500-10500

▶ **ASIAGO** VICENZA
Ekar ☎ 0424 455157
20 May-Sep & 15 Nov-15 Apr 3.5HEC ⊞ ♣ ℟ ⅃ ⅄ ⊙ ◻
⌀ ♨ ⌂ ⊞ lau
Prices: ⅄5000 pitch 14000

▶ **AURISINA** TRIESTE
Imperial Aurisina Cave 55 ☎ 040 200459
➲ *Access via SS14 in Sistiana-Aurisina direction.*
25 May-15 Sep 1.5HEC ⊞ ♣ ℟ ⅃ ⌀ ◻ ⌀ ⅂ P ⌂ ⊞ ♣ ✗
Prices: ⅄5500-8500 ⌘5500-7500 ⌘5500-7500 ▲5500-7500

▶ **BARDOLINO** VERONA
Continental ☎ 045 7210192
A pleasant site directly on the lake with good, modern facilities.
Apr-Sep 3.5HEC ⊞ ♣ ℟ ⅃ ⅄ ⊙ ◻ ⌀ ⌂ ⅂ ⅂ ⌂ ⊞ lau
Prices: ⅄7000-9500 pitch 13000-20000

Rocca S Pietro ☎ 045 7211111
Subdivided site in slightly sloping grassland broken up by rows of trees. Separated from the lake by a public path (no cars). Part of site on the other side of the main road is terraced amongst vines and olives with lovely view of lake.
➲ *Below the SS249 at Km40/IV*
May-28 Sep 80HEC ⊞ ♣ ℟ ⅃ ⅄ ⊙ ◻ ⌂ ⅂ LP ⌂ ⊞ lau
♣ ⌀
Prices: ⅄7000-9500 pitch 13000-20000

▶ **BIBIONE** VENEZIA
Villagio Turistico Internazionale via Colonie 2 ☎ 0431 439191
Mostly sandy terrain under pine trees. Some meadowland with a few deciduous trees. Wide sandy beach. Tennis court.
➲ *Access is well signed along approach.*
23 Apr-23 Sep 13HEC ⊞ ⁞⁞⁞ ⌀ ♣ ℟ ⅃ ⅄ ⊙ ◻ ⌀ ♨
⅂ PS ⌂ ⊞ lau
Prices: ⅄9000-14000 pitch 20000-34000

▶ **BRENZONE** VERONA
Primavera via Benaco 5 ☎ 045 7420421
Small site on the shore of Lake Garda.
Apr-10 Oct 0.8HEC ⊞ ♣ ℟ ⅃ ⅄ ✗ ⊙ ◻ ⌀ ♨ ⌂ ⅂ ⌂ lau
♣ ✗ ⊞
Prices: ⅄8000-9000 pitch 13000-15000

▶ **CA'NOGHERA** VENEZIA
Alba d'Oro via Triestina 214/B ☎ 041 5415102
On level ground directly on the lagoon with good, modern facilities including moorings for small boats. Regular bus service to Venice.
➲ *Access from SS14.*
15 Mar-31 Aug 5HEC ⊞ ♣ ℟ ⅃ ⅄ ✗ ⊙ ◻ ⌀ ♨ ⌂ ▲ ⅂ PR
⌂ lau
Prices: ⅄8000-9000 ⌘5000-6000 ⌘14000-16000 ▲6000-8000

▶ **CAORLE** VENEZIA
Falconera ☎ 0421 84282
Level site partially on sandy meadowland under tall poplars on the Porto di Falconera.
➲ *E on riverside road to Pizzeria Capri, then turn seawards.*
May-15 Sep 2.9HEC ⊞ ⁞⁞⁞ ♣ ℟ ⅃ ⅄ ✗ ⊙ ◻ ⌀ ♨ ⌂ ⌂ ♣
⅂ S ⊞

San Francesco via Selva Rosata ☎ 0421 299333
This generously laid-out site, on level lawns with shady poplars, lies in the midst of a holiday village.
➲ *Follow signs from Caorle for access.*
May-Sep 32HEC ⊞ ⁞⁞⁞ ♣ ℟ ⅃ ⅄ ✗ ⊙ ◻ ⌀ ♨ ⌂ ⌂ ⅂ PS
⌂ lau

▶ **CASSONE** VERONA
Bellavista ☎ 045 7420244
In a fine position in an olive grove overlooking Lake Garda with modern sanitary installations. Access to the lake is by an underpass and good watersports facilities are available.
All year 27HEC ⊞ ♣ ℟ ⅃ ⅄ ✗ ⊙ ◻ ⌀ ♨ ⌂ ⌂ ⌂ ⅂ ⌂ ⊞
⌀ lau ♣ ⅂ PR

▶ **CASTELLETTO DI BRENZONE** VERONA
Maior Loc Croce ☎ 045 7430333
A comfortable, modern site in a pleasant, quiet location.
Etr-10 Oct 8HEC ⊞ ♣ ℟ ⅃ ⅄ ✗ ⊙ ◻ ⌀ ♨ ⌂ ⌂ lau ♣ ✗
⅂ L ⊞
Prices: ⅄8000-9500 pitch 15000-19000

San Zeno via A.Vespucci 91 ☎ 045 7930231
Situated only a few metres from the lake surrounded by hundred year old olive groves.
➲ *Exit the southbound motorway from Rovereto at Trento. The site is 10km S of Malcesine.*
May-Sep 1.4HEC ⊞ ♣ ℟ ⅃ ⅄ ✗ ⊙ ◻ ⌀ ♨ ⌂ ⌂ ⌂ P ⊞ ♣ ✗ ⅂ L
Prices: ⅄6800-9000 pitch 11500-14500

▶ **CAVALLINO** VENEZIA
Cavallino via delle Batterie 164 ☎ 041 966133
In a pinewood close to the sea with plenty of recreational facilities.
Apr-Sep 8HEC ⊞ ♣ ℟ ⅃ ⅄ ✗ ⊙ ◻ ⌀ ♨ ⌂ ⌂ ⅂ PS ⌂ ⊞ ⌀ lau
Prices: ⅄5700-11000 pitch 13000-28000

Europa via Fausta 332 ☎ 041 968069
On grassland reaching to the sea, with some poplars.
Lunchtime siesta 13.00-15.00 hrs.
➲ *Well signposted on Punta Sabbioni road.*
Apr-Sep 11HEC ⊞ ⁞⁞⁞ ♣ ℟ ⅃ ⅄ ✗ ⊙ ◻ ⌀ ♨ ⌂ ⌂ ⌂ ⅂ S ⌂
lau
Prices: ⅄5500-10000 pitch 12000-25000

Italy via Fausta 272 ☎ 041 968090
Small family-type campsite 6km from Lido di Jesolo on a peninsula. Venice can be reached by public ferry.
⮑ *Brennero/Venezia motorway. Then follow signs for Jesolo-Cavallino.*
Etr-Sep 3.9HEC ⸬ ♣ ⋔ ⛱ ⛨ ✗ ⊙ ☒ ⌀ ⛺ ⛽ ⚓ PS ☎ ⚘ lau ♦ ⊞
Prices: ⚑6500-10500 pitch 12000-25000

Joker via Fausta 318 ☎ 041 5370766
Between coastal road and the sandy beach with tall poplars. Partially subdivided.
May-Sep 4.4HEC ⸬ ♣ ⋔ ⛱ ⛨ ✗ ⊙ ☒ ⌀ ⛺ ⛽ ⚓ PS ☎ ⊞ ⚘ lau

Residence via F-Baracca 47 ☎ 041 968027
Well laid out site on level, wooded grassland, by a sandy beach, between Jesolo and Cavallino. Lunchtime siesta 13.00-15.00 hrs.
⮑ *Signposted.*
24 Apr-24 Sep 7HEC ⸬ ♣ ⋔ ⛱ ⛨ ✗ ⊙ ☒ ⛽ ⚓ PRS ☎ ⊞ ⚘ lau ♦ ⌀ ♨
Prices: ⚑6200-11900 pitch 13000-27500

Sant' Angelo via F-Baracca 63 ☎ 041 968882
A large beach site decorated by trees and flower beds. Good entertainment, sports and eating facilities.
⮑ *Outside Venice follow signs for Caposile and Jesolo. Crossing the bridge just after Lido di Jesolo turn right and follow road round to coast.*
May-25 Sep 20HEC ⸬ ♣ ⋔ ⛱ ⛨ ✗ ⊙ ☒ ⌀ ⛺ ⛽ ⚓ ⛺ PS ☎ ⚘ lau ♦ ⛱ ⛨ ✗ ♨
Prices: ⚑6300-12500 pitch 29500-31000

Silva via F-Baracca 53 ☎ 041 968087
The site lies on sand and grassland and is located between road and beach, divided by a vineyard. The section of site near the beach is quiet.
15 May-15 Sep 3.3HEC ⸬ ♣ ⋔ ⛱ ⛨ ✗ ⊙ ☒ ⌀ ⛽ ⚓ S ☎ lau
Prices: ⚑6000-9000 ⛺3000-5000 ⛽13000-20000 ⚑12000-18000

Union-Lido via Fausta 258 ☎ 041 968080
This large site lies on a long stretch of land next to a 1km-long beach. Separate section for tents and caravans. Minimum stay during peak period is one week. Ideal for families.
⮑ *From Tarvisio follow motorway via Udine, San Dona di Piave then is signposted to Jesolo and Cavallino.*
May-Sep 60HEC ⸬ ♣ ⋔ ⛱ ⛨ ✗ ⊙ ☒ ⌀ ⛺ ⛽ ⚓ PS ☎ ⊞ ⚘ lau
Prices: ⚑9400-13000 pitch 16500-33000

Villa al Mare via del Faro 12 ☎ 041 968066
Level site divided into plots on a peninsula behind the lighthouse. Direct access to a long, sandy beach.
May-25 Sep 2.2HEC ⸬ ♣ ⋔ ⛱ ⛨ ✗ ⊙ ☒ ⛺ ⚓ S ☎ ⊞ ⚘ lau
Prices: ⚑6000-10500 pitch 12000-26000

▶ CHIOGGIA VENEZIA

Miramare via A-Barbarigo 103 ☎ 041 490610
Longish site reaching as far as the beach, clean and well-maintained.
⮑ *Access from Strada Romeo (SS309) in direction of Chioggia Sottomarina, turn right on reaching beach and continue 500m.*
May-20 Sep 4HEC ⸬ ⸬ ♣ ⋔ ⛱ ⛨ ✗ ⊙ ☒ ⛺ ⚓ PS ☎ ⊞ ⚘ lau

Villaggio Turistico Isamar via Isamar 9, Isolaverde ☎ 041 498100
The site lies on level grassland at the mouth of the River Etsch. Shade is provided by high poplars. Good beach.
⮑ *Access via the SS309. Caravans are advised to approach via Km84/VII near the Brenta village.*
8 May-19 Sep 33HEC ⸬ ♣ ⋔ ⛱ ⛨ ✗ ⊙ ☒ ⌀ ⛺ ⛽ ⚓ PRS ☎ ⊞ ⚘ lau
Prices: ⚑5300-15000 pitch 8000-35000

See advertisement under Colour Section

▶ CHIOGGIA SOTTOMARINA VENEZIA

Atlanta via Barbarigo 73 ☎ 041 491311
A woodland site directly on the seafront, less than 1km to Venice.
⮑ *W of town centre towards the beach.*
May-14 Sep 7HEC ⸬ ♣ ⋔ ⛱ ⛨ ✗ ⊙ ☒ ⌀ ♨ ⚓ PRS ☎ ⚘ lau ♦ ⛱ ⛨ ✗ ♨ ⚓ R ⊞

Oasi via A-Barbarigo 147 ☎ 041 490801
A well equipped site situated on a wooded peninsula near the mouth of the Brenta River with a wide private beach.
⮑ *W of town centre towards the river and the beach.*
All year 3HEC ⸬ ⸬ ♣ ⋔ ⛱ ⛨ ✗ ⊙ ☒ ⌀ ♨ ⛺ ⛽ ⚓ PRS ☎ lau ♦ ⊞
Prices: ⚑7000-11000 ⛽13000-24000 pitch 13000-24000

▶ CISANO VERONA

Cisano via Peschiera ☎ 045 6229098
Quiet, partly terraced site beside Lake Garda with good watersports facilities and entertainment.
⮑ *AFFI exit on Brenner-Verona motorway, access 4km further.*
20 Mar-4 Oct 14HEC ⸬ ♣ ⋔ ⛱ ⛨ ✗ ⊙ ☒ ⌀ ♨ ⛺ ⛽ ⚓ LP ☎ ⊞ ⚘ lau
Prices: ⚑6500-11000 pitch 15000-22000

San Vito via Pralesi 3 ☎ 045 6229026
A tranquil and shady site with many modern facilities.
⮑ *Off the Brennero motorway it is signposted to the south of Cisano.*
20 Mar-5 Oct 5HEC ⸬ ♣ ⋔ ⛱ ⛨ ✗ ⊙ ☒ ⌀ ⛺ ⛽ ⚓ LP ☎ ⊞ ⚘ lau

▶ CORTINA D'AMPEZZO BELLUNO

Cortina via Campo 2 ☎ 0436 867575
This site lies amongst pine trees, several hundred metres away from the edge of town, off the Dolomite road towards Belluno.
⮑ *Turn off road and drive 1km to the campsite which is situated by a small river.*
All year 45HEC ⸬ ⸬ ♣ ⋔ ⛱ ⛨ ✗ ⊙ ☒ ⌀ ⚓ P ☎ ⊞ lau
Prices: ⚑7000-10500 pitch 11500-17500

Dolomiti via Campo di Sotto ☎ 0436 2485
The site is beautifully situated on grassland with pine trees in a hollow, not far from the Olympic ski-jump.
⮑ *For access, follow the directions for Camping Cortina. The camp is then 500m further on 2.7km S of Cortina.*
20 May-20 Sep 5.4HEC ⸬ ⊕ ⋔ ⛱ ⛨ ✗ ⊙ ☒ ⌀ ♨ ⚓ PR ☎ lau ♦ ✗ ⚓L
Prices: ⚑7000-13000 pitch 9000-17000

Olympia Fiames 1 ☎ 0436 5057
A very beautiful site set in the centre of the centre of the magnificent Dolomite landscape.
⮑ *It lies N of town off the SS51.*
All year 4HEC ⸬ ⊕ ⋔ ⛱ ⛨ ✗ ⊙ ☒ ⌀ ⛺ ⛽ ⚓ R ☎ ⊞ lau ♦ ⚓L ⊞
Prices: ⚑7000-13000 ⛺9000-17000 ⚑9000-17000

Rocchetta via Campo 1 ☎ 0436 5063
In beautiful wooded surroundings.
➩ *Access S from Cortina via SS51.*
Jun-20 Sep 2.5HEC ⚏ ⬛ 👍 🏪 ⛱ ♀ ✕ ⊙ 🗗 ∅ 🏛 ⚒ R 🏦 lau ➡
✕ ⚒L

▶ **DUINO-AURISINA** TRIESTE

At **SISTIANA**

Marepinetá ☎ 040 299264
A modern site in a pleasant wooded location with a wide
range of recreational facilities. Free bus service to the beach.
➩ *On SS14 near the harbour and beach. Highway A4 Venice-
Trieste, exit Duino 1km on left.*
May-Sep 10.8HEC ✿ ♀ ⬛ 👍 🏪 ⛱ ♀ ✕ ⊙ 🗗 ∅ 🏛 🏠 ⚒ ⚒ P 🏦 ⊞
⚒ lau ➡ ∅ ⚒ ⚒S
Prices: ⚑5500-10000 pitch 10000-23000

▶ **ERACLEA MARE** VENEZIA

Porto Felice viale dei Fiori 15 ☎ 0421 66411
A well equipped family village site separated from the beach
by a pinewood. A wide variety of recreational facilities are
available.
8 May-20 Sep 17.9HEC ⚏ ♀ ⬛ 👍 🏪 ⛱ ♀ ✕ ⊙ 🗗 ∅ 🏛 🏠 ⚒ ⚒
PS 🏦 ⚒ lau
Prices: ⚑7500-12500 pitch 15500-29500

 See advertisement under Colour Section

▶ **FUSINA VENEZIA** VENEZIA

Fusina via Moranzani 79 ☎ 041 5470055
This well-equipped site is ideal for those visiting Venice and
the Venetian Lagoon.
All year 6HEC ⚏ ♀ ⬛ 👍 🏪 ⛱ ♀ ✕ ⊙ 🗗 ∅ 🏛 ⚒ 🅰 🏦 ⊞ lau
Prices: ⚑10000 pitch 20000

camping fusina venezia

Via Moranzani, 79 • I-30030 Fusina (VE)
Tel. 0039/0415470055 • Fax 0039/0415470050
Http://www.camping-fusina.com
E-mail: info@camping-fusina.com

Campsite at the mouth of the Brenta facing
Venice. All year round steamboat service to
the city centre.
Centre for trips to the Venetian lagoons, the Islands of Murano, Burano
and Torcello and the wonderful villas of Palladio on the banks of the
Brenta.
During the summer fast motor boat service to the beaches of Lido di
Venezia and Alberoni. Ideal centre for visits to Padua, Basilica of St.
Antonius, Euganei Hills, Treviso and Verona.
Campsite plus 500 beds in bungalows or caravans.
Tickets booked for ferries to Greece, Croatia, Slovenia and Turkey
— Campsite has its own harbour basin with 500 moorings
— Internet service for campsite visitors
— Bar with international TV programme

Open throughout
the year

▶ **GEMONA DEL FRIÚLI** UDINE

Ai Pioppi via del Bersaglio 44 ☎ 0432 980358
Quiet, well equipped site in a pleasant mountain setting.
➩ *1km from town centre via N13.*
15 Mar-Oct 1HEC ⚏ ♀ ⬛ 🏪 ⛱ ✕ ⊙ 🗗 ∅ 🏛 🏠 ⚒ 🏦 lau ➡ ⚒
✕ ⚒R ⊞
Prices: ⚑6000-7000 ⚘4000-5000 ⚗8000-10000 ▲6000-7000

▶ **GRADO** GORIZIA

Europa ☎ 0431 80877
In level terrain under half grown poplars. Partially in shade
in pine forest.
➩ *On road to Monfalcone, 20km from Palmanova via
Aquileia.*
10 Apr-20 Sep 22HEC ⚏ ⚏ ♀ ⬛ 👍 🏪 ⛱ ✕ ⊙ 🗗 ∅ 🏛 🏠 ⚒
⚒ PS 🏦 🏦 ⊞ lau

Tenuta Primero Loc Primero ☎ 0431 81523
The site lies in extensive level grassland between the road and
the dam, which is 2m high along the narrow and level beach.
Tennis court.
➩ *Access from Monfalcone road. Signposted.*
12 May-13 Sep 20HEC ⚏ ♀ ⬛ 👍 🏪 ⛱ ✕ ⊙ 🗗 ∅ 🏛 ⚒ PS 🏦
⊞ ⚒ lau
Prices: ⚑10000-15000 pitch 20000-25000

▶ **IÉSOLO**

See JÉSOLO, LIDO DI

▶ **JÉSOLO, LIDO DI** VENEZIA

At **JÉSOLO PINETA**(6km E)

Malibu Beach viale Oriente 78 ☎ 0421 362212
➩ *From Venezia via Cavallino on coast road to Cortellazzo.*
15 May-15 Sep 10HEC ⚏ ⚏ ♀ ⬛ 👍 🏪 ⛱ ✕ ⊙ 🗗 ∅ 🏛 🏠 ⚒
⚒ PS ⊞ ⊞ ⚒ lau
Prices: ⚑8000-13000 pitch 18500-30000

Waikiki viale Oriente 144 ☎ 0421 980186
15 May-15 Sep 5.2HEC ⚏ ⚏ ♀ ⬛ 👍 🏪 ⛱ ✕ ⊙ 🗗 ∅ 🏛 🏠
⚒ PS 🏦 🏦 ⚒ lau ➡ ⚒R
Prices: ⚑6500-12000 pitch 12500-25000

At **PORTO DI PIAVE VECCHIA**(8km S)

Jesolo International via a da Giussano 1 ☎ 0421 971826
The site lies ob a sandy beach, beside the coast road. It has
modern facilities and is ideal for a relaxing beach holiday.
➩ *Signposted from Cavallino. Opposite lighthouse.*
May-Sep 11HEC ⚏ ⚏ ♀ ⬛ 👍 🏪 ⛱ ✕ ⊙ 🗗 ∅ 🏛 ⚒ PS 🏦 ⊞
⚒ lau

▶ **LAZISE** VERONA

Ideal Loc Vanon ☎ 045 7580077
On the shore of Lake Garda with asphalt roads and access to
a safe, flat beach.
➩ *1km from the town centre near the Gardaland Amusement
Park.*
Etr-Sep 13HEC ⚏ ♀ ⬛ 👍 🏪 ⛱ ✕ ⊙ 🗗 ∅ 🏠 ⚒ ⚒ LP 🏦 ⊞ ⚒
lau ➡ 🏛

Parc Loc Sentieri ☎ 045 7580127
Well-kept, lakeside site off main road.
➩ *If approaching from Garda, the site is on S side of Lazise
just after turning for Verona.*
15 Mar-Oct 6HEC ⚏ ♀ ⬛ 🏪 ⛱ ✕ ⊙ 🗗 🏠 ⚒ ⚒ L 🏦 ⊞ lau
➡ ∅ 🏛
Prices: ⚑8000-10000 pitch 17000-23000

 See advertisement under Colour Section

Quercia ☎ 045 6470577
The site is divided into many large sections by tarred drives and lies on terraced ground that slopes gently down to the lake. There is a large private beach.
➲ *For access, turn off the main road SS49 at Km31/8 and drive for 400m.*
Apr-Sep 1.8HEC ▥ ⊞ 🏕 🛒 🍴 ✕ ☉ 🚽 🔊 🏪 ᗷ LP ☎ ⊞ lau

LIDO DI JÉSOLO
See JÉSOLO, LIDO DI

LIGNANO SABBIADORO UDINE
Sabbiadoro via Sabbiadoro 8 ☎ 0431 71455
May-Sep 13HEC ▥ ⋮⋮ ✦ 🏕 🛒 🍴 ✕ ☉ 🚽 🔊 🚿 🏪 🚻 ᗷ P
☎ ⊞ lau ✦ ᗷS
Prices: ★6500-12000 pitch 10500-19000

▶ MALCESINE VERONA
Claudia via Molini 2 ☎ 045 7400786
Flat grassy site only 30mtrs from the lake. Excellent facilities available, especially for water sports.
➲ *From Rome/Brennero motorway, continue via Trento, Arco, Torbole, and site is on outskirts of Malcesine.*
20 Mar-20 Oct 1HEC ▥ ⊞ 🏕 🛒 🍴 ✕ ☉ 🚽 🔊 ▲ ☎ ✦ 🛒
🛒 ✕ 🔊 ᗷL
Prices: ★8500-9500 pitch 14000-19000

▶ MALGA CIAPELA BELLUNO
Malga Ciapela Marmolada ☎ 0437 722064
A terraced site in tranquil wooded surroundings at the foot on Mt. Marmolada.
➲ *Take the Bozen exit off the Brenner/Verona motorway. Follow signs for Canazei, Malga Ciapela and finally the site, Marmolada.*
Jun-19 Sep & Dec-25 Apr 3HEC ▥ ♨ ⊞ 🏕 🛒 🍴 ☉ 🚽 🔊 🚿
ᗷ R ☎ lau ✦ ✕ ⊞
Prices: ★8000-10000 pitch 9000-12000

▶ MARGHERA VENEZIA
Jolly delle Querce via A-de-Marchi 7 ☎ 041 920312
The site lies on meadowland scattered with poplars.
➲ *For access, turn off into the Autostrada in Venezia in the direction of Chioggia on the SS309 and continue for 200m.*
Apr-Oct 3.6HEC ▥ ✦ 🏕 🛒 🍴 ✕ ☉ 🚽 🔊 🚿 🏪 🚻 ☎ ⊞ lau

▶ MASARÈ BELLUNO
Alleghe ☎ 0437 723737
Several terraces on a wooded incline below a road.
7 Jun-Sep & 7 Dec-1 May 2HEC ▥ ♨ ⊞ 🏕 🛒 ✕ ☉ 🚽 🔊 🚿
🔲 lau ✦ 🛒 ✕ ᗷLPR ⊞
Prices: ★10000-11000 🚐12000 ▲6000

▶ MESTRE VENEZIA
Venezia via Orlanda 8 ☎ 041 5312828
A well equipped site on the shore of the Lagoon close to the causeway with a regular bus service to Venice within easy reach.
15 Feb-Nov 1.8HEC ▥ ✦ 🏕 🛒 🍴 ✕ ☉ 🚽 🔊 🏪 ☎ lau
Prices: ★10000 pitch 16000

▶ MONFALCONE GORIZIA
Isola Panzano Lido via dei Bagni Nuova 171 ☎ 0481 411202
Well equipped family site close to the beach.
➲ *A4 (Venezia-Trieste) exit at Monfalcone/Lisert and follow signs for the sea. Site is signposted from coast.*
15 May-15 Sep 13HEC ▥ ✦ 🏕 🛒 🍴 ✕ ☉ 🚽 🔊 🚿 🏪 🚻 ᗷ S
☎ ⊞
Prices: ★9000-10000 🚐16000-18000 ▲16000-18000

CAMPING LIDO
I-37010 PACENGO (VR)
Tel: 0039/0457590611
Fax: 0039/0457590030
On the Verona side of Lake Garda. Right by the sea, private swimming pool. Well shaded site with pitches for tents and caravans. Brick built bungalow for hire.
Bungalows and mobile homes for letting

▶ MONTEGROTTO TERME PADOVA
Sporting Center ☎ 049 793400
A peaceful site in a pleasant setting in the Euganean hills with good facilities including a thermal treatment centre.
5 Mar-10 Nov 6.5HEC ▥ ⊞ 🏕 🛒 🍴 ✕ ☉ 🚽 ᗷ P ☎ lau ✦ 🛒 🔊
Prices: ★8800-12200 pitch 16500-22600

▶ ORIAGO VENEZIA
Serenissima via Padana 334 ☎ 041 920286
A well looked after site with shade provided by the local woodland. Local bus service every 20 minutes to Venice.
➲ *A4 to Venice, SS11 at Oriago.*
Etr-10 Nov 2HEC ▥ ✦ 🏕 🛒 🍴 ✕ ☉ 🚽 🔊 🏪 🚻 ᗷ R ☎ lau
Prices: ★10000 pitch 15000-18000

▶ PACENGO VERONA
Camping Lido via Peschiera 2 ☎ 045 7590611
Apr-Sep 10HEC ▥ ✦ 🏕 🛒 🍴 ✕ ☉ 🚽 🔊 🏪 ᗷ LP ☎ ⊞ lau

▶ PALAFAVERA BELLUNO
Palafavera ☎ 0437 788506
In a beautiful location in the heart of the Dolomites at an altitude of 1514mtrs. Good, modern sanitary installations and plenty of recreational facilities.
5HEC ▥ ⊞ 🏕 🛒 🍴 ✕ ☉ 🚽 🔊 🚿 ᗷ R ⊞ 🔲 ⊞ ⊘ lau
Prices: ★8000-10000 🚐10000-12000 ▲5000-6000

▶ PESCHIERA DEL GARDA VERONA
Bella Italia via Bella Italia 2 ☎ 045 6400688
Extensive lakeside site. No animals or motorcycles allowed.
➲ *Turn off Brescia road between Km276.2 and Km275.8 and head towards lake.*
20 Mar-3 Oct 20HEC ▥ ✦ 🏕 🛒 🍴 ✕ ☉ 🚽 🔊 🚿 🏪 🚻 ▲ ᗷ
P ☎ ⊞ ⊘ lau ✦ 🔊 ᗷLR
Prices: ★7000-12000 pitch 16000-23000

Bergamini via Bergamini 51 ☎ 045 7550283
Ideal for young families as site has two children's pools and extensive play areas.
➲ *Follow signs 'Porto Bergamini'.*
May-Sep 1.4HEC ▥ ✦ 🏕 🛒 🍴 ✕ ☉ 🚽 🏪 🚻 ᗷ LP ☎ ⊞ ⊘
lau ✦ 🔊
Prices: ★8000-12000 pitch 16000-23000

Garda via Marzan ☎ 045 7550540 & 7551899
A quiet, pleasant site with beach access on the shore of Lake Garda.
➲ *Near the town centre, 2km from Milan/Venice motorway exit.*

Apr-Sep 20.4HEC ▦ ♣ ⋔ 🏊 ⏺ ✗ ⊙ 🍴 ⌀ 🏕 ⌇ LP 🏪 ⊞ ⊘
lau ➧ 🛁 ⌇LR ⊞
Prices: ♦6000-11000 pitch 14000-24000

San Benedetto via Bergamini 14 ☎ 045 7550544
A family site in a fine position overlooking the lake.
Apr-Sep 22HEC ▦ ♣ ⋔ 🏊 ⏺ ✗ ⊙ 🍴 🏕 🏪 Å ⌇ LP 🏪 lau
➧ ⌀ 🛁
Prices: ♦5500-9200 pitch 11500-19700

▶ **PORTO SANTA MARGHERITA** VENEZIA

Pra'delle Torri ☎ 0421 299063
Extensive site on flat ground.
➲ *3km W at edge of beach.*
May-26 Sep 53HEC ▦ 🍴 ⋔ 🏊 ⏺ ✗ ⊙ 🍴 ⌀ 🏕 🏪 ⌇ PS 🏪
⊞ ⊘ lau
Prices: ♦5200-13500 🚐10500-29000 Å8500-26000

▶ **PUNTA SABBIONI** VENEZIA

Marina di Venezia via Montello 6 ☎ 041 5300955
Extensive, well-organised and well maintained holiday centre,
extremely well appointed, with ample shade by trees. A
section of the site is designated for dog owners, caravans and
tents.
➲ *Access from the coastal road, turn seawards about 500m
before the end then continue along narrow asphalt road. Well
signposted approach.*
Apr-Oct 80HEC ▦ ♣ ⋔ 🏊 ⏺ ✗ ⊙ 🍴 ⌀ 🏕 🏪 Å ⌇ PS 🏪 ⊞
lau ➧ 🛁

Miramare Lungomare D-Alighieri 29 ☎ 041 966150
In a magnificent location overlooking the lagoon.
27 Mar-18 Oct 1.8HEC ▦ 🍴 ⋔ 🏊 ⏺ ✗ ⊙ 🍴 ⌀ 🏕 ⊞ ⊘
lau ➧ ⌇S
Prices: ♦6500-8500 pitch 12500-21000

▶ **ROSOLINA MARE** ROVIGO

Margherita via Foci Adige 10 ☎ 0426 68212
A well equipped family site situated between the sea and a
pine wood in the Po Delta Park.
May-Sep 6.1HEC ▦ ⋮⋮ ♣ ⋔ 🏊 ⏺ ✗ ⊙ 🍴 ⌀ 🛁 🏕 ⌇ PS 🏪
⊞ lau
Prices: ♦7500-12000 🚗5000-7000 🚐10000-18500 Å10000-
18500

Rosapineta Strada Nord 24 ☎ 0426 68033
The site lies in the grounds of an extensive holiday camp.
Pitches for caravans and tents are separate.
➲ *Take Strada Romea towards Ravenna and drive to the
bridge over the River Adige. Continue for 800m, then turn off,
cross bridge and head towards Rosolina Mare and Rosapineta
(approx 8km).*
16 May-19 Sep 22HEC ▦ ⋮⋮ ♣ ⋔ 🏊 ⏺ ✗ ⊙ 🍴 ⌀ 🛁 🏕 🚐
⌇ PS ⊞ lau ➧ ⌇R
Prices: ♦6000-8700 🚐10900-15000 Å7300-10000

▶ **TREPORTI** VENEZIA

Cá Pasquali via Poerio 33 ☎ 041 966110
Sandy, meadowland site with poplar and pine trees.
➲ *Access from Cavallino-Punta Sabbioni coast road, along an
asphalt road for 400m.*
May-19 Sep 9HEC ⋮⋮ ♣ ⋔ 🏊 ⏺ ✗ ⊙ 🍴 🛁 🏕 🏪 Å ⌇ PS
🏪 ⊞ ⊘ lau ➧ ⌀ 🛁
Prices: ♦6500-10400 🚐11500-25000 pitch 11500-25000

Cá Savio via di Ca'Savio 77 ☎ 041 966017
A level site along the edge of the sea with private, sandy
beach. Separate pitches for caravans and tents.
➲ *From Cá Savio, at traffic lights, turn towards the sea and
continue for 500m to the beach.*

May-Sep 26.8HEC ⋮⋮ ♣ ⋔ 🏊 ⏺ ✗ ⊙ 🍴 🏕 🏪 ⌇ PS 🏪 ⊞ ⊘
➧ ⌀
Prices: ♦6900-10900 🚐13000-24500 Å13000-24500

Fiori via Pisani 52, Ca'vio ☎ 041 966448
The site stretches over a wide area of sand dunes and pine
trees with separate sections for caravans and tents.
➲ *From A4 at Venice follow coast road via Jesolo to Lideo del
Cavallino.*
May-Sep 10.6HEC ▦ ⋮⋮ ♣ ⋔ 🏊 ⏺ ✗ ⊙ 🍴 🏕 🏪 ⌇ PS 🏪
⊞ ⊘ lau ➧ ⌀ 🛁
Prices: ♦6900-13200 pitch 13000-31300

Mediterráneo via delle Batterie 38, Ca'Vio ☎ 041 966721
Slightly hilly grassland site with trees and sunshade roofs.
Lunchtime siesta 13.00-15.00 hrs.
➲ *Well signposted from Jesolo.*
May-Sep 17HEC ⋮⋮ ♣ ⋔ 🏊 ⏺ ✗ ⊙ 🍴 🏕 🏪 ⌇ PS 🏪 ⊞ ⊘
lau ➧ ⌀ 🛁 ⌇R
Prices: ♦5400-12600 Å8200-22500

Scarpiland via A-Poerio 14 ☎ 041 966488
In a beautiful area surrounded by a pinewood with direct
access to the beach and beautiful views of the sea.
22 Apr-19 Sep 4.5HEC ▦ ⋮⋮ ♣ ⋔ 🏊 ⏺ ✗ ⊙ 🍴 ⌀ 🛁 🏕 🚐
⌇ S 🏪 ⊞ lau

▶ **VERONA** VERONA

Romeo & Giulietta ☎ 045 8510243
Comfortable site in wooded surroundings. Shop open June
to September only.
➲ *Access via A22 exit 'Verona Nord' towards Borgo Trento.*
Mar-Nov 3.5HEC ▦ 🍴 ⋔ 🏊 ⊙ 🍴 ⌀ ⌇ P 🏪 lau ➧ ✗

▶ **VICENZA** VICENZA

Vicenza Strada Pelosa 239 ☎ 0444 582311
A modern, well-equipped site.
➲ *Access via A4 exit 'Vicenza-Est'.*
Apr-Sep 3HEC ▦ ⋔ 🏊 ⊙ 🍴 🏪 lau ➧ 🏊 ⏺ ✗ ⌀
Prices: ♦7600-10300 pitch 18000-24200

▶ **ZOLDO ALTO** BELLUNO

Pala Favera ☎ 0437 788506 & 789161
Site with some woodland, at the foot of Monte Pelmo.
Dec-Apr & Jun-Sep 5HEC ▦ ♦ 🍴 ⋔ 🏊 ⏺ ✗ ⊙ 🍴 ⌀ 🛁 ⌇ R
🏪 ⊘ lau ➧ ⊞

NORTH WEST/MED COAST

Liguria is known as the Italian Riviera, having many small harbours and a large and prosperous port, Genoa. Inland, the slopes of the Alps and Apennines, covered in lavender and herbs, provide the sheltering warmth in which carnations and chrysanthemums are grown as a major industry.
Tuscany stretches down the north western coast with medieval hill towns, towers and cultural centres such as Florence and Sienna, a medieval town famous for its fan shaped square Piazza del Campo and the Palio horse races run twice a year. Landscapes vary from oak and chestnut woods near the Apennines, tall cypresses and farmhouses, vineyards (red Chianti is produced here), olive groves, and the rugged hills of the Carrara marble. Jousting and archery competitions take place between rival towns and festivals are occasions for pageantry.
Elba, off the Tuscan coast, is a thriving holiday island with resorts around the coast, and inland you can find some attractive old villages with narrow alleyways or take the cable car from the village of Marciano to the top of Monte Capanne.

▷ **ALBENGA** SAVONA

Bella Vista Campochiesa, Reg Campore 23 ☎ 0182 540213
➲ *1km from Km613.5 on SS1.*
All year 0.8HEC ⸴⸴⸴ ⚐ ⟨ 🛒 ⟐ 🍴 ✕ ☉ 🛆 ⛺ 🚐 ⟐ P 🏧 ⊞ lau
🚻 ✕ ⌀ ⟐S
Prices: pitch 20000-38000 (incl 2 persons)

Green Village viale Che Guevara 14 ☎ 0182 559248
A modern site set among eucalyptus and pine trees with a private beach.
➲ *Signposted*
3 Apr-2 Oct & 23 Dec-7 Jan 1.8HEC ⸴⸴⸴ 🚻 ⟨ 🍴 ✕ ☉ 🛆 ⛺
⟐ S 🏧 lau 🚻 🛒 ⌀ ⟐PR ⊞
Prices: pitch 37000-70000 (incl 3 persons)

Roma Regione Foce ☎ 0182 52317
The site is divided into pitches and laid out with many flower beds.
➲ *N of bridge over Centa, turn left.*
Apr-Sep 0.8HEC ⸴⸴⸴⸴ ⸴⸴⸴ 🚻 ⟨ 🛒 ⟐ 🍴 ✕ ☉ 🛆 ⌀ ⛺ ⟐ RS 🏧 lau
🚻 ⸷ ⊞
Prices: ⚑7000-9500 pitch 17000-27000

▷ **ALBINIA** GROSSETO

Acapulco via Aurelia ☎ 0564 870165
Set on hilly terrain in pine woodland.
➲ *Take coast road from via Aurelia at Km155.*
15 May-15 Sep 2HEC ⸴⸴⸴ 🚻 ⟨ 🛒 ⟐ 🍴 ✕ ☉ 🛆 🚐 ⟐ S 🏧 ⊞
⸷ lau
Prices: ⚑6000-12000 🚐10000-19000 ▲10000-19000

Hawaii ☎ 0564 870164
The site lies in a pine forest on rather hilly ground.
➲ *Turn off via Aurelia at Km154/V and drive towards the sea.*
23 Apr-Sep 4HEC ⸴⸴⸴ 🚻 ⟨ 🛒 ⟐ 🍴 ✕ ☉ 🛆 ⸷ ⛺ ⟐ S
🏧 ⊞ ⸷ lau

International Argentario ☎ 0564 870302
Set in a pine forest on the shores of the Bay of Porto S Stefano. Mooring facilities.
Etr-Sep 10HEC ⸴⸴⸴⸴ 🚻 ⟨ 🛒 ⟐ 🍴 ✕ ☉ 🛆 ⌀ ⛺ 🚐 ⟐ S
🏧 ⊞ ⸷ lau

▷ **BIBBONA, MARINA DI** LIVORNO
See also Forte di Bibbona

Capannino via Cavalleggeri Sud 26 ☎ 0586 600252
Well tended park site in pine woodland with private beach.
➲ *On via Aurelia by Km272/VII turn towards sea.*
May-Sep 3HEC ⸴⸴⸴⸴ ⸴⸴⸴ 🚻 ⟨ 🛒 ⟐ 🍴 ✕ ☉ 🛆 ⌀ ⛺ ⸷ S 🏧 ⊞ ⸷
lau
Prices: ⚑8000-15600 🚗4000-5400 🚐18000-24400 ▲9000-12000

Casa di Caccia via del Mare 40, La Calafornia ☎ 0586 600000
A tranquil site by the sea direct access to a private beach.
➲ *From the A12 exit Rosignano and join SS follow signs for Cecina. 6km exit "La California" site in a further 3km south.*
Apr-15 Oct 3.5HEC ⸴⸴⸴ 🚻 ⟨ 🛒 ⟐ 🍴 ✕ ☉ 🛆 ⌀ ⛺ 🚐 ⸷ S 🏧 ⊞
⸷ lau

Free Beach via Cavalleggeri Nord 88 ☎ 0586 600388
Situated 300m from the sea through pine woods.
➲ *From the SS206 at Cecina follow signs to S. Guido.*
Etr-Sep 9HEC ⸴⸴⸴⸴ ⸴⸴⸴ ⚐ ⟨ 🛒 ⟐ 🍴 ✕ ☉ 🛆 ⛺ 🚐 ⸷ P ⟐ ⊞ lau
🚻 ⸷S
Prices: ⚑10000-16000 🚗5000 🚐15000-22000 ▲11000-15000

Il Gineprino via dei Platani ☎ 0586 600550
A modern site situated on the Tuscany coast and shaded by a pine wood. There are good recreational facilities and the beach is within 300mtrs.
➲ *Access via motorway exit 'La California' for Marina di Bibbona.*
Etr-Sep 1.5HEC ⸴⸴⸴⸴ 🚻 ⟨ 🛒 ⟐ 🍴 ✕ ☉ 🛆 ⌀ ⛺ 🚐 ▲ ⸷ P lau
🚻 ⸷S ⊞
Prices: ⚑8000-14000 pitch 14000-20000

▷ **BOGLIASCO** GENOVA

Genova Est via Marconi, Cassa ☎ 010 3472053
Quiet and shady site 1km from the sea. A free bus service operates from the site to the beaches.
➲ *Exit A12 at Nervi, then 8km east.*
Feb-Nov 1.2HEC ⸴⸴⸴⸴ 🚻 ⟨ 🛒 ⟐ 🍴 ✕ ☉ 🛆 ⌀ ⛺ 🚐 ▲ lau 🚻 ⸷
Prices: ⚑9000 🚗4500 🚐9000 ▲7500

▷ **BOTTAI** FIRENZE

Internationale Firenze via S Cristoforo 2 ☎ 055 2374704
Situated on the welcoming Florentine hills this site offers a restful atmosphere close to many historic places.
Apr-15 Oct 6HEC ⸴⸴⸴⸴ 🛆 ⚐ ⟨ 🛒 ⟐ 🍴 ✕ ☉ 🛆 ⛺ 🚐 ⸷ P 🏧
lau 🚻 ⸷LR ⊞
Prices: ⚑12000 🚐23000 ▲23000

▷ **CALENZANO** FIRENZE

Autosole via V-Emanuele 11 ☎ 055 8825576
All year 2.2HEC ⸴⸴⸴⸴ 🚻 ⟨ 🛒 ⟐ 🍴 ✕ ☉ 🛆 ⌀ ⛺ ⸷ P 🏧 ⊞ lau
🚻 ⸷

▷ **CAPANNOLE** AREZZO

Chiocciola via G-Cesare 14 ☎ 055 995776
15 Mar-30 Sept 1.5HEC ⸴⸴⸴⸴ 🚻 ⟨ 🛒 ⟐ 🍴 ✕ ☉ 🛆 ⌀ ⸷ ⛺ ▲ ⸷
PR 🏧 ⊞ lau 🚻 ⸷LR
Prices: ⚑11000 🚗4000 🚐12000 ▲10000

▷ **CASALE MARITTIMO** PISA

Valle Gaia ☎ 0586 681236
Site amongst pines and olive trees in a quiet rural location.
➲ *In Southern Cecina heading south from Livorno take the autostrada/superstrada then take 2nd exit for Cecina (Casale Marittimo - ignore first signpost for Cecina S Pietro). Camp is signposted.*

27 Mar-16 Oct 4HEC ⊞ ⌇ ⊞ ⌇ ⌇ × ⊙ ⊟ ⌀ ⌂ ⊞ ⌇ P ⌑
⊞ lau
Prices: ⚹8500-11500 pitch 14000-22000

CASTAGNETO CARDUCCI LIVORNO

Climatico Le Pianacce via Bolgherese ☎ 0565 763667
Terraced site on slopes of mountain in typical Tuscany
landscape, enhanced by site landscaping. Pleasant climate
due to height.
➲ *Turn off via Aurelia at Km344/VIII in direction of
Castagneto Carducci/Sassetta. In 3.2km to left in direction of
Bolgheri, in 500m turn right towards mountains.*
20 Mar-15 Oct 9HEC ⊞ ⌇ ⌇ ⊞ ⌇ ⌇ × ⊙ ⊟ ⌀ ⌂ ⌇ P ⌑ ⊞
lau ⌇ ⌂
Prices: ⚹7200-13000 pitch 12500-22000

CASTEL DEL PIANO GROSSETO

Amiata via Roma 15 ☎ 0564 955107
A grassland site with a separate section for dog owners.
➲ *On the outskirts of Castel del Piano, on the national road
(SS) 323, towards Arcidosso.*
All year 4.2HEC ⊞ ⌇ ⌇ ⊞ ⌇ ⌇ × ⊙ ⊟ ⌀ ⌂ ⌂ ⊞ ⌑ ⊞ lau ⌇
⌇P
Prices: ⚹7500-10600 pitch 7500-10600

CASTIGLIONE DELLA PESCAIA GROSSETO

Santa Pomata Strada della Rocchette ☎ 0564 941037
Site in hilly woodland terrain with some pitches amongst
bushes. Flat clean sandy beach.
➲ *Turn off the SS322 at Km20, then in direction of Le
Rocchette 4.5km NW and continue towards the sea for 1km to
site on left.*
Etr-20 Oct 6HEC ⊞ ⠿ ⌇ ⌇ ⊞ ⌇ ⌇ × ⊙ ⊟ ⌀ ⌂ ⌂ ⌂ ⌇ S
⌑ ⊞ lau
Prices: ⚹7000-12000 ⌷11000-20000 ▲11000-20000

CÉCINA, MARINA DI LIVORNO

Tamerici ☎ 0586 620629
Camping Card Compulsory.
All year 8.7HEC ⊞ ⌇ ⌇ ⊞ ⌇ ⌇ × ⊙ ⊟ ⌀ ⌂ ⌂ ⌑ ⊞ ⌇ lau ⌇
⌇PRS

CERIALE SAVONA

Baciccia via Torino 19 ☎ 0182 990743
An orderly site, lying inland off the via Aurelia, 500mtrs from
the sea.
➲ *Entrance 100m W of Km612/V.*
All year 1.2HEC ⊞ ⌇ ⌇ ⊞ ⌇ ⌇ × ⊙ ⊟ ⌀ ⌂ ⌇ P ⌑ lau ⌇
× ⌇ ⌇S
Prices: ⚹6400-11000 pitch 15800-28000

CERVO IMPERIA

Lino Via N Sauro 4 ☎ 0183 400087
A seaside site shaded by grape vines, which is clean and well
managed. There is a knee-deep lagoon suitable for children.
➲ *Turn off via Aurelia at Km637/V near the railway
underpass and follow via Nazionale Sauro towards sea.*
20 Mar-16 Oct 1.1HEC ⠿ ⌇ ⌇ ⊞ ⌇ ⌇ × ⊙ ⊟ ⌀ ⌂ ⌂ ⌑ ⊞
lau ⌇ ⌂ ⌇S
Prices: pitch 32000-42000 (incl 2 persons)

DEIVA MARINA LA SPEZIA

Costabella ☎ 0817 825343
Etr-Sep 1.5HEC ⊞ ⌇ ⌇ ⊞ ⌇ ⌇ × ⊙ ⊟ ⌂ ⌇ lau ⌇ ⌇S ⊞

La Sfinge Gea 5 ☎ 0187 825284
Partly terraced site in pleasant wooded surroundings. Ideal
for both nature lovers and families.
➲ *Access via A12 Genova-La Spezia.*

Camping LA SFINGE
Località Gea –
19013 Deiva Marina (SP)

The terraced site is located in an enchanting pine
wood between the famous "CINQUE TERRE" and
Portofino, only 3 km from the sea (free bus service).
Entertainment at the weekend in July and August.
Ideal for all types of water sports (diving, surfing,
fishing, rowing …). Good walking in the delightful
woods of Liguria.
For more information: Tel/Fax: 0187 82 54 64

Camping VILLAGGIO, Turistico ARENELLA

The site is located in a scenic peaceful valley about
1.5 kilometres from the sea. It offers its guests the
widest possible range of facilities such as hot water
for showers, wash basins, sinks for washing-up,
bidets, food market, bar, pizzeria and spaghetti
restaurant plus a children's play area and bowls,
free bus from campsite to the sea, place of interest
in the vicinity.
Camping Arenella, I-19013 Déiva Marina.
Tel: (0187) 825259 Fax: 815861

All year 1.8HEC ⊞ ⌇ ⌇ ⊞ ⌀ ⌂ ⌀ ⌇ ⌇ R ⌑ ⊞ ⌇ ⌇ ×
Prices: ⚹10000 ⌷10000 ▲10000

Villaggio Turistico Arenella Arenella ☎ 0187 825259
In a beautiful, quiet valley 1.5km from the sea with good
facilities.
➲ *Access via A12 (Genoa-La Spezia).*
Closed Nov 16.2HEC ⊞ ⌇ ⌇ ⊞ ⌇ ⌇ × ⊙ ⊟ ⌀ ⌂ ⌂ ⌑ lau ⌇
⌇S ⊞
Prices: ⚹10000-12000 ⌷3000 ⌷10000-12000 ▲10000-12000

ELBA, ISOLA D' LIVORNO

LACONA

Lacona Pineta Lacona CP 186 ☎ 0565 964322
Apr-Oct 4HEC ⊞ ⌇ ⌇ ⊞ ⌇ ⌇ × ⊙ ⊟ ⌀ ⌂ ⌇ S ⌑ ⊞ lau
Prices: ⚹10500-19000 ⌷3500-5000 ⌷14000-19500 ▲14000-
19500

NISPORTO

Sole e Mare ☎ 0565 934907
A well equipped, modern site in pleasant wooded
surroundings close to the beach. A wide variety of
recreational facilities are available.
➲ *From Portoferraio take Porto Azzurro road, then turn
towards Rio nell'Elba-Nisporto.*
Apr-15 Oct 1.5HEC ⊞ ⌇ ⌇ ⊞ ⌇ ⌇ × ⊙ ⊟ ⌀ ⌂ ⌂ ⌂ ⌇ S ⌑
lau
Prices: ⚹8000-19000 ⌷11500-30000 ▲11500-30000

ORTANO

Canapai Loc Ortano ☎ 0565 939165
Camping Card Compulsory.
Apr-Sep 4HEC ⊞ ⠿ ⌇ ⌇ ⊞ ⌇ ⌇ × ⊙ ⊟ ⌀ ⌂ ⌂ ⌇ P ⊞
⌇ ⌇S
⌇ ⌇S *Contd.*

Prices: ♦9000-18000 ➡2000-5000 ⬜10000-20000
▲8000-15000

OTTONE

Rosselba le Palme Ottone 3 ☎ 0565 933101
Pitches are on varying heights up from the beach. Shade is
provided by large palm trees.
➲ *8km from Portferraio around bay via Bivo Bagnaia.*
25 Apr-Sep 30HEC ⬛ ♦ ℝ ⅀ ⅂ ✕ ⊙ ◻ ∅ ⊞ ⬛ ⱬ PS 🏛 ⊞
lau ➡ ⱬS
Prices: ♦11000-20000 pitch 70000-120000

PORTO AZZURRO

Reale ☎ 0565 95678
Apr-Sep 2.5HEC ⬛ ♣ ℝ ⅀ ⅂ ✕ ⊙ ◻ ∅ ⬛ ⱬ S ⊞ lau

PORTOFERRAIO

Acquaviva Acquqviva ☎ 0565 930674
This seafront site is surrounded by trees and has excellent
facilities for scuba diving, watersports etc.
➲ *3km W of town.*
Etr-Oct 2HEC ⬛ ⋮⋮ ♦ ℝ ⅀ ⅂ ✕ ⊙ ◻ ∅ ⅂ ⬛ ⬛ ▲ ⱬ S
🏛 ◻ lau
Prices: ♦10000-19000 ➡3000-4000 ⬜11500-21000 ▲11500-
21000

Enfola Enfola ☎ 0565 939001
Located on the Isle of Elba, ideal for scuba-diving, sailing and
sunshine.
Apr-Sep 1HEC ⋮⋮ ♦ ℝ ⅀ ⅂ ✕ ⊙ ◻ ∅ ⬛ ⱬ S 🏛 lau
Prices: ♦11000-19500 ➡4000-4500 ⬜13500-22000 ▲11000-
20000

Scaglieri via Biodola 1, Casella Postale 158 ☎ 0565 969940
Sloping terraces 10mtrs from the sea make up this site.
Facilities such as tennis and golf are avaliable at the nearby
Hotel Hermitage.
➲ *The island is accessible by plane and ferry. The site is on
the north coast 7km from Portoferraio.*
Etr-Oct 1.7HEC ⋮⋮ ♦ ℝ ⅀ ⅂ ✕ ⊙ ◻ ∅ ⬛ ⱬ P ∅ lau
♦ ⱬS
Prices: ♦11000-21000 ➡4500 ⬜18000-23000 ▲17000-21000

FIÉSOLE FIRENZE

Panoramico via Peramonda 1 ☎ 055 599069
Site stretches over wide terraces on the Fiesole hillside
surrounded by a variety of tall evergreens.
➲ *Exit A1 at Firenze Sud, follow signs through the city to
Fiesole. Site is on SS Bolognese.*
All year 5.5HEC ⬛ ♦ ℝ ⅀ ⅂ ✕ ⊙ ◻ ∅ ⅂ ⬛ ⬛ 🏛 lau

FIGLINE VALDARNO FIRENZE

Norcenni Girasole via Norcenni 7 ☎ 055 959666
Terraced site on partial slope. Separate section for young
people.
➲ *3km W of village. Take Valdarno motorway exit and drive
N for 15km.*
20 Mar-Oct 11HEC ⬛ ∅ ♦ ℝ ⅀ ⅂ ✕ ⊙ ◻ ∅ ⬛ ⬛ ⱬ P 🏛
⊞ lau
Prices: ♦11800-13400 ➡6600-7600 ⬜10500-11800 ▲9700-
10800

FIRENZE (FLORENCE) FIRENZE

See also Troghi

At MARCIALLA

Toscana Colliverdi via Marcialla 349, Certaldo ☎ 0571
669334
A sloping, terraced site with good facilities, surrounded by
vineyards and olive groves.

➲ *Access via 'Firenze-Certosa' exit on Autostrada del Sole or
'Tavarnelle Valpesa' exit on Autostrada del Palio.*
20 Mar-10 Oct 2.2HEC ⬛ ⅃ ℝ ⊙ ◻ ∅ 🏛 ⊞ ♦ ⅀ ⅂ ✕

FLORENCE

See FIRENZE

FORTE DI BIBBONA LIVORNO

See also Bibbona, Marina di

Capanne via Aurelia ☎ 0586 600064
A pleasant family site situated in a spacious wooded park
amid magnificent Tuscan scenery. The pitches are well
defined and there is a wide variety of recreational facilities.
➲ *Access from Km273 via Aurelia travelling inland.*
May-10 Sep 6HEC ⬛ ♦ ℝ ⅀ ⅂ ✕ ⊙ ◻ ∅ ⬛ ⱬ P 🏛 ⊞
lau ♦ ⱬS
Prices: ♦6300-10900 ⬜12000-15000 ▲12000-15000

Esperidi ☎ 0586 600196
Site stretching to the sea with pines and other coniferous trees.
➲ *Turn off via Aurelia, at Km727.7.*
Apr-Sep 11HEC ⬛ ♦ ℝ ⅀ ⅂ ✕ ⊙ ◻ ∅ ⱬ S P ⊞ ⊞ ∅ lau

Forte via dei Platani 58 ☎ 0586 600155
Level site, grassy, sandy terrain.
4 Apr-20 Sep 8HEC ⬛ ♦ ℝ ⅀ ⅂ ✕ ⊙ ◻ ∅ ⱬ P 🏛 ⊞ ∅ ♦ ⱬS
Prices: ♦6700-11300 ➡3900-5000 ⬜12900-14800 ▲12900-
14800

GROSSETO, MARINA DI GROSSETO

La Marze ☎ 0564 35501
➲ *Access via SS322.*
May-15 Oct 20HEC ⋮⋮ ♦ ℝ ⅀ ⅂ ✕ ⊙ ◻ ∅ ⅂ ⬛ ⬛ ⱬ P ◻
⊞ lau
Prices: ♦10600-11000 pitch 15000-21500

CAMPING Via Castra, 71 - I-50050 Limite sull'Arno
Tel. + Fax 0039/0558712304

FIRENZE

SAN GIUSTO

The campsite is located on the verdant slopes of Montalbano in a protected area about to be declared a nature reserve. The position of the campsite provides ample opportunity to choose between sun and shade where you can relax in a quiet atmosphere and family environment. Its central location makes it quick and easy to reach the most beautiful towns of Tuscany.

During April, May, June, September and October 7=6 (stay for 7 nights and pay for only 6). Price reductions for groups.

Rosmarina via delle Colonie 37 ☎ 0564 36319
A modern site situated in a pine wood and close to the sea, with beautiful views. Various sports and entertainments for everyone to enjoy.
10 May-20 Sep 1.4HEC ⌁⌁ ♣ ⋒ 🐂 ⴾ ✕ ⊙ 🚱 ⌀ ⴱ ⵗ S 🖃 ⴾ lau
Prices: ♣9000-15000 ⛟12000-20000 ▲8000-10000

LERICI La spezia

Maralunga via Carpanini 61, Maralunga
☎ 0187 966589
This terraced site is directly on the seafront and surrounded by olive groves.
➔ *Access from Sarzana-La Spezia motorway.*
Jun-Sep 10HEC ◈ ♣ ⋒ 🐂 ⴾ ✕ ⊙ 🚱 ⌀ ⵗ S 🖃 ⴱ ⴾ ✕ ⴲ

LIMITE Firenze

San Giuspo via Castra 71 ☎ 055 8712304
A useful site on slightly sloping ground within easy reach of Florence by car or public transport.
Etr-Oct 2.5HEC ⌁⌁ ⴰ ⋒ 🐂 ✕ ⊙ 🚱 ⌀ ⴱ ⴿ
Prices: ♣8000 pitch 8000-15000

MASSA, MARINA DI Massa carrara

Giardino viale delle Pinete 382 ☎ 0585 869291
Site in pine woodland and on two meadows, shade provided by roof matting.
➔ *On the island side of the SS328 to Pisa.*
Apr-Sep 3.2HEC ⌁⌁ ♣ ⋒ 🐂 ⴾ ✕ ⊙ 🚱 ⴲ ⴱ ⴲ ⵗ lau ⴾ ⴾS ⴲ
Prices: ♣6000-9000 ⛟25000-35000 ▲25000-35000

MONEGLIA Genova

Villaggio Smeraldo Preata ☎ 0185 48375
A pleasant site in a pine wood overlooking the sea with good, modern facilities and direct access to the beach.
➔ *Access via A12/SS1.*
All year 1.5HEC ◈ ⴰ ⋒ 🐂 🐂 ⴾ ✕ ⊙ 🚱 ⴲ ⴱ ⵗ S 🖃 ⴿ lau
ⴾ ⌀
Prices: ♣8000-16000 pitch 20000-40000

MONTECATINI TERME Pistoia

Belsito via delle Vigne 1/A, Vico ☎ 0572 67396
A quiet site at an altitude of 250mtrs with good sized pitches.
All year 3.3HEC ⌁⌁⌁⌁ ♣ ⋒ 🐂 🐂 ⴾ ✕ ⊙ 🚱 ⌀ ⴱ ⴲ ⵗ
P ⴲ 🖃 lau
Prices: ♣9000 pitch 18000-22000

MONTE DI FO Firenze

Sergente ☎ 055 8423018
The site is at 780m above sea level on a hill. The pitches are flat. Ideal for walkers.
➔ *Exit the SS65 at Barberino Mugollo and follow signs for Monte di Fo.*
All year 3HEC ⌁⌁⌁⌁ ♣ ⋒ 🐂 🐂 ⴾ ✕ ⊙ 🚱 ⌀ ⴲ ⴱ ⴲ ⴲ 🖃 lau
Prices: ♣10000 pitch 17000

MONTERIGGIONI Siena

Piscina Luxor Quies Loc. Trasqua ☎ 0577 743043
Lies on a flat-topped hill, partly in an oak wood, partly in meadowland.
➔ *Turn off via Cassia (SS2) at Km239/II or Km238/IX and continue for further 2.5km, crossing railway line. Approach to site via very steep and winding road.*
25 May-12 Sep 1.5HEC ⌁⌁⌁⌁ ⁝⁝⁝ ♣ ⋒ 🐂 ⴾ ✕ ⊙ 🚱 ⌀ ⴾ P ⴲ
🖃 lau
Prices: ♣10500 ⇄4700 ⛟5700 ▲5300

MONTESCUDÁIO Livorno

Montescudáio via del Poggetto ☎ 0586 683477
This modern site is situated on a hill and is completely divided into individual pitches, some of which are naturally screened. Children under 2 years are not accepted.
➔ *From Cecina (on SS1, via Aurelia) follow road to Guardistallo for 2.5km.*
6 May-19 Sep 25HEC ⌁⌁⌁⌁ ♣ ⋒ 🐂 ⴾ ✕ ⊙ 🚱 ⌀ ⴲ ⴱ ⴲ ⴲ ⵗ
lau ⴾ ⴾS
Prices: ♣8200-10500 pitch 17800-24000

MONTICELLO AMIATA Grosseto

Lucherino Lucherino ☎ 0564 992975
A peaceful site 735m above sea level on the slopes of Mount Amiata. The shady but sloping site is ideal for walkers and historians.
➔ *Access via SS223 to Paganico then follow signs to Monte Amiata.*
May-15 Oct 2.6HEC ⌁⌁⌁⌁ ♣ ⋒ 🐂 ✕ ⊙ 🚱 ⌀ ⴲ ⴲ ▲ ⴾ P 🖃 ⴲ
lau ⴾ 🐂
Prices: ♣7000-10000 ⛟9000-13000 ▲9000-13000

PEGLI Genova

Villa Doria via al Campeggio 15n ☎ 010 6969600
Quiet site in pleasant wooded surroundings.
➔ *Access via SS1. Singposted.*
All year 0.5HEC ⌁⌁⌁⌁ ♣ ⋒ 🐂 ⴾ ✕ ⊙ 🚱 ⴱ 🖃 lau ⴾ ✕ ⌀ ⴾS
Prices: ♣8000 pitch 13000-17000

PISA PISA

Torre Pendente viale della Cascine 86 ☎ 050 561704
Pleasant, modern site on level ground in a rural setting. 1km
walk to the Leaning Tower.
➲ *Situated on the northern outskirts of Pisa.*
Apr-15 Oct 2.5HEC ⛺ ♠ ♟ ⚍ ♥ ✕ ⊙ ♨ ∅ 🏠 ♻ 🅿 ⊞ lau
♦ ♣ ₹R ⊞
Prices: ♦10000-11000 ♠6000 ♣11000 ▲10000

POPULÓNIA LIVORNO

Sant'Albínia via della Principessa ☎ 0565 29389
A good overnight stopping place with plenty of facilities.
Ideally placed for the ferry ports.
➲ *10km N of Piombino on the San Vincenzo road.*
May-15 Sep 3HEC ⛺ ♠ ♟ ⚍ ♥ ✕ ⊙ ♨ ∅ ♨ ▲ ₹ S 🅿
♨ lau
Prices: ♦7600-11000 ♠3200-4800 ♣8700-14000 ▲7600-
10000

RIOTORTO LIVORNO

Orizzonte Perelli ☎ 0565 28007
In a fine coastal position overlooking the island of Elba.
All year 10HEC ⛺ ♠ ♟ ⚍ ♥ ✕ ⊙ ♨ ∅ ♨ ♻ ⊞ lau
♦ ∅ ₹S

SAN BARONTO FIRENZE

Barco Reale via Nardini 11 ☎ 0573 88332
A well equipped site in a hilly, wooded location.
➲ *Signposted from Lamporecchio.*
Apr-Sep 10HEC ⛺ ♠ ♟ ⚍ ♥ ✕ ⊙ ♨ ∅ ♨ ▲ ₹ P 🅿 lau
Prices: ♦8500-11800 ♠4500-6500 ♣9500-12500
▲7400-9100

SAN GIMIGNANO SIENA

Boschetto di Piemma Santa Lucia ☎ 0577 940352
This small grassy site is well equipped and has many facilities
for both families and idividuals.
Apr-15 Oct 1.5HEC ⛺ ♠ ♟ ⚍ ✕ ⊙ ♨ ∅ ♨ ♻
₹ P 🅿 ⊞

SAN PIERO A SIEVE FIRENZE

Mugello Verde via Masso Rondinaio 2 ☎ 055 848511
Terraced site in wooded surroundings. Lunchtime siesta
14.00-16.00 hrs.
➲ *Leave motorway at exit 18 and follow signs.*
All year 12HEC ⛺ ♠ ♟ ⚍ ♥ ✕ ⊙ ♨ ∅ ♨ 🏠 ₹ P 🅿 ⊞ lau
Prices: ♦8500-13000 ♣10000-22000 ▲10000-22000 pitch
10000-22000

SAN REMO IMPERIA

Villaggio dei Fiori via Tiro a Volo 3 ☎ 0184 660635
➲ *1.5km from the town.*
All year 2.3HEC ⛺ ♠ ♟ ♥ ✕ ⊙ ♨ 🏠 ♻ ₹ PS 🅿 ♨ lau
♦ ⚍ ∅ ♨ ⊞
See advertisement under Colour Section

SAN VINCENZO LIVORNO

Park Albatros Pineta di Torre Nuova ☎ 0565 701018
The site lies amongst beautiful, tall pine trees. 1km from sea.
➲ *Turn off SP23 beyond San Vincenzo at Km7/III and drive
600m inland.*
29 Mar-5 Sep 11.4HEC ⛺ ♠ ♟ ⚍ ♥ ✕ ⊙ ♨ ∅ ♨ 🅿 ⊞
♨ lau ♦ ₹S
Prices: ♦7900-11700 pitch 11000-16900

SARTEANO SIENA

Bagno Santo via del Bagno Santo 29 ☎ 0578 26971
27 Mar-Sep 15HEC ⛺ ♠ ♟ ⚍ ♥ ✕ ⊙ ♨ ♨ ♻ ₹ 🅿 🅿 ⊞ ♨
lau ♦ ♟
Prices: ♦13000-17000 ♠5000 ♣13000-17000 ▲13000-17000

SARZANA LA SPEZIA

Iron Gate via XXV Aprile 54 ☎ 0187 676370
A modern site with good facilities attached to the Iron Gate
Marina.
All year 2HEC ⛺ ♟ ⚍ ♥ ✕ ⊙ ♨ ♨ ₹ PR 🅿 ⊞
♦ ∅ ♨
Prices: ♦7400-11900 ♠4600-7100 ♣8400-13400
▲7400-12800

SESTRI LEVANTE GENOVA

Fossa Lupara via Costa 31 ☎ 0185 43992
All year 1.5HEC ⛺ ♠ ♟ ⚍ ♥ ✕ ⊙ ♨ ∅ ♨ ♻ ⊞ lau
♦ ₹S

SIENA SIENA

Montagnola Sovicille ☎ 0577 314473
Quiet site in an oak wood with individual plots separated by
hedges. Facilities are modern and extensive.
➲ *From the A1 westbound, exit at Siena, campsite is
signposted towards Sovicille.*
7 Apr-Sep 2.5HEC ⛺ ∴ ♠ ♟ ⚍ ♥ ✕ ⊙ ♨ ∅ ♨ ♻ 🅿
♦ ✕ ⊞

Siena Colleverde Strada di Scacciapensieri 47 ☎ 0577 280044
The site offers both large areas for caravans and mobile
homes and a large grassy area for tents. There is a local bus
service to the centre of Siena.
➲ *The only campsite in Siena situated just to the north.*
21 Mar-10 Nov 4.5HEC ⛺ ♠ ♟ ♥ ✕ ⊙ ♨ ♨ ₹ P 🅿 lau
♦ ♟ ⊞

Soline Casciano di Murlo ☎ 0577 817410
Terraced hilly site surrounded by woodland. Offers a wide
variety of sports facilities and family entertainment.
➲ *Take the left turning at Fontazzi and ascend hill.*
All year 6HEC ⛺ ♠ ♟ ⚍ ♥ ✕ ⊙ ♨ ∅ ♨ 🏠 ♻ ▲ ₹ P 🅿 ⊞ lau
♦ ♨
Prices: ♦10000 ♠3000 ♣10500 ▲8000-9500

STELLA SAN GIOVANNI SAVONA

Stella via Rio Basco 62 ☎ 019 703269
In wooded surroundings with well defined pitches, 5.5km
from the coast.
➲ *Access via SS334.*
All year 3.3HEC ⛺ ♠ ♟ ✕ ⊙ ♨ ♨ ₹ PR 🅿 ⊞ lau
♦ ⊞
Prices: pitch 26000-34000 (incl 2 persons)

TALAMONE GROSSETO

International Camping Talamone ☎ 0564 887026
Some facilities may not be available before April and vehicles
must use a separate car park during the high season.
Etr-Sep 5HEC ⛺ ♨ ☼ ♟ ⚍ ✕ ⊙ ♨ ₹ P ♦ ₹S

TORRE DEL LAGO PUCCINI LUCCA

Burlamacca viale G-Marconi Int ☎ 0584 359544
In a beautiful wooded location 1km from the sea on the
Versilia Riviera and close to the former home of Puccini. A
wide variety of facilities are available.
Apr-Sep 4HEC ⛺ ♠ ♟ ⚍ ♥ ✕ ⊙ ♨ ∅ ♨ 🏠 ♻ ▲ ₹ P 🅿
♨ ♦ ₹LS ⊞
Prices: ♦5800-9800 ♠4000 ♣10500-18000 ▲10500-18000

Europa ☎ 0584 350707
Site in pine and poplar woodland.
➲ *On the land side of the viale dei Tigli, coming from Viareggio.*
27 Mar-Sep 60HEC ⊞⊞⊞ ♦ ⋔ ⋤ ⋩ ⋔ ⊙ ⊟ ⊘ ⚏ 🏠 🅿 ⊞ ⊗
♦ ⋩LS
Prices: ♠7000-11000 ⛺12000-16000 ▲12000-16000

Italia viale dei Tigli ☎ 0584 359828
This site is divided into pitches and lies in meadowland planted with poplar trees.
➲ *Inland from the Viareggio road (viale dei Tigli).*
9 Apr-13 Sep 9HEC ⊞⊞⊞ ♦ ⋔ ⋤ ⋩ ⋔ ⊙ ⊟ ⊘ ⚏ 🏠 🏕 ▲ ⊞ 🅿
⊞ ⊗ lau ♦ ⋤ ⋩ ⋔ ⊘ ⚏ ⋩LS
Prices: ♠7000-12000 pitch 13000-20000

Tigli Viale dei Tigli ☎ 0584 341278
Shady site close to a Regional Park, Lake Massaciuccoli, and the villa where Puccini wrote much of his music.
Apr-Sep 9HEC ⊞⊞⊞ ⋮⋮⋮ ♦ ⋔ ⋤ ⋩ ⋔ ⊙ ⊟ ⊘ ⚏ 🏠 ⋩ L ⊞ ⊞
lau ♦ ⋩S
Prices: ♠8800 ⛺12100 ▲12100

➤ **TROGHI** FIRENZE
Il Poggetto via il Poggetto 143 ☎ 055 8307323
A modern site with good facilities. Large, level, grassy pitches.
➲ *5km from exit 'Incisa Valdarno' on the A1.*
All year 4.5HEC ⊞⊞⊞ ⋔ ⋔ ⋤ ⋩ ⋔ ⊙ ⊟ ⊘ ⚏ 🏠 🏕 ▲ ⋩ P ⊞
⊞ lau
Prices: ♠9500-11000 pitch 17000-18500

➤ **VADA** LIVORNO
Flori ☎ 0586 770096
Level grassland surrounded by fields. Shade provided by roof matting.
➲ *Access from the SS1 S of Vada, after 1.5km turn right and continue for 500m.*
27 Mar-26 Sept 15HEC ⊞⊞⊞ ♦ ⋔ ⋤ ⋩ ⋔ ⊙ ⊟ ⊘ ⚏ 🏠 ⋩ P ⊞
⊞ lau ♦ ⋩S
Prices: ♠12000-18000 ⛺9000-15000 ▲9000-15000

➤ **VIAREGGIO** LUCCA
Paradiso via dei Tigli ☎ 0584 392005
Site with tall pine trees and firm terrain.
➲ *2.5km S off via Aurelia at Km354/V onto via Comparini towards the sea in 600m.*
May-15 Sep 4.8HEC ⊞⊞⊞ ♦ ⋔ ⋤ ⋩ ⋔ ⊙ ⊟ ⊘ ⚏ 🏠
♦ ⋩PS

Pineta via dei Lecci ☎ 0584 383397
May-20 Sep 3.2HEC ⊞⊞⊞ ♦ ⋔ ⋤ ⋩ ⋔ ⊙ ⊟ ⊘ ⚏ 🏠 🏕 🅿 ⊞
lau ♦ ⋩PS

Viareggio via Comparini 1 ☎ 0584 391012
The site lies in a poplar wood 700m from beach.
➲ *1.5km S of town. At Km354/V head towards coast.*
Apr-Sep 2HEC ⊞⊞⊞ ⋮⋮⋮ ♦ ⋔ ⋤ ⋩ ⋔ ⊙ ⊟ ⊘ ⚏ ⊞ lau
♦ ⋩S
Prices: ♠7000-12000 ⛺13000-20000 ▲13000-20000

➤ **ZINOLA** SAVONA
Buggi International via N S del Monte 15 ☎ 019 860120
A well equipped site with plenty of space for tents, approx. 900mtrs from the sea.
All year 3HEC ⊞⊞⊞ ♦ ⋔ ⋤ ⋩ ⋔ ⊙ ⊟ ⊘ ⚏ ⋩ S ⊞
♦ ⊘ ⚏ ⋩S ⊞
Prices: ♠8500 ⛺7500 ⛺10000 ▲8000

This area covers some very dissimilar regions east of the Apennine mountains on whose slopes the glaciers glint for much of the year. Fish from the Adriatic make specialities like the fish soup *brodetto* worth trying. Inland you may like to try Bologna's Mortadella sausage and the Lambrusco Frizzante wine. Emilia Romagna's varied geography - mountains, the river Po and the sea - allows winter skiing, and walking in pine forests in summer. Art lovers can see the mosaics in Ravenna, or Corrigio's paintings in Parma, a town which is famous for its dried ham and cheese.
In the rugged Marches you can find the splendid Renaissance palace of Urbino or perhaps visit the hill town of Maceratas which has a Roman arena where concerts and dramas are held, or go to Ascoli Piceno, enclosed by two rivers and with a delightful town centre.
The Abruzzo in the centre of Italy is dramatic with high mountains, and a National Park where bears, chamois and wolves live. Attractive towns like L'Aquila dominated by its castle, contrast with the flourishing seaside resorts such as Pescara.

➤ **ALBA ADRIATICA** TERAMO
➤ At **TORTORETO, LIDO**(4km S)
Salinello c da Piane a Mare ☎ 0861 786306
Well-tended meadowland site with numerous rows of poplars. Private beach, siesta 13.30-16.00 hrs.
➲ *On southern outskirts, signposted from Km405 of the SS16.*
15 May-20 Sep 15HEC ⊞⊞⊞ ♦ ⋔ ⋤ ⋩ ⋔ ⊙ ⊟ ⊘ ⚏ 🏠 ⋩ PRS
⊞ ⊞ ⊗ lau
Prices: ♠5000-10500 pitch 12000-23000

➤ **AQUILA, L'** L'AQUILA
Funivia del Gran Sasso Fonte Cerreto ☎ 0862 606163
1100m above sea level this mountainous site is near a medieval town and a National Park.
15 May-15 Sep 1HEC ⊞⊞⊞ ⋔ ⋔ ⋤ ⋩ ⋔ ⊙ ⊟ ⊘ ⚏ ▲ ⊞ ♦ ⊞
Prices: ♠7000-8000 ⛺2000 ⛺11000-13000 ▲7000-9000

➤ **ASSISI** PERUGIA
Internationale via San Giovanni, Campiglione 110
☎ 075 813710
At the foot of the hill on which Assisi stands, this modern campsite is well-equipped and a good touring centre.
➲ *W via SS147.*
Etr-Oct 3HEC ⊞⊞⊞ ⋔ ⋔ ⋤ ⋩ ⋔ ⊙ ⊟ ⊘ ⚏ 🏕 ▲ ⊞ ⊞ ♦ ⋩P
Prices: ♠8500 ⛺3500 ⛺9500 ▲7500

➤ **BARREA** L'AQUILA
Grenziana Parco Nazionale d'Abruzzo, Tre Croci
☎ 0864 88101
In picturesque wooded surroundings on the shore of a lake.
All year 2HEC ⊞⊞⊞ ⋮⋮⋮ ⋔ ⋔ ⋤ ⋩ ⋔ ⊙ ⊟ ⚏ ▲ ♦ ⋔ ⊘ ⚏ ⋩L
Prices: ♠8000 ⛺5000 ⛺12000 ▲12000

➤ **BELLARIA** FORLI
Happy via Panzini 228 ☎ 0541 346102
The campsite is in a quiet position on the sea shore close to the centre of town.
➲ *A14, SS16, exit for Bellaria Cagnona S. Mauro Mare, and follow signs for Acquabell. Over level crossing and site is on right.*
All year 4HEC ⊞⊞⊞ ⋮⋮⋮ ⋔ ⋔ ⋤ ⋩ ⋔ ⊙ ⊟ ⊘ ⚏ 🏠 ⋩ PS ⊞ ⊞
lau ♦ ⋤ ⋩ ⋔ ⋩LR ⊞
Prices: ♠8000-13000 pitch 16000-26000

> **BEVAGNA** PERUGIA

Pian di Boccio Pian di Boccio 10 ☎ 0742 360391
In wooded surroundings in the centre of the Umbria region
with good modern facilities. Popular with families.
Apr-Sep 8.5HEC ▥ ♨ ♠ ⋔ ⚡ ⍾ ✕ ⊙ ▨ ⌀ 🏕 ⛽ ⌕ LP ⌂
Prices: ♠9000 ♣3000 ⛽10000 ▲5000-9000

> **BOLOGNA** BOLOGNA

Citta di Bologna via Romita 12/IVA ☎ 03951 325016
Located in the northern part of this ancient town this site
offers a cheap and convenient alternative to hotels.
All year 6.3HEC ▥ ♠ ⋔ ⚡ ⍾ ✕ ⊙ ▨ 🏕 ⛽ ⌂ ⊞ lau ♦ ✕ ⌀ 🚿
⌕P
Prices: ♠6500-9000 pitch 14000-18000

> **BORGHETTO** PERUGIA

Badiaccia via Trasimenoi, no.91 ☎ 075 9659097
A well equipped site with large grassy pitches and direct
access to the lake.
➲ *From the A1 exit at Valdichiana and join the road to*
Perugia and follow signs for Lake Trasimeno.
Apr-Sep 5.5HEC ▥ ♠ ⋔ ⚡ ⍾ ✕ ⊙ ▨ ⌀ 🏕 ⛽ ⌕ LP lau ♦ 🚿
Prices: ♠8000-9500 ♣3000 ⛽9000-10000 ▲8000-9000

> **BRUCIATA** MODENA

Modena via Cave di Ramo 111 ☎ 059 332252
All year 2.6HEC ▥ ♨ ♠ ⋔ ⚡ ⍾ ✕ ⊙ ▨ ⌀ ⌕ PR ⌂ ⊞ lau
Prices: ♠9000 pitch 17000

> **CASALBORDINO, MARINA DI** CHIETI

Santo Stefano ☎ 0873 918118
Level terrain, below road, within agricultural area, adjoining
railway line. Open air disco. Lunchtime siesta 14.00-16.00 hrs.
Camping Card Compulsory.
➲ *Exit off Vastro-Nord of A14 and continue north via SS16 to*
Km498.
All year 2HEC ▥ ♠ ⋔ ⚡ ⍾ ✕ ⊙ ▨ ⌀ 🚿 🏕 ⌕ S ⌂ ⊘ lau ♦ ⊞

> **CASAL BORSETTI** RAVENNA

Adria via Spallazzi N30 ☎ 0544 445217
The site lies in a field behind the Ristorante Lugo.
➲ *Turn off the motorway at the Ravenna exit or take the*
SS309 (Romea) Km13 N of Ravenna.
May-20 Sep 4.4HEC ▥ ♠ ⋔ ⚡ ⍾ ✕ ⊙ ▨ ⌀ 🚿 ⌕ PS ⌂
⊞ lau

Reno via Spaccazzi 11 ☎ 0544 445020
Meadowland in sparse pine woodland and separated from
the sea by dunes.
➲ *Turn off SS309 at Km8 or 14.*
Apr-Sep 33HEC ▥ ♠ ⋔ ⚡ ⍾ ✕ ⊙ ▨ ⌀ 🏕 ⛽ ⊞ lau ♦ ⌕S
Prices: ♠6000-9000 pitch 12000-16000

> **CASTIGLIONE DEL LAGO** PERUGIA

Listro via Lungolago ☎ 075 951193
Attractive site on a peninsula in Lake Trasimeno.
Apr-Sep 1HEC ▥ ♠ ⋔ ⚡ ⍾ ✕ ⊙ ▨ 🚿 ⌕ L ⌂ lau ♦ ✕ ⌀
🚿P ⊞
Prices: ♠6000-7500 ♣2000-2500 ⛽6000-7500 ▲6000-7500

> **CERVIA** RAVENNA

Adriatico via Pinarella 90 ☎ 0544 71537
Level meadowland site with plenty of shade, pleasantly
landscaped with olives, willows, elms and maples.
➲ *Located shortly before Pinarella di Cervia. Access by via*
Caduiti per le Liberta (SS16) 600m from sea.
15 May-12 Sep 34HEC ▥ ♠ ⋔ ⚡ ⍾ ✕ ⊙ ▨ ⌀ 🚿 ⌕ P ⌂ ⊞
lau ♦ ⚡ ✕ ⌀ 🚿 ⌕S ⊞
Prices: ♠6500-9500 pitch 14000-19000

> **CESENATICO** FORLI

Cesenatico via Mazzini 182 ☎ 0547 81344
The site stretches over an area of land belonging to the
Azienda di Soggiomo e Turismo.
➲ *1.5km N at Km178 turn off the SS16 towards the sea.*
29 Mar-21 Sep 19HEC ▥ ┉ ♠ ⋔ ⚡ ⍾ ✕ ⊙ ▨ 🚿 ⌕ S ⌂ ⊞
lau ♦ ⌀ 🚿P

Zadina via Mazzini 184 ☎ 0547 82310
Very pleasant terrain in dunes on two sides of a canal.
23 Apr-16 Sep 10HEC ┉ ♠ ⋔ ⚡ ⍾ ✕ ⊙ ▨ ⌀ 🚿 ⌕ S ⌂ ⊞
lau

> **CITTA DI CASTELLO** PERUGIA

La Montesca ☎ 075 8521420
In a large, wooded park with excellent facilities. An ideal base
for exploring the surrounding area.
➲ *3km from the town, beside the River Tiber.*
May-Sep 5HEC ▥ ♠ ⋔ ⚡ ⍾ ✕ ⊙ ▨ ⌀ ⌕ P ⌂ ⊞ lau
Prices: ♠7500-8500 ♣3000 ⛽7500-8500 ▲6500-7500

> **CIVITANOVA MARCHE** MACERATA

Nuove Giare via Delle Fosse 46 ☎ 0733 70440
A modern family site with good recreational facilities.
➲ *Exit A14 at Civitanova Marche, signposted.*
15 May-15 Sep 6HEC ▥ ♠ ⋔ ⚡ ⍾ ✕ ⊙ ▨ 🚿 🏕 ⛽ ▲ ⌕
PS ⌂ ⊞ lau

> **CUPRAMARITTIMA** ASCOLI PICENO

Calypso via Boccabianca 8 ☎ 0735 778686
Apr-Sep 26HEC ▥ ♠ ⋔ ⚡ ⍾ ✕ ⊙ ▨ ⌀ 🚿 ⌕ PS ⊞ lau

> **DANTE, LIDO DI** RAVENNA

Classe viale Catone ☎ 0544 492005
Level meadowland in grounds of former farm.
➲ *Access from the SS16 turning towards the sea at Km154/V*
and continue 9km to site.
10 May-30 Sep 7.1HEC ▥ ♠ ⋔ ⚡ ⍾ ✕ ⊙ ▨ ⌀ 🚿 🏕 ⛽ ▲
⌕ PS ⌂ ⊞ lau

> **ESTENSI, LIDO DEGLI** FERRARA

International Mare Pineta via delle Acacie 67 ☎ 0533
330194 & 330110
Extensive site on slightly hilly ground under pines and
decidous trees, providing shade. Near the beach and has
numerous mobile homes.
➲ *2km SE of Port Garibaldi.*
24 Apr-20 Sep 16HEC ▥ ┉ ♠ ⋔ ⚡ ⍾ ✕ ⊙ ▨ ⌀ 🏕 ⛽
⌕ PS ⌂ lau
Prices: ♠6500-11600 pitch 11600-19000

See advertisement under Colour Section

> **FANO** PESARO & URBINO

Mare Blu ☎ 0721 884201
The site is surrounded by tall poplars with direct access to a
sandy beach. Facilities for most watersports and
entertainment for children and families.
➲ *Exit A14 at Fano and travel south for 3km.*
Apr-Sep 2.5HEC ▥ ♠ ⋔ ⚡ ⍾ ✕ ⊙ ▨ ⌀ 🚿 ⌕ S ⌂ ⊡ ⊞
lau
Prices: ♠8000-10000 pitch 17000-19500

> **FERRARA** FERRARA

Estense via Gramicia 80 ☎ 0532 752396
A good overnight stop on the way south.
➲ *NE outskirts of Ferrara*
All year 3.3HEC ▥ ♠ ⋔ ⊙ ▨ ⌂ ⊞ ♦ ⚡ ✕ ⌀ 🚿 ⌕PS ⊞

FIORENZUOLA DI FOCARA PESARO & URBINO

Panorama Strada Panoramica ☎ 0721 208145
Located in a park 100mtrs above sea level this site welcomes
families, animals, cyclists and those wishing to relax.
⮡ *Signposted off the SS16, 10km from Gabicce and 7km from
Pesaro.*
May-Sep 2.2HEC ⬛ ♦ ⋔ ⅏ ⟟ ✗ ⊙ ⬛ ⬦ ⅏ ⬛ ⟟ PS ⬛ ⊞
lau
Prices: ⚊8000-11000 ⬤4000-5000 ⬛9500-13000 ⚊9500-
13000

GATTEO MARE FORLI

Rose via Adriatica 29 ☎ 0547 86213
In a peaceful setting close to the sea and the town centre.
⮡ *Turn off SS16, at Km186.*
May-25 Sep 5HEC ⬛ ⬛ ⋙ ♦ ⋔ ⅏ ⟟ ✗ ⊙ ⬛ ⬦ ⬛ ⬛ ⟟
PS ⬛ ⊞ lau
Prices: ⚊6200-12500 pitch 14000-25000

GUBBIO PERUGIA

Villa Ortoguidone Ortoguidone 214 ☎ 075 9272037
One of two well equipped sites in the same location. Plenty
of space for tents.
⮡ *Access via SS298 (Gubbio-Perugia).*
Apr-Sep 0.5HEC ⬛ ♦ ⋔ ✗ ⊙ ⬛ ⬛ ⬛ ⬛ lau ♦ ⅏ ⟟ ✗ ⟟P
Prices: ⚊10000-14000 ⬤3000-4000 ⬛10000-13000
⚊8000-11000

MAGIONE PERUGIA

Polvese via Montivalle ☎ 075 848200
In a peaceful location beside Lake Trasimeno with plenty of
recreational facilities.
Apr-Sep 5HEC ⬛ ♦ ⋔ ⅏ ⟟ ✗ ⊙ ⬛ ⬦ ⅏ ⬛ ⟟ LP ⬛ lau
Prices: ⚊7500-9500 ⬤3000-4000 ⬛9000-10000 ⚊6000-7000

Villaggio Italgest via Martiri di Cefalonia ☎ 075 848238
Situated by a lake and surrounded by woodland. There are
good, modern facilities and all kinds of recreation are
available.
Apr-Sep 5.5HEC ⬛ ♦ ⋔ ⅏ ⟟ ✗ ⊙ ⬛ ⬦ ⅏ ⬛ ⟟ LP ⬛ ⊞
lau
Prices: ⚊10000-11500 ⬤3000-4000 ⬛10500-12500 ⚊8500-
10000

MARCELLI DI NUMANA ANCONA

Conero Azzurro via Litoranea ☎ 071 7390507
Well-equipped site situated between the Adriatic and Mount
Canero.
Jun-15 Sep 5HEC ⬛ ⬦ ♦ ⋔ ⅏ ⟟ ✗ ⊙ ⬛ ⬦ ⟟ PS ⊞ lau
♦ ⅏
Prices: ⚊8000-11000 ⬤4000-5000 ⬛13000-16000 ⚊13000-
16000

MAROTTA PESARO & URBINO

Gabbiano via Faa' di Bruno 95 ☎ 0721 96691
Quiet location surrounded by trees overlooking the sea.
⮡ *Exit A14 at Marotta, join SS16 and site is 2.5km in the
direction of Fano.*
May-Sep 1.9HEC ⬛ ♦ ⋔ ⅏ ⟟ ✗ ⊙ ⬛ ⬦ ⅏ ⟟ PS ⬛ ⊞ ⬤
lau ♦ ⊞
Prices: ⚊8000-9500 pitch 18000-21000

MARTINISCURO TERAMO

Duca Amedeo Lungomare Europa 158 ☎ 0861 797376
By the sea.
May-20 Sep 1.5HEC ⬛ ♦ ⋔ ⟟ ✗ ⊙ ⬛ ⬦ ⅏ ⬛ ⬛ ⟟ PS ⬛
⊞ lau ♦ ⅏ ✗
Prices: ⚊5000-10000 pitch 13000-23000

MILANO MARITTIMA RAVENNA

Romagna viale Matteotti 190 ☎ 0544 949326
Level and flat site with young trees.
⮡ *Access via the SS16 (Strada Adriatica) turn off beyond
Milano Marittima and follow signs.*
17 Apr-12 Sep 4HEC ⬛ ♦ ⋔ ⅏ ⟟ ✗ ⊙ ⬛ ⬦ ⟟ S ⬛ ⬦ lau
♦ ⟟PR ⊞
Prices: ⚊7000-10000 pitch 13000-19000

MONTENERO, MARINA DI CAMPOBASSO

Costa Verde ☎ 0873 803144
A level site with good facilities and direct access to the beach
E of San Salvo Marino.
⮡ *Leave the coast road, SS16, at Km525/VII and continue by
a farm road for 300m to the site.*
15 May-15 Sep ⬛ ⬦ ⋔ ⅏ ⟟ ✗ ⊙ ⬛ ⬦ ⅏ ⬛ ⚊ ⟟
PRS ⬛ ⊞ ⬦ lau ♦ ⊞
Prices: pitch 8000-16000 (incl 4 persons)

NAZIONI, LIDO DELLE FERRARA

Tahiti viale Libia 133 ☎ 0533 379500
Pleasantly laid out site 650m from sea. Has own private
beach accessible via a miniature railway. Lunchtime siesta
13.30-15.30 hrs.
⮡ *Turn off SS309 near Km32.5 then 2km to site. Signposted.*
10 May-21 Sep 8HEC ⬛ ⬛ ⬛ ♦ ⋔ ⅏ ⟟ ✗ ⊙ ⬛ ⬦ ⅏ ⬛ ⟟ P
⬛ ⊞ ⬦ lau ♦ ⟟S

OLMO PERUGIA

Rocolo strada Fontana la Trinita ☎ 075 5178550
15 Jun-15 Sep 2.4HEC ⬛ ⬦ ⋔ ⅏ ⟟ ✗ ⊙ ⬛ ⬦ ⬛ ⊞ lau ♦ ⅏ ⟟P

ORVIETO TERNI

Orvieto Lago di Corbara ☎ 0744 950240
A quiet site surrounded by large trees.
⮡ *Turn off SS448 at Km3.770.*
All year 1.6HEC ⬛ ♦ ⋔ ⅏ ⟟ ✗ ⊙ ⬛ ⬦ ⟟ LP ⬛

PARMA PARMA

Cittadella parco Cittadella ☎ 0521 961434
Camping Card Compulsory.
Apr-Oct 4HEC ⬛ ♦ ⋔ ⊙ ⬛ ⬛ ♦ ⅏ ⟟ ✗ ⊞
Prices: ⚊11000 pitch 18000

PASSIGNANO PERUGIA

Kursaal viale Europa 41 ☎ 075 828085
The site is situated between the road and the lake, near the
villa of the same name.
⮡ *Access from SS75, Arezzo to Perugia road, from Km35.2.*
Mar-Oct 2HEC ⬛ ♦ ⋔ ⅏ ⟟ ✗ ⊙ ⬛ ⬦ ⅏ ⬛ ⟟ LP ⬛ ⊞ lau
Prices: ⚊9000-10000 ⬤3000 ⬛11000-15000 ⚊11000-15000

CAMPING EUROPA ★★
Loc. San Donato
I-06055 Passignano sul Trasimeno (PG)

TRASIMENO LAKE

Quiet, friendly campsite, families also welcome, right on the lake with private beach and free sunshade. Also available: bar, shop, restaurant, pizzeria, own (compacted-sand) tennis courts overlooking the sea, beach volleyball, free hot water, (free) electricity, caravans and bungalows for hire.
Rail passengers (Inter-Rail) may telephone for free transport from station to campsite. Well served for Perugia (20 km), Assisi (30 km), Siena (90 km), Florence (120 km) and Rome (180 km).

Telephone number of campsite: 0039/075827405 or 075829200. Fax: 0039/0758296061.

PASSIGNANO SUL TRASIMENO PERUGIA

Europa Loc San Donato ☎ 075 827405
Situated by Lake Trasimeno with private beach.
➦ *From the motorway take exit Passignano Est and campsite is signposted.*
Etr-10 Oct 3HEC 〰 ♣ ♠ 🖢 🍴 ✕ ☉ 🗐 🔗 🏤 🛒 ⟡ L 🏬 ⊞ lau
Prices: ⚑8500-9500 ♠4000-5000 ♠9000-10000 ▲7500-8500
See advertisement on page 245.

PESARO PESARO & URBINO

Marinella via Adriatica 244 ☎ 0721 55795
A flat grassy site with a private beach. Modern and well maintained facilities.
➦ *Access is through railway underpass from Km244 of SS16.*
Apr-10 Oct 15HEC 〰 🖫 ♠ 🖢 🍴 ✕ ☉ 🗐 🔗 ♨ 🏤 🛒 ⟡ S 🏬
🏬 ⊞ lau ♣ 🖢 🍴 ✕

PIEVEPELAGO MODENA

Fra Dolcino ☎ 0536 71229
All year 3.6HEC 〰 ♨ ♣ ♠ 🖢 🍴 ✕ ☉ 🗐 ♨ 🏤 🏬 lau ♣ ✕
⟡PR ⊞

Rio Verde via M-de-Canossa 34 ☎ 0536 72204
All year 1.8HEC 〰 🖫 ♠ 🖢 🍴 ✕ ☉ 🗐 🏤 🛒 ⟡ R 🏬 lau ♣ 🖢 ♨
⟡P ⊞
Prices: ⚑8000-10000 ♠10000-12000 ▲6000-7000

PINARELLA RAVENNA

Pinarella viale Abruzzi 52 ☎ 0544 987408
Subdivided terrain surrounded by houses. Partially shaded, some young poplars. Private beach. Management request reservations day before arrival.
May-15 Sep 1.8HEC 〰 ♣ ♠ 🍴 ✕ ☉ 🗐 🏬 ⊞ ⊗ lau ♣ 🖢 ✕
🔗 ♨ ⟡S
Prices: ⚑6000-9000 ♠13500-18000 ▲12500-17000

Safari viale Titano 130 ☎ 0544 987356
The site is divided into several sections. Only families are accepted.
9 May-13 Sep 2.5HEC 〰 ♣ ♠ 🖢 🍴 ✕ ☉ 🗐 ♨ 🏬 ⊞ ⊗
lau ♣ ✕ ⟡S

PINETO TERAMO

Heliopolis Contrada Villa Fumosa ☎ 085
Situated near a golden sandy beach. Various activies for all to enjoy. Idyllic scenery for relaxing walks.
Apr-Sep 12HEC 〰 ⋯ ♣ ♠ 🖢 🍴 ✕ ☉ 🗐 🔗 ♨ 🛒 ▲ ⟡ PS
🏬 ⊞ lau
Prices: ⚑6000-11000 ♠8000-48000 ▲8000-13000

International Loc Torre Cerrano ☎ 085 930639
Site on level terrain with young poplars. Sunshade roofing on the beach.
➦ *Turn off SS16 at Km431.2 and continue under railway underpass. Adjoining railway line.*
May-Sep 1.5HEC 〰 ♣ ♠ 🖢 🍴 ✕ ☉ 🗐 ♨ 🏤 🛒 ⟡S 🏬 🏬
⊞ ⊗ lau
Prices: ⚑6500-11500 ♠13000-23000 ▲5000-10000

Pineto Beach ☎ 085 9492796
A well equipped site in wooded surroundings with direct access to the beach.
➦ *At Km425 on SS16 'Adriatica'.*
15 May-Sep 25HEC 〰 ⋯ ♣ ♠ 🖢 🍴 ✕ ☉ 🗐 🏤 🛒 ⟡ S 🏬
⊞ lau

POMPOSA FERRARA

International Tre Moschettieri via Capanno Garibaldi 22
☎ 0533 380376
Camp site set beneath pine trees next to sea.

➦ *Signposted from SS309.*
23 Apr-21 Sep 11HEC 〰 ♣ ♠ 🖢 🍴 ✕ ☉ 🗐 🔗 🏤 🛒 ⟡ PS 🏬 ⊞
lau ♣ 🖢 ⟡L ⊞
Prices: ⚑6000-11000 pitch 11000-18000

Vigna sul Mar via Capanno Garibaldi 20 ☎ 0533 380216
Well tended meadowland under poplars. Private beach of 1km beyond the dunes.
➦ *Well signposted from entrance to Lido.*
May-20 Sep 12HEC 〰 ♣ ♠ 🖢 🍴 ✕ ☉ 🗐 🔗 🛒 ⟡ P 🏬 ⊞ lau ♣
🔗

PORTO RECANATI MACERATA

Bellamare ☎ 071 976628
On the S side of the mouth of the Musone.
➦ *Access from the Autostrada exit Ancona Sud via the SS16 turn to S bank at Km324.*
May-Sep 5HEC 〰 🖫 ♠ 🖢 🍴 ✕ ☉ 🗐 🔗 🛒 ⟡ PS 🏬 ⊞ ⊗ lau

PORTO SANT'ELPÍDIO ASCOLI PICENO

Risacca via Gabbie 6 ☎ 0734 991423
Clean, well-kept site on level meadowland, with some trees surrounded by fields.
➦ *Access via main SS16 N of village, follow road seawards under railway (narrow underpass maximum height 3m), then 1.2km along field paths to site. Caravan access is 400m further S along SS16, then under railway and along field paths to site.*
22 May-11 Sep 8HEC 〰 ♣ ♠ 🖢 🍴 ✕ ☉ 🗐 ♨ 🏤 🛒 ⟡ PS
🏬 ⊞ ⊗ lau
Prices: ⚑4500-11500 pitch 10000-27000

PRECI PERUGIA

Il Collaccio Castelvecchio di Preci ☎ 0743 939005
In beautiful natural surroundings with plenty of roomy pitches and good recreational facilities.
➦ *Access via SS 209.*
Apr-1 Oct 10HEC 〰 🖫 ♠ 🖢 🍴 ✕ ☉ 🗐 🛒 ⟡ P 🏬 lau
Prices: ⚑9000-11000 ♠3000-5000 ♠11000-13000 ▲9000-11000

PUNTA MARINA RAVENNA

At ADRIANO, LIDO(4.5km S)

Adriano via dei Campeggi 7 ☎ 0544 437230
300m from the sea. A pleasantly landscaped site amidst the dunes of the Punta Marina.
➦ *On SS309 via Lido Adriano to Punta Marina.*
23 Apr-20 Sep 14HEC 〰 ⋯ ♣ ♠ 🖢 🍴 ✕ ☉ 🗐 🔗 🏤 🛒
⟡ PS 🏬 lau
Prices: ⚑6400-13000 pitch 13000-23000

Coop 3 via dei Campeggi 8 ☎ 0544 437353
300m to the sea. Level site under isolated high pines and poplars. Across flat dunes to the beach.
➦ *Signposted.*
24 Apr-12 Sep 7HEC 〰 ♣ ♠ 🖢 🍴 ✕ ☉ 🗐 🔗 🏤 🏬 lau ♣ 🔗
⟡PS ⊞
Prices: ⚑5800-10000 ♠2700-5500 ♠11800-18200 ▲3900-7800

RAVENNA, MARINA DI RAVENNA

International Piomboni via Lungomare 421 ☎ 0544 530230
Site on slightly undulating mainly grassy terrain with pines and poplars. Separate section for tents. Lunchtime siesta 14.00-15.30 hrs.
➦ *Access is 1km S from town centre off coast road.*
May-15 Sep 5HEC 〰 ♣ ♠ 🖢 🍴 ✕ ☉ 🗐 🔗 ♨ ⟡ S 🏬 ⊞ lau
Prices: ⚑6500-9000 pitch 12000-15000

RICCIONE FORLI

Alberello via Torino 80 ☎ 0541 615402
On the seafront connected to the beach by a private subway. Popular with families, with a wide range of recreational facilities.
⊃ *Access via A14 and SS16.*
May-20 Sep 4HEC ⸫⸫⸫ ♦ ⋔ ⴲ ♥ ✗ ⊙ ⬤ ∅ ⵎ ⌂ ⊞ ⊗ lau
♦ ⵚLS
Prices: ♦5600-10600 pitch 12100-18400

Fontanelle via Torino 56 ☎ 0541 615449
On southern outskirts separated from beach by coast road. Underpass to public beach.
Camping Card Compulsory.
⊃ *Turn off SS16 between Km216 and 217.*
Etr-20 Sep 6HEC ⸫⸫⸫ ⋔ ⴲ ♥ ✗ ⊙ ∅ ⵎ ⵚ S lau ♦ ⊞

Riccione via Marsala N10 ☎ 0541 690160
About 300m from sea. Extensive flat meadowland, with poplars of medium height.
⊃ *From SS16 turn seawards on the S outskirts of the town and continue for 200m. Alternative access from coast road, turn inland on S outskirts at sign and continue for 700m.*
May-20 Sep 6.5HEC ⸫⸫⸫ ♦ ⋔ ⴲ ♥ ✗ ⊙ ⬤ ∅ ⵎ ⵚ P ⊞ ⊞
lau ♦ ⵚS
Prices: ♦5600-10600 pitch 14200-32300

ROSETO DEGLI ABRUZZI TERAMO

Eurcamping-Roseto Lungomare Trieste Sud 90
☎ 085 8993179
A meadow site at the S end of the beach road.
⊃ *Leave the SS16 within the town, then continue for 500m to the site.*
All year 5HEC ⸫⸫⸫ ♦ ⋔ ⴲ ♥ ✗ ⊙ ⬤ ∅ ⵎ ⌂ ⵚ PS ⊞ ⊞ lau

Gilda viale Makarska ☎ 085 8941023
Jun-Aug 1.5HEC ⸫⸫⸫ ♦ ⋔ ⴲ ♥ ✗ ⊙ ⬤ ⵎ ⌂ ⴱ ⵚ S ⊞ ⊞ lau
♦ ∅ ⵚP
Prices: ♦5500-10000 ⛺14000-23000 ▲5000-9500

SALSOMAGGIORE TERME PARMA

Arizona via Tabiano 40 ☎ 0524 565648
Family site with plenty of activities, and close to two "thermal cures" establishments.
Apr-15 Oct 13HEC ⸫⸫⸫ ♦ ⋔ ⴲ ♥ ✗ ⊙ ⬤ ∅ ⴱ ⵚ P ▣ lau ♦ ⵎ
Prices: ♦8000-11000 ⛺13000-16000

SAN MARINO

Centro Turistico San Marino Strada San Michele 50
☎ 0549 903964
In a quiet, wooded location close to the centre of the Republic of San Marino.
⊃ *Access via 'Rimini Sud' exit on the A14.*
All year 100HEC ⸫⸫⸫ ⋔ ⴲ ♥ ✗ ⊙ ⬤ ∅ ⵎ ⴱ ⴲ ▲ ⵚ P ⊞
⊞ lau

SAN PIERO IN BAGNO FORLI

Altosavio strada per Alfero 37c ☎ 0543 917670
On level ground at an altitude of 600mtrs with good facilities.
⊃ *Exit E45 at Bagno di Romagna for San Piero in Bagno*
24 Apr-Sep 1.3HEC ⸫⸫⸫ ♦ ⋔ ⵚ ✗ ⊙ ⬤ ⊞ lau
Prices: ♦7500-8500 pitch 13000

SASSO MARCONI BOLOGNA

Piccolo Paradiso via Sirano, Marzabotto ☎ 051 842680
Pleasant site with plenty of trees. A new sport centre less than 100mtrs from the site provides excellent facilities for sports and recreation.

⊃ *Leave A1 autostrada (Milano-Roma) at town exit and continue towards Vado for 2km. Signposted.*
All year 6.5HEC ⸫⸫⸫ ♦ ⋔ ⴲ ♥ ✗ ⊙ ⬤ ∅ ⵎ ⴱ ⊞ lau ♦ ♥ ✗
ⵚLPR

At SAVIGNANO SUL RUBICONE

Rubicone via Matrice Destra 1 ☎ 0541 346377
An extensive, level site divided into two sections by a narrow canal. It extends to the beach.
⊃ *Situated about 0.8km from the road fork at Km187/0 off SS16 (Strada Adriatica).*
May-Sep 13HEC ⸫⸫⸫ ⋔ ♦ ⋔ ⴲ ♥ ✗ ⊙ ⬤ ∅ ⴱ ⵚ PS ⊞ ⊞ ⊗
lau
Prices: ♦8000-13400 pitch 16500-23500

SCACCHI, LIDO DEGLI FERRARA

Florenz via alpi Centrali 199 ☎ 0533 380193
Site with sand dunes extending to the sea.
⊃ *Turn off the Strada Romea in the direction of Lido Degli Scacchi, and continue along an asphalt road to the sandy beach.*
24 Apr-18 Sep 8HEC ⸫⸫⸫ ⸫⸫ ⋔ ♦ ⋔ ⴲ ♥ ✗ ⊙ ⬤ ∅ ⵎ ⴱ ⴲ ⵚ
PS ⊞ lau
Prices: ♦6000-12000 pitch 13000-19000

SENIGALLIA ANCONA

Summerland via Podesti 236 ☎ 071 7926816
A pleasant site with good facilities, 150mtrs from the sea.
⊃ *3km from Senigallia exit on SS16.*
Jun-15 Sep 4.5HEC ⸫⸫⸫ ♦ ⋔ ⴲ ♥ ✗ ⊙ ⬤ ∅ ⴱ ⊞ ⊞ lau
♦ ⵚPS
Prices: ♦5500-8250 pitch 15000-22000

SPINA, LIDO DI FERRARA

Spina via del Campeggio 99 ☎ 0533 330179
Widespread site on level meadowland and on slightly hilly sand dune terrain. Separate section for dog owners.
⊃ *Off SS309. Signposted.*
17 Apr-19 Sep 24HEC ⸫⸫⸫ ♦ ⋔ ⴲ ♥ ✗ ⊙ ⬤ ∅ ⴱ ⵚ PS ⊞
lau ♦ ⊞
Prices: ♦5000-9700 ⛺10000-19000 ▲10000-19000

SPOLETO PERUGIA

Monteluco S.Pietro ☎ 0743 220358
A modern site situated on the slopes of Monteluco.
⊃ *From the SS75 towards Foligno exit on to the SS3 towards Spoleto. The Monteluco road leads to the site.*
Apr-Sep 6HEC ⸫⸫⸫ ⟡ ♦ ⋔ ♥ ✗ ⊙ ⬤ ⴱ ⊞ ♦ ⴲ ⊞
Prices: ♦7000-8000 ⟡3000-4000 ⛺7000-8000 ▲7000-8000

TORINO DI SANGRO MARINA CHIETI

Belvedere ☎ 0873 911381
Jun-15 Sep 1.5HEC ⸫⸫⸫ ♦ ⋔ ⴲ ♥ ✗ ⊙ ⬤ ∅ ⵎ ⴱ ⵚ S ⊞
♦ ✗ ⵚP ⊞

VASTO CHIETI

Europa ☎ 0873 801988
Site on level terrain by the road with poplars.
⊃ *At Km522 of road SS16.*
May-Sep 2.3HEC ⸫⸫⸫ ♦ ⋔ ⴲ ♥ ✗ ⊙ ⬤ ∅ ⵎ ⴱ ⵚ S lau ♦ ∅
Prices: ♦7500-11200 pitch 12300-17200

Grotta del Saraceno via Osca 6, loc Vignola ☎ 0873 310213
Site in olive grove on steep coastal cliffs with lovely views. Steep path to beach. Siesta 14.00-16.00 hrs.
⊃ *Turn off SS16 at Km512.200.*
15 Jun-15 Sep 12HEC ⸫⸫⸫ ♦ ⋔ ⴲ ♥ ✗ ⊙ ⬤ ⵎ ⴱ ⵚ S lau
♦ ∅ ⵎ

Pioppeto ☎ 0873 801466
Camping Card Compulsory.
15 May-Sep 1HEC ﹏ ♦ ⋒ ⚊ ⍾ ⚐ ✕ ⊙ ⚑ ⬛ ♦ ⬗ ≟ ⟨S ⊞
Prices: ⚑8000-10000 ⬤5500-7000 ⚑11000-13000 ▲11000-13000

VILLALAGO L'AQUILA

I Lupi ☎ 0864 740100
All year 7HEC ﹏ ⊶ ⋒ ⚊ ⍾ ⊙ ⚑ ⬛ ⚑ ▥ ⊞ ♦ ⬗ ⟨LP

● ● ● ● ● **ROME** ● ● ● ● ●

Rome has affected western culture and attitudes for more than 2,000 years. The city is uniquely beautiful; from the famous Colosseum (a third of which is still intact) to the elegantly proportioned piazzas and churches, there are historic buildings which provide dramatic examples of changing architectural ideals. Of the 22 bridges which span the Tiber, some date from the first century BC.
Situated on the famous seven hills, the city is the focus of the province of Latium, which has been described as 'the cradle of Roman civilization'. Stretching from the Apennines to the Tyrrhenian sea, it is characterised by magnificent and beautiful scenery, especially in the volcanic regions, where long extinct volcanoes form the lakes of Albano, Bracciano, Bolsena and Vico. Viterbo, in the northern hills, is a large town with many fine examples of religious architecture, including the 13th-century Papal Palace. Rieti's Civic Museum houses an extensive collection of Roman artifacts, while Frosinone commands breathtaking views of surrounding countryside. The Latin Lido features sheltered harbours and sandy beaches.

ANGUILLARA-SABAZIA ROMA

Parco del Lago via Trevighahese ☎ 06 99802003
➲ *Alongside Lake Bracciano, off the Trevignano road, in beautiful countryside. A variety of watersports facilities are available.*
Apr-Sep 3HEC ﹏ ♦ ⋒ ⚊ ⍾ ⚐ ✕ ⊙ ⚑ ⬤ ≟ ⬛ ⚑ ⟨ L ▣ ⬥ lau
Prices: ⚑7500-9500 pitch 10000-12000

BOLSENA VITERBO

Lido via Cassia ☎ 0761 799258
A lakeside family site with good modern facilities.
➲ *Access via motorway exit 'Orvieto'.*
Apr-Sep 10HEC ﹏ ♦ ⋒ ⚊ ⍾ ⚐ ✕ ⊙ ⚑ ⬤ ≟ ⬛ ⟨ L ▣ ⬥ lau ♦ ⊞

BRACCIANO ROMA

Porticciolo via Porticciolo ☎ 06 99803060
A family site in a pleasant location on the shore of a lake.
➲ *Access via SS493 to Bracciano.*
Apr-Sep 2.8HEC ﹏ ♦ ⋒ ⚊ ⍾ ⚐ ✕ ⊙ ⚑ ⬤ ⚑ ⟨ L ▣ lau ♦ ⊞
Prices: ⚑8000-9000 ⬤2500-3000 ⚑9000-10000 ▲8000-9000

FORMIA LATINA

Gianola via delle Vigne ☎ 0771 720223
Situated in a narrow grassland area near a little stream and trees amidst agricultural land. Pleasantly sandy beach edged by rocks.
➲ *Access via Roma-Napoli road, from S Croce 800m.*
Apr-Sep 4HEC ﹏ ⦂⦂⦂ ♦ ⋒ ⚊ ⍾ ⚐ ✕ ⊙ ⚑ ⬤ ≟ ⬛ ⟨ RS ▣ ♦ ⊞

MINTURNO, MARINA DI LATINA

Golden Garden via Dunale 74 ☎ 0771 681425
Secluded quiet site within agricultural area by the sea.
Camping Card Compulsory.
➲ *Access from the SS7 across river bridge (Garigliano) and continue 4.6km changing direction. Last km sandy field track.*
All year 2.3HEC ﹏ ♦ ⋒ ⚊ ⍾ ⚐ ✕ ⊙ ⚑ ⬤ ≟ ⟨ S ⬛ ⊞ lau

MONTALTO DI CASTRO, MARINA DI VITERBO

Internazionale Pionier Etrusco via Vulsinia ☎ 0766 802199
Situated in a pine forest close to the beach. Various leisure and sports activities, also a relaxing aymosphere.
Camping Card Compulsory.
All year 3HEC ⦂⦂⦂ ♦ ⋒ ⚊ ⍾ ✕ ⊙ ⚑ ⬤ ≟ ⬛ ⟨ LPRS ⬛ ⬥ lau ♦ ⚊ ⟨PRS ⊞

PESCIA ROMANA, MARINA DI VITERBO

Gli Amici ☎ 0766 830250
A quiet, pleasantly situated site behind dunes. Clean wide beach.
➲ *Turn off via Aurelia seawards at Km118.5. After 4.3km turn right and continue on sandy tracks 900m.*
All year 2.6HEC ﹏ ♦ ⋒ ⚊ ⍾ ⚐ ✕ ⊙ ⚑ ≟ ⬛ ⚑ ⬛ lau ♦ ⟨PS

ROMA (ROME) ROMA

Flaminio via Flaminia 821 ☎ 06 3332604
An exstensive site with good facilities, which lies in a quiet valley on narrow terraces on a hill.
➲ *From ring road follow via Flaminia, SS3, for 2.5km towards city centre.*
15 Mar-8 Nov 8.4HEC ﹏ ♦ ⋒ ⚊ ⍾ ⚐ ✕ ⊙ ⚑ ⬤ ≟ ⚑ ⟨ P ▣ lau ♦ ⟨R ⊞
Prices: ⚑12000-13000 ⬤6000-7000 ⚑8000-9000 ▲7000-8000

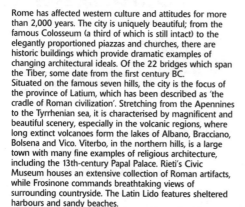

A real oasis with the correct balance between landscape, man and animals – only a stone's throw from the eternal city.

Camping Seven Hills
VILLAGGIO TURISTICO
for fun-loving people

4 km from Rome – via Cassia 1216
Tel: 06/30310826-30362751
Fax: 06/30310039
I-00191 ROMA

The campsite is located near Exit No. 3 of the city ring road with ample tree cover set in a delightful valley between the seven hills of Rome. Site has good transport links with the city centre and the Vatican: only 20 minutes in our own bus! The site has well-kept toilet facilities with cold and hot showers, food shop, shopping area, bar, restaurant, pizzeria, discotheque, camping gas, medical service, laundry service, ironing room, table tennis, **swimming pool with salted water, mini zoo**, volleyball court, horse riding, golf course (Olgiata 2 km). Excursions also to Capri and Pompei.

Also bungalows for hire on the site. Flats for 2 or 3 persons with bathroom and kitchen . On presentation of this guide 10% discount from 5th overnight. Special conditions for groups of 20 persons and over.
Open throughout the year. Facilities for riding.

An island of tranquillity outside the gates of the capital (peace). The TIBER campsite is located on the banks of the Tevere and is open from 01.03 to 10.11. Bar – Restaurant – Pizzeria – Supermarket – Swimming-pool – Playground for children – Sightseeing tours – Automatic washing machine. Rooms and caravans to let and accommodation for groups. Centre of Rome 20 minutes by public transport. **From the North: from A1, direction ROME NORTH exit FIANO ROMANO than on the Tiberina Road towards Rome. From Gran Raccordo Anulare: Exit Nr. 6 FLAMINIA – PRIMA PORTA than follows the signs to via Tiberina.**
Via Tiberina Km. 1,400.
Tel. 06/33610733.
Fax: 33612314
I-00188 PRIMA PORTA
ROMA, ITALY

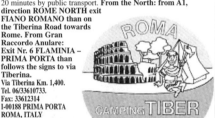

Happy via Prato della Corte 1915 ☎ 06 33626401
Conveniently placed in northern area of town. Modern installations, electricity and hot water free throughout.
➲ *Exit No.5 "Grande Raccordo Anulare" (ring road).*
15 Mar-Oct 3.6HEC ⬛ ♠ ⋔ ⛊ ⛯ ⛾ ✕ ⊙ ⬛ ∅ ⛺ ⋟ P ⛾ ⊞ lau

Roma via Aurelia 831 ☎ 06 6623018
The site lies on terraces on a hill near the AGIP Motel. All kinds of excursions can be arranged.
➲ *From ring road follow SS1 (via Aurelia) for 1.5km towards town centre turn off to site at Km8/11.*
All year 3HEC ⬛ ♠ ⋔ ⛊ ⛯ ⛾ ✕ ⊙ ⬛ ∅ ⛺ ⛊ lau ♠ ⛊ ⋟P ⊞
Prices: ⋔11000-12000 ⋒5500-6000 ⛺9500-10000 ⛁5500-6000

Seven Hills via Cassia 1216 ☎ 06 30310826
A fine, partly terraced site in beautiful rural surroundings yet ideally situated for access to the city by bus or underground.
➲ *2.5km NE of the outer ring road via exit '3'.*
All year 5HEC ⬛ ♦ ♠ ⋔ ⛊ ✕ ⊙ ⬛ ∅ ⛺ ⋟ P ⛾ lau
Prices: ⋔12500 ⋒6000 ⛺12000 ⛁8000

Tiber via Tiberina Km1400 ☎ 06 33612314
On level grassland, shaded by poplars beside the Tiber.
➲ *N of city. Signposted from ringroad. Access from N via exit '3' or from S follow signs 'Prima Porta'.*
Mar-4 Nov 5HEC ⬛ ♠ ⋔ ⛊ ⛯ ⛾ ✕ ⊙ ⬛ ∅ ⛺ ⛊ ⋟ PR ⛾ ⊞ lau
Prices: ⋔11000-12000 ⋒5500-6000 ⛺9000-9500 ⛁5500-6000

SALTO DI FONDI LATINA

Fondi Holiday Camp via Flacce Km 6800 ☎ 0771 555009
Well-shaded and well-equipped site only a few metres from the Mediterranean.

Apr-Sep 4HEC ⬛ ⁙ ♠ ⋔ ⛊ ⛯ ✕ ⊙ ⬛ ∅ ⛺ ⛺ ⛊ ⋟ LPS ⬛ ⊞ ⌀ lau

TERRACINA LATINA

Badino Porto Badino ☎ 0773 764430
Apr-15 Oct 1.8HEC ⬛ ⁙ ♠ ⋔ ⛊ ⊙ ⬛ ∅ ⛺ ⛺ ⛁ ⋟ S ⬛ ♠ ⛊ ✕
Prices: ⋔8000-12000 pitch 12000-22000

● ● ● ● SOUTH ● ● ● ●

The area known as the Mezzogiorno, takes in Campania and the 'toe and heel' provinces of Calabria (the toe), Basilicata, and Apulia (the heel).
From Naples, a port set in a beautiful bay with volcanic Vesuvius behind it, you travel south to an area in which you look back in time and where the language is different from northern Italian. Apulia is mountainous but has fertile plains producing olives, wines and tobacco. In the university town of Lecce you can see the exuberant 'Lecce Baroque' ornate stone carving while in Alberobella you find the circular 'trulli' houses made of drystone with cone shaped roofs. Equally intriguing is the abandoned city at Matera where semi-cave dwellings made of tufa used to house hundreds of families.
Baby octopus and other fish are part of a healthy diet of seafood, vegetables and pulses. Travel though the poorest region of Italy, Basilicata, before arriving in Calabria - also mountainous, with skiing in winter, but with 372 miles of coastline. Reggio di Calabria, right on the toe, has a mild climate in which exotic plants like the bergamot orange flourish.
....

ACCIAROLI SALERNO

Ondina ☎ 0974 904040
Delightful seaside site, full of flowers. Lunchtime siesta
14.00-16.00 hrs.
⮑ *Turn off towards the sea at Km35/VII.*
Apr-Oct 3HEC ⚏ ♣ ♠ ℥ 🏪 ⛽ ✕ ⊙ ☻ ∅ ≕ 🏕 ⛺ ⤢ S 🏧 ⊞
♣ ✕

BAIA DOMIZIA CASERTA

Baia Domizia Camping Villaggio Baia Domizia
☎ 0823 930164
Part of this extensive seaside site is laid out with flower beds.
Good sports and leisure facilities. Ideal for families. No
radios allowed.
⮑ *Turn off the SS7 (qtr) at Km6/V, then 3km seawards.*
May-Sep 35HEC ⚏ ∵ ♣ ♠ ℥ 🏪 ⛽ ✕ ⊙ ☻ ∅ ≕ 🏕 ⤢ PS 🏧
⊞ ≈ lau
Prices: ⚑5900-14000 ♠3500-7500 ⚑9000-19500

BATTIPAGLIA SALERNO

Lido Mediterraneo via Litoranea, Salerno Paestum
☎ 0828 624097
In a pinewood with direct access to a private beach.
15 Apr-Sept 1.5HEC ⚏ ♣ ♠ ℥ 🏪 ⛽ ✕ ⊙ ☻ ∅ ≕ 🏕 ⤢ S ⊞
⊞ ♣ ✕ ⤢P

BRIATICO CATANZARO

Dolomiti ☎ 0963 391355
The site is in a delightful setting on two terraces planted with
olive trees. It lies by the road and 50m from railway.
⮑ *Turn off road 522 between Km17 and Km18 and head
towards the sea.*
May-Sep 5HEC ⚏ ♣ ♠ ℥ 🏪 ⛽ ✕ ⊙ ☻ ∅ ≕ 🏕 ⛺ ⤢ S 🏧 ⏚
lau ♣
Prices: ⚑8000-14500 ♠4000-6000 ⚑9000-13500
⚑9000-13500

CAMEROTA, MARINA DI SALERNO

Happy Localita Arconte ☎ 0974 932326
The site lies on a park-like hill sloping down to the sea and is
scattered with olive trees.
⮑ *1km N of village just off the coast road.*
Jun-Sep 12HEC ⚏ ♣ ♠ ℥ 🏪 ⛽ ✕ ⊙ ☻ ≕ 🏕 ⛺ ⤢ S ⊞

Risacca via delle Barche 11, Lentiscella ☎ 0974 932415
On level ground, shaded by olive trees, with direct access to a
sandy beach.
⮑ *Approach via SS18.*
20 May-20 Sep 2HEC ⚏ ♣ ♠ ℥ 🏪 ⛽ ✕ ⊙ ☻ ∅ ≕ 🏕 ⛺
⤢ S ⏚ ⊞

CAMPORA SAN GIOVANNI COSENZA

Principessa ☎ 0982 46903
Modern motel with camp site annexed to it, lying 150m from
the sea and a fine sandy beach.
⮑ *2km S and inland from Campora on SS18.*
All year 30HEC ⚏ ∵ ♣ ♠ ℥ 🏪 ⛽ ✕ ⊙ ☻ ∅ ≕ 🏕 ⤢ PS
🏧 ⊞ lau

CAPO VATICANO CATANZARO

Gabbiano San Nicolo di Ricadi ☎ 0963 663159
Apr-Oct ⚏ ∵ ♣ ♠ ℥ 🏪 ⛽ ✕ ⊙ ☻ ∅ ≕ 🏕 ⛺ ⤢ PS ⏚ lau
♣ ⊞
Prices: ⚑9500-19000 pitch 11000-22500

Quattro Scogli San Nicolo di Ricadi
☎ 0963 663126 & 663115
The site is beautifully located in a quiet sandy bay
surrounded by rocks.

Camping Card Compulsory.
⮑ *Drive from San Nicolo di Ricardi to Capo Vaticano.*
All year 0.8HEC ∵ ♣ ♠ ℥ 🏪 ⛽ ✕ ⊙ ☻ ∅ ≕ 🏕 ⛺ ⤢ S ⏚ ⊞
Prices: ⚑10000-14000 ♠4000-6500 ⚑14000-18000
⚑12000-16000

CAROVIGNO BRINDISI

At SPECCHIOLLA, LIDO

Pineta al Mare Lido Specchiolla ☎ 0831 987821
Site in pine woodland with sandy beach and some rocks.
⮑ *E of Bari-Brindisi road at Km21.5.*
All year 5.5HEC ⚏ ♣ ♠ ℥ 🏪 ⛽ ✕ ⊙ ☻ ∅ ≕ 🏕 ⤢ PS ⊞ lau
Prices: ⚑8500-12500 ♠3000-4500 ⚑10000-12000
⚑8000-10000

CIRÒ MARINA CATANZARO

Punta Alice ☎ 0962 31160
The site lies on meadowland amidst lush Mediterranean
vegetation and borders a fine gravel beach, some 50m wide.
⮑ *2km from town. From SS106 (Strada Ionica) turn off at
Km290 seaward to Cira Marina. Pass through village and
follow beach road for 1.5m towards the lighthouse.*
Apr-Sep 5.5HEC ∵ ♣ ♠ ℥ 🏪 ⛽ ✕ ⊙ ☻ ∅ ≕ 🏕 ⤢ PS ⏚ ⊞
Prices: ⚑5300-10500 ♠3000-5400 ⚑5800-11300
⚑5300-10400

Villaggio Torrenova via Torrenova ☎ 0962 31482
Directly on sea, with on site facilities to suit all the family.
May-Sep 1.2HEC ∵ ♣ ♠ ℥ 🏪 ⛽ ✕ ⊙ ☻ ≕ 🏕 ⤢ S ⏚ lau
♣ ⊞
Prices: pitch 25000-67000 (incl 2 persons)

CORIGLIANO CÁLABRO COSENZA

Thurium Contrada Ricota Grande ☎ 0983 851955
The site is close to the beach and has all the facilites needed
for an enjoyable camping break. It is just a walk away from
the woodland and ideal for peaceful walks.
Jun-15 Sep 16HEC ∵ ◨ ♣ ♠ ℥ 🏪 ⛽ ✕ ⊙ ☻ ∅ ≕ 🏕 ⛺ ⤢ S ⏚
⏚ ⊞ lau
Prices: ⚑5000-12000 ♠2500-6000 ⚑5000-13000
⚑3500-10000

EBOLI SALERNO

Paestum Foce Sele ☎ 0828 691003
Sandy, meadowland site in tall poplar wood by river mouth.
Steps and bus service to private beach, 600m from site.
⮑ *Access from the Litoranea at Km20 from the road fork to
Santa Cecilia and continue for 0.3km. Signposted.*
Apr-10 Sep 8HEC ⚏ ♣ ♠ ℥ 🏪 ⛽ ✕ ⊙ ☻ ∅ ≕ 🏕 ⤢ P 🏧 ⊞
lau ♣ ⤢RS
Prices: ⚑4500-8300 pitch 13500-24500

GALLIPOLI LECCE

Baia di Gallipoli ☎ 0832 315542 or 358957
Camping Card Compulsory.
Jun-Sep 10HEC ⚏ ♣ ♠ ℥ 🏪 ⛽ ✕ ⊙ ☻ ∅ ≕ 🏕 ⤢ P ⊞ ♣ ⤢S

Vecchia Torre ☎ 0833 209083
This well-kept and clean site lies amidst sand dunes in a pine
wood. Small size pitches.
⮑ *5km N of Gallipoli and 200m S of Hotel Rivabella at
seaward side of coast road.*
Jun-Sep 8HEC ∵ ♣ ♠ ℥ 🏪 ⛽ ✕ ⊙ ☻ ∅ ≕ 🏕 ⤢ S ⏚ ⊞ ♣ ≈ lau
Prices: ⚑6000-7000 ⚑10000-25000 ⚑10000-25000

GIOVINAZZO BARI

Campofreddo ☎ 080 8942112
Site in level terrain by the sea, mainly under sunshade
roofing. Siesta 14.00-16.00 hrs.

➲ *Turn off the SS16, 20km N of Bari at Km784,300.*
May-Sep 34HEC ⊞ Ϥ ↿ ⅏ ⅀ ⅄ ✕ ⊙ ⬚ ⬚ ⬚ ⬚ ⬚ ✕ lau
➤ ✕ ⅂S

GUARDAVALLE, MARINA DI CATANZARO

Dello Ionio via Nazionale ☎ 0967 86002
Site is situated on the seafront and along 4km of sandy beach. All pitches are under the shade of tall trees and have large grassy areas.
➲ *Situated 2km from Santa Caterina dello Jonio on the SS106.*
Jun-15 Sep 5HEC ⊞ ➤ ↿ ⅏ ⅀ ⅄ ✕ ⊙ ⬚ ⬚ ⬚ ⬚ ⬚ ⬚ ⅂ S ⬚
⬚ lau
Prices: ↟6500-10900 ➥3000-4000 ⬚8000-12500
⬚5000-8000

LÁURA SALERNO

Hera Argiva ☎ 0828 851193
Site in sandy terrain in eucalyptus grove by the sea.
➲ *Signposted from Km88/VII SS18.*
Apr-Sep 40HEC ⸪ ➤ ↿ ⅏ ⅀ ⅄ ✕ ⊙ ⬚ ⬚ ⬚ ⬚ ⅂ S ⬚ ⬚ lau

LEPRANO, MARINA DI TARANTO

Porto Pirrone Litoranea Salentina ☎ 099 5334844
Set in a pine wood offering flat large plots for both tents and caravans. Good sports and entertainment. No Animals.
➲ *From A14 at Massafra towards Taranto and Leporano. Site is near marina.*
Jun-Sep 3.2HEC ⊞ ⸪ ➤ ↿ ⅏ ⅀ ⅄ ✕ ⬚ ⬚ ⅂ S ⬚ ⬚
⬚ ➤ ✕ ⬚ ⬚
Prices: ↟7000-10000 ➥3000-4500 ⬚7000-10000
⬚5000-7000

MÁCCHIA FOGGIA

Monaco ☎ 0884 530280
In a pleasant situation with good facilities and direct access to the beach.
Jun-Aug 5.3HEC ⊞ ➤ ↿ ⅏ ⅀ ⅄ ✕ ⊙ ⬚ ⬚ ⬚ ⅂ S ⬚ ⬚ ✕
lau
Prices: ↟5000-10000 pitch 7000-12000

MASSA LUBRENSE NAPOLI

Villa Lubrense via Partenope 31 ☎ 081 5339781
All year 2.5HEC ⊞ ➤ ↿ ⅏ ⅀ ⅄ ✕ ⊙ ⬚ ⬚ ⬚ ⅂ PS ⬚ ⬚

MATTINATA FOGGIA

Degli Ulivi ☎ 0884 550118
This well-kept grassland site lies in an old olive grove, facing a picturesque bay.
➲ *Off SS89, 0.6km N of turning to Mattinata.*
Jun-Sep 2HEC ⊞ ➤ ↿ ⅏ ⅀ ⅄ ✕ ⊙ ⬚ ⬚ ⬚ ⅂ PS ⬚ lau
➤ ✕ ⬚
Prices: ↟7500-19000

Villaggio Turistico San Lorenzo ☎ 0884 4152
The site is situated above the coast road in direction of Viesta. Bungalows for hire.
Camping Card Compulsory.
All year 5HEC ⊞ ➤ ↿ ⅏ ⅀ ⅄ ✕ ⊙ ⬚ ⬚ ⬚ ⅂ PS ⬚ ⬚ lau
➤ ⬚ ⬚

METAPONTO, LIDO DI MATERA

Camel Camping Club viale Magna Grecia ☎ 0835 741926
A modern, well organised site. Sports and entertainment avaliable all season. Ideal for both relaxing and sightseeing.
Jun-Sep 3.5HEC ⸪ ➤ ↿ ⅏ ⅀ ⅄ ✕ ⬚ ⬚ ⅂ P ➤ ⬚ ⅂S ⬚
Prices: ↟7000-16500 ➥3000-9000 ⬚7000-16500
⬚7000-16500

NICÓTERA MARINA CATANZARO

Sabbia d'Oro ☎ 0963 886395
Lies on level ground amidst farmland 100m from a beautiful lonely beach.
➲ *Turn off SS18 at Km453/VII and continue 15km.*
15 Jun-10 Sept 2.7HEC ⸪ ➤ ↿ ⅏ ⅀ ⅄ ✕ ⊙ ⬚ ⬚ ⬚ ⬚ ⬚ S
⬚ ⬚ lau
Prices: ↟8500 ➥4000 ⬚10000 ⬚7500

OTRANTO LECCE

Mulino d'Acqua via S Stefano ☎ 0836 802191
Shaded by olive trees, close to the beach and with plenty of organised activities.
Jun-5 Sep 10HEC ⊞ ➤ ↿ ⅏ ⅀ ⅄ ✕ ⊙ ⬚ ⬚ ⬚ ⬚ ⬚ ⅂ PS ⬚
⬚ lau

PAESTUM SALERNO

Vilaggio del Pini ☎ 0828 811030 & 811323
The site lies on hilly ground in a pine forest beside clean and sandy beach.
Camping Card Compulsory.
➲ *Turn off via Tirrenia at Km95/1X and continue 1km.*
All year 3HEC ⊞ ⸪ Ϥ ➤ ↿ ⅏ ⅀ ⅄ ✕ ⊙ ⬚ ⬚ ⬚ ⬚ ⬚ ⅂
PRS ⬚ ⬚ lau

PALMI REGGIO DI CALABRIA

San Fantino via S-Fantino ☎ 0966 479430
Site on several terraces with lovely views of the bay of Lido di Palmi. 200m to the beach. Siesta 13.00-16.00 hrs.
➲ *Turn off road SS18 seawards N of Palmi.*
All year 4HEC ⊞ ➤ ↿ ⅏ ⅀ ⅄ ✕ ⊙ ⬚ ⬚ ⬚ ⬚ ⬚ ⬚ lau
➤ ⅂PS ⬚

PESCHICI FOGGIA

Centro Turistico San Nicola Loc San Nicola ☎ 0884 964024
Terraced site in lovely situation by the sea, in a bay enclosed by rocks. Can become overcrowded.
➲ *Turn off coast road Peschici-Vieste, follow signs along winding road to site in 1km.*
Apr-15 Oct 14HEC ⊞ ➤ ↿ ⅏ ⅀ ⅄ ✕ ⊙ ⬚ ⬚ ⬚ ⬚ ⅂ S ⬚ ⬚
lau
Prices: ↟6700-14500 ➥5100-8800 ⬚8700-17500
⬚6700-14500

Internazionale Manacore ☎ 0884 911020
Meadowland with a few terraces in attractive bay, surrounded by wooded hills.
➲ *Turn off the coastal road (Peschici-Vieste) towards ths sea in a wide U bend.*
4 May-20 Oct 20HEC ⊞ ➤ ↿ ⅏ ⅀ ⅄ ✕ ⊙ ⬚ ⬚ ⅂ S ⬚
Prices: ↟7000-12000 ➥3000-5000 ⬚7000-13000
⬚6000-11000

PIZZO, MARINA DI CATANZARO

Pinetamare ☎ 0963 534871
A sandy site surrounded by tall pine trees. Most watersports are avaliable along the private beach and families are welcomed.
➲ *From the Salerno/Reggio motorway take the Pizzo exit and site is north of town.*
Jun-Sep 10HEC ⸪ ➤ ↿ ⅏ ⅀ ⅄ ✕ ⊙ ⬚ ⬚ ⬚ ⬚ ⅂ PS ⬚ ⬚
lau ➤ ⅂L

POMPEI NAPOLI

Spartacus via Plinio 127 ☎ 081 5369519
Site is on a level meadow with orange trees.
➲ *Lies near the motorway exit, Pompei and access is from the main Napoli road, opposite Scavi di Pompei near an IP petrol station.* *Contd.*

All year 9HEC ⚏ ♣🏠🕍♋️🍴✕⊙⚑∅♨ 🏕 💬🅿️⊞ lau ➡ ⏉S
Prices: 🏕7000-9000 🚐3000 🚏6000 🛆3000

POZZUOLI NAPOLI

Vulcano Solfatara via Solfatara 161 ☎ 081 5267413
Clean and orderly site situated in a deciduous forest near the crater of the extinct Solfatara volcano.
⮑ *Leave Nuova via Domiziana (SS7 qtr) at Km60/1 (at about 6km short of Napoli) and turn inland through stone gate.*
Apr-Oct 3HEC ⚏ ♣🏠🕍♋️✕⊙⚑∅🚿🏕💬🛆⏉P🅿️⊞ lau
Prices: 🏕11000-14000 🚐7500-10000 🚏11500-14000 🛆6500-9000

At VARCATURO, MARINA DI (12km N)

Partenope ☎ 081 5091076
Partially undulating terrain in woodland of medium height.
Camping Card Compulsory.
⮑ *Turn seawards for 300m at Km45/II of the SS7 (via Domiziana).*
May-15 Sep 5HEC ⚏ ♣🏠🕍♋️🍴✕⊙⚑∅♨🏕⏉RS🅿️⊞ 🎗 lau
Prices: 🏕10000-11500 pitch 13000-17000

PRAIA A MARE COSENZA

Internazionale sul Mare ☎ 0985 72211
In a beautiful location on the Gulf of Policastro with fine recreational facilities.
⮑ *Access via A3 to Falerna and then SS18.*
15 Jun-15 Sep 4HEC ⚏ ♨♣🏠🕍♋️🍴✕⊙⚑∅🚿🏕💬🛆 ⏉S🅿️⊞

RODI GARGANICO FOGGIA

Ripa Contrada Ripa ☎ 0884 965367
Well-equipped and attractive site close to the beach.
20 Jun-9 Sept 6HEC ⚏ ♣🏠🕍♋️🍴✕⊙⚑∅🏕⏉PS⊞ lau ➡ ⊞
Prices: 🏕8000-15000 pitch 8000-12000

ROSSANO SCALO COSENZA

Marina di Rossano Contrada Leuca ☎ 0983 516054
In wooded surroundings close to the beach, with good, modern facilities.
⮑ *Access via N106.*
10 Apr-26 Sep 7HEC ⚏ ♣🏠🕍♋️🍴✕⊙⚑🏕⏉PS🅿️⊞ lau ➡♨

SALVE, MARINA DI LECCE

Ionian Club ☎ 0833 741379
May-Oct 6HEC ⚏ ♣🏠🕍♋️✕⊙⚑∅🚿🏕💬🛆⏉P🅿️⊞ ➡⏉S

SAN MENÁIO FOGGIA

Valle d'Oro via Degli Ulivi ☎ 0884 991580
Site in olive grove surrounded by wooded hills with some terraces.
⮑ *Turn off the SS89 onto SS528 and to site at Km1.800. 2km from the sea.*
15 Jun-Sept 3HEC ⚏ ♣🏠🕍♋️✕⊙⚑∅🏕🅿️➡🕍∅⏉PS⊞
Prices: 🏕4000-7000 pitch 6000-10000

SAN NICOLO DI RICADI CATANZARO

Agrumeto ☎ 0963 663175
The access road leads over a dusty field track, then on to a steep ramp with large, wide bends. Because the trees are very close together, the pitches are rather narrow. Lying in a lemon grove beside the sea, this site looks more like a garden. Beautiful beach. Excursions by boat can be arranged.
Apr-Sep 3.7HEC ⚏ ♣🏠🕍♋️🍴✕⊙⚑∅🏕⏉S🅿️⊞ lau

SANTA CESÁREA TERME LECCE

Scogliera ☎ 0836 949802
Attractive site close to the sea.
⮑ *1km S on SS173.*
All year 8HEC ⦙⦙⦙ ♣🏠🕍♋️🍴✕⊙⚑∅🏕💬⏉PS ➡🚿⊞

SANTA MARIA DI CASTELLABATE SALERNO

Trezene ☎ 0974 965027
The site is partly divided into pitches and consists of two sections lying either side of the access road. Pitches between road and fine sandy beach are reserved for touring campers.
Apr-Oct 2.5HEC ⚏ ♣🏠🕍♋️🍴✕⊙⚑∅🚿🏕⏉S🅿️⊞⊘ lau ⏉P
Prices: 🏕7000-12000 pitch 20000-34000

SOLE, LIDO DEL FOGGIA

Lido del Mare c da Pantanello 27 ☎ 0884 917012
30 May-26 Sep 22HEC ⚏ ♣🏠🕍♋️🍴✕⊙⚑∅🏕💬⏉S🅿️ lau ➡🕍✕∅⏉LPS⊞

SORRENTO NAPOLI

Campogaio via Capo 39 ☎ 081 8073579
A well appointed, terraced site shaded by olive trees and with direct access to the sea.
⮑ *2km from town centre and 400m beyond the turning from the SS145 on road towards Massa Lubrense and 50m from sea.*
Apr-Sep 10HEC ⚏ ♣🏠🕍♋️🍴✕⊙⚑∅🚿🏕⏉PS🅿️⊞ lau
Prices: 🏕10000-15000 🚐5000-7000 🚏11000-15000 🛆9000-12000

Giardino delle Esperidi S.Agnello ☎ 081 8783255
In a pleasant park, surrounded by lemon and orange trees 2km from the centre of Sorrento and 250mtrs from La Marinella beach. There are good facilities and modern bungalows are available for hire.
Mar-Oct 3HEC ⚏ ♣🏠♋️🍴✕⊙⚑🏕💬⏉S🅿️⊞ lau ➡🕍∅

International Camping Nube d'Argento via Capo 21 ☎ 081 8781344
The site lies on narrow terraces just off a steep concrete road between the beach and the outskirts of the town.
⮑ *Access is rather difficult for caravans.*
All year 1.5HEC ⚏ ♣🏠🕍♋️🍴✕⊙⚑∅🏕💬⏉PS🅿️⊞
Prices: 🏕12000-16000 🚐5000-6000 🚏11000-14000 🛆6000-14000

Santa Fortunata via Capo ☎ 081 8073579
Extensive site lying on terraces in a shady olive grove with many small secluded pitches.
Camping Card Compulsory.
⮑ *1km from town and 50m from sea.*
Apr-Sep 12HEC ⚏ ♣🏠🕍♋️🍴✕⊙⚑∅🚿🏕💬🛆⏉PS🅿️⊞ lau

TORRE RINALDA LECCE

Torre Rinalda Litoranea Salentina ☎ 0832 652161
On an extensive level meadow, separated from the sea by dunes. Discotheque. Lunchtime siesta 13.30-16.00 hrs.
⮑ *Access via SS613 (Brindisi-Lecce) exit Trepuzzi then coastal road for 1.5km.*
All year 23HEC ⚏ ♣🏠🕍♋️🍴✕⊙⚑∅🚿🏕💬🏕⏉PS🅿️⊞
Prices: 🏕6700-11500 🚐3000-5000 🚏8000-15000 🛆4700-9000

UGENTO LECCE

Riva di Ugento Litoranea Gallipoli-SM di Leve
☎ 0833 933600
A well equipped site in wooded surroundings close to the beach.

16 May-27 Sep 32HEC ⊞⊞⊞ ː∷ː ♠ ⋔ ⊾ ⫪ ✕ ⊙ ⊟ ⌀ ⇞ ⊕ ⚲
⫪ PS 🅿 ⊞ ⊗ lau
Prices: pitch 26000-56000 (incl 3 persons)

◗ VICO EQUENSE NAPOLI

Sant' Antonio Marina d'Equa ☎ 081 8028570
A modern site set among fruit trees, close to the beach with
fine views over the Bay of Naples.
Camping Card Compulsory.
15 Mar-15 Oct 1HEC ⊞⊞⊞ ♠ ⋔ ⊾ ⫪ ✕ ⊙ ⊟ ⌀ ⇞ ⊞ ⫪ S 🅿 ⊞
lau ➠ ⫪PS
Prices: ♠11000-13000 ♠4000-5000 ♠11000-13000
⚲8000-9000

Seiano Spiaggia Marina Aequa ☎ 081 8028560
About 20m from the sea.
Apr-Sep 2.2HEC ⊞⊞⊞ ♠ ⋔ ⊾ ⫪ ✕ ⊙ ⊟ ⌀ ⇞ ⊞ 🏛 lau ➠ ✕
⫪PS ⊞

◗ VIESTE FOGGIA

Baia Turchese Lungomare Europa ☎ 0884 708587
Camping Card Compulsory.
➲ *1km N of Vieste on Strada Panoramica towards Peschici.*
May-Sep 3.6HEC ⊞⊞⊞ ♠ ⋔ ⊾ ⫪ ✕ ⊙ ⊟ ⌀ ⇞ ⊞ ⫪ S 🅿 ⊞
Prices: ♠4000-11000 ♠3500 ♠5000-15000 ⚲5000-15000

Capo Vieste ☎ 0884 706326
The site lies on a large area of unspoilt land, planted with a
few rows of poplar and pine trees. It is by the sea and has a
large bathing area.
➲ *Off coastal road to Peschici about 7km beyond Vieste.*
15 Mar-30 Oct 6HEC ⊞⊞⊞ ː∷ː ⊕ ♠ ⋔ ⊾ ⫪ ✕ ⊙ ⊟ ⌀ ⇞ ⊞
⫪ ⫪ S 🅿 ⊞ lau

Castello Lungomare E-Mattei 77 ☎ 0884 707415
Attractive and well-equipped site with access to the beach
and organised entertainment.
Etr-Sep 2HEC ⊞⊞⊞ ♠ ⋔ ⊾ ⫪ ✕ ⊙ ⊟ ⌀ ⇞ ⊞ ⫪ S 🅿 ⊗ lau
➠ ⊞

Umbramare Santa Maria di Merino ☎ 0884 706174
➲ *On A14 leave at Poggio Imperiale and take route via Rodi
Gargánico and Peschici.*
All year 1.3HEC ⊞⊞⊞ ː∷ː ♠ ⋔ ⊾ ⫪ ✕ ⊙ ⊟ ⌀ ⇞ ⫪ S 🅿 ⊞ ⊗
➠ ⇞

Vieste Marina Litoranea Vieste ☎ 0884 706471
Tree-lined level site adjacent to the coast road in a quiet
situation with good facilities.
➲ *5km N of Vieste, signposted.*
Jun-Sep 5.2HEC ⊞⊞⊞ ♠ ⋔ ⊾ ⫪ ✕ ⊙ ⊟ ⊞ ⫪ ⫪ P 🅿 ⊞
➠ ⌀ ⇞ ⫪S
Prices: ♠5700-13900 ♠3200-5900 ♠9000-18500

Village Punta Lunga Defensola, CP 339 ☎ 0884 706031
A terraced site in wooded surroundings encompassing two
sandy bathing bays and a rocky peninsula.
➲ *2km N of Vieste, signposted from coast road.*
6HEC ⊞⊞⊞ ː∷ː ⊕ ♠ ⋔ ⊙ ⊟ ⊞ ⫪ S 🅿 ⊗ lau
Prices: ♠5500-15000 ♠4500 ♠7000-16000 ⚲6000-14000

◗ ZAPPONETA FOGGIA

Ippocampo ☎ 0884 371121
In grounds of a holiday village.
Jun-Sep 8HEC ː∷ː ⊕ ♠ ⋔ ⊾ ⫪ ✕ ⊙ ⊟ ⌀ ⇞ ⊞ ⚲ 🅿 ⊞ lau
➠ ⫪PS
Prices: ♠6000-10000 ♠3000-5000 ⚲3500-4800

◗◗◗◗ ◗ **THE ISLANDS** ◗ ◗ ◗ ◗ ◗

Sardinia and Sicily are virtually the same size but Sardinia's
population is 1.5 million compared with Sicily's 5 million.
Sardinia's mountains are less dramatic, much of the coast is
deserted and the people with their distinctive dialect,
clothes and folklore, seem far removed from the 20th
century. The Costa Smeralda on the north-east coast is
luxuriously developed but elsewhere on the coast tourism is
increasing only slowly, and inland, the old town of Nuoro
set high on a 1500ft granite hill, remains mysterious.
Cagliari is the capital, a modern city, whilst Oristano is the
provincial capital with old streets and lively atmosphere.
Where Sardinia is an island on which to relax, in Sicily there
is much to see: classical sites at Taormina, Syracuse and
Agrigento; busy cities like Palermo and Catánia and the
dramatic, erupting volcano Etna in whose foothills oranges
and lemons grow profusely. There is also poverty and the
occasional outburst from the Mafia. The best beaches and
clearest waters are around the Aolian islands to the north,
but Sicily is not primarily a seaside resort island. Seafood,
vegetables and fresh fruit are in abundance, not forgetting
of course, the inimitable ice-cream.
....

◗ SARDEGNA (SARDINIA)
◗ AGLIENTU SASSARI

Baia Blu la Tortuga Pineta di Vignola Mare ☎ 079 602077
Site in pine forest by the sea.
6 Apr-3 Oct 17HEC ⊞⊞⊞ ː∷ː ♠ ⋔ ⊾ ⫪ ✕ ⊙ ⊟ ⌀ ⊞ ⫪ ⚲ ⫪
S 🅿 lau
Prices: ♠10000-17000 pitch 40000-90000

◗ ARBATAX NUORO

Telis Porto Frailis ☎ 0782 667261
Terraced site by the sea.
➲ *SS125 between Cagliari and Olbia.*
All year 3HEC ː∷ː ♠ ⋔ ⊾ ⫪ ✕ ⊙ ⊟ ⌀ ⊞ ⫪ ⫪ S 🅿 lau
Prices: ♠9000-14000 ♠12000-18000 ⚲8000-12000

◗ BARI SARDO NUORO

Domus de Janas Torri di Bari ☎ 0782 29361
Well equipped site in a sheltered position with good
recreational facilities.
All year 2.5HEC ⊞⊞⊞ ♠ ⋔ ⊾ ⫪ ✕ ⊙ ⊟ ⌀ ⇞ ⊞ ⫪ RS 🅿 lau

◗ CAGLIARI
◗ At SANT'ANTIOCO

Tonnara Loc Calasapone ☎ 0781 809058
Situated in the centre of Calasapone Bay with enclosed plots,
good sporting facilities and access to a sandy beach.
➲ *Access is by road, south of Carbonia, to the small island of
St Antioco.*
Apr-Oct 7HEC ⊞⊞⊞ ː∷ː ⊕ ⋔ ⊾ ⫪ ✕ ⊙ ⊟ ⌀ ⇞ ⊞ ⫪ ⫪ S 🅿
lau

◗ CALASETTA CAGLIARI

Sardi Le Saline Le Saline ☎ 0781 88615
In wooded surroundings close to the beach and 500mtrs
from the village with good recreational facilities.
All year 6HEC ⊞⊞⊞ ♠ ⋔ ⊾ ⫪ ✕ ⊙ ⊟ ⊞ ⫪ PS ⊞

◗ CANNIGIONE DI ARZACHENA SASSARI

Isuledda ☎ 0789 86003
Near the sea on the beautiful Costa Smeralda with good,
modern sanitary installations and plentiful sports and
entertainment facilities. *Contd.*

Apr-15 Oct 15HEC ⊞ ∷ ♣ ℝ ⚡ ♥ ✕ ⊙ 🅟 ⌂ ♨ ⚐ ⇗ S 🆎 ⊞
♨ lau
Prices: ♦8000-16000 ♣4000-7000 ♞9000-24000
▲9000-24500

▶ LOTZORAI NUORO

Cernie via Case Sparse 17 ☎ 0782 669472
Close to the beach with beautiful views on all sides. Varied
sports and leisure activities.
All year 1.5HEC ∷ ♣ ℝ ⚡ ♥ ✕ ⊙ 🅟 ⌂ ♨ ⚐ ⇗ S lau
♦ ⊞

▶ PORTO ROTONDO SASSARI

Cugnana Loc Cugnana ☎ 0789 33184
A well appointed family site with good recreational facilities
and offering free transport to the local beaches.
15 May-Sep 5HEC ⊞ ♣ ℝ ⚡ ♥ ✕ ⊙ 🅟 ⌂ ♨ ⇗ P 🅿
♦ ✕ ⇗ S ⊞
Prices: ♦11000-21000 ♣4000-6000

▶ SANTA LUCIA NUORO

Cala-Pineta St Statale Orientale Sarda 125 ☎ 0784 819184
Well-equipped site 1.5km from a white sand beach.
1 Jun-15 Sep 4.1HEC ⊞ ♣ ℝ ⚡ ♥ ✕ ⊙ 🅟 ⌂ ♨ ▲ ⇗ S 🆎 lau
Prices: ♦11000-16000 pitch 9000-15000

Selema ☎ 0784 819068
Wooded beach site on the island of Sardinia.
May-Oct 7.5HEC ⊞ ∷ ♣ ℝ ⚡ ♥ ✕ ⊙ 🅟 ⌂ ♨ ⇗ RS 🅿
lau ♦ ⌂ ⊞

▶ SAN TEODORO NUORO

San Teodoro la Cinta via del Tirreno ☎ 0784 865777
Situated in a large wooded, park the site faces the sea. Ideal
for families with small children.
⊃ *25km from Olbia.*
15 May-15 Oct 3HEC ⊞ ♣ ℝ ⚡ ♥ ✕ ⊙ 🅟 ⌂ ♨ ⚐ ⇗ S
🆎 ⊞ ♨ lau ♦ ✕ ⇗PR

▶ TEULADA CAGLIARI

Porto Tramatzu ☎ 070 9283027
With extensive facilities and large individual plots. The site is
less than 100mtrs from the beautiful Port Tramatzu.
⊃ *SS195 from Cagliari.*
Etr-Oct 3.5HEC ⊞ ⊛ ℝ ⚡ ♥ ✕ ⊙ 🅟 ⚐ ⇗ S lau
Prices: ♦8500-12000 ♞15000-18000 ▲15000-18000

▶ TORRE SALINAS CAGLIARI

Torre Salinas ☎ 070 999032
Apr-15 Oct 1.5HEC ∷ ♣ ℝ ⚡ ♥ ✕ ⊙ 🅟 ⚐ ▲ ⇗ S 🆎 lau
Prices: ♦6500-12000 pitch 11500-17500

▶ VALLEDORIA SASSARI

Foce via Ampurias ☎ 079 582109
In a delightful wooded setting separated from the main
beach by the River Coghinas which can be crossed by ferry.
Modern sanitary installations and plenty of recreational
facilities.
15 May-Sep 18HEC ⊞ ∷ ♣ ℝ ⚡ ♥ ✕ ⊙ 🅟 ⌂ ♨ ⚐ ⇗
PRS 🅿 lau ♦ ⊞
Prices: ♦12000-17000 ♞4000-8000

Valledoria ☎ 079 584070
Located in a pine wood, this site has both white sand beaches
and rocky cliffs.
Jun-Sep 10HEC ∷ ♣ ℝ ⚡ ♥ ✕ ⊙ 🅟 ⌂ ♨ ⇗ S 🅿 ♨ lau
Prices: ♦12000-17000 ♣3500-5000

▶ SICILIA (SICILY)
▶ ACIREALE
▶ At CARRUBA(10.2km N)

Praiola ☎ 095 964366
In idyllic location, very quiet.
⊃ *5km S of Riposto by the sea between orchards. 6km from
A18 exit Giarre.*
15 Mar-Sep 22HEC ⊛ ♣ ℝ ⚡ ♥ ✕ ⊙ 🅟 ⌂ ♨ ⚐ ♨ ▲ ⇗ S 🆎 lau

▶ AVOLA SIRACUSA

Pantanello Lungomare di Avola ☎ 0931 823275
All year 7.5HEC ⊞ ♣ ℝ ⊙ 🅟 🆎 ♦ ⚡ ♥ ✕ ⚐ ⇗S ⊞

Sabbia d'Oro ☎ 0931 822415
Situated close to the beach in a picturesque area surrounded
by trees with magnificient views.
All year 2HEC ⊞ ♣ ℝ ⚡ ♥ ✕ ⊙ 🅟 ⚐ ⌂ ♨ ⇗ S 🅿 lau
Prices: ♦8000 ♞10000 ▲10000

▶ BUONFORNELLO PALERMO

Himera ☎ 091 8140175
All year ♣ ℝ ⚡ ♥ ✕ ⊙ 🅟 ⚐ ⌂ ♨ ⚐ ▲ ⇗ PRS 🆎 ⊞ lau

▶ CASTEL DI TUSA MESSINA

Scoglio ☎ 0921 334345
A terraced site. No shade on the gravel beach.
Camping Card Compulsory.
⊃ *Turn off SS113 st Km164, 2km W of Castel di Tusa.*
May-Sep 1.5HEC ⊞ ♣ ℝ ⚡ ♥ ✕ ⊙ 🅟 ⚐ ⌂ ♨ ⇗ S 🆎 ⊞
Prices: ♦8000-12000 ♣4000 ♞10000 ▲8000-10000

▶ CATANIA CATANIA

Ionio via Villini a Mare 2 ☎ 095 491139
On a clifftop plateau. Access to beach via steps. Lunchtime
siesta 14.00-17.00 hrs.
⊃ *Turn off SS14 N of town towards sea.*
All year 1.2HEC ⊞ ♣ ℝ ⚡ ♥ ✕ ⊙ 🅟 ⚐ ⌂ ♨ ⚐ ⇗ S 🅿 ⊞ lau

▶ CEFALÚ PALERMO

Plaja degli Uccelli ☎ 0921 999068
In wooded surroundings with good, modern equippment
close to a fine sandy beach.
Apr-10 Oct 1.9HEC ⊞ ∷ ♣ ℝ ⚡ ♥ ✕ ⊙ 🅟 ⚐ ⌂ ♨ ⚐ ⇗
S 🆎
Prices: ♦8500 pitch 11500-19500

▶ FINALE DI POLLINA PALERMO

Rais Gerbi ☎ 0921 26570
A well equipped, modern site with its own private beach in
picturesque wooded surroundings.
⊃ *Take the SS113 Messina-Palermo road to Km172.9.*
May-Oct 4.5HEC ∷ ⊛ ♣ ℝ ⚡ ♥ ✕ ⊙ 🅟 ⚐ ⌂ ♨ ⚐ ▲ ⇗ PS
🆎 ⊞

▶ FONDACHELLO CATANIA

Mokambo ☎ 095 938731
Level terrain, thickly wooded in parts not directly next to the
sea.
⊃ *For access leave A18 (Messina-Catania) at Giarre exit,
through Giarre and via Máscali to Fondachello on coast.*
Apr-Sep 2.8HEC ∷ ♣ ℝ ⚡ ♥ ✕ ⊙ 🅟 ⚐ ⌂ ♨ ⚐ ⇗ S 🆎 ⊞
lau
Prices: ♦7500-8000 ♣4000 ♞8000-8500 ▲6000-6500

▶ FÚRNARI MARINA MESSINA

Village Bazia Contrada Bazia ☎ 0941 800130
Jun-Sep 4HEC ∷ ♣ ℝ ⚡ ♥ ✕ ⊙ 🅟 ⚐ ⌂ ♨ ⇗ PS 🆎 🅿 ♦ ⊞
Prices: ♦8000-10000 ♞2800-3500 ♞8800-11000 ▲8800-11000

GIARRE
At MILO(11km E)

Mareneve ETNA ☎ 095 7082163
Site in hilly terrain with lovely view of the sea.
Camping Card Compulsory.
➜ *Approach from the A18 exit Giarre direction Venerina and Milo about 10km.*
All year 2HEC ⊞ ♣ ♠ ⚌ ⚏ ✕ ☉ ⬛ ⬗ ⛺ ⬛ ⬛ ⟋ P
⚐ ⊞ lau

ÍSOLA DELLE FÉMMINE   PALERMO

La Playa viale Marino 55 ☎ 091 8677001
A ideal site for a relaxing holiday with beautiful views and quiet woodland walks. Direct access to the beach.
➜ *A29 Palermo to Trapini and SS113.*
21 Mar-30 Oct 2.2HEC ⠿ ♣ ♠ ⚌ ⚏ ✕ ☉ ⬛ ⬗ ⛺ ⟋ S ⚐
lau ♦ ✕ ⟋S ⊞
Prices: ♦6500-10000 pitch 11000-15000

MENFI   AGRIGENTO

Palma via delle Palme n 29 ☎ 0925 78392
Camping Card Compulsory.
➜ *6km S.*
All year 1HEC ⊞ ⠿ ♣ ♠ ⚌ ⚏ ✕ ☉ ⬛ ⬗ ⛺ ⬛
Å ⟋ S ⚐
Prices: ♦9000 ♦4000 ⬛13000 Å13000

NICOLOSI   CATANIA

Etna via Goethe ☎ 095 914309
All year 2.9HEC ⠿ ♣ ♠ ⚏ ✕ ☉ ⬛ ⬗ ⛺ ⬛ ⬛ Å ⟋ P ⚐ lau
♦ ⚌ ✕
Prices: ♦7000 ♦3500 ⬛10000 Å7000-8000

OLIVERI   MESSINA

Marinello Contrada Marinello ☎ 0941 313000
Campsite consists of small pitches set in a woodland area 100m from the sea. Dogs are not allowed during July and August.
➜ *On the A20 motorway exiting at Falcone.*
Apr-Oct 3.2HEC ⠿ ♣ ♠ ⚌ ⚏ ✕ ☉ ⬛ ⬗ ⛺ ⬛ ⟋ S ⬛ lau
♦ ⚌ ⊞

PACHINO
At PORTOPALO(6.6km SE)

Capo Palssero ☎ 0931 842333
Site slightly sloping towards the sea with view of fishing harbour of Portopalo. Discotheque.
➜ *Turn S on 115 in Noto or Iolspica in direction of Pachino.*
10 Mar-30 Oct 3.5HEC ⊞ ♣ ♠ ⚌ ⚏ ✕ ☉ ⬛ ⬗ Å ⚐ ⬛
♦ ✕ ⟋ ⟋S ⊞
Prices: ♦7500-9000 ♦4500-5000 ⬛10500-12000
Å7500-9000

PALAZZOLO ACREIDE   SIRACUSA

Torre Torre Tudica ☎ 0931 32694
All year 2HEC ⊞ ♣ ♠ ⚏ ✕ ☉ ⬛ ⬗ ⛺ ⟋ P ⚐ ♦ ⚌ ⊞
Prices: ♦4500-5000 ♦3000 ⬛7000 Å5000-7000

PUNTA BRACCETTO   RAGUSA

Rocca dei Tramonti ☎ 0932 918054
The site lies in a quiet setting on rather barren land near a beautiful sandy bay surrounded by cliffs.
➜ *From Marina di Ragusa 10km W on coast road to Punta Braccetto.*
Etr-15 Oct 3HEC ⊞ ⠿ ♣ ♠ ⚌ ⚏ ✕ ☉ ⬛ ⬗ ⛺ ⬛
⟋ S ⚐ ⊞

RAGUSA, MARINA DI   RAGUSA

Baia del Sole Lungomare A-Doria ☎ 0932 239844
Well tended level site. Pitches provided with roofs of straw matting.
All year 3.5HEC ⠿ ♣ ♠ ⚌ ⚏ ✕ ☉ ⬛ ⬗ ⛺ ⟋ PS ⚐ ♦ ⊞
Prices: ♦6000 ♦5000 ⬛10000 Å10000

SANT' ALESSIO SICULO   MESSINA

Focetta Sicula via Torrente Agrò ☎ 0942 751657
A well equipped site with a private beach in a quiet location.
➜ *From Messina take autostrada to 'Roccalumera' exit, then SS114 towards Sant' Alessio and follow signs.*
All year 1.2HEC ⠿ ♣ ♠ ⚏ ☉ ⬛ ⬗ ⛺ ⬛ ⟋ S ⊞ lau
Prices: ♦6600-9000 ♦4000-5000 ⬛9000-10400 Å6600-9000

SANT' ANTONIO DI BARCELLONA   MESSINA

Centro Vacanze Cantoni ☎ 090 9710165
All year 1HEC ⊞ ♣ ♠ ⚌ ⚏ ✕ ☉ ⬛ ⬗ ⛺ ⬛ ⟋ PS ⚐ ⊞
Prices: ♦8000-9000 ♦4000-4500 ⬛12000-14000
Å8000-9000

SCOPELLO   TRAPANI

Baia di Guidaloca via Modena ☎ 0924 541262
Apr-Sep 3HEC ⊞ ♣ ♠ ⚌ ⚏ ✕ ☉ ⬛ ⬗ ⛺ ⬛ ♦ ⟋S

SECCAGRANDE   AGRIGENTO

Kameni Camping Village ☎ 0925 69212
In wooded surroundings close to the beach with good recreational facilities.
All year 5HEC ⊞ ♣ ♠ ⚌ ⚏ ✕ ☉ ⬛ ⬛ Å ⟋ PS ⚐ lau
♦ ⬗ ⬛ ⊞
Prices: ♦6000-9000 ♦4000 ⬛9000-12000 Å5000-8000

TAORMINA
At CALATABIANO(5.2km SW)

Castello San Marco ☎ 095 641181
In lemon grove by an old castle, 9km S of Taormina.
➜ *Turn off SS114 between Calatabiano and Fiumefreddo in direction of the sea and continue for 1km.*
All year 3.5HEC ⊞ ♣ ♠ ⚌ ⚏ ✕ ☉ ⬛ ⬗ ⛺ ⚐ ⊞ lau
♦ ⟋S

LUXEMBOURG

Luxembourg, the tiny Grand Duchy only 999 square miles in size, offers a wide range of facilities to the visitor.

FACTS AND FIGURES
Capital: Luxembourg City
Language: Luxembourgeois, French and German
IDD code: 352. To call the UK dial 00 44
Currency: Franc (LUF) = 100 centimes. At the time of going to press £1 = LUF. 55.93. Belgian Franc is also accepted in Luxembourg.
Local time: GMT + 1 (summer GMT + 2)
Emergency Services: Fire and ambulance 112; police 113
Business hours-
Banks: Mon-Fri 09.00-12.00 and 13.30-16.30

Shops: Mon-Sat 09.00-18.00
Average daily temperatures:
Luxembourg City
Jan 1°C   Jul 19°C
Mar 6°C   Sep 15°C
May 13°C   Nov 5°C
Tourist Information: Luxembourg National

Tourist Office
UK 122 Regent Street London W1R 5FE
Tel 0171-434 2800
USA 17 Beckman Place New York, NY 10022
Tel (212) 935 8888
Camping card: Recommended. Few reductions offered.

Luxembourg is entirely landlocked by France, Belgium and Germany. One third of the country is occupied by the hills and forests of the Ardennes, while the rest is mostly wooded farmland or the rich wine-growing area around the Moselle. The climate is temperate, with summer often extending from May to late October. Luxembourgeois is the everyday language but the official languages are French and German. English is widely spoken and understood.

There are over 100 officially recognised campsites throughout the country. Most open from April to October, but some function throughout the year. A booklet containing details of campsites is obtainable from the National Tourist Office (B.P.1001, L-1010 Luxembourg). All campsites open to the public must be authorised by the Minister of Tourism.

Off-site camping Caravans may only be parked on campsites. Non-coupled caravans may not be parked on the public highway or used as living accommodation. Casual camping with a tent is permitted, but permission must be obtained from the landowner. The owner is not allowed to give permission for more than 2 tents to be erected on his/her land. Casual camping is not allowed on the banks of Esch-sur-Sure.

HOW TO GET THERE
Luxembourg is easily approached through either Belgium or France. Apart from crossing by Eurotunnel, the usual Continental Channel ports for this journey are Boulogne or Calais in France, and Oostende (Ostende) or Zeebrugge in Belgium. For details of the *AA European Routes Service* please consult the Contents Page.

Distance
Luxembourg City is just over 330km (205 miles) from the Belgian ports, or about 420km (260 miles) from the French ports, and is, therefore, within a day's drive of the Channel coast.
See Belgium for location map.

Motoring & General Information
The information given here is specific to Luxembourg. It **must** be read in conjunction with the Continental ABC at the front of the book, which covers those regulations which are common to many countries.

British Embassy/Consulate*
The British Embassy together with its consular section is located at L-2450 Luxembourg, 14 Boulevard Roosevelt ☎229864/65/66

Children in cars
Children under 12 and/or 1.5 metres in height are not permitted to travel as front seat passengers unless using suitable restraint system. Children in rear seats must use a child seat or restraint if fitted.

Currency
There are no restrictions on the amount of foreign or local currency which can be taken into or out of the country, but because of the limited market for Luxembourg notes in other countries, it is advisable to change them into Belgian or other foreign notes before leaving.

Dimensions and weight restrictions
Private cars and towed trailers or caravans are restricted to the following dimensions - height, 4 metres; width, 2.5 metres; length, 12 metres. The maximum permitted overall length of vehicle/trailer or caravan combination is 25 metres.

    The weight of a caravan must not exceed 75% of the weight of the towing vehicle.

Driving licence*
A valid UK or Republic of Ireland licence is acceptable in Luxembourg. The minimum age at which visitors from UK or Republic of Ireland may use a temporarily imported car or motorcycle is 17 years.

Foodstuffs*
There are no limits on the importation of foodstuffs obtained duty and tax paid within the EC. Up to 500g of coffee (200g of coffee extract) and 100g of tea (40g of tea extract) purchased duty-free or outside the EC may be imported free of duty and tax. However, coffee bought duty-free or outside the EC cannot be imported by visitors under 15 years of age.

Motoring club*
The **Automobile Club du Grand-Duché de Luxembourg** (ACL) has its head office at 8007 Bertrange, 54 route de Longwy ☎450045-1. ACL office hours are 08.30-12.00hrs and 13.30-18.00hrs from Monday to Friday; closed Saturday and Sunday.

Petrol
At the time of going to press both leaded and unleaded pettrol are available in Luxembourg. However, only one grade of leaded petrol is sold, 98 octane 'Super'.

Roads
There is a comprehensive system of good main and secondary roads. Luxembourg has 68 miles of toll-free motorway.

Speed limits*
Car
Built-up areas 50kph (31mph)
Other roads 90kph (55mph)
Motorways 120kph (74mph)
Car/caravan/trailer
Built-up areas 50kph (31mph)
Other roads 75kph (46mph)
Motorways 90kph (56mph)
All lower signposted speed limits must be adhered to.

Warning triangle*
The use of a warning triangle is compulsory in the event of accident or breakdown. The triangle must be placed on the road about 100 metres (109yds) behind the vehicle to on ordinary roads and 200-300 metres (219-328 yds) on motorways to warn following traffic of any obstruction.

*Additional information will be found in the Continental ABC at the front of the book.

BERDORF

Parc Martbusch 3 Baim Maartbesch ☎ 79545
A comfortable, modern site in picturesque wooded
surroundings.
⊃ *NW of town centre.*
All year 3HEC ᛃᚢ 🛆 🏕 🐦 ✕ ⊙ 🏪 🚿 ♨ 🚐 ⚑ ⚡ P 🏧 lau

CLERVAUX

Official de Clervaux 33 r Klatzewee ☎ 920042
Situated next to the sports stadium, between the La Clervé
stream and the railway in a forested area. Trains only run
during the day and there is little noise. Separate field for tents.
⊃ *0.5km SW from the village.*
21 Mar-10 Nov 3HEC ᛃᚢ ♣ 🏕 🐦 ⊙ 🏪 🚿 ♨ 🚐 ⚑ ⚡ P 🏧 🏧
lau ♣ 🚿 ✕
Prices: ♠140 pitch 140

CONSDORF

Bel Air Burgkapp 15 r Burgkapp ☎ 790353
The site is divided into pitches and lies on level meadowland
in the forest area of 'Petite Suisse Luxembourgeoise'.
⊃ *On W outskirts of village. Turn right off E42. 6km S of
Echternach.*
15/05-31 Aug 2.2HEC ᛃᚢ ♣ 🐦 ⊙ 🏪 🚿 ♨ 🏧 🏧 lau ♣ 🚿 🏕 ✕ ♨
Prices: ♠160 pitch 160

DIEKIRCH

Bleesbruck ☎ 803134
A modern site in tranquil wooded surroundings.
Apr-1 Nov 5HEC ᛃᚢ ♣ 🐦 🚿 ⊙ 🏪 🚿 ♨ ♨ ⚡ R 🏧 🏧 lau
♣ ✕

Op der Sauer rte de Gilsdorf ☎ 00352-808590
⊃ *500m from town centre on Gilsdorf road near the sports
stadium.*
All year 5HEC ᛃᚢ 🛆 🐦 🚿 🏕 ✕ ⊙ 🏪 🚿 ♨ 🚐 🏧 🏧 lau ♣ ⚡PR
Prices: ♠120 pitch 120

DILLINGEN

Benelux 1-3 chemin de la Forêt ☎ 836267
A terraced, grassland site partially in an orchard and divided
into pitches.
⊃ *Off N10, turn right before reaching the church.*
15 Apr-11 Nov 1.7HEC ᛃᚢ 🛆 🐦 ⊙ 🏪 🚿 ♨ 🚐 🏧 🏧 lau ♣ 🚿
🏕 ✕ ⚡R

Wies-Neu 12 r de la Sûre ☎ 836110
A comfortable family site on the bank of the River Sûre.
⊃ *Between Diekirch and Echternach.*
Apr-1 Nov 3HEC ᛃᚢ ♣ 🐦 ⊙ 🏪 🚿 ♨ 🚐 ⚡ R 🏧 🏧 lau ♣ 🏕
✕

ECHTERNACH

Official 5 rte de Diekirch ☎ 720272
⊃ *Take E42 to Echternach.*
15 Mar-15 Oct 7HEC ᛃᚢ ♣ 🐦 ⊙ 🏪 🚐 ⚑ 🅿 🏧 lau ♣ 🚿 🏕 ✕
♨ 🏕 ⚡LPR

ENSCHERANGE

Val d'Or ☎ 920691
Quiet family site in a beautiful natural setting beside the
River Clerve.
⊃ *8km S of Clervaux between Drauffelt and Wilwerwiltz.*
All year 3HEC ᛃᚢ 🛆 🐦 🏕 ✕ ⊙ 🏪 🚿 🚐 ⚑ ⚑ Å ⚡ R 🅿 🏧
Prices: ♠140 ⚑200 Å200

ESCH-SUR-ALZETTE

Gaalgebierg ☎ 541069
A level park-like site with lovely trees on a hillock.

⊃ *SE along N6 from the town centre in the direction of
Dudelange as far as the motorway underpass. Then turn right
and follow the steep climb uphill.*
All year 2.5HEC ᛃᚢ 🛆 🐦 🚿 🏕 ✕ ⊙ 🏪 🚿 ♨ 🚐 🏧 🏧 lau

HALLER

Relax r Henerecht 6 ☎ 86748
All year 2.3HEC ᛃᚢ ≋ 🛆 🐦 🚿 🏕 ✕ ⊙ 🏪 🚿 ⚡ P 🏧 🏧 lau ♣ 🚿

HEIDERSCHEID

Fuussekaul rte de Bastogne 2 ☎ 00352 839659
A level grassland family site adjoining a woodland area. Good
recreational facilities.
⊃ *Turn off the N15 (Ettelbruck-Wiltz/Bastogne) S of
Heiderscheid in a westerly direction.*
All year 12HEC ᛃᚢ 🛆 🐦 🚿 🏕 ✕ ⊙ 🏪 🚿 ♨ 🚐 ⚑ ⚑ Å ⚡ P 🏧 🏧
lau ♣ ⚡LRS
Prices: ♠190 pitch 360

INGLEDORF

Gritt r du Pont ☎ 802018
On southern bank of River Sûre between Ettelbruck and
Diekirch. In beautiful country setting ideal for fishing.
All year ᛃᚢ 🛆 🐦 🚿 ✕ ⊙ 🏪 🚿 ♨ ⚡ R 🏧 🏧 ♣ 🚿 ⚡LP
Prices: pitch 600 (incl 2 persons)

KOCKELSCHEUER

Kockelscheuer 22 rte de Bettembourg ☎ 471815
A modern site on the edge of a forest.
⊃ *4km from Luxembourg off N31.*
Etr-Oct 3.4HEC ᛃᚢ 🛆 🐦 🚿 ⊙ 🏪 🚿 ♨ 🏕 ⚡ P 🏧 🏧 lau ♣ 🏕 ✕
Prices: ♠120 pitch 140

LAROCHETTE

Kengert ☎ 837186
On gently sloping meadow in a pleasant, rural location.
⊃ *Take the N8 towards Mersch, then the CR119 towards
Nommern and turn right after approx 2km.*
20 Feb-8 Nov 8 Nov - 12 Feb 4HEC ᛃᚢ ♣ 🐦 🚿 🏕 ✕ ⊙ 🏪 🚿
🏕 ⚡ P 🏧 🏧 lau
Prices: ♠320-400 pitch 320-400

MERSCH

Krounebierg r de la Piscine 12 ☎ 329756
A clean, well-kept site on five terraces, split into sections by
hedges.
⊃ *Approx 0.5km W of village church.*
01/04-30/09 4HEC ᛃᚢ ♣ 🐦 🚿 🏕 ✕ ⊙ 🏪 🚿 ♨ 🏕 ⚡ P 🏧 🏧 lau
♣ 🏧
Prices: pitch 705-925 (incl 2 persons)

MONDORF-LES-BAINS

Risette 4 rte de Burmerange ☎ 660746
In pleasant wooded surroundings near the French and
German borders.
⊃ *1km from Mondorf-les-Bains.*
Mar-Oct ᛃᚢ 🛆 🐦 🚿 🏕 ✕ ⊙ 🏪 🚿 lau ♣ ⚡PR
Prices: ♠130 pitch 150

NOMMERN

Belle Vue 3 r Principale ☎ 878068
25 Apr-30 Oct 2HEC ᛃᚢ ♣ 🐦 🚿 🏕 ✕ ⊙ 🏪 🚿 ♨ 🚐 ⚑ Å ⚡ P 🏧
🏧 lau ♣ ✕

Europe Nommerlayen r Nommerlayen ☎ 878078
A terraced site in wooded surroundings with plenty of
recreational facilities.
Closed 8 Nov-14 Feb 15HEC ᛃᚢ 🛆 🐦 🚿 🏕 ✕ ⊙ 🏪 🚿 ♨ 🚐
Å ⚡ P 🏧 🏧 lau

OBEREISENBACH

Kohnenhof 1 Maison ☎ 929464
Quiet site in a rural setting in the River Our valley.
Mar-Nov 6HEC ⚏ ⌂ ⛬ ⚑ ☂ ✕ ☉ ⛱ ⌂ ⛴ ⚑ ☂ R ☎ ⊞ lau
➡ ☂LP
Prices: ♦120-150 pitch 200-250

REISDORF

Rivière rte de la Sûre ☎ 86398
The entire site is divided into pitches and lies on a field near
the church.
➲ *Between the River Sûre/Sauer and Km9.5 off the N19,
10km E of Diekrich.*
Mar-Sep 1.7HEC ⚏ ⌂ ⌂ ⛬ ✕ ☉ ⛱ ⌂ ⚑ ☂ R ☎ ⊞ lau ➡ ⛬

ROSPORT

Barrage rte d'Echternach ☎ 730160
Situated by Lake Sûre on the German border at the entrance
to Luxembourg's 'Little Switzerland'.
➲ *Main road from Echternach to Wasserbillig.*
Mar-Oct 3.2HEC ⚏ ⌂ ⌂ ☉ ⚑ ☂ LPR ☎ ⊞ lau ➡ ⛬ ✕ ⌂ ☂
Prices: ♦120 pitch 150

STEINFORT

Steinfort 72 rte de Luxembourg ☎ 398827
A small family site with good recreational and entertainment
facilities, well situated for exploring the 'Seven Castles' area.
➲ *Access via E25 Steinfort exit.*
All year 3.5HEC ⚏ ⌂ ⌂ ⛬ ⛬ ✕ ☉ ⛱ ⌂ ⚑ ☂ P ☎ ⊞ lau
➡ ⛬ ⛬ ✕ ☂P
Prices: ♦50-100 pitch 125-250

VIANDEN

Deich ☎ 84375
Etr-Oct 3HEC ⚏ ⌂ ⌂ ☉ ⚑ ☂ R ☎ ⊞ lau ➡ ⛬ ⛬ ✕ ⌂ ⛱
☂P

Moulin rte de Bettel ☎ 84501
➲ *On Bettel-Vianden road beside the river.*
10 May-2 Sep 2.8HEC ⚏ ➡ ⌂ ⌂ ☉ ⚑ ☂ R ☎ ⊞ lau ➡ ⌂ ⛱
☂P

At WALSDORF(2km SW)

Romantique Tandelerbaach ☎ 834464
A terraced grassland site in picturesque wooded
surroundings.
➲ *W of Diekirch-Vianden road, access from the N17 and
CR354.*
3 Mar-1 Nov 6HEC ⚏ ⌂ ⌂ ✕ ☉ ⚑ ☂ R ☎ ⊞ lau ➡
☂LP
Prices: pitch 470-700 (incl 2 persons)

WEILER-LA-TOUR

Ma Campagne 9 rte de Thionville ☎ 369497
Camp shop and bar available in August only.
➲ *Access via main road Luxembourg-Thionville.*
All year 0.5HEC ⚏ ⌂ ⌂ ⛬ ⛬ ☉ ⚑ ☂ ⌂ ⚑ ☎ ⊞ lau ➡ ✕
Prices: ♦150 pitch 150

NETHERLANDS

The Netherlands is bordered by two countries,
Belgium and Germany.

A fifth of this flat, level country criss-crossed by
rivers and canals lies below sea-level. The
areas reclaimed from the sea, known as *polders*, are
extremely fertile. The landscape is broken up by
the forests of Arnhem, the bulbfields in the west,
the lakes in the central and northern areas, and
the coastal dunes which are the most impressive
in Europe.

The climate is generally mild and tends to be
damp. The summers are moderate with
changeable weather and are seldom excessively
hot. The language, Netherlandish or Dutch, is
fairly guttural and closely allied to the low
German dialect. Other dialect forms exist
throughout the Netherlands.

There are some 900 officially recognised and
classifed campsites throughout the Netherlands. It
is not generally possible to book sites in advance.
Coastal sites tend to be crowded in June, July and
August when many of the Dutch take their
holidays. Local tourist information offices (VVV)
can provide detailed information about sites in
their area. The camping season is generally from
April to September, but some sites are open all
year.

Off-site camping is not possible outside
organised sites. Overnight stops are not
permitted.

HOW TO GET THERE
There are direct ferry services to the Netherlands.
Harwich to the **Hoek van Holland** takes 3hrs 40
mins by catamaran **Hull** to **Rotterdam**
(Eurosport) takes 12hrs 30mins. **Newcastle** to
Amsterdam takes 14hrs (terminal is at **Ijmuiden**
30km from Amsterdam). Alternatively, use the
Channel Tunnel, or take one of the short Channel
crossings and drive through France and Belgium.
For details of the *AA European Routes Service* please
consult the Contents Page.

Distance
From Calais to Den Haag (The Hague) is just
over 340km (211 miles) (within a day's drive).

MOTORING & GENERAL INFORMATION
The information given here is specific to The
Netherlands. It **must** be read in conjunction with
the European ABC at the front of the book,
which covers those regulations which are
common to many countries.

British Embassy/Consulate*
The British Embassy is located at 2514 ED Den
Haag, Lange Voorhout 10 ☎(070) 4270427, but
the Embassy has no consular section. The British
Consulate is located at 1075 AE Amsterdam,

Dam Square, Amsterdam

Koningslaan 44 ☎(020) 6764343.

Children in cars
Child under 12 and/or 1.5 metres* in height cannot travel as front seat passenger unless using a suitable restraint. Child under 3 in the rear does not have to wear a seat belt but must use child seat or restraint if fitted; child over 3 and under 12 must wear seat belt in the absence of such equipment.
*A child of 10 eg 1.6 metres in height may sit in the front wearing normal seat belts.

Currency
There are no restrictions limiting the import of currency. All imported currency may be freely exported, as well as any currency exchanged in, or drawn on, an account established in the Netherlands.

Dimensions and weight restrictions
Private cars and towed **trailers** or **caravans** are restricted to the following dimensions - height, 4 metres; width†, 2.55 metres; length, **car** 12 metres, **trailer/caravan with one axle** up to 3,500kg (empty weight and carrying capacity) 8 metres; between 3,500kg and 8,000kg 10 metres, over 8,000kg 11 metres; **trailer/caravan with two axles or more** 12 metres. The maximum permitted overall length of vehicle/trailer or caravan combination is 18 metres. The maximum weight of caravan/luggage trailers will be determined by the instructions of the manufacturer of the towing vehicle and/or the manufacturer of the caravan/luggage trailer.
†Some very small roads have a maximum width restriction of 2.2 metres.

Driving licence*
A valid UK or Republic of Ireland licence is acceptable in the Netherlands. The minimum age at which visitors from UK or Republic of Ireland may use a temporarily imported car or motorcycle is 18 years.

Firearms
Dutch laws concerning the possession of firearms are the most stringent in Europe. Any person crossing the frontier with any type of firearm will be arrested. The law applies also to any object which, on superficial inspection, shows any resemblance to real firearms (*eg* plastic imitations).

If you wish to carry firearms, real or imitation, of any description into the Netherlands, seek the advice of the Netherlands Consulate.

Foodstuffs*
There are no limits on the importation of foodstuffs obtained duty and tax paid within the EC. Up to 500g of coffee (200g of coffee extract) and 100g of tea (40g of tea extract) purchased duty-free or outside the EC may be imported free of duty and tax. However, coffee bought duty-free or outside the EC cannot be imported by visitors under 15 years of age. The importation of unpreserved meat products is forbidden.

Motoring club*
The **Koninklijke Nederlandse Toeristenbond** (ANWB) has its headquarters at 2596 EC 's-Gravenhage, Wassenaarseweg 220, and offices in numerous provincial towns. They will assist motoring tourists generally, and supply road and touring information. Offices are usually open 09.00-17.30hrs Mon-Fri and 09.00-14.00hrs on Saturday. Traffic information for the Netherlands can be obtained from the ANWB on ☎0900-9622 but only Dutch is spoken.

Petrol
Only unleaded petrol is sold in the Netherlands. However, the 98 octane 'Super' petrol (not Super Plus) contains additive making it suitable for vehicles designed to run on leaded petrol.

Roads
Main roads usually have only two lanes, but are well-surfaced. The best way to see the countryside is to tour along minor roads, often alongside canals.

The Netherlands has a network of motorways (*autosnelweg*) carrying most inter-city and long distance traffic. Yellow ANWB emergency telephone pillars are located every 2km along highways.

Speed limits*
Car
Built-up areas 50kph (31mph)
Other roads 80kph (49mph)
Motorways 120kph (74mph)
Car/caravan/trailer
Built-up areas 50kph (31mph)
Other roads 80kph (49mph)
Motorways 80kph (49mph)
The minimum speed on motorways for cars and vehicles towing a caravan or trailer is 80kph (49mph).

Warning triangle/Hazard warning lights*
In the event of accident or breakdown a motorist must use either a warning triangle or hazard-warning lights to warn approaching traffic of any obstruction. However, a warning triangle is recommended as hazard-warning lights may be damaged or inoperative. The triangle must be placed 30 metres (33yds) behind the vehicle on ordinary roads and 100 metres 109yds) on motorways: it must be visible at a distance of 100 metres (109yds).

*Additional information will be found in the Continental ABC at the front of the book.

● ● ● ● ● **NORTH** ● ● ● ●

The Dutch have been doing battle with the sea for centuries. It is part of their history, an essential element in the country's security and prosperity, and a large influence on the people's make-up. It is a battle the people have, for the most part, won. Where there once was nothing but water, we now find one of the most fertile countries in Europe; vast polders with peacefully grazing Frisian cattle, drainage mills along the canals, and drawbridges leading to farmhouses.
The West Frisian islands extend along the coast like a string of pearls, sheltering the mainland from the unpredictable and stormy North Sea, offering visitors long white beaches and many nature parks.
On the mainland, visit Dokkum, the small walled town where St Boniface was murdered in 754; Noordbergum, where clogmakers demonstrate their skills; Hindeloopen, famed for painted furniture; and Leeuwarden, the home of Mata Hari - whose statue stands on the Korfmakerspijp - and of the Princesshof, which houses a unique ceramic museum.

....

) AMELAND (ISLAND OF)
See **NES**

) AMEN DRENTHE
Reservaat Diana Heide 53 Amen ☎ 0592 389297
An ideal site for relaxation, which lies away from the traffic amongst forest and heathland.
➲ *If approaching from Assen along the E35, drive through Amen and on towards Hooghalen.*
1 Apr-1 Oct 30HEC ⬛ ⠿ ⚶ 🄰 ℝ 🖳 ⛊ ✕ ⊙ 🄮 ⌀ ⛺ 🄱 🄰 ⟨ P 🄿 🄴 lau ➧ ⟨LR
Prices: ⋏4.80-6 🚐10-12.50 🄰10-12.50

) ANNEN DRENTHE
Hondsrug Annerweg 3 ☎ 0592 271292
A family site in a pleasant rural setting with good recreational facilities.
➲ *Access via N34 to site SE of Annen.*
Apr-1 Oct 18HEC ⬛ ⠿ ⚶ ℝ 🖳 ✕ ⊙ 🄮 ⌀ ⌶ 🄱 🄰 ⟨ P 🄿 🄴 lau ➧ ⟨L
Prices: ⋏6.95 pitch 7.50

) ASSEN DRENTHE
Witterzomer Witterzomer 7 ☎ 0592 393535
A large site with asphalt internal roads, lying in mixed woodland near nature reserve. Separate sections for dog owners. Individual washing facilities for the disabled.

➲ *Turn off the E35 at Assen W exit into Europaweg Zuid and continue for 100m, then turn right. Continue through Witten and follow signs.*
All year 75HEC ⬛ 🄰 ℝ 🖳 ✕ ⊙ 🄮 ⌀ 🄱 🄰 ⟨ LP 🄿 🄿 lau ➧ ⌶
Prices: ⋏4-6 🚐9 🚐9 🄰4-6

) BERGUM FRIESLAND
Bergumermeer Solcamastr 30 ☎ 0511 461305
In pleasant wooded surroundings close to the marina on the Bergumermeer with good recreational facilities.
➲ *From N355 Groningen-Leeuwarden turn S via Bergum on N356 then exit E to Sumar towards Oostermeer.*
20 Mar-19 Oct ⬛ 🄰 ℝ 🖳 ⛊ ✕ ⊙ 🄮 ⌀ ⌶ 🄱 🄿 ⟨ LP 🄿 🄴 lau

) BORGER DRENTHE
Hunzedal De Drift 3 ☎ 0599 24698
The site is clean, well-kept and lies NE of the village.
➲ *For access, turn off the road towards Buinen, drive 200m E of the bridge over the Buinen-Schoondoord canal, then head S for a further 1km.*
4 Apr-31 Oct 30HEC ⬛ 🄰 ℝ 🖳 ⛊ ✕ ⊙ 🄮 ⌀ 🄱 ⟨ LP 🄿 🄴 lau ➧ ⌶

) DELFZIJL GRONINGEN
Delfzijl Zeebadweg 3 ☎ 0596 612318
In a wooded setting at the foot of the sea wall, adjoining a mini-golf course and attached to the AqcuriOm leisure complex.
Apr-Sep 1.4HEC ⬛ 🄰 ℝ ⊙ 🄮 🄱 🄿 🄿 🄴 ➧ 🖳 ⛊ ✕ ⟨PS
Prices: ⋏7 🚐3.50 🚐5.50 🄰4.50

) DIEVER DRENTHE
Hoeve aan de Weg Bosweg 12 ☎ 521 387269
In pleasant wooded surroundings with good recreational facilities.
Camping Card Compulsory.
1 Apr-31 Oct 9HEC ⬛ 🄰 ℝ 🖳 ⛊ ✕ ⊙ 🄮 ⌀ ⌶ 🄱 🄿 ⟨ P 🄿 🄿 🄴 lau ➧ ⟨L
Prices: ⋏2.50-5 🚐2.50-5 🚐2.50-5 🄰1.75-3.50

) DWINGELOO DRENTHE
Noordster Noordster 105 ☎ 521 597238
➲ *3km S on E35.*
All year 42HEC ⬛ ⚶ 🄰 ℝ 🖳 ⛊ ✕ ⊙ 🄮 ⌀ ⌶ 🄱 🄿 🄴 lau ➧ ⟨L
Prices: pitch 32-49 (incl 6 persons)

) EMMEN DRENTHE
Emmen Angelsloerdijk 31 ☎ 0591 612080
On several pitches of well-kept meadowland, near an indoor swimming pool.
Camping Card Compulsory.
➲ *From village drive towards Angelso for 1.5km, then follow signpots.*
All year 6HEC ⬛ 🄰 ℝ 🖳 ⛊ ✕ ⊙ 🄮 ⌀ ⌶ 🄱 🄿 🄿 🄴 lau ➧ ⟨P

) FORMERUM (ISLAND OF TERSCHELLING) FRIESLAND
Nieuw Formerum Formerum 13 ☎ 0562 448977
Apr-Sep 7HEC ⬛ 🄰 ℝ ⊙ 🄮 🄱 🄿 🄴 ⋙ lau ➧ 🖳 ⛊ ✕ ⌀ ⌶ ⟨S

) FRANEKER FRIESLAND
Bloemketerp Burg J Dykstraweg 3 ☎ 0517 395099
In a well equipped leisure centre near the historic old city centre of Franeker.
All year ⬛ 🄰 ℝ 🖳 ⛊ ✕ ⊙ 🄮 🄱 ⟨ PR 🄿 lau ➧ ✕ ⌀ 🄴
Prices: ⋏10 pitch 7-20

GASSELTE DRENTHE

Berken Borgerweg 23 ☎ 599 564255
Part of this site lies in wooded surroundings.
➲ *0.5km SW.*
Apr-25 Oct 3.5HEC ⬛ ⌘ ⌂ ⊙ ⊕ ⌀ 🏖 ⛉ ⊞ lau
➡ ☕ ♀ ✕

GROLLOO DRENTHE

Berenkuil De Pol 15 ☎ 0592 501242
Partly in a forest and partly on heathland.
➲ *On the western outskirts of the village towards Hooghalen.*
Drive a further 0.8km along a road which narrows at the end.
Apr-Sep 39HEC ⬛ ⌘ ⌂ ✕ ⊙ ⊕ ⌀ 🏖 ⌁ LP 🅿 ⊞ lau ➡ ☕

GRONINGEN GRONINGEN

Stadspark Campinglaan 6 ☎ 050 5251624
A well-kept site on patches of grass between rows of bushes
and groups of pine and deciduous trees. Some of its pitches
are naturally screened.
➲ *For access from the SW outskirts of the town, take the road*
towards Peize and Roden.
15 Mar-15 Oct 6HEC ⬛ ⌘ ⌂ ☕ ♀ ✕ ⊙ ⊕ ⌀ 🏖 🅿 ⊞ lau ➡
⌁LP
Prices: ⍏4.75 ⍕4.50 ⍖7 ⍗4.16

HARKSTEDE GRONINGEN

Grunopark Mooldweg 163 ☎ 050 416371
All year 23HEC ⬛ ⌘ ⌂ ☕ ♀ ✕ ⊙ ⊕ ⌀ 🏖 ⌁ L ⛉ ⊞ lau

HARLINGEN FRIESLAND

Zeehoeve ☎ 05178 413465
A well-kept meadow site which is divided into large sections
by rows of bushes.
➲ *1km S of Harlingen near a dyke.*
Apr-Sep 10HEC ⬛ ⌇ ⌂ ⊙ ⊕ ⌀ ⌁ S ⛉ ⊞ lau ➡ ☕

HINDELOOPEN FRIESLAND

Hindeloopen Westerdijk 9 ☎ 0514 521452
A peaceful site on the Ysselmeer with fishing and watersports
facilities.
➲ *1km S.*
1 Apr-1 Nov 16HEC ⬛ ⌘ ⌂ ☕ ♀ ✕ ⊙ ⊕ ⌀ 🏖 ⌁ L ⛉ 🅿 ⊞
lau
Prices: pitch 22.50-25 (incl 2 persons)

KOUDUM FRIESLAND

Nautic Park "De Kuilart" Kuilart 1 ☎ 0514 522221
A camping and watersports centre on the shores of 'De
Fluessen' lake.
➲ *Access via N359.*
All year 30HEC ⬛ ⌘ ⌂ ☕ ♀ ✕ ⊙ ⊕ ⌀ 🏖 ⚑ ⌁ LP ⛉ 🅿
⊞ lau ➡ ⌁S
Prices: pitch 41.50-47.50 (incl 2 persons)

See advertisement under Colour Section

LAUWERSOOG GRONINGEN

Lauwersoog Strandweg 7 ☎ 0159 349199
In a pleasant situation on the shores of Lauwersmeer. A good
excursion centre with fine water sports facilities.
Camping Card Compulsory.
All year 11HEC ⬛ ⠿ ⌘ ⌂ ☕ ♀ ✕ ⊙ ⊕ ⌀ 🏖 🏕 ⌁ 🅿
⊞ lau ➡ ⌁S

MAKKUM FRIESLAND

Holle Poarte Holle Poarte 2 ☎ 515 231344
A modern site with fine water sports facilities on the
Ijsselmeer.
All year 32HEC ⬛ ⠿ ⌘ ⌂ ☕ ♀ ✕ ⊙ ⊕ ⌀ 🏖 🏕 ⚑ ⍏ ⌁ L
⊞ lau

NES (ISLAND OF AMELAND) AMELAND

Duinoord J-van Eijckweg 4 ☎ 05191 42070
➲ *Take ferry at Holward, site left off road towards beach.*
Apr-Nov 17HEC ⬛ ⌇ ⌂ ☕ ♀ ✕ ⊙ ⊕ ⌀ ⍏ 🅿 ⊞ ⍣ lau ➡
⌁PS

ONNEN GRONINGEN

Fruitberg Dorpsweg 67 ☎ 50 4061282
A peaceful site situated in an orchard.
➲ *S of the village, and right of the Haren-Zuidlaren road.*
A28 Groningen-Assen-Haren,follow signs 15 Mar-1 Nov
5.5HEC ⬛ ⌘ ⌂ ☕ ♀ ✕ ⊙ ⊕ ⌀ 🏖 ⚑ ⌁ P ⛉ 🅿 ⊞ lau ➡ ☕ ✕
⌁L
Prices: pitch 20-25

OPENDE FRIESLAND

'T Strandheem Parkweg 2 ☎ 0594 659555
A family site with modern sanitary blocks and a wide variety
of recreational facilities.
➲ *Access from A7 (Groningen-Afsluitdijk) exit 31.*
1 Apr-1 Oct 15HEC ⬛ ⌘ ⌂ ☕ ♀ ✕ ⊙ ⊕ ⌀ 🏖 ⍏ ⌁ LP ⛉
🅿 ⊞ lau
Prices: pitch 22.50-30 (incl 2 persons)

RODEN DRENTHE

Cnossen Leekstermeer Meenweg 13 ☎ 05945 12073
On the S shores of the Leekstemeer.
➲ *For access, turn off the N13 about 1.6km SE of Leek*
(towards Roden) and drive NE. Then take a narrow paved
road, and continue for a further 2.7km.
Apr-Nov 3.8HEC ⬛ ⌇ ⌂ ✕ ⊙ ⊕ ⌀ ⛉ ⊞ lau ➡ ⌁L

RUINEN DRENTHE

Engeland Oude Benderseweg 11 ☎ 522 471770
1 Apr-5 Oct 26HEC ⬛ ⌇ ⌂ ☕ ♀ ✕ ⊙ ⊕ ⌀ ⌁ P ⛉ ⊞ lau ➡
☕ 🏖 ⌁LR

Wiltzangh Witteveen 2 ☎ 552 471227
N of the village in the middle of a coniferous and deciduous
forest, and within the grounds of a big holiday village.
Advance booking is necessary for the peak season.
➲ *For access, drive from Ruinen towards Ansen for 3km, then*
turn and head N.
1 Apr-31 Oct 13HEC ⬛ ⌘ ⌂ ☕ ♀ ✕ ⊙ ⊕ ⌀ 🏖 🏕 ⌁ P ⛉
lau ➡ ♀ ✕
Prices: pitch 25-36

SONDEL FRIESLAND

Sondel Beuckeswijkstr 26 ☎ 05140 2300
In a dense wood.
➲ *Just off the Sondel-Rijs road.*
29 Mar-Oct 6HEC ⬛ ⌘ ⌂ ♀ ✕ ⊙ ⊕ ⌁ LPRS ⛉ 🅿 ⊞ ⍣
lau ➡ ☕ ⌀ 🏖

TERSCHELLING (ISLAND OF)

See FORMERUM, HEE & WEST TERSCHELLING

WATEREN DRENTHE

Olde Lanschap Schurerslaan 4 ☎ 0521 387244
A spacious family site near the outskirts of a National Park.
Apr-Oct 13HEC ⬛ ⌘ ⌂ ☕ ♀ ✕ ⊙ ⊕ ⌀ 🏖 ⌁ LP ⛉ ⊞ lau

HEE (ISLAND OF TERSCHELLING) FRIESLAND

Kooi Hee 9 ☎ 562 442743
(5km from harbour) 25 Apr-10 Sep 7.2HEC ⬛ ⌘ ⌂ ♀ ✕ ⊙
⊕ 🅿 ⊞ lau ➡ ☕ ⌀ 🏖 ⌁LPS
Prices: ⍏6.50 ⍕3.50 ⍖7.50 ⍗4-7.50

WEDDE GRONINGEN

Wedderbergen Molenweg 2 ☎ 0597 561673
On meadowland divided by deciduous trees and bush hedges.
➲ *On the E outskirts of the village take a narrow asphalt road, and drive N for 3.2km. Then take Spanjaardsweg and Molenweg to the camp.*
All year 40HEC � ⌂ ♠ ⚊ ❤ ✕ ☉ 🖾 🅰 ⚒ ₹ L 🄴 ⊞ lau

WESTERBROEK GRONINGEN

Groningen International Woortmansdijk 1 ☎ 05904 1433
A pleasant site on the outskirts of Groningen.
➲ *From Groningen take A7 to Hoogezand and follow signs.*
All year 3HEC 架 ⌂ ⌂ ♠ ⚊ ❤ ✕ ☉ 🖾 ⚒ 🔲 🄴 ⊞ lau

WEST TERSCHELLING (ISLAND OF TERSCHELLING)

FRIESLAND

Cnossen Hoofdweg 8 ☎ 562 442321
Several patches of meadowland, left of the road towards Formerum, and right of the forest.
➲ *For access, take the ferry from Harlingen.*
Mar-1 Nov 2.5HEC ⋯⋯ ⌂ ⌂ ♠ ⚊ ❤ ✕ ☉ 🖾 ⚒ 🔲 🅰 🄿 ⊞
➧ ₹LPS
Prices: ⚑7.50 🚗3 🚐9 ▲5-9

● ● ● ● **CENTRAL** ● ● ● ●

In the heart of the Netherlands lies the country's largest nature reserve - the Hogwe Veluwe National Park. In addition to its many rare species, there are numerous museums and galleries, including the National Kröller-Müller Museum which houses a wonderful Van Gogh collection.
The Noord-Holland is *the* flower province of the Netherlands, with fields of daffodils, tulips, hyacinths and crocuses. Beautiful canals run through its capital, Amsterdam, with richly ornamental mansions on their banks. The most attractive and compact shopping centre in Holland, it is said you can buy anything in Amsterdam! In winter, the region of Overijsell is a paradise for those who enjoy long-distance skiing "langlauf". Alternatively, a visit in July to Dedomsvaart during its week-long festival will show you the largest open-air dinner and the largest shovel-board in the world.
Utrecht is truly unique; it combines a rich past and a dynamic present. It is the home of the tallest and finest church tower in Holland - the 'Dom'. Breathtaking views will reward those who climb its 465 steps.

⋯⋯⋯⋯⋯⋯⋯⋯⋯⋯⋯⋯⋯⋯⋯⋯⋯⋯⋯⋯

AALSMEER NOORD-HOLLAND

Amsterdamse Bos Kleine Noorddijk 1
☎ 020 6416868
The site is in a park-like setting in the Amsterdam wood. The camp is near the Airport flight path and is subject to noise depending on the wind direction.
➲ *If approaching from The Hague along the motorway, turn at the northern edge of the airport, and head towards Amstelveen. Then follow directions for Aalsmeer. Alternatively, if approaching from Utrecht, leave the motorway at the Amstelveen exit, and drive towards Aalsmeer, passing through Bovenkerk.*
(from Ag - Aalsmeer - camping signs) 1 Apr-14 Oct 6.8HEC
架 ⌂ ⌂ ♠ ⚊ ❤ ✕ ☉ 🖾 🅰 ⚒ 🄴 ⊞ lau ➧ ⚊ ₹LS
Prices: ⚑8.50 🚗4.25 🚐6.50 ▲5.50

Gaasper Camping Amsterdam
Loosdrechtdreef 7,
NL-1108 AZ Amsterdam
Tel: +31 20 696 73 26
Fax: +31 20 696 93 69

GAASPER CAMPING
AMSTERDAM

Just 20 minutes from the centre of Amsterdam there is a unique region of natural beauty, the "Gaasperpark" on the Gaasperplas. Within easy reach of a tube-station one of the finest camp sites of the Dutch capital is found: Gaasper Camping Amsterdam, situated on the verge of a park, with many trees and flowers.

ALKMAAR NOORD-HOLLAND

Alkmaar Bergerweg 201 ☎ 072 5116924
The site is well-kept and divided into many sections by rows of trees and bushes.
Camping Card Compulsory.
➲ *Lies on the NW outskirts of the town, off the Bergen road.*
(on NW outskirts of town) Apr-Oct 3HEC 架 ⌂ ⌂ ☉ 🖾 🔲
🄴 ⊞ lau ➧ ⚊ ❤ 🅰 ₹LPS
Prices: ⚑7 🚗4 🚐10 ▲7

AMSTERDAM NOORD-HOLLAND
See also Aalsmeer

Gaasper Loosdrechtdreef 7 ☎ 020 6967326
Situated on the edge the beautiful 'Gaasperpark' within easy reach of Amsterdam.
Camping Card Compulsory.
➲ *From A9 take Gaasperplas exit before city centre and follow camping signs.*
15 Mar-Dec 5.5HEC 架 ⌂ ⌂ ♠ ✕ ☉ 🖾 🅰 ⚒ 🄿 ⊞ lau
➧ ✕ ₹L
Prices: ⚑6.50 🚗6 🚐9 ▲7-9

Vliegenbos Meeuwenlaan 138 ☎ 0031 20 6368855
This is a tent site for young people.
➲ *From main railway station through tunnel, then right and right again at traffic lights, then follow signposts.*
1 Apr-30 Sep 25HEC 架 ♨ ⚶ ⌂ ♠ ⚊ ❤ ✕ ☉ 🖾 🅰 ⚒ 🔲 🄿 ⊞
⚇ lau ➧ ₹P
Prices: pitch 16 (incl 2 persons)

ANDIJK NOORD-HOLLAND

Vakantiedorp Het Grootslag Proefpolder 4 ☎ 228 592944
One of the most well equipped sites in the area, situated on the IJsselmeer. Individual bathrooms are allocated to each pitch and a wide range of recreational facilities are available.
➲ *From A7 exit Hoorn-Noord/Enkhuizen/Lelystad turn left for Andijk, then follow signs for Het Grootslag and Dijkweg.*
Mar-Nov 40HEC 架 ⌂ ⌂ ♠ ⚊ ❤ ✕ ☉ 🖾 🅰 ₹ LP 🄴 ⊞ lau ➧
🅰 ⚒

APPELTERN GELDERLAND

Het Groene Eiland Lutenkampstr 2 ☎ 0487 562130
➲ *A50 towards Druten, follow signs to Gouden Ham.*
15 Mar-Oct 16HEC 架 ⚶ ⌂ ♠ ⚊ ❤ ✕ ☉ 🖾 🅰 ⚒ 🔲 ₹ LR 🄿
⊞ lau
Prices: ⚑4.50-4.50 🚗3-3 🚐19.50-19.50 ▲8-8

ARNHEM GELDERLAND

Arnhem Kemperbegerweg 771 ☎ 026 4431600
The site lies on grassland and is surrounded by trees.
➲ *NW of town and S of E36.* *Contd.*

Apr-Oct 36HEC ⊞ lau ⇒ P
Prices: pitch 27 (incl 2 persons)

Hooge Veluwe Koningsweg 14 ☎ 026 4432272
Situated in a pleasant natural park with good facilities.
⊃ *From Apeldoorn exit on E36 drive NW towards Hooge Veluwe.*
28 Mar-25 Oct 18HEC ⊞ P ⊞
lau

Warnsborn Bakenbergseweg 257 ☎ 026 4423469
The site is surrounded by woodland and lies on slightly sloping meadowland. Near zoo and open-air museum.
⊃ *Near the E36 motorway NW of town in the direction of Utrecht. 200m S of SHELL filling station, continue in W direction for 0.7km.*
Apr-Oct 3.5HEC ⊞ lau ⇒
Prices: 6 ⇒5 ⇒5 ⇒3-5

BABBERICH GELDERLAND

Rivo Torto Beekseweg 8 ☎ 0316 247332
A riverside site with good recreational facilities.
⊃ *3km W on E36.*
15 Mar-31 Oct 8.5HEC ⊞ lau ⇒
L

BEEKBERGEN GELDERLAND

Bosgraaf Kanaal Zuid 444 ☎ 055 5051359
Situated on hilly grassland and woodland, but the woodland pitches are mainly used by residential caravans.
⊃ *For access from the N50, Arnhem-Apeldoorn road, turn N in West Hoeve onto the Loenen road, then follow signs for 2km.*
1 Apr-1 Oct 22HEC ⊞ P ⊞ lau

Lange Bosk Hoge Bergweg 16 ☎ 05765 1252
On level ground in a spruce forest. Divided into pitches.
⊃ *Turn off the Beekbergen-Loenen road at Km4.3 and drive N. Site about 3.5km from town.*
Apr-1 Nov 37.5HEC ⊞ P ⊞ lau
⇒L

BERKHOUT NOORD-HOLLAND

Westerkogge Kerkebuurt 202 ☎ 0229 551208
In a fine situation with well sheltered pitches and a good range of recreational facilities.
⊃ *Access via A7 (Amsterdam-Leeuwarden) exit Hoorn-Berkhout or Berkhout-Avenhorn.*
Apr-1 Oct 11HEC ⊞ P ⊞ lau
Prices: 4.20-5.25 ⇒3.60-4.50 ⇒11.60-14.50 ⇒6-7.50

BILTHOVEN UTRECHT

Biltse Duinen Burg.v.d Borchlaan 7 ☎ 030 2286777
Family site in wooded surroundings with asphalt drives.
⊃ *Signposted from town centre.*
Apr-1 Oct 20HEC ⊞ P ⊞ lau

BLOKZIJL OVERIJSSEL

Tussen de Diepen Duinigermeerweg 1A ☎ 0527 291565
Secluded site surrounded by water. Fishing, water-sports and sailing.
Apr-Oct 5HEC ⊞ R ⊞ lau
⇒P

BUURSE OVERIJSSEL

't Hazenbos Oude Buurserdijk 1 ☎ 053 5696338
On several meadows, partially surrounded by trees.
⊃ *7km from the German border.*
All year 6HEC ⊞ lau ⇒

CALLANTSOOG NOORD-HOLLAND

Recreatiecentrum de Nollen Westerweg 8 ☎ 0224 581281
A modern family site with plenty of facilities. Less than 1 mile from the beach.
⊃ *E of town towards N9.*
1 Apr-1 Nov 9HEC ⊞ lau ⇒S

Tempelhof Westerweg 2 ☎ 0224 581522
Well equipped site on level meadowland.
Apr-31 Oct 12.7HEC ⊞ P ⊞ lau ⇒LS

COCKSDORP, DE (ISLAND OF TEXEL) NOORD-HOLLAND

Krim Roggeslootweg 6 ☎ 0222 390111
A well kept site with easy access to the nearby beaches.
All year 30HEC ⊞ P ⊞ lau ⇒S

Sluftervallei Krimweg 102 ☎ 0222 316214
On sand-dunes. It is advisable to book in advance during the peak season.
⊃ *From the ferry landing stage, drive to the N tip of the island. Just before entering the village, turn left and head towards Vuurtoren (lighthouse). Turn left again after several hundred metres. The road leads directly to the site.*
Etr-Oct 10HEC ⊞ P ⊞ lau ⇒S

DALFSEN OVERIJSSEL

Buitenplaats Gerner Haersolteweg 9-17 ☎ 0529 431181
Camping Card Compulsory.
⊃ *Turn off at Dalfsen and take second road on the left.*
All year 14HEC ⊞ LP ⊞ lau

DELDEN OVERIJSSEL

Park Camping International De Mors 6 ☎ 074 3763420
On two grassy terraces at the edge of a wood, to the SE of town.
⊃ *Take A1 and exit at Hengelo-Zuid.*
15 Mar-Oct 5HEC ⊞ lau ⇒

DENEKAMP OVERIJSSEL

Papillon Kanaalweg 30 ☎ 05413 51670
Predominantly a chalet site on meadowland in a tall coniferous and deciduous forest, about 2km N of Denekamp. It has a few naturally screened pitches.
⊃ *For access, turn off the E72 towards Nordhorn (Germany), about 0.3km N of the signposts for Almelo-Nordhorn canal, and drive NE for 1.5km.*
All year 11HEC ⊞ P ⊞ lau ⇒

DIEPENHEIM OVERIJSSEL

Molnhofte Nyhofweg 5 ☎ 0547 351514
A family site in a rural setting with modern bungalows for hire.
⊃ *E of town.*
All year 6HEC ⊞ lau ⇒P
Prices: 5 ⇒4.50 ⇒5 ⇒5

DOESBURG GELDERLAND

Ijsselstrand Eekstr 18 ☎ 313 472797
On level meadow with trees and hedges beside the River Ijssel. Separate field for young people. Water sports.
↪ *NE across river. Signposted.*
All year 45HEC ⸺ 🏕️🛁🛒🍴🍽️⊙🚽∅🏊⛺🚿 LR ⊞⊞ lau

DOETINCHEM GELDERLAND

Wrange Rekhemseweg 144 ☎ 0314 324852
On the eastern outskirts of the town. It is set in meadowland and surrounded by bushes and deciduous trees.
↪ *200m E of link road between roads to Varsseveld and Terborg.*
1 Apr-1 Oct 10HEC ⸺ 🏕️🛒🛁🍴🍽️⊙🚽∅🏊⛺🚽 P ⊞⊞ lau
Prices: pitch 23-23 (incl 2 persons)

DOORN UTRECHT

Bonte Vlucht Leersumsestraatweg 23 ☎ 0343 473232
↪ *3km E.*
Apr-Oct 17HEC ⸺ ⋮⋮⋮ 🛒🍴🍴🍽️⊙🚽∅🏊🚿♦ ✝P

Het Grote Bos Hydeparklaan 24 ☎ 0343 513644
Well layed out site on wooded grassland. Varied leisure activities for children and adults.
Camping Card Compulsory.
↪ *About 1km NW of Doorn.*
All year 80HEC ⸺ ⋮⋮⋮ 🛁🛒🍴🍴🍽️⊙🚽∅🏊
⛺ ✝ P ⊞ lau
Prices: pitch 31-44 (incl 2 persons)

DRONTEN GELDERLAND

At BIDDINGHUIZEN(9km S)

Flevostrand Strandweg 1 ☎ 0320 288480
Plots of grassland separated by close belts of shrubs. Own marina.
↪ *On the Polder, 5km S of Biddinghuizen turn right near the Veluwemeer.*
Apr-Nov 25HEC ⸺ 🏕️🛒🛁🍴🍽️⊙🚽∅🏊⛺🚽 LP ⊞⊞ lau

Riviera Park Spijkweg 15 ☎ 0321 331344
Situated on grassland near a forest of deciduous trees and surrounded by shrubs.
↪ *On the Polder beside the Veluwemeer, 5km S of Biddinghuizen turn left.*
21 Mar-29 Oct 63HEC ⸺ 🛒🛁🍴🍽️⊙🚽∅🏊⛺🚽 ✝
LP ⊞⊞ lau

EDAM NOORD-HOLLAND

Strandbad Zeevangszeedijk 7a ☎ 0299 371994
Apr-1 Oct 4HEC ⸺ 🏕️🛒🛁🍴🍽️⊙🚽∅🏊⛺ ✝L ⊞⊞
🍽️ lau ♦ ✝P
Prices: ♠4.60 ♣5 ♠7.50 ▲5.50

EERBEEK GELDERLAND

Coldenhove Boshoffweg 6 ☎ 0313 659101
In woodland.
↪ *From Apeldoorn-Dieren road, drive 2km SW, then NW for 1km.*
All year 74HEC ⸺ 🛒🛁🍴🍽️⊙🚽∅🏊⛺🚽 ✝P ⊞⊞⊞
🍽️ lau

Robertsoord Doonweg 4 ☎ 0313 651346
In a wooded location with good recreational facilities.
↪ *1km SE.*
All year 2.5HEC ⸺ 🛒🛁✗⊙🚽∅⛺🚽⊞ lau ♦ 🛒
Prices: ♠3.50 ♣3.50 ♠10 ▲10

EMST GELDERLAND

Wildhoeve Hanendorperweg 102 ☎ 05787 1324
A picturesque, peaceful site within the confines of the Royal Forest with good, modern facilities.
↪ *3.5km W. Signposted.*
Apr-Oct 11HEC ⸺ 🏕️🛒🛁🍴🍽️✗⊙🚽∅🏊⛺ ✝ P ⊞⊞
🍽️ lau

ENSCHEDE OVERIJSSEL

De Twentse Es Keppelerdijk 200 ☎ 053 4611372
In a wooded location with good recreational facilities.
↪ *E towards Glanerbrug.*
All year 15HEC ⸺ 🛒🛁🍴🍽️✗⊙🚽∅🏊⛺ ✝ P ⊞⊞ lau
Prices: pitch 31 (incl 2 persons)

ERMELO GELDERLAND

Haeghehorst Fazantlaan 4 ☎ 0341 553185
Well equipped site in pleasant wooded surroundings.
Camping Card Compulsory.
↪ *Access via A28/E35 towards Amersfoort, then N303.*
All year 9.8HEC ⸺ 🏕️🛒🛁🍴🍽️✗⊙🚽∅🏊⛺⊞⊞⊞🍽️ lau
♦ ✝L
Prices: pitch 33.25-43.75 (incl 2 persons)

GROET NOORD-HOLLAND

Groede Hargerweg 8 ☎ 72 5091555
The site consists of a meadow enclosed by hedges.
15 Apr-15 Sep 3HEC ⸺ 🛒🛁🍴⊙🚽∅🏊⊞⊞🍽️ lau
♦ 🍴✗ ✝S

GROOTE KEETEN NOORD-HOLLAND

Callassande Voorweg 5A ☎ 0224 581663
A large tourist site with fine facilities close to the sea.
Apr-Oct 11.5HEC ⸺ 🛒🛁🍴🍽️✗⊙🚽∅🏊⛺ ✝ P ⊞⊞⊞ lau
♦✗∅🏊 ✝S
Prices: ♠6 ♣5 ♠23-31.50 ▲15.50-21.50

HAAKSBERGEN OVERIJSSEL

Scholtenhagen Scholtenhagenweg 30 ☎ 05427 22384
The internal site roads are asphalt.
↪ *Turn off by-pass W of town and drive towards Eilbergen for 0.7km, then turn right and follow Zwemmbad signposts.*
Apr-Oct 10HEC ⸺ 🛒🛁🍴✗⊙🚽∅🏊⛺⊞⊞ lau ♦ ✝P

't Stien'nboer Scholtenhagenweg 42 ☎ 053 5722610
A family site with good recreational facilities lying S of the town.
1 Apr-26 Oct 10.5HEC ⸺ 🛒🛁🍴🍴🍽️✗⊙🚽∅🏊⛺
▲ ✝ P ⊞⊞⊞ lau
Prices: pitch 21.50-32.50 (incl 2 persons)

HALFWEG NOORD-HOLLAND

Houtrak Zuickerweg 2 ☎ 0120 4972796
Grassy site on several levels subdivided by trees, hedges and shrubs. Separate section for young campers.
↪ *Signposted from Spaarwonde exit on A5.*
Apr-1 Oct 13HEC ⸺ 🛒🛁🍴⊙🚽∅🏊⛺ ✝ L ⊞⊞ lau

HATTEM GELDERLAND

Grandgoed Molecaten Koeweg 1 ☎ 038 4447044
Trailer caravans not admitted.
31 Mar-Sep 4HEC 🛒✗⊙🚽∅ ✝ P ⊞⊞ lau

Leemkule Leemkuilen 6 ☎ 038 4441945
A holiday centre situated in one of the largest nature reserves in the country.
↪ *2.5km SW.*
Apr-2 Nov 24HEC ⸺ 🛁🛒🍴🍽️✗⊙🚽∅⛺ ✝ P ⊞⊞🍽️
lau
Prices: pitch 39 (incl 2 persons)

HEILOO NOORD-HOLLAND

Heiloo De Omloop 24 ☎ 072 5355555
One of the best sites in the area. It is divided into many large squares by hedges.
Apr-Oct 4HEC ⚑ 🛁 ♠ ♔ ♥ X ⊙ 🅿 ⌀ ♨ 🚐 🅿 ⊞ ✗ lau ➡ ♨
⏏LPS
Prices: ⚑2 pitch 18-25.25

Klein Varnebroek De Omloop 22 ☎ 072 5331627
A grassy family campsite surrounded by trees.
➲ *Off the Alkmaar road towards the swimming pool.*
Apr-Oct 4.9HEC ⚑ ♠ ♔ ♥ X ⊙ 🅿 ⌀ ♨ 🅿 ⊞ ✗ lau ➡
⏏LPS
Prices: pitch 42.50

HELDER, DEN NOORD-HOLLAND

Donkere Duinen Jan Verfailleweg 616 ☎ 0223 614731
A quiet, pleasant site with good facilities.
➲ *800m towards the beach. Follow signs 'Nieuw-Den Helder' Strand.*
1 Apr-15 Sep 7HEC ⚑ ♠ ⊙ 🅿 ⌀ ♨ ⏏ P 🅿 ⊞ lau ➡ ♨ ♥
X ⏏S
Prices: ⚑7.10 pitch 15.75

Noorder Sandt Noorder Sandt 2, Julianadorp aan Zee
☎ 0223 641266
A flat, well-maintained site on meadowland, with good sanitary blocks.
➲ *Access from the Den Helder to Callantsoog coastal road.*
15 Mar-15 Sep 9.8HEC ⚑ ♠ ♔ X ⊙ 🅿 ⌀ ♨ 🚐 P 🅿 🅿
lau ➡ ♨ ♥ X ⏏S

HENGELO GELDERLAND

Kom-Es-An Handwijzersdijk 4 ☎ 0575 467242
➲ *NE of village in wooded area in the direction of Ruurlo.*
Apr-Oct 10.5HEC ⚑ ♠ ♔ X ⊙ 🅿 ⌀ ♨ ⏏ P 🅿 🅿 ⊞
lau
Prices: ⚑4.50-4.75 pitch 11.50-12.50

HENGELO OVERIJSSEL

Zwaaikom Kettingbrugweg 60 ☎ 074 2916560
A family site with good facilities situated on the Twente Canal.
➲ *SE towards Enschede between canal and road.*
15 Apr-15 Sep 4HEC ⚑ ♠ ♔ ♥ X ⊙ 🅿 ⌀ ♨ ⏏ P 🅿 ⊞
✗

HEUMEN GELDERLAND

Heumens Bos Vosseneindseweg 46 ☎ 024 3581481
One of the best sites in the area with good, modern facilities and spacious pitches.
➲ *NW of village, 100m N of the Wijchen road.*
1 Apr-31 Oct 16HEC ⚑ ♠ ♔ ♥ X ⊙ 🅿 ⌀ 🚐 🚐 ♠ ⏏ P
⊞ lau ➡ ⏏L
Prices: ⚑6 ♠10 🚐18

HOENDERLOO GELDERLAND

Pampel Woeste Hoefweg 33-35 ☎ 055 3781760
A most attractive site in pleasant wooded surroundings with good facilities for families.
All year 14.5HEC ⚑ ⁙⁙ ♠ ♔ ♥ X ⊙ 🅿 ⌀ ♨ ⏏ P 🅿 🅿
lau

't Veluws Hof Krimweg 154 ☎ 055 3781777
Comfortable site with good, modern facilities.
➲ *W of N93.*
All year 31HEC ⚑ ♠ ♔ ♥ X ⊙ 🅿 ⌀ ♨ 🚐 🚐 ⏏ P 🅿 🅿
lau
Prices: ⚑5 ♠3 🚐5 ⚑5

HOLTEN OVERIJSSEL

Prins Wildweg 2 ☎ 0031 0548 512272
A holiday complex operated by the Dutch ENNIA Company, in an area of attraction to the rambler. Swimming pool on edge of site.
➲ *Access from the E8 Deventer-Almelo road. Take the Holten/Rijssen exit then turn off.*
Apr-Oct 6HEC ⚑ ➡ ♠ ♨ ♥ X ⊙ 🅿 ⌀ 🚐 ⏏ P 🅿 🅿 ⊞ lau

HOORN, DEN (ISLAND OF TEXEL) NOORD-HOLLAND

Loodsmansduin Rommelpot 19 ☎ 0222 319203
Extensive site, numerous large and small hollows between dunes, connected by paved paths. Several sanitary blocks. At the highest part there is a bungalow village in amongst a shopping and administrative complex. A section is reserved for naturists and there is a naturists beach 2km away.
➲ *From the ferry drive N towards Den Burg, then turn left at crossroads towards Den Hoorn.*
1 Apr-25 Oct 38HEC ⚑ ✂ ♠ ♨ ♥ X ⊙ 🅿 ⌀ ♨ ⏏ PS ⊞
lau

KESTEREN GELDERLAND

Lede en Oudewaard Hogedijkseweg 40 ☎ 488 481477
On level meadowland surrounded by bushy hedges and divided into individual pitches. 100m from private beach and pool.
➲ *2km N of village, turn W off main Rhenen-Kesteren road, and continue for 2.7km.*
All year 30HEC ⚑ ♠ ♨ ♥ X ⊙ 🅿 ⌀ ♨ 🚐 ⏏ L 🅿 🅿
lau

KOOG, DE (ISLAND OF TEXEL) NOORD-HOLLAND

Shelter Boodklaan 93 ☎ 0222 317475
Small family site a short distance from the sea.
15 Mar-25 Oct 1.1HEC ⚑ ✂ ♠ ⊙ 🅿 🅿 ⊞ lau ➡ ♨ ♥ X ⌀
♨ ⏏S

KOOTWIJK GELDERLAND

Kerkendel Kerkendelweg 49 ☎ 0577 456224
A family site with good facilities situated in the heart of the Veluwe National Park.
27 Mar-Oct 7.5HEC ⚑ ♠ ♨ ♥ X ⊙ 🅿 ⌀ ♨ 🚐 ♠ ⏏ P 🅿
⊞ lau ➡ ⏏LR
Prices: pitch 32.50-51 (incl 2 persons)

LAAG-SOEREN GELDERLAND

Jutberg Jutberg 78 ☎ 0313 619220
A well equipped site in the woods of the South East Veluwezoom near Arnhem.
➲ *Access via A12 (Arnhem) towards Zulfa, then follow signposts.*
All year ⚑ ⁙⁙⁙ ♠ ♨ ♥ X ⊙ 🅿 ⌀ ♨ 🚐 🚐 ⏏ P 🅿 lau
Prices: pitch 41.40-51.40 (incl 4 persons)

LATHUM GELDERLAND

Honingraat Marsweg 2 ☎ 0313 633211
Site with modern facilities on an arm of the Ijssel with good boating facilities and its own marina.
➲ *For access, turn off Arnhem-Doesburg road and pass through the village to the site in 1.5km.*
mid Mar-mid Oct 17HEC ⚑ ✂ ♠ ♨ ♥ X ⊙ 🅿 ♨ ⏏ LP 🅿
⊞ lau ➡ ⌀

Mars Marsweg 6 ☎ 0313 631131
Divided into pitches on level meadowland beside a dammed tributary of River Ijssel.
➲ *Turn off Arnhem-Doesberg road N of village and continue W for 1.7km.*
Apr-Oct 10HEC ⚑ ✂ ♠ ♨ ♥ X ⊙ 🅿 ♨ ⏏ L 🅿 ⊞ lau

▶ **LOCHEM** GELDERLAND

Ruighenrode Vordenseweg 6 ☎ 0573 289400
Site among mixed woodland with tall spruce.
➲ *2km SW of town. For access, turn off the road to Zutphen at Km10.4 in S direction on the Vorden road for the site.*
All year 58HEC ⬛ ⚏ ⚅ ♨ ☂ ✕ ⊙ ⛺ ∅ ⛺ 🏪 ⋚ LP 🅿 ⊞ lau ◆
⛺

▶ **LUTTENBERG** OVERIJSSEL

Luttenberg Heuvelweg 9 ☎ 0572 301405
A large holiday park with spacious, well defined pitches separated by bushes. Wide variety of recreational facilities.
Camping Card Compulsory.
27 Mar-3 Oct 12HEC ⬛ ⚏ ⚅ ♨ ☂ ✕ ⊙ ⛺ ∅ 🏖 ⛺ ⛺ ⋚ P
🅿 🅿 ⊞ lau
Prices: 🏕6 pitch 20

▶ **MAARN** UTRECHT

Laag-Kanje Laan van Laag-Kanje 1 ☎ 0343 441348
Situated 500m from the lake.
➲ *2km NE.*
Apr-1 Oct 29HEC ⬛ ⚄ ⚅ ♨ ☂ ✕ ⊙ ⛺ ∅ 🅿 ⊞ ⚘ lau ◆ ⋚L
Prices: 🏕5.50 ♣3 ⛽9 🅰6.50-9

▶ **MARKELO** OVERIJSSEL

Hessenheem Potdijk 8 ☎ 0547 361200
Situated near a swimming pool.
➲ *3km NE.*
All year 30HEC ⬛ ⫶⫶ ⚄ ⚅ ♨ ☂ ✕ ⊙ ⛺ ∅ 🏖 🏖 ⛺ ⋚ P 🅿
⊞ lau

▶ **MIJNDEN** UTRECHT

Mijnden Bloklaan 22a ☎ 0294 233165
Situated directly on the Loosdrechtse Plassen lake with good sporting facilities.
1 Apr-10 Oct 25HEC ⬛ ⚏ ⚅ ♨ ☂ ✕ ⊙ ⛺ ∅ ⋚ P 🅿 🅿
⊞ lau

▶ **NEEDE** GELDERLAND

Eversman Bliksteeg 1 ☎ 0545 291906
Situated in a quiet position, surrounded by trees.
➲ *W of town.*
3 Apr-30 Oct 3HEC ⬛ ⚄ ⚅ ♨ ✕ ⊙ ⛺ ⛺ ⋚ P 🅿 ⊞ lau ◆
∅
Prices: 🏕5 ♣4.25 ⛽5.75 🅰8.75

▶ **NOORD SCHARWOUDE** NOORD-HOLLAND

Molengroet Molengroet 1 ☎ 0031 226393444
Site with modern facilities within easy reach of the beach and the 'Geestmerambacht' water park.
➲ *Signposted on N245.*
All year 11HEC ⚄ ⚅ ♨ ☂ ✕ ⊙ ⛺ ∅ ⛺ ⋚ L 🅿 ⊞ lau
Prices: pitch 33.50-60 (incl 2 persons)

▶ **NUNSPEET** GELDERLAND

Vossenberg Groenlaantje 25 ☎ 03412 252458
Apr-1 Nov 3.6HEC ⬛ ⚄ ⚅ ☂ ✕ ⊙ ⛺ ∅ ⛺ 🏖 ⊞ ⚘ ◆
⋚LP

▶ **OMMEN** OVERIJSSEL

Calluna Stouweweg 3 ☎ 05291 55553
➲ *NW on left off road to Zwolle.*
Apr-Nov 25HEC ⬛ ⚄ ⚅ ♨ ☂ ✕ ⊙ ⛺ ∅ ⛺ 🏖 ⛺ ⋚ LP 🅿 ⊞

▶ **OTTERLO** GELDERLAND

Beek en Hei Heldeweg 4 ☎ 0318 591483
Camping Card Compulsory.
All year 3HEC ⬛ ⚄ ⚅ ⊙ ⛺ 🏖 🅿 ⊞ lau ◆ ♨ ✕ ∅ ⛺ ⋚L

▶ **PETTEN** NOORD-HOLLAND

Corfwater Korfwaterweg 1a ☎ 02268 1981
15 Apr-Oct 5.5HEC ⫶⫶⫶ ⚄ ⚅ ⊙ ⛺ ⋚ S 🅿 ⊞ ⚘ lau ◆ ♨ ☂
✕ ∅ ⛺ ⋚P

▶ **PUTTEN** GELDERLAND

Strand Nulde Strandboulevard 27 ☎ 341 361304
1 Apr-31 Oct 8HEC ⬛ ⚄ ⚅ ♨ ☂ ✕ ⊙ ⛺ ∅ ⛺ 🅰 ⋚ L 🅿 ⊞
⚘ lau ◆ ⋚P
Prices: pitch 49.50 (incl 4 persons)

▶ **RHENEN** UTRECHT

Thymse Berg Nieuwe Veenendaalseweg 229 ☎ 317 612384
➲ *N of town.*
1 Apr-30 Sep 10HEC ⬛ ⚄ ⚅ ♨ ☂ ✕ ⊙ ⛺ ∅ ⛺ ⛺ ⋚ PS 🅿
⊞ ⚘ lau ◆ ⋚LR
Prices: 🏕6.95 ♣2 ⛽15 🅰15

▶ **RUURLO** GELDERLAND

't Sikkeler Sikkelerweg 8 ☎ 573 461221
In a beautiful wooded location with good, modern facilities. Popular with walkers.
➲ *4km SW.*
N315 Ruurlo-Doetinchem.4km from Ruurlo,right. All year
5HEC ⬛ ⚄ ⚅ ♨ ✕ ⊙ ⛺ ∅ 🏖 🅿 ⊞ lau ◆ ♨ ✕ ⛺ ⋚LP
Prices: pitch 10-36

▶ **ST MAARTENSZEE** NOORD-HOLLAND

St Maartenszee Westerduinweg 30 ☎ 0224 561401
Completely surrounded and divided into pitches by hedges, lying on meadowland on the edge of a wide belt of sand dunes.
➲ *For access, turn off the Alkmaar to Den Helder road at St Maartensvlotburg and drive towards the sea. Take the road over the dunes and follow it for about 1.5km, then turn right and continue for a further 300m.*
25 Mar-25 Sep 7HEC ⬛ ⚄ ⚅ ♨ ☂ ✕ ⊙ ⛺ ∅ ⛺ 🏖 ⊞ ⚘
lau ◆ ⋚LPS

▶ **SOEST** UTRECHT

King's Home Birkstr 136 ☎ 033 4619118
Well maintained site with modern facilities in a natural setting on the edge of woodland.
➲ *On N221 between Amersfoort and Soest.*
All year 5HEC ⬛ ⚄ ⚅ ♨ ☂ ✕ ⊙ ⛺ ∅ ⛺ ⛺ 🅿 ⊞ lau ◆ ♨

▶ **STEENWIJK** OVERIJSSEL

Kom Bultweg 25 ☎ 521 513736
Split into two sections, lying near a country house, and surrounded by a beautiful oak forest.
➲ *The access road off the Steenwijk-Frederiksoord road is easy to miss.*
1 Apr-1 Oct 12HEC ⬛ ⫶⫶⫶ ⚄ ⚅ ♨ ☂ ✕ ⊙ ⛺ ∅ ⛺ 🏖 ⛺
⋚ P 🅿 🅿 ⊞ lau
Prices: pitch 27 (incl 2 persons)

▶ **TEXEL (ISLAND OF)**

See **COCKSDORP, DE, HOORN, DEN & KOOG, DE**

▶ **UITDAM** NOORD-HOLLAND

Uitdam Zeedijk 2 ☎ 20 4031433
A well maintained site on the Markermeer adjoining the marina.
➲ *Access via N247 Amsterdam-Monnickendam.*
Mar-Oct 23HEC ⬛ ⚄ ⚅ ♨ ☂ ✕ ⊙ ⛺ ∅ ⛺ ⛺ ⋚ L 🅿 ⊞
lau
Prices: pitch 29-36.50 (incl 2 persons)

URK FLEVOLAND

Hazevreugd Vormtweg 9 ☎ 0527 681785
A modern family site in wooded surroundings with a wide
variety of recreational facilities.
➲ *Access via A6.*
Apr-Oct 12HEC ⛺ 🔌 🏕 🛁 ⚊ ✕ ⊙ 🖫 ⌀ ⚒ 🏪 🖭 ⚡ P 🏧 ⊞
lau ➧ ⚊S
Prices: ⚊5 ➧3.50 🚐6 ▲6

UTRECHT UTRECHT

Berekuil Arienslaan 5 ☎ 030 713870
In a wooded location beside a lake with well defined pitches
and good facilities.
➲ *On N outskirts near motorway to Hilversum.*
All year 4.5HEC ⛺ 🔌 🏕 🛁 ⚊ ✕ ⊙ 🖫 ⌀ ⚒ 🏪 ⚡ P 🖭 ⊞ lau
Prices: ⚊8 ➧5 🚐7.50-10 ▲8

VAASSEN GELDERLAND

Bosrand Elspeterweg 45 ☎ 0578 571343
In castle grounds surrounded by woods.
➲ *Access via A50 Vaassen exit.*
All year 3HEC ⛺ 🔌 🏕 ✕ ⊙ 🖫 ⌀ ⚒ 🏪 🖭 ⚡ P 🏧 ⊞ lau
➧ ⚊

VELSEN-ZUID NOORD-HOLLAND

Weltevreden ☎ 023 383726
Camping Card Compulsory.
Apr-Oct 10HEC ⛺ ➧ 🏕 🛁 ✕ ⊙ 🖫 ⌀ ⚒ 🏪 🖭 ⚡ LP ⊞
P ⊞ lau ➧ ✕ ⚊S

VOGELENZANG NOORD-HOLLAND

Vogelenzang Tweede Doodweg 17 ☎ 023 5847014
➲ *1km W.*
Etr-15 Sep 22HEC ⛺ 🔌 🏕 🛁 ⚊ ✕ ⊙ 🖫 ⌀ ⚒ ⚡ P 🏧 ⊞ ⌂
lau

WAGENINGEN GELDERLAND

Wielerbaan Zoomweg 7-9 ☎ 0317 413964
A friendly family site on the edge of a forest.
➲ *Access via A12, then follow signposts.*
All year 6.5HEC ⛺ 🔌 🏕 🛁 ✕ ⊙ 🖫 ⌀ 🏪 ⚡ PS 🏧 ⊞ lau
Prices: pitch 31.20-39.20 (incl 2 persons)

WEZEP GELDERLAND

Heidehoek Heidehoeksweg 7 ☎ 38 3761382
➲ *0.5km W of railway station.*
1 Apr-31 Oct 15HEC ⛺ 🔌 🏕 🛁 ⚊ ✕ ⊙ 🖫 ⌀ ⚒ ⚡ P 🏧 ⊞
lau ➧ ⚊L
Prices: pitch 25-45 (incl 2 persons)

WIJDENES NOORD-HOLLAND

Het Hof Zuideruitweg 64 ☎ 0229 501435
25 Mar-Oct 4HEC ⛺ 🔌 🏕 🛁 ⚊ ✕ ⊙ 🖫 ⌀ ⚒ 🏪 ⚡ LP P
⊞ lau
Prices: ⚊5 pitch 12.50

WINTERSWIJK GELDERLAND

Twee Bruggen Meenkmolenweg 11 ☎ 543 565366
A family site in pleasant wooded surroundings with good,
modern facilities.
All year 34HEC ⛺ 🔌 🏕 🛁 ⚊ ✕ ⊙ 🖫 ⌀ ⚒ 🏪 🖭 ⚡ LP 🏧 P
⊞ lau
Prices: pitch 37.50-45

The south of the Netherlands is the home of the traditional
Delft china and Gouda cheese, and is also the location of a
project which is the first of its kind in the world: the
building of a moveable marine floodgate across the outlet
of the Oostenschelde River.
One of the oldest cities in Holland, and the provincial
capital of Limburg, is Maastricht. Shaped through the ages
by art and culture, the city has a rich heritage and a wealth
of historic monuments.
The region also includes two prominent and very different
cities. The Hague, with its favourable reputation as the City
of Arts, has parliamentary buildings and stately palaces,
wide streets and spacious squares, giving an impression of
distinction and elegance.
The world's premier harbour has expanded to become the
dynamic metropolis of Rotterdam; a city full of vitality and
conviviality with a variety of architecture ranging from snug
Delfshaven to the futuristic pencil flats and cube houses.
....

AFFERDEN LIMBURG

Klein Canada Dorpsstr 1 ☎ 0485 531223
Situated among heath and woodland close to the River
Meuse.
All year 10HEC ⛺ 🔌 🏕 🛁 ⚊ ✕ ⊙ 🖫 ⌀ ⚒ ⚡ P 🏧 ⊞ lau
Prices: pitch 35 (incl 2 persons)

ARCEN LIMBURG

Maasvallei Dorperheideweg 34 ☎ 77 473 1564
In wooded surroundings near the beach, this family site has
varied sporting facilities and play areas for children.
➲ *Off the N271.*
All year 11HEC ⛺ 🔌 🏕 🛁 ⚊ ✕ ⊙ 🖫 ⌀ ⚒ 🏪 ⚡ LP 🏧 ⊞ ⌂
➧ ⚊
Prices: ⚊27.50-46

ARNEMUIDEN ZEELAND

Witte Raaf Muidenweg 3 ☎ 0118 601212
A modern well-maintained site in meadowland, divided into
sections by rows of shrubs, ideal for sailing and motor boat
enthusiasts with yacht marina.
➲ *Situated on the Veersmeer, N of the Goes-Vlissingen
motorway, from Arnemuiden exit follow signs for about 5km.*
Apr-Sep 20HEC ⛺ 🔌 🏕 🛁 ⚊ ✕ ⊙ 🖫 ⌀ ⚒ 🏪 ▲ ⚡ L 🏧 ⊞
⌂ lau

ASSELT LIMBURG

Maasterras Eind 4 ☎ 0475 501207
Well-kept site on terrace. Private beach.
➲ *W of Swalmen-2.3km W of the TEXACO petrol station on
the N273.*
15 Mar-15 Oct 5HEC ⛺ 🔌 🏕 🛁 ✕ ⊙ 🖫 ⚒ 🏧 P lau ➧ ⌀ ⚊

BAARLAND ZEELAND

Scheldeoord Landingsweg 1 ☎ 01193 9226
A popular family site in a beautiful location by the Scheldt
River.
➲ *S of town on the coast.*
All year 16HEC ⛺ 🔌 🏕 🛁 ⚊ ✕ ⊙ 🖫 ⌀ ⚒ 🏪 🖭 ⚡ PS P ⊞ lau

BAARLE NASSAU NOORD-BRABANT

Heimolen Heimolen 6 ☎ 507 9425
In a wooded location with good, modern facilities.
➲ *1.5km SW.*
All year 15HEC ⛺ 🔌 🏕 ⚊ ✕ ⊙ 🖫 ⌀ ⚒ 🏪 🖭 🏧 P ⊞ lau
Prices: ⚊5 ➧2.50 🚐6 ▲6

BARENDRECHT ZUID-HOLLAND

Jachthaven de Oude Maas Achterzeedijk 1a ☎ 78 6772445
On the banks of the Oude Maas, the site is particularly suitable for families and hikers.
All year 12HEC ⊞ ⌐ ⌐ ⌐ ⌐ ⌐ ⊙ ⌐ ⌐ ⌐ ⌐ ᎑ P ⊞ ⊞ lau
Prices: ⚲6.15 ⚲6.15 ⚲6.15 ⚲6.15

BERG EN TERBLIJT LIMBURG

Oriëntal Rijksweg 6 ☎ 043 6040075
⤷ On Maastricht-Valkenburg road 3km from Maastricht.
25 Apr-30 Oct 5.5HEC ⊞ ⌐ ⌐ ⌐ ⌐ ⌐ ⊙ ⌐ ⌐ ᎑ ⌐ ᎑ P ⊞
⊞ lau ➧ ✕

BERGEYK NOORD-BRABANT

Paal De Paaldreef 14 ☎ 0497 571977
⤷ Campsite especially catering for families with children.
Camping Card Compulsory.
⤷ Signposted.
Apr-1 Nov 31HEC ⊞ ⌐ ⌐ ⌐ ⌐ ⌐ ✕ ⊙ ⌐ ⌐ ᎑ ᎑ P ⊞ ⊞ lau
➧ ᎑LR
Prices: pitch 55 (incl 4 persons)

BLADEL NOORD-BRABANT

Achterste Hoef Troprijt 10 ☎ 04977 81579
⤷ S of town.
Apr-29 Oct 15HEC ⊞ ⌐ ⌐ ⌐ ⌐ ⌐ ✕ ⊙ ⌐ ⌐ ᎑ ᎑ P ⊞ ⊞ lau

BOXTEL NOORD-BRABANT

Dennenoord Dennendreef 5 ☎ 0411 601280
Level, grassy site with hedging and groups of trees. Leisure activities organised for adults and young people. Soundproof disco.
⤷ Turn off the N2 at Esch in direction of Osterwijk. Follow signs.
Apr-1 Oct 7HEC ⊞ ⌐ ⌐ ⌐ ⌐ ⌐ ✕ ⊙ ⌐ ⌐ ᎑ P ⊞ ⊞ lau
Prices: pitch 29

BRESKENS ZEELAND

Napoleon Hoeve Zandertje 30 ☎ 0117 383838
A family site with access to the beach.
All year 13HEC ⊞ ⌐ ⌐ ⌐ ⌐ ⌐ ✕ ⊙ ⌐ ⌐ ᎑ ᎑ ᎑ P ⊞ ⊞ ⊞
lau ➧ ᎑S

Schoneveld Schoneveld 1 ☎ 0117 383220
Camping Card Compulsory.
⤷ 3km S at the beach.
All year 14HEC ⊞ ⌐ ⌐ ⌐ ⌐ ⌐ ✕ ⊙ ⌐ ⌐ ᎑ ᎑ ᎑ PS ⊞ ⊞
lau
Prices: pitch 41-67 (incl 3 persons)

BRIELLE ZUID-HOLLAND

Krabbeplaat Oude Veerdam 4 ☎ 0181 412363
On level ground scattered with trees and groups of bushes. It has asphalt drives. Nearest campsite to the coast and ferries.
⤷ Signposted.
Apr-1 Oct 20HEC ⊞ ⌐ ⌐ ⌐ ⌐ ⌐ ✕ ⊙ ⌐ ⌐ ᎑ L ⊞ ⊞ ⌐ lau

BROEKHUIZENVORST LIMBURG

Kasteel Ooyen Blitterswijkseweg 2 ☎ 077 4631307
Apr-Oct 16HEC ⊞ ⌐ ⌐ ⌐ ⌐ ⌐ ✕ ⊙ ⌐ ⌐ ᎑ PR ⊞ ⊞ lau

BROUWERSHAVEN ZEELAND

Osse Blankersweg 4 ☎ 0111 691513
An attractive site with good watersports facilities.
Apr-Oct 8.3HEC ⊞ ⌐ ⌐ ⌐ ⌐ ⌐ ✕ ⊙ ⌐ ⌐ ᎑ ᎑ ᎑ P ⊞ ⊞ lau
➧ ᎑ ᎑L

BURGH-HAAMSTEDE ZEELAND

Zeelandcamping Duinoord Steenweg 16 ☎ 0111 658888
All year 4.1HEC ⊞ ⌐ ⌐ ⊙ ⌐ ⌐ ᎑ ⊞ ⊞ lau ➧ ᎑ ✕ ᎑S

CROMVOIRT NOORD-BRABANT

Vondst Pepereind 13 ☎ 04118 1431
⤷ 1km SE.
All year 8HEC ⊞ ⌐ ⌐ ⌐ ⌐ ✕ ⊙ ⌐ ⌐ ᎑ ᎑ ᎑ P ⊞ lau ➧
᎑L

DELFT ZUID-HOLLAND

Delftse Hout Korftlaan 5 ☎ 015 2130040
On a level meadow surrounded by woodland close to the lake.
Camping Card Compulsory.
⤷ 1 mile E of A13. Signposted.
All year 5.5HEC ⊞ ⌐ ⌐ ⌐ ⌐ ⌐ ✕ ⊙ ⌐ ⌐ ᎑ ᎑ ᎑ P ⊞ ⊞
⊞ lau ➧ ᎑L
Prices: pitch 40-50 (incl 2 persons)

DOMBURG ZEELAND

Domburg Schelpweg 7 ☎ 0118 588200
On meadowland divided into several sections, with asphalt drives. It is on the inland side of the road, along the dyke, with a belt of shrubs dividing it from the road. 2 tennis courts, small golf course, a children's swimming pool and play garden.
⤷ 500m on main road to Westkapelle.
All year 8HEC ⊞ ⌐ ⌐ ⌐ ⌐ ✕ ⊙ ⌐ ⌐ ᎑ ᎑ ᎑ Å ᎑ PS ⊞ ⊞
᎑ lau

DORDRECHT ZUID-HOLLAND

Bruggehof Rijksstraatweg 186 ☎ 078 183241
⤷ Near Moerdijkbrug.
Apr-15 Oct 21HEC ⊞ ⌐ ⌐ ⌐ ⌐ ⌐ ✕ ⊙ ⌐ ⌐ ᎑ P ⊞ ⊞ lau

ECHT LIMBURG

Marisheem Brugweg 89 ☎ 04754 481458
The site is well-kept and lies E of the village.
⤷ From town drive approx 2.2km towards Echterbosch and the border, then turn left.
Apr-Oct 12HEC ⊞ ⌐ ⌐ ⌐ ⌐ ⌐ ✕ ⊙ ⌐ ⌐ ᎑ ᎑ ᎑ P ⊞ ⊞ ⊞
᎑ lau

EERSEL NOORD-BRABANT

Ter Spegelt Postelseweg 88 ☎ 0497 512016
A large family-orientated site with good recreational facilities.
Mar-Nov 63HEC ⊞ ⌐ ⌐ ⌐ ⌐ ⌐ ✕ ⊙ ⌐ ⌐ ᎑ ᎑ ᎑ ᎑ LP ⊞
⊞ ᎑ lau

FLUSHING

See VLISSINGEN

'S-GRAVENZANDE ZUID-HOLLAND

Jagtveld Nieuwlandsedijk 41 ☎ 0174 413479
A quiet family site on level meadowland with good facilities.
⤷ Access via N220.
1 Apr-1 Oct 3.3HEC ⊞ ⌐ ⌐ ⌐ ⌐ ⌐ ✕ ⊙ ⌐ ⌐ ᎑ ᎑ ⊞ ⊞ ᎑
lau ➧ ᎑S
Prices: ⚲5 ⚲3 ⚲13.50 Å13.50

GROEDE ZEELAND

Groede Zeeweg 1 ☎ 0117 371384
16HEC ⊞ ⌐ ⌐ ⌐ ⌐ ✕ ⊙ ⌐ ⌐ ᎑ ᎑ ᎑ S ⊞ ⊞ lau

HAAG, DEN (THE HAGUE) ZUID-HOLLAND

K'hduinpark Machiel Vr"enhoehlaan 450 ☎ 070 4482100
A modern chalet and camping site in an extensive leisure park close to the beach with excellent recreational facilities.
All year 40HEC ⊞ ⌐ ⌐ ⌐ ⌐ ⌐ ✕ ⊙ ⌐ ⌐ ᎑ ᎑ ᎑ Å ⊞ ⊞ lau ➧
᎑S
Prices: pitch 35-65

⟩ **HANK** NOORD-BRABANT

Brabantse Biesbosch Kurenpolderweg 31 ☎ 0162 402787
Site in a nature park.
➭ *Take A27 and exit at Hank. Signposted.*
Apr-Sep 102HEC ⊞ ♦ ♠ ✗ ⊙ 🖳 𝄃 🗚 🛱 Å ⤢ L ⊡ ⊞ ✅
lau

⟩ **HELLEVOETSLUIS** ZUID-HOLLAND

'T Weergors Zuiddyk 2 ☎ 0181 312430
A pleasant, peaceful site on a level meadow close to the
beach. A good overnight stopping place or holiday site.
Apr-Oct 9.7HEC ⊞ ⋇ ⚓ ♠ ♣ ✗ ⊙ 🖳 𝄃 🛱 ☂ ⤢ PS
⊡ ⊡ ⊞ lau

⟩ **HENGSTDIJK** ZEELAND

Vogel Vogelweg 4 ☎ 0114 681625
All year 33HEC ⊞ ⚓ ♠ ♣ ✗ ⊙ 🖳 𝄃 🗚 🛱 ☂ ⤢ L ⊡ ⊡ ⊞
lau
Prices: pitch 22-45 (incl 2 persons)

⟩ **HERKENBOSCH** LIMBURG

Vrijetijdspark Elfenmeer Meinweg 1 ☎ 0475 531689
Hilly, well-maintained site in pine forest beside a small lake.
➭ *NE off Roermond road.*
A2 to Roermond-E. J. Roerstreek-Herkenbosch-E 26 Mar-01
Nov 37HEC ⊞ ⚓ ♠ ♣ ✗ ⊙ 🖳 𝄃 🛱 ☂ Å ⤢ P ⊡ ⊡ ⊞ lau
♦ 🗚 ⤢R
Prices: pitch 19.50-33.25

⟩ **HERPEN** NOORD-BRABANT

Herperduin Schaykseweg 12 ☎ 0486 411383
Situated in extensive woodland.
➭ *Access from the 'S-Hertogenbosch-Nijmegen motorway.
Take the Ravenstein exit and continue towards Herpen, then in
direction Bergheim/Oss.*
Apr-20 Oct 45HEC ⊞ ⚓ ♠ ♣ ✗ ⊙ 🖳 𝄃 ☂ ⤢ P ⊡ ⊞ ✅
lau
Prices: ♠4-4.50 pitch 12.50-20

⟩ **HILVARENBEEK** NOORD-BRABANT

Beekse Bergen Beekse Bergen 1 ☎ 0031 5360032
Situated in a holiday centre in the Brabant afforestation on
the edge of a safari park. Lake suitable for swimming. Various
other facilities.
➭ *10km S of Tilburg.*
3 Apr-7 Nov 400HEC ⊞ ⚓ ♠ ♣ ✗ ⊙ 🖳 𝄃 🗚 🛱 ☂ Å ⤢
LP ⊡ ⊡ ⊞ lau
Prices: ♠7 pitch 19.50-31.50

⟩ **HOEK** ZEELAND

Braakman Middenweg 1 ☎ 01152 1730
On meadowland between a wood and shrubs.
➭ *About 4km W of town and 40m N of expressway to
Breskens.*
All year 80HEC ⊞ ♦ ♠ ♣ ✗ ⊙ 🖳 𝄃 🛱 ☂ ⤢ LP ⊡
⊞ lau ♦ ⤢S
Prices: ♠27.50-60

⟩ **HOEK VAN HOLLAND** ZUID-HOLLAND

Hoek van Holland Wierstraat 101 ☎ 0174 382550
On grass, surrounded by bushes and paved drives.
➭ *If approaching from the N, turn off the E36 and drive to the
beach.*
1 Apr-11 Oct 5.5HEC ⊞ ⋇ ♠ ♣ ✗ ⊙ 🖳 𝄃 🗚 ⊡ ⊞ ✅
lau ♦ ⤢S
Prices: pitch 42.50

⟩ **HOEVEN** NOORD-BRABANT

Bosbad Hoeven Oude Antwerpse Postbaan 81b
☎ 165 502570
Extensive site with good, modern facilities.
➭ *Between Breda and Roosendaal W of Etten-Leur.*
1 Apr-24 Oct 35HEC ⋯ ♦ ♠ ♣ ♣ ✗ ⊙ 🖳 𝄃 🛱 ⤢ P ⊡ ⊞
✅ lau
Prices: pitch 24.50-36 (incl 2 persons)

⟩ **HOOGERHEIDE** NOORD-BRABANT

FamilyLand Groene Papegaai 19 ☎ 0164 613155
In pleasant wooded surroundings, the site, as its name
suggests has fine facilities for both adults and children with
all kinds of sports and entertainments available.
➭ *2km from junction of A30 and A58.*
All year 25HEC ⊞ ⋇ ♦ ♠ ♣ ✗ ⊙ 🖳 𝄃 🛱 ⤢ P ⊡ ⊞ lau
Prices: ♠8.75 pitch 12.50

⟩ **KAMPERLAND** ZEELAND

Roompot Mariapolderseweg 1 ☎ 01107 4000
A level, well-maintained site with a private beach.
➭ *Turn off Kamperland-Wissenkerke road and drive N for
0.5km.*
All year 33HEC ⊞ ⚓ ♠ ♣ ✗ ⊙ 🖳 𝄃 🛱 ☂ Å ⤢ PS ⊞
lau

Schotsman Schotsmanweg 1 ☎ 0113 371751
On a large, level meadow beside the Veerse Meer, next to a
Nature Reserve. Water sports.
➭ *Signposted.*
27 Mar-1 Nov 30HEC ⋯ ⚓ ♠ ♣ ✗ ⊙ 🖳 𝄃 🗚 ⤢ L ⊡
⊞ ✅ lau

⟩ **KATWIJK AAN ZEE** ZUID-HOLLAND

Noordduinen Campingweg 1 ☎ 071 4025295
Family site set among sand dunes close to the sea.
➭ *Access via Hoorneslaan.*
mid Mar-mid Oct 11HEC ⊞ ⋇ ♠ ♣ ✗ ⊙ 🖳 𝄃 🛱
S ⊡ ⊞ ✅ lau
Prices: pitch 37-45

⟩ **KORTGENE** ZEELAND

Paardekreek Havenweg 1 ☎ 0113 302051
A municipal site next to the Veerse Meer canal.
➭ *For access, turn off the Zierikzee-Goes trunk road at the
CHEVRON petrol station and drive towards Kortgene,
continue through the village and drive SW.*
Apr-30 Oct 10HEC ⊞ ⚓ ♠ ♣ ✗ ⊙ 🖳 𝄃 🛱 ⤢ LP ⊡ ⊞
lau
Prices: pitch 30-39 (incl 3 persons)

⟩ **KOUDEKERKE** ZEELAND

Dishoek Dishoek 2 ☎ 118 551348
➭ *W on Vlissingen-Dihoek road.*
Apr-Oct 4.5HEC ⊞ ⋯ ⚓ ♠ ✗ ⊙ 🖳 𝄃 🗚 ☂ ⤢ S ⊡ ⊞
lau ♦ ♣
Prices: pitch 48-52 (incl 4 persons)

Duinzicht Strandweg 7 ☎ 0118 551397
A small family site with good facilities.
➭ *1.5km SW of Koudekerke.*
1 Apr-1 Oct 6HEC ⊞ ⚓ ♠ ♣ ✗ ⊙ 🖳 𝄃 ☂ ⊡ ⊞ ♦ ♣ ✗ ⤢S
Prices: ♠6.25 ♠5 ♠5 Å5

★★★★★
VAKANTIECENTRUM

de hertenwei

WELLENSEIND 7-9
NL-5094 EG LAGE, MIERDE.
Tel: 013-5091295

Located 2km North of Lage Mierde, on the Tilburg-Reusel road (road No. N.269). Pleasantly wooded site. Ideal starting point for Efteling, Beekse Bergen, Theme Park "Land van Ooit" and Belgium. Modern, heated sanitary blocks with hot water and hot showers. Heated pool and paddling pool. Indoor pool with hot whirlpool, sauna, solarium, bar, supermarket, snackbar, washing machines, tennis-courts, children's play area. Restaurant and disco. Please ask for our brochure.

LAGE MIERDE NOORD-BRABANT

Vakantlecentrum de Hertenwei Wellenseind 7-9
☎ 013 5091295
Pleasant wooded site with modern facilities.
Camping Card Compulsory.
⮕ *2km N on N269 (Tilburg-Reusel).*
All year 20HEC ⊞ ⏚ 🅬 🛒 🍴 ✕ ⊙ 🕭 🔌 ᐱ 🏕 🖈 P 🔁 🆑 lau
Prices: pitch 40-50

LUYKSGESTEL NOORD-BRABANT

Zwarte Bergen Zwarte Bergen Dreef 1 ☎ 0497 541373
The site is isolated and very quiet, and lies in a pine forest.
⮕ *From Eindhoven through Valkenswaard and Bergiejkl. Signposted.*
All year 25.5HEC ⊞ ⏚ 🅬 🛒 🍴 ✕ ⊙ 🕭 🔌 ᐱ 🏕 🖈 P 🔁 🆑
lau ⮕ 🖈L
Prices: ♙5-6.40 ⛺20-27 ▲20-27

MAASBREE LIMBURG

BreeBronne Lange Heide ☎ 77 4652360
A family site in quiet surroundings with good facilities.
⮕ *On the E3 just before Venlo, on the border with Germany.*
Apr-Oct 24HEC ⊞ ⁙ ⏚ 🅬 🛒 🍴 ✕ ⊙ 🕭 🔌 ᐱ 🏕 🖈 LP 🔁
🆑 lau
Prices: pitch 42.75-53.75 (incl 4 persons)

MAASTRICHT LIMBURG

Dousberg Dousbergweg 102 ☎ 043 3432171
A modern site with good facilities.
⮕ *From the Eindhoven-Liège motorway follow sings for Hasselt, then pick up local signs to the site.*
25 Mar-1 Nov 10HEC ⊞ 🌤 🅬 🛒 🍴 ✕ ⊙ 🕭 🔌 ᐱ 🔁 🆑 lau
⮕ 🖈P

MIDDELBURG ZEELAND

Middelburg Koninginnelaan 55 ☎ 118 625395
On meadowlands surrounded by trees and bushes.
⮕ *On W outskirts of town.*
Etr-15 Oct 4.2HEC ⊞ 🌤 🅬 🛒 🍴 ✕ ⊙ 🕭 🔌 🏕 🔁 🆑 lau ⮕
🛒 ✕ 🖈LPS
Prices: ♙6.10 ⛺5 ⛺5.60 ▲5

MIERLO NOORD-BRABANT

Wolfsven Patrijslaan 4 ☎ 0492 661661
Large campsite with wooded areas and several lakes. Asphalt drives.
All year 80HEC ⊞ ⁙ 🌤 🅬 🛒 🍴 ✕ ⊙ 🕭 🔌 🏕 🖈 LP 🔁 🆑
🏊 lau

NIEUWVLIET ZEELAND

International St-Bavodk 2d ☎ 0117 371233
Well equipped family site close to the beach.
⮕ *On N outskirts, near a windmill on the road leading to the dyke.*
Apr-Oct 5.9HEC ⊞ ⏚ 🅬 🛒 🍴 ✕ ⊙ 🕭 🔌 🏕 🖈 🔁 🆑 lau ⮕ 🛒 🌊
🖈S

Pannenschuur Zeedijk 19 ☎ 0117 372300
A modern site with good facilities. Close to the beach.
⮕ *NW of town. Signposted.*
All year 14HEC ⊞ ⏚ 🅬 🛒 🍴 ✕ ⊙ 🕭 🔌 ᐱ 🏕 🖈 PS 🔁 🆑
lau

NOORDWIJK AAN ZEE ZUID-HOLLAND

Carlton Kraaierslaan 13 ☎ 0253 272783
A good centre for touring the surrounding area and visiting the famous bulb fields.
Camping Card Compulsory.
23 Mar-1 Nov 2HEC ⊞ 🅬 ⊙ 🕭 🏕 🖈 P 🔁 lau ⮕ 🛒 ✕ 🔌 🖈S

Jan de Wit Kapellebolaan 10 ☎ 252 372405
A well equipped family site in a wooded location 2km from the beach.
15 Mar-Sep 6HEC ⊞ ⏚ 🅬 🛒 🍴 ✕ ⊙ 🕭 🔌 ᐱ 🏕 🔁 🆑 🏊 lau
⮕ 🖈LPS
Prices: ♙9 ⛺10 ▲10

At NOORDWIJKERHOUT(5km NE)

Club Soleil Kraaierslaan 7 ☎ 0252 374225
In a pleasant situation near the bulb fields and the sea.
⮕ *Signposted.*
Apr-Nov 5.5HEC ⊞ ⏚ 🅬 🛒 🍴 ✕ ⊙ 🕭 🔌 ᐱ 🏕 🖈 P 🔁 🆑
lau ⮕ 🖈LS

OISTERWIJK NOORD-BRABANT

Reebok Duinenweg 4 ☎ 13 5282309
Situated in a large pine forest, hardly fenced off and impossible to overlook. In attractive surroundings with numerous small lakes.
⮕ *SE of town.*
15 Mar-Oct 8HEC ⊞ 🅬 ⏚ 🛒 🍴 ✕ ⊙ 🕭 🔌 ᐱ 🏕 🔁 🆑 lau ⮕
🖈LP
Prices: ♙5.25 ⛺5.25

OOSTERHOUT NOORD-BRABANT

Katjeskelder Katjeskelder 1 ☎ 162 453539
A large, modern family site with good sanitary and recreational facilities.
⮕ *Access via A27 (Breda-Utrecht) exit 17 and follow signs.*
Apr-1 Nov 25HEC ⊞ ⏚ 🅬 🛒 ✕ ⊙ 🕭 🔌 🏕 🖈 P 🔁
🆑 lau ⮕ ᐱ
Prices: pitch 41.50-62.50 (incl 4 persons)

OOSTKAPELLE ZEELAND

Dennenbos Duinweg 64 ☎ 118 581310
A well maintained family site in a wooded loaction, 500mtrs from the beach.
15 Mar-3 Nov 2.5HEC ⟑ ⚊ 🏕 🄟 ♋ ⚡ ⊙ 🚻 ⌀ ♨ 🏪 ☎ ✈ PS 🅿 🅗 lau ➧ ♋ ✕
Prices: pitch 30-37.50 (incl 2 persons)

In de Bongerd Brouwerijstr 13 ☎ 0118 581510
Well-kept in a meadow with hedges and apple trees. There are fine recreational facilities and the beach is within easy reach.
➲ 500m S.
26 Mar-1 Nov 7.3HEC ⟑ ⚊ 🏕 🄟 ♋ ⚡ ✕ ⊙ 🚻 ⌀ ♨ 🏪 ✈ P 🅿 🅗 lau ➧ ✕
Prices: pitch 30-45

Ons Buiten Aagtekerkeseweg 2a ☎ 0118 581813
In a beautiful location with a wide choice of recreational activities.
➲ From church drive S towards Grijpskerke, turn W and continue 400m.
27 Mar-31 Oct 7.7HEC ⟑ ⚊ 🏕 🄟 ♋ ⚡ ✕ ⊙ 🚻 ⌀ ♨ ✈ P 🅿 🅗 ⚯ lau
See advertisement on page 273.

Pekelinge Landmetersweg 1 ☎ 0118 582820
The on-site facilities have seasonal opening.
Apr-Oct 12HEC ⟑ ⚊ 🏕 🄟 ♋ ⚡ ✕ ⊙ 🚻 ⌀ ✈ P 🅿 🅗 ⚯ lau ➧ ⌀ ✈S

OOSTVOORNE ZUID-HOLLAND

Kruininger Gors Gorspl 2 ☎ 0181 482711
A small site, divided by hedges, close to the lake.
➲ Access via N15.
Apr-1 Oct 1.1HEC ⟑ ⚊ 🏕 🄟 ♋ ⚡ ✕ ⊙ 🚻 ⌀ ♨ 🅿 🅗 ⚯ lau ➧ ✈L

OUDDORP ZUID-HOLLAND

Klepperstee Vrijheidsweg 1 ☎ 187 681511
On level meadow divided by hedges and trees.
➲ Access via N57 (Rotterdam-Vlissingen) exit Ouddorp.
Apr-Oct 40HEC ⟑ ⚊ 🏕 🄟 ♋ ⚡ ✕ ⊙ 🚻 ⌀ ♨ ✈ P 🅿 🅗 ⚯ lau ➧ ✈PS

PLASMOLEN LIMBURG

Eldorado Witteweg 18 ☎ 024 6961914
Well equipped site in wooded surroundings on the Mooker See.
➲ S of N271.
Apr-Oct 6.5HEC ⟑ ⚊ 🏕 🄟 ♋ ⚡ ✕ ⊙ 🚻 ⌀ ♨ ✈ L 🅿 🅗 lau

RENESSE ZEELAND

Brem Hoogenboomlaan 11 ☎ 0111 461403
Well-kept site belonging to a trade union, but also accepting tourists. The last camping site in Hoogenboomlaan with numbered sections. It is advisable to reserve pitches between 21 Jun and 9 Aug.
Apr-25 Oct 12HEC ⟑ ⚊ 🏕 🄟 ♋ ✕ ⊙ 🚻 ⌀ ♨ 🏪 ✈ P 🅿 🅗 ⚯ lau ➧ ♋ ⌀

International Scharendijkseweg 8 ☎ 0111 461391
On grassland, between rows of tall shrubs and trees. Between dyke road and main road to Scharendijk on E outskirts of village.
Mar-Nov 3HEC ⟑ ⚊ 🏕 🄟 ♋ ⚡ ⊙ 🚻 ⌀ ♨ 🅿 🅗 lau ➧ ✕ ✈S

Vakantiepark 'Schouwen' Hoogenboomlaan 28
☎ 0111 461231
Mar-Oct 9HEC ⟑ ⚊ 🏕 🄟 ♋ ⚡ ✕ ⊙ 🚻 ⌀ ♨ 🏪 ☎ ✈ PS 🅿 🅗 ⚯ lau

Wyde Blick Hogezaam 12 ☎ 0111 461444
A family site with good facilities.
➲ Well signposted.
All year 8HEC ⟑ ⚊ 🏕 🄟 ♋ ⚡ ✕ ⊙ 🚻 ⌀ ♨ 🏪 ☎ ✈ P 🅿 🅗 ⚯ lau

RETRANCHEMENT ZEELAND

De Zwinhoeve Duinweg 1 ☎ 117 392120
In a beautiful position backed by sandunes with easy access to the fine beaches of the Zeeuws-Vlaanderen coast.
All year 9HEC ⟑ ⚊ 🏕 🄟 ♋ ⚡ ✕ ⊙ 🚻 ⌀ ♨ 🏪 ✈ S 🅿 🅗 lau ➧ ✈P
Prices: ⛺7.35 🚐10 ⛺10

RIJEN NOORD-BRABANT

D'n Mastendol Oosterhoutseweg 7-13 ☎ 0161 222664
A comfortable site in wooded surroundings.
➲ SW of town.
Apr-Oct 10.5HEC ⟑ ⚊ 🏕 🄟 ♋ ⚡ ✕ ⊙ 🚻 ⌀ ♨ 🏪 ✈ P 🅿 🅗 lau ➧ ✕ ⌀ ✈L

RIJNSBURG ZUID-HOLLAND

Koningshof Elsgeesterweg 8 ☎ 71 4026051
Modern site on level meadow near the flower fields.
➲ 1km N. Signposted
All year 8.8HEC ⟑ ⚊ 🏕 🄟 ♋ ⚡ ✕ ⊙ 🚻 ⌀ ♨ 🏪 ☎ ⛺ ✈ P 🅿 🅗 lau ➧ ✈S
Prices: pitch 38-42 (incl 2 persons)

ROCKANJE ZUID-HOLLAND

Itsoncamping C-G-Kleyburgweg 3 ☎ 0181 401200
A small site close to a North Sea beach, divided by hedges.
Motor caravans and tents only.
➲ Access via N15.
Apr-Aug 8HEC ⟑ ⚊ 🏕 🄟 ♋ ⚡ ✕ ⊙ 🚻 ⌀ ✈ S 🅿 🅗 ⚯ lau

Rondeweibos Schapengorsedijk 19 ☎ 0181 401944
15 Mar-Oct 32HEC ⟑ ⚊ 🏕 🄟 ♋ ⚡ ✕ ⊙ 🚻 ⌀ ♨ 🏪 ✈ P 🅿 🅗 lau ➧ ✈S

Waterboscamping Duinrand 11 ☎ 181 401900
A small, pleasant site near the beach. **Motor caravans and tents only.**
➲ Access via N15.
Apr-Sep 7HEC ⟑ ⚊ 🏕 🄟 ♋ ⚡ ⊙ 🚻 ⌀ ♨ 🅿 🅗 ⚯ lau ➧ ✕ ✈S
Prices: pitch 32.60 (incl 2 persons)

ROERMOND LIMBURG

Hatenboer Hatenboer 51 ☎ 475 336727
Situated in a 'Waterpark' with access to all watersports.
Camping Card Compulsory
➲ Leave A68 (Roermond-Eindhoven) at 'Hatenboer' exit.
Apr-1 Nov 15HEC ⟑ ⚊ 🏕 🄟 ♋ ⚡ ✕ ⊙ 🚻 ✈ LR 🅿 🅗 lau ➧ ♋ ⌀ ♨ ✈P
Prices: ⛺6 🚐5 🚐13 ⛺10

Marina Oolderhuuske Oolderhuuske 1 ☎ 475 588686
A well equipped site within the marina area on the Maasplassen.
28 Mar-1 Nov 6HEC ⟑ ⚊ 🏕 🄟 ♋ ⚡ ✕ ⊙ 🚻 ⌀ ♨ 🏪 ✈ LPR 🅿 🅗 lau

ROOSENDAAL NOORD-BRABANT

Zonneland Tufvaartsestr 6 ☎ 01656 365429
➲ *S of town towards the Belgian border.*
Mar-15 Oct 14HEC ⭤ ♠ ⋒ ⚘ ♖ ⊙ ⬛ ⤺ ⚒ P ⛁ ⊞ ⁓ lau

ROTTERDAM ZUID-HOLLAND

Rotterdam Kanaalweg 84 ☎ 10 4153440
A quiet, well appointed site in a rural setting within easy
reach of the city. Good facilities for walkers.
➲ *Leave motorway by-pass (roads E10/E36) at exit
Rotterdam-Centrum, then follow signs.*
All year 4HEC ⭤ ⭗ ⋒ ⚘ ✕ ⊙ ⬛ ⬛ ⤺ ⬛ ⛁ ⊞ lau
♦ ⚘ ⤻PS
Prices: ⚘8.50 ⬢5 ⬢9 ⬣6

ST ANTHONIS NOORD-BRABANT

Ullingse Bergen Bosweg 36 ☎ 485 388566
A family site in natural wooded surroundings with good
facilities for children.
➲ *W of town.*
Apr-Oct 11HEC ⭤ ⭗ ⋒ ⚘ ✕ ⊙ ⬛ ⬛ ⤺ ⬛ ⤻ P ⛁ ⛁ ⊞ ⁓
lau
Prices: pitch 26-34.50 (incl 2 persons)

ST OEDENRODE NOORD-BRABANT

Kienehoef Zwembadweg 35-37 ☎ 413 472877
An exceptionally well appointed site in a peaceful rural
setting.
➲ *NW towards Boxtel.*
All year ⭤ ⭗ ⋒ ⚘ ♖ ✕ ⊙ ⬛ ⬛ ⬢ ⬣ P ⛁ ⛁ ⊞ ⁓ lau ♦
✕
Prices: pitch 42

SCHAESBERG LIMBURG

Bousberg Boomweg 10 ☎ 045 311213
➲ *NW towards Kakert.*
Apr-Oct 7HEC ⭤ ⭗ ⋒ ⚘ ♖ ✕ ⊙ ⬛ ⬛ ⤺ ⬛ ⬛ ⤻ P ⛁ ⊞
lau ♦ ✕

SEVENUM LIMBURG

Schatberg Midden Peelweg 5 ☎ 77 4677777
➲ *SW towards Eindhoven.*
All year 86HEC ⭤ ⭗ ⋒ ⚘ ♖ ✕ ⊙ ⬛ ⬛ ⤺ ⬛ ⬛ ⤻ LP ⛁ ⛁
⊞ ⁓ lau
Prices: pitch 35.45-47.25 (incl 4 persons)

SLUIS ZEELAND

Meldoorn Hoogstr 68 ☎ 0117 461662
In a meadow surrounded by rows of deciduous trees.
➲ *N on the road to Zuidzande.*
All year 6.5HEC ⭤ ⭗ ⋒ ⚘ ♖ ⊙ ⬛ ⬛ ⤺ ⛁ ⛁ ⊞ lau ♦ ⚘
Prices: ⚘6.80 ⬢4.10 ⬢8.15 ⬣6.10

SOERENDONK LIMBURG

Soerendonk Strijperdijk 9 ☎ 0495 591652
A spacious site in wooded surroundings close to the Belgian
border. There are good recreational facilities and good fishing
is available in the lake.
All year 17.8HEC ⭤ ⭗ ⋒ ⚘ ♖ ✕ ⊙ ⬛ ⬛ ⤺ ⬛ ⬛
⤻ P ⛁ ⊞ lau

STRAMPROY LIMBURG

't Vosseven Lochstr 26 ☎ 0495 566023
A family site with adequate facilities.
➲ *Turn right at the church and continue for 5km.*
Apr-Oct 11HEC ⭤ ⭗ ⋒ ✕ ⊙ ⬛ ⬛ ⛁ ⊞ lau ♦ ⚘ ⤻P

VALKENBURG LIMBURG

Europa Couberg 29 ☎ 43 6013097
A quiet family site within easy reach of the town.
➲ *SW of town.*
Apr-Oct 10HEC ⭤ ⥿ ⋒ ⚘ ♖ ✕ ⊙ ⬛ ⬛ ⤺ ⤺ P ⛁ ⊞ lau
Prices: pitch 20-30

VENLO LIMBURG

Ons Buiten St-Urbansweg 120-122 ☎ 077 3515821
A pleasant family site with plenty of touring pitches in a
picturesque wooded location.
➲ *500mtrs from A67/E34.*
All year 12HEC ⭤ ⭗ ⋒ ⊙ ⬛ ⬛ ⤺ ⤻ P ⛁ ⛁ ⊞ lau ♦
⤻R
Prices: ⚘6 ⬢10 pitch 10

VENRAY LIMBURG

Oude Barrier Maasheseweg 93 ☎ 0478 582305
A quiet site recommended for young children.
➲ *NE of town.*
1 Apr-1 Oct 14HEC ⭤ ⭗ ⋒ ⊙ ⬛ ⬛ ⤻ P ⛁ ⊞ lau ♦ ⤺

VESSEM NOORD-BRABANT

Eurocamping Vessem BV Zwembadweg 1 ☎ 04979 1214
Apr-Sep 50HEC ⭤ ⭗ ⋒ ⚘ ♖ ✕ ⊙ ⬛ ⬛ ⤺ ⤻ P ⛁ ⊞ lau ♦ ✕

VLISSINGEN (FLUSHING) ZEELAND

Lange Pacht Boksweg 1 ☎ 01184 60447
Apr-Sep 1.2HEC ⭤ ⭗ ⋒ ⊙ ⬛ ⬛ ♦ ⚘ ✕
Prices: pitch 27.50 (incl 2 persons)

Nolle Woelderenlaan 1 ☎ 01184 14371
The site consists of five sections near two tennis courts.
15 Mar-2 Jan 1.2HEC ⭤ ⥿⥿ ♦ ⭗ ⋒ ⚘ ⊙ ⬛ ⬛ ⛁ ⊞ lau
♦ ⚘ ✕ ⤻S

VROUWENPOLDER ZEELAND

Oranjezon Koningin Emmaweg 16a ☎ 118 591549
Well-kept between tall, thick hedges and bushes. SW of the
village.
Camping Card Compulsory.
➲ *For access drive towards Oostkapelle for approx 2.5km, then
turn N and continue for 300m.*
Apr-Oct 5.3HEC ⭤ ⭗ ⋒ ⚘ ♖ ✕ ⊙ ⬛ ⬛ ⤺ ⬛ ⬣ ⤻ P ⛁ ⛁
lau ♦ ⤻S
Prices: pitch 30-60 (incl 4 persons)

WASSENAAR ZUID-HOLLAND

Duinhorst Buurtweg 135 ☎ 070 3242270
A peaceful site in wooded surroundings with modern
facilities and fine opportunities for sports and entertainment.
Apr-1 Oct 11HEC ⭤ ⥿⥿ ⭗ ⋒ ⚘ ♖ ✕ ⊙ ⬛ ⬛ ⤺ ⤻ P ⛁ ⊞
⁓ lau

Duinrell Duinrell 1 ☎ 70 5155255
Very well maintained site with additional recreation centre
which is free for campers. NW in area of same name. Some
noise from aircraft. Toilets for invalids. Area restricted to
cars. Naturist beach nearby.
➲ *Turn off A44 (Den Haag-Leiden) at traffic lights in
Wassenaar dorp' and camping signs.*
All year 20HEC ⭤ ⥿ ⋒ ⚘ ♖ ✕ ⊙ ⬛ ⬛ ⤺ ⬛ ⬛ ⬣ ⤻ P ⛁
⛁ ⊞ lau ♦ ⤻LS
Prices: ⚘18.50 pitch 25
See advertisement on page 276.

WEERT LIMBURG

Ijzeren Man Herenvennenweg 60 ☎ 495 533202
Well-kept with asphalt drives, in a big nature reserve with
zoo, heath and forest. *Contd.*

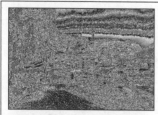

⊃ *Off E9.*
1 Apr-1 Oct 11.5HEC ⛺ ⋮⋮ ⊈ ⋔ ⛊ ⅄ ✕ ⊙ ⊕ ⌀ ⚏ ⊞ ⋨ P
⊠ ⏚ ⊞ lau
Prices: ♠6 ➾4 ⬛6 ▲6

WEMELDINGE ZEELAND

Linda Oostkanaalweg 4 ☎ 113 621259
On meadowland surrounded by rows of tall shrubs.
⊃ *Turn opposite bridge in town and continue 100m, over bridge to camp.*
1 Apr-1 Nov 8HEC ⛺ ⥾ ⋔ ⛊ ⅄ ✕ ⊙ ⊕ ⌀ ⚏ ⊕ ⋨ S ⊠
⊞ lau
Prices: ♠6.75 ➾5 ⬛5 ▲5

WESTKAPELLE ZEELAND

Boomgaard Domineeshofweg 1 ☎ 118 571377
A flat grassy site.
⊃ *For access turn off the Middleburg road on the S outskirts of the town, then follow signs.*
27 Mar-24 Oct 8HEC ⛺ ⋔ ⛊ ⅄ ✕ ⊙ ⊕ ⌀ ⚏ ⊕ ⋨ P ⏚
⊞ lau ➡ ⋨S
Prices: pitch 35.25 (incl 2 persons)

ZEVENHUIZEN ZUID-HOLLAND

Zevenhuizen Tweemanspolder 8 ☎ 0180 631654
Situated NW of the village, this site is surrounded by a wide belt of bushes.
⊃ *On NW outskirts follow signs . Site on right of the road beyond a car park.*
Apr-Oct 6HEC ⛺ ⊈ ⋔ ⛊ ⅄ ✕ ⊙ ⊕ ⌀ ⚏ ⊕ ⋨ PS ⏚ ⊞ lau
➡ ✕

ZOUTELANDE ZEELAND

Meerpaal Duinweg 133 ☎ 118 561300
On meadowland hidden behind bushy hedges at the end of a cul-de-sac.
⊃ *1km SE.*
27 Mar-1 Nov 2HEC ⛺ ⥾ ⋔ ⛊ ⅄ ⊙ ⊕ ⌀ ⚏ ⊕ ⋨ S ⏚
⊞ lau ➡ ✕ ⋨P
Prices: ♠9 ➾6.65 ⬛12.65 ▲12.65

Weltevreden Melseweg 1 ☎ 0118 561321
30 Mar-26 Oct 2.5HEC ⛺ ⊈ ⋔ ⛊ ⊙ ⊕ ⌀ ⊕ ⊕ ⋨ S ⊠ ⊞
⚙ lau ➡ ⅄ ✕

PORTUGAL

A relatively small country lying in the south western corner of the Iberian peninsula, Portugal's only land frontier is the Spanish border in the east.

FACTS AND FIGURES
Capital: Lisbon
Language: Portuguese
IDD code: 351. To call the UK dial 00 44
Currency: Escudo (PTE) = 100 centavos). At the time of going to press £1 = PTE 276.
Local time: GMT(summer GMT+1)

Emergency Services:
Police, Fire and Ambulance 112
Business hours-
Banks: Mon-Fri 08.30-15.00
Shops: Mon-Fri 09.00-13.00-and 15.00-19.00, Sat 09.00-13.00 (and 15.00-19.00 Dec); shopping centres Mon-Sun

10.00-24.00
Average daily temperature: Lisbon
Jan 11°C   Jul 21°C
Mar 13°C   Sep 20°C
May 17°C   Nov 14°C
Tourist Information:
Portuguese National Tourist Office
UK 22-25A Sackville Street London W1X 2LY

Tel 0171-494 1441
USA 4th Floor, 590 Fifth Avenue New York, NY 10036-4704
Tel (212) 354 4403
Camping card:
Compulsory at Federação Portuguesa de Campismo parks and camping clubs offering special prices. Recommended elsewhere.

The country is, perhaps, best known for its five hundred miles of coastline. The Algarve in the extreme south is one of the finest stretches of coastline in Europe, with unique caves and a remoteness which has been conserved despite the development of the area. Inland, the cool valleys and pastures of the Tagus contrast sharply with the wooded mountain slopes of the Minho area in the north.

Generally the country enjoys a mild climate with the Algarve being very hot in the summer. The language is Portuguese, which was developed from Latin and closely resembles Spanish, although English is often spoken in the Algarve.

Mainland Portugal has about 184 campsites most of which are on the coast. There are about 21 *Orbitur* parks in the country which are privately owned and of a high standard, as indeed are the municipal parks. Orbitur parks are open throughout the year and most of them offer fully-equipped bungalows which accommodate four people. A booklet containing details of officially classified parks is produced by the Direcção Geral de Turismo, Palácio Foz, Praça dos Restauradores, Lisboa ☎(01) 346 6307. The Oporto office is at Praça D João I, 25-4 ☎(02) 200 5805 and the Coimbra office is at Largo da Portagem. Otherwise ask for Comissao Municipal de Turismo, Junta de Turismo or Câmara Municipal.

Off-site camping is prohibited You must stay on an organised site. However, when stopping in a motorway rest or service area with a caravan, it is permissible to cook a meal.

HOW TO GET THERE
You can ship your vehicle to Spain, using either the Plymouth to Santander service (24hrs approx) - Poole to Santander in winter (28hrs approx) - or the Portsmouth to Bilbao service (27 hrs approx) and then travel onwards by road. For details of the *AA European Routes Services* please consult the Contents Page.

Distance
From Santander to Lisboa (Lisbon) is about 920km (570 miles), normally requiring one or two overnight stops. Using the Channel ports, or the Channel tunnel, driving through France and Spain (enter Spain on the Biarritz to San Sebastian (Donostia) road at the western end of the Pyrénées).

From the Channel ports to Lisboa (Lisbon) is about 2,157km (1,340 miles). This will require 3 or 4 overnight stops.

Car sleeper trains
Services are available from Calais to Biarritz, or Paris to Madrid. **See Spain for location map**

MOTORING & GENERAL INFORMATION

The information given here is specific to Portugal. It **must** be read in conjunction with the European ABC at the front of the book, which covers those regulations which are common to many countries. **Note** Portuguese law requires that everyone carries photographic proof of identity at all times.

British Embassy/Consulates*

The British Embassy is located at 1200 Lisboa, rua de São Bernardo 33 ☎(01) 2924000; consular section ☎(01) 3924159. There is a British Consulate in Porto (Oporto) and one with an Honorary Consul in Portimão.

Children in cars

Child under 3 cannot travel as front seat passenger unless seated in approved child seat; child over 3 and under 12 must use approved restraint system unless the car is a two seater.

Currency

Although unlimited amounts of Portuguese or foreign currency may be taken into or out of Portugal, amounts in axcess of PTE 2,500,000 must be declared on arrival or departure. Visitors are not required to exchange a certain amount per day but they must prove to be in possession of a minimum amount of PTE20,000 plus PTE6,000 per day. During the summer, currency exchange facilities are usually provided throughout the day in main tourist resorts, at frontier posts, airports and in some hotels.

Dimensions and weight restrictions

Private **cars** and towed **trailers** or **caravans** are restricted to the following dimensions - height, 4 metres; width, 2.5 metres; length, 12 metres. The maximum permitted overall length of vehicle/trailer or caravan combination is 18 metres.

There are no weight restrictions governing the temporary importation of trailers into Portugal. However, it is recommended that the following be adhered to: weight (unladen), up to 750kg if the towing vehicle's engine is 2,500cc or less; up to 1,500kg if the towing vehicle's engine is between 2,500cc and 3,500cc; up to 2,500kg if the towing vehicle's engine is more than 3,500cc.

Armação de Pera, Algarve

The Discovery Monument, Lisbon

open 09.00-16.45hrs Monday to Friday (to 17.30hrs from 1 April to 30 September); English and French are spoken. Offices are closed on Saturday and Sunday.

Petrol
At the time of going to press both leaded and unleaded petrol are available in Portugal. However, only one grade of leaded petrol is sold, 98 octane 'Super'.

Roads
Main roads and most of the important secondary roads are good, as are the mountain roads to the north-east.

Portugal has about 516 miles of motorway (*auto-estrada*) with tolls payable on most sections. Emergency telephones are located every 2km on most motorways.

Speed limits*
Car
Built-up areas 50kph (31mph)
Other roads 90kph (55mph) or 100kph (62mph)
Motorways min† 40kph (24mph)
max 120kph (74mph)
Car/caravan/trailer
Built-up areas 50kph (31mph)
Other roads 70kph (43mph) or 80kph (49mph)
Motorways min† 40kph (24mph)
max 100kph (62mph)

†Minimum speeds on motorways apply, except where otherwise signposted.

Both Portuguese residents and visitors to Portugal, who have held a full driving licence for less than one year, must not exceed 90kph (50mph) when driving on any road or motorway outside built-up areas.

Warning triangle*
The use of a warning triangle is compulsory in the event of accident or breakdown. The triangle must be placed on the road 30 metres (33yds) behind the vehicle and must be clearly visible from 100 metres (109yds).

Driving licence*
A valid UK or Republic of Ireland licence is acceptable in Portugal. The minimum age at which a visitor may use a temporarily imported motorcycle (over 50cc) or car is 18 years. See also Speed limits below.

Foodstuffs*
There are no limits on the importation of foodstuffs obtained duty and tax paid within the EC. Up to 500g of coffee (200g of coffee extract) and 100g of tea (40g of tea extract) purchased duty-free or outside the EC may be imported free of duty and tax. However, coffee bought duty-free or outside the EC cannot be imported by visitors under 15 years of age.

Motoring club*
The **Automóvel Club de Portugal** (ACP) which has its headquarters at Lisboa 1250 rua Rosa Araüjo 24 ☎(01) 3563931 has offices in a number of provincial towns. ACP offices are normally

*Additional information will be found in the Continental ABC at the front of the book.

SOUTH

Bordered by the Atlantic coast on two sides, by mountains in the north and by Spain in the east, the Algarve enjoys one of the most settled climates in the world. Though poorer than the rest of Portugal in art and architecture, the region is rich in subtropical vegetation; almond and orange groves, cotton plantations, and fields of rice and sugar cane. Beyond the mountains in the north, the land is predominantly agricultural, with low rolling hills stretching beyond the horizon. Cork oaks are grown to provide much-needed shade, making an important contribution to the region's economy.
Water is also a major source of income in the south; inland, the salt-pans of the Sado river maintain the pretty towns of narrow twisting lanes and whitewashed houses. On the coast, towns such as Faro, Lagos, and Cape St. Vincent, glory in a history of trade, shipbuilding, sea battles and exploration.

ALBUFEIRA ALGARVE

Albufeira ☎ 35189 587627
A modern, purpose-built site with excellent sanitary blocks and a wide variety of sports and entertainment facilities.
➲ *1.5km from Albufeira. Signposted from N125*
All year 29HEC ⛺ 🚿 📶 👤 💧 🍴 ✕ ⊙ 🏪 🅿 💈 PS 💈 🏢 lau
➧ ✕ 🌐 ⚓ ⚡ ⅃S 💈
Prices: ♣795 ⚓795 🚐795-895 ▲795-895

ALCANTARILHA ALGARVE

Turismovel - Parque Campismo de Canelas ☎ 082 312612
All year 6.5HEC 🏖 🚿 📶 👤 💧 🍴 ✕ ⊙ 🏪 🌐 🏪 ⅃ P 💈 🏢 lau
➧ 🏖 ⅃LRS

ALVITO BAIXO ALENTEJO

Markádia Barragem de Odivelas ☎ 084 763141
Open savannah terrain beside a lake with good, modern facilities.
➲ *Leave N121 (Beja-Lisboa) at Ferrera do Alentejo and continue N towards Torrão. From Odivelas follow signposts.*
All year 10HEC ⛺ 🏖 📶 👤 💧 🍴 ✕ ⊙ 🏪 🌐 🏖 🏪 ⅃ L 💈 🏢
lau ➧ ⅃P
Prices: ♣360-720 ⚓360-720 🚐360-720 ▲360-720

BEJA BAIXO ALENTEJO

CM de Beja av Vasco da Gama ☎ 084 324328
All year 1.2HEC ⋮⋮⋮ 📶 🌐 ⊙ 🏪 💈 🏢 lau ➧ 💧 🍴 ✕ 🌐 🏖
⅃LPRS 💈
Prices: ♣170-340 ⚓125-250 🚐175-500 ▲125-250

PORTIMÃO ALGARVE

Da Dourada Alvor ☎ 028 458002
In a parklike area close to the beach with good facilities.
➲ *N off Portimão-Lagos road.*
All year 40HEC ⛺ 📶 👤 💧 🍴 ✕ ⊙ 🏪 🌐 🏪 🏪 ▲ 💈 🏢 lau
➧ 🏖 ⅃PRS
Prices: ♣550-550 ⚓400-400 🚐600-600 ▲500-600

PRAIA DA LUZ ALGARVE
At VALVERDE

Orbitur Praia da Luz ☎ 082 789211
Well-equipped site with children's playground and tennis courts.
➲ *Off N125 Lagos-Cape St Vincent road. 4km from Lagos.*
All year 10HEC ⋮⋮⋮ 📶 👤 💧 🍴 ✕ 🏪 🌐 🏪 🏪 💈 🏢 lau
Prices: ♣730 ⚓620 🚐760-1030 ▲630-970

QUARTEIRA ALGARVE

Orbitur Barros da Fonte Santa ☎ 089 302826
A terraced site at the top of a hill.
➲ *Off M125 in Almoncil and follow signs to Quarteira. About 500m before reaching the sea turn left into the camp.*
All year 10.6HEC ⋮⋮⋮ 📶 👤 💧 🍴 ✕ 🏪 🌐 🏪 ⅃ P 💈 🏢 lau
➧ ⅃S
Prices: ♣740 ⚓610 🚐750-1020 ▲620-970

SAGRES ALGARVE

Parque de Campismo de Sagres Cerro das Moitas ☎ 082 64351
Closed Dec-2 Jan 6HEC ⋮⋮⋮ 📶 👤 💧 🍴 ✕ ⊙ 🏪 🌐 ⅃ P 💈 🏢
➧ 🏖 ⅃S

SANTO ANDRE BAIXO ALENTEJO

Lagoa de Santo Andre ☎ 069 79151
In wooded surroundings with good facilities.
➲ *Signposted.*
Jan-Nov 16HEC ⋮⋮⋮ 📶 👤 💧 🍴 ✕ ⊙ 🏪 🌐 💈 🏢 🏝 lau
➧ 💧 ✕ ⅃LS
Prices: ♣350-500 ⚓350-350 🚐720-720 ▲280-600

SÃO MIGUEL BAIXO ALENTEJO

São Miguel ☎ 082 94145
A well equipped site within a Nature Protected Area.
➲ *1.5km from Odeceixe, just before entering the Algarve.*
Closed Nov 4HEC ⋮⋮⋮ 🌿 📶 👤 💧 🍴 ✕ ⊙ 🏪 🌐 🏪 ⅃ P 💈 🏢 lau

SINES BAIXO ALENTEJO

Sines r di Farol ☎ 069 862531
Closed 16 Dec-14 Jan 4.5HEC ⛺ 📶 👤 💧 🍴 ✕ ⊙ 🏪 🌐 🏝 🏪
💈 🏢 lau ➧ ⅃S

S. Tonnes S. Tonnes ☎ 069 632105
In a pine wood on the Cabo de Sines peninsula, to the N of the town.
➲ *Follow signs for Algarve/ S. Tonnes.*
30 Jun-Sep 3.5HEC ⛺ 📶 👤 💧 🍴 ✕ ⊙ 🏪 🌐 🏝 🏪 ▲ 🏢 lau
➧ ⅃S

VILA DO BISPO ALGARVE
At PRAIA DE SALEMA(7.5km SE)

Quinta dos Carriços Praia da Salema ☎ 082 65201
A well equipped site with good facilities. There is a naturist section in a separate valley with its own facilities.
All year 20HEC ⛺ 📶 👤 💧 🍴 ✕ ⊙ 🏪 🌐 🏝 🏪 🏪 💈 🏢 lau
➧ ⅃S
Prices: ♣660 ⚓660 🚐910 ▲660-850

VILA NOVA DE MILFONTES BAIXO ALENTEJO

Parque de Campismo de Milfontes ☎ 083 96104
All year 6.5HEC 📶 👤 💧 🍴 ✕ ⊙ 🏪 🌐 🏝 🏪 💈 lau ➧ ⅃RS 💈

NORTH

Northern Portugal offers medieval castles perched on mountain crags, grey stone villages, and purple vineyards whose grapes produce the popular Vinho Verde, Mateus Rosé and Portugal's most famous product - port wine.
There are magnificent forests, spectacular lakes, long sandy beaches sheltered by pinewoods, and villages hidden by the springtime blossom of almond and chestnut trees.
A region of ancient human settlement, even the smallest towns are rich in architectural treasures, from palaces of the Renaissance period to prehistoric rock engravings. The region also boasts a wealth of traditional crafts of a variety and colour to match the splendid local costumes worn for

the many religious festivals and "romaries" celebrated with enormous enthusiasm and energy throughout the year. The capital of the region, Oporto, is Portugal's second largest city and also its most untypical - a lively port, a university town and a hub of industry and commerce in one.

CAMINHA MINHO

Orbitur Mata do Caminha ☎ 058 921295
On undulating sandy ground with trees.
➲ *Turn off N13 at Km89.7 and drive W, along the Rio Minho for about 800m, then turn left.*
16 Jan-Nov 2.8HEC ⫶⫶⫶ ⌼ ↾ ➋ ⏛ ✕ ⊙ 🖩 ⌀ 🗎 ⊞ lau ➧ ↺S
Prices: ↟600 ☛510 ⬛610-930 ▲500-840

CAMPO DO GERES MINHO

Cerdeira ☎ 053 351005
In a picturesque wooded location with mature oak trees surrounding the pitches.
Camping Card Compulsory.
All year 4.6HEC ⛭ ⫶⫶⫶ ⌼ ↾ ⊙ 🖩 ⌀ ⏛ 🗎 ⊞ ⤳ lau ➧ ➋ ⏛ ✕ ⛟ ↺LR
Prices: ↟600-700 ☛550-650 ⬛700-1000 ▲500-900

MATOSINHOS DOURO LITORAL
At ANGEIRAS(12km N)

Orbitur Angeiras ☎ 02 9270571
A modern, well-kept site in a pine wood on a hill overlooking the sea.
➲ *W of the N13 at the X-roads at Km12.1, E of Vila do Pinheiro and towards the sea for 5km.*
All year 9.6HEC ⛭ ⌼ ↾ ➋ ⏛ ✕ ⊙ 🖩 ⌀ ⏛ ↺ P 🗎 ⊞ lau ➧ ↺S
Prices: ↟710 ☛580 ⬛730-950 ▲580-950

MONDIM DE BASTO MINHO

Mondim de Basto ☎ 055 381650
In wooded surroundings beside the River Olo.
➲ *Signposted.*
Jan-Nov 4HEC ⫶⫶⫶ ⌼ ⌼ ↾ ➋ ⏛ ✕ ⊙ 🖩 ⌀ 🗎 ⊞ ⤳ lau ➧ ↺R
Prices: ↟350-500 ☛350-350 ⬛720-720 ▲280-600

PÓVOA DE VARZIM DOURO LITORAL

Rio Alto Estela-Rio Alto ☎ 052 615699
Situated near dunes 150m from the sea.
➲ *Off NX111 towards Viana.*
All year 7HEC ⛭ ⫶⫶⫶ ⌼ ↾ ➋ ⏛ ✕ ⊙ 🖩 ↺ P 🗎 ⊞ lau ➧ ⌀ ⏛ ↺S

VIANA DO CASTELO MINHO

Orbitur Matado Cabedelo ☎ 058 322167
A well equipped site with direct access to a sandy beach.
➲ *Approach via N13 Porto-Viana do Castelo.*
Closed Dec-15 Jan 3HEC ⫶⫶⫶ ➧ ↾ ➋ ⏛ ✕ ⊙ 🖩 ⌀ ⏛ 🗎 ⊞ lau ➧ ↺PRS

VILA NOVA DE GAIA DOURO LITORAL

Orbitur Praia da Madalena ☎ 02 7122520
Well equipped site in a pinewood 500mtrs from Madalena Beach.
All year 24HEC ⫶⫶⫶ ⌼ ↾ ➋ ⏛ ✕ ⊙ 🖩 ⌀ ⏛ ↺ P 🗎 ⊞ lau ➧ ↺S
Prices: ↟710 ☛580 ⬛730-950 ▲580-950

VILA REAL TRAS-OS-MONTES ALTO DOURO

Parque Campismo de Vila Real r Dr-Monuel Cardona
☎ 059 324724
➲ *In the E part of town off N2 by GALP petrol station. Site in 300m near new school.*
Closed Jan 4HEC ⫶⫶⫶ ⌼ ↾ ➋ ⏛ ✕ ⊙ 🖩 ⌀ 🗎 ⊞ lau ➧ ↺PR

CENTRAL

This is a vast and wonderful region of infinite variety; to the west, the popular Costa da Prata; the beautiful park-like landscape in the south; the dramatic mountains in the north and east; and the cattle-herding country in the centre, where the fighting bulls graze along the River Tejo, watched by mounted cattle herders in colourful local costume.
The highest town in Portugal is Guarda, the ideal base from which to explore the magnificent Serra da Estrala. Further west is the romantic town of Coimbra, whose university is amongst the oldest in the world and until 1911, was the only one in the country.
Portugal's capital, Lisbon, has the attraction of combining the charm of the past with the excitement of a progressive capital city. It is also the heart of the production of the famous Azulejos - the glazed ornamental tiles which are Portugal's favourite form of architectural decoration.

ABRANTES RIBATEJO

Castelo do Bode Martinchel ☎ 041 99262
In natural wooded surroundings.
➲ *Signposted.*
Jan-Nov 3HEC ⫶⫶⫶ ⌼ ↾ ➋ ⏛ ✕ ⊙ 🖩 ⌀ 🗎 ⊞ ⤳ lau ➧ ↺L
Prices: ↟350-500 ☛350-350 ⬛720-720 ▲280-600

ALENQUER ESTREMADURA

Alenquer ☎ 063 7103745
A modern well equipped terraced site surrounded by walnut trees.
Reductions available to campers presenting this publication.
Apr-Sep 1.5HEC ⫶⫶⫶ ⌼ ↾ ➋ ⏛ ✕ ⊙ 🖩 ⌀ ⏛ ⏛ ↺ P 🗎 ⊞ lau ➧ ↺R

ARGANIL BEIRA LITORAL

Orbitur Sarzedo ☎ 035 25706
In a pleasant situation among pine trees, close to the River Alva.
➲ *On N342-4.*
All year 2.5HEC ⛭ ⌼ ↾ ⏛ ✕ ⊙ 🖩 ⏛ ↺ R 🗎 ⊞ lau
Prices: ↟490 ☛440 ⬛510-780 ▲410-710

CASTRO DAIRE BEIRA ALTA

Orbitur Termas do Carvalhal ☎ 032 32803
In a beautiful peaceful location, 200mtrs from the sea.
➲ *Access via N2, Km144.2.*
Jun-Sep 2HEC ⫶⫶⫶ ⌼ ↾ ➋ ⏛ ✕ ⊙ 🖩 ⊞ lau ➧ ✕
Prices: ↟490 ☛440 ⬛510-780 ▲410-790

COIMBRA BEIRA LITORAL

CM de Coimbra Praça 25 de Abril ☎ 039 701497
Camping Gaz available summer only.
All year 1.1HEC ⛭ ⌼ ↾ ➋ ⏛ ✕ ⊙ 🖩 ⌀ 🗎 ⊞ lau ➧ ✕ ↺PR

COJA BEIRA LITORAL

Coja ☎ 035 99666
In a wooded location beside the River Alva.
➲ *Signposted.*
Mar-Oct 3HEC ⛭ ⫶⫶⫶ ⌼ ↾ ➋ ⏛ ✕ ⊙ 🖩 ⌀ 🗎 ⊞ ⤳ lau ➧ ↺R
Prices: ↟350-500 ☛350-350 ⬛720-720 ▲280-600

▶ COSTA DA CAPARICA ESTREMADURA

Orbitur ☎ 01 2903894
This site has a small touring section and is situated 200mtrs from a fine sandy beach.
➲ *After crossing the 'Ponte Sul' on the road to Caparica, turn right at first traffic light. Campsite is 1km on left.*
All year 5.7HEC ⁛ ⌂ ⋔ 🏊 ⚎ ✕ ⌀ 🏠 ⌸ 🎦 ⊞ lau
➡ ⚲S
Prices: ♠690 ♠620 ♙730-1030 ▲620-980

▶ ÉVORA ALTO ALENTEJO

Orbitur ☎ 066 25190
In wooded surroundings with good, modern facilities.
➲ *2km S right of road near Km94.5.*
All year 4HEC ⚎ ⁛ ⌂ ⋔ 🏊 ⚎ ✕ ⌀ 🏠 ⌸ ⚲ P 🎦 ⊞ lau
Prices: ♠600 ♠510 ♙610-930 ▲500-840

▶ ÉVORA DE ALCOBAÇA ESTREMADURA

Rural de Silveira Capuchos ☎ 062 509573
In a wooded, rural location.
➲ *3km from Alcobaça on N86.*
All year 0.5HEC ⚎ ⋔ ⌂ ⚎ ⚲ ⊙ 🏠 🎦 ⊞ lau ➡ 🏊 ⌀ ⚱
Prices: ♠400 ♠300 ♙500-650 ▲300-600

▶ FIGUEIRA DA FOZ BEIRA LITORAL

Foz do Mondego Cabedelo, Gala ☎ 033 31542
January-November 4HEC ⁛ ⚹ ⋔ 🏊 ⚎ ✕ ⊙ 🏠 ⌀ ⚲ S 🎦 ⊞
⚯ lau ➡ 🏊 ✕
Prices: ♠350-500 ♠350-350 ♙720-720 ▲280-600

Orbitur Gala ☎ 033 31492
In an enclosed area within a municipal park on top of Guarda Hill.
➲ *At Km177, on the NW outskirts of the town, turn left off the N16 Porto road and drive uphill for about 500m.*
All year 6.5HEC ⁛ ⌂ ⋔ 🏊 ⚎ ✕ 🏠 ⚎ 🎦 ⊞ lau ➡ ⚲S
Prices: ♠600 ♠510 ♙610≈930 ▲500-840

▶ GOUVEIA BEIRA LITORAL

Curral do Negro ☎ 038 491008
In a mountainous setting, surrounded by woodland.
➲ *Signposted.*
Jan-Nov 2HEC ⁛ ⚹ ⌂ ✕ ⊙ 🏠 ⌀ ⚲ P 🎦 ⊞ lau ➡ ⚎ ✕
Prices: ♠350-500 ♠350 ♙720 ▲280-600

▶ GUARDA BEIRA ALTA

Orbitur ☎ 071 211406
A well equipped site in a pleasant location.
Feb-Oct 2HEC ⚎ ⚹ ⌂ ⋔ 🏊 ⚎ ✕ ⌀ 🎦 ⊞ lau
Prices: ♠590 ♠500 ♙590-920 ▲480-820

▶ GUINCHO ESTREMADURA

Orbitur Crismina ☎ 01 4870450
On hilly ground amidst a pine wood in the Parque du Guincho, near the Boca do Inferno.
➲ *4km W of Cascais at Km98, turn right and follow road no 247-6 for 1km.*
All year 7HEC ⁛ ⚎ ⚹ ⌂ ⋔ 🏊 ⚎ ✕ ⌀ 🏠 🏠 🎦 ⊞ lau ➡ ⚲S
Prices: ♠700 ♠620 ♙740-1030 ▲630-980

▶ LISBOA (LISBON) ESTREMADURA

CM Monsanto Estrada da Circunvalação ☎ 01 7609620
On partly level terraced ground. Recently renovated to become one of the largest sites in the country.
➲ *Access well signposted from the motorway towards Estoril.*
All year 38HEC ⚎ ⚹ ⌂ ⋔ 🏊 ⚎ ✕ ⊙ 🏠 ⌀ ⚲ P 🎦 ⊞ lau
Prices: ♠800 ♠500 ♙1200 ▲1200
See advertisement under Colour section

▶ LOURIÇAL BEIRA LITORAL

De Klomp Casas Brancas ☎ 036 952551
In pleasant wooded surroundings.
➲ *Access via N109 or A1.*
All year 1.5HEC ⚎ ⌂ ⋔ 🏊 ⚎ ✕ ⊙ 🏠 🏠 ⌀ ⚲ P 🎦 lau
➡ 🏊 ⌀ ⊞
Prices: ♠400 ♠300 ♙400 ▲300

▶ MONTARGIL ALTO ALENTEJO

Orbitur Barragem de Montargil ☎ 042 91207
In a beautiful wooded location with good recreational facilities close to the River Alva.
➲ *N off N2.*
All year 7HEC ⚎ ⁛ ⌂ ⋔ 🏊 ⚎ ✕ ⌀ 🏠 ⌀ ⚲ L 🎦 ⊞ lau
➡ ⊞
Prices: ♠600 ♠510 ♙610-930 ▲500-840

▶ NAZARÉ ESTREMADURA

Orbitur Valado Valado ☎ 062 561111
In a pinewood 2km from the village with good facilities.
➲ *300m E of village, S of road 8-4 Nazaré-Alcobaça.*
Feb-Nov 6HEC ⁛ ⚹ ⌂ ⋔ 🏊 ⚎ ✕ ⊙ 🏠 ⌀ 🏠 🎦 ⊞ lau
Prices: ♠590 ♠500 ♙590-920 ▲480-820

Vale Paraiso ☎ 062 561800
Situated in a beautiful natural park amid tall pine trees, this site is exceptionally well appointed with very high standards of hygiene and varied recreational facilities.
All year 8HEC ⚎ ⚹ ⌂ ⋔ 🏊 ⚎ ✕ ⊙ 🏠 ⌀ 🏠 ▲ ⚲ P 🎦 ⊞ lau
➡ ⚲L
Prices: ♠370-595 ♠305-490 ♙365-790 ▲305-650

▶ PALHEIROS DE MIRA BEIRA LITORAL

Orbitur ☎ 031 471234
Site lies in a dense forest.
➲ *N off the N334 at KM2, towards Videira, opposite a road fork.*
16 Jan-30 Nov 3HEC ⁛ ⚹ ⌂ ⋔ 🏊 ⚎ ✕ 🏠 ⌀ 🎦 ⊞ lau
➡ ⚲LS
Prices: ♠600 ♠510 ♙610-930 ▲500-840

▶ PENACOVA BEIRA LITORAL

Penacova est da Carvoeira ☎ 039 477464
A pleasant riverside site in wooded surroundings.
➲ *Signposted.*
Jan-Dec 2HEC ⁛ ⚹ ⌂ ⋔ 🏊 ⚎ ✕ 🏠 ⌀ 🎦 ⊞ ⚯ lau
➡ ⚲R
Prices: ♠350-500 ♠350-350 ♙720-720 ▲280-600

▶ PENICHE ESTREMADURA

CM ☎ 062 789529
On a sandy hillock, partly wooded 0.5km from sea.
➲ *2km E.*
All year 12.6HEC ⚎ ⁛ ⚹ ⌂ ⋔ 🏊 ⚎ ✕ 🏠 ⌀ 🎦 ⊞ lau
➡ ⚱ ⚲PS
Prices: ♠350 ♠300 ♙450 ▲300-400

Peniche Praia ☎ 062 783460
On level ground 500mtrs from the sea.
➲ *N towards Cabo Carudeiro.*
All year 1.5HEC ⚎ ⁛ ⚹ ⌂ ⋔ 🏊 ⚎ ✕ ⊙ 🏠 ⌀ 🏠 🎦 ⊞ lau
➡ ⌀ ⚱ ⚲PS ⊞
Prices: ♠250-420 ♠220-360 ♙290-595 ▲250-420

▶ PORTALEGRE ALTO ALENTEJO

Orbitur Quinta da Saude ☎ 045 22848
A hilltop site commanding magnificent views.
➲ *Access via N18 Estremoz-Castelo Branco.*
Apr-Sep 2.5HEC ⚎ ⚹ ⌂ ⋔ 🏊 ⚎ ✕ ⊙ 🏠 ⌀ 🎦 ⊞ lau ➡ 🏊 ✕ ⚲P
Prices: ♠480 ♠430 ♙500-770 ▲400-700

PRAIA DE PEDRÓGÃO BEIRA LITORAL

Parque Municipal de Campismo ☎ 044 695403
Camping Card Compulsory.
15 Feb-15 Dec 9HEC ⊞ ⌗ ♠ ⋒ ➋ ⚼ ✕ ⊙ ➌ ⊘ ☷ ⌇ S ▣ ⊞
⊗

SALVATERRA DE MAGOS RIBATEJO

Parque de Campismo de Escaroupim Mata Florestal de
Escaroupim ☎ 063 55484
Closed Dec 4HEC ⋮⋮⋮ ♠ ⋒ ➋ ⚼ ✕ ⊙ ➌ ⊘ ⌇ P ☑ ⊞ ⊗ lau
⮕ ☷ ⌇RS
Prices: ⋔350-500 ⚗350 ⚕720 ▲280-600

SÃO JACINTO BEIRA LITORAL

Orbitur ☎ 034 48284
In a dense pine wood seawards from the uneven, paved road
from Ovar which runs alongside the lagoon.
➲ *1.5km from the sea.*
Feb-Nov 2.5HEC ⊞ ⋮⋮⋮ ⊘ ♠ ⋒ ➋ ⚼ ✕ ➌ ⊞ ☑ ⊞ lau
⮕ ⌇RS
Prices: ⋔590 ⚗500 ⚕560-920 ▲480-820

SÃO MARTINHO DO PORTO ESTREMADURA

Colina do Sol ☎ 062 989763
Closed 16 Dec-14 Jan 8.5HEC ⊞ ⚞ ⋒ ➋ ⚼ ✕ ⊙ ➌ ⊘ ⌇ P
☑ ⊞ lau ⮕ ➋ ☷ ⌇S

SÃO PEDRO DE MOEL ESTREMADURA

Orbitur ☎ 044 599168
On a hill amidst pine trees.
➲ *Off road No 242-2 from Marinha Grande at the
roundabout near the SHELL petrol station on the E outskirts of
the village and drive N for 100m.*
All year 7.5HEC ⋮⋮⋮ ♠ ⋒ ➋ ⚼ ✕ ➌ ⊘ ⊞ ➍ ⌇ P ☑ ⊞ lau
⮕ ⌇S
Prices: ⋔600 ⚗510 ⚕610-930 ▲500-840

SERRAZES BEIRA ALTA

Serrazes Santa Cruz da Trapa ☎ 032 711557
In wooded surroundings.
➲ *Signposted.*
Jan-Nov 1.5HEC ⋮⋮⋮ ♠ ⋒ ⊙ ➌ ⊘ ⌇ P ☑ ⊞ ⊗ lau
⮕ ➋ ⚼ ✕
Prices: ⋔350-500 ⚗350 ⚕720 ▲280-600

VAGOS BEIRA LITORAL

Vagueira ☎ 034 797618
In pleasant wooded surroundings with good, modern
sanitary blocks and a variety of recreational facilities.
All year 10HEC ⋮⋮⋮ ♠ ⋒ ➋ ⚼ ✕ ⊙ ➌ ⊘ ☑ ⊞ lau ⮕ ⌇LPRS

VISEU BEIRA ALTA

Orbitur Mata do Fontelo ☎ 058 322167
A pleasant, quiet site in a rural location.
➲ *Access via N2.*
16 Jan-Nov 3HEC ⋮⋮⋮ ⌗ ⋒ ➋ ⚼ ✕ ➌ ⊘ ⊞ ☑ ⊞ lau ⮕ ⌇PRS
Prices: ⋔600 ⚗510 ⚕610-930 ▲500-840

SPAIN

Rich in history and natural beauty, Spain is bordered by two countries, France in the north and Portugal in the west.

FACTS AND FIGURES
Capital: Madrid
Language: Spanish (Castilian), Catalan, Galician, Basque
IDD code: 34. To call the UK dial 00 44
Currency: Peseta (ESP). At press date, £1 = ESP 229
Local time: GMT + 1 (summer GMT + 2)

Emergency Services:
Madrid and Barcelona Police 091; Fire 080; Ambulance 068; in other towns call operator.112, the European emergency number is being introduced alongside existing numbers in some areas, e.g. Navarra. Dial 112 and request the service required.

Business hours:
Banks: Mon-Fri 08.30-14.30 (most banks are closed on Sats).
Shops: Mon-Sat 09.00-13.00 and 16.30-19.30.
Average daily temperatures: Madrid
Jan 4°C   Jul 24°C
Mar 9°C   Sep 19°C
May 16°C   Nov 8°C

Tourist Information:
UK Spanish National Tourist Office, 22-3 Manchester Sq., London W1M 5AP Tel 0171-486 8077
USA 35th Floor, 666 Fifth Ave, New York NY 10103 Tel (212) 265 8822
Camping card:
Not compulsory, but recommended

Central Spain is mountainous and barren while the coastline is mostly extremely rocky. Some of the most popular holiday areas in Europe are in Spain, the best known being the Costa Brava, the Costa Blanca, the Costa Dorada and the Costa del Sol. All these regions offer fine, sandy and safe beaches. Spain has a varied climate; temperate in the north, dry and hot in the south and in the Balearic Islands. Languages spoken are Spanish, Catalan, Basque and Galician. Spanish has developed from Castilian and there are many local dialects spoken throughout the provinces.

Sites are numerous on the Costa Brava and elsewhere along the coast, but there are not many inland. They are officially classified according to the facilities and services provided and their classification should be displayed at the site entrance and on any literature. If you intend visiting sites at popular resorts along the coast between late spring and mid-October, it is not generally possible to book in advance. The best advice is to arrive before midday when the new charge begins. Late spring is recommended, as the intense heat of mid-summer is avoided and sites and roads are less congested. Opening dates vary considerably and some sites are open all year. Information about campsites and a detailed guide

book are available from the Spanish National Tourist Office (see *Tourist Information*) and local tourist information offices.

Hire of equipment is not generally possible, but some campsites have bungalow accommodation.

Off-site camping is generally prohibited. Permission to camp off an official campsite must be obtained from the landowner or local police. **Camp fires are absolutely forbidden.** Free camping near to beaches, rivers, towns or established campsites is forbidden.

HOW TO GET THERE

You can ship your vehicle direct to Spain using either the Plymouth to Santander service (24hrs approx) - Poole to Santander in winter (28hrs approx) - or the Portsmouth to Bilbao service (27hrs approx). Using Eurotunnel, or the Channel ports, approach Spain through passing either end of the Pyrenean mountains. For **central and southern Spain** take the Biarritz to San Sebastian (Donostia) road or motorway at the western end. For **the Costa Brava and beyond** take the Perpignan to Barcelona road, or motorway, at the eastern end of the mountains. **For Andorra** from France via Pas de la Casa (6860ft) then over the Envalira Pass (7897ft). Nov - Apr roads through the central Pyréneés may sometimes be closed.

From Spain, the approach via La Seu d'Urgell is always open. For details of the *AA European Routes Service* please consult the Contents Page.

Distance
From Calais to Madrid is about 1,600km (994 miles), usually requiring two or three overnight stops.

Car sleeper trains
Calais to Narbonne; Calais to Biarritz; Paris to Madrid.

MOTORING & GENERAL INFORMATION
The information given here is specific to Spain and/or Andorra. It **must** be read in conjunction with the European ABC at the front of the book, which covers those regulations which are common to many countries.

Bail Bond
An accident in Spain can have serious consequences, including the impounding of car and property, and a Bail Bond is advisable. It provides a written guarantee that a cash deposit of usually up to £1500 will be paid to the Spanish court as surety for bail and for any fine which may be imposed. However, the Bond is not insurance cover as such, insofar as the insurers must be reimbursed. Bail Bonds are usually available from vehicle insurers. A Bail Bond guarantee of up to £1500 is available with the AA Five Star Breakdown Assistance, subject to suitable agreement for its repayment being received either from the Five Star holder's motor vehicle insurer or from the policy holder.

British Embassy/Consulates*
The British Embassy is located at Madrid 28010, Calle de Fernando el Santo 16 ☎913190200; consular section, 228004 Madrid, Centro Colón Marqués de la Ensenada 16 ☎913085201. There are British Consulates in Alicante, Barcelona, Bilbao, Granada, Malaga, Seville and Palma (Majorca); there are British Consulates with Honorary Consuls in Santander and Vigo. There is a British Vice-Consulate in Ibiza and a British Vice-Consulate with Honorary Vice-Consul in Menorca.

Children in cars
Child under 12 not permitted to travel as front seat passengers unless using suitable restraint system.

Currency
Visitors may import unlimited amounts of Spanish and foreign currency. Spanish currency up to ESP 1,000,000 or its equivalent in foreign currency, or any amount declared on arrival, may be exported.

Dimensions and weight restrictions
Private **cars** and towed **trailers** or **caravans** are restricted to the following dimensions - height, 4 metres; width 2.5 metres; length 12 metres. The maximum permitted overall length of private vehicle/trailer or caravan combinations is 18.35 metres.

Trailers with an unladen weight exceeding 750kg must have an independent braking system.

Driving licence
A valid UK or Republic of Ireland EC model licence is acceptable in Spain. The minimum age at which visitors from UK or Republic of Ireland may use a temporarily imported motorcycle (over 75cc) or car is 18 years.

The holder of an older all-green UK licence (in Northern Ireland any licence issued before 1 April 1991) should consider exchanging it for a new-style licence if time allows to avoid any local difficulties. Alternatively these older licences may be accompanied by an International Driving Permit (IDP).**Note** The licence of a Spanish driver who needs glasses to drive is endorsed accordingly. Such drivers must carry a spare pair of glasses in their vehicle. It is strongly recommended that visiting motorists do the same to avoid any misunderstandings with the local authorities.

Foodstuffs*
There are no limits on the importation of foodstuffs obtained duty and tax paid within the EC. Up to 500g of coffee (200g of coffee extract) and 100g of tea (40g of tea extract) purchased duty-free or outside the EC may be imported free of duty and tax. However, coffee bought duty-

free or outside the EC cannot be imported by visitors under 15 years of age.

Lights*
Visiting motorists must equip their vehicles with a spare set of vehicle bulbs.

Motoring club*
The **Real Automóvil Club de España (RACE)**, which has its headquarters at 28003 Madrid, Calle José Abascal 10 ☎915947400, is associated with local clubs in a number of provincial towns. The office hours of RACE in Madrid are 08.30-17.30hrs Mon-Thu and 08.30-14.30hrs Fri during the summer (15 Jun-15 Sep) and, for the rest of the year, 08.30-17.30hrs Mon-Fri.

Petrol*
At the time of going to press both leaded and un-leaded petrol are available in Spain. However only one grade of leaded petrol is sold, 97 octane 'Super'.

Roads, including holiday traffic
The surfaces of the main roads vary, but on the whole are good. The roads are winding in many places, and at times it is not advisable to exceed 30-35mph. Secondary roads are often rough and winding. Holiday traffic, particularly on the coast road to Barcelona and Tarragona and in the San Sebastian-Donostia area, causes congestion which may be severe at weekends.

Casares, Costa del Sol

In the *Basque* and *Catalan* areas some place names appear on signposts as alternative spellings *eg* San Sebastian-Donostia and Gerona-Girona. The current AA directories and maps show both names.

Spain has some 2,500 miles of dual carriageways, of which over 1,200 miles are motorway toll roads (*autopista*) and the rest are free (*autovías*). Emergency telephones are located every 2km on both.

Speed limits*
Car
Built-up areas 50kph (31mph)
Other roads †90kph (55mph)
††100kph (62mph)
Motorways 120kph (74mph)

ANDORRA

Andorra is an independent Principality located high in the Pyrenees between France and Spain.

FACTS AND FIGURES
Capital: Andorra la Vella
Language: Catalan, Spanish and French
IDD Code: 376. To call the UK dial 0044
Currency: French Franc (FRF = 100 centimes) and Spanish Peseta (EPS)

Local time: GMT + 1 (summer GMT + 2)
Emergency services: Fire & Ambulance 118; Police 110
Business hours: variable
Banks: Mon-Fri 09.00-13.00/15.00-17.00 Sat 09.00-12.00

Shops: Daily 09.00-20.00
Average daily temperatures: Andorra la Vella
Jan 3°C   Jul 19°C
Mar 9°C   Sep 16°C
May 11°C   Nov 6°C
Tourist Information:
UK Andorran Delegation

63 Westover Road
London SW18 2RF
Tel 0181-874 4806 (am if telephoning; personal visit by appointment only)
Camping card: Recommended.

Covering 180 square miles, it has a population of 60,000 and is administered by its own government and independent Legislative Assembly. The constitutional heads of state are its traditional co-princes, the President of France and the Bishop of Seu d'Urgell. Catalan is the official language, but French and Spanish are widely spoken. General regulations for France and Spain apply to Andorra with the following exceptions.

British Consulate*
The British Consulate with Honorary Consul is located at Prat de la Creu 22, Alt. 2, PO Box 1041, Andorra la Vella ☎867731.

Children in cars
Child under 10 not permitted as front-seat passenger.

Dimensions
The maximum height for vehicles going through tunnels is 3.5 metres.

Driving licence*
A valid UK or Republic of Ireland driving licence is acceptable. The minimum age at which a visitor may use a temporarily imported car or motorcycle is 18 years.

Motoring club*
The **Automobil Club d'Andorra** (ACA) has its head office at Andorra la Vella, Carrer Babot Camp 13 ☎820890.

Petrol*
At the time of going to press both leaded and unleaded petrol are available in Andorra. However, only one grade of leaded petrol is sold, 98 octane 'Super'.

Roads
The three main roads in Andorra are prefixed 'N' and numbered; side roads are prefixed 'V'. Andorra has no motorways.

Speed limits*
Car, car/caravan combinations
Built-up areas 60kph (37mph)
Other roads 90kph (55mph)
Some villages have a speed limit of 20kph (12mph).

Warning triangle*
The use of a warning triangle is compulsory in the event of an accident or breakdown.

***Additional information will be found in the Continental ABC at the front of the book.**

● ● ● NORTH EAST COAST ● ● ●

The brava, or 'wild' coast, and resorts such as Tossa and Lloret de Mar, have long been a favourite with sun-seekers. Low season can be a perfect time to visit the beautiful coastline, and art lovers are drawn year-long to Figueres' Salvador Dali Museum and historic Girona's impressive cathedral, interesting monuments and medieval Jewish quarter.

On the Mediterranean to the south lies Barcelona, capital of Catalonia. Catalonians are proud of their heritage and language. Host of the 1992 Olympics, this bustling, vital seaport has many faces: literary capital of Spain, shopper's paradise and beach town. Walk along its famous boulevards, the Ramblas, or visit Gaudí's monumental Church of the Holy Family - symbol of the city and its region. The site of the Olympic stadium at Montjuic also boasts several museums and shares spectacular views with its neighbouring hilltop, Tibidabo. The fiesta in September is a colourful carnival famed for its enormous papier-maché figures, its street celebrations and bullfights, and the local sardana dancing.

··

) ARENYS DE MAR BARCELONA

Carlitos Carretera 2 ☎ 93 7921355
The slightly sloping site has very friendly family atmosphere and is situated just 150mtrs from the sea on the Costa del Maresme.
May-Sep 3.5HEC ⬛ ♠ ⋒ ⛟ ⵬ ✗ ⊙ ⬛ ⬛ ⬛ ⬦ PS ⬛ ⬛ lau ♠ ⵬ ⵬S

) BAGUR
See **BEGUR**

) BEGUR GIRONA

Begur ☎ 972 623201
A terraced site in a wooded valley.
⮑ 1.4km SE of town and right of the road to Palafrugell, 400m after the turn towards Fornells and Aiguablava.
26 Apr-1 Sep 4HEC ⬛ ⬛ ♠ ⋒ ⛟ ⵬ ✗ ⊙ ⬛ ⬦ ⬛ ⵬ P ⬛ ⬛ lau ♠ ⵬S
Prices: ⭑475-610 ⬅460-590 ⬛475-610 ⬛455-570

Maset Playa de sa Riera ☎ 72 623023
A well-kept terraced site, divided into pitches in a beautiful valley, 300mtrs from the sea.
⮑ 2km N of Begur. If entering from the W, turn left just before reaching the town.
26 Mar-25 Sept 1.2HEC ⬛ ⬛ ♠ ⋒ ⛟ ⵬ ✗ ⊙ ⬛ ⬦ ⬛ ⵬ P ⬛ ⬛ ⬛ lau ♠ ⵬S
Prices: ⭑560-710 ⬅550-700 ⬛690-890 ⬛590-760

) BLANES GIRONA

Bella Terra av Villa de Madrid ☎ 972 348017
A large family site in a luxuriant pinewood beside the beach with good, modern facilities.
⮑ Access via main N11.
Apr-Sep 8HEC ⬛ ⬛ ♠ ⋒ ⛟ ⵬ ✗ ⊙ ⬛ ⬦ ⬛ ⬛ ⵬ PS ⬛ ⬛ lau ♠ ⵬R

Blanes ☎ 972 331591
In a pine forest bordering the beach, 1km from the town centre.
⮑ On left of the Paseo Villa de Madrid coast road towards town.
Apr-Sep 2HEC ⬛ ♠ ⋒ ⛟ ⵬ ✗ ⊙ ⬛ ⬦ ⵬ S ⬛ ⬛ lau
Prices: ⭑475-630 pitch 1500-1850

Masia c Colon 44, Los Pinos ☎ 972 331013
A pleasant family site on level ground with shady pitches, 150mtrs from the sea.
⮑ 50m inland from Paseo Villa de Madrid coast road.
May-Sep 9HEC ⬛ ♠ ⋒ ⛟ ⵬ ✗ ⊙ ⬛ ⬦ ⬛ ⵬ PRS ⬛ ⬛ lau
Prices: ⭑485-645 pitch 795-2175

Pinar av Villa de Madrid ☎ 72 331083
Divided into two by the coastal road. Partially meadow under poplars.
⮑ 1km on Paseo Villa de Madrid coast road.
May-Sep 4HEC ⬛ ⬛ ♠ ⋒ ⛟ ⵬ ✗ ⊙ ⬛ ⬦ ⬛ ⵬ S ⬛ ⬛ lau

S'Abanell av Villa Madrid s/n ☎ 972 331809
Within a pine wood, a section of which is inland and open to the public.
⮑ On either side of the Avenida Villa de Madrid road. Off coast road S of Blanes.
All year 3HEC ⬛ ♠ ⋒ ⛟ ⵬ ✗ ⊙ ⬛ ⬦ ⬛ ⵬ S ⬛ ⬛ lau

Vora Mar av de Madrid ☎ 972 330349
Level site with pine trees on sandy beach.
⮑ 1.5km from Blanes on seaward side of the Paseo Villa de Madrid coast road.
Mar-Sep 2.4HEC ⬛ ♠ ⋒ ⊙ ⬛ ⬦ ⬛ ⵬ R ⬛ ⬛ lau ♠ ⛟ ⵬ ✗ ⵬LPS

) CABRERA DE MAR BARCELONA

Costa de Oro ☎ 93 7591234
Quiet site bordered by cultivated fields. The beach is reached via a railway underpass.
⮑ Lies at Km650 of the N11, on the seaward side, between the road and the railway embankment.
15 May-11 Sep 2HEC ⬛ ♠ ⋒ ⛟ ✗ ⊙ ⬛ ⬛ ⵬ S ⬛ ⬛ ⬮ lau ♠ ⵬ ⬦ ⬛

) CALELLA DE LA COSTA BARCELONA

Botanic Bona Vista ☎ 93 7692488
Totally subdivided and well tended terraced site on a hillside, beautifully landscaped. Internal roads steep. Access to beach via pedestrian underpass.
Camping Card Compulsory.
⮑ Turn off the N11 at Km665.
All year 3.4HEC ⬛ ⬛ ⧉ ♠ ⋒ ⛟ ⵬ ✗ ⊙ ⬛ ⬦ ⬛ ⵬ S ⬛ ⬛ lau ♠ ⵬P
Prices: ⭑589 ⬅589 ⬛589 ⬛589

Far ☎ 93 7690967
Terraced site on a hillock under deciduous trees with lovely view of Calella and out to sea. Steep internal roads.
⮑ For access, travel S before reaching a major left hand bend at Km666 to the right of the N11.
Apr-Sep 2.5HEC ⬛ ♠ ⋒ ⛟ ⵬ ✗ ⊙ ⬛ ⬛ ⬛ ⬛ lau ♠ ⛟ ⵬ ✗ ⬦ ⵬ ⵬LPRS
Prices: ⭑560 ⬅560 ⬛560 ⬛560

) CASTELL D'ARO GIRONA

Castell d'Aro crta S'Agaro ☎ 972 819699
A quiet family site, 2km from the beach, with good recreational facilities.
⮑ Access at Km1 on S'Agaró road.
Semana Santa - 30 Sep Dec-Jan 8HEC ⬛ ⬛ ⬛ ♠ ⋒ ⛟ ⵬ ✗ ⊙ ⬛ ⬦ ⬛ ⵬ P ⬛ ⬛ lau ♠ ⵬S
Prices: ⭑453-600 pitch 1000-1300

) CASTELLÓ D'EMPURIES GIRONA

Castell-Mar Platja de la Rubina ☎ 972 450822
8 May-26 Sep 4HEC ⬛ ⬛ ⧉ ♠ ⋒ ⛟ ⵬ ✗ ⊙ ⬛ ⬦ ⬛ ⬛ ⬛ PS ⬛ ⬛ lau
Prices: ⭑350 pitch 1800-3695

Laguna ☎ 972 450553
Flat grassland site by the sea.
➲ *Turn right at Km11 Figueres-Roses road in direction of Sant Pere Pescador and continue, last 4km poorly surfaced lane.*
27 Mar-24 Oct 14.6HEC ﹏﹏ ♠ ⚑ ☎ ♨ ⚓ ✕ ⊙ 🛒 🚻 ⛺ ⇗ PRS ☎ ⊞ lau
Prices: ⚑540-875 ⛺540-875 🚐540-875 ▲540-875

Mas-Nou ☎ 972 454175
A family site with good recreational facilities, 2.5km from the coast.
➲ *Exit from the Figueres-Roses road at Km38.*
27 Mar-26 Sep 7.8HEC ﹏﹏ ♠ ⚑ ☎ ♨ ✕ ⊙ 🛒 🚻 ⛺ ⇗ P ☎ ⊞ lau ⇗ ☎ ⚓ ⇗S
Prices: ⚑524-722 ⛺524-722 🚐524-722 ▲524-722

Nautic Almanta ☎ 972 454477
Level meadowland, no shade, good facilities, reaching as far as the sea. Alongside the River Fluvia which has been made into a canal. Boating is possible in the canal which flows into the sea.
➲ *Turn S at Km11 on C260, approx, halfway along the road and turn E along the track and continue 2.2km.*
9 May-27 Sep 22HEC ﹏﹏ ⚑ ⚑ ☎ ♨ ✕ ⊙ 🛒 ⚓ ⛺ ▲ ⇗ PRS ☎ ⊞ lau
Prices: ⚑305-350 pitch 1665-3990

ESCALA, L' GIRONA

Escala ☎ 972 770084
Level site, partially under pines and close to the sea.
➲ *Within village on the left of the road towards Riells.*
4 Apr-27 Sep 1.8HEC ﹏﹏ ♠ ⚑ ☎ ♨ ✕ ⊙ 🛒 ⚓ 🚻 ⛺ ☎ ⊞ ⇗ ⛴ ⇗S

Maite Playa Riells ☎ 972 770544
An extensive site, lying inland, but near the sea, at a small lake. Partly on a hillock under pine trees.
➲ *The access is well signed from the outskirts of L'Escala on the road towards Cala Montgo.*
1 Jun-15 Sep 6HEC ﹏﹏ ♠ ⚑ ☎ ♨ ✕ ⊙ 🛒 ⚓ ⇗ LS ☎ ⊞

ESTARTIT, L' GIRONA

Castell·Montgri ☎ 972 751630
On a large terraced meadow in pine woodlands.
➲ *100m N of GE road from Torroella de Montgri and about 0.5km before L'Estartit on a hillock.*
8 May-10 Oct 25HEC ﹏﹏ ♠ ⚑ ☎ ♨ ✕ ⊙ 🛒 ⚓ 🚻 ⛺ ▲ ⇗ P ☎ ⊞ lau
Prices: ⚑350 pitch 1975-3975

Estartit Cap Villa Primavera 12 ☎ 972 758909
In a valley on sloping ground which is rather steep in places. Some terraces, shaded by pine trees.
➲ *It is located about 200m from the church and the road from Torroella de Montgri.*
Apr-Sep 1.5HEC ⠿⠿ ♠ ⚑ ☎ ♨ ✕ ⊙ 🛒 🚻 ▲ ⇗ PRS ☎ ⊞ lau ⇗ ⚓ ⇗L
Prices: ⚑419-600 ⛺410-588 🚐445-636 ▲392-583

Medes ☎ 972 751805
Quiet holiday site in rural surroundings with clearly marked pitches and good modern facilities.
➲ *Turn right off GE641 from Torroella di Montgri by Km5 and continue for 1.5km .*
All year 2.6HEC ﹏﹏ ⚑ ☎ ♨ ✕ ⊙ 🛒 ⚓ ⛺ ⇗ P ☎ ⊞ ⊘ lau
Prices: ⚑600 pitch 1350

Molino ☎ 972 750629
Divided into several sections of open meadowland near the beach on grassland with young poplars. The reconstructed mill is a landmark.
⮥ *Approaching from Torroella de Montgri turn right on entering L'Estartit and follow signs.*
Apr-Sep 10HEC ⚏ ⠿ ⌕ ♠ ⛟ ⛱ ✕ ⊙ ⛲ ∅ 🏕 🖼 🀫 lau ➧ ⭲S
Prices: ⚑475 ⛺475 ⛺475 ▲475

▶ GAVÁ BARCELONA

Albatros ☎ 93 6330695
In a shady pine wood divided into pitches on partly level, partly uneven terrain by the sea.
⮥ *For access, turn off the C246, dual carriageway at Km15 and drive towards the sea.*
May-27 Sep 15HEC ⠿ ♦ ⌕ ⛟ ⛱ ✕ ⊙ ⛲ ∅ 🀫 ⭲ PS 🖼 🀫
lau

Tortuga Ligera ☎ 93 6580504
Apr-Sep 22HEC ⚏ ⠿ ♦ ⌕ ⛟ ⛱ ✕ ⊙ ⛲ ∅ 🖫 🀫 🀫 ⭲ PS 🖼 🀫 lau

▶ GUARDIOLA DE BERGUEDA BARCELONA

El Bergueda ☎ 93 8227432
A peaceful site in the middle of a forest at an altitude of 900mtrs with a wide variety of sporting facilities.
⮥ *On B400.*
All year 3HEC ⚏ ⌕ ♠ ⛟ ⛱ ✕ ⊙ ⛲ ∅ 🖫 🀫 🀫 ⭲ PR 🖼 🀫
lau ➧ ⛟ ✕ ⭲L
Prices: ⚑492 ⛺492 ⛺492 ▲492

▶ GUILS DE CERDANYA GIRONA

Pirineus ctra Guils de Cerdanya ☎ 972 881062
In a fine, level location at an altitude of 1200mtrs affording fine views over the Cerdanya Valley.
⮥ *On the main Puigcerda-Guils de Cerdanya road.*
18 Jun-12 Sep 5HEC ⚏ ♠ ⌕ ⛟ ⛱ ✕ ⊙ ⛲ ∅ 🀫 ⭲ P 🖼 🀫
⚐ lau
Prices: ⚑696 pitch 2194

▶ LLANÇÁ GIRONA

Ombra ☎ 972 380335
A quiet site, 500mtrs from the sea.
⮥ *At Km16.5 on N260.*
All year 1.1HEC ⚏ ⠿ ♦ ⌕ ⛟ ⛱ ✕ ⊙ ⛲ ∅ 🀫 ▲ 🖼 🀫 lau ➧ 🖫 ⭲S
Prices: ⚑449-523 pitch 533-1168

▶ LLORET DE MAR GIRONA

Lloret ctra Vieja de Vidreras ☎ 972 365483
500m from the sea.
Jun-Sep 2.3HEC ⠿ ⌕ ♠ ⛟ ⛱ ✕ ⊙ ⛲ ∅ ⭲ P 🖼 🀫 lau ➧ ⛟
⛱ ✕ ∅ 🖫 ⭲S 🀫

▶ MALGRAT DE MAR BARCELONA

Naciones ☎ 93 7654153
Level site divided by a small stream. Partially dusty, another part in meadow under high poplars.
⮥ *Approach road passes through Camping Malgrat de Mar.*
Apr-Sep 9.6HEC ⚏ ⌕ ♠ ⛟ ⛱ ✕ ⊙ ⛲ ∅ 🖫 🀫 ⭲ S 🖼 🀫 lau ➧ 🖫

▶ MASNOU, EL BARCELONA

Masnou ctra Nac 2 ☎ 93 5551503
A well equipped site in wooded surroundings, 150mtrs from the beach on the Costa del Maresme.
⮥ *Inland from the N11 at Km633.*
All year 2HEC ⚏ ♦ ⌕ ⛟ ⛱ ✕ ⊙ ⛲ ∅ 🖫 🀫 ⭲ P 🖼 🀫 lau ➧ ⭲S
Prices: ⚑650 ⛺650 ▲650

LLAFRANC - PALAFRUGELL
CAMPING
Tel (34) 972 30 11 56
Fax (34) 972 61 08 94
Internet:
http://www.campingkims.com
E-mail: info@campingkims.com
1ª CATEGORIA ★★★

Bungalows and mobile homes for hire.
Open Easter-30.9. Friendly site 500 m from beach.
• One of the most beautifully situated camp sites on the Costa Brava in a landscaped green zone belt.
• 2 swimming pools, Children's playground, bar, restaurant, supermarket.
• Only 322 sites (60-70-100m²) on a surface of 50,000 sq. m.

▶ PALAFRUGELL GIRONA

▶ At LLAFRANC

Kim's Font d'En Xeco 1 ☎ 972 301156
Terraced site with winding drives, lying on the wooded slopes of a narrow valley leading to the sea.
⮥ *For access, turn right off the Palafrugell-Tamariu road, follow a wide tarred road for 1km, past the El Paranso Hotel and head towards Llafranc. 0.4km from sea.*
24 Jun-Aug 5.6HEC ⚏ ⠿ ♦ ⌕ ⛟ ⛱ ✕ ⊙ ⛲ ∅ 🀫 🀫 ⭲ P 🖼 🀫 ⚐ lau ➧ ⭲S
Prices: ⚑482-775 ⛺482-775 ⛺589-936 ▲589-829

▶ At MONTRÁS(3km SW)

Relax-Ge ☎ 972 301549
Level meadow under poplars and olive trees.
⮥ *Turn off the C255 at Km38.7. 4km to the sea.*
Jun-Aug 2.7HEC ⚏ ♦ ⌕ ⛟ ⛱ ✕ ⊙ ⛲ ∅ 🀫 ⭲ P 🖼 🀫 lau
Prices: ⚑535 pitch 1070-1498

▶ At PLAYA DE ENSUEÑOS

Tamariu ☎ 972 620422
Terraced site with mixture of high young pines. Direct access to the beach.
⮥ *Turn towards site at beach parking area and continue 300m.*
May-Sep 2HEC ⚏ ♦ ⌕ ⛟ ⛱ ✕ ⊙ ⛲ ∅ ⭲ PS 🖼 🀫 lau ➧ 🖫 ⛱ ✕ ∅ 🀫
Prices: ⚑480-610 ⛺480-610 ⛺530-690 ▲480-610

▶ PALAMÓS GIRONA

Castell Park ☎ 972 315263
Level and gently sloping meadow with poplars and pine woodland on a hill.
⮥ *At Km40 about 100m to the right of the C255 to Palamós and 3km S of Montras.*
Apr-Sep 4.5HEC ⚏ ♦ ⌕ ⛟ ⛱ ✕ ⊙ ⛲ ∅ 🀫 ⭲ P 🖼 🀫 lau
Prices: ⚑440-550 ⛺475-650 ▲475-650

Coma Cami Vell de la Fosca 2 ☎ 34972 314638
Sloping terraced terrain with young deciduous trees and isolated pines. 0.8km from the sea.
⮥ *In N outskirts turn seawards off the C255 near the RENAULT garage.*
Apr-Sep 5.2HEC ⚏ ♦ ⌕ ⛟ ⛱ ✕ ⊙ ⛲ ∅ ▲ ⭲ P 🖼 🀫 lau ➧ ⭲S
Prices: ⚑420-520 pitch 1450-2450

Internacional Palamós Playa de la Fosca ☎ 972 314736
⮥ *Signposted.*
Jun-Sept 5.2HEC ⚏ ♦ ⌕ ⛟ ⛱ ✕ ⊙ ⛲ 🀫 🀫 ▲ ⭲ PS 🖼 🀫 lau ➧ ∅
Prices: ⚑400-400 pitch 2025-2590

Palamós ctra la Fosca 12 ☎ 72 314296
In a picturesque situation on a wooded headland overlooking the sea.
27 Mar-Sep 5.5HEC ⊞⊞ ⠿ ♣ ⋔ ⅄ ⅀ ⚍ ✕ ⊙ ⬛ ∅ ⛺ ⌂ ⅄ PS ⊠ ⊞ lau ♦ ⛺
Prices: ♦589-589 pitch 1231-2060

Vilarromá calle del Mar ☎ 972 314375
Clean and tidy site, almost completely divided into pitches.
⟳ *Turn off on the eastern outskirts of Palamós near big petrol station.*
1 Apr-15 Sep 1.8HEC ⊞⊞ ♣ ⋔ ⅄ ⅀ ⚍ ✕ ⊙ ⬛ ∅ ⛺ ⊠ ⊞ lau ♦ ⅄S ⊞
Prices: ♦588-631 ⬤588-674 ⬛588-1006 ▲388-1006

At CALONGE(5km W)

Cala Gogo ☎ 972 651564
Terraced site in tall pine woodland and poplars with some good views of the sea. Underpass across to section of site with private beach. Some internal dusty roads
⟳ *Access from Palamós 4 km S on coastal road C253, entrance to site on right shortly after Km47.*
27 Mar-26 Sept 16HEC ⊞⊞ ♣ ⋔ ⅄ ⅀ ⚍ ✕ ⊙ ⬛ ∅ ⛺ ⌂ ▲ ⅄ PS ⊠ ⊞ ⅍ lau
Prices: ♦508-856 ⬤525-910 ⬛685-1300 ▲589-1150

Internacional de Calonge ☎ 972 651233
Set on a pine covered hill overlooking the sea within easy reach of a sandy beach.
⟳ *On the coast road between Platja d'Aro and Palamós.*
Apr-Oct 11HEC ⠿ ♣ ⋔ ⅄ ⅀ ⚍ ✕ ⊙ ⬛ ∅ ⛺ ▲ ⅄ PS ⊠ ⊞ lau
Prices: ♦445-775 pitch 1595-2295

CAMPING · CARAVANING
INTERNACIONAL DE CALONGE
E-17251 CALONGE
COSTA BRAVA
1st. CATEGORIE

Special fees (Oct-May)

Privileged situation in the very heart of the famous COSTA BRAVA, between Palamós and Platja d'Aro (follow indication signs "Sant Antoni, Platja d'Aro i Platges), on a beautiful pine-covered hill overlooking the sea, you will find one of the most beautiful campsites of Spain, 55 yards from a lovely beach, surrounded by rocks and with private access. Magnificent facilities including swimming pool, restaurant, bar, superm., tennis courts, hairdr., free hot water, etc.
A 2nd new swimming pool.
Reservations possible. **OPEN THROUGHOUT THE YEAR.**
English spoken. Guarded day & night.
Information and reservations:
Apto. correus 272, E-17250 Platja d'Aro, Spain.
Tel. (34) 972 65 12 33 & 972 65 14 44 • Fax 972 65 25 07.
Internet: http://www.intercalonge.com
E-mail: intercalonge@intercalonge.com
Or in G.B: John Worthington, 17 Waverley Road, Worsley, Manchester M28 5UW. Tel. (0161) 799 1274.
COMPLETELY EQUIPPED MOBILE HOMES AND TENTS FOR HIRE.

PALS GIRONA

Cypsela ☎ 972 667696
Well-kept grassy site in a pine wood.
⟳ *For access, turn towards the sea N of Pals and follow road towards Playa de Pals, then turn left after Km3.*
15 May-27 Sep 20HEC ⠿ ♣ ⋔ ⅄ ⅀ ⚍ ✕ ⊙ ⬛ ∅ ⛺ ⅄ P ⊠ ⊞ ⊞ ⅍ lau ♦ ⛺ ⅄RS
Prices: ♦642-802 pitch 2140-2675

Mas Patoxas ☎ 972 636928
A family site in a quiet location close to the sea. Good, modern sanitary blocks and plenty of recreational facilities.
⟳ *At Km5 on Palafrugell to Torroella.*
Apr-Oct 12HEC ⊞⊞ ♣ ⋔ ⅄ ⅀ ⚍ ✕ ⊙ ⬛ ∅ ⛺ ⌂ ⅄ ▲ ⅄ P ⊠ ⊞ lau
Prices: ♦400-700 pitch 1300-2150
See advertisement on page 292.

Playa Brava 17256 Platja De Pals ☎ 972 636894
On level terrain adjoining pine woodlands, golf course, rivers and sea.
⟳ *From N end of village of Pals turn towards sea and Playa de Pals.*
15 May-19 Sep 11HEC ⊞⊞ ⠿ ⚄ ⋔ ⅄ ⅀ ⚍ ✕ ⊙ ⬛ ∅ ⅄ PRS ⊠ ⊞ ⅍ lau
Prices: ♦225-321 pitch 2540-3630

PINEDA DE MAR BARCELONA

Camell Ada de los Naranjos 12 ☎ 93 7671520
Surrounded by deciduous trees next to a small wood owned by the Taurus Hotel.
⟳ *Turn off the N11 at Km670 and drive along av de los Naranjos in direction of sea.*
May-Oct 2.2HEC ⠿ ♣ ⋔ ⅄ ⅀ ⚍ ✕ ⊙ ⬛ ∅ ⅄ PS ⊠ ⊞ lau ♦ ⛺
Prices: ♦525 pitch 1400

Enmar ☎ 08397 7671730
⟳ *Leave autopista at exit 9 (Lloret and Malgrat) and continue towards Pineda de Mar.*
Mar-Oct 2.5HEC ⠿ ⚄ ⋔ ⅄ ⅀ ⚍ ✕ ⊙ ⬛ ∅ ⛺ ⅄ PS ⊠ ⊞ lau

PLATJA D'ARO, LA GIRONA

Valldaro ctra Santa Cristina 113 ☎ 72 817515
Extensive level meadowland under poplars, pines and eucalyptus trees. Some large pitches without shade.
⟳ *Site lies on the left of the GE662 towards Castell and Santa Cristina d'Aro at Km4.*
7 Mar-12 Oct 18HEC ⊞⊞ ⠿ ♣ ⋔ ⅄ ⅀ ⚍ ✕ ⊙ ⬛ ∅ ⅄ ⛺ ⌂ ⅄ PR ⊠ ⊞ lau ♦ ⅄S
Prices: ♦550 pitch 1675-2675

PUERTO DE LA SELVA GIRONA

Port de la Selva ☎ 972 387287
Level, grassland site with young poplar trees.
⟳ *1.5km from the village, in a valley off the Puerto de la Selva to Cadaques road.*
Jun-Sep 3HEC ⊞⊞ ♣ ⋔ ⅄ ⅀ ⚍ ✕ ⊙ ⬛ ∅ ⅄ P ⊠ ⊞ lau ♦ ⅄S

PUIGCERDÀ GIRONA

Stel ctra Llivia ☎ 972 882361
Modern campsite in the Pyrenees on level land. Has wonderful views of the mountains and surrounding area. First class sanitary installations.
⟳ *Access via N340 between Comarruga and Tarragona.*
18 Jun-26 Sep 7HEC ⠿ ⚄ ⋔ ⅄ ⅀ ⚍ ✕ ⊙ ⬛ ∅ ⛺ ⅄ P ⊠ ⊞ lau
Prices: ♦696 pitch 2194

Contd.

> **RIPOLL** GIRONA

Solana del Ter ☎ 972 701062
In a peaceful location close to the local ski resorts at the foot
of the Pyrenees. Part of a small hotel/restaurant complex.
May-Oct 8.5HEC ⊞ ⚐ ⛌ ≈ ⚑ ✕ ☉ ⚑ ⚐ ⊹ P ⊞ ⊞ lau ♦ ⚑ ⌀
Prices: ⚑650 pitch 1300

> **SALDES** BARCELONA

Repos del Pedraforca ☎ 093 8258044
A well equipped site sitauted in an area of natural beauty.
All year 4HEC ⊞ ♦ ⚐ ⚑ ⚑ ✕ ☉ ⚑ ⌀ ⚑ ⚑ ⚑ ⊹ P ⊞ ⊞ lau
Prices: ⚑510-680 ⚑510-680 ⚑510-680 ⚑510-680

> **SANT ANTONI DE CALONGE** GIRONA

Costa Brava ☎ 972 650222
Level site with tall pine woodland partially subdivided under
deciduous trees.
➲ *From Calonge de les Gavarres turn off C253 S of Calonge.
Site lies behind the hotel.*
Jun-Sep 2.4HEC ⊞ ♦ ⚐ ⚑ ⚑ ✕ ☉ ⚑ ⊹ P ⊞ ⊞ lau ♦ ⌀ ⊹S

Euro ☎ 72 650879
A family site in a peaceful location close to the sea with fine
recreational facilities.
➲ *Access via A7 exit 9.*
May-26 Sep 13HEC ⊞ ♦ ⚐ ⚑ ⚑ ✕ ☉ ⚑ ⌀ ⚑ ⊹ PS ⊞ ⊞
lau ♦ ⌀
Prices: ⚑300-530 pitch 2113-3300

Treumal ☎ 972 651095
A peaceful family site in a beautiful location between a pine
wood and the beach.
➲ *Entrance on Sant Feliú-Platja d'Aro-Palamós road.*

27 Mar-12 Oct 7HEC ⸺ ∷ ♠ ↑ ⬛ ♀ ✕ ⊙ ◨ ∅ ⬛ ⊀ PS ⊞ ⊞ lau
Prices: ♠780 ⬛2760 ▲2620

SANTA SUSANA BARCELONA

Bon Répos ☎ 93 7678475
In pine woodland between railway and the beach with some sunshade roofing.
⮕ *Turn off the N11 at Km681 and approach via the underpass (height 2.5m) just before reaching the beach.*
All year 60HEC ⸺ ∷ ⊙ ↑ ⬛ ♀ ✕ ⊙ ◨ ∅ ⬛ ⊀ PS ⊞ ⊞ lau ♦ ⬛ ♀ ⊀S

SANT CEBRIÁ DE VALLALTA BARCELONA

Verneda av Maresme ☎ 93 7631185
Inland and among tall trees.
⮕ *Leave the N11 Girona-Barcelona road at the far end of Sant Pol de Mar, turn inland at Km670. Continue for 2km to edge of the village and short of the bridge over the River Vallala turn right.*
Apr-Sep 1.6HEC ∷ ♠ ↑ ⬛ ♀ ✕ ⊙ ◨ ∅ ⊀ P ⊞ ⊞ lau
Prices: ♠500 ⬛500 ◨500 ▲500

SANT FELIU DE GUIXOLS GIRONA

Sant Pol ctra Palamos ☎ 972 321019
In wooded surroundings near the beach with good facilities.
⮕ *800m from the town centre towards Palamos.*
Apr-Sep 1.5HEC ⸺ ♠ ↑ ⬛ ♀ ✕ ⊙ ◨ ⬛ ⊀ PS ⊞ ⊞ lau ♦ ⊀S
Prices: ♠476-797 ⬛685-725 ◨535-882 ▲476-797

SANT PERE PESCADOR GIRONA

Amfora av J-Terradellas 2 ☎ 972 520540
A pleasant site, directly on the beach, with good modern sanitary facilities. There are plentiful leisure facilities and English is spoken.
9HEC ⸺ ⊙ ↑ ⬛ ♀ ✕ ⊙ ◨ ∅ ⬛ ⊀ PRS ⊞ ⊞ lau
Prices: ♠450-500 ◨1600-3500

Aquarius ☎ 972 520003
Level meadowland. Partially in shade, quiet well organised site by the lovely sandy beach of Bahia de Rosas.
⮕ *Travel in direction of L'Escala and turn towards the beach following signs.*
20 Mar-18 Oct 6HEC ⸺ ⊙ ↑ ⬛ ♀ ✕ ⊙ ◨ ∅ ⬛ ⊀ S ⊞ ⊞ lau
Prices: ♠400-700 ◨750-1400 ▲750-1400

Ballena Alegre 2 ☎ 972 520302
Extensive site near wide sandy beach with dunes. Large shopping complex. Washing and sanitary facilities have recently undergone extensive modernisation.
⮕ *Access from L'Escala to San Martin de Ampurias, then onward to site in 2km .*
15 May-Sep 24HEC ⸺ ⊙ ↑ ⬛ ♀ ✕ ⊙ ◨ ∅ ⬛ ⬛ ◨ ⊀ LPRS ⊞ ⊞ lau
Prices: ♠350 pitch 1700-3650

Dunas ☎ 972 520400
Level extensive grassland site with young poplars, some of medium height, on the beach, totally subdivided.
⮕ *It lies 5km SE of village. If approaching from L'Escala follow an asphalt road to San Martin, then follow a dusty earth track for 2.5km.*
9 May-25 Sep 30HEC ⸺ ⊙ ↑ ⬛ ♀ ✕ ⊙ ◨ ∅ ⬛ ◨ ▲ ⊀ PS ⊞ ⊞ lau

Palmeras ctra de la Platja ☎ 972 520506
On level grassland with plenty of shade. Recently installed modern sanitary blocks and heated swimming pool.
⮕ *Off the road from Sant Pere Pescador to the beach about 200m from the sea.*

27 Mar-17 Oct 3HEC ⸺ ⊙ ↑ ⬛ ♀ ✕ ⊙ ◨ ∅ ⬛ ⊀ PRS ⊞
⊞ lau
Prices: ♠321-428 pitch 1605-2889

SITGES BARCELONA

Roca av de Ronda ☎ 93 8940043
On three terraces with a view of Sitges. Shade is provided by pines and deciduous trees. Separate section for young people. 1km from the sea.
Camping Card Compulsory.
⮕ *Turn off the C246 (Barcelona-Tarragona) in the direction of Sant Pere de Ribes/San Pedro de Ribas. In 15m turn right to site.*
21 Mar-12 Oct 2HEC ∷ ♠ ↑ ⬛ ♀ ✕ ⊙ ◨ ∅ ⊞ lau ♦ ✕ ⊀PS

TARADELL BARCELONA

Vall Cami de la Vallmissand ☎ 93 8126336
In the mountains near the Guilleries-Montseny, with good recreational facilities.
All year 9HEC ⸺ ∅ ⊙ ↑ ⬛ ♀ ✕ ⊙ ◨ ∅ ⬛ ⬛ ⊀ P ⊞ lau
Prices: ♠458-500 pitch 1500-1800

TORROELLA DE MONTGRI GIRONA

Delfin Verde ☎ 972 758450
On undulating ground with some pine trees, and an open meadow beside the long sandy beach.
⮕ *Turn left off the road to Begur approx 2km S of Torroella de Montgri, and head towards Maspinell following a wide asphalt road 4.8km towards the sea.*
Apr-27 Sep 35HEC ⸺ ⊙ ↑ ⬛ ♀ ✕ ⊙ ◨ ∅ ⬛ ⊀ PRS ⊞ ⊞ lau
Prices: ♠375-400 pitch 1700-4100

See advertisement under Colour Section

Sirena ☎ 972 758542
Level site with some grass near the sea.
⮕ *Approaching from Toroella de Montgri turn right about 400m from 'Estartit' sign at Km1 and continue 300m.*
May-Oct 2HEC ⸺ ⊙ ↑ ⬛ ♀ ✕ ⊙ ◨ ∅ ⬛ ◨ ⊀ PS ⊞ ⊞ lau ♦ ⊀S

TOSSA DE MAR GIRONA

Cala Llevadó ☎ 72 340314
Magnificent terraced site with hairpin roads overlooking three bays, all suitable for bathing. Narrow, winding drives which are quite steep in parts. Separate section for caravans.
⮕ *Take the coast road for about 4km towards Lloret de Mar and turn towards the sea.*
May-Sep 14HEC ⸺ ♠ ↑ ⬛ ♀ ✕ ⊙ ◨ ∅ ⬛ ◨ ▲ ⊀ PS ⊞ ◨ ⊞ lau
Prices: ♠642-952 ⬛642-952 ◨738-1027 ▲642-952

See advertisement under Colour Section

Can Marti ☎ 972 340851
Pleasant, unspoilt site in a partly wooded location. Good modern facilities. English spoken.
⮕ *1km from the sea.*
16 May-13 Sep 10HEC ⸺ ♠ ↑ ⬛ ♀ ✕ ⊙ ◨ ∅ ⊀ PRS ⊞ ⊞ lau ♦ ⊀S
Prices: ♠625-775 ⬛400-500 ◨675-800 ▲675-800

Tossa ctra Llagostera ☎ 972 340547
On a meadow in a quiet, isolated valley, in a deciduous forest. 3km from the sea.
⮕ *3km SW near the GE681 (Tossa de Mar-Llagostera), in 600m to site along an unmade road.*
Apr-Sep 9.5HEC ∷ ♠ ↑ ⬛ ♀ ✕ ⊙ ◨ ∅ ⬛ ⬛ ⊀ PS ⊞ ⊞ lau

Contd.

293

VILADECANS BARCELONA

Ballena Alegre I ☎ 93 6330642
An exceptionally well run family site with a wide range of facilities and direct access to a fine, sandy beach.
➲ *Access cia C246. Before entering Barcelona follow signs for 'Airport'.*
Apr-Sep 25HEC ⸝⸝⸝⸝ ∷∷ ⌂ ⋔ ⅄ ⋔ ⅄ ✕ ☉ 🛢 ⌀ ☎ ⚡ PS ☎ ⊞ lau
Prices: ⚑575 pitch 1425-2650

Toro Bravo ☎ 93 6373462
Level site in extensive pine woodland area by the sea. To the left of the access road on the banks of a stagnant canal about 1km long is a leisure and sports complex with many facilities including evening entertainment in the season.
➲ *Leave the C246 (Barcelona-Castelldeféls), at Km11 and continue towards the sea for 1km.*
All year 30HEC ⸝⸝⸝⸝ ∷∷ ♠ ⋔ ⅄ ⋔ ⅄ ✕ ☉ 🛢 ⌀ ☎ ⚡ PS ☎ ⊞ lau

VILALLONGA DE TER GIRONA

Conca de Ter ctra Camprodon-Setcases ☎ 972 740629
All year 3.2HEC ⸝⸝⸝⸝ ⌂ ⋔ ⅄ ⋔ ⅄ ✕ ☉ 🛢 ⌀ ☎ ⚡ Å ⚡ PR ☎ ⊞ lau ♦ ⅃
Prices: ⚑590 pitch 1525

VILANOVA I LA GELTRÚ BARCELONA

Vilanova Park ☎ 93 8933402
A well equipped family site on the edge of a densely wooded area close to the coast in the heart Catalonian wine producing area. Modern sanitary block recently added.
➲ *Access via A7 exit 29.*
All year 40HEC ⸝⸝⸝⸝ ⌀ ♠ ⋔ ⅄ ⋔ ⅄ ✕ ☉ 🛢 ⌀ ☶ ☎ 🛢 Å ⚡ P ☎ ⊞ lau
Prices: ⚑540-860 ⛟540-860 ⛺540-860 Å540-860

See advertisement under Colour Section

CENTRAL

The La Mancha plains and Don Quixote's windmills, massive mountain ranges, pastures, wheatfields, vineyards, and ancient forests are some of the region's contrasts. Here are St Teresa's walled city of Avila, Cáceres' exceptional old quarter, Guadalajara's outstanding Renaissance palace, Salamanca, with its university and beautiful square and Segovia's dramatic Roman aqueduct and 14th-century palace.
Architectural and artistic riches continue with Cuenca's hanging houses and Teruel, part of which, like Toledo, belongs to the Heritage of Mankind. The framed walled city of Toledo, with its mosque, synagogue and medieval cathedral, has its associations with El Cid and contains El Greco's house and museum.
Spain's vital capital, Madrid, is home to the Prado and numerous other museums, a colourful old town, lovely parks, squares and palaces, while a short drive away lie the Sierra of Guadarrama with its forests, wild animals and birds of prey and the Pedriza del Manzanares' geological wonderland.

ALBA DE TORMES SALAMANCA

Tormes av Dehesa Boyal ☎ 923 160998
Camping Card Compulsory.
All year 2.2HEC ⸝⸝⸝⸝ ⸝⸝ ⋔ ⅄ ✕ ☉ 🛢 Å ⚡ R ☎ ⊞ lau ♦ ⅃ ✕ ⌀ ☶ ⚡PR
Prices: ⚑425 ⛟375 ⛺450 Å450-450

ALBARRACIN TERUEL

Ciudad de Albarracin Camino de Gea, Arrabal ☎ 978 710197
A modern site on mainly level ground with good facilities.
➲ *Signposted from A1512.*
Apr-Oct 1.4HEC ⸝⸝⸝⸝ ♠ ⋔ ⅄ ⋔ ⅄ ✕ ☉ 🛢 ⌀ ☎ ⊞ lau ♦ ⅃ ⚡PR
Prices: ⚑375 ⛟375 ⛺400 Å375

ALDEANUEVA DE LA VERA CÁCERES

Yuste ☎ 927 560910
Meadowland with dense woodland on a hill above two valleys.
➲ *300m S of C501 at Km47.1.*
Apr-Sep 3HEC ⸝⸝⸝⸝ ♠ ⋔ ⅄ ⋔ ⅄ ✕ ☉ 🛢 ⌀ Å ⚡ P ☎ ⊞ lau ♦ ⚡R

ARANJUEZ MADRID

Soto del Castillo ctra de Andalucia 1 ☎ 91 8911395
Site developed into two parts with trees and lawns in large castle park.
➲ *Turn off NIV at Km46. In the village 200m beyond FIRESTONE petrol station turn sharp NE and continue for 1km.*
All year 33HEC ⸝⸝⸝⸝ ♠ ⋔ ⅄ ⋔ ⅄ ✕ ☉ 🛢 ⌀ ☎ ⚡ PR ☎ ⊞ lau
Prices: ⚑475-625 ⛟400-525 ⛺550-700 Å425-550

CABRERA, LA MADRID

Pico de la Miel ☎ 91 8688082 & 8688541
Jun-15 Sep 10HEC ⸝⸝⸝⸝ ♠ ⋔ ⅄ ⋔ ⅄ ✕ ☉ 🛢 ⌀ ☎ ⚡ P ☎ ⊞ lau ♦ ⸋

CUENCA CUENCA

Cuenca ☎ 969 231656
A modern site in a peaceful wooded location.
➲ *N towards Mariana.*
15 Mar-15 Nov 23HEC ⸝⸝⸝⸝ ⌂ ⋔ ⅄ ⋔ ⅄ ✕ ☉ 🛢 ⌀ ⚡ P ☎ ⊞ lau ♦ ⚡R
Prices: ⚑490 ⛟450 ⛺550 Å450

ESCORIAL, EL MADRID

El Escorial ctra Guadarrama ☎ 91 8902412
In pleasant wooded surroundings with good recreational facilities.
All year 40HEC ⸝⸝⸝⸝ ♠ ⋔ ⅄ ⋔ ⅄ ✕ ☉ 🛢 ⌀ ☶ ☎ ⚡ P ☎ ⊞ lau
Prices: ⚑680 ⛟680 ⛺680 Å680

FUENTE DE SAN ESTEBAN, LA SALAMANCA

Cruce ☎ 923 440130
Useful transit site.
➲ *On N620 at Km291.*
15 Jun-15 Sep 0.5HEC ⸝⸝⸝⸝ ⌂ ⋔ ⅄ ⋔ ⅄ ✕ ☉ 🛢 ⌀ ☎ ⚡ P ☎ ⊞ lau ♦ ⅃ ⅄ ✕
Prices: ⚑400 ⛟400 ⛺500 Å375

GARGANTILLA DE LOZOYA MADRID

Monte Holiday ☎ 91 8695278
A terraced site with good modern facilities in a beautiful mountain setting.
➲ *Turn off N1 (Burgos-Madrid) at Km69 towards Cotos and continue for 10km.*
All year 30HEC ⸝⸝⸝⸝ ⌀ ⌂ ⋔ ⅄ ⋔ ⅄ ✕ ☉ 🛢 ⌀ ☎ ⚡ P ☎ ⊞ lau ♦ ⚡LR
Prices: ⚑640 ⛟640 ⛺640 Å640

GETAFE MADRID

Alpha ☎ 91 6958069
Surrounded by pine woods at approx. the geographical centre of Spain with well defined pitches and modern facilities. Direct bus service to Madrid.
➲ *Access via NIV at Km 12,400.*

All year 5HEC ∴∷ ♠ ⋒ ☂ ⏼ ✗ ☉ 🖳 ∅ ☎ ⅀ P 🄿 ⊞ lau
Prices: ♦690 �car690 🚐710 ▲710

MADRID MADRID

Arco Iris ☎ 91 6160387
➲ *From M40 (Madrid ring road) take exit 36 to Boadilla del Monte and continue towards Villaviciosa to Km12.*
All year 4HEC ⍟ ∴∷ ♠ ⋒ ☂ ⏼ ✗ ☉ 🖳 ∅ ⛌ ☎ 🖳 ⅀ P 🄿 ⊞ lau
Prices: ♦630 🚗650 🚐650 ▲650

See advertisement also in Colour Section

Osuna Av de Logrono s/n ☎ 91 7410510
On long stretch of land, shade being provided by pines, acacias and maple. Some noise from airfield, road and railway.
➲ *If approaching from the town centre take N11 road and drive towards Barajas for about 7.5km. At Km1 in 300m and after railway underpass turn right.*
All year 2.3HEC ⍟ ∴∷ ⍩ ⋒ ☂ ⏼ ✗ ☉ 🖳 🖳 ☎ 🄿 ⊞ lau ➤ ∅ ⛾ ⅀LP
Prices: ♦707 🚗707 🚐707 ▲707

MALPARTIDA DE PLASENCIA CÁCERES

Parque Natural de Monfrague ctra Trujillo ☎ 927 459220
A modern site with well defined pitches and good facilities.
➲ *10km from Plasencia on C524.*
All year 7HEC ∴∷ ⍟ ⍩ ⋒ ☂ ⏼ ✗ ☉ 🖳 ∅ ☎ ▲ ⅀ P 🄿 ⊞ lau ➤ ⛾
Prices: ♦450 🚗450 🚐450 ▲450

MÉRIDA BADAJOZ

Lago de Proserpina Apdo 121 ☎ 924 313236
1 Apr-15 Sep 5.5HEC ⍋ ∴∷ ⍩ ⋒ ☂ ⏼ ✗ ☉ 🖳 ∅ ⅀ L 🄿 ⊞ lau ➤ ⏼ ✗ ⅀P
Prices: ♦400-400 🚗400-400 🚐400-400 ▲400

NAVALAFUENTE MADRID

Camping Piscis ☎ 918 432253
Spacious pitches surrounded by oak trees.
➲ *Turn off N1/E5 (Madrid-Burgos) at exit 50 and continue towards Guadalix de la Sierra.*
All year 23HEC ⍟ ♠ ⋒ ☂ ⏼ ✗ ☉ 🖳 ∅ 🖳 ⅀ P
Prices: ♦560 🚗400 🚐560 ▲560

SANTA MARTA DE TORMES SALAMANCA

Regio ctra Salamanca/Madrid Km4 ☎ 923 138888
A pleasant site, divided into several fields, with good, modern facilities.
➲ *100m from the N501 (Salamanca-Avila) behind Hotel Jardin-Regio.*
All year 3HEC ⍋ ⍩ ⋒ ☂ ⏼ ✗ ☉ 🖳 ∅ ⅀ PR 🄿 ⊞ lau
Prices: ♦325-450 🚐325-450 ▲325-450

SEGOVIA SEGOVIA

Acueducto ☎ 921 425000
➲ *SE next to N601 at Km112*
Apr-Sep 3HEC ⍋ ♠ ⋒ ☂ ⏼ ✗ ☉ 🖳 ∅ ☎ ⅀ P ⊞ lau ➤ ✗
Prices: ♦465-500 🚗465-500 🚐558-600 ▲465-500

TOLEDO TOLEDO

Greco ☎ 925 220090
Few shady terraces on slope leading down to the River Tajo. On SW outskirts of town.
➲ *Approaching from the town centre take the C401, Carretera Comarcal and drive SW for about 2km. Turn right at Km28 and drive 300m towards Puebla de Montalban.*
All year 4HEC ∴∷ ⍩ ⋒ ☂ ⏼ ✗ ☉ 🖳 ∅ ⅀ PR 🄿 ⊞ lau ➤ ⛾
Prices: ♦595 🚗550 🚐635 ▲620

▶ **VALDEMAQUEDA** MADRID

El Canto la Gallina ☎ 091 8984820
In a wooded location at the foot of a mountain.
All year 12HEC ⚏ ⚑ ᐤ ⚏ ⚏ ⚏ ✕ ☉ ⚏ ⊘ ⚏ ⌇ P ⚏ ⊞ lau ➡ ⌇R
Prices: ⚏600 ⚏500 ⚏600

● ● ● **SOUTH EAST COAST** ● ● ●

The Costa Blanca is a household name; Benidorm a tourist
mecca. South of Alicante, tourism is less developed and,
inland, there are lemon and orange groves and picturesque
mountain towns.
A busy port and relatively unspoiled, Alicante has a
cathedral and museum of 20th-century art, and there are
tremendous views from its fascinating castle. Roman
remains surround Tarragona, whose medieval walled city
has a Gothic cathedral, interesting palace and architectural
museum. Journey can be to the Monastery of Poblet inside its
three perimeter walls and the Abbey of Santa Creus, burial
place of the kings of Aragon.
Valencia, home of paella, is Spain's third largest city with a
countryside criss-crossed by ancient irrigation channels.
Numerous historic buildings include a cathedral with the
legendary Holy Grail, beautiful bridges and gardens and
many museums. The Fallas - a fortnight of celebrations -
take place in mid-March. Inland, Requena has a moorish
castle, medieval walls and the house of El Cid.

....

▶ **ALCANAR** TARRAGONA

Mare Nostrum ☎ 977 737179
Gently sloping towards the sea with pines, olive and
deciduous trees.
➲ *Turn towards the sea off the N340 at Km58.3.*
All year 1.4HEC ⚏ ◆ ᐤ ⚏ ⚏ ✕ ☉ ⚏ ⊘ ⌇ S ⚏ ⊞ lau ➡ ✕

▶ **ALCOCEBER** CASTELLÓN

Playa Tropicana ☎ 964 412463
On a 500m long sandy beach 3km from the village.
➲ *For access, leave motorway at exit 44, then drive 3km N on
the CN340 and turn towards the sea at Km1018.*
15 Mar-Oct 3HEC ⚏ ◆ ᐤ ⚏ ⚏ ✕ ☉ ⚏ ⊘ ⚏ ⌇ PS ⚏ ⊞ ⚏
lau ➡ ⚏
Prices: ⚏905 pitch 3135-4500

Ribamar Partida Ribamar s/n ☎ 964 414165
Quiet wooded site between sea and mountains. Individual
pitches.
27 Mar-26 Sep 2.2HEC ⚏ ᐤ ⚏ ⚏ ⚏ ✕ ☉ ⚏ ⊘ ⚏ ⌇ PS ⚏ ⊞ lau
Prices: ⚏380-530 ⚏380-530 ⚏462-642 ⚏462-642

▶ **ALTEA** ALICANTE

Cap Blanch Playa del Cap-Blanch ☎ 96 5845946
A well equipped site on Albir beach backed by imposing
mountains. Good sporting and recreational facilities.
➲ *Access via A7 exit 65 (Benidorm-Callosa).*
All year 4HEC ⚏ ◆ ᐤ ⚏ ⚏ ✕ ☉ ⚏ ⊘ ⚏ ⌇ S ⚏ ⊞ lau ➡ ⚏ ⚏
✕ ⊘ ⊞
Prices: ⚏600 ⚏600 ⚏800 ⚏600

▶ **AMETLLA DE MAR, L'** TARRAGONA

L'Ametlla Village Platja Paratge Santes Creus ☎ 977 267784
A modern site with first class equipment. Direct access to two
beaches.
➲ *2km W, S of A7.*
Closed 15 Jan-Feb 8HEC ⚏ ⚏ ᐤ ⚏ ⚏ ⚏ ✕ ☉ ⚏ ⊘ ⚏ ⚏
⌇ P ⚏ ⊞ lau
Prices: ⚏696-749 ⚏696-749 ⚏749-803 ⚏749-803

Nautic c Libertad ☎ 977 456110
Terraced with pines, palms and olives and has uneven stony
ground. Has own beach.
➲ *Turn right off N340 (Tarragona-Valencia) at Km20.1, take
TV3025 and continue to railway station via flyover and level
crossing. Turn right and take third road on left. Access road has
10% gradient.*
15 Mar-15 Oct 8HEC ⚏ ⚏ ◆ ᐤ ⚏ ⚏ ⚏ ✕ ☉ ⚏ ⊘ ⚏ ⚏ ⚏
⌇ LPS ⚏ ⊞ lau

▶ **BENICARLÓ** CASTELLÓN

Alegria del Mar Playa Norte ☎ 964 470871
All year 10HEC ⚏ ⚑ ᐤ ⚏ ⚏ ⚏ ✕ ☉ ⚏ ⊘ ⚏ ⌇ PS ⚏ ⊞ lau
Prices: ⚏450 ⚏450 ⚏450

▶ **BENICASIM** CASTELLÓN

Bonterra av Barcelona 47 ☎ 964 300007
Between the railway line and avenida de Barcelona with a
number of deciduous trees.
➲ *300m N towards Las Villas de Benicasim.*
Closed 13 Oct-15 Apr 5HEC ⚏ ⚏ ◆ ᐤ ⚏ ⚏ ⚏ ✕ ☉ ⚏ ⊘ ⚏
⌇ P ⚏ ⊞ ⚏ lau ➡ ⚏ ⌇ ⚏
Prices: ⚏235-450 pitch 958-2357

▶ **BENIDORM** ALICANTE

Arena Blanca av Dr Severo Ochoa 44 ☎ 96 5861889
A modern site with plenty of good facilities.
➲ *Access via N332 Benidorm-Altea.*
All year 2.2HEC ⚏ ◆ ᐤ ⚏ ⚏ ✕ ☉ ⚏ ⊘ ⚏ ⚏ ⌇ PS ⚏ ⊞ lau
Prices: pitch 1819

Armanello av Comunidad ☎ 96 5853190
Divided by bushes with large pitches on terraces under olive
and palm trees next to a small orange grove.
➲ *For access turn off the N332 at Km123.1 N of the town.*
All year 16HEC ⚏ ◆ ᐤ ⚏ ⚏ ✕ ☉ ⚏ ⊘ ⚏ ⚏ ⌇ P ⚏ ⊞ lau
Prices: ⚏600 ⚏700 ⚏600

Benisol av de la Comunidad ☎ 96 5851673
A modern family site with plenty of facilities. The large
pitches are separated by hedges and the centre of Benidorm
is within easy reach.
➲ *NE of Benidorm off N332 towards Altea.*
All year ⚏ ◆ ᐤ ⚏ ⚏ ✕ ☉ ⚏ ⊘ ⚏ ⚏ ⚏ ⌇ P ⚏ ⊞ lau
Prices: ⚏550-600 pitch 1600-2000

▶ **BENISA** ALICANTE

Fanadix ctra Calpe-Moraira Km 5 ☎ 96 5747307
Terraced site completely divided into pitches.
➲ *10km E & 400m from the sea. Access off AV-1445.*
Apr-Sep 1.6HEC ⚏ ◆ ᐤ ⚏ ✕ ☉ ⚏ ⌇ P ⚏ ⊞ lau ➡ ⚏ ⊘ ⚏ ⌇S
Prices: ⚏525 pitch 1575

CALPE ALICANTE

Vinã de Calpe ☎ 96 5831551
Level site with sunshade roofing.
⤳ *1.5km towards Benisa and turn inland towards Cometa.*
All year 2HEC ♠ 🅿 ⚍ ⛱ ⚓ 🛒 ⊙ 🅿 ⚒ ⚓ ⚡ P ⚐ 🅿 ⊞ 🌳 lau
➡ ⌀ ⚡S

CAMBRILS TARRAGONA

Playa Cambrils Auda Diputacion 42 ☎ 977 361490
Divided into pitches, lying on both sides of the coast road in
a wooded location.
⤳ *Drive 2km N of the town towards Salou and W of the*
bridge over the river.
15 Mar-12 Oct 11HEC ⋰⋰⋰ ♠ 🅿 ⚍ 🛒 ⊙ 🅿 ⌀ 🛒 ⚡ PS ⚐ ⊞
lau
Prices: ♦430-625 ⇐430-625 ⇐430-625 ▲430-625

CAMPELLO ALICANTE

Costa Blanca c Convento s/n, Nacional 332 Km121.5
☎ 96 5630670
On most level ground scattered with old olive and eucalyptus
trees. The Alicante-Denia railway line runs behind the camp.
⤳ *For access turn off the N332 at Km94.2 next to the big*
petrol station, and drive along a narrow gravel track towards
the sea for 0.5km.
15 Apr-15 Sep 1.1HEC ⋰⋰⋰ ♠ 🅿 ⚍ 🛒 ⊙ 🅿 ⌀ 🛒 ⚓ ▲ ⚡ P
⚐ ⊞ lau ➡ ⚡S

CUNIT TARRAGONA

Mar de Cunit Playa Cunit ☎ 977 674058
A friendly site on level ground overlooking the beach.
Jun-Sep 2HEC ⋰⋰⋰ ⚍ 🅿 ⚍ 🛒 ⊙ 🅿 ⌀ 🛒 ⚡ S ⚐ ⊞ lau
➡ ⊞

DAIMUS VALENCIA

Aventura ctra Playa Daimus ☎ 96 2818330
Picturesque setting in wooded surroundings on a safe, sandy
beach.
⤳ *Access via N332 Alicante-Valencia.*
Mar-Sep 1.8HEC ⚍⚍⚍ ⋰⋰⋰ ♠ 🅿 ⚍ 🛒 ⊙ 🅿 ⌀ 🛒 ⚡ PS ⚐ ⊞
lau ➡ ⚡S
Prices: ♦492-642 pitch 1578-2194

DENIA ALICANTE

Marinas Les Bovetes ☎ 96 5781446
⤳ *For access turn off the N332 in Vergel and drive E on the*
Denia road for 4km . Turn N, cross the P1324, turn right near
the beach and continue for 200m.
Apr-Sep 12.7HEC ⋰⋰⋰ ♠ 🅿 ⚍ 🛒 ⊙ 🅿 ⌀ 🛒 ⚡ S ⚐ ⊞ lau
➡ ⚡P
Prices: ♦412-556 ⇐578-728 ▲433-583

ELCHE ALICANTE

Palmeral Prolongacion Curtidores s/n ☎ 96 5422766
Long narrow site in a palm forest. It has many pitches in
recesses between groups of trees.
Camping Card Compulsory.
⤳ *Off the N340 and continue for 200m. Signposted.*
All year 18HEC ⚍⚍⚍ ⚍ 🅿 ⚍ 🛒 ⊙ 🅿 ⌀ ⚡ P ⚐ ⊞ lau

GUARDAMAR DEL SEGURA ALICANTE

Mare Nostrum ☎ 96 5728073
Partially terraced meadow with some shade from roofing.
⤳ *Turn towards the sea off the N332 Alicante-Cartagena road*
at about Km38.5.
Apr-15 Sep 20HEC ⚭ ⚍ 🅿 ⚍ 🛒 ⊙ 🅿 ⌀ ⚍ 🛒 🛒 ⚡ PS ⚐ ⊞
lau ➡ ✕ ⚡LRS
Prices: ♦535 ⇐535 ⇐535 ▲535

Palm Mar ☎ 96 5728856
Jun-Sep 2HEC ⋰⋰⋰ ♠ 🅿 ⚍ 🛒 ⊙ 🅿 ⌀ ⚡ S ⚐ ⊞ lau ➡ ✕ ⚡P

HOSPITALET DE L'INFANT, L' TARRAGONA

El Templo del Sol Platja del Torn ☎ 977 810486
A new site with modern sanitary installations and good
recreational facilities on a 1.5km long beach. **This is a**
naturist site and only families or holders of an
International Naturism Carnet are allowed.
⤳ *Access via A3 (Barcelona-Valencia), 4km from exit 38*
towards the sea.
1 Jun - 30 Sep 15 Oct - 1 May ⚍⚍⚍ ⚍ 🅿 ⚍ 🛒 ⊙ 🅿 ⌀ 🛒 ⚡
PS ⚐ ⊞ 🌳 lau
Prices: 1850-2550 pitch 1850-2550

Masia Playa de la Almadraba ☎ 77 820588
All year 2.6HEC ⋰⋰⋰ ⚍ 🅿 ⚍ 🛒 ⊙ 🅿 ⌀ 🛒 🛒 ⚡ S ⚐ ⊞ lau

JARACO VALENCIA

San Vincente Playa Xeraio ☎ 96 2888188
Level subdivided site with some trees.
⤳ *On leaving Jaraco at Km332 turn off at Km304 (Valencia-*
Alicante) in the direction of Playa to the site in 3.5km.
All year 5HEC ⋰⋰⋰ ♠ 🅿 ⚍ 🛒 ⊙ 🅿 🛒 ⚡ S ⚐ ⊞ lau ➡ ⚍ ⌀ ⚍
⚡PR
Prices: ♦400-490 ⇐600-665 ▲400-490

MARINA, LA ALICANTE

International la Marina ☎ 96 5419051
A modern site in a wooded setting, 500 metres from a sandy
beach.
⤳ *At Km29 on Alicante-Cartagena road.*
All year 6.3HEC ⚍⚍⚍ ⚍ 🅿 ⚍ 🛒 ⊙ 🅿 ⌀ ⚍ 🛒 🛒 ⚡ PS ⚐ ⊞
lau
Prices: ♦182-642 pitch 599-2033

MIRAMAR PLAYA VALENCIA

Coelius av del Mar ☎ 96 2819574
A fine camp site 500m from the Miramar beach with good,
modern facilities.
⤳ *Access via N430.*
Apr-Sep 1.7HEC ⋰⋰⋰ ⚭ ♠ 🅿 ⚍ 🛒 ⊙ 🅿 ⚍ 🛒 🛒 ⚡ P ⚐ ⊞
lau ➡ ⚍ 🛒 ⌀ ⚡S
Prices: ♦425-575 ⚭425-575 ⇐975-1425 ▲975-1425

MONT-ROIG DEL CAMP TARRAGONA

Marius ☎ 977 810684
Pitches are planted with flowers and shrubs. Separate section
for dog owners.
⤳ *For access, leave the N340, Tarragona to Valencia road, at*
Km1137 and drive through a 4.9m-wide railway underpass
with a clearance of 3.65m, then head towards the beach.
Etr-15 Oct 4HEC ⚍⚍⚍ ⋰⋰⋰ ⚭ ♠ 🅿 ⚍ 🛒 ⊙ 🅿 ⌀ ⚡ S ⚐ ⊞
lau
Prices: ♦500-800 pitch 1400-2300

Playa Montroig ☎ 977 810637
An ideal holiday centre for the whole family with sanitary
installations of the highest quality. Situated on a fine sandy
beach and surrounded by tropical gardens, this award
winning site offers a wide range of sporting and recreational
facilities and is noted for its helpful and friendly staff.
⤳ *Turn left off the N340 at Km1136. Use motorway exit*
37 or 38.
Mar-Oct 35HEC ⚍⚍⚍ ♠ 🅿 ⚍ 🛒 ⊙ 🅿 ⌀ 🛒 ⚡ PS ⚐ ⊞ 🌳
lau
Prices: ♦450-800 pitch 4500

▶ **MORAIRA** ALICANTE

Moraira Camino Paellero 50 ☎ 96 5745249
0.3km from the sea in a pine forest. On several terraces and
divided into pitches.
➲ *1km S on AP1347, turn W and continue up a hill for 500m.*
All year 11HEC ⋮⋮⋮ ⊕ ⋔ ⋒ ⅀ ⅄ ✕ ⊙ ▢ ⊘ ⌸ ⊞ ▲ ⁺ P ⌷ ⊞
lau ➡ ⁺S

▶ **MUCHAMIEL** ALICANTE

Muchamiel ctra Veneteta 7 ☎ 96 5950126
Jul-Sep 1.7HEC ⋮⋮⋮ ⋔ ⋒ ⅀ ⅄ ✕ ⊙ ▢ ⊘ ⁺ P ⌷ ⊞ lau ➡ ⅀ ✕

▶ **NULES** CASTELLÓN

Huertas ☎ 964 675009
Clean, well-kept site, completely divided into pitches. Few
trees but equipped with straw mat roofs. Dancing every
Saturday and Sunday.
➲ *Turn off N340 at Km47.1 and drive towards sea for 5.3km.
Site about 20m from the sea.*
Jun-15 Sep 2HEC ▥▥▥ ⋮⋮⋮ ⊕ ⋔ ⋒ ⅀ ⅄ ✕ ⊙ ▢ ⊘ ⌸ ⌑ ⁺ PS
⌷ ⊞ lau

▶ **OLIVA** VALENCIA

Azul Partida Rabdells ☎ 96 2854106
A well equipped site with direct access to the beach.
Apr-Oct 2.5HEC ⋮⋮⋮ ⋔ ⋒ ⅀ ⅄ ✕ ⊙ ▢ ⊘ ⌸ ⌑ ⁺ S ⌷ ⊞ lau
➡ ⁺PR
Prices: ⋏550 ⇙600 ⇖900 ▲800

Euro Camping ☎ 96 2854098
On a wide sandy beach between orange groves and well
shaded with poplar and eucalyptus trees.
➲ *For access turn off the N332 at Km184.9, 600m from Oliva.
Following signs for camp drive towards the sea for 3.3km. The*
access road has narrow stretches and some blind corners so
beware of oncoming traffic.
All year 4.5HEC ⋮⋮⋮ ⊕ ⋔ ⋒ ⅀ ⅄ ✕ ⊙ ▢ ⊘ ⌸ ⌑ ▲ ⁺ S ⌷ ⊞ lau
➡ ⁺R

See advertisement under Colour Section

Ferienplatz Olé ☎ 96 2851180
An extensive site with some pitches amongst dunes.
➲ *Turn off the N332 at Km209.9 about 5km S of Oliva. In
about 3km continue to site on access road partially asphalt,
through an orchard.*
Apr-Sep 46HEC ⋮⋮⋮ ⋔ ⋒ ⅀ ⅄ ✕ ⊙ ▢ ⊘ ⌸ ⁺ S ⌷ ⊞ lau ➡ ⊞
Prices: ⋏615 ⇙615 ⇖899 ▲615

Kiko Playa de Oliva ☎ 96 2850905
Family holiday camp, divided into pitches, lying between
marshland and vineyard. The sea can be reached by crossing
a dyke and there are sunshade roofs.
➲ *Access from motorway A7 exit 61 and continue via CN332
towards Oliva.*
All year 4HEC ⋮⋮⋮ ⊕ ⋔ ⋒ ⅀ ⅄ ✕ ⊙ ▢ ⊘ ⌸ ⌑ ⁺ S ⌷ ⊞ lau ➡
⁺LPR ⊞
Prices: ⋏405-675 pitch 1020-2300

▶ **OROPESA DEL MAR** CASTELLÓN

Didota av de la Didota ☎ 964 319551
Mar-Oct 1.7HEC ⊕ ⋔ ⋒ ⅀ ⅄ ✕ ⊙ ▢ ⊘ ⌸ ⌑ ⁺ P ⌷ ⊞ lau ➡
⁺S

▶ **PEÑISCOLA** CASTELLÓN

Camping Eden ☎ 964 480562
All year 4HEC ▥▥▥ ⋔ ⋒ ⅀ ⅄ ✕ ⊙ ▢ ⊘ ⌑ ⁺ PRS ⌷ ⊞ lau ➡
⋒ ⅄ ✕
Prices: pitch 900-3000 (incl 2 persons)

▶ PUEBLA DE FARNALS VALENCIA

Brasa ☎ 96 1460388
Level meadowland site with poplars near village centre.
⮑ *For access leave motorway Barcelona-Valencia at exit 3,*
towards Playa Puebla de Farnals.
All year 3.9HEC ⚏ 👤 🏕 🍴 ✕ ⊙ 🅿 ⌀ ♨ 🚐 ⚲ PS 🏧 ⊞ lau
➡ 🛁

▶ RODA DE BERÁ TARRAGONA

Playa Bara ☎ 977 802701
Extensive site well kept and laid out in terraces. Separated
from the beautifully situated beach by railway line with an
underpass.
⮑ *For accesss turn off the N340 near the Arco de Berá*
(triumphant arch) and drive towards the sea for about 1.5 km.
10 Mar-Sep 14.5HEC ⚏ ∷∵ 👤 🏕 🛍 🍴 ✕ ⊙ 🅿 ⌀ ♨ 🚐 ⚲ P
🏧 ⊞ lau
Prices: ♠460-920 ⟵920 🚐920 🛆920

See advertisement under Colour Section

▶ SALOU TARRAGONA

Cambrils Park ☎ 977 351031
May-Sep 17HEC ⚏ 👤 🏕 🛍 🍴 ✕ ⊙ 🅿 ⌀ ⚲ P 🏧 ⊞ ⊞ 🏊 lau
➡ ⚲S
Prices: ♠404-674 pitch 2119-3959

Pineda de Salou Playa de la Pineda ☎ 977 372176
A well equipped site close to the sea.
⮑ *At Km5 on the Tarragona-Salou road.*
20 Jun-Aug 4HEC ⚏ ♠ 🏕 🛍 🍴 ✕ ⊙ 🅿 ⌀ ♨ 🚐 ⚲ P 🏧 ⊞
lau ➡ 🛍 🍴 ✕ ♨ ⚲S

Sanguli ☎ 977 381641
A large, family site in pleasant wooded surroundings, 50mtrs
from the beach, with extensive sports and entertainment
facilities.
⮑ *3km from Port Aventura on SW outskirts, 50mtrs inland*
from coast road to Cambrils
19 Mar-Oct 23HEC ⚏ ∷∵ ♠ 🏕 🛍 🍴 ✕ ⊙ 🅿 ⌀ 🚐 ⚲
PRS 🏧 ⊞ lau
Prices: ♠674-674 pitch 2247-4066
See advertisement under Colour section.

Siesta ☎ 977 380852
Divided into pitches and planted with young deciduous trees
and old olive trees. Sunshade roofs.
⮑ *If approaching from Tarragona, turn right off the main*
road on outskirts of Salou and drive a further 150mtrs to the
camp. The site is between the railway and road 0.4km from
the sea.
16 Mar-3 Nov 6HEC ∷∵ ♠ 🏕 🛍 🍴 ✕ ⊙ 🅿 ⌀ 🚐 ⚲ P 🏧 ⊞
lau ➡ ♨ ⚲S
Prices: ♠546-744 ⟵546-744 🚐546-744 🛆546-744

Union c Pompeu Fabra 37 ☎ 977 384816
A well equipped site in wooded surroundings, 350mtrs from
the sea.
⮑ *On southern outskirts, 1km from the Port Aventura theme*
park.
Apr-Sep 3.5HEC ⚏ 👤 🏕 🛍 🍴 ✕ ⊙ 🅿 ⌀ ⚲ P 🏧 ⊞ 🏊 lau
➡ ⚲S

▶ SANTA OLIVA TARRAGONA

Santa Oliva Jaume Balmes 122 ☎ 977 661252
⮑ *At Km3 on Vendrell-Santa Oliva road.*
All year 2HEC ∷∵ ♠ 🏕 🛍 🍴 ✕ ⊙ 🅿 ⌀ ♨ ⚲ P 🏧 ⊞ lau ➡ 🛍 ✕
Prices: ♠500-550 ⟵500-550 🚐500-550 🛆500-550

▶ TAMARIT TARRAGONA

Caledonia ☎ 77 650098
A well appointed site in wooded surroundings, 800mtrs from
the sea.
⮑ *At Km1172 on N340.*
18 Jun-30 Sept 3.5HEC ∷∵ 🛶 👤 🏕 🛍 🍴 ✕ ⊙ 🅿 ⌀ 🚐 ⚲ P 🏧
⊞ lau ➡ ⚲S
Prices: ♠481-588 🚐481-588 🛆481-588

Trillas Platja Tamarit ☎ 977 650249
About 50mtrs from the sea. On several terraces planted with
olive trees next to a farm.
⮑ *For access, turn off the N340 at Km1.172, about 8km N of*
Tarragona. Follow road and cross a narrow railway bridge.
(Beware of oncoming traffic).
22 Mar-Sep 4.5HEC ⚏ ♠ 🏕 🛍 🍴 ✕ ⊙ 🅿 ⌀ ⚲ S 🏧 ⊞ lau ➡ ♨
Prices: ♠440-575 pitch 880-1150
See advertisement under Colour Section

▶ TARRAGONA TARRAGONA

Gaya El Cattlar ☎ 977 653070
On level grassland with single poplars on the River Gaya.
⮑ *Turn N inland at Km259.7 off the N340 (Barcelona-*
Tarragona). Continue on metalled road in 7.5km via T202 and
T203 to just before the Gaia river bridge at El Cattlar. To site
via unmade road to right in 0.2km.
May-Sep 1HEC ∷∵ ♠ 🏕 🍴 ✕ ⊙ 🅿 ⌀ ⚲ PR 🏧 ⊞ lau

Tamarit-Park Platja Tamarit ☎ 977 650128
Well-kept site at the sea beneath Tamarit Castle. One section
lies under tall shady trees, and a new section lies in a meadow
with some trees.
⮑ *Turn off N340 and Km259.3 about 8km N of Tarragona*
and drive 800mtrs seaward along a narrow track. Contd.

All year 15HEC ⟨symbols⟩ lau
Prices: ⚡625-825 pitch 2300-2800

▶ **TORREBLANCA** CASTELLÓN

Mon Rossi Carrasa Mon Rossi, Torrenostra ☎ 964 425096
All year 0.8HEC ⟨symbols⟩
Prices: ⚡500 ⟨symbol⟩500 ⟨symbol⟩550 ▲450-500

▶ **VALENCIA** VALENCIA

Saler ☎ 96 1830023
Amongst pines providing shade with its own entrance to
sandy beach in 300mtrs. The site has recently undergone
many improvements and has modern sanitary and
recreational facilities.
⟳ *Access from Valencia via coastal road towards Cullera as far
as El Saler, then turn left at SE end of village and turn right.*
All year 80HEC ⟨symbols⟩ LS
Prices: ⚡535-575 ⟨symbol⟩585-630 ⟨symbol⟩585-630 ▲390-420

▶ **VENDRELL, EL** TARRAGONA

Franca's ☎ 77 680725
Slopes gently towards the sea, between the beach and the
railway line which separates the two sections. These are
connected by a pedestrian underpass.
⟳ *Lies about 100m away from the N340 on the seaward side
at Km273.*
Apr-Sep 3.5HEC ⟨symbols⟩ lau

San Salvador av Palfuriana 68 ☎ 77 680804
On two large grassy terraces and has some sunshade roofs.
Near the sea in the centre of the town.
⟳ *Access via A7 exit 31 (Barcelona-Tarragona). Site in centre
of Comarruga-Sant Salvador.*
4 Apr-Sep 3HEC ⟨symbols⟩ lau

Vendrell ☎ 77 694009
A large family site in a pleasant wooded location close to the
beach.
26 Mar-Sep 7HEC ⟨symbols⟩ lau
Prices: ⚡134-670 ⟨symbol⟩670 ⟨symbol⟩670 ▲670

▶ **VERGEL** ALICANTE

Llanos ☎ 96 6474488
In a field next to an orange grove and shaded by tall trees.
⟳ *Turn off N332 between Km203 and Km204 and continue
on gravel road for 200m.*
Jun-15 Sep 2HEC ⟨symbols⟩

▶ **VILANOVA DE PRADES** TARRAGONA

Serra de Prades Sant Antoni ☎ 977 869050
A fine site close to the beach and within easy reach of
Barcelona and the Port Aventura theme park.
All year 50HEC ⟨symbols⟩ lau
Prices: ⚡615 ⟨symbol⟩615 ⟨symbol⟩615 ▲615

▶ **VILLAJOYOSA** ALICANTE

Camping la Cala-Garoa Cala de Finestrat ☎ 96 5851461
On level ground on the seaward side of the N332. Large
pitches, asphalt interior roads. Different types of trees
provide shade.
⟳ *On N332 at Km143.*
All year 3.3HEC ⟨symbols⟩ lau
Prices: pitch 1525-1900

Hércules ☎ 96 5891343
Section near sea is well shaded. Asphalt interior road,
separate section for caravans with numbered pitches.
⟳ *Turn E off N332 near Km141 then turn S.*
All year 6.3HEC ⟨symbols⟩ lau
Prices: ⚡605 ⟨symbol⟩605 ⟨symbol⟩669 ▲605

Sertorium N332.PK 141 ☎ 96 5891599
On level ground on the seaward side of the N332. Small
stony beach, suitable for non-swimmers.
⟳ *On N332 at Km141.*
All year 69HEC ⟨symbols⟩ PS lau

▶ **VINAROZ** CASTELLÓN

Garoa-Sol de Riu Playa ☎ 964 454917
In wooded surroundings close to the sea with good, modern
facilities.
All year 5.5HEC ⟨symbols⟩ lau
Prices: ⚡450 pitch 1650

NORTH COAST

The region varies from the beaches of the Cantabrian coast
to mountain gorges, and attracts sun-lovers as well as
hikers, fishermen and outdoor enthusiasts. Of the two
coastal provinces, Cantabria has dairy farms and a huge
hunting reserve; its capital, Santander, has a cathedral and
spectacular beaches, with superb views from the
Magdalene peninsular. The Altamira caves, with wall-
paintings, are nearby. Asturias has a more rugged
countryside. Its capital, Oviedo, is a cathedral city with fine
buildings in the old quarter.
On the Pilgrim Way to Compostela lies Lugo, with its
cathedral and picturesque old quarter of ancient streets and
wrought-iron balconies. Walk around the city's perimeter
on top of encircling walls dating from Roman times.
Famous in both Spanish and British history is Corunna.
Now a bustling seaside resort and good touring centre, this
old town saw the departure of the ill-fated Spanish Armada
and has the tomb of Sir John Moore, killed in the
Napoleonic Wars. There is also a Roman lighthouse. North
east of Corunna is Ferrol, Franco's birthplace.

▶ **BARREIROS** LUGO

Gaivota Playa de Benquerencia ☎ 982 124451
Site leads down to a sandy beach with windsurfing. The main
buildings have been designed and built by the owner, who is
a painter.
15 Jun-15 Sep 1HEC ⟨symbols⟩ lau
Prices: ⚡475 ⟨symbol⟩475 ⟨symbol⟩550 ▲425

▶ **BERGONDO** LA CORUÑA

Santa Marta ☎ 981 795826
Apr-Sept 2.8HEC ⟨symbols⟩ lau
Prices: ⚡590 ⟨symbol⟩590 ⟨symbol⟩590 ▲590

▶ **CADAVEDO** ASTURIAS

Regalina ctra de la Playa ☎ 98 5645056
A modern site with good facilities noted for its mountain
and sea views.
⟳ *On N632 between Luarca and Avilés.*
Jun-12 Oct 1HEC ⟨symbols⟩ lau
Prices: ⚡440 ⟨symbol⟩440 ⟨symbol⟩550 ▲465

CÓBRECES CANTABRIA

Cóbreces Playa de Cóbreces ☎ 942 725120
➲ *50m from the beach.*
15 Jun-15 Sep 1.5HEC ⬛ 🌿 🚻 🛁 ⛽ ⊙ ⊘ ⌀ ⊀ S ⊡ lau
Prices: ♦535 ➡513 ⊞513 Å513

COMILLAS CANTABRIA

Comillas ctra M-Noriga ☎ 94242 720074
Level grassland site to the right of the road to the beach.
➲ *E on C6316 at Km23.*
Jun-Sep 3HEC ⬛ 🌿 🚻 🛁 🛒 ⛽ ✗ ⊙ ⊘ ⌀ ⊀ S ⊡ ⊞ lau ➡ ✗
Prices: ♦500 pitch 1600

CUDILLERO ASTURIAS

Amuravela El Pito ☎ 985 590995
Etr & Jun-15 Sep 2.8HEC ⬛ 🌿 🚻 🛁 🛒 ⛽ ✗ ⊙ ⊘ ⌀ ⊞ ⊞ Å ⊀ P
⊡ ⊞ lau ➡ 🍴 ⊀RS

FOZ LUGO

San Rafael Playa de Peizas ☎ 982 132218
May-15 Sep 1.5HEC ⬛ 🌿 🚻 🛁 🛒 ⛽ ✗ ⊙ ⊘ ⌀ ⊞ Å ⊀ S ⊡ ⊞
lau ➡ ⊀PRS
Prices: ♦485 ➡495 ⊞595 Å495

FRANCA, LA ASTURIAS

Las Hortensais Playa de la Franca ☎ 98 5412145
A well maintained site with good facilities beside the La
Franca Beach.
Jun-Sep 28HEC ⬛ 🌿 🚻 🛁 🛒 ⛽ ✗ ⊙ ⊘ ⌀ ⊀ RS ⊡ ⊞ lau ➡ 🍴
Prices: ♦525 ➡495 ⊞675 Å520

ISLARES CANTABRIA

Playa Arenillas ☎ 942 863152
Well equipped site in meadowland with some pine trees,
100mtrs from the beach.
➲ *On N634 at Km155.8 turn N and continue 100mtrs. The
entrance is rather steep.*
Apr-Sep 3HEC ⬛ 🌿 🚻 🛁 🛒 ⛽ ✗ ⊙ ⊘ ⌀ Å ⊡ ⊞ ⊘ lau ➡ ⊀S
Prices: ♦588 pitch 1445

LAREDO CANTABRIA

Carlos V pl de Carlos V ☎ 942 605593
Camp surrounded by walls and buildings on W outskirts of
Laredo.
➲ *Turn off N634 at Km171.6 into an avenue and drive
towards the sea. Turn left before reaching the beach and drive
around the roundabout on the plaza Carlos V.*
1 Mar-15 Oct 10HEC ⬛ 🌿 🚻 🛁 🛒 ⛽ ✗ ⊙ ⊘ ⌀ 🍴 ⊞ ⊡ ⊞ lau
➡ ✗ ⊀S
ⵊPrices: ♦500 ⊞500 Å450

LLANES ASTURIAS

Barcenas Antigua CN 634 ☎ 98 5402887
100mtrs from the town centre and beaches beside the
Carrocedo River.
➲ *SW of town beyond the hospital.*
Jun-Sep 2.2HEC ⬛ 🌿 🚻 🛁 🛒 ⛽ ✗ ⊙ ⊘ ⌀ 🛒 Å ⊡ ⊞ lau ➡ ✗
🍴 ⊀S
Prices: ♦782-508 ➡428-455 ⊞642-696

Brao ☎ 98 5400014
A terraced site surrounded by trees with magnificent
mountain and sea views
➲ *5.5km from the sea. At Km96.2 on N634 turn N for 1.8km
and turn towards Cue for 200m.*
Jun-Sep 27HEC ⬛ 🌿 🚻 🛁 🛒 ✗ ⊙ ⊘ ⌀ ⊀ PRS ⊡ ⊞ lau

Palacio de Garaña ☎ 98 5410075

Situated in the grounds of the former Palace of the Marquis
of Argüelles, the site is enclosed by stone walls and has good
facilities.
1 May-15 Sept 2.8HEC ⬛ 🌿 🚻 🛁 🛒 ✗ ⊙ ⊘ ⌀ ⊞ ⊞ ⊀ PS
⊡ ⊞ lau
Prices: ♦595 ➡575 ⊞790 Å615

LUARCA ASTURIAS

Cantiles ☎ 98 5640938
Meadowland beautifully situated high above the cliffs with
little shade from bushes. Footpath to bay 70mtrs below.
➲ *At Km308.5 turn off the N634 from Oviedo, turn towards
Faro de Luarca beyond the Firestone filling station. In Villar de
Luarca turn right and onwards 1km to site.*
All year 2.3HEC ⬛ 🌿 🚻 🛁 🛒 ✗ ⊙ ⊘ ⌀ ⊞ ⊞ ⊡ ⊞ lau ➡ ✗
⊀PS ⊞
Prices: ♦450 pitch 450-525

MOTRICO (MUTRIKU) GUIPÚZCOA

Aitzeta ☎ 943 603356
On two sloping meadows, partially terraced. Lovely view of
the sea 1km away.
➲ *0.5km NE on C6212 turn at KmSS56.1.*
All year 1.5HEC ⬛ 🌿 🚻 🛁 🛒 ✗ ⊙ ⊘ ⌀ ⊀ PS ⊡ ⊞ lau ➡ ✗

NOJA CANTABRIA

Los Molinos ctra al Faro ☎ 942 630426
In pleasant surroundings close to the Esmerald Coast with its
fine beaches. Various leisure and sports activities.
Jul-Aug 18HEC ⬛ 🌿 🚻 🛁 🛒 ✗ ⊙ ⊘ ⌀ ⊀ P ⊡ ⊞ lau
➡ ⊀S
Prices: ♦480-640 pitch 965-1390

Playa Joyel Playa de Ris ☎ 42 630081
On a level meadow on a peninsula with direct access to the
beach.
➲ *Between Laredo and Solares.*
Etr-Sep 25HEC ⬛ 🌿 🚻 🛁 🛒 ✗ ⊙ ⊘ ⌀ ⊀ PS ⊡ ⊞ ⊘ lau
➡ 🍴

Prices: ♦450-715 pitch 1475-1575

See advertisement under Colour Section

ORIO GUIPÚZCOA

CM Playa de Orio ☎ 943 834801
On two flat terraces along cliffs and surrounded by hedges.
➲ *Turn off the N634 San Sebastian-Bilbao road at about
Km12.5 in Orio. Shortly before the bridge over the River Orio
turn towards the sea and continue for 1.5km.*
Closed Nov & Dec 5.4HEC ⬛ 🌿 🚻 🛁 🛒 ✗ ⊙ ⊘ ⌀ ⊀ P ⊡
⊞ ⊘ lau ➡ ⊀RS

PECHÓN CANTABRIA

Arenas ☎ 942 717188
On numerous terraces between rocks, reaching down to the
sea.
➲ *Turn off N634 E of Unquera at Km74 towards sea and take
road towards S.*
Jun-Sep 10HEC ⬛ 🌿 🚻 🛁 🛒 ✗ ⊙ ⊘ ⌀ ⊞ ⊀ LRS ⊡ ⊞ lau

PERLORA-CANDAS ASTURIAS

Perlora ☎ 98 5870048
On top of a large hill on a peninsula with a few terraced
pitches.
➲ *Access 7km W of Gijon, turn off N632 in direction Luanco
and continue for 5km.*
All year 1.4HEC ⬛ 🌿 🚻 🛁 🛒 ✗ ⊙ ⊘ ⌀ ⊀ S ⊡ ⊞ lau
➡ 🍴

⟩ **REINANTE** LUGO

Reinante ☎ 982 134005
Longish site beyond a range of dunes on lovely sandy beach.
⮕ *On N634 at Km391.7.*
All year 2.2HEC ⛺ ♦ ⋔ ⛴ ⚥ ♀ ✕ ⊙ ▢ ∅ ⊞ ⛽ ⚓ ⟍ S 🅰 ⊞ lau
Prices: ♦425 ➡375 ⛺400 ▲400-475

⟩ **SAN SEBASTIAN (DONOSTIA)** GUIPÚZCOA

⟩ At **IGUELDO**

Garoa Camping Igueldo ☎ 943 214502
Terraced site on Monte Igualdo divided by hedges.
⮕ *Follow signs Monte Igualdo from town, and beach road, about 4.5km.*
All year 3HEC ⛺ ◑ ⋔ ⛴ ⚥ ✕ ⊙ ▢ ∅ 🅰 ⊞ lau
Prices: pitch 2750-3100 (incl 3 persons)

⟩ **SANTIAGO DE COMPOSTELA** LA CORUÑA

As Cancelas r do 25 de Xulls 35 ☎ 981 580266
All year 1.8HEC ⛺ ♦ ⋔ ⛴ ⚥ ✕ ⊙ ▢ ∅ ⚓ ⛽ ▲ ⟍ P 🅰 ⊞
lau

⟩ **SANTILLANA DEL MAR** CANTABRIA

Santillana ☎ 942 818250
Slightly sloping meadow with bushes on a hillock within the area of a restaurant adjoining a swimming pool.
⮕ *Access from Santander via C6316 turn off shortly after the Santillana sign and continue up the hill.*
All year 70HEC ⛺ ♦ ⋔ ⛴ ⚥ ✕ ⊙ ▢ ∅ ⚓ ⛽ ▲ ⟍ P 🅰 ⊞
lau ♦ ⟍RS
Prices: ♦575-675 ⛺650-750 ▲550-650

⟩ **VALDOVIÑO** LA CORUÑA

Valdoviño ctra Ferrol-Cederia ☎ 981 487076
Six gently sloping fields partly in shade. Located behind Cafeteria Andy and block of flats with several villas beyond.
⮕ *Turn off the C646 towards Cedeira seawards and continue 700m to site.*
All year 2HEC ⛺ ♦ ⋔ ⛴ ⚥ ✕ ⊙ ▢ ∅ ⚓ ⛽ ⊞ lau ♦
⟍LPRS
Prices: ♦600 ➡645 ⛺665 ▲645

⟩ **VEGA DE LIÉBANA** CANTABRIA

Molino ☎ 942 736009
In an orchard by river about 300m outside town.
Jun-Sep 1HEC ⛺ ♦ ⋔ ⛴ ⚥ ✕ ⊙ ▢ ∅ ⟍ PR 🅰 ⊞ lau ♦ ✕

⟩ **VIDIAGO** ASTURIAS

Paz Playa de Vidiago ☎ 98 5411012
⮕ *From N634 turn off at Km292 between Buelna and Vidiago towards the sea.*
Jun-17 Sep 10HEC ⛺ ◐ ⛵ ⋔ ⛴ ⚥ ✕ ⊙ ▢ ∅ ⟍ S 🅰 ⊞ lau
♦ ⚒

⟩ **VIVEIRO** LUGO

Vivero ☎ 982 560004
In tall woodland near beach road and sea.
⮕ *Turn off the C642 Barreois-Ortueire road at Km443.1 and follow signs.*
Jun-Sep 1.2HEC ⛺ ♦ ⋔ ⛴ ⊙ ▢ ∅ 🅰 ⊞ lau ♦ ✕ ⟍S
Prices: ♦475 ➡475 ⛺600 ▲475

⟩ **ZARAUZ (ZARAUTZ)** GUIPÚZCOA

Talai Mendi ☎ 943 830042
In meadowland on hillside divided by interior roads without shade. 0.5km from the sea.
⮕ *On outskirts of town at FIRESTONE filling station at Km17.5 on N634 turn towards the sea and continue for 350m along narrow asphalt road.*

24 Jun-10 Sep 38HEC ⛺ ◑ ⋔ ⛴ ⚥ ✕ ⊙ ▢ ∅ ⟍ S 🅰 ⊞
Prices: ♦470 pitch 2595

Zarauz ☎ 943 831238
Site with terraces separated by hedges.
⮕ *1.8km from the N634 San Sebastian-Bilbao road. Asphalt access road from Km15.5.*
All year 4.2HEC ⛺ ◑ ⋔ ⛴ ⚥ ✕ ⊙ ▢ ∅ ▲ 🅰 ⊞ lau ♦ ⟍PS
Prices: ♦540 ➡540 ⛺565 ▲565

NORTH EAST

Medieval villages, green valleys, forests, and arid gorges are some of this region's varied attractions.
Tranquil Burgos, with its pleasant river setting and old centre, was Franco's capital during the Civil War. The principal city of Castille has a magnificent Gothic cathedral which reflects its importance on the Pilgrim Way to Compostela and contains the tomb of the legendary El Cid. The city of Saragossa lies in a fertile pocket. Its basilica contains a national shrine to the Virgin of the Pillar. The province of the same name contains Spain's largest natural inland lake and is a great attraction for ornithologists.
Beautiful scenery surrounds the pleasant cathedral city of Huesca. Nearby Loarre Castle is a wonderful medieval fortress; superb views can be had from its rocky heights and the amazing grotto site of the Monastery of San Juan de la Peña.
Lush valleys and Pyrennean crags are just two faces of Navarre. Its ancient capital, Pamplona, is notorious for the Running of the Bulls each morning during its week-long fiesta celebrations in July. Wine lovers will be attracted to La Rioja - an area renowned for its fine wines.

⟩ **ARANDA DE DUERO** BURGOS

Costajàn ☎ 947 502070
In a wooded setting with good facilities.
⮕ *Turn off N1 (Burgos-Madrid) at Km162.1 N of town.*
All year 1.8HEC ⠸ ◑ ⋔ ⛴ ⚥ ✕ ⊙ ▢ ∅ ⚓ ⛽ ⟍ P 🅰 ⊞ lau
♦ ⛴ ⚥ ✕ ⚒ ⟍LR
Prices: ♦518-572 ➡518-572 ⛺518-572 ▲518-572

⟩ **BELLVER DE CERDANYA** LLEIDA

Solana del Segre ☎ 973 510310
A well equipped site on the River Segre, known for its trout fishing.
⮕ *Off N260.*
Closed 16-30 Nov 6.5HEC ⛺ ♦ ⋔ ⛴ ⚥ ✕ ⊙ ▢ ∅ ⚒ ⚓ ⟍
PR 🅰 ⊞ lau ♦ ⟍L

⟩ **BIESCAS** HUESCA

Edelweiss ☎ 974 485084
In meadow with deciduous trees on a hill in a pleasant situation.
⮕ *Turn right off C138 at Km97.*
15 Jun-15 Sep 30HEC ⛺ ♦ ⋔ ⛴ ⚥ ✕ ⊙ ▢ ∅ 🅰 ⊞ lau
♦ ⟍PR
Prices: ♦650 ➡650 ⛺650 ▲650

⟩ **BONANSA** HUESCA

Baliera Cruce ctra Castejon Desos ☎ 974 554016
A well equipped site in a beautiful Pyrenean location on the bank of a river.
⮕ *At Km365.5 on N260.*
All year 5HEC ⛺ ♦ ⋔ ⛴ ⚥ ✕ ⊙ ▢ ∅ ⚒ ⚓ ⟍ LPR 🅰 ⊞ lau
Prices: ♦600 ➡600 ⛺600 ▲600

▶ BORDETA, LA LLEIDA

Bedurá-Park ☎ 73 648293
A terraced site in the Aran Valley offering spectacular views over the surrounding mountains. The site, in wooded surroundings, offers all modern facilities and a wide variety of sporting opportunities.
➲ *Access via N230 Km174.4.*
1 Jun-30 Sep 3.5HEC ⸬⸬⸬ ✦ ⋔ ⛴ ⛱ ✗ ⊙ 🖭 ⌀ 🏕 🚽 ⚡ LPR
🅿 ⊞ ⚲ lau
Prices: 🛉590 pitch 1100-1550

Prado Verde ☎ 973 647172
Level meadowland on River Garona with sparse trees and sheltered by high hedges from traffic noise.
➲ *On the N230, Puente de Rey (French border)-Lleida road, at Km199 behind PIRELLI GENERAL filling station.*
All year 1.7HEC ⸬⸬⸬ ✦ ⋔ ⛴ ⛱ ✗ ⊙ 🖭 ⌀ 🏕 ⚡ LPR 🅿 ⊞ lau
Prices: 🛉550-570 ➡550-570 🚐550-570 🛆550-570

▶ CALATAYUD ZARAGOZA

Calatayud ctra Madrid-Barcelona ☎ 976 880592
15 Mar-15 Oct 1.7HEC ⸬⸬⸬ ⚲ ⋔ ⛴ ⛱ ✗ ⊙ 🖭 ⌀ ⚡ 🅿 🅿 ⊞
lau ✦ ✗

▶ CASTAÑARES DE RIOJA LA RIOJA

Rioja ctra Haro a Sto Domingo de la, Calzada ☎ 941 300174
A well appointed site on the banks of the River Oja with a private beach.
21 Jun-21 Sep 10HEC ⸬⸬⸬ ⚭ ✦ ⋔ ⛴ ⛱ ✗ ⊙ 🖭 ⌀ ⚡ PR 🅿 ⊞
lau ✦ ⚡PR

▶ ESPOT LLEIDA

Sol I Neu ctra d'Espot ☎ 973 624001
A peaceful site in a beautiful mountain setting with good, modern facilities. Organised Land Rover excursions available.
Jun-Sep 1.5HEC ⸬⸬⸬ ✦ ⋔ ⛴ ⛱ ✗ ⊙ 🖭 ⌀ ⚡ PR 🅿 ⊞ lau ✦ ✗
⚡L
Prices: 🛉575 🚐575 🛆575

▶ ESTELLA NAVARRA

Lizarra Paraje de Ordoiz ☎ 948 551733
All year 40HEC ⸬⸬⸬ ⚲ ⋔ ⛴ ⛱ ✗ ⊙ 🖭 ⌀ 🚐 ⚡ 🛆 🅿 ⊞ lau
Prices: 🛉535 pitch 1500

▶ GUINGUETA, LA LLEIDA

Vall d'Aneu ☎ 973 626390
In meadowland on rising ground on both sides of the road, partially in shade. No shade on terrace between road and lake.
➲ *On outskirts of town near the by-pass, C147.*
May-Sep 0.5HEC ⸬⸬⸬ ✦ ⋔ ⛱ ✗ ⊙ 🖭 ⚡ 🅿 ⊞ lau ✦ ⛴ ⛱ ✗
⌀ ⛺ ⚡LR
Prices: 🛉525 ➡525 🚐525 🛆525

▶ HECHO HUESCA

Selva de Osa Selva de Osa ☎ 974 375168
On meadowland, partly covered with pines and deciduous trees and between a dirt track and a mountain stream.
➲ *12.5km NE towards Espata.*
15 Jun-15 Sep 2HEC ⸬⸬⸬ ⚲ ⋔ ⛴ ⛱ ✗ ⊙ 🖭 ⌀ ⚡ R 🅿 ⊞ lau

▶ HUESCA HUESCA

San Jorge Ricardo del Arco ☎ 974 227416
Site with sports field surrounded by high walls. Subdivided by hedges, sparse woodland.
➲ *From town centre, about 1.5km along M123 towards Zaragoza direction and follow signs.*
Apr-15 Oct 0.7HEC ⸬⸬⸬ ⚲ ⋔ ⛱ ✗ ⊙ ⚡ 🅿 ⊞ lau ✦ ⛴ ⌀
Prices: 🛉535 🚐535 🛆535

▶ JACA HUESCA

At GUASA

Peña Oroel ctra Jaca-Sabiñanigo ☎ 974 360215
Grassland with rows of high poplars.
➲ *At Km13.8 of the C134 Jaca-Sabiñanigo road.*
15 Jun-15 Sep 50HEC ⸬⸬⸬ ✦ ⋔ ⛴ ⛱ ✗ ⊙ 🖭 ⌀
⚡ 🅿 ⊞ lau
Prices: 🛉650 ➡650 🚐650 🛆650

▶ LABUERDA HUESCA

Peña Montañesa ctra Aínsa-Bielsa ☎ 974 500730
A well equipped family site in a wooded location near the entrance to the Ordesa and Monte Perdido National Park.
All year 7HEC ⸬⸬⸬ ✦ ⋔ ⛴ ⛱ ✗ ⊙ 🖭 ⌀ 🏕 🚐 ⚡ PR 🅿 ⊞ lau
✦ ⚡R
Prices: 🛉660 pitch 1950

▶ MENDIGORRIA NAVARRA

El Molino ctra N111 ☎ 948 340604
All year 15HEC ⸬⸬⸬ ✦ ⋔ ⛴ ⛱ ✗ ⊙ 🖭 ⌀ 🏕 🚐 🛆 ⚡ PR 🅿 ⊞
lau ✦ ⚰ ⚡R

▶ NÁJERA LA RIOJA

Ruedo ps San Julian 24 ☎ 941 360102
Amongst poplars and the area of the bullring, almost no shade.
➲ *Turn off the N120 Logroño-Burgos road in Nájera and then continue along the river banks just before the stone bridge across the River Majerilla, then turn left.*
Apr-10 Oct 0.5HEC ⸬⸬⸬ ⚲ ⋔ ⛴ ⛱ ✗ ⊙ 🖭 ⌀ 🅿 ⊞ lau
✦ ⚡PR
Prices: 🛉575 ➡525 🚐575 🛆575

▶ NUEVALOS ZARAGOZA

Lago Park ctra Alhama de Aragón-Nuevalos ☎ 976 849038
In a pleasant location, 100mtrs from the Laguna de la Tranquera.
➲ *NE towards Alhama de Aragon.*
Apr-Sep 3HEC ⸬⸬⸬ ⚭ ✦ ⋔ ⛴ ⛱ ✗ ⊙ 🖭 ⌀ 🏕 ⚡ 🅿 ⊞ lau
✦ ⚡LR
Prices: 🛉650 ➡700 🚐700 🛆700

▶ ORICAIN NAVARRA

Ezcaba ctra Francia-Irun km7 ☎ 948 331665
Gently sloping meadowland and a few terraces on a flat topped hill.
➲ *N of Pamplona. Turn off N121 at Km7.3 and drive towards Berriosuso. Turn right and drive uphill after crossing the bridge over the River Ulzama.*
All year 2HEC ⸬⸬⸬ ⚲ ⋔ ⛴ ⛱ ✗ ⊙ 🖭 ⌀ ⚰ 🛆 ⚡ PR 🅿 ⊞ ✦
⚡R

▶ PANCORBO BURGOS

Desfiladero ☎ 947 354027
A well appointed site close to the river.
➲ *Off N1 at Km305.2.*
All year 13HEC ⸬⸬⸬ ⚭ ⚲ ⋔ ⛱ ✗ ⊙ 🖭 🚐 ⚡ 🅿 🅿 ⊞ lau
✦ ⛴ ⌀ ⚡R
Prices: 🛉455 ➡482 🚐450 🛆482

▶ PUEBLA DE CASTRO, LA HUESCA

Lago de Barasona crta Nacional 123 ☎ 974 545148
A well equipped, terraced site in a beautiful setting beside the lake and backed by mountains.
Apr-Sep 3HEC ⸬⸬⸬ ⚲ ⋔ ⛴ ⛱ ✗ ⊙ 🖭 ⌀ 🏕 🚐 ⚡ LP
🅿 ⊞ lau
Prices: 🛉481-631 ➡535-722 🚐535-722 🛆535-722

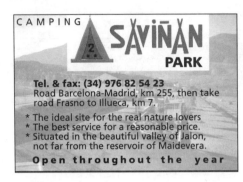

CAMPING

SAVIÑAN PARK

Tel. & fax: (34) 976 82 54 23
Road Barcelona-Madrid, km 255, then take
road Frasno to Illueca, km 7.

* The ideal site for the real nature lovers
* The best service for a reasonable price.
* Situated in the beautiful valley of Jalon,
  not far from the reservoir of Maidevera.

Open throughout the year

Another kind of quality of life

CAMPING LOS CAMEROS
(LA RIOJA)

BILBAO
LOGROÑO
CAMPING "LOS CAMEROS"
ZARAGOZA
SORIA
LERIDA
MADRID
BARCELONA
VALENCIA

Open throughout the year.
Genuine hunting district of the Cameros within
the national park of the Sierra Cebollera in the
Iberian mountain range.
**Activities: Hunting, fishing, climbing, cross-
country skiing, walking, hiking, taking pictures of
the wild animal world, rafting, canoeing, equitation
...according to the season.**

Ctra. La Virgen, km. 3
E-26125 Villoslada de Cameros
(La Rioja)
Tel. (34) 941 74 70 21
941 74 70 81
Fax (34) 941 74 70 91

— CAMPING LOS CAMEROS

RIBERA DE CARDÓS LLEIDA

Cardós ☎ 973 623112
Long stretch of meadowland divided by four rows of poplars.
Camping Card Compulsory.
⊃ *Near the electricity plant in Llavorsi turn NE onto the Ribera road and follow it for 9km. Entrance near hostel Soly Neu.*
Apr-Sep 2.2HEC ⊞ ⠇ ♦ ⋔ ⛟ ⚡ ✕ ⊙ 🇦 🇪 ⚡ ⁑ PR ⚐ ⊞
lau ➡ ⁑PR

SANTO DOMINGO DE LA CALZADA LA RIOJA

Bañares ☎ 941 342804
All year 11HEC ⊞ ♦ ⋔ ⛟ ⚡ ✕ ⊙ 🇦 ⚡ 🇦 ≙ 🇦 ⁑ P ⚐ ⊞ lau
Prices: ♠585 ➡585 🇦585 🇦585

SAVIÑAN ZARAGOZA

Saviñan Park ☎ 976 825423
On meadowland in the Jalón Valley with plenty of trees for shade.
⊃ *Access via NII Zaragoza-Calatayud, exit El Frasno towards Illueca.*
All year 6HEC ⊞ ♦ ⋔ ⛟ ⚡ ✕ ⊙ 🇦 🇪 ⁑ P

SOLSONA LLEIDA

Solsonès ☎ 973 482861
A well equipped site in a picturesque mountain setting with facilities for both summer and winter holidays.
All year 6.3HEC ⊞ ♦ ⋔ ⛟ ⚡ ✕ ⊙ 🇦 🇪 ≙ 🇦 🇦 ⁑ P ⚐ ⊞
lau ➡ ⁑LRS
Prices: ♠626 ➡626 🇦626 🇦626

TIERMAS ZARAGOZA

Mar del Pirineo ☎ 948 887009
On broad terraces sloping down to the banks of the Embalse de Yese. Roofing provides shade for tents and cars.
⊃ *Situated on the N240 Huesca-Pamplona road at Km317.7.*
Etr & May-Sep 2.9HEC ⊞ ⠇ ♦ 🇦 ⋔ ⛟ ⚡ ✕ ⊙ 🇦 🇪 ⁑
LP ⚐ ⊞ lau ➡ ⁑R
Prices: ♠550 ➡550 🇦625 🇦375-600

TORLA HUESCA

Ordesa ctra de Ordesa ☎ 974 486146
On three terraces between well-kept hedges.
⊃ *2km N of the village at Km96 and N of the C138.*
Closed Nov-Xmas 3.5HEC ⊞ ♦ ⋔ ⛟ ⚡ ✕ ⊙ 🇦 🇪 ⁑ P ⚐ ⊞
lau ➡ ⁑R

VILLOSLADA DE CAMEROS LA RIOJA

Los Cameros ctra La Virgen ☎ 941 468195
Situated in the National Park of the Sierra Cebollera in the Iberian mountain range.

⊃ *Access via N111, turn off 50km before Logroño towards Soria and on to Villoslada.*
All year 4HEC ⊞ ♦ ⋔ ⛟ ⚡ ✕ ⊙ 🇦 🇪 🇦
Prices: ♠465 ➡465 🇦490 🇦450

● ● ● ● ● NORTH WEST ● ● ● ●

In this region of contrasts are beautiful green valleys, rugged mountains still roamed by bears and wolves, a wealth of historic monuments, fine resorts such as Bayona, and quiet fishing villages. This is Galicia, a land of mild climate mostly bordered by the Atlantic - a celtic land with strong traditions, local costume, bagpipes and drums.
The regional capital, Santiago de Compostela, was once the most visited city in Europe, ranking alongside Rome and Jerusalem. The pilgrimage tradition lives on in its cathedral - one of the finest in the world - and the architecture it inspired on the Pilgrim Way.
This legacy has left a wealth of historic monuments, such as the magnificent cathedral at Léon, with its wonderful stained glass. Mountains form the backdrop to Orense, with its fine cathedral and interesting museums, while a green valley is the setting for Pontevedra. Here, in the old town, lie a fascinating museum and cathedral, and houses bearing armorial badges and narrow streets, just as they were hundreds of years ago.
....

BAIONA PONTEVEDRA

Baiona Playa ctra Vigo-Baionna ☎ 986 350035
On a long sandy peninsula on the Galicia coast with direct access to the beach. The site has good, modern facilities and a variety of watersports can be enjoyed there.

Jun-Sep 4HEC ▦ ♣ ⋒ ⛱ ♟ ✕ ⊙ ⊟ ⌀ ⛺ ☗ ☷
ᘐ PRS ☑ ⊞ lau
Prices: ⚑738 ⚓813 ⊟744 ⊠744

▶ Cubillas de Santa Marta Valladolid

Cubillas ☎ 983 585002
Meadowland with young trees, subdivided by hedges.
➲ *Entrance on the right of the N620 from Burgos between Km100 & 101.*
All year 4HEC ▦ ⊲ ⋒ ⛱ ♟ ✕ ⊙ ⊟ ⌀ ⛺ ☷ ⊠ ᘐ P ☑ ⊞ lau
♦ ᘐR

▶ Leiro Orense

Leiro ☎ 988 488036
On level meadow in a pine forest in a valley by a stream, behind the football ground.
Closed Nov 1.8HEC ▦ ⊲ ⋒ ⛱ ♟ ✕ ⊙ ⊟ ⌀ ☗ ᘐ R ☑ ⊞ lau

▶ Nigrán Pontevedra

Playa America rua Canido 7 ☎ 986 365404
A modern site in a poplar wood, 300mtrs from a magnificent beach.
➲ *Access at Km 9.250 on the Vigo-Bayona road.*
Apr-29 Oct 4HEC ▦ ♣ ⋒ ⛱ ♟ ✕ ⊙ ⊟ ⌀ ☷ ☗ ᘐ P ☑
lau ♦ ᘐRS
Prices: ⚑535-600 ⚓535-600 ⊟550-620 ⊠550-620

▶ Portonovo Pontevedra

Paxariñas ☎ 986 723055
Slightly sloping towards a bay, in amongst dunes, with high pines and young deciduous trees. Lovely beach.
Camping Card Compulsory.
All year 2HEC ▦ ⊲ ⋒ ⛱ ♟ ✕ ⊙ ⊟ ⌀ ⊠ ᘐ S ☑ ⊞ lau

▶ Santa Marina de Valdeon León

El Cares ☎ 987 742676
In a wooded mountain setting with good facilities.
➲ *N off N621 from Portilla de la Reina.*
Apr-15 Oct 2HEC ▦ ⊲ ⋒ ⛱ ♟ ✕ ⊙ ⌀ ☷ ☗ ☷ ⊠ ᘐ R ☑ ⊞
lau ♦ ᘐL
Prices: ⚑510 ⚓510 ⊟562 ⊠510-562

▶ San Vicente do Mar Pontevedra

Siglo XXI ☎ 986 738100
All year 1.6HEC ▦ ⊲ ⋒ ⛱ ♟ ✕ ⊙ ⊟ ⌀ ⛺ ☷ ᘐ PS ☑ ⊞
lau

▶ Simancas Valladolid

Plantió ☎ 983 590082
In a poplar wood, on the river bank.
➲ *On outskirts turn off N620 at Km132.2 and continue 500m on narrow asphalt road and a long single track stone bridge over the River Pisverga.*

CAMPING **EL ASTRAL**

Camino de Pollos, 8
E-47100 TORDESILLAS (Valladolid)
Tel. (34) 983 770 953
Fax (34) 983 238 193
Open: 1.4 - 30.9.

Situated in the very heart of the region, very suitable for overnight stops, but also for longer stays to visit CASTILLA and LEON; our tourist office will be happy to organize excursions for you. Our site is situated at 1km from Tordesillas, near the Duero river. It is very well kept, clean and quiet, with lots of shade. Very nice bungalows. Very helpful staff and a complete leisure programme. Restaurant with regional food. Off-season 20% discount. We admit reservations. Please, don't hesitate to contact us for more information. Access: Leave highways in direction Tordesillas and follow the signs to Camping or Parador Nacional.

15 Jun-22 Sep 1.5HEC ▦ ⠿ ♣ ⋒ ⛱ ♟ ✕ ⊙ ⊟ ⌀ ☷ ⊠ ᘐ
PR ☑ ⊞ lau ♦ ☷
Prices: ⚑475 ⚓475 ⊟500 ⊠475

▶ Tordesillas Valladolid

Astral Camino de Pollos 8 ☎ 983 770953
A well equipped site in a pleasant rural location close to the River Duero.
➲ *Leave motorway at Tordesillas exit and follow signs.*
Apr-Sep 3HEC ⠿ ⊲ ⋒ ⛱ ♟ ✕ ⊙ ⊟ ⌀ ⛺ ᘐ P ☑ ⊞ lau ♦
ᘐR
Prices: ⚑423-530 ⚓364-455 ⊟423-530 ⊠423-530

▶ Valencia de Don Juan León

Pico Verde c Santas Martas 18 ☎ 987 750525
➲ *Turn E off the N630 (Léon-Madrid) at Km32.2 and continue for 4km.*
15 Jun-13 Sep 2.7HEC ▦ ⊲ ⋒ ⛱ ♟ ✕ ⊙ ⊟ ⌀ ᘐ P ☑ ⊞ lau
♦ ⛱ ♟ ✕ ⌀ ☷ ᘐPR
Prices: ⚑450 ⚓450 ⊟450 ⊠450

▶ Villamejil León

Rio Tuerto ☎ 908 226998
Jun-Aug 0.6HEC ▦ ⋒ ♟ ✕ ⊙ ⊟ ⌀ ⊠ ᘐ R ☑ ⊞ lau ♦ ⛱ ✕

● ● ● ● ● **SOUTH** ● ● ● ● ●

Forbidding crags, dry river beds, spectacular snow-capped mountains, terraced olive groves, flamenco and some of Spain's finest historic cities, draw the visitor to the Andalusian south, a region with attractions as varied as itself.
The amazing backdrop of the Sierra Nevada towers over lovely Granada and its palace-fortress, the Alhambra. The Moorish heritage of ancient Córdoba is proclaimed by its astonishing mosque-cathedral - one of the glories of Spain. Inside the dazzlingly beautiful mosque's forest of archways and columns, sits a Gothic cathedral. The wonderful gardens of a 14th-century castle are nearby.
Bullfights and carnival are part of the excitement of Cádiz. In Seville, Easter week sees the procession of penitents while in May, colourful celebrations drawing vast numbers from throughout Spain, mark the El Rocío pilgrimage.
The isolation of much of Andalusia contrasts with the better-known hectic charms of the coast, which draws sun-seekers and pleasure-lovers to the resorts of Marbella, Málaga and many more.
....

▶ Adra Almeria

Las Gaviotas ☎ 950 400660
➲ *2km W on N340 (Almeria-Málaga)*
All year 2HEC ⠿ ⊲ ♣ ⋒ ⛱ ♟ ✕ ⊙ ⊟ ⌀ ☷ ⊠ ᘐ PS ☑ ⊞
lau ♦ ᘐPS
Prices: ⚑475 ⚓475 ⊟500 ⊠475

Habana ☎ 950 522127
A quiet site with good facilities and direct access to the sea.
➲ *2km W at Km58.3 on N340 (Almeria-Málaga).*
All year 1.5HEC ⠿ ♣ ⋒ ⛱ ♟ ✕ ⊙ ⊟ ⌀ ⊠ ᘐ S ☑ ⊞ lau
Prices: ⚑400-450 ⚓400-450 ⊟400-450 ⊠400-450

▶ Aguilas Murcia

Calarreona ctra de Aguilas a Vera ☎ 968 413704
A quiet site, 50m from the sea.
➲ *Near Km4 on N332 (Aguilas-Murcia).*
15 Jun-15 Sep 3.6HEC ⠿ ⊲ ⋒ ⛱ ♟ ✕ ⊙ ⊟ ⌀ ᘐ S ☑ ⊞ lau
♦ ᘐP
Prices: ⚑480 ⊟535 ⊠480

ALCALA DE GUADAIRA SEVILLA

Los Naranjos ☎ 954 5630354
All year 16HEC ⬢♦🏠⚡🍴✕⊙🛒🏪🚾🅰 ⚲ P 🏧⊞ lau ♦🚿🏊

ALCAZARES, LOS MURCIA

Cartagonova ☎ 968 575100
⟳ *On CN332 between Los Alcazares and La Union.*
15 Jun-Sep 30HEC ⋯ ⬢♦🏠⚡🍴✕🛒🏊🚾⚲ PS 🏧⊞ lau ♦✕

ALJARAQUE HUELVA

Las Vegas ☎ 959 318141
⟳ *From Huelva cross the bridge over the River Odiel and continue for 8km towards Punta Umbria. Signposted.*
All year 3HEC ⋯ ⬢♦🏠⚡🍴✕⊙🛒🏊⚲🅰⚲ PRS 🏧⊞ lau

BAÑOS DE FORTUNA MURCIA

Fuente ☎ 968 685454
⟳ *Take C3223 from Fortuna à Pinoso to Balncario de Fortuna. Signposted.*
Jun-15 Sep 0.9HEC ⬛ 🌿🏠⚡🍴✕⊙🛒🏊🚾🏧⊞ lau ♦🏊🚿⚲P

Las Palmeras ☎ 968 685123
Camping Card Compulsory.
All year ⋯ 🌿⬢🏠⚡🍴✕⊙🛒🚿🏊⚲ P 🏧⊞ lau

BOLNUEVO MURCIA

Garoa Camping Playa de Mazarrón ☎ 968 150660
On level ground divided by a footpath and partly bordered by palm trees.
⟳ *Turn W off N332 in Puerto de Mazarrón at approx Km111 and head towards Bolnuevo. Then take the MU road and drive 4.6km to site entrance which is 1km E of Punta Bela.*
All year 8HEC ⋯ ♦⬢🏠⚡🍴✕⊙🛒🏊⚲ S 🏧⊞ lau
Prices: pitch 1525-1650

CARCHUNA GRANADA

Don Cactus Carchuna-Motril ☎ 958 623109
Modern site adjoining the beach. Dogs not allowed in July and August.
⟳ *At Km343 on N340 (Carchuna-Motril).*
All year 4HEC ⋯ ♦🏠⚡🍴✕⊙🛒🏊🚾⚲ P 🏧⊞ lau ♦⚲S
Prices: ⛺530 pitch 985

CARLOTA, LA CORDOBA

Carlos III ☎ 957 300697
In wooded surroundings with modern facilities.
⟳ *Access via 'La Carlota' exit on NIV.*
All year 5HEC ⋯ ♦🏠⚡🍴✕⊙🛒🏊🏪🚾⚲ P lau ♦🚾⚲L ⊞

CASTILLO DE BAÑOS GRANADA

Castillo de Baños Castillo de Banos, La Mamola ☎ 958 829528
Well equipped site next to the beach.
⟳ *At Km360 on N340 (Castillo de Baños-La Mamola).*
15 Jun-15 Sep 2.7HEC ♦🏠⚡🍴✕⊙🛒🏊⚲ PS 🏧⊞ lau
Prices: ⛺515 pitch 950

CONIL DE LA FRONTERA CÁDIZ

Fuente del Gallo Fuente del Gallo ☎ 956 440137
A well equipped site in a wooded location 300m from the beach.
⟳ *Signposted from N340, Km21.6.*
15 Mar-1 Oct 3HEC ⬛ ⬢🏠⚡🍴✕⊙🛒🏊⚲ P 🏧⊞ lau ♦⚲S
Prices: ⛺545 🚐455 🏠530 🅰455

Roche Pago del Zorro ☎ 956 442216
Spread among pine groves with well defined pitches close to the beach.
All year 3HEC ⬛ ⋯ ♦🏠⚡🍴✕⊙🛒🏊⚲ P 🏧⊞ lau
♦🚿🍴✕⚲⚲S ⊞
Prices: ⛺510 🚐430 🏠495 🅰435

EJIDO, EL ALMERIA

Mar Azul Playa de San Miguel ☎ 950 497505
On level ground surrounded by palm trees and tamarins. Sports and recreational facilities available.
⟳ *6km from village.*
All year 22HEC ⬛ ♦🏠⚡🍴✕⊙🛒🏊⚲🅰⚲ PS 🏧⊞ lau
Prices: ⛺300-650 🚐300-650 🏠300-650 🅰300-650

ESTEPONA MÁLAGA

Parque Tropical ☎ 95 2793618
A modern site situated at the foot of the Sierra Bermeja mountains, five minutes walk from the sea.
⟳ *Access via N340 at Km162.*
All year 1.2HEC 🚿⬢🏠⚡🍴✕⊙🛒🏊🏪🚾⚲ PS 🏧⊞ lau ♦⚲S
Prices: ⛺401-562 🚐401-535 🏠524-642 🅰524-642

FUENGIROLA MÁLAGA

Calazul Mijas Costa ☎ 95 2493219
A level site in a pleasant rural location with good recreational facilities, 300mtrs from the sea.
⟳ *Exit from C340 at Km200.*
All year 5HEC ⋯ ⬢🏠⚡🍴✕⊙🛒🏊🚾⚲ PS 🏧⊞ lau ♦⚲S
Prices: ⛺348-535 🚐348-535 🏠348-910 🅰348-910

GALLARDOS, LOS ALMERIA

Gallardos ☎ 950 528324
Level site with individual pitches, 10 minutes from the sea and the old Moorish village of Mojacar. English management.
⟳ *500m from km 525 on CN340.*
All year 3.5HEC ⋯ ⬢🏠⚡🍴✕⊙🛒🏊🚾⚲ P 🏧⊞ lau ♦⚲S
Prices: ⛺190-475 🚐475 🏠190-475 🅰190-475

GRANADA GRANADA

Sierra Nevada ctra de Jaen 107 ☎ 958 150062
Almost level grassy site, in numerous sections, within motel complex.
Mar-1 Nov 4HEC ⬛ ♦🏠⚡🍴✕⊙🛒🏊🏪⚲ P 🏧⊞ lau
Prices: ⛺642 🚐642 🏠685 🅰535-642

GUIJAROSSA, LA CORDOBA

Campiña ☎ 957 315158
In a quiet location in a rural setting surrounded by olive trees and elms with good, modern facilities.
⟳ *Access via N4 turn off at Km424 or Km441 and follow signs to Santaella and campsite.*
All year 0.7HEC ⋯ ⬢🏠⚡🍴✕⊙🛒🏊🅰⚲ P 🏧⊞ lau
Prices: ⛺482 🚐482 🏠508 🅰455

ISLA PLANA MURCIA

Madrilles ctra de la Azohia Km45 ☎ 968 152151
All year 5.5HEC ⬛ ⬢🏠⚡🍴✕⊙🛒🏊🏪⚲ PS 🏧⊞🚫 lau ♦✕
Prices: ⛺460-540 pitch 1380-1620

MARBELLA MÁLAGA

Buganvilla ☎ 95 2831974
A well equipped site in a pine forest close to the beach.
Camping Card Compulsory.

➲ *E of Marbella off the N340 coast road towards Mijas.*
All year 4HEC ⏚ ∷ ⊶ ⋔ ⚑ ⛱ ✕ ⊙ ☰ ⌀ ⛺ ⛽ ⚑ ⛔ PS ⌂
⊞ lau

Marbella Playa ☎ 952 833998
On beach with large sports area.
➲ *Access is via N340 Cádiz-Málaga Km200.*
All year 5.5HEC ⏚ ∷ ⊶ ♦ ⋔ ⚑ ⛱ ✕ ⊙ ☰ ⌀ ⛔ P ⌂ ⊞ lau
♦ ⛔S

) **MAZAGÓN** HUELVA

Mazagón cuesta de la Barca s/n ☎ 959 376208
Undulating terrain amongst dunes in sparse pine forest. Long sandy beach.
➲ *Turn off the N431 Sevilla-Huelva road just before San Juan del Puerto in direction of Moguer and continue S via Palso de la Frontera.*
All year 80HEC ∷ ⊶ ⋔ ⚑ ⛱ ⊙ ☰ ⌀ ⛔ P ⌂ ⊞ lau
♦ ✕ ⛔S

) **MOJACAR** ALMERIA

Sopalmo Sopalmo ☎ 950 478413
All year 1.7HEC ∷ ⊶ ⚑ ⋔ ⚑ ⛱ ✕ ⊙ ☰ ⌀ ⌂ ⊞ lau ♦ ⛔S
Prices: ⚑375-481 ⛱375-481 ▲350-428

) **PELIGROS** GRANADA

Granada Cerro de la Cruz ☎ 958 340548
In a wooded location with panoramic views.
➲ *Access via N323 Jaen-Granada exit 123 towards Peligros.*
All year 2.2HEC ⏚ ⚑ ⊶ ⋔ ⚑ ✕ ⊙ ☰ ⌀ ⛔ P ⌂ ⊞ lau
Prices: ⚑562 ⛱562 ⛱605 ▲497

) **PUERTO DE SANTA MARÍA, EL** CÁDIZ

Playa Las Dunas de San Anton ps Maritimo de la Puntilla
☎ 9566 872210
Large site with good recreational facilities close to the beach.
All year 13.2HEC ∷ ♦ ⋔ ⚑ ⛱ ✕ ⊙ ☰ ⌀ ⛔ P ⌂ lau ♦
⚑ ⛱ ✕ ⛱ ⛔RS ⊞
Prices: ⚑546-605 ⛱471-519 ⛱589-658 ▲589-658

) **PUNTA UMBRIA** HUELVA

Derena Mar ☎ 959 312004
All year 12.5HEC ∷ ♦ ⋔ ⚑ ⛱ ✕ ⊙ ☰ ⌀ ▲ ⌂ ⊞ lau ♦ ⛔LS

) **RONDA** MÁLAGA

El Sur ctra de Algeciras ☎ 095 2875939
In a beautiful location in the heart of the Serrania of Ronda.
All year 4HEC ∷ ♦ ⋔ ⚑ ⛱ ✕ ⊙ ☰ ⌀ ⛺ ⛔ P ⌂ ⊞ lau
Prices: ⚑500 ⛱430 ⛱430 ▲430

) **ROQUETAS-DE-MAR** ALMERIA

Roquetas Los Parrales ☎ 950 343809
➲ *Access by road No 340. 1.7km from Km428.6.*
All year 8HEC ∷ ⊶ ⋔ ⚑ ⛱ ✕ ⊙ ☰ ⌀ ⛱ ⛺ ⛔ PS ⌂ ⊞ lau ♦
⛔L
Prices: ⚑525 ⛱525 ⛱525 ▲525

) **SAN ROQUE** CÁDIZ

Motel San Roque ☎ 956 780100
All year 4HEC ⏚ ♦ ⋔ ⚑ ⛱ ✕ ⊙ ☰ ⛺ ▲ ⛔ P ⌂ ⊞ lau ♦
⛔S

) **SANTA ELENA** JAÉN

Despeñaperros ☎ 953 664192
A clean, restful site, in a nature reserve with fine views of the surrounding mountains. *Contd.*

⮎ *At Km257 on NIV-E5.*
All year ☼ ⚒ 🏪 🛒 🍴 ⊙ 🚿 ⊘ ⚡ P ⊞ ⊞ lau ➡ ⚡R
Prices: 🛆410-460 🚗435-485 🚐435-485 ▲435-485

El Estanque ☎ 953 623093
15 May-15 Sep 1.5HEC ⚏ ⚒ 🏪 🍴 ✕ ⊙ 🚿 ⚑ ⊞ lau ➡ ⚡
⚡LPR

Sevilla ☎ 954 514379
Level site near airfield, road and railway.
⮎ *About 2km from airfield, 100m from the NIV (Madrid-Sevilla) at Km533.8.*
Apr-Sep 2HEC ☼ ⚒ 🏪 🛒 🍴 ✕ ⊙ 🚿 ⊘ 🏕 ⚡ P ⊞ ⊞ lau
Prices: 🛆475 🚗475 🚐460 ▲430

Paloma ☎ 956 684203
A modern site in a secluded situation 400mtrs from the beach and next to the Bronze Age Necrolopis de los Algarbes. Fine views of the African coast across the Straits of Gibraltar.
⮎ *Access via N340 Cádiz-Málaga at Km 74.*
All year 4.9HEC ⚏ ⚒ 🏪 🛒 🍴 ✕ ⊙ 🚿 ⚑ ⚡ P ⊞ ⊞ lau ➡
⚡RS

Rió Jara ☎ 956 680570
Extensive site on meadowland with good tree coverage. Long sandy beach.
⮎ *On the N340 Málaga-Cádiz road at Km79.7 turn towards the sea.*
All year 3HEC ⚏ ⚒ 🏪 🛒 🍴 ✕ ⊙ 🚿 ⊘ ⚡ RS ⊞ lau ➡ ⚡R

Tarifa ☎ 956 684778
A terraced site in wooded surroundings, 100mtrs from the sea.
⮎ *At Km78 on Málaga-Cádiz road.*
All year 32.5HEC ⚏ ☼ ⚒ 🏪 🛒 🍴 ✕ ⊙ 🚿 ⊘ ⚡ P ⊞ ⊞ lau
➡ ⚡RS
Prices: 🛆600 🚐475 ▲400

Torre de la Peña ☎ 956 684903
Terraced, on both sides of through road. Upper terraces are considerably quieter. Roofing provides shade. View of the sea, Tarifa and on clear days N Africa (Tangier).
⮎ *Entrance on the N340 Cádiz-Málaga, at Km76.5 turn inland by the old square tower.*
All year 3HEC ⚏ ☼ ⚒ ⚒ 🏪 🛒 🍴 ✕ ⊙ 🚿 ⊘ 🏕 🚐 ⚡ S ⊞ ⊞ lau

CAMPING TORRE DEL MAR
Paseo Maritimo s/n • E-29740 Torre del Mar (Prov. Málaga)

1st category holiday site, right on a beautiful beach of the Costa del Sol and not far from Torre del Mar. Restaurant with terrace and typical regional restaurant, swimming-pool and paddling-pool with aquatic toboggan, clean and modern sanitary installations, free hot water in showers. Satellite dish. No long-term campers. Special prices in low season (1.10.-31.3): up to 9 days 20%, up to 19 days 40%, 30 days or more 50%. Special fees in low season for pensioners.

Torre del Mar ☎ 95 2540224
A fine site on a beautiful beach, with good facilities. Shop open June-September only.
⮎ *SW of town. Access via N340 (Almeria-Málaga).*
All year 2.4HEC ⚏ ☼ ⚒ 🏪 🛒 🍴 ✕ ⊙ 🚿 ⊘ ⚡ P ⊞ ⊞ lau ➡
⚡S

Vejer ctra National (N340) ☎ 956 450098
A quiet family site in a pleasant shady location.
⮎ *At Km39.5 on N340 Cádiz-Málaga.*
15 Jun-15 Sep 0.8HEC ☼ ⚒ 🏪 🛒 🍴 ✕ ⊙ 🚿 ⊘ ⚡ P ⊞ ⊞ lau
➡ ✕ 🏕 ⚡S
Prices: 🛆1175-1275

Prices are in French Francs or Spanish Pesetas.

Huguet ctra de Fontaneda ☎ 07376 843718
On level strip of meadowland with rows of fruit and deciduous trees.
⮎ *Off La Seu d'Urgell road N1, S of village and drive W across river.*
All year 1.5HEC ⚏ ⚒ ☼ 🏪 ⊙ 🚿 ⚡ R ⊞ ⊞ lau ➡ 🛒 🍴 ✕ ⊘
🏕 ⚡LP

SWITZERLAND

Bordered by France in the west, Germany in the north, Austria in the east, and Italy in the south, Switzerland is considered by many to be one of the most beautiful countries in Europe.

FACTS AND FIGURES
Capital: Bern (Berne)
Language: German, French, Italian, Romansh
IDD code: 41. To call the UK dial 00 44
Currency: Franc (CHF) = 100 centimes). At the time of going to press £1 = CHF 2.22.

Local time: GMT + 1 (summer GMT + 2)
Emergency Services: Police 117; Fire 118; Ambulance 144.
Business Hours-
Banks: Mon-Fri 08.30-16.30 (in towns)
Shops: Mon-Fri 08.30-12.00 and 14.00-18.30; Sat 08.30-12.00 and 14.00-

16.00/17.00 (shops remain open all day in cities).
Average daily temperatures: Zurich
Jan 0°C   Jul 19°C
Mar 5°C   Sep 15°C
May 9°C   Nov 5°C
Tourist Information:
Switzerland Tourism

UK Swiss Centre, Swiss Court
London W1V 8EE
Tel 0171-734 1921 (recorded message)
USA 608 Fifth Avenue
New York, NY 10020
Tel (212) 757 5944
Camping card: recommended. Some reductions available.

It has the highest mountains in Europe and some of the most awe-inspiring waterfalls and lakes, features that are offset by picturesque villages set amid green pastures and an abundance of Alpine flowers covering the valleys and lower mountain slopes during the spring. The highest peaks are Monte Rosa (15,217ft) on the Italian border, the Matterhorn (14,782ft), and the Jungfrau (13,669ft). Some of the most beautiful areas are the Via Mala Gorge, the Falls of the Rhine near Schaffhausen, the Rhône Glacier, and the lakes of Luzern and Thun.

The Alps cause many climatic variations throughout Switzerland, but generally the climate is said to be the healthiest in the world. In the higher Alpine regions temperatures tend to be low, whereas the lower land of the northern area has higher temperatures and hot summers. French is spoken in the western cantons (regions), Swiss-German dialects (although German is understood) in the central and northern cantons and Italian in Ticino. Romansch is spoken in Grisons.

Switzerland has 350 campsites, 74 of them are run by the Touring Club Suisse (TCS) who publish details of classified sites annually. Information can also be obtained from tourist offices, which are to be found in most provincial towns and resorts. The season extends from April

or May to September or October, although some sites are open all year, particularly at winter sports resorts.

Off-site camping regulations differ from canton (region) to canton. However, permission to camp off an official campsite must be obtained from the landowner or local police. Overnight parking may be tolerated in rest areas of some motorways, but at all times the high standard of hygiene regulations must be observed. Make sure you do not contravene local laws.

HOW TO GET THERE
From Britain, Switzerland is usually approached via France. For details of the *AA European Routes Service* please consult the Contents Page.

Distance
From the Channel ports to Bern is approximately 810km (503 miles), a distance which will normally require only one overnight stop.

If you intend to use Swiss motorways, you will be liable for a tax of CHF 40 - see 'Motorway tax' below for full details.

MOTORING & GENERAL INFORMATION
The information given here is specific to Switzerland. It **must** be read in conjunction with the European ABC at the front of the book,

which covers those regulations which are common to many countries.

Boats*
Third party insurance is compulsory for craft used on the Swiss lakes.

British Embassy/Consulates*
The British Embassy together with its consular section is located at 3005 Berne, Thunstrasse 50 ☎(031) 3597700. There are British Consulates and agencies in Genève (Geneva), Lugano, Montreux/Vevey (St Légier), Valais (Mollens) and Zurich.

Children in cars
Children under seven not permitted to travel as front seat passengers unless using suitable restraint system. Children bewteen seven and 12 must use seat belts or restraints system appropriate to size when travelling in front or rear.

Currency
There are no restrictions on the import or export of foreign or Swiss currency. In addition to banks there are exchange offices at the border, railway stations in large towns, airports and in travel agencies and hotels which are usually open 08.00-20.00hrs.

Dimensions and weight restrictions
Private cars and towed trailers or caravans are restricted to the following dimensions - car height, 4 metres; width, 2.5 metres; length, 12 metres.
Trailer/caravan height, 4 metres; width, 2.5 metres; length, 12 metres (including tow bar). The maximum permitted overall length of vehicle/trailer or caravan combination is 18.35 metres.
Note It is dangerous or forbidden to use a vehicle towing a trailer or caravan on some mountain roads; motorists should ensure that roads on which they are about to travel are suitable for the conveyance of vehicle/trailer or caravan combinations.
 The fully-laden weight of trailers which do not have an independent braking system should

not exceed 50% of the unladen weight of the towing vehicle, but trailers which have an independent braking system can weigh up to 100% of the unladen weight of the towing vehicle.

Driving licence*
A valid UK or Republic of Ireland licence is acceptable in Switzerland. The minimum age at which visitors from UK or Republic of Ireland may use a temporarily imported car is 18 years and a temporarily imported motorcycle of between 50-125cc (not exceeding 40kph) 16 years, exceeding 125cc 18 years.

Foodstuffs*
Travellers over 17 years of age may import provisions for 1 day but a maximum of 500g of butter and a maximum of 1.5kg of meat and meat products, made up of no more than 500g of meat and/or no more than 1kg of meat products such as ham, sausages, canned/tinned meat and/or no more than 2.5kg of rabbit, poultry, game, fish and shellfish. The import of meat and meat products (except tins or preserves) of all animals from Africa, Asia (except Japan), Turkey and the former USSR is forbidden, as is the import of pork meat and pork products from Bosnia Herzogovina, Macedonia (FYROM), South America and Yugoslavia (Serbia & Montenegro).

Lights*
Driving on sidelights only is prohibited. Spotlights are forbidden. Fog lamps in front must be in pairs. Dipped headlights must be used in cities and towns. Dipped headlights are compulsory in tunnels, whether they are lit or not, and failure to observe this regulation can lead to a fine. Switzerland has a 'tunnel' road sign (a rectangular blue panel showing the entrance of the tunnel), which serves to remind drivers to turn on their dipped headlights. In open country, headlights must be dipped as follows: at least 200 metres (219yds) in front of any pedestrian or oncoming vehicle (including trains parallel to the road); when requested to do so by the driver of an oncoming vehicle flashing lights; or when reversing, travelling in lines of traffic or stopping. Parking lights must be used when waiting at level crossings,

or near roadworks. They must also be used in badly-lit areas when visibility is poor. It is recommended that *motorcyclists* use dipped headlights during the day.

Motoring club*

The **Touring Club Suisse** (TCS) has branch offices in all important towns, and has its head office at 1214 Vernier/Genève, Chemin de Blandonnet 4, ☎(022) 4172727. The TCS will extend a courtesy service to all motorists but their major services will have to be paid for. The opening hours of TCS offices vary according to location and time of year, but generally they are 08.00/09.00-11.45/12.30hrs and 13.30/14.00-17.00/18.30hrs Monday to Friday and 08.00/09.00-11.45/12.00hrs Saturday (summer only).

Motorway tax

The Swiss authorities levy an annual motorway tax. A vehicle sticker, costing CHF40 for vehicles up to 3.5 tonnes maximum total weight and known locally as a *vignette,* must be displayed by vehicles using Swiss motorways including motorcycles, trailers and caravans. Motorists may purchase the stickers at the Swiss frontier. Vehicles over 3.5 tonnes maximum total weight are taxed on all roads in Switzerland; a licence for one day, 10 days, one month and one year periods can be obtained. There are no stickers, and the tax must be paid at the Swiss frontier.

Petrol*

At the time of going to press both leaded and unleaded petrol are available in Switzerland. However, only one grade of leaded petrol is sold, 98 octane 'Super'.

Roads

The road surfaces are generally good, but some main roads are narrow in places. Traffic congestion may be severe at the beginning and end of the German school holidays.

On any stretch of mountain road, the driver of a private car may be asked by the driver of a postal bus which is painted yellow, to reverse, or otherwise manoeuvre to allow the postal bus to

pass. Postal bus drivers often sound a distinctive three note horn; no other vehicles may use this type of horn in Switzerland.

Switzerland has about 1,000 miles of motorway (*Autobahn* or *autoroute*). Tolls are not payable but see *Motorway Tax* above. Emergency telephones, which connect you to the motorway control police, are located every 2km.

Speed limits*
Car
Built-up areas 50kph (31mph)
Other roads 80kph (49mph)
semi-motorways 100kph (62mph)
Motorways 120kph (74mph)
Car/caravan/trailer
Built-up areas 50kph (31mph)
Other roads, including semi-motorways 80kph (49mph)†
Motorways 80kph (49mph)

These limits do not apply if another limit is indicated by signs, or if the vehicle is subject to a lower general speed limit.

†If the weight of the caravan or luggage trailer exceeds 1,000kg, a speed limit of 60kph (37mph) applies on roads outside built-up areas and semi-motorways, but 80kph (49mph) is still permissible on motorways.

Warning triangle/Hazard warning lights*

The use of a warning triangle is compulsory in the event of accident or breakdown. The triangle must be placed on the road at least 50 metres (55yds) behind the vehicle on ordinary roads, and at least 100 metres (109yds) on high speed roads. If in an emergency lane the triangle must be placed on the right. Hazard warning lights may be used in conjunction with the triangle or when traffic slows due to accident or traffic jam.

*Additional information will be found in the Continental ABC at the front of the book.

● ● ● ●   **NORTH**   ● ● ● ● ●

Basel owes its prosperity to its key geographical position - at the junction of the borders of France, Germany and Switzerland, and at the point on the Rhine where it becomes navigable. It has evolved into an important business and industrial centre. The old town has a great Gothic cathedral - with a fine view from the top of the towers, and a remarkable collection of art in the Fine Arts Museum, "Kunstmuseum". The town also has an extensive Zoological Garden, with an emphasis on breeding threatened species. The countryside of this area is one of medieval castles, quaint villages, thermal spas, dense forests, lush meadows and sparkling lakes. But above the charming Baroque town of Solothurn is the last ridge of the Jura - the giddy crests of the Weissenstein, from where, at over 4,000ft, there is an outstanding view over Berne and the lakes of Neuchâtel, Murten and Biel.

....

▶ **GRENCHEN** SOLOTHURN
▶ At **STAAD**

Strausak (TCS) ☎ 065 521133
12 Apr-Sep 1HEC � ⅄ ⋔ ⅏ ♀ ✕ ⊙ ⊕ ⅄ LR 🄿 ⊞ ➡ ⅄P

▶ **KÜNTEN** AARGAU

Sulz ☎ 056 4964879
Situated by a river.
➔ *From motorway A1 turn off at Baden in the direction of Bremgarten.*
15 Mar-Oct 2.5HEC � ⅄ ⋔ ⅏ ✕ ⊙ ⊕ ⅄ ⌀ ⅄ ⅄ PR 🄿 ⊞ lau
Prices: ♠5 🚐6-10 ▲4-10

▶ **LÄUFELFINGEN** BASEL

Läufelfingen ☎ 062 2991189
➔ *On road from Basel to Olten.*
Apr-Oct 0.5HEC � ⅄ ⋔ ⊙ ⊕ ⊕ ⊞ ⊞

▶ **MÖHLIN** AARGAU

Bachtalen (TCS) ☎ 061 8515095
A pleasant site in a wooded rural setting.
➔ *2km N towards the River Rhine.*
Apr-early Oct 1HEC � ⅄ℳ ⋔ ⊙ ⊕ ⅄ ⌀ ⊞ ⊞ lau ➡ ⅏ ♀ ✕ ⅄PR
Prices: ♠4.30-5.20 🚐9-13 ▲4.30-5.30

▶ **REINACH** BASEL

Waldhort Heideweg 16 ☎ 061 7116429
In pleasant wooded surroundings close to the Basle/Delémont road.
13Mar-16 Oct 2.9HEC ⎚⎚⎚ ⅄ ⋔ ⅏ ✕ ⊙ ⊕ ⌀ ⅄ ⅄ P ⊞ ⊞ lau
Prices: ♠7 🚐3.50 🚐8 ▲4-6

Waldhort Basel

at the motorway Basle-Delémont (exit Reinach-Nord), about 4 miles outside the city

Quiet and well equipped site: hot showers, shop, kitchen commodities. Swimming pool 10 x 4m. Good base for the -worthwhile-visit of Basle: cathedral, museums, fairs, Goetheanum, zoo, etc.

Information: Camping-Caravanning club beider Basel, P.O.B., CH-4002 Basel

---

▶ **ZURZACH** AARGAU

Oberfeld ☎ 56 2492575
Apr-Oct 2HEC ⎚⎚⎚ ⌀ ⅄ ⋔ ⅏ ✕ ⊙ ⊕ ⅄ ⌀ ⅄ ⅄ PR ⊞ ⊞
Prices: ♠5-5 🚐2-2 🚐9-12 ▲4.50-7 pitch 9-12

● ● ● ●   **NORTH EAST**   ● ● ● ● ●

At the northern gateway to Switzerland, the town of Schaffhausen falls in terraces from the 16th-century Munot Castle, and is the traditional starting point for a visit to the Rhine Falls, "Rheinfall". The most powerful waterfall in Europe, the Rhine makes a spectacular 70ft drop - one of the most famous sights in Europe. St Gallen is popular with visitors; the twin domed towers of the cathedral overlook the attractive old town. The cathedral's plain exterior belies a wonderfully rich Baroque interior, with mural paintings covering the central dome and nave, and there is a remarkable chancel with a huge high altar.
The largest city in Switzerland, cosmopolitan Zürich hums around the Bahnhofstrasse - a fine, wide, tree-lined boulevard of glittering shops and modern offices and banks. For more sedate pursuits visit the quays along the banks of Lake Zürich - lined with immaculate gardens and lawns, visit the old quarters with their cobbled streets, or take a boat trip on the lake. The Swiss National Museum, "Schweizerisches Landesmuseum" is a treasure-house of Swiss civilisation from prehistoric times to the present. The countryside of the region provides good walking, and the mountains and hills are dotted with attractive farms. Picturesque villages contain traditional colourful houses, and sparkling lakes adorn the valleys.
Between the borders of Switzerland and Austria is the principality of Leichtenstein, with its extensive tourist attractions, but retaining its own individual charm and appeal. The capital and main centre is Vaduz, overlooked by its 14th- century castle.

....

▶ **ALTNAU** THURGAU

Ruderbaum ☎ 071 6951885
A small tourist site with ample facilities.
➔ *Close to the railway station by Lake Bodensee between Constance and Romanshorn.*
Apr-Oct 7.5HEC ⎚⎚⎚ ⅄ ⋔ ⊙ ⊕ ⅄ ⅄ ⅄ L ⊞ ⊞ lau ➡ ⅏ ♀ ✕
Prices: ♠5.50-6.50 🚐3.50 🚐8 ▲7

▶ **ALT ST JOHANN** ST-GALLEN

3 Eidgenossen (TCS) ☎ 071 9991274
All year 0.5HEC ⎚⎚⎚ ⅄ ⋔ ✕ ⊙ ⊕ ⅄ 🄿 ⊞ lau ➡ ⅄R

▶ **APPENZELL** APPENZELL

Kau Appenzell ☎ 071 7875030
Camping Card Compulsory.
All year 2HEC ⎚⎚⎚ ⅄⅄ ⋔ ⅏ ✕ ⊙ ⊕ ⅄ ⊞ ⊞ ⅊ lau

▶ **EGNACH** THURGAU

Wiedehorn ☎ 071 661006
Etr-Sep 2.5HEC ⎚⎚⎚ ⅄⅄ ⋔ ⅏ ✕ ⊙ ⊕ ⌀ 🄿 ⊞ ➡ ⅄L

▶ **ESCHENZ** THURGAU

Hüttenberg ☎ 052 7412337
Terraced site lying above village.
➔ *1km SW.*
All year 6HEC ⎚⎚⎚ ⅄ ⋔ ⅏ ⊙ ⊕ ⌀ ⅄ ⅄ P ⊞ ⊞ lau ➡ ✕ ⊞

▶ **GOLDINGEN** ST-GALLEN

Atzmännig ☎ 055 2841235
Suitable for summer and winter holidays, the site is situated

---

close to the main cable car and ski lift stations and the the giant mountainside slide.
All year 1.5HEC ⚏ ⛷ 🏪 ✕ ⊙ 🚽 🔋 🖂 lau

KRUMMENAU ST-GALLEN

Adler ☎ 074 41030
On edge of village.
All year 0.8HEC ⚏ ⛷ 🏪 🍴 ✕ ⊙ 🚽 🖂 lau

LEUTSWIL BEI BISCHOFFZELL THURGAU

Sitterbrücke ☎ 071 4226398
➲ *Signposted from Bischoffzell on the Konstanz-St Gallen road.*
Apr-15 Oct 1HEC ⚏ 🔌 🏪 ⊙ 🚽 🔋 ⌐ R 🖂 lau ➧ 🍴 ✕
Prices: ⚑5 pitch 10

MAMMERN THURGAU

Guldifuss Guldifusstr 1 ☎ 052 7411320
A terraced site directly on the Untersee.
All year 1.5HEC ⚏ 🔌 🏪 ✕ ⊙ 🚽 🔋 ⌐ L 🖵 lau ➧ 🍴 ✕ ⌐ 🖂
Prices: ⚑8 ➜4 ⛺4 ▲4

OTTENBACH ZÜRICH

Reussbrücke (TCS) Muristr 32 ☎ 01 7612022
By river of same name.
➲ *Access from Zürich via road 126 in SW direction, via Affoltern to Ottenbach.*
Apr-Oct 1.5HEC ⚏ 🔌 🏪 ✕ ⊙ 🚽 🔋 ⌐ ▲ ⌐ R 🖂 lau ➧ 🍴 ✕
Prices: ⚑4.50-5.50 ➜3.50 ⛺8-11 ▲5

ST GALLEN ST-GALLEN

Leebrücke (TCS) ☎ 071 384969
29 Apr-1 Oct 1.5HEC ⚏ ⛷ 🏪 🍴 ✕ ⊙ 🚽 🔋 ⌐ R 🖵 🖂 lau ➧ ⌐P

SCHÖNENGRUND APPENZELL

Schönengrund ☎ 071 3611268
A comfortable, partly residential site with well defined touring pitches.
All year 1HEC ⚏ 🔌 ⊙ 🚽 🔋 ⌐ 🖂 lau ➧ 🍴 ✕ 🖂
Prices: ⚑5.50 ➜3.50 ⛺5-8 ▲4-6

STEIN AM RHEIN SCHAFFHAUSEN

Grenzstein Öhningerstr 75 ☎ 052 7415141
➲ *1.8km E.*
All year 1.1HEC ⚏ ⠿ 🔌 🏪 🍴 ✕ ⊙ 🚽 🔋 ⌐ P 🖂 lau

WAGENHAUSEN SCHAFFHAUSEN

Wagenhausen Hauptstr 82 ☎ 052 7414271
In a delightful wooded location beside the River Rhein.
Apr-Oct 4.5HEC ⚏ 🔌 🏪 ✕ ⊙ 🚽 🔋 ⌐ R 🖂 lau
Prices: ⚑7 ➜3 ⛺9 ▲8

WALENSTADT ST-GALLEN

See-Camping ☎ 081 7351212
Camping Card Compulsory.
mid May-mid Sep 2.2HEC ⚏ 🔌 🏪 ⊙ ⌐ L 🖵 lau ➧ 🍴 ✕ ⌐ 🖂
Prices: ⚑7 ➜3 ⛺5-7 ▲4-8

WILDBERG ZÜRICH

Weid ☎ 052 453388
On a terraced meadow in a very peaceful situation surrounded by woods.
➲ *In Winterthur, follow Tösstal signs, then turn right after spinning-mill in Turbenthal.*
All year 5.4HEC ⚏ 🔌 🏪 🍴 ✕ ⊙ 🚽 🔋 ⌐ 🖂 lau ➧ ⌐PR
Prices: ⚑5 pitch 10-13

WINTERTHUR ZÜRICH

Winterthur Eichliwaldstr 4 ☎ 052 2125260
➲ *To the left of the Schaffhausen road, near the Schützenhaus restaurant.*
All year 1HEC ⚏ 🔌 🏪 ⊙ 🚽 🔋 ⌐ 🖂 lau ➧ 🍴 ✕ ⌐P

NORTH WEST/CENTRAL

This region extends from the French border in the northwest, to Adermatt in the canton of Uri, in the heart of the St Gothard Massif at the crossroads of the Alps. The Province of Jura makes a lovely transition from the Saône plain to the Germanic 'middle country' - it is a gentle land of peaceful pastures and low houses, and is a favourite with cross-country skiers in winter. Neuchâtel, capital of its own canton, stands in a delightful position between the lake of Neuchâtel and the mountains, and has a picturesque old town. The lake offers good facilities for watersports and cruising, and a nearby funicular railway serves Chaumont, from where there is a vast panorama of the Bernese Alps and the Mont Blanc Massif.
Bern is a delight, with pretty arcaded buildings lining the streets of the old town, and a lovely setting facing the Alps. Lucerne has a superb site at the northwestern end of Lake Lucerne, and cruises on the lake offer breathtaking changing panoramas. The Transport Museum in Lucerne contains a fascinating story of the development of Swiss transport.
But the highlight of the central region must be the Alps, with the Jungfrau Massif reaching heights of over 13,600ft. Of course during the winter this is a paradise for winter sports, but during the summer there is good access to the most well-known peaks by road, rail or cable-car, with dizzy heights and spectacular views.
....

AESCHI BERN

Panorama ☎ 033 6544377
400m SE of Camping Club Bern.
15 May-15 Oct 1HEC ⚏ 🔌 🏪 ⊙ 🚽 🔋 🖂 lau ➧ 🍴 ✕ ⌐P
Prices: ⚑5-5.40 ➜2.50 ⛺9-10 ▲7-10

ALTDORF URI

Moosbad Flüerstr ☎ 041 8708541
In a delightful mountain setting.
➲ *Access via Altdorf exit on A2.*
All year 0.9HEC ⠿ 🔌 🏪 ⊙ 🚽 🔋 ⌐ 🖂 lau
Prices: ⚑6 ➜3 ⛺5-6 ▲4-5

BERN (BERNE) BERN
At WABERN

SC Eichholz Strandweg 49 ☎ 031 9612602
In municipal parkland. Separate section for caravans.
➲ *Approach via Gossetstr and track beside river.*
22 Apr-Sep 2HEC ⚏ 🔌 🏪 🍴 ✕ ⊙ 🚽 🔋 ⌐ R 🖵 🖂 lau ➧ 🍴 ✕ ⌐P
Prices: ⚑6.90 ➜12 ⛺9 ▲5-8.50

BRENZIKOFEN BERN

Wydeli (TCS) Wydeli 60 ☎ 031 7711141
➲ *8km N of Thun.*
May-Sep 1.3HEC ⚏ ⛷ 🏪 ✕ ⊙ 🚽 🔋 ⌐ P 🖵 lau ➧ 🏪 🖂
Prices: ⚑5.70-6.30 ⛺12-14 ▲5-14

BRUNNEN SCHWYZ

Hopfreben ☎ 041 8201373
On the right bank of the Muotta stream 100m before it flows into the lake.
➲ *1km W.*
May-29 Sep 1.5HEC ⚏ ♨ ⊕ ⋒ ⤬ ⊙ ⊡ ⊘ ⩱ ▲ ⤳ LR ⊞ ⊞

BURGDORF BERN

Waldegg (TCS) ☎ 034 4227943
➲ *On Oberburg road, turn left at petrol station.*
Etr-Sep 0.5HEC ⚏ ⊕ ⋒ ⊙ ⊡ ⊞ ⤳ ⊡ ⤬ ⊘ ⩱ ⤳PR ⊞

CHAUX-DE-FONDS, LA NEUCHÂTEL

Bois du Couvent ☎ 079 2405039
Partly on uneven ground.
➲ *Take turning off Neuchâtel road near the Zappella and Moeschier factory and drive for 200m.*
15 Jul-15 Aug 2.5HEC ⚏ ⊕ ⋒ ⊡ ⤬ ⊙ ⊡ ⊘ ⩱ ⊟ ⊡ ⤳ P ⊡ ⊞ lau

COLOMBIER NEUCHÂTEL

Paradis-Plage ☎ 038 8412446
In a delightful setting beside Lake Neuchâtel with good, modern facilities.
Mar-Oct 4HEC ⚏ ⊕ ⋒ ⊡ ⤬ ⊙ ⊡ ⊘ ⩱ ⊡ ⤳ L ⊞

ENGELBERG OBWALDEN

Eienwäldli Wasserfallstr 108 ☎ 041 6371949
➲ *1.5km SW behind restaurant Eienwäldli.*
Closed Nov 4HEC ⚏ ♨ ⊕ ⋒ ⊡ ⤬ ⊙ ⊡ ⊘ ⩱ ⤳ PR ⊡ ⊞ lau

ERLACH BERN

Mon Plaisir ☎ 032 3381358
Well equipped site beside the lake.
All year 0.6HEC ⚏ ⊕ ⋒ ⊡ ⤬ ⊙ ⊡ ⩱ ⊟ ⊡ ⤳ L ⊟ lau ⤳ ⤬ ⤳PR ⊞
Prices: pp8-11

EUTHAL SCHWYZ

Euthal ☎ 055 4122718
On the shore of the Sihlsee in a beautiful mountain setting.
The site is reserved for tents only.
Jun-Oct 1HEC ⚏ ✻ ⋒ ⤬ ⊙ ⊡ ⤳ L ⊟ ⊘ ⤳ ⊡ ⊘ ⩱
Prices: ⤳7 ⤳2.50 ▲6-8

FLÜELEN URI

Urnersee ☎ 041 8709222
15 Apr-Oct 4.5HEC ⚏ ✻ ⋒ ⊡ ⤬ ⊡ ⤬ ⊙ ⊡ ⤳ LR ⊡ ⊞ ⤳ ⊘ ⤳P

FRUTIGEN BERN

Grassi ☎ 033 6711149
Scattered with fruit trees beside a farm on the right bank of the River Engstilgern.
➲ *From the Haupstr, turn right at the Simplon Hotel.*
All year 1.5HEC ⚏ ⊕ ⋒ ⊡ ⊙ ⊡ ⊘ ⩱ ⊡ ⊡ ⊞ lau ⤳ ⤳P
Prices: ⤳6.20 pitch 6-12

GAMPELEN BERN

Fanel (TCS) ☎ 032 3132333
On the shore of Lake Neuchâtel.
26 Mar-5 Oct 11.5HEC ⚏ ⊕ ⋒ ⊡ ⤬ ⊙ ⊡ ⊘ ⩱ ⤳ L ⊡ ⊞ lau

GOLDAU SCHWYZ

Bernerhöhe ☎ 041 8551887
On the edge of a forest with a beautiful view of Lake Lauerz.
Separate field for tents.
➲ *1.5km SE and turn left.*
All year 2.5HEC ⚏ ♨ ✻ ⋒ ⊙ ⊡ ⊘ ⊡ ⊞ ⊗ lau

Buosingen ☎ 041 8553898
All year 1.5HEC ⚏ ⊕ ⋒ ⊡ ⤬ ⊙ ⊡ ⊘ ⩱ ⊟ ⊡ ⊡ lau ⤳ ⤬ ⤳LP

GRINDELWALD BERN

Aspen ☎ 036 8531124
Sunny hill terraces.
May-15 Oct 2.5HEC ⚏ ✻ ⋒ ⤬ ⊙ ⊡ ⤳ ⊘ ⊞
Prices: ⤳6 pitch 8-14

Eigernord 27 ☎ 036 534227
1.2HEC ⚏ ⊕ ⋒ ⊡ ⤬ ⊙ ⊡ ⊘ ⩱ ⊡ ⊞ lau ⤳ ⤳P

Camping FRUTIGEN

- Located off the road, alongside the Enstligen stream, surrounded by high pine trees, this is the location for the quiet and well equipped tent site in the summer holiday resort of Frutigen.
- Inexhaustible choice of excursions.
- Favourable starting point for the popular upland walks on the north and south approaches of the Lötschberg railway. Free cycle hire.
- Guided tours for mountain and touring bikes.

Winter Camping Ski-ing resort of Adelboden, Kandersteg, Elsigenalp. Swiss Ski School only 10-12km distant. Inf. W. Glausen, CH-3741 Frutigen.

GSTAAD BERN

Bellerive ☎ 033 4746330
All year 0.8HEC ⟅⟆ ⚙ 🛉 🏪 ✕ ⊙ 🚻 ⌀ 🍴 🚮 ⚓ R ⊞ lau ➡ ⚓P

INNERTKIRCHEN BERN

Aareschlucht Hauptstr 6/11 ☎ 033 9715332
In a beautiful Alpine location with superb mountain views.
All year 0.5HEC ⟅⟆ ⚙ 🛉 🏪 ⊙ 🚻 ⌀ 🚮 🚮 ⚓ ⊞ lau ➡ ⚓ ✕
⚓R
Prices: ⚓5.10-5.50 🚐10-13 ⚓6-10 pitch 8-13

Grund ☎ 033 9714409
Next to a farm on southern outskirts of village.
➲ *Turn S off main road in centre of village at hotel Urweider.*
Drive for 0.3km, turn right.
All year 80HEC ⟅⟆ ⚙ 🛉 ⊙ 🚻 🏪 ⚓ ⚓ ⊞ lau ➡ ⚓ ✕ ⌀ 🚮
⚓R
Prices: ⚓3.50-3.90 🚐13-18 ⚓10-15

INTERLAKEN BERN

Alpenblick Seestr 135, Neuhaus ☎ 033 227757
Well equipped family site on the left bank of the River
Lombach upstream from the bridge in a meadow bordering a
forest opposite the Neuhaus Motel and the Strandbad
Restaurant.
➲ *8km N.*
All year 2.3HEC ⟅⟆ ⚙ 🛉 🏪 ⊙ 🚻 ⌀ 🚮 ⚓ ⊞ lau ➡ ⚓ ✕ ⚓LR

Hobby 3 Lehnweg 16 ☎ 033 8229652
Family site with first class sanitary facilities, quietly situated
with fine views of the surrounding mountains and within
easy walking distance of Interlaken.
➲ *Access via A8 (Spiez-Interlaken) towards*
Gunten/Beatenberg.
Apr-Sep 1.2HEC ⟅⟆ ➡ 🛉 ⊙ 🚻 ⌀ 🚮 ⊞ lau ➡ ✕ ⚓LR
Prices: ⚓5.20-6.40 pitch 14.50-25

Jungfrau Steindlerstrasse 50 ☎ 033 8227107
Has a beautiful view of the Eiger, the Monch and the
Jungfrau.
➲ *Turn right at Unterseen, drive through the Schulhaus and*
Steiner Str to site.
15 Mar-Oct 2.5HEC ⟅⟆ ⚙ 🛉 🏪 ✕ ⊙ 🚻 ⌀ 🚮 ⚓ P ⚓
lau ➡ ⚓LR ⊞

Jungfraublick Gsteigstr 80 ☎ 033 8224414
A family site with clean, modern facilities in a fine central
situation.
➲ *Take Autobahn A8 through tunnel, leave at Lauterbrunnen-*
Grindelwald exit, site on left, 300m from A8 sliproad.
May-25 Sep 1.4HEC ⟅⟆ ⚙ 🛉 ⊙ 🚻 ⌀ ⚓ P ⚓ ⊞ lau
➡ 🍴 ⚓ ✕
Prices: ⚓7.20-8.10 pitch 10-28

Lazy Rancho 4 ☎ 822 8228716
A family campsite in a magnificent position with views of the
Eiger, Mönch and Jungfrau with fine facilities.
➲ *Motorway A8: exit Unterseen, turn toward Gunten. After*
2km turn right, then at Landhotel Golf turn left.
Apr-20 Sep 16HEC ⟅⟆ ⚙ 🛉 ⊙ 🚻 ⌀ ⚓ P ⚓ ⊞ lau
➡ 🍴 ✕ 🚮 ⚓LR
Prices: ⚓5.40-6.70 pitch 7-26

Manor Farm ☎ 033 8222264
A well equipped site in a beautiful mountain setting.
➲ *From motorway A8 (Bern-Spiez-Interlaken-Brienz), exit*
Gunten/Beatenberg; follow signposts.
All year 7.5HEC ⟅⟆ ⚙ 🛉 🏪 🍴 ✕ ⊙ 🚻 ⌀ 🚮 🏪 🚐 ⚓ ⚓ LR ⚓
⊞ lau
Prices: ⚓5.70-9.10 pitch 7-33

Sackgut (TCS) ☎ 036 8224434
Between a hill and the River Aare.
➲ *From Brienz turn left before Interlaken opposite the Ost*
railway station.
May-6 Oct 1.2HEC ⟅⟆ ⚙ 🛉 🏪 🍴 ✕ ⊙ 🚻 ⌀ ⚓ ⊞ lau
➡ ⚓P

KANDERSTEG BERN

Rendez-Vous ☎ 033 6751534
In a delightful mountain setting with good modern facilities.
➲ *750m E of town.*
All year 0.5HEC ⟅⟆ ⚙ 🛉 🏪 🍴 ✕ ⊙ 🚻 ⌀ 🚮 ⚓ ⊞ lau ➡ ⚓P
Prices: ⚓5 ➡3 🚐8-16 ⚓6-12

LANDERON, LE NEUCHÂTEL

Peches ☎ 032 7512900
A small site at the meeting point of the River Thielle and the
Lac de Bienne.
Apr-Sep 2.1HEC ⟅⟆ ☀ 🛉 🏪 🍴 ✕ ⊙ 🚻 ⌀ 🚮 🚐 ⚓ LPR ⚓ ⊞
lau ➡ 🍴 ✕ ⚓P
Prices: ⚓5.50-6.50 ➡3.50 🚐8.50-10 ⚓5.50-8.50

LAUTERBRUNNEN BERN

Jungfrau ☎ 036 552010
Widespread site in meadowland crossed by a stream. Partly
divided into pitches.
➲ *100m before the church turn right, drive a further 400m.*
All year 5HEC ⟅⟆ ⚙ 🛉 🏪 ✕ ⊙ 🚻 ⌀ 🚮 🏪 🚐 ⚓ ⊞ lau
➡ 🍴 ⚓P
See advertisement under Colour section.

Schützenbach (TCS) ☎ 036 551268
About 300m from the lake.
➲ *S of village to the left of road leading to Stechelberg opposite*
B50. 0.8km SE towards Stechelberg.
All year 2.5HEC ⟅⟆ ⚙ 🛉 🏪 🍴 ✕ ⊙ 🚻 ⌀ 🚮 🏪 🚐 ⚓ ⊞ lau
➡ ⚓P

LIGNIÈRES NEUCHÂTEL

Fraso-Ranch ☎ 07 514616
8.7HEC 🛉 🏪 ✕ ⊙ 🚻 ⚓ ⚓ P
Prices: ⚓8 pitch 15

LOCLE, LE NEUCHÂTEL

Communal (TCS) ☎ 032 9317493
3 May-19 Oct 1.2HEC ⟅⟆ 🛉 🍴 ✕ ⊙ 🚻 ⌀ 🚮 ⚓ P ⚓ ⊞ lau ➡ ✕

LUCERNE

See LUZERN

▶ LUNGERN OBWALDEN

Obsee ☎ 041 6781748
In a beautiful setting between the lake and the mountains with good facilities for watersports.
⮑ *1km W.*
All year 1.5HEC 🎪 ⚡ ♠ ⛱ ✕ ⊙ 🛒 ⊘ 🗻 ⇲ LR 🚻 ⊞ lau
➡ 🛁 ⇲P

▶ LÜTSCHENTAL BERN

Dany's Camp ☎ 036 531824
15 May-Sep 4HEC 🎪 ♠ ⛱ ⊙ 🛒 ⊘ 🚻 ⊞ lau ➡ 🛁 ⚡ ✕

▶ LUZERN (LUCERNE) LUZERN

At HORW

Steinibachried (TCS) ☎ 041 4601466
In gently sloping meadow next to the football ground and the beach, separated from the lake by a wide belt of reeds.
⮑ *3.2km S of Luzern.*
26 Mar-5 Oct 2HEC 🎪 ♠ ⛱ ⚡ ✕ ⊙ 🛒 ⊘ 🗻 🚻 ⊞ lau
➡ ✕ ⇲L

▶ MAUENSEE LUZERN

Sursee Waldheim ☎ 041 921 11 61
Next to Waldheim Country Estate.
⮑ *0.8km W of Sursee, 100m from Sursee-Basel road.*
Apr-Sept 1.7HEC 🎪 ♠ ⛱ ⚡ ✕ ⊙ 🛒 ⊘ 🗻 🚻 ⊞ lau ➡ ✕
⇲LP

▶ MOSEN LUZERN

Seeblick ☎ 041 851666
In two strips of land on edge of lake, divided by paths into several squares.
⮑ *N on the A26.*
Apr-Oct 3HEC 🎪 ⚡ ♠ ⛱ ⊙ 🛒 ⊘ 🚌 ⇲ L 🚻 ⊞ lau
➡ ✕
Prices: ♙6.40 ⛺3 🚐5 ⛺3-4

▶ NOTTWIL LUZERN

St Margrethen ☎ 045 541404
Natural meadowland under fruit trees, with own access to lakeside.
⮑ *Turn off road to Sursee 400m NW of Nottwil and drive towards lake for 100m.*
Apr-Oct 1HEC 🎪 ♠ ⛱ ⊙ 🛒 ⊘ ⇲ L 🚻 ⊞ ➡ ✕ ⇲L

▶ PRÊLES BERN

Prêles ☎ 032 3151716
On a wooded plateau overlooking Lake Biel.
⮑ *Turn off the main Biel-Neuchâtel road at Twann and follow signs for Prêles. Pass through village, site on left.*
All year 6HEC 🎪 ♠ ⛱ ✕ ⊙ 🛒 ⊘ ⇲ P 🚻 ⊞
Prices: ♙6.50-6.50 ⛺1-2 🚐7-11 ⛺4-9

▶ SAANEN BERN

Beim Kappeli (TCS) ☎ 033 7446191
In a long meadow between railway and River Saane.
⮑ *1km SE.*
Closed 29 Oct-2 Dec 0.8HEC 🎪 ♠ ⛱ ⊙ 🛒 ⊘ 🚻 ⊞ lau
➡ ✕ ⇲P

▶ SACHSELN OBWALDEN

Ewil ☎ 041 6663270
⮑ *On Lake Sarnersee.*
Apr-Sep 1.5HEC 🎪 ♠ ⛱ ⊙ 🛒 ⊘ 🚌 ⇲ L 🚻 ⊞ lau
Prices: ♙5-5.50 ⛺3-3 🚐6-6 ⛺3-6

▶ SARNER SEE

See SACHSELN

▶ SEMPACH LUZERN

Seeland (TCS) ☎ 041 4601466
Rectangular, level site on SW shore of lake.
⮑ *700m S on Luzern road by lake.*
26 Mar-5 Oct 5.2HEC 🎪 ♠ ⛱ ⚡ ✕ ⊙ 🛒 ⊘ 🚻 ⊞ lau

▶ STECHELBERG BERN

Breithorn ☎ 033 8551225
In a beautiful location in the Lauterbrunnen valley.
⮑ *3km S of Lauterbrunnen.*
All year 1HEC 🎪 ♠ ⛱ ⊙ 🛒 ⊘ 🚌 🚻 ⊞ lau ➡ ✕
Prices: ♙6.40 🚐8-10

▶ UNTERAEGERI ZUG

ZKZS Unteraegeri Wilbrunnenstr 81 ☎ 042 723928
All year 6HEC 🎪 ♠ ⛱ ⊙ 🛒 ⊘ ⇲ L 🚻 ⊞ ⊘ lau ➡ ⇲P

▶ VITZNAU LUZERN

Vitznau ☎ 041 3971280
Well tended terraced site, in lovely countryside with fine views of lake.
⮑ *Approaching from N, turn towards mountain at church and follow signs.*
Apr-5 Oct 1.8HEC 🎪 ♠ ⛱ ⚡ ⊙ 🛒 ⊘ 🗻 ⇲ P 🚻 ⊞ lau ➡ ⚡
✕ ⇲L
Prices: ♙8-9.50 pitch 13-17

▶ WILDERSWIL BERN

Oberei ☎ 036 8221335
A peaceful site in a picturesque village with fine views of the Jungfrau and surrounding mountains. There are good facilities and reservations are recommended during July and August.
Etr-15 Oct 0.6HEC 🎪 ♠ ⛱ ⚡ ⊙ 🛒 ⊘ 🗻 🚌 🚻 ⊞ lau ➡ ⚡ ✕
Prices: ♙5-5.60 pitch 9-17

▶ ZUG ZUG

Innere Lorzenallmend (TCS) Chamer Fussweg 36 ☎ 041 7418422
Pleasantly situated with beautiful view of Lake Zug and surrounding mountains. Much traffic on railway which passes the site.
⮑ *1km NW by lake.*
27 Apr-Sep 1.1HEC 🎪 ♠ ⛱ ✕ ⊙ 🛒 ⊘ 🗻 ⇲ L 🚻 ⊞ lau ➡
⚡ ✕

▶ ZWEISIMMEN BERN

Fankhauser ☎ 030 21356
All year 12HEC 🎪 ⚡ ♠ ⛱ ⊙ 🛒 ⊘ 🗻 🚻 ⊞ lau ➡ 🛁 ⚡ ✕
⇲LPR

Vermeille ☎ 030 21940
Well laid-out site along the River Simme.
⮑ *1km N towards Lake Thun.*
All year 1.3HEC ⚡ ♠ ⛱ ⊙ 🛒 ⊘ 🗻 🚻 lau ➡ ✕ ⇲P ⊞

 EAST

The cantons of Glarus and Grisons make up this region of eastern Switzerland. The town of Glarus still maintains the practice of direct democracy, when every spring all active citizens fill the great Zaunplatz, and in a highly ceremonial meeting decide all issues affecting the community by a show of hands.

Grisons, astride the Alps, is truly Switzerland's holiday corner. Superb road, railway and cable-car networks, run with usual Swiss efficiency, access the wonderful winter sports regions and well-equipped resorts - the elegant Arosa, Davos, Chur, Flims, the famous royal retreat of

Klosters and glittering St Moritz. This efficient transport makes the area a summer paradise for walkers and hikers - there are over 3,000 miles of unsignposted cross-country footpaths. Many areas of superb natural beauty are protected by law - the largest is the 65-square-mile Swiss National Park, reached from Zernez, where authorised roads and paths (and guided walks in season), give glimpses of a flora and fauna completely protected from man.

ANDEER GRAUBÜNDEN

Sut Baselgia (TCS) ☎ 081 6611453
In a pleasant, peaceful setting N towards Chur.
Nov 1.2HEC ⬛ ⚡ ♠ ✕ ⊙ ⌀ ⚑ lau ➡ ⚡ ♟ ✕ ⬍P

AROSA GRAUBÜNDEN

Arosa ☎ 081 311745
All year 0.6HEC ⬛ ⚡ ♠ ⊙ ⚑ ⬍ ➡ ♟ ✕ ⌀ ⬍LP ⊞

CHUR (COIRE) GRAUBÜNDEN

Camp Au (TCS) Felsenaustr 61 ☎ 081 242283
A summer and winter site on level ground with fine views of the surrounding mountains. Good recreational facilities.
➔ *Take exit Chur-Süd from A13. 2km NW of town centre on bank of Rhein. Access is via outskirts of town.*
All year 2.6HEC ⬛ ⚡ ♠ ♟ ✕ ⊙ ⌀ ⌀ ⬍ ⚑ ⬍ ⊞ lau ➡ ⬍P

CHURWALDEN GRAUBÜNDEN

Pradafenz ☎ 081 3821921
Closed 18 Apr-May 1.3HEC ⚡ ♠ ⊙ ⚑ ⌀ ⊞ lau ➡ ♟ ✕ ⬍
⬍PR

LENZ GRAUBÜNDEN

St Cassian ☎ 081 3842472
A level, shady site in a beautiful location at an altitude of 1415mtrs above sea level. There are good facilities and the site is 1km from the town.
➔ *Leave motorway at 'Chur-Süd' exit and follow signs for Lenzerheide/St.Moritz up a well constructed mountain road.*
All year 25HEC ⬛ ⬍ ♠ ♟ ✕ ⊙ ⚑ ⌀ ⬍ ⬍ ⊞ lau ➡ ♟
Prices: ♠6.50-7 ⬛2.50 ⬛8.50 ▲5.50-8.50

MÜSTAIR GRAUBÜNDEN

Clenga ☎ 082 85410
Next to small river near the Italian frontier.
15 May-20 Oct 1.5HEC ⬛ ⚡ ♠ ♟ ♟ ⊙ ⚑ ⌀ ⬍ ⚑ ⬍ R ⬍ ⊞ lau
Prices: ♠5.50-6 pitch 10-12

PONTRESINA GRAUBÜNDEN

Plauns (TCS) ☎ 081 8426285
Beautiful situation at foot of Pit Palü.
➔ *Access from road towards Bernina pass about 4.5km beyond Pontresina. Turn off main road 29 towards Hotel Morteratsch then 0.5km to site.*
25 May-15 Oct 4HEC ⬛ ⬍ ⬍ ⬍ ♠ ♟ ✕ ⊙ ⚑ ⌀ ⬍ ⚑
⬍ ⊞ lau

POSCHIAVO GRAUBÜNDEN

Boomerang ☎ 082 50713
In a quiet setting.
➔ *2km SE.*
All year 1.5HEC ⬛ ⚡ ♠ ⊙ ⚑ ⌀ ⬍ ⊞ lau ➡ ♟

SAMEDAN GRAUBÜNDEN

Punt Muragl (TCS) ☎ 081 8428197
A summer and winter site in a pleasant alpine setting.

➔ *Near Bernina railway halt, to the right of the fork of the two roads Samedan and Celerina/Schlarigna to Pontresina.*
1 Dec-15 Apr & 1 Jun-27 Sep 2HEC ⬛ ⚡ ♠ ♟ ♟ ✕ ⊙ ⚑ ⌀
⬍ ⬍ R ⬍ ⊞ lau ➡ ✕
Prices: ♠5.70-7.10 ⬛10.50-15 ⬛10.50-15 ▲4.20-10.50

SPLÜGEN GRAUBÜNDEN

Sand ☎ 081 6641476
On left bank of River Hinterrhein.
➔ *Turn off the main trunk road in the village and follow signposts.*
All year 0.8HEC ⬛ ➡ ♠ ♟ ♟ ⊙ ⚑ ⌀ ⬍ ⬍ R ⬍ ⊞ lau
➡ ✕ ⊞
Prices: ♠6.40 ⬛3.20 ⬛13-16 ▲6-7.20

STRADA IM ENGADIN GRAUBÜNDEN

Arina ☎ 081 8863212
➔ *At the foot of a mountain, SW of village.*
May-Oct 0.8HEC ⬛ ⚡ ♠ ⊙ ⚑ ⬍ PR ⬍ ⊞ lau ➡ ♟ ✕

SUR EN GRAUBÜNDEN

Sur En ☎ 081 8663544
A family site in a beautiful mountain setting surrounded by pine trees with good facilities.
All year 2HEC ⬛ ⚡ ♠ ♟ ♟ ✕ ⊙ ⚑ ⌀ ⬍ ⬍ ⚑ ⬍ PR ⬍ ⊞
lau

SUSCH GRAUBÜNDEN

Muglinas ☎ 081 8622744
➔ *200m W.*
Jun-15 Sep 1HEC ⬛ ⚡ ♠ ⊙ ⚑ ⌀ ⬍ R ⬍ ⊞ ➡ ♟ ♟
Prices: ♠5 ⬛2 ⬛5 ▲3

THUSIS GRAUBÜNDEN

Viamala ☎ 081 6512472
In pleasant wooded surroundings near the River Hinterrhein and close to the beautiful Viamala Gorge.
➔ *NE towards Chur.*
May-Sep 4.5HEC ⬛ ➡ ♠ ♟ ✕ ⊙ ⚑ ⌀ ⬍ ⊞ lau ➡ ♟ ⬍ ⬍PR

TSCHIERV GRAUBÜNDEN

Sternen (TCS) ☎ 081 8585628
In village behind the Sternen Hotel.
➔ *Between Ofen Pass and Santa Maria.*
All year 1HEC ⬛ ⚡ ♠ ♟ ♟ ✕ ⊙ ⚑ ⬍ PR ⬍ ⊞ lau
Prices: ♠4.50-5 ⬛8-8

VICOSOPRANO GRAUBÜNDEN

Mulina ☎ 081 8221035
May-Oct 1.5HEC ⬛ ⚡ ♠ ✕ ⊙ ⚑ ⬍ LR ⬍ ➡ ♟ ✕ ⌀ ⊞

ZERNEZ GRAUBÜNDEN

Cul ☎ 081 8561456
➔ *Off road 27 W of Zernez.*
May-15 Oct 3.6HEC ⬛ ⚡ ♠ ♟ ♟ ✕ ⊙ ⚑ ⌀ ⬍ R ⬍ ⊞
lau ➡ ✕ ⬍P
Prices: ♠5.80-6.50 ⬛2.50-2.50 ⬛7-7 ▲5-5

● ● ● ● **SOUTH** ● ● ● ●

Here, in the canton of Ticino, the German and Italian cultures mingle in a land where Alpine mountains and valleys fall towards the great lakes and the plain of Lombardy. The province is a climatic oasis: the Alpine chain protects it from strong winds, and even in winter there is a comparatively high number of sunny days. Alpine and Mediterranean plant species flourish side by side, giving Ticino a unique flora.

Contd.

In this area of outstanding beauty, Lugano remains a favourite with visitors. The town has a traditional atmosphere, with attractive lanes and shopping arcades, spacious parks and lakeside promenades. Excursions from Lugano lead to high mountains and some of the best views in the country - Mount San Salvatore, Mount Bré and Mount Generoso. Locarno, a lovely town on the shores of Lake Maggiore, is also popular, and the exceptionally mild southern climate produces lush vegetation and a wonderfully colourful display of flowers in early spring.

ACQUACALDA TICINO

Ai Cembri Lukmanierstr ☎ 091 8722610
Apr-Oct 5HEC ⟱ 🔧♠🛁🍴✕⊙🚐∅🚿🚮 ⫪ R 🏕🔲 🎿 lau

AGNO TICINO

Eurocampo ☎ 091 6052114
Part of site is near its own sandy beach and is divided by groups of trees.
⟳ *600m E on road from Lugano to Ponte Tresa. Entrance opposite Aeroport sign and Alfa Romeo building.*
Apr-Oct 6HEC ⟱ 🔧♠🛁🍴✕⊙🚐∅🚮 ⫪ L 🔲🏕 lau ⬆✕
Prices: ⚑7.50 🚗2.50-4 ⛺6-9 👤6

Golfo del Sole via Rivera 8 ☎ 091 6054802
By lake. Separate play area for children.
Etr-25 Oct 6HEC ⟱ 💧🔧♠🛁🍴✕⊙🚐∅🚮 ⫪ L 🔲🏕⬆✕
Prices: ⚑7-8 🚗2 ⛺9-16 👤7-13

AVEGNO TICINO

Piccolo Paradiso ☎ 093 811581
In the Maggia Valley between the main road and River Maggia.
⟳ *6km NW from Locarno on the Maggia Valley road.*
Mar-Oct 4HEC ⟱ 🔧♠🛁🍴✕⊙🚐∅🚮 ⫪ R 🔲 lau ⬆ ⫪P

CHIGGIOGNA TICINO

Gottardo ☎ 091 8661562
Open meadowland on mountain slope partly on natural terraces.
⟳ *1km S of Faido, 20m above A2.*
All year 0.8HEC ⟱ 🔧♠🛁🍴✕⊙🚐∅ ⫪ PR 🏕 lau

CLARO TICINO

Censo ☎ 091 8631753
Below a woodland slope.
⟳ *Off the A2 (E9).*
Apr-Sep 2HEC ⟱ ⬆♠🛁🍴✕⊙🚐∅🚮 ⫪ PR 🏕🔲 lau

CUGNASCO TICINO

Park-Camping Riarena ☎ 091 8591688
Beautiful park-like family site in level, natural woodland. All facilities are well maintained and Lake Maggiore is within easy reach.
⟳ *1.5km NW. Turn off road 13 at BP filling station 9km NE of Locarno and continue 0.5km.*
Apr-18 Oct 3.2HEC ⟱ ⁝⁝⁝ ⬆♠🛁🍴✕⊙🚐∅🚮🚐 ⫪ P 🏕🔲 lau ⬆ ⫪R
Prices: ⚑7-8 🚗2-3 ⛺11-16 👤11-16

GORDEVIO TICINO

Bellariva ☎ 093 871444
In quiet location between the road and the left bank of the River Maggia.
Apr-Oct 2.5HEC ⟱ 🔧♠🛁⊙🚐∅ ⫪ PR 🏕🔲 lau ⬆🍴✕

LOCARNO TICINO

Delta via Respini 7 ☎ 091 7516081
A beautiful, well-equipped and well-organised site at Lake Maggiore.
⟳ *2km away from the city.*
Mar-Oct 60HEC ⟱ ⁝⁝⁝ 🔧♠🛁🍴✕⊙🚐∅🚮🚐 ⫪ LR 🏕 🔲🎿 lau ⬆ ⫪P
Prices: ⚑10-15 pitch 20-30

At LOSONE(4km W)

Zandone ☎ 091 7916563
In a quiet, picturesque location beside the River Melezza with fine views of the Tessin mountains.
⟳ *Situated between the Losone-Golino road and the river.*
Etr-Oct 2.1HEC ⟱ 🔧♠🛁🍴✕⊙🚐∅🚮🚐 ⫪ R 🏕🔲⬆🍴✕
Prices: ⚑9.60 🚗4 ⛺16 👤11-15

MELANO TICINO

Pedemonte ☎ 091 6498333
Between railway and lake with own private beach.
⟳ *Turn off road no.2 in S outskirts of Maroggia towards lake.*
Apr-Oct 2HEC ⟱ 🔧♠🛁🍴✕⊙🚐∅ ⫪ L 🏕🔲 lau

MOLINAZZO DI MONTÉGGIO TICINO

Tresiana ☎ 091 6083342
A family site on meadowland with trees on riverbank.
⟳ *Turn right after bridge in Ponte Tresa, then 5km to site.*
Etr-Oct 1.5HEC ⟱ 🔧♠🛁✕⊙🚐∅🚮🚐 ⫪ PR 🏕 lau ⬆🍴✕⫪L
Prices: ⚑6 🚗2.50 ⛺10-13.50 👤4.50-13.50

ROVEREDO TICINO

Vera ☎ 091 8271857
⟳ *10km N of Bellinzona near A13 exit 'Chur-Bellinzona'.*
All year 4HEC ⟱ 🔧♠🛁🍴✕⊙🚐∅🚮 ⫪ PR 🏕 lau ⬆🛁🔲

TENERO TICINO

Campofelice Lago Maggiore ☎ 091 (0041) 745 14 17
Beautifully situated and extensive site completely divided into pitches, and crossed by asphalt drives.
⟳ *1.9km S. Signposted.*
27 Mar-24 Oct 15HEC ⟱ ⁝⁝⁝ ⬆♠🛁🍴✕⊙🚐∅🚮🚐 ⫪ LR 🏕🔲🎿 lau

Lido Mappo Via Mappo ☎ 091 7451437
Beautifully situated, well appointed site on lakeside. Teenagers not accepted on their own. Minimum stay, 1 week in Jul-Aug.
⟳ *700m SW. Signposted.*
19 Mar-24 Oct 6.5HEC ⟱ ⬆♠🛁🍴✕⊙🚐∅🚮 ⫪ L 🏕🔲 🎿 lau ⬆ ⫪PR
Prices: pitch 38-55 (incl 3 persons)

Miralago ☎ 093 671255
Situated in pleasant position by the lake. Caravans only.
⟳ *Access from main road TL 21 to via Pressighe to via Roncaccio.*
All year 2HEC ⟱ 🔧⬆♠🛁🍴✕⊙🚐∅🚐 ⫪ LP 🏕🔲 lau

Tamaro via Mappo ☎ 091 7452161
Well equipped site with direct access to the lake. Groups of young persons not admitted unless accompanied by adults.
⟳ *4km from Locano. Signposted from motorway.*
18 Mar-24 Oct 6HEC ⟱ 🔧♠🛁🍴✕⊙🚐∅🚮 ⫪ L 🏕🔲 🎿 lau ⬆ ⫪P
Prices: pitch 33-64 (incl 2 persons)

Verbano ☎ 093 671020
Site in two sections, of which one is on the lakeside. The larger section has access to the lake about 150m distance.
⮕ *Signposted.*
Apr-Oct 2.6HEC ⭤ ⌇⌇⌇ ▦ 🏕 🗻 ☉ 🟩 🚿 ⸌ LR ⊞ lau ➧ 🍴 ✗

 ## SOUTH WEST

Vaud, Fribourg, Valais and Geneva are the cantons in this south-west region. All these provinces have resorts at every altitude to welcome both summer and winter visitors - the mountains and glaciers are easily accessed in winter for skiers, and in summer mountain huts, chalets, and hotels provide facilities for walkers and hikers.

Valais has been a trading crossroads since Roman times, with its passes at St Bernard and Simplon. The Rhône, with its tributaries, cuts a lovely swathe through Valais on its way to the jewel of the south west - Lake Geneva. Resorts dot the lake shores - small towns like Crans, Nyon and Vevey, popular Montreux, cosmopolitan Lausanne, and, of course, the country's great international centre, Geneva. Art, culture and education are great traditions here, and there is a wealth of attractions for tourists - excellent shopping centres, renowned restaurants, an attractive old town, fascinating museums, and miles of attractive promenades along the shores of the lake with wonderful views of the mountains.

AGARN VALAIS

Gemmi Briannenstr ☎ 027 4731154
In a very pleasant location on the outskirts of the town, providing outstanding views of the surrounding mountains. There are clean, modern facilities and individual bathrooms are available for weekly hire.
⮕ *Exit from A9 at Agarn. Signposted*
23 Apr-09 Oct 0.9HEC ⭤ ⌇⌇⌇ ▦ 🏕 ✗ ☉ 🟩 🚿 ⛰ ☎ ⊞ lau ➧ 🍴 ✗ ⸌P
Prices: 🏕6.80-7.80 pitch 10-18

AIGLE VAUD

Glariers (TCS) ☎ 025 262660
Near railway line and the avenue des Glariers.
⮕ *800m NE off the A9 near SHELL/MIGROL petrol station.*
3 Apr-29 Sep 1HEC ⠿ ⌇⌇⌇ 🏕 🗻 🍴 ✗ ☉ 🟩 🚿 ⛰ ☎ lau ➧ ✗ ⸌P

AROLLA VALAIS

Petit Praz ☎ 027 2832295
In an imposing mountain setting.
Jun-Sep 1.2HEC ⭤ ⌇⌇⌇ ⬦ 🏕 🗻 ☉ 🟩 🚿 ➧ 🗻 🍴 ✗
Prices: 🏕5.60 🚗1.50 🚐6-8 ⛺3-6

BALLENS VAUD

Bois Gentil ☎ 021 8095120
⮕ *200m S of station.*
Apr-Sep 2.5HEC ⭤ 🏕 🗻 🗻 ☉ 🟩 🚿 ⸌ P ☎ ⊞

BOUVERET, LE VALAIS

Rive Bleue ☎ 024 4812161
Beside lake with a natural sandy beach and good, modern facilities.
⮕ *Turn off the A37 to Monthey in the SW district of Bouveret and drive NE for about 0.8km.*
Apr-Sep 2HEC ⭤ 🏕 🗻 🗻 ☉ 🟩 🚿 ⛰ 🏪 🟩 ⛺ ▲ ⸌ LP 🅿 ⊞ lau ➧ 🍴 ✗
Prices: 🏕7.20-8.70 🚗1.70 🚐7.80-10.60 ▲7.30-9.70

BULLET VAUD

Cluds ☎ 024 4541440
In beautiful mountain setting among pine trees with a private beach on Lake Neuchâtel.
⮕ *1.5km NE.*
All year 1.2HEC ⭤ 🌱 🏕 ✗ ☉ 🟩 🚿 ⛰ 🅿 ⊞ lau

CHÂTEAU-D'OEX VAUD

Berceau (TCS) La Place ☎ 029 47788
On level strip of grass between the mountain and the river bank.
⮕ *1km SE at junction of roads 77 and 76.*
All year 1HEC ⭤ 🏕 🗻 🍴 ✗ ☉ 🟩 🚿 ⸌ PR ☎ ⊞ lau

CHÂTEL-ST-DENIS FRIBOURG

Bivouac rte des Paccots ☎ 021 9487849
Beautiful views of the rolling Swiss countryside. Various sports and leisure activities.
⮕ *Turn E in Chatel-St Denis and continue for 2km.*
All year 2HEC ⭤ 🏕 🗻 🍴 ✗ ☉ 🟩 🚿 ⛰ ▲ ⸌ P ☎ ⊞ lau ➧ ✗ ⸌R
Prices: 🏕6 pitch 15

CHESSEL VAUD

Grands Bois ☎ 025 814225
On a level meadow close to a canal and only a few kilometres from Lake Geneva.
⮕ *N of town towards the lake.*
All year 3.5HEC ⭤ 🏕 🗻 🟩 🚿 ⸌ P lau ➧ 🗻 🍴 ✗
Prices: 🏕4.50-5.50 🚗3 🚐7-10 ▲5-8

CUDREFIN VAUD

Chablais ☎ 037 773277
500mtrs from the town centre, directly on the lake.
15 Mar-Oct 228HEC ⭤ 🏕 🗻 ☉ 🟩 ⸌ L 🅿 lau ➧ 🗻 🍴 ✗ 🚿 ⸌R ➧
Prices: 🏕8 🚗3 🚐8 ▲6-8

DÜDINGEN FRIBOURG

Schiffenensee ☎ 026 493486
⮕ *Leave the A12 (Bern-Fribourg) at Düdingen and proceed N towards Murten.*
Apr-Oct 9HEC ⭤ 🏕 🗻 🍴 ✗ ☉ 🟩 ⸌ LP ☎ ⊞ lau ➧ 🚿 ⛰
Prices: 🏕8 🚐10 ▲8

EPAGNY-GRUYÈRES FRIBOURG

Sapins ☎ 029 29575
⮕ *1km N on the edge of a forest.*
30 May-Sep 2.2HEC ⭤ 🏕 🗻 🗻 ✗ ☉ 🟩 🚿 ⛰ ☎ 🅿 ⊞ lau ➧ ⸌LPR

EVOLÈNE Valais

Evolène ☎ 027 2831144
➲ *200m from town*
May-Oct 10HEC 〜 ♨ lau ✦R
Prices: ♦4.50 ♦2 ♦6 ▲4-6

FOREL Vaud

Forel ☎ 021 7811464
A family site in a pleasant rural setting with good
recreational facilities.
➲ *Leave the A9 at Chexbres in the direction of Forel and take
left turning to Savigny.*
All year 4HEC 〜 P lau
Prices: ♦4.50-6.50 ♦6.50-12 ▲4-10

FOULY, LA Valais

Glaciers ☎ 027 7831735
At end of village in a beautiful Alpine location with fine
views of the surrounding mountains.
15 May-Sep 7HEC lau ✦
Prices: ♦6 pitch 10-16

GENÈVE (GENEVA) Genève

At SATIGNY(6km SW)

Bois-de-Bay ☎ 022 3410505
➲ *Leave A1 at Bernex and follow campsite signs.*
All year 2.8HEC
Prices: ♦7 ♦3.50 ♦8-14.50 ▲4-6

At VÉSENAZ(6km NE)

Pointe á la Bise (TCS) ☎ 022 7521296
Small pool for children. On shores of lake.
➲ *NE between Vésenaz and Bellerive.*
3 Apr-27 Oct 3.2HEC L
Prices: ♦5-6 ♦6.50-7 ♦6.50-12 ▲6.50-9

GRÄCHEN Valais

Grächbiel ☎ 027 9563202
A modern site with excellent facilities, in a good location for
access to Zermatt.
All year 6HEC lau

GRANDSON Vaud

Pécos C.P 515 ☎ 024 4454969
➲ *400m SW of railway station between railway and lake.*
Apr-Sep 2HEC L
lau
Prices: ♦6.70 ♦3 ♦6-12 ▲4.80-12

GUMEFENS Fribourg

Lac ☎ 026 9152162
On the borders of the lake.
15 May-15 Sep 1.5HEC L
lau
Prices: ♦6.40 ♦2.20 ♦8.50 ▲6.50-8.50

LAUSANNE Vaud

At OUCHY

Vidy chemin du Camping 3 ☎ 021 6242031
In a delightful location amid trees and flowerbeds overlook-
ing Lac Léman. Shop and restaurant open May-Sep only.
All year 4.5HEC L lau
Prices: ♦6.50 ♦2.50 ♦11 ▲7-11

LEUKERBAD Valais

Sport-Arena Leukerbad ☎ 027 4701037
➲ *On road N of Leuk.*
May-Oct 1HEC lau ✦PR

LEYSIN Vaud

Sémiramis ☎ 024 4941829
In a picturesque Alpine setting.
➲ *After entering the village turn left at SHELL filling station
and continue for 400mtrs.*
All year 1.1HEC lau
✦P

MORGES Vaud

Petit Bois (TCS) ☎ 021 8011270
➲ *Follow Geneva road from town. Site by lakeside.*
26 Mar-19 Oct 3.2HEC lau
✦LP

MORGINS Valais

Morgins (TCS) ☎ 025 4772361
A terraced site below pine forest.
➲ *Turn left at end of village towards Pas de Morgins near
Swiss Customs.*
All year 1.5HEC lau ✦LPR
Prices: ♦4.60 pitch 10

PAYERNE Vaud

Piscine de Payerne ☎ 037 614322
Camping Card compulsory
Apr-Sep 8HEC P lau
Prices: ♦4.50 ♦2 ♦6-8 ▲3.50-5.50

RARON Valais

Santa Monica ☎ 027 9342424
All year 4HEC P lau
✦LR
Prices: ♦5-6 ♦9.50-12 ▲7-8.50

Simplonblick ☎ 027 9341274
➲ *300m W of Turtig.*
Apr-Oct 6HEC P lau
✦

RECKINGEN Valais

Ellbogen (TCS) ☎ 028 731355
On an alpine meadow close to the River Rhône.
➲ *400m S on bank of Rhône.*
13 May-13 Oct 1.3HEC lau
✦P

RIED-BRIG Valais

Tropic ☎ 028 232537
➲ *To the left of Simplon road near entrance to village. 3km
above Brig.*
May-15 Sep 1.5HEC lau

RÔCHE Vaud

Clos de la George (TCS) Les Ecots ☎ 025 265828
➲ *4.5km from Aigle.*
All year 2.6HEC P
lau

SAAS-GRUND Valais

Kapellenweg ☎ 028 572989
On a level meadow in a picruresque mountain setting in the
Saas Valley. Good, modern facilities.
➲ *Turn right over bridge towards Saas-Almagell.*
May-Oct 1.5HEC R lau ✦
Prices: ♦4-5 ♦2.50-3 ♦3-3.50 ▲3-3.50

SALGESCH Valais

Swiss Plage ☎ 027 4556608
Situated beside a small lake and surrounded by vineyards.

Good recreational facilities.
Etr-1 Nov 10HEC ⬛ ⠿ ◊ ⚘ ⋔ ⌱ ♥ ✕ ⊙ ⊟ ∅ ⚏ ⌂ ⋈ ⋌
L ⌸ lau ➡ ⊞
Prices: ♠6.30 pitch 14

▶ SEMBRANCHER VALAIS

Prairie (TCS) ☎ 027 7852206
➲ *12km from Martigny and 500m from town.*
All year 50HEC ⬛ ⋇ ⋔ ⌱ ♥ ✕ ⊙ ⊟ ∅ ⚏ ⋌ R ⌸ lau

▶ SIERRE (SIDERS) VALAIS

Bois de Finges (TCS) ☎ 027 550284
Very beautiful site.
Camping Carnet Compulsory.
➲ *Access difficult for caravans.*
May-Sep 2HEC ⠿ ◆ ⋔ ⌱ ♥ ✕ ⊙ ⊟ ∅ ⋌ PR ⌸ ⊞ lau ➡ ✕
⚏ ⋌L

▶ SORENS FRIBOURG

Forêt ☎ 029 51882
➲ *Turn right off the A12 in Gumefens and drive on to the village.*
All year 4HEC ⬛ ⚘ ⋔ ⌱ ✕ ⊙ ⊟ ∅ ⋌ P ⌸ lau
Prices: ♠6.80 ⋈2.50 ⋈5 ▲5 pitch 3

▶ SUSTEN VALAIS

Bella Tola (TCS) ☎ 027 4731491
A peaceful, terraced site at an altitude of 750mtrs, sheilded by a belt of woodland. Good, clean modern facilities.
➲ *2km from village.*
12 May-30 Sep 3.6HEC ⬛ ⚘ ⋔ ⌱ ♥ ✕ ⊙ ⊟ ∅ ⚏ ⌂ ⋈ ⋌
P ⌸ ⊞ lau
Prices: ♠9.50 pitch 10-25

Rhodania Kantonstr ☎ 027 4731312
May-Oct 0.3HEC ⬛ ◆ ⋔ ⌱ ✕ ⊙ ⊟ ⊠ ➡ ⚏ ∅ ⋌PR ⊞
Prices: ♠5 ⋈2 ⋈4.50 ▲3.50

▶ ULRICHEN VALAIS

Nufenen ☎ 027 9731437
➲ *1km SE to right of road to Nufenen Pass.*
30 Jun-Sep 8HEC ⬛ ⚘ ⋔ ♥ ⊙ ⊟ ∅ ⋌ R ⌸ ⊞ ➡ ⌱ ✕
Prices: ♠5 ⋈3 ⋈4 ▲3.50

▶ VALLORBE VAUD

Pré sous Ville (TCS) ☎ 021 8432309
In a wooded riverside location. Neighbouring swimming pool available to campers free of charge.
➲ *On left bank of River Orbe.*
May-Oct 1HEC ⬛ ⚘ ⋔ ⊙ ⊟ ∅ ⋌ P ⌸ ⊞ lau ➡ ⌱ ✕
Prices: ♠6 ⋈8-9.50 ⋈8-9.50 ▲3-6

▶ VERS-L'ÉGLISE VAUD

Murée (TCS) ☎ 021 8011908
Partially terraced site by a stream.
➲ *Signposted on the right at the entry to the village.*
All year 1.1HEC ⬛ ⋇ ⚘ ⋔ ⊙ ⊟ ∅ ⋌ R ⌸ lau ➡ ✕

▶ VETROZ VALAIS

Botza (TCS) ☎ 027 3461940
All year 3HEC ⬛ ⚘ ⋔ ⌱ ♥ ✕ ⊙ ⊟ ∅ ⚏ ⌂ ⋌ P ⌸ ⊞

▶ YVONAND VAUD

Pointe d'Yvonand ☎ 024 4301655
6km NE of Yverdon bordering Lake Neuchâtel with private beach 1km away, boat moorings, private jetty and boat hire.
➲ *3km W. Signposted.*
Apr-Sep 5HEC ⬛ ⠿ ◆ ⋔ ⌱ ♥ ✕ ⊙ ⊟ ∅ ⚏ ⌂ ⋈ ⋌ L ⊡
⊞ ⌀ lau
Prices: ♠6.70 ⋈3 ⋈6-12 ▲4.80-12

Driving to Europe for your holiday this year

YOU NEED A ROUTE FROM **European Routes Service**

For more details
tel: 0117 930 8242

INDEX

INDEX

INDEX

INDEX

GERMANY

INDEX

INDEX

LUXEMBOURG

NETHERLANDS

INDEX

INDEX

INDEX

MAJOR ROAD & RAIL TUNNELS

ROAD TUNNELS
See Lights in the ABC. Minimum and maximum speed limits operate in the road tunnels.

During the winter wheel chains may occasionally be required on the approaches to some tunnels. However, you may not use them in tunnels. Use the laybys provided for removal and refitting. Charges listed below are a guide only.

BIELSA France-Spain
The trans-Pyrenean tunnel is 3km (2 miles) long, and runs nearly 1830 metres (6000ft) above sea level between Aragnouet and Bielsa.The Bielsa is open 24hrs a day.

CADI Spain
The tunnel is 5km (3 miles) long and runs about 1220 metres (4000ft) above sea level under the Sierra del Cadi mountain range between the villages of Bellver de Cerdanya and Baga, and to the west of the Toses (Tosas) Pass.

Charges (in Pesetas)

Motorcycles	1015
Cars	1260
Car/caravan	1260

FREJUS France-Italy
This tunnel is over 1220 metres (4000ft) above sea level and runs between Modane and Bardonecchia. The tunnel is 12.8km (8 miles) long, 4.5 metres (14ft 9in) high, and the single carriageway is 9 metres (29ft 6in) wide. The minimum speed is 60kph (37mph) and the maximum 80kph (49mph).

Charges (in French francs)

Motorcycles	99
Cars wheelbase less than 2.30 metres (7ft 6.5in)	99
Wheelbase from 2.30 metres to 2.63 metres (7ft 6.5in to 8ft 7.5in)	150
Wheelbase from 2.63 metres to 3.30 metres (8ft 7.5in to 10ft 10in)	196
Car/caravan	196
Wheelbase over 3.30 metres (10ft 10in)	472
Vehicles with three axles	718
With four or more axles	950

MONT BLANC Chamonix (France)-Courmayeur (Italy)
The tunnel is over 1220 metres (4000ft) above sea level and is 11.6km (7 miles) long. The single carriageway is 7 metres (23ft) wide. Permitted dimensions of vehicles are: height 4.30 metres (14ft 1in); length 20 metres (65ft 7in); width 2.80 metres (9ft 2in). Larger vehicles, up to 4.70 metres (15ft 5in) high, by special arrangement. Minimum speed is 50kph (31mph); maximum 80kph (49mph). Do not stop, overtake, sound your horn or make U-turns. Use only side/rear lights not headlights and keep 100 metres (110yds) distance between vehicles.

Make sure you have sufficient petrol for the journey, 30km (19 miles). There are breakdown bays with telephones. From November to March, wheel chains may be required on the approaches.

Charges (in French francs)

Motorcycles	100
Cars wheelbase less than 2.30 metres (7ft 6.5in)	100
Wheelbase from 2.30 metres but less than 2.63 metres (7ft 6.5in to 8ft 7.5in)	150
Wheelbase from 2.63 metres to a maximum of 3.30 metres (8ft 7.5in to 10ft 10in)	200
Car/caravan	200
Wheelbase over 3.30 metres (10ft 10in)	480
Vehicles with three axles	730
With four or more axles	970

GRAND ST BERNARD Switzerland - Italy
The tunnel is over 1830 metres (6000ft) above sea level. Although there are covered approaches, wheel chains may be needed in winter. Customs, passport control and toll offices are at the entrance. The tunnel is 5.9km (3.6 miles) long. Permitted maximum dimensions of vehicles are: height 4 metres (13ft 1in), width 2.5 metres (8ft 2.5in). Minimum speed is 40kph (24mph); maximum 80kph (49mph). Do not stop or overtake. Breakdown bays have telephones.

Charges* (in Swiss francs)

Motorcycles	15
Cars	27
Car/caravan	27
Minibus, camper van (2 axles)	56.50
Vehicles with three axles	90
with four axles	134
with five or more axles	139

*Motorway tax disc (see Switzerland Country Intro) must be displayed.

ST GOTTHARD Switzerland

The world's longest road tunnel at 16.3km (10 miles) is about 1159 metres (3800ft) above sea level; it runs under the St Gotthard Pass from Göschenen, on the northern side in the Alps, to Airolo in the Ticino. The tunnel is 4.5 metres (14ft 9in) high, and the single carriageway is 7.5 metres (25ft) wide. Maximum speed is 80kph (49mph). Forming part of the Swiss motorway network, the tunnel is subject to motorway tax, and the tax disc must be displayed (see Switzerland - Country Intro).

SAN BERNARDINO Switzerland

This tunnel is over 1525 metres (5000ft) above sea level. It is 6.6km (4 miles) long, 4.8 metres (15ft 9in) high; the carriageway is 7 metres (23ft) wide. Do not stop or overtake in the tunnel. Keep 100 metres (110yds) between vehicles. There are breakdown bays with telephones.

Forming part of the Swiss motorway network, the tunnel is subject to motorway tax; tax disc must be shown (see Switzerland - Country Intro).

ARLBERG Austria

This tunnel is 14km (8.75 miles) long and runs at about 1220 metres (4000ft) above sea level, to the south of and parallel to the Arlberg Pass.

Charges* (in Austrian schillings)

Motorcycles	100
Cars	130
Caravans	60

*Motorway tax disc (see Austria Country Intro) must be displayed.

BOSRUCK Austria

This tunnel is 742 metres (2434ft) above sea level. It is 5.8km (3.6 miles) long and runs between Spital am Pyhrn and Selzthal, to the east of the Pyhrn Pass. Maximum speed is 80kph (49mph). Do not overtake. Use of dipped headlights compulsory; occasional emergency laybys with telephones. With the Gleinalm Tunnel (see below) it forms part of the A9 Pyhrn Autobahn between Linz and Graz, being built in stages.

Charges* (in Austrian schillings)

Motorcycles	60
Cars	70
Car/caravan	100

*Motorway tax disc (see Austria Country Intro) must be displayed.

FELBERTAUERN Austria

This tunnel, over 1525 metres (5000ft) above sea level, runs between Mittersill and Matrei, west of and parallel to the Grossglockner Pass.

The tunnel is 5.3km (3.25 miles) long, 4.5 metres (14ft 9in) high, and the two-lane carriageway is 7 metres (23ft) wide. From November to April, wheel chains may be needed on the approach.

Charges (in Austrian schillings)

Motorcycles	110
Cars summer rate (May-Oct)	140
winter rate (Nov-Apr)	130
Car/caravan summer rate (May-Oct)	140
winter rate (Nov-Apr)	130

GLEINALM Austria

This tunnel, part of the A9 Pyhrn Autobahn, is 817 metres (2680ft) above sea level, 8.3km (5 miles) long and runs between St Michael and Friesach, near Graz.

Charges* (in Austrian schillings)

Motorcycles	100
Cars	110
Car/caravan	140

*Motorway tax disc (see Austria Country Intro) must be displayed.

KARAWANKEN Austria-Slovenia

This motorway tunnel under the Karawanken mountains between Rosenbach in Austria and Jesenice in Slovenia is about 610 metres (2000ft) above sea level and nearly 8km (5 miles) long.

Charges* (in Austrian schillings)

Motorcycles	90
Cars	90
Car/caravan	135

*Motorway tax disc (see Austria Country Intro) must be displayed.

TAUERN AUTOBAHN (Katschberg and Radstädter) Austria

Two tunnels, the Katschberg and the Radstädter Tauern, form the key elements of this toll motorway between Salzburg and Carinthia.

The Katschberg tunnel is 1110 metres (3642ft) above sea level. It is 5.4km (3.5 miles) long, 4.5 metres (14ft 9in) high, and the single carriageway is 7.5 metres (25ft) wide.

The Radstädter Tauern tunnel is 1340 metres (4396ft) above sea level and runs east of the Tauern railway tunnel (see below). The tunnel is 6.4km (4 miles) long, 4.5 metres (14ft 9in) high; the single carriageway is 7.5m (25ft) wide.

Charges* (for the whole toll section between Flachau and Rennweg:) **(in Austrian schillings)**

Motorcycles	100
Cars	140
Car/caravan	180

***Motorway tax disc (see Austria Country Intro) must be displayed.**

RAIL TUNNELS
CHANNEL TUNNEL See the Continental ABC

SWITZERLAND
Vehicles are conveyed throughout the year through the Lötschberg tunnel (Kandersteg-Goppenstein). Services are frequent with no advance booking necessary; actual transit time is 15-20 minutes, but loading and unloading formalities can take some time.

A full timetable and tariff is available from the Swiss National Tourist Office (see Switzerland - Tourist information for address) or at most Swiss frontier crossings.

ALBULA TUNNEL Switzerland
Thusis (723 metres, 2372ft) - Samedan (1722 metres, 5650ft).

The railway tunnel is 5.9km (3.5 miles) long. It will accept vehicles, but you must give notice. Thusis telephone 081 811113 and Samedan telephone 082 65404. Journey time 90 minutes.

Services
9 trains daily southbound; 6 trains daily northbound.

Charges (in Swiss francs; likely to increase)

Cars (including driver)	100
Additional passengers	24
Car/caravan	270

FURKA TUNNEL Switzerland
Oberwald (1367 metres, 4482ft)-Realp (1539 metres, 5046ft).

Railway tunnel is 15.4km (9.5 miles) long. Journey time 15 minutes.

Services
Hourly from 06.50-21.00.

Charges (in Swiss Francs)

| Cars (including passengers) | 34 |
| Car/caravan | 68 |

OBERALP RAILWAY Switzerland
Andermatt (1444 metres, 4737ft)-Sedrun (1441 metres, 4728ft). Journey duration 50 minutes.

Booking
Advance booking is necessary; Andermatt telephone 044 67220, Sedrun tel 086 91137.

Services
2-4 trains daily, winter only (from October-April).

Charges (in Swiss francs)

Cars (including driver)	73
Additional passengers	11
Car/caravan	146

TAUERN TUNNEL Austria
Bockstein (1131 metres, 3711ft)(near Badgastein)-Mallnitz, 8.5km (5.5 miles) long.
Maximum dimensions, caravans and trailers: height 8ft 10.5in, width 8ft 2.5in.

Booking
Advance booking unnecessary (except for request trains), but motorists must report at least 30 minutes before dparture. Drivers must drive their vehicles on and off the wagon.

Services
At summer weekends, trains run approximately every half-hour in both directions, 06.30-22.30hrs; and every half-hour at night. For the rest of the year, there is an hourly service from 06.30-22.30hrs (23.30hrs on Fri and Sat from 7 July-9 September). Journey time 12 minutes.

Charges (in Austrian schillings)

Motorcycles (with or without sidecar)	100
Cars (including passengers)	190
Caravans	80

LOCAL AND INTERNATIONAL CALLS

It is no more difficult to use the telephone abroad than it is at home. It only appears to be so because of unfamiliar language and equipment. The following chart may help with elementary principles when making local calls from public callboxes, but try to get help if you encounter language difficulties.

International Direct Dial (IDD) calls can be made from many public callboxes abroad, avoiding surcharges imposed by most hotels.

Types of callboxes from which IDD calls can be made are identified in the chart. You will need to dial the international code, international country code (for the UK it is 44), the telephone dialling code (omitting the initial 'O'), followed by the number. For example to call a Basingstoke number from Italy, dial 00 44 1256 followed by the number you require. Use higher-denomination coins for IDD calls to ensure reasonable periods of conversation before the coin expiry warning. The equivalent of £2 should allow for a reasonable amount of time.

Cardphones are in general use; phonecards may be purchased from a post office or shop in the vicinity, unless stated otherwise.

Country	Insert coin/card before or after lifting receiver	Dialling tone	Making local and national calls
	After (instructions in English in many callboxes)		
	After	Same as UK	Precede number with relevant area code where necessary
	After	Continuous tone	Dial 0 before the 9 digit-number
	After	Continuous tone	Precede number with relevant area code when necessary
	Before		Precede number with relevant area code when necessary
	After	Same as UK	There are no area codes
	After (instructions in English in all callboxes)		
	After	Same as UK	Precede number with relevant area code when necessary
	After (instructions in English in many callboxes)		Do not press button to left of the dial or you may lose your money
	After	Continuous tone	Precede number with relevant area code when necessary

Replacement for p.350 where country headings are missing from the table.

USING THE TELEPHONE ABROAD

LOCAL AND INTERNATIONAL CALLS

It is no more difficult to use the telephone abroad than it is at home. It only appears to be so because of unfamiliar language and equipment. The following chart may help with elementary principles when making local calls from public callboxes, but try to get help if you encounter language difficulties.

International Direct Dial (IDD) calls can be made from many public callboxes abroad, avoiding surcharges imposed by most hotels.

Types of callboxes from which IDD calls can be made are identified in the chart. You will need to dial the international code, international country code (for the UK it is 44), the telephone dialling code (omitting the initial 'O'), followed by the number. For example to call a Basingstoke number from Italy, dial 00 44 1256 followed by the number you require. Use higher-denomination coins for IDD calls to ensure reasonable periods of conversation before the coin expiry warning. The equivalent of £2 should allow for a reasonable amount of time.

Cardphones are in general use; phonecards may be purchased from a post office or shop in the vicinity, unless stated otherwise.

Country	Insert coin/card before or after lifting receiver	Dialling tone	Making local and national calls
AUSTRIA	After (instructions in English in many callboxes)		
BELGIUM	After	Same as UK	Precede number with relevant area code where necessary
FRANCE	After	Continuous tone	Dial 0 before the 9 digit-number
GERMANY	After	Continuous tone	Precede number with relevant area code when necessary
ITALY	Before		Precede number with relevant area code when necessary
LUXEMBOURG	After	Same as UK	There are no area codes
NETHERLANDS	After (instructions in English in all callboxes)		
PORTUGAL	After	Same as UK	Precede number with relevant area code when necessary
SPAIN	After (instructions in English in many callboxes)		Do not press button to left of the dial or you may lose your money
SWITZERLAND	After	Continuous tone	Precede number with relevant area code when necessary

COUNTRY MAP SECTION

AUSTRIA

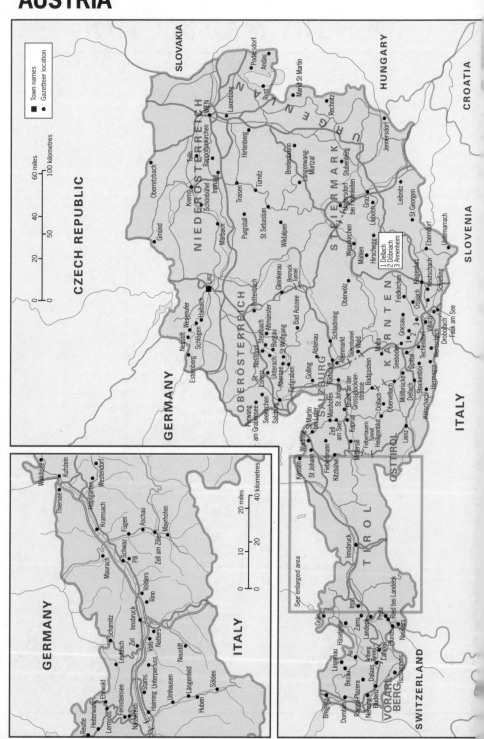

1

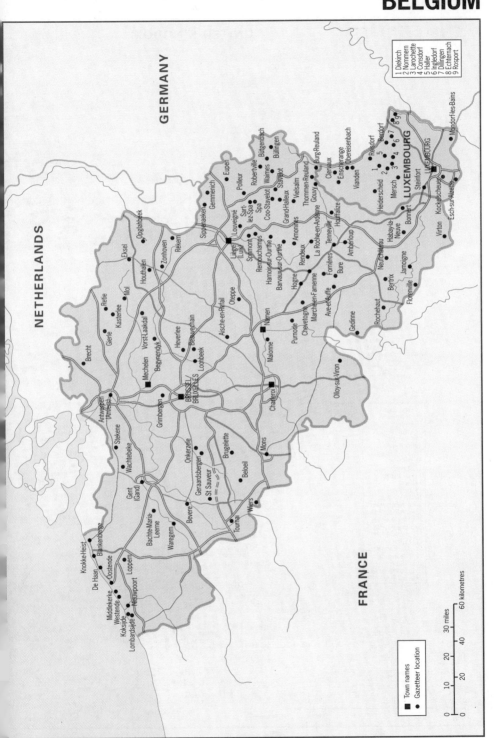

BELGIUM

GERMANY

NETHERLANDS

FRANCE

LUXEMBOURG

1 Diekirch
2 Nommern
3 Larochette
4 Consdorf
5 Haller
6 Ingeldorf
7 Dillingen
8 Echternach
9 Rosport

Knokke-Heist
De Haan
Blankenberge
Oostende
Middelkerke
Westende
Koksijde
Nieuwpoort
Lombardsijde
Loppem

Brecht
Gierle
Retie
Kasterlee
Mol
Eksel
Houthalen
Zonhoven
Rekem
Onglabbeek
Sippelbaeken

Antwerpen (Anvers)
Stekene
Wachtebeke
Gent (Gand)
Bachte-Maria-Leerne
Waregem
Bevere
Geraardsbergen
St Sauveur
Onkerzele
Tournai
Wiers
Beloeil
Brugelette
Mons

Grimbergen
Mechelen
Begijnendyk
VorsLaakdal
Heverlee
Beauvechain
Loonbeek
BRUSSEL/BRUXELLES
Aische-en-Refail
Oteppe
Malonne
Namen
Charleroi
Olloy-sur-Viron

Eupen
Gemmenich
Polleur
Roberville
Bütgenbach
Büllingen
Robertville
Warnes
Stavelot
Burg-Reuland
Louveigné
Sart-lez-Spa
Spa
Coo-Stavelot
Grand-Halleux
Velsalm
Clervaux
Liège (Luik)
Spimont
Rendeux
Anmonies
Gouvy
Vianden
Heiderscheid
Mersch
Renouchamps
Hamoir-sur-Ourthe
Banavaux-Ourthe
La Roche-en-Ardenne
Tenneville
Holffalize
Amberloup
Bomert
Kockelscheuer
Hogne
Marchien-Famenne
Torrières
Bure
Neufchâteau
Stenfort
Esch-sur-Alzette
Purnode
Chevetogne
Ave-et-Auffe
Habay-la-Neuve
Jamoigne
Virton
Gedinne
Rochehaut
Bertrix
Florenville
Mondorf-les-Bains

Thommen-Reuland
Einscherange
Obereisenbach

■ Town names
● Gazetteer location

0   10   20   30 miles
0   20   40   60 kilometres

FRANCE

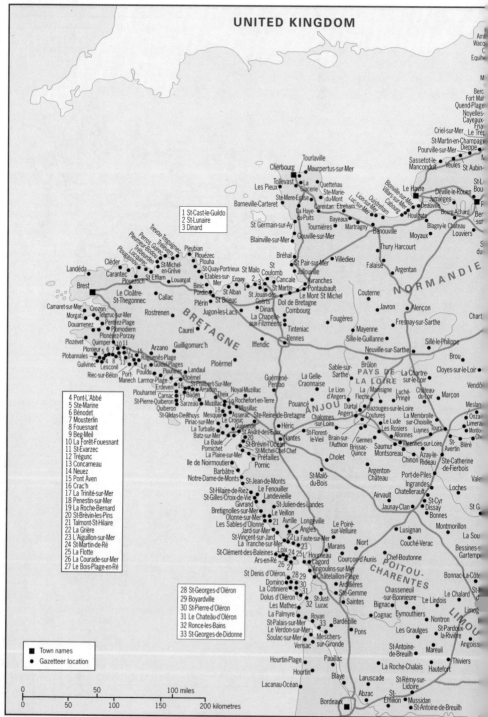

UNITED KINGDOM

1 St-Cast-le-Guildo
2 St-Lunaire
3 Dinard

4 Pont-L'Abbé
5 Ste-Marine
6 Bénodet
7 Mousterlin
8 Fouesnant
9 Beg-Meil
10 La Forêt-Fouesnant
11 St-Evarzec
12 Trégunc
13 Concarneau
14 Neuez
15 Pont Aven
16 Crac'h
17 La Trinité-sur-Mer
18 Penestin-sur-Mer
19 La Roche-Bernard
20 St-Brévin-les-Pins
21 Talmont-St-Hilaire
22 La Grière
23 L'Aiguillon-sur-Mer
24 St-Martin-de-Ré
25 La Flotte
26 La Couarde-sur-Mer
27 Le Bois-Plage-en-Ré

28 St-Georges-d'Oléron
29 Boyardville
30 St-Pierre-d'Oléron
31 Le Chateâu-d'Oléron
32 Ronce-les-Bains
33 St-Georges-de-Didonne

■ Town names
● Gazetteer location

0   50   100 miles
0   50   100   150   200 kilometres

3

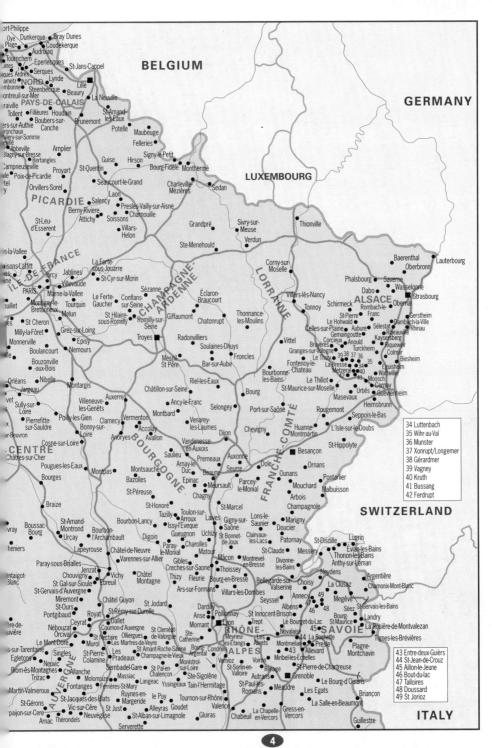

FRANCE

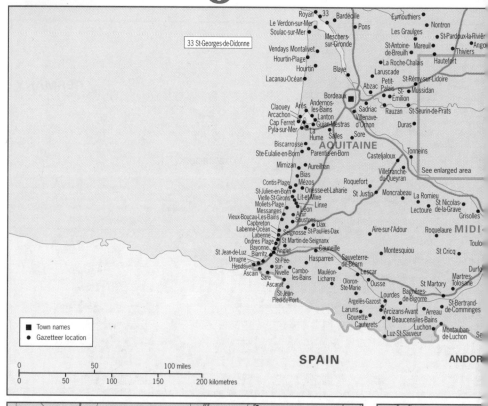

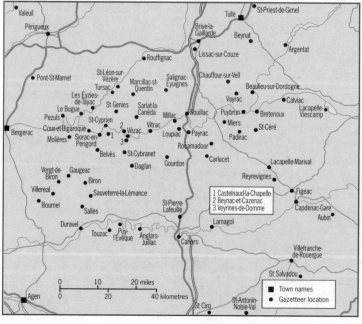

43 Entre-deux-Guiers
44 St-Jean-de-Crouz

49 Bessèges	57 Tarascon
50 St-Germain-de-	58 Fontvielle
Calberte	59 St Reim
51 St-Jean-de-Gard	60 Mouries
52 Arpaillargues	61 Orgon
53 Remoulins	62 St-Andiol
54 Pont-du-Gard	63 Salon-de-Provence
55 Villeneuve-les-	64 La Roque-
Avignon	d'Anthéron
56 Vallabrègues	65 Charleval

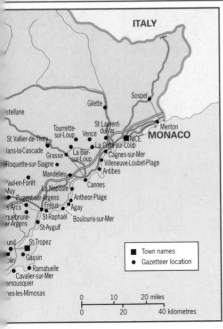

Town names ■
Gazetteer location ●

0   10   20 miles
0   20   40 kilometres

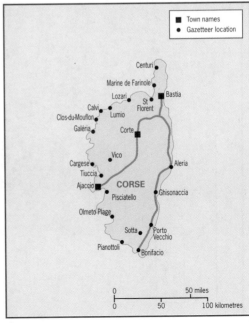

Town names ■
Gazetteer location ●

0   50 miles
0   50   100 kilometres

4

GERMANY

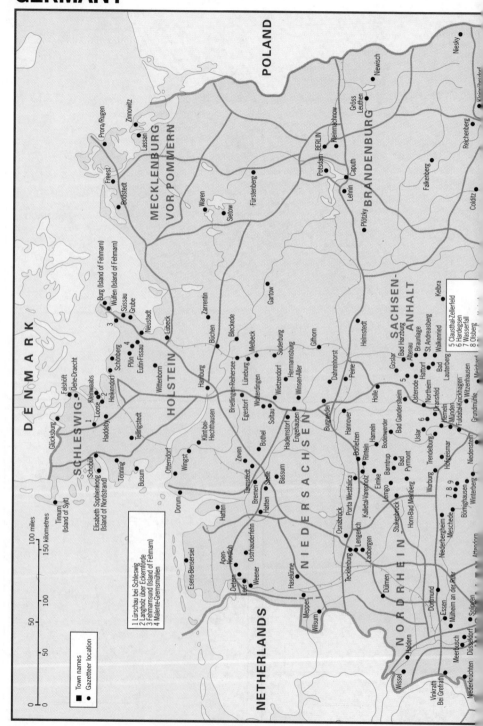

POLAND

Niesky

Niewisch

Gross Leuthen

Reichenberg

Colditz

Falkenberg

BRANDENBURG

Weinmachnow

BERLIN

Potsdam

Caputh

Lehnin

Plötzky

MECKLENBURG VOR POMMERN

Prora/Rügen

Zinnowitz

Lassan

Freest

Brodstedt

Waren

Sietow

Fürstenberg

Gartow

Zarrentin

Bleckede

Büchen

Lübeck

Neustadt

Grube

Süssau

Wulfen (Island of Fehmarn)

Burg (Island of Fehmarn)

Schönberg

3

Plön

4

Eutin-Fissau

Wittenborn

Harburg

Klint-bei-Hechthausen

Melbeck

Süderburg

Hermannsburg

Hammannsburg

Winsen-Aller

Lüneburg

Wietzendorf

Soltau

Egestorf

Briefingen-Reihersee

Gifhorn

Helmstedt

Dahrenhorst

Peine

Hannover

Holle

Burgwedel

Hademstorf

Engelhausen

SACHSEN-ANHALT

Kelbra

Bad Harzburg

Altenau

Braunlage

St. Andreasberg

Goslar

Northeim

Hattorf

Osterode

Mansfeld

Bad Lauterberg

Walkenried

5

Bad Gandersheim

Uslar

Hehlen

Münden

Fuldatal-Knickhagen

Grundmühle

Meinhart

Niedenstein

6

Witzenhausen

Hofgeismar

Trendelburg

Warburg

Meerhof

7 8 9

Bad Pyrmont

Bodenwerder

Rinteln

Börftlen

Hameln

Barntrup

Lemgo

Eimke

Kalletal-Varenholz

Hom-Bad Meinberg

Niederbergheim

Meschede

Börnighausen

Winterberg

Attendorn

Atteln

NORD RHEIN

Niedermarsberg

Dortmund

Essen

Mülheim an der Ruhr

Solingen

Düsseldorf

Meerbusch

Niederkrüchten

Vinkrath Bei Grefrath

Wisse

Haldern

Dülmen

Haltern

Meppen

Wilsum

NIEDERSACHSEN

Osnabrück

Tecklenburg

Lengerich

Ladbergen

Stukenbrock

Porta Westfalica

Haselünne

Leer

Detern

Weener

Ostrhauderfehn

Apen-Nordloh

Esens-Bensersiel

Hatten

Dorum

Hatten

Bremen

Stelle

Bassum

Tarmstedt

Zeven

Bothel

Wingst

Ottendorf

Busum

Tönning

Tellingstedt

Glückstadt

Haddeby

Loose

Hekendorf

2

1

Kleinwaabs

Gelle-Draecht

Falshöft

Schobüll

Elisabeth Sophienkoog (Island of Nordstrand)

Tinnum (Island of Sylt)

DENMARK

SCHLESWIG

HOLSTEIN

DE NM AR K

100 miles

150 kilometres

100

50

50

0   0

1 Lürschau bei Schleswig
2 Langhölz über Eckernförde
3 Fehmarnsund (Island of Fehmarn)
4 Malente-Gremsmühlen

5 Clausthal-Zellerfeld
6 Hardegsen
7 Wasserfall
8 Olsberg

NETHERLANDS

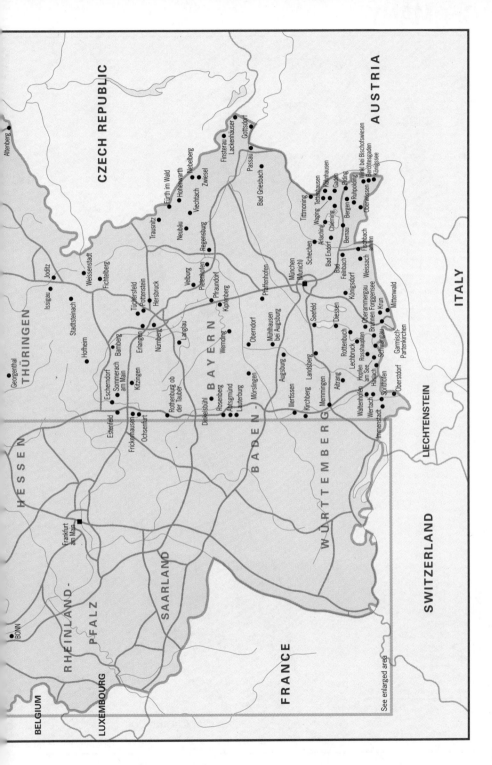

5

GERMANY

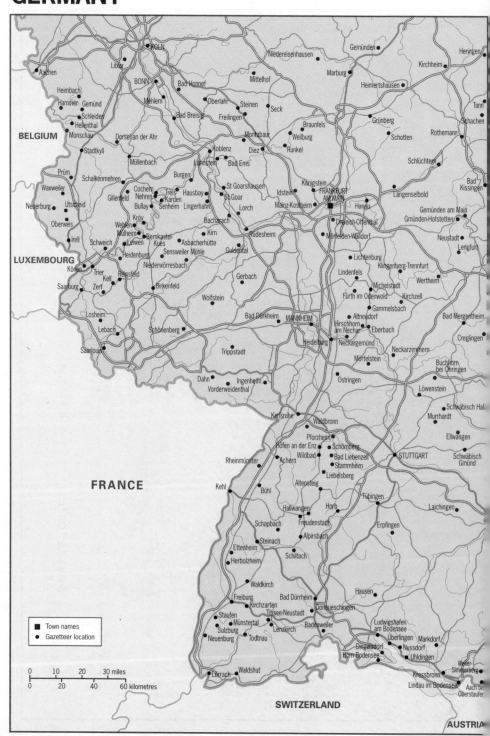

BELGIUM

LUXEMBOURG

FRANCE

SWITZERLAND

AUSTRIA

Aachen
KÖLN
Liblar
Niedereisenhausen
Gemünden
Heringen
Kirchheim
BONN
Bad Honnef
Mittelhof
Marburg
Heimertshausen
Tann
Schachen
Heimbach
Hammer
Gemünd
Mehlem
Oberlahr
Steinen
Seck
Braunfels
Grünberg
Schotten
Rothemann
Schleiden
Hellenthal
Bad Breisig
Freilingen
Montabaur
Weilburg
Monschau
Dorsel an der Ahr
Stadtkyll
Koblenz
Diez
Runkel
Schlüchtern
Prüm
Müllenbach
Lahnstein
Bad Ems
Waxweiler
Schalkenmehren
Burgen
St Goarshausen
Königstein
Idstein
FRANKFURT AM MAIN
Langenselbold
Bad Kissingen
Neuerburg
Utscheid
Cochem
Nehren
Treis
Karden
Hausbay
St Goar
Mainz-Kostheim
Hanau
Gillenfeld
Senheim
Lingerhahn
Lorch
Gemünden am Main
Gmünden-Hofstetten
Oberweis
Kröv
Bullay
Bacharach
Dreieich-Offenthal
Wehlen
Kirn
Rüdesheim
Mörfelden-Walldorf
Neustadt
Lengfurt
Irrel
Mülheim
Bernkastel-Kues
Asbacherhütte
Guldental
Lichtenburg
Klingenberg-Trennfurt
Schweich
Leiwen
Sensweiler Mühle
Lindenfels
Wertheim
Heidenburg
Niederwörresbach
Michelstadt
Kirchzell
Könen
Trier
Kell
Repsfeld
Gerbach
Fürth im Odenwald
Gammelsbach
Bad Mergentheim
Saarburg
Zerf
Birkenfeld
Altneudorf
Creglingen
Wolfstein
Bad Dürkheim
MANNHEIM
Hirschhorn am Nechar
Eberbach
Losheim
Neckargemünd
Neckarzimmern
Lebach
Schönenberg
Heidelburg
Mortelstein
Buchhorn bei Öhringen
Saarlouis
Trippstadt
Ostringen
Löwenstein
Dahn
Ingenheim
Schwäbisch Hall
Vorderweidenthal
Murrhardt
Karlsruhe
Waldbronn
Ellwangen
Pforzheim
Höfen an der Enz
Schömberg
Rheinmünster
Achern
Wildbad
Bad Liebenzell
STUTTGART
Schwäbisch Gmünd
Kehl
Bühl
Stammheim
Liebelsberg
Altensteig
Hallwangen
Horb
Tübingen
Laichingen
Schapbach
Freudenstadt
Erpfingen
Steinach
Alpirsbach
Ettenheim
Schiltach
Herbolzheim
Waldkirch
Hausen
Freiburg
Bad Dürrheim
Kirchzarten
Donaueschingen
Staufen
Titisee-Neustadt
Münstertal
Lenzkirch
Badenweiler
Ludwigshafen am Bodensee
Sulzburg
Überlingen
Markdorf
Neuenburg
Todtnau
Dingelsdorf
Nussdorf
Uhldingen
Horn Bodensee
Weiler-Simmerberg
Lörrach
Waldshut
Kressbronn
Lindau im Bodensee
Aach bei Oberstaufen

■ Town names
● Gazetteer location

0   10   20   30 miles
0   20   40   60 kilometres

6

NETHERLANDS

Town names
Gazetteer location

0   20   40   60 miles
0   50   100 kilometres

Nes
Formerum
Hee
West
Terschelling
Harlingen
Franeker
De Koog   De Cocksdorp
Den Helder
Den Hoorn
Groote Keeten
Callantsoog
St Maartenszee
Petten
Alkmaar
Helloo
Berkhout
Velsen-Zuid
Haarlem
Vogelenzang
Noordwijk aan Zee
Rijnsburg
Katwijk aan Zee
Wassenaar
's-Gravenzande
Hoek Van Holland

GRONINGEN
Lauwersoog   Delfzijl
Groningen   Harkstede
Bergum   Opende   Onnen
Roden   Annen   Wedde
Makkum   Assen   Gasselte
Hindeloopen   Wateren   Amen   Borger
Koudum   Diever   Grolloo
Sondel   Steenwijk   Dwingeloo   Emmen
Andijk   Ruinen
Noord Scharwoude   Urk   Blokzijl
Wijdenes   DRENTHE

FRIESLAND

Edam   Dronten
Uitdam   FLEVOLAND
Nunspeet   Hattem   Ommen
Wezep   Dalfsen
Luttenberg   Denekamp
Ermelo   Ernst   OVERIJSSEL   Delden   Hengelo
Putten   Vaassen   Holten   Markelo   Enschede
Kootwijk   Apeldoorn   Diepenheim   Buurse
Beekbergen   Lochem   Haaksbergen
Hoenderloo   Eerbeek   Hengelo   Neede
Otterlo   Laag-Soeren   Ruurlo   GELDERLAND
Arnhem   Lathum
Doorn   Winters Wijk
Rhenen   Wageningen   Doesburg   Doetinchem
Kesteren   Babberich
Appeltern

Halfweg   AMSTERDAM
Aalsmeer
Mijnden   UTRECHT
Leiden   Bilthoven   Soest
Utrecht   Maarn
DEN HAAG

Delft   Zevenhuizen
Oostvoorne   Brielle   Rotterdam
Rockanje   Barendrecht
Ouddorp   Hellevoetsluis   Dordrecht
Renesse   ZUID-HOLLAND
Burgh-Haamstede   Brouwershaven   Hank
Herpen   Heumen
Kamperland   Hoeven   Cromvoirt   NOORD-   Plasmolen
Westkapelle   Kortgene   Breda   Oosterhout   BRABANT   St Anthonis   Afferden
Zoutelande   ZEELAND   Roosendaal   Rijen   Tilburg   Boxtel   St Oedenrode   Broekhuizenvorst
Koudekerke   Arnemuiden   Wemeldinge   Oisterwijk   Eindhoven   Venray   Arcen
Nieuwvliet   Vlissingen   Baarle Nassau   Hilvarenbeek   Mierlo   LIMBURG   Venlo
Breskens   Hoogerheide   Vessem   Sevenum
Groede   Baarland   Lage Mierde   Eersel   Maasbree
Retranchement   Hoek   Hengstdijk   Bladel   Bergijk   Soerendonk   Asselt
Sluis   Luyksgestel   Weert   Roermond
Stramproy   Herkenbosch
Echt

Schinveld
Berg en Terblijt
Maastricht   Valkenburg

GERMANY

BELGIUM

FRANCE

NOORD-
HOLLAND

1 Domburg
2 Oostkapelle
3 Vrouwenpolder
4 Middelburg

7

ITALY

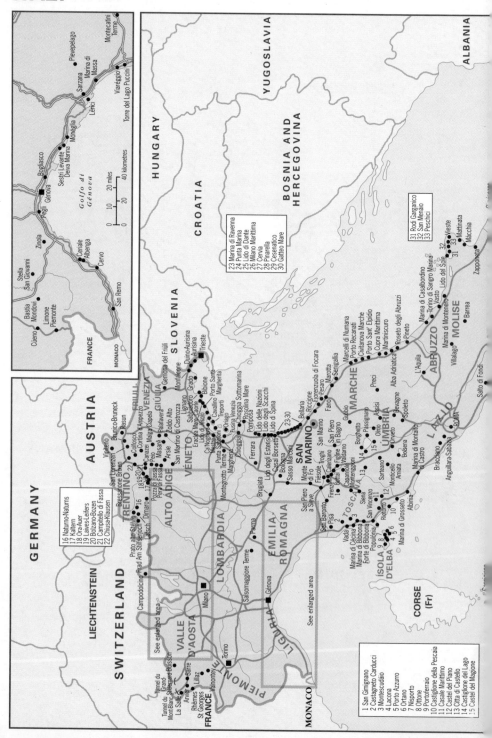

16 Naturno-Naturns
17 Kaltem
18 Ora-Auer
19 Laives-Leifers
20 Bolzano-Bozen
21 Campotello di Fassa
22 Chiusa-Klausen

23 Marina di Ravenna
24 Punta Marina
25 Lido di Dante
26 Milano Marittima
27 Cervia
28 Pinarella
29 Cesenatico
30 Gatteo Mare

31 Rodi Garganico
32 San Menaio
33 Peschici

1 San Gimignano
2 Castagneto Carducci
3 Montescudaio
4 Lacona
5 Porto Azzurro
6 Ortano
7 Nisporto
8 Ottone
9 Portoferraio
10 Castiglione della Pescaia
11 Casale Marittimo
12 Castel del Piano
13 Città di Castello
14 Castiglione del Lago
15 Castel del Magione

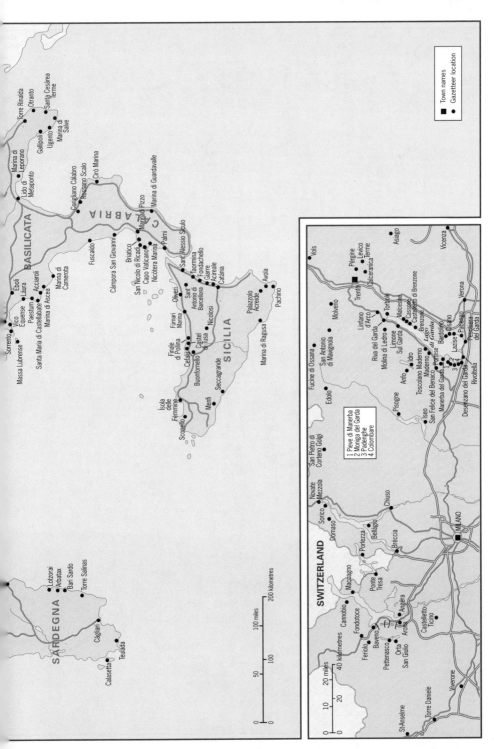

Town names ■

Gazetteer location ●

SARDEGNA

Calasetta
Teulada
Càgliari
Lotzorai
Arbatax
Bari Sardo
Torre Salinas

BASILICATA

Sorrento
Massa Lubrense
Vico Equense
Eboli
Làura
Paestum
Santa Maria di Castellabate
Marina di Camerota
Marina di Ascea
Acciaroli

Càmpora San Giovanni
Briatico
San Nicolo di Ricadi
Capo Vaticano
Nicotera Marina
Marina di Guardavalle
Marina di
Pizzo

CALABRIA

Gengliano Calabro
Rossano Scalo
Cirò Marina

Lido di
Metaponto
Marina di
Leporano
Gallipoli
Ugento
Marina di
Salve
Torre Rinalda
Otranto
Santa Cesàrea
Terme

Fuscaldo
Palmi
Sant' Alessio Siculo
Taormina
Fondachello
Giarre
Acireale
Catania
Oliveri
Sant'
Antonio di
Barcellona
Nicolosi
Palazzolo
Acreide
Avola
Pachino

Furnari
Marina
Finale
di Pollina
Castel
di Tusa
Cefalù
Buonfornello
Marina di Ragusa

SICILIA

Isola
delle
Fèmmine
Scopello
Seccagrande
Menfi

0   50   100 miles
0   100   200 kilometres

SWITZERLAND

Vols
Pérgine
Lévico
Trento
Calceranica Terme
Asiago
Vicenza
Verona

Molveno
Molina di Ledro
Linfano
d'Arco
Torbole
Malcesine
Cassone
Castelletto di Brenzone
Riva del Garda
Brenzone
Limone
Sul Garda
Bardolino
Làzise
Ùstano
Pacengo
Lago
di Garda
Peschiera
del Garda
Rivoltella
San
Antonio
di Mavignola
Vidro
Anfo
Toscolano Maderno
Maderno
Gardone
Gargnano
Manerba del Garda
San Felice del Benaco
Desenzano del Garda
Iseo

Fucine di Ossana
Edolo
Pisogne

San Pietro di
Corteno Golgi
Novate
Mèzzola
Sònico
Dòmaso
Pòrlezza
Bellagio
Brèscia
Chiuso

1 Pieve di Manerba
2 Moniga del Garda
3 Padenghe
4 Colombare

MILANO

Macàgnio
Ponte
Tresa
Angera
Castelletto
Ticino
Cannòbio
Fondotoce
Fèriolo
Baveno
Pettenasco
Orta
San Giulio
Arona
Arona

Viverone

St-Anselme
Torre Dàniele

0   10   20 miles
0   20   40 kilometres

8

SPAIN AND PORTUGAL

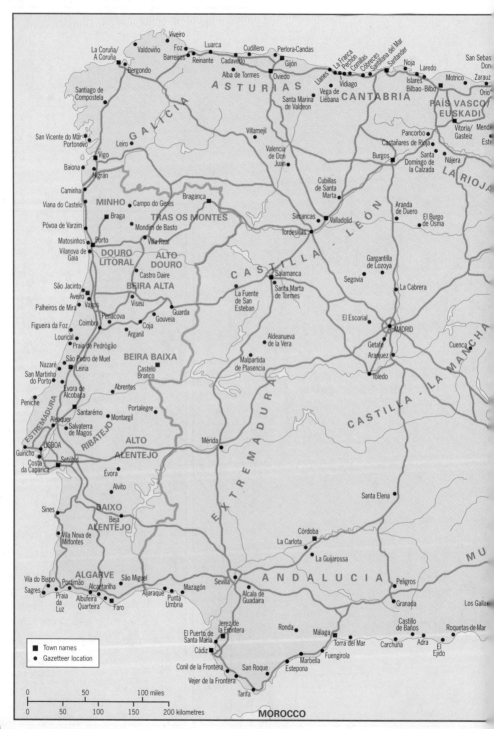

Legend:
■ Town names
● Gazetteer location

0   50   100 miles
0   50   100   150   200 kilometres

MOROCCO

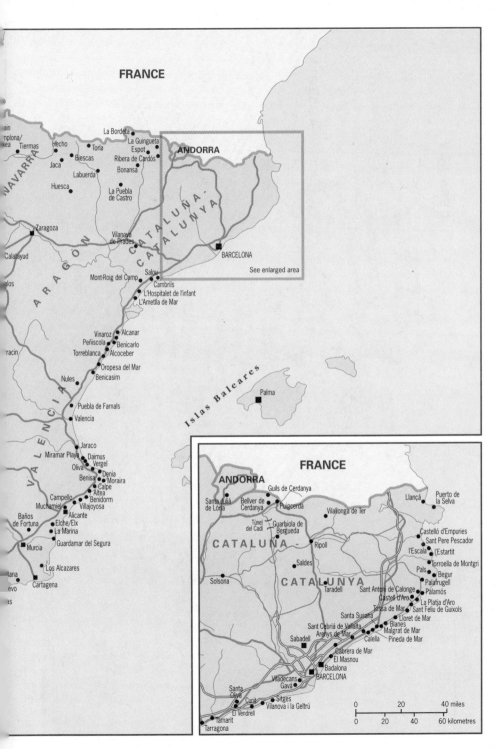

SWITZERLAND

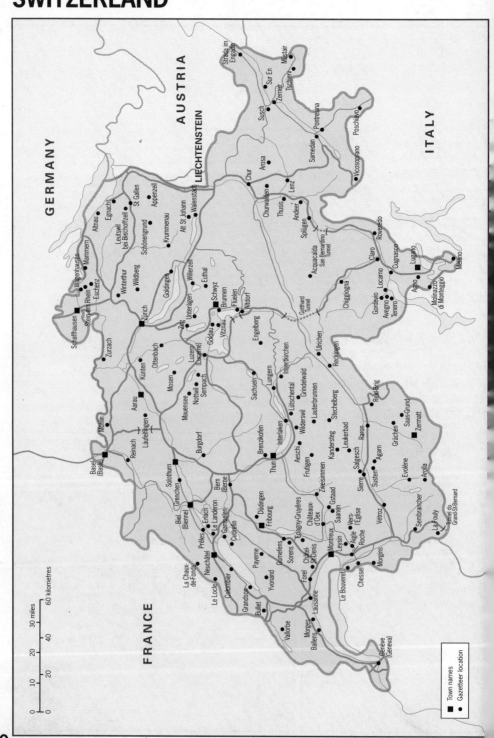

GERMANY

AUSTRIA

LIECHTENSTEIN

ITALY

FRANCE

Strada im Engadin
Mistair
Sur En
Tschierv
Zernez
Susch
Pontresina
Poschiavo
Samedan
Vicosoprano
Roveredo
Cugnasco
Arosa
Lugano
Chur
Lenz
Melino
Churwalden
Thusis
Ander
Splügen
Agno
San Bernardino Tunnel
Molinazzo di Monteggio
Acquacalda
Claro
Locarno
Walenstadt
Alt St Johann
Appenzell
St Gallen
Krummenau
Schönengrund
Egnach
Altnau
Leutswil bei Bischofzell
Mammern
Wilzezell
Euthal
Gordevio
Avegno
Tenero
Chiggiogna
Gotthard Tunnel
Ulrichen
Reckingen
Wagenhausen
Stein am Rhein
Eschenz
Winterthur
Wildberg
Goldingen
Schwyz
Brunnen
Flüelen
Altdorf
Engelberg
Zürich
Unterägeri
Goldau
Vitznau
Zug
Schaffhausen
Zurzach
Künten
Ottenbach
Luzern (Lucerne)
Lungern
Interlaichen
Reid-Brig
Mollin
Aarau
Mosen
Mauensee
Nottwil
Sempach
Sachseln
Widerswil
Grindelwald
Lauterbrunnen
Stechelberg
Saas-Grund
Zermatt
Grächen
Reinach
Laufelfingen
Burgdorf
Brenzikofen
Unterinken
Aeschi
Kandersteg
Leukerbad
Raron
Agarn
Basel (Basle)
Solothurn
Grenchen
Thun
Frutigen
Zweisimmen
Sierre
Salgesch
Susten
Evolène
Arolla
Biel (Bienne)
Erlach
Bern (Berne)
Gstaad
Le Landeron
Gampelen
Cudrefin
Düdingen
Epagny-Gruyères
Gruyères
Vétroz
Sembrancher
La Fouly
Prêles
Fribourg
Saanen
Châteaux-d'Oex
Vers-l'Église
Tunnel du Grand-St-Bernard
La Chaux-de-Fonds
Neuchâtel
Payerne
Sorens
Château-St-Denis
Montreux
Leysin
Aigle
Roche
Morgins
Le Locle
Colombier
Yvonand
Forel
Chessel
Grandson
Bullet
Lausanne
Le Bouveret
Vallorbe
Morges
Ballens
Genève (Geneva)
Gumefens

kilometres
miles
0 10 20 30 40 60
0 20 40 60

■ Town names
● Gazetteer location

10